The Environment Acts 1990–1995

Third Edition
of
The Environmental Protection Act 1990

AUSTRALIA
LBC Information Services
Brisbane ● Sydney ● Melbourne ● Perth

CANADA
Carswell
Ottawa ● Toronto ● Calgary ● Montreal ● Vancouver

AGENTS:
Steimatzky's Agency Ltd., Tel Aviv;
N. M. Tripathi (Private) Ltd., Bombay;
Eastern Law House (Private) Ltd., Calcutta;
M.P.P. House, Bangalore;
Universal Book Traders, Delhi;
Aditya Books, Delhi;
MacMillan Shuppan KK, Tokyo;
Pakistan Law House, Karachi

The Environment Acts 1990–1995

Third Edition

with annotations by

Stephen Tromans

M.A., FRSA, MCIWEM, Solicitor,
Partner and Head of Environmental Law Department,
Simmons & Simmons

assisted by

Mike Nash
Solicitor,
Environmental
Law Department,
Simmons & Simmons

Mark Poustie
Solicitor,
Lecturer in Law,
University of Strathclyde

LONDON
SWEET & MAXWELL
1996

Published in 1996 by
Sweet & Maxwell Limited of
100 Avenue Road
London NW3 3PF
Typeset by Mendip Communications Ltd,
Frome, Somerset
Printed and bound in Great Britain by
Butler & Tanner Ltd, Frome and London

**A CIP catalogue record for this book is available
from The British Library**

ISBN 0–421–55810–5

CONTENTS

Contents

PREFACE

Taken together, the Environmental Protection Act 1990 and the Environment Act 1995 provide a substantial part of the skeletal framework supporting UK environmental law. "Skeletal" however perhaps implies an absence of corporeal substance, which could be misleading when compared with the all too-evident bulk of the legislation. Putting on legislative weight is perhaps pardonable when one considers the rich and varied diet of policy which shaped these Acts. The 1990 Act coincided with a White Paper (Cm. 1200) on environmental policy which the then Secretary of State referred to as stretching "from the stratosphere to the street corner": it included measures on integrated and air pollution control, waste management, statutory nuisance, litter, and genetically modified organisms, amongst other delights. The 1995 Act reflects a further five years of prolific (and occasionally profound) policy-making prompted—rightly or wrongly—by an increasing sense of the need for urgent action to forestall little-understood consequences:

"And the world must be cleaned in the winter, or we shall have only
A sour spring, a parched summer, an empty harvest."
(T.S. Eliot, *Murder in the Cathedral*, Faber and Faber, 1935)

The 1995 Act made substantial amendments to the 1990 Act, including the addition of new provisions on waste and an entire new Part dealing with contaminated land: the 1990 Act is printed here with those amendments. The 1995 Act also changed the whole institutional structure for environmental protection by creating new agencies for England and Wales and for Scotland. Those parts of the 1995 Act dealing with environmental protection are also included.

The Acts themselves are of course only part of the picture without the relevant regulations and guidance; some provisions are so genuinely skeletal as to be unintelligible without reference to the secondary materials. All such materials as were available at the time of going to press are of course referred to in the annotations, and a few of the major organs which space permitted to be included have been reproduced as Appendices. Those wishing to have access to all secondary materials are recommended to refer to *The Encyclopedia of Environmental Law*, published by Sweet & Maxwell in six loose-leaf volumes. However, it is hoped that this book will provide, as the first two editions did, a convenient guide to the legislation and its underlying policy background.

Credit in full measure is due to the two people who assisted in preparation of the annotations. Mike Nash of Simmons & Simmons took responsibility for the annotations relating to the Environment Agency in Part I of the 1995 Act, and much of this material represents original thought on his part. He also assisted with many other parts of the text, in particular the material on abandoned mines. Mark Poustie of the Law School, University of Strathclyde, likewise must take the credit for the annotations on the Scottish

Environment Protection Agency, with Mike Nash for the material on abandoned mines, and for invaluable input throughout especially on the position in Scotland. As a result of his work, the text should be as helpful for readers north of the border as for those in less-favoured areas to the south.

Mr Poustie should also take the credit for drawing to my attention the potential aptness to the complex provisions of Part I of the 1995 Act (relating to the aims and duties of the new Agencies) of a quotation from the 1995 Report of General Sir John Learmont into *The Escape from Parkhurst Prison*:

> "Any organisation which boasts one Statement of Purpose, one Vision, five Values, six Goals, seven Strategic priorities and eight Key Performance Indicators without any clear correlation between them is producing a recipe for total confusion and exasperation".

Let us hope that this is not true of the Agencies, and that the highly able people within them are enabled in terms of resources and Government policy support to protect the environment in the way it deserves by effective and even-handed enforcement of the legislation.

Finally, this Preface would not be complete without a firm expression of thanks to the long-suffering Tromans family for their interested support during preparation of the text at a time of many other professional commitments. Let the message in a more modest publication of the three Misses Tromans (a loose-leaf text entitled "The Book of Pulution and Sewige" produced circa 1994) provide a final stern warning for all environmental miscreants: "If you pwlute you will go to jail." Caveat emittor.

Stephen Tromans
Simmons & Simmons
21 Wilson Street
London EC2M 2TX

February 2, 1996

TABLE OF CASES

Table of Cases

Table of Cases

Table of Cases

Table of Cases

Table of Cases

TABLE OF STATUTES

References are to the Introduction or the General Note to the specified section, Part or Schedule. References to the 1990 Act are preceded by 90/, and references to the 1995 Act are preceded by 95/.

Table of Statutes

TABLE OF STATUTORY INSTRUMENTS

References are to the Introduction or the General Note to the specified section, Part or Schedule. References to the 1990 Act are preceded by 90/, and references to the 1995 Act are preceded by 95/.

TABLE OF EUROPEAN LEGISLATION AND TREATIES

References are to the Introduction or the General Note to the specified section, Part or Schedule. References to the 1990 Act are preceded by 90/, and references to the 1995 Act are preceded by 95/.

ENVIRONMENTAL PROTECTION ACT 1990

(1990 c. 43)

ARRANGEMENT OF SECTIONS

PART I

INTEGRATED POLLUTION CONTROL AND AIR POLLUTION CONTROL BY LOCAL AUTHORITIES

Preliminary

PART II

WASTE ON LAND

Preliminary

GENERAL NOTE

The Environmental Protection Act ("the 1990 Act") was undoubtedly the most important piece of legislation in its field since the Control of Pollution Act 1974. On moving the second reading of the Bill in the House of Commons, the then Secretary of State for the Environment (Mr Chris Patten) stated his view that "Whatever the arguments about the Bill ... it will surely provide us with the basic framework for much of our pollution control in Britain well into the next century" (*Hansard*, H.C. Vol. 165 col. 32 January 15, 1990)

The passage of the Act coincided with the readily apparent growth of media and public interest and concern for the environment at all levels: local, national and global. The diversity of environmental issues is reflected in the heterogenous nature of the Act's provisions and it is possibly the lack of a completely coherent approach which aroused the strongest criticisms of the Act. Mr Bryan Gould, then the Labour Party's environment spokesman, described the Bill in the Second Reading debate as " ... little more than a rag-bag of measures drawn from disparate sources, many of which have been dusted down and brought to life again simply to be cobbled together to give it a lick of green paint and the impression of action and cohesion" (*Hansard*, H.C. Vol. 165, col. 50, January 15, 1990)

An attempt to provide an integrated system of environmental protection and conservation was provided by the Environmental Protection Bill of the Earl of Cranbrook (H.L. Bill 6 50/3), introduced shortly before the Government's Bill. This Bill, largely based on the model of the Health and Safety at Work, etc Act 1974, had the aim of the integration and progressive replacement of existing statutes dealing with environmental protection and conservation. This object was to be achieved by a number of very general statutory duties, amplified by regulations and codes of practice and enforced by inspectors acting under the authority of two new agencies—an Environmental Protection Commission and an Environmental Protection Executive. Lord Cranbrook ultimately withdrew his bill, but the need to ensure a genuinely integrated approach to environmental problems in the broad sense remains an important issue.

With the exception of that part of the Act dealing with the reorganisation and winding-up of the Nature Conservancy Council, relatively little major political controversy was engendered by the passage of the Act. Apart from the N.C.C. provisions, one of the most controversial (though non-party political) aspects related to proposals for the introduction of a scheme of compulsory dog registration. This proposal figured largely, and dramatically, in the Bill's final stages. At Lords' Committee stage an amendment moved by Lord Stanley of Alderley for the creation of a compulsory scheme of dog registration was carried by 155 votes to 83. The Government, opposing such a scheme, put forward an alternative set of proposals to deal with the problem of stray dogs. The Commons on that basis rejected the Lords' amendment by 274 votes to 271. The Bill therefore returned to the Lords on October 31, with Parliamentary time fast running out. In the event, a difficult situation for the Government was averted when Lord Stanley's amendment was defeated by 158 votes to 139, though it was clear that, even if the Lords had decided to require the Commons to reconsider the amendment, Lord Stanley would not have pressed the point further so as to jeopardise the Bill if the Commons had rejected the amendment again (see *Hansard*, H.C. Vol. 522 col. 1857).

The Bill was subject to many amendments in both the Commons' and the Lords' stages: particularly in the Lords, where some 436 amendments were carried. Many of these were of a technical nature, but a number of significant additions and modifications also resulted. In the course of its Parliamentary progress the Bill grew from an original 147 sections and 14 Schedules to 164 sections and 16 Schedules.

The Policy Background
It is possible to argue that a factor which contributed to the general consensus in relation to the Act was the long policy gestation period of a number of the Act's provisions. Some of these can be traced back in their antecedents to the work of Parliamentary Select and Standing Committees and of the Royal Commission on Environmental Pollution (RCEP). Others have emerged through lengthy consultative procedures in various proposals and consultation papers issued by the relevant departments. The following table illustrates the point by listing those sources in relation to some of the Act's main provisions.

Provision	*Relevant policy or consultative documents*
Integrated pollution control/best practicable environmental option (Pt. I)	RCEP Fifth Report, *Air Pollution Control, an Integrated Approach* (Cm. 6371, January 1976) DOE Pollution Paper No. 18: Response to the RCEP's Fifth Report (December 1982) RCEP Tenth Report, *Tackling Pollution—Experience and Prospects* (Cm. 9149, February 1984) DOE Pollution Paper No. 22: Response to RCEP's Tenth Report (December 1984) RCEP Twelfth Report, *Best Practicable Environmental Option* (Cm. 310, February 1988) DOE/Welsh Office, *Integrated Pollution Control—a Consultation Paper* (July 1988) DOE/Welsh Office, *Control of "Red List" Substances—a Consultation Paper* (July 1988)
Local Authority Air Pollution Control (Pt. I)	RCEP Fifth Report (above) DOE Pollution Paper No. 18 (above) DOE/Scottish Development Department/Welsh Office, *Air Pollution Control in Great Britain—Review and Proposals: a Consultation Paper* (December 1986) DOE/Scottish Development Department/Welsh Office, *Air Pollution Control in Great Britain—Follow up to Consultation Paper issued in December 01987* (December 1988) DOE/Scottish Development Department/Welsh Office, *Air Pollution Control in Great Britain—Works Proposed to be Scheduled for Prior Authorisation: a Consultation Paper* (December 1988)

Provision	Relevant policy or consultative documents
Waste (Pt. II)	*House of Lords Select Committee on Science and Technology 1st Report Session 1980–81, Hazardous Waste Disposal,* H.L. 273-I-III (July 1981) RCEP Eleventh Report, *Managing Waste, the Duty of Care* (Cm. 9675, December 1985) DOE Pollution Paper No. 24: Response to RCEP's Eleventh Report (September 1986) DOE/DOE (Northern Ireland)/Welsh Office/Scottish Office, Hazardous Waste Inspectorate Reports 1–3: First Report: *Hazardous Waste Management: an Overview* (June 1985); Second Report: *"Hazardous Waste Management Ramshackle and Antediluvian?"* (July 1986); Third Report (June 1988) DOE/Welsh Office, *Waste Office, Waste Disposal Law: Amendments—Consultation Paper* (September 1986) DOE/Welsh Office, *Waste Disposal Law Amendment: Decisions Following Public Consultation* (June 1988) DOE/Welsh Office, *The Role and Functions of Waste Disposal Authorities—a Consultation Paper* (January 1989) DOE/Welsh Office, *The Role and Functions of Waste Disposal Authorities—Conclusions* (September 1989) House of Commons Environment Committee Second Report Session 1988–89, *Toxic Waste,* H.C. 22-I-III (February 1989) DOE, Reply to the Second Report from the Environmental Committee, *Toxic Waste* (Cm 679, April 1989) DOE, Response to the Fourth Report from the House of Lords Select Committee on Science and Technology, *Hazardous Waste Disposal* (Cm. 763, July 1989) House of Commons Environment Committee First Report Session 1989–90, *Contaminated Land,* H.C. 170-I-III (January 1990) DOE/Welsh Office, *Waste Management—the Duty of Care,* Consultation Paper and Draft Code of Practice (February 1990) DOE/Welsh Office, *Control of Pollution Act 1974, The Special Waste Regulations 1980—a Consultation Paper, Special Waste and the Control of its Disposal* (January 1990)
Litter (Pt. IV)	DOE/Department of Transport/Scottish Office/Welsh Office, *Action on Litter: the Government's Proposals for Legislation* (July 1989) DOE/Department of Transport/Scottish Office/Welsh Office, *Environmental Protection Bill: Draft Code of Practice on Litter and Refuse—A Consultation Paper* (February 1990)
Control over Genetically Modified Organisms (Pt. VI)	RCEP Thirteenth Report, *The Release of Genetically Engineered Organisms to the Environment* (Cm. 720, July 1989) DOE, *Consultation Paper on Proposals for Additional Legislation on the Intentional Release of Genetically Manipulated Organisms* (June 1989)

Provision	*Relevant policy or consultative documents*
Nature Conservancy Council (Pt. VIII)	House of Lords Select Committee on Science and Technology, Session 1989–90 Second Report, *Nature Conservancy Council*, H.L. Paper 33-I and II (March 1990) House of Lords Session 1989–90, Sixth Report, the Government's Response to the Second Report H.L. Paper 60 (May 1990)
Public access to environmental information (various parts)	RCEP Second Report (Cm. 4894, March 1972), Tenth Report (Cm. 9149, February 1984) DOE Pollution Paper No. 23, *Public Access to Environmental Information* (1986) House of Lords Select Committee on the European Communities, Session 1989–90 First Report, *Freedom of Access to Information on the Environment*, H.L. Paper 2 (November 1989)

This does not represent an exhaustive list of relevant materials, but serves to illustrate the main strands of advice and consultation underlying the Act, the protracted periods during which many areas of environmental policy have been under debate, and the very significant input to the legislation provided by the valuable work of the Royal Commission and the relevant Parliamentary Committees. Reference to further materials are given in the Notes to the relevant parts of the Act.

The international and Community law background to the 1990 Act are discussed separately below, but the changing climate of enforcement and increased commercial awareness of environmental problems are also an important part of the backcloth against which the 1990 Act operates.

It is apparent that enforcing agencies at various levels are becoming less tolerant of lapses or inaction on the part of industry which threaten human life or health or the environment. This can be seen particularly in the sectors of health and safety legislation and in relation to water pollution. Both the Health and Safety Executive and the National Rivers Authority have expressed their willingness to take prosecutions to the Crown Court in appropriate cases, the most notable example to date being the prosecution of Shell U.K. at Liverpool Crown Court in February 1990 under Pt II of the Control of Pollution Act 1974 for oil pollution of the Mersey Estuary caused by a fracture in a pipeline at the company's Stanlow refinery. A fine of £1,000,000 was imposed by Mars-Jones J. This approach contrasts with the somewhat more lenient co-operative and pragmatic approach cultivated by the Industrial Air Pollution Inspectorate and Regional Water Authorities in earlier years and discussed in various studies such as G. Richardson, A. Ogus and P. Burrows, *Policing Pollution* (Clarendon Press, 1982), K. Hawkins, *Environment and Enforcement* (Clarendon Press, 1984) and P.Q. Watchman, C.R. Barker and J. Rowan-Robinson, *River Pollution: A Case for a Pragmatic Approach to Enforcement* [1988] J.P.L. 674.

The Government has supported such a change of attitude, raising a number of the maximum magistrates' court fines under the Act tenfold from £2,000 to £20,000 and emphasising the need for realistic fines related to resultant profits or savings from the offence: see *Crime, Justice and Protecting the Public* Cm. 965, para. 5.8; DOE News Release No. 720. December 20, 1989; Home Office News Release, June 4, 1990.

Secondly many companies and lending institutions are now paying much greater attention to environmental performance and compliance, again encouraged by the Government, and it may be expected that in the coming years environmental law will play an increasingly significant role in general corporate, commercial and property transactions. This has been borne out in practice since the passage of the 1990 Act, not only in the transactional context, but in the increased interest in the use of corporate environmental management and audit systems. The 1990 Act is thus likely to have long-standing repercussions in terms of commercial practice as well as regulatory activity.

Commencement and territorial extent
Details of commencement dates and territorial extent are given in the General Note of each Part of the Act in relation to that Part.
The following are details of sections in force:

TABLE OF SECTIONS IN FORCE

The following provisions of the Environmental Protection Act 1990 have been brought into force by commencement orders up to and including S.I. 1995 No. 2152 (C.43) or by section 164(2) of the Act:

Provision	Date of Commencement	S.I.
ss.1 and 2	01.01.1991	1990 No. 2635
s.3	19.12.1990	1990 No. 2635
ss.4–28	01.01.1991	1990 No. 2635
ss.29–32	31.05.1991	1991 No. 1319
s.33(1)(a) and (b) (partially)	01.05.1994	1994 No. 1096
s.33(1)(a) and (b) (partially)	01.04.1995	1994 No. 1096, 1994 No. 2487 and 1994 No. 3234
s.33(1)(a) and (b) (insofar as not already in force)	Various	1994 No. 1096, 1994 No. 2487 and 1994 No. 3234
s.33(1)(c)	01.04.1992	1991 No. 2829
s.33(2) (partially)	01.04.1992	1991 No. 2829
s.33(2) (partially)	01.05.1994	1994 No. 1096
s.33(2) (partially)	01.04.1995	1994 No. 1096, 1994 No. 2487 and 1994 No. 3234
s.33(2) (insofar as not already in force)	Various	1994 No. 1096, 1994 No. 2487 and 1994 No. 3234
s.33(3) and (4)	13.12.1991	1991 No. 2829
s.33(6)–(9) (partially)	01.04.1992	1991 No. 2829
s.33(6)–(9) (partially)	01.05.1994	1994 No. 1096
s.33(6)–(9) (partially)	01.04.1995	1994 No. 1096, 1994 No. 2487 and 1994 No. 3234
s.33(6)–(9) (insofar as not already in force)	Various	1994 No. 1096, 1994 No. 2487 and 1994 No. 3234
s.34(1)–(4)	01.04.1992	1991 No. 2829
s.34(5)	13.12.1991	1991 No. 2829
s.34(6)	01.04.1992	1991 No. 2829
s.34(7)–(9)	13.12.1991	1991 No. 2829
s.34(10)	01.04.1992	1991 No. 2829
s.34(11)	13.12.1991	1991 No. 2829
s.35(1)–(5) (partially)	01.05.1994	1994 No. 1096
s.35(1)–(5) (partially)	01.04.1995	1994 No. 1096, 1994 No. 2487 and 1994 No. 3234
s.35(1)–(5) (insofar as not already in force)	Various	1994 No. 1096, 1994 No. 2487 and 1994 No. 3234
s.35(6)	18.02.1993	1993 No. 274
s.35(7)–(12) (partially)	01.05.1994	1994 No. 1096
s.35(7)–(12) (partially)	01.04.1995	1994 No. 1096, 1994 No. 2487 and 1994 No. 3234
s.35(7)–(12) (insofar as not already in force)	Various	1994 No. 1096, 1994 No. 2487 and 1994 No. 3234
s.36(1)	18.02.1993	1993 No. 274
ss.36(2)–(10) and 37(1) and (2) (partially)	01.05.1994	1944 No. 1096
ss.36(2)–(10) and 37(1) and (2) (partially)	01.04.1995	1994 No. 1096, 1994 No. 2487 and 1994 No. 3234
ss.36(2)–(10) and 37(1) and (2) (insofar as not already in force)	Various	1994 No. 1096, 1994 No. 2487 and 1994 No. 3234
s.37(3) (partially)	18.02.1993	1993 No. 274

Provision	Date of Commencement	S.I.
ss.37(3)–(6) and 38(1)–(6) (partially)	01.05.1994	1994 No. 1096
ss.37(3)–(6) and 38(1)–(6) (partially)	01.04.1995	1994 No. 1096, 1994 No. 2487 and 1994 No. 3234
ss.37(3)–(6) and 38(1)–(6) (insofar as not already in force)	Various	1994 No. 1096, 1994 No. 2487 and 1994 No. 3234
s.38(7) (partially)	18.02.1993	1993 No. 274
ss.38(7)–(12) and 39(1) and (2) (partially)	01.05.1994	1994 No. 1096
ss.38(7)–(12) and 39(1) and (2) (partially)	01.04.1995	1994 No. 1096, 1994 No. 2487 and 1994 No. 3234
ss.38(7)–(12) and 39(1) and (2) (insofar as not already in force)	Various	1994 No. 1096, 1994 No. 2487 and 1994 No. 3234
s.39(3)	18.02.1993	1993 No. 274
ss.39(4)–(11) and 40(1) and (2) (partially)	01.05.1994	1994 No. 1096
ss.39(4)–(11) and 40(1) and (2) (partially)	01.04.1995	1994 No. 1096, 1994 No. 2487 and 1994 No. 3234
ss.39(4)–(11) and 40(1) and (2) (insofar as not already in force)	Various	1994 No. 1096, 1994 No. 2487 and 1994 No. 3234
s.40(3)	18.02.1993	1993 No. 274
s.40(4)–(6) (partially)	01.05.1994	1994 No. 1096
s.40(4)–(6) (partially)	01.04.1995	1994 No. 1096, 1994 No. 2487 and 1994 No. 3234
s.40(4)–(6) (insofar as not already in force)	Various	1994 No. 1096, 1994 No. 2487 and 1994 No. 3234
s.41(1)	16.03.1994	1994 No. 780
s.41(2)	18.02.1993	1993 No. 274
s.41(3)	16.03.1994	1994 No. 780
s.41(4) and (5)	18.02.1993	1993 No. 274
s.41(6)–(8)	16.03.1994	1994 No. 780
s.42(1)–(7) (partially)	01.05.1994	1994 No. 1096
s.42(1)–(7) (partially)	01.04.1995	1994 No. 1096, 1994 No. 2487 and 1994 No. 3234
s.42(1)–(7) (insofar as not already in force)	Various	1994 No. 1096, 1994 No. 2487 and 1994 No. 3234
s.42(8) (partially)	18.02.1993	1993 No. 274
ss.42(8) and 43(1)–(7) (partially)	01.05.1994	1994 No. 1096
ss.42(8) and 43(1)–(7) (partially)	01.04.1995	1994 No. 1096, 1994 No. 2487 and 1994 No. 3234
ss.42(8) and 43(1)–(7) (insofar as not already in force)	Various	1994 No. 1096, 1994 No. 2487 and 1994 No. 3234
s.43(8)	18.02.1993	1993 No. 274
s.44 (partially)	01.05.1994	1994 No. 1096
s.44 (partially)	01.04.1995	1994 No. 1096, 1994 No. 2487 and 1994 No. 3234
s.44 (insofar as not already in force)	Various	1994 No. 1096, 1994 No. 2487 and 1994 No. 3234
s.45(1)	01.04.1992	1992 No. 266
s.45(2) (Scotland)	01.04.1992	1992 No. 266
s.45(3) (partially)	14.02.1992	1992 No. 266
s.45(3)–(12) (insofar as not already inforce)	01.04.1992	1992 No. 266

11

Provision	Date of Commencement	S.I.
ss.46, 47 and 48(1)–(6)	01.04.1992	1992 No. 266
s.48(8) and (9)	01.04.1992	1992 No. 266
s.49	01.08.1991	1991 No. 1577
ss.50 and 51	31.05.1991	1991 No. 1319
s.52(1)	01.04.1992	1992 No. 266
s.52(3)–(7)	01.04.1992	1992 No. 266
s.52(8) (partially)	13.12.1991	1991 No. 2829
ss.52(9)–(11) and 53	01.04.1992	1992 No. 266
s.54(1)–(13)	01.05.1994	1994 No. 1096
s.54(14)	18.02.1993	1993 No. 274
s.54(15)–(17)	01.05.1994	1994 No. 1096
ss.55 and 56	01.04.1992	1992 No. 266
s.57 (partially)	01.05.1994	1994 No. 1096
s.57 (partially)	01.04.1995	1994 No. 1096, 1994 No. 2487 and 1994 No. 3234
s.57 (insofar as not already in force)	Various	1994 No. 1096, 1994 No. 2487 and 1994 No. 3234
ss.58 and 59	01.05.1994	1994 No. 1096
s.60 (partially)	31.05.1991	1991 No. 1319
s.60 (insofar as not already in force)	01.05.1994	1994 No. 1096
s.62	11.08.1995	1995 No. 2152
s.63(1)	18.02.1993	1993 No. 274
s.64(1)	18.02.1993	1993 No. 274
s.64(2) and (3)	01.05.1994	1994 No. 1096
s.64(4)	18.02.1993	1993 No. 274
s.64(5)–(7)	01.05.1994	1994 No. 1096
s.64(8)	18.02.1993	1993 No. 274
s.65(1)	01.05.1994	1994 No. 1096
s.65(2) (partially)	18.02.1993	1993 No. 274
s.65(2) (insofar as not already in force)	01.05.1994	1994 No. 1096
ss.65(3) and (4) and 66(1)–(6)	01.05.1994	1994 No. 1096
s.66(7) (partially)	18.02.1993	1993 No. 274
s.66(7) (insofar as not already in force)	01.05.1994	1994 No. 1096
ss.66(8)–(11) and 67	01.05.1994	1994 No. 1096
s.68	31.05.1991	1991 No. 1319
ss.69 and 70	01.04.1992	1991 No. 2829
ss.71 and 72	31.05.1991	1991 No. 1319
s.73(1)–(5)	01.04.1992	1992 No. 266
ss.73(6)–(9) and 74(1)–(5)	01.05.1994	1994 No. 1096
s.74(6)	18.02.1993	1993 No. 274
s.74(7)	01.05.1994	1994 No. 1096
s.75	31.05.1991	1991 No. 1319
s.77	31.05.1991	1991 No. 1319
s.78	13.12.1991	1991 No. 2829
ss.79–85	01.01.1991	s.164(2)
s.86(1) (England and Wales)	13.02.1991	1991 No. 96
s.86(1) (Scotland)	01.04.1991	1991 No. 1042
s.86(2)	14.01.1991	1991 No. 96
s.86(3)	01.04.1991	1991 No. 1042
s.86(4) and (5) (England and Wales)	13.02.1991	1991 No. 96
s.86(4) and (5) (Scotland)	01.04.1991	1991 No. 1042
s.86(6)–(8)	14.01.1991	1991 No. 96
s.86(9) (England and Wales)	13.02.1991	1991 No. 96
s.86(10)	01.04.1991	1991 No. 1042

Provision	Date of Commencement	S.I.
s.86(11)	14.01.1991	1991 No. 96
s.86(12)	01.06.1991	1991 No. 1042
s.86(13) (England and Wales)	13.02.1991	1991 No. 96
s.86(13) (Scotland)	01.04.1991	1991 No. 1042
s.86(14) and (15)	14.01.1991	1991 No. 96
s.87(1), (2) and (3)(a)–(e) (England and Wales)	13.02.1991	1991 No. 96
s.87(1), (2) and (3)(a)–(e) (Scotland)	01.04.1991	1991 No. 1042
s.87(3)(f)	01.06.1991	1991 No. 1042
s.87(4)–(6) (England and Wales)	13.02.1991	1991 No. 96
s.87(4)–(6) (Scotland)	01.04.1991	1991 No. 1042
s.87(7)	01.04.1991	1991 No. 1042
s.88(1)–(4) (England and Wales)	13.02.1991	1991 No. 96
s.88(1)–(4) (Scotland)	01.04.1991	1991 No. 1042
s.88(5)	14.01.1991	1991 No. 96
s.88(6) (England and Wales)	13.02.1991	1991 No. 96
s.88(6) (Scotland)	01.04.1991	1991 No. 1042
s.88(7)	14.01.1991	1991 No. 96
s.88(8) and (9)(a) (England and Wales)	13.02.1991	1991 No. 96
s.88(8) and (9)(a) (Scotland)	01.04.1991	1991 No. 1042
s.88(9)(b)	14.01.1991	1991 No. 96
s.88(9)(c) and (d) (Scotland)	01.04.1991	1991 No. 1042
s.88(9)(c)–(e) and (10) (England and Wales)	13.02.1991	1991 No. 96
s.88(10) (Scotland)	01.04.1991	1991 No. 1042
s.89(1)(a)–(f)	01.04.1991	1991 No. 1042
s.89(1)(g)	01.06.1991	1991 No. 1042
s.89(2) and (3)	01.04.1991	1991 No. 1042
s.89(4)	14.01.1991	1991 No. 96
s.89(5) and (6)	01.04.1991	1991 No. 1042
s.89(7)–(9)	13.11.1990	1990 No. 2243
s.89(10)	01.04.1991	1991 No. 1042
s.89(11)–(13)	13.11.1990	1990 No. 2243
s.89(14)	01.04.1991	1991 No. 1042
s.90(1) and (2)	14.01.1991	1991 No. 96
s.90(3)–(6)	01.06.1991	1991 No. 1042
s.90(7)	14.01.1991	1991 No. 96
s.91(1)(a)–(f)	01.04.1991	1991 No. 1042
s.91(1)(g)	01.06.1991	1991 No. 1042
s.91(2)–(13)	01.04.1991	1991 No. 1042
s.92(1)(a)–(c)	01.04.1991	1991 No. 1042
s.92(1)(d)	01.06.1991	1991 No. 1042
ss.92(2)–(10) and 93	01.04.1991	1991 No. 1042
s.94(1) and (2)	14.01.1991	1991 No. 96
ss.94(3)–(9), 95 and 96(1)	01.04.1991	1991 No. 1042
s.96(2) and (3)	14.01.1991	1991 No. 96
s.97	01.01.1991	s.164(2)
s.98(1) (Scotland)	01.04.1991	1991 No. 1042
s.98(1) and (2) (England and Wales)	13.02.1991	1991 No. 96
s.98(3) and (4)	01.04.1991	1991 No. 1042
s.98(5) and (6) (England and Wales)	13.02.1991	1991 No. 96
s.98(5) and (6) (Scotland)	01.04.1991	1991 No. 1042
s.99	01.01.1991	s.164(2)
ss.100–104	01.01.1991	1990 No. 2565 and 1990 No. 2635
s.105 (partially)	07.12.1990	1990 No. 2565

Provision	Date of Commencement	S.I.
s.105 (partially)	01.01.1991	s.164(2)
s.105 (insofar as not already in force)	01.01.1991	1990 No. 2565 and 1990 No. 2635
s.106(1)–(3)	01.02.1993	1992 No. 3253
s.106(4) and (5)	01.04.1991	1991 No. 1042
ss.106(6) and (7) and 107(1)–(7)	01.02.1993	1992 No. 3253
s.107(8)	01.04.1991	1991 No. 1042
s.107(9)–(11)	01.02.1993	1992 No. 3253
s.108(1)(a) (partially)	01.02.1993	1992 No. 3253
s.108(1)(b)	01.04.1991	1991 No. 1042
s.108(3)(b)	01.04.1991	1991 No. 1042
s.108(5)	01.04.1991	1991 No. 1042
s.108(7)	01.04.1991	1991 No. 1042
s.108(9)	01.04.1991	1991 No. 1042
s.108(10)	01.01.1993	1992 No. 3253
s.110 (partially)	01.02.1993	1992 No. 3253
s.111(1) and (2)	01.04.1991	1991 No. 1042
s.111(4) and (5)	01.04.1991	1991 No. 1042
s.111(6) and (6A)	01.02.1993	1992 No. 3253
s.111(7)	01.04.1991	1991 No. 1042
s.111(8)–(10)	01.02.1993	1992 No. 3253
s.111(11)	01.04.1991	1991 No. 1042
s.112(1) and (2)	01.02.1993	1992 No. 3253
s.112(5)–(7)	01.02.1993	1992 No. 3253
ss.113, 114(1)–(3)	01.04.1991	1991 No. 1042
ss.114(4) and (5) and 115(1)–(3)	01.02.1993	1992 No. 3253
s.115(4)	01.04.1991	1991 No. 1042
s.115(5)–(10)	01.02.1993	1992 No. 3253
s.116 (partially)	01.02.1993	1992 No. 3253
s.117	01.02.1993	1992 No. 3253
s.118(1)(a)	01.02.1993	1992 No. 3253
s.118(1)(c)	01.02.1993	1992 No. 3253
s.118(1)(e)–(l)	01.02.1993	1992 No. 3253
s.118(1)(m) (partially)	01.02.1993	1992 No. 3253
s.118(1)(n) and (o) and (2)–(10)	01.02.1993	1992 No. 3253
ss.119–121	01.02.1993	1992 No. 3253
s.122(1) (partially)	01.04.1991	1991 No. 1042
s.122(1)(c)–(h) (insofar as not already in force)	01.02.1993	1992 No. 3253
s.122(2) and (3)	01.02.1993	1992 No. 3253
s.122(4)	01.04.1991	1991 No. 1042
s.123(1)–(6)	01.02.1993	1992 No. 3253
s.123(7)	01.04.1991	1991 No. 1042
s.123(8)	01.02.1993	1992 No. 3253
s.123(9), 124–126	01.04.1991	1991 No. 1042
s.127	01.02.1993	1992 No. 3253
s.128 (partially)	05.11.1990	1990 No. 2226
s.128 (insofar as not already in force)	01.04.1991	1991 No. 685
s.129	05.11.1990	1990 No. 2226
s.130 (partially)	05.11.1990	1990 No. 2226
s.130 (insofar as not already in force)	01.04.1991	1991 No. 685
s.131	05.11.1990	1990 No. 2226
s.132 (partially)	05.11.1990	1990 No. 2226
s.132 (insofar as not already in force)	01.04.1991	1991 No. 685
ss.133–139	05.11.1990	1990 No. 2226

Provision	Date of Commencement	S.I.
ss.140–142	01.01.1991	s.164(2)
s.143(1) (England and Wales)	14.02.1992	1992 No. 266
s.143(5) and (6) (England and Wales)	14.02.1992	1992 No. 266
s.144 (partially)	01.01.1992	1991 No. 2829
s.144 (partially)	18.02.1993	1993 No. 274
s.144 (insofar as not already in force)	01.05.1993	1993 No. 274
ss.145 and 146	01.01.1991	s.164(2)
s.147	31.05.1991	1991 No. 1319
s.148	01.01.1991	s.164(2)
ss.149–151 (partially)	14.02.1992	1992 No. 266
ss.149–151 (insofar as not already in force)	01.04.1992	1992 No. 266
s.152	10.07.1991	1991 No. 1577
ss.153–155	01.01.1991	s.164(2)
s.156	01.04.1991	1991 No. 1042
s.157	01.01.1991	s.164(2)
s.158	01.04.1991	1991 No. 1042
s.159	01.01.1991	1990 No. 2635
ss.160 and 161	01.01.1991	s.164(2)
s.162(1) (partially)	14.01.1991	1991 No. 96
s.162(1) (partially)	01.04.1991	1991 No. 1042
s.162(1) (partially)	31.05.1991	1991 No. 1319
s.162(1) (partially)	01.04.1992	1991 No. 2829
s.162(1) (partially)	01.04.1992	1992 No. 266
s.162(1) (partially)	18.02.1993	1993 No. 274
s.162(1) (partially)	01.05.1994	1994 No. 1096
s.162(1) (partially)	01.10.1994	1994 No. 1096
s.162(1) (partially)	Various	1994 No. 1096, 1994 No. 2487 and 1994 No. 3234
s.162(2) (partially)	01.01.1991	1990 No. 2565 and 1990 No. 2635
s.162(2) (partially)	01.04.1991	1991 No. 685
s.162(2) (partially)	01.04.1991	1991 No. 1042
s.162(2) (partially)	31.05.1991	1991 No. 1319
s.162(2) (partially)	01.01.1992	1991 No. 2829
s.162(2) (partially)	01.04.1992	1991 No. 2829
s.162(2) (partially)	01.04.1992	1992 No. 266
s.162(2) (partially)	18.02.1993	1993 No. 274
s.162(2) (partially)	01.05.1993	1993 No. 274
s.162(2) (partially)	01.05.1994	1994 No. 1096
s.162(2) (partially)	01.04.1995	1994 No. 1096, 1994 No. 2487 and 1994 No. 3234
s.162(2) (partially)	Various	1994 No. 1096, 1994 No. 2487, 1994 No. 2854 and 1994 No. 3234
s.162(3)	01.04.1992	1992 No. 266
ss.162(5) and 163	01.01.1991	s.164(2)
s.164	01.11.1990	

PART I

INTEGRATED POLLUTION CONTROL AND AIR POLLUTION CONTROL BY LOCAL AUTHORITIES

GENERAL NOTE

The purpose of Pt. I of the Act is described in the Preamble as "to make provision for the improved control of pollution arising from certain industrial and other processes." The provisions of Pt. I establish two separate systems of control: integrated pollution control (IPC) and local authority air pollution control (LAAPC).

The two systems share a number of features, for example: the prescription of processes and substances for control; authorisations, which may be subject to conditions; enforcement powers; publicity provisions; and offences. However, IPC is to be exercisable "for the purpose of preventing or minimising pollution of the environment due to the release of substances into any environmental medium" (s.4(2)); LAAPC, by contrast, "shall be exercisable for the purpose of preventing or minimising pollution of the environment due to the release of substances into the air (but not into any other environmental medium)" (s.4(3)).

Since April 1, 1996, IPC has in England and Wales been administered by the Environment Agency, which, along with the Scottish Environment Protection Agency (SEPA), was created by the Environment Act 1995. On that date, the Agency took over (*inter alia*) the functions of HM Inspectorate of Pollution (HMIP) which, under its Chief Inspector, had previously administered IPC in England and Wales. By contrast, since its inception LAAPC has in England and Wales been operated by local authorities, and this remains the case. In Scotland, on the same date, SEPA took over from HM Industrial Pollution Inspectorate (HMIPI) and the river purification authorities the administration of IPC, and from local authorities the administration of LAAPC. Although the term "LAAPC" is still in common use, the Scottish changes render it inaccurate in its application to Pt. I generally. Therefore, in these notes the term LAPC (for "local air pollution control") is adopted, since air pollution control is still "prescribed for local control," albeit not in Scotland, for control by local authorities. The advent of the agencies brings more than merely administrative change, in that they have not only new powers, objectives and duties, but also powers and duties previously associated with their other constituent bodies (in the case of the Agency, the National Rivers Authority and waste regulation authorities) which now apply to their IPC and, for SEPA, LAPC functions. See further the introductory note to the 1995 Act, Pt. I. The 1995 Act also made other amendments to Part I of the 1990 Act, including in relation to variation notices (s.10(3A)), appeals (s.15), and sentencing for offences (s.23(2)). Provisions previously found in Part I are now to be found in the 1995 Act, notably in relation to the enforcing authorities' powers of entry.

Background

The background to the two systems can be traced through a number of consultation papers (references to HMIP and the NRA would now of course refer to the Agency):

(a) *Integrated Pollution Control* (DoE/Welsh Office, July 1988), reaffirming acceptance of the position of the RCEP that wastes should be disposed of according to the Best Practicable Environmental Option (BPEO) and proposing "that a system of integrated pollution control (IPC) should be introduced for certain types of industrial processes that discharge significant quantities of harmful wastes." Such processes would be scheduled by the Secretary of State and HMIP would examine, and where appropriate authorise, the process technology and methods of operation to be adopted, and the levels of discharge into all three environmental media in the context of the environment as a whole. Such control should recognise two basic concepts:

  (i) that pollutants have effects in media other than those into which they have been released; and

  (ii) that reducing opportunities to dispose of a waste to one medium often increases the need to dispose of the waste (or its modified components) into one of the other media. The proposed system was also intended to accord with the UK's E.C. and international obligations.

(b) *Inputs of Dangerous Substances to Water: Proposals for a Unified System of Control* (DoE/Welsh Office, July 1988) setting out the Government's proposals for tightening control over the input of the most dangerous substances to water. The paper proposed the use, for the first time, of technology-based emission standards, based on "best available technology not entailing excessive cost" (BATNEEC), applied to discharges to water of those substances identified as representing the greatest threat because of their toxicity, persistence and capacity for bio-accumulation. The paper identifies some 26 such substances ("the Red List") and makes the case for seeking to combine the environmental quality objectives (EQO) and uniform emission standards (UES) approaches. As with the IPC proposals, the suggestion was to introduce a system of "scheduling" of industrial processes discharging significant amounts of "Red List" substances, and the progressive application of technology-based emission standards to those processes. Possible models for the relationship between HMIP and the NRA were also discussed.

(c) *Trade Effluent Discharges to Sewers* (DoE/Welsh Office, April 1988) envisaged that the privatised sewerage utility companies would in future be responsible for granting consents in respect of discharges of most substances to sewers. However, dischargers of "Red List" substances would require authorisation from HMIP in addition to consent from the utility company. Two possible models for operating such a system were put forward.

(d) *Air Pollution Control in Great Britain: Review and Proposals* (DoE/Scottish Development Department/Welsh Office, December 1986) proposed retention of the principle of "best practicable means" (bpm) but allowing its use to be adapted to take account of existing and prospective E.C. legislation. The proposal was to establish a common system of control, giving local authorities powers of prior approval over certain processes, with a system of consents setting out "the main elements of the bpm agreement by the control authorities." A "middle tier" of industrial processes was identified, where existing controls were seen to be inadequate or inconsistent with emerging E.C. legislation: these included the small ferrous-metal industries, plants manufacturing asbestos-based products or producing bulk glass and ceramics, hospital incinerators and "plants disposing of non-toxic and non-dangerous waste by inciner-ation". "*Post facto*" control by nuisance powers was not regarded as suitable for such works; nor could planning conditions "enforce the ongoing good housekeeping and operational systems that are essential to proper control". Increasing account would need to be taken of E.C. and other air quality standards and emission limits.

(e) *Air Pollution Control in Great Britain: Follow-up to Consultation Paper of December 1986* (DoE/Scottish Development Department/Welsh Office, December 1988) sum-marised the responses to the 1986 Consultation Paper and indicated one major change in thinking on the part of the Government. This change was to combine the bpm and consent-based approaches, by setting conditions for certain aspects of a plant's control, while retaining the general bpm duty in respect of all residual matters.

(f) *Air Pollution Control in Great Britain: Works Proposed to be Scheduled for Prior Authorisation* (DoE/Scottish Development/Welsh Office, December 1988) sought comments on proposals for the precise definition of the processes to be scheduled for national and local control. A change of format in the designation of processes was proposed, having regard not only to the type of process (as previously) "but also to the end-product, in terms both of the commodity produced and the nature of the pollution". The intention was to make the new Schedule easier to use, and also to align it more closely in content with the provisions of E.C. Directive 84/360/EEC on the combating of air pollution from industrial plants (see later). That Directive requires that certain categories of plant be authorised before commencing operation and also subsequently if subject to significant modification. It also provides for the gradual improvement of existing plant to current standards, taking into account certain factors including "the desirability of not entailing excessive costs for the plant ... having regard in particular to the economic situation of undertakings belonging to the category in question".

The main strands of Part I of the Act may therefore be discerned: an integrated approach to pollution of all three media; concentration on the most difficult or potentially problematic processes and substances; control by prior approval; specific conditions combined with a residual duty; the use of best available technology (later techniques) not entailing excessive cost; and the need to comply with E.C. requirements, specifically Directive 84/360.

Implementation of E.C. and international requirements

The importance of certain E.C. directives in relation to Pt. I of the Act has already been mentioned. Section 3 of the Act provides the means by which those requirements may be translated into binding limits, quotas, objectives or standards under domestic law. At the present time the following directives are of most immediate general relevance. (The proposed directive on IPPC is considered separately immediately after this section.)

(a) *Directive 84/360/EEC on the combating of air pollution from industrial plants* (O.J. L188/20, July 16, 1984) as amended by Directive 91/692/EEC p. 48 (O.J. L377, December 31, 1991). This Directive lists in Annex I various categories of industrial plant and provides (Art. 3) that Member States must take the necessary measures to ensure that the operation of such plants requires prior authorisation by competent authorities, the necessity to meet any relevant requirements being taken into account at the design stage. Authorisation is also required (Art. 3(2)) for "substantial alterations" to such plants. Article 4 requires that an authorisation should only be issued upon the competent authority being satisfied that: (a) all appropriate preventive measures against air pollution have been taken, including the use of best available technology, provided that the application of such measures does not entail excessive cost; (b) the use of the plant will not cause significant air pollution, particularly from the emission of substances listed in Annex II (including sulphur dioxide, oxides of nitrogen, hydrocarbons, heavy metals, chlorine, asbestos and fluorine, and their respective compounds); (c) no applicable emission limit values will be exceeded; and (d) all applicable air quality limit values will be taken into account. By Article 8 the Council is given power, acting unanimously on a proposal from the Commission, to fix emission limit values. By Art. 12, Member States must follow developments "as regards the best available technology and the environmental situation" and in the light of this must, if necessary, impose appropriate conditions on the basis of those developments and the desirability of avoiding excessive costs, having regard to "the economic situation of the plants belonging to the category concerned". Article 13 requires policies to be implemented for the "gradual adaptation" of existing plants to the best available technology, taking into account in particular the plant's technical characteristics; its rate of utilisation and length of its remaining life; the nature and volume of polluting emissions from it; and the desirability of not entailing excessive costs for the plant concerned, having regard in particular to the economic situation of undertakings belonging to the category in question. "Existing plant" means a plant in operation before July 1, 1987 or built or authorised before that date (Art. 2(3)). The implementation date for the Directive is June 30, 1987.

(b) *Directive 88/609/EEC on the limitation of emissions of certain pollutants into the air from large combustion plants* (O.J. L336/1, December 12, 1988) as amended by Directive 94/66 (O.J. L357/83, December 24, 1994). By Art. 1 the Directive applies to combustion plants the rated thermal input of which is 50 MW or more, irrespective of the type of fuel used, be it solid, liquid or gaseous. Article 3 requires Member States, no later than July 1, 1990, to draw up appropriate programmes for the progressive reduction of total annual emissions from existing plants (*i.e.* those for which the original construction licence was granted before July 1, 1987). Such programmes are to be drawn up and implemented with the aim of complying with (at least) the emission ceilings and percentage reductions for sulphur dioxide and oxides of nitrogen in Annexes I and II. These reduction targets are to be reviewed by the Commission in 1994 (Art. 3(4)). By Art. 4, Member States must take appropriate measures to ensure that all licences for the construction or operation of new plant contain conditions relating to compliance with the emission limit values fixed in Annexes III to VII in respect of sulphur dioxide, oxides of nitrogen and dust. By Art. 10, waste gases from combustion plants must be discharged "in controlled fashion by means of a stack" and the competent authorities shall in particular ensure that the stack height is calculated in such a way as to safeguard health and the environment. By Art. 13, Member States must take the necessary measures to ensure monitoring of emissions in accordance with Annex IX: the methods and equipment used must correspond to "the best industrial measurement technology." The programmes drawn up in accordance with Art. 3(1) must be notified to the Commission not later than December 31, 1990 (Art. 16) and the relevant laws and provisions necessary to comply with the Directive must be in force no later than June 30, 1990.

(c) *Directive 76/464/EEC on pollution caused by dangerous substances discharged into the aquatic environment of the Community* (O.J. L129/32, May 4, 1976) as amended by Directive 91/692 on standardising and rationalising reports on the implementation of certain Directives relating to the environment (O.J. L337/48, December 31, 1991). This Directive applies to inland territorial, coastal and ground waters and by Art. 2 requires Member States to take the appropriate steps: (a) to eliminate pollution of such waters by dangerous substances in the families and groups of substances in List I of the Annex; and (b) to reduce pollution of such waters by the dangerous substances in the families and groups of List II of the Annex. The Annex contains the two lists.

List I ("the Black List") contains substances, families and groups selected mainly on the basis of their toxicity, persistence or bio-accumulation, with the exception of those that are biologically harmless or are "rapidly converted" into substances that are biologically harmless. List II ("the Grey List") is composed of two main classes of substance, namely: (a) substances within List I for which the limit values have not yet been determined under the Directive; and (b) certain listed substances and categories of substance, and which, in the case of both (a) and (b), have a deleterious effect on the aquatic environment which can, however, "be confined to a given area and which depend on the characteristics and location of the water into which they are discharged". All discharges "liable to contain" List I substances require prior authorisation laying down emission standards; where necessary to implement the Directive, emission standards must also be set for discharges to sewer (Art. 3). These emission standards must, by Art. 5, determine the permissible maximum concentration of the substances in question and the maximum permissible quantity over time. Articles 5(3) and (4) state unequivocally that authorisation for the discharge shall be refused where it appears that the discharge is unable to comply with such standards and that if the standards are not in fact complied with, appropriate steps must be taken to ensure that the discharge is prohibited. Under Art. 6 the Council, on a proposal from the Commission, shall lay down limit values for the various substances, which domestic emission standards must not exceed. Where appropriate, by Art. 6(1), limit values applicable to industrial effluents shall be established "according to sector and type of product".

Discharges liable to contain List II substances also require prior authorisation, with emission standards laid down (Art. 7(2)). Advice as to implementation of the Directive is contained in DoE Circ. 7/89 (W.O. 16/89): *Water and the Environment.* This points out that particular substances are, in the terms of the Directive, not confirmed as warranting List I methods of control until a "daughter" directive setting the limit values has been agreed, and that progress to agreeing such directives has been slow. It also points out that by Art. 6(3) the relevant limit values do not apply where a member state can prove to the Commission that quality objectives established by the Council under Art. 6(2) "are being met and continuously maintained throughout the area which might be affected by the discharges". The Government intends to make use of this provision "wherever possible" (para. 10). Where there are cases where exceptionally the appropriate quality objective cannot initially be met, "competent authorities may need to apply the limit value approach until such time as the quality objectives can be achieved" (para. 14). In relation to discharges to sewer, the Circular interprets the Directive as requiring that all discharges of List I substances to sewer must be controlled by authorisation, with specific emission standards, where these are likely to lead to or contribute towards any appreciable effect in the ultimate receiving waters (para. 16). Paragraphs 17 and 18 explain how the quality objective and limit value approaches apply to such discharges.

(d) *Directive 86/280/EEC on limit values and quality objectives for discharges of certain dangerous substances included in List I of the Annex to Directive 76/464/EEC* (O.J. L181/16, June 12, 1986) as amended by Directive 91/692 (O.J. L377/48, December 31, 1991), Directive 88/347 (O.J. L148/35, June 25, 1988) and Directive 90/415 (O.J. L213/3, August 9, 1990). This Directive lays down limit values and quality objectives for specified families or groups of substances (carbon tetrachloride, DDT and pentachlorophenol) in respect of discharges from industrial plant handling those substances. By Art. 3(4), Member States may grant authorisations for "new plants" only if those plants apply "the standards corresponding to the best technical means available when that is necessary for the elimination of pollution in accordance with Art. 2 of Directive 76/464/EEC or for the prevention of distortions of competition". "New plants" means: (a) plant becoming operational later than 12 months after notification of the Directive; and (b) existing industrial plant, whose capacity for handling the relevant substances is "substantially increased" after that date. This is interpreted by the UK government as an overall increase of 20 per cent or more in handling capacity for that substance (Circ. 7/89, para. 22).

It can be seen that many of the provisions of Pt. I of the Act are framed with a view to complying with the requirements of these and other Directives, and that those provisions will need to be read in the light of applicable E.C. law.

Increasingly, it may also be necessary to utilise Pt. I to implement wider international obligations under Conventions relating to, for example, the emission of greenhouse gases and ozone-depleting substances and the protection of marine ecosystems. The work of UNEP and the UN Conference on Environment and Development in Rio de Janeiro in 1992 is important, since one of the achievements of the Conference was to secure agreement to a convention on climate change. Other important areas of international co-operation are the 1985 Vienna Convention and 1987 Montreal Protocol on consumption and production of chlorofluorocarbons, the 1979 Geneva Convention on Long Range Transboundary Air Pollution and the 1988 Sofia No_x Protocol made thereunder, and the four North Sea Conferences.

Proposal for a Directive on Integrated Pollution Prevention and Control (IPPC)
The Commission proposal for a Council directive on IPPC (COM (93) 423 final) was submitted on September 30, 1993 (O.J. No. C311/6, 17.11.93). An amended proposal was subsequently published as COM(95)88 final (L.J. No. C165/9, 1.7.95), but by then the Environment Council had reached political agreement on a yet later text at its June 1995 meeting. The common position was published in March 1996 ((EC) No. 9/96, OJ C87/8, 25.3.96). The purpose of the proposed Directive is to provide procedures to prevent, wherever practicable, or to minimise, emissions from industrial installations within the Community.

The proposal has significant similarities to the United Kingdom system of IPC, involving as it does (in the common position text) an integrated permit regime based on a Best Available Techniques (BAT) concept similar to BATNEEC. However, one article comparing the draft with the existing IPC regime suggests that IPPC will cover perhaps 5,000 processes which at present are not governed by IPC, including intensive livestock units and food and drink plants and several hundred manufacturing processes currently governed by LAPC (*ENDS Report* [1995] 248, pp. 35–37).

Article 7 of the proposal, in order to facilitate an integrated approach, requires the Member State to take the measures necessary, where there is no single competent authority, to ensure the full co-ordination of the licensing procedure in respect of each category of installation. This leaves open the option of implementing IPC where appropriate through modifications to LAPC, rather than by transferring IPPC regulated processes from LAPC to IPC. Emissions other than to air, however, would then have to be regulated by local authorities in England and Wales. The draft requires Member States to ensure that no existing installation is operated later than eight years after their implementation of the Directive (which in turn must be completed within three years of its publication), without a permit issued in accordance with the Directive. The permit must include all necessary measures to achieve a high level of protection for the environment as a whole, and must include emission limit values or equivalent parameters or technical measures for pollutants, in particular those listed in Annex III, that are likely to be emitted in significant quantities (Art. 9). Emission limit values and equivalent parameters are to be based on BAT—that is, techniques signifying the "most effective and advanced stage in the development of activities and their methods of operation which indicate the practical suitability of particular techniques for providing in principle the basis for emission limit values designed to prevent and, where that is not practicable, generally to reduce emissions and the impact on the environment as a whole."Article 10 deals with the relationship between BAT and environmental quality standards: stricter conditions than those achievable by the use of BAT must be set where this is necessary to ensure that environmental quality standards are not breached.

By proposed Article 9.6, the permit must also govern "conditions other than normal operating conditions", including "definitive cessation of operations," if there is a risk to the environment. This would require a significant extension of the United Kingdom system of IPC to cover conditions as to decommissioning.

Annex I of the Proposal contains the categories of activities which it is proposed to prescribe for IPPC. Articles 18 and 20, and Annex II deal with the relationship between the proposed new system and the existing Community legislation dealing with specific substances or industry sectors. Annex III contains an indicative list of the most important polluting substances to be taken into account, where relevant, for fixing emission limit values. Annex IV lists the considerations to be taken in account in selecting best available techniques, "bearing in mind the likely costs and benefits and the principles of precaution and prevention".

Prescribed processes and prescribed substances
Processes may be prescribed for control by regulations, as may substances the release of which is subject to control (s.2). The Secretary of State prescribed two lists of processes, the "A list" being those subject to central control (IPC) and the "B list" being those subject to local control under LAPC. The lists were discussed in the consultative papers referred to above and issued for consultation in the context of the specific legislation in April 1990. The two lists are found in Sched. 1 to the Environmental Protection (Prescribed Processes and Substances) Regulations 1991 (S.I. 1991 No. 472) (see Appendix 1) as amended on several occasions to reflect either

experience in operating the regime or the Government's deregulation initiative. As well as prescribing the processes for central or local control, the regulations contain provision as to exceptions (reg. 4), rules for the interpretation of the prescriptive descriptions (Sched. 2), the date from which authorisation is required for the various processes (Sched. 3), and prescribed substances for release into the air, water and land (Scheds. 4–6). Sched. 1 to the regulations divides processes into six main industry sectors as follows:

Chapter 1: Fuel Production Processes, Combustion Processes (including power generation) and Associated Processes
Chapter 2: Metal Production and Processing
Chapter 3: Mineral Industries
Chapter 4: The Chemical Industry
Chapter 5: Waste Disposal and Recycling
Chapter 6: Other Industries.

Each Chapter is subdivided into main categories of process. For example, Chapter 3 (Mineral Industries) is divided into the following:

3.1   Cement and lime manufacture and associated processes
3.2   Processes involving asbestos
3.3   Other mineral fibres
3.4   Other mineral processes
3.5   Glass manufacture and production
3.6   Ceramic production.

Each sub-category is further divided into detailed descriptions of actual processes or operations falling within two sections: Pt. A (IPC) or Pt. B (LAPC). For example, category 3.1 (cement and lime manufacture) is divided into the following:

Part A (a) making cement clinker;
　　　　(b) grinding cement clinker;
　　　　(c) various named processes associated with (a) and (b);
　　　　(d) heating of calcium carbonate or calcium magnesium carbonate for the purpose of making lime;
　　　　(e) the slaking of lime when related to a process in (d).

Part B (a) storing cement in bulk prior to further transportation in bulk;
　　　　(b) various processes involving blending, loading and bagging of cement, the batching of ready mixed concrete and the manufacture of concrete blocks and cement products;
　　　　(c) the slaking of lime for the purpose of making calcium hydroxide.

Quite clearly, disputes may arise as to the category or categories into which a particular plant falls. Sched. 2 of the 1991 Regulations gives nine rules of interpretation, and indeed some of the sections of Sched. 1 themselves make specific provision to resolve such questions. Of particular importance are Rules 3 and 4 of Sched. 2.

Rule 3
This states that where processes falling within two or more descriptions set out in the same section of Sched. 1 under the heading "Pt. A" or the heading "Pt. B" are carried on by the same person at the same location those processes are to be treated as a single process falling within the description within which the principal process so carried on falls.

Rule 4
This states that where a process falls within two or more descriptions, the process shall be regarded as falling only within the description which fits it most aptly, but (a) if the possible descriptions include both Pt. A and Pt. B processes, no regard shall be had to Pt. B; and (b) special rules apply for determining the category of process to be applied in the case of Chapter 4 (the chemical industry).
　　Regulation 4 of the regulations contains excepting provisions which in particular provide that a process shall not be taken to fall within Sched. 1 if it *cannot* result:
　　　　(a) in the release to air of prescribed substances (or there is no likelihood that it will result in such releases except in a quantity "so trivial that it cannot result in any harm");
　　　　(b) in the release into water of prescribed substances except in a concentration which is greater than the "background concentration" as defined in reg. 4(7); and
　　　　(c) in the release into land of any prescribed substance.

The Government's original criteria for processes to be scheduled for IPC control are set out at para. 27 of the Consultation Paper of July 1988, *Integrated Pollution Control*. They are: (a) processes in Air Pollution Control List "A" (see above); (b) processes discharging "Red List" substances to water and sewers in significant quantities (see above); and (c) processes generating large amount of special wastes (see Pt. II of the Act). The long term aim is to evolve a single coherent set of criteria related to potential for harm of the substances discharged, judged on the basis of toxicity, persistence, difficulty of control and potential for cross-media transfers.

The substances prescribed in Scheds. 4–6 of the regulations largely follow the previous proposals in the case of air and water. The substances prescribed for air are those set out in the 1984 Air Framework Directive 84/360/EEC with the addition of a few others. For water, the prescribed substances follow the "Red List" (see above). In the case of substances prescribed for release to land, the expectation was that criteria based on special waste generally would be adopted. However, the list adopted is, in the event, much narrower than the list of special wastes and appears to be based on substances which are likely to be particularly hazardous if disposed of directly to landfill (see ENDS report 190, November 1990, pp. 31–32).

It will be seen that the systems involve a considerable number of processes and substances coming for the first time under prior control, though some were already controlled by HMIP or HMIPI for air quality purposes under s.5 of the Health and Safety at Work, etc. Act 1974 and the Health and Safety (Emissions in the Atmosphere) Regulations 1983 (S.I. 1983 No. 943).

Functions of the Secretary of State
Apart from prescribing the processes and substances to be controlled, the Secretary of State has considerable powers in relation to the IPC and LAPC systems. His functions include:
  (1) establishing standards, objectives or requirements (s.3(1));
  (2) making regulations to establish quantitative and qualitative standard limits on substances which may be released (s.3(2)(a));
  (3) prescribing standard requirements for the measurement or analysis of prescribed substances, or their release (s.3(2)(b));
  (4) prescribing standards or requirements as to any aspect of a prescribed process (s.3(2)(c));
  (5) establishing quality objectives or standards for any environmental medium in relation to substances to be released into that medium (s.3(4));
  (6) making plans to establish limits for the total amount of substances to be released into the environment in the UK or any area of the UK, for allocating quotas as to the release of substances to persons carrying on processes where such limits are prescribed, and using such limits so as to reduce pollution progressively and to achieve progressive improvements in quality objectives and standards (s.3(5));
  (7) directing that functions being exercised by local authorities should be exercised instead by the Environment Agency (s.4(4); not Scotland);
  (8) giving directions specifying conditions which are or are not to be included in authorisations (s.7(3));
  (9) issuing guidance as to the techniques and environmental options that are appropriate for any description of prescribed process (s.7(11));
  (10) making with the approval of the Treasury, schemes as to fees payable for applications for authorisations and variations, and charges in respect of the subsistence of authorisations in relation to LAPC only (s.8(2); not Scotland);
  (11) giving directions as to the exercise of variation powers, and what constitutes a "substantial change" in a prescribed process for the purpose of those powers (s.10(6) and (7));
  (12) giving directions as to the exercise of revocation powers (s.12(5));
  (13) giving directions as to the exercise of enforcement powers (s.13(3));
  (14) giving directions as to the exercise of powers relating to prohibition notices (s.14(4));
  (15) determining appeals or directing determination by an appointed person (s.15);
  (16) making regulations as to appeals (s.15(10));
  (17) requiring information from enforcing authorities and any other persons (s.19);
  (18) making regulations as to public registers of information to be maintained by the enforcing authorities (s.20(1));
  (19) giving directions as to the removal of information from registers (s.20(6));
  (20) determining whether the inclusion of information in a register would be contrary to national security and giving directions accordingly (s.21);

(21) determining appeals on whether information is commercially confidential so as not to require inclusion on the register, making regulations as to such appeals, and giving directions as to commercially confidential information which nonetheless should be included within the register on grounds of public interest (s.22);

(22) approval as to exercise of powers by the Environment Agency and SEPA to remedy harm caused by offences (s.27(2)).

Functions of the Agency, SEPA and local authorities
The enforcing authorities' role can be thought of as twofold: on the one hand, they must determine applications under Pt. I for the grant (s.6) or variation (s.11) of authorisations, and on the other hand, they must enforce the regimes and ensure that authorisations contain the appropriate conditions (s.7) and that no prescribed process is operated without an authorisation or in breach of authorisation conditions (s.6). To this latter, enforcement end, they have a wide range of enforcement powers at their disposal, both within Pt. I and by virtue of the 1995 Act. It is emphasised that the 1995 Act powers of entry, etc., do not precisely mirror, but in general are at least as wide as, the powers previously contained in Pt. I itself as ss.17 and 18. It should be noted that some of the Pt. I offence provisions formerly contained in s.23 have been replaced by provisions in s.110 of the 1995 Act and the two sections should accordingly be read together. The enforcement powers are as follows:

1. Variation of authorisation: s.10.
2. Revocation of authorisation: s.12.
3. Enforcement notices: s.13.
4. Prohibition notices: s.14.
5. Powers of entry, examination and investigation: 1995 Act, s.108.
6. Powers of seizure: 1995 Act, s.109.
7. Powers to require information: s.19.
8. Power to take civil proceedings in the High Court or, in Scotland, in the appropriate sheriff court or the Court of Session, to secure compliance with enforcement or prohibition notices: s.24.
9. (Arguably), power to take civil proceedings in other cases—for example where a process is operated without an authorisation: 1995 Act, s.37(1).
10. Power to take steps to remedy harm and recover the cost of such steps from the offender: s.27.

Additionally, where a person is convicted of carrying on a prescribed process without authorisation or of breaching authorisation conditions or an enforcement or prohibition notice, the court may order the offender to take steps to remedy matters which appear to the court to be within his power to remedy (s.26).

Authorisations, conditions and BATNEEC
Subject to transitional provisions made by regulations, authorisation is required to carry on a prescribed process after the date prescribed in the regulations (s.6(1)). The authorisation must contain such specific conditions as the enforcing authority considers appropriate for achieving certain stated objectives (s.7(1)(a)) and may contain such other conditions as appear to the enforcing authority to be appropriate (s.7(1)(c)). All authorisations will also be subject to a general condition as to the use of best available techniques not entailing excessive cost to minimise pollution (s.7(4)). These provisions are considered more fully in the relevant annotations, but the importance of the phrase "best available techniques not entailing excessive cost" (BATNEEC) should be noted. This phrase clearly requires more than simply the use of certain technology or equipment: it includes also adequate personnel and premises (s.7(10)).

Non-statutory guidance on the meaning of BATNEEC has been set out in the DoE's *Integrated Pollution Control: A Practical Guide* (1993, HMSO). In Scotland materially identical non-statutory guidance on the meaning of BATNEEC may be found in the Scottish Office Environment Department & Association of Directors and River Inspectors of Scotland's *Environmental Protection Act 1990—Part 1: A Practical Guide—Central Control* (1992, Scottish Office). The Secretary of State has also issued guidance on BATNEEC for LAPC: *GG1(91)—Introduction to Part I of the Act* which is discussed further in the General Note to s.7. This guidance applies both north and south of the border.

IPC and LAPC Guidance
Published guidance is issued to inspectors (now the Environment Agency/SEPA) and local authorities (or, in Scotland, SEPA) as to the application of IPC and LAPC for the various classes of process: this includes reference to BATNEEC. In considering the implications of any specific guidance it is important to bear in mind whether it is statutory or non-statutory in effect (see further below where the more important of the different kinds of guidance are discussed).

Since there is no statutory obligation on the Secretary of State to produce guidance for the purposes of s.7(11), equally he is under no duty to revise such guidance. However, the s.6(6) duty on enforcing authorities to review authorisations at least every four years means in practice that guidance is itself subjected to a review of that frequency, in order to provide a basis for consistency of review: thus, for processes for which authorisation applications had to be made in 1991, in general guidance was overhauled and reissued in 1995.

IPC Guidance
There are three main sources of guidance to inspectors for IPC. All relate only to England and Wales, being (originally) guidance from the Chief Inspector of HMIP to his inspectors. For the same reason, none constitute statutory guidance for the purposes of s.7(11). Environment Agency inspectors can be expected to continue in practice to have regard to the Chief Inspector's guidance until it is superseded. Although prepared for England and Wales, these guidance notes provide an important source of guidance in Scotland given that no specific Scottish guidance has been issued to date. The Scottish Office Environment Department & Association of Directors and River Inspectors of Scotland's *Environmental Protection Act 1990—Part 1: A Practical Guide—Central Control* (1992, Scottish Office) indicates that the enforcing authorities (now SEPA) will take note of the contents of the English and Welsh guidance but may also produce different or alternative guidance (para. 6.18).

The first such source of guidance was the sector-specific IPR Notes 1–5. Building on these came IPR Notes for each category of regulated process (revision of which carries not an IPR but a Series 2 (S2) reference). Finally there is the series of TG Notes as technical guidance. These, in so far as they relate to emissions to air, are commended by the DoE to LAPC enforcing authorities as potentially valuable. *Integrated Pollution Control: A Practical Guide* (1993, HMSO) and its Scottish equivalent, *Environmental Protection Act 1990—Part 1: A Practical Guide—Central Control* (1992, Scottish Office), should also be noted, as should DoE publications like *A Guide to Risk Assessment and Risk Management for Environmental Protection* (1995, HMSO).

IPR 1–5
The first step towards the provision of IPC guidance was the issue of five Chief Inspector's Guidance to Inspectors notes IPR 1–IPR 5 by HMIP. These cover the main industry sectors as follows:
 IPR 1. Fuel and Power Industry Sector
 IPR 2. Metal Industry Sector
 IPR 3. Mineral Industry Sector
 IPR 4. Chemical Industry Sector
 IPR 5. Waste Disposal Industry Sector
All five notes follow a common format of: (a) an introductory section; (b) details of the scheduled processes within the sector; (c) a list of relevant E.C. Directives and other international guidance and obligations; (d) further details of processes with reasons for scheduling, likely prescribed substances and major substances requiring control, and levels of release regarded as achievable with appropriate techniques under normal conditions; (e) details of available abatement technologies and techniques; and (f) emission sampling and monitoring.

Process-specific Guidance—IPR 1/1 onwards
Based upon this general guidance for industry sectors, detailed process guidance notes for over 200 individual processes are being produced and revised over time containing information about the characteristics of the process, why it is being prescribed and the particular features to which assessment, authorisation and subsequent enforcement have to have regard. The guidance also deals with the upgrading of existing processes and is introduced well in advance of the upgrading deadline for such processes.

The Notes are intended both to provide guidance to inspectors in their functions relating to IPC authorisations, and for use by applicants and other interested parties as to the criteria against which inspectors will judge the acceptability of applications or variations and the types of conditions to be imposed.
Each of the original IPR Guidance Notes follows a similar format, namely:
 (a) An introduction, including a full description of the process.
 (b) Standard general provisions on applications, authorisations and consultees.
 (c) A section on release levels. This section applies the Standards in the Notes to new plant from the prescribed date. For existing plant, minimum standards are given for immediate application, based in general on existing or former statutory requirements (the series 52 revisions are set out differently and employ, instead, "achievable release levels", acknowledging BATNEEC's site-specific nature). A deadline is also given by

which existing plant is to be upgraded to achieve the standards of the Note: earlier upgrading should be achieved where possible, for example where alterations are made to the plant. Only in "exceptional circumstances" should the deadline be extended, and as part of the first application for authorisation the applicant should provide the inspector with a detailed programme for upgrading or closing the plant.

(d) A section on releases into air, giving the technical reference conditions for concentrations of substances in emissions to air and stating detailed requirements for specific emissions (such as smoke, sulphur dioxides and oxides of nitrogen). The section also deals with monitoring; most figures are given for non-continuous monitoring, and for continuous monitors, the emission limit values are complied with if 95 per cent of the half-hourly average readings for each rolling 24-hour period do not exceed the emission limit values, and the peak value does not exceed three times the limit value.

(e) A section on releases into water. Typically this states the relationship with environmental quality objectives set for controlled waters. It also states that limits may be expressed either as absolute maxima or as percentiles requiring a number of measurements over a defined period; percentile limits, where appropriate, will normally be additional to absolute limits for which compliance may be tested by a single spot sample. The total load of a pollutant discharged in a given time period should be controlled and monitored where appropriate.

(f) A section on releases into land where applicable, bearing in mind that the disposal of controlled waste off site and the consignment of special waste are the subject of separate legislation and should not be covered by the authorisation.

(g) A section dealing with what constitutes a "substantial change", to be read in conjunction with s.10(7) of the EPA 1990 and with the DoE publication: *Integrated Pollution Control—A Practical Guide* (see Part F). Examples are given of substantial changes, contrasted with examples of changes that are not substantial but which will require a variation of the authorisation conditions.

(h) Annex 1, giving basic information on the nature of the prescribed processes covered by the Note currently employed in England and Wales. In some cases the description will be relatively simple, giving the characteristics of the process and noting the environmental problems which may arise. In other cases the description may be complex, especially where several separate types of process are covered.

(i) Annex 2, listing the prescribed substances for release to air, water and land. Those listed are the substances most likely to be present in releases and of principal concern; the Notes point out that it is for the applicant to identify all releases of prescribed substances.

(j) Annex 3, giving the required techniques for pollution abatement: these deal with materials handling generally, and with releases to the three environmental media.

(k) Annex 4 on compliance monitoring: the term including sampling, analysis and testing as well as periodic and continuous monitoring. Again, releases to the three media are dealt with separately, and there are sections on quality assurance and general monitoring requirements. For example, preference should be given, where available, to analytical methods published by the British Standards Institute and related committees, *e.g.* The Standing Committee of Analysis.

(l) Annex 5 on "additional requirements", a number of which are standard form (for example, requiring use of properly qualified staff, the provision of process and waste flow diagrams and commissioning or other trials, and requiring a generally high standard of housekeeping). In some cases, more specific requirements will be added to this section, for example relating to water cooling towers or storage tanks.

TECHNICAL GUIDANCE NOTES

HMIP has issued a series of Technical Guidance Notes (TGNs) to Inspectors; again, these are non-statutory in effect:

TGN A1   Guidance on Effective Flaming in the Gas, Petroleum, Petrochemical and Associated Industries (1993) ISBN 0-11-752916-8

TGN A2   Pollution Abatement Technology for the Reduction of Solvent Vapour Emissions (1994) ISBN 0-11-752925-7

TGN A3   Pollution Abatement Technology for Particulate and Trace Gas Removal (1994) ISBN 0-11-752983-4

TGN M1   Sampling Facility Requirements for the Monitoring of Particulates in Gaseous Releases to the Atmosphere (1993) ISBN 0-11-752777-7

TGN M2   Monitoring Emissions of Pollutants at Source (1994) ISBN 0-11-752922-2

TGN M3   Standards for IPC Monitoring: Pt. I—Standards organisations and the measurement infrastructure (1995) ISBN 0-11-753133-2
TGN M4   Standards for IPC Monitoring: Pt. II—Standards in support of IPC monitoring (1995) ISBN 0-11-753134-0
TGN D1   Guidelines on Discharge Stack Heights for Polluting Emissions (1993) ISBN 0-11-752794-7

LIST OF IPC PROCESS GUIDANCE NOTES

The IPC Process Guidance Notes in the IPR series are listed below in numerical order. The periodic revision of the IPR series is underway, and the absent Notes in the IPR 1 sector have been replaced as indicated by the Series 2 (S2) Notes listed at the end of the list for that sector.

(i) *Fuel and Power Sector*

IPR 1/2   Combustion processes: gas turbines (1992) ISBN 0-11-752569-3
S2 1.01   Combustion processes: lage boilers and furnaces 50 MW(th) and over (1995) ISBN 0-11-753206-1 (Replaces IPR 1/1)
S2 1.03   Combustion processes: compression ignition engines 50 MW(th) and over (1995) ISBN 0-11-753166-9 (Replaces IPR 1/3)
S2 1.04   Combustion processes: waste and recovered oil burners 3 MW(th) and over (1995) ISBN 0-11-753167-7 (Replaces IPR 1/4)
S2 1.05   Combustion processes: combustion of fuel manufactured from or comprised of solid waste in appliances 3 MW(th) and over (1995) ISBN 0-11-753168-5 (Replaces IPR 1/5, IPR 1/6, IPR 1/7, and IPR 1/8)
S2 1.06   Carbonisation processes: coke manufacture (1995) ISBN 0-11-753176-6 (Replaces IPR 1/9)
S2 1.07   Carbonisation and associated processes: smokeless fuel, activated carbon and carbon black manufacture (1995) ISBN 0-11-753177-4 (Replaces IPR 1/10)
S2 1.08   Gasification processes: gasification of solid and liquid feedstocks including gasification combined cycle (1995) ISBN 0-11-753202-9 (Replaces IPR 1/11)
S2 1.09   Gasification processes: refining of natural gas (1995) ISBN 0-11-753203-7 (Replaces IPR 1/12 and 1/13)
S2 1.10   Petroleum processes: oil refining and associated processes (1995) ISBN 0-11-753204-5 (Replaces 1/14 and 1/15)
S2 1.11   Petroleum processes: on-shore oil production (1995) ISBN 0-11-753205-3 (Replaces IPR 1/16)
S2 1.12   Combustion processes: reheat and heat treatment furnaces 50 MW(th) and over (1995) ISBN 0-11-753178-2 (Replaces IPR 1/17)

(ii) *Metals Sector*

IPR 2/1   Iron and steel making processes: integrated iron and steel works (1994) ISBN 0-11-752961-3
IPR 2/2   Ferrous foundry processes (1994) ISBN 0-11-752962-1
IPR 2/3   Processes for electric arc steelmaking, secondary steelmaking and special alloy production (1994) ISBN 0-11-752963-X
IPR 2/4   Processes for the production of zinc and zinc alloys (1994) ISBN 0-11-753024-7
IPR 2/5   Processes for the production of lead and lead alloys (1994) ISBN 0-11-753025-5
IPR 2/6   Processes for the production of refractory metals (1994) ISBN 0-11-753026-3
IPR 2/7   Processes for the production, melting and recovery of cadmium, mercury and their alloys (1994) ISBN 0-11-753027-1
IPR 2/8   Processes for the production of aluminium (1994) ISBN 0-11-753028-X
IPR 2/9   Processes for the production of copper and copper alloys (1994) ISBN 0-11-753029-8
IPR 2/10 Processes for the production of precious metals and platinum group metals (1994) ISBN 0-11-753030-1
IPR 2/11 The extraction of nickel by the carbonyl process and the production of cobalt and nickel alloys (1994) ISBN 0-11-753031-X
IPR 2/12 Tin and bismuth processes (1994) ISBN 0-11-753038-8

(iii) *Mineral Industry Sector*

IPR 3/1   Cement manufacture and associated processes (1992) ISBN 0-11-752681-9
IPR 3/2   Lime manufacture and associated processes (1992) ISBN 0-11-752682-7
IPR 3/3   Processes involving asbestos (1992) ISBN 0-11-752683-5
IPR 3/4   Glass fibres and non-asbestos mineral fibres (1992) ISBN 0-11-752684-3

IPR 3/5 Glass manufacture and production, glass frit and enamel frit (1992) ISBN 0-11-752685-1

IPR 3/6 Ceramic processes (1992) ISBN 0-11-752686-X

(iv) *Petrochemical and Pharmaceutical Industries Sector*

IPR 4/1 Petrochemical processes (1993) ISBN 0-11-752738-6

IPR 4/2 Processes for the production and use of amines, nitriles, isocyanates and pyridines (1993) ISBN 0-11-752739-4

IPR 4/3 Processes for the production or use of acetylene, aldehydes etc. (1993) ISBN 0-11-752740-8

IPR 4/4 Processes for the production or use of organic sulphur compounds, and production, use or recovery of carbon disulphide (1993) ISBN 0-11-752741-6

IPR 4/5 Batch manufacture of organic chemicals in multipurpose plant (1993) ISBN 0-11-752742-4

IPR 4/6 Production and polymerisation of organic monomers (1993) ISBN 0-11-752743-2

IPR 4/7 Processes for the manufacture of organo-metallic compounds (1993) ISBN 0-11-752744-0

IPR 4/8 Pesticide processes (1993) ISBN 0-11-752745-9

IPR 4/9 Pharmaceutical processes (1993) ISBN 0-11-752746-7

IPR 4/10 Processes for the manufacture, use or release of oxides of sulphur and the manufacture, recovery, condensation or distillation of sulphuric acid or oleum (1993) ISBN 0-11-752833-1

IPR 4/11 Processes for the manufacture or recovery of nitric acid and processes involving the manufacture or release of acid-forming oxides of nitrogen (1993) ISBN 0-11-752834-X

IPR 4/12 Processes for the sulphonation or nitration of organic chemicals (1993) ISBN 0-11-752835-8

IPR 4/13 Processes for the manufacture of, or which use or release halogens, mixed halogen compounds or oxohalocompounds (1993) ISBN 0-11-752836-6

IPR 4/14 Processes for the manufacture of, or which use or release hydrogen halides or any of their acids (1993) ISBN 0-11-752837-4

IPR 4/15 Processes for the halogenation of organic chemicals (1993) ISBN 0-11-752838-2

IPR 4/16 Processes for the manufacture of chemical fertilizers or their conversion into granules (1993) ISBN 0-11-752839-0

IPR 4/17 Bulk storage installations (1993) ISBN 0-11-752840-4

IPR 4/18 Processes for the manufacture of ammonia (1993) ISBN 0-11-752904-4

IPR 4/19 Processes involving the use, release or recovery of ammonia (1993) ISBN 0-11-752905-2

IPR 4/20 The production of, and the use of, in any process for the manufacture of a chemical, phosphorus and any oxide, hydride or halide of phosphorus (1993) ISBN 0-11-752906-0

IPR 4/21 Processes involving the manufacture, use or release of hydrogen cyanide or hydrogen sulphide (1993) ISBN 0-11-752907-9

IPR 4/22 Processes involving the use of release of antimony, arsenic, beryllium, gallium, indium, lead, palladium, platinum, selenium, tellurium, thallium or their compounds (1993) ISBN 0-11-752908-7

IPR 4/23 Processes involving the use or release of cadmium or any compound of cadmium (1993) ISBN 0-11-752909-5

IPR 4/24 Processes involving the use or release of mercury or any compound of mercury (1993) ISBN 0-11-752910-9

IPR 4/25 Processes for the production of compounds of chromium, magnesium, nickel and zinc (1993) ISBN 0-11-752911-7

(v) *Waste Disposal and Recycling Sector*

IPR 5/1 Merchant and in-house chemical waste incineration (1992) ISBN 0-11-752653-3

IPR 5/2 Chemical waste incineration (1992) ISBN 0-11-752652-5

IPR 5/3 Municipal waste incineration (1992) ISBN 0-11-752649-5

IPR 5/4 Animal carcass incineration (1992) ISBN 0-11-752654-1

IPR 5/5 Burning out of metal containers (1992) ISBN 0-11-752651-7

IPR 5/6 Making solid fuel from waste (1992) ISBN 0-11-752647-9

IPR 5/7 Cleaning and regeneration of activated carbon (1992) ISBN 0-11-752655-X

IPR 5/8 Recovery of organic solvents by distillation (1992) ISBN 0-11-752645-2

IPR 5/9 Regeneration of ion exchange resins (1992) ISBN 0-11-752650-9

IPR 5/10 Recovery of oil by distillation (1992) ISBN 0-11-752648-7
IPR 5/11 Sewage sludge incineration (1992) ISBN 0-11-752646-0

(vi) *Other Industries*

IPR 6/1 The application or removal of tributyltin or triphenyltin coatings at shipyards or boatyards (1995) ISBN 0-11-753079-4
IPR 6/2 Tar and bitumen processes (1995) ISBN 0-11-753080-8
IPR 6/3 Timber preservation processes (1995) ISBN 0-11-753081-6
IPR 6/4 Di-isocyanate manufacture (1995) ISBN 0-11-753082-4
IPR 6/5 Toluene di-isocyanate use and flame bonding of polyurethanes (1995) ISBN 0-11-753083-2
IPR 6/6 Textile treatment processes (1995) ISBN 0-11-753084-0
IPR 6/7 Processing of animal hides and skins (1995) ISBN 0-11-753085-9
IPR 6/8 The making of paper pulp by chemical methods (1995) ISBN 0-11-753105-7
IPR 6/9 Paper making and related processes including mechanical pulping, recycling fibre and de-inking (1995) ISBN 0-11-753106-5

SECRETARY OF STATE'S GUIDANCE ON PROCESSES PRESCRIBED FOR LOCAL AIR POLLUTION CONTROL

GENERAL NOTE
The Secretary of State has issued a range of Guidance Notes on "Part B" processes prescribed for local control by local authorities or, in Scotland, SEPA under Pt. I. The DoE produces updated briefing notes on LAPC which include lists of guidance and can be found on the Internet at the following address: http://www.open.gov.uk./doe/doehome.html. These notes fall into four categories: PG, GG, UG and AQ Notes.

1. PROCESS GUIDANCE (PG) NOTES—First and most important are PG Notes, which constitute statutory guidance to enforcing authorities for the purposes of s.7(11). The numbered PG Notes have in some cases been amended by unnumbered PG Notes. There are also unnumbered PG Notes for several categories of process which have been transferred from IPC to LAPC—these are extremely brief and refer the reader to the relevant parts of the relevant Chief Inspector's Guidance Note dating from before the transfer of the process.

PG Notes relate to specific processes and contain guidance on the techniques appropriate for air pollution control. Guidance is given for both new and existing processes, together with information about any directions, limits, requirements, quality objectives or quality standards in force at the date of publication. These notes are significantly less complex than those for processes prescribed for IPC with less detailed emission levels given and with a certain amount of common material, for example on "general operations".

Many process guidance notes contain requirements as to:
(a) emissions free from persistent mist and fume and free from droplets;
(b) emissions free from offensive odour outside the process boundary, as perceived by the local authority or SEPA inspector;
(c) emissions free from visible smoke in normal operation;
(d) proper materials handling;
(e) chimney height and efflux velocity.
The PG Notes issued by December 1995 are listed below.

2. GENERAL GUIDANCE (GG) NOTES—There is also a series of (at present) five GG Notes, which in general do not constitute statutory guidance—GG Notes 1–3 and 5 state this expressly. GG Note 4 is silent as to its status, and arguably, since it offers interpretation of terms used in PG Notes, which *are* statutory guidance, it should itself be treated as constituting statutory guidance for the purposes of s.7(11). On the other hand, para. 2 of Guidance Note UG 1 appears to draw a statutory/non-statutory distinction between PG Notes and the 5 GG Notes taken as a whole. The five GG Notes issued to date are as follows:

GG1 (91)—Introduction to Part I of the Act: This note contains a brief introduction to the relevant provisions of the Act and provides a certain amount of guidance on issues such as the meaning of BATNEEC, the meaning of "substantial change" and handling commercially confidential information.

GG2 (91)—Authorisations: This contains guidance on the content of authorisations and on the drafting of appropriate conditions; some 72 specimen conditions are given as an Appendix.

GG3 (91)—Applications and Registers: This provides guidance on the content of applications, the procedural requirements for handling applications, and on the public registers. A suggested form of application is given.

GG4 (91)—Interpretation of Terms Used in Process Guidance Notes: This Note provides interpretation of some of the terms commonly used in Process Notes (see below) for example: "colourless"; "offensive odour"; and "continuous monitoring".

GG5 (91)—Appeals: This contains guidance on the appeals procedures set out in the Environmental Protection (Applications, Appeals and Registers) Regulations 1991 (S.I. 1991 No. 507).

3. UPGRADING GUIDANCE (UG) NOTES—One upgrading guidance note has been issued by the Secretary of State to local authorities: *UG 1 (May 1992)—Revisions/Additions to Existing Process and General Guidance Notes.* Upgrading Guidance Notes revise and add to the advice that was given in previous Guidance Notes. It is intended that such notes will be published as the need arises. In so far as the guidance or advice which UG 1 revised or supplements is statutory, then so is UG 1, but where it is revising or supplementing non-statutory advice then it is itself non-statutory.

4. ADDITIONAL GUIDANCE (AQ) NOTES—Finally, there has been a large number of guidance notes issued by the Department of the Environment in the non-statutory AQ series. These tend to be brief and to suggest approaches to problems and issues which have emerged during the application of LAPC to the processes it governs. A number of these were subsequently replicated in UG 1 (something which may be repeated for others if any further UG Notes are issued), and this may have changed the status of the guidance concerned, since in so far as such guidance in UG 1 constitutes an addition or revision to a PG Note, then it has statutory effect. AQ Notes issued by November 1995 are listed below:

AQ1 (91)	S.I. 1991 No. 472, rule 3
AQ2 (91)	treatment of timber using a schedule 5 substance
AQ3 (91)	clause 17 of PG 3/2 (91) clarification
AQ4 (91)	waste oil burners, BS 4265:1972 (PG 1/1 (91))
AQ5 (91)	registers, Rehabilitation of Offenders Act
AQ6 (91)	BPM papers for processes passing from HMIP to LAs
AQ7 (91)	meaning of "existing process"
AQ8 (91)	specimen notice for obtaining further information
AQ9 (91)	VAT on charges
AQ10 (91)	DOE Circular 3/91 reminder
AQ1(92)	notification of processes passing from HMIP to LAs
AQ2 (92)	"EPA and You"—copies of leaflet still available
AQ3 (92)	radioactive substances
AQ4 (92)	list of PG notes
AQ5 (92)	foundries—triviality
AQ6 (92)	timescale for deciding applications
AQ7 (92)	amendments to applications
AQ8 (92)	rubber processes—meaning of "if carbon black is used"
AQ9 (92)	mobile plant
AQ10 (92)	monitoring particulates from timber processes
AQ11 (92)	emission limits for particleboard fibreboard processes (PG 6/4 (91))
AQ12 (92)	meaning of "use" of organic solvents
AQ13 (92)	vegetable matter drying—triviality
AQ14 (92)	pressure delivery of bulk cement, amended clause 22 (PG 3/1 (91))
AQ15 (92)	English Nature sub office list
AQ16 (92)	queries to Local Authority Unit and Air Quality Division
AQ1 (93)	explanation for operators of rights of appeal
AQ2 (93)	holding of spares and consumables
AQ3 (93)	zinc diecasters—triviality
AQ4 (93)	transfer of authorisations under section 9
AQ5 (93)	animal by-product rendering—clarification
AQ6 (93)	HMIP technical guidance—monitoring particulates
AQ7 (93)	small coal mines—triviality
AQ8 (93)	mobile plant—statutory consultation
AQ9 (93)	variation notices—consolidation of authorisations

AQ10 (93)   HMIP technical guidance—stack heights
AQ11 (93)   stand-by cremators
AQ12 (93)   obtaining additional information
AQ13 (93)   new address and telephone for LAU
AQ14 (93)   service of notices etc.
AQ15 (93)   appeals—costs and commercial confidentiality
AQ16 (93)   sending draft authorisations to operators
AQ17 (93)   notifying HMIP of determination of authorisations
AQ18 (93)   HMIP technical guidance note D1—corrections
AQ19 (93)   training of cremator operators
AQ20 (93)   index of additional guidance

AQ1 (94)   notification of triviality
AQ2 (94)   solvent substitution in vapour degreasing equipment
AQ3 (94)   animal by-product rendering [PG 6/1 (91)]
AQ4 (94)   HMIP technical guidance note M2—monitoring
AQ5 (94)   content of public registers
AQ6 (94)   HMIP technical guidance note A2—VOC abatement
AQ7 (94)   Appeals arrangements
AQ8 (94)   Coil coating processes
AQ9 (94)   HMIP Technical Guidance Note A3
AQ10 (94)   Knackers Yards: The relationship between local authorities and the State Veterinary Service
AQ11 (94)   Waste Management Licensing Regulations 1994
AQ12 (94)   Environmental Technology Best Practice Programme
AQ13 (94)   Advice on chimney height calculations and dispersion of emissions
AQ14 (94)   LAAPC statistical returns
AQ15 (94)   Appeals
AQ16 (94)   Fluoride emissions from processes for the manufacture of heavy clay goods and refractories
AQ17 (94)   Odour measurement and control
AQ18 (94)   Recirculation of workroom air and triviality
AQ19 (94)   Processes for the surface treatment of metals etc.
AQ20 (94)   Index of additional guidance

AQ1 (95)   Monitoring of wind direction and strength for cement processes
AQ2 (95)   Delays in deciding applications and considering upgrading submissions
AQ3 (95)   Refractory materials
AQ4 (95)   Inspection frequency—basic principles
AQ5 (95)   Reviews under section 6(6) of the Act
AQ6 (95)   Information about LAAPC on the Internet
AQ7 (95)   4-year time limit for commercially confidential information and Rehabilitation of Offenders Act 1974
AQ8 (95)   Index to additional guidance issued to local authorities by DOE and Welsh Office between March 1991 and April 1995
AQ9 (95)   Guidance on implementation of the Stage 1 EC petrol vapour recovery directive
AQ10 (95)   Standards for sewage sludge incinerators
AQ11 (95)   Amendments to LAAPC made by the Environment Act 1995
AQ12 (95)   Wood combustion processes and poultry litter combustion processes
AQ13 (95)   Timber treatment processes
AQ14 (95)   HMIP technical guidance note M4
AQ15 (95)   Respraying of road vehicles
AQ16 (95)   Authorisation conditions relating to odour
AQ17 (95)   Summary of recent appeal decisions
AQ18 (95)   Commencement of amendments to LAAPC made by the Environment Act 1995
AQ19 (95)   Animal feed compounding processes
AQ20 (95)   Monitoring of processes and emissions
AQ21 (95)   Stage 1 EC Petrol Vapour Recovery Directive

LAPC PROCESS GUIDANCE NOTES

Secretary of State's PG Guidance notes without a reference number (September to December 1994):

— Odorising of natural gas and liquefied petroleum gas (refers the reader to IPC guidance note IPR 1/14)

— Bulk chemical storage installations (refers the reader to IPC guidance note IPR 4/17)
— Small lime manufacturing processes (refers the reader to IPC guidance note IPR 3/2).
— Crucible and reverberatory furnaces (amending PG 2/3)
— Investment casting and various melting processes (amending PG 2/3 and PG 2/4)
— Magnesium oxide fume emissions from ferrous industries (amending PG 2/3 and PG 2/5)
— Manganese containing non-ferrous metal alloys (amending PG 2/4 and PG 2/8)
— Magnesium and magnesium alloy processes (amending PG 2/6)
— Pulverised fuel ash loading, etc., (amending PG 3/1)
— Salt glazing of ceramics (amending PG 3/2)
— Glass frit and enamel frit processes (amending PG 3/4)
— Petroleum coke loading etc. (amending PG 3/5)
— Coating in drum manufacturing and reconditioning processes (amending PG 6/15)
— Cold set web offset printing processes (amending PG 6/16)
— Sheet fed offset lithographic printing processes (amending PG 6/16)
— Coating of metal and plastic (amending PG 6/23)
— Di-isocyanate processes (amending PG 6/29)
— Wood coating processes (amending PG 6/33)
— Road vehicle re-finishing processes using 1–2 tonnes per annum of organic solvents (amending PG 6/34)
— Respraying of road vehicles (amending PG 6/34)

Numbered PG Notes
Those PG Notes which have been amended by one or more of the unnumbered PG Notes issued between September and December 1994 are indicated with one or more asterisks accordingly. The year of publication is apparent from the numbering system: PG 1/1 (91) was published in 1991, whilst PG 6/42 (94) was published in 1994.

PG 1/1 (95)
Waste oil burners, less than 0.4MW
net rated thermal input
ISBN 0-11-753194-4

PG 1/2 (95)
Waste oil or recovered oil burners,
less than 3MW net rated thermal
input
ISBN 0-11-753195-2

PG 1/3 (95)
Boilers and furnaces, 20–50MW net
rated thermal input
ISBN 0-11-753195-2

PG 1/4 (95)
Gas turbines, 20–50MW net rated
thermal input
ISBN 0-11-753147-2

PG 1/5 (91)
Compression ignition engines, 20–
50MW net rated thermal input
ISBN 0-11-752389-5

[PG 1/6 (91), PG 1/7 (91), PG 1/8
(91) and PG 1/9 (91) have been
superseded by PG 1/12 (95)]

PG 1/10 (91)
Waste derived fuel burning processes
less than 3MW net rated thermal
input
ISBN 0-11-752594-4

PG 1/11 (92)
Reheat and heat treatment furnaces,
20–50MW net rated thermal input
ISBN 0-11-752670-3

PG 1/12 (95) [replaces PG 1/6, 1/7,
1/8 and 1/9]
Combustion of fuel manufactured
from or comprised of solid waste in
appliances between 0.4 and 3MW net
rated thermal input
ISBN 0-11-753196-0

PG 2/1 (91)
Furnaces for the extraction of non-
ferrous metal from scrap
ISBN 0-11-752398-4

PG 2/2 (91)
Hot dip galvanising processes
ISBN 0-11-752479-4

PG 2/3 (91)***
Electrical and rotary furnaces
ISBN 0-11-752476-X

PG 2/4 (91)**
Iron, steel and non-ferrous metal
foundry processes
ISBN 0-11-752478-6

PG 2/5 (91)*
Hot and cold blast cupolas
ISBN 0-11-752474-3

PG 2/6 (91)*
Aluminium and aluminium alloy
processes
ISBN 0-11-752467-0

PG 2/7 (91)
Zinc and zinc alloy processes
ISBN 0-11-752460-3

PG 2/8 (91)*
Copper and copper alloy processes
ISBN 0-11-752473-5

PG 2/9 (91)
Metal decontamination processes
ISBN 0-11-752481-6

PG 3/1 (95)
Blending, packing, loading and use of
bulk cement
ISBN 0-11-753148-0

PG 3/2 (95)
Manufacture of heavy clay goods and
refractory goods
ISBN 0-11-753197-9

PG 3/3 (95)
Glass (excluding lead glass)
manufacturing processes
ISBN 0-11-753149-9

PG 3/4 (95)
Lead glass manufacturing processes
ISBN 0-11-753150-2

PG 3/5 (91)*
Coal, coke and coal product
processes
ISBN 0-11-752469-7

PG 3/6 (95)
Processes for the polishing or etching
of glass or glass products using
hydrofluoric acid
ISBN 0-11-753151-0

PG 3/7 (91)
Exfoliation of vermiculite and expan-
sion of perlite
ISBN 0-11-752459-X

PG 3/8 (91)
Quarry processes including roadstone
plants, and the size reduction of
bricks, tiles and concrete
ISBN 0-11-752463-8

PG 3/9 (91)
Sand drying and cooling
ISBN 0-11-752474-7

PG 3/10 (91)
China and ball clay
ISBN 0-11-752470-0

PG 3/11 (91)
Spray drying of ceramic materials
ISBN 0-11-752468-9

PG 3/12 (91)
Plaster processes
ISBN 0-11-752458-1

PG 3/13 (91)
Asbestos processes
ISBN 0-11-752482-4

PG 3/14 (91)
Lime slaking processes
ISBN 0-11-752480-8

PG 4/1 (94)
Processes for the surface treatment of
metals
ISBN 0-11-753072-7

PG 5/1 (95)
Clinical waste incineration processes
under 1 tonne an hour
ISBN 0-11-753152-9

PG 5/2 (95)
Crematoria
ISBN 0-11-753153-7

PG 5/3 (95)
Animal carcase incineration
processes under 1 tonne an hour
ISBN 0-11-753154-5

PG 5/4 (95)
General waste incineration processes
under 1 tonne an hour
ISBN 0-11-753155-3

PG 5/5 (1991)
Sewage sludge incineration processes
under 1 tonne an hour
ISBN 0-11-752641-1

PG 6/1 (91)
Animal by-product rendering
ISBN 0-11-752461-1

PG 6/2 (95)
Manufacture of timber and wood
based products
ISBN 0-11-753198-7

PG 6/3 (91)*
Chemical treatment of timber and
wood based products
ISBN 0-11-752402-6

PG 6/4 (95)
Processes for the manufacture of
particleboard and fibreboard
ISBN 0-11-753156-1

PG 6/5 (91)
Maggot breeding processes
ISBN 0-11-752396-8

[PG 6/6 (91)
Related to fur breeding processes
which were removed from Pt. I
control by S.I. 1993 No. 1749]

PG 6/7 (91)
Printing and coating of metal
packaging
ISBN 0-11-752462-X

PG 6/8 (91)
Textile and fabric coating and fin-
ishing processes
ISBN 0-11-752466-2

PG 6/9 (91)
Manufacture of coating powder
ISBN 0-11-752471-9

PG 6/10 (92)
Coating manufacturing process
ISBN 0-11-752595-2

PG 6/11 (92)
Manufacture of printing ink
ISBN 0-11-752596-0

PG 6/12 (91)
Production of natural sausage cas-
ings, tripe, chitterlings and other
boiled green offal products
ISBN 0-11-752465-4

PG 6/13 (91)*
Coil coating processes
ISBN 0-11-752472-7

PG 6/14 (91)
Film coating processes
ISBN 0-11-752477-8

PG 6/15 (91)*
Coating in drum manufacturing and
reconditioning processes
ISBN 0-11-752475-1

PG 6/16 (92)**
Printworks
ISBN 0-11-752597-9

PG 6/17 (92)
Printing of flexible packaging
ISBN 0-11-752598-7

PG 6/18 (92)
Paper coating processes
ISBN 0-11-752599-5

PG 6/19 (92)
Fish meal and fish oil processes
ISBN 0-11-752600-2

PG 6/20 (92)
Paint application in vehicle
manufacturing
ISBN 0-11-752601-0

PG 6/21 (92)
Hide and skin processes
ISBN 0-11-752602-9

PG 6/22 (92)
Leather finishing processes
ISBN 0-11-752603-7

PG 6/23 (94)
Coating of metal and plastic
ISBN 0-11-752604-5

PG 6/24 (92)
Pet food manufacturing processes
ISBN 0-11-752605-3

PG 6/25 (92)
Vegetable oil extraction and fat and
oil refining processes
ISBN 0-11-752606-1

PG 6/26 (82)
Animal feed compounding processes
ISBN 0-11-752607-X

PG 6/27 (92)
Vegetable matter drying processes
ISBN 0-11-752608-8

PG 6/28 (92)
Rubber processes
ISBN 0-11-752609-6

PG 6/29 (92)*
Di-isocyanate processes
ISBN 0-11-752610-X

PG 6/30 (92)
Production of compost for
mushrooms
ISBN 0-11-752611-8

PG 6/31 (92)
Powder coating processes, including
sheradising
ISBN 0-11-752612-6

PG 6/32 (92)
Adhesive coating processes
ISBN 0-11-752613-4

PG 6/33 (92)*
Wood coating processes
ISBN 0-11-752614-2

PG 6/34 (92)**
Respraying of road vehicles
ISBN 0-11-752615-0

PG 6/35 (92)
Metal and other thermal spraying
processes
ISBN 0-11-752616-9

PG 6/36 (92)
Tobacco processing
ISBN 0-11-752617-7

PG 6/37 (92)
February 1992
Knackers yards
ISBN 0-11-752618-5

PG 6/38 (92)
Blood processing
ISBN 0-11-752619-3

PG 6/39 (92)
Primal by-product dealers
ISBN 0-11-752620-7

PG 6/40 (94)
Coating and recoating of aircraft and
aircraft components
ISBN 0-11-753040-9

PG 6/41 (94)
Coating and recoating of rail vehicles
ISBN 0-11-753041-7

PG 6/42 (94)
Bitumen and tar processes
ISBN 0-11-753042-5

Operator and Pollution Risk Appraisal
In April 1995, HMIP issued a booklet for consultation, describing a new procedure for the assessment of plant operator and pollution risks, trialled by HMIP inspectors from the beginning of April 1995. The system, Operator and Pollution Risk Appraisal (OPRA) seeks to formalise the existing process by which IPC regulatory activity and the number of visits made to each particular process are based upon an assessment of the potential risk of pollution from the process. This in the past has been based upon "a skilled and professional assessment made by the relevant inspector". A long term project, OPRA is clearly intended to be carried over into IPC regulation under the Environment Agency.

The OPRA system seeks to provide scores against seven key indicators for operator performance appraisal and seven attributes of process to result in a Pollution Hazard Appraisal (PHA). Evaluating these two elements will provide a comparative measure to enable the regulator to target its activities on those processes with greatest pollution potential. The intention is that at the end of each compliance visit to a site, the inspector will complete an assessment for using the criteria set out in the booklet, and the contents of the form will be made known to the operator at the time. The possible use of the system as a basis for charging, noted at Section 4 of the consultation booklet, is considered under *Fees and Charges* below.

Fees and charges

Fees and charges for IPC and LAPC regulation are provided for under Pt. I itself only in relation to LAPC in England and Wales (s.8). The Agency and SEPA being the enforcing authorities for IPC and, in Scotland, for LAPC, fees and charges for those regimes are determined in accordance with schemes made by the Agency/SEPA under ss.41 and 42 of the Environment Act 1995. Fees and charges are payable to the enforcing authority in accordance with a scheme made by the Secretary of State (or by the Agency/SEPA in the case of IPC and Scottish LAPC), with the approval of the Treasury (ss.8(1), (2) of the 1990 Act and ss.41(9) and 42(7) of the 1995 Act). In framing a scheme under s.8 the Secretary of State must, so far as practicable, secure that fees and charges payable are sufficient to cover the expenditure incurred by the English and Welsh local enforcing authorities in exercising their regulatory functions. In approving a scheme prepared by the Agency/SEPA under s.41 of the 1995 Act, the Secretary of State need only have regard to the desirability of securing this end (s.42(2) of the 1995 Act).

The working of this cost recovery approach is illustrated by the fact that an underestimation of regulatory costs and expenses for IPC in England and Wales in the 1991/92 financial year, and consequent failure of that year's charging scheme to fully recover costs, led to a supplementary charge for recoupment being levied on businesses whose authorisations had been granted in that year. Spread over four years, the supplementary charge added £610 per component to the subsistence charge in each of the four years (£410 in the case of processes previously regulated by HMIP under other legislation).

The relatively unsophisticated structure of fees and charges schemes to date provides only a crude approximation to the amount of regulatory time spent in connection with a given regulated process, and thus to the "polluter pays" principle (something on which the HMIP Advisory Committee commented in its Interim Report of February 13, 1995). The OPRA system developed by HMIP if implemented, may ultimately be used as a basis for the fine-tuning of charging schemes, for IPC in England and Wales at least. In addition, the Environment Act 1995 gives greater flexibility to the Agency and SEPA (although not to local authorities) than their predecessors enjoyed, to charge (outside statutory charging schemes) for work done and advice given (see in particular ss.37(7) and 43 of the 1995 Act). In the context of Pt. I, this is likely to result in a fee being charged, in some cases at least, for the sometimes considerable amount of advice and assistance given by the Agency/SEPA to applicants prior to an application for the grant or variation of an authorisation.

Information

Part I of the Act, like other parts, contains provision for the maintenance of comprehensive public registers of applications, authorisations, notices, appeals, convictions and information obtained pursuant to conditions of authorisations (s.20; amended by the 1995 Act, Sched. 22, para. 57). The important implications of the availability of such information have already been mentioned in the General Note to the Act. Only two exemptions from public registration apply: information affecting national security (s.21) and certain confidential information (s.22; amended by the 1995 Act, Sched. 22, para. 58). The provisions of the 1995 Act, ss. 51 and 113 should be noted, on the provision of information to the Secretary of State and its sharing between enforcing authorities.

Relationship with other areas of control

IPC and LAPC inevitably raises issues of duplication or overlap with other pre-existing areas of control. Examples are matters of health and safety at work, statutory nuisances, water pollution and waste disposal.

(a) *Health and Safety at Work:* No condition may be imposed in an IPC or LAPC authorisation for the purpose only of securing the health of persons at work (within the meaning of Pt. I of the Health and Safety at Work etc. Act 1974 (s.7(1)).

(b) *Deposit, disposal or recovery of controlled waste:* No condition may be attached to an authorisation so as to regulate the final disposal by deposit in or on land of controlled waste, nor shall any condition apply to such a disposal (s.28(1)). The s.28(1) requirement, for the waste regulator (now the Agency or SEPA) to be notified where a prescribed process does involve the final disposal of controlled waste by deposit in or on land, was removed by the 1995 Act.

By paragraph 2 of Schedule 4 to the Waste Management Licensing Regulations 1994 (S.I.

1994 No. 1056, see Appendix 3), and subject to certain provisos therein, an enforcing authority, the Secretary of State or a person appointed under s.15(3)(b) are required to exercise their functions under Part I, in so far as they relate to the recovery or disposal of waste, with the "relevant objectives" as defined in that Schedule.

Under s.33(3), the Secretary of State may make regulations excluding the deposit, treatment, keeping or disposal of controlled waste from control under Pt. II of the Act. In exercising this power, the Secretary of State is to have regard to the expediency of excluding cases for which adequate controls are provided otherwise than by s.33: s.33(4)(c). Thus, forms of waste disposal activity other than incineration, *e.g.* landfill, may be brought within Pt. I of the Act. This may prove important in the implementation of the proposed IPPC Directive discussed above, since certain landfilled hazardous waste recovery operations are scheduled for inclusion within that regime.

(c) *Radioactive substances:* Where activities comprised within a prescribed process are regulated both by authorisation under Pt. I and by registration or authorisation under the Radioactive Substances Act 1993, then if different obligations are imposed as respects the same matter by the relevant conditions, those conditions imposed under Pt. I are not binding (s.28(2)). Thus, the supremacy of the Radioactive Substances Act conditions is secured.

(d) *Water pollution:* The foundation of the distinction between IPC and LAPC is that the former, but not the latter, governs processes which present a significant possible impact on environmental media other than the air. There is thus no express provision for the relationship between LAPC and water protection regimes. Section 28 formerly contained provisions for consultation between the IPC enforcing authority and the water pollution regulator (the NRA in England and Wales), but there is no need for such provision now that the NRA and HMIP in England and Wales have merged. In Scotland, the Environmental Protection (Determination of Enforcing Authority etc.) (Scotland) Regulations 1992 (S.I. 1992 No. 530) made provision for consultation arrangements between HMIPI and the relevant river purification authority which similarly is no longer needed now that the functions of HMIPI and the river purification authorities have been merged in SEPA. However the Agency and SEPA arrange matters internally, they will no doubt seek to take into account the same matters as would formerly have been the subject of consultation: the need to ensure that statutory water quality objectives under the Water Resources Act 1991 or, in Scotland, the Control of Pollution Act 1974 are attained and that their water pollution control functions under the 1991 Act or, in Scotland, the 1974 Act, the Environment Act 1995 and other relevant legislation are discharged.

The Environment Act 1995 introduced a power for the Agency/SEPA to serve works notices to secure the carrying out of remedial works in circumstances of actual or likely water pollution: 1995 Act, Sched. 22, paras. 29(22) and 162, inserting ss.46A–D into the Control of Pollution Act 1974 as regards Scotland and ss.161A–D into the Water Resources Act 1991 as regards England and Wales. Those sections contain no provision comparable to that noted at (g) below in relation to contaminated land remediation notices, restricting the service of a notice where powers exist under Pt. I of this Act. This was presumably seen as unnecessary in that the water pollution regulator is now also the IPC enforcing authority and may thus act as it deems appropriate in particular circumstances.

(e) *Trade effluent:* Under Chapter III of Pt. IV of the Water Industry Act 1991, the Environment Agency (formerly the Secretary of State) exercises ultimate control over the discharge of certain types of trade effluent to sewers. The Trade Effluent (Prescribed Processes and Substances) Regulations 1989 (S.I. 1989 No. 1156) prescribe the relevant substances and processes. Schedule 15, para. 28 of the 1990 Act amended the Water Act by providing that Sched. 9 (now Chapter III of Pt. IV of the Water Industry Act 1991) shall not apply in relation to trade effluent produced or to be produced in a process prescribed for central (IPC) control under Pt. I of the 1990 Act. The definition of release into water as including releases to sewers (s.1(11)(c)) enables the Agency/SEPA to control discharges to sewers from prescribed processes by means of conditions. However, the sewer and its contents are to be disregarded in determining whether there is pollution of the environment. Thus, plant subject to IPC which discharge trade effluent to sewer will be subject to IPC conditions in relation to that discharge. They will also require consent from the sewerage undertaker under s.118 of the Water Industry Act 1991, which may include conditions as to volume, composition, temperature and other matters, as well as setting the charge to be paid.

(f) *Statutory nuisances:* In the case of statutory nuisances consisting of smoke emitted from premises, dust, steam, smell or other effluvia arising on industrial, trade or business premises, or any accumulation or deposit, a local authority may not issue summary proceedings under Pt. III of the Act without the consent of the Secretary of State, if proceedings in respect thereof might be instituted under Pt. I of the Act: s.79(10). However, under the former Scottish statutory nuisance provisions in the Public Health (Scotland) Act 1897 a local authority could serve an abatement notice on a process subject to IPC or LAPC without the consent of the Secretary of State. This gave rise to a potential for double jeopardy, the removal of which was one of the reasons advanced in the Scottish Office Environment Department's consultation paper, *The Extension of Part III of the Environmental Protection Act 1990 to Scotland: A Consultation Paper* (August 1994), for extending Part III of the 1990 Act to Scotland replacing the provisions of the 1897 Act. The 1995 Act did so: hence the position in Scotland is now identical to that south of the border. Given the breadth of the definitions of "pollution of the environment" and "harm" contained in s.1 of the Act, control under Pt. I can clearly embrace matters of public health and, indeed, activities causing offence to man's olfactory or other senses. However, noise does not appear to be governed by Pt. I (see the note to s.1(11)), and therefore the statutory nuisance regime applies in its regard. The question of the framing of authorisation conditions so as to ensure compliance with statutory nuisance legislation is considered in the General Note to s.7.

(g) *Contaminated land:* Where it appears to the enforcing authority under the contaminated land regime in Pt. IIA (either the local authority or the Environment Agency/SEPA) that the Pt. I remedial powers of the Agency/SEPA under s.27 are exercisable, then that enforcing authority may neither serve a contaminated land remediation notice, nor exercise its own Pt. IIA remediation powers; ss.78YB(1) and 78N(2). The s.27 powers are exercisable where (a) harm is caused by the carrying on of a prescribed process, either without an authorisation or in breach of authorisation conditions, or of an enforcement or prohibition notice, (b) it is possible for that harm to be remedied, and (c) the Agency/SEPA has both the Secretary of State's written approval to do so, and (if the land is not the land on which the process in question is being carried on) the permission of the occupant. If the s.27 powers are exercisable, then it is irrelevant whether they are in fact exercised.

(h) *Planning control:* There is no explicit linkage between planning control and the provisions of Pt. I of the Act. Unlike a waste management licence under Pt. II, there is no requirement that planning permission be in force before authorisation is granted under Pt. I. Clearly there is a danger that conditions attached to planning permissions or terms contained in planning agreements could conflict with the conditions of the Pt. I authorisation. The traditional approach of the Secretary of State to planning conditions is that they will be unnecessary so far as they duplicate other, more specific, areas of control, and *ultra vires* in so far as they conflict with other such controls although there have been cases where planning conditions have been upheld, notwithstanding a degree of overlap with industrial air pollution controls, on the basis that they provide better protection than the more specifically-based controls: see, *e.g.* the *Ferro-Alloys and Metals Smelter, Glossop* decision noted at [1990] 1 LMELR 175.
  In July 1994 the Government published long-awaited guidance for England and Wales on the relationship between the functions of local planning authorities and the separate statutory responsibilities exercised by local and other authorities under pollution control legislation: *PPG23: Planning and Pollution Control.* It contains specific sections dealing with development plans, development control considerations, contaminated land and waste disposal. It super- sedes a number of existing circulars including most notably 21/87 on Development of Contaminated Land. The Scottish Office has yet to produce similar guidance although it has issued *NPPG10: Planning and Waste Management* (March 1996) which, in addition to providing advice on that area, provides limited guidelines on planning powers and pollution control powers generally in paras. 16–18. This is materially identical to the advice contained in *PPG23* discussed above. Para. 17 of *NPPG 10* indicates that further advice on planning and pollution controls is to be issued.
  The central thrust of the guidance is that the planning system should not be operated so as to duplicate controls which are the statutory responsibility of other bodies (para. 1.3 and passim). Planning controls are not seen as an appropriate means of regulating the detailed characteristics of potentially polluting activities. In this respect the advice follows the decision of the Court of Appeal in *Gateshead MBC v. Secretary of State for the Environment and Northumbrian Water Group* [1995] Env.L.R. 37, C.A. To the extent that the planning interest focuses on pollution, this must relate to effects on current and future uses of land and the weight which a planning authority is to attach to pollution issues when considering a planning application is "reduced to the extent that these are capable of being addressed by the pollution control authority in carrying out its statutory responsibilities" (para. 3.3).
  PPG 23 also aims to encourage close consultation between planning and pollution control authorities; in particular planning authorities will need to consult pollution control authorities in order to take account of the scope and requirements of the relevant pollution controls (para.

1.34) and, having done so, should work on the assumption that pollution control regimes will be properly enforced and should not seek to substitute their own judgment on pollution control issues for that of the specialist authority. "It is not the role of the planning authority to undertake detailed risk assessment of releases into the environment." (para. 3.19).

To further such consultation, in August 1995 HMIP issued a paper *Planning Liaison with Local Authorities*, which welcomes prior discussion of IPC (and Radioactive Substances Act 1993) authorisations and, where possible, simultaneous preparation of applications for IPC authorisation and planning permission. The IPC regulator's role as consultee in the planning process, as envisaged by HMIP, includes commenting on whether the proposed process constitutes BATNEEC and is likely to receive an authorisation, and providing details of likely releases, comparable plants in the area and the state of the local environment.

The proviso mentioned in the note to s.7(2), relating to the deposit of controlled waste and the "relevant objectives", is a good example of the Government's approach to avoiding the duplication of planning and pollution controls. It will be noted that the enforcing authority appears entitled to assume, where the planning authority is to have applied the relevant objectives, that the planning authority actually will have applied the relevant objectives as regards the issues for which it is responsible.

Implementation of Part I
Part I of the Act comes into force on such day or days as the Secretary of State may by order appoint: s.164(3). Section 3 (Emission, etc. limits and quality objectives) came into force on December 19, 1990. Sections 1, 2 and 4–28 came into force on January 1, 1990. See the Environmental Protection Act 1990 (Commencement No. 4) Order 1991 (S.I. 1991 No. 2635).

The original proposals for implementation were announced by the Minister of State for the Environment on April 26, 1990 (DoE News Release No. 271). The intention was to introduce the IPC system in England and Wales on January 2, 1991, from which date all new processes, and all existing processes to be substantially altered, would be required to apply for authorisation. Existing processes would be brought within the system by a sectoral phased programme. The first sector, combustion processes (including plant covered by the E.C. Large Combustion Plants Directive), would have been within the system from January 2, 1991.

That unofficial timetable was subsequently revised, as the Minister of State announced on July 24, 1990 (DoE News Release No. 441). The initial date for implementing IPC was postponed to April 1, 1991 for new prescribed processes, processes undergoing a substantial change and large combustion plant. Other prescribed processes are being phased in over four years from April 1, 1992, a process now almost complete.

In Scotland, implementation of IPC commenced on April 1, 1992 for new prescribed processes, processes undergoing a substantial change and large combustion plant. As in England and Wales, other prescribed processes are being phased in on a rolling timetable, a process which should be completed during 1996.

A more detailed and statutory timetable is set out in the Environmental Protection (Prescribed Processes and Substances) Regulations 1991 (S.I. 1991 No. 472), as amended (see Appendix 1).

IPC in practice—a review
A comprehensive survey of the workings of IPC in England and Wales has been published by Environmental Data Services Limited: Integrated Pollution Control—The First Three Years (January 1994, ISBN 0-907673-09-0, £64). No similar study has been carried out in Scotland.

The ENDS study, which is the most detailed yet carried out, involved scrutiny of public registers, focusing on authorisations and applications on the file at April 1, 1993; a questionnaire was also sent to operators of all 328 processes authorised by that date, responses being received in relation to 145 processes on 120 sites. The main findings of the survey are as follows:

Preparation of applications: Preparation of applications has clearly involved a significant effort on the part of applicants, most applications having taken between 100–500 man hours to prepare, at a cost of £2,000–£15,000. Many of the more recent applications for existing organic chemical processes appear to have required considerably more cost and effort, sometimes in excess of 100 man days per application. Most companies are adopting a team approach towards preparing the applications, involving three or four technical staff co-ordinated by an environmental manager; some multi-process chemical sites have appointed dedicated "IPC co-ordinators". The "arm's length" approach adopted by HMIP in 1989 proved to be "disastrous" and the policy was formally dropped in early 1993. The Report suggests however that in many ways the move has been beneficial, resulting in some improvement in the quality of applications: nonetheless, the much vaunted transparency of the new system has been "severely damaged" by the use of off-the-record meetings between HMIP and applicants.

Commercial confidentiality: Of the 666 applications submitted by April 1, 1993, 97 were accompanied by claims for exclusion for information from the public register on grounds of commercial confidentiality. 63 of these requests were accepted by HMIP in whole or in part, 21 were rejected, and the outcome of the remaining 13 was uncertain. Most applicants claiming confidentiality were within the combustion, organic chemical and minerals sectors. Many of the claims for confidentiality related to the technical details of the process, though some companies also sought to protect the identity of the product or raw materials used.

Quality of applications: The Report suggests that the initial applications for existing large combustion plants were generally of very poor quality, the main shortcomings being failure to provide information on background levels of pollutants, air pollution dispersion models and adequate assessment of the environmental impact of releases. Later applications were presented more clearly, though many firms submitted large amounts of unhelpful or irrelevant information. The Report suggests that many operators are still failing to demonstrate a clear understanding of some of the basic requirements of IPC and are not complying with clear official guidance. In particular, assessment of environmental impact and demonstration that releases will be "rendered harmless" remains a significant weakness of any applications, as does any meaningful discussion or evaluation of BATNEEC or BPEO. However, despite these shortcomings, in almost all cases, HMIP failed to force applicants to address the issues.

Upgrading programmes: The Report suggests that the real meat of most authorisations is contained in the upgrading programmes, but that in many cases HMIP has been forced to rely on the improvement programme simply to require operators to supply information which should properly have been considered before the authorisation was issued. This practice has led to doubts emerging as to whether information supplied under an improvement programme should be entered on the public register—the result being, according to the Report, that many key decisions have been kept out of the public domain.

Inspection and enforcement: The workload of dealing with authorisations has meant a fall in inspection rates and site visits, and the Report states that inspection rates in the period under study were still some way short of levels which were common during the 1980s. At least 70 per cent of the site visits made during 1992/93 were application-related and the concern is expressed that the move away from the "arm's length" approach, with HMIP devoting considerable effort to helping firms obtain their authorisations, has been at the expense of its enforcement role. It is also suggested by the report that HMIP could have taken a tougher stance on enforcement, in view of the fact that many operators continue to submit poor applications and that there have been several significant breaches of authorisation conditions.

Variation: The Report indicates that HMIP has not made use of its power to vary the terms of authorisations to ensure environmental protection or to secure technological improvements in line with BATNEEC. By contrast, many variations have been granted at the request of the operator, either to correct errors in the initial authorisation, or because of difficulties in meeting authorisation conditions. It also appears that many authorisations are being varied by way of "off the record discussions", and without written justification or entry on the public register. The Report also suggests that HMIP in some cases allowed large increases in releases from a process without categorising the change as being "substantial", which would result in the application of more stringent statutory procedures.

Appeals: An increasing number of firms have appealed against authorisation conditions. By October 1993, 19 firms had appealed in connection with 67 authorisations. It appears that for most appeals the formal appeal procedure has been waived in order to allow the complaints to be resolved by negotiation. A large proportion of appeals related to the wording and enforceability of conditions and could be dealt with simply by clarification. However, a number of appeals are now relating to "fundamental areas of HMIP policy", such as upgrading requirements and the setting of annual mass emission limits.

Cost of meeting authorisation conditions: The Report failed to find any authoritative estimates of the cost of implementing IPC: the results of the questionnaire survey revealed huge variations even within individual industrial sectors. On average, operators of existing processes authorised by April 1, 1993, expected to invest in the order of £720,000 in upgrading, half of which they attributed solely to IPC requirements. In the case of new processes, operators anticipated expenditure of £650,000 on average, £340,000 being attributable to IPC. In particular, the small differential in these figures between the expenditure on new and existing processes appears to indicate that even new processes authorised by HMIP fall some way behind the standards which would be expected for the new plant. ENDS believes that the detailed costs indicated by the survey should be viewed with caution, but feels that its general finding that IPC is likely to double the environmental expenditure on prescribed processes is robust.

Public registers: The Report suggests that public registers are failing to secure the transparency which the system was intended to provide. This is partly a result of private decision making by off-the-record discussions, partly by missing data resulting from poor maintenance of registers, partly by systematic failure to enter certain categories of information on the register (in particular, periodic returns about releases) and finally the common practice of requiring submission of important information after an authorisation has been issued, rather than as part of the application.

Is IPC making a difference? The Report concludes that in most cases it is too soon to assess the degree of environmental improvement arising from IPC, though clearly the system is acting as a driving force for investment in environmental improvements. It seems far from clear that standards laid down for new processes truly represent what is achievable using best available techniques. Another major area of concern identified is that much of the industrial focus continues to be on end-of-pipe abatement rather than minimisation of waste at source. It is also clear that those companies which are most enthusiastic about IPC are those which already had a commitment to make fundamental improvements in their environmental performance. The Report concludes that "unless more operators follow their lead, the perception of IPC as a burdensome regime will be with us for some years to come."

PRELIMINARY

Preliminary

1.—(1) The following provisions have effect for the interpretation of this Part.

(2) The "environment" consists of all, or any, of the following media, namely, the air, water and land; and the medium of air includes the air within buildings and the air within other natural or man-made structures above or below ground.

(3) "Pollution of the environment" means pollution of the environment due to the release (into any environmental medium) from any process of substances which are capable of causing harm to man or any other living organisms supported by the environment.

(4) "Harm" means harm to the health of living organisms or other interference with the ecological systems of which they form part and, in the case of man, includes offence caused to any of his senses or harm to his property; and "harmless" has a corresponding meaning.

(5) "Process" means any activities carried on in Great Britain, whether on premises or by means of mobile plant, which are capable of causing pollution of the environment and "prescribed process" means a process prescribed under section 2(1) below.

(6) For the purposes of subsection (5) above—

"activities" means industrial or commercial activities or activities of any other nature whatsoever (including, with or without other activities, the keeping of a substance);

"Great Britain" includes so much of the adjacent territorial sea as is, or is treated as, relevant territorial waters for the purposes of [Part III of the Water Resources Act 1991] or, as respects Scotland, Part II of the Control of Pollution Act 1974; and

"mobile plant" means plant which is designed to move or to be moved whether on roads or otherwise.

(7) The "enforcing authority", in relation to England and Wales, is [the

Environment Agency or the local authority by which], under section 4 below, the functions conferred or imposed by this Part otherwise than on the Secretary of State are for the time being exercisable in relation respectively to releases of substances into the environment or into the air; and "local enforcing authority" means any such local authority.

[(8) In relation to Scotland, references to the "enforcing authority" and a "local enforcing authority" are references to the Scottish Environment Protection Agency (in this Part referred to as "SEPA").]

(9) "Authorisation" means an authorisation for a process (whether on premises or by means of mobile plant) granted under section 6 below; and a reference to the conditions of an authorisation is a reference to the conditions subject to which at any time the authorisation has effect.

(10) A substance is "released" into any environmental medium whenever it is released directly into that medium whether it is released into it within or outside Great Britain and "release" includes—

(a) in relation to air, any emission of the substance into the air;
(b) in relation to water, any entry (including any discharge) of the substance into water,
(c) in relation to land, any deposit, keeping or disposal of the substance in or on land;

and for this purpose "water" and "land" shall be construed in accordance with subsections (11) and (12) below.

(11) For the purpose of determining into what medium a substance is released—

(a) any release into—
  (i) the sea or the surface of the seabed,
  (ii) any river, watercourse, lake, loch or pond (whether natural or artificial or above or below ground) or reservoir or the surface of the riverbed or of other land supporting such waters, or
  (iii) ground waters,
  is a release into water;
(b) any release into—
  (i) land covered by water falling outside paragraph (a) above or the water covering such land; or
  (ii) the land beneath the surface of the seabed or of other land supporting waters falling within paragraph (a)(ii) above,
  is a release into land; and
(c) any release into a sewer (within the meaning of the [Water Industry Act 1991] or, in relation to Scotland, of the Sewerage (Scotland) Act 1968) shall be treated as a release into water;

but a sewer and its contents shall be disregarded in determining whether there is pollution of the environment at any time.

(12) In subsection (11) above "ground waters" means any waters contained in underground strata, or in—

(a) a well, borehole or similar work sunk into underground strata, including any adit or passage constructed in connection with the well, borehole or work for facilitating the collection of water in the well, borehole or work; or
(b) any excavation into underground strata where the level of water in the excavation depends wholly or mainly on water entering it from the strata.

(13) "Substance" shall be treated as including electricity or heat and "prescribed substance" has the meaning given by section 2(7) below.

[(14) In this Part "the appropriate Agency" means
(a) in relation to England and Wales, the Environment Agency; and
(b) in relation to Scotland, SEPA.]

COMMENCEMENT
January 1, 1991 (S.I. 1990 No. 2635).

AMENDMENTS
The words in square brackets in subss. (6) and (11)(c) were substituted by the Water Consolidation (Consequential Provisions) Act 1991, s.2, Sched. 1. Subs. (7) was amended, subs. (8) was substituted and subs. (14) was added by the Environment Act 1995, Sched. 22, para. 45.

GENERAL NOTE
This section contains a series of definitions which are of central importance to the systems of control instituted by Pt. I.

Subs. (2)
The environment. It should be noted that the definition includes the medium of air within buildings and other structures above or below ground.

Subs. (3)
Pollution of the environment. The term "pollution" is not directly defined, but one well-known definition runs as follows:

> "The introduction by man into the environment of substances or energy liable to cause hazards to human health, harm to living resources and ecological systems, damage to structures or amenity, or interference with legitimate use of the environment." M. W. Holdgate, *A Perspective on Environmental Pollution* (Cambridge, 1979).

It is the likelihood of undesirable effects that distinguishes pollution from contamination, in the sense of the introduction of alien substances into the environment: see RCEP Tenth Report Cm. 9149, paras. 1.9–1.13.

However, subs. (3) refers to the release of substances *capable* of causing harm as defined: pollution as the term is used in the subsection does not require proof of *actual* harm but simply the potential to cause harm.

Subs. (4)
Harm. This subsection extends considerably the definition of "pollution of the environment" by reference to the health of all living organisms, the ecological systems supporting them, offence to any human senses and harm to property.

Subs. (5)
Process. The term is given a wide meaning to include any activities capable of causing pollution of the environment. Such activities may either be carried out on premises or by means of mobile plant. In other statutory contexts the term "process" has been held to involve some degree of continuity and repetition of acts, albeit not of long duration: see *Nurse v. Morganite Crucible* [1989] 2 A.C. 692 (H.L.); *Vibroplant v. Holland (Inspector of Taxes)* (1982) 126 S.J. 82 (C.A.). The definition in subs. (5), however, does not appear to be qualified in that way. The burning of rubbish on a demolition site has been held to fall within the Clean Air Act 1968 as being "in connection with an industrial or trade process," namely demolition: *Sheffield City Council v. A.D.H. Demolition* (1984) 82 L.G.R. 177.

Subs. (6)
Activities. The term is given an extremely wide interpretation to cover activities of any nature and also to cover the passive keeping of substances. This avoids any doubt as to whether pure storage, whether of materials or of waste, could constitute an "activity": see *Hillil Property & Investment Co. v. Naraine Pharmacy* (1979) 123 S.J. 437.

Great Britain. The relevant "territorial waters" for the purposes of Pt. III of the Water Resources Act 1991 are "waters which extend seaward and for three miles from the baselines from which the breadth of the territorial sea adjacent to England and Wales is measured": Water Resources Act 1991, s.104(1)(a). The Control of Pollution Act 1974, s.30A(1) defines the territorial waters adjacent to Scotland in identical terms. It is possible for the Secretary of State to extend this jurisdiction to other areas of territorial sea up to the general 12 mile territorial limit by order made under s.104(4) of the Water Resources Act or, in Scotland, under s.30A(5) of the 1974 Act. The Water Resources Act expressly deals with the situation of trade or sewage effluent which is discharged from land in England and Wales through a pipe, into the sea outside the relevant seaward limits (s.85(3)(b)). Section 30F(3)(b) of the 1974 Act makes equivalent position for Scotland. Such a provision is not necessary for the purposes of Pt. I of the Environmental Protection Act, for the reason that territoriality is only relevant for the purposes of the location of the process (subs. 1(5)), and not for the concept of pollution (subss. 1(3) and (10)).

Mobile plant. The crucial test is whether the plant is "designed" to move or be moved. The word "designed" is ambiguous and in the context of Town and Country Planning legislation has been said to mean "intended" rather than technically designed: *Wilson v. West Sussex County Council* [1963] 2 Q.B. 764, 780, 783.

Subss. (7) and (8)
The original division of responsibility between a central regulator and local authorities, for IPC and LAPC respectively, remains true in England and Wales following the transfer of IPC regulation to the Agency by the 1995 Act. However, in Scotland local authorities no longer play a part, as SEPA is the "local enforcing authority" for LAPC as well as the enforcing authority for IPC.

Subs. (10)
Release. As mentioned above, Pt. I is concerned with releases into the environment both within and outside Great Britain.

Subs. (11)
Medium of release. This subsection contains important rules for the purpose of determining whether a substance is released into water or into land. It also establishes that release into a sewer can be controlled as a release into water, though on determining whether there is pollution of the environment any effect on the sewer and its contents is to be disregarded. However, the definition of "sewer" in this sense would not extend to sewage treatment works, so it would seem that the effect on such works and the effluent they treat could be considered.

Subs. (12)
Ground waters. The definition of ground waters here is identical to that contained in the Control of Pollution Act 1974, s.30A(1)(d) in respect of Scotland. The definition in s.104(1)(d) of the Water Resources Act 1991 refers to "any waters contained in underground strata" only. It may be contrasted with that contained in the E.C. Groundwaters Directive (80/68/EEC) which reads as follows:

> "All water which is below the surface of the ground in the saturation zone and in direct contact with the ground or subsoil."

See also DoE Circ. 20/90 (W.O. 34/90), para. 6.

Subs. (13)
Substance. "Substance," as well as including electricity or heat as expressly stated, would include natural or artificial substances, whether in solid or liquid form or in the form of a gas or vapour.

Noise is not a "substance" (something confirmed by the Secretary of State in his Appeal Decision letter dated April 8, 1994 on *the appeal by Yeoman Bulk Cargoes against Great Yarmouth Borough Council's refusal to vary an authorisation*).

Prescribed processes and prescribed substances

2.—(1) The Secretary of State may, by regulations, prescribe any description of process as a process for the carrying on of which after a prescribed date an authorisation is required under section 6 below.

(2) Regulations under subsection (1) above may frame the description of a process by reference to any characteristics of the process or the area or other circumstances in which the process is carried on or the description of person carrying it on.

(3) Regulations under subsection (1) above may prescribe or provide for the determination under the regulations of different dates for different descriptions of persons and may include such transitional provisions as the Secretary of State considers necessary or expedient as respects the making of applications for authorisations and suspending the application of section 6(1) below until the determination of applications made within the period allowed by the regulations.

(4) Regulations under subsection (1) above shall, as respects each description of process, designate it as one for central control or one for local control.

(5) The Secretary of State may, by regulations, prescribe any description of substance as a substance the release of which into the environment is subject to control under sections 6 and 7 below.

(6) Regulations under subsection (5) above may—

    (a) prescribe separately, for each environmental medium, the substances the release of which into that medium is to be subject to control; and

    (b) provide that a description of substance is only prescribed, for any environmental medium, so far as it is released into that medium in such amounts over such periods, in such concentrations or in such other circumstances as may be specified in the regulations;

and in relation to a substance of a description which is prescribed for releases into the air, the regulations may designate the substance as one for central control or one for local control.

(7) In this Part "prescribed substance" means any substance of a description prescribed in regulations under subsection (5) above or, in the case of a substance of a description prescribed only for releases in circumstances specified under subsection (6)(b) above, means any substance of that description which is released in those circumstances.

DEFINITIONS
    "authorisation": s.1(9).
    "environment": s.1(2).
    "environmental medium": s.1(2).
    "prescribed process": s.1(5).
    "process": s.1(5).
    "release": s.1(10).
    "substance": s.1(13).

COMMENCEMENT
January 1, 1991 (S.I. 1990 No. 2635).

GENERAL NOTE
This section deals with the prescription of processes and substances for (a) central or (b) local control. (See also the General Note to Pt. I.) In relation to processes wide discretion is given as to how the description of the process is framed, to provide different prescribed dates for different descriptions of operator, and to make transitional provisions (subs. (2) and (3)).

    Schedule 2 to the Environmental Protection (Prescribed Processes and Substances) Regulations 1991 (S.I. 1991 No. 472) (see Appendix 1) provides that the description of a prescribed process in the authorisation of that process includes any other process carried on at the same location by the same person as part of that process. *Her Majesty's Inspectorate of Pollution v. Safety Kleen UK Ltd* (Rotherham Magistrates' Court, September 5, 1994, reported in *HMIP Bulletin*, November 1994), considered the implications of this. The literal description in the authorisation of the solvent recovery process in question ended at the point where the solvent was loaded into tanker vehicles at a tanker terminal. However, when the solvent subsequently escaped from the tanker, which had been parked on the site since loading, and made its way into a brook nearby, the operator of the process was successfully prosecuted for breaching an authorisation condition precluding discharges to controlled waters.

    In relation to substances, prescription may relate to a specific environmental medium and may incorporate thresholds as to quantities over time, concentrations, or indeed, other circumstances (subs. (6)). "Prescribed substance" is then construed by reference to such thresholds.

    In the case of prescribed processes, designation as to central or local control will, in relation to England and Wales, determine whether control is exercised by the Agency over releases to all media, or by local authorities over releases to the air (subs. (4)). In relation to a substance prescribed for releases into the air, the substance may be designated as one for either central or local control. Where the substance is prescribed in relation to releases to all media, or to the media of water or land, the inference is that the designation must be for central control. It would appear theoretically possible, though it might be technically undesirable, for the same substance to be prescribed for central control if released into water or land, but for local control if released into the air. However, in Scotland, controls over prescribed processes and substances designated for central and local control are all now exercised by SEPA.

Further details on prescription, proposals for prescribed processes and substances, and for the prescribed dates are given in the General Note to Pt. I.

The Environmental Protection (Prescribed Processes and Substances) Regulations 1991 (S.I. No. 472) as amended by S.I. 1991 No. 836 and S.I. 1992 No. 614 were made under these powers. Regulation 4 provides that various exceptions may apply. Section 101 of the Magistrates' Courts Act 1980 indicates that the burden of proving that one of these exceptions applies rests upon the defendants: *Tandridge District Council v. P & S Civil Engineering Ltd & Others* [1995] Env.L.R. 67. The same would be true in Scotland by virtue of the Criminal Procedure (Scotland) Act 1995, Sched. 3, para. 16.

Emission etc. limits and quality objectives

3.—(1) The Secretary of State may make regulations under subsection (2) or (4) below establishing standards, objectives or requirements in relation to particular prescribed processes or particular substances.

(2) Regulations under this subsection may—
  (a) in relation to releases of any substance from prescribed processes into any environmental medium, prescribe standard limits for—
    (i) the concentration, the amount or the amount in any period of that substance which may be so released; and
    (ii) any other characteristic of that substance in any circumstances in which it may be so released;
  (b) prescribe standard requirements for the measurement or analysis of, or of releases of, substances for which limits have been set under paragraph (a) above; and
  (c) in relation to any prescribed process, prescribe standards or requirements as to any aspect of the process.

(3) Regulations under subsection (2) above may make different provision in relation to different cases, including different provision in relation to different processes, descriptions of person, localities or other circumstances.

(4) Regulations under this subsection may establish for any environmental medium (in all areas or in specified areas) quality objectives or quality standards in relation to any substances which may be released into that or any other medium from any process.

(5) The Secretary of State may make plans for—
  (a) establishing limits for the total amount, or the total amount in any period, of any substance which may be released into the environment in, or in any area within, the United Kingdom;
  (b) allocating quotas as respects the release of substances to persons carrying on processes in respect of which any such limit is established;
  (c) establishing limits of the descriptions specified in subsection (2)(a) above so as progressively to reduce pollution of the environment;
  (d) the progressive improvement in the quality objectives and quality standards established by regulations under subsection (4) above;
and the Secretary of State may, from time to time, revise any plan so made.

(6) Regulations or plans under this section may be made for any purposes of this Part or for other purposes.

(7) The Secretary of State shall give notice in the London, Edinburgh and Belfast Gazettes of the making and the revision of any plan under subsection (5) above and shall make the documents containing the plan, or the plan as so revised, available for inspection by members of the public at the places specified in the notice.

(8) Subject to any Order made after the passing of this Act by virtue of subsection (1)(a) of section 3 of the Northern Ireland Constitution Act 1973, the making and revision of plans under subsection (5) above shall not be a transferred matter for the purposes of that Act but shall for the purposes of

subsection (2) of that section be treated as specified in Schedule 3 to that Act.

DEFINITIONS
"environment": s.1(2).
"environmental medium": s.1(2).
"pollution of the environment": s.1(3).
"prescribed processes": s.1(5).
"processes": s.1(5).
"releases": s.1(10).
"substances": s.1(13).

COMMENCEMENT
December 19, 1990 (S.I. 1990 No. 2635).

GENERAL NOTE
The general purpose of this provision is to allow the Secretary of State power to achieve uniformity of approach and to further national strategies for pollution abatement. At the same time, considerable discretion as to making different provision for different cases is given by subs. (3).

In practice the use of such powers will be driven by obligations under European Community law (for example in the case of emission limits, quality objectives and quality standards) or obligations to the wider international community (for example, limits on the total amounts of substances released within the UK and plans for the progressive reduction of pollution). See further General Note to Pt. I, under the heading *Implementation of E.C. and International Requirements*.

Subs. (5)
Plans. The UK Programme and National Plan for Reducing Emissions of SO_2 and NO_x was made under this section on December 20, 1990, and subsequently amended in July 1994 and again in October 1995. The plan sets yearly targets for SO_2 and NO_x emissions from 1990–2003 and 1990–1998 respectively, for existing large plants in three separate sectors: power stations; refineries; and "other industry". The plan was made to implement the Large Combustion Plants Directive 88/609/EEC, which is also implemented by means of directions under ss.7, 10 and 165. The Directive was amended in December 1994 by Directive 94/66/EC.

Discharge and scope of functions

4.—(1) This section determines the authority by whom the functions conferred or imposed by this Part otherwise than on the Secretary of State are exercisable and the purposes for which they are exercisable.

(2) Those functions, in their application to prescribed processes designated for central control, shall be functions of [the appropriate Agency], and shall be exercisable for the purpose of preventing or minimising pollution of the environment due to the release of substances into any environmental medium.

(3) Subject to subsection (4) below, those functions, in their application to prescribed processes designated for local control, shall be functions of—

[(a) in the case of a prescribed process carried on (or to be carried on) by means of a mobile plant, where the person carrying on the process has his principal place of business—

    (i) in England and Wales, the local authority in whose area that place of business is;

    (ii) in Scotland, SEPA;

(b) in any other cases, where the prescribed processes are (or are to be) carried on—

    (i) in England and Wales, the local authority in whose area they are (or are to be) carried on;

    (ii) in Scotland, SEPA;]

and the functions applicable to such processes shall be exercisable for the purpose of preventing or minimising pollution of the environment due to the release of substances into the air (but not into any other environmental medium).

(4) The Secretary of State may, as respects the functions under this Part being exercised by a local authority specified in the direction, direct that those functions shall be exercised instead by [the Environment Agency] while the direction remains in force or during a period specified in the direction.

[(4A) In England and Wales, a local authority, in exercising the functions conferred or imposed on it under this Part by virtue of subsection (3) above, shall have regard to the strategy for the time being published pursuant to section 80 of the Environment Act 1995.]

(5) A transfer of functions under subsection (4) above to [the Environment Agency] does not make them exercisable by [that Agency] for the purpose of preventing or minimising pollution of the environment due to releases of substances into any other environmental medium than the air.

(6) A direction under subsection (4) above may transfer those functions as exercisable in relation to all or any description of prescribed processes carried on by all or any description of persons (a "general direction") or in relation to a prescribed process carried on by a specified person (a "specific direction").

(7) A direction under subsection (4) above may include such saving and transitional provisions as the Secretary of State considers necessary or expedient.

(8) The Secretary of State, on giving or withdrawing a direction under subsection (4) above, shall—

    (a) in the case of a general direction—

        (i) forthwith serve notice of it on [the Environment Agency] and on the local enforcing authorities affected by the direction; and

        (ii) cause notice of it to be published as soon as practicable in the London Gazette [...] and in at least one newspaper circulating in the area of each authority affected by the direction;

    (b) in the case of a specific direction—

        (i) forthwith serve notice of it on [the Environment Agency], the local enforcing authority and the person carrying on or appearing to the Secretary of State to be carrying on the process affected, and

        (ii) cause notice of it to be published as soon as practicable in the London Gazette [...] and in at least one newspaper circulating in the authority's area;

and any such notice shall specify the date at which the direction is to take (or took) effect and (where appropriate) its duration.

[(8A) The requirements of sub-paragraph (ii) of paragraph (a) or, as the case may be, of paragraph (b) of subsection (8) above shall not apply in any case where, in the opinion of the Secretary of State, the publication of notice in accordance with that sub-paragraph would be contrary to the interests of national security.

(8B) Subsections (4) to (8A) above shall not apply to Scotland.]

[(9) It shall be the duty of local authorities to follow such developments in technology and techniques for preventing or reducing pollution of the environment due to releases of substances from prescribed processes as concern releases into the air of substances from prescribed processes designated for local control.]

(10) It shall be the duty of [the Environment Agency, SEPA] and the local enforcing authorities to give effect to any directions given to them under any provision of this Part.

(11) In this Part "local authority" means, subject to subsection (12) below—

    (a) in Greater London, a London borough council, the Common Council of the City of London, the Sub-Treasurer of the Inner Temple and the Under Treasurer of the Middle Temple;

    (b) [in England and Wales,] outside Greater London, a district council and the Council of the Isles of Scilly.

    (c) [...]

(12) Where, by an order under section 2 of the Public Health (Control of Disease) Act 1984, a port health authority has been constituted for any port health district, the port health authority shall have by virtue of this subsection, as respects its district, the functions conferred or imposed by this Part and no such order shall be made assigning those functions; and "local authority" and "area" shall be construed accordingly.

DEFINITIONS
"appropriate Agency": s.1(14).
"environment": s.1(2).
"local authority": subs. (11).
"local enforcing authority": s.1(7) and (8).
"mobile plant": s.1(6).
"pollution of the environment": s.1(3).
"prescribed processes": s.1(5).
"process": s.1(5).
"release": s.1(10).
"SEPA": s.1(8).
"substances": s.1(13).

COMMENCEMENT
January 1, 1991 (S.I. 1990 No. 2635).

AMENDMENTS
The Environment Act 1995, Sched. 22, para. 46, amended subss. (2), (3), (4), (5), (8), (10) and (11), inserted subss. (4A), (8A) and (8B) and substituted subs. (9). The Local Government (Wales) Act 1994, Sched. 9, para. 17, amended subs. (11). (*N.B.*—the combined effects of the amendments to subs. (11), if inserted literally, would mean that para. (b) begins "in England in England and Wales ... ". The wording employed in the text above reflects the editor's understanding of their intended effect).

GENERAL NOTE
This section explains the distinction between centrally and locally controlled processes. The functions conferred or imposed by Pt. I of the Act fall, in the case of centrally controlled processes, to the Environment Agency in England and Wales and to SEPA in Scotland. The functions relating to locally controlled processes fall in England and Wales to the relevant local authority at district level (see subs. (11)) and in Scotland to SEPA. Prior to the Environment Act 1995, and the introduction of the Agency and SEPA, Scottish local authorities at district and islands council level were the regulators for locally-controlled processes in their area, as was and is the case in England and Wales. The transfer of such processes to SEPA control appears to have been prompted by the perception that very few Scottish local authority areas contained a significant number of prescribed processes, that as a result Scottish local authorities might lack the technical expertise required of the LAPC regulator, and that it was desirable to centralise the technical expertise which did exist in the local authorities. See further in the General Introduction to the 1995 Act, Pt. I, which effected the change.

    The functions are to be exercised for the purpose of preventing or minimising pollution of the environment due to the release of substances into any medium in the case of centrally-controlled processes (subs. (2)). For locally-controlled processes, the functions are exercisable for preventing or minimising pollution of the environment due to the release of substances into the air. It should be noted that the functions are not limited to reducing or preventing pollution of the air: they could be used in relation to pollution of soil or water caused by substances originally released into the air.

Subs. (4)
Transfer of functions. It is possible for the Secretary of State to transfer functions from English and Welsh local authorities to the Environment Agency by means of a general or specific direction given under subss. (4) and (6). Such a transfer does not, however, widen control beyond the release of substances to the air (subs. (5)).

Subs. (4A): Air quality strategy
The Environment Act 1995, Pt. IV, provides for the preparation by the Secretary of State of a national air quality strategy, implementation of which is essentially a matter for local authorities: see the General Note to that Part of the 1995 Act. Subsection (4A), inserted by the 1995 Act, requires local authorities to have regard to the strategy in their capacity as LAPC regulators, and thus enables them to exercise their powers under Pt. I in furtherance of the strategy and their own action plans (if any) prepared under Pt. IV of the 1995 Act.

Subs. (9)
Developments in technology and techniques. Local authorities are under a statutory duty to follow developments in pollution abatement technology and techniques in relation to the relevant processes. This duty is important in relation to the concept of use of best available techniques not entailing excessive cost. The Environment Agency and SEPA are under a comparable but broader duty by virtue of the 1995 Act, ss.5(4) and 33(4).

Further provision as to discharge and scope of functions: Scotland

5. [...]

Section 5, which enabled the Secretary of State to allocate functions in Scotland as appropriate between HMIPI and river purification authorities (and which the Secretary of State had done by means of the Environmental Protection (Determination of Enforcing Authority etc.) (Scotland) Regulations 1992 (S.I. 1992 No. 530)), was repealed by the Environment Act 1995, Sched. 24, since the functions of those bodies have now been transferred to SEPA.]

Authorisations

Authorisations: general provisions

6.—(1) No person shall carry on a prescribed process after the date prescribed or determined for that description of process by or under regulations under section 2(1) above (but subject to any transitional provision made by the regulations) except under an authorisation granted by the enforcing authority and in accordance with the conditions to which it is subject.

(2) An application for an authorisation shall be made to the enforcing authority in accordance with Part I of Schedule 1 to this Act and shall be accompanied by

[(a) in a case where, by virtue of section 41 of the Environment Act 1995, a charge prescribed by a charging scheme under that section is required to be paid to the appropriate Agency in respect of the application, the charges so prescribed; or

(b) in any other case,] the fee prescribed under section 8(2)(a) below.

(3) Where an application is duly made to the enforcing authority, the authority shall either grant the authorisation subject to the conditions required or authorised to be imposed by section 7 below or refuse the application.

(4) An application shall not be granted unless the enforcing authority considers that the applicant will be able to carry on the process so as to comply with the conditions which would be included in the authorisation.

(5) The Secretary of State may, if he thinks fit in relation to any application for an authorisation, give to the enforcing authority directions as to whether or not the authority should grant the authorisation.

(6) The enforcing authority shall, as respects each authorisation in respect of which it has functions under this Part, from time to time but not less frequently than once in every period of four years, carry out a review of the conditions of the authorisation.

(7) The Secretary of State may, by regulations, substitute for the period for the time being specified in subsection (6) above such other period as he thinks fit.

(8) Schedule 1 to this Act (supplementary provisions) shall have effect in relation to authorisations.

DEFINITIONS
"appropriate Agency": s.1(14).
"enforcing authority": s.1(7) and (8).
"prescribed process": s.1(5).
"process": s.1(5).

COMMENCEMENT
January 1, 1991 (S.I. 1990 No. 2635).

AMENDMENT
The Environment Act 1995, Sched. 22, para. 48, amended subs. (2).

GENERAL NOTE
The effect of this section is that a prescribed process may only be lawfully carried on after the relevant prescribed date (see General Note to Pt. I) if an authorisation has been granted and if the process is carried on in accordance with the conditions to which the authorisation is subject.

Carry on. Questions may arise as to what constitutes the "carrying on" of a process. Cases on the expression "carry on business" suggests that: (a) a repetition or series of acts is required (*Smith v. Anderson* (1880) 15 Ch.D. 247, 277, 278 (C.A., *per* Brett L.J.)); and (b) the person carrying on the process must have control and direction with regard to it (*Lewis v. Graham* (1888) 22 Q.B.D. 1, 5 (C.A., *per* Fry L.J.)).

Subs. (1): Fees and charges
As amended by the 1995 Act, subs. (1) reflects the fact that any charging scheme for regimes governed by the Agency/SEPA are made under that Act.

Subs. (2)
Applications for authorisation. By Pt. I of Sched. 1 to the Act the form of application, the information it must contain, and the advertisement required, may be prescribed by regulations (see below). The application itself will be subject to the publicity provisions of s.20, by which prescribed particulars of the application will be contained in the public register.

Subs. (4)
Ability of applicant. Whilst Pt. I does not contain any provisions equivalent in sophistication to the concept of "fit and proper person" contained in Pt. II in relation to waste management licensing, it is clear from this subsection that the enforcing authority must have regard to characteristics of the applicant in so far as they are relevant to the applicant's ability to comply with the proposed conditions.

The interpretation of subs. (4) was considered by the Secretary of State in determining the *appeal by R. J. Compton and Sons against West Wiltshire District Council's refusal to grant an LAPC authorisation*: Appeal Decision Letter dated August 22, 1995. He considered the subs. to give rise to two questions: (a) if an authorisation were to be granted, what conditions would be granted, and (b) would it be possible for the applicant to carry on the process in compliance with those conditions? The existence of enforcement powers under the regime should conditions be breached following grant of an authorisation led him to the view that "the test provided by section 6(4) is whether a process operator is *able* to comply, not whether he is *likely* to comply". (It has since been reported that the local authority has succeeded, in a judicial review application, in having this decision quashed on the ground that the Secretary of State had failed to justify his conclusion that the firm would be able to comply—see [1996] ENDS 254, p.7).

The tenor of this decision is reflected also in his Appeal Decision Letter dated June 27, 1995 upholding an *appeal by Wildriggs Proteins Ltd against Eden District Council's refusal to grant an LAPC authorisation*, in which the focus is on the competence of the operator, although there he unfortunately appears to conflate ability and likely conduct: "the likelihood of [compliance] is an important factor in deciding whether to grant an authorisation, and . . . a genuine conviction on the part of the authority that an operator would not be able to comply . . . would be grounds for a refusal to authorise the process."

However, his decision (dated August 1, 1995) on the *appeal by Smith Brothers (Hyde) Ltd against Tameside Metropolitan Borough Council's refusal to grant an LAPC authorisation* suggests that only in circumstances where there is "evidence of a management failing or lack of competence in the history of the operation of the appellant which could not be addressed by [authorisation] conditions, the enforcement of which would then be a matter for the authority", would it be appropriate to refuse an authorisation. In upholding the latter appeal and directing the grant of an authorisation subject to conditions which, on the facts, the applicant would not be able to meet for some time, he appears to have taken the view that present physical incapacity of the site is also no ground for refusing an authorisation unless the site is physically incapable of being upgraded so as to comply with the conditions. The Appeal Decision Letter is ambiguous as to whether the applicant's financial means are relevant: "The Inspector concludes that the appellant could not afford such a reorganisation [as would be necessary to comply with the conditions]. However, the Secretary of State is not satisfied that there is sufficient evidence that the appellant would be unable to do so, nor that the appeal should be dismissed on those grounds." (The Appeal Decision letter imposed two conditions on the LAPC authorisation to be granted to the appellant, and enforcement action and litigation followed, including an application by Smith Brothers for judicial review of the decision—see [1996] ENDS 253, p8–9).

Subs. (6)
Review of authorisations. The conditions of an authorisation must be reviewed from time to time and at least once every four years. No doubt the frequency of review will be affected by the use made by the Secretary of State of his powers under s.3, and by requirements of European Community law.

Supplementary provisions. Sched. 1 contains supplementary provisions as to the grant and variation of authorisations. These provisions deal with:
    (a) form of applications;
    (b) advertisement of applications;
    (c) requests for further information;
    (d) consultation;
    (e) representations by other persons;
    (f) transmission of applications to the Secretary of State for determination;
    (g) public inquiries or hearings in transmitted cases;
    (h) directions to enforcing authorities by the Secretary of State;
    (i) period for determination and deemed refusal (four months);
    (j) procedure for variation of authorisations, both by the enforcing authority and on application by the person carrying on the process.

Regulations on applications. Regulations dealing with (*inter alia*) applications were made on March 6, 1991 and came into force on April 1, 1991 in England and Wales and on April 1, 1992 in Scotland (Environmental Protection (Applications, Appeals and Registers) Regulations 1991 (S.I. 1991 No. 507 as amended: see Appendix 2). These provide that applications for authorisation shall be made in writing and shall contain the following information (reg. 2(1)):
    (a) the name and address of the applicant and, if the applicant is a body corporate, its registered or principal office address, its registered number and registered office;
    (b) in a case where the prescribed process will be carried on by means of mobile plant, the name of the local authority in whose area the applicant has his principal place of business and, in any other case, the name of any local authority in whose area the prescribed process will be carried on;
    (c) in a case where the prescribed process will not be carried on by means of mobile plant, the address of the premises where the prescribed process will be carried on, a map or plan showing the location of those premises and, if only part of those premises will be used for carrying on the process, a plan or other means of identifying that part;
    (d) a description of the prescribed process;
    (e) a list of prescribed substances (and any other substances which might cause harm if released into any environmental medium) used in connection with or resulting from the prescribed process;
    (f) a description of the techniques to be used for preventing the release into any environmental medium of such substances, for reducing the release of such substances to a minimum and for rendering harmless any such substances which are released;
    (g) details of any proposed release of such a substance into any environmental medium and an assessment of the environmental consequences;
    (h) proposals for monitoring any release of such substances, the environmental consequences of any such release and the use of techniques mentioned in sub-para. (f) above;

    (i) the matters on which the applicant relies to establish that the objectives mentioned in section 7(2) of the Act (including the objective referred to in s.7(7) of the Act) will be achieved and that he will be able to comply with the condition implied by s.7(4) of the Act;

    (j) any additional information which he wishes the enforcing authority to take into account in considering his application.

In relation to LAPC processes, by reg. 2(3), the reference to release of substances relates only to releases to air.

Consultations and advertisement. The same regulations provide for the following persons to be consulted on applications and variation by the enforcing authority (reg. 4(1)):

    (a) the Health and Safety Executive, in all cases;

    (b) the Minister of Agriculture, Fisheries and Food or, in relation to Wales, the Secretary of State for Wales, in the case of all IPC processes carried on in England and Wales;

    (c) the Secretary of State for Scotland, in the case of all IPC processes carried on in Scotland;

    (d) the sewerage undertaker or, in relation to Scotland, the new water and sewerage authority (established by the Local Government etc. (Scotland) Act 1994) in cases which may involve the release of any substance into a sewer vested in the undertaker or, in Scotland, a water and sewerage authority or a private undertaking by virtue of the Build, Own, Operate scheme;

    (e) English Nature, Scottish Natural Heritage, or the Countryside Council for Wales, in cases which may involve a release of any substance which affects a site of special scientific interest within the Council's area;

    (f) a harbour authority into whose harbour an IPC process may discharge; and

    (g) a Scottish local authority in the case of certain IPC-related waste disposal and recovery processes.

Regulation 5 deals with the required advertisement procedures. By reg. 6, neither reg. 4 nor 5 applies to waste oil burners with a net rated thermal input of less than 0.4 MW.

A consultation paper published in 1994 on the regulations included the possibility that HSE no longer be a statutory consultee for LAPC applications, together with a number of other proposed amendments.

Period for consideration of applications. The general period given for consideration and determination of applications is four months (Sched. 1, para. 5(1)). This period has been extended to 18 months for existing processes involving the use of waste oil as fuel in appliances having a thermal input of less than 0.4 MW and to 12 months in the case of all other Pt. B existing processes: Environmental Protection (Authorisation of Processes) (Determination of Periods) Order 1991 (S.I. 1991 No. 513). However, for processes which became subject to LAPC on December 1, 1994, an extended period of nine months applies unless the process is waste oil burners with a net rated thermal input of less than 0.4 MW: S.I. 1994 No. 2847 amending S.I. 1991 No. 513 above.

Conditions of authorisation

    7.—(1) There shall be included in an authorisation—

    (a) subject to paragraph (b) below such specific conditions as the enforcing authority considers appropriate, when taken with the general condition implied by subsection (4) below, for achieving the objectives specified in subsection (2) below;

    (b) such conditions as are specified in directions given by the Secretary of State under subsection (3) below; and

    (c) such other conditions (if any) as appear to the enforcing authority to be appropriate;

but no conditions shall be imposed for the purpose only of securing the health of persons at work (within the meaning of Part I of the Health and Safety at Work etc. Act 1974).

    (2) Those objectives are—

    (a) ensuring that, in carrying on a prescribed process, the best available techniques not entailing excessive cost will be used—

      (i) for preventing the release of substances prescribed for any environmental medium into that medium or, where that is not practicable by such means, for reducing the release of such substances to a minimum and for rendering harmless any such substances which are so released; and

(ii) for rendering harmless any other substances which might cause harm if released into any environmental medium;

(b) compliance with any directions by the Secretary of State given for the implementation of any obligations of the United Kingdom under the Community Treaties or international law relating to environmental protection;

(c) compliance with any limits or requirements and achievement of any quality standards or quality objectives prescribed by the Secretary of State under any of the relevant enactments;

(d) compliance with any requirements applicable to the grant of authorisations specified by or under a plan made by the Secretary of State under section 3(5) above.

(3) Except as respects the general condition implied by subsection (4) below, the Secretary of State may give directions to the enforcing authorities as to the conditions which are, or are not, to be included in all authorisations, in authorisations of any specified description or in any particular authorisation.

(4) Subject to subsections (5) and (6) below, there is implied in every authorisation a general condition that, in carrying on the process to which the authorisation applies, the person carrying it on must use the best available techniques not entailing excessive cost—

(a) for preventing the release of substances prescribed for any environmental medium into that medium or, where that is not practicable by such means, for reducing the release of such substances to a minimum and for rendering harmless any such substances which are so released; and

(b) for rendering harmless any other substances which might cause harm if released into any environmental medium.

(5) In the application of subsections (1) to (4) above to authorisations granted by a local enforcing authority references to the release of substances into any environmental medium are to be read as references to the release of substances into the air.

(6) The obligation implied by virtue of subsection (4) above shall not apply in relation to any aspect of the process in question which is regulated by a condition imposed under subsection (1) above.

(7) The objectives referred to in subsection (2) above shall, where the process—

(a) is one designated for central control; and

(b) is likely to involve the release of substances into more than one environmental medium;

include the objective of ensuring that the best available techniques not entailing excessive cost will be used for minimising the pollution which may be caused to the environment taken as a whole by the releases having regard to the best practicable environmental option available as respects the substances which may be released.

(8) An authorisation for carrying on a prescribed process may, without prejudice to the generality of subsection (1) above, include conditions—

(a) imposing limits on the amount or composition of any substance produced by or utilised in the process in any period; and

(b) requiring advance notification of any proposed change in the manner of carrying on the process.

(9) This section has effect subject to section 28 below [...].

(10) References to the best available techniques not entailing excessive cost, in relation to a process, include (in addition to references to any technical means and technology) references to the number, qualifications,

training and supervision of persons employed in the process and the design, construction, lay-out and maintenance of the buildings in which it is carried on.

(11) It shall be the duty of enforcing authorities to have regard to any guidance issued to them by the Secretary of State for the purposes of the application of subsections (2) and (7) above as to the techniques and environmental options that are appropriate for any description of prescribed process.

(12) In subsection (2) above "the relevant enactments" are any enactments or instruments contained in or made for the time being under—

(a) section 2 of the Clean Air Act 1968;
(b) section 2 of the European Communities Act 1972;
(c) Part I of the Health and Safety at Work etc. Act 1974;
(d) Parts II, III or IV of the Control of Pollution Act 1974;
(e) [the Water Resources Act 1991];
(f) section 3 of this Act; and
[(g) section 87 of the Environment Act 1995].

DEFINITIONS
"enforcing authority": s.1(7) and (8).
"environment": s.1(2).
"environmental medium": s.1(2).
"harm": s.1(4).
"harmless": s.1(4).
"pollution of the environment": s.1(3).
"prescribed process": s.1(5).
"process": s.1(5).
"release": s.1(10).
"relevant enactments": subs. (12).
"substances": s.1(13).

COMMENCEMENT
January 1, 1991 (S.I. 1991 No. 2635).

AMENDMENTS
The words in square brackets in subs. (12)(e) were substituted by the Water Consolidation (Consequential Provisions) Act 1991, s.2 and Sched. 1. Subs. (12)(g) was added by the Environment Act 1995, Sched. 22, para. 49, which also amended subs. (9). Subsection (12)(a) was not amended by the Clean Air Act 1993, an apparent oversight since the 1968 Act, s.2, was consolidated into the 1993 Act, s.5.

GENERAL NOTE
This section is of central importance to Pt. I of the Act, dealing with the conditions to be imposed on authorisations, and introducing the key concepts of best available techniques not entailing excessive cost (BATNEEC) and best practicable environmental option (BPEO). Each authorisation incorporates a general implied condition (subs. (4)) and in addition may contain specific express conditions (subs. (1)) falling into one of three categories:

(a) conditions considered appropriate by the enforcing authority for achieving objectives stated in subs. (2) (to which air quality standards and objectives prescribed under the air quality strategy provisions in the Environment Act 1995, Pt. IV, have been added);
(b) conditions specified by direction of the Secretary of State (subs. (3)); and
(c) such other conditions, if any, as appear to the enforcing authority to be appropriate.

The validity of all conditions (and perhaps particularly those in category (c)) will no doubt be subject to general principles of administrative law and *ultra vires*. For example, a condition imposed by a local enforcing authority in England and Wales which purported to control emissions to media other than air would appear to be *ultra vires*. It may be possible to draw analogies from the general principles evolved by the courts in relation to conditions attached to planning permissions.

Some guidance as to the attitude of the Secretary of State to conditions is to be found in general guidance note *GG2: Authorisations*. In relation to air pollution control, GG2 suggests tests based on clarity, relevance and workability. It is possible for the Secretary of State, under subs. (3) to give directions as to the conditions which are not to be included in authorisations as well as those that are. This power could be used to prevent an authority from including unjustified or irrelevant conditions: see Standing Committee H, Seventh Sitting, February 1, 1990, col. 227.

All specific conditions are subject to the statutory principle in subs. (1) that they shall not be imposed for the purpose *only* of securing the health of persons at work; however, it would be possible to have a valid condition which secures that purpose along with that of preventing or minimising pollution. In relation to the objectives contained in subs. (2) the linkage with s.3, by which the Secretary of State may prescribe limits requirements, standards, objectives and plans, should be noted.

The Secretary of State has indicated (in determining the *appeal by Wildriggs Proteins Ltd against Eden District Council's refusal of an authorisation, June 27, 1995*) that an LAPC authorisation condition requiring operation in compliance with the Clean Air Act 1993 and statutory nuisance legislation should be replaced, since this end should be achieved by "specific conditions, rather than broad statements".

Subss. (2) and (4): BATNEEC

The concept of BATNEEC runs throughout s.6. Subsection (10) makes it clear that the term is not restricted to the application of technology, but also takes in matters of staffing, training, building layout and maintenance. As to the Government's guidance as to the meaning of BATNEEC, see *Integrated Pollution Control: A Practical Guide* (HMSO 1993), non-statutory guidance published by the DoE/Welsh Office and, in relation to Scotland, *Environmental Protection Act 1990—Part 1: A Practical Guide—Central Control* (1992, Scottish Office); see also (for LAPC) GG1 (91): *Secretary of State's Guidance—Introduction to Part I of the Act* (HMSO, 1991) for LAPC. All three sets of guidance make clear that BATNEEC is envisaged as offering a measure of flexibility: "the inspector/[local authority inspector] concerned will take into account variable factors such as configuration, size, other individual characteristics of the process and local environmental factors" in deciding what is BATNEEC for a particular process.

"Available", according to the guidance, does not mean in general use, "but it does require general accessibility". This could be from abroad or from a monopoly supplier. It "includes a technique which has been developed (or proven) at a scale which allows its implementation in the relevant industrial context with the necessary business confidence". This notion was examined further by the Secretary of State in determining an appeal against a local authority's refusal to grant an LAPC authorisation: *appeal by Triplex Foundry Ltd against conditions in authorisation from City of Bradford Metropolitan Council*, Appeal Decision Letter dated May 11, 1995. The Secretary of State endorsed the Inspector's view that although "experience in Germany indicates that the ['dry bag' technology in question] has been proven in principle", nevertheless it may not be "reliable for general application in the UK, where foundries generally melt [poorer quality scrap than their German counterparts]". It was thus appropriate in that case to defer an upgrading condition until the results of a Department of Trade and Industry DEMOS project on the dry bag system were available, since it was not yet known to be BAT. Its existence, however, meant that rival technologies which all parties accepted were "available", and which could achieve compliance with the emission limits in the relevant PG Note, would not be appropriate to employ (as would be necessary to comply with the upgrading deadline which the Council sought to impose), since the dry bag system was expected to achieve far greater emission abatement.

"Not entailing excessive cost" needs to be considered separately for new processes (where BAT is expected to equal BATNEEC), but the guidance adds that the greater the environmental damage at stake, the greater the costs of BAT which can be required before costs become "excessive". That BATNEEC can be attained by a given process does not necessarily mean that an authorisation should be granted: if serious harm would still result then the requirement to prevent or minimise pollution (subs. (2)(a)(i)) would not be met by granting the authorisation. Although the notion of excessive cost should be considered in relation to the economic circumstances of the industrial sector concerned, the profitability or otherwise of the particular plant or business under consideration should not affect the determination of what is BATNEEC. Site-specific factors are, however, a legitimate consideration, and the guidance (mainly non-statutory IPR Notes for IPC and statutory PG Notes for LAPC—see subs. (11)) on attainable performance standards should only be taken as a material consideration (to which, in the case of PG Notes, the authority must have regard), but not necessarily as conclusive as to the BATNEEC for the process in question.

Having determined the BATNEEC for the process in question, the guidance suggests that the enforcing authority should not then be overly prescriptive and simply stipulate that those techniques be adopted. Rather, the performance standards yielded by the identified BAT-NEEC should be determined and any technique which does at least as well in terms of release levels attained should be accepted as BATNEEC.

Both in relation to specific conditions and the general implied condition, BATNEEC is to be used for two purposes, namely:

(1) preventing the release of substances prescribed for any environmental medium into that medium (or in the case of LAPC preventing the release of substances prescribed for air into the air) or, where that is not practicable by the application of BATNEEC, reducing release to a minimum and rendering any releases harmless; and

(2) rendering harmless any other (non-prescribed) substances that might cause harm if released into any environmental medium (or, in the case of LAPC, into the air).

The dichotomy created by the Alkali etc. Works Regulation Act 1906 (and earlier legislation) between: (a) preventing release where practicable; and (b) rendering releases harmless where prevention is not practicable is thereby preserved in the case of prescribed substances. The first step would therefore appear to be to identify those techniques which do not entail excessive cost for preventing the release of such substances and then to ask whether it is practicable to prevent release by those means. Traditional judicial interpretations of the term "practicable" have brought in questions of cost and risk: see, *e.g. Adsett v. K. and L. Steelfounders and Engineers* [1953] 1 W.L.R. 773; *Edwards v. National Coal Board* [1949] 1 K.B. 704; *Coltness Iron Co. v. Sharp* [1938] A.C. 90. This has also been the view expressed by HMIP in its Note on *Best Practicable Means: general principles and practice* (BPM 1/88, January 1988) paras. 10–16. It is therefore not entirely clear how BATNEEC relates to practicability in this sense: in particular if a technique which could prevent release has been identified as one not entailing excessive cost, is it still possible to argue that it is not practicable to prevent release by that technique?

With non-prescribed substances, the position is clearer. It should be asked whether the substance might cause harm if released, and if so BATNEEC is to be used to render it harmless, but not necessarily to prevent its release.

Where an enforcing authority grants or varies an authorisation in respect of activities which include the disposal of waste, the authorisation must cover the types and quantities of waste; the technical requirements; the security precautions to be taken; the disposal site; and the treatment method (paragraph 6 of Schedule 4 to the Waste Management Licensing Regulations 1994 (S.I. 1994 No. 1056), see Appendix 3).

Subs. (2)

In addition to the subs. (2) objectives, where a prescribed process involves the disposal or recovery of waste then an enforcing authority must exercise its functions under Pt. I for the purpose of achieving the "relevant objectives" implied into Pt. I by paragraph 8 of Schedule 4 to the Waste Management Licensing Regulations 1994 (S.I. 1994 No. 1056). However, prevention of detriment to a locality's amenities need not be taken into account, under this obligation, provided that the relevant objectives are to have been taken into account by an action of the planning authority.

Subs. (7)

BPEO. Where a process is subject to central control and is likely to involve the release of substances into more than one environmental medium, the concept of BPEO comes into play. BATNEEC is to be used to minimise pollution caused to the environment as a whole (not just the receiving medium) having regard to the best practicable environmental option available as respects the substances that may be released. The complex process envisaged by the subsection therefore appears to be:

(1) identification of the substances that may be released;

(2) deciding what is the best practicable environmental option in relation to such substance or substances (or possibly combinations of substances);

(3) "having regard" to the BPEO so identified, identifying the BATNEEC which will minimise the pollution which may be caused to the environment as a whole, focusing here on the carrying on of the process rather than simply on the substances.

It appears therefore on the wording of the subsection that the crucial concept is still BATNEEC: the objective is to minimise pollution by the application of BATNEEC, having regard to BPEO.

Meaning of BPEO. BPEO is not defined in the Act but was considered at length by the Royal Commission on Environmental Pollution in their Eleventh Report of that name (Cm. 310). The RCEP's definition is given at para. 2.1 of the Report, as follows:

> "A BPEO is the outcome of a systematic consultative and decision-making procedure which emphasises the protection and conservation of the environment across land, air and

water. The BPEO procedure establishes, for a given set of objectives, the option that provides the most benefit or least damage to the environment as a whole, at acceptable cost, in the long term as well as in the short term."

The Report stresses:
(a) the width of options to be considered (para. 2.3);
(b) the evaluation of options for their environmental effects early in the decision-making process (para. 2.4);
(c) that "practicable" entails the option being in accordance with current technical knowledge and must not have disproportionate financial implications (para. 2.6);
(d) that local derogations to BPEO should not be admitted for social or political reasons (para. 2.7); and
(e) that it is doubtful whether there is ever an absolute best (para. 2.9).

Chapter 3 of the Report gives the RCEP's views on the procedure for arriving at BPEO, including the importance of maintaining a properly recorded "audit trail". The Report is generally an extremely full and careful examination of the concept, which defies concise summary.

HMIP have developed for consultation a methodology on evaluating the BPEO for IPC processes. This was first issued in draft in April 1994: *Environmental, Economic and BPEO Assessment Principles for Integrated Pollution Control.* Subsequent drafts in the form of draft Technical Guidance Note E1 (in 3 volumes) were at the time of writing being assessed by an ad hoc advisory group. The draft introduces the notion of an Integrated Environmental Index as part of the methodology.

Subs. (8)
Under this subsection, conditions may: (a) impose limits on the amount or composition of input and output substances in relation to a process; and (b) require advance notification of proposed changes in the manner of carrying on a process. The Government's thinking behind (a) is shown clearly by the following comments from Mr David Trippier in Committee:

"It is not our intention that enforcing authorities should in the normal course of events restrict the production capacity of a process, or the nature of the products that it produces, or set requirements as to inputs. Unless overriding considerations prevail, decisions on these matters are for industry itself. Enforcing authorities have no basis for getting involved, and no need to. But there will be some cases where such controls have to be exercised, if emissions are to be properly controlled. It might help if I give a couple of examples. If a certain piece of hardware is to be used to control emissions, it may be that there needs to be a limit on the throughput in the process, because that hardware is only effective up to certain levels of throughput. Higher throughput would require more sophisticated control technology. Therefore, it is important that limits can be set on the throughput. Conditions might be required in similar circumstances to regulate the type of feedstock. Such controls can be regarded as interim measures before more suitable emission control equipment is installed.

We also need to provide against cases where, for example, a combustion plant using high sulphur fuel causes significant air pollution. Enforcing authorities need to be able to limit the amount of such fuel that is used, or to specify less polluting fuel.

But I emphasise that that power is intended to be used infrequently, and only when necessary. Wherever possible, industry will have full flexibility to make its own decisions on inputs and throughputs within the parameters required by the necessary controls over releases." (H.C. Standing Committee H, Seventh Sitting, February 1, 1990, cols. 228–299.)

Subs. (11)
Guidance. The Secretary of State may achieve consistency as to BATNEEC for LAPC and as to BATNEEC and BPEO for IPC by means of guidance as to techniques and environmental options relating to any description of prescribed process. The enforcing authorities are under a statutory duty to have regard to such guidance. Further detail as to guidance proposed and issued is given in the General Note to Pt. I, under the heading *Authorisations, Conditions and BATNEEC.*

Fees and charges for authorisations

8.—(1) There shall be charged by and paid to the [local enforcing authority] such fees and charges as may be prescribed from time to time by a scheme under subsection (2) below (whether by being specified in or made calculable under the scheme).

(2) The Secretary of State may, with the approval of the Treasury, make, and from time to time revise, a scheme prescribing—

(a) fees payable in respect of applications for authorisations;

(b) fees payable by persons holding authorisations in respect of, or of applications for, the variation of authorisations; and

(c) charges payable by such persons in respect of the subsistence of their authorisations.

(3) The Secretary of State shall, on making or revising a scheme under subsection (2) above, lay a copy of the scheme or of the alterations made in the scheme or, if he considers it more appropriate, the scheme as revised, before each House of Parliament.

(4) [...]

(5) A scheme under subsection (2) above may, in particular—

(a) make different provision for different cases, including different provision in relation to different persons, circumstances or localities;

(b) allow for reduced fees or charges to be payable in respect of authorisations for a number of prescribed processes carried on by the same person;

(c) provide for the times at which and the manner in which the payments required by the scheme are to be made; and

(d) make such incidental, supplementary and transitional provision as appears to the Secretary of State to be appropriate.

(6) The Secretary of State, in framing a scheme under subsection (2) above, shall, so far as practicable, secure that the fees and charges payable under the scheme are sufficient, taking one financial year with another, to cover the relevant expenditure attributable to authorisations.

(7) The "relevant expenditure attributable to authorisations" is the expenditure incurred by the [local enforcing authorities] in exercising their functions under this Part in relation to authorisations. [...]

(8) If it appears to the [local enforcing authority] that the holder of an authorisation has failed to pay a charge due in consideration of the subsistence of the authorisation, it may, by notice in writing served on the holder, revoke the authorisation.

(9) [...]

[(10) The foregoing provisions of this section shall not apply to Scotland.]

(11) [...]

DEFINITIONS
"authorisation": s.1(9).
"local enforcing authority": s.1(7) and (8).
"prescribed processes": s.1(5).

COMMENCEMENT
January 1, 1991 (S.I. 1990 No. 2365).

AMENDMENTS
Subss. (1), (7) and (8) were amended, subss. (4) and (9) were deleted, and a new subs. (10) was substituted for the former subss. (10) and (11), by the Environment Act 1995, Sched. 22, para. 50.

GENERAL NOTE
This section gives wide power to the Secretary of State, with Treasury approval, to set a scheme of fees and charges for LAPC in England and Wales. The equivalent charging schemes for IPC and for Scottish LAPC, formerly governed by this section, are now made under ss.41 and 42 of the Environment Act 1995. Fees are payable on applications for authorisation and in respect of variation or applications for variation.

The essential concept is that of "relevant expenditure attributable to authorisations," defined in subs. (7).

The sanction for non-payment of charges for subsistence of the authorisation is notice revoking the authorisation (subs. (8)). If the fee is not paid in respect of an application for authorisation or for variation, then the application is not duly made, and need not be considered by the local enforcing authority (ss.6(2) and (3) and 11(9)).

Further information on the charging regime is given in the General Note to Pt. I under the heading *Fees and Charges*. The charging schemes current at the time of writing for England and Wales (both in fact made under this section prior to the amendments) are set out in:

(i) *Fees and Charges for Integrated Pollution Control 1995/96.*

The application fee for 1995/96 is £2,750 per component for processes previously regulated by HMIP for air releases under previous legislation (the Alkali etc. Works Regulation Act 1906 and Health and Safety at Work, etc., Act 1974), and £3,860 per component for processes coming under regulation by the Agency for the first time. The substantial variation fee is £1,290 per component, and the annual subsistence charge is £1,805 per component. Factors described in the publication may vary these figures in certain cases, so this summary oversimplifies somewhat.

(ii) *Fees and Charges for Local Authority Air Pollution Control 1995/96.*

The application fee for 1995/96 is £990, the annual subsistence charge fee is £605, and where a substantial change is made the fee is £635. Where such a change is made for the purpose of implementing a programme for upgrading an existing process the fee is £100. The application and subsistence fee for small waste oil burners is £100 and the application fee for processes registered under the Alkali etc. Works Regulation Act 1906 is £595.

The current charging schemes for Scotland are set out in the Integrated Pollution Control Fees and Charges (Scotland) Scheme 1995 and the Local Authority Air Pollution Control Fees and Charges (Scotland) Scheme 1995 as revised.

Transfer of authorisations

9.—(1) An authorisation for the carrying on of any prescribed process may be transferred by the holder to a person who proposes to carry on the process in the holder's place.

(2) Where an authorisation is transferred under this section, the person to whom it is transferred shall notify the enforcing authority in writing of that fact not later than the end of the period of 21 days beginning with the date of the transfer.

(3) An authorisation which is transferred under this section shall have effect on and after the date of the transfer as if it had been granted to that person under section 6 above, subject to the same conditions as were attached to it immediately before that date.

DEFINITIONS
"authorisation": s.1(9).
"enforcing authority": s.1(7) and (8).
"prescribed process": s.1(5).

COMMENCEMENT
January 1, 1991 (S.I. 1990 No. 2635).

GENERAL NOTE
This section deals with transfer of authorisations. It is open to the holder of an authorisation to transfer it to any person who proposes to carry out the process in the holder's place. This wording appears to imply that the transfer may only be made prospectively and not once control of the process itself has been transferred. There is no requirement that the transfer of the authorisation be effected in writing, though this may in practice be prudent. By subs. (3) the effect of the transfer is that the authorisation forthwith takes effect as if granted to the transferee, and subject to the same conditions as before.

There is no obligation to obtain the prior consent of the enforcing authority to a transfer, but simply for the transferee to notify the authority in writing of the fact of transfer not later than 21 days beginning with the date of the transfer. Failure to give such notice is an offence (s.23(1)(b)). The authority have no specific power to object to the transfer, despite the fact that on grant of an authorisation they must have regard to the capability of the applicant (see s.6(4) and notes thereto.) If the authority entertained serious doubts as to the ability or intentions of the transferee to carry on the process in accordance with the conditions, then it could serve an enforcement notice (s.13), or in an extreme case serve a prohibition notice (s.14) or revoke the authorisation (s.12).

Variation of authorisations by enforcing authority

10.—(1) The enforcing authority may at any time, subject to the requirements of section 7 above, and, in cases to which they apply, the requirements of Part II of Schedule 1 to this Act, vary an authorisation and shall do so if it appears to the authority at that time that that section requires conditions to be included which are different from the subsisting conditions.

(2) Where the enforcing authority has decided to vary an authorisation under subsection (1) above the authority shall notify the holder of the authorisation and serve a variation notice on him.

(3) In this Part a "variation notice" is a notice served by the enforcing authority on the holder of an authorisation—

(a) specifying variations of the authorisation which the enforcing authority has decided to make; and

(b) specifying the date or dates on which the variations are to take effect;

and, unless the notice is withdrawn [or is varied under subsection (3A) below], the variations specified in a variation notice shall take effect on the date or dates so specified.

[(3A) An enforcing authority which has served a variation notice may vary that notice by serving on the holder of the authorisation in question a further notice—

(a) specifying the variations which the enforcing authority has decided to make to the variation notice; and

(b) specifying the date or dates on which the variations specified in the variation notice, as varied by the further notice, are to take effect;

and any reference in this Part to a variation notice, or to a variation notice served under subsection (2) above, includes a reference to such a notice as varied by a further notice served under this subsection.]

(4) A variation notice served under subsection (2) above shall also—

(a) require the holder of the authorisation, within such period as may be specified in the notice, to notify the authority what action (if any) he proposes to take to ensure that the process is carried on in accordance with the authorisation as varied by the notice; and

[(b) require the holder to pay, within such period as may be specified in the notice,—

(i) in a case where the enforcing authority is the Environment Agency or SEPA, the charge (if any) prescribed for the purpose by a charging scheme under section 41 of the Environment Act 1995; or

(ii) in any other case, the fee (if any) prescribed by a scheme under section 8 above.]

(5) Where in the opinion of the enforcing authority any action to be take by the holder of an authorisation in consequence of a variation notice served under subsection (2) above will involve a substantial change in the manner in which the process is being carried on, the enforcing authority shall notify the holder of its opinion.

(6) The Secretary of State may, if he thinks fit in relation to authorisations of any description or particular authorisations, direct the enforcing authorities—

(a) to exercise their powers under this section, or to do so in such circumstances as may be specified in the directions, in such manner as may be so specified; or

(b) not to exercise those powers, or not to do so in such circumstances or such manner as may be so specified;

and the Secretary of State shall have the corresponding power of direction in respect of the powers of the enforcing authorities to vary authorisations under section 11 below.

(7) In this section and section 11 below a "substantial change", in relation to a prescribed process being carried on under an authorisation, means a substantial change in the substances released from the process or in the amount or any other characteristic of any substance so released; and the Secretary of State may give directions to the enforcing authorities as to what does or does not constitute a substantial change in relation to processes generally, any description of process or any particular process.

(8) In this section and section 11 below—

"prescribed" means prescribed in regulations made by the Secretary of State;

"vary", [(a)] in relation to the subsisting conditions or other provisions of an authorisation, means adding to them or varying or rescinding any of them; [and (b) in relation to a variation notice, means adding to, or varying or rescinding the notice or any of its contents,]

and "variation" shall be construed accordingly.

DEFINITIONS
"authorisation": s.1(9).
"enforcing authority": s.1(7) and (8).
"prescribed process": s.1(5).
"process": s.1(5).
"released": s.1(10).
"substances": s.1(13).

COMMENCEMENT
January 1, 1991 (S.I. 1990 No. 2635).

AMENDMENTS
The Environment Act 1995, Sched. 22, para. 51, amended subss. (3), (4) and (8), and inserted subs. (3A).

GENERAL NOTE
This section gives enforcing authorities power to vary authorisations. "Variation" can include the addition or rescission of conditions (subs. (8)). Subsection (1) gives authorities a general power of variation at any time, subject to the general objectives and provisions of s.7. It also places a duty on authorities to vary conditions if it appears that s.7 would require different conditions to be imposed from those subsisting. As mentioned in the notes to s.6, authorities are under a continuing duty to keep authorisations under review.

Part II of Sched. 1 contains provisions which apply where an enforcing authority is of the view that action to be taken in consequence of a variation will involve "a substantial change in the manner in which the process is being carried on". In such cases the authority is required to advertise the action, give notice of it to prescribed persons, and consider any representations received.

Variation is effected by means of a variation notice served on the holder of the authorisation. The variations take effect from the date or dates specified in the notice (subs. (3)). If the authority is of the opinion that any action to be taken in consequence of the variation notice will involve a substantial change in the manner in which the process is being carried on, this opinion is to be notified to the holder of the authorisation (subs. (5)). "Substantial change" in this context is defined in subs. (7) by reference to the amount or other characteristics of substances released from the process; the Secretary of State may additionally give directions as to what does or does not constitute such a change. "Substantial" has been said to mean "considerable, solid, or big"; it will be a question for the discretion of the judge of fact, applying as much precision as is attainable in the context of the subject-matter being considered (see *Palser v. Grinling, Property Holding Co. v. Mischeff* [1948] 1 All E.R. 1, 11, H.L., *per* Viscount Simon and also *Atkinson v. Bettison* [1955] 3 All E.R. 340, 342, C.A., *per* Denning L.J.; [1955] 1 W.L.R. 1127). In the context of E.C. Directive 76/464/EEC on limit values and quality objectives for discharges of dangerous substances to the aquatic environment, the Government interprets "substantial change" as meaning an overall increase in capacity of 20 per cent or more (see Circ. 7/89, para. 2, referred to in the General Note to Pt. I).

Subss. (3) and (3A): varying a variation notice
Amendments introduced by the Environment Act 1995 provide for an enforcing authority which has issued a variation notice to serve a further notice varying that variation notice. Previously the only course would have been to withdraw the first notice and serve a new one.

Variation of conditions etc.: applications by holders of authorisations

11.—(1) A person carrying on a prescribed process under an authorisation who wishes to make a relevant change in the process may at any time—
  (a) notify the enforcing authority in the prescribed form of that fact, and
  (b) request the enforcing authority to make a determination, in relation to the proposed change, of the matters mentioned in subsection (2) below;
and a person making a request under paragraph (b) above shall furnish the enforcing authority with such information as may be prescribed or as the authority may by notice require.

(2) On receiving a request under subsection (1) above the enforcing authority shall determine—
  (a) whether the proposed change would involve a breach of any condition of the authorisation;
  (b) if it would not involve such a breach, whether the authority would be likely to vary the conditions of the authorisation as a result of the change;
  (c) if it would involve such a breach, whether the authority would consider varying the conditions of the authorisation so that the change may be made; and
  (d) whether the change would involve a substantial change in the manner in which the process is being carried on;
and the enforcing authority shall notify the holder of the authorisation of its determination of those matters.

(3) Where the enforcing authority has determined that the proposed change would not involve a substantial change, but has also determined under paragraph (b) or (c) of subsection (2) above that the change would lead to or require the variation of the conditions of the authorisation, then—
  (a) the enforcing authority shall (either on notifying its determination under that subsection or on a subsequent occasion) notify the holder of the authorisation of the variations which the authority is likely to consider making; and
  (b) the holder may apply in the prescribed form to the enforcing authority for the variation of the conditions of the authorisation so that he may make the proposed change.

(4) Where the enforcing authority has determined that a proposed change would involve a substantial change that would lead to or require the variation of the conditions of the authorisation, then—
  (a) the authority shall (either on notifying its determination under subsection (2) above or on a subsequent occasion) notify the holder of the authorisation of the variations which the authority is likely to consider making; and
  (b) the holder of the authorisation shall, if he wishes to proceed with the change, apply in the prescribed form to the enforcing authority for the variation of the conditions of the authorisation.

(5) The holder of an authorisation may at any time, unless he is carrying on a prescribed process under the authorisation and wishes to make a relevant change in the process, apply to the enforcing authority in the prescribed form for the variation of the conditions of the authorisation.

(6) A person carrying on a process under an authorisation who wishes to make a relevant change in the process may, where it appears to him that the change will require the variation of the conditions of the authorisation, apply to the enforcing authority in the prescribed form for the variation of the conditions of the authorisation specified in the application.

(7) A person who makes an application for the variation of the conditions of an authorisation shall furnish the authority with such information as may be prescribed or as the authority may by notice require.

(8) On an application for variation of the conditions of an authorisation under any provision of this section—

    (a) the enforcing authority may, having fulfilled the requirements of Part II of Schedule 1 to this Act in cases to which they apply, as it thinks fit either refuse the application or, subject to the requirements of section 7 above, vary the conditions or, in the case of an application under subsection (6) above, treat the application as a request for a determination under subsection (2) above; and

    (b) if the enforcing authority decides to vary the conditions, it shall serve a variation notice on the holder of the authorisation.

[(9) Any application to the enforcing authority under this section shall be accompanied—

    (a) in a case where the enforcing authority is the Environment Agency or SEPA, by the charge (if any) prescribed for the purpose by a charging scheme under section 41 of the Environment Act 1995; or

    (b) in any other case, by the fee (if any) prescribed by a scheme under section 8 above.]

(10) This section applies to any provision other than a condition which is contained in an authorisation as it applies to a condition with the modification that any reference to the breach of a condition shall be read as a reference to acting outside the scope of the authorisation.

(11) For the purposes of this section a relevant change in a prescribed process is a change in the manner of carrying on the process which is capable of altering the substances released from the process or of affecting the amount or any other characteristic of any substance so released.

DEFINITIONS
    "authorisation": s.1(9).
    "enforcing authority": s.1(7) and (8).
    "prescribed": s.10(8).
    "prescribed process": s.1(5).
    "process": s.1(5).
    "released": s.1(10).
    "SEPA": s.1(8).
    "substances": s.1(13).
    "substantial change": s.10(7).
    "variation": s.10(8).
    "vary": s.10(8).

COMMENCEMENT
January 1, 1991 (S.I. 1990 No. 2635).

AMENDMENT
The Environment Act 1995, Sched. 22, para. 52, substituted subs. (9).

GENERAL NOTE
This section provides a number of means by which conditions of an authorisation may be varied at the instigation of the holder of the authorisation. The section applies not only to variation of conditions but also limitations or other provisions contained in an authorisation (subs. (10)).

    (1) The first method, where the holder of the authority wishes to make a "relevant change" in the process, is to notify the authority of that fact and to request the authority to make a determination on various matters (subs. (1)). The matters for determination are set out in subs. (2). The authority may determine that the change would not involve breach of any condition

and would not lead the authority to vary the conditions—in that case the holder of the licence is presumably free to make the change, though it appears this would not preclude the authority from keeping the conditions under review and exercising its own powers of variation under s.10. Alternatively, the authority may determine that the change would not involve any breach but that the authority would be likely to vary the conditions as a result of the change; or that it would involve a breach but that the authority would consider varying the conditions to allow the change to be made. In either case the authority should notify the variations it would be likely to consider making, and the holder of the authorisation may then apply for the relevant variations (subs. (3)). If the applicant disagrees with the determination, there is no right of appeal under s.15. In such circumstances the options open to the applicant would appear to be to make the relevant change (in which case enforcement action might follow) or to make an application for variation and then to appeal if refused. A separate procedure applies where the authority determines under subs. (2)(d) that the change would involve a substantial change in the manner of the process (as defined in s.10(7)). See subs. (4) and Sched. 1, Pt. II. Here the holder of the authorisation, if he wishes to proceed with the change, must apply for variation (subs. (4)(b)).

(2) The second method applies to the holder of an authorisation who does not wish to make a relevant change in the process he is carrying on. Here the procedure is a straightforward application for variation under subs. (5). This procedure could therefore be used either: (a) where no prescribed process is actually being carried on; or (b) where the proposed change is not "relevant" as defined in subs. (11).

(3) The third method applies to the person carrying on a process and who wishes to make a relevant change. Where it appears to him that the change will require variation of the conditions, an application for variation may be made under subs. (6), thus bypassing the complex provisions involving determination by the authority under subss. (1) and (2) as described above.

It is perhaps easier to compare these alternative procedures diagrammatically: see below.

Regulations. Regulations have been made dealing with variation procedures: Environmental Protection (Applications, Appeals and Registers) Regulations 1991 (S.I. 1991 No. 507, as amended, see Appendix 2). These deal with the information to be given on applying for a determination or variation.

Sched. 1, Part II, para. 7
Procedure for substantial changes. Where the authority has determined that a proposed change would be substantial and an application is subsequently made under s.11(4)(b) for variation, para. 7(1) of the Schedule applies requirements of consultation, advertisement and consideration of representations. These procedures appear not to apply where an application for variation is made which involves a substantial change, but has not been the subject of a previous determination to that effect. It is however, open to the authority to treat the application for variation as an application for a determination and proceed accordingly (subs. 8(a)).

Relevant change and *substantial change.* The differing effects of these expressions should be noted. A "relevant change" is one that triggers the procedures under subs. (1) (notification and request for determination) and (6) (application for variation). "Relevant change" is defined by subs. (11) as one which is capable of altering the substances released or their amount or other characteristics. A "substantial change" is one that triggers the procedure of subs. (4) and consequently the requirements of Sched. 1, para. 7 as to advertisement and consultation. A "substantial change" is defined by s.10(7) as one leading to a substantial change in the substances released or in their amounts or characteristics. Thus not all "relevant" changes will be "substantial", but all "substantial" changes will be "relevant".

Appeals
Appeal against refusal of a variation lies to the Secretary of State under s.15(1)(c).

Revocation of authorisation

12.—(1) The enforcing authority may at any time revoke an authorisation by notice in writing to the person holding the authorisation.

(2) Without prejudice to the generality of subsection (1) above, the enforcing authority may revoke an authorisation where it has reason to believe that a prescribed process for which the authorisation is in force has not been carried on or not for a period of 12 months.

(3) The revocation of an authorisation under this section shall have effect from the date specified in the notice; and the period between the date on

PERSON CARRYING ON PROCESS UNDER AUTHORISATION
AND WISHING TO MAKE A RELEVANT CHANGE

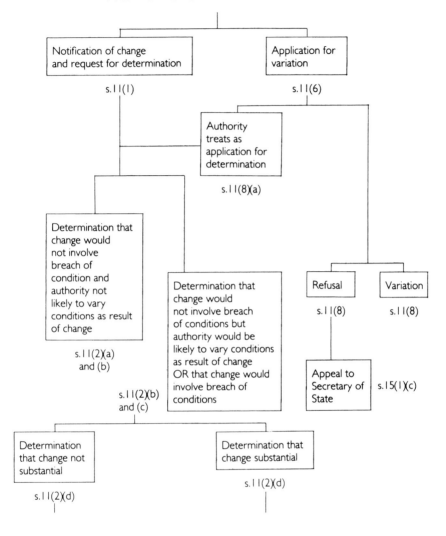

PERSON CARRYING ON PROCESS UNDER AUTHORISATION
AND WISHING TO MAKE A RELEVANT CHANGE—*cont.*

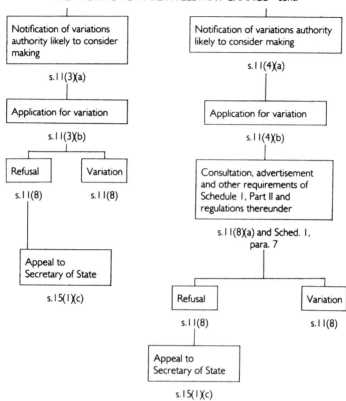

HOLDER OF AUTHORISATION (UNLESS CARRYING
ON PROCESS AND WISHING TO MAKE A
RELEVANT CHANGE)

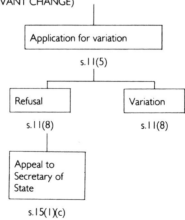

which the notice is served and the date so specified shall not be less than 28 days.

(4) The enforcing authority may, before the date on which the revocation of an authorisation takes effect, withdraw the notice or vary the date specified in it.

(5) The Secretary of State may, if he thinks fit in relation to an authorisation, give to the enforcing authority directions as to whether the authority should revoke the authorisation under this section.

DEFINITIONS
"authorisation": s.1(9).
"enforcing authority": s.1(7) and (8).
"prescribed process": s.1(5).

COMMENCEMENT
January 1, 1991 (S.I. 1990 No. 2635).

GENERAL NOTE
In addition to the general power of revocation conferred by subs. (1), a specific power of revocation is given by subs. (2) where the relevant process has not been carried on for a period of 12 months (presumably ending with the date of the revocation notice, though the subsection does not say this). There is obviously a drafting slip in subs. (2): presumably what is intended is that the authorisation may be revoked if the process has not been carried on at all or has not been carried on for a period of 12 months. The question of whether a process is or is not being "carried on" is therefore important (see note to s.6).

Revocation notices have so far been used in the following circumstances: (1) where an authorisation holder had failed to comply with an improvement programme set out in their IPC authorisation despite a number of extensions to the timescale for implementing the programme (HMIP Bulletin, Issue 34, February 1995, *revocation notice served on A. W. Stokes & Sons (Drums) Ltd*); and (2) to prevent the re-opening of a plant which an authorisation holder had closed because it could not reach the upgrading standards (HMIP Bulletin, Issue 35, March 1995, p. 20, *revocation notice served on Beacon Waste*).

Enforcement

Enforcement notices

13.—(1) If the enforcing authority is of the opinion that the person carrying on a prescribed process under an authorisation is contravening any condition of the authorisation, or is likely to contravene any such condition, the authority may serve on him a notice ("an enforcement notice").

(2) An enforcement notice shall—
   (a) state that the authority is of the said opinion;
   (b) specify the matters constituting the contravention or the matters making it likely that the contravention will arise, as the case may be;
   (c) specify the steps that must be taken to remedy the contravention or to remedy the matters making it likely that the contravention will arise, as the case may be; and
   (d) specify the period within which those steps must be taken.

(3) The Secretary of State may, if he thinks fit in relation to the carrying on by any person of a prescribed process, give to the enforcing authority directions as to whether the authority should exercise its powers under this section and as to the steps which are to be required to be taken under this section.

[(4) The enforcing authority may, as respects any enforcement notice it has issued to any person, withdraw the notice.]

DEFINITIONS
"authorisation": s.1(9).
"enforcing authority": s.1(7) and (8).
"prescribed process": s.1(5).

COMMENCEMENT
January 1, 1991 (S.I. 1990 No. 2635).

AMENDMENT
The Environment Act 1995, Sched. 22, para. 53, inserted subs. (4).

GENERAL NOTE
Enforcement notices under this section may be served not only where a condition or conditions is being contravened, but also where contravention appears likely to take place.

Failure to comply with the notice is an offence under s.23(1)(c). The requirements as to the matters to be contained in an enforcement notice under subs. (2) are mandatory and it appears that any notice which on its face does not comply with those requirements will be a nullity and, as such, so much waste paper that can be ignored or challenged in proceedings: *Miller-Mead v. Minister of Housing and Local Government* [1963] 2 Q.B. 196, 226 (C.A., *per* Upjohn L.J.). In practice, it is perhaps unlikely that many notices will fail to comply with these requirements on their face: rather, the question is likely to be whether the notice is bad for failure to specify the required matters with sufficient accuracy and precision. The most widely accepted test as to these matters in the case of planning enforcement notices is whether the notice tells the recipient "fairly what he has done wrong and what he must do to remedy it": *Miller-Mead v. Minister of Housing and Local Government* [1963] 2 Q.B. 196, 232 (C.A., *per* Upjohn L.J.). There seems no reason why the same test should not be applied to notices under s.13.

It should be noted that on an appeal against an enforcement notice (which may only be made where the notice does not implement a direction of his: s.15(2)), the Secretary of State may by s.15(7) either quash or affirm the notice and, if affirming it, do so either in its original form or with such modifications as he thinks fit. Though it does not say so explicitly, this power may well allow the Secretary of State to correct defects in a notice, but it is questionable whether it will be possible to cure fundamental defects that make the notice a nullity. Reference to the considerable body of case-law on defective enforcement notices under the Town and Country Planning Acts may provide some degree of assistance as to the likely attitude of the courts on this question, and in general the courts have become increasingly reluctant to hold that notices must be treated as a nullity.

HMIP's *1994/95 Annual Report* indicated that HMIP served 78 enforcement notices in 1994/95.

Subs. (4): withdrawal of notice
The insertion of subs. (4) by the 1995 Act provides a mechanism whereby an enforcement notice, once complied with (or perhaps where issued in error) may be withdrawn. This wording may be compared with s.14(5) in relation to prohibition notices, which *must* be withdrawn when complied with.

Prohibition notices

14.—(1) If the enforcing authority is of the opinion, as respects the carrying on of a prescribed process under an authorisation, that the continuing to carry it on, or the continuing to carry it on in a particular manner, involves an imminent risk of serious pollution of the environment the authority shall serve a notice (a "prohibition notice") on the person carrying on the process.

(2) A prohibition notice may be served whether or not the manner of carrying on the process in question contravenes a condition of the authorisation and may relate to any aspects of the process, whether regulated by the conditions of the authorisation or not.

(3) A prohibition notice shall—
   (a) state the authority's opinion;
   (b) specify the risk involved in the process;
   (c) specify the steps that must be taken to remove it and the period within which they must be taken; and
   (d) direct that the authorisation shall, until the notice is withdrawn, wholly or to the extent specified in the notice cease to have effect to authorise the carrying on of the process;
and where the direction applies to part only of the process it may impose

conditions to be observed in carrying on the part which is authorised to be carried on.

(4) The Secretary of State may, if he thinks fit in relation to the carrying on by any person of a prescribed process, give to the enforcing authority directions as to—

(a) whether the authority should perform its duties under this section; and

(b) the matters to be specified in any prohibition notice in pursuance of subsection (3) above which the authority is directed to issue.

(5) The enforcing authority shall, as respects any prohibition notice it has issued to any person, by notice in writing served on that person, withdraw the notice when it is satisfied that the steps required by the notice have been taken.

DEFINITIONS
"authorisation": s.1(9).
"enforcing authority": s.1(7) and (8).
"pollution of the environment": s.1(3).
"prescribed process": s.1(5).
"process": s.1(5).

COMMENCEMENT
January 1, 1991 (S.I. 1990 No. 2635).

GENERAL NOTE
The power conferred by this section to serve a prohibition notice is not limited to cases where a condition is being contravened, and extends to any aspect of the process, whether regulated by a condition or not (subs. (2)). The issue is whether the process involves "an imminent risk of serious pollution of the environment." Under the definition in ss.1(3) and (4) this would include harm to human health or property and offence to human senses, though it will no doubt be questionable whether offence to senses would be "serious" in the sense contemplated by the section. An example of the circumstances where a prohibition notice might be appropriate was given by Lord Reay in the following extract:

"Prohibition notices are slightly different. They are not designed primarily to be served when an operator is breaching or is likely to breach the conditions of an authorisation. They are designed to cover circumstances in which a process is being operated in a perfectly reasonable manner and within the conditions of the authorisation but where some event external to the process requires quick and decisive action. For example, an accident at one process could release substances which could react with those normally allowed to be released by a nearby process, so causing serious pollution. In those circumstances it would be right to close down temporarily the second process even though it was operating within its authorisation." (*Hansard*, H.L. Vol. 520, col. 897.)

See also H.C. Standing Committee H, Eighth Sitting, February 6, 1990, cols. 249–250.

As with enforcement notices, breach of a prohibition notice is an offence (s.23(1)(c)) and an appeal against the notice lies to the Secretary of State unless, the notice implements a direction of his (s.15(2)). There are mandatory requirements as to the matters to be included in a notice (subs. (3)) and the comments made in the note to s.13 as to the effect of non-compliance with those requirements would appear to apply equally.

HMIP's *1994/95 Annual Report* indicated that HMIP issued two prohibition notices during 1994/95. In both cases the problems prompting the issuing of the notice appear to have been resolved within a couple of months and the notice presumably therefore withdrawn.

Appeals as respects authorisations and against variation, enforcement and prohibition notices

15.—(1) The following persons, namely—

(a) a person who has been refused the grant of an authorisation under section 6 above;

(b) a person who is aggrieved by the conditions attached, under any provision of this Part, to his authorisation;

(c) a person who has been refused a variation of an authorisation on an application under section 11 above;

(d) a person whose authorisation has been revoked under section 12 above;

may appeal against the decision of the enforcing authority to the Secretary of State (except where the decision implements a direction of his).

(2) A person on whom a variation notice, an enforcement notice or a prohibition notice is served may appeal against the notice to the Secretary of State [(except where the notice implements a direction of his)].

[(3) This section is subject to section 114 of the Environment Act 1995 (delegation or reference of appeals etc.)]

(4) An appeal under this section shall, if and to the extent required by regulations under subsection (10) below, be advertised in such manner as may be prescribed by regulations under that subsection.

[(5) Before determining an appeal under this section, the Secretary of State may, if he thinks fit

(a) cause the appeal to take or continue in the form of a hearing (which may, if the person hearing the appeal so decides, be held, or held to any extent, in private): or

(b) cause a local inquiry to be held;

and the Secretary of State shall act as mentioned in paragraph (a) or (b) above if a request is made by either party to the appeal to be heard with respect to the appeal.]

(6) On determining an appeal against a decision of an enforcing authority under subsection (1) above, the Secretary of State—

(a) may affirm the decision;

(b) where the decision was a refusal to grant an authorisation or a variation of an authorisation, may direct the enforcing authority to grant the authorisation or to vary the authorisation, as the case may be;

(c) where the decision was as to the conditions attached to an authorisation, may quash all or any of the conditions of the authorisation;

(d) where the decision was to revoke an authorisation, may quash the decision;

and where he exercises any of the powers in paragraphs (b), (c) or (d) above, he may give directions as to the conditions to be attached to the authorisation.

(7) On the determination of an appeal under subsection (2) above the Secretary of State may either quash or affirm the notice and, if he affirms it, may do so either in its original form or with such modifications as he may in the circumstances think fit.

(8) Where an appeal is brought under subsection (1) above against the revocation of an authorisation, the revocation shall not take effect pending the final determination or the withdrawal of the appeal.

(9) Where an appeal is brought under subsection (2) above against a notice, the bringing of the appeal shall not have the effect of suspending the operation of the notice.

(10) Provision may be made by the Secretary of State by regulations with respect to appeals under this section and in particular—

(a) as to the period within which and the manner in which appeals are to be brought; and

(b) as to the manner in which appeals are to be considered;

[and any such regulations may make different provision for different cases or different circumstances.]

DEFINITIONS
"authorisation": s.1(9).
"enforcing authority": s.1(7) and (8).

COMMENCEMENT
January 1, 1991 (S.I. 1990 No. 2635).

AMENDMENTS
The Environment Act 1995, Sched. 22, para. 54, amended subss. (2) and (10), and substituted subss. (3) and (5).

GENERAL NOTE
This section, together with the regulations to be made under it, but subject to s.114 of the 1995 Act, as regards the delegation or reference of appeals, governs all appeals under Pt. I of the Act. (However, where appeal is against a decision under s.22, the modification to this section effected by s.22(5) should be noted.) There is power for the Secretary of State either to determine the appeal himself or to transfer jurisdiction to an inspector or, in Scotland, to a reporter (1995 Act, s.114, by virtue of subs. (3)). The three modes of appeal contemplated are written representations, a hearing, either in public or in private, and a local inquiry. Either party is entitled as of right to a hearing: whether the forum is a public or private hearing or a local inquiry is at the Secretary of State's discretion: subs. (5). The position is comparable under the 1995 Act, s.114. Wide discretion is given as to the disposition of appeals, including substitution of new conditions and modification of notices, but by paragraph 2 of Schedule 4 to the Waste Management Licensing Regulations 1994 (S.I. 1994 No. 1056, see Appendix 3), the Secretary of State and any person to whom he transfers jurisdiction under the 1995 Act, s.114 are required to exercise their functions under Part I in so far as they relate to the recovery or disposal of waste, with the "relevant objectives" as defined in that Schedule. In addition, where jurisdiction is transferred, the appointed person is bound by any direction given to the Agency/SEPA in determining an appeal from an Agency/SEPA decision: 1995 Act, s.40(5).

Whoever hears the appeal must, if the authorisation covers activities including the disposal of waste and if the appeal results in a decision to vary the authorisation, ensure that the authorisation covers the types and quantities of waste; the technical requirements; the security precautions to be taken; the disposal site; and the treatment method (paragraph 6 of Schedule 8 to the Waste Management Licensing Regulations 1994 (S.I. 1994 No. 1056)).

Appeals regulations
Regulations dealing with appeals were made on March 6, 1991 and came into force on April 1, 1991 in England and Wales and, in Scotland, on April 1, 1992: Environmental Protection (Applications, Appeals and Registers) Regulations 1991 (S.I. 1991 No. 507, see Appendix 2). Regulation 9 provides for written notices of appeal and for the following documents to be included with any notice of appeal:
    (a) a statement of the grounds of appeal;
    (b) a copy of any relevant application;
    (c) a copy of any relevant authorisation;
    (d) a copy of any relevant correspondence between the appellant and the enforcing authority;
    (e) a copy of any decision or notice which is the subject-matter of the appeal;
    (f) a statement indicating whether the appellant wishes the appeal to be in the form of a hearing or to be disposed of on the basis of written representations.
Regulation 10 gives a two or six month time limit for the bringing of appeals, depending on the decision being appealed against. Regulations 11–13 provide for the procedure to be followed on appeals. There is no provision for the award of costs.

A consultation paper on a number of procedural changes in respect of appeals was published by the DoE in 1994, but at the time of writing regulations implementing the proposals had not been laid.

Effect of appeal
An appeal against revocation of an authorisation has the effect of suspending the revocation until final determination or withdrawal of the appeal (subs. (8)). An appeal against a variation, prohibition or enforcement notice, by contrast, does not have the effect of suspending the operation of the notice (subs. (9)).

Challenge to decisions
No express means or grounds for challenging a decision on appeal are provided by the Act (*cf.* Town and Country Planning Act 1990, s.288).

Guidance on appeals
Explanatory guidance to local authoritities on the regulations dealing with appeals has been issued by the Secretary of State (GG5/91). That guidance is reproduced in Part F as a useful indication of how the system is likely to work in practice.

ss. 16–18 [...]

The Environment Act 1995, Sched. 24, revoked ss.16–18. Section 16 (appointment of inspectors) was rendered unnecessary by the transition from the two inspectorates (HMIP and HMIPI) to the Agency and SEPA. Sections 17 and 18 (various powers of inspectors, including entry, questioning, and seizure of articles) are superseded for all of the enforcing authorities under Pt. I by ss.108 and 109 of the Environment Act 1995, to which the reader is referred both for text and for commentary. The ss.108 and 109 powers do not precisely mirror the powers previously available under ss.17 and 18.

Obtaining of information from persons and authorities

19.—(1) For the purposes of the discharge of his functions under this Part, the Secretary of State may, by notice in writing served on an enforcing authority, require the authority to furnish such information about the discharge of its functions as an enforcing authority under this Part as he may require.

(2) For the purposes of the discharge of their respective functions under this Part, the following, that is to say—
    (a) the Secretary of State,
    (b) a local enforcing authority,
    [(c) the Environment Agency, and
    (d) SEPA,]
may, by notice in writing served on any person, require that person to furnish to the authority such information which the authority reasonably considers that it needs as is specified in the notice, in such form and within such period following service of the notice [, or at such time,] as is so specified.

(3) For the purposes of this section the discharge by the Secretary of State of an obligation of the United Kingdom under the Community Treaties or any international agreement relating to environmental protection shall be treated as a function of his under this Part.

DEFINITIONS
    "enforcing authority": s.1(7) and (8).
    "local enforcing authority": s.1(7) and (8).
    "SEPA": s.1(8).

COMMENCEMENT
January 1, 1991 (S.I. 1990 No. 2635).

AMENDMENT
The Environment Act 1995, Sched. 22, para. 56, amended subs. (2) in two places.

GENERAL NOTE
This section gives power to the Secretary of State to obtain information from enforcing authorities in furtherance of his functions under Pt. I, including the discharge of any obligations of the UK under European Community or other treaty obligations relating to environmental protection (subs. (1)). This power is supplemented by that in the Environment Act 1995, s.51. That section requires the Agency and SEPA (but not local authorities) to furnish the Secretary of State, and additionally in the case of the Agency, the Minister of Agriculture, Fisheries and Food, with all such information as he may reasonably require relating to (*inter alia*) their responsibilities generally and the carrying out and proposed carrying out of their functions. Section 51 expressly requires the Agency/SEPA where reasonable to obtain such information, in so far as it is not in their possession.

Also, the Secretary of State and central and local enforcing authorities are empowered to require any person to furnish them with such information as they reasonably consider is needed in the discharge of their functions (subs. (2)). Failure to comply with such a requirement is an offence (s.23(1)(g)), as is the giving of false or misleading information knowingly or recklessly (s.23(1)(h)(i)).

Publicity

Public registers of information

20.—(1) It shall be the duty of each enforcing authority, as respects prescribed processes for which it is the enforcing authority, to maintain, in accordance with regulations made by the Secretary of State, a register containing prescribed particulars of or relating to—

(a) applications for authorisations made to that authority;

(b) the authorisations which have been granted by that authority or in respect of which the authority has functions under this Part;

(c) variation notices, enforcement notices and prohibition notices issued by that authority;

(d) revocations of authorisations effected by that authority;

(e) appeals under section 15 above;

(f) convictions for such offences under section 23(1) below as may be prescribed;

(g) information obtained or furnished in pursuance of the conditions of authorisations or under any provision of this Part;

(h) directions given to the authority under any provision of this Part by the Secretary of State; and

(i) such other matters relating to the carrying on of prescribed processes or any pollution of the environment caused thereby as may be prescribed;

but that duty is subject to sections 21 and 22 below.

(2) Subject to subsection (4) below, the register maintained by a local enforcing authority [in England and Wales] shall also contain prescribed particulars of such information contained in any register maintained by [the Environment Agency] as relates to the carrying on in the area of the authority of prescribed processes in relation to which [the Environment Agency] has functions under this Part; and [the Environment Agency] shall furnish each authority with the particulars which are necessary to enable it to discharge its duty under this subsection.

(3) […]

(4) Subsection (2) above does not apply to port health authorities but each local enforcing authority [in England and Wales] whose area adjoins that of a port health authority shall include corresponding information in the register maintained by it; and [the Environment Agency] shall furnish each such local enforcing authority with the particulars which are necessary to enable it to discharge its duty under this subsection.

(5) Where information of any description is excluded from any register by virtue of section 22 below, a statement shall be entered in the register indicating the existence of information of that description.

(6) The Secretary of State may give to enforcing authorities directions requiring the removal from any register of theirs of any specified information not prescribed for inclusion under subsection (1) or (2) above or which, by virtue of section 21 or 22 below, ought to have been excluded from the register.

(7) It shall be the duty of each enforcing authority—

(a) to secure that the registers maintained by them under this section are available, at all reasonable times, for inspection by the public free of charge; and

(b) to afford to members of the public facilities for obtaining copies of entries, on payment of reasonable charges.

[and, for the purposes of this subsection, places may be prescribed by the Secretary of State at which any such registers or facilities as are mentioned in paragraph (a) or (b) above are to be available or afforded to the public in pursuance of the paragraph in question.]

(8) Registers under this section may be kept in any form.

(9) […]

(10) In this section "prescribed" means prescribed in regulations under this section.

DEFINITIONS

"authorisation": s.1(9).
"enforcing authority": s.1(7) and (8).
"prescribed processes": s.1(5).

COMMENCEMENT

January 1, 1991 (S.I. 1990 No. 2635).

AMENDMENTS

The Environment Act 1995, Sched. 22, para. 57, amended subss. (2), (4) and (7), and revoked subss. (3) and (9).

GENERAL NOTE

As mentioned in the General Note to Pt. I of the Act, public access to information is an important aspect of environmental policy, and ss.20–22 deal with the public registers to be created. These provisions need to be read in conjunction with E.C. Directive 90/313/EEC of June 7, 1990 on the freedom of access to information on the environment (O.J. L158/56 June 23, 1990). Under this Directive, as from December 31, 1992, Member States are to ensure that public authorities are required to make available information relating to the environment to any natural or legal person at his request and without his having to prove an interest. It is questionable whether these obligations can be fully satisfied by a system of registers: see House of Lords Select Committee on the European Communities, 1st Report Session 1989–90 on *Freedom of Access to Information on the Environment* (H.L. Paper November 22, 1989) paras. 40–42 and 77–80. The Government issued a consultation paper in January 1992 setting out how Directive 90/313/EEC will be implemented in the UK and giving the public a right to information beyond that on registers (The Government's Proposals for the Implementation in the UK Law of the EC Directive on Freedom of Access to Information on the Environment, DoE, W.O.) Subsequently the Environmental Information Regulations 1992 (S.I. 1992 No. 3240) were made to implement the Directive with effect from December 31, 1992.

Contents of registers

The matters to be covered in the registers are set out in subs. (1) and the relevant particulars to be included are prescribed in regulations. Of particular significance and sensitivity to holders of authorisations is likely to be information contained in authorisations about the relevant processes (sub-para. (a)), details of authorisations and conditions attached thereto (sub-para. (b)), convictions (sub-para. (f)) and information obtained or furnished in pursuance of conditions (sub-para. (g)). The list does not include data obtained by enforcing authorities under their general powers of sampling, but it seems likely that such information will be prescribed for inclusion under sub-para. (i) as relating to the carrying on of prescribed processes or pollution caused thereby—certainly the E.C. Directive 90/313 referred to above would require this. The Environmental Protection (Application, Appeals and Registers) Regulations 1991 (S.I. 1991 No. 507, see Appendix 2) state that all particulars of the following matters should be contained within the registers (reg. 15(1)):

"(a) any application for an authorisation made to the authority;

(b) any notice to the appellant by the enforcing authority under paragraph 1(3) of Schedule 1, and any information furnished in response to the notice;

(c) any representations made by any person registered to be consulted under paras. 2, 6 or 7 of Sched. 1 to the 1990 Act pursuant to reg. 4(1).

(d) any authorisation granted by the authority;

(e) any variation notice, enforcement notice, or prohibition notice issued by the authority;

(f) any notice issued by the authority withdrawing a prohibition notice;

(g) any notification of the holder of an authorisation by the authority under section 10(5);

(h) any application for the variation of the conditions of an authorisation under section 11(4)(b);

(i) any revocation effected by the authority;

(j) any notice of appeal under section 15, any decision letter of the Secretary of State relating to such an appeal and any report by an inspector, or in Scotland, a reporter, accompanying any such decision letter;

(k) details of any conviction for any offence under section 23(1), including the name of the offender, the date of conviction, the penalty imposed and the name of the Court;

(l) any monitoring information relating to a prescribed process obtained by the authority as a result of its own monitoring or furnished to the authority in writing by virtue of a condition of the authorisation or section 19(2);

(m) in a case where any such monitoring information is omitted from the register by virtue of section 22, a statement by the authority, based on the monitoring information from time to time obtained by or furnished to them, indicating whether or not there has been compliance with any relevant condition of the authorisation; and

(n) any report published by an enforcing authority relating to an assessment of the environmental consequences of the carrying on of a prescribed process in the locality of premises where the prescribed process is carried on under an authorisation granted by the authority.

(o) any direction given to the authority by the Secretary of State under any provision of Pt. I, other than a direction given under s.21(2) (national security).

It is stated (reg. 17) that monitoring information need not be kept on the register for more than four years (but presumably may be if the authority chooses). Registers may be kept in any form, including electronically: subs. (8).

Who keeps the registers, and where?
Registers are maintained by the Environment Agency, SEPA, local authorities in England and Wales, and port health authorities in relation to prescribed processes for which they are the enforcing authority. In addition, local authorities keep on their registers information from the register of the Agency relating to IPC processes in their area, thereby making such information available locally (see subs. (2)). The 1995 Act amendment to subs. (7) allows the Secretary of State to stipulate where registers are to be publicly available.

Exclusion from registers of information affecting national security

21.—(1) No information shall be included in a register maintained under section 20 above if and so long as, in the opinion of the Secretary of State, the inclusion in the register of that information, or information of that description, would be contrary to the interests of national security.

(2) The Secretary of State may, for the purpose of securing the exclusion from registers of information to which subsection (1) above applies, give to enforcing authorities directions—

(a) specifying information, or descriptions of information, to be excluded from their registers; or

(b) specifying descriptions of information to be referred to the Secretary of State for his determination;

and no information referred to the Secretary of State in pursuance of paragraph (b) above shall be included in any such register until the Secretary of State determines that it should be so included.

(3) The enforcing authority shall notify the Secretary of State of any information it excludes from the register in pursuance of directions under subsection (2) above.

(4) A person may, as respects any information which appears to him to be information to which subsection (1) above may apply, give a notice to the Secretary of State specifying the information and indicating its apparent nature; and, if he does so—

(a) he shall notify the enforcing authority that he has done so; and

(b) no information so notified to the Secretary of State shall be included in any such register until the Secretary of State has determined that it should be so included.

DEFINITION
"enforcing authority": s.1(7) and (8).

COMMENCEMENT
January 1, 1991 (S.I. 1990 No. 2635).

GENERAL NOTE
The Secretary of State may give directions under subs. (2) as to the exclusion of information on grounds of national security. Such information is to be excluded from the register for so long as the Secretary of State is of the opinion that inclusion would be contrary to the interests of national security. Any person may notify to the Secretary of State their view that information should be excluded under the section, and such information may then not be included on the register until the Secretary of State determines otherwise (subs. 4(b)).

For the procedures, see reg. 7 of the Environmental Protection (Applications, Appeals and Registers) Regulations 1991 (S.I. 1991 No. 507, see Appendix 2).

Exclusion from registers of certain confidential information

22.—(1) No information relating to the affairs of any individual or business shall be included in a register maintained under section 20 above, without the consent of that individual or the person for the time being carrying on that business, if and so long as the information—

(a) is, in relation to him, commercially confidential; and
(b) is not required to be included in the register in pursuance of directions under subsection (7) below;

but information is not commercially confidential for the purposes of this section unless it is determined under this section to be so by the enforcing authority or, on appeal, by the Secretary of State.

(2) Where information is furnished to an enforcing authority for the purpose of—

(a) an application for an authorisation or for the variation of an authorisation;
(b) complying with any condition of an authorisation; or
(c) complying with a notice under section 19(2) above;

then, if the person furnishing it applies to the authority to have the information excluded from the register on the ground that it is commercially confidential (as regards himself or another person), the authority shall determine whether the information is or is not commercially confidential.

(3) A determination under subsection (2) above must be made within the period of 14 days beginning with the date of the application and if the enforcing authority fails to make a determination within that period it shall be treated as having determined that the information is commercially confidential.

(4) Where it appears to an enforcing authority that any information (other than information furnished in circumstances within subsection (2) above) which has been obtained by the authority under or by virtue of any provision of this Part might be commercially confidential, the authority shall—

(a) give to the person to whom or whose business it relates notice that that information is required to be included in the register unless excluded under this section; and
(b) give him a reasonable opportunity—
    (i) of objecting to the inclusion of the information on the ground that it is commercially confidential; and
    (ii) of making representations to the authority for the purpose of justifying any such objection;

and, if any representations are made, the enforcing authority shall, having taken the representations into account, determine whether the information is or is not commercially confidential.

(5) Where, under subsection (2) or (4) above, an authority determines that information is not commercially confidential—

(a) the information shall not be entered [in the register] until the end of the period of 21 days beginning with the date on which the determination is notified to the person concerned;

(b) that person may appeal to the Secretary of State against the decision;

and, where an appeal is brought in respect of any information, the information shall not be entered [in the register until the end of the period of seven days following the day on which the appeal is finally determined or withdrawn].

[(6) Subsections (5) and (10) of section 15 above shall apply in relation to an appeal under subsection (5) above as they apply in relation to an appeal under that section, but

(a) subsection (5) of that section shall have effect for the purposes of this subsection with the substitution for the words from "(which may" onwards of the words "(which must be held in privacy)"; and

(b) subsection (5) above is subject to section 114 of the Environment Act 1995 (delegation or references of appeals etc).]

(7) The Secretary of State may give to the enforcing authorities directions as to specified information, or descriptions of information, which the public interest requires to be included in registers maintained under section 20 above notwithstanding that the information may be commercially confidential.

(8) Information excluded from a register shall be treated as ceasing to be commercially confidential for the purposes of this section at the expiry of the period of four years beginning with the date of the determination by virtue of which it was excluded; but the person who furnished it may apply to the authority for the information to remain excluded from the register on the ground that it is still commercially confidential and the authority shall determine whether or not that is the case.

(9) Subsections (5) and (6) above shall apply in relation to a determination under subsection (8) above as they apply in relation to a determination under subsection (2) or (4) above.

(10) The Secretary of State may, by order, substitute for the period for the time being specified in subsection (3) above such other period as he considers appropriate.

(11) Information is, for the purposes of any determination under this section, commercially confidential, in relation to any individual or person, if its being contained in the register would prejudice to an unreasonable degree the commercial interests of that individual or person.

DEFINITIONS
"authorisation": s.1(9).
"enforcing authority": s.1(7) and (8).

GENERAL NOTE
The general principle of the section is that information which is commercially confidential shall not be included within a register without the consent of the person or business to whose affairs it relates: subs. (1). However, information is not commercially confidential in this sense merely because the relevant person claims that it is, but only if determined to be so by the enforcing authority or the Secretary of State. Commercial confidentially is defined in subs. (11) by reference to the prejudice caused to the relevant commercial interests, and whether that prejudice would be unreasonable. The Government has indicated that it will look on claims to commercial confidentiality sceptically: in DoE News Release No. 56 (January 30, 1990) Mr David Trippier, Minister for the Environment, was quoted as saying that "cogent and specific

evidence" would be required to substantiate such claims. Draft Guidance on commercial confidentiality was issued with that News Release and contains the following paragraph:

"If the Secretary of State receives an appeal against a decision by an enforcing authority not to withhold information from the IPC register, he will require cogent and specific evidence to substantiate the claim that disclosure would prejudice to an unreasonable degree some person's commercial interests. This would need to demonstrate that disclosure of information would negate or significantly diminish the commercial advantage that one operator has over another. This might for instance relate to preserving the secrecy of a new process technology, or of a particular raw material or catalyst, or of the capacity of the process, or some other specific feature which if known to competitors might diminish a legitimate commercial advantage. Arguments based on general claims, for instance, that disclosure might damage the reputation of the operator and hence his commercial competitiveness, are unlikely to be given weight. Where information is withheld from the register, the register will indicate that there has been an omission. The authority will periodically include a statement indicating whether the operator has complied with terms and conditions of the authorisation which are withheld from the register."

The issue of confidentially can arise in various ways. Where information is furnished to the enforcing authority for the purpose of an application for authorisation or variation, in pursuance of a condition, or pursuant to a statutory requisition, the person furnishing the information may apply on grounds of commercial confidentiality for exclusion of the information (subs. (2)). The argument as to confidentiality can relate to the commercial interests of the person furnishing the information, or to those of some other person.

Where information is obtained by an authority in other circumstances and it appears that it might be confidential, under subs. (4) the authority must notify the relevant person or business and give them a reasonable opportunity of objecting to inclusion and making representations in support of such objection.

In either case the authority will determine whether or not the information is commercially confidential and in the event of an adverse determination, a 21 day period is given for an appeal to the Secretary of State. The information may not be entered on the register whilst the appeal is pending: subs. (5).

Included in 67 applications for exemption on grounds of commercial confidentiality noted by HMIP's *1991/92 Annual Report* to have been made were a number which went to appeal. The Secretary of State released his decision on the Confidentiality Appeals by PowerGen (against inclusion of forecast schedules of emissions for 1991) and by National Power (against inclusion of data about the type and quality of fuel it planned to burn) on November 19, 1992. The appeal by PowerGen was dismissed (after a 12 day private hearing) on the basis of the "significance of the information to the processes of application and authorisation and the consequent importance of its being available to the public, and my conclusions on the likelihood and extent of prejudice". The disputed information is now on the public registers. The National Power appeal (conducted by way of written representation) was allowed on the basis that the Secretary of State was satisfied that "the information is not directly relevant to determination of the applications for authorisation themselves or to any of the conditions which are likely to be imposed in the authorisations, and is not necessary to enable the public to comment effectively on the applications". No comparable figures were given in HMIP's *1994/95 Annual Report*, which does however make reference to an HMIP approach which "strongly resists attempts by operators to regard details of releases to the environment as confidential" (p. 90).

Public interest
It is possible for the Secretary of State to override the confidentiality exemption on public interest grounds by a direction given under subs. (7).

Review of confidentiality
A determination of confidentiality lapses after a period of four years and application may be made by "the person who furnished it" (who may of course be different to the person later carrying on the prescribed process) for the information to remain excluded on the ground it is still commercially confidential" (subs. (8)).

Provisions as to offences

Offences
23.—(1) It is an offence for a person—
    (a) to contravene section 6(1) above;
    (b) to fail to give the notice required by section 9(2) above;

(c) to fail to comply with or contravene any requirement or prohibition imposed by an enforcement notice or a prohibition notice;

(d)–(f) [...]

(g) to fail, without reasonable excuse, to comply with any requirement imposed by a notice under section 19(2) above;

(h) to make a statement which he knows to be false or misleading in a material particular, or recklessly to make a statement which is false or misleading in a material particular, where the statement is made—

    (i) in purported compliance with a requirement to furnish any information imposed by or under any provision of this Part; or

    (ii) for the purpose of obtaining the grant of an authorisation to himself or any other person or the variation of an authorisation;

(i) intentionally to make a false entry in any record required to be kept under section 7 above;

(j) with intent to deceive, to forge or use a document issued or authorised to be issued under section 7 above or required for any purpose thereunder or to make or have in his possession a document so closely resembling any such document as to be likely to deceive;

(k) [...]

(l) to fail to comply with an order made by a court under section 26 below.

(2) A person guilty of an offence under paragraph (a), (c) or (l) of subsection (1) above shall be liable:

(a) on summary conviction, to a fine not exceeding £20,000 [or to imprisonment for a term not exceeding three months or to both];

(b) on conviction on indictment, to a fine or to imprisonment for a term not exceeding two years, or to both.

(3) A person guilty of an offence under paragraph (b), (g), (h), (i) or (j) of subsection (1) above shall be liable—

(a) on summary conviction, to a fine not exceeding the statutory maximum;

(b) on conviction on indictment, to a fine or to imprisonment for a term not exceeding two years, or to both.

(4)–(5) [...]

DEFINITION
"authorisation": s.1(9).

COMMENCEMENT
January 1, 1991 (S.I. 1990 No. 2635).

AMENDMENTS
The Environment Act 1995, Sched. 22, para. 59, revoked subss. (4) and (5) and amended subss. (1) and (2).

GENERAL NOTE
This section creates some of the various offences under Pt. I and prescribes the various penalties.

The main offence of carrying on a prescribed process except under an authorisation and in accordance with its conditions (subs. (1)(a)) is subject to a maximum fine of £20,000 and/or imprisonment not exceeding three months on summary conviction and to an unlimited fine and/or imprisonment not exceeding two years on conviction on indictment (subs. (2)). The potential prison sentence on summary conviction was added by the Environment Act 1995. The offence appears to be one of strict liability, and ignorance that a condition was being contravened would not provide a defence. Nor is there any defence of "reasonable excuse", such as applies to some of the other offences. It would appear that the subs. (1)(a) offence of carrying on a process without authorisation or without complying with conditions may take place "whether continuously or intermittently, over a period of time" (*Hodgetts v. Chiltern*

District Council [1983] 2 A.C. 120, 128, *per* Lord Roskill). It can still, according to that case, constitute a single offence and it appears could be charged either "on and since" a specific date, or between two specified dates, without the charge being bad for duplicity. Each case will need careful consideration, however, especially where breach of conditions has been intermittent: in some cases it may be appropriate to frame the charge as relating to "divers days" between two specified dates, or in some cases as specimen charges related to single days.

1995 Act offences
A number of offences previously found in this section have been replaced by Environment Act 1995 offences, as follows:

Subsection (1)(d) (failing to comply with a requirement imposed by an authorised person) is now s.110(2)(a) of the 1995 Act. Subsection (1)(e) (preventing another person from answering questions) is now s.110(2)(c). Subsection (1)(f) (intentionally obstructing an authorised person) is now s.110(1), and subs. (1)(k) is now s.110(3).

Similarly, penalty provisions for those offences are now found at s.110(4) and (5) of the 1995 Act: these remain at £5,000 on summary conviction, save that the offence of intentional instruction is now triable either way in cases where the obstructed person is attempting to deal with the cause of an imminent danger of serious harm—in that events on trial by indictment the maximum penalty is an unlimited fine and/or two years' imprisonment.

According to HMIP's *1994/95 Annual Report*, HMIP took 15 prosecutions under Pt. I in 1994/95, all of which resulted in a guilty verdict. Fines totalled £136,500, ranging between £22,500 and £4,000, whilst costs totalled £104,225, ranging between £1,540 and £13,716. In two cases the costs were more than double the fine awarded. The figures do not necessarily relate to single charges: one prosecution can involve a number of charges. This point is strikingly illustrated in the case of *Coal Products Ltd* (ENDS Report 238, November 1993, p. 41), whose fines totalling £22,500 were imposed at a rate of £300 per offence on a total of no less than 75 charges. Essentially the charges related to 25 discharges of ammonia into controlled waters: in respect of each discharge HMIP charged the company with one offence of discharging in excess of authorisation limits, and one offence of failing to notify HMIP and one offence of failing to notify the NRA.

The prosecution of UML, a Unilever subsidiary, should also be noted here (ENDS Report 250, November 1995, p. 44). HMIP indicated that this case involved 998 discharges in breach of the company's authorised pH limit for liquid discharges over a 12 month period. A potential 2,994 charges could have been laid in respect of these breaches given a failure to notify HMIP and the NRA on each and every occasion a breach occurred. However, six specimen charges were brought, two relating to breaches of authorised discharge limits and the other four relating to failure to notify HMIP and the NRA on each of the two occasions. A fine of £35,000 was imposed.

In Scotland it appears that there have only been two IPC prosecutions to date (ENDS Report 247, August 1995, p.43). These prosecutions of Scottish Hydro-Electric plc and Scottish Power plc resulted in an admonishment and a fine of £250 respectively. It is not possible to recover costs in Scottish prosecutions.

Enforcement by High Court

24.—If the enforcing authority is of the opinion that proceedings for an offence under section 23(1)(c) above would afford an ineffectual remedy against a person who has failed to comply with the requirements of an enforcement notice or a prohibition notice, the authority may take proceedings in the High Court or, in Scotland, in any court of competent jurisdiction for the purpose of securing compliance with the notice.

DEFINITIONS
"enforcement notice": s.13(1).
"enforcing authority": s.1(7) and (8).
"prohibition notice": s.14(1).

COMMENCEMENT
January 1, 1991 (S.I. 1990 No. 2635).

GENERAL NOTE
This section gives an alternative remedy for non-compliance with an enforcement or prohibition notice where the enforcing authority believes that criminal proceedings would be an ineffectual remedy, for example where urgent action is required or where the criminal

penalties available might not be an adequate deterrent. (It should be noted that, in England and Wales at least, any public or private body may apply for an injunction with the consent of the Attorney-General. The position in Scotland is less clear: for a fuller discussion, see the General Note to s.37 of the 1995 Act). This section provides a power to do so without such consent. In England and Wales the authority may take High Court proceedings to secure compliance in such cases. The advantage of such proceedings is that they may result in an injunction, breach of which constitutes contempt of court, for which imprisonment and sequestration of assets might follow. Judicial guidance on the meaning of s.24 and the circumstances in which resort may be had to this power has been provided in *Tameside Metropolitan Borough Council v. Smith Brothers (Hyde) Ltd.* October 4, 1995, QBD; ENDS Report 250, November 1995, p. 42. In this case the enforcing authority applied for an interlocutory injunction after serving an enforcement notice which was not complied with within the specified time limit. However, the company is reported to have informed the authority that although it was not appealing against the enforcement notice it was going to seek judicial review of the Secretary of State's decision to grant an authorisation subject to certain conditions, the authority's decision to serve the notice and the notice itself. Firstly, the court held that "ineffectual" in s.24 meant that a criminal prosecution would not have the effect of securing compliance with the notice, but that s.24 could be invoked without any need for there to have been a prosecution. However, the court held that it had to follow the general principles laid down in *City of London Corporation v. Bovis Construction* (1988) 86 L.G.R. 666, C.A. (civil injunctions should be used sparingly as an aid to enforcing criminal law and should be confined to situations where nothing less than an injunction would restrain a defendant from continuing unlawful operations) and *American Cyanamid v. Ethicon* [1975] A.C. 396 (there must be a serious issue to be tried and the balance of convenience must favour the plaintiffs). Although there was an arguable case that the notice had not been complied with, there was also an arguable case that the notice was invalid and Kershaw J. was of the view that at the time the notice was served the evidence did not suggest that authority had had strict regard to the conditions in s.24, *i.e.* that the notice had not been complied with and that criminal proceedings would be an ineffectual remedy. This was the crucial issue for the court in deciding not to grant an interlocutory injunction. However, the court also considered balance of convenience issues including the unpleasant smells from the plant, the possibility the action might cause the closure of a business performing a socially useful function and cause the loss of over 40 jobs, the fact the authority refused to give an undertaking in damages and the possibility that the plaintiffs might lose at the trial. Interestingly, the court also considered that the plaintiffs had not had regard to s.26 which gives the court the power, where a person has been convicted of an offence under Part I of the 1990 Act, to order the cause of an offence to be remedied in addition to or as an alternative to any other penalty in the context of whether or not a criminal prosecution would have provided an ineffectual remedy or not.

In Scotland, SEPA likewise may take civil proceedings under this section for interdict to secure compliance with an enforcement or prohibition notice. This may be done either in the Court of Session or in the sheriff court which has jurisdiction.

The circumstances covered by s.24 are not the only circumstances in which the enforcing authority might wish to seek an injunction or, in Scotland, an interdict. Other circumstances include where a process is being operated without an authorisation at all. Local authorities in England and Wales can in certain circumstances rely on their powers under s.222, Local Government Act 1972, to seek an injunction in such a case. The Court of Appeal in *City of London Corporation v. Bovis Construction* (1988) 86 L.G.R. 66 has examined the use of the power under that section. The position for the Agency and SEPA is less clear, and turns on the interpretation of a general power bestowed upon them by the Environment Act 1995, s.37(1)(a). This in turn, if certain conditions are met, may involve a court in recourse to a relevant *Hansard* extract to elucidate Parliament's intention in introducing s.37(1)(a). See further the note to that subsection of the 1995 Act.

Onus of proof as regards techniques and evidence

25.—(1) In any proceedings for an offence under section 23(1)(a) above consisting in a failure to comply with the general condition implied in every authorisation by section 7(4) above, it shall be for the accused to prove that there was no better available technique not entailing excessive cost than was in fact used to satisfy the condition.

(2) Where—
    (a) an entry is required under section 7 above to be made in any record as to the observance of any condition of an authorisation; and
    (b) the entry has not been made;

that fact shall be admissible as evidence that that condition has not been observed.

[(3) Subsection (2) above shall not have effect in relation to any entry required to be made in any record by virtue of a condition of a relevant licence, within the meaning of section 111 of the Environment Act 1995 (which makes corresponding provision in relation to such licences).]

DEFINITION
"authorisation": s.1(9)

AMENDMENT
Subsection (3) was added by the Environment Act 1995, s.111(6).

COMMENCEMENT
January 1, 1991 (S.I. 1990 No. 2635).

GENERAL NOTE
This section is of great importance in that it deals with the onus of proof as to certain matters in prosecutions under Pt. I. Where the alleged offence is failure to comply with the *general* condition as to the use of BATNEEC implied by s.7(4), the onus rests with the accused to show that there was no better available technique not entailing excessive cost than that actually employed (subs. (1)).

It is important to note that the presumption does not apply to *specific* conditions requiring the use of BATNEEC. This is significant when read in conjunction with s.7(6), which provides that the general condition does not apply in relation to any aspect of the process which is regulated by a specific condition. Thus the impact of subs. (1) may be less than appears at first sight.

Secondly, if an express condition requires records to be kept as to the observance of conditions, the absence of a relevant entry is admissible (though not conclusive) as evidence that the condition has not been observed (subs. (2)).

Subs. (3): "relevant licence"
Section 111(4) of the Environment Act 1995 introduces, for "relevant licences" as there defined, a provision equivalent to that in subs. (2). However, "relevant licences", as far as it relates to Pt. I, includes only authorisations granted by the Agency or SEPA. Subsection (2) is therefore disapplied by subs. (3) in relation to such licences, but continues to apply to LAPC authorisations in England and Wales, for which local authorities are the enforcing authority.

Power of court to order cause of offence to be remedied

26.—(1) Where a person is convicted of an offence under section 23(1)(a) or (c) above in respect of any matters which appear to the court to be matters which it is in his power to remedy, the court may, in addition to or instead of imposing any punishment, order him, within such time as may be fixed by the order, to take such steps as may be specified in the order for remedying those matters.

(2) The time fixed by an order under subsection (1) above may be extended or further extended by order of the court on an application made before the end of the time as originally fixed or as extended under this subsection, as the case may be.

(3) Where a person is ordered under subsection (1) above to remedy any matters, that person shall not be liable under section 23 above in respect of those matters in so far as they continue during the time fixed by the order or any further time allowed under subsection (2) above.

COMMENCEMENT
January 1, 1991 (S.I. 1990 No. 2635).

GENERAL NOTE
This section allows a court to order a person convicted of certain offences under Pt. I to take specified steps in respect of matters which appear to be within his power to remedy. The

relevant offences are carrying on a prescribed process without authorisation or without complying with conditions, or contravention of an enforcement notice or prohibition notice. It is not clear whether such an order is limited to steps required to comply with the conditions or notice, or whether it can extend to more general remedial measures, perhaps for example in relation to contamination occurring after the date of the relevant notice. The strict test appears to be that the matters ordered to be remedied must be matters in respect of which the offender was convicted, not, as suggested by the marginal note, the cause of the offence.

Failure to comply with the order is an offence (s.23(1)(*l*)): presumably, in the case of an order made by the High Court, it may also be contempt. No offence is committed in respect of matters continuing during the time fixed by the order for the relevant remedial measures (subs. (3)).

Section 26 was apparently used in a prosecution of Enichem Elastomers by HMIP (ENDS Report 238, November 1994, pp. 40–41), a case involving the overflow of chemicals from a storage tank into a bund and their escape from the bund through an open valve into a site's surface water drainage system. It is reported that magistrates imposed a fine of £5,000 and ordered the company under s.26 to fit alarms to the storage tanks involved by July 1995.

Power of [appropriate Agency] to remedy harm

27.—(1) Where the commission of an offence under section 23(1)(a) or (c) above causes any harm which it is possible to remedy, [the appropriate Agency] may, subject to subsection (2) below—

    (a) arrange for any reasonable steps to be taken towards remedying the harm; and

    (b) recover the cost of taking those steps from any person convicted of that offence.

(2) [The Environment Agency or SEPA, as the case may be, shall not exercise its] powers under this section except with the approval in writing of the Secretary of State and, where any of the steps are to be taken on or will affect land in the occupation of any person other than the person on whose land the prescribed process is being carried on, with the permission of that person.

DEFINITION
"harm": s.1(4).

COMMENCEMENT
January 1, 1991 (S.I. 1990 No. 2635).

AMENDMENTS
Subsections (1) and (2) were amended by the Environment Act 1995, Sched. 22, para. 60.

GENERAL NOTE
This section gives an important general power to the Environment Agency, or SEPA in Scotland, to remedy harm caused by the commission of certain offences and to recover the cost of any reasonable steps from the person or persons convicted. The relevant offences are, first, carrying on a prescribed process without an authorisation or in breach of conditions and, secondly, non-compliance with an enforcement or prohibition notice.

The power may be used in conjunction with the wide powers of entry now contained in s.108 of the 1995 Act, but if any of the steps are to be taken on or will affect land in the occupation of anyone other than the owner of the land on which the prescribed process is being carried on, then the permission of that person is necessary (subs. (2)).

It does not appear that the Agency/SEPA must wait for a conviction before exercising the powers, though no cost can be recovered until conviction, and the written approval of the Secretary of State is necessary before taking any steps.

The power is only to remedy actual harm and does not cover anticipatory or preventive measures.

The power does not extend to English and Welsh local authorities in their enforcement role, though it seems that the Agency/SEPA can exercise their powers under the section in respect of offences relating to both centrally and locally controlled processes.

Where the power is exercisable, then the enforcing authority under Pt. IIA (contaminated land) may neither serve a remediation notice in respect of the harm, where it results from "contaminated land", nor undertake remediation itself under that Part: ss.78YB(1) and 78N(2).

Authorisation and other statutory controls

Authorisations and other statutory controls

28.—(1) No condition shall at any time be attached to an authorisation so as to regulate the final disposal by deposit in or on land of controlled waste (within the meaning of Part II), nor shall any condition apply to such a disposal. [. . .]

(2) Where any of the activities comprising a prescribed process are regulated both by an authorisation granted by the enforcing authority under this Part and by a registration or authorisation under the [Radioactive Substances Act 1993], then, if different obligations are imposed as respects the same matter by a condition attached to the authorisation under this Part and a condition attached to the registration or authorisation under that Act, the condition imposed by the authorisation under this Part shall be treated as not binding the person carrying on the process.
[. . .]

DEFINITIONS
"authorisation": s.1(9).
"enforcing authority": s.(7) and (8).
"prescribed process": s.1(5).
"process": s.1(5).
"release": s.1(10).
"substances": s.1(13).

AMENDMENTS
In subs. (2) the words in square brackets were substituted by the Radioactive Substances Act 1993, s.49(1). Reference previously had been to the Radioactive Substances Act 1960, which was consolidated into the 1993 Act. Subsection (1) was amended, and subss. (3) and (4) revoked, by the Environment Act 1995, Sched. 22, para. 61.

GENERAL NOTE
This section deals with the relationship between authorisations under Pt. I and other systems of statutory control. See the General Note to Pt. I under the heading *Relationships with Other Areas of Control.*

PART II

WASTE ON LAND

GENERAL NOTE
Part II of the Act deals with the collection, recycling, deposit and other forms of disposal of waste. It replaces, with various amendments, the provisions of Pt. I of the Control of Pollution Act 1974 and is itself amended by the Environment Act 1995. However, Pt. II is more than simply a re-enactment of previous law, and introduces significant innovations, which in some cases implement long-standing proposals for reform from the Royal Commission on Environmental Pollution and various Parliamentary and Departmental committees.

The reforms can perhaps be marshalled into two broad groups: (a) changes to the waste management licensing system; and (b) re-casting of the institutional local framework for waste regulation and disposal. Relevant background materials include:

(1) Report of The House of Lords Select Committee on Science and Technology, *Hazardous Waste Disposal* (Session 1980–81, 1st Report, July 1981).
(2) Reports 1–3 of the Hazardous Waste Inspectorate (June 1985, July 1986, June 1988).
(3) Report of a Review of the Control of Pollution (Special Waste) Regulations 1980 (April 1985).
(4) DoE Consultation Papers on Waste Disposal Law Amendment (September 15, 1986 and November 23, 1988) and Decisions following Consultation (June 29, 1988 and September 26, 1989).
(5) DoE Consultation Paper on the Role and Functions of Waste Disposal Authorities (January 24, 1989) and Decisions following Consultation (September 26, 1989).
(6) Report on the House of Lords Select Committee on Science and Technology, *Hazardous Waste Disposal* (Session 1988–89, Fourth Report, April 19, 1989).

(7) Government's Response to the Select Committee on Science and Technology, Fourth Report (Cm. 763, July 1989).
(8) Report of Commons Environment Committee, *Toxic Waste* (Session 1988–89, Second Report, February 1989).
(9) Government's Response to the House of Commons Environment Committee Second Report (Cm. 679, April 1989).
(10) Royal Commission on Environmental Pollution, Eleventh Report, *Managing Waste*: *The Duty of Care* (Cm. 9675, December 1985).
(11) Pollution Paper No. 24 (response to RCEP Eleventh Report, 1986).
The innovative features of Pt. II included:
(1) reorganisation of waste functions, including the separation of operational and regulatory functions within local authorities, and power to create regional authorities;
(2) the imposition of a duty of care upon persons importing, producing, carrying, keeping, treating or otherwise disposing of controlled waste;
(3) greater powers of discrimination in the grant of waste management licences, by reference to the concept of "fit and proper person";
(4) the holders of licences are no longer able to surrender them at will, but only if the authority accepts the surrender;
(5) greater emphasis is placed on waste recycling with greater powers, mandatory waste recycling plans and a system of credits for waste recycled by collection authorities;
(6) a duty is placed on authorities to monitor and remedy closed landfills in respect of matters such as leachate contamination and methane generation;
(7) more comprehensive provision is made for the provision of information on public registers.
Part II of the Act is modified by the Environment Act 1995, and must be read in conjunction with the Waste Management Licensing Regulations 1994 No. 1056 ("the 1994 Regulations") as amended by S.I. 1995 No. 288 (see Appendix 3). Save in relation to activities involving scrap metal, the provisions on waste management licensing were brought into force on May 1, 1994 by the Environmental Protection Act (Commencement No. 15) Order 1994 No. 1096. The system and its relationship to E.C. law are explained by Circular 11/94, *Environmental Protection Act 1990 Part II. Waste Management Licensing, The Framework Directive on Waste.* (Scottish Office Environment Department 10/94, Welsh Office 26/94), and the amendments introduced by S.I. 1995 No. 288 are explained by Circular 6/95.
Significant amendments were introduced by the Environment Act 1995. In part these were in consequence of the creation of the Environment Agencies, and in part in order to ensure conformity with the relevant E.C. legislation (see below). However, there are also a number of other amendments. These include a new procedure (s.35A) for third party compensation where a third party is required to give consent or grant rights to the holder of a licence in order to comply with licence conditions. A new procedure to allow third parties to make representations in relation to such conditions before they are imposed is also introduced by ss.36A and 36B.
The other noteworthy change effected by the 1995 Act concerns the replacement of section 61 dealing with problems caused by closed landfill sites with the more comprehensive régime for contaminated land inserted as Part IIA of the 1990 Act. Section 61 was repealed without ever having come into force.

EC and international law
As with many other Parts of the 1990 Act, it is important to view Pt. II against the backcloth of European Community strategies and directives on waste, a subject which has become an increasing preoccupation within the Community. EEC law and policy relating to waste includes the following:
(1) Directive 75/442/EEC on Waste (as amended by 91/156/EEC, O.J. L78/32, 26.3.91 p. 38).
(2) Directive 78/319/EEC on Toxic and Dangerous Wastes; superseded by Directive 91/689/EEC on hazardous waste, item (10) below. (O.J. 1978 L84, p. 43, March 31, 1978).
(3) Directive 86/278/EEC on the use of sewage sludge in agriculture (O.J. 1986 L181, p. 6, July 4, 1986).
(4) Directive 75/439/EEC on the disposal of waste oils (O.J. 1975 L194, p. 23, June 16, 1975) amended by Directive 87/101 (O.J. 1987 L42, p. 43, January 2, 1987).
(5) Directive 76/403 on disposal of PCBs and PCTs (O.J. 1976 L108, p. 41, April 25, 1976). Proposal for a Council Directive on the Disposal of PCBs and PCTs (O.J. 88/C319/06);

Amended Proposal for a Council Directive on the Disposal of PCBs and PCTs (O.J. 91/C299/05).
(6) Directive 78/176/EEC on waste from the titanium dioxide industry (O.J. 1978 L54, p. 19, February 25, 1976) amended by Directive 82/883 (O.J. 1982 L378 p. 1, December 31, 1982) and amended by Directive 83/29 (O.J. 1983 L32, p. 28, February 3, 1983).
(7) Regulation (EEC) No.259/93 on the shipment of waste within, into and out of the EEC. (O.J. 1993 L30, p. 1, February 2, 1993).
(8) Directive 80/68/EEC on the protection of groundwater against pollution by certain dangerous substances (O.J. 1980 L20, p. 43, January 26, 1980).
(9) Directive 91/156/EEC amending Directive 75/442/EEC on waste (O.J. 1991 L78, p, 32, March 26, 1991).
(10) Directive 91/689/EEC on hazardous waste (O.J. 1991 L377, p. 20, December 31, 1991) as amended by Directive 94/31/EC (O.J. 1994 L168, p. 28, July 2, 1994).
(11) Directive 91/157/EEC on batteries and accumulators containing certain dangerous substances (O.J. 1991 L78, March 26, 1991).
(12) Commission Decision 94/3/EC (O.J. 1994 L5, p. 15, January 7, 1994) establishing a list of wastes.
(13) Directive 94/67/EC on the incineration of hazardous waste (O.J. 1994 L365, p. 34, December 31, 1994).
(14) Directive 94/62/EC on packaging and packaging waste (O.J. 1994 L365, p. 10, December 31, 1994).
Current EC proposals on waste include:
(1) Amended Proposal for a Directive on the landfill of waste submitted on June 10, 1993 COM (93) 279. (O.J. C212, p. 33, August 5, 1994). (Informal Common Position reached in June 1994.)
(2) Amended proposal for a Directive on civil liability for damage caused by waste submitted on June 28, 1991 COM (91) 219 (O.J. 1991 C192, p. 6, July 23, 1991).
(3) *Community Strategy for Waste Management* SEC (89) 934, September 18, 1989.
(4) Amended Proposal for a Directive on the disposal of PCBs and PCTs (O.J. C299 p. 9, November 20, 1991).
Reference is made to the various EC measures and proposals in the annotations to the relevant sections of Pt. II.
International law is also of growing importance in relation to waste policy; specifically the Basel Convention of 1989 on The Control of Transboundary Movements of Hazardous Wastes and their Disposal (Cm 984) which came into force on May 5, 1992 and which led to the Regulation at (7) above, having been signed and ratified by the E.C. and the U.K.

Organisation of functions
Sections 30–32 dealt with the reorganisation of waste regulation, collection and disposal functions. Three types of authority were constituted, namely: (1) waste regulation authorities; (2) waste disposal authorities; and (3) waste collection authorities. Their composition and functions were as follows:

(1) Waste regulation authorities
In England, county councils were the waste regulation authorities (WRAs) save for Greater London and the metropolitan areas, where the authority was either a statutorily constituted waste authority or the district council. District councils were the WRAs in Wales, and islands or district councils in Scotland. The main regulatory functions are:
(a) waste management licensing (s.35);
(b) supervision of the new duty of care as to waste (s.34);
(c) inspecting land before accepting surrender of licences (s.39);
(d) supervision of licensed activities (s.42);
(e) powers to require removal of waste unlawfully deposited (s.59);
(f) maintenance of public registers (s.64); and
(g) publication of annual reports (s.67).
The amendments made by the Environment Act 1995 transfer these regulatory functions to the Environment Agencies established for England and Wales, and for Scotland. A consultation paper on the arrangements for waste disposal planning under the Agency and in the interim period before its creation was issued by the Department of Environment on August 17, 1992. DoE Circular 15/95 deals with the transfer of property, rights and liabilities from Waste Regulation Authorities to the Agency. Save for the London Waste Regulation Authority

(to be abolished), English WRAs must prepare transfer schemes for the transfer of appropriate property, rights and liabilities. Scottish Office Environment Department Circular 19/95 entitled "Transfer of Property, Rights and Liabilities from District and Islands Councils to the Scottish Environment Protection Agency" (October 12, 1995) makes similar provision for Scotland.

(2) Waste Disposal Authorities
Waste disposal authorities (WDAs) are the county councils in non-metropolitan areas; special arrangements at present apply in some metropolitan counties and in London, and in other metropolitan areas the district councils are the WDAs. In Wales the district councils are the WDAs and in Scotland the functions fall to islands or district councils and, from April 1, 1996, to the new unitary councils established by the Local Government etc. (Scotland) Act 1994.
  The functions, powers and duties of WDAs under Pt. II in England and Wales are:
  (a) formation of waste disposal companies and transfer of relevant parts of their undertakings to such companies (s.32);
  (b) direction of waste collection authorities as to places to which collected waste is to be delivered (s.51(4)(a));
  (c) arranging for the disposal of controlled waste collected in the area by waste collection authorities (s.51(1)(a));
  (d) arrangement for the provision of places at which residents of the area may deposit household waste and for the disposal of waste so deposited (s.51(1)(b));
  (e) arrangement for the provision of places where collected waste may be treated or kept prior to removal for treatment or disposal (*e.g.* transfer stations) (s.51(4)(b));
  (f) making payments to waste collection authorities for savings in disposal costs in respect of waste retained for recycling (s.52(1)); and
  (g) waste recycling (s.55).
Separate provisions apply to waste disposal authorities in Scotland in relation to a number of these matters (ss.53, 54 and 56).
  In exercising these functions, the scheme of the Act is that regulatory and disposal functions shall be kept separate (s.30(7)). Operational disposal functions are not carried out by the disposal authorities themselves, but through "waste disposal contractors" defined as companies formed for the purpose of collection, keeping, treating or disposing of waste in the course of a business (s.30(5)). Such companies may either be private sector businesses or companies formed by waste disposal authorities. Section 32 and Sched. 2, Pt. I make provision for the transition of undertakings of waste disposal authorities to such local authority waste disposal companies (LAWDCs). The intention is that LAWDCs and private sector waste disposal companies will compete for business on equal terms, and Sched. 2, Pt. II contains detailed provisions as to contracts and putting such contracts to tender.
  It should be noted that in Scotland, Pt. II made no provision for the formation of local authority waste disposal companies and that waste disposal functions continued to be carried out by district and islands councils until April 1, 1996, when these functions were transferred to the new unitary councils established by the Local Government etc. (Scotland) Act 1994. It should also be noted that waste disposal authorities in Scotland also acted as waste regulation authorities until the transfer of their waste regulation function to SEPA although administrative arrangements were put in place to keep the functions separate.

(3) Waste Collection Authorities
Waste collection functions fall to district councils in England and Wales, London boroughs, the Common Council of the City or the Temple authorities in Greater London, and the new unitary councils in Scotland established by the Local Government etc. (Scotland) Act 1994 (formerly the function fell to district and islands councils in Scotland). The functions of such authorities are:
  (a) to arrange for the collection of household waste in their area and to arrange for the collection of commercial or industrial waste on request (s.45);
  (b) to arrange for the emptying of privies or cesspools in their areas (s.45);
  (c) to determine the nature and source of receptacles in which household waste is to be placed for collection (s.46);
  (d) to supply receptacles for commercial or industrial waste (s.47);
  (e) to deliver for disposal waste collected to such places as the waste disposal authority directs (s.48);
  (f) to carry out investigations as to appropriate arrangements for dealing with waste for the purpose of recycling and to prepare a statement of such arrangements (s.49); and

(g) to retain waste which the authority has decided to recycle and to make arrangements for recycling it (s.48).

It should be noted that s.48 does not apply to Scotland. Section 53 makes equivalent provision for Scotland reflecting the fact that north of the border district and islands councils and, from April 1, 1996, the new unitary councils established by the Local Government etc. (Scotland) Act 1994 act both as waste collection authorities and waste disposal authorities.

Central control and national strategy

Central Government control over the activities of waste regulation, disposal and collection authorities is provided by a variety of powers conferred on the Secretary of State to give directions on a wide range of matters, including:

    (1) arrangements for transition to waste disposal companies (England and Wales only) (s.32(2));

    (2) exercise of licensing functions, both specific directions and general guidance (s.35(7) and (8));

    (3) modification and variation of licences (s.37(3));

    (4) revocation and suspension of licences (s.38(7));

    (5) supervision of licensed activities (s.42(8));

    (6) content and preparation of waste recycling plans (s.49(4) and (7)); and

    (7) acceptance of waste by holders of licences and delivery of waste by persons keeping control of it (s.57(1) and (2)).

Additionally, the Secretary of State makes the various Regulations required under Pt. II (including those regulating special waste), issues the Code of Practice on the duty of care relating to waste (s.34(7)) and exercises the appellate functions in matters of licensing (s.43) and exclusion of information from registers (s.66(5)).

The Secretary of State also has power to issue guidance to waste regulation authorities on their functions in relation to licences (s.35(8)). The Secretary of State has produced various waste management papers giving guidance of a technical nature on waste management and the exercise of regulatory functions. The waste management papers are listed below.

An important development, prompted in part by E.C. requirements, in the introduction by s.92 of the Environment Act 1995 of the requirement of national waste strategies for England and Wales (s.44A) and for Scotland (s.44B). The strategy must contain policies in relation to the recovery and disposal of waste and may comprise either a single statement or a number of separate statements. These provisions are expressly stated by the legislation to be for the purpose of implementing the requirements of Article 7 of the waste framework Directive 91/156/EEC, amending directive 75/442/EEC. As such, the objectives provided by the Directive are related to the national strategies by Schedule 2A of the Act (inserted by s.92 and Sched. 12 of the 1995 Act) which incorporates the E.C. objectives relating to protection of human health and the environment, an integrated and adequate network of disposal installations, self-sufficiency, proximity, waste prevention and reduction, and the encouragement of waste recovery and the use of waste as a source of energy. A non-statutory national waste strategy for England and Wales was published in December 1995: *Making Waste Work* (Cm. 3040).

LIST OF WASTE MANAGEMENT PAPERS (HMSO PUBLICATIONS)

Number   *Title*

    1 A review of Options; Second Edition 1992. (ISBN 0117526444)

    2 Waste Disposal Surveys; 1976. (ISBN 0117510033)

    3 Guidelines for the Preparation of a Waste Disposal Plan; 1976. (ISBN 0117511242) [* WMPs 2 and 3 have been replaced by WMP 2/3, Waste Disposal Plans]

    4 The Licensing of Waste Facilities; Third Edition 1994. (ISBN 0117527270)

  4A Licensing of Metal Recycling Sites; 1995. (ISBN 0117530646)

    5 The Relationship between Waste Disposal Authorities and Private Industry; 1976. (ISBN 0117509205) (out of print)

    6 Polychlorinated Biphenyl (PCB) Wastes—a Technical Memorandum on Reclamation, Treatment and Disposal; 1976. (ISBN 011751009) (a second edition was due to be published in December 1994, ISBN 0117529524)

    7 Mineral Oil Wastes—a Technical Memorandum on Arisings, Treatment and Disposal; 1976. (ISBN 0117510602) (out of print)

  8 Heat Treatment Cyanide Wastes—a Technical Memorandum on Arisings, Treatment and Disposals; Second Edition 1985. (ISBN 0117518131)
  9 Halogenated Hydrocarbon Solvent Wastes from Cleaning Processes—a Technical Memorandum on Reclamation and Disposal; 1976. (ISBN 011751103X)
 10 Local Authority Waste Disposal Statistics 1974/75; 1976. (ISBN 011751120X)
 11 Metal Finishing Wastes—a Technical Memorandum on Arisings, Treatment and Disposal; 1976. (ISBN 0117511226)
 12 Mercury Bearing Wastes—a Technical Memorandum on Storage, Handling, Treatment, Disposal and Recovery; 1977. (ISBN 0117511269)
 13 Tarry and Distillation Wastes and other Chemical Based Wastes—a Technical Memorandum on Arisings, Treatment and Disposal; 1977. (ISBN 0117511277)
 14 Solvent Wastes (excluding Halogenated Hydrocarbons)—a Technical Memorandum on Reclamation and Disposal; 1977. (ISBN 0117511285) (out of print)
 15 Halogenated Organic Wastes—a Technical Memorandum on Arisings, Treatment and Disposal; 1979. (ISBN 0117513709)
 16 Wood Preserving Wastes—a Technical Memorandum on Arisings, Treatment and Disposal; 1980. (ISBN 0117514764)
 17 Wastes from Tanning, Leather Dressing and Fellmongering—a Technical Memorandum on Recovery, Treatment and Disposal; 1978. (ISBN 0117513202) (out of print)
 18 Asbestos Waste—a Technical Memorandum on Arisings and Disposal; 1979. (ISBN 0117513849) (out of print)
 19 Wastes from the Manufacture of Pharmaceuticals, Toiletries and Cosmetics—a Technical Memorandum on Arisings, Treatment and Disposal; 1978. (ISBN 0117513180) (out of print)
 20 Arsenic Bearing Wastes—a Technical Memorandum on Recovery, Treatment and Disposal; 1980. (ISBN 0117514721)
 21 Pesticide Wastes—a Technical Memorandum on Arisings and Disposal; 1980. (ISBN 0117514845) (out of print)
 22 Local Authority Waste Disposal Statistics 1974/75 to 1977/78; 1978. (ISBN 0117514535)
 23 Special Wastes—a Technical Memorandum Providing Guidance on their Definition; 1981. (ISBN 0117515558) (out of print)
 24 Cadmium Bearing Wastes—a Technical Memorandum on Arisings, Treatment and Disposal; 1984. (ISBN 011751716X)
 25 Clinical Wastes—a Technical Memorandum on Arisings, Treatment and Disposal; 1983. (ISBN 0117517194)
 26 Landfilling Wastes—a Technical Memorandum for the Disposal of Wastes on Landfill Sites; 1986. (ISBN 0117518913)
26A Landfill Completion. A Technical Memorandum Providing Guidance on Assessing the Completion of Licensed Landfill Facilities; 1994. (ISBN 0117528072)
26B Landfill Design, Construction and Operational Practice: 1995. (ISBN 0117531855).
 27 Landfill Gas—a Technical Memorandum on the Monitoring and Control of Landfill Gas; Second Edition 1991. (ISBN 0117524883)
 28 Recycling—a Memorandum providing Guidance to Local Authorities on recycling; 1991. (ISBN 011752445X)

As at November 1995, a number of developments were anticipated. Consultation on a new edition of WMP 25 had been completed; and it was understood that several other WMPs were in preparation. These included: WMP 2/3 on waste disposal plans (amalgamating existing WMPs 2 and 3); and new editions of WMPs 16 and 23. Further subdivisions of WMP 26 are to be: 26C on landfill operation and processes; 26D on landfill monitoring; 26E on landfill restoration; and 26F on landfill co-disposal. It was understood that these were also in preparation.

The Duty of Care
Section 34 contains a new duty of care as to the keeping, control and transfer of waste. The case for such a duty was put cogently by the RCEP in their Eleventh Report, *Managing Waste: The Duty of Care* (Cm. 9675, December 1985). Paras. 3.4–3.7 of that Report state as follows:

"The first task is for society to identify where the responsibility lies for ensuring that wastes are properly handled and disposed of. In our judgment this must rest with the individual organisation who controls the wastes. The producer incurs a *duty of care* which is owed to society, and we would like to see this duty reflected in public attitudes and enshrined in legislation and codes of practice ... we believe that the waste producer's or handler's legal obligations towards the environment need to be classified and strengthened, with particular reference to the requirement to satisfy himself, when passing on the waste to somebody else, that it will be correctly dealt with. ... We believe that, within the framework of the duty of care, a waste producer may assign responsibility to a person who he had good reason to believe is competent to handle the waste safely ... "

The broad thrust of these recommendations was accepted by the Government in Pollution Paper No. 24 (1986) and the Government agreed that "this duty of care should find its main expression in ensuring the integrity of the waste stream on its journey from producer to disposer and beyond this to its safe containment or disposal over time" (para. 5).

The duty covers all those responsible for the arising or importation of controlled waste and those who have control of such waste at whatever point in the chain from arising to final disposal.

The standard is based on reasonableness in the light of the measures applicable to the relevant person in their particular capacity. Reasonable steps are required: (a) to prevent any other person contravening the law as to unauthorised deposit, treatment or disposal of the waste; (b) to prevent escape of the waste; (c) to secure that the waste is transferred only to an authorised person; and (d) to secure that a sufficient written description of the waste accompanies it on transfer.

The duty does not, however, apply to occupiers of domestic property in respect of their own household wastes (s.34(2)). Central to the operation of s.34 is the Code of Practice issued by the Secretary of State; such a code is admissible and relevant evidence in any proceedings as to whether the duty of care has been fulfilled (s.34(10)). The Code of Practice was issued in December 1991 and a revised version was issued in March 1996 following consultation.

In considering the duty of care, attention should also be directed to the proposals of the European Commission for strict civil liability for damage caused by waste. Amended proposals for a directive were submitted on June 28, 1991 COM (91) 219 (O.J. 1991 C192 p. 6, July 23, 1991). If adopted, which appears increasingly unlikely, such proposals when implemented would in many cases create a parallel liability on a producer or controller of waste, with no-fault civil liability as distinct from criminal liability based on a test of reasonableness. Furthermore, the draft directive proposes a system of joint and several liability on producers whose wastes are mixed or disposed of together, and cause damage. On the other hand, liability under s.34 would arise whether or not damage resulted from the breach, whereas under the directive either personal injury, property damage, or injury to the environment would be a prerequisite of liability.

The possible relationship between the duty of care and the directive were considered in evidence before the House of Lords European Communities Committee, Sub-Committee F and in the Report of that Committee, *Paying for Pollution: Civil Liability for Damage caused by Waste* (House of Lords, Session 1989–90, 25th Report, H.L. paper 84–I).

The meaning of "waste"
The regulatory controls of Part II rest upon the concept of "controlled waste" defined by s.75(4) as household, industrial or commercial waste, or any such waste. This in turn rests upon the meaning of "waste". Section 75(2) as originally drafted contained a definition of waste taken from the Control of Pollution Act 1974 which stated that it included:
    (a) any substance which constitutes a scrap material or an effluent or other unwanted substance arising from the application of any process; and
    (b) any substance or article which requires to be disposed of as being broken, worn out, contaminated or otherwise spoiled.
Section 75(3) provided a presumption that any thing which is discarded or otherwise dealt with as if it were waste shall be presumed to be waste unless the contrary is proved. A certain amount of case-law built up around these provisions, but the definition came to be seen increasingly as an unsatisfactory and potentially inaccurate method of implementing the relevant requirements of E.C. legislation on waste. The definition was therefore modified by the Waste Management Licensing Regulations 1994, effectively to bring it into conformity with the E.C. definition of waste. Having to read the primary legislation in conjunction with the Regulations was complex and confusing, and the opportunity has been taken in the 1995 Act to bring the amendments onto the face of the legislation. The previous definition referred to above is replaced by a definition taken from the waste framework directive 75/442/EEC as amended by Directive 91/156/EEC based upon the concept of substances or objects being discarded by their holder. A new Schedule 2B is inserted into the Act to incorporate the relevant categories of materials and objects which may be waste from the Directive. The presumption contained in s.75(3) is repealed. So as to leave no doubt as to the legislative purpose behind these amendments, a new subsection (s.75(11)) states that the purpose is to assign to "waste" the meaning which it has in the waste framework directive, and that the relevant provisions shall be construed accordingly.

Waste management licensing

A waste management licence authorises the treatment, keeping or disposal of any specified description of controlled waste (see previous section) in or on specified land, or the treatment or disposal of any specified description of controlled waste by means of mobile plant (s.35(1)). The licence shall be granted on such terms and subject to such conditions as the authority thinks appropriate (s.35(3)) and continues in force until revoked or surrendered (s.35(11)).

Where planning permission is required for the use of land authorised by the licence, the licence may not be issued unless either: (a) such permission is in force; or (b) an established use certificate or certificate of lawful use or development is in force (s.36(2) as modified by the 1994 Regulations). Subject to this requirement, and to obligations to refer the proposal to the local planning authority and the Health and Safety Executive, the waste regulation authority may not reject an application unless either: (a) they are not satisfied that the applicant is a "fit and proper person"; or (b) they are satisfied that rejection is necessary for the prevention of harm to the environment, harm to human health, or serious detriment to the amenities of the locality (s.36(3)). This last ground of refusal does not apply where planning permission is in force in relation to the proposed use, presumably on the basis that in such a case, issues of amenity will have been addressed at the planning application or appeal stage. These grounds of refusal are different from the equivalent provisions under the Control of Pollution Act 1974, Pt. I. The question whether the applicant is "fit and proper" is completely new, and brings in considerations of technical competence, financial standing and the absence of relevant convictions (s.74). The previous consideration of pollution of water is widened to cover pollution of the environment generally, defined broadly by reference to the capability of causing harm to man or other living organisms (s.39(3)).

Part II contains provisions as to variation of licences (s.37), revocation and suspension of licences (s.38) and surrender and transfer of licences (ss.39 and 40 respectively). Under s.39 it is no longer possible to surrender a licence at will, but only if the authority accepts the surrender—this process involves inspection of the land and the issue of a "certificate of completion" if the authority is satisfied that the condition of the land is unlikely to cause pollution of the environment or harm to human health. Appeal to the Secretary of State lies against the various decisions of waste regulation authorities under the licensing system (s.43).

Under s.62 the Secretary of State may make provision by regulations for the treatment, keeping, or disposal of controlled waste that may be difficult or dangerous: such waste is known as "special waste". Detailed control is at present exercised over such waste by the Control of Pollution (Special Waste) Regulations 1980 No. 1709. This involves a system of documentation of the waste and of pre-notification to the relevant waste authorities of disposal of the waste. The Government is considering proposals for the reform of the Special Waste Regulations and a consultation document on *Special Waste and the Control of its Disposal* was issued in February 1990.

The deposit, treatment or disposal of controlled waste is an offence except under and in accordance with a waste management licence (s.33). Other offences include: the deposit of waste other than controlled waste in certain circumstances (s.63(2) as substituted by the 1995 Act); the making of false statements in relation to licence applications (s.44); breach of the regulations on special waste (authority to create an offence by delegated legislation being given by s.62(2)(g)); failure to comply with requirements to deal with pollution when a licence is suspended (s.38(10) and (11)); forging or using a licence with intent to deceive (s.35(7B)(b)); intentionally making a false entry in any record required to be kept under a licence condition; and failure to comply with a requirement to remove unauthorised waste deposited on land (s.59(5)). Also, damage caused by waste unlawfully deposited on land may give rise to civil liability under s.73(6).

Waste Management Licensing (Amendment etc.) Regulations 1995

These Regulations came into force on April 1, 1995 and establish the permanent exemption from waste management licensing of scrap metal recycling activities. They follow the consultation paper setting out the proposed exemptions issued in November 1994. The Government's expressed policy relating to the exemptions is that the controls applied to waste should be proportionate to the risks involved and the benefits to be obtained, and should not impose unjustifiable or disproportionate burdens on those subject to control, especially small businesses. The Government regards the scrap metal and waste motor vehicle dismantling industries as playing an important role in the recovery of waste: see further DoE Circular 6/95 (W.O. 25/95, S.O.E.D. 8/95).

The Regulations add a number of new categories of exemption to Schedule 3 of the Waste Management Licensing Regulations 1994. These are:

1. Heating iron, steel or any ferrous-alloy, non-ferrous metal or non-ferrous metal alloy in one or more furnaces or other appliances the primary combustion chambers of which have in aggregate a net rated thermal input of less than 0.2 megawatts, for the purpose of removing grease, oil or other non-metallic contaminant.
2. The carrying on, at any secure place, designed or adapted for the recovery of scrap metal or for the dismantling of waste motor vehicles, in respect of types of waste described in tabular form in the new Regulations, of any of the activities specified in the Table in relation to that kind of waste, provided that the total quantity does not exceed the limits stated in the table. The Table categorises various types of waste, various activities, and provides quantitative limits of waste which may be dealt with in any period of seven days. The storage of waste in relation to these activities is also exempted, subject to maximum total quantities set out in a separate Table. These activities are only exempted on certain conditions, including the activity and storage being carried out on a surfaced area with an impermeable pavement provided with a sealed drainage system. Other conditions relate to the administrative arrangements, monthly audits to confirm compliance with the terms and conditions of the exemption, and the keeping of records.
3. The temporary storage of non-scrap waste delivered together with a consignment of waste consisting of at least 70 per cent by weight of waste motor vehicles or at least 95 per cent by weight of other scrap metal wastes is also exempted, again subject to conditions.

These exemptions must be registered by those relying on them with the Waste Regulation Authority, including plans of the location showing boundaries, and the location and specifications of impermeable pavements, drainage systems or hard standings as are required under the relevant conditions. Initial registration must be accompanied by a fee of £300, and an annual fee of £100 is thereafter payable.

Details are specified as to inspection by Waste Regulation Authorities of scrap yards subject to the exemption; the authority must carry out an initial inspection within two months of having received the relevant notice of exemption, plan and fee and thereafter must carry out periodic inspections at intervals not exceeding 12 months.

The duty of care was delayed in its application to scrap metal. The 1995 Regulations, by amending the Controlled Waste Regulations 1992 No. 588, also provided for scrap metal to be subject to the duty of care from October 1, 1995.

The 1995 Regulations make some further amendments to the Waste Management Licensing Regulations 1994. In particular, a number of further categories of mobile plan are added to those specified at Regulation 12. The new categories are plant for the recovery of waste oil from electrical equipment, for the destruction by dechlorination of waste PCBs or PCTs, for the vitrification of waste, or for the treatment by microwave of clinical waste.

The 1995 Regulations also, by reg. 4, extend the transitional provisions exempting certain persons from the requirement to demonstrate technical competence under reg. 4 of the Waste Management Licensing Regulations 1994. The new transitional provisions apply to the person who applies for a certificate of technical competence before July 10, 1995 and at any time in the 23 months ending on that date acted as manager of the facility of a listed type. The exemption extends until August 10, 1999.

Control of Pollution (Amendment) Act 1989
Part II of the Act needs to be read in conjunction with the Control of Pollution (Amendment) Act 1989. The 1989 Act creates a scheme for the registration of carriers of controlled waste with related offences and powers. As such, the 1989 Act is an important component of the statutory framework for controlling and regulating waste, in conjunction with the 1990 Act. In particular, registration of carriers is a vital precondition to the statutory duty of care on waste producers (see above).

Waste recycling
Current policy both at domestic level and within the European Community is beginning to give greater priority to waste recycling and reclamation, and this is reflected in the terms of Pt. II of the Act. The Government's views and policies on recycling are conveniently summarised at paras. 2.59–2.92 of the December 1995 White Paper, *Making Waste Work* (Cm. 3040). The Government has set the target of recycling or composting 25 per cent of *recyclable* household waste by the year 2000. para. 1.48.

The Government has pressed hard for the sectors of industry primarily responsible for the production and scale of packaging to produce a voluntary "industry-led" scheme for increasing the recovery of packaging waste. The alternative to a voluntary scheme would be legislation. An industry body set up as a result, the Producer Responsibility Group (PRG), produced a report

Real Value from Packaging: the PRG Plan in November 1994, but urged the Government to underpin such a scheme with legislation to prevent "free-riders" from taking advantage of those businesses which were complying with the scheme. The Government conceded that legislation would be needed and the Environment Act 1995 provides power for the Secretary of State to make regulations accordingly (ss.93–95). How any scheme will operate is at the time of writing unclear.

Under s.46(2) a waste collection authority may require household waste to be placed in separate receptacles or compartments according to whether the waste is to be recycled or not. Waste collection and disposal authorities may make arrangements for the recycling of waste under express powers in s.55 (s.56 for Scotland). In England and Wales, in respect of waste which the collection authority decides to recycle, the usual requirement of delivery to such place as the disposal authority directs does not apply (s.48(2)) and there is provision for the disposal authority to make payments to the collection authority in respect of net savings in disposal costs (s.52(1)). Provision for determination of net savings of expenditure is made by the Environmental Protection (Waste Recycling Payments) Regulations 1992 (S.I. 1992 No. 462, amended most recently by S.I. 1995 No. 476) and the system is explained in Circ. 4/92 (Welsh Office 10/92).

Waste collection authorities are under a duty to carry out investigations as to the appropriate arrangements to facilitate recycling and to prepare waste recycling plans as to such arrangements (s.49). Finally, in England and Wales, in determining the contents of waste disposal contracts they enter into with contractors, and in the tendering process for such contracts, waste disposal authorities must have regard to the desirability of including terms designed to maximise the recycling of waste (Sched. 2, para. 19(1)(b)).

Closed landfills
Considerable public concern has been expressed as to the problems caused by the methanogenic properties of landfilled domestic and other wastes: see for example the Report of the Non Statutory Inquiry of Gerrard Ryan Q.C. on behalf of Derbyshire County Council into the explosion at Loscoe in 1986, and Waste Management Paper No. 27 on *The Control of Landfill Gas* (see note to s.61). Similarly, the accumulation of leachate, which may escape from the site and pollute ground or surface waters, is a cause for concern: see, for example, RCEP Eleventh Report (Cm. 9675) paras. 7.5–7.12.

An attempt is made to address these issues for the future by the new and more stringent provisions on surrender of site licences (see above). In relation to sites no longer in operation, new duties and powers were to be provided by s.61 under which waste regulation authorities would have been under a duty to inspect their area to detect whether deposits of controlled waste on the land had led or were leading to noxious gases or liquids being concentrated or accumulated, and emitted or discharged so as to cause possible pollution of the environment or harm to human health. It would have been the duty of the authority to do works or take steps (whether on the land affected or on adjacent land) as necessary to avoid such pollution or harm, the cost of such measures then being recovered, in whole or in part, from the person for the time being the owner of the land, except where the surrender of the relevant waste management licence had already been accepted by the authority under s.39. In the event, s.61 was never implemented, the issue of closed waste sites being subsumed within the Government's general review of contaminated land (see General Note to Part IIA). The type of problems with old sites referred to above will be dealt with under those provisions, and s.61 was repealed by the 1995 Act, Sched. 24.

Public information
As with Pt. I and indeed the rest of the Act, Pt. II contains comprehensive provisions for the disclosure of information on public registers (s.64). The relevant information relates predominantly to the exercise of licensing powers, and there are provisions as to the exclusion of information on grounds of national security (s.65) and commercial confidentiality (s.66). Each waste collection authority must maintain a register containing particulars from the main register relating to the treatment, keeping or disposal of waste within its area: such information is to be furnished to the waste collection authority by the waste regulation authority.

Relationship of waste licensing with other powers
Waste management licensing may to some extent be duplicated by other statutory controls. The relevant principles are as follows:

(a) *Integrated Pollution Control:* Conditions attached to IPC authorisations may not be framed so as to regulate the final disposal of controlled waste by deposit in or on land: other forms of disposal may be so regulated (s.28(1)). The Secretary of State may, by regulations, exclude the deposit, keeping treatment or disposal of waste from licensing requirements and from the offence of treating, keeping or disposing in a manner likely to cause pollution of the environment or harm to human health (s.33(3)). In exercising that power, the adequacy of other statutory controls (for example, IPC) is relevant (s.33(4)(c)).

The Waste Management Licensing Regulations 1994, reg. 16 (as amended), make provision for excluding from the requirement for a waste management licence, the deposit in or on land, recovery or disposal of waste under an IPC authorisation, save in relation to the final deposit of controlled waste by deposit in or on land; a similar exemption exists for waste management in connection with the carrying on of a process prescribed for IPC where the prescribed date has not yet arrived (again subject to the qualification as to final disposal by deposit on land).

(b) *Statutory nuisances:* The provisions of Pt. III of the Act on statutory nuisances could apply to accumulations of controlled waste (s.79(1)(e), but see new s.79(1A)) or to smell or other effluvia from such waste (s.79(1)(d)). The relationship of waste licensing powers and control over statutory nuisances was considered by the Court of Appeal in *Att.-Gen.'s Reference (No. 2 of 1988)* [1989] 3 W.L.R. 397, which held that:

  (i) the primary purpose of waste disposal licensing powers under Pt. I of the Control of Pollution Act 1974 was to avoid water pollution, serious detriment to the amenities of the locality and harm to public health; therefore the power to impose conditions under s.6(2) of the 1974 Act was not wide enough to allow a condition prohibiting public nuisances of all kinds, whether or not they had one of those three effects; and

  (ii) if such condition were valid, there would be no need to trace a nuisance back to a particular failure of management or operation in order to establish a breach.

It is questionable how far proposition (i) remains correct under Pt. II of the Act, where protection of water from pollution has been broadened to protection of the environment generally, and where "harm" to the environment receives a very broad statutory definition to include human senses.

(c) *Water pollution:* A waste site or installation that involves the discharge of effluent into controlled waters (for example a leachate treatment plant), or which results in polluting matter entering such waters, will require consent from the Environment Agency under the Water Resources Act 1991 or, in Scotland, from SEPA under the Control of Pollution Act 1974. Formerly, the NRA or, in Scotland, the relevant river purification authority had to be consulted before a waste management licence was issued (s.36(4)–(6)), in relation to a proposal for modification of licences (s.37(5)) and in relation to a proposal to accept the surrender of a licence (s.39(7)–(8)). However, these provisions are no longer required since the functions of the NRA and the river purification authorities have been transferred to the Agency and SEPA respectively and accordingly they have been repealed. In practice, however, it may be that administrative arrangements within the agencies require such proposals to be referred by the section dealing with waste regulation to a different section dealing with water issues.

The Waste Management Licensing Regulations, reg. 16, exclude from the need for a waste management licence the disposal of liquid waste under a discharge consent under the Water Resources Act 1991 or the Control of Pollution Act 1974. Whether the keeping and treatment of liquid effluent prior to such discharge requires a waste management licence largely depends on whether such effluent is to be regarded as "waste waters" (as opposed to "waste in liquid form") within article 2(1)(b)(iv) of the Waste Framework Directive; if so then it will not be Directive Waste as defined in the 1994 Regulations and accordingly will not be controlled waste. This issue aroused much confusion and controversy in 1995 when the Department of the Environment indicated that in its view effluent treatment plant was licensable under Pt. II, and that the appropriate course was to frame exemptions (see S.I. 1995 No. 1950).

(d) *Radioactive Substances:* By s.78, nothing in Pt. II of the Act applies to radioactive waste, but regulations may apply some or all of the provisions of Pt. II, with or without modification, for the purpose of dealing with such waste.

(e) *Town and Country Planning:* The prerequisite of either planning permission or an established use certificate or certificate of lawful use or development before a waste management licence can be granted has already been referred to (see above and the notes to s.36(2)). Another question which can arise is the relationship between planning and waste management licence conditions.

Guidance on this issue is provided by PPG 23 *Planning and Pollution Control*, Annexes 4 and 5 (England and Wales only) and in Waste Management Paper No. 4, *Licensing of Waste Facilities* paras. 1.17–1.22 (for the whole of Great Britain). Guidance for Scotland on this issue is provided by *NPPG 10, Planning and Waste Management* (Scottish Office Development Department, March 1996). It should be noted that many types of waste facility may require environmental assessment both south and north of the border under the Town and Country

Planning (Assessment of Environmental Effects) Regulations 1988 (S.I. 1988 No. 1199) or, in Scotland, the Environmental Assessment (Scotland) Regulations 1988 (S.I. 1988 No. 1221) prior to the grant of planning permission.

The Planning and Compensation Act 1991 amended the Town and Country Planning Act 1990 so as to require (s.38(2)) local planning authorities to prepare either a waste local plan or waste policies contained in their minerals local plan: in formulating such policies the local planning authority must have regard to any waste disposal plan for its area prepared under s.50 of EPA 1990 (Development Plan Regulations 1991, reg. 9(2)). Paragraph 7 of Sched. 4 to the Waste Management Licensing Regulations 1994 (S.I. 1994 No. 1056) amends ss.5(3)(a) and 9(3)(a) of the Town and Country Planning (Scotland) Act 1972 to the effect that local and structure plans in Scotland must include policies in respect of suitable waste disposal sites or installations. The waste disposal plan will consider the types and quantities of waste arising in the area, the availability of disposal facilities and the need for further provision, while the waste local plan addresses the land use implications of waste policies, such as suitable locations and the criteria likely to apply (PPG 12 para. 3.14).

In relation to their planning functions, planning authorities are placed under a duty to discharge those functions with specified objectives in relation to the disposal and recovery of waste: 1994 Regulations, regs. 2–4.

(f) *Health and Safety at work:* The Waste Management Regulations 1994, reg. 13, provide that no condition may be imposed in a waste management licence for the purpose only of securing the health of persons at work.

(g) *Deposits at Sea:* Reg. 16 of the 1994 Regulations excludes from the requirement for a waste management licence the recovery or disposal of waste where the activity is or forms part of an operation which is the subject of a licence under Part II of the Food and Environment Protection Act 1985 or which does not require a licence by virtue of s.7 of the 1985 Act.

(h) *Contaminated land:* Activities licensed by waste regulation authorities under Pt.II may have the potential to contaminate land: also they may be carried out on land which is already subject to contamination from previous uses or earlier deposits of waste. The provisions of Pt. IIA dealing with contaminated land are not intended to apply to activities regulated by a site licence and s.78YB(2) provides that Pt. IIA shall not apply to any land in respect of which a site licence under Pt. II is in force, except to the extent that the relevant harm or water pollution which results in the land being identified as contaminated is attributable to causes other than breach of licence conditions (the remedy there being under Pt. II) or to the carrying on of any activity authorised by the licence in accordance with its conditions.

Territorial extent
Only s.62(2)(e) (keeping of records as to special waste) applies to Northern Ireland and only in relation to imports of waste (s.164(4)).

COMMENCEMENT
The provisions of Pt. II of EPA 1990 on waste management are gradually being implemented. Sections 29–32 on waste regulation authorities, the Secretary of State's power to create regional waste regulation authorities, and waste disposal companies came into force on May 31, 1991. Section 34 on the Duty of Care came into force on April 1, 1992 along with the offence of treating, keeping, or disposing of controlled waste, in a manner likely to cause pollution of the environment or harm to human health (s.33(1)(c)). Sections 45–48 on the collection, disposal and treatment of controlled waste came into force on April 1, 1992. Section 49 on waste recycling plans came into force on August 1, 1991. Sections 50 and 51 on waste disposal plans and the functions of waste disposal authorities respectively came into force on May 31, 1991. Section 52 on payments for recycling and disposal of waste and s.55 on powers for recycling waste came into force on April 1, 1992. Section 75 on the definition of waste, including household, commercial and industrial waste and special waste come into force on May 31, 1991. The provisions relating to waste management licensing came into force on May 1, 1994 (see Commencement Order No. 15, S.I. 1994 No. 1096) subject to certain transitional provisions. However, the scrap metal industry, that is, activities involving the treating, keeping or disposing of scrap metal or motor vehicles which are to be dismantled, was temporarily exempted from both the waste management licensing provisions and the section 34 duty of care in respect of waste: first until October 1, 1994, then (by S.I. 1994 No. 2487) until January 1, 1995. Finally (by S.I. 1994 No. 3234) these activities were made subject to the licensing provisions as from April 1, 1995. S.I. 1995 No. 288 provides exemptions for a range of scrap metal activities (see Appendix

3) which had to be registered by operators by October 1, 1995, the date on which, also by S.I. 1995 No. 288, scrap metal became subject to the duty of care. See further, the Table in the General Introduction to this Act for the full list of Commencement Orders and dates.

Preliminary

Preliminary

29.—(1) The following provisions have effect for the interpretation of this Part.

(2) The "environment" consists of all, or any, of the following media, namely land, water and the air.

(3) "Pollution of the environment" means pollution of the environment due to the release or escape (into any environmental medium) from—

    (a) the land on which controlled waste is treated,

    (b) the land on which controlled waste is kept,

    (c) the land in or on which controlled waste is deposited,

    (d) fixed plant by means of which controlled waste is treated, kept or disposed of,

of substances or articles constituting or resulting from the waste and capable (by reason of the quantity or concentrations involved) of causing harm to man or any other living organisms supported by the environment.

(4) Subsection (3) above applies in relation to mobile plant by means of which controlled waste is treated or disposed of as it applies to plant on land by means of which controlled waste is treated or disposed of.

(5) For the purposes of subsections (3) and (4) above "harm" means harm to the health of living organisms or other interference with the ecological systems of which they form part and in the case of man includes offence to any of his senses or harm to his property; and "harmless" has a corresponding meaning.

(6) The "disposal" of waste includes its disposal by way of deposit in or on land and, subject to subsection (7) below, waste is "treated" when it is subjected to any process, including making it re-usable or reclaiming substances from it and "recycle" (and cognate expressions) shall be construed accordingly.

(7) Regulations made by the Secretary of State may prescribe activities as activities which constitute the treatment of waste for the purposes of this Part or any provision of this Part prescribed in the regulations.

(8) "Land" includes land covered by waters where the land is above the low water mark of ordinary spring tides and references to land on which controlled waste is treated, kept or deposited are references to the surface of the land (including any structure set into the surface).

(9) "Mobile plant" means, subject to subsection (10) below, plant which is designed to move or be moved whether on roads or other land.

(10) Regulations made by the Secretary of State may prescribe descriptions of plant which are to be treated as being, or as not being, mobile plant for the purposes of this Part.

(11) "Substance" means any natural or artificial substance, whether in solid or liquid form on in the form of a gas or vapour.

DEFINITIONS
    "controlled waste": s.75(4).
    "waste": s.75(2).

COMMENCEMENT
May 31, 1991 (S.I. 1991 No. 1319).

Pollution of the Environment: subss. (3) and (4)
This is an important definition in the light of the powers and duties contained later in Pt. II. The essential features are:

(a) land, fixed plant or mobile plant on or by means of which controlled waste is treated, kept, deposited or disposed of;

(b) the release or escape from such land or plant into any environmental medium of substances or articles constituting or resulting from the waste;

(c) those substances or articles must be capable of causing harm to man or other living organisms supported by the environment;

(d) "harm" in this sense is defined widely by subs. (5) to include harm to health, interference with ecological systems, offence to human senses and harm to property; and

(e) the escape or release must result in "pollution of the environment", being all or any of the media of land, water or air.

Disposal: subs. (6)
The definition makes it clear that "disposal" is a wider term than "deposit" and that disposal includes deposit in or on land as a means of disposal. It does not, however, appear to follow that every deposit of waste on land will constitute disposal: if the waste is not deposited as a means of disposing of it the act will simply be a deposit and not a disposal. As to the meaning of "deposit", see notes to s.33.

Some statutory provisions make reference to "final disposal" (for example s.28(1) of this Act). It therefore seems to be contemplated that there may be temporary, or interim, disposal of waste as opposed to final disposal.

The Queen's Bench Divisional Court decision in *R. v. Metropolitan Stipendiary Magistrate, ex p. London Waste Regulation Authority*; *Berkshire County Council* v. *Scott* [1993] 3 All E.R. 113 held that the decision in *Leigh Land Reclamation Limited v. Walsall Metropolitan Borough Council* [1991] J.P.L. 867 was wrongly decided and the *Leigh* case should no longer be followed on this point. The Court concluded that "deposit" as used in s.3(1) of the Control of Pollution Act 1974 was not to be applied to final deposits or disposals only. The defendants in the case had been operating a waste transfer station which was not licensed under the Act.

Treatment: subss. (6) and (7)
Treatment is defined to mean the subjection of waste to any process. "Process" has been judicially defined in other contexts: see notes to s.1(5). It is expressly stated that making waste re-usable or reclaiming substances from it constitutes treatment, so that waste recycling activities such as solvent or scrap metal recovery could be included. In practice, the definition of what constitutes "waste" will also be important here, and reference should be made to the definition in s.75 in that respect. Schedule 3 to the Waste Management Licensing Regulations 1994 creates various exemptions from the need for a waste management licence, a number of which relate to processes in connection with recovery, recycling or re-use. These exemptions further the Government's policy to envisage re-use and recycling and to exempt such activities so far as is consistent with environmental protection; see Circular 11/94 paras. 9–11.

Land: subs. (8)
See notes to s.33 under the heading "Deposit."

Mobile Plant: subss. (9) and (10)
The Waste Management Licensing Regulations 1994, reg. 12 (as substituted by S.I. 1995 No. 288), provides that plant fitting one of a number of descriptions shall be treated as mobile plant, provided that *either* it is designed to move or be moved by any means from place to place with a view to being used at each such place, *or*, if not so designed, it is readily capable of moving or being so moved. The descriptions are as follows: an incinerator which is an exempt incinerator for the purposes of Sched. 1, Chap. 5, s.5.1 to the Environmental Protection (Prescribed Processes and Substances) Regulations 1991 (S.I. 1991 No. 472, see Appendix 1) (*i.e.* an incinerator designed to incinerate waste, including animal remains, at a rate of not more than 50 kg per hour, other than one employed to incinerate clinical waste, sewage storage, sewage screenings or municipal waste); plant for the recovery, by filtration or heat treatment, of waste oil from electrical equipment; plant for the destruction by dechlorination of waste PCBs or PCTs; plant for the vitrification of waste; and plant for the treatment by microwave of clinical waste (*i.e.* "clinical waste" as defined in regulation 1(2) of the Controlled Waste Regulations 1992 (S.I. 1992 No. 588)). Regulation 12 expressly provides that no other plant shall be treated as such. Any other forms of such plant will either need to be expressly provided for or will require a site licence for each location at which they operate.

The 1995 amending regulations came into force on April 1, 1995. Prior to that date, only plant of the first description (exempt incinerators) was to be treated as mobile plant, and then only if designed to be mobile. Where the pre-April 1, 1995 regulation 12 is applicable, it should be noted that whether plant is "designed" to move or be moved on roads will be a question of fact, and is a different question from whether it is movable. "Designed" may mean either intended or alternatively designed in structural or engineering terms: see *Wilson v. West Sussex County Council* [1963] 2 Q.B. 764.

Authorities for purposes of this Part

30.—[(1) Any reference in this Part to a waste regulation authority—
- (a) in relation to England and Wales, is a reference to the Environmental Agency; and
- (b) in relation to Scotland, is a reference to the Scottish Environment Protection Agency;

and any reference in this Part to the area of a waste regulation authority shall accordingly be taken as a reference to the area over which the Environment Agency or the Scottish Environment Protection Agency, as the case may be, exercises its functions or, in the case of any particular function, the function in question.]

(2) For the purposes of this Part the following authorities are waste disposal authorities, namely—
- (a) for any non-metropolitan county in England, the county council;
- (b) in Greater London, the following—
  - (i) for the area of a London waste disposal authority, the authority constituted as the waste disposal authority for that area;
  - (ii) for the City of London, the Common Council;
  - (iii) for any other London borough, the council of the borough;
- (c) in the metropolitan county of Greater Manchester, the following—
  - (i) for the metropolitan district of Wigan, the district council;
  - (ii) for all other areas in the county, the authority constituted as the Greater Manchester Waste Disposal Authority;
- (d) for the metropolitan county of Merseyside, the authority constituted as the Merseyside Waste Disposal Authority;
- (e) for any district in any other metropolitan county in England, the council of the district;
- (f) for any district in Wales, the council of the district;
- (g) in Scotland, [a council constituted under section 2 of the local Government etc. (Scotland) Act 1994].

(3) For the purposes of this Part the following authorities are waste collection authorities—
- (a) for any district in England and Wales not within Greater London, the council of the district;
- (b) in Greater London, the following—
  - (i) for any London borough, the council of the borough;
  - (ii) for the City of London, the Common Council;
  - (iii) for the Temples, the Sub-Treasurer of the Inner Temple and the Under Treasurer of the Middle Temple respectively;
- (c) in Scotland, [a council constituted under section 2 of the local Government etc. (Scotland) Act 1994].

(4) In this section references to particular authorities having been constituted as waste disposal [...] authorities are references to their having been so constituted by the Waste Regulation and Disposal (Authorities) Order 1985 made by the Secretary of State under section 10 of the Local Government Act 1985 and the reference to London waste disposal authorities is a reference to the authorities named in Parts I, II, III, IV and V of Schedule 1 to that Order and this section has effect subject to any order made under the said section 10 [...].

(5) In this Part "waste disposal contractor" means a person who in the

course of a business collects, keeps, treats or disposes of waste, being either—

(a) a company formed for all or any of those purposes by a waste disposal authority whether in pursuance of section 32 below or otherwise; or

(b) either a company formed for all or any of those purposes by other persons or a partnership or an individual;

and "company" has the same meaning as in the Companies Act 1985 and "formed," in relation to a company formed by other persons, includes the alteration of the objects of the company.

[...]

DEFINITIONS
"disposes": s.29(6).
"treats": s.29(6).
"waste": s.75(2).

COMMENCEMENT
May 31, 1991 (S.I. 1991 No. 1319).

AMENDMENTS
Subs. (1) was substituted, words in subs. (4) were deleted, and subss. (6)–(8) were repealed entirely by the Environment Act 1995, Sched. 22, para. 62. Subss. (2)(g) and (3)(c) were amended by the Local Government etc. (Scotland) Act 1994.

Waste authorities
This section makes provision for the various waste authorities, namely:

(a) waste regulation authorities (the Agency and SEPA after the Environment Act 1995);

(b) waste disposal authorities; and

(c) waste collection authorities.

Their respective roles and functions are summarised at the General Note to Pt. II of the Act.

"Waste Disposal Contractor": subs. (5)
Waste disposal functions are to be discharged through waste disposal contractors as defined in subs. (5). Such a contractor may either be a private business operating through the medium of sole trader, partnership, or limited company or alternatively may be a company formed by the waste disposal authority (see also s.32 below). In either case, the contractor must be a person who collects, keeps, treats or disposes of waste "in the course of a business". The expression implies at least a degree of continuity of activity. "Business" has been said to be a wider term than "trade" and while naturally it will usually be carried on with a view to profit, this is not always an essential prerequisite (see *Stroud's Judicial Dictionary* (5th ed., 1986), Vol. I, pp. 323 *et seq.*). Clearly it is contemplated that the local authority companies will be run on a commercial profit-making basis.

Separation of regulation and disposal functions
One of the main objects of Pt. II of the Act was the separation of waste regulation and waste disposal functions, and the general duty formerly contained in subss. (7) and (8) to make administrative arrangements for that purpose reflected this. With the transfer of waste regulation functions to the Agency and SEPA, these provisions are no longer necessary and have accordingly been repealed.

Details of the administrative arrangements regarding the separation of functions of the waste regulation authority and the waste disposal authority were formerly provided in DoE Circ. 10/91 (Welsh Office 27/91) dated 31.5.91 entitled "Separation of Local Authority Waste Regulation and Waste Disposal Functions". With the transfer of waste regulation functions to the Agency the guidance contained in the Circular has been rendered unnecessary. It should be noted that the Circular did not apply to Scotland since, until the transfer of waste regulation functions to SEPA, district and islands councils continued to act both as waste regulation authorities and as waste disposal authorities although within each council administrative arrangements were put in place to keep each function separate.

Power to create regional authorities for purposes of waste regulation

31. [...]

Section 31, relating to the creation of regional waste authorities, was repealed by the Environment Act 1995, Sched. 22, para. 63.

Transition to waste disposal companies etc.

32.—(1) In this section "existing disposal authority" means any authority (including any joint authority) constituted as a waste disposal authority for any area before the day appointed for this section to come into force.

(2) The Secretary of State shall, subject to subsection (3) below, give directions to existing disposal authorities or, in the case of joint authorities, to the constituent authorities requiring them, before specified dates, to—

(a) form or participate in forming waste disposal companies; and

(b) transfer to the companies so formed, by and in accordance with a scheme made in accordance with Schedule 2 to his Act, the relevant part of their undertakings;

and a waste disposal authority shall accordingly have power to form, and hold securities in, any company so established.

(3) Subject to subsection (4) below, the Secretary of State shall not give any direction under subsection (2) above to an existing disposal authority, or to the constituent authorities of an existing disposal authority, as respects which or each of which he is satisfied that the authority—

(a) has formed or participated in forming a waste disposal company and transferred to it the relevant part of its undertaking;

(b) has, in pursuance of arrangements made with other persons, ceased to carry on itself the relevant part of its undertaking;

(c) has made arrangements with other persons to cease to carry on itself the relevant part of its undertaking; or

(d) has, in pursuance of arrangements made with other persons, ceased to provide places at which and plant and equipment by means of which controlled waste can be disposed of or deposited for the purposes of disposal.

(4) Subsection (3) above does not apply in a case falling within paragraph (a) unless it appears to the Secretary of State that—

(a) the form of the company and the undertaking transferred are satisfactory; and

(b) the requirements of subsections (8) and (9) below are fulfilled;

and "satisfactory" means satisfactory by reference to the corresponding arrangements to which he would give his approval for the purposes of a transfer scheme under Schedule 2 to this Act.

(5) Where the Secretary of State is precluded from giving a direction under subsection (2) above to any authority by reason of his being satisfied as to the arrangements mentioned in subsection (3)(c) above, then, if those arrangements are not implemented within what appears to him to be a reasonable time, he may exercise his power to give directions under subsection (2) above as respects that authority.

(6) Part I of Schedule 2 to this Act has effect for the purposes of this section and Part II for regulating the functions of waste disposal authorities and the activities of waste disposal contractors.

(7) Subject to subsection (8) below, the activities of a company which a waste disposal authority has formed or participated in forming (whether in pursuance of subsection (2)(a) above or otherwise) may include activities which are beyond the powers of the authority to carry on itself, but, in the case of a company formed otherwise than in pursuance of subsection (2)(a)

above, only if the Secretary of State has determined under subsection (4)(a) above that the form of the company and the undertaking transferred to it are satisfactory.

(8) A waste disposal authority shall, for so long as it controls a company which it has formed or participated in forming (whether in pursuance of subsection (2)(a) above or otherwise), so exercise its control as to secure that the company does not engage in activities other than the following activities or any activities incidental or conducive to, or calculated to facilitate, them, that is to say, the disposal, keeping or treatment of waste and the collection of waste.

(9) Subject to subsection (10) below, a waste disposal authority shall, for so long as it controls a company which it has formed or participated in forming (whether in pursuance of subsection (2)(a) above or otherwise), so exercise its control as to secure that, for the purposes of Part V of the Local Government and Housing Act 1989, the company is an arm's length company.

(10) Subsection (9) above shall not apply in the case of a company which a waste disposal authority has formed or participated in forming in pursuance of subsection (2)(a) above until after the vesting date for that company.

(11) In this section and Schedule 2 to this Act—

"control" (and cognate expressions) is to be construed in accordance with section 68 or, as the case requires, section 73 of the Local Government and Housing Act 1989;

"the relevant part" of the undertaking of an existing disposal authority is that part which relates to the disposal, keeping or treatment or the collection of waste;

and in this section "securities" and "vesting date" have the same meaning as in Schedule 2.

(12) This section shall not apply to Scotland.

DEFINITIONS
"disposal": s.29(6).
"treatment": s.29(6).
"waste": s.75(2).

COMMENCEMENT
May 31, 1991 (S.I. 1991 No. 1319).

GENERAL NOTE
Together with Sched. 2, this complex section provides the framework for the transition of waste disposal functions from disposal authorities to disposal contractors (see s.30 above). The Secretary of State is under a duty by subs. (2) to direct disposal authorities in existence on the appointed day to form waste disposal companies (LAWDCs) and to transfer the relevant part of their undertakings to such companies (the relevant part being that relating to the collection, disposal or treatment of waste: subs. (11)).

Disposal authorities may avoid being given such a direction by making their own arrangements to form waste disposal companies, transferring the relevant part of their undertaking and ceasing to carry on such parts themselves or making arrangements to do so (subs. (3)). However, authorities making such arrangements may still be subject to a direction if the Secretary of State is not satisfied that the arrangements are satisfactory, or if they are not implemented within what appears to be a reasonable time (subs. (4) and (5)).

The arrangements are explained in DoE Circ. 8/91 *Competition for Local Authority Waste Disposal Contracts and New Arrangements for Disposal Operations* (Welsh Office 24/91). Notices of intention to direct the formation of LAWDCs were issued by the Secretary of State in May/June 1991, following which timetables were given to authorities to put in place the necessary arrangements. The first transfer schemes were approved by the Secretary of State during the Summer of 1992.

Formation of LAWDCs
Guidance as to the formation of LAWDCs and their constitution and management is given at paras. 26–34 and Annex C of Circ. 8/91. The main restrictions relating to LAWDCs concern the objects of the company and "arm's length" requirements.

Objects of Company: A "private sector" waste disposal contracting company may have any objects, so long as its business is defined in s.30(5). A waste contracting company formed by a waste disposal authority may have objects and engage in activities beyond the authority's own powers (subs. (7)), but so long as the authority controls the company it must exercise its control so as to secure that the company does not engage in activities other than the collection, disposal, keeping or treatment of waste, and ancillary activities (subs. (8)). The company may seek such business from any source.

Arm's length requirements: subsection (9): Part V of the Local Government and Housing Act 1989 deals with companies in which local authorities have interests. Section 68(1) of the 1989 Act defines a company "under the control of a local authority" as being one which by virtue of s.736 of the Companies Act 1985 is a subsidiary of the local authority if the authority have power to control a majority of votes at a general meeting, or power to appoint or remove a majority of the board of directors, or if the company is under the control of an intermediate company which is itself under the control of the authority. Notwithstanding that a company is under the control of an authority in that sense, by s.68(6) of the 1989 Act it is still an "arm's length company" for the purposes of Pt. V:

> "In relation to any financial year if, at a time before the beginning of that year, the authority resolved that the company should be an arm's length company and, at all times from the passing of that resolution up to the end of the financial year in question the following conditions have applied while the company has been under the control of the local authority:
>
> (a) that each of the directors of the company was appointed for a fixed term of at least two years;
> (b) that, subject to subs. (7) below, no director of the company has been removed by resolution under s.303 of the Companies Act 1985;
> (c) that not more than one-fifth of the directors of the company have been members or officers of the authority;
> (d) that the company has not occupied (as tenant or otherwise) any land in which the authority have an interest other than for the best consideration reasonably obtainable;
> (e) that the company has entered into an agreement with the authority that the company will use its best endeavours to produce a specified positive return on its assets;
> (f) that except for the purpose of enabling the company to acquire fixed assets or to provide it with working capital, the authority have not lent money to the company or guaranteed any sum borrowed by it or subscribed for any securities in the company;
> (g) that the authority have not made any grant to the company the amount of which is in any way related to the financial results of the company in any period."

The importance of being an "arm's length company" lies in the controls exercised by the Government over companies established by local authorities. The general philosophy is that local authority controlled companies or local authority influenced companies are extensions of local authorities, should observe the same principles of conduct as local authorities, and should be subject to the same statutory controls as local authorities. By s.70 of the 1989 Act, the Secretary of State may regulate the activities of such companies by orders, but different provision may be made in such orders for companies which are arm's length companies.

Control: The four ways in which a company may, by s.68 of the 1989 Act, be regarded as under the control of a local authority are referred to in the previous paragraph. Detailed provisions deal with what is meant by power to control a majority of votes at a general meeting, the right to appoint or remove a majority of the board of directors, and the circumstances in which a person's shareholding in the company is under the control of a local authority. Section 73 of the 1989 Act applies in cases where authorities act jointly to constitute or control a company, so that the company is not under the control of any one authority but is under the control of the authorities acting as one.

Transfer of undertaking

Waste disposal authorities are not required, in all cases, to set up LAWDCs. They may choose to make alternative arrangements for waste disposal to be carried out by the private sector (Circ. 8/91, para. 17). However, in either case the authority will need to divest itself of its waste disposal undertaking.

The disposal authority may continue to own the freehold of waste sites, but the leasehold interest would have to be vested in the LAWDC (or in a private contractor in the absence of a LAWDC) for the life of the site (see s.51(4)(d) and (5)(c)). The disposal authority must transfer all plant and equipment used for treatment, recycling or disposing of waste, but may own plant or equipment used for waste disposal contractors for enabling them to keep collected waste prior to its removal for disposal, or to treat such waste in connection with its keeping, or to facilitate its transportation, *e.g.* transfer station facilities such as balers and compactors (see s.51(4)(c) and (5)(b)). In any event, any transfer scheme will be subject to the approval of the Secretary of State, who will wish to ensure that the new companies will be financially viable.

The transfer scheme must also be supported by assurances from the directors of the LAWDC that the scheme does not withhold any staff, property or rights from the company which it would need to perform the disposal contracts it has won.

Transfer scheme
It is not necessary for assets to be transferred to a LAWDC by way of a transfer scheme under Sched. 2, though there are advantages in doing so, particularly in relation to capital allowances (Sched. 2, para. 9), the benefit of deemed planning permission (Sched. 2, para. 10) and the transfer of rights under otherwise unassignable agreements (Sched. 2, paras. 13 and 14).

The procedure for preparation submission and approval of transfer schemes is set out at Sched. 2, paras. 6–8 and at Annex D of Circ. 4/92. The effect of the scheme, when approved by the Secretary of State is to transfer to the company the assets, rights and liabilities specified in the scheme (Sched. 2, para. 6(7)). As a consequence of that vesting, the company issues to the authority such securities as are specified in the scheme (Sched. 2, para. 6(8)); these are treated as issued fully paid and as if paid up by virtue of payment to the company of their normal value in cash (Sched. 2, para. 9(1)).

The scheme will identify the property, rights and liabilities to be transferred (Sched. 2, para. 7), so that in general no separate conveyance or assignment will be necessary. However, the Scheme may make supplemental, necessary and consequential provisions, and the authority and company are under the duty to enter into such other written agreements as may be necessary to afford mutual rights and safeguards (Sched. 2, para. 8(4) and (5)). These may, for example, deal with indemnities for environmental impairment or other damage resulting from waste disposal operations prior to or after vesting, operational leases of sites, and provisions to allow the authority to participate in "windfall" profits which may accrue from future disposals of assets.

The DoE requires each transfer scheme to be supported by written assurances from the directors of the LAWDC and the authority, in the form, or substantially the form, set out at Annex E of Circ. 4/92.

Any provision fettering the right to transfer securities of a waste disposal contractor (not just a LAWDC) from disposing of those securities is void, so long as it relates to securities of a waste disposal contractor controlled by a waste disposal authority or to which the authority has transferred the relevant part of its undertaking (Sched. 2, para. 23).

Waste Disposal Contracts
Schedule 2, Pt. II deals with the terms of waste disposal contracts and the procedure for putting such contracts out to tender. Those provisions are explained and amplified at Annex A of Circ. 4/92.

The key principle is the avoidance of undue discrimination between "local authority" and "private sector" companies (para. 18). This is qualified by para. 19 which requires waste disposal authorities to have regard to the desirability of including in any contract terms designed to minimise pollution of the environment or harm to human health and to maximise the recycling of waste. Acceptance or refusal of tenders may be justified on such grounds, presumably even if the result is discrimination between classes of waste contractor. The procedural requirements for putting waste contracts to tender are set out in detail at para. 20, and by para. 21 the fact of whether a waste disposal contract is or is not controlled by the authority is to be disregarded. Once entered into, a waste disposal contract may not be varied so as to result in undue discrimination between classes of waste contractors (para. 22).

Reference is made at Circ. 4/92, Annex A, paras. A17–18 to the relevant existing and proposed E.C. requirements on competitive tendering, in particular the services directive proposal (COM (90) 372) on which further advice is to be issued.

Practical considerations
Disposal authorities have therefore been faced with a choice between the options of setting up a LAWDC or withdrawing completely from operational activities and disposing of assets by sale or lease to the private sector. If the first option is selected, the authority will need to decide how the LAWDC is to be controlled and whether it is to continue to be wholly owned by the authority. Which option proves to be appropriate will depend on the particular circumstances of the authority, the extent of private sector competition, and how viable a LAWDC is perceived to be. If a LAWDC is formed, there may be advantages in the disposal authority not retaining control. One advantage is the ability to diversify activities (s.32(8); see above). Another possible advantage is that where the authority's voting rights in the LAWDC are less than 20 per

cent, the capital borrowings of the LAWDC will not count against credit approvals with respect to the credit arrangements and capital expenditure of the authority under Pt. IV of the Local Government and Housing Act 1989 (see s.69 of the 1989 Act). The Government's view on this issue was stated as follows by Baroness Blatch:

> "I do not intend to go over the same grounds at great length today. Suffice it to say that a major part of any government's economic policy must be to control public expenditure. Current local authority waste disposal operations are already subject to the capital finance regime, so these controls on local authorities are not new. LAWDCs will be set up as arm's length companies controlled by local authorities. It is only right and proper therefore that while LAWDCs continue to be controlled or influenced by local authorities they should be subject to the local authority capital finance rules. This general point was made, and accepted, during the passage of the Local Government and Housing Bill; and, again, because these companies are, to some extent, underwritten by the local authorities.
>
> It should also be remembered that if an authority chooses to relinquish control or influence of its LAWDC, the capital finance rules no longer apply. In this way, significant new private investment can be brought into waste disposal to meet the new higher standards which public sector regulators will concentrate on enforcing." (*Hansard*, H.L. Vol. 522, col. 308).

The risk attending loss of control is whether the authority is thereby exposed to the possibility of exploitation in the future, whether by the LAWDC or the private sector.

Tender procedures: The Terry Adams Case
R. v. Avon County Council, ex parte Terry Adams Ltd [1994] Env. L.R. 442, deals with the procedure for awarding waste disposal contracts under Schedule 2, Part II. Judicial review proceedings were brought by Terry Adams Ltd, a waste disposal company, against Avon County Council for the authority's decision in February 1993 to award to Avon Waste Management Limited (AWM) five contracts for the disposal of all waste arising within the County. AWM was a local authority waste disposal company set up and owned by Avon under the Environmental Protection Act 1990. The main complaint of Terry Adams was that the statutory tendering process provided by the 1990 Act had at various stages been unlawfully distorted, leading to the rejection of their tender.

The Court of Appeal referred to the obligation in paragraph 18 of Schedule 2 on waste disposal authorities to avoid undue discrimination in favour of one waste disposal company as against another, when determining the terms and conditions of any contract which the authority proposes to enter into. As the Court of Appeal stated, if the contract terms were unduly discriminatory there would be distortion of competition, and indeed there might be no competition at all, either because the potential tenderers would find it impossible or prohibitively expensive to make a bid or because any bid made would be inevitably uncompetitive. As appears from the full transcript of the decision Ralph Gibson L.J. stated:

> "The WDA may thus be misinformed; and fail to 'identify the full cost of waste disposal'; and the ability of the WDA then, in the public interest, and decide whether or not to accept any tender which has been received will be impaired. A particular vice of the presence of unduly discriminatory conditions in a proposed contract is that the effect of such conditions in deterring potential tenders is likely to be unknown and undiscernable."

In this case Terry Adams had put in a tender for only one of the six contracts, for the disposal of about 250,000 tonnes a year, this being the balance of the estimated 400,000 tonnes of domestic waste produced in the County after deduction of 150,000 tonnes a year covered by existing contractors. Terry Adams' tender had quoted prices approximately one half of the prices per tonne quoted in AWM's successful tender. Avon sought to explain this decision on the basis that AWM's tender was based upon continuing use of an existing incinerator until 1996 and thereafter either upon a new incinerator or, in default, upon disposal to landfill. Avon's policy, based upon environmental protection considerations, was to secure as best it could re-cycling of appropriate waste, and the production of energy by incineration of the remainder. Paragraph 19 of Schedule 2 provides that a waste disposal authority shall have regard to the desirability of including in any contract terms and conditions designed to minimise the pollution of the environment or harm to human health and to maximise the re-cycling of waste.

Ralph Gibson L.J. (with whom McCowan L.J. agreed) held that Avon was entitled to decide which bid to prefer for the various contracts under tender according to the honest judgment of the councillors to whom fell the task of decision. The only limitation was that the decision should be rational in the *Wednesbury* sense ([1948] 1 K.B. 223) and was reached in accordance with any statutory requirements. Avon was not only entitled to have regard to environmental factors with regard to arrangements for waste disposal, but was in effect bound to have such regard as a responsible waste disposal authority. This duty was not limited to environmental factors specifically mentioned in the tender documentation. The Court of Appeal held that the preparation of a transfer scheme is a distinct exercise to the award disposal contracts and that nothing in a transfer scheme could legitimise contracts which were unduly discriminatory. In particular, the scheme could be revised in the light of the outcome of the tender process. Whilst therefore it might be difficult in practice to avoid discrimination in the process of reviewing or replacing contracts after assets had already vested in the LAWDC, that potential future problem "does not permit a WDA to frame proposed contracts so as to discriminate unduly in favour of the proposed LAWDC when it is neither difficult nor impossible to avoid so doing."

It was held that the terms of the contract for transfer and loading operations for a scheme for the transfer of waste by rail to landfill in Buckinghamshire were unduly discriminatory, in that there was no prospect of any contractor other than AWM providing such facilities: indeed advice had been given to Avon by its officers and advisers that the transfer of the crucial assets to AWM ran the risk of being held to be unduly discriminatory. The result was that AWM were the only tenderer and that its tender was "much in excess of a competitive price". The discrimination was "undue" in that it was likely to have had a significant effect on the competitive tendering for the contract: the terms were prescriptive in that "they required the servicing of the particular British Rail Contract through particular rail heads for which transfer stations suitably placed were necessary and which, in the time allowed, were available to AWM only." No justification for such discrimination could be found.

A further point was that a change made to the requirements of the tender by Avon had not been advertised: if, as Avon argued, that change meant that the terms were no longer discriminatory then the trade and prospective tenderers should have been informed.

With regard to the issue of the waste disposal contract it was held that undoubtedly it was permitted for a waste disposal authority to have a policy favouring disposal by incineration, to the extent that it was reasonable to do so. It was, however, in the interest of the waste disposal authority and the public served by that authority, to have accurate information for comparing the cost of that preferred option against the cost, over a comparable period of time, of other legitimate means of disposal. Parliament was taken to have intended that WDAs should have such information. On that basis the proposed contract, which required the tenderer to provide not only the new incinerator but also the site for it, was probably discriminatory by preventing any company other than AWM form tendering for disposal by that method since the site for the incinerator was to be made available only to that company under the terms of the transfer scheme to AWM. However, this aspect of the case was not pursued and on balance the Court of Appeal was not satisfied that the contract was unduly discriminatory: the necessity to use specific transfer station facilities was not demonstrated clearly, as it had been for the rail contract.

Therefore, in relation to the proposed contract for landfill operation, the Court of Appeal accepted the conclusion at first instance (*The Times*, July 7, 1993) that the terms were not unduly discriminatory. The appeal on that particular ground was therefore dismissed.

It was also held that it was not open to Avon to accept the interdependent bids of AWM for all the contracts. The WDA had invited separate bids capable of acceptance, and that was not a matter of "mere form". AWM "was thereby purporting to enter into separate contracts by the acceptance of tenders which were not made in the course of, and in consequence of, the statutory tendering process but in breach of an important express requirement of the tendering process in respect of each contract." AWM had submitted contracts which did not comply with the requirement of the tender documents and Avon could only have supposed that they did comply if they thought the stipulation of interdependency was irrelevant. Avon had not taken steps to negotiate with AWM, as they could have done, to bring the tenders into compliance with the tender documents.

The case was distinguished from the decision of the Court of Appeal in *R. v. Birmingham City Council, ex parte Mass Energy* [1993] Env. L.R. 298 that there it was open to a WDA to negotiate an alternative mode of performance with a successful tenderer whose tender was in compliance with the requirements of the tender documents.

The applicant was held to have standing to seek judicial review despite having sought to qualify its own tender in two respects, nor was there any good reason to refuse relief as a matter of discretion—indeed substantial public benefit might result from Avon being forced to re-tender. Hobhouse L.J., agreeing, said that there were undoubtedly difficulties for local authorities in carrying out their obligations under Part II of the 1990 Act as a result of a combination of various potentially conflicting strategy objectives: *i.e.* environmental consider-ations, the requirement of divestment of the waste disposal undertaking and, thirdly competitive tendering in the open market. The drafting of Schedule 2 of the 1990 Act did not provide unequivocal guidance as to the ranking of those objectives.

It seems clear from the decision that the Courts will be unwilling to intervene on decisions made on tendering, unless those decisions fall foul of the statutory requirements or are irrational in the administrative law sense. The difficulty is, however, that since the statutory requirements conflict, it may always be possible to make out a case that the outcome has fallen foul of one or other of those requirements. In particular, it is clear that it is not open to the waste disposal authority to regard securing the environmental objectives referred to in paragraph 19 of Schedules as being an overriding consideration. Indeed this would appear to follow from the express wording of paragraph 19 which simply provides that a waste disposal authority "shall have regard to the desirability" of including such terms in its contracts. It is also clear that authorities will need to exercise care in framing the terms of the contracts and the structure of the tender to avoid discrimination in favour of an operator who has a monopoly situation in terms of a particular asset: this may be particularly important in the case of a local authority waste disposal company which has been vested with strategic assets such as transfer stations or incinerators. Finally, the decision points out the dangers in awarding contracts to a tenderer who had not submitted their tender in accordance with the tendering process: AWM in this case had submitted their bid on an "all or nothing" basis whereby the contracts were inter-dependent. This conflicted with the process as laid down by Avon, and steps should have been taken by Avon to ensure conformity with the tender requirements before accepting the bid. Avon initially appealed but is understood to have withdrawn that appeal: the Court of Appeal ruling therefore stands.

Cardiff City Council v. Gooding Investments Limited
In this unreported case (April 7, 1995) the waste disposal authority invited tenders for private sector parties to enter into a joint venture with the authority. The applicant submitted a tender, knowing from the details supplied that the successful tenderer would be awarded shares in the company which would enter into the waste disposal contract. Nonetheless, the proposal put forward by the applicant did not accord with the council's preferred solution. Having been successful in its tender, the applicant then challenged the process by way of judicial review. The main question was whether the proposed arrangements were in accordance with s.51 and Sched. 2. Owen J. held that s.51 did not require the authority to contract directly or at all with the waste disposal contractor, but simply to arrange with the contractor for the disposal of waste. The word "arrange" contemplated a relationship which might not be as formal or binding as a contract. Paras. 18 and 19 of Sched. 2 contemplated a contract, but not necessarily with the successful tenderer. It was therefore lawful for a waste disposal authority to contract with a company and require the successful tenderer to acquire shares in the company. In proposing these arrangements, the authority was trying to avoid the difficulties encountered in the *Terry Adams* case and to prevent any unfair advantage to one tenderer as against the others.

Scotland
Section 32 and Sched. 2 do not apply to Scotland, where authorities continued to exercise both regulatory and disposal functions until the transfer of their waste regulation function to SEPA.

Prohibition on unauthorised or harmful depositing, treatment or disposal of waste

Prohibition on unauthorised or harmful deposit, treatment or disposal etc. of waste

33.—(1) Subject to subsection (2) and (3) below […] a person shall not—
  (a) deposit controlled waste, or knowingly cause or knowingly permit controlled waste to be deposited in or on any land unless a waste management licence authorising the deposit is in force and the deposit is in accordance with the licence;
  (b) treat, keep or dispose of controlled waste, or knowingly cause or knowingly permit controlled waste to be treated, kept or disposed of—
    (i) in or on any land, or
    (ii) by means of any mobile plant,
  except under and in accordance with a waste management licence;

(c) treat, keep or dispose of controlled waste in a manner likely to cause pollution of the environment or harm to human health.

(2) Subsection (1) above does not apply in relation to household waste from a domestic property which is treated, kept or disposed of within the curtilage of the dwelling by or with the permission of the occupier of the dwelling.

(3) Subsection (1)(a), (b) or (c) above do not apply in cases prescribed in regulations made by the Secretary of State and the regulations may make different exceptions for different areas.

(4) The Secretary of State, in exercising his power under subsection (3) above, shall have regard in particular to the expediency of excluding from the controls imposed by waste management licences—

(a) any deposits which are small enough or of such a temporary nature that they may be so excluded;

(b) any means of treatment or disposal which are innocuous enough to be so excluded;

(c) cases for which adequate controls are provided by another enactment than this section.

(5) Where controlled waste is carried in and deposited from a motor vehicle, the person who controls or is in a position to control the use of the vehicle shall, for the purposes of subsection (1)(a) above, be treated as knowingly causing the waste to be deposited whether or not he gave any instructions for this to be done.

(6) A person who contravenes subsection (1) above or any condition of a waste management licence commits an offence.

(7) It shall be a defence for a person charged with an offence under this section to prove—

(a) that he took all reasonable precautions and exercised all due diligence to avoid the commission of the offence; or

(b) that he acted under instructions from his employer and neither knew nor had reason to suppose that the acts done by him constituted a contravention of subsection (1) above; or

[(c) that the acts alleged to constitute the contravention were done in an emergency in order to avoid danger to human health in a case where

(i) he took all such steps as were reasonably practicable in the circumstances for minimising pollution of the environment and harm to human health; and

(ii) particulars of the acts were furnished to the waste regulation authority as soon as reasonably practicable after they were done.]

(8) Except in a case falling within subsection (9) below, a person who commits an offence under this section shall be liable—

(a) on summary conviction, to imprisonment for a term not exceeding six months or a fine not exceeding £20,000 or both; and

(b) on conviction on indictment, to imprisonment for a term not exceeding two years or a fine or both.

(9) A person who commits an offence under this section in relation to special waste shall be liable—

(a) on summary conviction, to imprisonment for a term not exceeding six months or a fine not exceeding £20,000 or both;

(b) on conviction on indictment, to imprisonment for a term not exceeding five years or a fine or both.

Definitions
"controlled waste": s.75(2) and (4).
"disposal": s.29(6).

"harm": s.29(5).
"household waste": s.75(5).
"mobile plant": s.29(9).
"pollution of the environment": s.29(3).
"special waste": s.75(9).
"treat": s.29(6).
"waste": s.75(2) and (4).

AMENDMENT
Subs. 7(c) was substituted by the Environment Act 1995 Sched. 22, para. 64. Words in subs. (1) were deleted by Sched. 24 of the 1995 Act.

COMMENCEMENT
Subsection 33(3) and (4): December 12, 1991 (S.I. 1991 No. 2829). Subsection 33(1)(c): April 1, 1992 (S.I. 1991 No. 2829). Subsection 33(2) and (6)(a) so far as relating to s.33(1)(c): April 1, 1992 (S.I. 1991 No. 2829). Remainder: May 1, 1994 (S.I. 1994 No. 1096).

GENERAL NOTE

Causing and knowingly permitting: The section forms the foundation of the waste licensing system by prohibiting the deposit, treatment, keeping or disposal of controlled waste in or on land, or by means of mobile plant, except under and in accordance with a waste management licence. It is an offence not only to carry out such activities, but also to "knowingly cause or knowingly permit" them. The different wording implies distinct offences, "permit" being a "looser and vaguer" term than "cause": see *McLeod v. Buchanan* [1940] 2 All E.R. 179, 187 (H.L., *per* Lord Wright).

The term "cause" should be approached in its everyday common sense, and does not imply intention or negligence: *Alphacell v. Woodward* [1972] A.C. 824. To "cause" a deposit or other act does, however, involve some positive participation on the defendant's part and where the defendant's role is entirely passive, a charge of "knowingly permitting" will be the more appropriate course: see *Price v. Cromack* [1975] 1 W.L.R. 988. Such a charge might, for example, be appropriate in the case of a waste producer who consigns waste to a contractor knowing that the latter intends to dispose of the waste unlawfully. Consequences following from some active operation involving the use, production or storage of material can be said to be caused by the person carrying out that operation, and the question of causation is to be decided in a commonsense way: *Southern Water Authority v. Pegrum and Pegrum* (1989) 153 J.P. 581. As to the distinction between causing and permitting, see also *Shave v. Rosner* [1954] 2 Q.B. 113. Unlike some provisions, "cause" is prefaced by "knowingly", so something more than a simple causal link is required.

The word "knowingly" has been construed as referring to knowledge of the deposit or other act involving the waste, and not to knowledge that such deposit is outside or is not in accordance with the terms of the licence: *Ashcroft v. Cambro Waste Management* [1981] 1 W.L.R. 1349. In the same case it was said that the prosecution simply has to prove that waste has been knowingly permitted to be deposited on land and it is then for the defence to establish that the deposit was in accordance with terms and conditions of a licence.

Changes from Control of Pollution Act 1974: Section 33 makes a number of changes from the equivalent section of s.3 the 1974 Act. In particular, the offences under the 1974 Act were confined to:
    (a) the deposit of controlled waste on land; and
    (b) the use of plant or equipment for the purpose of disposing of controlled waste or dealing with it in a prescribed manner.

The power to make regulations under s.6(1) of the 1974 Act as to conditions to be disregarded for certain offences, but contravention of which would be an offence *per se* (s.6(3)), was never exercised.

The main changes brought about by the 1990 Act are as follows:
    (a) widening of offences to include treatment, keeping and disposal of controlled waste (subs. (1)(b));
    (b) treatment, keeping or disposal of controlled waste in a manner likely to cause pollution of the environment or harm to human health is itself an offence (subs. (1)(c)); and
    (c) contravention of a condition of a waste management licence is itself an offence (subs. (6)).

Meaning of "deposit": As to the relationship of "disposal" to "deposit", see notes to s.29. Unlike "disposal", "deposit" is not defined. The verb "to deposit" has been said by the Court of

Appeal to be a term of wide connotation, which could be used in a limitless number of contexts, but unless the context required should be used in a broad sense: *Scott v. Westminster City Council, The Times,* February 9, 1995.

The DoE has generally expressed the view that "deposit" includes both permanent and temporary deposit, *i.e.* final deposit in landfill or temporary deposit on land or in containers pending final disposal, treatment or recovery elsewhere: see Circular 13/88 (Welsh Office 19/88), Annex I para. 2.10. On the other hand, Regulation 14 of the Control of Pollution (Special Waste) Regulations 1980 (S.I. 1980 No. 1709) appears to envisage "deposit" as meaning the final resting place of waste. In *Leigh Land Reclamation v. Walsall Metropolitan Borough Council* [1991] J.P.L. 867, the Divisional Court, considering the word "deposit" in the context of the 1974 Act, took the view that it is a colourable word and in the context of the 1974 Act is concerned, primarily at least, with the manner in which the waste is disposed of:

> "Its provisions and the conditions in the licence, are directed towards the mode of final disposal and not to the intermediate processes. For the purposes of this Act, waste is, in my view, to be regarded as deposited when it is dumped on the site with no realistic prospect of further examination or inspection to reject goods of which deposit is not allowed under the licence" (Bingham L.J.)

However, a different view appears to have been reached in *Lancashire County Council v. Dodd, Dodd and Dugdale* (written judgment of Preston Crown Court, February 19, 1992; summarised at *IWM Journal,* May 1992). The case did not concern a licensed site as did the *Leigh* case, but rather the tipping of waste onto unlicensed land. It was held that the *Leigh* case was to be distinguished on its facts and that in the absence of any statutory definition the word "deposit" was to be given its ordinary and natural meaning, which the court was satisfied included both a temporary and permanent disposal or setting down. Similarly in another Crown Court decision, *Berridge Incinerators v. Nottinghamshire County Council* (Nottingham Crown Court, June 12, 1992) the term "deposit" was equated with the activity simply of bringing waste onto land and putting it down there (a case on a notice requiring the removal of unlawfully deposited waste under s.16 of the 1974 Act).

A gloss is added to the term "deposit" by Sched. 4, para. 9(3) of the Waste Management Licensing Regulations 1994 (see Appendix 3) which provides that any reference to the deposit of waste on land includes a reference to any operation listed in Part III or IV of the Schedule which involves such a deposit. Parts III and IV replicate, respectively, Annexes IIA and IIB of the waste framework directive (categories D1–D15 of Disposal Operations and R1–R13 of Recovery Operations).

Treatment: This term is defined: see notes to s.29(6) and (7). References to treatment are taken to be references to submitting waste to any of the operations listed in Parts III or IV of Schedule 4 to the 1994 Regulations: Sched. 4, para. 9(4) and (5).

Keeping: The term is not defined but DoE Circ. 11/94 on the Waste Management Licensing Regulations, Annex 1, para. 1.5, suggests that it covers situations where waste is retained in the lands of the holder, whether it can be said to be deposited or not. Whilst it is clearly a wider term than disposal or deposit, it would seem to import retention of waste with at least some degree of continuity. For example, one could query whether an isolated incident where waste remained on premises for a short period by an oversight would constitute "keeping": compare *Blue v. Pearl Assurance Co.* [1940] 3 W.W.R. 13, 19, 20 (a Canadian case on the "keeping" of gasoline). Storage of waste on the producer's premises pending disposal would constitute keeping, but may fall within one of a number of exemptions from the requirement of a licence provided by the Waste Management Licensing Regulations 1994 (see Appendix 3).

Other offences: As well as the offences referred to above, the section creates two other offences. The first is that of treating, keeping or disposing of controlled waste "in a manner likely to cause pollution of the environment or harm to human health" (s.33(1)(c)). The width of these words has already been noted. The fact that a waste management licence is in force and that all conditions are being complied with would not preclude a prosecution for this offence.

The second offence is that of contravening any condition of a licence (s.33(6)). This has the effect, long urged from various quarters, of making breach of any condition *per se* an offence, whether or not the breach involves the disposal, keeping, treatment, etc. of waste and whether or not the condition relates to such matters. As was pointed out by the RCEP Eleventh Report (Cm. 9675, para. 840) relatively few conditions of licences relate to the actual deposit of waste and most relate to the proper management of the site as a whole, covering matters such as fencing, monitoring and record-keeping. This problem emerged for judicial consideration in *Leigh Land Reclamation v. Walsall Metropolitan Borough Council* [1994] J.P.L. 867. The Divisional Court held that under s.3(1)(a) of the 1974 Act, deposits made properly and in accordance with licence conditions could not be said to constitute an offence simply because there was some improper deposit previously or because, for example, there was no signboard on the site as required by a condition. This, in the view of the Court, would strain the language of the statute "beyond the limits acceptable in a criminal statute and ... a statute creating potentially serious indictable offence."

The position under s.33 is different. Even if actual deposit of waste on a site has ceased, permanently or temporarily, it would still be possible to prosecute for inactivity, for example failure to fulfil a restoration, landscaping or fencing condition. Similarly, the task of waste regulation authorities bringing prosecutions will be made easier in that they will simply have to identify breach of a licence condition by the holder and not prove an attendant deposit, disposal or other act by the licence-holder or knowingly permitted by him.

Identity of defendant: In *Shanks & McEwan (Midlands) Limited v. Wrexham Maelor Borough Council, The Times*, April 10, 1996, the Divisional Court held that the words "a person" in s.33(6) connotes the person who actually infringed the licence condition, which may not necessarily be the licence-holder.

Relevant offences: All of the offences created by this section are relevant offences for the purposes of the "fit and proper person" test which any applicant for a waste management licence must pass: Waste Management Licensing Regulations 1994, reg. 3.

Special waste: Under s.3(3) of the 1974 Act, separate offences carrying substantially enhanced penalties were created where the waste in question was of a kind which was "poisonous, noxious or polluting" and where its presence on land was likely to give rise to an "environmental hazard". This language has now been replaced by a distinction between controlled waste and special waste in that the maximum term of imprisonment on conviction on indictment is greater in the case of an offence in relation to special waste (s.33(9)). It may be noted that maximum penalties on summary conviction are substantially increased from those in the 1974 Act (subss. (8) and (9)). Breach of the Control of Pollution (Special Waste) Regulations 1996 (S.I. 1996 No. 972) will constitute a separate offence in its own right.

Deposit from motor vehicles: Special provision is made by subs. (5) for the case where waste is carried in and deposited from a motor vehicle. The person controlling the use of the vehicle or who is in a position to do so is treated as knowingly causing the waste to be deposited, whether or not any instructions were given to that effect. This provision is no doubt intended to make it easier to bring prosecutions in the case of fly-tipping, where the exact circumstances, beyond the fact of tipping and the identity of the vehicle, may be obscure. Powers also exist in s.6 of the Control of Pollution (Amendment) Act 1989 to seize and dispose of vehicles used for illegal waste disposal.

Relationship with goods vehicle licensing: Fly-tipping or other offences involving waste can now lead to loss of the goods vehicle operator's licence under the Transport Act 1968, s.69 (see Sched. 15, para. 10 and notes to s.162).

Exceptions: household waste: By subs. (2) the requirement of a licence does not apply to household waste from a domestic property which is treated, kept or disposed of within the curtilage of the dwelling by or with the permission of the occupier. However, by reg. 3(1) of the Controlled Waste Regulations 1992 (S.I. 1992 No. 588) waste of the following descriptions shall not be treated as household waste for that purpose:

    (a) any mineral or synthetic oil or grease;
    (b) asbestos; and
    (c) clinical waste.

By Sched. 4, para. 9(6) of the Waste Management Licensing Regulations 1994, subs. (2) does not apply to the treatment, keeping or disposal of household waste by an establishment or undertaking.

Exceptions: prescribed categories: By subs. (3) and (4) the Secretary of State may create exceptions to the requirements of s.33(1)(a), (b) and (c). The exceptions (there called "exemptions") are provided by reg. 17 of and Sched. 3, to the Waste Management Licensing Regulations 1994 and are explained at Annex 5 to Circ. 11/94. As the Circular points out there are significant changes to the exemptions prescribed under s.3 of the 1974 Act; these arise from the expanded scope of licensing and from the Government's policies of encouraging recycling and in favour of deregulation; "the net effect will be a considerable increase in the activities exempted." Furthering this approach, various activities in relation to scrap metal or motor vehicles which are to be dismantled have been added to the list of exempt activities in Schedule 3 to the Waste Management Licensing Regulations 1994 by the Waste Management Licensing (Amendment etc.) Regulations 1995 (S.I. 1995 No. 288), as from April 1, 1995 (see Appendix 3).

This is the date at which the 1995 Regulations finally bring the treatment, keeping or disposal of scrap metal and such motor vehicles within the scope of waste management licensing, following their exclusion whilst the possibility and scope of the exemptions was discussed with representatives of the industry. Guidance on the new exemptions is provided by Circular 6/95 on the 1995 Regulations.

However, the requirements of Directive 91/156/EEC have meant that the exceptions generally are more heavily qualified than before and that in some cases registration is required by the person wishing to claim the benefit of an exemption. The new exemptions established by the 1995 Regulations are even more heavily qualified: that in the new paragraph 45 of Sched. 3 to the 1994 Regulations includes conditions relating, for instance, to the payment of an annual fee, annual inspection by the Waste Regulation Authority and annual submission of a site plan.

It is conceivable that a waste regulation authority may overlook an applicable exemption, or may take the view that an exemption is inapplicable to particular circumstances when in fact it is; and on that basis may purport to grant a licence. DoE Circular 11/94 states at para. 4.80 the Government's view that where there is no requirement in law for a licence (*e.g.* because of an exemption) a document which on its face purports to be a licence for that activity cannot in fact be a licence: see also Circ. 6/95, para. 1.39.

Defences: Subsection (7) provides three defences:
 (a) The defendant took all reasonable precautions and exercised all due diligence to avoid commission of the offence. As to the term "reasonable" in this context, *cf. Austin Rover Group v. H.M. Inspector of Factories* [1989] 3 W.L.R. 520, 527 (H.L.), *per* Lord Goff of Chieveley. As to due diligence, see the statement of Willmer L.J. in *Riverstone Meat Co. v. Lancashire Shipping Co.* [1960] 1 All E.R. 193, 219, equating it to an obligation to exercise reasonable care. The 1974 Act, s.3(4) contained the defence, not repeated in the 1990 Act, that the defendant took care to inform himself as to whether the deposit was lawful. That defence was held not to be available in the case of *Durham County Council v. Peter Connors Industrial Services* (Divisional Court, May 19, 1992) where a skip was provided for the use of the waste producer with no information being provided on specific consignments. It is also arguable that the requirements of the s.34 duty of care are relevant, by analogy, to this defence.
 (b) The defendant acted under instructions from his employer and neither knew nor had reason to suppose his acts were in contravention of the section. The defence of having taken care to inform himself, from persons in a position to provide the information, as to whether the deposit was unlawful (s.3(4)(a) of the 1974 Act) is no longer available;
 (c) The acts were done in an emergency to avoid danger to human health and particulars were furnished to the waste regulation authority as soon as reasonably practicable thereafter. Obviously as a matter of practice, except in cases of extreme emergencies such as road accidents, it will be prudent to obtain the advice and permission of a waste disposal officer in advance of taking any action in reliance on this provision. In any event, all reasonably practicable steps must be taken for minimising pollution of the environment and harm to human health. On the issue of emergency, see *Waste Incineration Services Ltd v. Dudley Metropolitan Borough Council* [1992] 1 Envir. L.R. 29.

Use of injunctions/interdicts
 Waste regulation authorities in England and Wales and in Scotland may in certain circumstances use civil proceedings to enforce waste management legislation, *e.g.* to secure compliance with licence conditions under s.42(6A). Section 33 does not provide express powers to take civil proceedings where no site licence is in force so as to prevent unlawful deposit or other activities. Nonetheless, there is nothing to prevent an injunction being sought on general principles by law. This approval was successfully used by Lancashire County Council and Blackpool Borough Council in 1992 when injunctions were obtained against Mr Owen Baguley for the unlawful deposit of waste and related waste activities in connection with a mini-skip business. Mr Baguley was ultimately sentenced in 1994 to 12 months' imprisonment for contempt of court (five 12 month sentences, one six month sentence and two one month sentences, all to run concurrently: information supplied by Lancashire County Council, County Surveyor).
 An injunction was also obtained by Kent County Council against Mr Martin Frank Poole for operating an illegal waste disposal operation at Sheerness, where waste was tipped over a cliff into the sea. The operation was continued for over three years during which time Mr Poole made eight separate court appearances. In 1992 he was sentenced to six months' imprisonment for contempt of court (information supplied by Kent Waste Regulation Group).
 In Scotland, it is less certain that an interdict could be sought on general principles of law. In

Buckhaven and Methil Magistrates v. Wemyss Coal Company Ltd 1932 S.C. 201, a case involving an attempt to obtain an interdict to prevent the dumping of colliery waste on the foreshore in circumstances in which the burgh had a statutory duty to prevent the deposit of rubbish under the Burgh Police (Scotland) Act 1892 which was reinforced with criminal sanctions against offending waste tippers, it was held that interdict was not available as a remedy under general common law principles where a statutory scheme of regulation with its own penalties existed. The principle in *Buckhaven and Methil Magistrates* may have been modified in subsequent legislation, which provides that local authorities may institute legal proceedings where they "consider it expedient for the promotion or protection of the interests of the inhabitants of their area" (Local Government (Scotland) Act 1973, s.189). SEPA does not, however benefit from s.189 of the 1973 Act. The Government has nevertheless agreed that s.37(1)(a) of the 1995 Act enables the Agency (and, presumably, by implication, SEPA—although this was not expressly indicated) to take civil proceedings (*Hansard*, H.L., Vol. 562, col. 1035). The absence of express language to that effect in s.37(1)(a) may, however, pose problems for SEPA in the light of the *Buckhaven and Methil Magistrates* case. Nonetheless, it may be possible to obtain an interdict on the basis that the unlawful deposit of waste constitutes a nuisance at common law: *Forth River Purification Board v. Adam Robertson, The Scotsman*, December 7, 1990.

Duty of care etc. as respects waste

Duty of care etc. as respects waste

34.—(1) Subject to subsection (2) below, it shall be the duty of any person who imports, produces, carries, keeps, treats or disposes of controlled waste or, as a broker, has control of such waste, to take all such measures applicable to him in that capacity as are reasonable in the circumstances—

    (a) to prevent any contravention by any other person of section 33 above;

    (b) to prevent the escape of the waste from his control or that of any other person; and

    (c) on the transfer of the waste, to secure—

        (i) that the transfer is only to an authorised person or to a person for authorised transport purposes; and

        (ii) that there is transferred such a written description of the waste as will enable other persons to avoid a contravention of that section and to comply with the duty under this subsection as respects the escape of waste.

(2) The duty imposed by subsection (1) above does not apply to an occupier of domestic property as respects the household waste produced on the property.

(3) The following are authorised persons for the purpose of subsection (1)(c) above—

    (a) any authority which is a waste collection authority for the purposes of this Part;

    (b) any person who is the holder of a waste management licence under section 35 below or of a disposal licence under section 5 of the Control of Pollution Act 1974;

    (c) any person to whom section 33(1) above does not apply by virtue of regulations under subsection (3) of that section;

    (d) any person registered as a carrier of controlled waste under section 2 of the Control of Pollution (Amendment) Act 1989;

    (e) any person who is not required to be so registered by virtue of regulations under section 1(3) of that Act; and

    (f) a waste disposal authority in Scotland.

[(3A) The Secretary of State may by regulations amend subsection (3) above so as to add, whether generally or in such circumstances as may be prescribed in the regulations, any person specified in the regulations, or any description of person so specified, to the persons who are authorised persons for the purposes of subsection (1)(c) above.]

(4) The following are authorised transport purposes for the purposes of subsection (1)(c) above—

    (a) the transport of controlled waste within the same premises between different places in those premises;

    (b) the transport to a place in Great Britain of controlled waste which has been brought from a country or territory outside Great Britain not having been landed in Great Britain until it arrives at that place; and

    (c) the transport by air or sea of controlled waste from a place in Great Britain to a place outside Great Britain;

and "transport" has the same meaning in this subsection as in the Control of Pollution (Amendment) Act 1989.

[(4A) For the purposes of subsection (1)(c)(ii) above—

    (a) a transfer of waste in stages shall be treated as taking place when the first stage of the transfer takes place, and

    (b) a series of transfers between the same parties of waste of the same description shall be treated as a single transfer taking place when the first of the transfers in the series takes place.]

(5) The Secretary of State may, by regulations, make provision imposing requirements on any person who is subject to the duty imposed by subsection (1) above as respects the making and retention of documents and the furnishing of documents or copies of documents.

(6) Any person who fails to comply with the duty imposed by subsection (1) above or with any requirement imposed under subsection (5) above shall be liable—

    (a) on summary conviction, to a fine not exceeding the statutory maximum; and

    (b) on conviction on indictment, to a fine.

(7) The Secretary of State shall, after consultation with such persons or bodies as appear to him representative of the interests concerned, prepare and issue a code of practice for the purpose of providing to persons practical guidance on how to discharge the duty imposed on them by subsection (1) above.

(8) The Secretary of State may from time to time revise a code of practice issued under subsection (7) above by revoking, amending or adding to the provisions of the code.

(9) The code of practice prepared in pursuance of subsection (7) above shall be laid before both Houses of Parliament.

(10) A code of practice issued under subsection (7) above shall be admissible in evidence and if any provision of such a code appears to the court to be relevant to any question arising in the proceedings it shall be taken into account in determining that question.

(11) Different codes of practice may be prepared and issued under subsection (7) above for different areas.

DEFINITIONS

    "controlled waste": s.75(4).
    "disposes": s.29(6).
    "household waste": s.75(5).
    "treats": s.29(6).

AMENDMENTS

Subs. (3A) was inserted by the Environment Act 1995, Sched. 22, para. 65. Subs. (4A) was inserted by the Deregulation and Contracting Out Act 1994 and came into force on November 3, 1994.

COMMENCEMENT

Subsections (5), (7), (8), (9) and (11): December 13, 1991 (S.I. 1991 No. 2829). Remainder: April 1, 1992 (S.I. 1991 No 2829).

GENERAL NOTE
This new provision can be seen as flowing from various calls for enhanced responsibility on the part of persons producing or having control of waste (see the General Note to Pt. II).

Under s.34 it is no longer possible for the producer of waste to rid himself of responsibility for it simply by consigning the waste to an agent or contractor. However, the section does not create complete "cradle to grave" responsibility for waste as urged by some sources.

Responsibility is primarily focused on the control of waste prior to transfer and the steps and precautions to be taken on transfer. However, it is also possible for a person to commit a breach of the duty of care after having transferred the waste, for example by failing to take reasonable steps to detect and prevent breaches by the transferee.

The provisions are explained in DoE Circ. 19/91 (Welsh Office 63/91 and Scottish Office 25/91).

It should be noted that the subs. (6) offence is a relevant offence for the purposes of the "fit and proper person" test which any applicant for a waste management licence must pass: Waste Management Licensing Regulations 1994, reg. 3.

Scope of duty
The duty applies to any person who imports, produces, carries, keeps, treats or disposes of controlled waste. As to the meaning of "waste" and "controlled waste" see notes to s.75. As to the meaning of "keeps", "treats" and "disposes", see notes to ss.29 and 33.

The view of the Departments is that the starting point for identifying the producer is to decide how the material became waste. The producer may be the person taking the action which causes the material to become waste or who takes the decision that it is waste; Circ. 19/91, para. 16. In the context of works of construction or demolition, the view of the Departments is that the person undertaking the works will be producer, not the person who let the contract or commissioned the works: however, a client or contractor may be regarded as a broker (see further, Circ. 19/91, para. 17).

In *Gotech Industrial and Environmental Services Ltd. & Anr. v. Friel*, 1994 G.W.D. 40–2389; 1995 S.C.C.R. 22; ENDS Report 242, March 1995, p. 44 the Scottish High Court of Justiciary held that an asbestos stripping firm, subcontracted to remove asbestos lagging from pipework in a church boiler house was the producer of the waste, rather than the main contractor or the church authorities. It was the sub-contractor's operations which had broken up the asbestos so as to result in waste.

Brokers
The duty applies to a person who, as a broker has control of the waste.

Brokers have been said to be, "Those that contrive, make, and conclude bargains and contracts between merchants and tradesmen for which they have a fee or reward": *Milford v. Hughes* (1846) 16 M. & W. 174, 177, *per* Alderson B. Waste brokerage can clearly take a wide variety of contractual forms, but the broker will only be liable under the duty of care to the extent that he has control of what happens to the waste.

The Departments regard transfers where a broker is involved as being tripartite in nature: Circ. 19/91, para. 19 and the revised Code of Practice, Annex B, para. B.12.

Article 12 of the E.C. Framework Directive on Waste (91/156/EEC) requires that undertakings which arrange for the disposal or recovery of waste on behalf of others (dealers or brokers) where not subject to authorisation, shall be registered. The Waste Management Licensing Regulations 1994 set up a scheme for the registration of brokers.

Exemptions
Subsection (2) exempts from the duty of care the occupier of domestic property as regards the household waste produced on that property. As to the meaning of "household waste" see notes to s.75. Waste from construction work on domestic premises is household waste for this purpose (Controlled Waste Regulations 1992 (S.I. 1992 No. 588), reg. 2(2), and see Circ. 14/92, para. 1.19. Where a contractor carries out works of construction or demolition, the waste will constitute household rather than commercial or industrial waste (see the Controlled Waste Regulations 1992, regs. 2(2) and 5(2)), but the occupier of the property will not usually be the producer (see above). The contractor will thus not benefit from the exemption; nor will a householder who disposes of waste from his neighbour's property or from his workplace (see the revised Code of Practice, Annex A, para. A.9).

Scrap metal
Scrap metal was until October 1, 1995 excluded from the scope of the duty of care by virtue of regs. 3 and 7 of the Controlled Waste Regulations 1992 (S.I. 1992 No. 588). It became subject to the duty of care as from that date by virtue of amendments to the 1992 Regulations made by reg. 2(1) of the Waste Management Licensing (Amendment etc.) Regulations 1995 (S.I. 1995 No.

288). October 1, 1995, is also the date by which operators of various activities relating to scrap metal must register exemptions from the waste management licensing regime in respect of those activities. This is again by virtue of S.I. 1995 No. 288 which brings activities in relation to scrap metal within the licensing regime as from April 1, 1995.

Nature of duty
The duty is to take all measures applicable to the relevant person in their actual capacity and in the circumstances to prevent or secure the four matters at paras. (a)–(c)(ii) of subs. (1). The first two of these apply at all times; the third and fourth specifically on the transfer of the waste. "Transfer in this sense appears to indicate physical transfer, rather than transfer to the title in the waste. DoE Circ. 19/19, para. 8 suggests that holders' obligations are not confined to the transfer in which they hand waste on to another party; they are also under obligations to take reasonable steps with regard to any transfers in which they receive waste."

By analogy with the House of Lords decision in *Seaboard Offshore Limited v. Secretary of State for Transport* [1994] 2 All E.R. 99 it may be that the wording of s.34 requires a lack of care to be shown on the part of the defendant itself (if a company) and that the defendant will not be vicariously liable for failure by a subordinate employee who cannot be equated with the company itself.

Simplified procedures: Subsection 4A
This subs. was inserted by the Deregulation and Contracting Out Act 1994. The subsection came into force on November 3, 1994.

The apparent intention of the subsection is to simplify the requirements for provision of a written description of waste and completion of a transfer note in cases where waste is transferred into stages, or where there are a series of transfers. The suggestion had already been made by the Department of Environment in the Code of Practice under section 34 (December 1991) that whilst transfers of waste must be documented, nothing in the Regulations requires each individual transfer to be separately documented: Annex C, paragraph C.4. This is re-affirmed in the revised Code of Practice (Annex C, para. (4) which refers to "season ticket provisions", *i.e.* one transfer note covering a series of transfers. The guidance suggests that in the case of, for example, weekly or daily collections waste from outside shops or commercial premises, or the removal of a large heap of waste by multiple lorry trips, separate documentation would be unrealistic and that it would be reasonable for a single transfer note to cover multiple consignments of waste transferred at the same time or over a period not exceeding a year, provided that the description and all the other details on the transfer note are all the same for all consignments, and that the parties to the transfer and the description of the waste remain the same.

However, this interpretation was not fully consistent with the wording of section 34 under the Environmental Protection (Duty of Care) Act Regulations 1991 (S.I. 1991 No. 2839), which required a written description to be transferred "on the transfer of the waste" (section 31(1)(c)(ii)) and for a transfer note to be completed and signed at the same time as the written description of the waste is transferred (regulation 2(1)).

The new subsection contemplates two separate situations. The first is where there is "a transfer of waste in stages": here the transfer is treated as taking place when the first stage of the transfer takes place. On that basis, the requirements of the Act and Regulation are complied with if a written description is provided, and transfer note completed and signed, on the first stage of the transfer. The difficulty lies in what exactly is meant by "a transfer of waste in stages", and how this differs from "a series of transfers", which is the other situation contemplated by the new subsection. Quite clearly, the provision cannot have been intended to apply in cases where the separate stages of the transfer involved the waste being passed on to different persons (for example, where waste is removed to a transfer station, and hence to a final disposal facility). In such a case, limitation of the obligation to provide a written description to only the first stage of the transfer would negate the whole purpose of section 34. Perhaps what the draftsman had in mind by "a transfer of waste in stages" was the situation referred to in the Code of Practice of "the removal of a large heap of waste by multiple lorry trips", however, the wording used does not seem entirely apt for that particular situation.

The second circumstance contemplated by the new subsection is that of a series of transfers between the same parties of waste of the same description. This seems much more clearly to cover the situation contemplated in the revised Code of Practice where weekly or daily collections of waste are made from shops or other commercial premises. Under the new subsection, as proposed, the series of transfers shall be treated as a single transfer taking place when the first of the transfers in the series takes place, provided that the series of transfers is made between the same parties and are of waste of the same description. In that circumstance, a single written description and transfer note, provided at the time of the first transfer, will satisfy the duty of care. The section contains no time limit provision as to the series of the transfers, whereas the revised Code of Practice refers to a period not exceeding one year.

Finally, it may be noted that the Deregulation and Contracting Out Act 1994, subs. 33(2) provides that the new subsection shall be deemed always to have had effect, except in relation to any proceedings for failure to comply with the duty which were commenced before coming into force of the new subsection on November 3, 1994. Effectively, therefore, actions which were in breach of section 34 prior to the amendment are legitimised, save where a prosecution has already been commenced. In the case where a prosecution has been commenced, subs. 33(2) of the 1994 Act provides that where any such proceedings have not been disposed of before the commencement of the new provision, it shall be a defence to show that the conduct in question would not have constituted a breach of the duty, had the new provision been in force at the time. This leaves open the possibility that a person or company who had already been convicted of an offence under the old law, prior to the new subsection taking effect, would be prejudiced by having a criminal conviction against them which could potentially disqualify them as a "fit and proper person" under section 73 of the Act. It would be logical, therefore, for a consequential amendment to be made providing that any such conviction should be disregarded for those purposes, though no such amendment appears to be contemplated at present.

Code of Practice: subss. (7)–(11)
Of central importance to the duty of care is the Code of Practice issued by the Secretary of State for the purpose of providing practical guidance on how persons subject to the duty may discharge it. Whilst not conclusive, the Code will be admissible and relevant in proceedings. The current Code of Practice was issued by the Department of Environment, Scottish Office and Welsh Office in March 1996, replacing the version issued in December 1991. It contains step by step advice on following the duty, a summary checklist of the main steps and annexes on the relevant law, responsibilities on various parties, record-keeping requirements and other legal controls. Apart from general updating, the revised code contains extra guidance relating to the metals recycling industry.

Documentation: subs. (5)
Regulations have been made as to the making and retention of documents: the Environmental Protection (Duty of Care) Regulations 1991 (S.I. 1991 No. 2839). These require the transferee of controlled waste (as defined in the Regulations), at the same time as the written description of waste required by s.34(1)(c)(ii) is transferred, to ensure that a transfer note is completed and signed (reg. 2(1)). The transfer note must contain the information specified at reg. 2(2) and the Table to the Regulations. Both parties must keep the written description and transfer note for a period of two years from the transfer (reg. 3) and furnish the authority with a copy on demand (reg. 4).

Circular 19/91, paras. 18–25, explains these requirements. In particular, para. 21 suggests that it would be reasonable for a single transfer note to cover multiple consignments of waste transferred at the same time or over a period (not exceeding a year) provided that all the relevant details as to the waste and the parties remain in the same throughout.

Written contracts: Neither s.34 nor the revised Code of Practice expressly requires contracts to be entered into between producers or other holders of waste and those to whom the waste is transferred. However, it is difficult to see how either party could effectively discharge the duty of care without a contract properly describing the waste and its destination and without being consistent in other respects with the duty of care.

Special waste: Special provisions apply to the more difficult and intractable wastes: see note to s.62. Such wastes remain subject to the duty of care in addition to the more specific controls of the Special Waste Regulations.

Prosecutions for inadequate description
A successful prosecution was recently brought in Leicester Magistrates' Court against Simons Construction Limited, a Lincoln based building firm, for failing to transfer an adequate description with waste removed from one of their construction sites (ENDS Report 226, November 1993, pp. 45–46).

The material was described as "builders waste" but tins of paints had been placed in the bottom of the skip in which the waste was contained and then covered by soil and rubble prior to collection. The transfer note completed between Simons and the waste carrier described the waste as "builders waste" and a similar description was entered on the transfer note provided to the landfill operator where the waste was deposited. Simons attempted to argue, in relation to the charge under section 34(6) that "builders waste" could contain a range of materials, including paint. They also argued that there was insufficient space on the standard form transfer note to complete a comprehensive description of the waste. Both of these arguments were rejected by the magistrates and the company was fined £1,500.

Another successful prosecution involved Hales Waste Control, who were fined £750 at Peterborough Magistrates' Court in May 1995 for delivering asbestos pipe waste described as "general construction waste" to a landfill. This description was held to be inadequate. Other section 34 cases include *Surrey County Council v. J. McArdle (Haulage) Ltd* (1994) (£2,000 fine for inadequate description of waste from motorway resurfacing contract), and *Surrey County Council v. Kingston NHS Trust* (1995) (£6,000 fine for clinical waste described as "domestic and kitchen waste").

Prosecutions for not transferring waste to an authorised person
In *Cleveland County Council v. Earth Mover Tyres (Yorkshire) Ltd* ENDS Report 218, March 1993, p. 44, a prosecution involving a waste producer who carried out inadequate checks into whether a disposal facility was licensed which resulted in waste being transferred to a person who did not hold a waste disposal licence, the producer was convicted and fined £200.

Prosecutions for failing to prevent the escape of waste
In *West Yorkshire WRA v. Darrington Quarries* ENDS Report 220, May 1993, p. 39 a successful prosecution was brought against a landfill operator for failing to make the site secure as chemically treated timber which posed a serious fire hazard was not covered over at the end of the day as it should have been and the site perimeter fence was insecure. This resulted in a fine of £1,500 for the s.34 offence together with a fine of £4,000 for a s.33(1)(c) offence.

Waste Management Licences

Waste management licences: general

35.—(1) A waste management licence is a licence granted by a waste regulation authority authorising the treatment, keeping or disposal of any specified description of controlled waste or in or on specified land or the treatment or disposal of any specified description of controlled waste by means of specified mobile plant.

(2) A licence shall be granted to the following person, that is to say—
(a) in the case of a licence relating to the treatment, keeping or disposal of waste in or on land, to the person who is in occupation of the land; and
(b) in the case of a licence relating to the treatment or disposal of waste by means of mobile plant, to the person who operates the plant.

(3) A licence shall be granted on such terms and subject to such conditions as appear to the waste regulation authority to be appropriate and the conditions may relate—
(a) to the activities which the licence authorises, and
(b) to the precautions to be taken and works to be carried out in connection with or in consequence of those activities;
and accordingly requirements may be imposed in the licence which are to be complied with before the activities which the licence authorises have begun or after the activities which the licence authorises have ceased.

(4) Conditions may require the holder of a licence to carry out works or do other things notwithstanding that he is not entitled to carry out the works or do the thing and any person whose consent would be required shall grant, or join in granting, the holder of the licence such rights in relation to the land as will enable the holder of the licence to comply with any requirements imposed on him by the licence.

(5) Conditions may relate, where waste other than controlled waste is to be treated, kept or disposed of, to the treatment, keeping or disposal of that other waste.

(6) The Secretary of State may, by regulations, make provision as to the conditions which are, or are not, to be included in a licence; and regulations under this subsection may make different provision for different circumstances.

(7) The Secretary of State may, as respects any licence for which an application is made to a waste regulation authority, give to the authority directions as to the terms and conditions which are, or are not, to be included in the licence; and it shall be the duty of the authority to give effect to the directions.

[(7A) In any case where—

(a) an entry is required under this section to be made in any record as to the observance of any condition of a licence, and

(b) the entry has not been made,

the fact shall be admissible as evidence that that condition has not been observed.

(7B) Any person who—

(a) intentionally makes a false entry in any record required to be kept under any condition of a licence, or

(b) with intent to deceive, forges or uses a licence or makes or has in his possession a document so closely resembling a licence as to be likely to deceive,

shall be guilty of an offence.

(7C) A person guilty of an offence under subsection (7B) above shall be liable—

(a) on summary conviction, to a fine not exceeding the statutory maximum;

(b) on conviction on indictment, to a fine or to imprisonment for a term not exceeding two years, or to both.]

(8) It shall be the duty of waste regulation authorities to have regard to any guidance issued to them by the Secretary of State with respect to the discharge of their functions in relation to licences.

(9) A licence may not be surrendered by the holder except in accordance with section 39 below.

(10) A licence is not transferable by the holder but the waste regulation authority may transfer it to another person under section 40 below.

(11) A licence shall continue in force until it is revoked entirely by the waste regulation authority under section 38 below or it is surrendered or its surrender is accepted under section 39 below.

(12) In this Part "licence" means a waste management licence and "site licence" and "mobile plant licence" mean, respectively, a licence authorising the treatment, keeping or disposal of waste in or on land and a licence authorising the treatment or disposal of waste by means of mobile plant.

DEFINITIONS
"controlled waste": s.75(2) and (4).
"disposal": s.29(6).
"mobile plant": s.29(9).
"treatment": s.29(6).
"waste": s.75(2) and (4).

AMENDMENT
Subss. (7A)–(7C) were introduced by the Environment Act 1995, Sched. 22, para. 66(2).

COMMENCEMENT
Subsection (6): February 18, 1993 (S.I. 1993 No. 274). Remainder: May 1, 1994 (S.I. 1994 No. 1096).

GENERAL NOTE
The term "waste management licence" replaces "waste disposal licence" as used in the 1974 Act. This change in terminology reflects the greater range of activities now embraced by licensing (see s.29). There are two types of waste of waste management licence: those related to activity on land ("site licences") and those related to treatment or disposal carried out by mobile plant ("mobile plant licences").

The provisions on waste management licence are amplified by the Waste Management Licensing Regulations 1994 and are explained in the accompanying DoE Circ. 11/94 and in

Waste Management Paper No. 4, *The Licensing of Waste Facilities* (revised 1994) as well as in new WMP No. 26A on *Landfill Completion.*

Licence conditions

The licence will specify the land or mobile plant and the description of controlled waste covered by the licence: additionally it may be granted "on such terms and subject to such conditions as appear to the authority to be appropriate" (subs. (3)). These conditions may relate not only to the authorised activities but also consequential or connected precautions or works. The relationship between licence conditions and planning conditions is discussed in the General Note to Pt. II.

Though the discretion to impose conditions is ostensibly very wide, such conditions must comply with ordinary principles of administrative law, that is to say they must be related to the underlying purpose of the legislation. For example, in the case of *Att.-Gen.'s Reference (No. 2 of 1988)* [1989] 3 W.L.R. 397, it was held that a condition prohibiting the creation of public nuisances of all kinds could not be lawfully imposed under s.6(2) of the 1974 Act. (See further General Note to Pt. II.) The view that the licensing provisions of the 1974 Act were primarily intended to ensure that waste disposal takes place without risk of water pollution or danger to human health was also frequently expressed by the Secretary of State in appeals against conditions under s.10 of the 1974 Act.

The wording of the 1990 Act is different from that used in the 1974 Act, which at s.5(3) referred to "pollution of water or danger to public health" as grounds for rejecting a disposal licence application. The equivalent s.36(3) in the 1990 Act refers to (a) "pollution of the environment"; (b) "harm to human health" (which will include offence to senses and harm to property); and (c) (where planning permission is not in force) "serious detriment to the amenities of the locality." It appears therefore that the purposes for which licence conditions may be imposed are widened correspondingly.

It is also to be noted that s.6(2) of the 1974 Act contained a list of specific matters to which conditions might relate, without prejudice to the general words of the section. These were: (a) the duration of the licence; (b) supervision by the holder of activities to which the licence relates; (c) kinds and quantities of waste, methods of dealing with waste, and recording of information; (d) precautions to be taken on the site; (e) steps to facilitate compliance with any relevant planning conditions; (f) hours; and (g) works to be carried out before licensed activities commence or while they are continuing.

No doubt, although s.35 contains no such specific list, those matters will fall within the general words of the section and will continue to form the subject-matter of conditions in appropriate cases.

Conditions as to specific matters

By the Waste Management Licensing Regulations 1994, reg. 14, licences which authorise the regeneration or keeping of waste oils must contain conditions to the effect specified in that regulation.

Similarly, in appropriate cases, conditions must be imposed to safeguard groundwater against List I and List II substances under Directive 80/68/EEC (Waste Management Licensing Regulations 1994, reg. 15). In *R. v. Vale of Glamorgan Borough Council and Associated British Ports, ex parte James* (August 10, 1995) an attempt to challenge the grant of a licence based on reg. 15 failed. It was held (a) that in fact failure to consider reg. 15 specifically had not vitiated the decision, (b) that water entering a site which has listed substances in it is probably not covered by the phrase "the entry of substances into groundwater" and (c) the authority were not in breach of reg. 15(2) or (4) in failing to consider the need to maintain a pumping system in perpetuity.

No condition may be imposed solely for the purpose of securing the health of persons at work: Waste Management Licensing Regulations 1994, reg. 13.

The meaning of "empty" in licence conditions

In *Durham County Council v. Thomas Swan & Co. Limited,* [1995] Env.L.R. 72 the Queen's Bench Divisional Court considered the issue of whether drums containing a small residue of solid phenol waste could be described as empty when deposited at a transfer station licensed to dispose of a quantity of empty used drums each week. The drums were collected from Thomas Swan and stored at the transfer station. On inspection they were found to contain a slurry mixture of free phenol and rainwater. Both Thomas Swan and the transfer station licensee were prosecuted; the licensee pleaded guilty but Thomas Swan were acquitted on the basis that at the time the drums were deposited at the transfer station, containing a small residue of solid phenol, they could be said to be empty. The Justices had dismissed the prosecution on the basis that the drums could be regarded as empty in such circumstances. An appeal by the waste regulation authority by way of case stated was dismissed by the Divisional Court, which held that a reasonable bench of magistrates was entitled on the facts to find that drums containing less than 1 per cent of original volume were to be treated as empty at the relevant time: the defendant led evidence that such drums were empty in accordance with industry standards and that "empty" was not to be equated with "clinically clean". If the drums were totally uncontaminated there would be no need to consign them to a licensed transfer station at all.

Departmental guidance on conditions
In appeals under s.10 of the 1974 Act the Secretary of State has also frequently stated his view that, whilst high standards with regard to waste handling and disposal are a desirable objective, conditions should be reasonable in that: (a) they should reflect the nature and scale of operations on, and the circumstances of, the particular site; (b) they should afford adequate protection to local amenities from operations on the site; and (c) they should not impose an unreasonable burden on the operator. Waste Management Paper No. 4 on The Licensing of *Waste Facilities* contains further guidance on licence conditions and in particular their relationship to the Working Plan prepared by the operator, describing the site and how it is to be operated. Appendix A gives a checklist of conditions to be considered.

Authorities must have regard to this, and to any other, departmental guidance (subs. (8)).

Waste management papers constitute an important source of such guidance. Whereas in the past such papers tended to focus on technical guidance as to the problems presented by different types of waste, the tendency with more recent papers has been to provide guidance on regulation, given the growing complexity of the regulatory framework.

Waste Management Papers are published by HMSO. A full list of current waste management papers is set out in the general note to Part II of the Act.

Subs. (4): effect on third parties
This subsection merits specific mention because of its uncertain potential effect on third parties. As originally drafted, the clause simply read: "Conditions may require the holder of a licence to carry out works or do other such things notwithstanding that he is not entitled to carry out the works or do the thing." This was similar to the wording which appeared in s.6(2) of the 1974 Act, save that the earlier wording used the term "entitled as of right." In Committee stage in the Commons, Mr Malcolm Bruce MP introduced an amendment (No. 407), inserting the words "and the owner of the land shall grant to the licence-holder any necessary rights to carry out such works or do such things," the object of which was, in the words of Mr Bruce as follows:

> "To clarify the arrangements of the management of sites so that an operator of a site who does not own the site but is a licensee can still do the work and that any contractual obligations he may have with the owner of the site will not prevent him from doing so. If a site has been closed, but continues to be a responsibility, there could be contractual obligations between the owner and the licensee that interfere with this duty of care. I am seeking clarification and pressing the point that a licensee should not be prevented by the owner from carrying out the necessary work." (Standing Committee H, Thirteenth sitting, February 13, 1990, cols. 462–3.)

The amendment was opposed by the Government and was withdrawn, Mr Heathcoat-Amory putting the Government position as follows:

> "Under the Bill the regulatory authority can impose conditions that the landowner might seem powerless to implement, possibly because he does not own the adjoining land. This possibility demonstrates the strength and depth of our provisions because it is up to the licensee in such conditions to negotiate with the neighbouring landowner. If it proves impossible for him to return to the waste regulation authority to ask for the conditions to be modified or, in extremis, the licence may have to be surrendered. Giving a private person automatic rights to go on to land that is not his and carry out work that is perhaps to its detriment without any kind of notice, appeal or limitation does not solve the problem. I therefore reject the Draconian powers implicit in amendment No. 407. The conditions in the Bill are important, but it is up to the licensee to satisfy those conditions by negotiation or purchase of the land in question." (*ibid.*, col. 463).

However, the Government subsequently brought forward the present wording of the sub-subsection as Amendment No. 70 on Third Reading, without comment (see *Hansard*, H.C. Vol. 17, col. 1153). This wording appears to go even further than that proposed by Mr Bruce. On the plain wording of the subsection it appears that if a condition is imposed requiring the licence-holder to carry out works or do other things which he is not entitled to do without the consent of another person, then that person is under a duty to grant the licence-holder such rights "in relation to the land" as will enable the licence-holder to comply with the requirements imposed on him by the licence. DoE Circ. 11/94 on Waste Management Licensing, para. 4.25, suggests that it is not desirable to rely on this power more often than is strictly necessary.

As originally drafted, the Act did not confer any protection on third parties affected by conditions imposed under subs. (4) either by way of notification, consultation, or compensation. That deficiency is rectified by s.35A, dealing with compensation, and s.36A, dealing with consultation. See further the note to those sections.

Subs. (5): waste other than controlled waste
This provision is useful where a site receives a mixture of controlled waste and waste which is not controlled; the non-controlled waste may be subject to licence conditions.

Subs. (6): provision as to conditions to be included
See the reference to waste oils and groundwater protection, above.

Bonds and financial provision
Though it has not been settled by the courts, it has been conceded in proceedings by the Secretary of State for the Environment that it is within the powers of s.6 of the 1974 Act (and no doubt therefore within the powers of the 1990 Act) to impose conditions requiring the licence-holder to: (a) enter into a financial bond before depositing waste at the site; and (b) take out a third party and public liability insurance policy.

It is now frequent practice to require financial assurance by way of bonds, deposit accounts or other provision by the prospective operator: and see the notes to s.74 on "fit and proper person".

[Compensation where rights granted pursuant to section 35(4) or 38(9A)

35A.—(1) This section applies in any case where—
   (a) the holder of a licence is required—
      (i) by the conditions of the licence; or
      (ii) by a requirement imposed under section 38(9) below,
     to carry out any works or do any other thing which he is not entitled to carry out or do;
   (b) a person whose consent would be required has, pursuant to the requirements of section 35(4) above or 38(9A) below, granted, or joined in granting, to the holder of the licence any rights in relation to any land; and
   (c) those rights, or those rights together with other rights, are such as will enable the holder of the licence to comply with any requirements imposed on him by the licence or, as the case may be, under section 38(9) below.

(2) In a case where this section applies, any person who has granted, or joined in granting, the rights in question shall be entitled to be paid compensation under this section by the holder of the licence.

(3) The Secretary of State shall by regulations provide for the descriptions of loss and damage for which compensation is payable under this section.

(4) The Secretary of State may by regulations—
   (a) provide for the basis on which any amount to be paid by way of compensation under this section is to be assessed;
   (b) without prejudice to the generality of subsection (3) and paragraph (a) above, provide for compensation under this section to be payable in respect of—
      (i) any effect of any rights being granted, or
      (ii) any consequence of the exercise of any rights which have been granted;
   (c) provide for the times at which any entitlement to compensation under this section is to arise or at which any such compensation is to become payable;
   (d) provide for the persons or bodies by whom, and the manner in which, any dispute—
      (i) as to whether any, and (if so) how much and when, compensation under this section is payable; or
      (ii) as to the person to or by whom it shall be paid,

(e) provide for when or how applications may be made for compensation under this section;

(f) without prejudice to the generality of paragraph (d) above, provide for when or how applications may be made for the determination of any such disputes as are mentioned in that paragraph;

(g) without prejudice to the generality of paragraphs (e) and (f) above, prescribe the form in which any such applications as are mentioned in those paragraphs are to be made;

(h) make provision similar to any provision made by paragraph 8 of Schedule 19 to the Water Resources Act 1991;

(j) make different provision for different cases, including different provision in relation to different persons or circumstances;

(k) include such incidental, supplemental, consequential or transitional provision as the Secretary of State considers appropriate.]

DEFINITION
"licence": s.35(12).

GENERAL NOTE
This provision was inserted by the Environment Act 1995, Sched. 22, para. 67. It deals with the situation where a third party is required to grant rights to the holder of a waste management licence in order to carry out works required under the licence. Such a requirement on the third party may arise from subs. (4) in relation to licence conditions, or from s.38(9A) in relation to measures required to be taken when a licence is suspended.

The section simply confers by subs. (2) a right to compensation in the circumstances set out in subs. (1) and leaves the detail to be provided in Regulations.

Grant of licences

36.—(1) An application for a licence shall be made—
(a) in the case of an application for a site licence, to the waste regulation authority in whose area the land is situated; and
(b) in the case of an application for a mobile plant licence, to the waste regulation authority in whose area the operator of the plant has his principal place of business;
[and shall be made on a form provided for the purpose by the waste regulation authority and accompanied by such information as that authority reasonably requires and the charge prescribed for the purpose by a charging scheme under section 41 of the Environment Act 1995.

(1A) Where an applicant for a licence fails to provide the waste regulation authority with any information required under subsection (1) above, the authority may refuse to proceed with the application, or refuse to proceed with it until the information is provided.]

(2) A licence shall not be issued for a use of land for which planning permission is required in pursuance of the Town and Country Planning Act 1990 or the Town and Country Planning (Scotland) Act 1972 unless—
(a) such planning permission is in force in relation to that use of the land, or
(b) an established use certificate is in force under section 192 of the said Act of 1990 or section 90 of the said Act of 1972 in relation to that use of the land.

(3) Subject to subsection (2) above and subsection (4) below, a waste regulation authority to which an application for a licence has been duly made shall not reject the application if it is satisfied that the applicant is a fit and proper person unless it is satisfied that its rejection is necessary for the purpose of preventing—
(a) pollution of the environment;
(b) harm to human health; or
(c) serious detriment to the amenities of the locality;

but paragraph (c) above is inapplicable where planning permission is in force in relation to the use to which the land will be put under the licence.

(4) Where the waste regulation authority proposes to issue a licence, the authority must, before it does so,—

(a) refer the proposal to the [appropriate planning authority] and the Health and Safety Executive; and

(b) consider any representations about the proposal which the [authority] or the Executive makes to it during the allowed period.

(5)–(6) [...]

(7) Where any part of the land to be used is land which has been notified under section 28(1) of the Wildlife and Countryside Act 1981 (protection for certain areas) and the waste regulation authority proposes to issue a licence, the authority must, before it does so—

(a) refer the proposal to the appropriate nature conservation body; and

(b) consider any representations about the proposal which the body makes to it during the allowed period;

and in this section any reference to the appropriate nature conservation body is a reference to the Nature Conservancy Council for England, [Scottish Natural Heritage] or the Countryside Council for Wales, according as the land is situated in England, Scotland or Wales.

(8) Until the date appointed under section 131(3) below any reference in subsection (7) above to the appropriate nature conservation body is a reference to the Nature Conservancy Council.

(9) If within the period of four months beginning with the date on which a waste regulation authority received an application for the grant of a licence, of within such longer period as the authority and the applicant may at any time agree in writing, the authority has neither granted the licence in consequence of the application nor given notice to the applicant that the authority has rejected the application, the authority shall be deemed to have rejected the application.

[(9A) Subsection (9) above—

(a) shall not have effect in any case where, by virtue of subsection (1A) above, the waste regulation authority refuses to proceed with the application in question, and

(b) shall have effect in any case where, by virtue of subsection (1A) above, the waste regulation authority refuses to proceed with it until the required information is provided, with the substitution for the period of four months there mentioned of the period of four months beginning with the date on which the authority received the information.]

[(10) The period allowed to the appropriate planning authority, the Health and Safety Executive, or the appropriate nature conservancy body for the making of representations under subsection (4) or (7) above about a proposal is the period of twenty-eight days beginning with the day on which the proposal is received by the waste regulation authority or such longer period as the waste regulation authority, the appropriate planning authority, the Executive or the body, as the case may be, agree in writing.]

[(11) In this section

"the appropriate planning authority" means

(a) where the relevant land is situated in the area of a London borough council, that London borough council;

(b) where the relevant land is situated in the City of London, the Common Council of the City of London;

(c) where the relevant land is situated in a non-metropolitan county in England, the council of that county;

(d) where the relevant land is situated in a National Park or the Broads, the National Park authority for that National Park or, as the case may be, the Broads Authority;

(e) where the relevant land is situated elsewhere in England or Wales, the council of the district or, in Wales, the county or county borough, in which the land is situated;

(f) where the relevant land is situated in Scotland, the council constituted under section 2 of the Local Government etc. (Scotland) Act 1994 for the area in which the land is situated;

"the Broads" has the same meaning as in the Norfolk and Suffolk Broads Act 1988;

"National Park authority", subject to subsection (12) below, means a National Park authority established under section 63 of the Environment Act 1995 which has become the local planning authority for the National Park in question;

"the relevant land" means

(a) in relation to a site licence, the land to which the licence relates; and

(b) in relation to a mobile plant licence, the principal place of business of the operator of the plant to which the licence relates.]

[(12) As respects any period before a National Park authority established under section 63 of the Environment Act 1995 in relation to a National Park becomes the local planning authority for that National Park, any reference in this section to a National Park authority shall be taken as a reference to the National Park Committee or joint or special planning board for that National Park.]

[(13) The Secretary of State may by regulations amend the definition of "appropriate planning authority" in subsection (11) above.]

[(14) This section shall have effect subject to section 36A below.]

<small>DEFINITIONS</small>
"fit and proper person": s.74.
"harm": s.29(5).
"licence": s.35(12).
"mobile plant licence": s.35(12).
"pollution of the environment": s.29(3).
"site licence": s.35(12).

<small>AMENDMENTS</small>
Subs. (1) was amended and subs. (1A) added by the Environment Act 1995, Sched. 2, para. 68(2). Subs. (4) was amended by Sched. 2, para. 68(3). Subss. (5) and (6) (which dealt with disagreements between waste and water authorities over the grant of licences) were repealed by para. 68(4). Subs. (7) was amended by the Natural Heritage (Scotland) Act 1991, Sched. 3, para. 10(2), para. 68(5). Subs. (9A) was inserted by the Environment Act 1995, Sched. 2. Subs. (10) was replaced and subss. (11)–(14) added by para. 68(6).

<small>COMMENCEMENT</small>
Subsection (1): February 18, 1993 (S.I. 1993 No. 274). Remainder: May 1, 1994 (S.I. 1994 No. 1096).

<small>GENERAL NOTE</small>
This section, which deals with applications for, and the grant of, waste management licences, contains a number of modifications of the equivalent section in the 1974 Act. By far the most important of these is the introduction of the concept of "fit and proper person", a much recommended reform giving the licensing authority power to have regard to the personal character, experience, record and capability of the applicant. The phrase is amplified in s.74 and further reference should be made to that section and the notes thereto.

Subs. (1): application form and fee
As to the form, the Waste Management Licensing Regulations 1994, reg. 2, simply provides that the application is to be in writing. It is therefore a matter for the authority to devise its own forms having regard to the advice in Waste Management Paper No. 4 as to the information desirable (Circ. 11/94, Annex 4, para. 4.34). Subsection (1A) allows the authority to refuse to proceed with an application where information which is reasonably required is not provided. The effect of subs. (9A) is that no appeal lies against such a refusal.
As to fees, see the note to s.41.

Subs. (1)(b)
Principal place of business: It may be a difficult question as to where the principal place of business of a company is located: see *Grant v. Anderson & Co.* [1892] 1 Q.B. 108 (C.A.). Presumably where a company carrying on waste management activities in this country is domiciled overseas, the intention must be for the principal place of business in Great Britain to be the relevant one.

Subs. (2)
Planning status of land: If planning permission is required for the use to be made of the land under a site licence, then the licence shall not be issued unless either such permission is in force or an established use certificate is in force. Planning permission will not be needed for uses of land commenced prior to July 1, 1948 or for those for which permission has been granted by a special or general development order. Nor will planning permission be required for the use of Crown land where the Crown is the occupier. Also, by s.191(7) of the Town and Country Planning Act 1990 (as substituted by s.10 of the Planning and Compensation Act 1991) a certificate of lawful use or development under s.191 of the 1990 Act shall have effect for the purpose of s.36(2)(a) as if it were a grant of planning permission. (For Scotland, see s.90(7) of the Town and Country Planning (Scotland) Act 1972 as substituted by s.42 of the Planning and Compensation Act 1991.)
   It should be noted that subs. (2) is framed in terms of uses of land. Land may not require planning permission to be used for waste disposal for one or other of the reasons given above. Nonetheless, the proposed activities may involve operational development which does require planning permission. This was the situation in *Berridge Incinerators v. Nottinghamshire County Council* (High Court, 1987, unreported but cited at para. 2.7 of DoE Circ. 13/88) Judge P. J. Crawford Q.C.). In that case the Deputy Judge held that the issue of the use of land had to be considered separately from that of development on the land by the installation of plant or equipment. On that basis he found that planning permission was not required for the use of land but was required in respect of the plant or equipment, and on that basis the applicants would not satisfy the conditions precedent to the grant of a licence. However, whereas the Deputy Judge's reasoning was based on the wording of s.5(2) of the 1974 Act in referring to "a use of land, *plant or equipment* for which planning permission is required", subs. (2) of the 1990 Act omits the italicised words.
   The Waste Management Licensing Regulations 1994, Sched. 4, imposes duties on planning authorities in relation to development control and plan-making decisions, consistent with the requirements of the Waste Framework Directive.

Subs. (3)
Grounds for refusal: This subsection effectively restricts the grounds on which a waste regulation authority may reject a licence application which has been duly made and where the conditions precedent as to planning permission in subs. (2) have been complied with. The equivalent provision in the 1974 Act (s.5(3)) was held in *Berridge Incinerators v. Nottingham-shire County Council* not to apply in a case where planning permission for the use was not required and where consequently no permission was in force: this problematic result is obviated by the new wording.
   The significance of the introduction of the requirement that the authority be satisfied that the applicant is a "fit and proper person" has been already mentioned: and see notes to s.74.
   The only other grounds on which the authority may lawfully reject an application are that rejection is necessary for the purpose of preventing: (a) pollution of the environment; or (b) harm to human health. The width of meaning given to these expressions by the legislation means that effectively the grounds for refusal are widened considerably beyond those in the 1974 Act. Further, where no planning permission is in force in relation to the proposed use, "serious detriment to the amenities of the locality" forms a further reason for rejection, presumably on the basis that there will have been no planning application stage where such matters could have been considered.
   If the evils referred to in the subsection can be effectively prevented by the imposition of conditions, then it will not be, in the words of the subsection, "necessary" to reject the application.
   By the Waste Management Licensing Regulations 1994, Sched. 4, para. 9(7), the reference to planning permission in subsection (3) shall be taken to be a reference to planning permission resulting from the taking of a specified action (essentially, determination of a planning application or appeal) after April 30, 1994. The objective of this change is to ensure that the issue of serious detriment to amenity is properly considered as required by the waste framework

directive—such issues may not have been explicitly addressed in planning permissions granted before the 1994 Regulations: see Circ. 11/94, paras. 1.57–1.58 and 1.62–1.63.

Subss. (4), (7) and (8)
Reference to other regulatory authorities: These subsections contain procedures whereby licence proposals are to be referred to the relevant authorities, and any representations made by such authorities within 28 days or such longer period as may be agreed in writing (subs. (10)) are to be considered. The obligation is simply to consider any representations made within the allowed period.

Subs. (9)
Deemed rejection: This subsection provides a means by which an applicant may appeal to the Secretary of State if the waste regulation authority fails to issue a decision within four months or such longer period as may be agreed in writing.
 It is subject by subs. (9A) to the right of the authority not to proceed with an application which is not supported by the appropriate information.

[Consultation before the grant of certain licences

36A.—(1) This section applies where an application for a licence has been duly made to a waste regulation authority, and the authority proposes to issue a licence subject (by virtue of section 35(4) above) to any condition which might require the holder of the licence to—
 (a) carry out any works, or
 (b) do any other thing,
which he might not be entitled to carry out or do.
 (2) Before issuing the licence, the waste regulation authority shall serve on every person appearing to the authority to be a person falling within subsection (3) below a notice which complies with the requirements set out in subsection (4) below.
 (3) A person falls within this subsection if—
 (a) he is the owner, lessee or occupier of any land; and
 (b) that land is land in relation to which it is likely that, as a consequence of the licence being issued subject to the condition in question, rights will have to be granted by virtue of section 35(4) above to the holder of the licence.
 (4) A notice served under subsection (2) above shall—
 (a) set out the condition in question;
 (b) indicate the nature of the works or other things which that condition might require the holder of the licence to carry out or do; and
 (c) specify the date by which, and the manner in which, any representations relating to the condition or its possible effects are to be made to the waste regulation authority by the person on whom the notice is served.
 (5) The date which, pursuant to subsection (4)(c) above, is specified in a notice shall be a date not earlier than the date on which expires the period—
 (a) beginning with the date on which the notice is served, and
 (b) of such length as may be prescribed in regulations made by the Secretary of State.
 (6) Before the waste regulation authority issues the licence it must, subject to subsection (7) below, consider any representations made in relation to the condition in question, or its possible effects, by any person on whom a notice has been served under subsection (2) above.
 (7) Subsection (6) above does not require the waste regulation authority to consider any representations made by a person after the date specified in the notice served on him under subsection (2) above as the date by which his representations in relation to the condition or its possible effects are to be made.

(8) In subsection (3) above—
"owner", in relation to any land in England and Wales, means the person who–
(a) is for the time being receiving the rack-rent of the land, whether on his own account or as agent or trustee for another person; or
(b) would receive the rack-rent if the land were let at a rack-rent, but does not include a mortgagee not in possession; and
"owner", in relation to any land in Scotland, means a person (other than a creditor in a heritable security not in possession of the security subjects) for the time being entitled to receive or who would, if the land were let be entitled to receive, the rents of the land in connection with which the word is used and includes a trustee, factor, guardian or curator and in the case of public or municipal land includes the persons to whom the management of the land is entrusted.]

DEFINITIONS
"licence": s.35(12).
"waste regulation authority": s.30.

GENERAL NOTE
This section was inserted by the Environment Act 1995, Sched. 22, para. 69. Its purpose is to protect third parties who might be affected by conditions imposed on a site licence, in that they might be required by s.35(4) to grant rights to the licence holder to allow him to carry out works which he would not otherwise be entitled to do. The procedures set out in the section only apply where the authority proposes to impose conditions which might require the holder to do things which he might not be entitled to do, *e.g.* offsite monitoring. The section would therefore not apply if the licence applicant could demonstrate to the authority that he already had the necessary rights.
The procedure also applies only if rights are likely to have to be granted in relation to land (subs. (3)). The section requires notice to be served on any owner, lessee or occupier of such land, and for any representation made by such person as to the proposed condition to its possible effects to be taken into account by the waste regulation authority before granting the licence.

Variation of licences

37.—(1) While a licence issued by a waste regulation authority is in force, the authority may, subject to regulations under section 35(6) above and to subsection (3) below,—
(a) on its own initiative, modify the conditions of the licence to any extent which, in the opinion of the authority, is desirable and is unlikely to require unreasonable expense on the part of the holder; and
(b) on the application of the licence holder accompanied by [the change prescribed for the purpose by a charging scheme under section 41 of the Environment Act 1995], modify the conditions of his licence to the extent requested in the application.
(2) While a licence issued by a waste regulation authority is in force, the authority shall, except where it revokes the licence entirely under section 38 below, modify the conditions of the licence—
(a) to the extent which in the opinion of the authority is required for the purpose of ensuring that the activities authorised by the licence do not cause pollution of the environment or harm to human health or become seriously detrimental to the amenities of the locality affected by the activities; and
(b) to the extent required by any regulations in force under section 35(6) above.
(3) The Secretary of State may, as respects any licence issued by a waste regulation authority, give to the authority directions as to the modifications which are to be made in the conditions of the licence under subsections

(1)(a) or (2)(a) above; and it shall be the duty of the authority to give effect to the directions.

(4) Any modification of a licence under this section shall be effected by notice served on the holder of the licence and the notice shall state the time at which the modification is to take effect.

(5) Section 36(4) [...], (7) [...] and (10) above shall with the necessary modifications apply to a proposal by a waste regulation authority to modify a licence under subsection (1) or (2)(a) above as they apply to a proposal to issue a licence, except that—

    (a) the authority may postpone the reference so far as the authority considers that by reason of an emergency it is appropriate to do so; and

    (b) the authority need not consider any representations as respects a modification which, in the opinion of the waste regulation authority, will not affect any authority mentioned in the subsections so applied.

(6) If within the period of two months beginning with the date on which a waste regulation authority received an application by the holder of a licence for a modification of it, or within such longer period as the authority and the applicant may at any time agree in writing, the authority has neither granted a modification of the licence in consequence of the application nor given notice to the applicant that the authority has rejected the application, the authority shall be deemed to have rejected the application.

[(7) This section shall have effect subject to section 37A below.]

DEFINITIONS
"harm": s.29(5).
"licence": s.35(12).
"pollution of the environment": s.29(3).

AMENDMENTS
Subss. (1) and (5) were amended by the Environment Act 1995, Sched. 2, para. 70(1) and (2). Subs. (7) was added by para. 70(3).

COMMENCEMENT
Subsection (3): February 18, 1993 (S.I. 1993 No. 274). Remainder: May 1, 1994 (S.I. 1994 No. 1096).

GENERAL NOTE
This section provides the power by which licences may be varied so as to modify the conditions, either: (a) on the initiative of the waste regulation authority (where the modification, in the opinion of the authority, is desirable and is unlikely to require unreasonable expense on the part of the holder); or (b) on the application of the licence-holder.

Subs. (2)
This imposes a duty upon waste regulation authorities to modify licence conditions in certain circumstances. The provisions as to consultation with other regulatory authorities which apply on the grant of licences also apply to variations, with slight changes (subs. (5)). Appeal lies against modifications under s.43(1)(c) and against rejection of an application for modification under s.43(1)(a).

Subs. (6)
Deemed refusal. Failure by a waste regulation authority to issue a decision on an application for modification within two months constitutes deemed rejection, against which the applicant may appeal under s.43(1)(a). This should obviate the practical difficulties caused by the absence of any such provision in the 1974 Act.

Existing licences
The provisions as to variation of licences apply to subsisting licences issued under the 1974 Act (s.77(2)).

Guidance as to review of conditions
The need to review licence conditions in the light of regs. 13, 14 and 15 of the Waste Management Licensing Regulations 1994 (see notes to s.35) is emphasised by the accompanying Circ. 11/94, Annex 4, para. 4.39.

Protection of groundwater
Circular 20/90 (W.O. 34/90) suggests (para. 3) that waste regulation authorities should review the disposal licences for landfill site involving the disposal of wastes containing substances within List I of the Groundwater Directive 80/68/EEC. Where the NRA advises that discharges are liable to affect groundwater adversely and that such water is not permanently unusable, the disposal licence should be reviewed. This may require the prohibition of the deposit of waste containing List I substances (para. 4). Para. 4.39 of Annex 4 to Circ. 11/94 on Waste Management Licensing Regulations states that authorities should review current licences in the light of reg. 15 of the Waste Management Licensing Regulations 1994 (protection of groundwater) as to which see notes to s.35. See also the decision in *R. v. Vale of Glamorgan Borough Council and Associated British Ports, ex p. James* referred to in the notes to s.35.

[Consultation before certain variations

37A.—(1) This section applies where—
    (a) a waste regulation authority proposes to modify a licence under section 37(1) or (2)(a) above; and
    (b) the licence, if modified as proposed, would be subject to a relevant new condition.

(2) For the purposes of this section, a "relevant new condition" is any condition by virtue of which the holder of the licence might be required to carry out any works or do any other thing
    (a) which he might not be entitled to carry out or do, and
    (b) which he could not be required to carry out or do by virtue of the conditions to which, prior to the modification, the licence is subject.

(3) Before modifying the licence, the waste regulation authority shall serve on every person appearing to the authority to be a person falling within subsection (4) below a notice which complies with the requirements set out in subsection (5) below.

(4) A person falls within this subsection if
    (a) he is the owner, lessee or occupier of any land; and
    (b) that land is land in relation to which it is likely that, as a consequence of the licence being modified so as to be subject to the relevant new condition in question, rights will have to be granted by virtue of section 35(4) above to the holder of the licence.

(5) A notice served under subsection (3) above shall
    (a) set out the relevant new condition in question;
    (b) indicate the nature of the works or other things which that condition might require the holder of the licence to carry out or do but which he could not be required to carry out or do by virtue of the conditions (if any) to which, prior to the modification, the licence is subject; and
    (c) specify the date by which, and the manner in which, any representations relating to the condition or its possible effects are to be made to the waste regulation authority by the person on whom the notice is served.

(6) The date which, pursuant to subsection (5)(c) above, is specified in a notice shall be a date not earlier than the date on which expires the period—
    (a) beginning with the date on which the notice is served, and
    (b) of such length as may be prescribed in regulations made by the Secretary of State.

(7) Before the waste regulation authority issues the licence it must, subject to subsection (8) below, consider any representations made in relation to the condition in question, or its possible effects, by any person on whom a notice has been served under subsection (3) above.

(8) Subsection (7) above does not require the waste regulation authority to consider any representations made by a person after the date specified in the notice served on him under subsection (3) above as the date by which his representations in relation to the condition or its possible effects are to be made.

(9) A waste regulation authority may postpone the service of any notice or the consideration of any representations required under the foregoing provisions of this section so far as the authority considers that by reason of an emergency it is appropriate to do so.

(10) In subsection (3) above, "owner" has the same meaning as it has in subsection (3) of section 36A above by virtue of subsection (8) of that section.]

DEFINITION
    "licence": s.35(12).

GENERAL NOTE
This section was inserted by the Environment Act 1995, Sched. 22, para. 71. It parallels s.36A so as to require consultation with third parties who may be affected by conditions imposed when a licence is modified. See general note to s.36A.

Revocation and suspension of licences

38.—(1) Where a licence granted by a waste regulation authority is in force and it appears to the authority—
    (a) that the holder of the licence has ceased to be a fit and proper person by reason of his having been convicted of a relevant offence; or
    (b) that the continuation of the activities authorised by the licence would cause pollution of the environment or harm to human health or would be seriously detrimental to the amenities of the locality affected; and
    (c) that the pollution, harm or detriment cannot be avoided by modifying the conditions of the licence;
the authority may exercise, as it thinks fit, either of the powers conferred by subsections (3) and (4) below.

(2) Where a licence granted by a waste regulation authority is in force and it appears to the authority that the holder of the licence has ceased to be a fit and proper person by reason of the management of the activities authorised by the licence having ceased to be in the hands of a technically competent person, the authority may exercise the power conferred by subsection (3) below.

(3) The authority may, under this subsection, revoke the licence so far as it authorises the carrying on of the activities specified in the licence or such of them as the authority specifies in revoking the licence.

(4) The authority may, under this subsection, revoke the licence entirely.

(5) A licence revoked under subsection (3) above shall cease to have effect to authorise the carrying on of the activities specified in the licence or, as the case may be, the activities specified by the authority in revoking the licence but shall not affect the requirements imposed by the licence which the authority, in revoking the licence, specify as requirements which are to continue to bind the licence holder.

(6) Where a licence granted by a waste regulation authority is in force and it appears to the authority—
    (a) that the holder of the licence has ceased to be a fit and proper person by reason of the management of the activities authorised by

the licence having ceased to be in the hands of a technically competent person; or

(b) that serious pollution of the environment or serious harm to human health has resulted from, or is about to be caused by, the activities to which the licence relates or the happening or threatened happening of an event affecting those activities; and

(c) that the continuing to carry on those activities, or any of those activities, in the circumstances will continue or, as the case may be, cause serious pollution of the environment or serious harm to human health;

the authority may suspend the licence so far as it authorises the carrying on of the activities specified in the licence or such of them as the authority specifies in suspending the licence.

(7) The Secretary of State may, if he thinks fit in relation to a licence granted by a waste regulation authority, give to the authority directions as to whether and in what manner the authority should exercise its powers under this section; and it shall be the duty of the authority to give effect to the directions.

(8) A licence suspended under subsection (6) above shall, while the suspension has effect, be of no effect to authorise the carrying on of the activities specified in the licence or, as the case may be, the activities specified by the authority in suspending the licence.

(9) Where a licence is suspended under subsection (6) above, the authority, in suspending it or at any time while it is suspended, may require the holder of the licence to take such measures to deal with or avert the pollution or harm as the authority considers necessary.

[(9A) A requirement imposed under subsection (9) above may require the holder of a licence to carry out works or do other things notwithstanding that he is not entitled to carry out the works or do the thing and any person whose consent would be required shall grant, or join in granting, the holder of the licence such rights in relation to the land as will enable the holder of the licence to comply with any requirements imposed on him under that subsection.

(9B) Subsections (2) to (8) of section 36A above shall, with the necessary modifications, apply where the authority proposes to impose a requirement under subsection (9) above which may require the holder of a licence to carry out any such works or do any such thing as is mentioned in subsection (9A) above as they apply where the authority proposes to issue a licence subject to any such condition as is mentioned in subsection (1) of that section, but as if—

(a) the reference in subsection (3) of that section to section 35(4) above were a reference to subsection (9A) above; and

(b) any reference in those subsections—

(i) to the condition, or the condition in question, were a reference to the requirement; and

(ii) to issuing a licence were a reference to serving a notice, under subsection (12) below, effecting the requirement.

(9C) The authority may postpone the service of any notice or the consideration of any representations required under section 36A above, as applied by subsection (9B) above, so far as the authority considers that by reason of an emergency it is appropriate to do so.]

(10) A person who, without reasonable excuse, fails to comply with any requirement imposed under subsection (9) above otherwise than in relation to special waste shall be liable—

(a) on summary conviction, to a fine of an amount not exceeding the statutory maximum; and

(b) on conviction on indictment, to imprisonment for a term not exceeding two years or a fine or both.

(11) A person who, without reasonable excuse, fails to comply with any requirement imposed under subsection (9) above in relation to special waste shall be liable—

    (a) on summary conviction, to imprisonment for a term not exceeding six months or a fine not exceeding the statutory maximum or both; and

    (b) on conviction on indictment, to imprisonment for a term not exceeding five years or a fine or both.

(12) Any revocation or suspension of a licence or requirement imposed during the suspension of a licence under this section shall be effected by notice served on the holder of the licence and the notice shall state the time at which the revocation or suspension or the requirement is to take effect and, in the case of suspension, the period at the end of which, or the event on the occurrence of which, the suspension is to cease.

[(13) If a waste regulation authority is of the opinion that proceedings for an offence under subsection (10) or (11) above would afford an ineffectual remedy against a person who has failed to comply with any requirement imposed under subsection (9) above, the authority may take proceedings in the High Court or, in Scotland, in any court of competent jurisdiction for the purpose of securing compliance with the requirement.]

DEFINITIONS
    "fit and proper person": s.74.
    "harm": s.29(5).
    "licence": s.35(12).
    "pollution of the environment": s.29(3).
    "relevant offence": s.74(6).
    "special waste": s.75(9).

COMMENCEMENT
Subsection (7): February 18, 1993 (S.I. 1993 No. 274). Remainder: May 1, 1994 (S.I. 1994 No. 1096).

AMENDMENTS
Subss. (9A)–(9C) were inserted by the Environment Act 1995, Sched. 22, para. 72(1). Subs. (13) was added by Sched. 22, para. 72(2).

GENERAL NOTE
This section allows waste regulation authorities to revoke licences in whole or in part and to suspend the licence in relation to all or some of the licensed activities. By s.77(2) these provisions apply by subsisting licences granted under the 1974 Act.

Revocation of licences
There are two main powers of revocation:

    (a) *Revocation of authorisation as to licensed activities.* Under subs. (3), the authority may revoke the licence so far as it authorises the licensed activities, or such of them as the authority specifies. The effect of such revocation is that the relevant activities are no longer authorised, but the authority may specify licence requirements which are to continue to bind the licence-holder (subs. (5)); and

    (b) *Total revocation.* Under subs. (4) the authority may revoke the licence entirely, in which case the licence ceases to have effect for all purpose.

The grounds for revocation appear in subss. (1) and (2):

    (a) that the holder of the licence has ceased to be a fit and proper person by reason of conviction for a relevant offence (see s.74 and notes thereto);

    (b) that the continuation of the licensed activities would cause pollution of the environment or harm to human health or that they would be seriously detrimental to the amenities of the locality, and that, in each case, the pollution, harm or detriment could not be avoided by modifying the licence conditions; and

    (c) that the holder of the licence has ceased to be a fit and proper person by reason of the management of the activities having ceased to be in the hands of a technically competent person (see s.74 and notes thereto).

Grounds (1) and (2) allow the authority to exercise either of the powers of revocation mentioned above, whereas ground (3) does not allow total revocation under subs. (4).

Appeal against revocation lies to the Secretary of State under s.43(1)(e), and whilst the appeal is pending the revocation is ineffective (s.43(4)) unless a statement is made that immediate revocation is necessary for preventing or minimising pollution of the environment or harm to human health (s.43(6)).

Further powers of revocation exist under s.42(5)(a) and (b) where licence conditions are not being complied with, following notice by the authority.

Suspension of licences
Subsection (6) allows an authority to suspend a licence so far as it authorises the licensed activities or such of them as the authority specifies.

There are two grounds of suspension:
(a) that the licence-holder has ceased to be a fit and proper person by reason of the licensed activities having ceased to be in the hands of a technically competent person (see s.74 and notes thereto); and
(b) that serious pollution of the environment or serious harm to human health has resulted from the licensed activities or is about to be caused by those activities (or in either case, some event affecting those activities) and that continuance of all or any of the licensed activities will lead to such serious pollution or harm.

The problems justifying suspension therefore have to be of a serious and continuing nature.

The effect of suspension is that the relevant activities are no longer authorises during the period of suspension (subs. 8)). Additionally, the authority can require the licence-holder to take necessary measures to deal with, or avert, the pollution or harm (subs. (9)). Failure to comply with such a requirement is an offence (subss. (10) and (11)) or the authority may be entitled to take civil proceedings under subs. (13) to secure compliance. Any necessary third party consent must be granted, subject to provision for compensation (s.35A) and consultation (s.36A, by virtue of subs. (9B) (subss. (9A)–(9C)).

Appeal against suspension lies to the Secretary of State under s.43(1)(d) and, unlike revocation, a pending appeal does not affect the validity of the suspension (s.43(5)). A further power of suspension exists where licence conditions are not complied with following notice by the authority (s.42(6)(c)).

Surrender of licences

39.—(1) A licence may be surrendered by its holder to the authority which granted it but, in the case of a site licence, only if the authority accepts the surrender.

(2) The following provisions apply to the surrender and acceptance of the surrender of a site licence.

(3) The holder of a site licence who desires to surrender it shall make an application for that purpose to the authority [on a form provided by the authority for the purpose, giving such information and accompanied by such evidence as the authority reasonably requires and accompanied by the charge prescribed for the purpose by a charging scheme under section 41 of the Environment Act 1995.]

(4) An authority which receives an application for the surrender of a site licence—
(a) shall inspect the land to which the licence relates, and
(b) may require the holder of the licence to furnish to it further information or further evidence.

(5) The authority shall determine whether it is likely or unlikely that the condition of the land, so far as that condition is the result of the use of the land for the treatment, keeping or disposal of waste (whether or not in pursuance of the licence), will cause pollution of the environment or harm to human health.

(6) If the authority is satisfied that the condition of the land is unlikely to cause the pollution or harm mentioned in subsection (5) above, the authority shall, subject to subsection (7) below, accept the surrender of the licence; but otherwise the authority shall refuse to accept it.

(7) Where the authority proposes to accept the surrender of a site licence, the authority must, before it does so,—
(a) refer the proposal to the [appropriate planning authority]; and

(b) consider any representations about the proposal which the [appro-
priate planning authority] makes to it during the allowed period;
(8) […]
(9) Where the surrender of a licence is accepted under this section the
authority shall issue to the applicant, with the notice of its determination, a
certificate (a "certificate of completion") stating that it is satisfied as
mentioned in subsection (6) above and, on the issue of that certificate, the
licence shall cease to have effect.

(10) If within the period of three months beginning with the date on which
an authority receives an application to surrender a licence, or within such
longer period as the authority and the applicant may at any time agree in
writing, the authority has neither issued a certificate of completion nor given
notice to the applicant that the authority has rejected the application, the
authority shall be deemed to have rejected the application.

(11) Section 36(10) above applies for the interpretation of the "allowed
period" in subsection (7) above.

[(12) In this section
"the appropriate planning authority" means
(a) where the relevant land is situated in the area of a London
borough council, that London borough council;
(b) where the relevant land is situated in the City of London, the
Common Council of the City of London;
(c) where the relevant land is situated in a non-metropolitan county
in England, the council of that county;
(d) where the relevant land is situated in a National Park or the
Broads, the National Park authority for that National Park or, as
the case may be, the Broads Authority;
(e) where the relevant land is situated elsewhere in England or
Wales, the council of the district or, in Wales, the county or
county borough, in which the land is situated;
(f) where the relevant land is situated in Scotland, the council
constituted under section 2 of the Local Government etc.
(Scotland) Act 1994 for the area in which the land is situated;
"the Broads" has the same meaning as in the Norfolk and Suffolk
Broads Act 1988;
"National Park authority", subject to subsection (13) below, means a
National Part authority established under section 63 of the
Environment Act 1995 which has become the local planning
authority for the National Park in question;
"the relevant land", in the case of any site licence, means the land to
which the licence relates.

(13) As respects any period before a National Park authority established
under section 63 of the Environment Act 1995 in relation to a National Park
becomes the local planning authority for that National Park, any reference
in this section to a National Park authority shall be taken as a reference to
the National Park Committee or joint or special planning board for that
National Park.

(14) The Secretary of State may by regulations amend the definition of
"appropriate planning authority" in subsection (12) above.]

DEFINITIONS
"the appropriate planning authority": subs. (12).
"disposal": s.29(6).
"harm": s.29(5).
"licence": s.35(12).
"pollution of the environment": s.29(3).
"site licence": s.35(12).
"treatment": s.29(6).
"waste": s.75(2).

AMENDMENTS
Subss. (3), (7) and (11) were amended by the Environment Act 1995, Sched. 22, para. 73(2), (3) and (5). Subs. (8) was deleted and subss. (12)–(14) added by para. 73(4) and (6).

COMMENCEMENT
Subsection (3): February 18, 1993 (S.I. 1993 No. 274). Remainder: May 1, 1994 (S.I. 1994 No. 1096).

GENERAL NOTE
This section makes significant amendments to the provisions on surrender of licences contained in the 1974 Act under which it was possible for the licence-holder to cancel the licence unilaterally. Such surrender is still possible for licences for mobile plant, but for site licences acceptance of the surrender by the authority is necessary.

Whether such acceptance is forthcoming depends upon where the condition of the land is likely or unlikely to cause pollution of the environment or harm to human health, as far as that condition is the result of waste being treated, kept or disposed of on the land (subss. (5) and (6)). The reference to "(whether or not in pursuance of the licence)" means that historic deposits of waste, or contamination caused by waste treatment, predating the current licensed activities will be relevant. This may be a particular problem in relation to activities such as transfer stations which may be established on old industrial land.

Detailed guidance as to the criteria for acceptance of surrender is provided under s.35(8) by Waste Management Paper No. 26A, *Landfill Completion* (HMSO, 1993) and more generally by Waste Management Paper No. 4. This guidance seeks to distinguish sites which have taken only inert waste and those which are isolated from sensitive targets from other sites, which will require more stringent monitoring.

There is a right of appeal against refusal to accept surrender of a licence (s.43(1)(f)) or against deemed refusal if no decision is given by the authority within three months of the application to surrender (s.39(10)).

Applications and information requirements
By the Waste Management Licensing Regulations 1994, reg. 2(2), applications for surrender are to be made in writing and are to be accompanied by the evidence prescribed by Sched. 1: this includes in particular details of all significant engineering works of an anti-pollution and restoration nature, and geological, hydrological, hydrogeological and monitoring data. One practical problem with the drafting of s.39 is the apparent inability to surrender a licence in relation to part only of the land which it covers: this may present problems with large sites, parts of which may be completed and stabilised long before others.

Existing licences
The new provisions on surrender apply to subsisting licences granted under the 1974 Act (s.77(2)).

Transfer of licences

40.—(1) A licence may be transferred to another person in accordance with subsections (2) to (6) below and may be so transferred whether or not the licence is partly revoked or suspended under any provision of this Part.

(2) Where the holder of a licence desires that the licence be transferred to another person ("the proposed transferee") the licence holder and the proposed transferee shall jointly make an application to the waste regulation authority which granted the licence for a transfer of it.

(3) An application under subsection (2) above for the transfer of a licence shall be made [on a form provided by the authority for the purpose, accompanied by such information as the authority may reasonably require, the charge prescribed for the purpose by a charging scheme under section 41 of the Environment Act 1995] and the licence.

(4) If, on such an application, the authority is satisfied that the proposed transferee is a fit and proper person the authority shall effect a transfer of the licence to the proposed transferee.

(5) The authority shall effect a transfer of a licence under the foregoing provisions of this section by causing the licence to be endorsed with the name

and other particulars of the proposed transferee as the holder of the licence from such date specified in the endorsement as may be agreed with the applicants.

(6) If within the period of two months beginning with the date on which the authority receives an application for the transfer of a licence, or within such longer period as the authority and the applicants may at any time agree in writing, the authority has neither effected a transfer of the licence nor given notice to the applicants that the authority has rejected the application, the authority shall be deemed to have rejected the application.

DEFINITIONS
"fit and proper person": s.74.
"licence": s.35(12).

COMMENCEMENT
Subsection (3): February 18, 1993 (S.I. 1993 No. 274). Remainder: May 1, 1994 (S.I. 1994 No. 1096).

AMENDMENT
Subs. (3) was amended by the Environment Act 1995, Sched. 22, para. 74.

GENERAL NOTE
In order to transfer a licence, a joint application by the licence-holder and proposed transferee is necessary, and the authority may only effect the transfer on being satisfied that the proposed transferee is "a fit and proper person" (as to which, see s.74). By reg. 2(5) of the Waste Management Licensing Regulations 1994, the application must be made in writing and be accompanied by the information prescribed at Sched. 2 as to the proposed transferee, any relevant convictions and the identity of the proposed technically competent person or persons.

There is a right of appeal against refusal to effect a transfer, or failure either to effect a transfer or to reject the application within two months (ss.40(6) and 43(1)(g)).

Existing licences
Subsisting licences granted under COPA may only be transferred under s.40 (s.77(2)).

Fees and charges for licences

41. [...].

[Section 41 (dealing with fees and charges for licences) was repealed by the Environment Act 1995, Sched 2, para. 75. Charges for waste management licensing are now dealt with by the general provisions of s.41 of the 1995 Act.]

Supervision of licensed activities

42.—(1) While a licence is in force it shall be the duty of the waste regulation authority which granted the licence to take the steps needed—
    (a) for the purpose of ensuring that the activities authorised by the licence do not cause pollution of the environment or harm to human health or become seriously detrimental to the amenities of the locality affected by the activities; and
    (b) for the purpose of ensuring that the conditions of the licence are complied with.

(2) [...]

(3) For the purpose of performing the duty imposed on it by subsection (1) above, any officer of the authority authorised in writing for the purpose by the authority may, if it appears to him that by reason of an emergency it is necessary to do so, carry out work on the land or in relation to plant or equipment on the land to which the licence relates or, as the case may be, in relation to the mobile plant to which the licence relates.

(4) Where a waste regulation authority incurs any expenditure by virtue of subsection (3) above, the authority may recover the amount of the

expenditure from [the holder, or (as the case may be) the former holder, of the licence], except where the holder or former holder of the licence shows that there was no emergency requiring any work or except such of the expenditure as he shows was unnecessary.

(5) Where it appears to a waste regulation authority that a condition of a licence granted by it is not being complied with [or is likely not to be complied with], then, without prejudice to any proceedings under section 33(6) above, the authority may—

[(a) serve on the holder of the licence a notice—
(i) stating that the authority is of the opinion that a condition of the licence is not being complied with or, as the case may be, is likely not to be complied with;
(ii) specifying the matters which constitute the non-compliance or, as the case may be, which make the anticipated non-compliance likely;
(iii) specifying the steps which must be taken to remedy the non-compliance or, as the case may be, to prevent the anticipated non-compliance from occurring; and
(iv) specifying the period within which those steps must be taken; and].
(b) if in the opinion of the authority the licence holder [has not taken the steps specified in the notice within the period so specified], exercise any of the powers specified in subsection (6) below.

(6) The powers which become exercisable in the event mentioned in subsection (5)(b) above are the following—

(a) to revoke the licence so far as it authorises the carrying on of the activities specified in the licence or such of them as the authority specifies in revoking the licence;
(b) to revoke the licence entirely; and
(c) to suspend the licence so far as it authorises the carrying on of the activities specified in the licence or, as the case may be, the activities specified by the authority in suspending the licence.

[(6A) If a waste regulation authority is of the opinion that revocation or suspension of the licence, whether entirely or to any extent, under subsection (6) above would afford an ineffectual remedy against a person who has failed to comply with any requirement imposed under subsection (5)(a) above, the authority may take proceedings in the High Court or, in Scotland, in any court of competent jurisdiction for the purpose of securing compliance with the requirement.]

(7) Where a licence is revoked or suspended under subsection (6) above, [subsections (5) and (12) or, as the case may be, subsections (8) to (12) of section 38] above shall apply with the necessary modifications as they respectively apply to revocations or suspensions of licences under that section. [...]

(8) The Secretary of State may, if he thinks fit in relation to a licence granted by a waste regulation authority, give to the authority directions as to whether and in what manner the authority should exercise its powers under this section; and it shall be the duty of the authority to give effect to the directions.

DEFINITIONS
"harm": s.29(5).
"licence": s.35(12).
"pollution of the environment": s.29(3).

AMENDMENTS
Subs. (2) (dealing with consultation with the NRA or river purification authority) was repealed by the Environment Act 1995, Sched. 22, para. 76(2). Subss. (4), (5) and (7) were amended by para. 76(3)–(6) and (8). Subs. (6A) was added by para. 76(7).

COMMENCEMENT
Subsection (8): February 18, 1993 (S.I. 1993 No. 274). Remainder: May 1, 1994 (S.I. 1994 No. 1096).

GENERAL NOTE
Under this section, waste regulation authorities are under a duty to take a supervisory rôle as to licences, to ensure that pollution, harm or detriment as mentioned in subs. (1)(a) do not occur, and to ensure that the conditions of the licence are complied with. Two main powers arise in the event of default:

(1) to carry out necessary work in the event of an emergency and to recover the expenditure (s.42(3) and (4)). The reference to recovery of expenditure from a former holder of a licence means that expenditure can be recovered for work done prior to the termination of the licence by surrender or revocation; it does not allow work to be carried out after the licence has come to an end, as in that case there would be no licence "in force" (subs. (1)); and

(2) in the case of actual or likely non-compliance with conditions, to serve notice specifying the steps required to comply and, in the event of default, to revoke the licence (subss. (5) and (6)), or to take civil proceedings under subs. (6A).

Waste Management Paper 4, *The Licensing of Waste Management Facilities*, provides guidance as to this inspecting and monitoring function. Appendix B of that Paper suggests site inspection frequencies for various types of sites; para. B.6 suggests that inspections should include random visits, though it is reasonable to inform the operator that a visit is being made where a specific problem or modification to the licence is being considered.

Appendix C to Waste Management Paper No. 4 deals with the monitoring of landfills. A continued regime of monitoring is suggested throughout the licensed life of the site up until the point at which surrender of the licence is contemplated. Such a regime should provided a complete position of the pollution potential of the site over most of its licensed life. Appendix C seeks to balance best practice with regard to monitoring and the costs to site operators.

Appeals to Secretary of State from decisions with respect to licences

43.—(1) Where, except in pursuance of a direction given by the Secretary of State,—

(a) an application for a licence or a modification of the conditions of a licence is rejected;

(b) a licence is granted subject to conditions;

(c) the conditions of a licence are modified;

(d) a licence is suspended;

(e) a licence is revoked under section 38 or 42 above;

(f) an application to surrender a licence is rejected; or

(g) an application for the transfer of a licence is rejected;

then, except in the case of an application for a transfer, the applicant for the licence or, as the case may be, the holder or former holder of it may appeal from the decision to the Secretary of State and, in the case of an application for a transfer, the proposed transferee may do so.

(2) Where an appeal is made to the Secretary of State—

(a) [...]

(b) [...]

(c) if a party to the appeal so requests, or the Secretary of State so decides, the appeal shall be or continue in the form of a hearing (which may, if the person hearing the appeal so decides, be held or held to any extent in private).

[(2A) This section is subject to section 114 of the Environment Act 1995 (delegation or reference of appeals etc.)]

(3) Where, on such an appeal, the Secretary of State or other person determining the appeal determines that the decision of the authority shall be altered it shall be the duty of the authority to give effect to the determination.

(4) While an appeal is pending in a case falling within subsection (1)(c) or (e) above, the decision in question shall, subject to subsection (6) below, be ineffective; and if the appeal is dismissed or withdrawn the decision shall

become effective from the end of the day on which the appeal is dismissed or withdrawn.

(5) Where an appeal is made in a case falling within subsection (1)(d) above, the bringing of the appeal shall have no effect on the decision in question.

(6) Subsection (4) above shall not apply to a decision modifying the conditions of a licence under section 37 above or revoking a licence under section 38 or 42 above in the case of which the notice effecting the modification or revocation includes a statement that in the opinion of the authority it is necessary for the purpose of preventing or, where that is not practicable, minimising pollution of the environment or harm to human health that that subsection should not apply.

(7) Where the decision under appeal is one falling within subsection (6) above or is a decision to suspend a licence, if, on the application of the holder or former holder of the licence, the Secretary of State or other person determining the appeal determines that the authority acted unreasonably in excluding the application of subsection (4) above or, as the case may be, in suspending the licence, then—

> (a) if the appeal is still pending at the end of the day on which the determination is made, subsection (4) above shall apply to the decision from the end of that day; and
>
> (b) the holder or former holder of the licence shall be entitled to recover compensation from the authority in respect of any loss suffered by him in consequence of the exclusion of the application of that subsection or the suspension of the licence;

and any dispute as to a person's entitlement to such compensation or as to the amount of it shall be determined by arbitration or in Scotland by a single arbiter appointed, in default of agreement between the parties concerned, by the Secretary of State on the application of any of the parties.

(8) Provision may be made by the Secretary of State by regulations with respect to appeals under this section and in particular—

> (a) as to the period within which and the manner in which appeals are to be brought; and
>
> (b) as to the manner in which appeals are to be considered.

DEFINITIONS
   "harm": s.29(5).
   "licence": s.35(12).
   "pollution of the environment": s.29(3).

AMENDMENT
Subs (2A) was added by the Environment Act 1995, Sched. 22 , para. 77. Paras. (a) and (b) of subs. (2) were repealed by Sched. 24 of the 1995 Act, being no longer necessary in view of the powers under s.114 applied by subs. (2A)

COMMENCEMENT
Subsection (8): February 18, 1993 (S.I. 1993 No. 274). Remainder: May 1, 1994 (S.I. 1994 No. 1096).

GENERAL NOTE
This section provides rights of appeal in relation to licensing decisions. Appeal is to the Secretary of State. Section 114 of the Environment Act 1995 (applied by subs. (2A)) gives the Secretary of State general powers to delegate and refer appellate functions. The appeal is conducted in writing, unless either party requests a hearing, which may be either public or private at the discretion of the inspector (subs. (2)(c)).

Effect of appeal
Where a licence is modified or revoked, and an appeal is made, the modification or revocation is ineffective until the appeal is dismissed or withdrawn (subs. (4)). The position is different in the case of appeal against suspension of licences, where the bringing of an appeal has no effect on the suspension (subs. (5)).

If an authority is of the view that modification or revocation should have immediate effect notwithstanding any appeal, a statement may be inserted in the modification or revocation notice excluding subss. (4) and (6). However, this course carries the risk of the authority having to pay compensation in the event that the authority is found to have acted unreasonably by the Secretary of State or inspector (subs. (7)(b)). The same risk applies to a decision to suspend a licence.

Form and manner of appeals
See the Waste Management Licensing Regulations 1994, regs. 6–19 as to appeals procedure. Notice of appeal must be given in writing before the expiry of a period of six months beginning with the date of the relevant decision or deemed rejection, or within such longer period as the Secretary of State may allow.

[Offences of making false or misleading statements or false entries

44.—(1) A person who—
 (a) in purported compliance with a requirement to furnish any information imposed by or under any provision of this Part, or
 (b) for the purpose of obtaining for himself or another any grant of a licence, any modification of the conditions of a licence, any acceptance of the surrender of a licence or any transfer of a licence,
makes a statement which he knows to be false or misleading in a material particular, or recklessly makes any statement which is false or misleading in a material particular, commits an offence.
 (2) A person who intentionally makes a false entry in any record required to be kept by virtue of a licence commits an offence.
 (3) A person who commits an offence under this section shall be liable—
 (a) on summary conviction, to a fine not exceeding the statutory maximum;
 (b) on convicted on indictment, to a fine or to imprisonment for a term not exceeding two years, or to both.]

DEFINITION
 "licence": s.35(12).

COMMENCEMENT
April 1, 1996 (S.I. 1996 No. 186).

GENERAL NOTE
The essentials of the offences created by this section are (1) knowingly or recklessly making a materially false or misleading statement in the circumstances identified in subs. (1)(a) and (b), and (2) intentionally making a false entry in a record which a licence condition requires to be kept.
 The section was substituted by Sched. 19, para. (4) to the Environment Act 1995, which also deleted the s.71(3)(b) offence relating to the making of false or misleading statements, now covered by this section. Sched. 19 to the 1995 Act also makes comparable amendments to the Control of Pollution Act 1974 the Water (Scotland) Act 1980, the Control of Pollution (Amendment)Act 1989, the Water Resources Act 1991 and the Radioactive Substances Act 1993.
 The former s.44 (unlike the repealed s.71(3)(b)) covered only false, and not merely misleading statements, and then only if these statements were in an application for the grant, etc., of a licence. The phase "for the purpose of obtaining ... " in subs. (1)(b) is clearly not limited to statements made in the application.
 The offences in this section are relevant offences for the purposes of the "fit and proper person" test which any applicant for a waste management licence must pass: Waste Management Licensing Regulations 1994, reg. 3.

 Material particular: This suggests that the statement must relate to matters which would have the tendency, or natural and probable result, of inducing the authority to act on the faith of it in such a way as might affect the outcome of the decision. It does not appear to be an ingredient of the offence that the authority should *actually* have relied on the statement or that it should *actually* have influenced the decision, if any. In the context of waste licensing this would no doubt involve matters relating to whether the applicant is fit and proper (for example, as to the absence of relevant convictions or as to financial resources) and, in the context of surrender of licences, the condition of the site.

[National waste strategy: England and Wales

44A.—(1) The Secretary of State shall as soon as possible prepare a statement ("the strategy") containing his policies in relation to the recovery and disposal of waste in England and Wales.

(2) The strategy shall consist of or include—

    (a) a statement which relates to the whole of England and Wales; or

    (b) two or more statements which between them relate to the whole of England and Wales.

(3) The Secretary of State may from time to time modify the strategy.

(4) Without prejudice to the generality of what may be included in the strategy, the strategy must include—

    (a) a statement of the Secretary of State's policies for attaining the objectives specified in Schedule 2A to this Act;

    (b) provisions relating to each of the following, that is to say—

        (i) the type, quantity and origin of waste to be recovered or disposed of;

        (ii) general technical requirements; and

        (iii) any special requirements for particular wastes.

(5) In preparing the strategy or any modification of it, the Secretary of State—

    (a) shall consult the Environment Agency,

    (b) shall consult—

        (i) such bodies or persons appearing to him to be representative of the interests of local government, and

        (ii) such bodies or persons appearing to him to be representative of the interests of industry,

    as he may consider appropriate, and

    (c) may consult such other bodies or persons as he considers appropriate.

(6) Without prejudice to any power to give directions conferred by section 40 of the Environment Act 1995, the Secretary of State may give directions to the Environment Agency requiring it—

    (a) to advise him on the policies which are to be included in the strategy;

    (b) to carry out a survey of or investigation into—

        (i) the kinds or quantities of waste which it appears to that Agency is likely to be situated in England and Wales,

        (ii) the facilities which are or appear to that Agency likely to be available or needed in England and Wales for recovering or disposing of any such waste,

        (iii) any other matter upon which the Secretary of State wishes to be informed in connection with his preparation of the strategy or any modification of it,

    and to report its findings to him.

(7) A direction under subsection (6)(b) above—

    (a) shall specify or describe the matters or the areas which are to be the subject of the survey or investigation; and

    (b) may make provision in relation to the manner in which—

        (i) the survey or investigation is to be carried out, or

        (ii) the findings are to be reported or made available to other persons.

(8) Where a direction is given under subsection (6)(b) above, the Environment Agency shall, in accordance with any requirement of the direction—

    (a) before carrying out the survey or investigation, consult—
        (i) such bodies or persons appearing to it to be representative of
            local planning authorities, and
        (ii) such bodies or persons appearing to it to be representative of
            the interests of industry,
        as it may consider appropriate; and
    (b) make its findings available to those authorities.
  (9) In this section—
    "local planning authority" has the same meaning as in the Town and
        Country Planning Act 1990;
    "strategy" includes the strategy as modified from time to time and
        "statement" shall be construed accordingly.
  (10) This section makes provision for the purpose of implementing Article
7 of the directive of the Council of the European Communities, dated 15th
July 1975, on waste, as amended by—
    (a) the directive of that Council, dated 18th March 1991, amending
        directive 75/442/EEC on waste; and
    (b) the directive of that Council, dated 23rd December 1991, stan-
        dardising and rationalising reports on the implementation of
        certain Directives relating to the environment.]

DEFINITIONS
  "disposal": s.29(6).
  "local planning authority": subs. (9); Town and Country Planning Act 1990.
  "statement": subs. (9).
  "strategy": subs. (9).
  "the strategy": subs. (1).
  "waste": s.75(2).

COMMENCEMENT
April 1, 1996 (S.I. 1996 No. 186).

GENERAL NOTE
This section (for England and Wales) and s.44B (for Scotland) were both inserted into the 1990
Act by s.92 of the Environment Act 1995, and provide for the preparation "as soon as possible"
of a national waste strategy and its subsequent modification. It is anticipated that each strategy
will be informed by a survey or investigation by the Environment Agency/SEPA into the
circumstances of waste production and management in their respective areas. A process of
consultation is required in the course of such a survey and in the course of the preparation or
modification of a strategy.
    The strategy for England and Wales is to be prepared by the Secretary of State, with a
significant role in its preparation envisaged for the Environment Agency. The Scottish strategy,
by contrast, is to be prepared by SEPA itself, overseen by the Secretary of State.
    This contrast is considered further below. It accounts for most of the differences in the
wording of the two sections: the content of each is essentially the same, which is unsurprising
since both were inserted in order to implement provisions in Article 7 of Directive 75/442/EEC
(as amended, generally known as the Waste Framework Directive). Accordingly, the discussion
below refers to both sections except where the contrary is indicated.
    Despite the EC dimension to the provisions, the national waste strategies can be expected to
be wider in scope than that dimension and these provisions would strictly require: see the
discussion below of the draft Waste Strategy for England and Wales.

Policy Background
Sections 44A and 44B can be seen as drawing together five inter-related EC and domestic
developments:

—Article 7
Article 7 of the Waste Framework Directive, the provisions in which relating to the drawing up
of waste management plans are in part to be implemented under ss.44A and 44B.

—Waste disposal plans
The duty of waste regulation authorities to prepare waste disposal plans. This duty was imposed
by s.50 of this Act in order to implement the same provisions in Article 7, through a network of

plans at local level, rather than through national level plans. Section 50 is repealed by the 1995 Act, subject to important transitional provisions at Sched. 23, paras. 16 and 17, which keep s.50 plans in force until they are replaced by a statutory waste strategy under these provisions. This shift in waste disposal strategy to national level thus mirrors the transfer of waste regulation from local to national level effected by Pt. I of the 1995 Act. Operational waste disposal itself, however, remains the responsibility of local waste disposal authorities.

—The Waste Strategy for England and Wales
In December 1995, the DoE and Welsh Office published a non-statutory waste strategy for England and Wales, entitled *Making Waste Work: A Strategy for Sustainable Waste Management in England and Wales* (Cm. 3040, HMSO £16.00). Its significance for the waste strategies to be drawn up under ss.44A and 44B is essentially twofold:
— it is "an advisory and non-statutory document" but it "prepares the way for" the s.44A waste strategy (paras. 183 and 185). Thus its key policy approaches can be expected to feature also in the s.44A strategy;
— it applies only to England and Wales: however, it is likely that the Secretary of State for Scotland will ensure (note s.44B(5)) that SEPA takes a policy approach which is broadly in line with that taken by the Secretary of State in the England and Wales strategy.
The aims of the strategy include to set out the Government's policy framework for waste management, to identify ways in which waste can be managed in a more sustainable way, to set targets for achieving that aim, and to enable industry, regulators and public authorities to plan ahead with a common understanding of the longer term objectives for waste management. It is based on three key objectives:
— to reduce the amount of waste that society produces (waste reduction);
— to make best use of the waste that is produced; and
— to choose waste management practices which minimise the risks of immediate and future environmental pollution and harm to human health.
This is turn leads the Government to adopt a "waste hierarchy" (which it first set out in *Sustainable Development: The UK Strategy* (January 1994)), and an overall policy aim of increasing the proportion of waste managed by the options towards the top of the hierarchy. The hierarchy is (from top down):
— *waste reduction* (giving priority to reducing or eliminating production of hazardous wastes);
— *reuse* (for example, reusing bottles);
— *recovery* (which consists of, from top down, *recycling* (putting materials back into use), *composting* and *energy recovery* (either from incineration or through the burning of methane emitted from landfilled waste)
— *disposal* (landfill or incineration without energy recovery: no benefit obtained from materials in the waste).

The Strategy comprises five complementary strategies for achieving its aims (a "five point plan"): a regulatory strategy, a market based strategy (for example, the landfill tax), a planning (as in land-use planning) strategy, a promotion strategy (promoting both the message of the strategy and good practice by waste producers which favours options such as waste reduction) and an information strategy (to develop sound information on which the strategy itself and individual decisions can be based).
The Strategy broadly endorses the use of targets in policy, and accordingly contains a number of targets which, together with "action points" are summarised in an Annex, and include the stabilisation of household waste production at 1995 levels and the recycling of 25 per cent of household waste by the year 2000.
As regards the wastes to which the draft Strategy applies, they are principally non-radioactive solid wastes and may well be "substances which are not waste at all under the new E.C. definition of waste [now in s.75(2) of this Act]". This latter point is significant since, without it, aspects of the Strategy become impossible to fulfil: in Circular 11/94 the DOE argues that in many cases reuse of an item means that it does not become waste within the EC definition; and it follows that achieving higher rates of reuse, as the Strategy seeks to do, does not achieve higher levels of the reuse of *waste* (as thus defined).

—The draft UK Plan for Imports and Exports of Waste
A draft of a separate United Kingdom waste management plan for imports and exports of waste was published in a separate consultation exercise in June 1994. When finalised it is to have statutory force under the Transfrontier Shipment of Waste Regulations 1994 as a waste management plan for the purposes of Article 7 of the Waste Framework Directive.
The ss.44A and 44B waste strategies will therefore combine with the imports and exports plan

(and with aspects of the land use planning system: see the note to ss.44A(4) and 44(B)(3) below) to implement Article 7. The imports and exports plan, it should be noted, also serves to implement aspects of the 1993 EC Waste Shipments Regulation (EEC) No. 295/93 and 1989 Basel Convention on the Control of Transboundary Movements of Hazardous Wastes and their Disposal.

—the EU Policy for waste
EU policy specifically on waste, on which much EC waste legislation has subsequently been based, is contained in the 1990 Council Resolution on the subject (O.J. C122/2, 18.5.90), although the role of the Community's Action Programmes on the Environment, of which the fifth (O.J. No. C138/1, 17.5.93) runs until the year 2000, and the Commission's Communication on a Community Strategy for Waste Management (SEC (89) 934 final) which led to the 1990 Resolution, should also be noted. The Council Resolution is currently under review, and as the draft Strategy for England and Wales suggests, "Having decided on its overall objectives for waste management policy, the United Kingdom should therefore be in a position to make a positive contribution in the forthcoming discussions about a European Union Waste strategy" para. 1.75).

—ss.44A(1) and 44B(1): Strategy to be prepared
Each strategy governing policies for the disposal and recovery of waste is to be prepared "as soon as possible": this phrase is borrowed from Article 7 of the Waste Framework Directive, which the strategies are to play a part in implementing.

As noted above, the Scottish strategy is to be prepared by SEPA rather than by the Secretary of State as in England and Wales. Rejecting a proposed amendment during the House of Lords debate on the Government Bill, which sought to require the Secretary of State to prepare the strategy in Scotland, the Government gave the explanation that "Unlike the Department of the Environment, the Scottish Office will not have the appropriate staff available to it to prepare a waste strategy for Scotland. SEPA, on the other hand, will be well placed to undertake that task, as it would be staffed in part by those expert staff who previously prepared plans for their local authorities." *Hansard*, H.L., Vol. 561 No. 38, February 9, 1995, col. 347, per the Earl of Lindsay. As regards SEPA, the explanation is, it will be noted, equally applicable to the Agency. The Earl of Lindsay went on to reassure the House of Lords Committee that "the Secretary of State will ultimately remain responsible for waste management policy in Scotland", and that he envisaged "that SEPA will wish to ensure that due regard is paid to the strategy for England and Wales, so that where possible there will be a common framework across Great Britain" (col. 347).

—Disposal and recovery
The strategies relate to the disposal and recovery of waste. As to the three kinds of recovery distinguished by the DOE in its "waste hierarchy", see the discussion of the draft Waste Strategy above. Section 29 provides an inclusive definition of "disposal" for the purposes of this Part of the Act, which definition now by virtue of Schedule 4 to the Waste Management Licensing Regulations 1994, includes reference to the operations listed in Annex II of the Waste Framework Directive.

"Recovery" is not defined. However, it is submitted that, since ss.44A(10) and 44B(9) make express reference to the provisions implementing part of the Waste Framework Directive, "recovery", as well as "disposal" and any other terms used in ss.44A and 44B which are also employed in the Directive, should where the context permits bear the meaning which they have in the Directive. "Recovery" is defined in the Directive by reference to the list of recovery operations set out in its Annex IIB. That list is also to be found at Part IV of Sched. 3 to the Waste Management Licensing Regulations 1994.

—ss.44A(2): Strategy or strategies
The only provision in s.44A with no counterpart in s.44B is subs. (2), which provides for the possibility of separate strategies for geographical areas within England and Wales. Viscount Ullswater explained this in the House of Lords during debate on the Environment Bill as follows:

> "The issues which need to be covered in a waste strategy are generally common to both Wales and England, and our approach to waste management policy in each country is the same. The Government therefore believe that a single waste strategy covering the whole of England and Wales is the most effective means of presenting their policies. However, circumstances may change, and the Bill accordingly makes provision ... for the preparation of separate statements for different areas of England and Wales. If it

appeared appropriate at the time one of those could relate to the whole of Wales"
(*Hansard* H.L., Vol. 561 No. 38, February 9, 1995, col. 339).

—ss.44A(3) and 44B(2): Modifications
Each of the strategies may be modified from time to time. The Government rejected a proposed
amendment to the Environment Bill which would have required their annual review: "The
production of such a strategy is a major undertaking. Annual review would be inappropriate for
many of the targets it will contain, which will need an implementation period of longer than one
year—in some cases considerably longer. Moreover, annual review would sit uncomfortably
with the timescale required for a national waste strategy" (*Hansard*, H.L., Vol. 561 No. 38,
February 9, 1995, Col. 399, per Viscount Ullswater).

—ss.44A(4) and 44B(3): Content of strategies
Each of the strategies may include any policies of the kind specified in each subs. (1), but each of
them must at least contain both (a) a statement of policies to attain specified objectives and (b)
certain specified provisions.

    Schedule 2A: Specified objectives—the objectives to be attained are set out in Sched. 2A,
which the 1995 Act inserted into this Act. All of the objectives are reproduced from the Waste
Framework Directive as follows:
— Para. 1 (avoiding harm to human health or the environment, nuisance and adverse
    effects on conservation interests): most of Article 4;
— Paras. 2 and 3(a) (integrated, BATNEEC network of disposal installations, and EC and
    eventual Member State self-sufficiency in waste disposal): Article 5(1);
— Para. 3(b) (ensuring environmental and health protection through the appropriate
    means of waste disposal in one of the nearest appropriate installations): Article 5(2);
— Para. 4 (encouraging the prevention or reduction of waste production and its
    harmfulness): Article 3(1)(a);
— Para. 5 (encouraging waste recovery and its use as a source of energy): Article 3(1)(b).
It will be noted that the para. 1 (Article 4) objectives are also the "relevant objectives" of the
Agency/SEPA in its waste licensing functions, and of planning authorities in their planning
functions in relation to the recovery and disposal of waste: Waste Management Licensing
Regulations 1994, Sched. 4.

Provisions to be contained in the strategies
The provisions set out in ss.44A(4) (b) (i)–(iii) and 44B (3)(b)(i)–(iii), as required to be
contained in each strategy, are essentially reproduced from Article 7(1) of the Waste
Framework Directive as provisions required to be contained in waste management plans under
that Article. However, Article 7(1) contains a fourth required provision ("suitable disposal sites
or installations") which is not reproduced in ss.44A or 44B, and an amendment was moved in
the House of Lords during the passage of the Environment Bill to rectify this perceived failure
to fully implement the Directive. The Government's response is a useful clarification of the
relationship between the waste strategies and the planning process.
    "... the omission ... is deliberate, and reflects the existing arrangements for
implementing Article 7 ... which will be partly superseded by [what are now ss.44A and
44B].
    At present, Article 7 is implemented jointly by waste disposal plans drawn up by waste
regulation authorities under Section 50 [of this Act], and by development plans drawn up
by local planning authorities. The precise arrangements for implementing the directive
are contained in Schedule 4 to the Waste Management Licensing regulations 1994.
Paragraph 7 specifically requires the waste policies in development plans to include
policies in respect of suitable disposal sites or installations. This is because the siting—and
criteria for siting—new waste facilities is a matter for the planning rather than the waste
regulation authority.
    In drawing up the waste strategy provisions we have been careful to retain this
distinction ... " (*Hansard*, H.L., Vol. 562 No. 54, March 9, 1995, col. 455, per Viscount
Ullswater).

ss.44A (5)–(8) and 44B (4)–(7): Consultation, reports and directions
Each of the Agency and SEPA may be directed to carry out a waste survey or investigation
(ss.44A(6)(b) and 44B(5)(b)). Such surveys and investigations will no doubt play an important
part in the "information strategy" aspect of the "five point plan" referred to above in the
discussion of the draft Waste Strategy for England and Wales.

Each of the sections contains two separate requirements for consultation, which must take place both when the strategy is being drawn up or modified, and before the Agency/SEPA carries out such a survey or investigation.

It will be noted that Secretary of State must consult the Agency in drawing up the strategy for England and Wales: s.44A(5)(a). The difference in terminology employed in s.44B(4)(b), from that employed in ss.44A(5)(b)(i), 44A(8)(a)(ii) and 44B(7)(a)(i) should be noted: it appears to require SEPA, in preparing the Scottish Waste Strategy, to consult directly with the affected local authorities, rather than with a representative body such as the Convention of Scottish Local Authorities (CoSLA) as appears to be envisaged in the other provisions.

It will also be noted that, whilst the provisions for consultation on the strategy itself refer to "local" government or authorities, consultation prior to the carrying out of an investigation or survey is to be with planning authorities. Viscount Ullswater explained to the House of Lords that:

> "The reason for providing a statutory duty to consult planning authorities in relation to a survey is their requirement for data on waste to enable them to draw up their development plan policies for waste. It is essential that the survey is carried out in a way which will enable disaggregation of results to a local level for the same reason it is essential that planning authorities receive the results of a Survey" (*Hansard*, H.L., Vol. 561 No. 38, February 9, 1995, col. 344).

In this regard the reference to directions to the Agency/SEPA making provision regarding the manner in which the findings are reported or made available to other persons is significant (ss.44A(7)(b)(ii) and 44B(6)(b)(ii)). It is clearly appropriate for the Agency and SEPA to have regard to the needs of planning authorities in carrying out their survey or investigation and to provide their findings to such authorities in an appropriate manner.

There was an attempt in the House of Lords to extend the s.44(b)(7)(a)(i) requirement, for consultation prior to SEPA's carrying out a waste survey or investigation, to refer to "local" rather than merely planning authorities. However the Earl of Lindsay responded that, following local government reorganisation in Scotland, all local authorities become planning authorities, and, "although CoSLA would be consulted in its capacity as a representative of planning authorities, there would be nothing to stop it responding for its wider interests [such as] environmental health . . . or its responsibilities for waste disposal" (*Hansard*, H.L., Vol. 561 No. 38, February 9, 1995, col. 349).

ss.44A(9) and 44B(8): Planning Authorities
The Town and Country Planning Act 1990, s.1, defines "local planning authority" as the county and county borough councils in Wales, the metropolitan district council in metropolitan districts, the London borough council in London boroughs and the county and district councils in English non-metropolitan counties. In the House of Lords, Viscount Ullswater noted that "that includes all principal councils in England and Wales, as well as certain other authorities such as the National park authorities and urban development corporations" (*Hansard*, H.L., Vol. 561 No. 38, February 9, 1995, col. 343). As regards Scotland, the Local Government (Scotland) Act 1973, s.172 (as substituted by the Local Government etc. (Scotland) Act 1994, Sched. 13, para. 92(57)) defines "planning authority" as a local authority. This reflects the reorganisation of local government in Scotland as from April 1, 1996 which involves the replacement of the two-tier system of local government which applied in most areas with a single-tier system. The two-tier planning system which operated in most parts of Scotland with responsibility divided between the district and regional councils (with the exception of Highland, Borders, Dumfries and Galloway Regions along with the islands councils areas which acted as general planning authorities) is accordingly replaced by a single-tier system of planning authorities.

ss.44A(10) and 44B(9): Waste Framework Directive
These subsections state the EC provisions which the sections make provision for implementing. It will be noted that the sections themselves do not implement the Directive: they make provision for the production of strategies which will do so. It is perhaps in anticipation of protracted periods during which strategies would be produced across the Community that Article 7, unusually, requires implementation only "as soon as possible", rather than by a specific date. Paras. 16 and 17 of Sched. 23 to the 1995 Act ensure continuity of implementation by providing for s.50 waste disposal plans to remain in force until replaced by a statutory national waste strategy.

[**National Waste Strategy: Scotland**

44B.—(1) SEPA shall as soon as possible prepare a statement ("the strategy") containing its policies in relation to the recovery and disposal of waste in Scotland.

(2) SEPA may from time to time modify the strategy.

(3) Without prejudice to the generality of what may be included in the strategy, the strategy must include—

    (a) a statement of SEPA's policies for attaining the objectives specified in Schedule 2A to this Act;

    (b) provisions relating to each of the following, that is to say—

        (i) the type, quantity and origin of waste to be recovered or disposed of;

        (ii) general technical requirements; and

        (iii) any special requirements for particular wastes.

(4) In preparing the strategy or any modification of it SEPA shall consult—

    (a) such bodies or persons appearing to it to be representative of the interests of industry as it may consider appropriate;

    (b) such local authorities as appear to it to be likely to be affected by the strategy or modification,

and may consult such other bodies or persons as it considers appropriate.

(5) Without prejudice to any power to give directions conferred by section 40 of the Environment Act 1995, the Secretary of State may give directions to SEPA—

    (a) as to the policies which are to be included in the strategy;

    (b) requiring it to carry out a survey or investigation into—

        (i) the kinds or quantities of waste which it appears to it is likely to be situated in Scotland,

        (ii) the facilities which are or appear to it likely to be available or needed in Scotland for recovering or disposing of any such waste,

        (iii) any other matter which the Secretary of State considers appropriate in connection with its preparation of the strategy or any modifications of it.

(6) A direction under subsection (5)(b) above—

    (a) shall specify or describe the matters or the areas which are to be the subject of the survey or investigation; and

    (b) may make provision in relation to the manner in which—

        (i) the survey or investigation is to be carried out, or

        (ii) the findings are to be reported or made available to other persons.

(7) Where a direction is given under subsection (5)(b) above SEPA shall, in accordance with any requirement of the direction—

    (a) before carrying out the survey or investigation, consult—

        (i) such bodies or persons appearing to it to be representative of planning authorities, and

        (ii) such bodies or persons appearing to it to be representative of the interests of industry,

        as it may consider appropriate; and

    (b) make its findings available to those authorities.

(8) In this section—

"planning authority" means an authority within the meaning of section 172 of the Local Government (Scotland) Act 1973;

"strategy" includes the strategy as modified from time to time and "statement" shall be construed accordingly.

(9) This section makes provision for the purpose of implementing Article 7 of the directive of the Council of the European Communities dated 15th July 1975 on waste, as amended by—
  (a) the directive of that Council dated 18th March 1991 amending directive 75/442/EEC on waste; and
  (b) the directive of that Council dated 23rd December 1991 standardising and rationalising reports on the implementation of certain Directives relating to the environment."]

DEFINITIONS
  "disposal": s.29(6).
  "planning authority": subs. (8).
  "statement": subs. (8).
  "strategy": subs. (8).
  "the strategy": subs. (1).
  "waste": s.75(2).

COMMENCEMENT
April 1, 1996 (S.I. 1996 No. 186).

GENERAL NOTE
This and the preceding section 44A were inserted into the 1990 Act by s.92 of the Environment Act 1995, subs. (2) of which inserted Sched. 2A into the 1990 Act.
  This section provides for the preparation of a national waste strategy for Scotland, and with the notable difference that it requires SEPA rather than the Secretary of State to prepare the strategy, it closely parallels s.44A. See the general note to that section for a discussion of the two sections.

Collection, disposal or treatment of controlled waste

Collection of controlled waste
  45.—(1) It shall be the duty of each waste collection authority—
  (a) to arrange for the collection of household waste in its area except waste—
    (i) which is situated at a place which in the opinion of the authority is so isolated or inaccessible that the cost of collecting it would be unreasonably high, and
    (ii) as to which the authority is satisfied that adequate arrangements for its disposal have been or can reasonably be expected to be made by a person who controls the waste; and
  (b) if requested by the occupier of premises in its area to collect any commercial waste from the premises, to arrange for the collection of the waste.
  (2) Each waste collection authority may, if requested by the occupier of premises in its area to collect any industrial waste from the premises, arrange for the collection of the waste; but a collection authority in England and Wales shall not exercise the power except with the consent of the waste disposal authority whose area includes the area of the waste collection authority.
  (3) No charge shall be made for the collection of household waste except in cases prescribed in regulations made by the Secretary of State; and in any of those cases—
  (a) the duty to arrange for the collection of the waste shall not arise until a person who controls the waste requests the authority to collect it; and
  (b) the authority may recover a reasonable charge for the collection of the waste from the person who made the request.
  (4) A person at whose request waste other than household waste is collected under this section shall be liable to pay a reasonable charge for the collection and disposal of the waste to the authority which arranged for its

collection; and it shall be the duty of that authority to recover the charge unless in the case of a charge in respect of commercial waste the authority considers it inappropriate to do so.

(5) It shall be the duty of each waste collection authority—

(a) to make such arrangements for the emptying, without charge, of privies, serving one or more private dwellings in its area as the authority considers appropriate;

(b) if requested by the person who controls a cesspool serving only one or more private dwellings in its area to empty the cesspool, to remove such of the contents of the cesspool as the authority considers appropriate on payment, if the authority so requires, of a reasonable charge.

(6) A waste collection authority may, if requested by the person who controls any other privy or cesspool in its area to empty the privy or cesspool, empty the privy or, as the case may be, remove from the cesspool such of its contents as the authority consider appropriate on payment, if the authority so requires, of a reasonable charge.

(7) A waste collection authority may—

(a) construct, lay and maintain, within or outside its area, pipes and associated works for the purpose of collecting waste;

(b) contribute towards the cost incurred by another person in providing or maintaining pipes or associated works connecting with pipes provided by the authority under paragraph (a) above.

(8) A waste collection authority may contribute towards the cost incurred by another person in providing or maintaining plant or equipment intended to deal with commercial or industrial waste before it is collected under arrangements made by the authority under subsection (1)(b) or (2) above.

(9) Subject to section 48(1) below, anything collected under arrangements made by a waste collection authority under this section shall belong to the authority and may be dealt with accordingly.

(10) In relation to Scotland, sections 2, 3, 4 and 41 of the Sewerage (Scotland) Act 1968 (maintenance of public sewers etc.) shall apply in relation to pipes and associated works provided or to be provided under subsection (7)(a) above as those sections apply in relation to public sewers but as if—

(a) the said section 2 conferred a power and did not impose a duty on a local authority to do the things mentioned in that section;

(b) in the said section 4, the words from "but before any person" to the end were omitted,

and the Pipe-lines Act 1962 shall not apply to pipes and associated works provided or to be provided under the said subsection (7)(a).

(11) In the application of this section to Scotland, subsection (5)(b) and the references to a cesspool occurring in subsection (6) shall be omitted.

(12) In this section "privy" means a latrine which has a moveable receptacle and "cesspool" includes a settlement tank or other tank for the reception or disposal of foul matter from buildings.

DEFINITIONS

"commercial waste": s.75(7).
"household waste": s.75(5).
"industrial waste": s.75(6).
"waste": s.75(2).

COMMENCEMENT

Partially: February 14, 1992 (S.I. 1992 No. 266). Subsections (1) and (3)–(12): April 1, 1992 (S.I. 1992 No. 266). Subsection (2) (Scotland): April 1, 1992 (S.I. 1992 No. 266).

GENERAL NOTE
This section replaces s.12 of the 1974 Act which was implemented in England and Wales by the Collection and Disposal of Waste Regulations 1988 (S.I. 1988 No. 819), and which in turn replaced ss.77–74 of the Public Health Act 1936.

Collection of household waste: subs. (3)
No charge may be made for collection except in prescribed cases. The cases were prescribed by the Controlled Waste Regulations 1992 (S.I. 1992 No. 588), reg. 4 and Sched. 2; see also DoE Circ. 14/92, Annex 1, paras. 1.23–1.46.

Subs. (9)
Title to waste: It is expressly provided that waste or anything else collected by the waste collection authority under s. 45 belongs to the authority, *not* to the employees or agents of the authority.

Receptacles for household waste

46.—(1) Where a waste collection authority has a duty by virtue of section 45(1)(a) above to arrange for the collection of household waste from any premises, the authority may, by notice served on him, require the occupier to place the waste for collection in receptacles of a kind and number specified.

(2) The kind and number of the receptacles required under subsection (1) above to be used shall be such only as are reasonable but, subject to that, separate receptacles or compartments of receptacles may be required to be used for waste which is to be recycled and waste which is not.

(3) In making requirements under subsection (1) above the authority may, as respects the provision of the receptacles—
 (a) determine that they be provided by the authority free of charge;
 (b) propose that they be provided, if the occupier agrees, by the authority on payment by him of such a single payment or such periodical payments as he agrees with the authority;
 (c) require the occupier to provide them if he does not enter into an agreement under paragraph (b) above within a specified period; or
 (d) require the occupier to provide them.

(4) In making requirements as respects receptacles under subsection (1) above, the authority may, by the notice under that subsection, make provision with respect to—
 (a) the size, construction and maintenance of the receptacles;
 (b) the placing of the receptacles for the purpose of facilitating the emptying of them, and access to the receptacles for that purpose;
 (c) the placing of the receptacles for that purpose on highways or, in Scotland, roads;
 (d) the substances or articles which may or may not be put into the receptacles or compartments of receptacles of any description and the precautions to be taken where particular substances or articles are put into them; and
 (e) the steps to be taken by occupiers of premises to facilitate the collection of waste from the receptacles.

(5) No requirement shall be made under subsection (1) above for receptacles to be placed on a highway or, as the case may be, road, unless—
 (a) the relevant highway authority or roads authority have given their consent to their being so placed; and
 (b) arrangements have been made as to the liability for any damage arising out of their being so placed.

(6) A person who fails, without reasonable excuse, to comply with any requirements imposed under subsection (1), (3)(c) or (d) or (4) above shall be liable on summary conviction to a fine not exceeding level 3 on the standard scale.

(7) Where an occupier is required under subsection (1) above to provide any receptacles he may, within the period allowed by subsection (8) below,

appeal to a magistrates' court or, in Scotland, to the sheriff by way of summary application against any requirement imposed under subsection (1), subsection (3)(c) or (d) or (4) above on the ground that—

(a) the requirement is unreasonable; or

(b) the receptacles in which household waste is placed for collection from the premises are adequate.

(8) The period allowed to the occupier of premises for appealing against such a requirement is the period of 21 days beginning—

(a) in a case where a period was specified under subsection (3)(c) above, with the end of that period; and

(b) where no period was specified, with the day on which the notice making the requirement was served on him.

(9) Where an appeal against a requirement is brought under subsection (7) above—

(a) the requirement shall be of no effect pending the determination of the appeal;

(b) the court shall either quash or modify the requirement or dismiss the appeal; and

(c) no question as to whether the requirement is, in any respect, unreasonable shall be entertained in any proceedings for an offence under subsection (6) above.

(10) In this section—

"receptacle" includes a holder for receptacles; and

"specified" means specified in a notice under subsection (1) above.

DEFINITION
"household waste": s.75(5).

COMMENCEMENT
April 1, 1992 (S.I. 1992 No. 266).

GENERAL NOTE
This section gives waste collection authorities the power to specify collection arrangements for household waste and the nature of the receptacles to be used in collection. The three options available under subs. (3) are: (a) provision of receptacles by the authority free of charge; (b) provision by the authority on payment by the occupier; and (c) provision by the occupier. Where the occupier is required to provide receptacles, he may appeal under subs. (7) to a magistrates' court (or, in Scotland, the Sheriff) on the ground that either: (a) the requirement is unreasonable; or (b) the receptacles already used are adequate. If an appeal is made, the first argument cannot subsequently be raised as a defence in criminal proceedings for failure to comply with the requirements (subs. (9)(c)).

Subs. (5)
Placing of receptacles on highways or roads: If a receptacle is placed on a highway or road otherwise than in accordance with arrangements made under this subsection, an unlawful obstruction will result: see *Wandsworth Corporation v. Baines* [1906] 1 K.B. 470.

Receptacles for commercial or industrial waste

47.—(1) A waste collection authority may, at the request of any person, supply him with receptacles for commercial or industrial waste which he has requested the authority to arrange to collect and shall make a reasonable charge for any receptacle supplied unless in the case of a receptacle for commercial waste the authority considers it appropriate not to make a charge.

(2) If it appears to a waste collection authority that there is likely to be situated, on any premises in its area, commercial waste or industrial waste of a kind which, if the waste is not stored in receptacles of a particular kind, is likely to cause a nuisance or to be detrimental to the amenities of the locality,

the authority may, by notice served on him, require the occupier of the premises to provide at the premises receptacles for the storage of such waste of a kind and number specified.

(3) The kind and number of the receptacles required under subsection (2) above to be used shall be such only as are reasonable.

(4) In making requirements as respects receptacles under subsection (2) above, the authority may, by the notice under that subsection, make provision with respect to—

(a) the size, construction and maintenance of the receptacles;

(b) the placing of the receptacles for the purpose of facilitating the emptying of them, and access to the receptacles for that purpose;

(c) the placing of the receptacles for that purpose on highways or, in Scotland, roads;

(d) the substances or articles which may or may not be put into the receptacles and the precautions to be taken where particular substances or articles are put into them; and

(e) the steps to be taken by occupiers of premises to facilitate the collection of waste from the receptacles.

(5) No requirement shall be made under subsection (2) above for receptacles to be placed on a highway or, as the case may be, road unless—

(a) the relevant highway authority or roads authority have given their consent to their being so placed; and

(b) arrangements have been made as to the liability for any damage arising out of their being so placed.

(6) A person who fails, without reasonable excuse, to comply with any requirements imposed under subsection (2) or (4) above shall be liable on summary conviction to a fine not exceeding level 3 on the standard scale.

(7) Where an occupier is required under subsection (2) above to provide any receptacles he may, within the period allowed by subsection (8) below, appeal to a magistrates' court or, in Scotland, to the sheriff by way of summary application against any requirement imposed under subsection (2) or (4) above on the ground that—

(a) the requirement is unreasonable; or

(b) the waste is not likely to cause a nuisance or be detrimental to the amenities of the locality.

(8) The period allowed to the occupier of premises for appealing against such a requirement is the period of 21 days beginning with the day on which the notice making the requirement was served on him.

(9) Where an appeal against a requirement is brought under subsection (7) above—

(a) the requirement shall be of no effect pending the determination of the appeal;

(b) the court shall either quash or modify the requirement or dismiss the appeal; and

(c) no question as to whether the requirement is, in any respect, unreasonable shall be entertained in any proceedings for an offence under subsection (6) above.

(10) In this section—

"receptacle" includes a holder for receptacles; and

"specified" means specified in a notice under subsection (2) above.

DEFINITIONS

"commercial waste": s.75(7).

"industrial waste": s.75(6).

"waste": s.75(2).

COMMENCEMENT

April 1, 1992 (S.I. 1992 No. 266), except subs. (7) which is not yet in force.

GENERAL NOTE
The subs. (6) offence is a relevant offence for the purposes of the "fit and proper person" test which any applicant for a waste management licence must pass: Waste Management Licensing Regulations 1994, reg. 3.

Duties of waste collection authorities as respects disposal of waste collected

48.—(1) Subject to subsections (2) and (6) below, it shall be the duty of each waste collection authority to deliver for disposal all waste which is collected by the authority under section 45 above to such places as the waste disposal authority for its area directs.

(2) The duty imposed on a waste collection authority by subsection (1) above does not, except in cases falling within subsection (4) below, apply as respects household waste or commercial waste for which the authority decides to make arrangements for recycling the waste; and the authority shall have regard, in deciding what recycling arrangements to make, to its waste recycling plan under section 49 below.

(3) A waste collection authority which decides to make arrangements under subsection (2) above for recycling waste collected by it shall, as soon as reasonably practicable, by notice in writing, inform the waste disposal authority for the area which includes its area of the arrangements which it proposes to make.

(4) Where a waste disposal authority has made with a waste disposal contractor arrangements, as respects household waste or commercial waste in its area or any part of its area, for the contractor to recycle the waste, or any of it, the waste disposal authority may, by notice served on the waste collection authority, object to the waste collection authority having the waste recycled; and the objection may be made as respects all the waste, part only of the waste or specified descriptions of the waste.

(5) Where an objection is made under subsection (4) above, subsection (2) above shall not be available to the waste collection authority to the extent objected to.

(6) A waste collection authority may, subject to subsection (7) below, provide plant and equipment for the sorting and baling of waste retained by the authority under subsection (2) above.

(7) Subsection (6) above does not apply to an authority which is also a waste disposal authority; but, in such a case, the authority may make arrangements with a waste disposal contractor for the contractor to deal with the waste as mentioned in that subsection.

(8) A waste collection authority may permit another person to use facilities provided by the authority under subsection (6) above and may provide for the use of another person any such facilities as the authority has power to provide under that subsection; and—

    (a) subject to paragraph (b) below, it shall be the duty of the authority to make a reasonable charge in respect of the use by another person of the facilities, unless the authority considers it appropriate not to make a charge;

    (b) no charge shall be made under this subsection in respect of household waste; and

    (c) anything delivered to the authority by another person in the course of using the facilities shall belong to the authority and may be dealt with accordingly.

(9) This section shall not apply in Scotland.

DEFINITIONS
"commercial waste": s.75(7).
"household waste": s.75(5).
"waste": s.75(2).
"waste disposal contractor": s.30(5).

COMMENCEMENT
April 1, 1992 (S.I. 1992 No. 266).

GENERAL NOTE
The general duty on waste collection authorities by subs. (1) to deliver all waste collected to such places as the waste disposal authority directs for disposal is qualified by subs. (2) so as to allow collection authorities to retain household or commercial waste (but not industrial waste) for recycling. Collection authorities (but not disposal authorities) are given express powers (subs. (6)) to provide plant or equipment for the sorting and baling of waste retained for recycling. Where there is a single collection and disposal authority therefore, as in some metropolitan areas and in Wales, the authority may need instead to make use of its powers as a disposal authority to make arrangements with a disposal contractor to carry out the sorting and baling. The section does not prevent, in the Government's view, disposal authorities from providing receptacles for the collection of waste for recycling, such as bottle banks: *Hansard*, H.L. Vol. 522, col. 1274.

It should be noted that this section does not apply to Scotland and that the comparable Scottish provisions are contained in s.53.

Waste recycling plans by collection authorities

49.—(1) It shall be the duty of each waste collection authority, as respects household and commercial waste arising in its area—
(a) to carry out an investigation with a view to deciding what arrangements are appropriate for dealing with the waste by separating, baling or otherwise packaging it for the purpose of recycling it;
(b) to decide what arrangements are in the opinion of the authority needed for that purpose;
(c) to prepare a statement ("the plan") of the arrangements made and proposed to be made by the authority and other persons for dealing with waste in those ways;
(d) to carry out from time to time further investigations with a view to deciding what changes in the plan are needed; and
(e) to make any modification of the plan which the authority thinks appropriate in consequence of any such further investigation.

(2) In considering any arrangements or modification for the purposes of subsection (1)(c) or (e) above it shall be the duty of the authority to have regard to the effect which the arrangements or modification would be likely to have on the amenities of any locality and the likely cost or saving to the authority attributable to the arrangements or modification.

(3) It shall be the duty of a waste collection authority to include in the plan information as to—
(a) the kinds and quantities of controlled waste which the authority expects to collect during the period specified in the plan;
(b) the kinds and quantities of controlled waste which the authority expects to purchase during that period;
(c) the kinds and quantities of controlled waste which the authority expects to deal with in the ways specified in subsection (1)(a) above during that period;
(d) the arrangements which the authority expects to make during that period with waste disposal contractors or, in Scotland, waste disposal authorities and waste disposal contractors for them to deal with waste in those ways;
(e) the plant and equipment which the authority expects to provide under section 48(6) above or 53 below; and
(f) the estimated costs or savings attributable to the methods of dealing with the waste in the ways provided for in the plan.

(4) It shall be the duty of a waste collection authority, before finally

determining the content of the plan or a modification, to send a copy of it in draft to the Secretary of State for the purpose of enabling him to determine whether subsection (3) above has been complied with; and, if the Secretary of State gives any directions to the authority for securing compliance with that subsection, it shall be the duty imposed by this section specified in the direction; and it shall be the duty of the authority to comply with the direction.

(5) When a waste collection authority has determined the content of the plan or a modification it shall be the duty of the authority—

  (a) to take such steps as in the opinion of the authority will give adequate publicity in its area to the plan or modification; and

  (b) to send to the waste disposal authority and waste regulation authority for the area which includes its area a copy of the plan or, as the case may be, particulars of the modification.

(6) It shall be the duty of each waste collection authority to keep a copy of the plan and particulars of any modifications to it available at all reasonable times at its principal offices for inspection by members of the public free of charge and to supply a copy of the plan and of the particulars of any modifications to it to any person who requests one, on payment by that person of such reasonable charge as the authority requires.

(7) The Secretary of State may give to any waste collection authority directions as to the time by which the authority is to perform any duty of the authority to comply with the direction.

DEFINITIONS
  "commercial waste": s.75(7).
  "controlled waste": s.75(4).
  "household waste": s.75(5).
  "waste": s.75(2).
  "waste disposal contractors": s.30(5).

COMMENCEMENT
August 1, 1991 (S.I. 1991 No. 1577).

GENERAL NOTE
This section introduces new duties as to planning for waste recycling. Waste recycling plans do not require the approval of the Secretary of State before adoption, but under subs. (4) must be submitted in draft to the Secretary of State, who may give directions to ensure compliance with the statutory requirements as to the content of plans.

Waste disposal plans of waste regulation authorities

50. [...]

[Section 50, which required the preparation of waste disposal plans by waste regulation authorities, was repealed by the Environment Act 1995, Sched. 22, para. 78. See ss.44A and 44B dealing with national waste strategy, and Sched. 23, paras. 16 and 17 to the 1995 Act which provide for plans made under s.50 which existed at the date on which waste regulation was transferred to the Agency/SEPA to remain in force until the national strategy is determined.

Offshore waste management plans
A new duty to prepare offshore waste management plans setting out policies relating to the disposal or recovery of waste below the low water mark is imposed on the Ministry of Agriculture Fisheries and Food by Sched. 4, para. 5 of the Waste Management Licensing Regulations 1994. These plans are explained in Annex 3 to Circular 11/94.]

Functions of waste disposal authorities

51.—(1) It shall be the duty of each waste disposal authority to arrange—

  (a) for the disposal of the controlled waste collected in its area by the waste collection authorities; and

(b) for places to be provided at which persons resident in its area may deposit their household waste and for the disposal of waste so deposited;

in either case by means of arrangements made (in accordance with Part II of Schedule 2 to this Act) with waste disposal contractors, but by no other means.

(2) The arrangements made by a waste disposal authority under subsection (1)(b) above shall be such as to secure that—

    (a) each place is situated either within the area of the authority or so as to be reasonably accessible to persons resident in its area;

    (b) each place is available for the deposit of waste at all reasonable times (including at least one period on the Saturday or following day of each week except a week in which the Saturday is December 25 or January 1);

    (c) each place is available for the deposit of waste free of charge by persons resident in the area;

but the arrangements may restrict the availability of specified places to specified descriptions of waste.

(3) A waste disposal authority may include in arrangements made under subsection (1)(b) above arrangements for the places provided for its area for the deposit of household waste free of charge by residents in its area to be available for the deposit of household or other controlled waste by other persons on such terms as to payment (if any) as the authority determines.

(4) For the purpose of discharging its duty under subsection (1)(a) above as respects controlled waste collected as mentioned in that paragraph a waste disposal authority—

    (a) shall give directions to the waste collection authorities within its area as to the persons to whom and places at which such waste is to be delivered;

    (b) may arrange for the provision, within or outside its area, by waste disposal contractors of places at which such waste may be treated or kept prior to its removal for treatment or disposal;

    (c) may make available to waste disposal contractors (and accordingly own) plant and equipment for the purpose of enabling them to keep such waste prior to its removal for disposal or to treat such waste in connection with so keeping it or for the purpose of facilitating its transportation;

    (d) may make available to waste disposal contractors (and accordingly hold) land for the purpose of enabling them to treat, keep or dispose of such waste in or on the land;

    (e) may contribute towards the cost incurred by persons who produce commercial or industrial waste in providing and maintaining plant or equipment intended to deal with such waste before it is collected; and

    (f) may contribute towards the cost incurred by persons who produce commercial or industrial waste in providing or maintaining pipes or associated works connecting with pipes provided by a waste collection authority within the area of the waste disposal authority.

(5) For the purpose of discharging its duties under subsection (1)(b) above as respects household waste deposited as mentioned in that paragraph a waste disposal authority—

    (a) may arrange for the provision, within or outside its area, by waste disposal contractors of places at which such waste may be treated or kept prior to its removal for treatment or disposal;

    (b) may make available to waste disposal contractors (and accordingly own) plant and equipment for the purpose of enabling them to keep such waste prior to its removal for disposal or to treat such waste in connection with so keeping it or for the purpose of facilitating its transportation; and

(c) may make available to waste disposal contractors (and accordingly hold) land for the purpose of enabling them to treat, keep or dispose of such waste in or on the land.

(6) Where the arrangements made under subsection (1)(b) include such arrangements as are authorised by subsection (3) above, subsection (5) above applies as respects household or other controlled waste as it applies as respects household waste.

(7) Subsection (1) above is subject to section 77.

(8) This section shall not apply to Scotland.

DEFINITIONS
"commercial waste": s.75(7).
"controlled waste": s.75(4).
"disposal": s.29(6).
"household waste": s.75(5).
"industrial waste": s.75(6).
"treatment": s.29(6).
"waste": s.75(2).
"waste disposal contractors": s.30(5).

COMMENCEMENT
May 31, 1991 (S.I. 1991 No. 1319).

GENERAL NOTE
This section imposes two main duties on waste disposal authorities: (a) to arrange for the disposal of controlled waste collected within their areas; and (b) to arrange for the provision of places at which residents may deposit their household waste free of charge.

Such duties may only be discharged through arrangements made with waste disposal contractors, but waste disposal authorities may hold land and own plant or equipment to be made available to waste disposal contractors in relation to those functions (subss. (4)(c) and (d) and (5)(b) and (c)). See also the note to s.32 and para. D7 of Annex D to Circ. 8/91, entitled "Competition for Local Authority Waste Disposal Contracts and New Arrangements for Disposal Operations." The equivalent Scottish provision is s.53.

Payments for recycling and disposal etc. of waste

52.—(1) Where, under section 48(2) above, a waste collection authority retains for recycling waste collected by it under section 45 above, the waste disposal authority for the area which includes the area of the waste collection authority shall make to that authority payments, in respect of the waste so retained, of such amounts representing its net saving of expenditure on the disposal of the waste as the authority determines.

(2) Where, by reason of the discharge by a waste disposal authority of its functions, waste arising in its area does not fall to be collected by a waste collection authority under section 45 above, the waste collection authority shall make to the waste disposal authority payments, in respect of the waste not falling to be so collected, of such amounts representing its net saving of expenditure on the collection of the waste as the authority determines.

(3) Where a person other than a waste collection authority, for the purpose of recycling it, collects waste arising in the area of a waste disposal authority which would fall to be collected under section 45 above, the waste disposal authority may make to that person payments, in respect of the waste so collected, of such amounts representing its net saving of expenditure on the disposal of the waste as the authority determines.

(4) Where a person other than a waste collection authority, for the purpose of recycling it, collects waste which would fall to be collected under section 45 above, the waste collection authority may make to that person payments, in respect of the waste so collected, of such amounts representing

its net saving of expenditure on the collection of the waste as the authority determines.

(5) The Secretary of State may, by regulations, impose on waste disposal authorities a duty to make payments corresponding to the payments which are authorised by subsection (3) above to such persons in such circumstances and in respect of such descriptions or quantities of waste as are specified in the regulations.

(6) For the purposes of subsections (1), (3) and (5) above the net saving of expenditure of a waste disposal authority on the disposal of any waste retained or collected for recycling is the amount of the expenditure which the authority would, but for the retention or collection, have incurred in having it disposed of less any amount payable by the authority to any person in consequence of the retention or collection for recycling (instead of the disposal) of the waste.

(7) For the purposes of subsections (2) and (4) above the net saving of expenditure of a waste collection authority on the collection of any waste not falling to be collected by it is the amount of the expenditure which the authority would, if it had had to collect the waste, have incurred in collecting it.

(8) The Secretary of State shall, by regulations, make provision for the determination of the net saving of expenditure for the purposes of subsections (1), (2), (3), (4) and (5) above.

(9) A waste disposal authority shall be entitled to receive from a waste collection authority such sums as are needed to reimburse the waste disposal authority the reasonable cost of making arrangements under section 51(1) above for the disposal of commercial and industrial waste collected in the area of the waste disposal authority.

(10) A waste disposal authority shall pay to a waste collection authority a reasonable contribution towards expenditure reasonably incurred by the waste collection authority in delivering waste, in pursuance of a direction under section 51(4)(a) above, to a place which is unreasonably far from the waste collection authority's area.

(11) Any question arising under subsection (9) or (10) above shall, in default of agreement between the two authorities in question, be determined by arbitration.

DEFINITIONS
"disposal": s.29(6).
"waste": s.75(2).

COMMENCEMENT
Subsections (1), (3)–(7), (9)–(11): April 1, 1992 (S.I. 1992 No. 266). Subsection (8) (partially): December 13, 1991 (S.I. 1991 No. 2829).

GENERAL NOTE
This section makes provision for various financial adjustments in relation to the collection, recycling and disposal of waste (sometimes loosely referred to as "waste recycling credits").

The most significant payments contemplated by the section relate to recycling and are as follows:

    (1) waste disposal authorities must pay to waste collection authorities who retain waste for recycling a sum representing their "net saving of expenditure on the disposal of the waste" (subs. (1));

    (2) where a waste disposal authority so discharges its functions that waste does not fall to be collected by the collection authority, the collection authority must pay to the disposal authority a sum representing "its net saving of expenditure on the collection of the waste" (subs. (2));

    (3) where some other person collects waste for recycling which would otherwise fall to be collected, the waste disposal authority *may* make payments representing the net saving of expenditure on disposal and the collection authority *may* make payments representing the net saving of expenditure on collection (subss. (3) and (4)).

The reasoning behind the decision to make payments falling into category (3) above voluntary rather than compulsory, initially at least, was explained by Baroness Blatch as follows:

"We do not believe that there is yet a need for the Secretary of State to make use of this power. It follows that we do not think it timely to place a duty on disposal authorities to pay credits to third parties.

It may take some time for local authorities to identify all those third parties in their area who have a claim to receive recycling credits. When they have identified all those bodies undertaking recycling in their area, they may decide that it would not be desirable for credits to be paid in every case. There may be instances where economies of scale make it more appropriate for the waste collection authority to undertake recycling rather than it being done by voluntary bodies. There may be other cases where a number of different bodies are undertaking similar schemes in the same area. It would not necessarily be appropriate for an authority to be required to pay recycling credits to a number of competing schemes in the same area, particularly where some of the schemes yielded only small quantities of waste. Giving disposal authorities discretion to pay credits will allow them to make sensible judgments about the type of third party recycling scheme which should be encouraged in their area." (*Hansard*, H.L. Vol. 522, col. 363.)

Net Saving of Expenditure
Provision as to the determination of net saving of expenditure for the purposes of subss. (1) and (3) is made by the Environmental Protection (Waste Recycling Payments) Regulations 1992 (S.I. 1992 No. 462) as amended by S.I. 1993 No. 445, S.I. 1994 No. 522 and S.I. 1995 No. 476. Net saving is defined as an amount equal to the expenditure which the authority would have incurred in disposing of the waste at a cost per tonne equal to its average cost per tonne at the relevant time of disposing of similar waste using its most expensive disposal method for waste collected in the relevant area.

Various factors are to be taken into account in determining the average cost of disposing of similar waste (reg. 2(3)). These are: market value of assets, including land; expenditure in operating sites or transfer stations; transport costs; site closure and post-closure expenditure; and any other expenditure. If it is impossible to determine the net saving because accurate information is not available or could only be obtained at disproportionate cost, net saving is to be determined by reference to the figures at the Schedule to the Regulations (reg. 2(5))—ranging from £34·52 per tonne for inner London Boroughs to £16·74 for shire counties with no transport costs.

Guidance
Circular 4/92 (Welsh Office 10/92) *Environmental Protection Act 1990. The Environmental Protection (Waste Recycling Payments) Regulations* provides guidance on the statutory provisions and regulations, including eligibility for credits, calculation of credit values, and arrangements to prevent error or fraud.

Duties of authorities as respects disposal of waste collected: Scotland

53.—(1) It shall be the duty of each waste disposal authority to arrange for the disposal of any waste collected by it, in its capacity as a waste collection authority, under section 45 above; and without prejudice to the authority's powers apart from the following provisions of this subsection, the powers exercisable by the authority for the purpose of performing that duty shall include power—

(a) to provide, within or outside its area, places at which to deposit waste before the authority transfers it to a place or plant or equipment provided under the following paragraph; and

(b) to provide, within or outside its area, places at which to dispose of or recycle the waste and plant or equipment for processing, recycling or otherwise disposing of it.

(2) Subsections (7) and (10) of section 45 above shall have effect in relation to a waste disposal authority as if the reference in paragraph (a) of the said subsection (7) to the collection of waste included the disposal of waste in pursuance of this section and the disposal of anything produced from waste belonging to the authority.

(3) A waste disposal authority may permit another person to use facilities provided by the authority under the preceding provisions of this section and may provide for the use of another person any such facilities as the authority has power to provide under those provisions, and—
  (a) subject to the following paragraph, it shall be the duty of the authority to make a reasonable charge in respect of the use by another person of the facilities unless the authority considers it appropriate not to make a charge;
  (b) no charge shall be made under this section in respect of household waste; and
  (c) anything delivered to the authority by another person in the course of using the facilities shall belong to the authority and may be dealt with accordingly.

(4) References to waste in subsection (1) above do not include matter removed from privies under section 45(5)(a) or (6) above, and it shall be the duty of a waste collection authority [...] by which matter is so removed—
  (a) to deliver the matter, in accordance with any directions of the [sewerage authority], at a place specified in the directions (which must be in or within a reasonable distance from the waste collection authority's area), to the [sewerage authority] or another person so specified;
  (b) to give to the [sewerage authority] from time to time a notice stating the quantity of the matter which the waste collection authority expects to deliver to or as directed by the [sewerage authority] under the preceding paragraph during a period specified in the notice.

(5) Any question arising under paragraph (a) of the preceding subsection as to whether a place is within a reasonable distance from a waste collection authority's area shall, in default of agreement between the waste collection authority and the [sewerage authority] in question, be determined by a single arbiter appointed, in default of agreement between the parties concerned, by the Secretary of State on the application of any of the parties; and anything delivered to a [sewerage authority] under that subsection shall belong to the [sewerage authority] and may be dealt with accordingly.

[(5A) In this section "sewerage authority" shall be construed in accordance with section 62 of the Local Government *etc.* (Scotland) Act 1994.]

(6) This section applies to Scotland only.

DEFINITIONS
  "disposal": s.29(6).
  "household waste": s.75(4).
  "privies": s.45(12).
  "waste": s.75(2).

AMENDMENTS
Subss. (4) and (5) were amended by, and subs. (5A) was inserted by, the Local Government etc. (Scotland) Act 1994, Sched. 13, para. 167(8).

COMMENCEMENT
April 1, 1992 (S.I. 1992 No. 266).

GENERAL NOTE
This section applies only to Scotland and specifies the duties of waste disposal authorities with regard to disposal of waste collected by them in their capacity as waste collection authorities. Separate arrangements apply (subss. (4) and (5)) to matter removed from privies (but not cesspools).

Special provisions for land occupied by disposal authorities: Scotland

54.—[...]

[Section 54, which made special provision for land occupied by disposal authorities in

Scotland, was repealed by the Environment Act 1995, Sched. 24 (although by what appears to be an oversight in the drafting of Sched. 22 to the 1995 Act, no parallel provision indicates that s.54 ceases to have effect). Transitional provisions in Sched. 23, para. 18 to the 1995 Act provide that resolutions under s.54 which were in force at the date of the transfer of waste regulation to SEPA continue in force for 6 months if no application is made for a waste management licence, or until such an application, were made, is withdrawn or determined. In relation to such continuing resolutions, s.54 continues to apply but as amended by Sched. 23, para. 18.]

Powers for recycling waste

55.—(1) This section has effect for conferring on waste disposal authorities and waste collection authorities powers of recycling waste.

(2) A waste disposal authority may—

(a) make arrangements with waste disposal contractors for them to recycle waste as respects which the authority has duties under section 51(1) above or agrees with another person for its disposal or treatment;

(b) make arrangements with waste disposal contractors for them to use waste for the purpose of producing from it heat or electricity or both;

(c) buy or otherwise acquire waste with a view to its being recycled;

(d) use, sell or otherwise dispose of waste as respects which the authority has duties under section 51(1) above or anything produced from such waste.

(3) A waste collection authority may—

(a) buy or otherwise acquire waste with a view to recycling it;

(b) use, or dispose of by way of sale or otherwise to another person, waste belonging to the authority or anything produced from such waste.

(4) This section shall not apply to Scotland.

DEFINITIONS
"disposal": s.29(6).
"treatment": s.29(6).
"waste": s.75(2).
"waste disposal contractors": s.30(5).

COMMENCEMENT
April 1, 1992 (S.I. 1992 No. 266).

GENERAL NOTE
This section contains express powers connected with the recycling of waste. Both disposal and collection authorities are given powers, which are in some respects different. Disposal authorities are given power to use, sell or otherwise dispose of waste collected in their area (subs. (2)(d)). Collection authorities have, by subs (3)(b), similar powers in respect of waste belonging to them (as to which, see s.45(9)).

Powers for recycling waste: Scotland

56.—(1) Without prejudice to the powers of waste disposal authorities apart from this section, a waste disposal authority may—

(a) do such things as the authority considers appropriate for the purpose of—

(i) enabling waste belonging to the authority, or belonging to another person who requests the authority to deal with it under this section, to be recycled; or

(ii) enabling waste to be used for the purpose of producing from it heat or electricity or both;

(b) buy or otherwise acquire waste with a view to its being recycled;

(c) use, sell or otherwise dispose of waste belonging to the authority or anything produced from such waste.

(2) This section applies to Scotland only.

DEFINITION
"waste": s.75(2).

COMMENCEMENT
April 1, 1992 (S.I. 1992 No. 266).

GENERAL NOTE
This section provides specific powers to Scottish waste disposal authorities in relation to recycling of waste.

Power of Secretary of State to require waste to be accepted, treated, disposed of or delivered

57.—(1) The Secretary of State may, by notice in writing, direct the holder of any waste management licence to accept and keep, or accept and treat or dispose of, controlled waste at specified places on specified terms.

(2) The Secretary of State may, by notice in writing, direct any person who is keeping controlled waste on any land to deliver the waste to a specified person on specified terms with a view to its being treated or disposed of by that other person.

(3) A direction under this section may impose a requirement as respects waste of any specified kind or as respects any specified consignment of waste.

(4) A direction under subsection (2) above may require the person who is directed to deliver the waste to pay to the specified person his reasonable costs of treating or disposing of the waste.

(5) A person who fails, without reasonable excuse, to comply with a direction under this section shall be liable on summary conviction to a fine not exceeding level 5 on the standard scale.

(6) A person shall not be guilty of an offence under any other enactment prescribed by the Secretary of State by regulations made for the purposes of this subsection by reason only of anything necessarily done or omitted in order to comply with a direction under this section.

(7) The Secretary of State may, where the costs of the treatment or disposal of waste are not paid or not fully paid in pursuance of subsection (4) above to the person treating or disposing of the waste, pay the costs or the unpaid costs, as the case may be, to that person.

(8) In this section "specified" means specified in a direction under this section.

DEFINITIONS
"controlled waste": s.75(4).
"dispose of": s.29(6).
"treat": s.29(6).

COMMENCEMENT
May 1, 1994 (S.I. 1994 No. 1096).

GENERAL NOTE
This is a comprehensive power allowing the Secretary of State to give directions as to the disposition of any specified kind or consignment of controlled waste. The direction can apply to licence-holders requiring them to accept the waste, and to keepers of waste, requiring them to deliver it for treatment or disposal. Failure to comply with a direction is an offence.
    The power is intended to be used only in exceptional circumstances, if at all, as a matter of last resort, where attempts to secure agreement between the relevant parties have failed and where the waste regulation authority has been consulted (*Hansard*, H.L. Vol. 520, col. 1511).
    The subs. (5) offence is a relevant offence for the purposes of the "fit and proper person" test

which any applicant for a waste management licence must pass: Waste Management Licensing Regulations 1994, reg. 3.

Power of Secretary of State to require waste to be accepted, treated, disposed of or delivered: Scotland

58. In relation to Scotland, the Secretary of State may give directions to a waste disposal authority to accept and keep, or accept and treat or dispose of, controlled waste at specified places on specified terms; and it shall be the duty of the authority to give effect to the directions.

DEFINITIONS
"controlled waste": s.75(4).
"dispose of": s.29(6).
"treat": s.29(6).

COMMENCEMENT
May 1, 1994 (S.I. 1994 No. 1096).

GENERAL NOTE
This section applies to Scotland in addition to s.57, allowing direction to be given to waste disposal authorities, requiring them to accept waste.

Powers to require removal of waste unlawfully deposited

59.—(1) If any controlled waste is deposited in or on any land in the area of a waste regulation authority or waste collection authority in contravention of section 33(1) above, the authority may, by notice served on him, require the occupier to do either or both of the following, that is—

(a) to remove the waste from the land within a specified period not less than a period of 21 days beginning with the service of the notice;

(b) to take within such a period specified steps with a view to eliminating or reducing the consequences of the deposit of the waste.

(2) A person on whom any requirements are imposed under subsection (1) above may, within the period of 21 days mentioned in that subsection, appeal against the requirement to a magistrates' court or, in Scotland, to the sheriff by way of summary application.

(3) On any appeal under subsection (2) above the court shall quash the requirement if it is satisfied that—

(a) the appellant neither deposited nor knowingly caused nor knowingly permitted the deposit of the waste; or

(b) there is a material defect in the notice;

and in any other case shall either modify the requirement or dismiss the appeal.

(4) Where a person appeals against any requirement imposed under subsection (1) above, the requirement shall be of no effect pending the determination of the appeal; and where the court modifies the requirement or dismisses the appeal it may extend the period specified in the notice.

(5) If a person on whom a requirement imposed under subsection (1) above fails, without reasonable excuse, to comply with the requirement he shall be liable, on summary conviction, to a fine not exceeding level 5 on the standard scale and to a further fine of an amount equal to one-tenth of level 5 on the standard scale for each day on which the failure continues after conviction of the offence and before the authority has begun to exercise its powers under subsection (6) below.

(6) Where a person on whom a requirement has been imposed under subsection (1) above by an authority fails to comply with the requirement the authority may do what that person was required to do and may recover from him any expenses reasonably incurred by the authority in doing it.

(7) If it appears to a waste regulation authority or waste collection

authority that waste has been deposited in or on any land in contravention of section 33(1) above and that—

    (a) in order to remove or prevent pollution of land, water or air or harm to human health it is necessary that the waste be forthwith removed or other steps taken to eliminate or reduce the consequences of the deposit or both; or

    (b) there is no occupier of the land; or

    (c) the occupier neither made nor knowingly permitted the deposit of the waste;

the authority may remove the waste from the land or take other steps to eliminate or reduce the consequences of the deposit or, as the case may require, to remove the waste and take those steps.

(8) Where an authority exercises any of the powers conferred on it by subsection (7) above it shall be entitled to recover the cost incurred by it in removing the waste or taking the steps or both and in disposing of the waste—

    (a) in a case falling within subsection (7)(a) above, from the occupier of the land unless he proves that he neither made nor knowingly caused nor knowingly permitted the deposit of the waste;

    (b) in any case, from any person who deposited or knowingly caused or knowingly permitted the deposit of any of the waste;

except such of the cost as the occupier or that person shows was incurred unnecessarily.

(9) Any waste removed by an authority under subsection (7) above shall belong to that authority and may be dealt with accordingly.

DEFINITIONS
    "controlled waste": s.75(4).
    "deposited": s.29(6).
    "harm": s.29(5).
    "waste": s.75(2).

COMMENCEMENT
May 1, 1994 (S.I. 1994 No. 1096).

GENERAL NOTE
This section gives waste regulation and collection authorities power to deal with controlled waste which has been fly-tipped, or otherwise unlawfully deposited, within their areas. The procedure involves service of notice on the occupier of the land, requiring removal of the waste and steps to eliminate or reduce the consequences of the deposit. In the event of non-compliance the authority may take the necessary steps itself and recover the reasonable costs of doing so from the recipient of the notice.

    Subsection (3) in effect provides the defence of "innocent occupier," in that the notice will be quashed on appeal if the occupier neither deposited the waste nor knowingly caused or knowingly permitted the deposit (as to which, see notes to s.33).

    The subs. (5) offence is a relevant offence for the purposes of the "fit and proper person" test which any applicant for a waste management licence must pass: Waste Management Licensing Regulations 1994, reg. 3.

    Powers to act immediately in certain cases to remove the waste or reduce the consequences of its deposit are given by subs. (7). The circumstances are: (a) where immediate action is necessary to prevent pollution of land, water or air (*cf.* "pollution of the environment") or harm to human health; or (b) where there is no occupier of the relevant land; or (c) where the occupier is innocent in relation to the deposit.

    Under subs. (8), reasonable costs so incurred may be recovered in case (a) from the occupier unless he or she can prove their innocence and, in any of the cases, from any person who deposited the waste or knowingly caused or knowingly permitted the deposit.

    For a case on the corresponding provision in the 1974 Act, see *Berridge Incinerators v. Nottinghamshire County Council* (Crown Court, Nottingham, June 12, 1992) where conviction for failure to comply with a notice was quashed on the grounds, *inter alia*, that the notice was unreasonable and unfair.

See also *R. v. Metropolitan Stipendiary Magistrate, ex p. London Waste Regulation Authority; Berkshire County Council v. Scott, The Times,* January 14, 1993, where the validity of a notice under s.16 of the 1974 Act was upheld notwithstanding an argument that the description of the waste to be removed was too vague.

Interference with waste sites and receptacles for waste

60.—(1) No person shall sort over or disturb—

  (a) anything deposited at a place for the deposit of waste provided by a waste collection authority, by a waste disposal contractor under arrangements made with a waste disposal authority or by any other local authority or person or, in Scotland, by a waste disposal authority;

  (b) anything deposited in a receptacle for waste, whether for public or private use, provided by a waste collection authority, by a waste disposal contractor under arrangements made with a waste disposal authority, by a parish or community council or by a holder of a waste management licence or, in Scotland, by a waste disposal authority or a roads authority; or

  (c) the contents of any receptacle for waste which, in accordance with a requirement under section 46 or 47 above, is placed on any highway or, in Scotland, road or in any other place with a view to its being emptied;

unless he has the relevant consent or right to do so specified in subsection (2) below.

(2) The consent or right that is relevant for the purposes of subsection (1)(a), (b) or (c) above is—

  (a) in the case of paragraph (a), the consent of the authority, contractor or other person who provides the place for the deposit of the waste;

  (b) in the case of paragraph (b), the consent of the authority, contractor or other person who provides the receptacle for the deposit of the waste;

  (c) in the case of paragraph (c), the right to the custody of the receptacle, the consent of the person having the right to the custody of the receptacle or the right conferred by the function by or under this Part of emptying such receptacles.

(3) A person who contravenes subsection (1) above shall be liable on summary conviction to a fine of an amount not exceeding level 3 on the standard scale.

DEFINITIONS
  "deposited": s.29(6).
  "waste": s.75(2).
  "waste disposal contractor": s.30(5).

COMMENCEMENT
In part: May 31, 1991 (S.I. 1991 No. 1319), "in part" meaning in so far as it relates to anything deposited at a place for the deposit of waste, or in a receptacle for waste, provided by a waste disposal contractor under arrangements made with a waste disposal authority; the remainder, May 1, 1994 (S.I. 1994 No. 1096).

GENERAL NOTE
This section creates the summary offence of sorting over or disturbing waste at waste sites or in bins or other receptacles for waste. No offence is committed if the sorting or disturbance takes place with the consent of the relevant person, as specified in subs. (2).

Duty of waste regulation authorities as respects closed landfills

61.—[...]

[Section 61 contained provisions dealing with the inspection and remediation of closed landfills and other land affected by deposits of controlled waste. The section never came into force and was repealed by the Environment Act 1995, Sched. 22, para. 79. See General Note to Pt. II.]

Special waste and non-controlled waste

Special provision with respect to certain dangerous or intractable waste

62.—(1) If the Secretary of State considers that controlled waste of any kind is or may be so dangerous or difficult to treat, keep or dispose of that special provision is required for dealing with it he shall make provision by regulations for the treatment, keeping or disposal of waste of that kind ("special waste").

(2) Without prejudice to the generality of subsection (1) above, the regulations may include provision—

    (a) for the giving of directions by waste regulation authorities with respect to matters connected with the treatment, keeping or disposal of special waste;

    (b) for securing that special waste is not, while awaiting treatment or disposal in pursuance of the regulations, kept at any one place in quantities greater that those which are prescribed and in circumstances which differ from those which are prescribed;

    (c) in connection with requirements imposed on consignors or consignees of special waste, imposing, in the event of non-compliance, requirements on any person carrying the consignment to re-deliver it as directed;

    (d) for requiring the occupier of premises on which special waste is situated to give notice of that fact and other prescribed information to a prescribed authority;

    (e) for the keeping of records by waste regulation authorities and by persons who import, export, produce, keep, treat or dispose of special waste or deliver it to another person for treatment or disposal, for the inspection of the records and for the furnishing by such persons to waste regulation authorities of copies of or information derived from the records,

    (f) for the keeping in the register under section 64(1) below of copies of such of those records, or such information derived from those records, as may be prescribed;

    (g) providing that a contravention of the regulations shall be an offence and prescribing the maximum penalty for the offence, which shall not exceed, on summary conviction, a fine at level 5 on the standard scale and on conviction on indictment, imprisonment for a term of two years or a fine or both.

(3) Without prejudice to the generality of subsection (1) above, the regulations may include provision—

    [(a) for the supervision by waste regulation authorities

        (i) of activities authorised by virtue of the regulations or of activities by virtue of carrying on which persons are subject to provisions of the regulations, or

       (ii) of persons who carry on activities authorised by virtue of the regulations or who are subject to provisions of the regulations, and for the recovery from persons falling within sub-paragraph (ii) above of the costs incurred by waste regulation authorities in performing functions conferred upon those authorities by the regulations,]

    (b) as to the recovery of expenses or other charges for the treatment, keeping or disposal or the re-delivery of special waste in pursuance of the regulations;

    (c) as to appeals to the Secretary of State from decisions of waste regulation authorities under the regulations.

"(3A) This section is subject to section 114 of the Environment Act 1995 (delegation or reference of appeals etc.)."

(4) In the application of this section to Northern Ireland "waste regulation authority" means a district council established under the Local Government Act (Northern Ireland) 1972.

DEFINITIONS
"controlled waste": s.75(4).
"dispose of": s.29(6).
"special waste": s.75(9).
"treat": s.29(6).
"waste": s.75(2).

AMENDMENTS
Subs. (3)(a) was substituted and subs. (3A) added by the Environment Act 1995, Sched. 22, para. 80(2) and (3).

COMMENCEMENT
Section 62 came into force on August 11, 1995: The Environmental Protection Act 1990 (Commencement No. 17) Order 1995 No. 2152.

GENERAL NOTE
Until replaced by the new Special Waste Regulations discussed below, the current regulations dealing with special waste are the Control of Pollution (Special Waste) Regulations 1980 No. 1709 as amended by S.I. 1988 No. 1790. Amendments to these Regulations relating to ships' tank washings and garbage which are special waste were made by the Control of Pollution (Landed Ships' Waste) Regulations 1987 No. 402 and the Control of Pollution (Landed Ships' Waste) (Amendment) Regulations 1989 No. 65. These Regulations are the means by which the E.C. Directive 78/319/EEC on *Toxic and Dangerous Waste* (O.J. L84, March 31, 1978) is implemented.

Separate controls attach to the transfrontier movement of toxic or hazardous wastes, both under Community law (Regulation 259/93 (O.J. L30/1, 6.2.93), 85/469/EEC (O.J. L272, October 12, 1985), 86/279/EEC (O.J. L181 July 4, 1986) and 87/112/EEC (O.J. L48 February 17, 1987)) and under UK law by the Transfrontier Shipment of Waste Regulations 1994 No. 1137.

Within the E.C., Directive 91/689/EEC on hazardous waste, including a new definition of such waste superseding that of Directive 78/319/EEC, is to be implemented by Member States by June 27, 1995. On March 27, 1995 the DoE issued a consultation paper entitled "The Special Waste Regulations 1995 and the Hazardous Waste Directive" on proposed regulations to implement Directive 91/689/EEC. The proposed regulations also make other changes including modifications to the consignment note system. See also the interim technical guidance on the identification and categorisation of special waste published on May 10, 1995.

The main changes apparent between s.62 and the equivalent section under the 1974 Act, s.17, is that the regulations made under s.62 may provide for the keeping of information in public registers and may impose requirements upon carriers of special waste to redeliver it in the event of non-compliance with the relevant requirements.

New Special Waste Regulations
New regulations on special waste come into force on September 1, 1996: The Special Waste Regulations 1996 (S.I. 1996 No. 972). The new Regulations were issued too late to allow for detailed analysis and comment in these annotations, but are significantly more complex than the 1976 Regulations which they replace. Among the innovations introduced is a requirement for the Agency to supply to each consignment or round of waste a unique code to enable the consignment to be identified.

Waste other than controlled waste

63.—(1) The Secretary of State may, after consultation with such bodies as he considers appropriate, make regulations providing that prescribed provisions of this Part shall have effect in a prescribed area—

(a) as if references in those provisions to controlled waste or controlled waste of a kind specified in the regulations included references to such waste as is mentioned in section 75(7)(c) below which is of a kind so specified; and

(b) with such modifications as may be prescribed;

and the regulations may make such modifications of other enactments as the Secretary of State considers appropriate.

[(2) A person who deposits, or knowingly causes or knowingly permits the deposit of, any waste—
  (a) which is not controlled waste, but
  (b) which, if it were controlled waste, would be special waste,
in a case where he would be guilty of an offence under section 33 above if the waste were special waste and any waste management licence were not in force, shall, subject to subsection (3) below, be guilty of that offence and punishable as if the waste were special waste.]

(3) No offence is committed by virtue of subsection (2) above if the act charged was done under and in accordance with any consent, licence, approval or authority granted under any enactment (excluding any planning permission under the enactments relating to town and country planning).

(4) Section 45(2) and section 47(1) above shall apply to waste other than controlled waste as they apply to controlled waste.

DEFINITIONS
"controlled waste": s.75(4).
"deposits": s.29(6).
"special waste": s.75(9).
"waste": s.75(2).

AMENDMENT
Subs. (2) is substituted by the Environment Act 1995, Sched. 22, para. 81.

COMMENCEMENT
Subsection (1): February 18, 1993 (S.I. 1993 No. 274). Remainder: no date has been set for commencement.

GENERAL NOTE
Subsection (1) allows the Secretary of State to make regulations applying prescribed provisions of Pt. II to mine and quarry wastes and agricultural waste within a prescribed area and subject to such modifications as may be prescribed.

Subsection (2), as substituted by the 1995 Act, creates an offence of depositing waste which is not controlled waste but which, if it were, would be special waste because of its hazardous properties; or knowingly causing or knowingly permitting such deposit. The more severe penalties of s.33 relating to special waste (s.33(9)) apply to such offences. It is a defence that the act was done under and in accordance with any statutory consent or other statutory approval, but planning permission is not sufficient authorisation for this purpose. The offence is a relevant offence for the purposes of the "fit and proper person" test which any applicant for a waste management licence must pass: Waste Management Licensing Regulations 1994, reg. 3.

The original wording of subs. (2) was infelicitous and almost certainly did not succeed in creating the offence intended: the effect of the substituted provision is much clearer in this respect.

Publicity

Public registers

64.—(1) Subject to sections 65 and 66 below, it shall be the duty of each waste regulation authority to maintain a register containing prescribed particulars of or relating to—
  (a) current or recently current licences ("licences") granted by the authority;
  (b) current or recently current applications to the authority for licences;
  (c) applications made to the authority under section 37 above for the modification of licences;
  (d) notices issued by the authority under section 37 above effecting the modification of licences;
  (e) notices issued by the authority under section 38 above effecting the revocation or suspension of licences or imposing requirements on the holders of licences;

(f) appeals under section 43 above relating to decisions of the authority;

(g) certificates of completion issued by the authority under section 39(9) above,

(h) notices issued by the authority imposing requirements on the holders of licences under section 42(5) above;

(i) convictions of the holders of licences granted by the authority for any offence under this Part (whether in relation to a licence so granted or not);

(j) the occasions on which the authority has discharged any function under section 42 or 61 above;

(k) directions given to the authority under any provision of this Part by the Secretary of State;

(l) [...]

(m) such matters relating to the treatment, keeping or disposal of waste in the area of the authority or any pollution of the environment caused thereby as may be prescribed;

and any other document or information required to be kept in the register under any provision of this Act.

(2) Where information of any description is excluded from any register by virtue of section 66 below, a statement shall be entered in the register indicating the existence of information of that description.

[(2A) The Secretary of State may give to a waste regulation authority directions requiring the removal from any register of its of any specified information not prescribed for inclusion under subsection (1) above or which, by virtue of section 65 or 66 below, ought to be excluded from the register.]

(3) For the purposes of subsection (1) above licences are "recently" current for the period of 12 months after they cease to be in force and applications for licences are "recently" current if they relate to a licence which is current or recently current or, in the case of an application which is rejected, for the period of 12 months beginning with the date on which the waste regulation authority gives notice of rejection or, as the case may be, on which the application is deemed by section 36(9) above to have been rejected.

(4) It shall be the duty of each waste collection authority in England or Wales [...] to maintain a register containing prescribed particulars of such information contained in any register maintained under subsection (1) above as relates to the treatment, keeping or disposal of controlled waste in the area of the authority.

[(5) The waste regulation authority in relation to England and Wales shall furnish any waste collection authorities in its area with the particulars necessary to enable them to discharge their duty under subsection (4) above.] Each waste regulation authority and waste collection authority:

(a) shall secure that any register maintained under this section is open to inspection at its principal office by members of the public free of charge at all reasonable hours;

(b) and shall afford to members of the public reasonable facilities for obtaining, on payment of reasonable charges, copies of entries in the register

[and, for the purposes of this subsection, places may be prescribed by the Secretary of State at which any such registers or facilities as are mentioned in paragraph (a) or (b) above are to be available or afforded to the public in pursuance of the paragraph in question.]

(7) Registers under this section may be kept in any form.

(8) In this section "prescribed" means prescribed in regulations by the Secretary of State.

DEFINITIONS
"controlled waste": s.75.
"disposal": s.29(4).
"licences": s.35(12).
"treatment": s.29(6).

AMENDMENTS
Subss. (2A) and (5) were respectively inserted and substituted by the Environment Act 1995, Sched. 22, para. 82(2) and (4). Subss. (4) and (6) were amended by para. 82(3) and (5). Para. (1) of subs. (1) was deleted by the Environment Act 1995 Sched. 24.

COMMENCEMENT
Subsections (1), (4), (8): February 18, 1993 (S.I. 1993 No. 274). Remainder: May 1, 1994 (S.I. 1994 No. 1096).

GENERAL NOTE
This section makes provision for the keeping of registers by waste regulation authorities relating to waste management licences and other matters. The obligation extends only to "current or recently current" licences and applications. A licence is "current" while in force and "recently current" for 12 months after it ceases to be in force (subs. (3)). Applications are current, so long as the licence granted remains in force or is recently current or, in cases of rejection of the application, for 12 months from rejection (subs. (3)). Broad discretion is given for the Secretary of State to prescribe further matters for inclusion in relation to treatment, keeping or disposal of waste or pollution thereby caused (subs. (1)(m)). Registers must also be kept at waste collection authority level, on the basis of particulars supplied by the waste regulation authority (subss. (4) and (5)).

Regulations
By reg. 10 of the Waste Management Licensing Regulations 1994 the register must contain full particulars of specified matters including current and recently current licences and applications, including supporting information, statutory notices, notices of appeal, relevant convictions, reports and monitoring information, special waste consignment notes and other documentation and, in Scotland, s.54 resolutions in so far as they continue in force (see General Note to s.54.)

Exclusion from registers of information affecting national security

65.—(1) No information shall be included in a register maintained under section 64 above (a "register") if and so long as, in the opinion of the Secretary of State, the inclusion in the register of that information, or information of that description, would be contrary to the interests of national security.

(2) The Secretary of State may, for the purpose of securing the exclusion from registers of information to which subsection (1) above applies, give to the authorities maintaining registers directions—

   (a) specifying information, or descriptions of information, to be excluded from their registers; or

   (b) specifying descriptions of information to be referred to the Secretary of State for his determination;

and no information referred to the Secretary of State in pursuance of paragraph (b) above shall be included in any such register until the Secretary of State determines that it should be so included.

(3) An authority maintaining a register shall notify the Secretary of State of any information it excludes from the register in pursuance of directions under subsection (2) above.

(4) A person may, as respects any information which appears to him to be information to which subsection (1) above may apply, give a notice to the Secretary of State specifying the information and indicating its apparent nature; and, if he does so—

   (a) he shall notify the authority concerned that he has done so; and

   (b) no information so notified to the Secretary of State shall be included in the register kept by that authority until the Secretary of State has determined that it should be so included.

COMMENCEMENT
Subsection (2): February 18, 1993 (S.I. 1993 No. 274). Remainder: May 1, 1994 (S.I. 1994 No. 1096).

GENERAL NOTE
This section provides for information to be excluded from the registers kept under s.64 where inclusion of the information would be contrary to the interests of national security. The Secretary of State may direct the removal of information from the register if it ought to be excluded under s.65: see subs. 64(2A).

"Cogent and specific evidence" will be required to substantiate claims for exemption on this ground (see *Hansard*, H.L. Vol. 522, col. 380).

Exclusion from registers of certain confidential information

66.—(1) No information relating to the affairs of any individual or business shall be included in a register maintained under section 64 above (a "register"), without the consent of that individual or the person for the time being carrying on that business, if and so long as the information—

(a) is, in relation to him, commercially confidential; and

(b) is not required to be included in the register in pursuance of directions under subsection (7) below;

but information is not commercially confidential for the purposes of this section unless it is determined under this section to be so by the authority maintaining the register or, on appeal, by the Secretary of State.

(2) Where information is furnished to an authority maintaining a register for the purpose of—

(a) an application for, or for the modification of a licence;

(b) complying with any condition of a licence; or

(c) complying with a notice under section 71(2) below;

then, if the person furnishing it applies to the authority to have the information excluded from the register on the ground that it is commercially confidential (as regards himself or another person), the authority shall determine whether the information is or is not commercially confidential.

(3) A determination under subsection (2) above must be made within the period of 14 days beginning with the date of the application and if the authority fails to make a determination within that period it shall be treated as having determined that the information is commercially confidential.

(4) Where it appears to an authority maintaining a register that any information (other than information furnished in circumstances within subsection (2) above) which has been obtained by the authority under or by virtue of any provision of this Part might be commercially confidential, the authority shall—

(a) give to the person to whom or whose business it relates notice that that information is required to be included in the register unless excluded under this section; and

(b) give him a reasonable opportunity—

(i) of objecting to the inclusion of the information on the grounds that it is commercially confidential; and

(ii) of making representations to the authority for the purpose of justifying any such objection;

and, if any representations are made, the authority shall, having taken the representations into account, determine whether the information is or is not commercially confidential.

(5) Where, under subsection (2) or (4) above, an authority determines that information is not commercially confidential—

(a) the information shall not be entered in the register until the end of the period of 21 days beginning with the date on which the determination is notified to the person concerned;

(b) that person may appeal to the Secretary of State against the decision;

and, where an appeal is brought in respect of any information, the information shall not be entered in the register [until the period of seven days following the day on which the appeal is finally determined or withdrawn].

[(6) Subsections (2) and (8) of section 43 above shall apply in relation to appeals under subsection (5) above as they apply in relation to appeals under that section; but

(a) subsection (2)(c) of that section shall have effect for the purposes of this subsection with the substitution for the words from "(which may"' onwards of the words "(which must be held in private)"; and

(b) subsection (5) above is subject to section 114 of the Environment Act 1995 (delegation or reference of appeals etc.).]

(7) The Secretary of State may give to the authorities maintaining registers directions as to specified information, or descriptions of information, which the public interest requires to be included in the registers notwithstanding that the information may be commercially confidential.

(8) Information excluded from a register shall be treated as ceasing to be commercially confidential for the purposes of this section at the expiry of the period of four years beginning with the date of the determination by virtue of which it was excluded; but the person who furnished it may apply to the authority for the information to remain excluded from the register on the ground that it is still commercially confidential and the authority shall determine whether or not that is the case.

(9) Subsections (5) and (6) above shall apply in relation to a determination under subsection (8) above as they apply in relation to a determination under subsection (2) or (4) above.

(10) The Secretary of State may, by order, substitute for the period for the time being specified in subsection (3) above such other period as he considers appropriate.

(11) Information is, for the purposes of any determination under this section, commercially confidential, in relation to any individual or person, if its being contained in the register would prejudice to an unreasonable degree the commercial interests of that individual or person.

DEFINITION
"licence": s.35(12).

AMENDMENTS
Subs. (5) was amended and subs. (6) substituted by the Environment Act 1995, Sched. 22, para. 83(1) and (2).

COMMENCEMENT
Subsection (2): February 18, 1993 (S.I. 1993 No. 274). Remainder: May 1, 1994 (S.I. 1994 No. 1096).

GENERAL NOTE
This section provides for the exclusion from the public registers kept under s.64 of information which is commercially confidential (as defined in subs. (11)) to an individual or business without their consent. As with the equivalent provision under Pt. I of the Act, s.22, the issue of confidentiality may be raised either by the person furnishing the information (subs. (2)) or by the authority maintaining the register (subs. (4)).

Again, as with registers under Pt. I, confidential information may be included if the Secretary of State so directs on the grounds that the public interest requires it (subs. (7)). Confidentiality lapses after four years and a new application will be necessary for continued exclusion (subs. (8)).

Guidance and procedures
The procedures for commercial confidentiality appeals are explained at Annex 10 to Circular 11/94. By reg. 6 of the Waste Management Licensing Regulations 1994 the notice of appeal must be in writing and accompanied by a statement of the grounds of appeal and other particulars.

Annual reports

67. […].
[This section, which required the preparation and publication of annual reports by waste regulation authorities, was repealed by the Environment Act 1995, Sched. 22, para. 84. See now s.52 of the 1995 Act.]

Supervision and enforcement

Functions of Secretary of State and appointment etc. of inspectors

68. […].
[Section 68, dealing with the supervisory functions of the Secretary of State and the appointment of inspectors, was repealed by the Environment Act 1995, Sched. 22, para. 85.]

Powers of entry etc. of inspectors

69. […].
[This section, providing for powers of entry and other powers for inspectors, was repealed by the Environment Act 1995, Sched. 22, para. 84. The general powers of enforcing authorities under ss.108–110 of the 1995 Act now apply.]

Power to deal with cause of imminent danger of serious pollution, etc.

70. […].
[This section, containing powers to deal with causes of imminent danger of serious pollution, was repealed by the Environment Act 1995, Sched. 22, para. 85. See now s.109 of the 1995 Act.]

Obtaining of information from persons and authorities

71. (1) […].
(2) For the purpose of the discharge of their respective functions under this Part—
(a) the Secretary of State, and
(b) a waste regulation authority,
may, by notice in writing served on him, require any person to furnish such information specified in the notice as the Secretary of State or the authority, as the case may be, reasonably considers he or it needs, in such form and within such period following service of the notice [, or at such time,] as is so specified.
(3) A person who—
(a) fails, without reasonable excuse, to comply with a requirement imposed under subsection (2) above
(b) […]
shall be liable—
(i) on summary conviction, to a fine not exceeding the statutory maximum;
(ii) on conviction on indictment, to a fine or to imprisonment for a term not exceeding two years, or to both.

COMMENCEMENT
May 31, 1991 (S.I. 1991 No. 1319).

AMENDMENT
Subs. (1) was repealed and subs. (2) amended by the Environment Act 1995, Sched. 22, para. 86(1) and (2). Para. (b) of subs. (3) was deleted by the Environment Act 1995 Sched. 24. Sched. 19 to the 1995 Act substituted a new s.44 into the 1990 Act which is comparable to the old s.71(3)(b) but wider in scope.

GENERAL NOTE

Subsection (1), which gave the Secretary of State power to require waste regulation authorities to furnish information about the discharge of their functions was repealed by the Environment Act 1995 which supersedes it.

Subsection (2) gives power to the Secretary of State and waste regulation authorities to require any person to furnish information that the Secretary of State or authority reasonably consider they need.

Subsection (3): Statutory maximum is currently £5,000. The subs. (3) offences is a relevant offence for the purposes of the "fit and proper person" test which any applicant for a waste management licence must pass: Waste Management Licensing Regulations 1994, reg. 3.

Default powers of Secretary of State

72. [...].

[This section provided the Secretary of State with default powers in relation to waste regulation authorities, and was repealed by the Environment Act 1995, Sched. 22, para. 86.]

Supplemental

Appeals and other provisions relating to legal proceedings and civil liability

73.—(1) An appeal against any decision of a magistrates' court under this Part (other than a decision made in criminal proceedings) shall lie to the Crown Court at the instance of any party to the proceedings in which the decision was given if such an appeal does not lie to the Crown Court by virtue of any other enactment.

(2) In Scotland an appeal against any decision of the sheriff under this Part (other than a decision made in criminal proceedings) shall lie to the Court of Session at the instance of any party to the proceedings in which the decision was given if such an appeal does not lie to the Court of Session by virtue of any other enactment.

(3) Where a person appeals to the Crown Court or the Court of Session against a decision of a magistrates' court or the sheriff dismissing an appeal against any requirement imposed under this Part which was suspended pending determination of that appeal, the requirement shall again be suspended pending the determination of the appeal to the Crown Court or Court of Session.

(4) Where an appeal against a decision of any authority lies to a magistrates' court or to the sheriff by virtue of any provision of this Part, it shall be the duty of the authority to include in any document by which it notifies the decision to the person concerned a statement indicating that such an appeal lies and specifying the time within which it must be brought.

(5) Where on an appeal to any court against or arising out of a decision of any authority under this Part the court varies or reverses the decision it shall be the duty of the authority to act in accordance with the court's decision.

(6) Where any damage is caused by waste which has been deposited in or on land, any person who deposited it, or knowingly caused or knowingly permitted it to be deposited, in either case so as to commit an offence under section 33(1) or 63(2) above, is liable for the damage except where the damage—

   (a) was due wholly to the fault of the person who suffered it; or

   (b) was suffered by a person who voluntarily accepted the risk of the damage being caused;

but without prejudice to any liability arising otherwise than under this subsection.

(7) The matters which may be proved by way of defence under section 33(7) above may be proved also by way of defence to an action brought under subsection (6) above.

(8) In subsection (6) above—

"damage" includes the death of, or injury to, any person (including any disease and any impairment of physical or mental condition); and

"fault" has the same meaning as in the Law Reform (Contributory Negligence) Act 1945.

(9) For the purposes of the following enactments—

    (a) the Fatal Accidents Act 1976;

    (b) the Law Reform (Contributory Negligence) Act 1945; and

    (c) the Limitation Act 1980;

and for the purposes of any action of damages in Scotland arising out of the death of, or personal injury to, any person, any damage for which a person is liable under subsection (6) above shall be treated as due to his fault.

DEFINITIONS
"deposited": s.29(6).
"waste": s.75(2).

COMMENCEMENT
Subsections (1)–(5): April 1, 1992 (S.I. 1992 No. 266). Remainder: May 1, 1994 (S.I. 1994 No. 1096).

GENERAL NOTE
Appeals from decisions of magistrates' and sheriff courts: Subsections (1)–(5) deal with appeals from decisions of magistrates' and sheriff courts made under Pt. II of the Act other than in criminal proceedings. Appeal lies to the Crown Court or, in Scotland, the Court of Session. The relevant decisions that may be appealed against in this way are : (1) provision of receptacles for collection of waste (s.46(7)); (2) provision of receptacles for collection of commercial or industrial waste (s.47(7)); and (3) requirements to remove waste deposited on land (s.59(2)).

Civil liability: Subsections (6)–(9) deal with civil liability for damage caused by waste deposited on land without a licence, in contravention of licence conditions, or in breach of s.63(2). "Damage," as well as damage to property, includes death or personal injury or impairment (subs. (8)). These provisions should be read in the light of emerging E.C. proposals for a Directive on *Strict Civil Liability for Damage Caused by Waste* which in some respects would go much further than subss. (6)–(9).

Meaning of "fit and proper person"

74.—(1) The following provisions apply for the purposes of the discharge by a waste regulation authority of any function under this Part which requires the authority to determine whether a person is or is not a fit and proper person to hold a waste management licence.

(2) Whether a person is or is not a fit and proper person to hold a licence is to be determined by reference to the carrying on by him of the activities which are or are to be authorised by the licence and the fulfilment of the requirements of the licence.

(3) Subject to subsection (4) below, a person shall be treated as not being a fit and proper person if it appears to the authority—

    (a) that he or another relevant person has been convicted of a relevant offence;

    (b) that the management of the activities which are or are to be authorised by the licence are not or will not be in the hands of a technically competent person; or

    (c) that the person who holds or is to hold the licence has not made and either has no intention of making or is in no position to make financial provision adequate to discharge the obligations arising from the licence.

(4) The authority may, if it considers it proper to do so in any particular case, treat a person as a fit and proper person notwithstanding that subsection (3)(a) above applies in his case.

(5) It shall be the duty of waste regulation authorities to have regard to any guidance issued to them by the Secretary of State with respect to the discharge of their functions of making the determinations to which this section applies.

(6) The Secretary of State may, by regulations, prescribe the offences that are relevant for the purposes of subsection (3)(a) above and the qualifications and experience required of a person for the purposes of subsection (3)(b) above.

(7) For the purposes of subsection (3)(a) above, another relevant person shall be treated, in relation to the licence holder or proposed licence holder, as the case may be, as having been convicted of a relevant offence if—

(a) any person has been convicted of a relevant offence committed by him in the course of his employment by the holder or, as the case may be the proposed holder of the licence or in the course of the carrying on of any business by a partnership one of the members of which was the holder or, as the case may be, the proposed holder of the licence;

(b) a body corporate has been convicted of a relevant offence committed when the holder or, as the case may be, the proposed holder of the licence was a director, manager, secretary or other similar officer of that body corporate; or

(c) where the holder or, as the case may be, the proposed holder of the licence is a body corporate, a person who is a director, manager, secretary or other similar officer of that body corporate—
   (i) has been convicted of a relevant offence; or
   (ii) was a director, manager, secretary or other similar officer of another body corporate at a time when a relevant offence for which that other body corporate has been convicted was committed.

COMMENCEMENT
Subsection (6): February 18, 1993 (S.I. 1993 No. 274). Remainder: May 1, 1994 (S.I. 1994 No. 1096).

GENERAL NOTE
This extremely important section expands on the meaning of "fit and proper person" for the purposes of s.36. Under s.36 a waste regulation authority "shall not reject the application [for a waste management licence] if it is satisfied that the applicant is a fit and proper person unless it is satisfied that its rejection is necessary for [one or other of a number of specified purposes]." It follows therefore that an authority may reject a licence application on the ground that it is not satisfied that the applicant is a fit and proper person. There are three circumstances where the applicant shall be treated as not being a fit and proper person (s.74(3)). These are: (a) the applicant or a "relevant person" has been convicted of a "relevant offence"; (b) the management of the licensed activities is not or will not be in the hands of a technically competent person; and (c) the applicant has not made and has not the intention or means of making adequate financial provision to discharge the obligations arising from the licence.

In addition to the grant of licences, the concept of "fit and proper person" is also relevant to s.38 on the revocation and suspension of licences (see s.38(1)(a), (2) and (6)(a) and notes thereto).

The concept can be traced back to various calls for greater discrimination in the grant of waste licences; see for example the Eleventh Report on the Royal Commission on Environmental Pollution, *Managing Waste: the Duty of Care* (Cm. 9675, December 1985) at para. 8.41. Similarly, in his address to the 92nd Annual Conference of the Institute of Wastes Management (June 12, 1990) Lord Gregson put the position prior to the Act as follows:

"At present any person irrespective of their competence, knowledge or training or their financial or personal profit can set themselves up as waste managers. This is an absurd and dangerous situation to be in."

The present provisions have evolved through various Government announcements and consultation papers including Pollution Paper No. 24 (July 1986), Consultation Paper on *Waste*

Disposal Law: Amendments (September 1986) and Paper on *Decisions following Public Consultations* (June 1988).

General considerations
It is clear that consideration of whether an applicant or licence-holder is fit and proper is to be made in the context of the activities authorised or to be authorised by the licence, and the fulfilment of the requirements of the licence (subs. (2)). Subsection (3) gives three instances where a person is to be treated as not being fit and proper, subject to the discretion of the authority to treat him as being so in one case (subs. (4)). However, it is questionable whether these three instances are exhaustive of the cases which can justify concluding a person not to be fit and proper, and there may be other factors that are of relevance to whether it is proper to grant a licence to a specific applicant. In any event, it seems clear that the authority must apply its mind in each case to the particular circumstances and may not fetter its discretion by applying general rules in a hard-and-fast way: see *R. v. Holborn Licensing Justices, ex p. Stratford Catering Company* (1927) 136 L.T. 278.
    The Secretary of State may issue guidance to waste regulation authorities in making the relevant determinations, and such guidance will be crucial to achieving national consistency. The guidance is contained in Chap. 3 of the Waste Management Paper No. 4, *Licensing of Waste Management Facilities.*

Relevant offence
Conviction of a relevant offence means that the offender will not be a fit and proper person, unless the authority considers it proper to treat the offender as fit and proper under subs. (4), notwithstanding the conviction. The offences that are "relevant" for this purpose are prescribed in Regulations made under subs. (6). The relevant provision is made by the Waste Management Licensing Regulations 1994, reg. 6, which specifies not only offences relating to waste but also a number of other pollution offences, as follows:
    (a) Public Health (Scotland) Act 1897, s.22 (repealed by the 1995 Act, s.120 and Sched. 24);
    (b) Public Health Act 1936, s.95(1);
    (c) Control of Pollution Act 1974, ss.3, 5(6), 16(4), 18(2), 31(1), 32(1), 34(5), 78, 92(6) or 93(3);
    (d) Refuse Disposal (Amenity) Act 1978, s.2;
    (e) Control of Pollution (Special Waste) Regulations 1980;
    (f) Food and Environmental Protection Act 1985, s.9(1);
    (g) Transfrontier Shipment of Hazardous Waste Regulations 1988;
    (h) Merchant Shipping (Prevention of Pollution by Garbage) Regulations 1988;
    (i) Control of Pollution (Amendment) Act 1989, ss.1, 5, 6(9) or 7(3);
    (j) Water Act 1989, ss.107, 118(4) or 175(1);
    (k) Environmental Protection Act 1990, ss.23(1), 33, 34(6), 44, 47(6), 57(5), 59(5), 63(2), 69(9), 70(4), 71(3) or 80(4);
    (l) Water Resources Act 1991, ss.85 202(4) or 206.
    It should be noted that relevant convictions are not limited to those relating to incidents at the site in question. Thus in the case of a company operating a number of sites, a conviction in respect of any of those sites would potentially affect the position of the company as a fit and proper person in relation to the other sites. It may be, therefore, that waste companies will tend increasingly to separate out operations at different sites between different companies. Whilst common directors of the companies could result in conviction of one company affecting the position of others (see below), control of shares in the companies, or the fact that they are part of the same group, would not appear to have that effect under the legislation.
    As to the significance of such offences, see below.

Relevant person
Subsection (7) contains complex provisions as to the persons who are "relevant" in that their convictions are imputed to the applicant or licence-holder. Broadly, the categories are:
    (a) employees of the applicant or licence-holder where the offence was committed in the course of their employment (subs. (7)(a));
    (b) business partners of the applicant or licence-holder where the offence was committed in the course of the partnership business (subs. (7)(a));
    (c) companies, where the offence was committed at a time where the applicant or licence-holder was a director, manager, secretary or other similar officer (subs. (7)(b));
    (d) directors, managers, secretaries and other similar officers of the applicant company or licence-holding company who were convicted of a relevant offence at any time (subs. (7)(c)(i)); and

(e) directors, managers, secretaries and other similar officers of the applicant company or licence-holding company, where they held one or other of those offices in another company at a time when an offence was committed for which the company was convicted (subs. (7)(c)(ii)).

Whilst similar to the categories of "relevant person" in s.3(5) of the Control of Pollution (Amendment) Act 1989 (relating to registration of waste carriers), there is one important difference. Section 3(6) of the 1989 Act provides that the authority shall have regard to the degree of complicity of the applicant or carrier in the offence, if the offence was committed by some other relevant person. No such provision appears in s.74, though it would still appear to be a relevant consideration.

Spent convictions

The Rehabilitation of Offenders Act 1974 would not be of assistance in the majority of likely situations, since it applies only to convictions of individuals, and not companies. However, para. 3.33 of Waste Management Paper No. 4 suggests that where the person convicted of the offence is a company the authority should normally have regard to whether the conviction would have become spent if committed by an individual.

Disregard of conviction

Subsection (4) allows an authority to treat a person as fit and proper despite a conviction or convictions of him or of a relevant person. Paras. 3.27–3.35 provide guidance as to the factors which an authority should take into account in reaching that decision. Three factors are relevant:

(a) Whether it was the applicant/licence-holder or another relevant person who was convicted (despite any express provision to that effect as in the Control of Pollution (Amendment) Act 1989. Different considerations may apply as between individuals, companies and partnerships.

(b) The nature and gravity of the relevant offences—whether they involved controlled or special waste, whether they caused serious pollution, and the penalty imposed.

(c) The number of relevant offences.

Technical competence

By subs. (3)(b) a person will be treated as not being fit and proper if the management of the licensed activities is not or will not be "in the hands of a technically competent person". The Secretary of State may, by regulations, prescribe the requisite qualifications and experience necessary to attain technical competence.

The criteria for technical competence were considered by the Waste Management Industry Training and Advisory Board (WAMITAB), a company limited by guarantee and founded by the Institute of Wastes Management, the National Association of Waste Disposal Contractors and the Road Haulage Association; an agreed programme for developing the qualification was drawn up and an agreement commencing on October 1, 1990 was entered into between the DoE and WAMITAB (see *Hansard*, H.L. Vol. 522, col. 290).

This work largely formed the basis of the provisions contained in reg. 4 of the Waste Management Licensing Regulations 1994.

Under this provision, a person is technically competent in relation to the types of facility listed at Table 1 to the regulation if they hold the certificate of technical competence appropriate to that type of facility awarded by WAMITAB. Types of facilities are categorised by reference to their general nature (*e.g.* landfill, treatment, transfer, civic amenity) and by reference to the type of waste dealt with. Three main types of certificate, with different levels, are referred to, *i.e.* managing landfill sites, managing treatment plants, and managing civic amenity sites.

Technical competence: transitional provisions

WAMITAB proposed "grandfather rights" for those with five years' or more relevant experience and introduction of the scheme on a voluntary basis with the aim of ensuring sufficient qualified managers in place to implement the scheme and relevant provisions by what was then the target date for implementation, April 1, 1992.

Regulation 5 of the Waste Management Licensing Regulations 1994 in fact provides for more limited transitional provisions. Regulation 5(1) allows facility managers to register with WAMITAB as an applicant for a certificate by August 10, 1994 and to be treated as technically competent until August 10, 1999 in relation to the type of facility for which they were manager at any time in the preceding 12 months.

Regulation 5(2) makes limited provision for "grandfather rights" in that a person aged 55 or over on August 10, 1994, who in the previous 10 years has had at least five years' experience as the manager of a facility, will be treated as technically competent in relation to that type of facility until August 10, 2004.

Regulation 4 of the Waste Management Licensing (Amendment etc.) Regulations 1995 (S.I. 1995 No. 288) extends the transitional provisions to two further classes of persons with effect from April 1, 1995. These new transitional provisions allow managers of two further kinds of facility to register with WAMITAB as an applicant for a certificate by a certain date and to be treated as technically competent until August 10, 1999 in relation to their kind of facility. The first kind of facility is those governed by Part I of this Act and operated under an IPC or LAPC authorisation (deadline for applications July 10, 1995 and applicants must have managed such a site at some point in the 23 months prior to that date). The second kind of facility is those which did not require to be licensed under the waste disposal licensing provisions of the Control of Pollution Act 1974 but do require to be licensed under the waste management licensing regime, and therefore enjoy a transitional exemption from waste management licensing by virtue of paragraph 43 of Schedule 3 to the Waste Management Licensing Regulations 1994. For this kind of facility, the manager's deadline for application is July 31, 1995 and he must have managed the facility in question at some point in the 15 months prior to that date—it should be noted that, unlike the first of the two new transitional exemptions, this one only enables the manager in question to be treated as technically competent in relation to the site managed—not others of that type.

Technical competence: guidance
Guidance as to technical competence is contained in Waste Management Paper No. 4, paras. 3.36–3.67.

This suggests that the technically competent manager (TCM) will be the person responsible for the proper management of the site and should normally be expected to be present on the site during the working day to control operations and make management decisions; absences and changes of personnel should be notified to the waste regulation authority. Paragraph 3.15 suggests that acceptance of a new TCM should be permitted without written WRA approval (*i.e.* negative approval rather than positive confirmation). For larger, more complex operations, or continuous operations, an operator should designate more than one TCM and the authority should accept a reasonable number of duplicating and deputising TCMs. It is also suggested that the decisions taken by the TCM should not be capable of being overruled (for example on cost grounds) where this would compromise the competent management of the site. Normally the authority should expect there to be at least one TCM per site allocated on a full-time basis. The Working Plan should contain a list of the current TCMs (see paras. 3.36–3.46).

Sites outside the WAMITAB Scheme
Some sites will not be covered by the WAMITAB scheme for certificates of technical competence, *e.g.* small sites and scrap metal sites. Here the waste regulation authority will need to make an individual assessment of the TCM's fitness based on formal qualifications and experience: this should not involve the authority in accepting a lower standard of operation. The Waste Management Paper suggests some of the types of qualification that may be acceptable and provides specific guidance for sites taking small amounts of waste and for scrap metal facilities (paras. 3.56–3.59 of Waste Management Paper No. 4). (See also Chapter 4 of Waste Management Paper 4A on the licensing of metal recycling sites).

Adequate financial provision
By subs. (3)(c) the authority must consider whether the applicant or licence holder has made, has the intention of making, and is in a position to make, "financial provision adequate to discharge the operations arising from the licence". Subsection (6) does not give power to make Regulations as to what constitutes adequate financial provision, but guidance is given under subs. (5) by way of the Waste Management Paper No. 4, paras. 3.68–3.122.

Unlike relevant offences and technical competence, adequate financial provision is not a matter which needs to be kept under review as a possible basis for revocation or suspension of a licence: however, in the circumstances of an individual licence it will usually be appropriate to include a condition specifying the maintenance of an appropriate form of financial cover (Waste Management Paper No. 4, para. 3.79).

The DoE's guidance is that assessment of financial capability needs to be closely related to the various stages of a licensed operation and to the terms of the licence, for which provision is to be made. Without specific provision, it is extremely unlikely that an applicant can demonstrate his ability and intention to cover financially his activities more than a few years into the future.

Financial provision: landfill operations
The DoE suggests that four major difficulties may arise in relation to landfill site operations (Waste Management Paper No. 4):
     (a) working risks to life, limb and property as may arise in any industrial operation;
     (b) technical operational risks such as litter, odour, infestation and nuisance;
     (c) short-term hazards relating to spillages, leaks or inappropriate mixing of wastes; and
     (d) environmental hazards associated and escape of polluting leachate or migration of gas.
These risks need to be addressed through the four stages of:
     (a) site acquisition and preparation;
     (b) site operation;
     (c) restoration and landscaping or aftercare; and
     (d) post closure control and monitoring.
Guidance is provided as to possible appropriate financial mechanisms for each of these stages, such as insurance, self insurance, guarantees, provision for contingent liabilities, charges on assets, bonds and escrow accounts.

The possibility remains open of a suitable mutual scheme being agreed to provide joint protection (for example, the scheme considered by the National Association of Waste Disposal Contractors). The guidance suggests that any such scheme would need to be clear and binding in order to ensure the build-up of sufficient reserves. The requirements of the proposed E.C. Directive on Landfill (COM (91) 102) as to financial guarantees for closure and aftercare (Art. 17) and a landfill aftercare fund or funds (Art. 18) are also relevant.

See also the Report of the DoE Working Group on *Financial Guarantees against Environmental Damage in the Waste Management Industry (1991)*.

Meaning of "waste" and household, commercial and industrial waste and special waste

75.—(1) The following provisions apply for the interpretation of this Part.
[(2) "Waste" means any substance or object in the categories set out in Schedule 2B to this Act which the holder discards or intends or is required to discard; and for the purposes of this definition—
     "holder" means the producer of the waste or the person who is in possession of it; and
     "producer" means any person whose activities produce waste or any person who carries out pre-processing, mixing or other operations resulting in a change in the nature or composition of this waste]
     (3) [...].
(4) "Controlled waste" means household, industrial and commercial waste or any such waste.
(5) Subject to subsection (8) below, "household waste" means waste from—
     (a) domestic property, that is to say, a building or self-contained part of a building which is used wholly for the purposes of living accommodation;
     (b) a caravan (as defined in section 29(1) of the Caravan Sites and Control of Development Act 1960) which usually and for the time being is situated on a caravan site (within the meaning of that Act);
     (c) a residential home;
     (d) premises forming part of a university or school or other educational establishment;
     (e) premises forming part of a hospital or nursing home.
(6) Subject to subsection (8) below, "industrial waste" means waste from any of the following premises—
     (a) any factory (within the meaning of the Factories Act 1961);

(b) any premises used for the purposes of, or in connection with, the provision to the public of transport services by land, water or air;

(c) any premises used for the purposes of, or in connection with, the supply to the public of gas, water or electricity or the provision of sewerage services; or

(d) any premises used for the purposes of, or in connection with, the provision to the public of postal or telecommunications services.

(7) Subject to subsection (8) below, "commercial waste" means waste from premises used wholly or mainly for the purposes of a trade or business or the purposes of sport, recreation or entertainment excluding—

(a) household waste;

(b) industrial waste;

(c) waste from any mine or quarry and waste from premises used for agriculture within the meaning of the Agriculture Act 1947 or, in Scotland, the Agriculture (Scotland) Act 1948; and

(d) waste of any other description prescribed by regulations made by the Secretary of State for the purposes of this paragraph.

(8) Regulations made by the Secretary of State may provide that waste of a description prescribed in the regulations shall be treated for the purposes of provisions of this Part prescribed in the regulations as being or not being household waste or industrial waste or commercial waste; but no regulations shall be made in respect of such waste as is mentioned in subsection (7)(c) above and references to waste in subsection (7) above and this subsection do not include sewage (including matter in or from a privy) except so far as the regulations provide otherwise.

(9) "Special waste" means controlled waste as respects which regulations are in force under section 62 above.

[(10) Schedule 2B to this Act (which reproduces Annex I to the Waste Directive) shall have effect.]

[(11) Subsection (2) above is substituted, and Schedule 2B to this Act is inserted, for the purpose of assigning to "waste" in this Part the meaning which it has in the Waste Directive by virtue of paragraphs (a) to (c) of Article 1 of, and Annex I to, that Directive, and those provisions shall be construed accordingly.]

[(12) In this section "the Waste Directive" means the directive of the Council of the European Communities, dated 15th July 1975, on waste, as amended by—

(a) the directive of that Council, dated 18th March 1991, amending directive 75/442/EEC on waste; and

(b) the directive of that Council, dated 23rd December 1991, standardising and rationalising reports on the implementation of certain Directives relating to the environment.]

DEFINITION
"substance": s.29(11).

AMENDMENTS
Subs. (2) was substituted and subss. (10)–(12) added by the Environment Act 1995, Sched. 22. paras. 88(2) and (4).

Subs. (3), which provided that any thing which was discarded or otherwise dealt with as if it were waste was to be presumed to be waste unless the contrary was proved, was repealed by para. 88(3).

COMMENCEMENT
May 31, 1991 (S.I. 1991 No. 1319).

The previous definition of "waste": subss. (2) and (3) and previous case law
As originally drafted, s.75(2) repeated the definition of waste originally found in s.30 of the Control of Pollution Act 1974, in the following terms:

(2) "Waste" includes—

(a) any substance which constitutes a scrap material or an effluent or other unwanted surplus substance arising from the application of any process; and

(b) any substance or article which requires to be disposed of as being broken, worn out, contaminated or otherwise spoiled;

but does not include a substance which is an explosive within the meaning of the Explosives Act 1875.

Subs. (3) provided a presumption that any thing which is discarded or otherwise dealt with as if it were waste should be presumed to be waste unless the contrary is proved.

"Waste" was thus formerly given a wide definition, though as was pointed out by para. 12 of Circ. 14/92 *The Environmental Protection Act 1990—Parts II and IV; The Controlled Waste Regulations 1992* (Welsh Office 30/92, Scottish Office 24/92), not an exhaustive definition. It included within the ordinary meaning of the word waste certain substances, materials and articles about which there might otherwise have been doubt. The starting point was therefore the ordinary and natural meaning of the term "waste," subject to the gloss provided by subs. (2) and the presumption of subs. (3) which applies to material discarded or otherwise dealt with as if it were waste.

In considering the meaning of "waste" within the context of s.30 of the Control of Pollution Act 1974 (framed in identical terms) the courts took the view that waste is defined by reference to the point of view of the person producing or discarding it. On that basis the fact that material may have a use or value to the person removing or receiving it will not of itself prevent the material being waste. The three judicial decisions to that effect are referred to at paras. 14–17 of Circ. 14/92: *Long v. Brooke* [1980] Crim.L.R. 109; *Berridge Incinerators v. Nottinghamshire County Council* (1987, unrep.); *Kent County Council v. Queensborough Rolling Mill Co. Ltd* (1990) 154 J.P.N. 442. A similar approach has been adopted in relation to Town and Country Planning legislation: *R. v. Rotherham Metropolitan Borough Council, ex p. Rankin* [1990] J.P.L. 503, citing also *Charles Neil Ashcroft v. Michael McErlain Ltd.* (Divisional Court, January 30, 1985). The Scottish courts also adopted an approach which is consistent with the foregoing judicial decisions: *H.L. Friel & Son Ltd v. Inverclyde District Council* 1994 S.C.L.R. 561 (Ex. Div., Court of Session); 1994 GWD 13–859.

Changes to the original definition

Various changes to the original definition of waste have been made with a view to ensuring conformity with the requirements of E.C. law and in particular the definition and objectives contained in the waste framework directive (see below). These changes were initially effected by the introduction of the concept of "Directive waste" in the Waste Management Licensing Regulations 1994 (S.I. 1994 No. 1056) (see Appendix 3), but change to the primary legislation itself had to await the 1995 Act.

The key changes are:

(1) the replacement of subs. (2) with a new definition following that in the directive;

(2) repeal of the presumption in subs. (3)

(3) insertion of a new Schedule 2B, reproducing Annex I of the directive; and

(4) an express statement of intention (subs. (11)) to assign to waste the meaning given in the waste framework directive, those provisions to be construed accordingly.

The E.C. law, discussed below, is therefore of central significance, given the statutory requirement in subs. (11) to construe the definition to conform with the directive.

E.C. law

The early Directives on waste, 75/442/EEC (the waste framework directive) and 78/319/EEC (the hazardous waste directive), defined waste as meaning "any substance or object which the holder disposes of or is required to dispose of pursuant to the provisions of the national law in force." Circular 4/92 (paras. 5–8 and Annex 7) refers to the decisions of the European Court of Justice in joined cases C–206/88 and C–207/88 (*Vessoso* and *Zanetti* [1990] I E.C.R. 1461) and case C–359/88 (*Zanetti and others* [1990] I E.C.R. 1509). The decision in C–206/88 and C–207/88 was that these E.C. definitions of waste did not exclude substances or objects capable of economic re-utilisation; it was also held that the intention of the holder to exclude all economic re-utilisation by others is not a necessary component of the definition. The European Court held in case C–359/88 that national legislation which defines waste so as to exclude substances or objects capable of economic re-utilisation is not compatible with Directives 75/442 and 78/319.

Directive 91/156/EEC, amending 75/442 defines waste by reference to a list of categories Q1–Q16 at Annex I of the Directive; any substance or object in those categories which the holder discards or intends or is required to discard is within the definition. The "holder" is defined as the producer of the waste or the natural or legal person who is in possession of it. The directives definitions of "producer" and "holder" are incorporated into subs. (2). The various categories Q1–Q16 are reproduced at Sched. 2B.

Determining whether something is waste
The first step in deciding whether something is waste under s.75 as amended is to consider whether is falls within the list of substances and items as Sched. 2B. Whilst it may be possible to identify the material as falling squarely within one of the categories there, failure to do so is of little consequence, since the Schedule begins with the category (1) "production or consumption residues not otherwise specified below" and ends with category (16) "any materials, substances or products which are not contained in the above categories."
    The next step is to identify the "holder" of the material, *i.e.* the producer of it or person in possession of it, and to consider whether that person discards, or intends to discard or is required to discard it. It is here that the central conundrum identified in the early cases on the original U.K. definition presents itself: the producer and a subsequent holder may not necessarily have the same intention as regards the material. The original producer may well wish to discard or rid himself of the material, but the person in receipt of it may intend its economic re-utilisation or reclamation. The U.K. case law (and the E.C. case-law referred to above) were clear that the potential for economic re-utilisation or value would not preclude material being waste. This result would be achieved under the new s.75 definition by reading the word "or" in the definition of holder to mean that if either the producer or possessor of the material has the relevant intention to discard, then the material will be waste. To focus on the actions or intention of the possessor above might well produce a different conclusion, and DoE guidance on the new definition is considered below.

Directive Waste
The Waste Management Licensing Regulations 1994 introduced a new concept of "Directive Waste" into the legislation; this means any substance or object in the categories set out in Part II of Schedule 4 to the Regulations (see Appendix 3) (corresponding to categories Q1–Q16 of the Directive, as set out above) which the producer or the person in possession of it discards or intends to discard or is required to discard but with the exception of anything excluded from the scope of the Directive by Article 2. Any reference to waste in Part II of the 1990 Act includes a reference to Directive Waste (Sched. 4, para. 9(2)).
    Waste which is not Directive Waste shall not be treated as household, industrial or commercial waste under the Collection and Disposal of Waste Regulations 1988 (1994 Regulations, regs. 22(4), inserting reg. 7A), nor under the Controlled Waste Regulations 1992 (1994 Regulations, regs. 24(8), inserting reg. 7A). Accordingly, the waste will not be controlled waste and will not be subject to mainstream waste management licensing controls. As to controlled waste, see below.

Excluded Wastes
By art. 2(1)(a) gaseous emissions released to the atmosphere are excluded from the Directive and consequently are not Directive Waste. But see Circ. 11/94 para. 1.13 and 4.95–4.103, dealing with the deliberate release of ozone-depleting substances.
    Also excluded from the scope of the Directive are five categories of waste where they are already covered by other legislation. These are radioactive waste, certain mineral wastes, specified types of agricultural wastes, waste waters (with the exception of waste in liquid form) and decommissioned explosives. The Government's views on the scope of these exemptions are set out at paras. 1.12–1.18 of Circ. 11/94.
    Originally, subs. (2) expressly excluded explosives within the meaning of the Explosives Act 1875. No such express exclusion now appears in subs. (2). However, as mentioned above, art. 2.1(b)(v) of directive 91/156/EEC excludes "decommissioned explosives" where these are covered by other legislation.

Explosives: subs. (2)
Substances which are explosives within the meaning of the Explosives Act 1875 are not included within the definition of waste. The term is defined by s.3 of the 1875 Act to mean:

    "(1) Gunpowder, nitro-glycerine, dynamite, gun-cotton, blasting powders, fulminate of mercury or other metals, coloured fires, and every other substance, whether similar to those above mentioned or not, used or manufactured with a view to produce a practical effect by explosion or a pyrotechnic effect; and

(2) includes fog-signals, fireworks, fuses, rockets, percussion caps, detonators, cartridges, ammunition of all descriptions, and every adaptation or preparation of an explosive as above defined."

By s.104 of the 1875 Act, any substance appearing to be specially dangerous to life or property by reason either of its explosive properties or of any such properties in its manufacturing processes, may be declared to be an explosive by Order in Council.

However, Directive 91/156/EEC excludes from the scope of the Directive only "decommissioned explosives" (Art. 2.1(b)(v)) and where they are covered by other legislation.

Controlled waste: subs. (4)
The three categories of controlled waste are defined in subss. (5)–(7) and by the Controlled Waste Regulations 1992 (S.I. 1992 No. 588) and the Waste Management Licensing Regulations 1994. The Controlled Waste Regulations are explained in Circ. 14/92 (Welsh Office 30/92; Scottish Office 24/92). As mentioned above, Reg. 24 of the Waste Management Licensing Regulations 1994/1056 inserts a new reg. 7A into the Controlled Waste Regulations 1992 which states that waste which is not "Directive waste" shall not be treated as household waste, industrial waste or commercial waste.

Household waste: subs. (5)
The primary definition of household waste is contained in subs. (5) but in addition waste of the descriptions set out in Sched. 1 to the Controlled Waste Regulations 1992 is to be treated as household waste. These are waste from:

(a) a hereditament on premises exempted from local non-domestic voting;
(b) premises occupied by a charity and wholly or mainly used for charitable purposes;
(c) any land belonging to or used in connection with domestic property, a caravan or a residential home;
(d) a private garage which either has a flow area of 25m² or less or is used wholly or mainly for the accommodation of a private motor vehicle;
(e) storage premises used wholly or mainly for the storage of articles of domestic use;
(f) moored vessel used wholly for the purposes of living accommodation;
(g) a camp site;
(h) a prison or other penal institution;
(i) a hall, or other premises used wholly or mainly for public meetings;
(j) a royal palace;
(k) arising from the discharge by a local authority of its duty under s.89(2) (duty to keep roads and highways clean).

Two categories of waste are treated as household waste for the purposes of the exemption from the duty of care under s.34(2) but for no other purpose: Controlled Waste Regulations 1992, reg. 2(2). These are:

(a) waste arising from works of construction or demolition, including preparatory works;
(b) septic tank sludge.

Domestic property: The building or the self-contained part of a building in question must be used wholly for the purposes of living accommodation; mixed use buildings would therefore be excluded in the absence of a self-contained domestic part.

Caravan: The terms "caravan" and "caravan site" are defined in the Caravan Sites and Control of Development Act 1960, s.29(1) as follows:

"any structure designed or adapted for human habitation which is capable of being moved from one place to another (whether by being towed, or by being transported on a motor vehicle or trailer) and any motor vehicle so designed or adapted, but does not include:

(a) any railway rolling-stock which is for the time being on rails forming part of a railway system, or
(b) any tent."

The express reference to caravans should avoid some of the difficulties encountered in *Gordon v. Kirkcaldy District Council* 1990 S.C.L.R. 104 (Court of Session) as to whether a caravan can be described as a dwelling-house. See also on the meaning of "caravan" *Wyre Forest District Council v. Secretary of State for the Environment* [1990] 2 W.L.R. 517 (H.L.).

By reg. 3 of the Controlled Waste Regulations 1992 certain types of waste are excluded from the definition of household waste so as not to fall within the exemption from waste management licensing for household waste from domestic property disposed of within the curtilage of the dwelling. These are:

(a) mineral or synthetic oil or grease;

(b) asbestos;

(c) clinical waste.

By reg. 3(2) scrap metal is not to be treated as household waste for the purposes of the s.34 duty of care at any time before the waste management licensing provisions of Pt. II of the 1990 Act come into effect.

Industrial waste: subs. (6)

Waste from a factory: An extended definition of "factory" is provided by s.175 of the Factories Act 1961:

"(1) Subject to the provisions of this section, the expression 'factory' means any premises in which, or within the close or curtilage or precincts of which, persons are employed in manual labour in any process for or incidental to any of the following purposes, namely:

(a) the making of any article or of part of any article; or

(b) the altering, repairing, ornamenting, finishing, cleaning, or washing or the breaking up or demolition of any article; or

(c) the adapting for sale of any article; or

(d) the slaughtering of cattle, sheep, swine, goats, horses, asses or mules; or

(e) the confinement of such animals as aforesaid while awaiting slaughter at other premises, in a case where the place of confinement is available in connection with those other premises, is not maintained primarily for agricultural purposes within the meaning of the Agriculture Act 1947, or, as the case may be, the Agriculture (Scotland) Act 1948, and does not form part of premises used for the holding of a market in respect of such animals;

being premises in which, or within the close or curtilage or precincts of which, the work is carried on by way of trade or for purposes of gain and to or over which the employer of the persons employed therein has the right of access or control.

(2) The expression 'factory' also includes the following premises in which persons are employed in manual labour (whether or not they are factories by virtue of subs. (1) of this section), that is to say,—

(a) any yard or dry dock (including the precincts thereof) in which ships or vessels are constructed, reconstructed, repaired, refitted, finished or broken up;

(b) any premises in which the business of sorting any articles is carried on as a preliminary to the work carried on in any factory or incidentally to the purposes of any factory;

(c) any premises in which the business of washing or filling bottles or containers or packing articles is carried on incidentally to the purposes of any factory;

(d) any premises in which the business of hooking, plaiting, lapping, making-up or packing of yarn or cloth is carried on;

(e) any laundry carried on as ancillary to another business, or incidentally to the purposes of any public institution;

(f) except as provided in subs. (10) of this section, any premises in which the construction, reconstruction or repair of locomotives, vehicles or other plant for use for transport purposes is carried on as ancillary to a transport undertaking or other industrial or commercial undertaking;

(g) any premises in which printing by letterpress, lithography, photogravure, or other similar process, or bookbinding is carried on by way of trade or for purposes of gain or incidentally to another business so carried on;

(h) any premises in which the making, adaptation or repair of dresses, scenery or properties is carried on incidentally to the production, exhibition or presentation by way of trade or for purposes of gain of cinematograph films or theatrical performances, not being a stage or dressing-room of a theatre in which only occasional adaptations or repairs are made;

(j) any premises in which the business of making or mending nets is carried on incidentally to the fishing industry;

(k) any premises in which mechanical power is used in connection with the making or repair of articles of metal or wood incidentally to any business carried on by way of trade or for purposes of gain;

(l) any premises in which the production of cinematograph films is carried on by way of trade or for purposes of gain, so, however, that the employment at any such premises of theatrical performers within the meaning of the Theatrical Employers Registration Act 1925 and of attendants on such theatrical performers shall not be deemed to be employment in a factory;

(m) any premises in which articles are made or prepared incidentally to the carrying on of building operations or works of engineering construction, not being premises in which such operations or works are being carried on;

(n) any premises used for the storage of gas in a gasholder having a storage capacity of not less than [140 cubic metres].

(3) Any line or siding (not being part of a railway or tramway) which is used in connection with and for the purposes of a factory, shall be deemed to be part of the factory; and if any such line or siding is used in connection with more than one factory belonging to different occupiers, the line or siding shall be deemed to be a separate factory.

(4) A part of a factory may, with the approval in writing of the chief inspector, be taken to be a separate factory and two or more factories may, with the like approval, be taken to be a single factory.

(5) Any workplace in which, with the permission of or under agreement with the owner or occupier, two or more persons carry on any work which would constitute the workplace a factory if the persons working therein were in the employment of the owner or occupier, shall be deemed to be a factory for the purposes of this Act, and, in the case of any such workplace not being a tenement factory or part of a tenement factory, the provisions of this Act shall apply as if the owner or occupier of the workplace were the occupier of the factory and the persons working therein were persons employed in the factory.

(6) Where a place situate within the close, curtilage, or precincts forming a factory is solely used for some purpose other than the processes carried on in the factory, that place shall not be deemed to form part of the factory for the purposes of this Act, but shall, if otherwise it would be a factory, be deemed to be a separate factory.

(7) Premises shall not be excluded from the definition of a factory by reason only that they are open air premises.

(8) Where the Minister by regulations so directs as respects all or any purposes of this Act, different branches or departments of work carried on in the same factory shall be deemed to be different factories.

(9) Any premises belonging to or in the occupation of the Crown or any municipal or other public authority shall not be deemed not to be a factory, and building operations or works of engineering construction undertaken by or on behalf of the Crown or any such authority shall not be excluded from the operation of this Act, by reason only that the work carried on thereat is not carried on by way of trade or for purposes of gain.

(10) Premises used for the purpose of housing locomotives or vehicles where only cleaning, washing, running repairs or minor adjustments are carried out shall not be deemed to be a factory by reason only of para. (f) of subs. (2) of this section, unless they are premises used for the purposes of a railway undertaking where running repairs to locomotives are carried out."

The question will ultimately be one of fact and common sense: see *Wood v. L.C.C.* [1948] 2 K.B. 232 (C.A.); also *Nash v. Hollinshead* [1901] 1 K.B. 700 (C.A.). In any event the definition of household waste as including waste from a number of institutional premises avoids any doubt as to the status of such premises.

Waste to be treated as industrial waste: By reg. 5(1) of the Controlled Waste Regulations 1992, waste of the descriptions set out at Sched. 3 is to be treated as industrial waste. These are waste from:

(1) premises used for maintaining vehicles, vessels or aircraft, not being waste from a private garage which falls under domestic waste by virtue of Sched. 1;

(2) a laboratory;

(3) a workshop or similar premises not being a factory within the meaning of s.175 of the Factories Act 1961 because the people working there are not employees or because the work there is not carried on by way of trade or for purposes of gain, excluding premises at which the principal activities are computer operations or the copying of documents by photographic or lithographic means;

(4) premises occupied by a scientific research association approved by the Secretary of State under s.508 of the Income and Corporation Taxes Act 1988;

(5) dredging operations;

(6) tunnelling on any other excavation;

(7) sewage not falling within a description in reg. 7 which—

(a) is treated, kept on disposed of in or on land, other than by means of a privy, cesspool or septic tank;

(b) is treated, kept on disposal of by means of mobil plant; or

(c) has been removed from a privy or cesspool.

(8) clinical waste other than—
    (a) clinical waste from a domestic property, caravan, residential home or from a moored vessel used wholly for the purposes of living accommodation;
    (b) waste collected under s.22(3) of the Control of Pollution Act 1974 (waste collected by a local authority under arrangement with any person who has an interest in or is the occupier of any relevant land);
    (c) waste collected under s.89 (local authority's duty to keep land and highways clear of litter; s.92(9) (waste collected by a local authority after a failure by any person to obey a litter abatement notice) or s.93 (power to serve street litter control notices).
(9) any aircraft vehicle or vessel which is not occupied for domestic purposes;
(10) waste which has previously formed part of any aircraft vehicle, or vessel and which is not household waste;
(11) waste, removed from land on which has previously been deposited and any soil with which such waste has been in contact, other than—
    (a) waste collected under s.22(3) of the Control of Pollution Act 1974 (see No. 8 above); or
    (b) waste collected under ss.89, 92(9) or 93 (see No. 8 above).
(12) leachate from a deposit of waste;
(13) poisonous or noxious waste arising from any of the following processes undertaken on premises used for the purposes of a trade or business—
    (a) mixing or selling paints;
    (b) sign writing;
    (c) laundering or dry cleaning;
    (d) developing photographic film or making photographic prints;
    (e) selling petrol, diesel fuel, paraffin kerosene, heating oil or similar substances; or
    (f) selling pesticides herbicides or fungicides.
(14) premises used for the purpose of breedings, boarding, stabling or exhibiting animals;
(15) waste oil, waste solvent, or (subject to reg. 7(2)) scrap metal, other than—
    (a) waste from a domestic property, caravan or residential house;
    (b) waste falling within paras. 3 to 6 of Sched. 1 (see further notes to subs. (5)).
(16) waste arising from the discharge by the Secretary of State of his duty under s.89(2) (duty to keep clean any trunk road which is a special road and relevant highways or roads for which he is responsible);
(17) waste imported into Great Britain;
(18) tank washings and garbage landed in Great Britain.

Commercial waste: subs. (7)
Premises used for trade or business: As to case law on this phrase, see annotations to ss.79 and 80.

Waste to be treated as commercial waste: By reg. 6 of the Controlled Waste Regulations 1992, waste of the descriptions set out in Sched. 4 is to be treated as commercial waste. These are waste from—
    (1) an office or showroom;
    (2) a hotel within the meaning of—
        (a) in England and Wales, s.1(3) of the Hotel Proprietors Act 1956; and
        (b) in Scotland, s.139(1) of the Licensing (Scotland) Act 1976.
    (3) any part of a composite hereditament or, in Scotland, or part residential subjects, which is used for the purposes of a trade or business;
    (4) a private garage which either has a floor area exceeding 25 square metres or is not used wholly or mainly for accommodation of a private motor vehicle;
    (5) premises occupied by a club, society or any association of persons (whether incorporated or not) in which activities are conducted for the benefit of the members;
    (6) premises (not being premises from which waste is by virtue of the Act or any other provision of these Regulations to be treated as household waste or industrial waste) occupied by—
        (a) a court;
        (b) a government department;
        (c) a body corporate or an individual appointed by or under any enactment to discharge any public functions; or
        (d) a body incorporated by a Royal Charter.
    (7) waste from a tent pitched on land other than a camp site;

(8) a market or fair;

(9) waste collected under s.22(3) of the Control of Pollution Act 1974 (local authority's power to collect waste under an arrangement with the person who has an interest in or is the occupier of relevant land).

Waste not to be treated as industrial or commercial waste
Waste of the following descriptions is not to be treated as industrial or commercial waste (Controlled Waste Regulations 1992, reg. 7(1)):

(a) sewage, sludge or septic tank sludge which is treated, kept or disposed of (otherwise than by mobile plant) within the curtilage of a sewage treatment works as an integral part of the operation of those works;

(b) sludge supplied or used in accordance with the Sludge (Use in Agriculture) Regulations 1989 (S.I. 1989 No. 1263, amended by S.I. 1990 No. 880); and

(c) septic tank sludge used in accordance with the same regulations.

Also, by reg. 7(2) scrap metal is not to be treated as industrial or commercial waste for the purposes of the section 34 duty of care until a day to be appointed. No such date has yet been set, but on November 8, 1994, the Government published for consultation draft Waste Management Licensing (Amendment, etc.) Regulations in which it was proposed that the date should be October 1, 1995.

Non-controlled wastes
By s.75(7)(c) two categories of waste are specifically excluded from the definition of commercial waste and consequently from control. These are:

(a) waste from any mine or quarry; and

(b) waste from premises used for agriculture.

The definition of "agriculture" in the Agriculture Act 1947, s.109(3) includes:

"horticulture, fruit growing, seed growing, dairy farming and livestock breeding and keeping, the use of land as grazing land, meadow land, osier land, market gardens and nursery grounds, and the use of land for woodlands where that use is ancillary to the farming of land for other agricultural purposes ... and 'agricultural' shall be construed accordingly."

However, see the notes relating to Directive Waste above; it is uncertain that these exclusions will be able to continue in their current form.

Sewage: subs. (8)
Subsection (8) excludes "sewage" from the definition of commercial waste; nor can such waste be prescribed as being within one or other of the other categories of waste by regulations unless the regulations expressly so provide. However, it appears there is nothing to prevent sewage being classified as household or industrial waste. The treatment, keeping and disposal of sewage within the curtilage of a sewage treatment works as an integral part of the operation of those works is dealt with by reg. 7(1)(a) of the Controlled Waste Regulations 1992, which provides that such sewage shall not be treated as industrial or commercial waste. It seems doubtful whether that exemption would apply to liquid effluent conveyed to the works by means other than a sewer, *e.g.* road tanker.

Special waste: subs. (9)
See notes to s.62.

Guidance as to the meaning of waste
The Government's views as to the definition of waste and its application to various factual circumstances are set out at length in Annex 2 of Circ. 11/94. Areas covered include the distinction between wastes and by-products, those operations which the Government regards as specialised recovery operations, the use of objects by their producer, and how waste may cease to be waste. For further comment and explanation, see the *Environmental Law Bulletin* No. 1 (January 1994) and No. 5 (May 1994) (*Sweet & Maxwell*).

The Guidance views the preambles of the EEC Waste Directives as being significant in relation to interpreting the definitions contained in the amended Framework Directive. The preambles suggest that waste is perceived as posing a particular threat to human health or the environment which is different from the threat posed by other substances or objects. This threat arises from the fact that the producer of the substance or object concerned will normally no longer have the self interest necessary to ensure the provision of appropriate safeguards. This leads the Government to the view that the purpose of the Framework Directive is to treat as waste, and accordingly to supervise the collection, transport, storage, recovery and disposal of "those substances or objects which fall out of the commercial cycle or out of the chain of utility." The "chain of utility" is regarded as an important consideration because the issues which need to be addressed will not always arise within a commercial context. The paper also points out that it is necessary to be clear as to what is meant by the "commercial cycle" and to draw a distinction between the normal commercial cycle and the commercial cycle which exists for the purpose of collecting, transporting, storing, recovering or disposing of waste. A central feature of the definition under European Community law is seen as the concept of discarding, intending to discard or being required to discard substances or objects. The Government takes the view that in reaching a judgment on the meaning of "discard" the determining consideration would be that interpretation which in the opinion of the European Court of Justice best furthers the purpose of the Framework Directive. This leads to the view that the concept of discarding should be interpreted as meaning also "disposing of" or "getting rid of."

Further points which arise from the guidance are as follows.

(a) in order for a substance or object to be waste it must not only fall within one of the categories specified in the Directive (and to be specified in the 1994 Regulations), but must also be discarded, disposed of or got rid of, or be intended or required to be discarded, disposed of or got rid of. Thus the inclusion of a substance or object in one of the relevant categories does not of itself mean that it is waste.

(b) To determine whether a substance or object has been discarded the question to be asked should be: "Has the substance or object been discarded so that it is no longer part of the normal commercial cycle or chain of utility?" An answer of "no" should provide a reasonable indication that the substance or object concerned is not waste. The example is given of glass bottles subject to a deposit, which are returned and which have not fallen outside the normal commercial cycle; on the other hand glass bottles which are placed in bottle banks for recycling have passed out of the normal commercial cycle (although in the process, they may have passed into the specifically waste-related commercial cycle).

(c) Annex IIA of the Framework Directive sets out a list of disposal operations as they occur in practice. Objects which are consigned to a disposal operation within that list should be considered to have been discarded and, therefore, to be waste.

(d) Annex IIB to the Framework Directive is intended to set out a list of operations which may lead to the recovery of waste. However, some of the recovery operations listed there are not sufficiently distinguishable from operations within the normal commercial cycle or chain of utility: the example is given of the use of materials principally as fuel, or the spreading of materials on land for the benefit of agriculture, both of which would be operations carried out within the normal commercial cycle or chain of utility. The fact that a substance or object is used for one of the operations described in that list (for example as a fuel) does not necessarily mean that it is waste. It would therefore be inappropriate to conclude that a substance or object is waste simply because it has been consigned to a recovery operation listed in the Framework Directive and as transposed into the 1994 Regulations.

(e) In the light of these considerations on recovery operations, the Government suggests that to help determine whether a substance or object has been discarded, further questions may be asked:

"(a) can the substance or object be used in its present form (albeit after repair) or in the same way as any other raw material without being subject to a specialised recovery operation and is it likely to be so used; or
(b) can the substance or object be used only after it has been subjected to a specialised recovery operation?"

An answer of "yes" to question (a) may provide a reasonable indication that the substance or object concerned has not been discarded, whereas an answer of yes to question (b) should provide a reasonable indication that the substance or object concerned has not been discarded. The concept of "specialised recovery operation" does not appear in the Framework Directive and for that reason it is not proposed to define it. The concept is introduced by the Government to help distinguish between those operations which could either be within the normal commercial cycle or could be recovery operations depending on the circumstances and, on the other hand, those operations which are of their nature recovery operations since they wholly or partly devise their justification from the recovery of waste.

(f) Further guidance is given as to this approach which it is claimed will, for example, enable a viable distinction to be drawn between useful by-products and waste. Some substances or objects may be capable of being put to immediate use otherwise than by a specialised waste recovery establishment, an example being by-products from the food and drink processing industries or animal by-products from abattoirs. Such substances are contrasted with degenerated substances or objects which can be put to use only by establishments or undertakings specialising in waste recovery: the example is given of contaminated solvents or scrap metal which are consigned to specialised recovery operations and which are no longer part of the normal commercial cycle or chain of utility.

(g) The guidance suggests that where the holder of a substance is paying someone to provide the service of removing something which the holder does not want and wishes to get rid of, then the substance or object should be regarded as waste. However, where the substance is fit for use in its present form (albeit after repairs) the fact that a payment is made by the producer may be evidential in relation to intent, but is not necessarily crucial. The presence or absence of such a payment may simply be a reflection of fluctuations in market conditions.

(h) The guidance also addresses the issue of intent and common interest, on the basis that in some cases the status of a substance or object as waste will depend on the holder's intent. In particular, it is suggested that the holder of a substance or object does not discard it when he transfers it to another person knowing and intending that the person to whom he transfers it intends to use it (rather than dispose of it) in the form in which it was transferred or in the same way as any other raw material, without its being subjected to a specialised recovery operation. In such a case, a substance or object should not be considered as having fallen out of the commercial cycle or chain of utility, nor as having been consigned to the processes of waste disposal or recovery. An example would be the transfer of old clothes to an identified charity or other organisation or person: in those circumstances the holder is doing no more than exercising their right as owner to determine the disposition and use of their possessions.

(i) However, there may be circumstances where the intent of transferring a substance or object purports to be its beneficial use by another person, but the intent of that other person appears to be to subject the substance or object to a recovery operation or to dispose of it. An example would be where the holder claims to be transferring a by-product for use as fuel or for agricultural land spreading, but the recipient appears to be treating it as waste and as surplus to his own requirements. The guidance suggests that in such cases it may be helpful to ask whether the purpose of the proposed use is wholly or mainly to relieve the holder or user of the substance or object of the burden of otherwise disposing of it and whether the user would be likely to seek a substitute for the substance or object if it ceased to become available to him.

(j) The guidance also refers to the use of substances or objects by their producer, and it is suggested that where a producer puts the substance or object to beneficial use he should not be regarded as producing waste, because the substance or object has not fallen out of the commercial cycle or chain of utility. The example is given of a horse riding stable operated in association with a market garden, where the operator may use manure either to produce compost for the market garden or for sale as fertiliser to customers of the business. In such circumstances, the guidance suggests, neither use would constitute disposal or recovery within the terms of the Framework Directive. However, there may be cases where the beneficial use to which the substance is put by the producer appears to be purely incidental, and is essentially for the purpose of relieving the producer of disposing of the substance or oject in any other way. Again, here it would be relevant to ask whether the producer would be likely to seek a substitute for the substance or object if it ceased to become available.

(k) The guidance considers the issue of how waste can cease to be waste and concludes that transport or consignment of waste to a recovery facility will not of itself cause the material to cease to be waste. The guidance suggests that the recovery of waste occurs when its processing produces a material of sufficient beneficial use to eliminate or diminish sufficiently the threat opposed by the original production of the waste. This will generally take place when the recovered material can be used as raw material in the same way as raw materials of non-waste origin by a person other than a specialised recovery establishment or undertaking.

[Application to the Isles of Scilly

76.—(1) Subject to the provisions of any order under this section, this Part shall not apply in relation to the Isles of Scilly.

(2) The Secretary of State may, after consultation with the Council of the Isles of Scilly, by order provide for the application of any provisions of this Part to the Isles of Scilly; and any such order may provide for the application of those provisions to those Isles with such modifications as may be specified in the order.

(3) An order under this section may—
  (a) make different provision for different cases, including different provision in relation to different persons, circumstances or localities; and
  (b) contain such supplemental, consequential and transitional provision as the Secretary of State considers appropriate, including provision saving provision repealed by or under any enactment.]

COMMENCEMENT
February 1, 1996 (S.I. 1996 No. 186).

GENERAL NOTE
This section was substituted by the Environment Act 1995, s.118(3), for the previous s.76, which stated that Pt. II would apply to the Isles of Scilly with such modifications as the Secretary of State by order specified, but which was never brought into force.

Transition from Control of Pollution Act 1974 to this Part

77.—(1) This section has effect for the purposes of the transition from the provisions of Part I of the Control of Pollution Act 1974 ("the 1974 Act") to the corresponding provisions of this Part of this Act and in this section—
  "existing disposal authority" has the same meaning as in section 32 above;
  "existing disposal licence" means a disposal licence under section 5 of the 1974 Act subsisting on the day appointed under section 164(3) below for the repeal of sections 3 to 10 of the 1974 Act and "relevant appointed day for licences" shall be construed accordingly;
  "existing disposal plan" means a plan under section 2 of the 1974 Act subsisting on the day appointed under section 164(3) below for the repeal of that section and "relevant appointed day for plans" shall be construed accordingly;
  "relevant part of its undertaking," in relation to an existing disposal authority, has the same meaning as in section 32 above; and
  "the vesting date," in relation to an existing disposal authority and its waste disposal contractors, means the vesting date under Schedule 2 to this Act.

(2) An existing disposal licence shall, on and after the relevant appointed day for licences, be treated as a site licence until it expires or otherwise ceases to have effect; and accordingly it shall be variable and subject to revocation or suspension under this Part of this Act and may not be surrendered or transferred except under this Part of this Act.

(3) The restriction imposed by section 33(1) above shall not apply in relation to land occupied by an existing disposal authority for which a resolution of the authority subsists under section 11 of the 1974 Act on the relevant appointed day for licences until the following date, that is to say—
  (a) in the case of an authority which transfers the relevant part of its undertaking in accordance with a scheme under Schedule 2 to this Act, the date which is the vesting date for that authority; and
  (b) in any other case, the date on which the authority transfers, or ceases itself to carry on, the relevant part of its undertaking or ceases to provide places at which and plant and equipment by means of which controlled waste can be disposed of or deposited for the purposes of disposal.

(4) Any existing disposal plan of an existing disposal authority shall, on and after the relevant appointed day for plans, be treated as the plan of that authority under section 50 above and that section shall accordingly have

effect as if references in it to "the plan" included the existing disposal plan of that authority.

(5) Subsection (4) above applies to Scotland and, for the purposes of that application, "existing disposal authority" means any authority constituted as a disposal authority for any area before the day appointed for this section to come into force and "that authority" means the waste disposal authority for that area under section 30(2) above.

(6) Subject to subsection (7) below, as respects any existing disposal authority—

    (a) the restriction imposed by section 51(1) of this Act on the means whereby the authority arranges for the disposal of controlled waste shall not apply to the authority—

        (i) in the case of an authority which transfers the relevant part of its undertaking in accordance with a scheme under Schedule 2 to this Act, until the date which is the vesting date for that authority; and

        (ii) in any other case, until the date on which the authority transfers, or ceases itself to carry on, the relevant part of its undertaking or ceases to provide places at which and plant and equipment by means of which controlled waste can be disposed of or deposited for the purposes of disposal; and

    (b) on and after that date, section 14(4) of the 1974 Act shall not authorise the authority to arrange for the disposal of controlled waste except by means of arrangements made (in accordance with Part II of Schedule 2 to this Act) with waste disposal contractors.

(7) The Secretary of State may, as respects any existing disposal authority, direct that the restriction imposed by section 51(1) above shall not apply in the case of that authority until such date as he specifies in the direction and where he does so paragraph (a) of subsection (6) above shall not apply and paragraph (b) shall be read as referring to the date so specified.

(8) In section 14(4) of the 1974 Act, after the words "this subsection," there shall be inserted the words "but subject to subsection (6) of section 77 of the Environment Protection Act 1990 as respects any time after the date applicable to the authority under paragraph (a) or (b) of that subsection."

(9) As respects any existing disposal authority, until the date which is, under subsection (6)(a) above, the date until which the restriction imposed by section 51(1) of this Act is disapplied,—

    (a) the powers conferred on a waste disposal authority by section 55(2)(a) and (b) of this Act as respects the recycling of waste and the use of waste to produce heat or electricity shall be treated as powers which the authority may exercise itself; and

    (b) the power conferred on a waste disposal authority by section 48(4) of this Act to object to a waste collection authority having waste recycled where the disposal authority has made arrangements with a waste disposal contractor for the contractor to recycle the waste shall be available to the waste disposal authority where it itself has the waste recycled.

<small>Definitions</small>
    "controlled waste": s.75(4).
    "disposed of": s.29(6).
    "site licence": s.35(12).
    "waste disposal contractors": s.30(5).

<small>Commencement</small>
May 31, 1991 (S.I. 1991 No. 1319).

<small>General Note</small>
This section makes various transitional provisions as to site licences and disposal authorities.

Subs. (2)
Existing disposal licences. Disposal licences granted under the 1974 Act effectively become site licences under Pt. II of the Act as from the appointed day, and therefore are subject to the same provisions on variation, revocation, suspension, transfer and surrender.

Subs. (3)
Land occupied by existing disposal authorities. This subsection ensures that until the date of transfer of its disposal undertaking to a waste disposal company, or until the date of cessation of that part of its undertaking, a waste disposal authority may continue to carry on its disposal activities lawfully under a resolution granted under s.11 of the 1974 Act.

Subs. (6)
Existing disposal authorities. This subsection allows for transition of disposal functions from disposals authorities to waste disposal contractors. The relevant date is the vesting date under a Sched. 2 scheme of transfer or alternatively, if there is no such scheme, the date of actual transfer. Until that date the authority is not restricted from dealing with the waste itself, but after that date the waste may only be disposed of by waste disposal contractors. Further, until that date, the disposal authority enjoys the ancillary powers related to disposal referred to in subs. (9).

This Part and radioactive substances

78. Except as provided by regulations made by the Secretary of State under this section, nothing in this Part applies to radioactive waste within the meaning of the [Radioactive Substances Act 1993]; but regulations may—

 (a) provide for prescribed provisions of this Part to have effect with such modifications as the Secretary of State considers appropriate for the purposes of dealing with such radioactive waste;

 (b) make such modifications of the [Radioactive Substances Act 1993] and any other Act as the Secretary of State considers appropriate.

COMMENCEMENT
December 13, 1991 (S.I. 1991 No. 2829).

AMENDMENTS
The words in square brackets were substituted by the Radioactive Substances Act 1993. Reference previously had been to the Radioactive Substances Act 1960, which is now consolidated into the 1993 Act.

GENERAL NOTE
The effect of s.78 is that Pt. II of the Act does not apply to radioactive waste as defined in the Radioactive Substances Act 1993 save to the extent the Secretary of State so provides in regulations.
  The definition of radioactive waste in the 1993 Act, s.2 is:

"Waste which consists wholly or partly of—
 (a) a substance or article which, if it were not waste, would be radioactive material, or
 (b) a substance or article which has been contaminated in the course of the production, keeping or use of radioactive material, or by contact with or proximity to other waste falling within paragraph (a) or this paragraph."

"Radioactive material" is defined by s.1 of the 1993 Act and by reference to the elements specified in the First Schedule.
  "Waste" is defined at s.47 of the 1993 Act in terms consistent with the definition contained in s.75 of the 1990 Act before its modification by the Waste Management Licensing Regulations 1994 and subsequently the Environment Act 1995. Thus there is now a discrepancy between the two definitions.
  On the Government's policy as to radioactive waste management generally, see Cm. 2919 (July 1995): *Review of Radioactive Waste Management Policy in Final Conclusions.*

[PART IIA

CONTAMINATED LAND

GENERAL NOTE
This Part of the Act was inserted by s.57 of the Environment Act 1995. It represents the Government's attempt to formulate a new regime for dealing with the problems arising from contaminated land. While existing provisions such as those on statutory nuisance (Part III of the Environmental Protection Act 1990), the removal of unlawfully deposited waste (s.59 of the 1990 Act) and works to prevent or remedy water pollution (s.161 of the Water Resources Act 1991 or, in Scotland, s.46 of the Control of Pollution Act 1974) were capable of application to contaminated land situations, they were in some respects inadequate and did not provide a comprehensive framework for the identification, assessment and remediation of the wide variety of contaminated sites in Great Britain.

Policy background
Concern was focused on contaminated land by two reports of the House of Commons Select Committee on the Environment dealing with toxic waste and contaminated land: House of Commons Session 1988–89; Second Report, *Toxic Waste* (22 I–III); Session 1989–90, First Report, *Contaminated Land* (170 I–III). See also S. R. Tromans and R. T. F. Turrall-Clarke, *Contaminated Land* (Sweet & Maxwell, 1994) in particular, Chap. 1.
  In the second of these Reports, the Select Committee recognised the difficult policy issues raised by any statutory scheme of liability but suggested that nonetheless action was needed:

" ... urgent attention [must] be given to the question of creating statutory liability for damage caused by contamination to land—particularly where this causes damage to neighbouring property or the environment. We recognise that this will raise complex questions as to retrospection, insurance cover and limitation periods in particular, but we believe that that present lack of clarity in relation to civil liability hampers the development of appropriate policies on the issue of contaminated land."

The initial response of the Government was not to address the issue of statutory liability directly, but to introduce a provision (s.143 of the Environmental Protection Act 1990) for public registers of land which had been subject to a "contaminative use": a use which might cause land to be contaminated with noxious substances. This approach was intended, with "minimal demands" on local authority resources (*Hansard*, H.L. Vol. 520, col. 2269), to provide a means of alerting interested parties to the possible existence of contamination without "extending planning blight in those areas of the country with a legacy of industrial land use". (DoE News Release No. 279, April 30, 1990.)
  This proved to be a somewhat optimistic assumption. Section 143 was intended to be implemented late in 1991. But, following an initial consultation exercise as to the range of uses to be prescribed as "contaminative", the Government announced on March 10, 1992 that it was postponing the introduction of the registers in view of the concerns that had been expressed over them, relating to the likelihood of serious blight in an already depressed property market.
  A second consultation process ensued, with a markedly reduced list of contaminative uses, and with a proposed timetable leading to the opening of the registers to public inspection in about April 1994. This exercise enabled the Government to identify three serious grounds for criticism of the proposed registers. Being based on current or former use of land rather than actual contamination, they would include a number of sites which were not actually contaminated, whilst excluding others which were. Furthermore, the logical consequence of a register based on historical fact as to land use would have been the inability to have land removed from the register following completion of clean-up. Finally, the system would have left it unclear what action should be taken and by whom, *i.e.* whether the land should be cleaned up and, if so, who should pay and how much.
  These misgivings led the Government to withdraw the proposal for registers, a decision announced by the then Secretary of State for the Environment, Michael Howard, on March 24, 1993. Mr Howard announced the institution of a "wide-ranging review" of the legal powers of public bodies to control and tackle contaminated land, to be conducted by an inter-departmental group under the chairmanship of the Department of Environment. Following similar consultation exercises in Scotland, the Secretary of State for Scotland announced an equivalent review on the same date.
  As part of this review process, the Government's first step was to issue the consultation paper, *Paying for Our Past: the Arrangements for Controlling Contaminated Land and Meeting the Cost of Remedying Damage to the Environment* (March 1994). In Scotland, a similar though not identical consultation paper entitled *Contaminated Land Clean-up and Control* (March 1994)

was issued by the Scottish Office Environment Department. Its conclusions did not differ in any material respect from those of the consultation paper issued in England and Wales. Neither Paper presented any firm proposals but rather set out a number of "preliminary conclusions" and posed a series of questions for respondents, grouped under seven issues:

   A. What should the objectives be within policy?
   B. How should the statutory framework meet the objectives?
   C. What relationship should the statutory framework have with the common law?
   D. Should there be any extension of strict liability?
   E. Who should pay for putting right environmental damage?
   F. How should markets be provided with information?
   G. What other roles should public sector bodies have?

These Papers, inconclusive even by consultation paper standards, instituted another phase of the debate, which culminated on November 24, 1994 with the publication of the outcome of the review, *Framework for Contaminated Land* (and in Scotland, *Contaminated Land Clean-up and Control: Outcome of Review*), and the subsequent passage of the Environment Act 1995, s. 57 of which introduced into this Act a new Part IIA dealing with contaminated land.

The central planks of the *Framework*, which were substantially mirrored by those of its Scottish counterpart, were said to be:

   (1) The maintenance of the "suitable for use" approach, requiring remedial action only where the contamination poses unacceptable actual or potential risks to health or the environment, and where there are "appropriate and cost-effective means to do so, taking into account the actual or intended use of the site".

   (2) To deal with "urgent and real problems, but in an orderly and controlled fashion with which the economy at large and individual businesses and land-owners can cope".

   (3) The creation of greater clarity and certainty than the law currently provides, so as to assist in the development of an efficient market in land which is contaminated and in land which has been subject to remedial works.

   (4) Replacing the existing statutory nuisance powers, which "have provided an essentially sound basis for dealing with contaminated land", with a modern, specific contaminated land power. Here the position in Scotland differs, and the *Outcome of Review* indicated that the introduction of the contaminated land regime was to coincide with the extension to Scotland of the statutory nuisance provisions already existing in England and Wales, replacing existing provisions. This is achieved by s.107 of and Sched. 17 to the 1995 Act.

Time will no doubt tell to what extent the actual drafting of the relevant provisions achieves those objectives. Substantial amendments were made to the provisions during the Parliamentary process, in response to concerns expressed by the industrial, financial, land-owning and legal communities: taken together, these amendments have had the effect of mitigating somewhat the harshness of the proposed liability regime and of making its provisions more palatable. Nonetheless the fact remains that the new sections constitute a regime of strict and retroactive liability for historic contamination, and that liability can extend in certain circumstances not only to the original polluter, but also to an "innocent" landowner or occupier.

As mentioned below, much reliance is placed on Government guidance as a means of mitigating the potentially harsher operations of the legislation, for example what degree of contamination or risk is sufficient to justify action, and how liability is to be apportioned between a number of potentially liable parties. At the time of the passage of the 1995 Act, none of this guidance was in final form, and much had not emerged even in draft form.

The Scheme of the Provisions

The new provisions follow through a sequence from the identification of contaminated land to securing its remediation. Primary responsibility for this process rests with local authorities, though both the Secretary of State and the Environment Agency/SEPA also have very important roles to play, as explained below.

   1. *Identifying Contaminated Land.* "Contaminated Land" is defined at s.78A(2) by reference to the subjective opinion of the local authority in whose area it is situated as to whether it is in such a condition by reason of substances in, on or under it, that significant harm is being caused or there is a significant possibility of such harm being caused, *or* that pollution of controlled waters is being or is likely to be caused. The local authority is under a statutory duty to cause its area to be inspected from time to time for the purpose of identifying such land (s.78B(1)). In making the determination as to whether the land is contaminated or not, the local authority is required to act in

accordance with guidance from the Secretary of State as to the manner in which the determination is to be made (s.78A(2)).

2. *Notification.* Upon identifying contaminated land, the local authority is required give notice of that fact to:
   (a) the Agency or SEPA;
   (b) the owner of the land;
   (c) any person who appears to be the owner or occupier of all or part of the land; and
   (d) the person who appears to be the "appropriate person", *i.e.* who caused or knowingly permitted the contamination, and as such may be served with a remediation notice.

3. *Special Sites.* As well as identifying contaminated land, the local authority must decide whether such land is required to be designated as a "special site": ss.78B(1)(b) and 78C(1). The significance of this distinction is that in the case of special sites the Agency/SEPA is the enforcing authority rather than the local authority (s.78A(9)). Before making this decision, the local authority must request the advice of the Agency/SEPA and have regard to the advice received (s.78C(3)). Land is, however, only required to be designated as a special site if it falls within a description prescribed for this purpose by the Secretary of State (s.78C(8)). The Agency/SEPA may itself consider that contaminated land falls within such a description, and may give notice of that fact to the local authority (s.78C(4)). Disagreements between the Agency/SEPA and the local authority are resolved by referral to the Secretary of State (s.78D).

4. *Duty to require remediation.* Where land has been identified as contaminated or has been designated as a special site, then the relevant enforcing authority falls under a duty to serve on the "appropriate person" a remediation notice, specifying what is to be done by way of remediation and within what period (s.78E(1)). In this context remediation can mean either works to assess the situation, or actual remedial or mitigating measures, or subsequent inspections (s.78A(10)). This duty is, however, qualified in four important respects:
   (a) the requirement of prior consultation under s.78H (see below);
   (b) restrictions on service of a notice under s.78H;
   (c) the requirement that remediation may only comprise those things the authority considers reasonable, having regard to the cost likely to be involved and the seriousness of the harm in question (s.78E(4)); and
   (d) the requirement to have regard to guidance issued by the Secretary of State (s.78E(5)).

5. *Determination of the "appropriate person".* Section 78F deals with the vital issue of who is the appropriate person or persons to bear responsibility to comply with the remediation notice. As might be expected, the section was extremely controversial at the Parliamentary stage, and has been heavily amended. Responsibility rests primarily with the person or persons who caused or knowingly permitted the contaminating substances to be in, on or under the land: s.78F(2). However, the current owner or occupier may also be liable where, after reasonable inquiry, no such person can be found: s.78F(4) and (5). Specific provision is made with regard to those acting in the context of insolvency (e.g. receivers): s.78X(3). No special provision is, however, made for lenders, other than the definition of "owner", which makes it clear that a mortgagee or, in Scotland, a creditor in a heritable security not in possession, is not within the definition: s.78A(9). One very difficult issue is that of joint and several liability. The starting point is that where a number of persons have contributed the same, or different, contaminating substances liability may be joint and several: s.78F(2). However, this potential liability is mitigated in two respects: first, by the requirement that the remedial action required to be taken by any appropriate person be "referable" to the substances he contributed (s.78F(3)) and, secondly, by the obligation of the enforcing authority in determining who is the appropriate person, to act in accordance with guidance issued by the Secretary of State: s78F(6) and (7). Special provision is also made for the situation where substances migrate from their original source, so as to cause other land to become contaminated: s.78K.

6. *Consultation.* One of the numerous amendments to the original provisions is the requirement for the enforcing authority to use reasonable endeavours to consult with the person who appears to be the responsible person, and with the owner and the occupier of the relevant land: s.78H(I). The consultation must relate to what is to be done by way of remediation and no remediation notice may be served during a three month period from the original notification (see (2) above): s.78H(3). Certain

circumstances are Specified where no remediation notice may be served at all, for example where the authority is satisfied that there is nothing that could reasonably be required, having balanced cost considerations against the seriousness of the contamination, or where the authority is satisfied that appropriate steps are being or will be taken by way of remediation voluntarily, without the need for service of a remediation notice: s.78H(5) In such cases, the outcome will be the preparation and publication of either a remediation declaration (by the authority) or a remediation statement (by the responsible person): s.78H(6) and (7).

7. *Appeals against remediation notices.* Where a remediation notice is served, the recipient has a right of appeal: s.78L. Notices served by local authorities are appealed to the magistrates' court, or in Scotland, to the sheriff by way of summary application. Appeals against notices served by the Agency/SEPA are determined by the Secretary of State.

8. *Offences.* Failure, without reasonable excuse, to comply with any of the requirements of a remediation notice is an offence: s.78M(1). The offence is punishable, on summary conviction only, by a maximum fine of £5,000 and a further fine of £500 per day for which failure continues after conviction. Where the contaminated land in question is "industrial, trade or business premises", the respective figures are £20,000 and £2,000. In England and Wales, the enforcing authorities may bring their own prosecutions, whereas in Scotland, enforcing authorities have no prosecution powers: they must report any alleged offences to the Procurator Fiscal who may bring a prosecution (see note to s.37 of the 1995 Act).

9. *Default powers.* As well as instigating a prosecution, an enforcing authority may itself carry out remediation works in a number of cases, for example, where works are urgently required to prevent serious harm of which there is imminent danger, or where the responsible person has entered into a written agreement for the authority to carry out the works, or where the recipient of a remediation notice fails to comply with it: s.78N. In a number of these cases, the authority is entitled to recover its reasonable costs, subject to considerations of hardships and guidance issued by the Secretary of State: s.78P. Additionally, in England and Wales (but not in Scotland) the authority may serve a charging notice, the effect of which is that the sums expended carry interest and that the cost and accrued interest form a charge on the premises.

10. *Registers.* Section 143 of this Act is repealed by Schedule 24 of the Environment Act 1995. Whilst the registers envisaged by s.143 have thus come to nothing, the new provisions include the maintenance of public registers of remediation notices and other matters (such as appeals and convictions): s.78R. Provisions deal with the exclusion of information from the register on grounds of national security and commercial confidentiality: ss.78S and 78T.

The role of statutory guidance

A number of the provisions on contaminated land require the exercise of discretion in making difficult decisions: Is land contaminated? What should be required by way of remediation? On whom should the remediation notice be served? Such issues are not susceptible to ready answers being given in the primary legislation; yet consistency and equity could be said to require something more than non-statutory guidance. The Government's solution has been to create a strong form of statutory guidance which the enforcing authority is required to follow, and which is itself subject to a negative resolution type of Parliamentary procedure: s.78YA. In other cases, the guidance is not subject to this special procedure and does not have prescriptive effect.

In February 1996 the Department of the Environment informally circulated for consultation working drafts of much of the guidance provided for by the contaminated land provisions. The intention at the time was to lay finalised guidance before Parliament (where required by s.78YA) late in 1996, following formal consultation. Since the working drafts appeared likely to be subject to significant revision, this commentary does not consider them further.

The types of guidance for which provision is made are as follows:

Type of Guidance	Provision	Effect of Guidance
Whether land is "contaminated"	s.78A(2) and 78A(8)	Local authority required to act in accordance with it

Type of Guidance	Provision	Effect of Guidance
Inspection of area to identify contaminated land	s.78B(2)	Local authority required to act in accordance with it
What is to be done by way of remediation; standard of remediation in terms of cost	s.78E(5)	Enforcing authority to have regard to it. (*N.B.:* guidance not issued under s.78YA)
Which of two or more persons who may be "appropriate" is to be treated as not being appropriate	s.78F(6)	Enforcing authority to make determination in accordance with it
Where two or more persons are "appropriate" in what proportions they are to bear the cost of remediation	s.78F(7)	Enforcing authority to make determination in accordance with it
Whether to recover all or part of remediation costs incurred by enforcing authority from the appropriate person	s.78P(2)	Enforcing authority to have regard to guidance (*N.B.:* guidance not issued under s.78YA)
Inspection and review of special sites and termination of designation as special sites	s.78Q(6)	Agency/SEPA to act in accordance with it
Site specific guidance by Agency/SEPA with regard to exercise or performance of local authority's functions in relation to any particular contaminated land	s.78V(1) and (2)	Local authority to have regard to it except in so far as it is inconsistent with any guidance issued by the Secretary of State
Guidance to Agency/SEPA with respect to the exercise or performance of its powers or duties	s.78W(1)	Agency/SEPA to have regard to it

Regulations, orders and directions
Quite apart from the wealth of guidance provided for by the new Part IIA of this Act, there is also bestowed on the Secretary of State in a number of places the power to make regulations or orders or to give directions, and for ease of reference these are listed below:

Type of Regulations	Provision
Designating descriptions of land required to be designated as a special site	s.78C(8)
Prescribing procedure for service of a remediation notice	s.78E(1)
Prescribing procedure for application for compensation, and determining the amount of such compensation, where rights granted enabling compliance with a remediation notice	s.78G(5)
Prescribing manner of consultation prior to service of a remediation notice	s.78H(2)
Making provision in respect of appeals against a remediation notice	s.78L(4)

Type of Regulations	Provision
Making provision in respect of appeals against a charging notice	s.78P(10)
Prescribing the offences and other additional matters to be included on registers of contaminated land	s.78R(1)
Prescribing the form in which certain notifications may be included on such registers	s.78R(2)
Prescribing the places at which such registers are to be made available to the public	s.78R(8)
Applying Part IIA provisions (modified as appropriate) to apply to radioactive contamination, and modifying Radioactive Substances Act 1993	s.78YC
N.B. s.78X(5) provides that regulations may make different provision for difference cases or circumstances	

Type of Order	Provision
Order increasing maximum fine for s.78M(1) offence in relation to industrial, trade or business premises	s.78M(4)
Order extending provisions (modified as appropriate) to the Isles of Scilly	s.78Y(2)

Type of Direction	Provision
Direction to exclude information from the registers, or refer it to Secretary of State for determination, on grounds of national security	s.78S(2)
Direction to include commercially confidential information on the registers, on grounds of public interest	s.78T(7)

Relationship of Part IIA and previous law

The Government has been anxious to stress on a number of occasions that the provisions on contaminated land are not intended to create new categories of liability, and simply reflect the pattern of powers and duties under previous law, most notably statutory nuisance. See for example, H.L. Vol. 560, col. 1461 and H.L. Vol. 562, col. 1054. Certainly the scheme of liability bears many striking similarities to statutory nuisance, with the primary responsibility resting with the originator of the contamination and residual liability with the current owner or occupier.

Specifically, steps have been taken to restrict liability where the harm or risk presented by the contaminated land takes the form of water pollution: s.78J. Here, liability does not extend to the owner or occupier purely in their capacity as owner or occupier; thereby according broadly with the position under s.161 of the Water Resources Act 1991 (or, in Scotland, under s.46 of the Control of Pollution Act 1974) which refers to those causing or knowingly permitting pollution, but not to the owner or occupier. See H.C. Standing Committee B, 11th sitting, col. 354, May 23, 1995. Similarly, restrictions apply in relation to remediation in respect of water from abandoned mines, so as to reflect the position under the Water Resources Act (or, in Scotland, under the Control of Pollution Act), as modified by the Environment Act 1995.

Indeed, the Government can with some justice point out that there are safeguards such as the requirements for consultation before service of a notice, the role of Government guidance and the provisions on financial hardship, which make Part IIA preferable to statutory nuisance from the perspective of anyone facing potential liability. See H.L. Vol. 562, col. 1055. There is also no provision in Part IIA corresponding to that in s.82 of this Act which permits any person aggrieved by the existence of a statutory nuisance to make a complaint direct to a magistrates' court.

Despite these similarities and safeguards, Part IIA cannot with total credibility be presented as nothing more than incremental change to previous law. The provisions on liability exist within an overarching framework of statutory duties to seek out, identify, prioritise and remediate contaminated land as such. If those duties are not performed, or are perceived by a non-governmental environmental organisation as being performed inadequately they may well provide the basis for actual or threatened judicial review proceedings. Overall, it seems unlikely simply to be "business as usual" so far as contaminated land is concerned. See for example the views of Baroness Hilton of Eggardon at H.L. Vol. 565, col. 1499:

> "For the first time local authorities will have an explicit duty to inspect their areas in order to identify contaminated land. The existing provisions, which are much more vague and tenuous, require only that they identify nuisances."

One measure of the significance of this new explicit duty is the extent to which local authorities had active programmes to identify contaminated land prior to the introduction of the regime. A survey of local authorities in England and Wales by the Chartered Institute of Environmental Health (CIEH), to which 303 out of a total of 405 responded, indicated that only 64 out of the 303 respondents had such a programme in 1993/94: CIEH *Report on Environmental Health 1993/94.*

Relationship with other relevant areas of law
Provision is made as to the relationship between the provisions on contaminated land and other potentially relevant areas of law, so as to avoid duplication or conflict of regulation.
  (a) *Part I 1990 Act.* Where it appears that clean up powers exist under s.27 of this Act in respect of contamination caused by breach of IPC or LAPC provisions, a remediation notice may not be served: s.78YB(1).
  (b) *Part II 1990 Act.* Where a waste site licence is in force in relation to land, Part IIA is inapplicable, except to the extent that the relevant harm or pollution is attributable to causes other than breach of the site licence, or the carrying on of any activity authorised by the licence and in accordance with its conditions: s78YB(2). Contamination which results from carrying on the licensed activities, or from breach of the licence conditions, is therefore outside the scope of Part IIA.
  (c) *Clean up powers under s.59 1990 Act.* A remediation notice may not be served where the contamination results from the deposit of controlled waste and powers exist under s.59 to secure the removal of unlawfully deposited controlled waste: s.78YB(3).
  (d) *Consented discharges to water.* A remediation notice may not require a person to do anything which would impede the making of a discharge to controlled waters pursuant to a consent under Chapter II of Part III of the Water Resources Act 1991 (or, in Scotland, Part II of the Control of Pollution Act 1974): s.78YB(4).
  (e) *Radioactive substances.* The provisions on contaminated land do not apply in relation to harm or pollution of controlled waters, so far as attributable to radioactivity: s.78YC. However, regulations may apply the provisions of Part IIA to such radioactivity, with such modifications as the Secretary of State considers appropriate.
  (f) *Statutory nuisance.* No matter shall constitute a statutory nuisance to the extent that it consists of, or is caused by, any land being in a contaminated state: s.79(1A) and (1B), as inserted by the 1995 Act, Sched. 22, para. 89(3). Statutory nuisance powers are thus disapplied in relation to contaminated land situations. It should be noted, however, that for this purpose the test of land being in a "contaminated state" is simply that of harm or risk of harm, not significant harm or significant risk. The practical effect of this is to avoid the prospect of land which presented a risk of harm, but fell short of the significant harm test, being subject to statutory nuisance liability, which would have circumvented the policy decision to confine clean-up to cases of significant harm. If contaminated land is presenting a statutory nuisance in some way unrelated to the contamination (*e.g.* by noise from operations carried out on the land) then of course statutory nuisance provisions remain applicable. The independent overhaul of statutory nuisance in Scotland is effected by s.107 of the 1995 Act.
  (g) *Water pollution clean-up powers.* Powers exercisable by the NRA in relation to anti-pollution measures under s.161 of the Water Resources Act 1991 (or, in Scotland, by river purification authorities under s.46 of the Control of Pollution Act 1974) were generally regarded as inadequate to deal with complex and contentious problems such as those presented by contaminated land. Those provisions have now been supplemented by the more powerful means of works notices requiring clean-up under s.161A (inserted by Sched. 22, para. 162 to the 1995 Act) (or, in Scotland, under s.46A of the 1974 Act (inserted by Sched. 22, para. 29(22) to the 1995 Act)). There appears to be nothing to prevent s.161A (or, in Scotland, s.46A), being used in relation to

contaminated land, thus presenting the possibility of dual enforcement. See further the general note to s.78YB.

Preliminary

78A.—(1) The following provisions have effect for the interpretation of this Part.

(2) "Contaminated land" is any land which appears to the local authority in whose area it is situated to be in such a condition, by reason of substances in, on or under the land, that—

    (a) significant harm is being caused or there is a significant possibility of such harm being caused; or

    (b) pollution of controlled waters is being, or is likely to be, caused;

and, in determining whether any land appears to be such land, a local authority shall, subject to subsection (5) below, act in accordance with guidance issued by the Secretary of State in accordance with section 78YA below with respect to the manner in which that determination is to be made.

(3) A "special site" is any contaminated land—

    (a) which has been designated as such a site by virtue of section 78C(7) or 78D(6) below; and

    (b) whose designation as such has not been terminated by the appropriate Agency under section 78Q(4) below.

(4) "Harm" means harm to the health of living organisms or other interference with the ecological systems of which they form part and, in the case of man, includes harm to his property.

(5) The questions—

    (a) what harm is to be regarded as "significant",

    (b) whether the possibility of significant harm being caused is "significant",

    (c) whether pollution of controlled waters is being, or is likely to be caused,

shall be determined in accordance with guidance issued for the purpose by the Secretary of State in accordance with section 78YA below.

(6) Without prejudice to the guidance that may be issued under subsection (5) above, guidance under paragraph (a) of that subsection may make provision for different degrees of importance to be assigned to, or for the disregard of,—

    (a) different descriptions of living organisms or ecological systems;

    (b) different descriptions of places; or

    (c) different descriptions of harm to health or property, or other interference;

and guidance under paragraph (b) of that subsection may make provision for different degrees of possibility to be regarded as "significant" (or as not being "significant") in relation to different descriptions of significant harm.

(7) "Remediation" means—

    (a) the doing of anything for the purpose of assessing the condition of—

        (i) the contaminated land in question;

        (ii) any controlled waters affected by that land; or

        (iii) any land adjoining or adjacent to that land;

    (b) the doing of any works, the carrying out of any operations or the taking of any steps in relation to any such land or waters for the purpose—

        (i) of preventing or minimising, or remedying or mitigating the effects of, any significant harm, or any pollution of controlled waters, by reason of which the contaminated land is such land; or

    (ii) of restoring the land or waters to their former state; or
  (c) the making of subsequent inspections from time to time for the purpose of keeping under review the condition of the land or waters;

and cognate expressions shall be construed accordingly.

(8) Controlled waters are "affected by" contaminated land if (and only if) it appears to the enforcing authority that the contaminated land in question is, for the purposes of subsection (2) above, in such a condition, by reason of substances in, on or under the land, that pollution of those waters is being, or is likely to be caused.

(9) The following expressions have the meaning respectively assigned to them—

"the appropriate Agency" means—
  (a) in relation to England and Wales, the Environment Agency;
  (b) in relation to Scotland, the Scottish Environment Protection Agency;

"appropriate person" means any person who is an appropriate person, determined in accordance with section 78F below, to bear responsibility for any thing which is to be done by way of remediation in any particular case;

"charging notice" has the meaning given by section 78P(3)(b) below;

"controlled waters"—
  (a) in relation to England and Wales, has the same meaning as in Part III of the Water Resources Act 1991; and
  (b) in relation to Scotland, has the same meaning as in section 30A of the Control of Pollution Act 1974;

"creditor" has the same meaning as in the Conveyancing and Feudal Reform (Scotland) Act 1970;

"enforcing authority" means—
  (a) in relation to a special site, the appropriate Agency;
  (b) in relation to contaminated land other than a special site, the local authority in whose area the land is situated;

"heritable security" has the same meaning as in the Conveyancing and Feudal Reform (Scotland) Act 1970;

"local authority" in relation to England and Wales means—
  (a) any unitary authority;
  (b) any district council, so far as it is not a unitary authority;
  (c) the Common Council of the City of London and, as respects the Temples, the Sub-Treasurer of the Inner Temple and the Under-Treasurer of the Middle Temple respectively;

and in relation to Scotland means a council for an area constituted under section 2 of the Local Government etc. (Scotland) Act 1994;

"notice" means notice in writing;

"notification" means notification in writing;

"owner", in relation to any land in England and Wales, means a person (other than a mortgagee not in possession) who, whether in his own right or as trustee for any other person, is entitled to receive the rack rent of the land, or, where the land is not let at a rack rent, would be so entitled if it were so let;

"owner", in relation to any land in Scotland, means a person (other than a creditor in a heritable security not in possession of the security subjects) for the time being entitled to receive or who would, if the land were let, be entitled to receive, the rents of the land in connection with which the word is used and includes a trustee, factor, guardian or curator and in the case of public or municipal land includes the persons to whom the management of the land is entrusted;

"pollution of controlled waters" means the entry into controlled waters of any poisonous, noxious or polluting matter or any solid waste matter;

"prescribed" means prescribed by regulations;

"regulations" means regulations made by the Secretary of State;

"remediation declaration" has the meaning given by section 78H(6) below;

"remediation notice" has the meaning given by section 78E(1) below;

"remediation statement" has the meaning given by section 78H(7) below;

"required to be designated as a special site" shall be construed in accordance with section 78C(8) below;

"substance" means any natural or artificial substance, whether in solid or liquid form or in the form of a gas or vapour;

"unitary authority" means—

    (a) the council of a county, so far as it is the council of an area for which there are no district councils;

    (b) the council of any district comprised in an area for which there is no county council;

    (c) the council of a London borough;

    (d) the council of a county borough in Wales.

COMMENCEMENT

September 21, 1995 in so far as this section confers power on the Secretary of State to issue guidance or makes provision with respect to the exercise of such power (S.I. 1995 No. 1983). The remainder will be brought into force by a commencement order made under s.125(3) of the Environment Act 1995.

GENERAL NOTE

This section contains the various definitions relating to this Part of the Act.

"Contaminated land"

The starting point of the definition is whether land appears to the local authority in whose area it is situated to be in a certain condition. The words "appears to the local authority" are subjective in effect, though the appearance of subjectivity is deceptive. In determining whether land appears to it to be contaminated, the local authority must act in accordance with the Secretary of State's guidance: s.78(2).

The definition of contaminated land must be read together with the supplementary provisions in s.78X, which allow the effects of two or more sites to be considered together, and deals with the situation where land adjoining or adjacent to the local authority's area causes the relevant problems within its area.

"Substances in, on or under the land"

The adverse environmental condition of the land must result from "substances in, on or under the land". The definition of "substance" is wide and includes both natural and artificial substances, as well as gases: s.78B(9). There is nothing in the legislation which expressly confines it to substances the presence of which results from human activity, as opposed to substances naturally present: however, the draftsman clearly had it in mind, in s.78F(2), that someone would have caused or knowingly permitted them to be present. The substances may be within the land, or on its surface. In most cases, the substances will be present in the sub-surface or underlying strata. However, since "land" itself is not defined for the purpose of the provisions, its definition in Sched. 1 to the Interpretation Act 1978 is applicable:

> " 'Land' includes buildings and other structures, land covered with water, and any estate, interest, easement, servitude or right in or over land."

Thus the words of the definition are also wide enough to catch substances which are present in underground or surface structures or containers, if the relevant conditions of harm or risk of harm are fulfilled: for example chemicals stored in corroded drums, or friable asbestos in a building. There is in principle no restriction on where in the building in question the substances which render the land contaminated are located. The words would also cover substances present in groundwater beneath land, or present in the soil beneath inland waters (for example, contaminated sediments under a river bed; see also "controlled waters" below).

One issue which arose in debate was that of deep contamination, for example in underground mine workings. Lord Northbourne posed the question: "Is a landowner to be made responsible for whatever goes on under his land, however deep down?" (H.L. Vol. 560, col. 1424). In answering, Viscount Ullswater indicated that the Government's intention in including the word "under" in the definition was to ensure that there were no undesirable omissions and that substrata and contaminated silts under streams or ponds were covered: H.L. Vol. 560, col. 1425. In relation to mineral workings, Viscount Ullswater referred to the Interpretation Act 1978 definition noted above, whereby land includes any estate, interest, easement, servitude or right in or over land. The Government's intention was that in general, the owner of the mine or mineral rights, not the surface owner, would be liable:

> "The primary responsibility for remediation of any mines identified as contaminated land would obviously fall on anyone who caused or knowingly permitted the contaminating substances to be there. But any residual responsibility passing to the 'owner' of the land would, as a result of the definition of land in the Interpretation Act [1978] fall to the owner of the mine or mineral rights, and not to the owner of the surface land where he is a different person" (H.L. Vol. 562, col. 1038.) See also H.L. Vol. 562, cols. 165–166.

"Harm"
One limb of the test relates to significant harm or the significant possibility of significant harm. Originally, the term "harm" had not been qualified in any way. At Lords Committee Stage the test of "serious" harm was proposed by Lord Northbourne: this was however rejected by the Government as too narrow and restrictive: H.L. Vol. 560, cols. 1427–1428, January 31, 1995.

"Harm" is defined by s.78A(7). Unlike other definitions of harm contained in this Act, it does not include offence to man's senses. This was a deliberate decision as the Government did not wish land to be regarded as contaminated for example on the basis of odours which were not harmful to health, and in respect of which statutory nuisance powers would be available. See H.L. Vol. 560, col. 1440. The word "significant" was introduced at the Lords Report Stage and is used in two separate contexts, relating both to the harm itself and to the possibility of the harm. "Significant" is clearly a word which may have various shades of meaning, and the precise meaning to be placed upon it in this context is determined by the guidance to be issued by the Secretary of State (s.78A(2), as to which, see below).

Pollution of controlled waters
Pollution of ground or surface water is one of the most serious problems presented by contaminated land and provides a second limb of the test. "Controlled waters" are given the same meaning as in the Water Resources Act 1991 in England and Wales and the Control of Pollution Act 1974 in Scotland (see below). "Pollution" is defined to mean the entry of poisonous, noxious or polluting matter, or any waste matter. This does not mean that harm must be shown to have resulted from that entry: see *R. v. Dovermoss Limited*, [1995] Env.L.R. 258 (C.A.), where it was held that the likelihood or capability of causing harm was sufficient.

By s.78A(8) controlled waters are only to be treated as affected by contaminated land if the condition of the land is such that pollution of the waters is being, or is likely to be, caused. As with the "harm" limb of the test, under s.78A(2) guidance by the Secretary of State is crucial to what is regarded as pollution or the likelihood of pollution (see below).

Guidance on determining whether land is contaminated
Subsections (2) and (8) of s.78A make reference to guidance by the Secretary of State on the manner in which the determination is to be made and on the question of whether harm or the possibility of harm are to be regarded as significant. The relevant determinations are to be made in accordance with that guidance. The Government took the view that it would not be possible to prescribe for all possible circumstances what answers should be given on the detailed technical judgements required for each individual site: H.L. Vol. 562 col. 138.

Guidance for England and Wales was published in draft form on May 5, 1995, for information during passage of the Environment Bill. Draft guidance had, at the time of writing, to be issued for Scotland although it is likely to be very similar to the draft guidance for England and Wales. The draft is to be developed further for consultation, before being laid before Parliament under the procedure set out in s.78YA. The guidance may therefore change in the course of being finalised, but the first draft indicates the following approach:

(a) The local authority should disregard harm or interference other than certain types, *i.e.* harm to human users or occupiers of the land in its current use, or to the health of current human users or occupiers of other land, harm to or interference with ecosystems protected under the Wildlife and Countryside Act 1981 or the EC Directives on wild birds (79/409/EEC) and habitats (92/43/EEC), or harm to property in relation to the present use of the land or other land. In relation to wildlife protection, the Government indicated in debate that its intention was not to introduce new requirements for the protection of habitats and ecological systems over and above those already in place under existing legislation: H.L. Vol. 562, col. 138.

(b) The authority should disregard any harm or interference other than certain types, *i.e.* death, serious injury or clinical toxicity in the case of harm to human health, a significant change in the functioning of ecosystems in protected areas, or physical damage to property which cannot be rectified without substantial works and which, in the case of livestock and crops, causes loss in value.

(c) The authority should disregard harm to living organisms or interference with ecosystems where the harm or interference is an intended and legal result of the addition of substances to the land, *e.g.* the controlled use of pesticides.

(d) The approach to the determination should be based on the fundamental principles of risk assessment, which will usually involve identification of a source-pathway-target relationship, with risk estimation as a final stage.

(e) The same approach is applicable to the question of whether pollution of controlled waters is being or is likely to be caused, though the sensitivity of the relevant controlled waters and the effectiveness of any possible preventive measures will also be relevant.

(f) The guidance deals in tabular form with the significance to be attached to the various combinations of possibility and degree of harm (covering "severe, moderate, mild and minimal harm", and "high, medium, low and very low" degrees of possibility).

"Remediation"

Subsection (7) defines remediation, *i.e.* those actions which may be required by a remediation notice. It covers three types of activity:

(a) Assessment of the condition of the contaminated land, any controlled waters "affected by" the land (see subs. (8)), and any land adjoining or adjacent to the contaminated land. This will cover, for example, the taking and analysis of soil or water samples, on-site or off-site.

(b) Works, operations or steps in relation to such land or waters (*i.e.* the contaminated land itself, controlled waters affected by it, and adjoining or adjacent land). Those works may be for the purpose of preventing, minimising, mitigating or remedying the relevant harm or pollution, or of restoring the land or waters to their former state. "Former state" must presumably refer to the condition of the land or water prior to the introduction of the relevant harmful substances or pollutants, though precisely what that condition was may be difficult to establish.

(c) Subsequent inspections from time to time for the purpose of keeping under review the condition of the land or waters. "Inspection" in this context must presumably mean more than visual inspection and would cover works required to review the condition of soil or water; in many cases this will mean a continued regime of sampling.

As will be appreciated, the definition of remediation is a comprehensive one, which makes it important to note the restrictions, contained elsewhere, on what may be required by way of remediation, particularly s.78E(4) and (5).

"Controlled waters"

The definition is by reference to the Water Resources Act 1991 for England and Wales (s.104) and to the Control of Pollution Act 1974 for Scotland (s.30A as inserted by Sched. 23 to the Water Act 1989). Both definitions cover essentially:

(a) territorial waters, *i.e.* those extending seaward for three miles from the relevant baseline (and areas of territorial sea beyond that limit up to a maximum of 12 miles fixed by the Territorial Sea Act 1987 if added by order of the Secretary of State);

(b) coastal waters, *i.e.* those inland from that baseline as far as the highest tide or freshwater limit;

(c) inland waters, *e.g.* relevant lochs, lakes and ponds, and relevant rivers and watercourses above the fresh water limit; and

(d) groundwaters, *i.e.* any waters contained in underground strata.

However, the definitions differ in certain details, which may or may not be significant. The definition applying to Scotland includes within the definition of groundwater, water in wells, boreholes and other excavations. The definition applying to England and Wales states that references to waters of lakes, ponds or watercourses include reference to the bottom, channel or bed which is for the time being dry: s.104(2).

"Creditor"

Section 9(8)(c) of the Conveyancing and Feudal Reform (Scotland) Act 1970 reads as follows:

" '*debt*' means any obligation due, or which will or may become due, to repay or pay money, including any such obligation arising from a transaction or part of a transaction in the course of any trade, business or profession, and any obligation to pay an annuity or *ad factum praestandum*, but does not include an obligation to pay any feuduty, ground annual, rent or other periodical sum payable in respect of land, and 'creditor' and 'debtor', in relation to a standard security, shall be construed accordingly."

The Government's intention was that the definition of owner in terms of lenders should be of similar effect in Scotland as in England and Wales: see H.L. Vol. 562, col. 1040.

"Heritable security"
Section 9(8)(a) of the Conveyancing and Feudal Reform (Scotland) Act 1970 reads as follows:

" 'heritable security' ... means any security capable of being constituted over any interest in land by disposition or assignation of that interest in security of any debt and of being recorded in the Register of Sasines."

Identification of contaminated land

78B.—(1) Every local authority shall cause its area to be inspected from time to time for the purpose—
  (a) of identifying contaminated land; and
  (b) of enabling the authority to decide whether any such land is land which is required to be designated as a special site.
  (2) In performing its functions under subsection (1) above a local authority shall act in accordance with any guidance issued for the purpose by the Secretary of State in accordance with section 78YA below.
  (3) If a local authority identifies any contaminated land in its area, it shall give notice of that fact to—
  (a) the appropriate Agency;
  (b) the owner of the land;
  (c) any person who appears to the authority to be in occupation of the whole or any part of the land; and
  (d) each person who appears to the authority to be an appropriate person;
and any notice given under this subsection shall state by virtue of which of paragraphs (a) to (d) above it is given.
  (4) If, at any time after a local authority has given any person a notice pursuant to subsection (3)(d) above in respect of any land, it appears to the enforcing authority that another person is an appropriate person, the enforcing authority shall give notice to that other person—
  (a) of the fact that the local authority has identified the land in question as contaminated land; and
  (b) that he appears to the enforcing authority to be an appropriate person.

DEFINITIONS
  "appropriate Agency": s.78A(9).
  "appropriate person": s.78A(9).
  "contaminated land": s.78A(9).
  "enforcing authority": s.78A(9).
  "functions": s.124(1).
  "local authority": s.78A(9).
  "notice": s.78A(9).
  "owner": s.78A(9).
  "required to be designated as a special site": s.78C(8).
  "special site": s.78A(3).

COMMENCEMENT
September 21, 1995 in so far as this section confers power on the Secretary of State to issue guidance or makes provision with respect to the exercise of such power (S.I. 1995 No. 1983). The remainder will be brought into force by a commencement order made under s.125(3) of the Environment Act 1995.

GENERAL NOTE

This section creates a statutory duty on local authorities to cause their area to be inspected for the purpose of identifying contaminated land and enabling a decision to be made as to whether any contaminated land identified is required to be designated as a special site.

"Cause its area to be inspected"

The language here is the same as that used in relation to statutory nuisance, though whereas a typical statutory nuisance is likely to be self-evident, a very different approach will be necessary to identify contaminated land, the risks and problems of which will not necessarily be apparent on visual inspection. The Government rejected an amendment imposing a requirement for quinquennial review, stating that local authorities should concentrate resources on areas where there were likely to be problems: H.L. Vol. 562, col. 167. No express power is provided to cover default by local authorities in their statutory duties. An amendment proposing the inclusion of such a power was rejected on the basis that default was a matter for "local political judgments and remedies": H.L. Vol. 562, col. 229.

Secretary of State's guidance

As with other issues, guidance issued by the Secretary of State is determinative of how a local authority is to exercise its function of inspection. The draft guidance issued for information in May 1995 (see notes to s.78A above) includes guidance as to the issue of inspection. This stresses that different local authorities will inevitably face different levels of problems associated with contaminated land in their areas, resulting from different historical factors and underlying geology. The preliminary draft states that each authority should prepare an "appropriate local strategy", making effective use of resources and ensuring effort is concentrated first on the areas where the chance of discovery of significant harm is greatest. This strategy should include:

— the use of existing information held by the authority;
— the identification of those areas in which vulnerable targets are present, as a first priority for inspection; and
— the way in which new information on the condition or circumstances of land in its area can be taken into account.

The draft guidance lists various factors which the authority should consider in preparing its strategy. These include: the extent to which information is already available; the extent to which vulnerable targets are likely to be in contact with contaminated land; and history, scale and nature of former industrial use; the relative likelihood of different descriptions of harm; the extent to which action has already been taken to deal with contamination; geological and hydrogeological features; and the nature and timing of redevelopment in different parts of the area.

The draft guidance also highlights the fact that some authorities will already have information about the condition of land in their area which will inform their views on the general likelihood of contaminated land being found; other authorities may be assisted by a pilot study of a representative part of their area. Some authorities may already be aware of specific sites which give cause for concern, or may become aware of such sites by reason of third party complaints, or through the planning process. Other authorities may have already collated information on past uses of land in readiness for compilation of the registers under s.143 of this Act, at the time when it seemed that the section would be brought into force.

Powers of entry

The rights of entry, testing, etc., available to local authorities in pursuance of their statutory duties are provided by s.108 of the 1995 Act, the provisions on contaminated land being one of the "pollution control functions" set out in that section (s.108(15)). See the note to s.108 of the 1995 Act for further discussion, which includes consideration of whether the power to carry out experimental borings and install, keep or maintain monitoring and other apparatus (s.108(5)) is available for the purpose of establishing whether land is contaminated.

Notification

By s.78B(4) a local authority which identifies contaminated land is required to give notice of that fact (no form of notice is specified) to various parties, including the person who appears to have caused or knowingly permitted the contaminating substances to be in, on or under the land (if such person can be found). By subs. (5), where after notice has been given to a person who appears to be the "appropriate person", it appears that some other person or persons is or are the appropriate person or persons, a fresh notice must be given to that person or persons. No provision is made for withdrawal of a notice where it no longer appears that the recipient is the appropriate person, though it presumably is possible for the authority to do this.

Somewhat surprisingly, s.78R does not provide for the inclusion on the registers established under that section of notices served under s.78B(4). Regulations under s.78R(1)(l) may however require their inclusion on such registers. If not, then such notices are presumably publicly available under the Environmental Information Regulations 1992, and it would appear to be wise for prospective purchasers of land to ask the local authority whether any such notice has been served, as well as to inspect the register.

Identification and designation of special sites

78C.—(1) If at any time it appears to a local authority that any contaminated land in its area might be land which is required to be designated as a special site, the authority—

    (a) shall decide whether or not the land is land which is required to be so designated; and

    (b) if the authority decides that the land is land which is required to be so designated, shall give notice of that decision to the relevant persons.

(2) For the purposes of this section, "the relevant persons" at any time in the case of any land are the persons who at that time fall within paragraphs (a) to (d) below, that is to say—

    (a) the appropriate Agency;

    (b) the owner of the land;

    (c) any person who appears to the local authority concerned to be in occupation of the whole or any part of the land; and

    (d) each person who appears to that authority to be an appropriate person.

(3) Before making a decision under paragraph (a) of subsection (1) above in any particular case, a local authority shall request the advice of the appropriate Agency, and in making its decision shall have regard to any advice given by that Agency in response to the request.

(4) If at any time the appropriate Agency considers that any contaminated land is land which is required to be designated as a special site, that Agency may give notice of that fact to the local authority in whose area the land is situated.

(5) Where notice under subsection (4) above is given to a local authority, the authority shall decide whether the land in question—

    (a) is land which is required to be designated as a special site, or

    (b) is not land which is required to be so designated,

and shall give notice of that decision to the relevant persons.

(6) Where a local authority makes a decision falling within subsection (1)(b) or (5)(a) above, the decision shall, subject to section 78D below, take effect on the day after whichever of the following events first occurs, that is to say—

    (a) the expiration of the period of twenty-one days beginning with the day on which the notice required by virtue of subsection (1)(b) or, as the case may be, (5)(a) above is given to the appropriate Agency; or

    (b) if the appropriate Agency gives notification to the local authority in question that it agrees with the decision, the giving of that notification;

and where a decision takes effect by virtue of this subsection, the local authority shall give notice of that fact to the relevant persons.

(7) Where a decision that any land is land which is required to be designated as a special site takes effect in accordance with subsection (6) above, the notice given under subsection (1)(b) or, as the case may be, (5)(a) above shall have effect, as from the time when the decision takes effect, as the designation of that land as such a site.

(8) For the purposes of this Part, land is required to be designated as a special site if, and only if, it is land of a description prescribed for the purposes of this subsection.

(9) Regulations under subsection (8) above may make different provision for different cases or circumstances or different areas or localities and may, in particular, describe land by reference to the area or locality in which it is situated.

(10) Without prejudice to the generality of his power to prescribe any description of land for the purposes of subsection (8) above, the Secretary of State, in deciding whether to prescribe a particular description of contaminated land for those purposes, may, in particular, have regard to—

(a) whether land of the description in question appears to him to be land which is likely to be in such a condition, by reason of substances in, on or under the land that—
   (i) serious harm would or might be caused, or
   (ii) serious pollution of controlled waters would be, or would be likely to be, caused; or
(b) whether the appropriate Agency is likely to have expertise in dealing with the kind of significant harm, or pollution of controlled waters, by reason of which land of the description in question is contaminated land.

DEFINITIONS
"appropriate Agency": s.78A(9).
"appropriate person": s.78A(9).
"contaminated land": s.78A(2).
"harm": s.78A(4).
"local authority": s.78A(9).
"notice": s.78A(9).
"owner": s.78A(9).
"regulations": s.78A(9).
"relevant persons": subs. (2).
"required to be designated as a special site": s.78C(8).
"significant": s.78A(5).
"special site": s.78A(3).

COMMENCEMENT
September 21, 1995 in so far as this section confers power on the Secretary of State to make regulations or makes provision with respect to the exercise of such power (S.I. 1995 No. 1983). The remainder will be brought into force by a commencement order made under s.125(3) of the Environment Act 1995.

GENERAL NOTE
This section deals with the designation of special sites: the importance of such designation is that the Agency or SEPA, rather than the local authority, is the enforcing authority (s.78A(9)). Land is only required to be designated as a special site if it is of a description prescribed by regulations (s.78C(8)). The criteria for prescribing descriptions of land for this purpose may, in particular have regard to:

(a) whether the harm or pollution that might be caused by the substances in, on or under the land are "serious" as opposed to "significant"; and
(b) whether the Agency/SEPA is likely to have expertise in dealing with the type of harm or pollution in question (s.78C(10)).

As initially drafted, the Bill proposed the creation of a special category of "closed landfills" so as to give this type of site a "more tailored approach": H.L. Vol. 560 col. 1432. However, the Government ultimately acceded to the arguments against such a distinction, which were compellingly put by Lord Crickhowell on the basis that it was not clear why a closed steelworks or gasworks should be seen as posing less serious problems than a closed landfill: see H.L. Vol. 562, cols. 156, 158, 160.

Procedure for designation

The initial onus is with the local authority to decide, following inspection, whether land is required to be designated as a special site: ss.78B(1)(b) and 78C(1)(a). In making its decision, the local authority must request the advice of the Agency/SEPA and have regard to any advice given: subs. (3). If the local authority decides that the land is required to be designated as a special site, then notice of that fact must be given to the persons specified at subs. (2); it appears that this notification may be combined with that required by subs. (3) (that the land has been identified as contaminated land) or may be given separately.

The Agency/SEPA may itself form the view that land is required to be designated as a special site, in which case it may give notice of that fact to the local authority, which must then decide whether or not this is the case: subss. (4) and (5). The outcome of that decision must be notified to the relevant persons including the Agency/SEPA: subs. (5).

A decision that land is required to be designated as a special site takes effect, under subs. (6), twenty-one days from the date of notification to the Agency/SEPA (subject to the referral procedure under s.78D) or upon notification by the Agency/SEPA of agreement with the decision. The notice given of the decision to the relevant persons then takes effect as the designation (subs. (7)) and notice that the decision has taken effect must be given by the authority to the relevant persons: subs. (6).

It should be noted that a site can be designated as a special site even after service of a remediation notice by the local authority. Provisions covering this eventuality are to be found in s.78Q.

Referral of special site decisions of the Secretary of State

78D.—(1) In any case where—

(a) a local authority gives notice of a decision to the appropriate Agency pursuant to subsection (1)(b) or (5)(b) of section 78C above, but

(b) before the expiration of the period of twenty-one days beginning with the day on which that notice is so given, that Agency gives the local authority notice that it disagrees with the decision, together with a statement of its reasons for disagreeing,

the authority shall refer the decision to the Secretary of State and shall send to him a statement of its reasons for reaching the decision.

(2) Where the appropriate Agency gives notice to a local authority under paragraph (b) of subsection (1) above, it shall also send to the Secretary of State a copy of the notice and of the statement given under that paragraph.

(3) Where a local authority refers a decision to the Secretary of State under subsection (1) above, it shall give notice of that fact to the relevant persons.

(4) Where a decision of a local authority is referred to the Secretary of State under subsection (1) above, he—

(a) may confirm or reverse the decision with respect to the whole or any part of the land to which it relates; and

(b) shall give notice of his decision on the referral—

(i) to the relevant persons; and

(ii) to the local authority.

(5) Where a decision of a local authority is referred to the Secretary of State under subsection (1) above, the decision shall not take effect until the day after that on which the Secretary of State gives the notice required by subsection (4) above to the persons there mentioned and shall then take effect as confirmed or reversed by him.

(6) Where a decision which takes effect in accordance with subsection (5) above is to the effect that at least some land is land which is required to be designated as a special site, the notice given under subsection (4)(b) above shall have effect, as from the time when the decision takes effect, as the designation of that land as such a site.

(7) In this section "the relevant persons" has the same meaning as in section 78C above.

DEFINITIONS
"appropriate Agency": s.78A(9).
"local authority": s.78A(9).
"notice": s.78A(9).
"relevant persons": subs. (7); s.78C(2).
"required to be designated as a special site": s.78C(8).

COMMENCEMENT
These provisions will be brought into force by a commencement order made under s.125(3) of the Environment Act 1995.

GENERAL NOTE
This section provides a mechanism for resolving disagreement between the local authority and the Agency/SEPA as to whether land is required to be designated as a special site. The disagreement may arise either where the authority makes the initial decision under s.78C(1), or where the Agency/SEPA has notified the authority of its view that the land is required to be designated, but the authority decides under s.78C(5) that it does not. In either case the Agency/SEPA has a 21 day period from being notified of the decision to give notice to the authority that it disagrees with the decision, together with a statement of its reasons for disagreeing (subs. (1)(b)). The authority must then refer the decision to the Secretary of State.

The relevant persons (referred to in s.78C as including the owner, occupier and appropriate person) must be notified of the referral to the Secretary of State and must also be notified of the final decision: subss. (3) and (4)(b). There is no statutory right for them to make representations to the Secretary of State, though there is nothing to prevent them doing so.

The Secretary of State has a wide discretion in making his determination and may decide, for example, that part only of the relevant land is to be designated as a special site: subss. (4) and (6).

Duty of enforcing authority to require remediation of contaminated land etc.

78E.—(1) In any case where—
    (a) any land has been designated as a special site by virtue of section 78C(7) or 78D(6) above, or
    (b) a local authority has identified any contaminated land (other than a special site) in its area,
the enforcing authority shall, in accordance with such procedure as may be prescribed and subject to the following provisions of this Part, serve on each person who is an appropriate person a notice (in this Part referred to as a "remediation notice") specifying what that person is to do by way of remediation and the periods within which he is required to do each of the things so specified.

(2) Different remediation notices requiring the doing of different things by way of remediation may be served on different persons in consequence of the presence of different substances in, on or under any land or waters.

(3) Where two or more persons are appropriate persons in relation to any particular thing which is to be done by way of remediation, the remediation notice served on each of them shall state the proportion, determined under section 78F(7) below, of the cost of doing that thing which each of them respectively is liable to bear.

(4) The only things by way of remediation which the enforcing authority may do, or require to be done, under or by virtue of this Part are things which it considers reasonable, having regard to—
    (a) the cost which is likely to be involved; and
    (b) the seriousness of the harm, or pollution of controlled waters, in question.

(5) In determining for any purpose of this Part—
    (a) what is to be done (whether by an appropriate person, the enforcing authority or any other person) by way of remediation in any particular case,

(b) the standard to which any land is, or waters are, to be remediated pursuant to the notice, or

(c) what is, or is not, to be regarded as reasonable for the purposes of subsection (4) above,

the enforcing authority shall have regard to any guidance issued for the purpose by the Secretary of State.

(6) Regulations may make provision for or in connection with—

(a) the form or content of remediation notices; or

(b) any steps of a procedural nature which are to be taken in connection with, or in consequence of, the service of a remediation notice.

<small>DEFINITIONS</small>
"appropriate person": s.78A(9).
"contaminated land": s.78A(2).
"enforcing authority": s.78A(9).
"harm": s.78A(4).
"local authority": s.78A(9).
"notice": s.78A(9).
"pollution of controlled waters": s.78A(9).
"regulations": s.78A(9).
"remediation notice": subs. (1).
"special site": s.78A(3).
"substance": s.78A(9).

<small>COMMENCEMENT</small>
September 21, 1995 in so far as this section confers power on the Secretary of State to issue guidance or make regulations or makes provision with respect to the exercise of such power (S.I. 1995 No. 1983). The remainder will be brought into force by a commencement order made under s.125(3) of the Environment Act 1995.

<small>GENERAL NOTE</small>
The section imposes a duty on the relevant enforcing authority, when contaminated land has been identified or a special site has been designated, to serve a remediation notice on each person who is an appropriate person, as determined under s.78F.

Suspicion not a ground for serving notice
During debates the question arose as to whether an enforcing authority might form the view that land was likely to be contaminated by virtue of its past use, and then serve a notice requiring detailed investigation. This is clearly not the Government's intention, as Viscount Ullswater indicated that the Government believed that the enforcing authority "... should have to be able to demonstrate that actual contamination existed on any site, and that there was sufficient contamination for the site to qualify as contaminated land, before it could require any remediation work, including further assessment." (H.L. Vol. 562, col. 175: see also H.C. Standing Committee B, 11th sitting, Pt I, col. 341).

Form of notice
No form is prescribed in the section for a remediation notice, though form and content and procedures for service may be prescribed by regulations: subss. 78E(1) and (6). The notice must specify:

(a) what is to be done by way of remediation by the person on whom it is served; and

(b) the periods within which he is to do each of the things so specified.

"Remediation" is widely defined (see note to s.78A) and can include a variety of actions. Difficult questions may arise as to the degree of exactitude with which the remedial actions required by the notice must be specified, and the risk is that a notice which does not give sufficient detail may be held void for uncertainty. The wording of s.78E(1) itself, referring to "each of the things so specified" is indicative that some precision is required. Case law also suggests that a notice which may have penal consequences if not complied with should tell the recipient what works are to be carried out so that he can be clear that he has complied with the notice: see *Network Housing Association v. Westminster City Council, The Times,* November 8, 1994 (noise nuisance); *Berridge Incinerators v. Nottinghamshire County Council* (Nottingham Crown Court, June 12, 1992, unreported—notice under s.59 of the 1990 Act); *R. v. Fenny Stratford Justices, ex parte Watney Mann Midlands Ltd* [1976] 1 W.L.R. 110 (noise nuisance); *R. v. East Northamptonshire District Council, ex p. Brian Fossett* [1994] Env. L.R.388. For a Scottish case on the clarity required in a notice, see *McNaughton v. Peter McIntyre (Clyde) Ltd.* 1981 SPLP 15 in which a planning enforcement notice requiring removal of stone from the foreshore was invalid because it was impossible to tell from the notice which stone was to be removed. However, the Government gave an indication in debate that they intended that remediation notices "should generally be phrased in terms of objectives to be achieved rather than specific works which have to be undertaken" (H.L. Vol. 562, col. 1047, Viscount Ullswater).

Multiple notices
The section contemplates two separate situations where multiple notices may be served in relation to the same land. The first is where there is more than one person who is the appropriate person in relation to the remedial action required, and in this respect the section needs to be read in conjunction with s.78F. In this situation, a remediation notice must be served on each appropriate person (s.78E(1)) but each notice must state the proportion, determined under s.78F(7), of the cost which each of them respectively is liable to bear in doing the thing for which they are the appropriate persons: s.78E(3). The second situation is where different contaminating substances are present and require the doing of different things by way of remediation. In this case, different remediation notices may be served on different persons: s.78E(2).

Consecutive notices
The remediation of contaminated land may require a phased approach, involving sampling, trials and feasibility studies prior to remedial action, which in turn may be followed by post-operational monitoring. If land continues to fall within the definition of "contaminated land" after one notice has been served and complied with, there would be nothing to prevent a subsequent notice being served. For example, the enforcing authority may know that land is contaminated but may not be able to specify what should be done to clean it up until further monitoring has been completed. There seems no reason why a first notice should not be served requiring such monitoring, followed by a second notice containing the clean up requirements, since the land will still be contaminated after the monitoring has been completed. Indeed, if those clean up requirements proved to be inadequate to the extent that after their completion the land still fell within the definition of contaminated land, the authority would be obliged to determine whether service of a further notice is required.

There is no provision for a civil remedy against the authority if the cost of remediation in such a case proves to be greater than it would have been had the initial clean up requirements been worded so as to secure adequate remediation without the service of a further notice. Although the possibility remains of an action against the authority on common law principles of negligence, the practical likelihood of success for such an action is limited both by the hurdles which are required to be overcome in establishing the liability of a public authority for the negligent exercise of its statutory functions and by the opportunity which the appropriate person had to influence the content of the remediation notice during the three month period before its service. Clearly, this latter factor will not weigh against the plaintiff where by virtue of s.78H(4) the consultation period was not observed in a case of imminent danger of serious harm or where the plaintiff's (in Scotland, the pursuer's) views were ignored by the local authority in its formulation of the notice requirements.

Restriction on content of remediation notice: subs. (4)
This subsection represents an overriding restriction on what may be required by way of remediation. The test is subjective, referring to what is reasonable in the opinion of the authority, which must have regard to the likely cost involved and the seriousness of the harm. The authority will presumably already have formed a view on the second issue (*i.e.* seriousness of harm) in the course of determining whether the land is contaminated. The first consideration will however involve the authority in taking steps to inform itself of the likely cost of what it proposes to require: failure to take adequate steps to do so may result in the notice being challenged.

It should be noted that the factors expressly referred to relate simply to the objective cost and seriousness of harm, and not to more specific issues such as the value of the land or financial hardship to the appropriate person (compare in the latter respect, s.78P(2)(a)). However, it could be argued that the two matters expressly referred to at (a) and (b) are not exclusive and do not preclude the authority having regard to other considerations in determining what is reasonable. This may be clarified in the guidance referred to in s.78E(5) (see below).

Secretary of State's guidance: subs. (5)
In determining the three issues referred to in this subsection, the authority must have regard to any guidance issued by the Secretary of State. This guidance is not required to be issued under the special Parliamentary procedure of s.78YA(2)–(4) and is therefore subject simply to the consultation and publication requirements of s.78YA(1) and (5). The guidance is not prescriptive but the enforcing authority must have regard to it. The guidance is relevant not only to determining what should be considered as reasonable under subs. (2) but in determining for any purpose under Part IIA what is to be done by way of remediation by any person, and the standard to which land or waters are to be remediated.

Remediation declarations
Where subss. (4) or (5) apply so as to preclude the inclusion of some thing within a remediation notice, the authority must serve a remediation declaration under s.78H(6).

Determination of the appropriate person to bear responsibility for remediation

78F.—(1) This section has effect for the purpose of determining who is the appropriate person to bear responsibility for any particular thing which the enforcing authority determines is to be done by way of remediation in any particular case.

(2) Subject to the following provisions of this section, any person, or any of the persons, who caused or knowingly permitted the substances, or any of the substances, by reason of which the contaminated land in question is such land to be in, on or under that land is an appropriate person.

(3) A person shall only be an appropriate person by virtue of subsection (2) above in relation to things which are to be done by way of remediation which are to any extent referable to substances which he caused or knowingly permitted to be present in, on or under the contaminated land in question.

(4) If no person has, after reasonable inquiry, been found who is by virtue of subsection (2) above an appropriate person to bear responsibility for the things which are to be done by way of remediation, the owner or occupier for the time being of the contaminated land in question is an appropriate person.

(5) If, in consequence of subsection (3) above, there are things which are to be done by way of remediation in relation to which no person has, after reasonable inquiry, been found who is an appropriate person by virtue of subsection (2) above, the owner or occupier for the time being of the contaminated land in question is an appropriate person in relation to those things.

(6) Where two or more persons would, apart from this subsection, be appropriate persons in relation to any particular thing which is to be done by way of remediation, the enforcing authority shall determine in accordance with guidance issued for the purpose by the Secretary of State whether any, and if so which, of them is to be treated as not being an appropriate person in relation to that thing.

(7) Where two or more persons are appropriate persons in relation to any particular thing which is to be done by way of remediation, they shall be liable to bear the cost of doing that thing in proportions determined by the enforcing authority in accordance with guidance issued for the purpose by the Secretary of State.

(8) Any guidance issued for the purposes of subsection (6) or (7) above shall be issued in accordance with section 78YA below.

(9) A person who has caused or knowingly permitted any substance ("substance A") to be in, on or under any land shall also be taken for the purposes of this section to have caused or knowingly permitted there to be in, on or under that land any substance which is there as a result of a chemical reaction or biological process affecting substance A.

(10) A thing which is to be done by way of remediation may be regarded for the purposes of this Part as referable to the presence of any substance notwithstanding that the thing in question would not have to be done—

(a) in consequence only of the presence of that substance in any quantity; or

(b) in consequence only of the quantity of that substance which any particular person caused, or knowingly permitted to be present.

DEFINITIONS

"appropriate person": s.78A(9).
"contaminated land": s.78A(2).
"enforcing authority": s.78A(9).
"owner": s.78A(9).
"remediation": s.78A(7).
"substance": s.78A(9).
"substance A": subs. (9).

COMMENCEMENT

September 21, 1995 in so far as this section confers power on the Secretary of State to issue guidance or makes provision with respect to the exercise of such power (S.I. 1995 No. 1983). The remainder will be brought into force by a commencement order made under s.125(3) of the Environment Act 1995.

GENERAL NOTE

This is a vitally important section. Its purpose, as indicated by subs. (1), is the determination of who is the appropriate person to bear responsibility for remediation. It is important to note that the concept of appropriate person is referable to the particular thing which the enforcing authority determines is to be done by way of remediation: it is not simply a case of saying that there is one person responsible for everything required by way of remediation in relation to a given piece of land. The significance of guidance to be issued under subss. (6) and (7) should also be noted: this may address some of the potentially harsh consequences to which attention is drawn below.

Subs. (2): primary responsibility

Primary responsibility rests with the person, or any of the persons, who either caused or knowingly permitted all or any of the contaminating substances to be in, on or under the land in question. Where two or more persons fall within this category then the prescriptive guidance to be issued by the Secretary of State will determine which of them is responsible, and in what proportions: subss. (6) and (7). Liability is also limited by the concept of referability under subss. (3) and (10) (see below). Apart from these provisions, the starting point of subs. (2) is that of joint and several liability, as indicated by the words "any of the persons" and "any of the substances".

Subs. (2): "caused"

The question of which person or persons caused a contaminating substance to be present will generally be a question of fact. The issue is likely to be approached by the courts in a commonsense way but without knowledge, fault or any other state of mind being required to be shown: See *Alphacell v. Woodward* [1972] A.C. 824 (H.L.) and (in relation to Scotland) *Lockhart v. NCB* 1981 S.L.T. 161 in the context of causing water pollution. In that context, it has been held that causation may be attributable to an operation or chain of operations which result in the water pollution: *Alphacell v. Woodward* (cited above); see also *NRA v. Yorkshire Water Services Ltd* [1994] 3 W.L.R. 1202 (H.L.). More than one person may be held to have caused the same event, even where they executed different and separate acts: *Attorney General's Reference (No. 1) of 1994* [1995] 2 All E.R. 1007. However the causal link between a person and the polluting incident may in some cases be broken by intervening factors such as natural forces (although see *Southern Water Authority v. Pegrum* [1989] Crim.L.R. 442), the act of a third party or an Act of God: *Lockhart v. NCB* (cited above); *Impress (Worcester) Ltd v. Rees* [1971] 2

All E.R. 357 (although note Lord Wilberforce's remarks in *Alphacell* on this case: p. 834H); *NRA v. Wright Engineering Co. Ltd* [1994] Env.L.R. 186.

It seems unlikely that someone will be regarded as having caused the substances to be on land where their role has been an entirely passive one: the question of a party's "passivity" may also be a factor where multiple parties are involved (subject to the judgment in *Attorney-General Reference (No. 1 of 1994)* noted above): *Price v. Cromack* [1975] 2 All E.R. 113; *Northwest Water Authority v. McTay Construction Ltd* Q.B.D. April 14, 1986, unreported; *Welsh Water Authority v. Williams Motors (Cwmdu) Ltd*, *The Times*, December 5, 1988. However, the House of Lords in *NRA v. Yorkshire Water Services Ltd*, whilst declining to overrule *Price v. Cromack* and *Wychavon District Council v. NRA* [1993] 1 W.L.R. 125, indicated *obiter* that those cases are not to be read as having established any general principle that a positive act is required before causation may be established. In "passivity" cases, the issue of "knowingly permitted" will then become relevant, and this term is considered below.

Where substances have migrated from one piece of land to another, the rules under s.78K will be relevant.

Subs. (2): Consignment to landfill
Whilst landfill sites which still have a licence will not be subject to Part IIA, the question may arise in the case of closed sites which constitute contaminated land as to which of the myriad parties involved could be said to have caused the substances to be there. The Government expressly indicated that it did not intend the words "caused or knowingly permitted" to be construed as including persons "merely on the grounds that they had consigned materials to an authorised waste stream"; they believed that such was already the effect of the words without the need for amendment. See H.L. Vol. 562, col. 182.

However, comments made in the Commons Standing Committee Stage indicate that the Government was not necessarily as sympathetic to those transporting waste to sites: "When individual lorry drivers or companies deliver material, they bear some responsibility for the quality of the material." (H.C. Standing Committee B, 11th Sitting, col. 341, May 23, 1995).

Subs. (2): "knowingly permitted": case law generally and meaning of "permitted"
The concept of "knowingly permitted" presents greater problems than the straightforward notion of causing. Case law on the phrase is limited, but it is clear that two elements are necessary. These are knowledge as to the presence of the substances, and failure to take steps to prevent or terminate their presence: *Berton v. Alliance Economic Investment Co. Ltd* [1922] 1 K.B. 742 (C.A.); *Commercial General Administration v. Thomsett* (1979) 250 E.G. 547; *Webb v. Maidstone & District Motor Services* 78 S.J. 336. See also *Carmichael v. L.A.W. Mining Ltd* 1995 Env.L.B. 9–10 (Sh.Ct.).

Such case law as there is on "knowingly permitting" in other contexts such as water pollution should be treated with caution, perhaps more so than with regard to "causing". There is a potentially important distinction between permitting an *event*, such as the entry of polluting matter into controlled waters, and permitting a *state of affairs*, such as the presence of substances under land. In this context the Government's rejection of a proposed amendment to the "knowingly permitting" provisions should be noted (see "*in, on or under the land*," below).

"Permitting" may involve giving permission, leave or licence for something to be done: in this sense it might include for example the owner of land who knowingly allows another to carry out a contaminating activity there, aware that contaminating substances are being introduced into the land. However, it can carry another sense, that of failure to take steps within one's power, and it is in this sense that it might be construed as applying to a subsequent owner or occupier who becomes aware that contamination is present and fails to take action.

If that interpretation were upheld, the consequences for future owners would be serious, in that they could be held primarily liable together with the original polluter (and not just in their capacity as a subsequent owner). Thus they would be potentially liable even if the original polluter could be found, and they would not benefit from the specific protections which apply to persons liable simply as owner or occupier. Indeed it does not appear out of the question that the notice required to be served under s.78B(3) might render an owner or occupier capable of being described as having "knowingly permitted" by the time the authority decides the appropriate persons on whom to serve remediation notices.

General principles of corporate liability will apply to determine whose state of knowledge may be attributed to a company: see, for example, *Tesco Supermarkets v. Nattrass* [1972] A.C. 153 (H.L.)

Subs. (2): "knowingly permitted": what must be known?
Another issue is what knowledge needs to be shown in order to establish that a person knowingly permitted something. There is clearly a difference between knowing that a substance

is present on or is being introduced into land and knowing in addition that it is a contaminative substance or is rendering the land contaminated. These two levels of knowledge correspond to what appear to be the only two possible readings of the relevant part of subs. (2) in relation to "knowingly permitting", which are described here and followed by an example which illustrates the practical significance of the issue:

    (a) one possibility is that one is an appropriate person if the substances are in fact contaminative and (whether or not one knows that fact) one "knowingly permitted the substances ... to be in, on or under the land".

    (b) the alternative is that one is only an appropriate person if one permits their presence in, on or under the land knowing that they fit the description of "substances, by reason of which the contaminated land in question is such land".

There does not appear to be available a "middle" reading whereby one is only an appropriate person if one permits the substances' presence in, on or under the land knowing that the substances are, in the ordinary sense of the word, contaminative: "contaminated land" is a precisely defined term, which involves the land "appearing" in a certain way to a local authority, incorporates the equally technical definition of "harm" and depends for its application on prescriptive guidance, so ordinary senses of the term would appear irrelevant.

The difficulty with the possible reading (b) above also follows from this. It seems absurd to argue that Parliament can have intended subs. (2) to require that, to be an appropriate person by virtue of having "knowingly permitted" something, the relevant knowledge is knowledge both that substances are in, on or under the land and also that those substances are contaminative in the very technical sense required by the Act. Indeed, if this were the reading, then the provision would be toothless against anyone whose alleged state of knowledge relates to a time prior to the point at which the land first appeared to the authority to be contaminated.

Yet if (as is submitted) reading (a) is correct then the scope of subs. (2) is very wide and injustice may conceivably result, with the increased likelihood of future owners being liable as having "knowingly permitted".

The implications of the distinction between interpretations (a) (in which liability follows from mere knowledge that one is permitting substances to be present) and (b) (in which one must also know that the substances render the land contaminated within the meaning of Part IIA) may be illustrated by the following example.

Prior to the advent of waste disposal licensing (so that s.78YB(2) or (3) do not disapply Part IIA), person X allows his land to be used by person Y for the disposal of waste. He does not at the time realise that the substances being disposed of have contaminative potential. Many years later, after Part IIA comes into force, the local authority identifies the land as having been contaminated by those substances. On reading (a) person X may well be an appropriate person as having knowingly permitted the substances to be present. On reading (b), person X's state of mind at the time when the substances were deposited does not make him an appropriate person in this capacity, since at the time he could not have had knowledge that the land "appeared" to the local authority to be in particular condition as a result of the substances: the authority had not yet formed that view.

However, having formed that view, if the authority then notifies its view to person X under s.78B(3) then from that point on, person X does have the requisite knowledge to be an appropriate person even under reading (b). If person X still has control over the land, perhaps as owner or occupier, then he may after that time become liable for knowingly permitting the continuing presence on the land of the substances. If in the intervening years X had relinquished control over the land, however, then his subsequent knowledge does not render him an appropriate person under reading (b), although he remains an appropriate person under reading (a).

If person Y deposited on person X's land substances of a kind which person X had prohibited or which had not been contemplated by person X when agreeing to allow person Y to use his land, then even on the harsher reading (a), it could not be said that person X had knowingly permitted the presence on his land of those substances.

Subs. (2): "knowingly permits": what constitutes "knowledge"?
There is authority, again from water pollution law, to suggest that "constructive knowledge" will suffice: that is, that one may be held to know that which one could in the circumstances reasonably be expected to know: *Schulmans Incorporated Limited v. NRA* [1993] Env.L.R. D.1. In the context of knowingly permitting unlicensed entertainments, wilful blindness (closing one's eyes to the obvious or failing to make enquiries which would have confirmed one's suspicions) has been held to constitute knowledge: *Westminster City Council v. Croyalgrange Ltd* [1986] 2 All E.R. 353.

Subs. (2): creating a "target" for contamination
A somewhat clearer case for liability may arise where a subsequent owner has redeveloped the site but has failed to remove contamination; or indeed by changing the use of the land has increased the risks presented by the substances. It seems clear that the Government had the responsibilities of such a person in mind in the drafting:

> "We believe that it would be reasonable for somebody who has had active control over contaminants on a site, for example when redeveloping it, to become responsible for any harm to health or the environment that may result, even if he did not originally cause or knowingly permit the site to become contaminated" (H.L. Vol. 560, col. 1461, Viscount Ullswater).

In this context the risk-orientated approach to contamination required by the definition is particularly important: although development or otherwise creating or knowingly permitted contamination may not of itself constitute causing or knowingly permitting contamination, it is clear from Viscount Ullswater's comments, that, where such a developer could be described as having also knowingly permitted the presence or continued presence of the substances, the Government would not find the consequent attachment of liability an unpalatable result.

Subs. (2): "in on or under the land"
A substance may be present on land before it makes its way into or under the land. An example would be chemicals which are stored in a surface installation at an industrial plant, but then are accidentally released and contaminate the subsurface: the chemicals were originally "on" the land, but are now "in" or "under" the land. The person (whom we might call A) who caused or knowingly permitted the chemicals to be placed originally on the land may be a different person to the person (B) who caused or knowingly permitted them to escape and to be in or under the land. Since the chemical which was in the tank or the surface is the same substance by reason of which the land is now contaminated, a strict and literal reading of subs. (2) would indicate that person A, as well as person B, is an "appropriate person". Such a result could obviously be unjust to person A, and might be avoided by construing the subsection so that the presence of the substance in, on or under the land is read as referable only to the point at which the land is in such a condition that harm or pollution of controlled waters (or the possibility or likelihood thereof) occur. On that basis the presence of the substances on land in a safe storage installation would not be relevant so as to fix person A with liability. Such a reading is difficult to reconcile with the wording of the subsection, and in any event would not benefit person A who had placed the chemical in a defective storage installation which presented the significant possibility of a harmful escape—there A would have caused the substances to be on land *and* the land thereby to come within the definition of contaminated land in s.78A.

The point was not addressed directly in debate, though at one point an amendment was proposed to replace the words "be in, on or under land" with "come into, onto or under land" as defining more accurately the polluter: H.L. Vol. 562, col. 189. Such an amendment would also have limited scope for subsequent owners to be liable, and was rejected by the Government on the basis that it would ignore the responsibility of those who "... genuinely and actively permit the continued presence of contaminating substances in land" (H.L. Vol. 562, col. 189, Viscount Ullswater).

One implication of the storage installation scenario is that a seller of land on which potentially contaminative substances are stored should consider emptying such installations on sale or seeking indemnities from any purchaser whose activities or failure to maintain such installations might result in the escape of substances originally brought onto the land by the seller.

Subss. (3) and (10): the referability limitation
As mentioned above, subs. (3) is intended to soften what would otherwise be the harsh consequences of joint and several liability which might otherwise arise under subs. (2). A person will only be "appropriate" if the relevant things required to be done by way of remediation are to any extent referable to substances which he caused or knowingly permitted to be in, on or under the land. It is necessary therefore to identify the substances which the person in question caused or knowingly permitted to be there, and to ask whether the specific remedial action is to any extent (however small) referable to those substances. For example, to take an extreme case, if two separate persons (A and B) have caused land to be contaminated with different substances (say, oil and asbestos), it would not be possible for the authority to impose a single remediation obligation for both substances so making A and B jointly and severally liable—unless, that is, the clean-up operations necessary for the oil could be said to be referable to the asbestos, and vice-versa. However, the position may also be affected by subss. (9) (see below) and (10).

Subsection 10 clarifies the meaning of the term "referable" under subs. (3). It should be remembered that subs. (3) requires the remedial action to be referable to the substances in question only "to any extent". Subsection (10) essentially avoids arguments by a potentially appropriate person that the type or amount of the substance they introduced would not of itself necessitate the relevant remedial action. The operation of paragraphs (a) and (b) of the subsection may perhaps best be illustrated by example:—

  (a) Persons A and B each introduce different substances into land. Each substance is individually harmless and would not of itself require remedial action. However, the combined presence of the two substances necessitates remediation. Subsection (10)(a) would prevent any argument by either A or B that the remediation was not referable to their substance. Note, however, that where a chemical reaction or biological process has occurred between the two substances, resulting in a third substance being formed, subs. (9) may also be relevant (see below).

  (b) Persons A and B each introduce different quantities of the same substance into land. Neither quantity of the substance would itself require remediation, but their combined quantity makes it necessary. The effect of subs. (10)(b) is that neither A or B can argue that the clean-up is not referable to the quantity of the substance for which they are responsible.

Subss. (4) and (5): liability of owner and occupier
Government policy is that the owner and occupier of land, even if "innocent" in relation to the presence of the contaminating substances, should bear responsibility for the condition of their land. Lord Northbourne, in debate, put extreme examples of cases where it would be unjust to regard an innocent owner as liable: for example an owner whose land was contaminated by a crashed tanker, or by migrating dust or particles. (H.L. Vol. 562, col. 1052). The Government's response was that it was not justifiable to relieve owners of liabilities which they might already incur under existing legislation and that it was reasonable for owners to bear responsibility for their property and its effects on others and the wider environment in cases where no original polluter can be found: H.L. Vol. 562, col. 1052.

As originally drafted, there were three circumstances where the current owner or occupier would be the appropriate person to bear responsibility for remediation. Two of these circumstances were dropped in the course of the passage of the Bill: namely cases where the owner/occupier refused consent for remediation works to be carried out on their land and, secondly, cases where the liability of the original "polluter" had been directly or indirectly transferred. The original provisions on transfer of liability were particularly difficult to understand, though they were basically prompted by the Government's wish to respect contractual provisions: see H.L. Vol. 562, cols. 1048–1051. On looking at the matter more closely, however, the Government concluded that it would be more practical to leave the question to be dealt with through the normal contractual means of guarantees and indemnities rather than detailed statutory provisions: H.L. Vol. 565, col. 1498.

Two circumstances now remain where the owner or occupier is liable under this provision; namely where after "reasonable inquiry" no person has been found who bears responsibility as an appropriate person under subs. (2) or where something to be done by way of remediation cannot be regarded as "referable" to anyone under subs. (3).

Subss. (4) and (5): "no person ... has been found"
Where the identity of the original person or company causing contamination is known but that person or company no longer exists (*i.e.* because of death or liquidation) the question is whether it can be said that no person "has been found". The Government's view is that circumstances where a polluter cannot be found would include cases where the relevant company has gone into liquidation: H.L. Vol. 562, col. 209. It is submitted, however, that where a person or company is located but dies or goes into liquidation during the s.78H(3) consultation period so that a remediation notice may no longer be served on them, they have nevertheless been "found" and subs. (4) cannot operate to make the owner or occupier of the land liable as such.

Owners and occupiers may well be prompted by the attentions of the authority themselves to seek to locate others who may have caused or knowingly permitted the presence of the substances in question. If they are successful in doing so, but liquidation of the located company or, in the case of a person, their death or disappearance, follows before the authority establishes contact with them, it is a moot point whether they can be described as having been "found".

Subss. (4) and (5): "owner"
The term "owner" is defined separately for England and Wales and for Scotland at s.78A(9).

Subss. (4) and (5): lenders as "owners"
The question of potential liability of lenders under the new provisions aroused considerable interest in debate. The Government did not regard it as likely that the act of lending money to a polluter would of itself constitute causing or knowingly permitting contamination: H.L. Vol. 565, col. 1497.

The definition of "owner" adopted in the Act expressly excludes a mortgagee not in possession and the Scottish equivalent. The Government expressed the view that banks should not be treated as "deep pockets", that the simple act of lending should not result in liability and that the lender should retain the right to walk away from security without taking possession if the costs of remediation appeared to exceed its ultimate value: H.L. Vol. 560, col. 1448.

However, the banks and other institutions such as the Council of Mortgage Lenders were still concerned as to the possibilities for a lender to find itself in possession by default where the borrower abandoned the property and sent the keys to the lender: H.L. Vol. 560, col. 1445; Vol. 562, col. 1040. Although it agreed to look into the issue the Government concluded that no changes were necessary to protect lenders in this situation: they were already exposed to similar liabilities under existing legislation on public health, highways and building standards: H.L. Vol. 562, col. 165.

Similarly the Government were not sympathetic to the argument that special provision was needed to protect lenders who took possession to a limited extent to secure property or deal with obvious hazards: see H.L. Vol. 562, cols. 1042–1043.

Subs. (4) and (5): trustees as "owners"
The possible hardship of the provisions to trustees was drawn to the attention of the Government in debate: H.L. Vol. 562, col. 163. The response was that to provide an exemption for trustees would be to open up an easy route for evasion: H.L. Vol. 562, col. 165; Vol. 560, col. 1448.

Subss: (4) and (5): the innocent fly-tipped owner
One problem for which the Government did have evident sympathy was that of the owner or occupier who suffers from fly-tipping on their land. Imposing liability for clean-up of such contamination on the owner or occupier on the basis that the fly-tipper could not be found would have resulted in significantly harsher liabilities than under s.59 of this Act, which deals with the removal of unlawfully deposited waste. The Government's view was that the best way of dealing with the problem was to disapply Part IIA in cases where s.59 could be used: H.L. Vol. 562, col. 182. This was achieved by an amendment at third reading stage in the Lords. Full responsibility for dealing with unlawfully deposited waste would thereby be placed with the Agency/SEPA as waste regulation authority and the exemption for innocent victims of fly-tipping retained: H.L. Vol. 562, col. 1045.

Certainly in relation to contamination occurring after controls over waste deposits on land were introduced the availability of s.59 as a remedy could be a significant restriction on the use of Part IIA powers.

Subss. (4) and (5) "occupier"
The term "occupier" is not defined in Part IIA and the question of whether a person is in occupation will have to be determined on the facts of each case. The test is that of the degree of control exercised over the land rather than exclusivity of rights of occupation: *Wheat v. E. Lacon & Co. Ltd* [1966] A.C. 552. A licence entitling a person to possession may make someone an "occupier": *Stevens v. London Borough of Bromley* [1972] 1 All E.R. 712 (C.A.). Similarly it appears that a statutory tenant is an "occupier" (*Brown v. Ministry of Housing and Local Government* [1953] 2 All E.R. 1385, but there is authority to suggest that a person who entered premises forcibly and unlawfully is not: *Woodcock v. South Western Electricity Board* [1975] 2 All E.R. 545.

In Scotland it has been established that receivers may become occupiers: *Lord Advocate v. Aero Technologies Ltd (in receivership)* 1991 SLT 134. Thus, those receivers acting in a management capacity may conceivably find themselves regarded as occupiers for the purposes of the contaminated land provisions, although the specific protection afforded to them by s.78(3)–(4) should be noted.

Subss. (4) and (5): protection of owner and occupier
Persons liable under subss. (4) and (5) are in a better position than persons liable under subs. (2) in one respect. This relates to the situation where the contamination results or is likely to result in pollution of controlled waters: see notes to s.78J below.

Subss. (2), (4) and (5): insolvency practitioners and similar persons
Persons acting in certain capacities in relation to insolvency enjoy specific protection: see s.78X(3)–(4).

Subss. (6) and (7): apportionment of liability
It will be appreciated that notwithstanding the Government's aversion to creating joint and several liability, there are a number of potential instances where more than one person could be held responsible for a particular remediation requirement. These include:
  (a) persons who at the same time or at different times have contributed the same substance to contaminated land;
  (b) persons who have contributed different substances that have combined or reacted together;
  (c) a person who has caused and a person or persons who have knowingly permitted contaminating substances to be in land (possibly the original polluter plus a subsequent owner);
  (d) where no polluter can be found, the owner and the occupier (if different persons) or possibly co-owners or co-occupiers.
The existence of such potential situations of joint and several liability (and there may well be others) means that guidance issued under subss. (6) and (7) on apportionment of liability is likely to be important. Such guidance will have prescriptive and decisive effect.

Under subs. (6) the authority may exempt one or more persons entirely. Where a number of persons fall into the first category of liability, it is questionable whether subs. (6) allows *all* of them to be treated as not being an appropriate person. The effect of so doing could be to make liability shift to owners and occupiers by subs. (4); they, however, might argue that persons liable by subs. (2) have in fact been "found" within the meaning of subs. (4) but having been found have simply been treated as not appropriate. Under subs. (7) the authority may determine the proportions in which such persons are to bear the responsibility. Again, various questions arise here. Can someone be attributed a nil share under this provision? This could have a different effect on persons liable under subs. (4) as owners and occupiers than excluding that person under subs. (6). Do the shares have to add up to 100 per cent of the cost? And where both subss. (6) and (7) operate, in which order do they operate? It is to be hoped that guidance will address these issues.

The proportions of responsibility in such cases are to be stated in the remediation notice: s.78E(3). In that case the defence under s.78M(2) should be noted, *i.e.* that non-compliance with the notice was due solely to the refusal or inability of the others involved to comply with the requirement.

The only indication given in debate as to the Government's views on apportionment was given by Viscount Ullswater at H.L. Vol. 562, col. 215. He rejected any suggestion that liability should be joint and several where different persons have separately contributed to an overall problem and went on to say that where one person caused substances to be present but another in knowingly permitting them to remain brought about the circumstances in which they came to result in significant harm it may be "... entirely appropriate for the whole responsibility for remediation to rest on the person with the most recent involvement with the contamination."

Subs. (9): Chemical and biological reactions and processes
The harm or risk arising from contaminated land may in some cases derive from a reaction or process affecting the substances within the land. Examples are the synergistic effect of chemicals which react together, or the biological processes resulting in the formation of poisonous or explosive gases from putrescible materials. Subsection (9) deals with this situation by providing that the person who caused or knowingly permitted the original substance to be present will also be regarded as having caused or knowingly permitted such harmful products to be present.

To take an example: A deposits substance X in land which reacts to form noxious substance Y; B then unwittingly purchases the land. A will be regarded as having *caused* substance Y to be present. B might also be liable for having *knowingly permitted* substance Y to be present, as he now has control of the land.

Grant of, and compensation for, rights of entry etc.

78G.—(1) A remediation notice may require an appropriate person to do things by way of remediation, notwithstanding that he is not entitled to do those things.

(2) Any person whose consent is required before any thing required by a remediation notice may be done shall grant, or join in granting, such rights in

relation to any of the relevant land or waters as will enable the appropriate person to comply with any requirements imposed by the remediation notice.

(3) Before serving a remediation notice, the enforcing authority shall reasonably endeavour to consult every person who appears to the authority—

    (a) to be the owner or occupier of any of the relevant land or waters, and

    (b) to be a person who might be required by subsection (2) above to grant, or join in granting, any rights,

concerning the rights which that person may be so required to grant.

(4) Subsection (3) above shall not preclude the service of a remediation notice in any case where it appears to the enforcing authority that the contaminated land in question is in such a condition, by reason of substances in, on or under the land, that there is imminent danger of serious harm, or serious pollution of controlled waters, being caused.

(5) A person who grants, or joins in granting, any rights pursuant to subsection (2) above shall be entitled on making an application within such period as may be prescribed and in such manner as may be prescribed to such person as may be prescribed, to be paid by the appropriate person compensation of such amount as may be determined in such manner as may be prescribed.

(6) Without prejudice to the generality of the regulations that may be made by virtue of subsection (5) above, regulations by virtue of that subsection may make such provision in relation to compensation under this section as may be made by regulations by virtue of subsection (4) of section 35A above in relation to compensation under that section.

(7) In this section, "relevant land or waters" means—

    (a) the contaminated land in question;

    (b) any controlled waters affected by that land; or

    (c) any land adjoining or adjacent to that land or those waters.

DEFINITIONS

    "appropriate person": s.78A(9).
    "contaminated land": s.78A(2).
    "controlled waters": s.78A(9).
    "enforcing authority": s.78A(9).
    "harm": s.78A(4).
    "owner": s.78A(9).
    "pollution of controlled waters": s.78A(9).
    "regulations": s.78A(9).
    "relevant land or waters": subs. (7).
    "remediation": s.78A(7).
    "remediation notice": s.78E(1).

COMMENCEMENT

September 21, 1995 in so far as this section confers power on the Secretary of State to make regulations or makes provision with respect to the exercise of such power (S.I. 1995 No. 1983). The remainder will be brought into force by a commencement order made under s.125(3) of the Environment Act 1995.

GENERAL NOTE

This section governs the situation where the appropriate person has no right to carry out the remediation works required, *e.g.* because he is no longer in ownership or occupation of the land, or the works are off-site.

    This fact is not a bar to service of a remediation notice (subs. (1)) and any person whose consent is required is obliged to grant, or join in granting such rights as are necessary (subs. (2)). This may of course involve cost, disruption and inconvenience. The owner or occupier affected is protected by:

    (a) the requirement on the enforcing authority to use reasonable endeavours to consult before serving the remediation notice (subs. (3)), save in cases of imminent danger of serious harm (subs. (4)).

(b) the entitlement, on application, to be paid compensation by the appropriate person, to be determined in such manner as may be prescribed (subs. (5)).

No offence is created of failing to grant the necessary rights: the onus would appear to be on the appropriate person to secure that the rights are in fact granted so as to allow remediation to be carried out, through civil action if necessary.

Restrictions and prohibitions on serving remediation notices

78H.—(1) Before serving a remediation notice, the enforcing authority shall reasonably endeavour to consult—

    (a) the person on whom the notice is to be served,

    (b) the owner of any land to which the notice relates,

    (c) any person who appears to that authority to be in occupation of the whole or any part of the land, and

    (d) any person of such other description as may be prescribed,

concerning what is to be done by way of remediation.

(2) Regulations may make provision for, or in connection with, steps to be taken for the purposes of subsection (1) above.

(3) No remediation notice shall be served on any person by reference to any contaminated land during any of the following periods, that is to say—

    (a) the period—

        (i) beginning with the identification of the contaminated land in question pursuant to section 78B(1) above, and

        (ii) ending with the expiration of the period of three months beginning with the day on which the notice required by subsection (3)(d) or, as the case may be, (4) of section 78B above is given to that person in respect of that land;

    (b) if a decision falling within paragraph (b) of section 78C(1) above is made in relation to the contaminated land in question, the period beginning with the making of the decision and ending with the expiration of the period of three months beginning with—

        (i) in a case where the decision is not referred to the Secretary of State under section 78D above, the day on which the notice required by section 78C(6) above is given, or

        (ii) in a case where the decision is referred to the Secretary of State under section 78D above, the day on which he gives the notice required by subsection (4)(b) of that section;

    (c) if the appropriate Agency gives a notice under subsection (4) of section 78C above to a local authority in relation to the contaminated land in question, the period beginning with the day on which that notice is given and ending with the expiration of the period of three months beginning with—

        (i) in a case where notice is given under subsection (6) of that section, the day on which that notice is given;

        (ii) in a case where the authority makes a decision falling within subsection (5)(b) of that section and the appropriate Agency fails to give notice under paragraph (b) of section 78D(1) above, the day following the expiration of the period of twenty-one days mentioned in that paragraph; or

        (iii) in a case where the authority makes a decision falling within section 78C(5)(b) above which is referred to the Secretary of State under section 78D above, the day on which the Secretary of State gives the notice required by subsection (4)(b) of that section.

(4) Neither subsection (1) nor subsection (3) above shall preclude the service of a remediation notice in any case where it appears to the enforcing authority that the land in question is in such a condition, by reason of substances in, on or under the land, that there is imminent danger of serious harm, or serious pollution of controlled waters, being caused.

(5) The enforcing authority shall not serve a remediation notice on a person if and so long as any one or more of the following conditions is for the time being satisfied in the particular case, that is to say—

    (a) the authority is satisfied, in consequence of section 78E(4) and (5) above, that there is nothing by way of remediation which could be specified in a remediation notice served on that person;

    (b) the authority is satisfied that appropriate things are being, or will be, done by way of remediation without the service of a remediation notice on that person;

    (c) it appears to the authority that the person on whom the notice would be served is the authority itself; or

    (d) the authority is satisfied that the powers conferred on it by section 78N below to do what is appropriate by way of remediation are exercisable.

(6) Where the enforcing authority is precluded by virtue of section 78E(4) or (5) above from specifying in a remediation notice any particular thing by way of remediation which it would otherwise have specified in such a notice, the authority shall prepare and publish a document (in this Part referred to as a "remediation declaration") which shall record—

    (a) the reasons why the authority would have specified that thing; and

    (b) the grounds on which the authority is satisfied that it is precluded from specifying that thing in such a notice.

(7) In any case where the enforcing authority is precluded, by virtue of paragraph (b), (c) or (d) of subsection (5) above, from serving a remediation notice, the responsible person shall prepare and publish a document (in this Part referred to as a "remediation statement") which shall record—

    (a) the things which are being, have been, or are expected to be, done by way of remediation in the particular case;

    (b) the name and address of the person who is doing, has done, or is expected to do, each of those things; and

    (c) the periods within which each of those things is being, or is expected to be, done.

(8) For the purposes of subsection (7) above, the "responsible person" is—

    (a) in a case where the condition in paragraph (b) of subsection (5) above is satisfied, the person who is doing or has done, or who the enforcing authority is satisfied will do, the things there mentioned; or

    (b) in a case where the condition in paragraph (c) or (d) of that subsection is satisfied, the enforcing authority.

(9) If a person who is required by virtue of subsection (8)(a) above to prepare and publish a remediation statement fails to do so within a reasonable time after the date on which a remediation notice specifying the things there mentioned could, apart from subsection (5) above, have been served, the enforcing authority may itself prepare and publish the statement and may recover its reasonable costs of doing so from that person.

(10) Where the enforcing authority has been precluded by virtue only of subsection (5) above from serving a remediation notice on an appropriate person but—

    (a) none of the conditions in that subsection is for the time being satisfied in the particular case, and

    (b) the authority is not precluded by any other provision of this Part from serving a remediation notice on that appropriate person,

the authority shall serve a remediation notice on that person; and any such notice may be so served without any further endeavours by the authority to consult persons pursuant to subsection (1) above, if and to the extent that that person has been consulted pursuant to that subsection concerning the things which will be specified in the notice.

DEFINITIONS
"appropriate Agency": s.78A(9).
"appropriate person": s.78A(9).
"contaminated land": s.78A(2).
"enforcing authority": s.78A(9).
"harm": s.78A(4).
"local authority": s.78A(9).
"notice": s.78A(9).
"pollution of controlled waters": s.78A(9).
"regulations": s.78A(9).
"remediation": s.78A(7).
"remediation declaration": subs. (6).
"remediation notice": s.78A(9).
"responsible person": subs. (8).

COMMENCEMENT
September 21, 1995 in so far as this section confers power on the Secretary of State to make regulations or makes provision with respect to the exercise of such power (S.I. 1995 No. 1983). The remainder will be brought into force by a commencement order made under s.125(3) of the Environment Act 1995.

GENERAL NOTE
This section contains various restrictions and prohibitions on service of a remediation notice, designed in part to meet concerns expressed by various interested organisations during the passage of the Bill.

Subss. (1)–(4): Consultation as to remediation requirements
The enforcing authority is subject to a general requirement that before serving a remediation notice it should use reasonable endeavours to consult the persons specified in subs. (1) concerning what is to be done by way of remediation. Such a requirement was initially opposed by the Government on the basis that it would impose a considerable bureaucratic burden for little benefit: H.L. Vol. 562, col. 171. This obligation is coupled with an embargo on service of a remediation notice during a period running from the date of identification of the contaminated land until three months from the date of notification of identification under s.78B or notification of designation as a special site under ss.78C or 78D (subs. (3)).

However, the requirement and restriction will not prevent a remediation notice being served in cases where it appears to the enforcing authority that the condition of the land presents a risk of imminent danger of serious land or serious water pollution (subs. (4)).

Subs. (5): Cases where enforcing authority is restrained from serving notice
Subsection (5) gives four cases (a)–(d) where the authority may not serve a remediation notice so long as the conditions specified there are applicable. Note that the section does not create a permanent restriction on service of a notice: circumstances may change so that the restriction no longer applies. In such a case, if no other restriction applies, a remediation notice must be served, and no further consultation many be necessary if this has already taken place with the appropriate person: subs. (10). The four cases are as follows:—

para. (a)—the authority is satisfied that nothing could reasonably be specified by way of remediation, having regard to cost, seriousness of harm and Secretary of State's guidance.
para. (b)—the authority is satisfied that appropriate remedial action will be undertaken voluntarily, without a remediation notice being served. Whilst the intended recipient of the notice may offer assurances that remedial action will be taken, in order to be satisfied that those things will be done (or completed if they have already been commenced), it is submitted that the authority may be prudent to require the appropriate person or persons to enter into a binding written agreement.
para. (c)—the authority itself is the appropriate person, *e.g.* because the site is owned by the authority, or was operated by the authority in the past as a landfill site or similar facility.
para. (d)—the effect of this paragraph is complex. The authority will be precluded from serving notice so long as it is satisfied that it could exercise its s.78N powers to carry out remediation. Section 78N(3) lists six cases (a)–(f) where the authority has power to act itself. Specifically these include cases where the authority considers it necessary to act to avoid to occurrence of serious harm or pollution in cases of imminent danger ((a)); where an appropriate person has entered into a written agreement for the authority to carry out the work at the cost of that person ((b)) (though presumably the authority would then

anyway be satisfied under s.78H(5)(b) that the appropriate things would be done); where ss.78J or 78K operate to preclude something being included in a remediation notice ((d)); or—most importantly—where there are circumstances of hardship ((e)); or where no appropriate person has been found after reasonable inquiry ((f)). In all of these cases the authority will not be able to serve notice: its remedy will lie in carrying out the works itself and then seeking (if possible) to recover its expenses under the procedures contained in s.78P.

Hardship

One of the most important practical effects of subs. (5) as outlined above is that before serving notice the authority must consider the question of hardship: H.C. Standing Committee B, 11th Sitting, cols. 361–362, May 23, 1995; H.L. Vol. 565, col. 1496. Apart from taking blanket policy decisions such as not to serve notices on residential owners, it is difficult to see how the authority could consider the issue adequately without eliciting information from the intended recipient of the notice. Yet any adoption of such a blanket policy would have to remain sufficiently flexible to avoid the threat of judicial review perhaps by another appropriate person on the basis that the enforcing authority has fettered its discretion.

Subs. (6): Remediation declarations

Where the authority is precluded by s.78E(4) or (5) from requiring some particular thing by way of remediation it must prepare and publish a remediation declaration recording the reasons why the thing would have been specified were it not for s.78E(4) and (5), and the grounds on which the authority is satisfied it is precluded from specifying the relevant thing. The declaration must be placed on the public register: s.78R(1)(c).

For the owner of land, the remediation declaration is something of a two-edged sword: on the one hand the polluter or owner may welcome the public recognition that the authority cannot require a particular type of remediation. On the other hand the notice will make it clear that but for considerations of cost or Government guidance, such action would be required. A prospective purchaser may be understandably nervous that the circumstances which led the authority to be satisfied that the action cannot be required may change: the seriousness of the risk of harm may increase, possibly due to factors outside the owner's control; the cost of remedial techniques may fall, or cheaper techniques may become available; or Government guidance may change. Such factors, and others, may lead the authority to reconsider its decision under s.78E(4) or (5).

Where an owner does not consider that the land should be the subject of a remediation declaration (*e.g.* because it is not within the definition of contaminated land at all) there is no statutory mechanism for appeal, though the declaration could no doubt be challenged by way of judicial review.

Subs. (7): Remediation statements

Where the authority is precluded from serving a remediation notice by s.78H(5)(b)–(d) (see above), an obligation falls on the "responsible person" (see subs. (8)) to prepare and publish a remediation statement recording the matters specified at subs. (7)(a)–(c). This will, where the remediation is to be carried out voluntarily, be the person who is to do the works; in all other cases, it will be the authority itself (either in its capacity as original polluter or current owner/occupier or because it is entitled to carry out the work itself under s.78N).

As with a remediation declaration, the remediation statement must be placed on the public register: s.78R(1)(c). Where the responsible person is someone other than the authority and fails to produce a remediation statement within a reasonable time then the authority may itself prepare and publish the statement and may recover its reasonable costs of so doing: subs. (9). There is no express remedy or sanction in cases of failure to carry out the steps contained in a remediation statement when this has been prepared; nor does s.78N appear to contain any reserve power for the authority to carry out the works itself in such a case. The remedy of the authority would be to serve a remediation notice on the basis that it is no longer satisfied (under subs. (5)(b)) that the works will be carried out.

There is no express sanction or default power where the authority itself is the responsible person, although the Agency/SEPA has the power under s.78V to issue site-specific guidance. Ordinary principles of judicial review would no doubt apply in the case of failure to take necessary action.

Restrictions on liability relating to the pollution of controlled waters

78J.—(1) This section applies where any land is contaminated land by virtue of paragraph (b) of subsection (2) of section 78A above (whether or not the land is also contaminated land by virtue of paragraph (a) of that subsection).

(2) Where this section applies, no remediation notice given in consequence of the land in question being contaminated land shall require a person who is an appropriate person by virtue of section 78F(4) or (5) above to do anything by way of remediation to that or any other land, or any waters, which he could not have been required to do by such a notice had paragraph (b) of section 78A(2) above (and all other references to pollution of controlled waters) been omitted from this Part.

(3) If, in a case where this section applies, a person permits, has permitted, or might permit, water from an abandoned mine or part of a mine—

(a) to enter any controlled waters, or

(b) to reach a place from which it is or, as the case may be, was likely, in the opinion of the enforcing authority, to enter such waters,

no remediation notice shall require him in consequence to do anything by way of remediation (whether to the contaminated land in question or to any other land or waters) which he could not have been required to do by such a notice had paragraph (b) of section 78A(2) above (and all other references to pollution of controlled waters) been omitted from this Part.

(4) Subsection (3) above shall not apply to the owner or former operator of any mine or part of a mine if the mine or part in question became abandoned after 31st December 1999.

(5) In determining for the purposes of subsection (4) above whether a mine or part of a mine became abandoned before, on or after 31st December 1999 in a case where the mine or part has become abandoned on two or more occasions, of which—

(a) at least one falls on or before that date, and

(b) at least one falls after that date,

the mine or part shall be regarded as becoming abandoned after that date (but without prejudice to the operation of subsection (3) above in relation to that mine or part at, or in relation to, any time before the first of those occasions which falls after that date).

(6) Where, immediately before a part of a mine becomes abandoned, that part is the only part of the mine not falling to be regarded as abandoned for the time being, the abandonment of that part shall not be regarded for the purposes of subsection (4) or (5) above as constituting the abandonment of the mine, but only of that part of it.

(7) Nothing in subsection (2) or (3) above prevents the enforcing authority from doing anything by way of remediation under section 78N below which it could have done apart from that subsection, but the authority shall not be entitled under section 78P below to recover from any person any part of the cost incurred by the authority in doing by way of remediation anything which it is precluded by subsection (2) or (3) above from requiring that person to do.

(8) In this section "mine" has the same meaning as in the Mines and Quarries Act 1954.

DEFINITIONS
"appropriate person": s.78A(9).
"contaminated land": s.78A(2).
"controlled waters": s.78A(9).
"enforcing authority": s.78A(9).
"mine": subs. (8).
"pollution of controlled waters": s.78A(9).
"remediation": s.78A(7).
"remediation notice": s.78E(1).

COMMENCEMENT
These provisions will be brought into force by a commencement order made under s.125(3) of the Environment Act 1995.

GENERAL NOTE
This section places certain restrictions on liability under Part IIA which relates to pollution of controlled waters. The first is a general restriction under subs. (2), the second is a specific restriction relating to water from abandoned mines in subs. (3). Both restrictions apply where land is regarded as contaminated because pollution of controlled waters is being caused or is likely to be caused, even if the land is also regarded as contaminated on the basis of the separate "harm" test: subs. (1).

Subs. (2): general restriction
The effect of this restriction is that a person who is regarded as an appropriate person by virtue of s.78F(4) or (5), *i.e.* as an owner or occupier where the original polluter cannot be found, shall not be required to do anything which he could not have been required to do if the water pollution limb of the definition of contaminated land did not exist. In other words, the remediation required may relate only to the general "harm" limb of the definition of contamination, *i.e.* significant harm to health of living organisms, interference with ecological systems, or harm to property. It is submitted that contamination of percolating groundwater so as to render it unfit for a purpose for which it is abstracted could constitute "harm to property", abstraction being a natural right incidental to the ownership of land.
    The object of this restriction is to avoid any additional liability accruing to an owner or occupier of land, beyond that which could already attach in relation to the clean up of water pollution under s.161 of the Water Resources Act 1991 (or, in Scotland, under s.46 of the Control of Pollution Act 1974). Section 161/s.46 liability is based upon causing or knowingly permitting pollution and subs. (2) seeks to mirror this concept. The extent to which it provides protection to an owner or occupier will however depend upon the interpretation placed on the word "knowingly permitted" in s.78F(2): a current owner may find they are liable on that basis and unable to take advantage of s.78J(2). Their only comfort in that situation is that they might well also have been liable under the law as it stood under s.161/s.46 the difference being, of course, that those sections imposed only a power, rather than a duty to act, on the enforcing authority. It should also be noted in this respect that those sections have been amended by the 1995 Act to allow a "works notice" to be served, with similar effect to a remediation notice, requiring clean up or anti-pollution operations: s.161A as inserted by Sched. 22, para. 162; and s.46A as inserted by para. 29(22) of that Schedule.

Subs. (3): Abandoned mines
The issue of who is an appropriate person in relation to contamination present in underground mine workings is discussed above in relation to s.78A.
    The effect of subs. (3) is to mirror the position as to liability for pollution from abandoned mines, contained in the Water Resources Act 1991 (or, in Scotland, the Control of Pollution Act 1974) as amended by the 1995 Act. The exemption is applicable to a person who permits, has permitted, or might permit, water from an abandoned mine to enter controlled waters, or to reach a place from which it is likely to do so. As with the defence/exception under the 1991 Act (or, in Scotland, the 1974 Act), it will not apply to owners or former operators of mines which become abandoned after December 31, 1999: subs. (4). As to the meaning of "mine" see subs. (8)—the definition in the 1954 Act, s.180 is as follows:

> "... an excavation or system of excavations, including all such excavations to which a common system of ventilation is provided, made for the purpose of, or in connection with, the getting, wholly or substantially by means involving the employment of persons below ground, of minerals (whether in their natural state or in solution or suspension) or products of minerals."

The question of when abandonment is to be regarded as occurring is dealt with by subss. (5) and (6). See further the notes to ss.58 and 59 of the 1995 Act.
    The effect of subs. (3) is that the person who is responsible for knowingly permitting under s.78F(2) (as opposed to causing) can only be required to remediate contamination which is harmful within the first limb of the section 78A test, and not that which results or is likely to result in water pollution without causing harm in that sense: see note to subs. (2) above.

Liability in respect of contaminating substances which escape to other land

78K.—(1) A person who has caused or knowingly permitted any substances to be in, on or under any land shall also be taken for the purposes of this Part to have caused or, as the case may be, knowingly permitted those substances to be in, on or under any other land to which they appear to have escaped.

(2) Subsections (3) and (4) below apply in any case where it appears that any substances are or have been in, on or under any land (in this section referred to as "land A") as a result of their escape, whether directly or indirectly, from other land in, on or under which a person caused or knowingly permitted them to be.

(3) Where this subsection applies, no remediation notice shall require a person—

    (a) who is the owner or occupier of land A, and

    (b) who has not caused or knowingly permitted the substances in question to be in, on or under that land,

to do anything by way of remediation to any land or waters (other than land or waters of which he is the owner or occupier) in consequence of land A appearing to be in such a condition, by reason of the presence of those substances in, on or under it, that significant harm is being caused, or there is a significant possibility of such harm being caused, or that pollution of controlled waters is being, or is likely to be caused.

(4) Where this subsection applies, no remediation notice shall require a person—

    (a) who is the owner or occupier of land A, and

    (b) who has not caused or knowingly permitted the substances in question to be in, on or under that land,

to do anything by way of remediation in consequence of any further land in, on or under which those substances or any of them appear to be or to have been present as a result of their escape from land A ("land B") appearing to be in such a condition, by reason of the presence of those substances in, on or under it, that significant harm is being caused, or there is a significant possibility of such harm being caused, or that pollution of controlled waters is being, or is likely to be caused, unless he is also the owner or occupier of land B.

(5) In any case where—

    (a) a person ("person A") has caused or knowingly permitted any substances to be in, on, or under any land,

    (b) another person ("person B") who has not caused or knowingly permitted those substances to be in, on or under that land becomes the owner or occupier of that land, and

    (c) the substances, or any of the substances, mentioned in paragraph (a) above appear to have escaped to other land,

no remediation notice shall require person B to do anything by way of remediation to that other land in consequence of the apparent acts or omissions of person A, except to the extent that person B caused or knowingly permitted the escape.

(6) Nothing in subsection (3), (4) or (5) above prevents the enforcing authority from doing anything by way of remediation under section 78N below which it could have done apart from that subsection, but the authority shall not be entitled under section 78P below to recover from any person any part of the cost incurred by the authority in doing by way of remediation anything which it is precluded by subsection (3), (4) or (5) above from requiring that person to do.

(7) In this section, "appear" means appear to the enforcing authority, and cognate expressions shall be construed accordingly.

DEFINITIONS
"enforcing authority": s.78A(9).
"harm": s.78A(4).
"land A": subs. (2).
"land B": subs. (4).
"owner": s.78A(9).
"person A": subs. (5)(a).
"person B": subs. (5)(b).
"pollution of controlled waters": s.78A(9).
"remediation": s.78A(7).
"remediation notice": s.78E(1).
"significant": s.78A(5).
"substance": s.78A(9).

COMMENCEMENT
These provisions will be brought into force by a commencement order made under s.125(3) of the Environment Act 1995.

GENERAL NOTE
This complex section attempts to deal with the complex situations which can arise where contamination migrates from its original location to other land. So far as this commentator is aware (at least in relation to environmental legislation) it sets the precedent for a new drafting style by its references to "land A", "person B", etc.

Subs. (1): Migrating contaminants—primary liability
The effect of this subsection is that a person who has caused or knowingly permitted substances to be in, on or under land shall also be taken to have caused or knowingly permitted them (as the case may be) to be in, on or under any other land to which they appear ("appear" in this context means appear to the enforcing authority) to have escaped: subs. (1) and (7). The result is that such a person will be an appropriate person under s.78F(2) in relation to the land to which the substances have escaped. It is possible, as discussed under s.78F, that the words "knowingly permit" could apply to a subsequent owner or occupier. The correct construction of subs. (1) appears to be that it will only apply to substances which escaped to the other land after the time by which the owner could be said to have knowingly permitted them to be on the first land: this would avoid the inconsistency which could otherwise arise with subs. (5) which envisages an "innocent" owner or occupier being liable only to the extent that they caused or knowingly permitted the escape to the other land.

Subs. (3): Responsibility of owner and occupier of land to which contaminants migrate
Subs. (3) is applied by subs. (2) to any case where it appears that substances are in, on or under any land (land A) as a result of their escape directly or indirectly from other land in, on or under which a person knowingly permitted them to be. Again, "appears" is to be construed by reference to what appears to the enforcing authority: subs. (7). The subsection refers to a direct or indirect escape, which is wide enough language to cover subsurface percolation or transport by wind or flowing water; it could therefore cover, for example, the situation where land A is contaminated by the fall-out of airborne emissions from other land.
   In such cases, the remediation notice may not require the owner or occupier of land A to do anything by way of remediation to any land or waters, other than the land or waters of which he is owner or occupier. The inference is that he may be required to carry out remediation of land or waters of which he is in ownership or occupation: however, by virtue of subs. (1) the person who originally caused or knowingly permitted the substances to escape onto land A will bear primary responsibility in relation to land A under s.78F(2), and the owner or occupier of land A should only be liable under s.78F(4) if that person cannot be found.
   The only problem with this logical scheme lies in the words "knowingly permitted" in s.78K(3)(b) in relation to the owner or occupier of land A: if such a person becomes aware that their land has become contaminated by substances from other land and fails to take action which is within his power he might be said to be knowingly permitting the substances to be there, in which case he would:
   (a) lose the protection of subs. (3); and
   (b) potentially be jointly liable with the person responsible for the escape, subject to apportionment under s.78F, and to any civil remedies available.

Subs. (4): Liability in respect of onward migration
Having escaped from other land to land A, contamination may then migrate on to land B. In this situation the effect of subs. (4) in that the owner or the occupier of land A—provided he may not be said to have caused or knowingly permitted the substances to be in, on or under their land—will not be responsible for the remediation of land B unless he is also the owner or occupier of that land.

In such circumstances the authority should be able to pursue either the original polluter who caused or knowingly permitted the substances to escape to land A (see s.78K(1)) or, if such person cannot be found, the owner or occupier of land B.

Subs. (5): Escapes prior to acquiring land
The effect of subs. (5) is that a purchaser or new occupier of contaminated land should not be responsible for the remediation of other land in respect of contaminants which have previously escaped from his land to that land. In this way the purchaser/occupier (person B) is not responsible for the acts or omissions of their predecessor (person A) except to the extent that person B caused or knowingly permitted the escape. Person B may thus be responsible for remediation works necessary to prevent further escapes, or for remediation to clean up contamination which escapes after they acquired ownership or occupation. Remediation liability in respect of person B's own land may be based on being a knowing permitter or an owner/occupier; remediation liability in respect of other land can only arise where person B caused or knowingly permitted the escape. It is submitted that, in this respect, the specific drafting of subs. (5) should prevail over the more general principle of subs. (1), which might indicate that if person B is knowingly permitting the substances to be under his land after acquisition, he will be treated also as having knowingly permitted them to be under the land to which they appear to have escaped, even though he did not cause or knowingly permit the escape itself.

Subs. (6): Remediation by authority
Subss. (3)–(5) may preclude a remediation notice being served or restrict what may be required, but they will not prevent the authority taking action itself under s.78N. The authority will, however, be restricted in the exercise of its cost recovery powers if it does take such action.

Appeals against remediation notices

78L.—(1) A person on whom a remediation notice is served may, within the period of twenty-one days beginning with the day on which the notice is served, appeal against the notice—

(a) if it was served by a local authority, to a magistrates' court or, in Scotland, to the sheriff by way of summary application; or

(b) if it was served by the appropriate Agency, to the Secretary of State;
and in the following provisions of this section "the appellate authority" means the magistrates' court, the sheriff or the Secretary of State, as the case may be.

(2) On any appeal under subsection (1) above the appellate authority—

(a) shall quash the notice, if it is satisfied that there is a material defect in the notice; but

(b) subject to that, may confirm the remediation notice, with or without modification, or quash it.

(3) Where an appellate authority confirms a remediation notice, with or without modification, it may extend the period specified in the notice for doing what the notice requires to be done.

(4) Regulations may make provision with respect to—

(a) the grounds on which appeals under subsection (1) above may be made;

(b) the cases in which, grounds on which, court or tribunal to which, or person at whose instance, an appeal against a decision of a magistrates' court or sheriff court in pursuance of an appeal under subsection (1) above shall lie; or

(c) the procedure on an appeal under subsection (1) above or on an appeal by virtue of paragraph (b) above.

(5) Regulations under subsection (4) above may (among other things)—

(a) include provisions comparable to those in section 290 of the Public Health Act 1936 (appeals against notices requiring the execution of works);

(b) prescribe the cases in which a remediation notice is, or is not, to be suspended until the appeal is decided, or until some other stage in the proceedings;

(c) prescribe the cases in which the decision on an appeal may in some respects be less favourable to the appellant than the remediation notice against which he is appealing;

(d) prescribe the cases in which the appellant may claim that a remediation notice should have been served on some other person and prescribe the procedure to be followed in those cases;

(e) make provision as respects—

    (i) the particulars to be included in the notice of appeal;

    (ii) the persons on whom notice of appeal is to be served and the particulars, if any, which are to accompany the notice; and

    (iii) the abandonment of an appeal;

(f) make different provision for different cases or classes of case.

(6) This section, so far as relating to appeals to the Secretary of State, is subject to section 114 of the Environment Act 1995 (delegation or reference of appeals etc).

DEFINITIONS

"appellate authority": s.78L(1).
"appropriate Agency": s.78A(9).
"local authority": s.78A(9).
"notice": s.78A(9).
"regulations" s.78A(9).
"remediations": s.78A(7).
"remediation notice": s.78(E)(1).

COMMENCEMENT

September 21, 1995 in so far as this section confers power on the Secretary of State to make regulations or makes provision with respect to the exercise of such power (S.I. 1995 No. 1983). The remainder will be brought into force by a commencement order made under s.125(3) of the Environment Act 1995.

GENERAL NOTE

This section refers a right of appeal against a remediation notice. Appeal is to the magistrates' court (or sheriff court in Scotland: see further below) where the notice is served by a local authority, or to the Secretary of State where it is served by the Agency/SEPA. Regulations will be required as to the grounds of appeal and appeal procedure. One point of particular interest is subs. (4)(b), which allows the regulations to provide for appeals from the decision of the magistrates' or sheriff court other than on points of law.

It can be anticipated that, given the complexity of the issues involved, and the substantial sums likely to be at stake, the costs incurred in appeal proceedings in the magistrates' court may be considerable. The magistrates have a wide jurisdiction as to the award of costs under the Magistrates' Court Act 1980 and a court is unlikely to interfere with their decision by way of judicial review unless it is perverse: see *R. v. The Stipendiary Magistrate for Southend, ex p. Rochford District Council* [1995] Env. L.R.1 (£75,000 costs awarded against authority in statutory nuisance case).

Scotland

The procedure for summary applications to the sheriff court in Scotland is currently governed by the Sheriff Court Summary Application Rules 1993 (S.I. 1993 No. 3240) which came into force on January 1, 1993. It appears that the regulations to be made under s.78L(4) with respect to appeals from the sheriff court will include a right of appeal to the Sheriff Principal and thence to the Inner House of the Court of Session (*per* Sir Hector Monro, Standing Committee B, May 23, 1995, col. 371).

Offences of not complying with a remediation notice

78M.—(1) If a person on whom an enforcing authority serves a remediation notice fails, without reasonable excuse, to comply with any of the requirements of the notice, he shall be guilty of an offence.

(2) Where the remediation notice in question is one which was required by section 78E(3) above to state, in relation to the requirement which has not been complied with, the proportion of the cost involved which the person charged with the offence is liable to bear, it shall be a defence for that person to prove that the only reason why he has not complied with the requirement is that one or more of the other persons who are liable to bear a proportion of that cost refused, or was not able, to comply with the requirement.

(3) Except in a case falling within subsection (4) below, a person who commits an offence under subsection (1) above shall be liable, on summary conviction, to a fine not exceeding level 5 on the standard scale and to a further fine of an amount equal to one-tenth of level 5 on the standard scale for each day on which the failure continues after conviction of the offence and before the enforcing authority has begun to exercise its powers by virtue of section 78N(3)(c) below.

(4) A person who commits an offence under subsection (1) above in a case where the contaminated land to which the remediation notice relates is industrial, trade or business premises shall be liable on summary conviction to a fine not exceeding £20,000 or such greater sum as the Secretary of State may from time to time by order substitute and to a further fine of an amount equal to one-tenth of that sum for each day on which the failure continues after conviction of the offence and before the enforcing authority has begun to exercise its powers by virtue of section 78N(3)(c) below.

(5) If the enforcing authority is of the opinion that proceedings for an offence under this section would afford an ineffectual remedy against a person who has failed to comply with any of the requirements of a remediation notice which that authority has served on him, that authority may take proceedings in the High Court or, in Scotland, in any court of competent jurisdiction, for the purpose of securing compliance with the remediation notice.

(6) In this section, "industrial, trade or business premises" means premises used for any industrial, trade or business purposes or premises not so used on which matter is burnt in connection with any industrial, trade or business process, and premises are used for industrial purposes where they are used for the purposes of any treatment or process as well as where they are used for the purpose of manufacturing.

(7) No order shall be made under subsection (4) above unless a draft of the order has been laid before, and approved by a resolution of, each House of Parliament.

DEFINITIONS
    "enforcing authority": s.78A(9).
    "industrial trade or business premises": subs. (6).
    "remediation notice" s.78E(1).

COMMENCEMENT
September 21, 1995 in so far as this section confers power on the Secretary of State to make orders or makes provision with respect to the exercise of such power (S.I. 1995 No. 1983). The remainder will be brought into force by a commencement order made under s.125(3) of the Environment Act 1995.

GENERAL NOTE
This section creates the offence of failure to comply, without reasonable excuse, with any of the requirements of a remediation notice.

The main penalty is a fine, but a daily fine is also payable for each day that the offence continues between conviction and the date (if any) on which the authority begins to exercise its own default clean up powers under s.78N. Separate penalties are prescribed for cases where the contaminated land to which the notice relates is industrial, trade or business premises (see below).

Subs. (1): "without reasonable excuse"
Lack of funds to complete the work required to comply with the notice is unlikely to constitute "reasonable excuse": see *Saddleworth U.D.C. v. Aggregate and Sand* (1990) 114 S.J. 931. The same case leaves it unclear whether reliance on the advice of an expert can be a reasonable excuse. Where access to land for remediation purposes is required but refused, the appropriate person will presumably have to resort to legal action on the basis of s.78G(2) to secure the grant of the necessary rights: in the absence of such efforts it may be difficult for an appropriate person to argue that such refusal of access constitutes a reasonable excuse.

Subs. (2): Defence of non-co-operation by other liable persons
Subsection (2) recognises that in cases where two or more persons are appropriate persons in relation to a single aspect of remediation and are liable each to pay a proportion of the cost it may be impossible for one party alone to comply with the notice if the other does not pay their proportion. In many cases compliance with the notice will presumably involve entering into contracts with consultants, engineers or contractors. A responsible party will not wish to be committed contractually to the cost of remediation until he is satisfied that a contribution is likely to be forthcoming from the other responsible parties. The onus of making out this defence rests with the defendant, since as it is worded he has to "prove" certain matters. The standard of proof which he has to meet is that of the balance of probabilities: *Islington Borough Council v. Panico* [1973] All E.R. 485 and, in Scotland, *Neish v. Stevenson* 1969 SLT 229. It would therefore be prudent for the recipient of a remediation notice seeking to rely on the defence to demonstrate that tenders have been obtained for the works, that attempts have been made to invite the other responsible party or parties to contribute, and that the defendant is willing and able to contribute his share.

Subss. (3) and (4): Penalties where land is industrial, trade or business premises
Where the contaminated land in question is industrial, trade or business premises (as defined in subs. (6)) the maximum fine and daily fine on summary conviction are both higher than those applicable to other contaminated land. The maximum fine is £20,000, and this figure may be increased by the Secretary of State. It should be noted that the court has discretion over the initial fine but no discretion over the level of the daily fine of £2,000; in principle, therefore, it would appear that a conviction could result in a fine of as little as £500 plus a daily fine of £2,000.
For other land, the maximum fine is £5,000, and accordingly the daily fine is a fixed £500.

Subs. (5): Civil proceedings
The authority may enforce compliance with a remediation notice by civil proceedings where it is of the opinion that a criminal prosecution would provide an ineffectual remedy. This is a common form provision, the usual purpose of which is to allow an authority to use injunctive proceedings.
Given that a remediation notice will normally impose positive requirements, the appropriate civil remedy would appear to be a mandatory injunction.
In Scotland, civil proceedings may be brought in either the appropriate sheriff court or the Court of Session for securing compliance with a remediation notice. Since a remediation notice is unlikely to impose negative requirements, the proceedings brought would usually be for specific implement or *ad factum praestandum* rather than interdict.

Powers of the enforcing authority to carry out remediation

78N.—(1) Where this section applies, the enforcing authority shall itself have power, in a case falling within paragraph (a) or (b) of section 78E(1) above, to do what is appropriate by way of remediation to the relevant land or waters.
(2) Subsection (1) above shall not confer power on the enforcing authority

to do anything by way of remediation if the authority would, in the particular case, be precluded by section 78YB below from serving a remediation notice requiring that thing to be done.

(3) This section applies in each of the following cases, that is to say—

(a) where the enforcing authority considers it necessary to do anything itself by way of remediation for the purpose of preventing the occurrence of any serious harm, or serious pollution of controlled waters, of which there is imminent danger;

(b) where an appropriate person has entered into a written agreement with the enforcing authority for that authority to do, at the cost of that person, that which he would otherwise be required to do under this Part by way of remediation;

(c) where a person on whom the enforcing authority serves a remediation notice fails to comply with any of the requirements of the notice;

(d) where the enforcing authority is precluded by section 78J or 78K above from including something by way of remediation in a remediation notice;

(e) where the enforcing authority considers that, were it to do some particular thing by way of remediation, it would decide, by virtue of subsection (2) of section 78P below or any guidance issued under that subsection,—

(i) not to seek to recover under subsection (1) of that section any of the reasonable cost incurred by it in doing that thing; or

(ii) to seek so to recover only a portion of that cost;

(f) where no person has, after reasonable inquiry, been found who is an appropriate person in relation to any particular thing.

(4) Subject to section 78E(4) and (5) above, for the purposes of this section, the things which it is appropriate for the enforcing authority to do by way of remediation are—

(a) in a case falling within paragraph (a) of subsection (3) above, anything by way of remediation which the enforcing authority considers necessary for the purpose mentioned in that paragraph;

(b) in a case falling within paragraph (b) of that subsection, anything specified in, or determined under, the agreement mentioned in that paragraph;

(c) in a case falling within paragraph (c) of that subsection, anything which the person mentioned in that paragraph was required to do by virtue of the remediation notice;

(d) in a case falling within paragraph (d) of that subsection, anything by way of remediation which the enforcing authority is precluded by section 78J or 78K above from including in a remediation notice;

(e) in a case falling within paragraph (e) or (f) of that subsection, the particular thing mentioned in the paragraph in question.

(5) In this section "the relevant land or waters" means—

(a) the contaminated land in question;

(b) any controlled waters affected by that land; or

(c) any land adjoining or adjacent to that land or those waters.

DEFINITIONS

"appropriate person": s.78A(9).
"contaminated land": s.78A(2).
"controlled waters": s.78A(9).
"harm": s.78A(4).
"enforcing authority": s.78A(9).
"notice": s.78A(9).

"pollution of controlled waters": s.78A(9).
"the relevant land or waters": subs. (5).
"remediation": s.78A(7).
"remediation notice": s.78E(1).

COMMENCEMENT
These provisions will be brought into force by a commencement order made under s.125(3) of the Environment Act 1995.

GENERAL NOTE
This section confers upon the local authority (or Agency/SEPA, in relation to special sites) power to carry out appropriate remediation itself, provided that:
  (a) the land has been identified as contaminated land or designated as a special site (subs. (1));
  (b) service of a remediation notice would not be precluded by s.78YB (subs. (2)); and
  (c) one of the cases specified in subs. (3) applies.

Subs. (3): Cases where the section applies
These cases (a)–(f) are generally self-explanatory and do not require comment. Para. (b) provides a potentially useful method of securing voluntary remediation, though whether such agreements will be popular with responsible persons remains to be seen; enforcing authorities may themselves also be concerned at the potential liability implications of assuming responsibility for clean-up, and such an agreement may be more appropriate where the remediation action in question consists of monitoring. Para. (c) clearly provides an important default power, and para. (f) can be used for "orphan sites" where no appropriate person at all (including an owner) can be found. It should be noted in relation to para. (e), which deals with hardship, that the authority may itself act in cases not only where there is "total hardship" (*i.e.* the authority would not seek to recover any of its costs) but also "partial hardship" where it would seek to recover its costs in part.

Subs. (4): Appropriate action
The subsection defines those things which it will be appropriate for the authority to do in each case. The precise wording is important, since this may limit the authority's power to recover its costs subsequently under s.78P. For example, if under para. (c) the authority in carrying out remediation goes beyond the requirements of the remediation notice it may not be able to recover its costs (or at least not its full costs).

Recovery of, and security for, the cost of remediation by the enforcing authority

78P.—(1) Where, by virtue of section 78N(3)(a), (c), (e) or (f) above, the enforcing authority does any particular thing by way of remediation, it shall be entitled, subject to sections 78J(7) and 78K(6) above, to recover the reasonable cost incurred in doing it from the appropriate person or, if there are two or more appropriate persons in relation to the thing in question, from those persons in proportions determined pursuant to section 78F(7) above.

(2) In deciding whether to recover the cost, and, if so, how much of the cost, which it is entitled to recover under subsection (1) above, the enforcing authority shall have regard—
  (a) to any hardship which the recovery may cause to the person from whom the cost is recoverable; and
  (b) to any guidance issued by the Secretary of State for the purposes of this subsection.
(3) Subsection (4) below shall apply in any case where—
  (a) any cost is recoverable under subsection (1) above from a person—
    (i) who is the owner of any premises which consist of or include the contaminated land in question; and

      (ii) who caused or knowingly permitted the substances, or any of the substances, by reason of which the land is contaminated land to be in, on or under the land; and

   (b) the enforcing authority serves a notice under this subsection (in this Part referred to as a "charging notice") on that person.

(4) Where this subsection applies—

   (a) the cost shall carry interest, at such reasonable rate as the enforcing authority may determine, from the date of service of the notice until the whole amount is paid; and

   (b) subject to the following provisions of this section, the cost and accrued interest shall be a charge on the premises mentioned in subsection (3)(a)(i) above.

(5) A charging notice shall—

   (a) specify the amount of the cost which the enforcing authority claims is recoverable;

   (b) state the effect of subsection (4) above and the rate of interest determined by the authority under that subsection; and

   (c) state the effect of subsections (7) and (8) below.

(6) On the date on which an enforcing authority serves a charging notice on a person, the authority shall also serve a copy of the notice on every other person who, to the knowledge of the authority, has an interest in the premises capable of being affected by the charge.

(7) Subject to any order under subsection (9)(b) or (c) below, the amount of any cost specified in a charging notice and the accrued interest shall be a charge on the premises—

   (a) as from the end of the period of twenty-one days beginning with the service of the charging notice, or

   (b) where an appeal is brought under subsection (8) below, as from the final determination or (as the case may be) the withdrawal, of the appeal,

until the cost and interest are recovered.

(8) A person served with a charging notice or a copy of a charging notice may appeal against the notice to a county court within the period of twenty-one days beginning with the date of service.

(9) On an appeal under subsection (8) above, the court may—

   (a) confirm the notice without modification;

   (b) order that the notice is to have effect with the substitution of a different amount for the amount originally specified in it; or

   (c) order that the notice is to be of no effect.

(10) Regulations may make provision with respect to—

   (a) the grounds on which appeals under this section may be made; or

   (b) the procedure on any such appeal.

(11) An enforcing authority shall, for the purpose of enforcing a charge under this section, have all the same powers and remedies under the Law of Property Act 1925, and otherwise, as if it were a mortgagee by deed having powers of sale and lease, of accepting surrenders of leases and of appointing a receiver.

(12) Where any cost is a charge on premises under this section, the enforcing authority may by order declare the cost to be payable with interest by instalments within the specified period until the whole amount is paid.

(13) In subsection (12) above—

   "interest" means interest at the rate determined by the enforcing authority under subsection (4) above; and

   "the specified period" means such period of thirty years or less from the date of service of the charging notice as is specified in the order.

(14) Subsections (3) to (13) above do not extend to Scotland.

DEFINITIONS
"appropriate person": s.78A(9).
"charging notice": subs. (3)(b).
"contaminated land": s.78A(2).
"enforcing authority": s.78A(9).
"interest": subs. (13).
"regulations": s.78A(9).
"specified period": subs. (13).
"substance": s.78A(9).

COMMENCEMENT
September 21, 1995 in so far as this section confers power on the Secretary of State to issue guidance or make regulations or makes provision with respect to the exercise of such power (S.I. 1995 No. 1983). The remainder will be brought into force by a commencement order made under s.125(3) of the Environment Act 1995.

GENERAL NOTE
This section provides the "teeth" in relation to s.78N, namely a power in certain cases for the enforcing authority to recover its reasonable costs of taking appropriate remedial action under that section, together with charging powers in relation to property. The provisions do not apply in all cases where action is taken under s.78N (nor would it be appropriate for them to do so). In particular they do not apply where the specific immunities in ss.78J and K are applicable or where there is a written agreement for the authority to carry out remediation (since, obviously, the authority can recover its costs under that agreement).

Limitations on costs recovery
The costs recoverable will be limited by:
   (a) whether the notice was "appropriate" action under s.78N;
   (b) whether the costs incurred were reasonable (subs. (1));
   (c) apportionments where there are two or more appropriate persons involved (subs. (1));
   (d) hardship which recovery might cause (subs. (2)(a)); and
   (e) any guidance issued by the Secretary of State (subs. (2)(b)).

Charging notice
Under subs. (3) the authority may serve a charging notice in certain circumstances. These provisions do not apply to Scotland (subs. (14): see the note to that subsection). The notice may only he served on a person from whom costs are recoverable who is:
   (a) the owner of any premises consisting of or including the contaminated land; and
   (b) who caused or knowingly permitted the contaminating substances to he in, on or under the land.
Such notice cannot therefore be served on an occupier, or on an original polluter who is no longer owner. Whether it can be served on an owner who acquires already contaminated property depends on whether they can he said to have knowingly permitted the substances to be in the land; a question discussed under subs. 78F.

Effect of charging notice
A charging notice has three effects:
   (a) the remedial cost then carries interest (subs. (4)(a));
   (b) the cost and accrued interest are a statutory charge on the premises (subss. (4)(b) and (7)); and
   (c) the authority may by order declare the cost to be payable by instalments (subs. (12)) over a period of up to 30 years (subs. (13)).

Procedure for charging notices
A charging notice must specify the amount of the cost which the authority claims is recoverable, together with the explanatory matters referred to in subs. (5). A copy must be served contemporaneously on every other person who, to the knowledge of the authority, has an interest in the premises capable of being affected by the charge (subs. (6)). There is no express obligation on the authority to make inquiry to discover such persons, though many such interests could presumably be discovered readily enough by a land registry or land charges search.
   A right of appeal against a charging notice (to the county court) is provided by subs. (8), on such grounds and under such procedures as may be provided for by regulations: subs. (10).

Effect and priority of statutory charge
A statutory charge under s.78P may be enforced by the powers and remedies of sale, lease and receivership available to a mortgagee by deed under the Law of Property Act 1925 (subs. (11)). The statutory charge is a charge on "the premises" (subs. (6)) "consisting of or including" (subs. (3)(a)(i)) the contaminated land. This raises the question of what constitutes "the premises" where these may be greater in extent than the contaminated area—a possibility which subs. (3)(a)(i) acknowledges. Where a charging notice may be served, there appears to be nothing to prevent the enforcing authority serving a notice charging the whole of any premises in the ownership of the same person, provided that those premises include the previously contaminated land. Such premises may be far more valuable than the part of it which had been contaminated, and this is an important protection for the enforcing authority.

The second question is how the statutory charge rates in terms of priority with existing mortgages. If the wording were a charge "on the land", on the authority of *Westminster City Council v. Haymarket Publishing Ltd* [1981] 2 All E.R. 555 it could be said that the charge is on all the estates and interests in the land, including prior mortgages. The wording here is "premises", but in fact this phraseology was used in earlier statutes and was held to have the effect of charging all proprietary interests in a series of cases followed in the *Westminster City Council* case: see *Birmingham Corpn. v. Baker* (1881) 17 Ch. D. 782, *Tendring Union Guardians v. Dowton* [1891] 3 Ch. 265, *Paddington Borough Council v. Finucane* [1928] Ch. 567. The conclusion thus seems inescapable that the statutory charge will affect, and take priority over, all existing mortgages, charges, options and other legal or equitable estates or interests in land, and this is another important protection for the enforcing authority.

Subs. (14): Scotland
Although the cost recovery provisions (subss. (1)–(2)) extend to Scotland, the charging powers in relation to property do not. However, there seems in principle no reason why subss. (3)–(13) should not have been extended to Scotland and amendments were introduced in Parliament to that effect albeit unsuccessfully: *e.g. Hansard*, H.L. Vol. 562 col. 250. Explaining its refusal to accept these amendments, the Government stated that existing mechanisms for recovering sums due under Scots law were adequate and that the amendments would require Scotland to change its system of conveyancing: *Hansard* H.L. Vol. 562, col. 221 *per* the Earl of Lindsay; see also Standing Committee B, May 23, 1995, col. 368 *per* Sir Hector Monro, Parliamentary Under-Secretary of State for Scotland; and *Hansard*, H.C., Vol. 262, col. 959 *per* Sir Paul Beresford. This reasoning appears to be highly unsatisfactory as statutory charging orders are by no means a new concept in Scots law as was indeed pointed out in Parliament: Standing Committee B May 23, 1995, col. 364 *per* Sam Galbraith. For example, the Building (Scotland) Act 1959, Sched. 6; the Sewerage (Scotland) Act 1968, s.47; the Water (Scotland) Act 1980, s.65; the Civic Government (Scotland) Act 1982, s.102; and the Housing (Scotland) Act 1987, Sched. 9 all make provision for charging orders. Primarily these charges may be created by local authorities in relation to works carried out as, for example, under the Building (Scotland) Act 1959 and the Housing (Scotland) Act 1987. Since their existence has not required the reform of the system of conveyancing in Scotland, it is not easy to understand the Government's refusal to give Scottish local authorities the power to make charging orders for remediation costs in relation to contaminated land. It may as a result be significantly more difficult for enforcing authorities to recover their costs in Scotland than in England and Wales although this would to a degree have been true in any event: unlike the English provisions which as noted above give the enforcing authority the same power as a mortgagee under the Law of Property Act 1925, the charging order provisions in the Scottish statutes do not put the enforcing authority in the same position as a heritable creditor under the Conveyancing and Feudal Reform (Scotland) Act 1970. They merely provide, where the charge is appropriately registered, for the burdening of the property concerned with an annuity to pay the amount due. In the absence of contaminated land charging order provisions in Scotland, local authorities will be required to rely on standard court procedures and methods of diligence such as inhibition and adjudication, which are not ideal. For example, inhibition may only be used against the owner of the property and is merely a means of preventing its sale until payment of the debt secured. Furthermore, adjudication involves a lengthy and complex process.

Special sites

78Q.—(1) If, in a case where a local authority has served a remediation notice, the contaminated land in question becomes a special site, the appropriate Agency may adopt the remediation notice and, if it does so,—
    (a) it shall give notice of its decision to adopt the remediation notice to the appropriate person and to the local authority;

    (b) the remediation notice shall have effect, as from the time at which the appropriate Agency decides to adopt it, as a remediation notice given by that Agency; and

    (c) the validity of the remediation notice shall not be affected by—

        (i) the contaminated land having become a special site;

        (ii) the adoption of the remediation notice by the appropriate Agency; or

        (iii) anything in paragraph (b) above.

(2) Where a local authority has, by virtue of section 78N above, begun to do any thing, or any series of things, by way of remediation—

    (a) the authority may continue doing that thing, or that series of things, by virtue of that section, notwithstanding that the contaminated land in question becomes a special site; and

    (b) section 78P above shall apply in relation to the reasonable cost incurred by the authority in doing that thing or those things as if that authority were the enforcing authority.

(3) If and so long as any land is a special site, the appropriate Agency may from time to time inspect that land for the purpose of keeping its condition under review.

(4) If it appears to the appropriate Agency that a special site is no longer land which is required to be designated as such a site, the appropriate Agency may give notice—

    (a) to the Secretary of State, and

    (b) to the local authority in whose area the site is situated,

terminating the designation of the land in question as a special site as from such date as may be specified in the notice.

(5) A notice under subsection (4) above shall not prevent the land, or any of the land, to which the notice relates being designated as a special site on a subsequent occasion.

(6) In exercising its functions under subsection (3) or (4) above, the appropriate Agency shall act in accordance with any guidance given for the purpose by the Secretary of State.

DEFINITIONS

"appropriate Agency": s.78A(9).
"appropriate person": s.78E(1).
"contaminated land": s.78A(2).
"local authority": s.78A(9).
"notice": s.78A(9).
"remediation": s.78A(7).
"remediation notice" s.78E(1).
"required to be designated as a special site": s.78C(8).
"special site": s.78A(3).

COMMENCEMENT

September 21, 1995 in so far as this section confers power on the Secretary of State to issue guidance or makes provision with respect to the exercise of such power (S.I. 1995 No. 1983). The remainder will be brought into force by a commencement order made under s.125(3) of the Environment Act 1995.

GENERAL NOTE

This section contains provisions dealing specifically with special sites and the change in status of land as regards that designation.

Subss. (1)–(2): Transition to special site

These subsections make provision for the case where land has been identified as contaminated and enforcement action has begun, either under s.78E or s.78N, and the land then becomes designated as a special site. The Agency/SEPA becomes the enforcing authority and may elect to adopt any remediation notice served (subs. (1)), but the local authority may continue to do things which have already been commenced under s.78N and recover costs under s.78P in respect of such things.

It may be a collorary of subs. (1)(c)(ii) that the validity of a remediation notice served by the local authority prior to a site's designation as a special site *is* affected by the Agency/SEPA choosing *not* to adopt the notice. Even if this is not the case, the local authority, no longer the enforcing authority, cannot enforce the notice. However, there are two ways in which a remediation notice served by the local authority prior to the site becoming a special site might continue to affect the appropriate person under the notice. First, if in fact the site becoming a special site does *not* affect the validity of the notice, then nothing in s.78M (the offences section of Part IIA) prevents a private individual or a local or environmental group bringing a private prosecution against an appropriate person for failure to comply with the remediation notice. (In Scotland, however, the consent of the Lord Advocate would be required for such a prosecution and hence it is a remote possibility north of the border). It may be, however, that the unusual circumstances envisaged here would have a bearing on whether the courts accepted that that person had a "reasonable excuse" (s.78M(1)) for the non-compliance.

Secondly, subs. (2), which gives the local authority the power to continue remediation it has already commenced, gives a limited scope for continued involvement by a local authority with a special site. Subsection (2) does not appear to distinguish between circumstances where the Agency/SEPA has and has not adopted any notice. Subject to the power of the Agency/SEPA to give the local authority site specific guidance under s.78V, it would appear that the local authority could press on with remediation which was already underway when the site became a special site, and then seek to recover its costs under subs. (2)(b). Such remediation work might, although it need not, have been commenced following non-compliance with the notice by the appropriate person, and the cost recovery position appears unaffected by whether or not the Agency/SEPA subsequently adopts the notice. As to how far the local authority can continue, it will be noted that it is allowed to continue any "series of things" it has begun to do: subs. (2)(a).

Subs. (3): Inspection of special sites
The Agency/SEPA has the power to inspect special sites for keeping their condition under review. The power is to be exercised in accordance with guidance from the Secretary of State (subs. (6)).

Subss. (4)–(5): Termination of designation as special site
These subsections provide a procedure whereby designation of land as a special site may be terminated at the instigation of the Agency/SEPA. Following termination of such designation, the land may of course continue to be contaminated land. Termination of designation will not prevent redesignation as a special site subsequently (subs. (5)). The power to terminate designation is to be exercised in accordance with the Secretary of State's guidance (subs. (6)).

Registers

78R.—(1) Every enforcing authority shall maintain a register containing prescribed particulars of or relating to—

(a) remediation notices served by that authority;

(b) appeals against any such remediation notices;

(c) remediation statements or remediation declarations prepared and published under section 78H above;

(d) in relation to an enforcing authority in England and Wales, appeals against charging notices served by that authority;

(e) notices under subsection (1)(b) or (5)(a) of section 78C above which have effect by virtue of subsection (7) of that section as the designation of any land as a special site;

(f) notices under subsection (4)(b) of section 78D above which have effect by virtue of subsection (6) of that section as the designation of any land as a special site;

(g) notices given by or to the enforcing authority under section 78Q(4) above terminating the designation of any land as a special site;

(h) notifications given to that authority by persons—

(i) on whom a remediation notice has been served, or

(ii) who are or were required by virtue of section 78H(8)(a) above to prepare and publish a remediation statement,

of what they claim has been done by them by way of remediation;

(j) notifications given to that authority by owners or occupiers of land—

(i) in respect of which a remediation notice has been served, or

(ii) in respect of which a remediation statement has been prepared and published,

of what they claim has been done on the land in question by way of remediation;

(k) convictions for such offences under section 78M above as may be prescribed;

(l) such other matters relating to contaminated land as may be prescribed;

but that duty is subject to sections 78S and 78T below.

(2) The form of, and the descriptions of information to be contained in, notifications for the purposes of subsection (1)(h) or (j) above may be prescribed by the Secretary of State.

(3) No entry made in a register by virtue of subsection (1)(h) or (j) above constitutes a representation by the body maintaining the register or, in a case where the entry is made by virtue of subsection (6) below, the authority which sent the copy of the particulars in question pursuant to subsection (4) or (5) below—

(a) that what is stated in the entry to have been done has in fact been done; or

(b) as to the manner in which it has been done.

(4) Where any particulars are entered on a register maintained under this section by the appropriate Agency, the appropriate Agency shall send a copy of those particulars to the local authority in whose area is situated the land to which the particulars relate.

(5) In any case where—

(a) any land is treated by virtue of section 78X(2) below as situated in the area of a local authority other than the local authority in whose area it is in fact situated, and

(b) any particulars relating to that land are entered on the register maintained under this section by the local authority in whose area the land is so treated as situated,

that authority shall send a copy of those particulars to the local authority in whose area the land is in fact situated.

(6) Where a local authority receives a copy of any particulars sent to it pursuant to subsection (4) or (5) above, it shall enter those particulars on the register maintained by it under this section.

(7) Where information of any description is excluded by virtue of section 78T below from any register maintained under this section, a statement shall be entered in the register indicating the existence of information of that description.

(8) It shall be the duty of each enforcing authority—

(a) to secure that the registers maintained by it under this section are available, at all reasonable times, for inspection by the public free of charge; and

(b) to afford to members of the public facilities for obtaining copies of entries, on payment of reasonable charges;

and, for the purposes of this subsection, places may be prescribed by the Secretary of State at which any such registers or facilities as are mentioned in paragraph (a) or (b) above are to be available or afforded to the public in pursuance of the paragraph in question.

(9) Registers under this section may be kept in any form.

DEFINITIONS
"appropriate Agency": s.78A(9).
"charging notice": s.78P(3)(b).
"enforcing authority": s.78A(9).
"local authority": s.78A(9).

"notification": s.78A(9).
"prescribed": s.78A(9).
"remediation": s.78A(7).
"remediation declaration": s.78H(6).
"remediation notice": s.78E(1).
"remediation statement": s.78H(7).
"special site": s.78A(3).

COMMENCEMENT
September 21, 1995 in so far as this section confers power on the Secretary of State to make regulations or makes provision with respect to the exercise of such power (S.I. 1995 No. 1983). The remainder will be brought into force by a commencement order made under s.125(3) of the Environment Act 1995.

GENERAL NOTE
Registers are to be maintained by local authorities (or the Agency/SEPA in the case of special sites) containing particulars relating to the matters specified in subs. (1). Particulars relating to special sites are also to be kept on the relevant local register: subss. (4) and (6).

Details of remedial action
Most of the matters to be contained in the registers relate to notices, notifications and the like, and are self-explanatory. However, paras. (h) and (j) of subs. (1) stand on a somewhat different footing. They require the authority to place on the register notifications by appropriate persons and owners or occupiers of what they claim has been done by way of remediation.

These paragraphs were inserted by a Government amendment in response to an amendment proposed by the Law Society of England and Wales and provide a means by which an appropriate person, owner or occupier can record in a public form what has been done to comply with a remediation notice or remediation statement. In this way some of the blight which might otherwise affect the land may be alleviated. However, it is important to note subs. (3), which negatives any implied representation by the authority that what is stated on the register as having been done has in fact been done, or has been done adequately. The authority's role is therefore simply one of a "postbox", recording notification which it receives: as it was put in debate, it is not the responsibility of the enforcing authority to indicate that the land has "a clean bill of health" (H.L. Vol. 562, col. 1047, Viscount Ullswater).

There is no requirement, at least in s.78R itself, that original notifications under s.78B(4) be included on the register. The implications of this are commented on in the general note to that section.

Exclusion from registers of information affecting national security

78S.—(1) No information shall be included in a register maintained under section 78R above if and so long as, in the opinion of the Secretary of State, the inclusion in the register of that information, or information of that description, would be contrary to the interests of national security.

(2) The Secretary of State may, for the purpose of securing the exclusion from registers of information to which subsection (1) above applies, give to enforcing authorities directions—

(a) specifying information, or descriptions of information, to be excluded from their registers; or

(b) specifying descriptions of information to be referred to the Secretary of State for his determination;

and no information referred to the Secretary of State in pursuance of paragraph (b) above shall be included in any such register until the Secretary of State determines that it should be so included.

(3) The enforcing authority shall notify the Secretary of State of any information which it excludes from the register in pursuance of directions under subsection (2) above.

(4) A person may, as respects any information which appears to him to be information to which subsection (1) above may apply, give a notice to the Secretary of State specifying the information and indicating its apparent nature; and, if he does so—

    (a) he shall notify the enforcing authority that he has done so; and

    (b) no information so notified to the Secretary of State shall be included in any such register until the Secretary of State has determined that it should be so included.

DEFINITIONS
"enforcing authority": s.78A(9).
"notice": s.78A(9).

COMMENCEMENT
September 21, 1995 in so far as this section confers power on the Secretary of State to give directions or makes provision with respect to the exercise of such power (S.I. 1995 No. 1983). The remainder will be brought into force by a commencement order made under s.125(3) of the Environment Act 1995.

GENERAL NOTE
This section provides a means of excluding from the public registers under s.78R information the disclosure of which would be contrary to national security.

Exclusion from registers of certain confidential information

78T.—(1) No information relating to the affairs of any individual or business shall be included in a register maintained under section 78R above, without the consent of that individual or the person for the time being carrying on that business, if and so long as the information—

    (a) is, in relation to him, commercially confidential; and

    (b) is not required to be included in the register in pursuance of directions under subsection (7) below;

but information is not commercially confidential for the purposes of this section unless it is determined under this section to be so by the enforcing authority or, on appeal, by the Secretary of State.

(2) Where it appears to an enforcing authority that any information which has been obtained by the authority under or by virtue of any provision of this Part might be commercially confidential, the authority shall—

    (a) give to the person to whom or whose business it relates notice that that information is required to be included in the register unless excluded under this section; and

    (b) give him a reasonable opportunity—

        (i) of objecting to the inclusion of the information on the ground that it is commercially confidential; and

        (ii) of making representations to the authority for the purpose of justifying any such objection;

and, if any representations are made, the enforcing authority shall, having taken the representations into account, determine whether the information is or is not commercially confidential.

(3) Where, under subsection (2) above, an authority determines that information is not commercially confidential—

    (a) the information shall not be entered in the register until the end of the period of twenty-one days beginning with the date on which the determination is notified to the person concerned;

    (b) that person may appeal to the Secretary of State against the decision;

and, where an appeal is brought in respect of any information, the information shall not be entered in the register until the end of the period of seven days following the day on which the appeal is finally determined or withdrawn.

(4) An appeal under subsection (3) above shall, if either party to the appeal so requests or the Secretary of State so decides, take or continue in the form of a hearing (which must be held in private).

(5) Subsection (10) of section 15 above shall apply in relation to an appeal under subsection (3) above as it applies in relation to an appeal under that section.

(6) Subsection (3) above is subject to section 114 of the Environment Act 1995 (delegation or reference of appeals etc.).

(7) The Secretary of State may give to the enforcing authorities directions as to specified information, or descriptions of information, which the public interest requires to be included in registers maintained under section 78R above notwithstanding that the information may be commercially confidential.

(8) Information excluded from a register shall be treated as ceasing to be commercially confidential for the purposes of this section at the expiry of the period of four years beginning with the date of the determination by virtue of which it was excluded; but the person who furnished it may apply to the authority for the information to remain excluded from the register on the ground that it is still commercially confidential and the authority shall determine whether or not that is the case.

(9) Subsections (3) to (6) above shall apply in relation to a determination under subsection (8) above as they apply in relation to a determination under subsection (2) above.

(10) Information is, for the purposes of any determination under this section, commercially confidential, in relation to any individual or person, if its being contained in the register would prejudice to an unreasonable degree the commercial interests of that individual or person.

(11) For the purposes of subsection (10) above, there shall be disregarded any prejudice to the commercial interests of any individual or person so far as relating only to the value of the contaminated land in question or otherwise to the ownership or occupation of that land.

DEFINITIONS
  "contaminated land": s.78A(2).
  "enforcing authority": s.78A(9).
  "owner": s.78A(9).

COMMENCEMENT
September 21, 1995 in so far as this section confers power on the Secretary of State to give directions or makes provision with respect to the exercise of such power (S.I. 1995 No. 1983). The remainder will be brought into force by a commencement order made under s.125(3) of the Environment Act 1995.

GENERAL NOTE
This section provides safeguards against disclosure on the register of information which is determined to be commercially confidential in relation to the affairs of any individual or business. Information which is excluded from the register on that basis will only be treated as confidential for a period of four years, subject to any application for it to remain excluded: subs. (8).

The meaning of commercial confidentiality
The test of what is commercially confidential is set out at subs. (10) and depends on whether entry on the register would prejudice the commercial interests of the relevant person or business to an unreasonable degree. One of the most likely ways in which such prejudice might be expected to occur is a negative effect of the value of the land or on its use or development. However, prejudice relating solely to land value or to the ownership or occupation of the land is to be disregarded (subs. (11)).

Reports by the appropriate Agency on the state of contaminated land

78U.—(1) The appropriate Agency shall—
(a) from time to time, or
(b) if the Secretary of State at any time so requests,
prepare and publish a report on the state of contaminated land in England and Wales or in Scotland, as the case may be.

(2) A local authority shall, at the written request of the appropriate Agency, furnish the appropriate Agency with such information to which this subsection applies as the appropriate Agency may require for the purpose of enabling it to perform its functions under subsection (1) above.

(3) The information to which subsection (2) above applies is such information as the local authority may have, or may reasonably be expected to obtain, with respect to the condition of contaminated land in its area, being information which the authority has acquired or may acquire in the exercise of its functions under this Part.

DEFINITIONS
"appropriate Agency": s.78A(9).
"contaminated land": s.78A(2).
"local authority": s.78A(9).

COMMENCEMENT
These provisions will be brought into force by a commencement order made under s.125(3) of the Environment Act 1995.

GENERAL NOTE
The Agency/SEPA is given the responsibility of producing and publishing reports on the state of contaminated land on a national basis. Local authorities are required to co-operate in this by providing relevant information: subss. (2) and (3).

Site specific guidance by the appropriate Agency concerning contaminated land

78V.—(1) The appropriate Agency may issue guidance to any local authority with respect to the exercise or performance of the authority's powers or duties under this Part in relation to any particular contaminated land; and in exercising or performing those powers or duties in relation to that land the authority shall have regard to any such guidance so issued.

(2) If and to the extent that any guidance issued under subsection (1) above to a local authority is inconsistent with any guidance issued under this Part by the Secretary of State, the local authority shall disregard the guidance under that subsection.

(3) A local authority shall, at the written request of the appropriate Agency, furnish the appropriate Agency with such information to which this subsection applies as the appropriate Agency may require for the purpose of enabling it to issue guidance for the purposes of subsection (1) above.

(4) The information to which subsection (3) above applies is such information as the local authority may have, or may reasonably be expected to obtain, with respect to any contaminated land in its area, being information which the authority has acquired, or may acquire, in the exercise of its functions under this Part.

DEFINITIONS
"appropriate Agency": s.78A(9).
"contaminated land": s.78A(2).
"local authority": s.78A(9).

COMMENCEMENT
These provisions will be brought into force by a commencement order made under s.125(3) of the Environment Act 1995.

This section allows the Agency/SEPA to issue site specific guidance to local authorities with regard to the local authority's functions: such guidance is not prescriptive but the local authority must have regard to it: subs. (1). Subsection (2) makes it clear that in the event of any conflict between Agency/SEPA and Secretary of State's guidance the latter will prevail.

The appropriate Agency to have regard to guidance given by the Secretary of State

78W.—(1) The Secretary of State may issue guidance to the appropriate Agency with respect to the exercise or performance of that Agency's powers or duties under this Part; and in exercising or performing those powers or duties the appropriate Agency shall have regard to any such guidance so issued.

(2) The duty imposed on the appropriate Agency by subsection (1) above is without prejudice to any duty imposed by any other provision of this Part on that Agency to act in accordance with guidance issued by the Secretary of State.

DEFINITION
"appropriate Agency": s.78A(9).

COMMENCEMENT
September 21, 1995 in so far as this section confers power on the Secretary of State to issue guidance or makes provision with respect to the exercise of such power (S.I. 1995 No. 1983). The remainder will be brought into force by a commencement order made under s.125(3) of the Environment Act 1995.

GENERAL NOTE
This section provides a general reserve power to the Secretary of State to issue guidance (which may be generic or site-specific) to the Agency/SEPA.

Supplementary provisions

78X.—(1) Where it appears to a local authority that two or more different sites, when considered together, are in such a condition, by reason of substances in, on or under the land, that—

  (a) significant harm is being caused or there is a significant possibility of such harm being caused, or

  (b) pollution of controlled waters is being, or is likely to be, caused,

this Part shall apply in relation to each of those sites, whether or not the condition of the land at any of them, when considered alone, appears to the authority to be such that significant harm is being caused, or there is a significant possibility of such harm being caused, or that pollution of controlled waters is being or is likely to be caused.

(2) Where it appears to a local authority that any land outside, but adjoining or adjacent to, its area is in such a condition, by reason of substances in, on or under the land, that significant harm is being caused, or there is a significant possibility of such harm being caused, or that pollution of controlled waters is being, or is likely to be, caused within its area—

  (a) the authority may, in exercising its functions under this Part, treat that land as if it were land situated within its area; and

  (b) except in this subsection, any reference—

    (i) to land within the area of a local authority, or

    (ii) to the local authority in whose area any land is situated,

    shall be construed accordingly;

but this subsection is without prejudice to the functions of the local authority in whose area the land is in fact situated.

(3) A person acting in a relevant capacity—

  (a) shall not thereby be personally liable, under this Part, to bear the whole or any part of the cost of doing any thing by way of remediation, unless that thing is to any extent referable to substances whose presence in, on or under the contaminated land in question is a result of any act done or omission made by him which it was unreasonable for a person acting in that capacity to do or make; and

(b) shall not thereby be guilty of an offence under or by virtue of section 78M above unless the requirement which has not been complied with is a requirement to do some particular thing for which he is personally liable to bear the whole or any part of the cost.

(4) In subsection (3) above, "person acting in a relevant capacity" means—

(a) a person acting as an insolvency practitioner, within the meaning of section 388 of the Insolvency Act 1986 (including that section as it applies in relation to an insolvent partnership by virtue of any order made under section 421 of that Act);

(b) the official receiver acting in a capacity in which he would be regarded as acting as an insolvency practitioner within the meaning of section 388 of the Insolvency Act 1986 if subsection (5) of that section were disregarded;

(c) the official receiver acting as receiver or manager;

(d) a person acting as a special manager under section 177 or 370 of the Insolvency Act 1986;

(e) the Accountant in Bankruptcy acting as permanent or interim trustee in a sequestration (within the meaning of the Bankruptcy (Scotland) Act 1985);

(f) a person acting as a receiver or receiver and manager—
   (i) under or by virtue of any enactment; or
   (ii) by virtue of his appointment as such by an order of a court or by any other instrument.

(5) Regulations may make different provision for different cases or circumstances.

DEFINITIONS
"contaminated land": s.78A(2).
"harm": s.78A(4).
"local authority": s.78A(9).
"pollution of controlled waters": s.78A(9).
"remediation": s.78A(7).
"significant": s.78A(5).
"substance": s.78A(9).

COMMENCEMENT
September 21, 1995 in so far as this section confers power on the Secretary of State to make regulations or makes provision with respect to the exercise of such power (S.I. 1995 No. 1983). The remainder will be brought into force by a commencement order made under s.125(3) of the Environment Act 1995.

GENERAL NOTE
This section contains a number of important supplementary provisions dealing with various matters.

Subs. (1): Combined effect of sites
This subsection covers the situation where a number of sites taken together present the conditions of harm or pollution necessary for land to be regarded as contaminated, even though each site of itself would not be sufficiently significant to be regarded as contaminated. An example might be where a number of sites together contribute a significant pollution load to a watercourse flowing past them, or to groundwater resources. The subsection allows each site in its own right to be regarded as contaminated: the correct procedure is therefore to serve separate remediation notices in relation to each site.

Subs. (2): Land outside local authority's area
Contamination is no respecter of local government boundaries, and land situated outside a local authority's area may quite conceivably represent a threat of harm within the area. An example would be the migration of landfill gas across a boundary so as to affect residential property. The authority in whose area the residential property is located would be able under this subsection to take enforcement action against the land from which the gas emanates. A similar provision applies to statutory nuisances under s.81(2) of this Act.

The relevant land must be "adjoining or adjacent to" the authority's area. If the use of the two terms together were not sufficient to indicate that the land can be adjacent to an authority's area without adjoining it, then case law confirms this: "'Adjacent' is not a word to which a precise and uniform meaning is attached by ordinary usage. It is not confined to places adjoining, and it includes places close to or near. What degree of proximity would justify the application of the word is entirely a question of circumstance" (*Wellington v. Lower Hutt* [1904] A.C. 773, in which two New Zealand boroughs were held to be adjacent for the purpose of making statutory contributions to the cost of building a bridge, despite being nowhere closer to each other than six miles apart); see also *Stanward Corpn. v. Denison Mines Ltd*, 67 D.L.R. (2d) 743, in which a similar approach was taken but two mining claims 1¼ miles apart were held *not* to be adjacent. In Scotland, it has similarly been held that the word does not require actual contact: *Anderson v. Lochgelly Iron & Coal Co. Ltd* (1904) 7 F. 187, where an accident which took place on a private railway connecting a mine to the public railway some 800 yards from the mine was held (with the Lord Justice-Clerk dissenting) to be "adjacent to" the mine in terms of the statutory definition in the Coal Mines Regulation Act 1887; see also *Dunbeath Estate Ltd v. Henderson* 1989 S.L.T. (Land Ct.) 99.

The power of an affected local authority to take action under this section is without prejudice to the functions of the local authority in whose area that land is in fact located. That authority may itself be required to take enforcement action because of harm or pollution within its own area; indeed, there seems to be nothing in the legislation to limit the consideration by the local authority to harm or pollution within its own area. Accordingly there must be the risk of an appropriate person being faced with possibly conflicting remediation requirements by two local authorities. It is suggested that to avoid this situation, any authority considering exercising its powers under s.78X(2) should as a matter of good practice consult the local authority in whose area the relevant land is located.

Subs. (3)-(4): Insolvency
Subsection (3) is intended to protect persons acting in various capacities (specified in subs. (4)) in insolvency situations. The provisions cover liquidators, administrators, administrative receivers, supervisors of voluntary arrangements, trustees in bankruptcy, the official receiver, and any person acting as a receiver under an enactment (*e.g.* the Law of Property Act 1925) or appointed as such by a court, or by any instrument. The protection is twofold:

(a) the person is not liable in a personal capacity for remediation costs unless the remediation requirement is referable (see s.78F(10) for the meaning of this) to substances whose presence in, on or under the land is a result of any act done or omission made by him, which was unreasonable for a person acting in his capacity; and

(b) he shall not be guilty of an offence of failing to comply with a remediation notice unless the relevant requirement relates to a thing for which he is personally responsible under (a).

This wording is potentially difficult. It seems unlikely that the presence of contamination is likely to be the result of the positive act of an insolvency practitioner or similar person, but its presence might well be said to result from an omission on his part, *i.e.* failure to remove it, or failure to take steps which would have prevented it occurring. The concept of an unreasonable omission is a difficult one, raising issues of what it is or is not reasonable to expect an insolvency practitioner to do as regards land which is or might be contaminated. It might be questioned to what extent a person should investigate for possible contamination, or to expend money on remedial measures, in order to avoid being held to have acted (or failed to act) unreasonably. In this respect, the case of *John Willment (Ashford) Limited* [1979] 2 All E.R. 615 may be relevant, in that it was suggested there that a receiver could not exercise his discretion in such a way as to lead the company to act unlawfully.

Application to the Isles of Scilly

78Y.—(1) Subject to the provisions of any order under this section, this Part shall not apply in relation to the Isles of Scilly.

(2) The Secretary of State may, after consultation with the Council of the Isles of Scilly, by order provide for the application of any provisions of this

Part to the Isles of Scilly; and any such order may provide for the application of those provisions to those Isles with such modifications as may be specified in the order.

(3) An order under this section may—

    (a) make different provision for different cases, including different provision in relation to different persons, circumstances or localities; and

    (b) contain such supplemental, consequential and transitional provision as the Secretary of State considers appropriate, including provision saving provision repealed by or under any enactment.

COMMENCEMENT

September 21, 1995 in so far as this section confers power on the Secretary of State to make orders or makes provision with respect to the exercise of such power (S.I. 1995 No. 1983). The remainder will be brought into force by a commencement order made under s.125(3) of the Environment Act 1995.

Supplementary provisions with respect to guidance by the Secretary of State

78YA.—(1) Any power of the Secretary of State to issue guidance under this Part shall only be exercisable after consultation with the appropriate Agency and such other bodies or persons as he may consider it appropriate to consult in relation to the guidance in question.

(2) A draft of any guidance proposed to be issued under section 78A(2) or (5), 78B(2) or 78F(6) or (7) above shall be laid before each House of Parliament and the guidance shall not be issued until after the period of 40 days beginning with the day on which the draft was so laid or, if the draft is laid on different days, the later of the two days.

(3) If, within the period mentioned in subsection (2) above, either House resolves that the guidance, the draft of which was laid before it, should not be issued, the Secretary of State shall not issue that guidance.

(4) In reckoning any period of 40 days for the purposes of subsection (2) or (3) above, no account shall be taken of any time during which Parliament is dissolved or prorogued or during which both Houses are adjourned for more than four days.

(5) The Secretary of State shall arrange for any guidance issued by him under this Part to be published in such manner as he considers appropriate.

DEFINITION

    "appropriate Agency": s.78A(9).

COMMENCEMENT

September 21, 1995 since this entire section makes provision with respect to the exercise by the Secretary of State of his power to issue guidance (S.I. 1995 No. 1983).

GENERAL NOTE

This section provides the special procedure (subss. (2)–(4)) by which the prescriptive guidance, with which enforcing authorities must act in accordance, is to be issued. The Parliamentary procedure is one of negative resolution (subs. (3)).

    Additionally, for *all* guidance, there are more general requirements of consultation (subs. (1)) and publication (subs. (5)).

Interaction of this Part with other enactments

78YB.—(1) A remediation notice shall not be served if and to the extent that it appears to the enforcing authority that the powers of the appropriate Agency under section 27 above may be exercised in relation to—

    (a) the significant harm (if any), and

    (b) the pollution of controlled waters (if any),

by reason of which the contaminated land in question is such land.

(2) Nothing in this Part shall apply in relation to any land in respect of which there is for the time being in force a site licence under Part II above, except to the extent that any significant harm, or pollution of controlled waters, by reason of which that land would otherwise fall to be regarded as contaminated land is attributable to causes other than—

(a) breach of the conditions of the licence; or

(b) the carrying on, in accordance with the conditions of the licence, of any activity authorised by the licence.

(3) If, in a case falling within subsection (1) or (7) of section 59 above, the land in question is contaminated land, or becomes such land by reason of the deposit of the controlled waste in question, a remediation notice shall not be served in respect of that land by reason of that waste or any consequences of its deposit, if and to the extent that it appears to the enforcing authority that the powers of a waste regulation authority or waste collection authority under that section may be exercised in relation to that waste or the consequences of its deposit.

(4) No remediation notice shall require a person to do anything the effect of which would be to impede or prevent the making of a discharge in pursuance of a consent given under Chapter II of Part III of the Water Resources Act 1991 (pollution offences) or, in relation to Scotland, in pursuance of a consent given under Part II of the Control of Pollution Act 1974.

DEFINITIONS
"appropriate Agency": s.78A(9).
"contaminated land": s.78A(2).
"enforcing authority": s.78A(9).
"harm": s.78A(4).
"pollution of controlled waters": s.78A(9).
"remediation notice": s.78E(1).
"significant": s.78A(5).

COMMENCEMENT
These provisions will be brought into force by a commencement order made under s.125(3) of the Environment Act 1995.

GENERAL NOTE
This important section governs the relationship between the contaminated land provisions and other forms of environmental control so as to avoid duplication or conflict. For completeness reference should also be made to Sch. 22, para. 89, which deals with the relationship with statutory nuisance provisions. The relationship with works notices for water pollution is not addressed, and this situation is commented on briefly below.

Subs. (1): IPC and LAPC
Where contamination results from the commission of an offence under Part I of this Act (integrated pollution control and LAPC) action should be taken under s.27 powers (powers of enforcing authority to remedy harm) rather than under Part IIA.

Subs. (2): Waste site licences
The implementation of a waste management licence for the deposit of waste may inevitably involve the contamination of that land, though the risk of harm to health and the environment and to controlled waters should be managed through the imposition and enforcement of licence conditions and the strict requirements relating to surrender of licences under s.39 of this Act.

The provisions on contaminated land are generally disapplied to land in respect of which a waste site licence is in force. However, they can be used in cases where the harm or pollution is attributable to causes other than:

(a) breach of licence conditions; or

(b) carrying on activities authorised by the licence, in accordance with the licence conditions.

The rationale appears to be that if contamination results from breach of licence conditions, then enforcement should be under Part II of this Act, *i.e.* prosecution, or under s.59 (see below). Where the contamination results from the carrying on of authorised activities in accordance with conditions, then the intention is that the contaminated land provisions should not be used. So to take the example of a landfill site, if waste deposited lawfully results in contamination, a remediation notice cannot be served and the licensing authority can take whatever action is appropriate and possible under the provisions of Part II. Rather more problematic is the case of, say, a waste transfer station or treatment plant operating on land subject to contamination from a previous use. Remedial action may be taken under Part IIA in relation to the previous contamination, but not in relation to any contamination caused by operation of the treatment plant or transfer station; provided that the later contamination was caused by the lawful carrying on of authorised activities, or by breach of a licence condition.

Subs. (3): Removal of unlawful waste deposits
1. Powers exist under s.59 of this Act to deal with controlled waste which has been fly-tipped or otherwise unlawfully deposited. In relation to such waste and contamination caused by its deposit, a contaminated land remediation notice may not be served if and to the extent it appears that s.59 powers may be exercised.
   The Government's intention in giving precedence to the s.59 powers is partly to preserve the effect of the defence of innocent occupiers which arises under s.59(3). See note to s.78F above.

Subs. (4): Consented discharges to controlled waters
By subs. (4) no remediation notice shall require a person to do anything which would impede or prevent the making of a consented discharge to controlled waters.

Water pollution: remediation notices and works notice
It will be noted that there is no express provision dealing with the relationship between the contaminated land regime and the Agency/SEPA powers in respect of water pollution.
   The Environment Act 1995 gives the Agency (and SEPA in Scotland) the power to serve a "works notice" requiring works to be carried out remediating or preventing pollution of controlled waters: Sched. 22, paras. 22 and 162, respectively inserting ss.46A–46D into the Control of Pollution Act 1974 for Scotland and ss.161A–161D into the Water Resources Act 1991 for England and Wales. See the note to s.120 and Sched. 22 to the 1995 Act.
   There is the possibility, without adequate co-operation between the relevant local authority and the Agency/SEPA, that someone may be served with both a remediation notice and a works notice containing different requirements, although it will be noted that:
   — the Agency/SEPA is not under a duty to serve a works notice: it merely has a power to do so;
   — in some cases where a works notice may be served, the land may also have been designated as a "special site" under s.78C, in which case the Agency/SEPA is the enforcing authority;
   — the Agency/SEPA has power under s.78V to give site specific guidance to which the local authority must have regard unless it conflicts with Secretary of State's guidance; and
   — a works notice, once served, may satisfy the local authority that appropriate things are being, or will be, done by way of remediation in which case it cannot serve a remediation notice: s.78H(5)(b).

This Part and radioactivity

78YC. Except as provided by regulations, nothing in this Part applies in relation to harm, or pollution of controlled waters, so far as attributable, to any radioactivity possessed by any substance; but regulations may—

(a) provide for prescribed provisions of this Part to have effect with such modifications as the Secretary of State considers appropriate for the purpose of dealing with harm, or pollution of controlled waters, so far as attributable to any radioactivity possessed by any substances; or

(b) make such modifications of the Radioactive Substances Act 1993 or any other Act as the Secretary of State considers appropriate."]

DEFINITIONS
   "harm": s.78A(4).
   "prescribed": "significant": s.78A(5).
   "pollution of controlled waters": "significant": s.78A(5).
   "regulations": "significant": s.78A(5).

COMMENCEMENT
September 21, 1995 in so far as this section confers power on the Secretary of State to make regulations or makes provision with respect to the exercise of such power (S.I. 1995 No. 1983). The remainder will be brought into force by a commencement order made under s.125(3) of the Environment Act 1995.

GENERAL NOTE
Part IIA does not apply to harm or pollution so far as attributable to the radioactive properties of any substance, except where those provisions are applied by regulations. The fact that the substance in question is radioactive will not prevent the application of contaminated land powers in relation to other properties of the substance (*e.g.* toxicity) if these result in significant harm or pollution.

The Government in debate indicated that it saw Part IIA as providing a suitable basis for dealing with radioactive contamination on old industrial sites, *e.g.* old radium luminescing works. But because of the particular scientific problems involved, some changes to the detail might be needed: H.C. Standing Committee B, 11th Sitting, Pt. II, col. 386, May 23, 1995.

PART III

STATUTORY NUISANCES AND CLEAN AIR

INTRODUCTORY AND GENERAL NOTE
Part III of the Act deals primarily with statutory nuisances (ss.79–82: see below). It also provides for the phasing out of specific controls over "offensive trades", which are now largely governed by this Part and Pt. I of this Act (s.84). The now-repealed s.85 made certain provisions in relation to clean air which have now been superseded by the Clean Air Act 1993.

Statutory nuisance
In relation to statutory nuisances, ss.79–82 replace the provisions of the Public Health Act 1936 and the Public Health (Recurring Nuisances) Act 1969 with a more streamlined system of summary procedures. The new procedures are similar to those contained in Pt. III of the Control of Pollution Act 1974 relating to noise nuisances, and are set out diagrammatically below.

PROCEDURE UNDER PART III OF ENVIRONMENTAL PROTECTION ACT 1990 (EPA 1990)

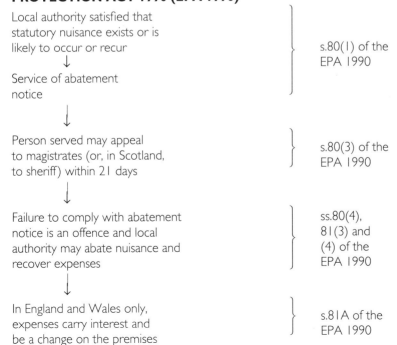

Local authority satisfied that statutory nuisance exists or is likely to occur or recur   s.80(1) of the EPA 1990

↓

Service of abatement notice

↓

Person served may appeal to magistrates (or, in Scotland, to sheriff) within 21 days   s.80(3) of the EPA 1990

↓

Failure to comply with abatement notice is an offence and local authority may abate nuisance and recover expenses   ss.80(4), 81(3) and (4) of the EPA 1990

↓

In England and Wales only, expenses carry interest and be a change on the premises   s.81A of the EPA 1990

NOTE:

1. Commencement of summary proceedings requires consent of the Secretary of State in certain cases: s.79(10).

2. A complaint (or, in Scotland, a summary application) may be made to a magistrates' court (or, in Scotland, a sheriff court) by any person aggrieved by the existence of a statutory nuisance. The court must make an order requiring abatement or prohibiting recurrence, if satisfied the nuisance exists or, if abated, is likely to recur and may also impose a fine. Breach of such an order is an offence: s.82.

3. Local authorities may take abatement, prohibition or restriction proceedings in the High Court (or, in Scotland, any court of competent jurisdiction) if of the opinion that a prosecution for failure to comply with the authority's abatement notice would afford an inadequate remedy: s.81(5).

The relationship between statutory nuisance and other regulatory regimes is considered below.
Since the introduction of the remodelled procedures with effect from January 1, 1991 (s.164(2)), there have been three significant alterations to their scope:
    (a) its extension in relation to *noise nuisance*, effected by the Noise and Statutory Nuisance Act 1993;
    (b) the exclusion of the statutory nuisance regime in relation to *land contamination*, effected upon the introduction by the Environment Act 1995, s.57, of the new contaminated land regime which forms Pt. IIA of this Act, and
    (c) the extension of the regime to *Scotland* by the 1995 Act, s.107 and Sched. 17, to replace as from April 1, 1996 Scottish provisions contained in the Public Health (Scotland) Act 1897 and Part III of the Control of Pollution Act 1974 (see notes to s.83, which provided that Pt. III of the 1990 Act did not apply to Scotland and has therefore been repealed, and to s.107 of the 1995 Act).

(a) Noise and Statutory Nuisance Act 1993
The Noise and Statutory Nuisance Act 1993 received Royal Assent on November 5, 1993 and came into force on January 5, 1994 (with the exception of s.9 and Sched. 3 dealing with audible intruder alarms, which come into force on a day to be appointed). The 1993 Act amended Part III of the 1990 Act to make provision in relation to street noise from vehicles, machinery of equipment; it also makes amendments to the procedure for abating statutory nuisances in relation to expenses incurred by local authorities.
A draft Circular on the 1993 Act was published for consultation in 1993 and it is understood that the Circular is to be published during the course of 1996.
The 1993 Act also contained a number of provisions which do not operate by way of amendment to Pt. III, and which are summarised here. The 1993 Act amended the Control of Pollution Act 1974 in order to introduce into Scottish law provisions analogous to those noted above on street noise from vehicles, machinery or equipment: those provisions are now repealed by the 1995 Act, Sched. 24, having been rendered unnecessary by the extension of Pt. III of the 1990 Act to Scotland (see (c)). In addition, ss.7–9 of the 1993 Act introduced new legislation for England, Wales and Scotland governing noise from loudspeakers and audible intruder alarms (*i.e.*, burglar alarms). Part of the loudspeaker legislation thus effected amended the Control of Pollution Act 1974, s.62, to modify its existing provisions with regard to loudspeakers, which remain in effect throughout Great Britain. The other aspect of the loudspeaker provisions, and the provisions on audible intruder alarms, stand alone in the 1993 Act and are described briefly here.

Loudspeakers. New provisions on the operation of loudspeakers in streets or roads are introduced by Schedule 2 of the 1993 Act. A local authority may resolve that these provisions are to apply to its area, in which case Schedule 2 comes into force in its area on such date as may be specified in the resolution. These provisions allow the local authority, on an application made by any person, to consent to the operation in its area of a loudspeaker which would otherwise be in contravention of section 62 of the Control of Pollution Act 1974. Consent may not be given to the operation of a loudspeaker in connection with any election or for the purpose of advertising any entertainment, trade or business. Consent may be granted subject to such conditions that the local authority considers appropriate. Where the authority grants consent, it may publicise this fact by way of notice in a local newspaper.

Audible intruder alarms. By section 9 of the 1993 Act a local authority may, after consulting the Chief Officer of Police, resolve that Schedule 3 is to apply to its area. As with Schedule 2, the relevant provisions will then come into force on such a date as may be specified in the resolution.

Schedule 3 requires the person who installs a new audible intruder alarm on or in any premises to ensure that the alarm complies with any prescribed requirements and that the local authority is notified within 48 hours of its installation. In relation to existing or new audible intruder alarms, the occupier of the premises where they are installed must not permit the alarm to be operated unless the requirements of paragraph 5 are satisfied: these require the alarm to comply with any prescribed requirements, for the police to have been informed in writing of the names, addresses and telephone numbers of the current key holders, and for the local authority to have been informed of the address of the police station to which notification has been given. This requirement applies not only to the person who was occupier when the alarm was installed, but also to persons who after the appointed day become the occupier of such premises.

Powers are given for officers of the local authority to enter premises where an intruder alarm is operating audibly more than one hour after it was activated and where the audible operation is such as to give persons living or working in the vicinity of the premises reasonable cause for annoyance. Where force is required to enter the premises, then an application must be made to the Justices of the Peace for a warrant, before which a notice must be left at the premises stating that such an application is to be made. When entering under the warrant, the officer must be accompanied by a police constable. Where the officer enters premises which are unoccupied or from which the occupier is temporarily absent the officer must after the alarm has been turned off, reset it if reasonably practicable, leave a notice at the premises stating what action has been taken and leave the premises, so far as reasonably practicable, as effectually secured against trespassers as he found them. The authority may recover (from the occupier of the premises) its reasonable expenses incurred in entering the premises, turning off the alarm, and complying with the requirements as to leaving the premises secure.

Section 9 and Sched. 3 are not yet in force, and so a local authority is not yet able to resolve that it apply in an area. However, on July 24, 1995, the DoE announced its intention of bringing the provisions into force, and published for consultation draft Audible Intruder Alarms Regulations 1995 and a draft Noise and Statutory Nuisance Act 1993 (Commencement) Order 1995. The draft regulations would prescribe, as a requirement with which all such alarms must comply, that they must be fitted with an automatic cut-out device so that the alarm stops sounding within 20 minutes of its first sounding. It was understood, as at December 1995, that the bringing into force of the provisions was being held back pending resolution of concerns about the demands it might place on police officers.

(b) Contaminated land

The Environment Act 1995, s.57, inserts into the 1990 Act a new Pt. IIA (ss.78A–78YC) on contaminated land: see further the general introductory note to Pt. IIA. That new regime is intended to replace statutory nuisance for land contamination problems, and accordingly the 1995 Act inserts into Pt. III a new s.79(1A) which disapplies statutory nuisance where the matter in question consists of or is caused by land being in a contaminated state. The circumstances in which the contaminated land provisions apply and those in which the statutory nuisance provisions have been disapplied are deliberately different, however: see *Relationship with other areas of control* below. The outcome is that there are conceivable situations in which an abatement notice could formerly have been served under Pt. III but in which now neither such an abatement notice, nor a remediation notice under Pt. IIA, can be served.

(c) Scotland

Pt. III did not originally apply to Scotland, but the Environment Act 1995, s.107 and Sched. 17 amend Pt. III so that the provisions apply throughout Great Britain. One important consequence of this change is that the case law on Pt. III developed since its introduction in England and Wales is now relevant to its application in Scotland, superseding the existing Scottish case law on the repealed Scottish provisions. See the note to s.107 of the 1995 Act for the reasons why Pt. III was extended to Scotland. As noted at (a) above, the 1993 Act and the relevant provisions of the Control of Pollution Act 1974 also apply throughout Great Britain.

Relationship with other areas of control

(a) *Integrated pollution control and local air pollution control (Pt. I of this Act):* In the case of statutory nuisances consisting of smoke emitted from premises, dust, steam, smell or other effluvia arising on industrial, trade or business premises, or any accumulation or deposit, a local authority may not issue summary proceedings under Pt. III without the consent of the Secretary of State, if proceedings in respect thereof might be instituted under Pt. I (s.79(10)). Given the breadth of the definitions of "pollution of the environment" and "harm" for the purposes of Pt. I (s.1), control under Pt. I can clearly embrace matters of public health and, indeed, activities causing offence to man's olfactory or other senses. (However, noise does not appear to be governed by Pt. I (see the note to s.1(11)), and therefore the statutory nuisance regime applies in its regard). It should be noted that the s.79(10) requirement does not apply to all statutory nuisances: only to those listed. Nor does it apply to summary proceedings commenced by an aggrieved person under s.82, which therefore do not require the Secretary of State's consent.

The general note to s.7 considers the question of the framing, in authorisations granted under Pt. I, of conditions designed to avoid prescribed processes causing statutory nuisance.

(b) *Waste on land (Pt. II of this Act):* The provisions of Pt. III could apply to accumulations of controlled waste (s.79(1)(e)) or to smell or other effluvia from such waste (s.79(1)(d), although the scope for such application is considerably reduced by s.79(1A) with the advent of the contaminated land regime (see further (c) below).

The relationship of waste licensing powers and control over statutory nuisance was considered by the Court of Appeal in *Att.-Gen.'s Reference (No. 2 of 1988)* [1989] 3 W.L.R. 397. It was held in that case that:

(i) the primary purpose of waste disposal licensing powers under Pt. I of the Control of Pollution Act 1974 (the predecessor to Pt. II of this Act) was to avoid water pollution, serious detriment to the amenities of the locality and harm to public health; therefore the power to impose conditions under s.6(2) of the 1974 Act was not wide enough to allow a condition prohibiting public nuisances of all kinds, whether or not they had one of those three effects; and

(ii) if such condition were valid, there would be no need to trace a nuisance back to a particular failure of management or operation in order to establish a beach.

It is questionable how far proposition (i) remains correct under Pt. II, where protection of water from pollution has been broadened to protection of the environment generally, and where "harm" to the environment receives a very broad statutory definition to include human senses.

(c) *Contaminated land (Pt. IIA of this Act):Section 79(1A) provides that no matter shall constitute a statutory nuisance to the extent that it consists of, or is caused by, any land being in a "contaminated state". Statutory nuisance powers are thus disapplied in relation to land contamination situations: if land which is in a contaminated state is presenting a statutory nuisance in some way unrelated to the contamination (e.g. by noise from operations carried out on the land) then of course statutory nuisance provisions remain applicable.*

The definition of "contaminated state" in s.79(1B) refers (in part) to harm being caused or the possibility of harm being caused. This terminology does not mirror the definition of contaminated land in s.78A(2). The relevant part of the latter refers to "*significant*" harm being caused or the "*significant*" possibility of "*such*" harm being caused. It follows that statutory nuisance powers are disapplied in wider circumstances than those in which contaminated land powers are introduced. For example, where a possibility exists, but not a significant possibility, of significant harm being caused by land in a contaminated state, then no contaminated land remediation notice may be served, yet neither may any statutory nuisance abatement notice be served or abatement order sought, even if the harm in question is prejudicial to health or a nuisance. The thinking behind this appears to be that, without such provision, statutory nuisance powers could be used in ways which circumvent or undermine the risk-based, "suitable for use" policy approach underlying the contaminated land provisions.

(d) *Radioactive substances:* For the purposes of the operation and enforcement of Pt. III, no account is to be taken of any radioactivity possessed by any substance or article or by any part of any premises: Radioactive Substances Act 1993, s.40(2)(a) and Sched. 3.

(e) *Air pollution investigations and research:* The Clean Air Act 1993, s.45, allows local authorities to exempt any chimney from certain provisions of that Act and from Pt. III of this

Act where it is satisfied, on application from any person interested, that it is expedient to do so to enable investigations or research relevant to air pollution problems to take place.

(f) *Colliery spoilbanks:* The Clean Air Act 1993, s.42, provides that statutory nuisance provisions do not apply in relation to smoke, grit or dust from the combustion of refuse deposited from any "mine" or "quarry" (as defined in the Mines and Quarries Act 1954) from which coal or shale has been, is being or is to be got.

(g) *Water pollution:* Pt. III contains no express provision on the relationship between Pt. III and the various enforcement measures existing elsewhere (notably in the Water Resources Act 1991 or, in Scotland, in the Control of Pollution Act 1974) in relation to water pollution. It should be noted that s.79(1)(h) includes as statutory nuisances for the purposes of Pt. III matters declared to be statutory nuisances by any other enactment. These include the statutory nuisance set out at the Public Health Act 1936, s.259(1)(a) and (b): pools, ponds, ditches, gutters and watercourses which for various reasons are prejudicial to health or a nuisance. However, the scope for statutory nuisance provisions to be applied in water pollution cases is curtailed by s.79(1A) (discussed at (c) above): it will be noted that land being in a "contaminated state" so as to exclude statutory nuisance provisions, as defined in s.79(1B), includes reference to pollution or likely pollution of controlled waters.

(h) *Construction works and other Control of Pollution Act 1974 noise controls:* Various defences to a prosecution under s.80(4) for non-compliance with a statutory nuisance abatement notice are provided by s.80(9). All are based on the principle that it is unreasonable for a local authority to institute such proceedings in relation to a level of noise to which, under other provisions (relating to construction sites or the noise abatement zone procedure), it has consented: see further the general note to s.80(9).

Notices under previous legislation
Despite the absence of any express transitional or saving provision in the 1990 Act, it has been held that a notice served under the Control of Pollution Act 1974 remained valid after the 1990 Act came into force, so that a conviction could lie for breach of the notice: see *Aitken v. South Hams District Council* ([1994] Env.L.R. 373). The decision was based on s.16(1) of the Interpretation Act 1978, and overrules the Divisional Court decision in *R. v. Folkstone Magistrates' Court, ex p. Kibble* ([1993] Env.L.R. 400).

Further developments
At the end of 1995, two further developments affecting the statutory law relating to nuisance were moving towards fruition, although the extent to which those developments would impinge directly on Pt. III was unclear at that point.

(a) *Domestic noise nuisance:* In October 1994 the Government set up a working party to review the effectiveness of Pt. III in addressing the problem of "neighbour noise" in residential properties. The DoE published the recommendations of the working party for consultation on March 27, 1995. On December 12, 1995, Environment Minister James Clappison announced in response to a written question in Parliament that the Government proposed to accept the recommendations in full.

The announcement grouped the nine recommendations into four areas: (i) the promotion, through the dissemination of best practice and professional guidance, of consistency in the approach to enforcement taken by different local authorities; (ii) the drawing up of a code of practice on effective liaison between the police and local authority environmental health officers; (iii) the creation of a specific power for local authorities to temporarily confiscate noise-making equipment (the working party found that different local authorities took different views on whether existing provisions allowed for this, and were acting differently as a result); and (iv) the creation of a new offence (in relation to noise at night only) of continuing to breach an objective statutory noise standard following a warning from a local authority officer to reduce the noise below that standard (the subjective and circumstantial nature of noise nuisance has often made it difficult for officers to prove the existence of a nuisance). The standard envisaged was a double one in that, to breach it, noise at night would, in the complainant's house, need both to exceed 35 decibels and to exceed the background level of noise by 10 decibels.

On December 13, 1995, a Private Member's Bill entitled the Noise Bill had its first reading, with a long title as follows: "A Bill to make provision about noise emitted from dwellings at night; about the forfeiture and confiscation of equipment used to make noise unlawfully; and for connected purposes." The Noise Bill had Government backing and it was envisaged as the means by which the proposals would be transposed into law. At the time of writing it had apparently not been decided whether or not it would operate by way of amendment to existing legislation. The Government was understood to be concerned to ensure that the new standard when introduced would both be, and be treated by courts as, entirely separate from existing statutory and common law nuisance in that a matter would be able to constitute a noise nuisance without necessarily exceeding the limit it established, and noise to which the standard did not apply could exceed it without necessarily constituting a nuisance.

(b) *Nuisance neighbours:* An entirely separate initiative related to nuisance problems from tenants in local authority housing (with "nuisance" here being used in a non-legal sense which could nevertheless encompass some forms of statutory or common law nuisance—most obviously noise nuisance). In July 1995 the Government announced its intention to legislate to introduce probationary (or "introductory") tenancies which would enable local authorities to terminate new tenancies within the first year: following that, the tenancies would convert to secure tenancies. On October 18, a package of further measures were announced including the strengthening of the grounds for repossession of local authority domestic property and the attachment of a power of arrest to injunctions taken out by local authorities to prevent antisocial behaviour. On December 4, 1995, the Government published *Notes for Guidance— How to get the best out of the courts system,* guidance intended to bolster local authority use of the legal sanctions available to them. The legislative measures were, as at the end of 1995, anticipated as part of a Housing Bill.

Statutory nuisances

Statutory nuisances and inspections therefor

79.—(1) Subject to subsections [(1A)] to [(6A)] below, the following matters constitute "statutory nuisances" for the purposes of this Part, that is to say—

(a) any premises in such a state as to be prejudicial to health or a nuisance;

(b) smoke emitted from premises so as to be prejudicial to health or a nuisance;

(c) fumes or gases emitted from premises so as to be prejudicial to health or a nuisance;

(d) any dust, steam, smell or other effluvia arising on industrial, trade or business premises and being prejudicial to health or a nuisance;

(e) any accumulation or deposit which is prejudicial to health or a nuisance;

(f) any animal kept in such a place or manner as to be prejudicial to health or a nuisance;

(g) noise emitted from premises so as to be prejudicial to health or a nuisance;

[(ga) noise that is prejudicial to health or a nuisance and is emitted from or caused by a vehicle, machinery or equipment in a street [or in Scotland, road];]

(h) any other matter declared by any enactment to be a statutory nuisance;

and it shall be the duty of every local authority to cause its area to be inspected from time to time to detect any statutory nuisances which ought to be dealt with under section 80 [and 80A] below and, where a complaint of a statutory nuisance is made to it by a person living within its area, to take such steps as are reasonably practicable to investigate the complaint.

[(1A) No matter shall constitute a statutory nuisance to the extent that it consists of, or is caused by, any land being in a contaminated state.

(1B) Land is in a "contaminated state" for the purposes of subsection (1A) above if, and only if, it is in such a condition, by reason of substances in, on or under the land, that—

(a) harm is being caused or there is a possibility of harm being caused; or

(b) pollution of controlled waters is being, or is likely to be caused;

and in this subsection "harm", "pollution of controlled waters" and "substance" have the same meaning as in Part 2A of this Act.]

(2) Subsection (1)(b) and (g) above do not apply in relation to premises—

  (a) occupied on behalf of the Crown for naval, military or air force purposes or for the purposes of the department of the Secretary of State having responsibility for defence, or

  (b) occupied by or for the purposes of a visiting force;

and "visiting force" means any such body, contingent or detachment of the forces of any country as is a visiting force for the purposes of any of the provisions of the Visiting Forces Act 1952.

(3) Subsection (1)(b) above does not apply to—

  (i) smoke emitted from a chimney of a private dwelling within a smoke control area,

  (ii) dark smoke emitted from a chimney of a building or a chimney serving the furnace of a boiler or industrial plant attached to a building or for the time being fixed to or installed on any land,

  (iii) smoke emitted from a railway locomotive steam engine, or

  (iv) dark smoke emitted otherwise than as mentioned above from industrial or trade premises.

(4) Subsection (1)(c) above does not apply in relation to premises other than private dwellings.

(5) Subsection (1)(d) above does not apply to steam emitted from a railway locomotive engine.

(6) Subsection (1)(g) above does not apply to noise caused by aircraft other than model aircraft.

[(6A) Subsection (1)(ga) above does not apply to noise made—

  (a) by traffic,

  (b) by any naval, military or air force of the Crown or by a visiting force (as defined in subsection (2) above), or

  (c) by a political demonstration or a demonstration supporting or opposing a cause or campaign.]

(7) In this Part—

"chimney" includes structures and openings of any kind from or through which smoke may be emitted;

"dust" does not include dust emitted from a chimney as an ingredient of smoke;

["equipment" includes musical instrument;]

"fumes" means any airborne solid matter smaller than dust;

"gas" includes vapour and moisture precipitated from vapour;

"industrial, trade or business premises" means premises used for any industrial, trade or business purposes or premises not so used on which matter is burnt in connection with any industrial, trade or business process, and premises are used for industrial purposes where they are used for the purposes of any treatment or process as well as where they are used for the purposes of manufacturing;

"local authority" means, subject to subsection (8) below,—

  (a) in Greater London, a London borough council, the Common Council of the City of London and, as respects the Temples, the Sub-Treasurer of the Inner Temple and the Under-Treasurer of the Middle Temple respectively;

  (b) [in England] outside Greater London, a district council;

  [(bb) in Wales, a county council or county borough council;]

  (c) the Council of the Isles of Scilly; [and]

  [(d) in Scotland, a district or islands council or a council constituted under section 2 of the Local Government etc. (Scotland) Act 1994;

"noise" includes vibration;

["person responsible"—

(a) in relation to a statutory nuisance, means the person to whose act, default or sufferance the nuisance is attributable;

(b) in relation to a vehicle, includes the person in whose name the vehicle is for the time being registered under the Vehicles (Excise) Act 1971 and any other person who is for the time being the driver of the vehicle;

(c) in relation to machinery or equipment, includes any person who is for the time being the operator of the machinery or equipment;]

"prejudicial to health" means injurious, or likely to cause injury, to health;

"premises" includes land and, subject to subsection (12) [and[, in relation to England and Wales, section 81A(9)] below, any vessel;

"private dwelling" means any building, or part of a building, used or intended to be used, as a dwelling;

["road" has the same meaning as in Part IV of the New Roads and Street Works Act 1991;]

"smoke" includes soot, ash, grit and gritty particles emitted in smoke;

["street" means a highway and any other road, footway, square or court that is for the time being open to the public;]

and any expressions used in this section and in [the Clean Air Act 1993] have the same meaning in this section as in that Act and [section 3 of the Clean Air Act 1993] shall apply for the interpretation of the expression "dark smoke" and the operation of this Part in relation to it.

(8) Where, by an order under section 2 of the Public Health (Control of Disease) Act 1984, a port health authority [or in Scotland where by an order under section 172 of the Public Health (Scotland) Act 1897 a port local authority or a joint port local authority has been constituted for the whole or part of a port,] has been constituted for any port health district, the port health authority[, port local authority or joint port local authority, as the case may be] shall have by virtue of this subsection, as respects its district, the functions conferred or imposed by this Part in relation to statutory nuisances other than a nuisance falling within paragraph (g) [or (ga)] of subsection (1) above and no such order shall be made assigning those functions, and "local authority" and "area" shall be construed accordingly.

(9) In this Part "best practicable means" is to be interpreted by reference to the following provisions—

(a) "practicable" means reasonably practicable having regard among other things to local conditions and circumstances, to the current state of technical knowledge and to the financial implications;

(b) the means to be employed include the design, installation, maintenance and manner and periods of operation of plant and machinery, and the design, construction and maintenance of buildings and structures;

(c) the test is to apply only so far as compatible with any duty imposed by law;

(d) the test is to apply only so far as compatible with safety and safe working conditions, and with the exigencies of any emergency or unforeseeable circumstances;

and, in circumstances where a code of practice under section 71 of the Control of Pollution Act 1974 (noise minimisation) is applicable, regard shall also be had to guidance given in it.

(10) A local authority shall not without the consent of the Secretary of State institute summary proceedings under this Part in respect of a nuisance falling within paragraph (b), (d) or (e) [and, in relation to Scotland, paragraph (g) or (ga),] of subsection (1) above if proceedings in respect thereof might be instituted under Part I or the Alkali &c. Works Regulation Act 1906 or section 5 of the Health and Safety at Work, etc., Act 1974.

(11) The area of a local authority which includes part of the seashore shall also include for the purposes of this Part the territorial sea lying seawards from that part of the shore; and subject to subsection (12)[, in relation to England and Wales,] [and 81A(9)] below, this Part shall have effect, in relation to any area included in the area of a local authority by virtue of this subsection—

    (a) as if references to premises and the occupier of premises included respectively a vessel and the master of a vessel; and

    (b) with such other modifications, if any, as are prescribed in regulations made by the Secretary of State.

(12) A vessel powered by steam reciprocating machinery is not a vessel to which this Part of this Act applies.

COMMENCEMENT
January 1, 1991 (s.164(2)). In relation to Scotland, April 1, 1996 (S.I. 1996 No. 186).

AMENDMENTS
This section is printed as amended (a) by ss.2 and 10 of the Noise and Statutory Nuisances Act 1993, the relevant provisions of which came into force on January 5, 1994; (b) as regards the references to the Clean Air Act 1993, by s.67 of the Clean Air Act 1993; (c) as to the insertion of subss. (1A) and (1B), and the reference to subs. (1A) in subs. (1), by the Environment Act 1995, Sched. 22, para. 89; (d) as to the definition of "road", and the distinctions drawn between the application of the provisions in England and Wales and in Scotland, by the 1995 Act, Sched. 17, para. 2; (e) in subs. (7) ("person responsible") by the Vehicle Excise and Registration Act 1994, Sched. 3, para. 27; (f) as to local authorities in Wales in subs. (7), by the Local Government (Wales) Act 1994, Sched. 9, para. 17; (g) as to local authorities in Scotland in subs. (7) by the 1995 Act, Sched. 17, para. 2; and (h) as to the references to port local authorities in subs. (8) by the 1995 Act, Sched. 17, para. 2.

GENERAL NOTE
This section has various functions. Subsections (1)–(6A) provide the definition of "statutory nuisances" for the purposes of the Part. By subs. (1), every local authority is under a duty to cause its area to be inspected for statutory nuisances. Subsections (1A) and (1B) operate to exclude the application of this Part in situations of land contamination: see further the general note to these subsections. Subsection (7) gives a series of other definitions. Subsection (8) deals with the position of certain port health authorities, and subs. (9) provides the important definition of "best practicable means". Subsections (10)–(12) contain ancillary provisions.

Subs. (1): definition of "statutory nuisance"
This subsection draws together various statutory nuisances which were formerly to be found in a number of different pieces of legislation. In some cases the opportunity has been taken to amend or clarify the definition and, in particular, noise nuisance which was formerly covered by ss.58 and 59 of the Control of Pollution Act 1974 has been defined as a statutory nuisance. However, given the many similarities of expression with the previous legislation, no doubt much of the substantial body of case law that has built up around the Public Health Act 1936, and other legislation, will remain relevant.

    (a) *Any premises in such a state as to be prejudicial to health or a nuisance:* This is a straight re-enactment of s.91(1)(a) of the Public Health Act 1936 and corresponds broadly to s.16(1) of the Public Health (Scotland) Act 1897.

    Premises. This is defined so as to include land and vessels other than those powered by steam reciprocating machinery (subss. (7) and (12)). There can therefore be no doubt that, for example, houseboats (*West Mersea Urban District Council v. Fraser* [1950] 2 K.B. 119) and caves (*Gardiner v. Sevenoaks Rural District Council* [1950] W.N. 260) would potentially be covered. Section 109 of the Public Health Act 1936 contained a saving provision excluding mines and smelting works, but the 1990 Act gives no such exemption. As to the case of premises rendered prejudicial to health by problems emanating from other premises, see *Pollway Nominees v. Havering London Borough Council* (1989) 21 H.L.R. 462. A limited Crown exemption applies by subs. (2). Premises which are insufficiently insulated against noise and vibration may fall within this category of statutory nuisance: *Southwark London Borough Council v. Ince* (1989) 153 JP 587.

    Prejudicial to health. The definition (subs. (7)) repeats that in the 1936 Act, s.343(1). In the Public Health (Scotland) Act 1897 the corresponding wording in s.16 was "injurious or dangerous to health". It is not necessary to show that the activity is prejudicial to health in order for it to constitute a statutory nuisance: in *Betts v. Penge Urban District Council* [1942] 2 K.B. 154 (Div. Ct.) it was held that it is sufficient to show that the premises in question are such as to interfere with personal comfort and thus constitute a nuisance. The case appears to remain good authority for that proposition, though it has been argued in relation to the Public Health Acts that the "nuisance" limb is itself to be qualified by reference to the general spirit and intention of the legislation as dealing with matters appertaining to health, disease or vermin: see *Salford City Council v. McNally* [1976] A.C. 379, 389, 394; *Coventry City Council v. Cartwright* [1975] 1 W.L.R. 845 at 848 and *National Coal Board v. Neath Borough Council* [1976] 2 All E.R. 478 at 482; and *cf. Wivenhoe Port v. Colchester Borough Council* [1985] J.P.L. 175, 178 (affirmed [1985] J.P.L. 396).

Nuisance. In *Betts v. Penge Urban District Council* (above) it was held that premises which were in such a state as to interfere with the reasonable comfort of the occupier (the front door and some of the window-sashes having been removed by the landlord) constituted a statutory nuisance. However, the decision was not followed in *National Coal Board v. Neath Borough Council* (above) on the basis that a "nuisance" coming within the meaning of the Public Health Act must be either a private or public nuisance as understood by common law. On that basis, interference with the enjoyment of neighbouring property is a prerequisite, and "a nuisance cannot arise if what has taken place affects only the person or person occupying the premises where the nuisance is said to have taken place" (p. 482). See also *Bishop Auckland Local Board v. Bishop Auckland Iron and Steel Co.* (1882) 10 Q.B.D. 138, 140–141 and *Salford City Council v. McNally* [1976] A.C. 379, 389, 392. See also the discussion of "nuisance" below in the context of dust (para. (d)).

(b) *Smoke emitted from premises so as to be prejudicial to health or a nuisance:* This is a category of statutory nuisance which did not appear in the Public Health Act, which by s.110(1) excluded from the meaning of "dust", dust emitted from a chimney as an ingredient of smoke. For the meaning of "premises", "prejudicial to health" and "nuisance", see (a) above. "Smoke" is defined at subs. (7). The scope of this category of statutory nuisance is restricted by subss. (2) (various military circumstances and (3) (smoke or dark smoke emitted from certain sources). The effect of subs. (10) should also be noted.

(c) *Fumes or gases emitted from premises so as to be prejudicial to health or a nuisance:* Again, this is a new category of statutory nuisance. It corresponds broadly to s.16(5A) of the Public Health (Scotland) Act 1897 which was inserted by s.83(2) of the 1990 Act. "Dust" and "fumes" are defined in subs. (7), and see (a) above generally. The category applies only to fumes and gases from private dwellings (subs. (4)). Emissions from commercial or industrial premises might well be caught under (d) below and in any event, may be subject to local authority air pollution control under Pt. I.

(d) *Any dust, steam, smell or other effluvia arising on industrial, trade or business premises and being prejudicial to health or a nuisance:* This corresponds broadly, though not exactly, to para. (d) of s.92(1) of the 1936 Act ("any dust or effluvia caused by any trade, business, manufacture or process and injurious, or likely to cause injury, to the public health or a nuisance") and to s.16(5B) of the Public Health (Scotland) Act 1897 which was inserted by s.83(2) of the 1990 Act ("any dust caused by any trade, or business, manufacture or process, being a nuisance or injurious or dangerous to health"). "Dust" does not include chimney smoke, that being dealt with under para. (b) above. Steam from railway engines is excluded by subs. (5). The effect of subs. (10) should also be noted.

Section 92(1)(d) of the 1936 Act was considered in *Wivenhoe Port v. Colchester Borough Council* [1985] J.P.L. 175 (Chelmsford Crown Court) (affirmed [1985] J.P.L. 396) in relation to an alleged statutory nuisance by dust arising from the handling of soya meal. Whilst recognising the great uncertainty of this area of law, Butler J. said that:

"To be within the spirit of the Act a nuisance to be statutory nuisance had to be one interfering materially with the personal comfort of the residents, in the sense that it materially affected their wellbeing although it might not be prejudicial to their health. Thus, dust falling on motor cars might cause inconvenience to their owners; it might even diminish the value of their motor car; but this would not be a statutory nuisance. In the same way, dust falling on gardens or trees, or on stock held in shop would not be a statutory nuisance. But dust in eyes or hair, even if not shown to be prejudicial to health, would be so as an interference with personal comfort."

How far the reference to "the spirit of the Act" is relevant now that the relevant provisions are contained in Pt. III of a general environmental protection statute is open to question, but certainly if the above statement of the law is correct, the use of the provisions to effect environmental quality improvements or to protect flora or fauna would, in the absence of interference with human comfort, be limited.

Paragraph (d) is the only category of statutory nuisance specifically confined to "industrial, trade or business premises". The expression is defined in subs. (7).

Trade. This has been the subject of the following judicial definitions:

> "No doubt in many contexts the word 'trade' indicates a process of buying and selling, but that is by no means an exhaustive definition of its meaning. It may also mean a calling or industry or class of skilled labour." (*Skinner v. Jack Breach* [1927] 2 K.B. 220, 225–227). "A trade is an organised seeking after profits as a rule with the aid of physical assets" (*Aviation & Shipping Co. v. Murray* [1961] 1 W.L.R. 974).

It seems clear that in the context of Pt. III the term would not be confined to buying and selling, but would include manufacture and processing.

Business. This again must be construed in its context, but has been said to be a wider term than "trade": see, *e.g. Debtor, Re A (No. 490 of 1935)* [1936] Ch. 237. It has been said to mean:

> "... almost anything which is an occupation, as distinguished from a pleasure—anything which is an occupation or duty which requires attention is a business" (*Rolls v. Miller* (1894) 27 Ch.D. 71, 88).

It seems clear that the term can include professional activities: *Wilkinson, Re* [1922] 1 K.B. 584, 587; *Williams' Will Trusts Re*; *Chartered Bank of India, Australia and China v. Williams* [1953] Ch. 138, 141; *R. v. Breeze* [1973] 1 W.L.R. 994. Purely domestic or recreational activities would not appear to fall within the term: see *Abernethie v. Kleiman* [1970] 1 Q.B. 10; *Town Investments v. Department of Environment* [1976] 3 All E.R. 479, 496 (C.A.); *Customs & Excise Commissioners v. Fisher (Lord)* [1981] 2 All E.R. 147; neither would an isolated transaction undertaken with no intention that it be repeated: *Griffin, Re, ex p. Board of Trade* (1890) 60 L.J. Q.B. 235, 237.

(e) *Any accumulation or deposit which is prejudicial to health or a nuisance:* This paragraph corresponds verbatim with s.93(1)(c) of the 1936 Act and corresponds approximately to s.16(5) of the Public Health (Scotland) Act 1897. In *Coventry City Council v. Cartwright* [1975] 1 W.L.R. 845 this paragraph was held by the Divisional Court to have the underlying conception of "an accumulation of something which produces a threat to health in the sense of a threat of disease, vermin or the like". It was held therefore not to extend to an accumulation of inert matter (building materials, scrap iron, broken glass and tin cans) merely because that matter may cause physical injury to persons who come into the land and walk on it. For a case relating to sewage debris on beaches under s.79(1)(e), see *R. v. Carrick District Council, ex p. Shelley, The Times,* April 15, 1996 (referred to below).

As to "prejudicial to health" and "nuisance," see (a) above. The effect of subs. (10) should also be noted.

(f) *Any animal kept in such a place or manner as to be prejudicial to health or a nuisance:* The corresponding provision of the 1936 Act, with identical wording, is s.92(1)(b). The provision also corresponds approximately to s.16(4) of the Public Health (Scotland) Act 1897. In *Morrisey v. Galer* [1955] 1 W.L.R. 110 Lord Goddard C.J., in considering a case concerning noise from the keeping of greyhounds, suggested that statutory nuisance provisions would not apply to such a noise nuisance, though they would cover smell from animals. However, Lord Widgery C.J. in *Coventry City Council v. Cartwright* (above) thought the wording was equally apt to catch noise made by animals.

See generally para. (a) as to "prejudicial to health" and "nuisance".

(g) *Noise emitted from premises so as to be prejudicial to health or a nuisance:* This paragraph defines noise, previously covered by ss.58 and 59 of the Control of Pollution Act 1974, as a statutory nuisance. "Noise" includes vibration (subs. (7)). As with other categories of statutory nuisance, it appears that noise may fall into this category either because it is prejudicial to health or because it is a nuisance in the sense of interfering unduly with the comfort and convenience of neighbouring occupiers (see Note to para. (a) above). A single event may constitute a noise nuisance and therefore a statutory nuisance: no element of repetition is necessary (*East Northamptonshire) District Council v. Fossett* [1994] Env.L.R. 388 (all-night "rave").

The noise must be emitted from premises. In a case decided under s.58 of the 1974 Act, the word "premises" was held not to cover noise made in streets or public places (see *Tower Hamlets London Borough Council v. Manzoni and Walder* (1984) J.P. 123 and the article by Macrory at [1984] J.P.L. 388). However, "premises" is now expressly defined to include land (s.79(7)), though it might still be arguable whether noise made by a person or group of persons at large in a public place could be said to be "emitted from land". In any event, the problem of street noise is now expressly addressed by para. (ga), added by the Noise and Statutory Nuisance Act 1993. There is an important exception by virtue of subs. (6), which is that the provision does not apply to aircraft noise other than model aircraft. Subsection (2) disapplies the provision in relation to premises occupied in various military circumstances.

Noise which affects premises, though emanating elsewhere, can make the premises affected themselves a statutory nuisance under para. (a) if the noise is such as to be injurious to health: *Southwark London Borough Council v. Ince* (1989) 153 J.P. 597.

(ga) *Noise emitted from or caused by a vehicle, machinery or equipment in a street:* This additional head of nuisance, introduced by the Noise and Statutory Nuisance Act 1993 and covering noise or vibration from equipment, machinery or vehicles in a street, overcomes some of the difficulties which arose under para. (g) (noise from premises) in cases of street noise The special procedures introduced in respect of such nuisances, contained in ss.80A and 81(1A) and (1B), should be noted, as should the fact that this category of statutory nuisance is disapplied in various circumstances (traffic noise, noise from certain military sources, and noise from demonstrations), by subs. (6A).

(h) *Any other matter declared by any enactment to be a statutory nuisance:* This paragraph widens the category in para. (f) of s.92(1) of the 1936 Act which was limited to matters declared by provisions of that Act to be a statutory nuisance. The matters now covered include: s.141 of the Public Health Act 1936 (insanitary cisterns, etc.); s.259 of the 1936 Act (nuisances in connection with watercourses, etc.); s.268 of the 1936 Act (nuisances relating to tents, vans, etc.); and s.151 of the Mines and Quarries Act 1954 (fencing of abandoned and disused mines and quarries).

Nuisance at workplaces
Subsection (1) does not re-enact the provisions of s.92(1)(e) of the 1936 Act relating to nuisance at workplaces (see also s.16(8) of the Public Health (Scotland) Act 1897). Such matters are now covered adequately by Health and Safety at work legislation.

Duty to inspect areas
By subs. (1), local authorities are under a duty to cause their areas to be inspected from time to time to detect statutory nuisances which ought to be dealt with according to the summary procedures under s.80. Schedule 3, para. 4 contains procedures to be followed in England and Wales in the event of default in this duty, which may lead to an order of direction by the Secretary of State enforceable by mandamus, or an order of the Secretary of State transferring the relevant functions to himself (para. 4(4)). In the light of these special procedures it is questionable whether other remedies are available: see, *e.g. Pasmore v. Oswaldtwistle Urban District Council* [1898] A.C. 387; *Clark v. Epsom Rural District Council* [1929] 1 Ch. 287; *R. v. Kensington and Chelsea (Royal) London Borough Council, ex p. Birdwood* (1976) 74 L.G.R. 424. Since these special default procedures do not apply to Scotland it would appear that the duty imposed on local authorities may only be enforced by way of a judicial review petition seeking specific performance of statutory duty in the Court of Session: Court of Session Act 1988, s.45(b).

Subss. (1A) and (1B): contaminated land
Subsection (1A) disapplies Pt. III (and, indeed, those other enactments referred to at subs. (1)(h) in so far as they identify statutory nuisances) to the extent that any statutory nuisance consists of or is caused by land being in a contaminated state as defined in subs. (1B). The exercise by local authorities of statutory nuisance powers in relation to contaminated land was not unknown prior to this (see for example the well-known Minister of Defence military and industrial waste site at the Lumsden Road Estate at Eastleigh, Hampshire—abatement notices were served there first to prohibit the re-occupation of housing which was evacuated as a result of concerns about the site, until specified protection measures were taken, and subsequently to enable the local authority to retain control over remedial works being carried out under a planning permission or, in Scotland, *Clydebank District Council v. Monaville Estate Ltd* 1982 S.L.T. (Sh.Ct.) 2 under the Public Health (Scotland) Act 1897 which concerned a site contaminated with asbestos). However, such cases were the exception rather than the rule; the

evolution of the contaminated land provisions which prompted this disapplication of statutory nuisance, and the provisions themselves, are discussed in the general introductory note to Pt. IIA above.

The relationship between the two regimes is considered above: it is noted there that the relationship between the term "contaminated state" in subs. (1B) and the definition of "contaminated land" at s.78A(1) is such that the statutory nuisance regime is disapplied by subs. (1A) in wider circumstances than those in which the contaminated land regime comes into play. It is arguable that further "mis-match" results from the fact that "contaminated land" is defined by s.78A(1) in purely subjective terms ("... appears to the local authority ...") whilst "contaminated state" is defined objectively.

The three Pt. IIA terms incorporated into the subs. (1B) definition are defined at s.78A(4) and (9).

Subs. (9): defence of best practicable means
This subsection defines the defence of best practicable means (bpm) which applies to some categories of statutory nuisance (see s.80(7) and (9)). The defence existed under s.94(5) of the Public Health Act 1936 and s.58(5) of the Control of Pollution Act 1974. The definition in subs. (8) follows that in s.72 of the 1974 Act.

The defence was raised in *Wivenhoe Port v. Colchester Borough Council* [1985] J.P.L. 175 (affirmed [1985] J.P.L. 396), where it was argued that the avoidance of dust nuisance by vacuum machinery was not practicable because it would render the operation uneconomic. It was accepted by the Crown Court that profitability was a relevant factor, but that it was for the company to establish the defence, the onus of proof as to practicability lying on them. The mere fact of increased expenditure, or even unprofitability, was not sufficient to establish the defence.

In the case of noise nuisance, any codes of practice promulgated under s.71 of the 1974 Act will be relevant. These include codes on:

Construction and open sites	— S.I. 1984 No. 1992
	— S.I. 1987 No. 1730
Construction and open sites (Scotland)	— S.I. 1982 No. 601
Audible intruder alarms	— S.I. 1981 No. 1829
Ice cream van chimes	— S.I. 1981 No. 1828
Model aircraft	— S.I. 1981 No. 1830

Subs. (10): relationship with air pollution control legislation
Subsection (10) restricts the scope of a local authority to take action under s.80 (although not, it will be noted, the scope of an aggrieved person to do so under s.82) where proceedings could be instituted under one of the three regimes cited. The restriction applies only in relation to three of the statutory nuisance categories: smoke; dust, steam, smell or other effluvia arising on industrial, trade or business premises; and accumulations or deposits. Even in relation to those, it is not absolute: proceedings may be taken with the consent of the Secretary of State. The purpose of the restriction is to avoid overlap between Pt. III and the other provisions, which govern prescribed processes under the IPC and LAPC systems in Pt. I of the Act, and scheduled processes under the Alkali etc. Works Regulation Act 1906 and Health and Safety at Work etc. Act 1974 (residual controls being superseded by Pt. I). Prior to the extension of Pt. III to Scotland there was a potential overlap of statutory nuisance controls and controls in Pt. I and the 1906 and 1974 Acts. The removal of this potential overlap was one of the Government's reasons for replacing the controls in the Public Health (Scotland) Act 1897 with those in Pt. III.

Summary proceedings for statutory nuisances

80.—(1) Where a local authority is satisfied that a statutory nuisance exists, or is likely to occur or recur, in the area of the authority, the local authority shall serve a notice ("an abatement notice") imposing all or any of the following requirements—
  (a) requiring the abatement of the nuisance or prohibiting or restricting its occurrence or recurrence;
  (b) requiring the execution of such works, and the taking of such other steps, as may be necessary for any of those purposes,
and the notice shall specify the time or times within which the requirements of the notice are to be complied with.

(2) [Subject to s.80A below, the] abatement notice shall be served—
  (a) except in a case falling within paragraph (b) or (c) below, on the person responsible for the nuisance;
  (b) where the nuisance arises from any defect of a structural character, on the owner of the premises;
  (c) where the person responsible for the nuisance cannot be found or the nuisance has not yet occurred, on the owner or occupier of the premises.

(3) [A person served with an abatement notice] may appeal against the notice to a magistrates' court [or in Scotland, the sheriff] within the period of 21 days beginning with the date on which he was served with the notice.

(4) If a person on whom an abatement notice is served, without reasonable excuse, contravenes or fails to comply with any requirement or prohibition imposed by the notice, he shall be guilty of an offence.

(5) Except in a case falling within subsection (6) below, a person who commits an offence under subsection (4) above shall be liable on summary conviction to a fine not exceeding level 5 on the standard scale together with a further fine of an amount equal to one-tenth of that level for each day on which the offence continues after the conviction.

(6) A person who commits an offence under subsection (4) above on industrial, trade or business premises shall be liable on summary conviction to a fine not exceeding £20,000.

(7) Subject to subsection (8) below, in any proceedings for an offence under subsection (4) above in respect of a statutory nuisance it shall be a defence to prove that the best practicable means were used to prevent, or to counteract the effects of, the nuisance.

(8) The defence under subsection (7) above is not available—
  (a) in the case of a nuisance falling within paragraph (a), (d), (e), (f) or (g) of section 79(1) above except where the nuisance arises on industrial, trade or business premises;
  [(aa) in the case of a nuisance falling within paragraph (ga) of section 79(1) above except where the noise is emitted from or caused by a vehicle, machinery or equipment being used for industrial, trade or business purposes;]
  (b) in the case of a nuisance falling within paragraph (b) of section 79(1) above except where the smoke is emitted from a chimney; and
  (c) in the case of a nuisance falling within paragraph (c) or (h) of section 79(1) above.

(9) In proceedings for an offence under subsection (4) above in respect of a statutory nuisance falling within paragraph (g) [or (ga)] of section 79(1) above where the offence consists in contravening requirements imposed by virtue of subsection (1)(a) above is shall be a defence to prove—
  (a) that the alleged offence was covered by a notice served under section 60 or a consent given under section 61 or 65 of the Control of Pollution Act 1974 (construction sites, etc.); or
  (b) where the alleged offence was committed at a time when the premises were subject to a notice under section 66 of that Act (noise reduction notice), that the level of noise emitted from the premises at that time was not such as to constitute a contravention of the notice under that section; or
  (c) where the alleged offence was committed at a time when the premises were not subject to a notice under section 66 of that Act, and when a level fixed under section 67 of that Act (new buildings liable to abatement order) applied to the premises, that the level of noise emitted from the premises at that time did not exceed that level.

(10) Paragraphs (b) and (c) of subsection (9) above apply whether or not the relevant notice was subject to appeal at the time when the offence was alleged to have been committed.

DEFINITIONS
  "abatement notice": subs. (1).
  "best practicable means": s.79(9).
  "chimney": s.79(7).
  "industrial trade or business premises": s.79(7).
  "local authority": s.79(7).
  "noise": s.79(7).
  "person responsible": s.79(7).
  "premises": s.79(7).
  "smoke": s.79(7).
  "statutory nuisance": s.79(1).

COMMENCEMENT
January 1, 1991 (s.164(2)). In relation to Scotland, April 1, 1996 (S.I. 1996 No. 186).

AMENDMENTS
This section is printed as amended by the Noise and Statutory Nuisance Act 1993, the relevant parts of which came into force on January 5, 1994. The reference in subs. (3) to the sheriff in Scotland was inserted by the Environment Act 1995, Sched. 17, para. 3.

GENERAL NOTE
This section deals with the procedures for action by local authorities for the abatement of statutory nuisances. The procedure draws together those contained in the Public Health Act 1936 and in the Public Health (Recurring Nuisances) Act 1969. The 1990 Act remodelled the procedures in three chief respects:
  (1) The procedure is streamlined. Under the former legislation, the local authority had first to serve an abatement notice. If that notice was not complied with, the authority then had to obtain a nuisance order in the Magistrates' Court. If that order was not complied with the authority then had to go back to court and prosecute for non-compliance. Complaints were made by local authorities that this procedure was cumbersome, time-consuming and ineffective. It may be noted that the procedure under the Public Health (Scotland) Act 1897 (ss.20–23) was similar to that described above. The new procedure is modelled on that found in s.58 of the Control of Pollution Act 1974 for noise nuisances. This procedure cuts out the middle nuisance order stage, so that the abatement notice becomes the main step, on which a prosecution may be founded. See also the comparative diagrams at the General Note to Pt. III.
  (2) The new section gives local authorities a power, similar to that existing in s.58 of the Control of Pollution Act 1974 in relation to noise nuisances, to take action in anticipation of a statutory nuisance occurring. The Government envisages that this power will be particularly useful in dealing with transient nuisances, such as dust from construction, demolition or cleaning operations, or certain agricultural operations such as the spreading of slurry.
  (3) The availability of the defence of best practicable means is widened so as to make it available for nuisances arising on industrial, trade or business premises where the nuisance falls within paras. (a), (d), (e), (f) and (g) of s.79(1). Under the 1936 Act, the defence was only available in trade, business and manufacturing cases for two categories of statutory nuisance, *i.e.* accumulations or deposits (s.92(1)(c)) and dust or effluvia (s.92(1)(d)). The effect of the change is to remove the anomaly whereby a business had the bpm defence available to it if the proceedings related to a smell nuisance under s.92(1)(d) relating to "effluvia", but not if the proceedings were taken under s.92(1)(a) relating to premises in such a state as to be a nuisance.
  (4) A distinction is drawn between statutory nuisances committed on industrial, trade or business premises, and those arising on other premises. The maximum fine on summary conviction for the former is increased to £20,000.

Duty to serve notice
Once it is found that a statutory nuisance exists, there is a duty, not a discretion, to serve an abatement notice. Accordingly, in *R. v. Carrick District Council, ex p. Shelley* (*The Times*, April

15, 1996) a local authority was held to have acted wrongly in resolving that it was "not appropriate" to serve notice in relation to pollution of a beach by sewage debris from local outfalls.

Service of notice: The wording of subs. (1) appears to impose a duty on local authorities to serve an abatement notice when satisfied that a statutory nuisance exists or is likely to occur or recur. However, in the housing context it has been suggested that where alternative remedies are open to a local authority, the word "shall" does not mean that the authority are bound to follow the abatement notice route in preference to all others open to them: *Nottinghamshire City District Council v. Newton* [1974] 1 W.L.R. 923. The notice should be served in accordance with s.233 of the Local Government Act 1972 or s.192 of the Local Government (Scotland) Act 1973.

Form of notice: No form of notice is prescribed, nor is there provision for regulations to prescribe the form. However, the notice must include a statement informing the recipient of his right of appeal under s.80(3) and giving the time limit for such appeal (Sched. 3, para. 6). It appears, on general principles, that the notice must at least identify clearly and precisely the nuisance complained of and tell the recipient clearly what is required of him. Thus, if works or steps are necessary to abate or prevent the recurrence of the nuisance, those works or steps must be specified with some particularity: see *Salford City Council v. McNally* [1976] A.C. 379, 389; *R. v. Wheatley* (1885) 16 Q.B. 34; *Millard v. Wastall* [1898] 1 Q.B. 342; *Whatling v. Rees* (1914) 84 L.J.K.B. 1122. If the nuisance can be abated without taking steps or executing works, then none need be specified (*ibid.*). The Divisional Court has suggested that the key is whether the abatement notice stipulates that the nuisance be abated or that works be done or other steps taken to achieve that end: "As the law stands, local authorities are not, in any event, obliged to require works to be done or other steps to be taken; they can, consonant with *R. v. Wheatley* [see above], simply require the nuisance to be abated: see *McGillivray v. Stephenson* [1950] 1 All E.R. 942; the obligation to specify the 'works' and the 'steps' only arises if they choose to include in their notices a requirement for works to be done or steps to be taken." *Sterling Homes (Midlands) Ltd v. Birmingham City Council* (unreported, Divisional Court, July 5, 1995), *per* McCullough J. This analysis does not form part of the *ratio* of that case, however.

It is arguable whether a notice can direct the recipient how to carry on day-to-day operations: see *Wivenhoe Port v. Colchester Borough Council* [1985] J.P.L. 175, 178; affirmed [1985] J.P.L. 396.

By analogy with the abatement orders made by magistrates under the old procedure, it can be suggested that any notice should be: (a) practical in its effect; (b) easily understood by the recipient and by persons aggrieved by the notice; and (c) specify, where appropriate, the action to be taken to comply (see *R. v. Fenny Stratford Justices, ex p. Watney Mann (Midlands)* [1976] 1 W.L.R. 1101, 1106). Where modern science allows requirements to be stated precisely, *e.g.* by giving decibel levels, this should be done (*ibid.*, p. 1107) but a notice specifying decibel levels without saying where they are to be measured will be void for uncertainty (*ibid.*). In Scotland it has been held that a notice requires to be precise and practicable in its terms: *Strathclyde Regional Council v. Tudhope* 1983 S.L.T. 22; [1983] J.P.L. 536.

In *Network Housing Association Ltd v. Westminster City Council* [1995] Env.L.R. 176 a notice in relation to noise nuisance in a block of flats was held to be invalid for failure to specify the nature of the work required; the notice simply required alterations to be made to reduce noise levels to a certain level of decibels. The notice could have led to the need to undertake a succession of works until the desired result was achieved; this was not acceptable.

Time for compliance
In cases under s.58 of the Control of Pollution Act, on identical wording as to notices, it has been held that there is no necessity to specify a time for compliance and that in appropriate cases an extremely short time may suffice: see *Strathclyde Regional Council v. Tudhope* 1983 S.L.T. 22; [1983] J.P.L. 536. In that case the notice required road-breaking equipment not to be used until fitted with effective dampeners. In the absence of a stated date for compliance, the notice was held to come into effect at midnight following the day of service. It was not unreasonable that the equipment should not be used thereafter unless fitted with dampeners. The prohibition of recurrence continues in effect indefinitely: see *R. v. Birmingham Justices, ex p. Guppy* (1988) 152 J.P. 159; *R. v. Tunbridge Wells Justices, ex p. The Tunbridge Wells Borough Council* (unreported, Divisional Court, May 1, 1995).

Subs. (2): on whom notice may be served
The notice will in most cases be served on the "person responsible" for the nuisance: this means the person to whose act, default or sufferance the nuisance is attributable (s.79(7)). The wording

in s.93 of the Public Health Act 1936 referred to the person by whose act default or sufferance the nuisance "arises or continues". In *Clayton v. Sale Urban District Council* [1926] 1 K.B. 415 it was held that an owner of land may be liable under those words for failure to abate a nuisance existing on his land in consequence of the activities or defaults of another, and regardless of whether the owner is under any contractual or other obligation to take remedial action. An analogy may possibly be drawn with the cases on "continuation" of nuisances in private law: see *Sedleigh-Denfield v. O'Callaghan* [1940] A.C. 880; *Leanse v. Lord Egerton* [1943] 1 K.B. 323. Formerly in Scotland, under s.20 of the Public Health (Scotland) Act 1897 the notice requiring the removal of the nuisance could be served on the author of the nuisance ("the person through whose act or default the nuisance is caused, exists, or is continued, whether he be the owner or occupier or both"—s.3) or, if the author could not be found, on the owner or occupier of the premises on which the nuisance arose or continued.

If the nuisance arises from a defect "of a structural character" the notice is to be served on the owner of the premises. This appears to mean some defect which affects a structure: *Granada Theatres v. Freehold Investment (Leytonstone)* [1958] 2 All E.R. 551, 552, 553. "Structure" has been said to mean "... something which is constructed in the way of being built up as is a building; it is in the nature of a building" (*South Wales Aluminium Co. v. Neath Assessment Committee* [1943] 2 All E.R. 587, 592) and "... something which is constructed. It is not everything which is 'constructed' that would ordinarily be called a building, but every building is a structure" (*Mills & Rockleys v. Leicester City Council* [1946] 1 All E.R. 424, 427). See also *Cardiff Rating Authority v. Guest Keen Baldwin's Iron and Steel Co.* [1949] 1 K.B. 385, 396. A landlord may be required to carry out works to abate a statutory nuisance even where no other statutory duty nor any contractual duty such as a repairing obligation in a lease could have obliged him to do so: *Birmingham District Council v. Kelly* (1985) 17 H.L.R. 572; see also *R. v. Highbury Corner Magistrates' Court, ex p. Edwards* (1995) 26 H.L.R. 682 (cases under s.82 and its predecessor).

Also, where the person who is responsible for the nuisance cannot be found, the notice maybe served on the owner or occupier of the premises. "Owner" was defined at length in the 1936 Act by reference to the person receiving or entitled to receive the rack rent of the premises, but no such definition is found in the 1990 Act. For cases under the old legislation on "owner", see *Walford v. Hackney Board of Works* (1894) 43 W.R. 110 (mesne tenant); *Kensington London Borough Council v. Allen* [1926] 1 K.B. 576 (mesne tenant); *St. Helen's Corporation v. Kirkham* (1885) 16 Q.B.D. 403 (agent); *Bacup Corporation v. Smith* (1890) 44 Ch.D. 395 (receiver); *Midland Bank v. Conway Corporation* [1965] 1 W.L.R. 1165 (bank); *Poplar Board of Works v. Love* (1874) 29 L.T. 915 (lessee at ground rent); *Holland (Lady) v. Kensington Vestry* (1867) L.R. 2 C.P. 565 (tenant under building agreement); *Blackburn Corporation v. Micklethwaite* (1886) 54 L.T. 539 (mortgagee); *Ebor Land & Development Co. v. Benfield* (1969) 68 L.G.R. 237 (vendor under Law Society's Conditions of Sale). See also *Environment Law Brief* (1990) Vol. 1, No. 9, p. 102 (owner responsible for noise nuisance by trespassers).

In Scotland "owner" was also defined at length in s.3 of the Public Health (Scotland) Act 1897 *inter alia* as the person entitled to receive the rents of the premises. In the absence of a statutory definition of owner, it is submitted that general case law on the definition of the term in Scotland is relevant. See *e.g. Jack's Exrx. v. Falkirk District Council* 1992 S.L.T. 5; *Northern Rock Building Society v. Wood* 1990 S.L.T.(Sh.Ct.) 109; *Kerr v. Robertson* (1952) 68 Sh.Ct.Rep. 247 (beneficiary under a lapsed trust); *Maclachlan v. Seafield's Trustees* 1940 J.C. 12 (trustees); *Pollock v. Park* (1951) 67 Sh.Ct. Rep. 96 (person entitled to receive the rents).

It appears from one case that a person who converts a building into flats may be a "person responsible" for nuisance resulting from inadequate soundproofing: see article by Bettle [1988] J.P.L. 79 and the case of *Rossall v. London Borough of Southwark* (November 1985, unreported) referred to therein. See also *Network Housing Association Ltd v. Westminster City Council* ([1994] Env.L.R. 176) where notice in relation to inadequate sound insulation was held to be correctly served on the landlord, a housing association.

Subs. (4): failure to comply with notice

Failure to comply with an abatement notice without reasonable excuse is an offence.

"Reasonable excuse" was argued as a defence in a case under the 1936 Act in *Saddleworth Urban District Council v. Aggregate and Sand* (1970) 114 S.J. 931. The argument was that an expert had advised certain works be carried out but funds were exhausted before the work could be completed. The Divisional Court held that lack of finance was not a reasonable excuse and that it would be difficult to rely on the advice of an independent expert as a defence when his recommendations had not been fully implemented. *Obiter* remarks in *Sterling Homes*

(*Midlands*) *Ltd v. Birmingham City Council* (unreported, Divisional Court, July 5, 1995) suggest that a defendant can properly rely, in support of a plea of "reasonable excuse", on attempts made to comply with it. As to the distinction between the defence of reasonable excuse and matters of mitigation, see *Wellingborough Borough Council v. Gordon* [1993] Env.L.R. 218 (birthday celebration held not to be "reasonable excuse" to offence caused by loud reggae music, air horns and whistles).

Where premises are in such a state as to be prejudicial to health or a nuisance, it has been suggested that simply removing the occupants does not constitute abatement of the nuisance: *Coventry City Council v. Doyle* [1981] 1 W.L.R. 1325. However, in the same case it was held that different considerations might apply if the premises had effectively been rendered incapable of being occupied.

Although the procedure for statutory nuisances is now different, on the principles discussed in *Coventry City Council v. Doyle*, it appears that the relevant date for deciding whether the nuisance has been abated and the notice complied with is the date of the information being laid, not the date of the hearing: see also *Northern Ireland Trailers v. Preston Corporation* [1972] 1 W.L.R. 203 and *Lambeth London Borough Council v. Stubbs* [1980] J.P.L. 517.

As to proof in noise cases, see *Cooke v. Adatia* (1989) J.P. 129 D.C.—it may be sufficient to present evidence of decibel levels from an environmental health officer without calling neighbouring occupiers to testify as to interference with their reasonable comfort or enjoyment.

Defence that notice contains no lawful requirement
In England and Wales it has been held that even where the defendant does not appeal against an abatement notice, it is still open to him to defend a prosecution for failure to comply with it on the ground that it contained no lawful requirement: *Sterling Homes (Midlands) Ltd v. Birmingham City Council* (unreported, Divisional Court, July 5, 1995). In that case the notice required the recipient to carry out such works and take such steps as were necessary to abate the alleged nuisance but failed to specify the works and steps required (see generally *Form of notice* above). The recipient did not appeal the notice, and on appeal by way of case stated from the ruling of the justices in the resulting prosecution for non-compliance, the case was remitted by the Divisional Court to the justices with a direction to acquit. However, in Scotland the opposite conclusion was reached by the High Court of Justiciary in *Stagecoach Ltd v. McPhail* 1988 S.C.C.R. 289, a noise nuisance case under the Control of Pollution Act 1974, in which the court held that failure to appeal against a notice deprived the accused of the right to challenge its terms at any subsequent trial.

The subs. (4) offence is a relevant offence for the purposes of the "fit and proper person" test which any applicant for a waste management licence under Pt. II of the Act must pass: Waste Management Licensing Regulations 1994, reg. 3.

Subss. (5) and (6): penalties
The current maximum penalty for nuisance offences on non-industrial, trade or business premises is £5,000, plus £500 for each day the offence continues after conviction. For nuisances arising on industrial, trade or business premises, the maximum penalty is £20,000 and there is no provision for further daily fines. For the definition of "industrial", trade or business premises", see s.79(7). The definition includes land on which matter is burnt in connection with any trade or business process, and so would catch, for example, construction site bonfires or cable-burning. For the meaning of "trade" and "business" see Note to s.79.

Subs. (8)
This subsection states in what circumstances the defence of best practicable means (bpm) is available (see s.79(9)). The defence is not available at all in the case of fumes or gases emitted from premises (s.79(1)(c)) and any matters declared by other enactments to be a statutory nuisance (s.79(1)(h)). In relation to smoke nuisances it is only available where smoke is emitted from a chimney as defined in s.79. In other cases it is only available where the nuisance arises on industrial, trade or business premises (see above).

Subs. (9)
This subsection contains provisions, relating to noise nuisance only, which reproduce the provisions of s.58(6) of the Control of Pollution Act 1974. It provides three further defences, all of which are based on the principle that it is unreasonable for the local authority to institute statutory noise nuisance proceedings where under some other provision they have effectively

given consent for a particular level of noise, and the person concerned is not exceeding that level. Perhaps as a result, the defences do not apply in relation to summary proceedings brought by an aggrieved person under s.82. The particular cases are:

(a) noise covered by a notice served under s.60 of the Control of Pollution Act 1974 (specifying maximum levels of noise for construction works) and consents given under s.61 or 65 of the 1974 Act (s.61 relates to orders under which local authorities agree to specified noise levels from construction works and s.65 relates to orders under which premises may be allowed to increase their noise levels above the originally measured level with the written consent of the local authority);

(b) noise where the premises are subject to a notice under s.66 of the 1974 Act, not constituting a contravention of that notice (s.66 of the 1974 Act deals with notices requiring a reduction in the levels of noise emanating from premises); and

(c) noise from premises in respect of which a level has been fixed under s.67 of the 1974 Act where the noise does not exceed that level (s.67 allows a local authority to determine the noise level for a new building before the building is complete).

Paragraphs (b) and (c) apply whether or not the relevant notice was subject to appeal at the time (subs. (10)).

The parallel, but narrower, set of defences to civil proceedings brought by a local authority under s.81(5) should be noted: s.81(6).

Nuisance and change of character of a neighbourhood
The High Court decision in *Gillingham Borough Council v. Medway (Chatham) Dock Co. Ltd* [1992] Env.L.R. 98 is particularly relevant to the potential availability of the statutory nuisance provisions although it dealt with a common law action based on public nuisance. Residents in the area complained to the environmental health officer about the noise associated with the use of the access roads to the dockyard and the Council sought an injunction to restrict night-time lorry movements on the grounds that the disturbance amounted in law to a public nuisance. The Council were unsuccessful as the Court found that the planning permission granted by Gillingham Borough Council for the dockyard use in 1983 had changed the character of the neighbourhood. Instead of considering the nuisance in the context of a residential area the Court considered it in the context of a commercial port and concluded that the noise and disturbance could not be a nuisance in law. However, not every grant of planning permission will change the character of a neighbourhood. The Court of Appeal reached this conclusion in *Wheeler v. JJ Saunders Ltd* [1995] Env.L.R. 286, a case involving an alleged odour nuisance resulting from the implementation of a grant of planning permission for pig rearing units. The Court of Appeal held that it was only strategic planning decisions, as in the case of the commercial port in *Gillingham* (above), where the public interest had to be balanced against interference with private rights, which could result in a change to a character of a neighbourhood and hence act as a defence to a nuisance action. However, the pig rearing development was not a strategic development and hence the grant of planning permission for it did not act as a defence to a nuisance action and did not deprive the plaintiffs of the right to bring a nuisance action. The Court also concluded that it was not the grant of planning permission which could change the character of a locality but the implementation of the grant of planning permission.

[Abatement notice in respect of noise in street

80A.—(1) In the case of a statutory nuisance within section 79(1)(ga) above that—

(a) has not yet occurred, or

(b) arises from noise emitted from or caused by an unattended vehicle or unattended machinery or equipment,

the abatement notice shall be served in accordance with subsection (2) below.

(2) The notice shall be served—

(a) where the person responsible for the vehicle, machinery or equipment can be found, on that person;

(b) where that person cannot be found or where the local authority determines that this paragraph should apply, by fixing the notice to the vehicle, machinery or equipment.

(3) Where—

(a) an abatement notice is served in accordance with subsection (2)(b) above by virtue of a determination of the local authority, and

(b) the persons responsible for the vehicle, machinery or equipment can be found and served with a copy of the notice within an hour of the notice being fixed to the vehicle, machinery or equipment,

a copy of the notice shall be served on that person accordingly.

(4) Where an abatement notice is served in accordance with subsection (2)(b) above by virtue of a determination of the local authority, the notice shall state that, if a copy of the notice is subsequently served under subsection (3) above, the time specified in the notice as the time within which its requirements are to be complied with is extended by such further period as is specified in the notice.

(5) Where an abatement notice is served in accordance with subsection (2)(b) above, the person responsible for the vehicle, machinery or equipment may appeal against the notice under section 80(3) above as if he had been served with the notice on the date on which it was fixed to the vehicle, machinery or equipment.

(6) Section 80(4) above shall apply in relation to a person on whom a copy of an abatement notice is served under subsection (3) above as if the copy were the notice itself.

(7) A person who removes or interferes with a notice fixed to a vehicle, machinery or equipment in accordance with subsection (2)(b) above shall be guilty of an offence, unless he is the person responsible for the vehicle, machinery or equipment or he does so with the authority of that person.

(8) A person who commits an offence under subsection (7) above shall be liable on summary conviction to a fine not exceeding level 3 on the standard scale.]

DEFINITIONS
    "abatement notice": s.80(1).
    "equipment": s.79(7).
    "local authority": s.79(7).
    "noise": s.79(7).
    "person responsible": s.79(7).
    "statutory nuisance": s.79(1).

COMMENCEMENT
The section was inserted by the Noise and Statutory Nuisance Act 1993 s.3(6) and came into force on January 5, 1994. In relation to Scotland, this section came into force on April 1, 1996 (S.I. 1996 No. 186).

GENERAL NOTE
The section provides procedures to deal with the specific problem of street noise emanating from unattended vehicles or equipment—for example, vehicle alarms. Additional enforcement powers are given by amendments to Schedule 3 of the Act to allow any person authorised by local authority on production (if so required) of his authority to enter or open a vehicle, machinery or equipment, if necessary by force, or to remove a vehicle, machinery or equipment from a street to a secure place for the purpose of taking any action or executing any work authorised or required in order to abate a nuisance. Having exercised such powers, the authorised person is required on leaving the unattended vehicle, machinery or equipment to leave it secure against interference or theft, or to immobilise it or to remove it from the street to a secure place.

Supplementary provisions

81.—(1) [Subject to subsection 1A below, where] more than one person is responsible for a statutory nuisance section 80 above shall apply to each of those persons whether or not what any one of them is responsible for would by itself amount to a nuisance.

[(1A) In relation to a statutory nuisance within section 79(1)(ga) above for which more than one person is responsible (whether or not what any one of those persons is responsible for would by itself amount to such nuisance), section 80(2)(a) above shall apply with the substitution of "any one of the persons" for "the person".

(1B) In relation to a statutory nuisance within section 79(1)(ga) above caused by noise emitted from or caused by an unattended vehicle or unattended machinery or equipment for which more than one person is responsible, section 80A above shall apply with the substitution—

(a) in subsection (2)(a), of "any of the persons" for "the person" and of "one such person" for "that person",

(b) in subsection (2)(b), of "such a person" for "that person",

(c) in subsection (3), of "any of the persons" for "the person" and of "one such person" for "that person",

(d) in subsection (5), of "any person" for "the person", and

(e) in subsection (7), of "a person" for "the person" and of "such a person" for "that person".]

(2) Where a statutory nuisance which exists or has occurred within the area of a local authority, or which has affected any part of that area, appears to the local authority to be wholly or partly caused by some act or default committed or taking place outside the area, the local authority may act under section 80 above as if the act or default were wholly within that area, except that any appeal shall be heard by a magistrates' court [or in Scotland, the sheriff] having jurisdiction where the act or default is alleged to have taken place.

(3) Where an abatement notice has not been complied with the local authority may, whether or not they take proceedings for an offence [or, in Scotland, whether or not proceedings have been taken for an offence,] under section 80(4) above, abate the nuisance and do whatever may be necessary in execution of the notice.

(4) Any expenses reasonably incurred by a local authority in abating, or preventing the recurrence of, a statutory nuisance under subsection (3) above may be recovered by them from the person by whose act or default the nuisance was caused and, if that person is the owner of the premises, from any person who is for the time being the owner thereof; and the court [or sheriff] may apportion the expenses between persons by whose acts or defaults the nuisance is caused in such manner as the court consider [or sheriff considers] fair and reasonable.

(5) If a local authority is of opinion that proceedings for an offence under section 80(4) above would afford an inadequate remedy in the case of any statutory nuisance, they may, subject to subsection (6) below, take proceedings in the High Court [or, in Scotland, in any court of competent jurisdiction,] for the purpose of securing the abatement, prohibition or restriction of the nuisance, and the proceedings shall be maintainable notwithstanding the local authority have suffered no damage from the nuisance.

(6) In any proceedings under subsection (5) above in respect of a nuisance falling within paragraph (g) [or (ga)] of section 79(1) above, it shall be a defence to prove that the noise was authorised by a notice under section 60 or a consent under section 61 (construction sites) of the Control of Pollution Act 1974.

(7) The further supplementary provisions in Schedule 3 to this Act shall have effect.

DEFINITIONS
  "abatement notice": s.80(1).
  "local authority": s.79(6).

"noise": s.79(7).
"premises": s.79(6).
"statutory nuisance": s.79(1).

COMMENCEMENT
January 1, 1991 (s.164(2)). In relation to Scotland, April 1, 1996 (S.I. 1996 No. 186).

AMENDMENTS
This section is printed as amended by s.4 of the Noise and Statutory Nuisance Act 1993, the relevant parts of which came into force on January 5, 1994. References to proceedings in Scotland were inserted by the Environment Act 1995, Sched. 17, para. 4.

GENERAL NOTE
This section, together with Sched. 3, contains various supplementary provisions.

Subs. (1)
This provision, modelled on s.73(3) of the Control of Pollution Act 1974, provides for the situation where more than one person is responsible for a statutory nuisance. Action may be taken against each such person regardless of whether or not the matters for which each is responsible would, taken in isolation, constitute a statutory nuisance.

Subs. (2)
This provision allows a local authority to take action in respect of a statutory nuisance wholly or partly caused by some act or default outside their area, but which affects their area. The provision replaces s.98 of the Public Health Act 1936 and is modelled on s.58(7) of the Control of Pollution Act 1974. By way of contrast under s.149 of the Public Health (Scotland) Act 1897, a local authority whose area suffered the effects of a nuisance caused outside its area could only call upon the local authority within whose district it was situated to take all competent steps for its removal and could seek any expenses incurred from that authority. If any appeal is made against the abatement notice in such cases, it is the magistrates' court (or, in Scotland, the sheriff court) for the area in which the relevant act or default took place that has jurisdiction.

Subss. (3) and (4)
These subsections give authorities powers comparable to those in ss.95 and 96 of the Public Health Act 1936 to take action themselves to abate statutory nuisances and to recover reasonable expenses incurred in so doing or, as regards Scotland, ss.24 and 26 of the Public Health (Scotland) Act 1897. The power arises where an abatement notice has not been complied with, whether or not criminal proceedings are taken under s.80(4).

The expenses of abating the nuisance or preventing its recurrence are to be recovered from the person by whose act or default the nuisance was caused. If that person happens to have been the owner of the premises, the expenses may be recovered from any person who is the owner for the time being. As to the meaning of "owner", see notes to s.80(2).

The court has wide power to apportion expenses between persons by whose acts or defaults the nuisance arose, in such manner as it considers fair and reasonable. For a recent apportionment case in a different statutory context, see *Watney Combe Reid & Co. v. Westminster (City) Council* (1970) 214 E.G. 1631 (fire precautions). On the question as to how far the power of apportionment can be excluded by agreement, for example in a lease, see *Monk v. Arnold* [1902] 1 K.B. 761, *Monro v. Lord Burghclere* [1918] 1 K.B. 291 and *Horner v. Franklin* [1905] 1 K.B. 479.

Subs. (5)
This subsection enables proceedings to be taken by local authorities in the High Court in England and Wales or in any court of competent jurisdiction, *i.e.* the appropriate sheriff court or Court of Session in Scotland to secure abatement, prohibition or restriction of statutory nuisances. The precondition is that the authority must be satisfied that proceedings for an offence under s.80(4) would afford an inadequate remedy. The provision follows s.100 of the Public Health Act 1936 and s.58(8) of the Control of Pollution Act 1974.

For an example of successful injunctive proceedings in relation to noise, see *Hammersmith London Borough Council v. Magnum Automated Forecourts* [1978] 1 W.L.R. 50, where the criteria for granting such relief were discussed. It was held there that the remedy is in addition to summary proceedings and that it is not a bar to relief that summary remedies have not been exhausted. In England and Wales interlocutory injunctive relief may be obtained where appropriate on the principles of *American Cyanamid Co. v. Ethicon* [1975] A.C. 396. In Scotland, an interim interdict may be obtained where there is a *prima facie* case to be tried, a matter which is settled on the balance of convenience: *Scottish Milk Marketing Board v. Paris*

1935 S.C. 287; and *NWL Ltd v. Woods* [1979] 1 W.L.R. 1294. See also *Lloyds Bank v. Guardian Assurance and Trollope & Colls* (1986) 35 Build.L.R. 38 (C.A.) for the relationship between statutory procedures and private nuisance actions. Civil proceedings may also be instituted by a local authority under s.222 of the Local Government Act 1972 (see *Mayor and Commonalty of the City of London v. Bovis Construction* [1989] J.P.L. 263) or, in Scotland, under s.189 of the Local Government (Scotland) Act 1973.

Subs. (6)
This re-enacts the proviso to s.58(8) of the Control of Pollution Act 1974. In relation to noise nuisances it is a defence to proceedings under subs. (5) to prove that the noise was authorised by a notice under s.60 of the 1974 Act (control of noise on construction sites) or a consent under s.61 (prior consent for work on construction sites). The parallel, but wider, set of defences to summary proceedings under s.80(4) for non-compliance with an abatement notice should be noted: s.80(9).

Subs. (7) and Sched. 3
Schedule 3 contains further ancillary provisions dealing with the procedure for appeals against abatement notices, powers of entry and related powers, offences of obstructing entry, procedures where local authorities default in their duties under Pt. III and protection of officers against personal liability.

The regulations governing appeals in England and Wales against abatement notices are the Statutory Nuisance (Appeals) Regulations 1995 (S.I. 1995 No. 2644), which revoked and replaced the 1990 regulations of the same name with effect from November 8, 1995. These Regulations follow in many respects those under the 1974 Act in relation to noise: the Control of Noise (Appeals) Regulations 1975 (S.I. 1975 No. 2116) and the Control of Noise (Appeals) (Scotland) Regulations 1983 (S.I. 1983 No. 1455). The grounds of appeal are identical in many respects. The 1995 Regulations give some ten separate grounds of appeal (reg. 2(2)) and give the court wide discretion in dealing with appeals (reg. 2(3)–(7)). By reg. 3 the effect of an appeal does not in general have the effect of suspending the notice unless compliance with it would require expenditure on carrying out works before the hearing of the appeal, or where the alleged nuisance is noise caused in the course of the appellant performing some duty imposed by law. For cases on the 1975 Regulations, see *Wycombe District Council v. Jeffways and Pilot Coaches* (1983) 81 L.G.R. 662 (C.A.) and *Johnsons News of London v. Ealing London Borough Council* (1989) 154 J.P. 33. In the latter case it was held that where an appeal is made on what, in the 1995 regulations, is ground (e) (use of best practicable means), steps taken by the appellant to abate the nuisance after the issue of the notice must be taken into account. As regards Scotland, the Statutory Nuisance (Appeals) (Scotland) Regulations 1996 (S.I. 1996 No. 1076) govern appeals against abatement notices with effect from May 1, 1996.

Paragraph 6 of Sched. 3 was introduced as a House of Lords amendment, and requires local authorities to include in notices served under Pt. III a statement (if that be the case) that appeal lies to a magistrates' court or, in Scotland, to the sheriff and to specify the time within which such an appeal must be brought.

[Expenses recoverable from owner to be a charge on premises

81A.—(1) Where any expenses are recoverable under section 81(4) above from a person who is the owner of the premises there mentioned and the local authority serves a notice on him under this section—

(a) the expenses shall carry interest, at such reasonable rate as the local authority may determine, from the date of service of the notice until the whole amount is paid, and

(b) subject to the following provisions of this section, the expenses and accrued interest shall be a charge on the premises.

(2) A notice served under this section shall—

(a) specify the amount of the expenses that the local authority claims is recoverable,

(b) state the effect of subsection (1) above and the rate of interest determined by the local authority under that subsection, and

(c) state the effect of subsections (4) to (6) below.

(3) On the date on which a local authority serves a notice on a person under this section the authority shall also serve a copy of the notice on every other person who, to the knowledge of the authority, has an interest in the premises capable of being affected by the charge.

(4) Subject to any order under subsection (7)(b) or (c) below, the amount of any expenses specified in a notice under this section and the accrued interest shall be a charge on the premises—

    (a) as from the end of the period of twenty-one days beginning with the date of service of the notice, or

    (b) where an appeal is brought under subsection (6) below, as from the final determination of the appeal,

until the expenses and interest are recovered.

(5) For the purposes of subsection (4) above, the withdrawal of an appeal has the same effect as a final determination of the appeal.

(6) A person served with a notice or copy of a notice under this section may appeal against the notice to the county court within the period of twenty-one days beginning with the date of service.

(7) On such an appeal the court may—

    (a) confirm the notice without modification,

    (b) order that the notice is to have effect with the substitution of a different amount for the amount originally specified in it, or

    (c) order that the notice is to be of no effect.

(8) A local authority shall, for the purpose of enforcing a charge under this section, have all the same powers and remedies under the Law of Property Act 1925, and otherwise, as if it were a mortgagee by deed having powers of sale and lease, of accepting surrenders of leases and of appointing a receiver.

(9) In this section—

"owner", in relation to any premises, means a person (other than a mortgagee not in possession) who, whether in his own right or as trustee for any other person, is entitled to receive the rack rent of the premises or, where the premises are not let at a rack rent, would be so entitled if they were so let, and

"premises" does not include a vessel.]

[(10) This section does not apply to Scotland.]

DEFINITIONS
"local authority": s.79(7).
"owner": subs. (9).
"premises": subs. (9) and s.79(7).

COMMENCEMENT
This section was added by the Noise and Statutory Nuisance Act 1993 s.10(2) and came into force on January 5, 1994.

AMENDMENT
Subsection (10) was added by the Environment Act 1995, Sched. 17, para. 5.

GENERAL NOTE
Section 81A provides that where under section 81(4) any expenses incurred by a local authority in abating or preventing the occurrence of a statutory nuisance are recoverable from a person who is the owner of the premises, then the local authority may serve notice on him under section 81A. The effect of such notice is that the expenses carry interest, at such reasonable rates as the local authority may determine, from the date of service of the notices until the whole amount is paid; also, the expenses and accrued interest are a charge on the premises. The section contains requirements as to the form and service of such notices and allows for appeal against the notice to the County Court within the period of 21 days beginning with the date of service.

By section 81A(8) the local authority, for the purpose of enforcing a charge imposed under the section, has all the same powers and remedies under the Law of Property Act 1925 as if it were a mortgagee by deed having powers of sale and lease.

The term "owner" is defined in relation to any premises as "a person (other than a mortgagee not in possession) who, whether in his own right or as trustee for any other person, is entitled to receive the rack rent of the premises or, where the premises are not let at a rack rent, would be so entitled if they were so let". It should be noted that the definition of owner is specifically provided only in relation to the term as it occurs in section 81(A): it is not therefore binding in relation to the term "owner" as it occurs elsewhere in the 1990 Act.

The section does not apply to Scotland. However, there seems no reason in principle why the provision could not have been extended to Scotland since there are already many statutory provisions in Scots law which do permit the imposition of a charge on property *e.g.* by local authorities for recovery of expenses incurred in carrying out works *e.g.* under the Building (Scotland) Act 1959 or the Housing (Scotland) Act 1987. It should nevertheless be noted that these existing provisions do not put the local authority in the same position as a heritable creditor under the Conveyancing and Feudal Reform (Scotland) Act 1970. In relation to similar charging provisions under Part IIA of the 1990 Act introduced by the 1995 Act, the Government argued that extending such provisions to Scotland would require fundamental changes to the system of conveyancing in Scotland. See also the note to s.78P(14).

Payment of expenses by instalments

81B.—(1) Where any expenses are a charge on premises under section 81A above, the local authority may by order declare the expenses to be payable with interest by instalments within the specified period, until the whole amount is paid.

(2) In subsection (1) above—

"interest" means interest at the rate determined by the authority under section 81A(1) above, and

"the specified period" means such period of thirty years or less from the date of service of the notice under section 81A above as is specified in the order.

(3) Subject to subsection (5) below, the instalments and interest, or any part of them, may be recovered from the owner or occupier for the time being of the premises.

(4) Any sums recovered from an occupier may be deducted by him from the rent of the premises.

(5) An occupier shall not be required to pay at any one time any sum greater than the aggregate of—

(a) the amount that was due from him on account of rent at the date on which he was served with a demand from the local authority together with a notice requiring him not to pay rent to his landlord without deducting the sum demanded, and

(b) the amount that has become due from him on account of rent since that date.

[(6) This section does not apply to Scotland.]

DEFINITIONS

"interest": subs. (2).
"premises": s.79(7).
"local authority": s.79(7).
"the specified period": subs. (2).

COMMENCEMENT

This section was inserted by the Noise and Statutory Nuisance Act 1993, s.10(2) and came into force on January 5, 1994.

AMENDMENT

Subsection (6) was added by the Environment Act 1995, Sched. 17, para. 5.

GENERAL NOTE

Section 81B deals with the payment of those expenses which are a charge on premises under section 81A. The local authority may by order declare the expenses to be payable with interest by instalments within a specified period, until the whole amount is paid. The specified period means such a period of 30 years or less from the date of service of the notice under section 81A as is specified in the order.

Section 81B(3) provides that the instalments and interest, or any part of them, may be recovered from the owner or occupier of the premises. However, the occupier may not be required to pay at any one time any sum greater than the aggregate of the amount due from him on account of rent on the date on which he was served with a demand by the local authority and any amount which has become due from him on account of rent since that date. Section 81B(4) provides that any sums recovered from an occupier may be deducted by him from the rent of the premises, and it appears from section 81B(5)(a) that the demand from the local authority to the occupier must be accompanied by a notice requiring him not to pay rent to his landlord without deducting the sum demanded.

Summary proceedings by person aggrieved by statutory nuisances

82.—(1) A magistrates' court may act under this section on a complaint [or, in Scotland, the sheriff may act under this section on a summary application,] made by any person on the ground that he is aggrieved by the existence of a statutory nuisance.

(2) If the magistrates' court [or, in Scotland, the sheriff,] is satisfied that the alleged nuisance exists, or that although abated it is likely to recur on the same premises [or, in the case of a nuisance within section 79(1)(ga) above, in the same street [or, in Scotland, road]], the court [or the sheriff] shall make an order for either or both of the following purposes—

(a) requiring the defendant [or, in Scotland, defender,] to abate the nuisance, within a time specified in the order, and to execute any works necessary for that purpose;

(b) prohibiting a recurrence of the nuisance, and requiring the defendant [or defender], within a time specified in the order, to execute any works necessary to prevent the recurrence,

and[, in England and Wales,] may also impose on the defendant a fine not exceeding level 5 on the standard scale.

(3) If the magistrates' court [or the sheriff] is satisfied that the alleged nuisance exists and is such as, in the opinion of the court [or of the sheriff], to render premises unfit for human habitation, an order under subsection (2) above may prohibit the use of the premises for human habitation until the premises are, to the satisfaction of the court [or of the sheriff], rendered fit for that purpose.

(4) Proceedings for an order under subsection (2) above shall be brought—

(a) except in a case falling within paragraph (b), (c) or (d) below, against the person responsible for the nuisance;

(b) where the nuisance arises from any defect of a structural character, against the owner of the premises;

(c) where the person responsible for the nuisance cannot be found, against the owner or occupier of the premises.

[(d) in the case of a statutory nuisance within section 79(1)(ga) above caused by noise emitted from or caused by an unattended vehicle or unattended machinery or equipment, against the person responsible for the vehicle, machinery or equipment.]

(5) [Subject to subsection 5A below, where] more than one person is responsible for a statutory nuisance, subsections (1) to (4) above shall apply to each of those persons whether or not what any one of them is responsible for would by itself amount to a nuisance.

[(5A) In relation to a statutory nuisance within section 79(1)(ga) above for which more than one person is responsible (whether or not what any one of those persons is responsible for would by itself amount to such a nuisance), subsection (4)(a) above shall apply with the substitution of "each person responsible for the nuisance who can be found" for "the person responsible for the nuisance".

(5B) In relation to a statutory nuisance within section 79(1)(ga) above caused by noise emitted from or caused by an unattended vehicle or unattended machinery or equipment for which more than one person is responsible, subsection (4)(d) above shall apply with the substitution of "any person" for "the person".]

(6) Before instituting proceedings for an order under subsection (2) above against any person, the person aggrieved by the nuisance shall give to that

person such notice in writing of his intention to bring the proceedings as is applicable to proceedings in respect of a nuisance of that description and the notice shall specify the matter complained of.

(7) The notice of the bringing of proceedings in respect of a statutory nuisance required by subsection (6) above which is applicable is—

(a) in the case of a nuisance falling within paragraph (g) [or (ga)] of section 79(1) above, not less than three days' notice; and

(b) in the case of a nuisance of any other description, not less than 21 days' notice;

but the Secretary of State may, by order, provide that this subsection shall have effect as if such period as is specified in the order were the minimum period of notice applicable to any description of statutory nuisance specified in the order.

(8) A person who, without reasonable excuse, contravenes any requirement or prohibition imposed by an order under subsection (2) above shall be guilty of an offence and liable on summary conviction to a fine not exceeding level 5 on the standard scale together with a further fine of an amount equal to one-tenth of that level for each day on which the offence continues after the conviction.

(9) Subject to subsection (10) below, in any proceedings for an offence under subsection (8) above in respect of a statutory nuisance it shall be a defence to prove that the best practicable means were used to prevent, or to counteract the effects of, the nuisance.

(10) The defence under subsection (9) above is not available—

(a) in the case of a nuisance falling within paragraph (a), (d), (e), (f) or (g) of section 79(1) above except where the nuisance arises on industrial, trade or business premises;

[(aa) in the case of a nuisance falling within paragraph (ga) of section 79(1) above except where the noise is emitted from or caused by a vehicle, machinery or equipment being used for industrial, trade or business purposes;]

(b) in the case of a nuisance falling within paragraph (b) of section 79(1) above except where the smoke is emitted from a chimney; and

(c) in the case of a nuisance falling within paragraph (c) or (h) of section 79(1) above; and

(d) in the case of a nuisance which is such as to render the premises unfit for human habitation.

(11) If a person is convicted of an offence under subsection (8) above, a magistrates' court [or the sheriff] may, after giving the local authority in whose area the nuisance has occurred an opportunity of being heard, direct the authority to do anything which the person convicted was required to do by the order to which the conviction relates.

(12) Where on the hearing of proceedings for an order under subsection (2) above it is proved that the alleged nuisance existed at the date of the making of the complaint [or summary application], then, whether or not at the date of the hearing it still exists or is likely to recur, the court [or the sheriff] shall order the defendant [or defender] (or defendants [or defenders] in such proportions as appears fair and reasonable) to pay to the person bringing the proceedings such amount as the court [or the sheriff] considers reasonably sufficient to compensate him for any expenses properly incurred by him in the proceedings.

(13) If it appears to the magistrates' court [or to the sheriff] that neither the person responsible for the nuisance nor the owner or occupier of the premises [or (as the case may be) the person responsible for the vehicle, machinery or equipment] can be found the court [or the sheriff] may, after giving the local authority in whose area the nuisance has occurred an opportunity of being heard, direct the authority to do anything which the court [or the sheriff] would have ordered that person to do.

DEFINITIONS
  "best practicable means": s.79(9).
  "chimney": s.79(7).
  "local authority": s.79(7).
  "premises": s.79(7).
  "smoke": s.79(7).
  "statutory nuisance": s.79(1).

COMMENCEMENT
January 1, 1991 (s.164(2)). In relation to Scotland, April 1, 1996 (S.I. 1996 No. 186).

AMENDMENTS
This section is printed as amended by s.5 of the Noise and Statutory Nuisance Act 1993 which
came into force on January 5, 1994. References to proceedings in Scotland were inserted by the
Environment Act 1995, Sched. 17, para. 6.

GENERAL NOTE
This section provides a right for any person aggrieved by the existence of a statutory nuisance to
make a complaint direct to a magistrates' court or, in Scotland, to the sheriff. A similar right
existed under s.99 of the Public Health Act 1936; s.81 is, however, based on the model of s.59 of
the Control of Pollution Act 1974 which applies to noise nuisance. However, in Scotland, in
relation to nuisances other than noise nuisances under the Control of Pollution Act 1974, it was
not possible for an individual alone to commence proceedings to abate a nuisance: s.146 of the
Public Health (Scotland) Act 1897 required ten council tax payers living in the local authority
district affected to take action collectively. The magistrates or the sheriff may, by subs. (2),
make an order either requiring abatement of the nuisance or prohibiting its recurrence; they
may also impose a fine. In each case, the defendant (in Scotland, the defender) may be required
to execute necessary works. Failure to comply with the order without reasonable excuse is an
offence (subs. (8)). The section contains ancillary provisions similar to those relating to
proceedings by local authorities, including the defence of best practicable means (subss. (9) and
(10)).
  Person aggrieved. There is an important difference from s.59 of the Control of Pollution Act,
under which the remedy was available only to an occupier of premises aggrieved by the noise in
his capacity as occupier. Under s.82 the complainant merely has to be a person aggrieved by the
existence of the nuisance.
  Clearly a person whose own health, or that of their family, is being prejudicially affected by
the nuisance would be a person aggrieved: see *Sandwell Metropolitan Borough Council v.
Bujok* [1990] 3 All E.R. 385. A person whose reasonable enjoyment of their property is
materially affected would similarly be a person aggrieved, and there seems no reason why
interference with commercial interests should not similarly provide standing.
  One of the best known definitions of "person aggrieved" is that given by Lord Denning M.R.
in *Att.-Gen. (Gambia) v. N'Jie* [1961] 2 All E.R. 504 at 511:

  "The words 'person aggrieved' are of wide import and should not be subjected to a
  restricted interpretation. They do not include, of course, a mere busybody who is
  interfering in things that do not concern him; but they do include a person who has a
  genuine grievance because an order has been made which prejudicially affects his interest."

  In *Birmingham District Council v. McMahon* (1987) 151 J.P. 709 (Div. Ct.) it was held that a
council tenant in a block of flats who complained of a statutory nuisance affecting the block in
general, but not his flat, was not a "person aggrieved". It appears that the important
consideration is to relate the grievance to the existence of the relevant category of statutory
nuisance and the interpretation to be placed on the qualifying words in s.79(1)(a)–(g)
"prejudicial to health or a nuisance": see note to s.79.
  In *Sandwell Metropolitan Borough Council v. Bujok* (above) the House of Lords held (p. 391)
that an adversely affected individual is a person aggrieved under s.99 of the Public Health Act
1936, irrespective of whether or not he has given prior notice of the nuisance to the proposed
defendant. See, however, the requirement, introduced by this Act, for notice under subss. (6)
and (7) (below).

Use of provisions against local authorities
It became well established that s.99 of the Public Health Act could be used against local
authorities responsible for statutory nuisances: *R. v. Epping (Waltham Abbey) JJ., ex p.
Burlinson* [1948] 1 K.B. 79. The section came to be used extensively in housing cases as a means

of forcing local authority landlords to carry out repairs or to remedy defects resulting in problems such as excessive condensation or inadequate sound insulation. In *Sandwell Metropolitan Borough Council v. Bujok* [1990] 3 All E.R. 385, 392 the House of Lords was told that the authority in question had been served with no less than 632 summonses under s.99 in just over two years since June 1988.

Procedure
Procedure under s.99 of the Public Health Act 1936 has been considered in a number of reported cases. Proceedings under s.99, read in conjunction with s.94(2), could result in a fine being imposed in addition to the making of a nuisance order. On that basis such proceedings have been held to be criminal in nature, and as such to be commenced by information and summons rather than complaint: see *Northern Ireland Trailers v. Preston Corporation* [1972] 1 W.L.R. 203; *R. v. Newham East Justices, ex p. Hunt*; *R. v. Oxted Justices, ex p. Franklin* [1976] 1 W.L.R. 420; *R. v. Inner London Crown Court, ex p. Bentham* [1989] 1 W.L.R. 408. However, in Scotland proceedings under s.146 of the Public Health (Scotland) Act 1897 were regarded as civil proceedings.

Proceedings under s.59 of the Control of Pollution Act, however, could not lead to an immediate fine and so on the same test were of the nature of civil proceedings, instigated by complaint. As originally drafted, s.82 of the 1990 Act like s.59 of the 1974 Act, contained no reference to a fine and indeed an express Government amendment altered the reference to an "information laid" to "complaint made". However, the section was subject to a late amendment on Third Reading in the Lords to allow magistrates to impose a fine in conjunction with the abatement order. The amended reference to "complaint made", however, anomalously remains. The reason for the amendment to "criminalise" the complaint was expressed as follows by Lord Byron in moving the amendment:

"Where a landlord is convicted of an offence under that section, the court may, and in most cases will, award compensation to the tenant for any personal injury, loss or damage caused by the offence. The magistrates will also order necessary work to be done. As drafted, the Bill will replace the current criminal procedure with a civil one, although still in the magistrates' court. No offence will be committed until a nuisance order made by the court has been breached, which issue will be determined by a second, later hearing. The power to award compensation to tenants will therefore be severely limited.

"The purpose of the amendment is to restore the current power in relation to proceedings brought by individuals where, by ss.99 and 94 of the 1936 Act, the existence of a statutory nuisance amounts to an offence and a court may fine a defendant and make an award of compensation in favour of the tenant under s.35 of the Powers of Criminal Courts Act 1973. The amendment will reproduce those arrangements in the Bill. Thus, under Clause 81, where the court is satisfied that a nuisance exists, the court shall make an order and, if the amendment is accepted, may impose a fine. The court may also in those circumstances make an award of compensation in favour of the tenant under s.35 of the Powers of Criminal Courts Act. That is possible only if, as is currently the case, a criminal offence has been committed.

"It is the power to award compensation which will be lost, or at least substantially diminished, unless the amendment is accepted. There is no doubt that as the law stands at present the nature of proceedings under s.99 is criminal and the offence is that of permitting the nuisance to exist. Magistrates' courts throughout England and Wales, especially in the metropolitan areas, are familiar with the criminal proceedings brought by individuals under s.99 and would similarly be able to apply the law as set out in Clause 82 if the amendment were accepted.

"The issue raised by the amendment is of great importance to tenants and other individual occupiers. Under the present arrangement, where a defendant is convicted in proceedings brought under s.99 of the 1936 Act, the power to award compensation is used widely by the courts. In many of the busy magistrates' courts in metropolitan areas it is now common for awards of between £1,500 and £2,000 to be made in favour of individuals aggrieved by nuisance.

"As presently drafted, the clause will reduce substantially the sums available for compensation in the event of the court choosing to exercise its discretion. This is because no offence is committed other than under Clause 81(5) where a nuisance order made at the first hearing has been breached and a tenant has proved the breach at the second subsequent hearing, once the time allowed for the work has expired. The time usually available for works in nuisance orders currently made depends on the nature of the works ordered. It could perhaps be eight weeks if the works are simple and up to six months for substantial works. The tenant having brought the matter back to court, there may be conviction at the second hearing. The individual may then seek to persuade the court to exercise its discretion to make an award of compensation in his favour.

"However, in contrast to the present arrangements, the courts can have in mind only any personal injury, loss or damage flowing from the offence: that is, any such loss occurring as a result of the breach of the order. The court will have no choice about that. It will be unlawful to relate an award of compensation to any period of time before the commission of the offence. Evidence relating to injury and loss during the period before conviction in which the premises are prejudicial to health and nuisance will be inadmissible.

"There are other reasons for and other major advantages to the present criminal process. Briefly, these are that the conviction and the discretion of the court to impose a fine allows the court to show its disapproval to the community. Further, landlords who allow premises to become dangerously unhealthy—and unhappily this also includes landlords in the public sector—take criminal proceedings seriously. The response to what is initially a civil claim may simply be to treat the matter as a commercial risk.

"Finally, the powers to fine and make an award of compensation are entirely discretionary. It is therefore hard to identify any objection in principle to the amendment. Furthermore—and perhaps the most powerful point—there is no case for a change in the law. Proceedings by individuals for statutory nuisance have been criminal in nature for over 50 years. Lawyers, advisers and all other organisations involved in this type of matter all favour the retention of the existing criminal procedures. I beg to move." (*Hansard*, H.L. Vol. 522, cols. 1279–1280.)

The essentially criminal nature of proceedings under section 82 has been confirmed by the Divisional Court in *Bottross v. London Borough of Hammersmith and Fulham* 27 H.L.R. 179, and by the Crown Court in *London Borough of Lewisham v. Fenner* (ENDS Report 248, September 1995, pp. 44–45). It follows that the standard of proof required to establish the existence of a statutory nuisance and the identity of the person responsible under s.82 is the criminal standard of "beyond reasonable doubt", unlike in proceedings under s.80 where the civil standard of proof on the balance of probabilities applies. The dominant indication of Parliament's intention was held in both cases to be the references to fines and the standard scale in s.82(2). Reference was also made in the *Bottross* case to the Hansard material mentioned above under *Pepper v. Hart* [1993] A.C. 593. Thus a compensation order under s.35 of the Powers of Criminal Courts Act 1973 could be made. As to the circumstances in which it is appropriate for the court to make a compensation order, see *Herbert v. London Borough of Lambeth* 24 H.L.R. 299 (on the predecessor to s.82(2), the Public Health Act 1936, s.94(2)) and *Davenport v. Walsall Metropolitan Borough Council* (unreported, Divisional Court, March 17, 1995): the usual principles applicable to the making of such orders under other legislation appear to apply; an order will usually only be appropriate in clear and simple cases where no great amount is at stake; and the absence or difficulty of obtaining alternative, civil forms of redress for the aggrieved person is relevant but by no means conclusive in favour of the aggrieved person. Indeed, in another case where the magistrates' decision not to make a compensation order was judicially reviewed, the existence of a concurrent civil action by the applicant against the person responsible for the nuisance in respect of the matters in question encouraged the High Court to decline to remit the case to the justices for an order to be made: *R. v. Horseferry Road Magistrates, ex p. Prophet* [1995] Env.L.R. 104. It has also been held that compensation may only be ordered in respect of the period of the nuisance indicated in the summary: *R. v. Liverpool Crown Court, ex p. Cooke* (*The Times*, April 22, 1996).

It has been held that an information laid under s.99 of the 1936 Act should disclose, at least in summary form, the same details as would have been contained in a s.93 abatement notice, as to the capacity in which the defendant is being served and the steps it is alleged he should take in order to abate the nuisance: *Warner v. Lambeth London Borough Council* (1984) 15 H.L.R. 42. The same principles may well apply to proceedings under s.82.

In Scotland, on the application of an individual, a sheriff who is satisfied that an alleged nuisance exists may only order the abatement of the nuisance or prohibit its recurrence and cannot impose a fine on the defender in contrast to the position south of the border: s.82(2). Criminal penalties only apply where an order imposed by the sheriff is contravened: s.82(8). The reason for this is that a summary application by an individual which could result in the imposition of a criminal penalty would be akin to a private prosecution and, in Scotland, the consent of the Lord Advocate is required for such a prosecution. Therefore, it appears that since criminal penalties are not available in Scotland on a summary application by an individual, the proceedings should be regarded as civil in nature and accordingly the civil standard of proof should apply.

However, where an order by the sheriff has been contravened and criminal penalties are available, such proceedings should be regarded as criminal in nature. This is because it would be unfair to the person alleged to be responsible for the nuisance to apply the civil standard of proof rather than the criminal standard. The foregoing discussion is also applicable to proceedings under s.91 in Pt. IV (Summary proceedings by persons aggrieved by litter); see the note to s.91.

Notice before action
In *Sandwell Metropolitan Borough Council v. Bujok* [1990] 3 All E.R. 385 (H.L.) it was held that s.99 of the 1936 Act did not require an aggrieved person to give notice equivalent to an abatement notice before commencing summary proceedings. However, the House of Lords made it clear that failure to give reasonable notice requiring the defect or nuisance to be remedied is to be deplored, endorsing the following passage from the judgment of Watkins L.J. at (1989) 88 L.G.R. 521, 534:

"... it is surely repugnant to common sense that in the area of legal activity a local authority should be prosecuted by one of its tenants without first being given the opportunity by that tenant to remedy the consequences of a neglect to repair the dwelling that tenant occupies. In law there is no doubt that [the respondent] was entitled to commence proceedings without giving notice of the state of the dwelling to the local authority. But in every other conceivable way I regard that action as entirely wrong. Endless trouble to many people in courts and local authority offices and much money could be saved by the giving of notice of disrepair which it is to be supposed a local authority would appropriately react to. If they did not, then would be the time for a tenant to exercise the right to prosecute. I doubt whether there is anyone, a ratepayer especially, giving proper thought to such a situation as we have been confronted with who would disagree with that approach to what surely is a commonplace problem."

That problem has now been addressed by late amendments to the Bill, forming subss. (6) and (7). These provisions require the person aggrieved to give at least 21 days' written notice (three days' in the case of noise nuisance) of intention to bring proceedings.

Abatement order by magistrates or sheriff
If satisfied as to the matters stated in subs. (2), the magistrates (in Scotland, the sheriff) have a duty to make an abatement order, but have wide discretion as to the terms of such order: *Nottingham Corporation v. Newton* [1974] 1 W.L.R. 923; *Salford City Council v. McNally* [1976] A.C. 379. In particular, in housing cases, any relevant proceedings under the Housing Acts may be taken into consideration: *ibid.*
As to the precision and clarity required in an order, see *R. v. Fenny Stratford Justices, ex p. Watney Mann (Midlands)* [1976] 1 W.L.R. 1101 (D.C.) and *Strathclyde Regional Council v. Tudhope* 1983 S.L.T. 22; [1983] J.P.L. 536 noted under s.80 above. As to whether an order may regulate day to day operational matters, see *Wivenhoe Port v. Colchester Borough Council* [1985] J.P.L. 396 (also noted above).
Where a person is convicted of contravention of the abatement notice, there is a residual power under subs. (11) for the court to direct the local authority for the area to do what is required to abate the nuisance, rather than the person convicted.

Subs. (3): unfit dwellings
Where the magistrates (in Scotland, the sheriff) are satisfied that the alleged nuisance is such as to render premises unfit for human habitation, the abatement order may prohibit the use of the premises for human habitation until rendered fit for that purpose. Whether a house is unfit for habitation is a question of fact for the magistrates: see *Hall v. Manchester Corporation* (1915) 84 L.J. Ch. 732, 741 and 742. Nor does it appear that non-compliance with any statutory requirements or standards means that premises are necessarily unfit: *Birchall v. Wirrall Urban District Council* (1953) 117 J.P. 384. In the context of the implied statutory obligation on landlords that dwelling-houses should be reasonably fit for human habitation it has been said that:

"If the state ... of a house is such that by ordinary use damage may naturally be caused to the occupier, either in respect of personal injury to life or limb or injury to health, then the house is not in all respects reasonably fit for human habitation" (*Morgan v. Liverpool Corporation* [1927] 2 K.B. 131, 144 and 145 (C.A., *per* Atkin L.J.)).

Subs. (12): costs
The summary procedure under s.99 of the Public Health Act contained no provision as to costs, which were at the discretion of the court: see *Sandwell Metropolitan Borough Council v. Bujok* [1990] 3 All E.R. 385, 392.
However, subs. (12) now provides that costs must be awarded in favour of the complainant where it is proved that the alleged nuisance existed at the date of the complaint, whether or not

it has ceased or been abated by the time of the hearing. It is the "alleged nuisance" that must be proved, *i.e.* the nuisance alleged in the complaint and specified in the notice before proceedings. If some different nuisance is found to exist rather than the one alleged, it would appear that subs. (12) does not apply and that costs are at the discretion of the court.

Expenses may be "properly incurred" for the purposes of this subsection even where they relate to an aspect of the proceedings which was instigated unsuccessfully by the aggrieved person: *Davenport v. Walsall Metropolitan Borough Council* (unreported, Divisional Court, March 17, 1995; justices ordered to award costs under this subsection in respect of an application for a compensation order (see above) which was unsuccessful but not "doomed from the outset").

Statutory nuisances: Scotland

83. [...]
[Section 83, which extended the scope of the Scottish statutory nuisance provisions which at that time were to be found in the Public Health (Scotland) Act 1897, was revoked by the Environment Act 1995, Sched. 24. Section 107 of and Scheds. 17 and 24 to the 1995 Act amended Pt. III so as to apply its provisions to Scotland, repealing the relevant provisions of the 1897 Act. See the general note to this Part and the note to s.107 of the 1995 Act.]

Termination of existing controls over offensive trades and businesses

Termination of Public Health Act controls over offensive trades etc.

84.—(1) Where a person carries on, in the area or part of the area of any local authority—
  (a) in England or Wales, a trade which—
      (i) is an offensive trade within the meaning of section 107 of the Public Health Act 1936 in that area or part of that area, and
      (ii) constitutes a prescribed process designated for local control for the carrying on of which an authorisation is required under section 6 of this Act; or
  (b) in Scotland, a business which—
      (i) is mentioned in section 32(1) of the Public Health (Scotland) Act 1897 (or is an offensive business by virtue of that section) in that area or part of that area; and
      (ii) constitutes a prescribed process designated for local control for the carrying on of which an authorisation is required under the said section 6,
subsection (2) below shall have effect in relation to that trade or business as from the date on which an authorisation is granted under section 6 of this Act or, if that person has not applied for such an authorisation within the period allowed under section 2(1) above for making applications under that section, as from the end of that period.

(2) Where this subsection applies in relation to the trade or business carried on by any person—
  (a) nothing in section 107 of the Public Health Act 1936 or in section 32 of the Public Health (Scotland) Act 1897 shall apply in relation to it, and
  (b) no byelaws or further byelaws made under section 108(2) of the said Act of 1936, or under subsection (2) of the said section 32, with respect to a trade or business of that description shall apply in relation to it;
but without prejudice to the continuance of, and imposition of any penalty in, any proceedings under the said section 107 or the said section 32 which were instituted before the date as from which this subsection has effect in relation to the trade or business.

(3) Subsection (2)(b) above shall apply in relation to the trade of fish frying as it applies in relation to an offensive trade.

(4) When the Secretary of State considers it expedient to do so, having regard to the operation of Part I and the preceding provisions of this Part of this Act in relation to offensive trades or businesses, he may by order repeal—

(a) sections 107 and 108 of the Public Health Act 1936; and

(b) section 32 of the Public Health (Scotland) Act 1897;

and different days may be so appointed in relation to trades or businesses which constitute prescribed processes and those which do not.

(5) In this section—

"prescribed process" has the same meaning as in Part I of this Act; and

"offensive trade" or "trade" has the same meaning as in section 107 of the Public Health Act 1936.

DEFINITION
"local authority": s.79(6).

COMMENCEMENT
January 1, 1991 (s.164(2)).

GENERAL NOTE
Existing controls over "offensive trades": This section makes provision for the gradual disapplication and eventual termination of existing statutory controls over the so-called "offensive trades" in ss.107 and 108 of the Public Health Act 1936 and s.32 of the Public Health (Scotland) Act 1897. Sections 107 and 108 have now been repealed although s.32 of the 1897 Act has not yet been repealed: see the note below to subs. (4).

Under s.107 of the 1936 Act, the consent of the local authority was required for offensive trades carried on within their area. No such trade could be lawfully established without such consent in writing: *Epping Forest District Council v. Essex Rendering* [1983] 1 W.L.R. 158 (H.L.). Such trades were defined by s.107 of the 1936 Act, as amended by Sched. 14, para. 11 of the Local Government Act 1972. (There was provision for other trades or processes to come under control by designation by the local authority, confirmed by the Secretary of State, and for local authorities to make by-laws relating to offensive trades under s.108(2) of the 1936 Act, a power still existing in Scotland, under the 1897 Act, s.32(3), for the purpose of prevention or diminishing the noxious or injurious effects of the trade.)

Subsections (1) and (2): disapplication of present controls: The subsections together provide for the disapplication of the controls described above. The general effect is that the offensive trade or offensive business controls cease to have effect in relation to trades or businesses as they fall under the local authority air pollution controls of Pt. I of the Act. The relevant date is that on which the individual trade or business is granted an authorisation under Pt. I, or if no application is made, the end of the period allowed for such applications. By subs. (2) the requirements for consent mentioned above cease to have effect in relation to the trade or business, as do any bye-laws made by the authority. This does not, however, affect proceedings instituted under the previous controls in relation to the trade or business before the relevant date.

Subsection (3): fish frying: This subsection has the same effect of disapplication in relation to by-laws made under s.108(1) of the 1936 Act in relation to fish frying. Fish frying is not an offensive trade in England and Wales, but can be the subject of analogous by-laws. In Scotland, fish frying may be declared an offensive trade under s.32(1) of the 1897 Act.

Subsection (4): termination of controls: This subsection gives the Secretary of State power, when he considers it expedient to do so, to repeal entirely the offensive trade provisions in England and Wales and in Scotland. The Secretary of State must have regard to the operation of Pts I and III of the 1990 Act in making this decision, the intention being that such activities will in future be controlled under those provisions. The majority of such processes are scheduled for control under Pt. I. As regards England and Wales, the power was exercised with effect from September 1, 1995 with the repeal of ss.107 and 108 of the 1936 Act by the Repeal of Offensive Trades or Business Order 1995 (S.I. 1995 No. 2054). As regards Scotland, the power has not yet been exercised in relation to s.32 of the 1897 Act.

Application to gases of certain Clean Air Act provisions

85. [...]

[s.85 was repealed by the Clean Air Act 1993, which repealed the Clean Air Act 1968 which s.85 amended.]

PART IV

LITTER ETC.

GENERAL NOTE

Part IV of the Act introduced new provisions relating to litter and to abandoned shopping and luggage trolleys. The Government issued a Consultation Paper on July 20, 1989, *Action on Litter: The Government's Proposals for Legislation* (DoE, Department of Transport and Welsh Office). The Paper pointed out (paras. 2 and 3):

"More and more people are concerned that in spite of increased efforts by many local authorities, private land owners, voluntary groups and individuals, the problem of litter shows no signs of abating. At the same time, public awareness, and the demand from both local authorities and individuals for tougher action, are growing. The Government shares this concern, and is determined to take the measures needed to ensure that the problem can be, and is, tackled effectively."

Various initiatives were mooted in the paper, a number of which are included in Pt. IV of the Act, with or without subsequent amendments:

(1) an increase in the maximum fine for littering to £1,000;

(2) power to introduce fixed penalty schemes for littering offences;

(3) a duty on local authorities to clean and keep clean of litter "all land in their beneficial occupancy or control, open to the air and to which the public have access";

(4) a rationalisation of the current division of responsibility for road cleaning between different tiers of authority;

(5) the issue of a Code of Practice on cleaning, to which local authorities would be required to have regard in discharging their duties;

(6) the ability for any "person aggrieved" by failure of a local authority to keep land clean to apply to the magistrates' court for a "litter abatement order" directed to the authority;

(7) obligations on statutory undertakers and private owners or occupiers of land to which the public have access (*e.g.* car parks, shopping precincts and sports grounds) to keep the land clean, and extension of littering offences to such areas;

(8) a reserve power to require local authorities to remove graffiti in public places, for possible implementation when the necessary technology is proven and the financial implications clearer; and

(9) cleaning up dog faeces to be included within the duty on local authorities to keep public areas clean.

These proposals have been translated into the following provisions of the Act:

(1) a widened offence of leaving litter, subject to a maximum £2,500 fine on summary conviction (s.87);

(2) power to issue fixed penalty notices to a person believed to have committed the new littering offence (s.88);

(3) duties on the Crown, local authorities, highway authorities (in Scotland roads authorities) designated statutory undertakers and the occupiers of "relevant land" to ensure land is, so far as practicable, kept clear of litter and refuse (s.89);

(4) power for the Secretary of State to issue a Code or Codes of Practice on the duty (s.89(7)–(13)). The Code was issued in November 1990: see Note to s.89. The operative (statutory) part of the Code is reproduced, without the non-statutory Appendix, as Appendix 8 at the end of these annotations;

(5) power to designate "litter control areas" (s.90);

(6) provision for summary proceedings by persons aggrieved by litter on highways (in Scotland, roads), Crown and local authority land, other relevant land, and litter

control areas designated under s.90 (s.91). The proceedings may lead to a "litter abatement order" under s.91(6), non-compliance with which is an offence;

(7) provision for summary proceedings by litter authorities, with power to serve litter abatement notices (s.92);

(8) power for litter authorities to issue "street litter control notices" on occupiers of premises adjacent to streets or fronting on to streets (s.93);

(9) power to apply provisions as to the seizure, removal, retention, return and disposal of abandoned shopping and luggage trolleys, with power to levy charges on the return of the trolleys (s.99 and Sched. 4).

Territorial extent
Part IV does not extend to Northern Ireland (s.164(4)).

COMMENCEMENT
Section 97 (transitional provisions) and s.99 (shopping and luggage trolleys) came into force after two months from passage of the Act, *i.e.* on January 1, 1991 (s.156(2)). The remainder of the provisions are also in force, the various sections and subsections having come into force on an appointed day or days as follows. Section 89(7), (8), (9), (11), (12) and (13) came into force on November 13, 1990 (S.I. 1990 No. 2243). Sections 86(2), (6)–(8), (11), (14) and (15), 88(5), (7) and 9(b), 89(4), 90(1), (2) and (7), 94(1) and (2) and 96(2) and (3) came into force in England and Wales and Scotland on January 14, 1991 (S.I. 1991 No. 96). Sections 86(1), (4), (5), (9) and (13), 87(1), (2), (3)(a)–(e) and (4)–(6), 88(1)–(4), (6), (8), 9(a) and (c)–(e) and (10) came into force in England and Wales only on February 13, 1991 (S.I. 1991 No. 96). The new duties on local authorities have been brought into force (Commencement Order No. 7 (S.I. 1991 No. 1042) and Commencement Order No. 5 (S.I. 1991 No. 96). Orders have also been made designating statutory undertakers and prescribing relevant land for litter control purposes. The Litter (Statutory Undertakers) (Designation and Relevant Land) Order 1991 (S.I. No. 1043 as amended by S.I. 1992 No. 406); the Litter Control Areas Order 1991 (S.I. No. 1325); and the Street Litter Control Notices Order 1991 (S.I. No. 1324). For the full list of sections in force see the Table of Sections In Force in the General Note to Pt. I.

Provisions relating to litter

Preliminary

86.—(1) The following provisions have effect for the purposes of this Part.

(2) In England and Wales the following are "principal litter authorities"—
(a) a county council,
(b) a district council,
(c) a London borough council,
(d) the Common Council of the City of London, and
(e) the Council of the Isles of Scilly;
but the Secretary of State may, by order, designate other descriptions of local authorities as litter authorities for the purposes of this Part; and any such authority shall also be a principal litter authority.

(3) In Scotland the following are "principal litter authorities"—
[(a) a council constituted under section 2 of the Local Government etc. (Scotland) Act 1994;
(b) ...]
(c) a joint board.

(4) Subject to subsection (8) below, land is "relevant land" of a principal litter authority if, not being relevant land falling within subsection (7) below, it is open to the air and is land (but not a highway or in Scotland a public road) which is under the direct control of such an authority to which the public are entitled or permitted to have access with or without payment.

(5) Land is "Crown land" if it is land—
(a) occupied by the Crown Estate Commissioners as part of the Crown Estate,
(b) occupied by or for the purposes of a government department or for naval, military or air force purposes, or

(c) occupied or managed by any body acting on behalf of the Crown; is "relevant Crown land" if it is Crown land which is open to the air and is land (but not a highway or in Scotland a public road) to which the public are entitled or permitted to have access with or without payment; and "the appropriate Crown authority" for any Crown land is the Crown Estate Commissioners, the Minister in charge of the government department or the body which occupies or manages the land on the Crown's behalf, as the case may be.

(6) Subject to subsection (8) below, land is "relevant land" of a designated statutory undertaker if it is land which is under the direct control of any statutory undertaker or statutory undertaker of any description which may be designated by the Secretary of State, by order, for the purposes of this Part, being land to which the public are entitled or permitted to have access with or without payment or, in such cases as may be prescribed in the designation order, land in relation to which the public have no such right or permission.

(7) Subject to subsection (8) below, land is "relevant land" of a designated educational institution if it is open to the air and is land which is under the direct control of the governing body of or, in Scotland, of such body or of the education authority responsible for the management of, any educational institution or educational institution of any description which may be designated by the Secretary of State, by order, for the purposes of this Part.

(8) The Secretary of State may, by order, designate descriptions of land which are not to be treated as relevant Crown land or as relevant land of principal litter authorities, of designated statutory undertakers or of designated educational institutions or of any description of any of them.

(9) Every highway maintainable at the public expense other than a trunk road which is a special road is a "relevant highway" and the local authority which is, for the purposes of this Part, "responsible" for so much of it as lies within its area is, subject to any order under subsection (11) below—

    (a) in Greater London, the council of the London borough or the Common Council of the City of London;

    (b) [in England] outside Greater London, the council of the district;

   [(bb) in Wales, the council of the county or county borough;] and

    (c) the Council of the Isles of Scilly.

(10) In Scotland, every public road other than a trunk road which is a special road is a "relevant road" and the local authority which is, for the purposes of this Part, "responsible" for so much of it as lies within [their] area is, subject to any order under subsection (11) below, [the council constituted under section 2 of the Local Government etc. (Scotland) Act 1994.]

(11) The Secretary of State may, by order, as respects relevant highways or relevant roads, relevant highways or relevant roads of any class or any part of a relevant highway or relevant road specified in the order, transfer the responsibility for the discharge of the duties imposed by section 89 below from the local authority to the highway or roads authority; but he shall not make an order under this subsection unless—

    (a) (except where he is the highway or roads authority) he is requested to do so by the highway or roads authority;

    (b) he consults the local authority; and

    (c) it appears to him to be necessary or expedient to do so in order to prevent or minimise interference with the passage or with the safety of traffic along the highway or, in Scotland, road in question;

and where, by an order under this subsection, responsibility for the discharge of those duties is transferred, the authority to which the transfer is made is, for the purposes of this Part, "responsible" for the highway, road or part specified in the order.

(12) Land is "relevant land within a litter control area of a local authority"

if it is land included in an area designated by the local authority under section 90 below to which the public are entitled or permitted to have access with or without payment.

(13) A place on land shall be treated as "open to the air" notwithstanding that it is covered if it is open to the air on at least one side.

(14) The Secretary of State may, by order, apply the provisions of this Part which apply to refuse to any description of animal droppings in all or any prescribed circumstances subject to such modifications as appear to him to be necessary.

(15) Any power under this section may be exercised differently as respects different areas, different descriptions of land or for different circumstances.

DEFINITIONS
"educational institution": s.98(2) and (3).
"highway": s.98(5).
"public road": s.98(5).
"special road": s.98(5).
"statutory undertaker": s.98(5).
"trunk road": s.98(5).

COMMENCEMENT
In force: See the Commencement section on p. 289.

AMENDMENT
Subsection (3) was amended by the Local Government etc. (Scotland) Act 1994, Sched. 13, para. 167(10)(a). Subsection (9) was amended by the Local Government (Wales) Act 1994, Sched. 9, para. 17. Subsection (10) was amended by the Local Government etc. (Scotland) Act 1994, Sched. 13, para. 167(10)(b).

GENERAL NOTE

Subs. (4): "relevant land" of principal litter authorities
Essentially there are three ingredients of such land (although see the note below to subs. (8)):
   (a) it must be open to the air (see subs. (13)), but not a highway or public road;
   (b) it must be "under the direct control" of the principal litter authority. "Control" appears to be a wide expression including many types of possession not commensurate with full ownership: *Johnstone Fear & Kingham v. Commonwealth* (1943) 67 C.L.R. 314 at 324. It would seem to include land under the superintendence and management of, though not owned by, the authority: see *Pardoe v. Pardoe* (1900) 82 L.T. 547 at 549; and
   (c) the public are entitled or permitted to have access to it with or without payment.

Subs. (6): "relevant land" of statutory undertakers
This comprises land "under the direct control" of a statutory undertaker designated by the Secretary of State (see above). As well as land to which the public have access, land to which there is no such access may be prescribed in the relevant order: this is to leave open the ability to extend the regime to areas such as railway embankments which are highly visible and particularly prone to litter. The Government's July 1989 Consultative Paper (para. 30) recognised that the burden on the landowners concerned "may not be a light one." See the Litter (Statutory Undertakers) (Designation and Relevant Land) Order 1991 (S.I. 1991 No. 1043) (as amended by S.I. 1992 No. 406). This designates the following statutory undertakers:
   — the British Railways Board and London Regional Transport, and certain other specified railway operators;
   — persons authorised to carry on any road transport undertaking other than taxi or car hire operators;
   — persons authorised to carry on canal, inland navigation, dock, harbour or pier undertakings; and
   — any relevant airport operator.

The Regulations prescribe operational land which is within a 100 metres of a railway station platform to which the public is permitted or entitled to have access. The Regulations also prescribe land which is not to be treated as relevant land for these purposes notwithstanding that the public are permitted or entitled to have access to it.

Subs. (7): "relevant land" of educational institutions
This covers land under the direct control of designated educational institutions and which is open to the air (see subs. (13)) whether or not the public has access thereto. See the Litter (Designated Educational Institutions) Order 1991 (S.I. 1991 No. 561) designating the institutions in s.98(2) and (3).

Subs. (8): land not to be treated as relevant land
Subsection (8) allows the Secretary of State to designate descriptions of land which are not to be treated as relevant land under such of subss. (4) to (7) as the designation specifies. The Litter (Relevant Land of Principal Litter Authorities and Relevant Crown Lands) Order 1991 (S.I. 1991 No. 476) provides that land below the place to which the tide flows at mean high water springs is not to be treated as relevant land of principal litter authorities (subs. (4) about) or as relevant Crown land (subs. (5)).

Subss. (9)–(11): highways and public roads
In England and Wales, responsibility for litter on highways falls to district and London Borough Councils (subs. (9)). In Scotland, the new councils constituted under the local Government etc. (Scotland) Act 1994 are responsible (subs. (10)). In both cases, motorways are excluded, responsibility lying with the Department of Transport in England and Wales and the Secretary of State in Scotland. Also, in each case the Secretary of State may, by order, transfer responsibility to highway or roads authorities (subs. (11)). The duties to keep highways and roads clean of litter are created by s.89(1)(a) and (b). See the Highway Litter Clearance and Cleaning (Transfer of Duties) Order 1991 (S.I. 1991 No. 337) which transfers responsibility from named councils to the Secretary of State for Transport.

Subs. (12): litter control area
This subsection defines "relevant land within a litter control area," to which duties under Pt. IV apply: see ss. 89(1)(g) and 91(1)(g). Designation of such areas is under s.90.

Subs. (13): open to the air
This provision was added on amendment to make it clear that partially covered areas, such as bus stations, precincts and sports stadiums, can still be regarded as open to the air.

Subs. (14): animal droppings
This subsection, much debated in the House of Lords, allows the Secretary of State to apply any of the provisions of the Act on litter to animal droppings. The mischief prompting this provision is that of dog faeces (see para. 41 of the July 1989 Consultative Paper) or, as less delicately put by Lord Macintosh of Haringey in the House of Lords, "dogshit". An assurance has been given by the Government that the subsection will be used to deal with that problem: *Hansard*, H.L. Vol. 522, col. 631. See the Litter (Animal Droppings) Order 1991 (S.I. 1991 No. 961) which applies the litter control provisions of this part to dog faeces on prescribed land such as public walks, pleasure grounds, frequented sea shores and picnic sites. For discussion of the existing law on this problem, see Peter Alldridge, *Incontinent Dogs and the Law* [1990] New L.J. 1067: see also the report in the same issue of the New L.J. of the first prosecution of a dog owner under bye-laws by Westminster City Council for dog fouling: [1990] New L.J. 1063. The Home Office has produced model bye-laws on dog fouling.

Offence of leaving litter

87.—(1) If any person throws down, drops or otherwise deposits in, into or from any place to which this section applies, and leaves, any thing whatsoever in such circumstances as to cause, or contribute to, or tend to lead to, the defacement by litter of any place to which this section applies, he shall, subject to subsection (2) below, be guilty of an offence.

(2) No offence is committed under this section where the depositing and leaving of the thing was—

(a) authorised by law, or

(b) done with the consent of the owner occupier or other person or authority having control of the place in or into which that thing was deposited.

(3) This section applies to any public open place and, in so far as the place is not a public open place, also to the following places—

   (a) any relevant highway or relevant road and any trunk road which is a special road;

   (b) any place on relevant land of a principal litter authority;

   (c) any place on relevant Crown land;

   (d) any place on relevant land of any designated statutory undertaker;

   (e) any place on relevant land of any designated educational institution;

   (f) any place on relevant land within a litter control area of a local authority.

(4) In this section "public open place" means a place in the open air to which the public are entitled or permitted to have access without payment; and any covered place open to the air on at least one side and available for public use shall be treated as a public open place.

(5) A person who is guilty of an offence under this section shall be liable on summary conviction to a fine not exceeding level 4 on the standard scale.

(6) A local authority, with a view to promoting the abatement of litter, may take such steps as the authority think appropriate for making the effect of subsection (5) above known to the public in their area.

(7) In any proceedings in Scotland for an offence under this section it shall be lawful to convict the accused on the evidence of one witness.

DEFINITIONS
   "educational institution": s.98(2) and (3).
   "highway": s.98(5).
   "principal litter authority": s.86(2).
   "relevant Crown land": s.86(5).
   "relevant highway": s.86(9).
   "relevant land of any designated educational institution": s.86(7).
   "relevant land of any designated statutory undertaker": s.86(6).
   "relevant land within a litter control area of a local authority": s.86(12).
   "relevant road": s.86(10).
   "special road": s.98(5).
   "statutory undertaker": s.98(6).
   "trunk road": s.98(5).

COMMENCEMENT
In force: See the Commencement section on p. 289.

GENERAL NOTE
The offence created by the section is similar in effect to that of s.1 of the Litter Act 1983, as are the specific circumstances described in subs. (2) where the offence is not committed. The land in relation to which an offence is committed is extended beyond the "free public open place" to which the Litter Act 1983 applied: the relevant places are defined in subs. (3) as any public open place (subs. (4)) and also a list of other places (a)–(f) in so far as they are not public open places. The definition can include land in the open air to which the public have access by permission or entitlement without making payment. This covers land in private as well as public ownership, and by subs. (4) can include covered places open to the air on at least one side such as railway stations, concert arenas and sports grounds and stadiums.

   Throwing down, dropping or otherwise depositing something is not in itself an offence under this section; it must also be left: *Vaughan v. Briggs* [1960] 2 All E.R. 473 (on its predecessor, the Litter Act 1958, s.1). The offence was considered further in *Westminster City Council v. Riding* (Q.B., *The Times*, July 21, 1995), where it was held that there was no clear dichotomy between the undefined term "litter" and "controlled waste" for the purposes of Pt. II of this Act: "the word should be given its natural meaning of miscellaneous rubbish left lying about, [which] can consist of all manner of things including domestic household waste, commercial waste, street waste and no doubt other waste not falling within such description". The same article can therefore be subject to both Pt. II and Pt. IV. If an article has been deposited (or presumably thrown down or dropped) without any intention to remove it, then the court "may conclude that after a short time it has been left there": *Witney v. Cattanach* [1979] Crim.L.R. 461. Such intention is, however, a question of fact and it may be that where there is no evidence as to when the article was deposited, etc., the offence cannot be made out: *Westminster City Council v. Riding* (above).

Subs. (4): "public open place"
In *R. v. Binns* and *R. v. Mallon* (Southwark Crown Court, March 15, 1995; appeals heard together), a telephone kiosk enclosed at the top and on all sides save for a small gap at the bottom on three sides was held not to be a place in the open air, nor a covered place open to the air on at least one side, and was accordingly not a public open place.

Subs. (5): penalties
The maximum penalty is a fine of £2,500.

Subs. (6): public awareness
The power to take steps for making the penalties for littering known to the public extends to all local authorities, not just principal litter authorities under Pt. IV. It replaces s.2 of the Litter Act 1983.

Subs. (7): no need for corroboration
The general rule of law in Scotland that evidence must be corroborated is modified to an extent by this subs. However, the rule may not have been rendered redundant given that it is possible for there to be corroboration otherwise than by the evidence of a second witness *e.g.* by means of circumstantial evidence or self-corroborating evidence.

Fixed penalty notices for leaving litter

88.—(1) Where on any occasion an authorised officer of a litter authority finds a person who he has reason to believe has on that occasion committed an offence under section 87 above in the area of that authority, he may give that person a notice offering him the opportunity of discharging any liability to conviction for that offence by payment of a fixed penalty.

(2) Where a person is given a notice under this section in respect of an offence—

   (a) no proceedings shall be instituted for that offence before the expiration of 14 days following the date of the notice; and
   (b) he shall not be convicted of that offence if he pays the fixed penalty before the expiration of that period.

(3) A notice under this section shall give such particulars of the circumstances alleged to constitute the offence as are necessary for giving reasonable information of the offence and shall state—

   (a) the period during which, by virtue of subsection (2) above, proceedings will not be taken for the offence;
   (b) the amount of the fixed penalty; and
   (c) the person to whom and the address at which the fixed penalty may be paid;

and, without prejudice to payment by any other method, payment of the fixed penalty may be made by pre-paying and posting to that person at that address a letter containing the amount of the penalty (in cash or otherwise).

(4) Where a letter is sent in accordance with subsection (3) above payment shall be regarded as having been made at the time at which that letter would be delivered in the ordinary course of post.

(5) The form of notices under this section shall be such as the Secretary of State may by order prescribe.

(6) The fixed penalty payable to a principal litter authority in pursuance of a notice under this section shall, subject to subsection (7) below, be £10; and as respects the sums received by the authority, those sums—

   (a) if received by an authority in England and Wales, shall be paid to the Secretary of State;
   (b) if received by an authority in Scotland, shall be treated as if the penalty were a fine imposed by a district court.

(7) The Secretary of State may by order substitute a different amount for the amount for the time being specified as the amount of the fixed penalty in subsection (6) above.

(8) In any proceedings a certificate which—
  (a) purports to be signed by or on behalf of—
    (i) in England and Wales, he chief finance officer of the litter authority; or
    (ii) in Scotland, the proper officer; and
  (b) states that payment of a fixed penalty was or was not received by a date specified in the certificate,
shall be evidence of the facts stated.
  (9) For the purposes of this section the following are "litter authorities"—
  (a) any principal litter authority, other than [an English county] council, [...] or a joint board;
  (b) any [English] county council, [...] or joint board designated by the Secretary of State, by order, in relation to such area as is specified in the order (not being an area in a National Park);
  [...]
  (e) the Broads Authority.
  (10) In this section—
"authorised officer" means an officer of [...] a litter authority who is authorised in writing by the authority for the purpose of issuing notices under this section;
"chief finance officer", in relation to a litter authority, means the person having responsibility for the financial affairs of the authority;
  [...]
"proper officer" means the officer who has, as respects the authority, the responsibility mentioned in section 95 of the Local Government (Scotland) Act 1973 (financial administration).

DEFINITIONS
  "authorised officer": subs. (10).
  "chief finance officer": subs. (10).
  "litter authorities": subs. (9).
  "principal litter authority": s.86(2).
  "proper officer": subs. (10).

COMMENCEMENT
In force: See the Commencement section on p. 289.

AMENDMENT
Subsection (9) was amended by the Local Government (Wales) Act 1994, Sched. 9, para. 17 by the Local Government etc. (Scotland) Act 1994, Sched. 13, para. 167(11) and Sched. 14. Subsections (9) and (10) were amended by the Environment Act 1995, Sched. 24.

GENERAL NOTE
This section gives power to litter authorities, as defined in subs. (9), to operate fixed penalty schemes for littering. National Park authorities and the Broads Authority are included within the definition of litter authorities. Originally the litter authorities for National Parks were the Park board and National Park Committee, but with the introduction by Pt. III of the Environment Act 1995 of "National Park authorities," reference to those bodies was deleted. The 1995 Act, Sched. 9, para. 12, provides that this section shall have effect as if a National Park authority were a litter authority, and the relevant Park were its area. By subs. (6), the fixed penalty is £10, but may be reviewed by the Secretary of State under subs. (7).
  The period for payment of the penalty is 14 days (subs. (2)) and payment means the person concerned cannot then be convicted of a litter offence (subs. (2)(b)).
  The 1989 Consultation Paper gives details of the Government's background thinking on this issue (paras. 6 and 7):

  "6. The model for such a scheme already exists in the City of Westminster, as provided for by the City of Westminster Act 1988. Many other local authorities are anxious to adopt this model. Following close monitoring of the Westminster scheme's first year of operation the Government concurs in Westminster's view that the scheme is a helpful and workable tool in the authority's efforts to fight litter and improve public awareness of the problem. Almost all approaches made by authorised officers resulted in the person concerned picking up the litter rather than the officer issuing a ticket. This bears out that the value of the scheme is above all one of education and persuasion, and that the demand of operating the scheme on the resources of the local authority and, ultimately, the courts is modest. 7. The Government has considered the case for retention of fines by the local authority, but does not accept that this particular instance merits a departure from the general principle that all such fines should be passed on to the Exchequer. Similarly, the Government has concluded that the Police should not be given the same power as authorised officers of the local authority to issue fixed penalty tickets, since this additional burden would effectively detract resources from serious crime prevention and detection."

The form of notice to be given to a person believed to have committed an offence has now been prescribed under subs. (5) by the Litter (Fixed Penalty Notices) Order 1991 (S.I. 1991 No. 111).

Duty to keep land and highways clear of litter etc.

89.—(1) It shall be the duty of—
(a) each local authority, as respects any relevant highway or, in Scotland, relevant road for which it is responsible,
(b) the Secretary of State, as respects any trunk road which is a special road and any relevant highway or relevant road for which he is responsible,
(c) each principal litter authority, as respects its relevant land,
(d) the appropriate Crown authority, as respects its relevant Crown land,
(e) each designated statutory undertaker, as respects its relevant land,
(f) the governing body of each designated educational institution or in Scotland such body or, as the case may be, the education authority responsible for the management of the institution, as respects its relevant land, and
(g) the occupier of any relevant land within a litter control area of a local authority,
to ensure that the land is, so far as is practicable, kept clear of litter and refuse.
(2) Subject to subsection (6) below, it shall also be the duty of—
(a) each local authority, as respects any relevant highway or relevant road for which it is responsible,
(b) the Secretary of State, as respects any trunk road which is a special road and any relevant highway or relevant road for which he is responsible,
to ensure that the highway or road is, so far as is practicable, kept clean.
(3) In determining what standard is required, as respects any description of land, highway or road, for compliance with subsections (1) and (2) above, regard shall be had to the character and use of the land, highway or road as well as the measures which are practicable in the circumstances.
(4) Matter of any description prescribed by regulations made by the Secretary of State for the purposes of subsections (1)(a) and (2) above shall be litter or refuse to which the duties imposed by those subsections apply as respects relevant highways or relevant roads whether or not it would be litter or refuse apart from this subsection.
(5) It shall be the duty of a local authority, when discharging its duty under subsection (1)(a) or (2) above as respects any relevant highway or relevant road, to place and maintain on the highway or road such traffic signs and barriers as may be necessary for giving warning and preventing danger to traffic or for regulating it and afterwards to remove them as soon as they cease to be necessary for those purposes; but this subsection has effect subject to any directions given under subsection (6) below.

(6) In discharging its duty under subsection (1)(a) or (2) above to keep clear of litter and refuse or to clean any relevant highway or relevant road for which it is responsible, the local authority shall comply with any directions given to it by the highway or roads authority with respect to—

    (a) the placing and maintenance of any traffic signs or barriers;

    (b) the days or periods during which clearing or cleaning shall not be undertaken or undertaken to any extent specified in the direction;

and for the purpose of enabling it to discharge its duty under subsection (1)(a) or (2) above as respects any relevant highway or relevant road the local authority may apply to the highway authority or roads authority for that authority to exercise its powers under section 14(1) or (3) of the Road Traffic Regulation Act 1984 (temporary prohibition or restriction of traffic).

(7) The Secretary of State shall prepare and issue a code of practice for the purpose of providing practical guidance on the discharge of the duties imposed by subsections (1) and (2) above.

(8) Different codes of practice may be prepared and issued under subsection (7) above for different areas.

(9) The Secretary of State may issue modifications of, or withdraw, a code issued under subsection (7) above; but where a code is withdrawn, he shall prepare and issue a new code under that subsection in substitution for it.

(10) Any person subject to any duty imposed by subsection (1) or (2) above shall have regard to the code of practice in force under subsection (7) above in discharging that duty.

(11) A draft code prepared under subsection (7) above shall be laid before both Houses of Parliament and shall not be issued until after the end of the period of 40 days beginning with the day on which the code was so laid, or if the draft is laid on different days, the later of the two days.

(12) If, within the period mentioned in subsection (11) above, either House resolves that the code the draft of which was laid before it should not be issued, the Secretary of State shall not issue that code.

(13) No account shall be taken in reckoning any period of 40 days for the purposes of this section of any time during which Parliament is dissolved or prorogued or during which both Houses are adjourned for more than four days.

(14) In this section "traffic sign" has the meaning given in section 64(1) of the Road Traffic Regulation Act 1984.

DEFINITIONS

    "appropriate Crown authority": s.86(5).
    "educational institution": s.98(2) and (3).
    "highway": s.98(5).
    "principal litter authority": s.86(2) and (3).
    "relevant Crown land": s.86(5).
    "relevant highway": s.86(9).
    "relevant land": s.86(4).
    "relevant land of designated educational institution": s.86(6).
    "relevant land of designated statutory undertaker": s.86(6).
    "relevant land within a litter control area of a local authority": s.86(12).
    "relevant road": s.86(10).
    "special road": s.98(5).
    "statutory undertaker": s.98(6).
    "trunk road": s.98(5).

COMMENCEMENT
In force: See the Commencement section on p. 289.

GENERAL NOTE
This section creates a new duty on the authorities and persons specified to ensure that their land is so far as practicable kept clear of litter and refuse (subs. (1)). A further duty is created by subs.

(2) on local authorities and trunk road authorities to keep highways and roads clean, so far as is practicable.

Standard of cleanliness

Two matters are relevant in relation to the standard of cleanliness and freedom from litter to be excepted. These are: (a) the character and use of the land, highway or road and the measures which are practicable in the circumstances (subs. (3)): (b) the Code of Practice prepared by the Secretary of State under subs. (7), to which regard must be had under subs. (10).

A draft code was issued for consultation on February 23, 1990, after work by an Advisory Group comprising representatives from local authority associations, statutory undertakers, commercial property owners and cleaning contractors. The Code was formally laid before Parliament in November 1990. The Code, which was published in January 1991, falls into two parts. The first part, the Statutory Code, describes four standards of cleanliness from Grade A (litter free) to Grade D (heavily littered) and divides land into 11 zones according to use and volume of traffic, describing the expected standards and the time by which those standards should be restored if the standard falls. Photographic examples are given. It will be for local authorities or the other body under the relevant duty to allocate to the various zones and to publicise such allocations. The second, non-statutory, part of the Code contains advice on "best practice" dealing with appraisal, implementation, campaigning, education and community involvement, litter bins, fly-tipping and grass cutting.

Special criteria have been applied to beaches, taking into account matters such as action of the tides, difficult access for machinery, unsuitability of terrain for mechanical cleaning and ecological sensitivity.

Highways/roads

As mentioned above, the new duties apply to roads and highways. The two duties are (a) to ensure that highways and roads (including motorways and trunk roads) are, so far as is practicable, kept clear of litter and refuse (s.89(1)(a) and (b)); and (b) to ensure that highways and roads (including motorways and trunk roads) are, so far as is practicable, kept clean (s.89(2)).

The duties fall to the Secretary of State in relation to motorways and trunk roads for which he is responsible. Otherwise, the responsibility is that of district and London borough councils in England, county and county borough councils in Wales and the new councils constituted under the Local Government etc. (Scotland) Act 1994 in Scotland (s.86(9) and (10)). The object is to achieve a clear allocation of responsibility for street and road cleaning. The system of divided responsibility under s.22(1) and (2) of the Control of Pollution Act 1974 had proved to cause friction and to have blurred accountability.

Under the new provisions, the responsibilities of highway and roads authorities are limited to their duties to maintain the highway under s.41 of the Highways Act 1980 or, in Scotland, ss.1 and 2 of of the Roads (Scotland) Act 1984. The only exception is where responsibility is transferred to the highway or roads authority by order under s.86(11). The local authority must, in discharging its cleaning duties, take the necessary traffic warning precautions (subs. (5)) and comply with any directions as to such matters given by the highway or roads authority under subs. (6). Compliance with such directions is a defence to summary proceedings in respect of the s.89 duty, under s.91 (see s.91(8)). Additional powers of temporary prohibition or restriction of traffic are given by Sched. 15 para. 23, amending the Road Traffic Regulation Act 1984.

Subs. (4): matter to be treated as litter or refuse

The Secretary of State may make regulations as to whether any matter is litter or refuse for the purpose of the provisions on highways and roads. This is a reserve power intended to enable the Secretary of State to resolve disputes as to whether specific matter (for example leaves) falls to the highway or roads authority as a road safety issue or is also a litter issue for the principal litter authorities.

Costs

In DoE News Release No. 418 (July 11, 1990) the Government, in commenting on a report prepared by Coopers & Lybrand Deloitte on the new litter duties, suggested that the additional costs involved for local authorities were likely to be in the range of 7–30 per cent. But *cf. Hansard*, H.L. Vol. 522, cols. 622–3.

Litter control areas

90.—(1) The Secretary of State may, by order, prescribe descriptions of land which may be designated under subsection (3) below as, or as part of, a litter control area.

(2) The power of the Secretary of State to prescribe descriptions of land under subsection (1) above includes power to describe land by reference to the ownership or occupation of the land or the activities carried on on it.

(3) Any principal litter authority other than [an English] county council, [a] [...] or [a] joint board may, in accordance with the following provisions of this section, by order designate any land in their area as, or as part of, a litter control area.

(4) No order under subsection (3) above designating any land shall be made unless the authority is of the opinion that, by reason of the presence of litter or refuse, the condition of the land is, and unless they make a designation order is likely to continue to be, such as to be detrimental to the amenities of the locality.

(5) The power to make a designation order under subsection (3) above shall be excluded from the functions to which section 101 of the Local Government Act 1972 (functions capable of delegation) applies.

(6) An authority proposing to make a designation order in relation to any land shall—

   (a) notify persons who appear to the authority to be persons who will be affected by the proposed order;

   (b) give them an opportunity to make representations about it within the period of 21 days beginning with the service of the notice; and

   (c) take any representations so made into account in making their decision.

(7) A designation order under subsection (3) above shall identify the land to which it applies and shall be in such form as the Secretary of State may by order prescribe.

DEFINITION
"principal litter authority": s.86(2) and (3).

COMMENCEMENT
In force: See the Commencement section on p. 289.

AMENDMENTS
Subsection (3) was amended by the Local Government (Wales) Act 1994, Sched. 9, para. 17 and by the Local Government etc. (Scotland) Act 1994, Sched. 13, para. 167(12) and Sched. 14.

GENERAL NOTE
This section makes provision for the designation of litter control areas. The Secretary of State may prescribe descriptions of land under subs. (1) which may be designated as such. The descriptions of such land could include, for example, car parks, beaches, shopping precincts, and industrial estates. Alternatively the land may be designated by reference to its ownership or occupation or the activities carried out on it (subs. (2)). Principal litter authorities may then make orders designating any land in their area as, or as part of, a litter control area (subs. (3)). County councils cannot make such orders, nor can the power to make orders be delegated (subs. (5)).

The condition precedent to making an order is by reference to detriment to the amenities of the area caused by the condition of the land due to the presence of litter or refuse (subs. (4)).

Persons who appear to be affected by any prospective order must be notified and given an opportunity to comment (subs. (6)). See the Litter Control Areas Order 1991 (S.I. 1991 No. 1325) which prescribes the descriptions of land which may be designated as litter control areas under subs. (3). These include car parks, shopping areas, cinemas, theatres, amusement centres, frequented beaches, motorway service stations, markets, camping and caravan sites, and a trunk road picnic area. The Regulations also prescribe the form of designation orders.

Summary proceedings by persons aggrieved by litter

91.—(1) A magistrates' court may act under this section on a complaint made by any person on the ground that he is aggrieved by the defacement, by litter or refuse, of—

(a) any relevant highway;

(b) any trunk road which is a special road;

(c) any relevant land of a principal litter authority;

(d) any relevant Crown land;

(e) any relevant land of a designated statutory undertaker;

(f) any relevant land of a designated educational institution; or

(g) any relevant land within a litter control area of a local authority.

(2) A magistrates' court may also act under this section on a complaint made by any person on the ground that he is aggrieved by the want of cleanliness of any relevant highway or any trunk road which is a special road.

(3) A principal litter authority shall not be treated as a person aggrieved for the purposes of proceedings under this section.

(4) Proceedings under this section shall be brought against the person who has the duty to keep the land clear under section 89(1) above or to keep the highway clean under section 89(2) above, as the case may be.

(5) Before instituting proceedings under this section against any person, the complainant shall give to the person not less than five days' written notice of his intention to make the complaint and the notice shall specify the matter complained of.

(6) If the magistrates' court is satisfied that the highway or land in question is defaced by litter or refuse or, in the case of a highway, is wanting in cleanliness, the court may, subject to subsections (7) and (8) below, make an order ("a litter abatement order") requiring the defendant to clear the litter or refuse away or, as the case may be, clean the highway within a time specified in the order.

(7) The magistrates' court shall not make a litter abatement order if the defendant proves that he has complied, as respects the highway or land in question, with his duty under section 89(1) and (2) above.

(8) The magistrates' court shall not make a litter abatement order where it appears that the matter complained of is the result of directions given to the local authority under section 89(6) above by the highway authority.

(9) A person who, without reasonable excuse, fails to comply with a litter abatement order shall be guilty of an offence and liable on summary conviction to a fine not exceeding level 4 on the standard scale together with a further fine of an amount equal to one-twentieth of that level for each day on which the offence continues after the conviction.

(10) In any proceedings for an offence under subsection (9) above it shall be a defence for the defendant to prove that he has complied, as respects the highway or land in question, with his duty under section 89(1) and (2) above.

(11) A code of practice under section 89(7) above shall be admissible in evidence in any proceedings under this section and if any provision of such a code appears to the court to be relevant to any question in the proceedings it shall be taken into account in determining that question.

(12) Where a magistrates' court is satisfied on the hearing of a complaint under this section—

(a) that, when the complaint was made to it, the highway or land in question was defaced by litter or refuse or, as the case may be, was wanting in cleanliness, and

(b) that there were reasonable grounds for bringing the complaint,

the court shall order the defendant to pay such reasonable sum to the complainant as the court may determine in respect of the expenses incurred by the complainant in bringing the complaint and the proceedings before the court.

(13) In the application of this section to Scotland—

(a) for any reference to a magistrates' court there shall be substituted a reference to the sheriff;

(b) for any reference to a complaint there shall be substituted a reference to a summary application, and "complainant" shall be construed accordingly;

(c) for any reference to the defendant there shall be substituted a reference to the person against whom the proceedings are taken;

(d) for any reference to a highway and a relevant highway there shall be substituted a reference to a road and a relevant road; and

(e) for any reference to a highway authority there shall be substituted a reference to a roads authority.

and any person against whom proceedings are brought may appeal on a point of law to the Court of Session against the making of a litter abatement order.

DEFINITIONS
"educational institution": s.98(2) and (3).
"highway": s.98(5).
"principal litter authority": s.86(2) and (3).
"relevant Crown land": s.86(5).
"relevant highway": s.86(9).
"relevant land of a designated educational institution": s.86(7).
"relevant land of a designated statutory undertaker": s.86(6).
"relevant land of a principal litter authority": s.86(4).
"relevant land within a litter control area of a local authority": s.86(12).
"special road": s.98(5).
"statutory undertaker": s.98(6).
"trunk road": s.98(5).

COMMENCEMENT
In force: See the Commencement section on p. 289.

GENERAL NOTE
This section provides a remedy for members of the public aggrieved by breach of the duties imposed by s.89. The remedy is by way of complaint to magistrates' courts in England and Wales, or by summary application to the sheriff in Scotland (subs. (13)). For a discussion of the nature of these proceedings see the General note to s.82. The proceedings must be preceded by not less than five days' written notice to the authority or other person alleged to be in breach of duty of intention to make the complaint, specifying the nature of the complaint (subs. (5)).

The Code of Practice (see s.89 above) is admissible in evidence (subs. (11)). If the complaint is successful, a litter abatement order will be made, failure to comply with which is an offence (subss. (6)–(9)). No offence can result in the case of the Crown (s.159(2)). Compliance with the relevant duty under s.89 is a defence to the original complaint (subs. (7)) and also to subsequent proceedings for non-compliance with a litter abatement order (subs. (10)).

Subs. (1): person aggrieved
In the context of duties relating to the state and cleanliness of public places, this expression is naturally likely to be construed widely and might therefore cover local residents, visitors, travellers, persons occupying property overlooking the relevant land, pupils at the relevant educational institutions, and no doubt their parents.

The Government's view, in some respects rather narrower, is expressed in the July 1989 Consultation Paper (para. 26):

"The Government's view is that a 'person aggrieved' might be a local resident, someone who worked in the area, or a regular visitor to it—in other words, anyone who had a bona fide interest in that locality and hence a particular right to demand proper standards of cleanliness there. The person could equally be an individual representing a local community organisation or voluntary body with such an interest in the locality."

Subs. (12): costs
Where, on hearing a complaint, the court is satisfied that there was cause for complaint at the time the complaint was made, and that there were reasonable grounds for bringing the complaint, the court may order the defendant to pay a reasonable sum in respect of the complainant's costs. This is necessary because, if by the time the complaint was heard, the litter had been cleared away or the lack of cleanliness rectified, no order could be made under subs. (6), and there would be no power to award costs.

Summary proceedings by litter authorities

92.—(1) Where a principal litter authority other than [an English] county council, [a] [...] or [a] joint board are satisfied as respects—
   (a) any relevant Crown land,
   (b) any relevant land of a designated statutory undertaker,
   (c) any relevant land of a designated educational institution, or
   (d) any relevant land within a litter control area of a local authority,
that it is defaced by litter or refuse or that defacement of it by litter or refuse is likely to recur, the authority shall serve a notice (a "litter abatement notice") imposing either the requirement or the prohibition or both the requirement and the prohibition specified in subsection (2) below.
   (2) The requirement and prohibition referred to in subsection (1) above are as follows, namely—
   (a) a requirement that the litter or refuse be cleared within a time specified in the notice;
   (b) a prohibition on permitting the land to become defaced by litter or refuse.
   (3) The litter abatement notice shall be served—
   (a) as respects relevant Crown land, on the appropriate Crown authority;
   (b) as respects relevant land of a designated statutory undertaker, on the undertaker;
   (c) as respects relevant land of a designated educational institution, on the governing body of the institution or in Scotland on such body or, as the case may be, on the education authority responsible for the management of the institution;
   (d) in any other case, on the occupier of the land or, if it is unoccupied, on the owner of the land.
   (4) The person served with the notice may appeal against the notice to a magistrates' court or, in Scotland, to the sheriff by way of summary application within the period of 21 days beginning with the date on which the notice was served.
   (5) If, on any appeal under subsection (4) above, the appellant proves that, as respects the land in question, he has complied with his duty under section 89(1) above, the court shall allow the appeal.
   (6) If a person on whom a litter abatement notice is served, without reasonable excuse, fails to comply with or contravenes the requirement or prohibition imposed by the notice, he shall be guilty of an offence and liable on summary conviction to a fine not exceeding level 4 on the standard scale together with a further fine of an amount equal to one-twentieth of that level for each day on which the offence continues after the conviction.
   (7) In any proceedings for an offence under subsection (6) above it shall be a defence for the person charged to prove that he has complied, as respects the land in question, with this duty under section 89(1) above.

(8) A code of practice under section 89(7) above shall be admissible in evidence in any proceedings under this section and if any provision of such a code appears to the court to be relevant to any question in the proceedings it shall be taken into account in determining that question.

(9) If a person on whom a litter abatement notice is served fails to comply with the requirement imposed by the notice in respect of any land, the authority may, subject to subsection (10) below—

(a) enter on the land and clear the litter or refuse; and

(b) recover from that person the expenditure attributable to their having done so, except such of the expenditure as that person shows was unnecessary in the circumstances.

(10) Subsection (9) above does not apply in relation to relevant Crown land or relevant land of statutory undertakers.

DEFINITIONS

"appropriate Crown authority": s.86(5).
"education institution": s.98(2) and (3).
"joint board": s.98(4).
"principal litter authority": s.86(2) and (3).
"relevant Crown land": s.86(5).
"relevant land of a designated educational institution": s.86(7).
"relevant land of a designated statutory undertaker": s.86(6).
"relevant land within a litter control area of a local authority": s.86(12).
"statutory undertaker": s.98(6).

COMMENCEMENT

In force: See the Commencement section on p. 289.

AMENDMENTS

Subsection (1) was amended by the Local Government (Wales) Act 1994, Sched. 9, para. 17 and by the Local Government etc. (Scotland) Act 1994, Sched. 13, para. 167(13) and Sched. 14.

GENERAL NOTE

Principal litter authorities have no right to take summary action under s.91 in respect of litter, refuse or want of cleanliness (s.91(3)). However, s.92 provides a specific remedy for such authorities (except county councils or joint boards) in respect of some categories of land as listed in subs. (1). Such land does not include, for obvious reasons, principal litter authorities' own land; nor does it include highway or road land.

The procedure is that the authority may serve notice (a litter abatement notice) on the relevant authority or in the case of private land on the occupier or, if the land is unoccupied, the owner. There is a right of appeal against the notice to a magistrates' court or to the sheriff in Scotland (subs. (4)).

Failure to comply with the notice is an offence (subs. (6)). The maximum penalty is a £2,500 fine, plus a daily fine of £175 for each day the offence continues after conviction. No offence is committed in the case of the Crown, but a declaration of unlawfulness may be obtained from the High Court or Court of Session (s.159(2)).

Default powers are given to enter and clear the relevant land of litter in the event of non-compliance, and to recover the costs from the person served with the notice (subs. (9)). This power does not, however, apply in relation to Crown land or land of statutory undertakers (subs. (10)).

Street litter control notices

93.—(1) A principal litter authority other than [an English] county council, [a] [...] or a joint board may, with a view to the prevention of accumulations of litter or refuse in and around any street or open land adjacent to any street, issue notices ("street litter control notices") imposing requirements on occupiers of premises in relation to such litter or refuse, in accordance with this section and section 94 below.

(2) If the authority is satisfied, in respect of any premises which are of a description prescribed under section 94(1)(a) below and have a frontage on a street in their area, that—

(a) there is recurrent defacement by litter or refuse of any land, being part of the street or open land adjacent to the street, which is in the vicinity of the premises, or

(b) the condition of any part of the premises which is open land in the vicinity of the frontage is, and if no notice is served is likely to continue to be, detrimental to the amenities of the locality by reason of the presence of litter or refuse, or

(c) there is produced, as a result of the activities carried on on the premises, quantities of litter or refuse of such nature and in such amounts as are likely to cause the defacement of any part of the street, or of open land adjacent to the street, which is in the vicinity of the premises,

the authority may serve a street litter control notice on the occupier or, if the premises are unoccupied, on the owner of the premises.

(3) A notice shall, subject to section 94(2), (3) and (4) below—

(a) identify the premises and state the grounds under subsection (2) above on which it is issued;

(b) specify an area of open land which adjoins or is in the vicinity of the frontage of the premises on the street;

(c) specify, in relation to that area or any part of it, such reasonable requirements as the authority considers appropriate in the circumstances;

and, for the purposes of paragraph (b) above, an area which includes land on both sides of the frontage of the premises shall be treated as an area adjoining that frontage.

(4) In this section and section 94 below—

"notice" means a street litter control notice;

"open land" means land in the open air;

"the premises," in relation to a notice, means the premises in respect of which the notice is issued;

"specified area" means the area specified in a notice under subsection (3)(b) above; and

"street" means a relevant highway, a relevant road or any other highway or road over which there is a right of way on foot.

DEFINITIONS
"highway": s.96(5).
"joint board": s.98(4).
"principal litter authority": s.86(2) and (3).
"relevant highway": s.86(9).
"relevant road": s.86(10).
"road": s.96(5).

COMMENCEMENT
April 1, 1991 (S.I. 1991 No. 1042).

AMENDMENTS
Subsection (1) was amended by the Local Government (Wales) Act 1994, Sched. 9, para. 17 and by the Local Government etc. (Scotland) Act 1994, Sched. 13, para. 167(14) and Sched. 14.

GENERAL NOTE
This section gives new powers to principal litter authorities (but not English county councils, or joint boards) to issue street litter control notices, with a view to preventing accumulations of litter or refuse in and around any street or open land adjacent to any street. Such notices are served on the occupier of premises which could loosely be described as being connected with street litter problems. The case for imposing a duty on the owners of commercial premises to keep clean any frontage land within their ownership and also the adjoining pavement was

considered and rejected in the July 1989 Consultation Paper, para. 38. The provisions in s.93 directly address that problem.

The types of premises on which, and the conditions under which, notice can be served are set out in subs. (2) and are essentially:

(a) premises having a frontage to a street where there is a recurrent defacement by litter or refuse of part of the street or of open land adjacent to the street, which is in the vicinity of the premises;

(b) premises having a frontage to a street, where open land forming part of the premises in the vicinity of the frontage is in a condition detrimental to the amenities of the locality because of litter or refuse, and is likely to continue to be so;

(c) premises having a frontage to a street, on which activities are carried on so as to produce litter or refuse likely in nature, quantities or amounts to cause the defacement of the street or of open land in the vicinity of the premises and adjacent to the street. The obvious examples are fast-food retail outlets.

The notice is served on the occupier or, in the case of unoccupied premises, on the owner. The notice must specify appropriate and reasonable requirements in relation to an area of open land which adjoins or is in the vicinity of the frontage of the premises on the street (subs. (3)), and for this purpose land on both sides of the frontage can be included as an area adjoining the frontage. It is not clear how the provisions apply to first floor premises, perhaps with simply a common entrance at ground level: would such premises "have a frontage on a street"?

Further provisions and requirements as to such notices are contained in s.94.

Street litter: supplementary provisions

94.—(1) The Secretary of State may by order prescribe—

(a) the descriptions of commercial or retail premises in respect of which a street litter control notice may be issued;

(b) the descriptions of land which may be included in a specified area; and

(c) the maximum area of land which may be included in a specified area;

and different descriptions or maximum dimensions may be prescribed under paragraph (b) or (c) above for different cases or circumstances.

(2) The power to describe premises or land under subsection (1)(a) or (b) above includes power to describe the premises or land by reference to occupation or ownership or to the activities carried on there.

(3) The land comprised in a specified area—

(a) shall include only land of one or more of the descriptions prescribed under subsection (1)(b) above;

(b) shall not include any land which is not—

(i) part of the premises,

(ii) part of a street,

(iii) relevant land of a principal litter authority, or

(iv) land under the direct control of any other local authority; and

(c) shall not exceed any applicable maximum area prescribed under subsection (1)(c) above;

but a specified area shall not include any part of the premises which is or is part of a litter control area.

(4) The requirements which may be imposed by a notice shall relate to the clearing of litter or refuse from the specified area and may in particular require—

(a) the provision or emptying of receptacles for litter or refuse;

(b) the doing within a period specified in the notice of any such thing as may be so specified; or

(c) the doing (while the notice remains in force) at such times or intervals, or within such periods, of any such thing as may be so specified;

but a notice may not require the clearing of litter or refuse from any carriageway, except at a time when the carriageway is closed to all vehicular traffic.

(5) In relation to so much of the specified area as is not part of the premises the authority shall take account, in determining what requirements to impose, of their own duties under this Part or otherwise, and of any similar duties of any other local authority, in relation to that land.

(6) An authority proposing to serve a notice shall—

(a) inform the person on whom the notice is to be served;

(b) give him the opportunity to make representations about the notice within the period of 21 days beginning with the day on which he is so informed; and

(c) take any representations so made into account in making their decision.

(7) A person on whom a notice is served may appeal against the notice to a magistrates' court or, in Scotland, to the sheriff by way of summary application; and the court may quash the notice or may quash, vary or add to any requirement imposed by the notice.

(8) If it appears to the authority that a person has failed or is failing to comply with any requirement imposed by a notice the authority may apply to a magistrates' court or, in Scotland, to the sheriff by way of summary application for an order requiring the person to comply with the requirement within such time a may be specified in the order.

(9) A person who, without reasonable excuse, fails to comply with an order under subsection (8) above shall be guilty of an offence and liable on summary conviction to a fine not exceeding level 4 on the standard scale.

DEFINITIONS
"notice": s.93(4).
"relevant land of a principal litter authority": s.86(4).
"specified area": s.93(4).
"street": s.93(4).

COMMENCEMENT
In force: See the Commencement section on p. 289.

GENERAL NOTE
This section contains further and supplementary provisions as to street litter notices as follows:

Matters to be prescribed
Various matters are to be prescribed by the Secretary of State including the types of commercial and retail premises that may be issued with a notice, and the descriptions and maximum areas of land that may be included within specified areas in notices (subs. (1)).

Subs. (3): land to be comprised in specified area
As well as the prescribed limitations as to description and area of land to be comprised in a specified area, such land may not include any land unless it is either: (a) part of the premises; or (b) part of a street; or (c) relevant land of a principal litter authority; or (d) land under the direct control of any other local authority. Nor can such areas include any land which is part of a litter control area (see s.90).

Subs. (4): requirements of the notice
Such requirements relate to the clearing of litter or refuse from the specified area and may contain the specific requirements listed in subs. (4).

Rights of occupier/owner: The occupier or owner has the right under subs. (6) to be informed of the authority's intention to serve a notice, and to make representations. There is a right of appeal to the magistrates' court or to the sheriff under subs. (7) against a notice served.

Enforcement: This is by way of application to the magistrates' court or to the sheriff for an order requiring compliance with the notice (subs. (8)). It appears that objections to the notice may not be raised at this stage, but should be the subject of an appeal under subs. (7). Breach of an order is an offence punishable with a maximum £2,500 fine on summary conviction (subs. (9)).

Public registers

95.—(1) It shall be the duty of each principal litter authority other than [an English] county council, [a] [...] or [a] joint board to maintain, in accordance with this section, a register containing copies of—

(a) all orders made by the authority under section 90(3)) above; and

(b) all street litter control notices issued under section 93(1) above.

(2) Where the requirements of a street litter control notice are varied or added to on an appeal under section 94(7) above a copy of the order making the variation or addition shall be included in the register.

(3) Copies of the orders and notices required to be kept in the register shall be so kept for so long as the order or notice is in force.

(4) It shall be the duty of each authority maintaining a register under this section—

(a) to secure that the register is available, at all reasonable times, for inspection by the public free of charge; and

(b) to afford to members of the public facilities for obtaining copies of the documents kept in the register, on payment of reasonable charges.

(5) A register under this section need not be kept in documentary form.

DEFINITION
"principal litter authority": s.86(2) and (3).

COMMENCEMENT
April 1, 1991 (S.I. 1991 No. 1042).

AMENDMENTS
Subsection (1) was amended by the Local Government (Wales) Act 1994, Sched. 9, para. 17 and by the Local Government etc. (Scotland) Act 1994, Sched. 13, para. 167(15) and Sched. 14.

GENERAL NOTE
This section imposes an obligation on district and London borough councils, and councils in Scotland, to keep public registers of: (a) orders designating litter control areas; and (b) street litter control notices.

Application of Part II

96.—(1) This section applies to litter and refuse collected—

(a) by an authority or person in pursuance of section 89(1) above;

(b) by a principal litter authority in pursuance of section 92(9) above; or

(c) by any person in pursuance of section 93 above.

(2) The Secretary of State may make regulations providing that prescribed provisions of Part II shall have effect, with such modifications (if any) as may be prescribed—

(a) as if references to controlled waste or controlled waste of a prescribed description included references to litter and refuse to which this section applies or any description of such litter and refuse;

(b) as if references to controlled waste or controlled waste of a prescribed description collected under section 45 above included references to litter and refuse collected as mentioned in subsection (1) above or any description of such litter and refuse.

(3) The powers conferred by this section are exercisable in relation to litter and refuse to which it applies whether or not the circumstances are such

that the litter or refuse would be treated as controlled waste apart from this section and this section is not to affect the interpretation of the expressions defined in section 75 above.

DEFINITION
"principal litter authority": s.86(2) and (3).

COMMENCEMENT
In force: See the Commencement section on p. 289.

GENERAL NOTE
This section applies to litter and refuse collected by litter authorities and other persons pursuant to the duties and power in Pt. IV. It allows the Secretary of State to make regulations applying provisions of Pt. II of the Act (with or without modifications) to such litter or refuse as if it were controlled waste and as if it were such waste collected by the waste collection authority. Such waste might not otherwise fall within any of the categories of controlled waste in s.75(4)–(7), which are concerned essentially with waste from premises. The provisions would, for example, make it clear that such items belong to the litter authority and may be recycled or otherwise dealt with under Pt. II.

Transitional provision relating to section 89

97.—(1) The Secretary of State may, for the purposes of the transition to the duties imposed by section 89 above on local authorities and educational bodies, by regulations, make provision—
   (a) modifying that section, or
   (b) modifying Part I of the Local Government Act 1988 (competition rules for functional work or works contracts).
   (2) Regulations under this section may make different provision for different descriptions of authorities, different areas or other different circumstances or cases.
   (3) In this section—
   "educational bodies" means the governing bodies and education authorities mentioned in section 89(1)(f) above; and
   "local authorities" means the local authorities mentioned in section 89(1)(a) and (c) and (2)(a) above.

COMMENCEMENT
January 1, 1991 (s.164(2)).

GENERAL NOTE
This section is designed to assist the transition to the new duties as to litter and public cleanliness contained in s.89. The Secretary of State is given power to make regulations: (a) modifying those duties: and (b) modifying the provisions on competitive tendering in Pt. I of the Local Government Act 1988. The Regulations may make different provisions for different authorities or for different cases. The purpose of the provision was explained by Baroness Blatch in the House of Lords at Report Stage as follows:

> "The new clause gives the Secretary of State the power to make transitional provisions to protect the position of authorities who had already assigned contracts for the provision of the relevant services under the competitive tendering legislation before the new litter code was published.
> We appreciate that such contracts are likely to have to be modified in many cases to take account of the standards of litter clearance now required by the code. Indeed, so far as concerns future contracts, we have already taken action by postponing the rounds of competition due to be completed by January 1 and August 1 next year to August 1, 1991 and January 1, 1992 respectively, so as to make it possible for authorities to take full account of the code when drawing up their specifications.
> Where contracts had already been let before the code was promulgated, the new clause will give the Secretary of State the power to make the necessary transitional arrangements. These will provide for any additional work which may be necessary to be taken on board.

They will also protect the position of authorities until such time as this can be done. They will cover cases in which contracts have been let to the private sector and also those in which work has been assigned to the authority's own direct service organisation following competition under the terms of the Local Government Act 1988. We intend to announce the nature of the provision to be made as soon as possible, once the details have been finalised" (*Hansard*, H.L. Vol. 522, cols. 667–668).

Definitions

98.—(1) The following definitions apply for the interpretation of this Part.
(2) "Educational institution," in relation to England and Wales, means—
  (a) any university (within the meaning of the Education Reform Act 1988) funded by the Universities Funding Council under section 131 of that Act;
  (b) the Open University;
  (c) any institution which provides higher education or further education (or both) which is full-time education being an institution which—
    (i) is maintained by grants made by the Secretary of State under section 100(1)(b) of the Education Act 1944;
    (ii) is designated by or under regulations under section 218 of the Education Reform Act 1988 as an institution dependent for its maintenance on assistance from local education authorities; or
    (iii) is maintained by a local education authority;
  (d) any higher education institution funded by the Polytechnics and Colleges Funding Council under section 132 of the Education Reform Act 1988;
  (e) any city technology college or city college for the technology of the arts (within the meaning of section 105 of the Education Reform Act 1988);
  (f) any county school, voluntary school or maintained special school;
  (g) any grant-maintained school.
(3) "Educational institution," in relation to Scotland, means—
  (a) any university within the meaning of the Education Reform Act 1988 funded by the Universities Funding Council under section 131 of that Act;
  (b) the Open University;
  (c) a college of further education—
    (i) as defined in section 80(1) of the Self Governing Schools (Scotland) Act 1989 ("the 1989 Act"); or
    (ii) managed by a company by virtue of section 65(1) of the 1989 Act;
  (d) a grant-aided college within the meaning of section 77(5) of the Education (Scotland) Act 1980 ("the 1980 Act");
  (e) a technology academy within the meaning of section 68(1) of the 1989 Act;
  (f) a public school as defined in section 135(1) of the 1980 Act;
  (g) a grant-aided school as defined in section 135(1) of the 1980 Act;
  (h) a self-governing school within the meaning of section 1(3) of the 1989 Act.
(4) "Joint board", in relation to Scotland, has the meaning given by section 235(1) of the Local Government (Scotland) Act 1973.
(5) "Highway" (and "highway maintainable at the public expense"), "special road" and "trunk road," in relation to England and Wales, have the same meaning as in the Highways Act 1980 and "public road," "special road" and "trunk road," in relation to Scotland, have the same meaning as in the Roads (Scotland) Act 1984.
(6) "Statutory undertaker" means—

(a) any person authorised by any enactment to carry on any railway, light railway, tramway or road transport undertaking;
(b) any person authorised by any enactment to carry on any canal, inland navigation, dock, harbour or pier undertaking; or
(c) any relevant airport operator (within the meaning of Part V of the Airports Act 1986).

COMMENCEMENT
In force: See the Commencement section on p. 289.

GENERAL NOTE

Subs. (4): joint board
Section 235(1) of the Local Government (Scotland) Act 1973 defines this term as any body set up by two or more local authorities to further their purposes and consisting entirely of members appointed by them. Examples are the Board for Lothian and Borders Police and the Board for the Forth Road Bridge.

Subs. (5): highways
The relevant definitions from the Highways Act 1980 are as follows:
(1) "Highway" means the whole or part of a highway other than a ferry or waterway.
(2) Where a highway passes over a bridge or through a tunnel, that bridge or tunnel is to be taken ... to be a part of the highway (s.328).
"Special road" means a highway, or a proposed highway, which is a special road in accordance with s.16 [of the 1980 Act].
"Trunk road" means a highway, or a proposed highway, which is a trunk road by virtue of s.10(1) or s.19 [of the 1980 Act] or by virtue of an order or direction under s.10 [of the 1980 Act] or under any other enactment (s.239(1)).
As regards Scotland, the definition of "road", "special road" and "trunk road" may be found in s.151(1) of the Roads (Scotland) Act 1984.
Privately-maintained or "unadopted" roads are therefore not included in the relevant litter clearing and cleaning duties of Pt. IV.

Statutory undertakers
The relevant classes of statutory undertakers are all those with transport-related functions: *e.g.* railways, underground railways, ports, harbours, airports, bus stations and canals.

Abandoned trolleys
Powers in relation to abandoned shopping and luggage trolleys

99.—(1) A local authority may, subject to subsection (3) below, resolve that Schedule 4 to this Act is to apply in its area; and if a local authority does so resolve, that Schedule shall come into force in its area on the day specified in the resolution, which must not be before the expiration of the period of three months beginning with the day on which the resolution is passed.

(2) A local authority shall publish in at least one newspaper circulating in its area a notice that the authority has passed a resolution under this section and indicating the general effect of that Schedule.

(3) It shall be the duty of the local authority, before making any resolution for the application of Schedule 4 to this Act in its area, to consult with the persons or representatives of persons who appear to the authority to be persons who will be affected by the application of that Schedule.

(4) It shall be the duty of a local authority from time to time to consult about the operation of Schedule 4 to this Act with the persons or representatives of persons who appear to be affected by its operation.

(5) In this section "local authority" means—
(a) the council of a district;
(b) the council of a London borough;
(c) the Common Council of the City of London;
(d) the council of the Isles of Scilly;

[(dd) in Wales the council of a county or county borough;] and
   (e) in Scotland, [a council constituted under section 2 of the Local
        Government etc. (Scotland) Act 1994].
(6) In Schedule 4 to this Act "the local authority" means any local
authority which has resolved that that Schedule is to apply in its area.

COMMENCEMENT
January 1, 1991 (s.164(2)).

Amendment
Subsection (5) was amended by the Local Government (Wales) Act 1994, Sched. 9, para. 17 and
by the Local Government etc. (Scotland) Act 1994, Sched. 13, para. 167(16).

GENERAL NOTE
This section allows local authorities at district level to resolve to apply to their area the
provisions of Sched. 4, relating to abandoned shopping and luggage trolleys.
    There is a general duty to consult about the operation of Sched. 4 from time to time with
persons or representatives of persons who appear to be affected by its operation (subs. (3)). The
main elements of Sched. 4 are:
    (1) it applies to any shopping or luggage trolley (defined in para. 5) found on any land in
         the open air by an authorised officer of the authority and appearing to him to be
         abandoned (para. 1);
    (2) it does not apply to trolleys found on land within the descriptions of para. 1(2);
    (3) trolleys to which the Schedule applies may be seized and removed to a place under the
         control of the authority (para. 2(1));
    (4) the power of removal is subject to consent or notification requirements where the
         trolley is found on land which appears to be occupied (para. 2(2));
    (5) trolleys seized must be kept for six weeks and may then be sold or otherwise disposed
         of (para. 3(1));
    (6) this is subject to the obligation to serve notice on any person believed to be the owner
         (para. 3(2)) and to make reasonable enquiries to ascertain who owns it (para. 3(5));
    (7) owners have the right to delivery of their trolleys, subject to payment of such charge as
         the authority requires (para. 3(3) and (4));
    (8) the authority, in setting charges, shall secure that the sums payable are sufficient,
         taking one year with another, to cover the cost of removal, storage and disposal (para.
         4(1));
    (9) the authority may agree a scheme for collection with owners of trolleys, and in such
         cases no charge may be demanded under para. 3 (para. 4(2)).
    For a case on obstruction of the highway by supermarket trolleys (parked rather than
abandoned), see *Devon County Council v. Gateway Foodmarkets* [1990] LMELR Issue 3, Vol.
21, p. 96; *The Daily Telegraph*, March 22, 1990, D.C.

PART V

AMENDMENT OF THE RADIOACTIVE SUBSTANCES ACT 1960

[Part V was repealed by the Radioactive Substances Act 1993 with effect from August 27, 1993]

PART VI

GENETICALLY MODIFIED ORGANISMS

This part of the Act contains new provisions imposing control over various activities involving
genetically modified organisms (GMOs). Section 106(1) states the purpose of the provision as
"preventing or minimising any damage to the environment which may arise from the escape or
release from human control of genetically modified organisms."
    It is helpful to appreciate from the outset that the activities governed by this Part are
importing, acquiring, keeping, releasing and marketing genetically modified organisms. Their
contained use is, in general though not entirely, governed by a separate regime under the Health
and Safety at Work etc. Act 1974: see further below.

Royal Commission Report

The issues raised by the possibility of genetically modified or engineered organisms being released into the environment were considered by the Royal Commission on Environmental Pollution in its Thirteenth Report, *The Release of Genetically Engineered Organisms into the Environment* (Cm. 720, July 1989). The benefits and risks of the new technology were stated by the Royal Commission as follows (paras. 1.2, 1.3, 4.2 and 5.8).

"1.2 Genetic engineering offers the prospect of major improvements in medicine, in industry and in agricultural quality and efficiency. It is also likely to help in dealing with problems of environmental pollution and to lead to new commercial products. The UK is well fitted scientifically to make advances in genetic engineering.

1.3 As in many other fields of technological innovation, potential benefits bring potential risks. The risks that genetic engineering may entail, and the associated ethical considerations, have been debated since the technology came into existence in the early 1970s. There can rarely have been a new technology which has attracted so much intense discussion of its potential risks from such an early point in its development. To some extent this reflects the nature of the science. There is a natural apprehension stemming from the belief that scientists are now manipulating something as fundamental as life itself. The discussion also reflects an awareness that the relationship between living things and their environment is complex and imperfectly understood. Changes to one may have unknown, widespread and lasting effects on the other. Consideration of the environmental implications of releasing GEOs forms the main thrust of this Report.

4.2 Organisms which survive and become established could affect the environment in a variety of ways—both beneficial and undesirable. Some releases may alter the diversity of species in the environment, including changing the composition of existing communities. Such effects could produce noticeable changes in the countryside, locally or more widely, and could also have an economic impact, for example if the new organisms proved to be successful predators, competitors, parasites or pathogens of crop plants. Some organisms could pose a threat to human health. At the most extreme, new organisms could conceivably affect major environmental processes such as weather patterns, the nitrogen cycle or other regenerative soil processes.

5.8 We conclude that, although the environment is generally resilient, resistant to invasion by alien organisms and robust to biological perturbations, it is probable that some organisms, once released to the environment will become established. Most are likely to pose no hazard but others may cause varying degrees of disturbances which, in the extreme, could have serious environmental consequences."

The Commission, in the light of these conclusions, proposed "a precautionary but realistic system of regulation" (para. 5.4.7). The Commission's main recommendations were:

(1) statutory control of releases of genetically engineered organisms (GEOs) to the environment;

(2) involvement of both the Secretary of State for the Environment and the Health and Safety Commission (acting on behalf of the Secretary of State for Employment) in decisions on release but with the Secretary of State for the Environment taking primary responsibility with regard to the environmental consequences of releases:

(3) a general statutory duty of care on all those responsible for release of a GEO to take all reasonable steps for protection of human health and safety and that of the environment;

(4) a "release licence" to be required before release of a GEO could take place, with powers of revocation and amendment of licences;

(5) proposed releases of GEOs to be notified to the licensing authorities, with full details including the results of a safety assessment;

(6) each stage in the development of a GEO to be the subject of a licence with the appropriate licensing authorities to be informed and consulted in relation to applications for product licensing involving GEOs;

(7) wide additional and ancillary regulatory powers to be given to the Secretary of State for the Environment;

(8) every proposed release to be screened by a local committee and then, if passed, thoroughly scrutinised by a national committee of experts;

(9) referral of each application for a release licence or product approval to a committee of experts for assessment with regard to environmental protection and human health and safety;

(10) arrangements to be made for the registration of companies or other organisations carrying out trial releases;

(11) statutory strict liability on any person, or the directors of any company or other organisation, responsible for carrying out the release of a GEO without the necessary licence and registration;

(12) power to impose licence conditions as to monitoring the released GEOs and their environmental impacts;

(13) public registers of applications and licences and authorised releases, and general public access to information forming the basis of decisions on release;

(14) extension of controls over contained work on GEOs to minimise the risk of damage to the environment, for example in relation to waste disposal, storage and transport.

Some, but by no means all, of these recommendations are embodied in Pt. VI of the Act.

Previous arrangements

Prior to the introduction of statutory controls in Pt. VI of the Act, release of GMOs was covered by a variety of arrangements, some statutory and some non-statutory. Following the reports of two working parties on *Experimental Manipulation of the Genetic Composition of Micro-Organisms* (Cm. 5880, 1975, "the Ashby Working Party") and *The Laboratory Use of Dangerous Pathogens* (Cm. 6054, 1975, "the Godber Working Party"), a further working party was established "to draft a central code of practice and to make recommendations for the establishment of a central advisory service for laboratories using the techniques available for genetic manipulation." This working party reported in 1976: *Report of the Working Party on the Practice of Genetic Manipulation* (Cm. 6600, "the Williams Working Party"). The recommendations of this report led to the establishment of the Genetic Manipulation Advisory Group (GMAG) with a risk assessment and advisory rôle. GMAG produced various reports and a series of guidance notes.

At that stage, concern was mainly focused upon the risks arising from contained work with GMOs, primarily in the laboratory. The relevant statutory powers were therefore those under the Health and Safety at Work, etc. Act 1974, and in 1978 regulations were made under that Act requiring notification to the HSE of intention to carry out genetic manipulation: Health and Safety (Genetic Manipulation) Regulations 1978 No. 752. Using Health and Safety at Work Act powers, HSE inspectors could therefore exercise control over work activities involving GMOs including, where appropriate, their release. The HSE took the view, however, that because their powers derived from health and safety at work legislation, they could not be used to prevent damage to the natural environment.

Advisory Committee on Genetic Manipulation

In 1984 the Health and Safety Commission established an Advisory Committee on Genetic Manipulation (ACGM) to replace GMAG. ACGM was given an advisory rôle to the Health and Safety Commission and Executive, and to related Ministers, including environment, on various aspects of genetic manipulation. Again, the main concern of the Committee was on contained experimental and industrial work and the health and safety aspects, and it continues to advise and publish guidance on these issues and the UK legislation implementing EC legislation on the contained use of certain GMOs. However, the ACGM also took a close interest in the planned release of GMOs and established a working group on that subject which later became the Planned Release Sub-Committee (later the Intentional Introductions Sub-Committee or IISC). In 1986, guidance prepared by that Sub-Committee was issued as ACGM/HSE/Note 3, *The Planned Release of Genetically Manipulated Organisms for Agricultural and Environmental Purposes: Guidelines for Risk Assessment and for the Notification of Proposals for Such Work*. The recommendations of ACGM in the Guidelines were that:

(1) in the absence of any statutory requirements, all proposals for the release of GMOs should nonetheless be notified to the ACGM for its consideration;

(2) the notifier should be advised on the possible environmental consequences of release by an appropriately constituted local body including relevant scientific expertise and, where appropriate, a local environmental health officer;

(3) various listed factors should be taken into account when making the initial local risk assessment;

(4) it was premature to devise a single, broadly applicable risk assessment scheme, though material was available to achieve a measure of consistency. All proposals to release GMOs should therefore be considered by ACGM on a case-by-case basis.

These arrangements were originally implemented by the HSE on a voluntary basis. However, the arrangements were put on to a statutory basis by the Genetic Manipulation Regulations 1989 No. 1810, in force from November 1, 1989 (see also the HSE Guidance Notes on the Regulations). The effect of the Regulations is to require at least 30 days' advance notice of intention to carry out activities involving genetic manipulation to be given to the HSE (reg. 5(1)). In the case of activities involving an international introduction into the environment, the period is 90 days. The Regulations also require the establishment by persons carrying out such activities of a risk assessment committee (reg. 6(2)). The risk assessment of the activity determines the type of notification required, according to the hazard groupings of Sched. 1 (reg. 5(4) and (5)). Further work of ACGM involving release to the environment includes ACGM/HSE/Note 6—*Large Scale Use of Genetically Manipulated Organisms* (October, 1990), Appendix IV of which deals with environmental aspects of risk assessment in arriving at "good large-scale practice."

In addition to these controls, specific legislation applicable to products comprising or including GMOs include the Food and Environment Protection Act 1985 (pesticides), the Medicines Acts 1968 and 1971, the Plant and Health (Great Britain) Act 1967, the Animals (Scientific Procedures) Act 1986, the Food and Environment Protection Act 1985, Pt. II (deposits at sea), the Food Act 1984 and the Consumer Protection Act 1987.

The conclusion of the Royal Commission, in considering these measures, was that, whilst many could in principle be used to control the release of GMOs to the environment, even taken together all the measures did not appear to cover all possible circumstances. Even the regulations made under the Health and Safety at Work, etc. Act, whilst referring specifically to GMOs, presented problems in controlling releases which presented a risk to the natural environment but which do not affect human health or safety. The Commission's conclusion was that "there is a clear need for fresh legislation to provide specifically for the control of releases of all categories of genetically engineered organism" (para. 7.23).

See also Neil Hawke, *Man-made micro-organisms and the environment* [1988] New L.J. 628.

The Introduction of Part VI
In June 1989 the DoE, Welsh Office and Scottish Office issued a Consultation Paper on *Proposals for Additional Legislation on the Intentional Release of Genetically Modified Organisms*. The Paper was published in advance of the Royal Commission's Report. In the light of existing controls, the Government concluded that there were good reasons for considering further environmental safety measures to control the release of GMOs; any such system, it was suggested, would need to be compatible both with general environmental protection measures and the human health and safety regulatory system.

Various approaches were canvassed and it was proposed (para. 6) that the augmented system should provide a comprehensive régime for environmental protection with four main elements: (1) a general duty of care on those releasing GMOs to protect the environment; (2) notification to Ministers by those proposing to release GMOs; (3) authorisation by Ministers of proposed releases; and (4) appropriate enforcement of the provisions.

At the stage of the Government introducing such measures in the Environmental Protection Bill, the Health and Safety Executive and DoE issued a useful explanatory leaflet on the workings of Pt. VI, entitled *Biotechnology and Genetically Modified Organisms: The Proposed New Controls*.

The Scheme of Pt. VI
The main features of Pt. VI of the Act are as follows:—
   (1) Sections 106 and 107 contain a series of definitions of key terms and concepts.
   (2) Section 108 contains a general prohibition on importation, acquisition, release and marketing of GMOs without carrying out a risk assessment of possible damage to the environment and notifying the Secretary of State of the intention to carry out the activity. Persons keeping GMOs are also under an obligation to carry out a risk assessment and to notify the Secretary of State of the keeping of the GMOs.
   (3) Section 109 places a series of duties of care relating to the risk of environmental damage on persons proposing to import or acquire GMOs, persons keeping GMOs and persons proposing to release GMOs.
   (4) Section 110 gives the Secretary of State power to serve prohibition notices in relation to acts or activities involving GMOs which would entail a risk of causing damage to the environment.
   (5) By s.111, in certain cases to be prescribed, the importation, acquisition, keeping, release or marketing of GMOs is prohibited, except in pursuance of a consent granted

by the Secretary of State and in accordance with any limitations and conditions to which the consent is subject. In such cases the requirements of ss.108 and 109 do not apply. Section 112 contains provisions as to express and implied conditions and limitations on such consents. Such conditions may not be imposed for the sole purpose of securing the health and safety of workers (s.112(1)). Consents will contain a series of conditions implied by statute as to reasonable measures for risk assessment, notification and use of best available techniques not entailing excessive cost for the purpose of preventing damage to the environment.

(6) By s.113 a scheme of fees and charges for consents may be instituted.

(7) Sections 114–117 provide for the appointment of inspectors and give various powers of entry, inspection, obtaining information, and dealing with imminent dangers.

(8) Section 118 creates various offences in relation to contravention of the requirements of Pt. VI.

(9) Sections 119–121 contain ancillary provisions on offences, including the onus of proof and powers to order matters to be remedied, or to recover the costs of remedial steps.

(10) Sections 122 and 123 make provision for public registers of information relating to matters under Pt. VI of the Act.

(11) Section 124 provides for the appointment of a committee to advise the Secretary of State on the exercise of his powers.

(12) Section 125 allows the delegation of certain enforcement functions to officers of public authorities.

Public access to information

Originally Pt. VI did not provide on its face for public access to information, save in relation to the advertising of applications for consent. However, the Government gave an assurance (DoE News Release No. 140, March 1, 1990) that it was committed to allowing access to information as for other Parts of the Act under the Secretary of State's inherent powers of disclosure. In the event, express statutory provisions to that effect were inserted as ss.122 and 123.

Relationship to Royal Commission proposals

At the House of Lords Second Reading stage, the Chairman of the RCEP, Lord Lewis of Newnham, voiced the following reservation about how the Act might operate in practice:

"I have a certain reservation. The Bill makes provision for releases and other activities not involved in releases to be the subject of one of three different levels of control. First, it involves specific consent of the authorities. That is very much a recommendation for the Beringer Committee which we are all very happy to see enforced. However, there are two other possibilities: namely, notifying the authorities in advance of a release or following a special procedure for risk assessment. I have no quarrel with those in principle. However, I am anxious as to whether the Government, when drawing up regulations under the Bill may immediately allow certain classes of releases to be subject only to the second and third categories.

My belief—and it is also the belief of the Royal Commission—is that that would be premature. At present, every prospective release of a GMO should be subject to the full consultative procedure. I believe that to be very important not only for the safety of the community but also for the sensitivity of industry as a whole. We have not enough knowledge of the possible impact of such organisms on the environment to allow exceptions to that rule." (*Hansard*, H.L. Vol. 519, cols. 517–518.)

The Government did not follow the suggestions of the RCEP on strict liability for activities involving GMOs (see above). This was regarded as a wider and more complex issue than general regulation, and one that needs to be considered on an international basis: *Hansard*, H.L. Vol. 522, cols. 704–706.

Advisory Committee on Releases to the Environment

In acknowledgment of the need for expert advice as to questions both of environmental and human safety in relation to GMOs, in 1990 the Government established a single expert committee to advise on both aspects in relation to the introduction of GMOs to the environment. The committee is known as the Advisory Committee on Releases to The Environment (ACRE). Section 124 deals with the appointment of that committee. The Government announced that the new committee would be chaired by Professor John Beringer of the Unit of Molecular Genetics at the University of Bristol (its chairman at the time of its Annual Report No. 2, 1994/95, was Professor M.H. Williamson of the University of York) and that it will have representatives from various areas of expertise (see further, note to s.124).

The DoE/ACRE produce a number of publications. These include the following:

The ACRE's Annual Reports (known as the "red series", the second of which covered 1994/95);

The DoE and ACRE Newsletter (an occasional free publication, of which No. 4 was published in December 1994).

DoE/ACRE Guidance Notes (known as the "green series"), obtainable from DoE Publications Sales Unit, Block 3, Spur 7, Government Buildings, Lime Grove, Eastcote HA4 8SF, as follows:

No. 1   The Regulation and Control of the Deliberate Release of Genetically Modified Organisms (1993)

No. 2   Fast Track Procedures for Certain GMO Releases (1994)

[No. 3   has been withdrawn]

No. 4   Guidance for Experimental Releases of Genetically Modified Plants (1994)

No. 5   Guidance for Experimental Releases of Genetically Modified Micro-organisms (excluding viruses and similar agents) (1994)

No. 6   Guidance for Experimental Releases of Genetically Modified Baculoviruses (1995)

No. 7   Guidance to the Genetically Modified Organisms (Deliberate Release) Regulations 1995 (1995).

In preparation at the end of 1995 was No. 8: Guidance for Experimental Releases of Genetically Modified Fish.

The DoE additionally produces a "blue series" of Research Reports on topics such as risk assessment of various forms of release, and the U.K. perspective on certain issues, available from the DoE Publications Sales Unit (details above).

European Community and international obligations, UK implementation
The Council of the European Community has promulgated two directives on GMOs. These govern, respectively, the contained use of genetically modified micro-organisms, and the deliberate release of genetically modified organisms.

Contained Use
Directive 90/219/EEC (O.J. L117, May 8, 1990, p. 1) deals with *The Contained Use of Genetically Modified Micro-Organisms*. This Directive is not, it will be appreciated, implemented primarily by or under Pt. VI. A brief review of its implementation and development is perhaps of some value, however. The Directive lays down common measures for the "contained use" of GMOs with a view to protecting human health and the environment. The measures include prior risk assessment based on a list of "parameters" set out in the Directive. Others relate to the observation of "good microbiological practice", containment measures, information and notification, emergency plans and reporting of accidents.

Implementation of Directive 90/219/EEC is through the Genetically Modified Organisms (Contained Use) Regulations 1992 (as amended by S.I. 1993 No. 15 and S.I. 1996 No. 967). The 1992 Regulations were made under the Health and Safety at Work, etc., Act 1974 and the European Communities Act 1972, but the 1993 Regulations were made under Pt. VI (ss.108 and 126), demonstrating the potential for overlap and interplay between the two regimes. As is the case in a number of other Member States, the U.K. implementing measures govern the contained use of genetically modified organisms generally, rather than merely of *micro*-organisms.

As noted below E.C. policy on biotechnology and the control of GMOs generally has been undergoing change, and this is reflected in the development of Directive 90/219/EEC. At the end of 1995 the position was as follows. Commission Directive 94/51/EC (O.J. L297/29, 18.11.94), made under article 21 of Directive 90/219/EEC, substituted into the 1990 Directive a revised Annex II containing simplified criteria for classifying GMOs into Group I or Group II. Risk assessment and other procedures for Group II GMOs are more stringent than those for Group I GMOs. The key to the simplified criteria is an explicitly risk-based approach: the likelihood of the GMOs in question causing disease to humans, animals or plants or having adverse effects on the environment. The date for implementation in Member States of Directive 94/51/EC was April 30, 1995, but it was eventually implemented in the U.K. by S.I. 1996 No. 967. Implementation depended in practice on the European Commission producing revised guidelines for applying the new criteria (which guidelines are to be included in a revision of the Health and Safety Executive's Guide to the Genetically Modified Organisms (Contained Use) Regulations 1992 (L29, 1993)). Those revised guidelines (replacing Commission Decision 91/448/EEC, O.J. L239, 28.08.91) eventually appeared as Commission Decision 96/134 (O.J. L31, 9.2.96), but the HSE's revised guide had not appeared at the time of writing. Meanwhile, a major overhaul of Directive 90/219/EEC which would abandon the distinction between Groups I and II and would simplify the notification procedures involved is underway (COM(95)640).

Directive 90/220/EEC (O.J. L117, May 8, 1990, p. 15) on *The Deliberate Release into the Environment of Genetically Modified Organisms* deals with deliberate releases of GMOs and the marketing of products containing GMOs. This Directive is implemented in the U.K. by Pt. VI and regulations made under this Part (see below). In the case of GMOs released in the course of research and development (as opposed to marketing) the release must be pre-notified to the competent authority, together with information specified in the Directive and a risk evaluation statement in relation to human health and the environment. The authority is then under an obligation to check the notification, carry out its own evaluation and any necessary tests, and record its decision in writing. Release may not take place without the authority's written consent. Products containing GMOs must similarly be pre-notified before being placed on the market. Written consent of the competent authority must be obtained and the product must comply with all other applicable Community legislation. The dossiers relating to approved products must be forwarded to the Commission and circulated to all Member States. The Directive was adapted to technical progress by Directive 94/15/EC which distinguishes between genetically modified higher plants and other genetically modified organisms. Directive 90/220/EC provides for simplified application procedures to be established regarding the release of genetically modified plants, and Decision 94/730/EC (O.J. L292/31, 12.11.94) established those procedures on the basis of criteria established by Commission Decision 93/584/EEC (O.J. L279/42, 12.11.93).

Directive 90/220/EEC is implemented by Pt. VI and the Genetically Modified Organisms (Deliberate Release) Regulations 1992 (S.I. 1992 No. 3280, as amended by S.I. 1993 No. 152). The subsequent adaptation to technical progress by Directive 94/15/EC was implemented with effect from March 8, 1995, through further amendments to the Deliberate Release Regulations by S.I. 1995 No. 304, which also introduced amendments to take account of Decision 94/730/EC. Guidance on the regulations has been issued and is noted above, at *Advisory Committee on Releases to the Environment.*

Subsequent developments in E.C. policy
E.C. policy on biotechnology and GMOs has been responding to pressures of competition from elsewhere in the world (notably Japan and the USA) in this potentially enormous market. The concern that the E.C. may be, or be perceived to be, over-regulated is considered in the White Paper on Growth, Competitiveness and Employment (COM(93)700 final) and the subsequent Commission Communication on Biotechnology (COM(94)219 final, O.J. C175/2, 28.6.94). There has also been considerable controversy over the related issue of the intellectual property rights to GMOs, particularly where human genetic material is involved: the Proposal for a Directive on this issue failed to reach adoption despite the efforts of a conciliation committee under the Co-decision procedure for its adoption, in the face of European Parliament opposition to it.

Work on safety issues relating to GMOs in the workplace and in the environment has also been carried out by an ad hoc group of government, scientific and industry experts under the OECD. This group made recommendations on risk assessment criteria in its 1986 Report, *R—DNA Safety Considerations.*

Further discussion on the international aspects of the control and regulation of GMOs can be found in the article by Richard B. Stewart and Maria A. Martinez, *International Aspects of Biotechnology: Implications for Environmental Law and Policy* [1989] J.E.L. Vol. 1, No. 2, p. 157.

Territorial extent
By s.127(2), Pt. VI, except as to importation of GMOs, applies to the territorial sea adjacent to Great Britain, and to the designated British Continental Shelf. Pt. VI applies to Northern Ireland so far as it relates to importation of GMOs. Section 127(2) applies to Northern Ireland without that restriction, in so far as it relates to the Continental Shelf (s.164(4)). It is intended in due course to make an Order in Council replicating Pt. VI in Northern Ireland (*Hansard*, H.L. Vol. 522, col. 716).

COMMENCEMENT
Part VI came into force on January 1, 1993 and February 1, 1993 (S.I. 1992 No. 3253) later than the October 1991 date required by the relevant E.C. Directives (*Hansard*, H.L. Vol. 522, col. 1261).

Preliminary

Purpose of Part VI and meaning of "genetically modified organisms" and related expressions

106.—(1) This Part has effect for the purpose of preventing or minimising any damage to the environment which may arise from the escape or release from human control of genetically modified organisms.

(2) In this Part the term "organism" means any acellular, unicellular or multicellular entity (in any form), other than humans or human embryos; and, unless the context otherwise requires, the term also includes any article or substance consisting or including biological matter.

(3) For the purpose of subsection (2) above "biological matter" means anything (other than an entity mentioned in that subsection) which consists of or includes—

(a) tissue or cells (including gametes or propagules) or subcellular entities, of any kind, capable of replication or of transferring genetic material, or

(b) genes or other genetic material, in any form, which are so capable,

and it is immaterial, in determining if something is or is not an organism or biological matter, whether it is the product of natural or artificial processes of reproduction and, in the case of biological matter, whether it has ever been part of a whole organism.

(4) For the purposes of this Part an organism is "genetically modified" if any of the genes or other genetic material in the organism—

(a) have been modified by means of an artificial technique prescribed in regulations by the Secretary of State; or

(b) are inherited or otherwise derived, through any number of replications, from genes or other genetic material (from any source) which were so modified.

(5) The techniques which may be prescribed for the purposes of subsection (4) above include—

(a) any technique for the modification of any genes or other genetic material by the recombination, insertion or deletion of, or of any component parts of, that material from its previously occurring state, and

(b) any other technique for modifying genes or other genetic material which in the opinion of the Secretary of State would produce organisms which should for the purposes of this Part be treated as having been genetically modified,

but do not include techniques which involve no more than, or no more than the assistance of, naturally occurring processes of reproduction (including selective breeding techniques or *in vitro* fertilisation).

(6) It is immaterial for the purposes of subsections (4) and (5) above whether the modifications of genes or other genetic material effected by a prescribed technique are produced by direct operations on that genetic material or are induced by indirect means (including in particular the use of viruses, microbial plasmids or other vector systems or of mutation inducing agents).

(7) In this Part, where the context permits, a reference to "reproduction", in relation to an organism, includes a reference to its replication or its transferring genetic material.

GENERAL NOTE

Subsection (1) states the purpose of Pt. VI, whilst subss. (2)–(7) provide a series of highly technical definitions dealing with what constitutes a "genetically modified organism".

Subs. (2)

Organism. The term is defined to include all living things, except humans or human embryos. It also includes "biological matter", which is defined in subs. (3) to include tissues, cells, subcellular material, genes or genetic material, which in each case is capable of replication or of transferring genetic material. The qualification in respect of replication or transfer is to ensure that matter is covered in situations where it might spontaneously hand on genetic material to other organisms which in turn might damage the environment. It is expressly provided that the origin of the organism or biological matter is immaterial, so that an organism reproduced by artificial processes is still an organism for the purposes of Pt. VI.

Subs. (4)

Genetically modified. Genetic modification means the modification of any genes or genetic material in the organism by the various artificial techniques to be prescribed in Regulations made by the Secretary of State. These are prescribed in the Genetically Modified Organisms (Deliberate Release) Regulations 1992 (S.I. 1992 No. 3280), reg. 3. By subs. 4(b) the definition also extends to cases where the genes or genetic material in the organism have not been directly modified but were inherited or otherwise derived from genes or genetic material which were so modified. This provision as to the inheritance of modified genes is crucial because the effects of genetic modification on the properties of an organism might not become apparent for several generations after the original modification. Subsection (5) describes the techniques which may be prescribed for the purposes of subs. (4) and, importantly, excludes techniques involving only naturally occurring processes of reproduction (including selective breeding and *in vitro* fertilisation). By subs. (6) it is immaterial whether the genetic modification operations are direct or indirect, so for example including the introduction of genetic material by means of vector viruses.

Subs. (7)

Reproduction. This term is given an extended meaning to include not only the replication of an organism, but also the transferral of genetic material.

Scientific terms

Section 106 uses a number of scientific terms which are not defined and the meaning of which as terms of art may not be familiar to all lawyers. The following definitions are therefore set out below for convenience (adapted from *Chambers Science and Technology Dictionary*, Cambridge 1988).

Acellular: Not partitioned into cells.

Cell: The unit, consisting of nucleus and cytoplasm, of which plants and animals are composed.

Gametes: Reproductive cells which will unite in pairs to form zygotes; germ cells.

Microbial plasmid: A plasmid is a genetic element containing nucleic acid and able to replicate independently of its host's chromosome. "Microbial" connotes that the plasmid is sub-microscopic and would therefore include, for example, bacteria and yeasts.

Multicellular: Consisting of a number of cells.

Organisms: Animals, plants, fungi and micro-organisms.

Propagule: Any structure, sexual or asexual, and independent from the parent, which serves as a means of reproduction.

Tissue: An aggregate of similar cells forming a definite and continuous fabric, and usually having a comparable and definable function.

Unicellular: Consisting of a single cell.

Vector systems: A vector is an agent of transmission; in the context of genetic engineering it means a DNA molecule that can accept inserted DNA and can be used to transfer it from one organism to another. "Systems" appears to be used to incorporate the various types of vectors used in practice.

Meaning of "damage to the environment", "control" and related expressions in Part VI

107.—(1) The following provision have effect for the interpretation of this Part.

(2) The "environment" consists of land, air and water or any of those media.

(3) "Damage to the environment" is caused by the presence in the environment of genetically modified organisms which have (or of a single such organism which has) escaped or been released from a person's control and are (or is) capable of causing harm to the living organisms supported by the environment.

(4) An organism shall be regarded as present in the environment notwithstanding that it is present in or on any human or other organism, or any other thing, which is itself present in the environment.

(5) Genetically modified organisms present in the environment are capable of causing harm if—

    (a) they are individually capable, or are present in numbers such that together they are capable, of causing harm; or

    (b) they are able to produce descendants which will be capable, or which will be present in numbers such that together they will be capable, of causing harm;

and a single organism is capable of causing harm either if it is itself capable of causing harm or if it is able to produce descendants which will be so capable.

(6) "Harm" means harm to the health of humans or other living organisms or other interference with the ecological systems of which they form part and, in the case of many, includes offence caused to any of his senses or harm to his property.

(7) "Harmful" and "harmless" mean respectively, in relation to genetically modified organisms, their being capable or their being incapable of causing harm.

(8) The Secretary of State may by regulations provide, in relation to genetically modified organisms of any description specified in the regulations, that—

    (a) the capacity of those organisms for causing harm of any description so specified, or

    (b) harm of any description so specified,

shall be disregarded for such purpose of this Part as may be so specified.

(9) Organisms of any description are under the "control" of a person where he keeps them contained by any system of physical, chemical or biological barriers (or combination of such barriers) used for either or both of the following purposes, namely—

    (a) for ensuring that the organisms do not enter the environment or produce descendants which are not so contained; or

    (b) for ensuring that any of the organisms which do enter the environment, or any descendants of the organisms which are not so contained, are harmless.

(10) An organism under a person's control is "released" if he deliberately causes or permits it to cease to be under his control or the control of any other person and to enter the environment; and such an organism "escapes" if, otherwise than by being released, it ceases to be under his control or that of any other person and enters the environment.

(11) Genetically modified organisms of any description are "marketed" when products consisting of or including such organisms are placed on the market.

D<small>EFINITIONS</small>
   "descendant": s.127(1).
   "genetically modified organisms": s.106.
   "organism": s.106.

Subs. (3)

Damage to the environment. A number of components make up the definition of "damage to the environment". These are: (1) the presence of GMOs in the environment (see subs. (4)); (2) such GMOs have either been released from or have escaped from a person's control (see subs. (9)); (3) such GMOs are capable of causing harm to the living organisms supported by the environment (see subs. (5)).

Subs. (5)

Capable of causing harm. It is the capability of GMOs to cause harm rather than actual harm which is the crucial concept, in view of the difficulty or impossibility of recovering or rendering harmless many forms of GMO once they are outside human control. GMOs can be capable of causing harm either individually, collectively, or in their ability to produce descendants capable of causing such harm.

Subs. (6)

Harm. The expression is given an extended meaning consistent with that given in other parts of the Act. It appears that the harm could be direct or indirect, so that, for example, it would cover the situation where material produced by a GMO reached a watercourse and thus affected organisms present in or dependent on the water.

Subs. (8)

The Secretary of State has power to provide by regulations that certain descriptions of harm are to be disregarded for the purposes of Pt. VI. The Genetically Modified Organisms (Deliberate Release) Regulations 1992 (S.I. 1992 No. 3280), reg. 4, so provide in relation to harm caused to any organisms by GMOs which control the number and/or activity of any organisms or control toxic wastes, and in relation to the capacity of such GMOs to cause such harm. This disregard applies only where the GMOs have been released or marketed in pursuance of and in accordance with a consent granted under s.111(1) below or by another competent authority under Article 23(4) of Directive 90/220/EEC; and applies only for the purposes of ss.110(1), 112(5) and (7)(a) and 117(1) below.

Subs. (9)

Control. This subsection deals with the crucial distinction between GMOs which are under human control and GMOs which have entered the environment at large. "Control" means that the GMOs are contained by physical, chemical or biological barriers so as to ensure that: (a) they or their descendants do not enter the environment; or (b) if they or their descendants do enter the environment, they are harmless. A simple example of the first type of control would be a fence or cage preventing the escape of a genetically modified animal. An example of the second type of control would be the insertion of a gene that would ensure the death of the GMO on exposure to sunlight, so that the organism would not survive in the open.

Subs. (10)

Release; escape. This subsection distinguishes the two means by which a GMO may cease to be under human control and enter the environment. The first is deliberate "release", and the second is non-intentional "escape". "Release" would include the discharge of waste from an industrial process which contains GMOs.

General controls

Risk assessment and notification requirements

    108.—(1) Subject to subsections (2) and (7) below, no person shall import or acquire, release or market any genetically modified organisms unless, before that act—

(a) he has carried out an assessment of any risks there are (by reference to the nature of the organisms and the manner in which he intends to keep them after their importation or acquisition or, as the case may be, to release or market them) of damage to the environment being caused as a result of doing that act; and

(b) in such cases and circumstances as may be prescribed, he has given the Secretary of State such notice of his intention of doing that act and such information as may be prescribed.

(2) Subsection (1) above does not apply to a person proposing to do an act mentioned in that subsection who is required under section 111(1)(a) below to have a consent before doing that act.

(3) Subject to subsections (4) and (7) below, a person who is keeping genetically modified organisms shall, in such cases or circumstances and at such times or intervals as may be prescribed—

(a) carry out an assessment of any risks there are of damage to the environment being caused as a result of his continuing to keep them;

(b) give the Secretary of State notice of the fact that he is keeping the organisms and such information as may be prescribed.

(4) Subsection (3) above does not apply to a person who is keeping genetically modified organisms and is required under section 111(2) below to have a consent authorising him to continue to keep the organisms.

(5) It shall be the duty of a person who carries out an assessment under subsection (1)(a) or (3)(a) above to keep, for the prescribed period, such a record of the assessment as may be prescribed.

(6) A person required by subsection (1)(b) or (3)(b) above to give notice to the Secretary of State shall give the Secretary of State such further information as the Secretary of State may by notice in writing require.

(7) Regulations under this section may provide for exemptions, or for the granting by the Secretary of State of exemptions to particular persons or classes of person, from the requirements of subsection (1) or (3) above in such cases or circumstances, and to such extent, as may be prescribed.

(8) The Secretary of State may at any time—

(a) give directions to a person falling within subsection (1) above requiring that person to apply for a consent before doing the act in question; or

(b) give directions to a person falling within subsection (3) above requiring that person, before such date as may be specified in the direction, to apply for a consent authorising him to continue keeping the organisms in question;

and a person given directions under paragraph (a) above shall then, and a person given directions under paragraph (b) above shall from the specified date, be subject to section 111 below in place of the requirements of this section.

(9) Regulations under this section may—

(a) prescribe the manner in which assessments under subsection (1) or (3) above are to be carried out and the matters which must be investigated and assessed;

(b) prescribe minimum periods of notice between the giving of a notice under subsection (1)(b) above and the doing of the act in question;

(c) make provision allowing the Secretary of State to shorten or to extend any such period;

(d) prescribe maximum intervals at which assessments under subsection (3)(a) above must be carried out;

and the regulations may make different provision for different cases and different circumstances.

(10) In this section "prescribed" means prescribed by the Secretary of State in regulations under this section.

DEFINITIONS
  "acquire": s.127(1).
  "consent": s.127(1).
  "damage to the environment": s.107(3).
  "genetically modified organisms": s.106.
  "import": s.127(1).
  "market": s.107(11).
  "release": s.107(10).

GENERAL NOTE
The effect of this section is that all persons proposing to import, acquire, keep, release or market GMOs (other than those who require express consent under s.111) must assess the risks to the environment. The risks are to be assessed by reference to the nature of the GMOs and the proposed activity (subs. (1)(a)). In addition, in prescribed cases notice must be given to the Secretary of State of intention to carry out the activity, together with such information as may be prescribed (subs. (1)(b)). Similar obligations apply to persons keeping, or continuing to keep, GMOs (subs. (3)).

It is possible for the Secretary of State to give directions requiring express consent to be applied for and obtained (subs. (8)), in which case the requirements of s.111 as to consent will apply, and conditions may be imposed. If no such direction is given, then after a prescribed period from notification the act in question may be carried out (subs. (9)(b)).

The section has been used to make risk-assessment related amendments to the Genetically Modified Organisms (Contained Use) Regulations 1992 although the 1992 Regulations were not themselves made under Pt. VI: S.I. 1993 No. 15.

General duties relating to importation, acquisition, keeping, release or marketing of organisms

109.—(1) A person who—
  (a) is proposing to import or acquire any genetically modified organisms, or
  (b) is keeping any such organisms, or
  (c) is proposing to release or market any such organisms,
shall, subject to subsection (5) below, be subject to the duties specified in subsection (2), (3) or (4) below, as the case may be.

(2) A person who proposes to import or acquire genetically modified organisms—
  (a) shall take all reasonable steps to identify, by reference to the nature of the organisms and the manner in which he intends to keep them (including any precautions to be taken against their escaping or causing damage to the environment), what risks there are of damage to the environment being caused as a result of their importation or acquisition; and
  (b) shall not import or acquire the organisms if it appears that, despite any precautions which can be taken, there is a risk of damage to the environment being caused as a result of their importation or acquisition.

(3) A person who is keeping genetically modified organisms—
  (a) shall take all reasonable steps to keep himself informed of any damage to the environment which may have been caused as a result of his keeping the organisms and to identify what risks there are of damage to the environment being caused as a result of his continuing to keep them;
  (b) shall cease keeping the organisms if, despite any additional precautions which can be taken, it appears, at any time, that there is a risk of damage to the environment being caused as a result of his continuing to keep them; and
  (c) shall use the best available techniques not entailing excessive cost for keeping the organisms under his control and for preventing any damage to the environment being caused as a result of his continuing to keep the organisms;

and where a person is required by paragraph (b) above to cease keeping the organisms he shall dispose of them as safely and as quickly as practicable and paragraph (c) above shall continue to apply until he has done so.

(4) A person who proposes to release genetically modified organisms—

(a) shall take all reasonable steps to keep himself informed, by reference to the nature of the organisms and the extent and manner of the release (including any precautions to be taken against their causing damage to the environment), what risks there are of damage to the environment being caused as a result of their being released;

(b) shall not release the organisms if it appears that, despite the precautions which can be taken, there is a risk of damage to the environment being caused as a result of their being released; and

(c) subject to paragraph (b) above, shall use the best available techniques not entailing excessive cost for preventing any damage to the environment being caused as a result of their being released;

and this subsection applies, with the necessary modifications, to a person proposing to market organisms as it applies to a person proposing to release organisms.

(5) This section does not apply—

(a) to persons proposing to import or acquire, to release or to market any genetically modified organisms, in cases or circumstances where, under section 108 above, they are not required to carry out a risk assessment before doing that act;

(b) to persons who are keeping any genetically modified organisms and who—

(i) were not required under section 108 above to carry out a risk assessment before importing or acquiring them;

(ii) have not been required under that section to carry out a risk assessment in respect of the keeping of those organisms since importing or acquiring them; or

(c) to holders of consents, in the case of acts authorised by those consents.

DEFINITIONS
"acquire": s.127(1).
"consent": s.127(1).
"control": s.107(9).
"damage to the environment": s.107(3).
"escaping": s.107(10).
"genetically modified organisms": s.106.
"import": s.127(1).
"market": s.107(11).
"release": s.107(10).

GENERAL NOTE
This section imposes separate duties on: (a) persons proposing to import or acquire GMOs; (b) persons keeping GMOs; (c) persons proposing to release or market GMOs.

Subs. (2): persons importing or acquiring GMOs
Such persons are: (a) under a duty to take reasonable steps to identify the risks of damage to the environment from the import or acquisition; and (b) may not import or acquire the GMOs if it appears there are such risks despite any precautions that could be taken.

Subs. (3): persons keeping GMOs
Such persons are under a duty: (a) to take all reasonable steps to identify past damage to the environment and what risks there are of damage being caused as a result of their continuing to keep the GMOs; (b) to cease keeping the organisms if it appears at any time that there is a risk of damage to the environment despite any additional precautions that can be taken; and (c) to use the best available techniques not entailing excessive cost (BATNEEC) for keeping the GMOs under their control and preventing damage to the environment.

Subs. (4): persons proposing to release or market GMOs
Such a person: (a) is under a duty to take all reasonable steps to identify the risks of damage from the release or marketing; (b) shall not release or market the GMOs if it appears there is a risk of such damage; and (c) shall, if the GMOs are released or marketed, use BATNEEC for preventing any such damage.

BATNEEC
This term is not defined, though by s.119(1) in any proceedings for the offence of failing to use BATNEEC, the onus of showing there was no better available technique not entailing excessive cost than that used lies with the defendant. It appears that the expression is likely to be interpreted by the Secretary of State in the same way as in Pt. I of the Act in that it involves not only technology but also the way in which the technology is applied, for example training of personnel and the layout of premises. Similarly, what is "excessive cost" seems likely to be judged objectively, balancing the benefits of risk reduction against the costs. It will not depend on the financial resources of the person involved, the philosophy being that persons who cannot afford to apply the approximate techniques should not operate with GMOs. It was intended that the Advisory Committee on Releases to the Environment (ACRE) would issue expert guidance on good practice "in an easily-updated form" (see *Hansard*, H.L. Vol. 520, col. 1983), and this they have done: see the list of Guidance Notes set out above.

Subs. (5): exclusions
The subsection disapplies the requirements of the section: (a) to persons who are not, and have not been, required to carry out a risk assessment under s.108; and (b) to persons holding consents under s.111, in relation to acts authorised by such consents.

Prohibition notices

110.—(1) The Secretary of State may serve a notice under this section (a "prohibition notice") on any person he has reason to believe—

(a) is proposing to import or acquire, release or market any genetically modified organisms; or

(b) is keeping any such organisms;

if he is of the opinion that doing any such act in relation to those organisms or continuing to keep them, as the case may be, would involve a risk of causing damage to the environment.

(2) A prohibition notice may prohibit a person from doing an act mentioned in subsection (1)(a) above in relation to any genetically modified organisms or from continuing to keep them; and the prohibition may apply in all cases or circumstances or in such cases or circumstances as may be specified in the notice.

(3) A prohibition notice shall—

(a) state that the Secretary of State is, in relation to the person on whom it is served, of the opinion mentioned in subsection (1) above;

(b) specify what is, or is to be, prohibited by the notice; and

(c) if the prohibition is not to be effective on being served, specify the date on which the prohibition is to take effect;

and a notice may be served on a person notwithstanding that he may have a consent authorising any act which is, or is to be, prohibited by the notice.

(4) Where a person is prohibited by a prohibition notice from continuing to keep any genetically modified organisms, he shall dispose of them as quickly and safely as practicable or, if the notice so provides, as may be specified in the notice.

(5) The Secretary of State may at any time withdraw a prohibition notice served on any person by notice given to that person.

DEFINITIONS
   "acquire": s.127(1).
   "consent": s.127(1).
   "damage to the environment": s.107(3).

"genetically modified organisms": s.106.
"import": s.127(1).
"market": s.107(11).
"release": s.107(10).

GENERAL NOTE

This section empowers the Secretary of State to prohibit a person from importing, acquiring, continuing to keep, releasing or marketing GMOs, if he is of the opinion that there is a risk of causing damage to the environment. The notice of prohibition may forbid the doing of the proposed act, or may prohibit the continued keeping of the GMOs (subs. (2)): in the latter case the person must then dispose of the GMOs as quickly and safely as possible, or in accordance with any requirements specified in the notice (subs. (4)).

The Secretary of State regards the power to prohibit the import of GMOs as being potentially of particular value in cases involving especially hazardous GMOs.

Consents

Consents required by certain persons

111.—(1) Subject to subsection (7) below, no person shall import or acquire, release or market any genetically modified organisms—

    (a) in such cases or circumstances as may be prescribed in relation to that act, or

    (b) in any case where he has been given directions under section 108(8)(a) above,

except in pursuance of a consent granted by the Secretary of State and in accordance with any limitations and conditions to which the consent is subject.

(2) Subject to subsection (7) below, no person who has imported or acquired any genetically modified organisms (whether under a consent or not) shall continue to keep the organisms—

    (a) in such cases or circumstances as may be prescribed, after the end of the prescribed period, or

    (b) if he has been given directions under section 108(8)(b) above, after the date specified in the directions,

except in pursuance of a consent granted by the Secretary of State and in accordance with any limitations or conditions to which the consent is subject.

(3) A person who is required under subsection (2) above to cease keeping any genetically modified organisms shall dispose of them as quickly and safely as practicable.

(4) An application for a consent must contain such information and be made and advertised in such manner as may be prescribed and shall be accompanied by the fee required under section 113 below.

(5) The applicant shall, in prescribed circumstances, give such notice of his application to such persons as may be prescribed.

(6) The Secretary of State may by notice to the applicant require him to furnish such further information specified in the notice, within such period as may be so specified, as he may require for the purpose of determining the application; and if the applicant fails to furnish the information within the specified period the Secretary of State may refuse to proceed with the application.

[(6A) Where an applicant for consent for releasing or marketing genetically modified organisms becomes aware, before his application is either granted or rejected, of any new information with regard to any risks there are of damage to the environment being caused as a result of the organisms being released or marketed, he shall notify the Secretary of State of that new information forthwith.]

(7) Regulations under this section may provide for exemptions, or for the granting by the Secretary of State of exemptions to particular persons or classes of person, from—

(a) any requirement under subsection (1) or (2) above to have a consent, or

(b) any of the requirements to be fulfilled under the regulations by an applicant for a consent,

in such cases or circumstances as may be prescribed.

(8) Where an application for a consent is duly made to him, the Secretary of State may grant the consent subject to such limitations and conditions as may be imposed under section 112 below or he may refuse the application.

(9) The conditions attached to a consent may include conditions which are to continue to have effect notwithstanding that the holder has completed or ceased the act or acts authorised by the consent.

(10) The Secretary of State may at any time, by notice given to the holder of a consent, revoke the consent or vary the consent (whether by attaching new limitations and conditions or by revoking or varying any limitations and conditions to which it is at that time subject).

(11) Regulations under this section may make different provision for different cases and different circumstances; and in this section "prescribed" means prescribed in regulations under this section.

DEFINITIONS
"acquire": s.127(1).
"consent": s.127(1).
"genetically modified organisms": s.106.
"import": s.127(1).
"market": s.107(11).
"release" s.107(10).

AMENDMENTS
Subsection 6A was inserted by the Genetically Modified Organisms (Deliberate Release) Regulations 1992 (S.I. 1992 No. 3280) reg. 13(1).

GENERAL NOTE
This section contains provisions as to the requirement of consent for the import, acquisition, keeping, release or marketing of GMOs. The consent requirements apply in two circumstances: (a) cases or circumstances prescribed in regulations; and (b) where the Secretary of State has given a direction under s.108(8) requiring consent to be applied for. In such cases the activity or keeping may only be carried out or continued, as the case may be, in pursuance of the consent and in accordance with any condition or limitations to which it is subject. The consent requirements might well apply to the release of GMOs as waste or as a part of waste, as well as to releases for commercial or trial purposes.

Matters to be dealt with by regulations include: (a) (subs. (1)) the cases or circumstances in which consent is required; (b) (subs. (4)) information to be contained in an application for consent; (c) (subs. (4)) requirements as to advertisement of consents; (d) (subs. (5)) circumstances in which notification of applications are required and the persons to whom such notice should be given; and (e) (subs. (7)) exemptions from the consent requirement or from the requirements of regulations as to applications. All of these matters are addressed in relation to the release or marketing of GMOs by Parts II and III respectively of the Genetically Modified Organisms (Deliberate Release) Regulations 1992 (S.I. 1992 No. 3280) as amended. No regulations under this Part have been made in relation to the import, acquisition or keeping of GMOs: it appears to be the Government's view that none are necessary in view of the existence of S.I. 1992 No. 3280 taken in conjunction with the Genetically Modified Organisms (Contained Use) Regulations (S.I. 1992 No. 3217) made under the Health and Safety at Work etc. Act 1974.

Subs. (11) allows regulations to make different provision for different cases and circumstances: S.I. 1995 No. 304 (amending S.I. 1992 No. 3280) in particular does so in implementing Directive 94/15/EC. As a result, applications for consent to market or release genetically modified higher plants are subject to entirely separate information requirements from those required for applications in respect of other GMOs.

Fees
Applications must be accompanied by the appropriate fee (subs. (4) and s.113) and will not be regarded as "duly made" unless the fee is paid (subs. (8)).

The fee is paid in accordance with a scheme made under s.113: the Genetically Modified Organisms (Deliberate Release) Fees and Charges Scheme 1995 took effect on April 1, 1995.

Conditions
The consent may be granted subject to conditions or limitations (subs. (8)). The detailed requirements for conditions are contained in s.112, and it should be noted that these include a number of general conditions which are implied into every relevant consent.

Revocation and variation
The Secretary of State is given wide powers by subs. (10) to give notice revoking or varying consents.

Appeals
There is no appeal from decisions of the Secretary of State (see *Hansard*, H.L. Vol. 520, cols. 1989–1993). The Government proposes that the advice of ACRE to the Secretary of State should be made public and that there should be a period for the applicant and the public to make representations thereon to the Secretary of State before he reaches a decision.

Consents: limitations and conditions

112.—(1) The Secretary of State may include in a consent such limitations and conditions as he may think fit; [...].

(2) Without prejudice to the generality of subsection (1) above, the conditions included in a consent may—

    (a) require the giving of notice of any fact to the Secretary of State; or

    (b) prohibit or restrict the keeping, releasing or marketing of genetically modified organisms under the consent in specified cases or circumstances;

and where, under any condition, the holder of a consent is required to cease keeping any genetically modified organisms, he shall dispose of them, if no manner is specified in the conditions, as quickly and safely as practicable.

(3) Subject to subsection (6) below, there is implied in every consent for the importation or acquisition of genetically modified organisms a general condition that the holder of the consent shall—

    (a) take all reasonable steps to keep himself informed (by reference to the nature of the organisms and the manner in which he intends to keep them after their importation or acquisition) of any risks there are of damage to the environment being caused as a result of their importation or acquisition; and

    (b) if at any time it appears that any such risks are more serious than were apparent when the consent was granted, notify the Secretary of State forthwith.

(4) Subject to subsection (6) below, there is implied in every consent for keeping genetically modified organisms a general condition that the holder of the consent shall—

    (a) take all reasonable steps to keep himself informed of any damage to the environment which may have been caused as a result of his keeping the organisms and of any risks there are of such damage being caused as a result of his continuing to keep them;

    (b) if at any time it appears that any such risks are more serious than were apparent when the consent was granted, notify the Secretary of State forthwith; and

    (c) use the best available techniques not entailing excessive cost for keeping the organisms under his control and for preventing any damage to the environment being caused as a result of his continuing to keep them.

(5) Subject to subsection (6) below, there is implied in every consent for

releasing or marketing genetically modified organisms a general condition that the holder of the consent shall—

    (a) take all reasonable steps to keep himself informed (by reference to the nature of the organisms and the extent and manner of the release or marketing) of any risks there are of damage to the environment being caused as a result of their being released or, as the case may be, marketed;

    [(b) notify the Secretary of State of—

        (i) any new information which becomes available with regard to any risks there are of damage to the environment being so caused, and

        (ii) the effects of any releases by him for the assessment of any risks there are of damage to the environment being so caused by such organisms being released or marketed;]

    (c) use the best available techniques not entailing excessive cost for preventing any damage to the environment being caused as a result of their being released or, as the case may be, marketed.

(6) The general condition implied into a consent under subsection (3), (4) or (5) above has effect subject to any conditions imposed under subsection (1) above; and the obligations imposed by virtue of subsection (4)(c) or (5)(c) above shall not apply to any aspect of an act authorised by a consent which is regulated by such a condition.

(7) There shall be implied in every consent for keeping, releasing or marketing genetically modified organisms of any description a general condition that the holder of the consent—

    (a) shall take all reasonable steps to keep himself informed of developments in the techniques which may be available in his case for preventing damage to the environment being caused as a result of the doing of the act authorised by the consent in relation to organisms of that description; and

    (b) if it appears at any time that any better techniques are available to him than is required by any condition included in the consent under subsection (1) above, shall notify the Secretary of State of the fact forthwith.

But this general condition shall have effect subject to any conditions imposed under subsection (1) above.

DEFINITIONS

    "acquire": s.127(1).
    "consent": s.127(1).
    "control": s.107(9).
    "damage to the environment": s.107(3).
    "genetically modified organisms": s.106.
    "import": s.127(1).
    "market": s.107(1).
    "release": s.107(10).

AMENDMENTS

The words missing in the square brackets in subs. (1) were deleted by the Environmental Protection Act 1990 (Modification of s.112) Regulations 1992 (S.I. 1992 No. 2617). The words in square brackets in subs. (5)(b) were substituted by the Genetically Modified Organisms (Deliberate Release) Regulations 1992 (S.I. 1992 No. 3280).

GENERAL NOTE

This section contains detailed provisions on conditions or limitations imposed on consents under s.111 (see s.111(8)). These may be express or implied. Such express limitations or conditions may be included as the Secretary of State thinks fit (subs. (1)). By s.111(9) such conditions may include those which continue to have effect notwithstanding completion or cessation of the acts authorised by the consent: this could allow, for example, a condition requiring continued monitoring following a release.

Further general conditions are implied by subss. (3)–(7). These in general correspond with the obligations as to risk identification and use of BATNEEC contained in s.109, which do not apply to authorised acts done under consents.

Subsection (3) contains the implied conditions for consents for the import or acquisition of GMOs, subs. (4) those on the keeping of GMOs, and subs. (5) those on release or marketing.

Subsection (6) makes clear that such general conditions have effect subject to any express conditions and that the obligations as to BATNEEC are disapplied in the case of aspects of activities dealt with by express conditions.

There is also by subs. (7) a general duty in the case of keeping, release or marketing of GMOs to take reasonable steps to remain informed as to developments in the relevant techniques for preventing harm to the environment and to notify the Secretary of State where it appears that better techniques than those specified in conditions have become available. This unusual provision reflects the fact that those carrying out work on GMOs are likely to be at the forefront of developing techniques for control and containment in their own specialist fields.

Fees and charges

113.—(1) The Secretary of State may, with the approval of the Treasury, make and from time to time revise a scheme prescribing—
 (a) fees payable in respect of applications for consents; and
 (b) charges payable by persons holding consents in respect of the subsistence of their consents;
and it shall be a condition of any such consent that any applicable prescribed charge is paid in accordance with that scheme.

(2) A scheme under this section may, in particular—
 (a) provide for different fees or charges to be payable in different cases or circumstances;
 (b) provide for the times at which and the manner in which payments are to be made; and
 (c) make such incidental, supplementary and transitional provision as appears to the Secretary of State to be appropriate.

(3) The Secretary of State shall so frame a scheme under this section as to secure, so far as practicable, that the amounts payable under it will be sufficient, taking one financial year with another, to cover the expenditure of the Secretary of State in discharging his functions under this Part in relation to consents.

(4) The Secretary of State shall, on making or revising a scheme under this section, lay a copy of the scheme or of the scheme as revised before each House of Parliament.

Definition
 "consent": s.127.

Genereal Note
This section provides for a scheme of fees for applications for consents and of charges for the subsistence of consents. It accords with the general policy, apparent in the Act, that the cost of regulatory functions should be borne by the persons regulated rather than by the public at large. The Genetically Modified Organisms (Deliberate Release) Fees and Charges Scheme 1995 took effect on April 1, 1995, replacing the previous (1993) Scheme.

Inspectors

Appointment etc. of inspectors

114.—(1) The Secretary of State may appoint as inspectors, for carrying this Part into effect, such number of persons appearing to him to be qualified for the purpose as he may consider necessary.

(2) The Secretary of State may make to or in respect of any person so appointed such payments by way of remuneration, allowances or otherwise as he may with the approval of the Treasury determine.

(3) An inspector shall not be personally liable in any civil or criminal proceedings for anything done in the purported exercise of any power under section 115 or 117 below if the court is satisfied that the act was done in good faith and that there were reasonable grounds for doing it.

(4) In England and Wales an inspector, if authorised to do so by the Secretary of State, may, although not of counsel or a solicitor, prosecute before a magistrates' court proceedings for an offence under section 118(1) below.

(5) In this Part "inspector" means, subject to section 125 below, a person appointed as an inspector under subsection (1) above.

GENERAL NOTE
This section allows the Secretary of State to appoint suitably qualified inspectors for the purposes of Pt. VI. Provision is made for remuneration, immunity from suit and standing to prosecute in magistrates' courts. Enforcement of Pt. VI is in fact carried out by Health and Safety Executive inspectors under an agency agreement with the Secretary of State, made under s.125.

Rights of entry and inspection

115.—(1) An inspector may, on production (if so required) of his authority, exercise any of the powers specified in subsection (3) below for the purposes of the discharge of the functions of the Secretary of State under this Part.

(2) Those powers are exercisable—
   (a) in relation to premises—
      (i) on which the inspector has reason to believe a person is keeping or has kept any genetically modified organisms, or
     (ii) from which he has reason to believe any such organisms have been released or have escaped; and
   (b) in relation to premises on which the inspector has reason to believe there may be harmful genetically modified organisms or evidence of damage to the environment caused by genetically modified organisms;
but they are not exercisable in relation to premises used wholly or mainly for domestic purposes.

(3) The powers of an inspector are—
   (a) At any reasonable time (or, in a situation in which in his opinion there is an immediate risk of damage to the environment, at any time)—
      (i) to enter premises which he has reason to believe it is necessary for him to enter and to take with him any person duly authorised by the Secretary of State and, if the inspector has reasonable cause to apprehend any serious obstruction in the execution of his duty, a constable; and
     (ii) to take with him any equipment or materials required for any purpose for which the power of entry is being exercised;
   (b) to carry out such tests and inspections (and to make such recordings), as may in any circumstances be necessary;
   (c) to direct that any, or any part of, premises which he has power to enter, or anything in or on such premises, shall be left undisturbed (whether generally or in particular respects) for so long as is reasonably necessary for the purpose of any test or inspection;
   (d) to take samples of any organisms, articles or substances found in or on any premises which he has power to enter, and of the air, water or land in, on, or in the vicinity of, the premises;

    (e) in the case of anything found in or on any premises which he has power to enter, which appears to him to contain or to have contained genetically modified organisms which have caused or are likely to cause damage to the environment, to cause it to be dismantled or subjected to any process or test (but not so as to damage or destroy it unless this is necessary);

    (f) in the case of anything mentioned in paragraph (e) above or anything found on premises which he has power to enter which appears to be a genetically modified organism or to consist of or include genetically modified organisms, to take possession of it and detain it for so long as is necessary for all or any of the following purposes, namely—

       (i) to examine it and do to it anything which he has power to do under that paragraph;

      (ii) to ensure that it is not tampered with before his examination of it is completed; and

     (iii) to ensure that it is available for use as evidence in any proceedings for any offence under section 118 below;

    (g) to require any person whom he has reasonable cause to believe to be able to give any information relevant to any test or inspection under this subsection to answer (in the absence of persons other than a person nominated to be present and any persons whom the inspector may allow to be present) such questions as the inspector thinks fit to ask and to sign a declaration of the truth of his answers;

    (h) to require the production of, or where the information is recorded in computerised form, the furnishing of extracts from, any records which are required to be kept under this Part or it is necessary for him to see for the purposes of any test or inspection under this subsection and to inspect, and take copies of, or of any entry in, the records;

    (i) to require any person to afford him such facilities and assistance with respect to any matters or things within that person's control or in relation to which that person has responsibilities as are necessary to enable the inspector to exercise any of the powers conferred on him by this section;

    (j) any other power for the purpose mentioned in subsection (1) above which is conferred by regulations made by the Secretary of State.

  (4) The Secretary of State may by regulations make provision as to the procedure to be followed in connection with the taking of, and the dealing with, samples under subsection (3)(d) above.

  (5) Where an inspector proposes to exercise the power conferred by subsection (3)(e) above, he shall, if so requested by a person who at the time is present on and has responsibilities in relation to those premises, cause anything which is to be done by virtue of that power to be done in the presence of that person.

  (6) Before exercising the power conferred by subsection (3)(e) above, an inspector shall consult such persons as appear to him appropriate for the purpose of ascertaining what dangers, if any, there may be in doing anything which he proposes to do under the power.

  (7) Where under the power conferred by subsection (3)(f) above an inspector takes possession of anything found on any premises, he shall leave there, either with a responsible person or, if that is impracticable, fixed in a conspicuous position, a notice giving particulars sufficient to identify what he has seized and stating that he has taken possession of it under that power; and before taking possession under that power of—

    (a) any thing that forms part of a batch of similar things, or

    (b) any substance,

an inspector shall, if it is practical and safe for him to do so, take a sample of it and give to a responsible person at the premises a portion of the sample marked in a manner sufficient to identify it.

(8) No answer given by a person in pursuance of a requirement imposed under subsection (3)(g) above shall be admissible in evidence—

(a) in any proceedings in England and Wales against that person; or

(b) in any criminal proceedings in Scotland against that person.

(9) The powers conferred by subsection (3)(a), (b), (c), (d), (e) and (h) above shall also be exercisable (subject to subsections (4), (5) and (6) above) by any person authorised for the purpose in writing by the Secretary of State.

(10) Nothing in this section shall be taken to compel the production by any person to a document of which he would on grounds of legal professional privilege be entitled to withhold production on an order for discovery in an action in the High Court or, in relation to Scotland, on an order for the production of documents in an action in the Court of Session.

DEFINITIONS
"damage to the environment": s.107(3).
"escape": s.107(10).
"genetically modified organisms": s.106.
"harmful": s.107(7).
"inspector": s.114(5).
"premises": s.127(1).
"release": s.107(10).

GENERAL NOTE
The section confers wide powers on inspectors including powers of entry, testing, sampling, seizure, requesting information and the production of records. The powers are exercisable in relation to premises (including any land) where the inspector has reason to believe GMOs are being or have been kept, or from which they have been released or have escaped (subs. (2)(a)). They are also exercisable in relation to premises on which there may be harmful released or escaped GMOs or where there may be evidence of damage to the environment caused by GMOs (subs. (2)(b)). In either event, they are not exercisable in relation to premises used wholly or mainly for domestic purposes.

Enforcement powers and offences

Obtaining of information from persons

116.—(1) For the purposes of the discharge of his functions under this Part, the Secretary of State may, by notice in writing served on any person who appears to him—

(a) to be involved in the importation, acquisition, keeping, release or marketing of genetically modified organisms; or

(b) to be about to become, or to have been, involved in any of those activities;

require that person to furnish such relevant information available to him as is specified in the notice, in such form and within such period following service of the notice as is so specified.

(2) For the purposes of this section "relevant information" means information concerning any aspects of the activities in question, including any damage to the environment which may be or have been caused thereby; and the discharge by the Secretary of State of an obligation of the United Kingdom under the Community Treaties or any international agreement concerning the protection of the environment from harm caused by

genetically modified organisms shall be treated as a function of his under this Part.

DEFINITIONS
"acquisition": s.127(1).
"damage to the environment": s.107(3).
"harm": s.107(6).
"genetically modified organisms": s.106.
"importation": s.127(1).
"marketing": s.107(11).
"release": s.107(10).

GENERAL NOTE
This section provides that the Secretary of State may, by notice in writing, obtain information from persons involved or about to be involved in activities relating to GMOs. It should be noted that this power is not restricted to the actual or proposed keeper, importer, releaser, marketer, etc. but applies to anyone involved in, or connected with, such operations.

By subs. (2) the power may be used not only in the discharge of functions under Pt. VI but in fulfilment of any E.C. or international obligation concerning the protection of the environment from damage caused by GMOs. For the Community and international aspects, see the General Note to Pt. VI.

Power to deal with cause of imminent danger of damage to the environment

117.—(1) Where, in the case of anything found by him on any premises which he has power to enter, an inspector has reason to believe that it is a genetically modified organism or that it consists of or includes genetically modified organisms and that, in the circumstances in which he finds it, it is a cause of imminent danger of damage to the environment, he may seize it and cause it to be rendered harmless (whether by destruction, by bringing it under proper control or otherwise).

(2) Before there is rendered harmless under this section—

    (a) any thing that forms part of a batch of similar things; or

    (b) any substance,

the inspector shall, if it is practicable and safe for him to do so, take a sample of it and give to a responsible person at the premises a portion of the sample marked in a manner sufficient to identify it.

(3) As soon as may be after anything has been seized and rendered harmless under this section, the inspector shall prepare and sign a written report giving particulars of the circumstances in which it was seized and so dealt with by him, and shall—

    (a) give a signed copy of the report to a responsible person at the premises where it was found by him; and

    (b) unless that person is the owner of it, also serve a signed copy of the report on the owner;

and if, where paragraph (b) above applies, the inspector cannot after reasonable inquiry ascertain the name or address of the owner, the copy may be served on him by giving it to the person to whom a copy was given under paragraph (a) above.

DEFINITIONS
"damage to the environment": s.107(3).
"genetically modified organism": s.106.
"harmless": s.107(3).
"inspector": s.114(5).
"premises": s.127(1).

GENERAL NOTE
This section is complementary to the power to serve prohibition notices contained in s.110, in that it enables speedy action to be taken to seize and render harmless GMOs which present an imminent danger to the environment. The power could be used either in situations where

GMOs presently under control appear to be a cause of danger, or where GMOs are at large in the environment.

Offences

118.—(1) It is an offence for a person—

(a) to do anything in contravention of section 108(1) above in relation to something which is, and which he knows or has reason to believe is, a genetically modified organism;

(b) to fail to comply with section 108(3) above when keeping something which is, and which he knows or has reason to believe is, a genetically modified organism;

(c) to do anything in contravention of section 111(1) or (2) above in relation to something which is, and which he knows or has reason to believe is, a genetically modified organism;

(d) to fail to comply with any requirement of subsection (2), (3)(a), (b) or (c) or (4) of section 109 above in relation to something which is, and which he knows or has reason to believe is, a genetically modified organism;

(e) to fail, without reasonable excuse, to comply with section 108(5) or (6) [or section 111(6A)] above;

(f) to contravene any prohibition imposed on him by a prohibition notice;

(g) without reasonable excuse, to fail to comply with any requirement imposed under section 115 above;

(h) to prevent any other person from appearing before or from answering any question to which an inspector may, by virtue of section 115(3) above, require an answer;

(i) intentionally to obstruct an inspector in the exercise of performance of his powers or duties, other than his powers or duties under section 117 above;

(j) intentionally to obstruct an inspector in the exercise of his powers or duties under section 117 above;

(k) to fail, without reasonable excuse, to comply with any requirement imposed by a notice under section 116 above;

(l) to make a statement which he knows to be false or misleading in a material particular, or recklessly to make a statement which is false or misleading in a material particular, where the statement is made—

(i) in purported compliance with a requirement to furnish any information imposed by or under any provision of this Part; or

(ii) for the purpose of obtaining the grant of a consent to himself or any other person or the variation of a consent;

(m) intentionally to make a false entry in any record required to be kept under section 108 or 111 above;

(n) with intent to deceive, to forge or use a document purporting to be issued under section 111 above or required for any purpose thereunder or to make or have in his possession a document so closely resembling any such document as to be likely to deceive;

(o) falsely to pretend to be an inspector.

(2) It shall be a defence for a person charged with an offence under paragraph (a), (b), (c), (d) or (f) of subsection (1) above to prove that he took all reasonable precautions and exercised all due diligence to avoid the commission of the offence.

(3) A person guilty of an offence under paragraph (c) or (d) of subsection (1) above shall be liable—

    (a) on summary conviction, to a fine not exceeding £20,000 or to imprisonment for a term not exceeding six months, or to both;

    (b) on conviction on indictment, to a fine or to imprisonment for a term not exceeding five years, or to both.

  (4) A person guilty of an offence under paragraph (f) of subsection (1) above shall be liable—

    (a) on summary conviction, to a fine not exceeding £20,000 or to imprisonment for a term not exceeding six months, or to both;

    (b) on conviction on indictment, to a fine or to imprisonment for a term not exceeding two years, to to both.

  (5) A person guilty of an offence under paragraph (a) or (b) of subsection (1) above shall be liable—

    (a) on summary conviction, to a fine not exceeding the statutory maximum or to imprisonment for a term not exceeding six months, or to both;

    (b) on conviction of indictment, to a fine or to imprisonment for a term not exceeding five years, or to both.

  (6) A person guilty of an offence under paragraph (e), (j), (k), (l), (m) or (n) of subsection (1) above shall be liable—

    (a) on summary conviction, to a fine not exceeding the statutory maximum or to imprisonment for a term not exceeding six months, or to both;

    (b) on conviction on indictment, to a fine or to imprisonment for a term not exceeding two years, or to both.

  (7) A person guilty of an offence under paragraph (g), (h) or (i) of subsection (1) above shall be liable on summary conviction to a fine not exceeding the statutory maximum or to imprisonment for a term not exceeding three months, or to both.

  (8) A person guilty of an offence under paragraph (o) of subsection (1) above shall be liable on summary conviction to a fine not exceeding level 5 on the standard scale.

  (9) Where a person is convicted of an offence under paragraph (b) of subsection (1) above in respect of his keeping any genetically modified organism, then, if the contravention in respect of which he was convicted is continued after he was convicted he shall be guilty of a further offence and liable on summary conviction to a fine of one-fifth of level 5 on the standard scale for each day on which the contravention is so continued.

  (10) Proceedings in respect of an offence under this section shall not be instituted in England and Wales except by the Secretary of State or with the consent of the Director of Public Prosecutions or in Northern Ireland except with the consent of the Director of Public Prosecutions for Northern Ireland.

DEFINITIONS
"genetically modified organism": s.106.
"inspector": s.114(5).
"prohibition notice": s.127(1).

AMENDMENTS
The words in square brackets in s.118(1)(e) were inserted by the Genetically Modified Organisms (Deliberate Release) Regulations 1992 (S.I. 1992 No. 3280), reg. 13(2).

GENERAL NOTE
Subsection (1) establishes the various offences in relation to the requirements of Pt. VI. Subsections (3)–(9) prescribe the various penalties, which reflect the relative seriousness of the separate offences.

  The most serious offences are those of engaging in GMO activities without the necessary consent or in breach of consent conditions (s.111(1) and (2)), failure to comply with general duties as to risk assessment and use of BATNEEC (s.109(2), (3) and (4)) and contravention of a prohibition notice (s.118(1)(f)). Such offences are subject to a maximum fine of £20,000 or to imprisonment for a term not exceeding six months on summary conviction. On conviction on indictment the fine may be unlimited, and the maximum term of imprisonment is five years, or two years for breach of a prohibition notice (subss. (3) and (4)).

Subs. (10): restriction on prosecutions
Prosecutions under s.118 may only be brought by the Secretary of State in England and Wales or with the consent of the Director of Public Prosecutions. The editor is not aware of any having been brought.

Defence of all reasonable precautions and all due diligence
This defence is available in relation to certain offences (subs. (2)). "All reasonable precautions" has been said to be related to those risks of harm reasonably foreseeable when a prudent and competent person applies his mind seriously to the situation: see *Colpron v. Canadian National Rly. Co.* [1934] S.C.R. 189 and 192.
    An obligation to exercise due diligence has been said to be "indistinguishable from an obligation to exercise reasonable care": *Riverstone Meat Co. Pty. v. Lancashire Shipping Co.* [1960] 1 All E.R. 193 at 219, Willmer L.J.; reversed [1961] A.C. 807.

Onus of proof as regards techniques and evidence

119.—(1) In any proceedings for either of the following offences, that is to say—
    (a) an offence under section 118(1)(c) above consisting in a failure to comply with the general condition implied by section 112(4)(c) or (5)(c) above; or
    (b) an offence under section 118(1)(d) above consisting in a failure to comply with section 109(3)(c) or (4)(c) above;
it shall be for the accused to prove that there was no better available technique not entailing excessive cost than was in fact used to satisfy the condition or to comply with that section.
    (2) Where an entry is required by a condition in a consent to be made in any record as to the observance of any other condition and the entry has not been made, that fact shall be admissible as evidence that that other condition has not been observed.

Definition
    "consent": s.127(1).

General Note
The effect of this provision is to put the onus of proof as to the use of BATNEEC on the accused and to make admissible as evidence the failure of the accused to produce appropriate records in respect of compliance with conditions, where such records are required by conditions.

Power of court to order cause of offence to be remedied

120.—(1) Where a person is convicted of an offence under section 118(1)(a), (b), (c), (d), (e) or (f) above in respect of any matters which appear to the court to be matters which it is in his power to remedy, the court may, in addition to or instead of imposing any punishment, order him, within such time as may be fixed by the order, to take such steps as may be specified in the order for remedying those matters.
    (2) The time fixed by an order under subsection (1) above may be extended or further extended by order of the court on an application made before the end of the time as originally fixed or as extended under this subsection, as the case may be.
    (3) Where a person is ordered under subsection (1) above to remedy any matters, that person shall not be liable under section 118 above in respect of those matters, in so far as they continue during the time fixed by the order or any further time allowed under subsection (2) above.

General Note
This section enables a court to order a person convicted of certain offences under Pt. VI to take specified steps to remedy such matters as it appears to be within his power to remedy.

By subs. (3) where such an order is made, no further criminal liability may arise during the period allowed by the order for taking the steps.

Power of Secretary of State to remedy harm

121.—(1) Where the commission of an offence under section 118(1)(a), (b), (c), (d), (e) or (f) above causes any harm which it is possible to remedy, the Secretary of State may, subject to subsection (2) below—
  (a) arrange for any reasonable steps to be taken towards remedying the harm; and
  (b) recover the cost of taking those steps from any person convicted of that offence.

(2) The Secretary of State shall not exercise his powers under this section, where any of the steps are to be taken on or will affect land in the occupation of any person other than a person convicted of the offence in question, except with the permission of that person.

DEFINITION
"harm": s. 107(6).

GENERAL NOTE
By this section, where commission of certain offences under Pt. VI has caused harm, which it is possible to remedy, the Secretary of State may arrange for reasonable steps to be taken towards remedying the harm, and may recover the cost from any person convicted of the offence. Where the steps have to be taken on land occupied by a person other than the offender, the permission of that person must be obtained.

Publicity

Public register of information

122.—(1) The Secretary of State shall maintain a register ("the register") containing prescribed particulars of or relating to—
  (a) notices given or other information furnished under section 108 above;
  (b) directions given under section 108(8) above;
  (c) prohibition notices;
  (d) applications for consents (and any further information furnished in connection with them) and any advice given by the committee appointed under section 124 below in relation to such applications;
  (e) consents granted by the Secretary of State and any information furnished to him in pursuance of consent conditions;
  (f) any other information obtained or furnished under any provision of this Part;
  (g) convictions for such offences under section 118 above as may be prescribed;
  (h) such other matters relating to this Part as may be prescribed;
but that duty is subject to section 123 below.

(2) It shall be the duty of the Secretary of State—
  (a) to secure that the register is open to inspection by members of the public free of charge at all reasonable hours; and
  (b) to afford to members of the public facilities for obtaining copies of entries, on payment of reasonable charges.

(3) The register may be kept in any form.

(4) The Secretary of State may make regulations with respect to the keeping of the register; and in this section "prescribed" means prescribed in regulations made by the Secretary of State.

DEFINITIONS
  "consents": s.127(1).
  "prohibition notices": s.127(1).

GENERAL NOTE
This section makes provision for public registers of information as to consent, notices and other matters under Pt. VI. See also General Note to Pt. VI.

Subs. (4): regulations
By subs. (1), the register is to contain such particulars, of or in relation to a number of matters there listed, as are prescribed in regulations. These particulars are prescribed by the Genetically Modified Organisms (Deliberate Release) Regulations 1992 (S.I. 1992 No. 3280), reg. 17, and include particulars of prohibition notices; applications for consent under s.111(1); consents (including details of conditions on, or reasons for refusal of, consent); information supplied in connection with conditions imposed; revocation and variation notices; new information on risks; and convictions under s.118. Regulation 17 has been amended by S.I. 1995 No. 304 so that where, by virtue of other amendments, the proposed location and foreseen dates of release of GMOs need not be contained in the application for consent to the release, neither need that information appear on the register. Regulation 18 (as amended by S.I. 1995 No. 304) prescribes time limits with which the Secretary of State must comply in placing information onto the register.

Exclusion from register of certain information

123.—(1) No information shall be included in the register under section 122 above if and so long as, in the opinion of the Secretary of State, the inclusion of the information would be contrary to the interests of national security.

(2) No information shall be included in the register if and so long as, in the opinion of the Secretary of State, it ought to be excluded on the ground that its inclusion might result in damage to the environment.

(3) No information relating to the affairs of any individual or business shall be included in the register without the consent of that individual or the person for the time being carrying on that business, if the Secretary of State has determined that the information—

(a) is, in relation to him, commercially confidential; and

(b) is not information of a description to which subsection (7) below applies;

unless the Secretary of State is of the opinion that the information is no longer commercially confidential in relation to him.

(4) Nothing in subsection (3) above requires the Secretary of State to determine whether any information is or is not commercially confidential except where the person furnishing the information applies to have it excluded on the ground that it is (in relation to himself or another person) commercially confidential.

(5) Where an application has been made for information to be excluded under subsection (3) above, the Secretary of State shall make a determination and inform the applicant of it as soon as is practicable.

(6) Where it appears to the Secretary of State that any information (other than information furnished by the person to whom it relates) which has been obtained under or by virtue of any provision of this Part might be commercially confidential, the Secretary of State shall—

(a) give to the person to whom or to whose business it relates notice that the information is required to be included in the register unless excluded under subsection (3) above; and

(b) give him a reasonable opportunity—

(i) of objecting to the inclusion of the information on the ground that it is commercially confidential; and

(ii) of making representations to the Secretary of State for the purpose of justifying any such objection;

and the Secretary of State shall take any representations into account before determining whether the information is or is not commercially confidential.

(7) The prescribed particulars of or relating to the matters mentioned in section 122(1)(a), (d) and (e) above shall be included in the register notwithstanding that they may be commercially confidential if and so far as they are of any of the following descriptions, namely—

    (a) the name and address of the person giving the notice or furnishing the information;

    (b) the description of any genetically modified organisms to which the notice or other information relates;

    (c) the location at any time of those organisms;

    (d) the purpose for which those organisms are being imported, acquired, kept, released or marketed (according to whichever of those acts the notice or other information relates);

    (e) results of any assessment of the risks of damage to the environment being caused by the doing of any of those acts;

    (f) notices under section 112(3), (4), (5) or (7) above;

and the Secretary of State may by regulations prescribe any other description of information as information which the public interest requires to be included in the register notwithstanding that it may be commercially confidential.

(8) Information excluded from the register under subsection (3) above shall be treated as ceasing to be commercially confidential for the purposes of that subsection at the expiry of a period of four years beginning with the date of the determination by virtue of which it was excluded; but the person who furnished it or to whom or to whose business it relates may apply to the Secretary of State for the information to remain excluded on the ground that it is still commercially confidential.

(9) The Secretary of State may by order substitute for the period for the time being specified in subsection (8) above such other period as he considers appropriate.

DEFINITION
    "damage to the environment": s.107(3).

GENERAL NOTE
This section provides for the categories of information to be excluded from the register kept under s.122. Broadly, these are:

    (1) information the inclusion of which would, in the opinion of the Secretary of State, be contrary to the interests of national security (subs. (1));

    (2) information the inclusion of which might result in damage to the environment (subs. (2)), *e.g.* by giving information which could facilitate sabotage or other illegal action (see *Hansard*, H.L. Vol. 522, col. 711);

    (3) information which is commercially confidential (subs. (3)). Applications for the commercial confidentiality exemption will no doubt be scrutinised closely: see note to s.22. Further, even where the confidentiality exemption is successfully claimed, certain information will still be included (subs. (7)) and the confidentiality lapses after four years, so a fresh application for exemption must be made (subs. (8)).

Supplementary

Advisory committee for purposes of Part VI

    124.—(1) The Secretary of State shall appoint a committee to provide him with advice—

    (a) on the exercise of his powers under sections 111, 112 and 113 above;

    (b) on the exercise of any power under this Part to make regulations;

and on such other matters concerning his functions under this Part as he may from time to time direct.

(2) The chairman and other members of the committee shall hold and vacate office in accordance with the terms of their appointment.

(3) The Secretary of State shall pay to the members of the committee such remuneration (if any) and such allowances as he may, with the consent of the Treasury, determine.

GENERAL NOTE

This section provides for the appointment of an expert committee to provide the Secretary of State with advice as to his consent and regulation-making functions, and on any other matters as he may from time to time direct. The Committee, which had already existed but was put on to a statutory footing by s.124 (see *Hansard*, H.L. Vol. 520, col. 1964), is known as the Advisory Committee on Releases to the Environment (ACRE). The Committee offers integrated advice on both the environmental and health and safety aspects of activities involving GMOs. See also General Note to Pt. VI, where published Guidance by ACRE is listed.

ACRE's terms of reference include advising not only the Secretaries of State for the Environment, Scotland and Wales, but also the Minister of Agriculture, Fisheries and Food (see s.126 below) and the Health and Safety Commission and Executive (see s.125) and other bodies as appropriate. Further, they include advising the Secretaries of State and other bodies on releases into the environment in Great Britain of non-indigenous animals and plants covered by the Wildlife and Countryside Act 1981, s.14, and advising the DoE (Northern Ireland) on releases into the environment for the purposes of the Genetically Modified Organisms (Deliberate Release) Regulations (Northern Ireland) 1993.

ACRE's Annual Report No. 2: 1994/95 notes that ACRE advised on 29 consent applications during that period, of which 27 were for experimental release of GMOs and two were for the marketing of GMOs. ACRE advised in all of these cases that a consent be issued subject to conditions. Membership includes representatives of scientists in the fields of ecology, molecular biology, virology, microbiology and medicine, the bio-technology industry, agriculture and environmental groups.

As to the relationship between ACRE and the ACGM, see *Hansard*, H.L. Vol. 522, col. 702, where Baroness Blatch put the matter as follows:

"ACGM and ACRE serve distinct purposes. Both committees have the advantage of having not only pure scientists as representatives but also representatives from both sides of industry. Of course the main function of ACGM is to advise on general standards of safe working with GMOs and in particular on the suitability of facilities in which they are produced and the competence of the individuals handling them.

Since the committee is established under the health and safety legislation, its remit concentrates on the protection of human health and safety. On the other hand, ACRE is specifically concerned with the effect of GMOs on the environment. The expertise and experience of those composing ACRE reflect that particular and distinct function."

Delegation of enforcement functions

125.—(1) The Secretary of State may, by an agreement made with any public authority, delegate to that authority or to any officer appointed by an authority exercising functions on behalf of that authority any of his enforcement functions under this Part, subject to such restrictions and conditions as may be specified in the agreement.

(2) For the purposes of this section the following are "enforcement functions" of the Secretary of State, that is to say, his functions under—
　　section 110;
　　section 114(1) and (4);
　　section 116;
　　section 118(10); and
　　section 121;
and "inspector" in sections 115 and 117 includes, to the extent of the delegation, any inspector appointed by an authority other than the Secretary of State by virtue of an agreement under this section.

(3) The Secretary of State shall, if and so far as an agreement under this section so provides, make payments to the authority to reimburse the authority the expenses incurred in the performance of functions delegated under this section; but no such agreement shall be made without the approval of the Treasury.

DEFINITION
"inspector": s.114(5).

GENERAL NOTE
This section allows "enforcement functions" of the Secretary of State under Pt. VI to be delegated by agreement to any public authority or to an officer of such authority. The relevant functions that may be delegated are prohibition notices (s.110), appointment of inspectors and authorisation of inspectors to prosecute (s.114), obtaining information (s.116), prosecuting (s.118(10)) and remedying harm (s.121). Functions of direction under s.108(8) and determination of consents under ss.111 and 112 are not amongst those that may be delegated.

The expression "inspector" in ss.115 and 117 applies to public authorities' inspectors where functions have been delegated (subs. (2)), so that such inspectors have the same powers of entry, etc. as those enjoyed by inspectors appointed by the Secretary of State.

The Health and Safety Executive is the enforcing agency for Pt. VI initially, by arrangements made under this section.

Exercise of certain functions jointly by Secretary of State and Minister of Agriculture, Fisheries and Food

126.—(1) Subject to subsection (2) below, any reference in this Part to a function exercisable by the Secretary of State shall, in any case where the function is to be exercised in relation to a matter with which the Minister of Agriculture, Fisheries and Food is concerned, be exercisable by the Secretary of State and that Minister acting jointly.

(2) The validity of anything purporting to be done in pursuance of the exercise of any such function shall not be affected by any question whether that thing fell, by virtue of this section, to be done by the Secretary of State and the Minister of Agriculture, Fisheries and Food.

GENERAL NOTE
Powers under Pt. VI are to be exercisable jointly by the Secretary of State for the Environment and the Minister of Agriculture, Fisheries and Food in relation to matters with which the latter is concerned. Activities with GMOs will frequently be connected with matters of agriculture, plants, animals, pest control and fisheries.

By subs. (2) the question as to whether a function should have been exercised jointly does not affect the validity of anything done under Pt. VI.

Definitions

127. In this Part—
"acquire", in relation to genetically modified organisms, includes any method by which such organisms may come to be in a person's possession, other than by their being imported;
"consent" means a consent granted under section 111 above, and a reference to the limitations or conditions to which a consent is subject is a reference to the limitations or conditions subject to which the consent for the time being has effect;
"descendant", in relation to a genetically modified organism, means any other organism whose genes or other genetic material is derived, through any number of generations, from that organism by any process of reproduction;
"import" means import into the United Kingdom;
"premises" includes any land;
"prohibition notice" means a notice under section 110 above.

(2) This Part, except in so far as it relates to importations of genetically modified organisms, applies to the territorial sea adjacent to Great Britain, and to any area for the time being designated under section 1(7) of the Continental Shelf Act 1964, as it applies in Great Britain.

GENERAL NOTE
Subsection (2): territorial application: Pt. VI applies to the territorial sea adjacent to Great Britain and to any area designated under the Continental Shelf Act 1964. This provision does not however apply in relation to imports of GMOs.

PART VII

NATURE CONSERVATION IN GREAT BRITAIN AND COUNTRYSIDE MATTERS IN WALES

GENERAL NOTE
Part VII was undoubtedly the most politically controversial part of the Environmental Protection Bill. Its effect is to reorganise the institutional structure for nature conservation matters in England, Scotland and Wales.
   The Nature Conservancy Council was the statutory body with responsibility for nature conservation throughout Great Britain until the reforms under Pt. VII. The NCC was created by the Nature Conservancy Council Act 1973 to replace the committee of the National Environment Research Council known as the Nature Conservancy. Under that Act (s.1) the NCC had the following main functions: (1) establishment, maintenance and management of nature reserves; (2) provision of advice on nature conservation matters to ministers; (3) provision of advice and dissemination of knowledge about nature conservation matters generally; and (4) the commissioning or support of research on nature conservation matters.
   The NCC also fulfilled important functions under the later Wildlife and Countryside Act 1981, including the notification of sites of special scientific interest (s.28) and entering into management agreements relating to such sites.
   The NCC also had a role as a statutory consultee in a variety of statutory contexts, most importantly in relation to certain applications for planning permission under the Town and Country Planning Act 1990 (in Scotland, under the Town and Country Planning (Scotland) Act 1972), including development proposals subject to the requirements of environmental assessment.
   The background to the proposals for reorganisation was considered in depth by the House of Lords Select Committee on Science and Technology in its report, *Nature Conservancy Council* (H.L. Paper 33–I and II, Session 1989–90, Second Report, March 1, 1990) under the Chairmanship of Lord Carver ("the Carver Report"). The Carver Report summarised this background as follows (paras. 1.2–1.9):

   "1.2 On July 11, 1989 the Nature Conservancy Council (NCC) met to put the final touches to a proposal for reorganising itself on a federal model. The object was to devolve more of the executive functions for nature conservation to its three regions, England, Scotland and Wales. On the same day the Government announced, without consultation and to the surprise of the NCC and everyone else, that the NCC would be split into three autonomous country agencies.
      1.3 The Government statements also announced that nature conservation and country-side responsibilities would be integrated in a single body in Scotland and in Wales.
      1.4 The reasons for the reorganisation were the 'increasing feelings that [existing] arrangements are inefficient, insensitive and mean that conservation issues in both Scotland and Wales are determined with too little regard for the particular requirements in these countries.' The new arrangements, combining the functions of the NCC and the Countryside Commission in Scotland and Wales will, according to the Government, 'allow a more comprehensive approach to pursuing the special inheritances of wildlife and natural beauty in those two countries'. (H.C. Deb. July 11, 1989, c.482W).
      1.5 The then Secretary of State for the Environment, Mr Ridley, stated that he would continue to be responsible for representing the United Kingdom's interests on nature conservation matters within the European Community and under international conventions.

1.6 He also said that in England the NCC and Countryside Commission would remain separate 'in view of the much greater density of population and consequent pressure upon the land'.

1.7 The Secretary of State for Scotland, Mr Rifkind, stated (H.C. Deb. July 11, 1989, c.436W) that Scottish reorganisation would take place in two stages. First a separate NCC in Scotland would be set up, and then it would be merged later with the Countryside Commission for Scotland into a single national heritage body, reporting directly to him. The new body would have full executive responsibility for its work in Scotland and the Government's proposals would 'result in substantial improvements in the effectiveness, accountability and, most important of all, in the sensitivity of administration in the vital task of conserving and managing Scotland's national heritage'. A consultation paper for Scotland, in broad terms, was issued after the announcement.

1.8 The Secretary of State for Wales, Mr Walker, announced (H.C. Deb. July 11, 1989, c.433W) that he would be appointing an executive Countryside Council for Wales, taking on the functional responsibilities of the offices in Wales of the NCC and Countryside Commission (whose present remit covers England and Wales). 'Decisions affecting Wales will in future be taken in Wales [by] a single body attuned to the needs of the Principality.' No consultation paper was issued.

1.9 No mention was made of the scientific base for these new agencies. Subject to parliamentary approval, the changes proposed for England and Wales, and the establishment of the new Scottish NCC, were to take effect in April 1991."

Discussion then followed on how best to secure the ability to take "a Great Britain over-view", and to ensure that the work of the new national councils continued to be underpinned by a sound science base, utilising the data and experience accumulated by the NCC. The proposed solution was a duty on the successor councils to form a joint advisory committee for that purpose.

The Carver Committee did not take up a position on the merits of reorganising the NCC but felt obliged to say that 'the reorganisation could have been better handled' (para. 3.2). A number of recommendations were made as to the new structure, with the object of ensuring scientific effectiveness, maintaining a national as well as a local perspective and supporting the independent commitment to nature conservation of the successor councils.

The Government's response to the Carver Report was published in May 1990 (H.L. Paper 60, Session 1989–90, 6th Report, May 17, 1990). The Government expressed agreement with or accepted, many of the Carver Committee's recommendations and in some cases assurances were given to introduce amendments to the Bill. The only significant reservation expressed by the Government was that it saw no need to extend the statutory remit of the Joint Committee to cover countryside and landscape conservation matters under the Countryside Acts:

"In the Government's view that remit should remain focused firmly on nature conservation. But the presence of the Chairman of the Countryside Commission will ensure that the Committee is well placed to take account of countryside matters in its deliberations." (DoE News Release No. 306, May 17, 1990.)

Nevertheless, in the debates on Second Reading of the Bill in the House of Lords, Lord Carver expressed continued reservations, the main ones being as to the cost and resourcing of the new arrangements, and the power of the Joint Committee to settle decisively conflicts with the County Councils over jurisdiction (*Hansard*, H.L. Vol. 519, cols. 502–503, May 18, 1990).

Lord Hesketh, on introducing Pt. VII on Second Reading and in Committee in the House of Lords, referred to "six fundamental objectives which lie at the root of reorganisation" (*Hansard*, H.L. Vol. 520, cols, 2119–2120, July 4, 1990).

"First, clearer accountability to Ministers; secondly, improved sensitivity to local circumstances; thirdly, a reduction in bureaucracy; fourthly, retention of the existing legal framework for wildlife conservation created by the 1981 Act; fifthly, effective coverage of national and global nature conservation issues, and, finally, protection of the Nature Conservancy Council's science base built up over 40 years."

The basic scheme of the reorganisation, as effected by Pt. VII, is as follows:—

(1) creation of three councils, the Nature Conservancy Council for England (more commonly known as English Nature), the Nature Conservancy Council for Scotland and the Countryside Commission for Wales ("the Councils") (s.128);

(2) transfer of nature conservation functions from the NCC to the Councils (ss.131–133);

(3) establishment by the Councils of the Joint Nature Conservation Committee ("the Joint Committee") (s.128(4)), to whose advice the Councils must have regard (s.132(1) and (3));

(4) the making of a transfer scheme or schemes by the NCC for the division of property, rights and liabilities between the Councils (s.135);

(5) entitlement by employees of the NCC to an offer of employment with one of the Councils (s.137); and

(6) dissolution of the NCC (s.138).

SSSIs
Some substantive amendments are also made to the law relating to sites of special scientific interest by Sched. 9: see note to s.132.

Wales
The Countryside Council for Wales takes over not only the functions of the NCC, but also a number of countryside functions of the Countryside Commission so far as concerns Wales (s.130 and Sched. 8).

Scotland
While nature conservation and countryside functions remained separate in Scotland under Pt. VII of the Act, the Natural Heritage (Scotland) Act 1991 integrated the functions of the Nature Conservancy Council for Scotland and the Countryside Commission for Scotland within a single body, Scottish Natural Heritage, as from April 1, 1992. This completed the Government's strategy for integrated agencies in Scotland and Wales. The funding of the new body has moved from the Department of Environment to the Scottish Office. See Scottish Development Department, *Scotland's Natural Heritage: The Way Ahead* (1990).

Territorial extent
Part VII applies to England and Wales and only applies to Scotland as regards the joint committee within the meaning of Part VII (s.164(4)).

COMMENCEMENT
Part VII came into force, save for the amendments made by ss.128, 130 and 132 on November 5, 1990 (The Environmental Protection Act 1990 (Commencement No. 1) Order 1990 No. 2226). The Environmental Protection Act 1990 (Commencement No. 6 and Appointed Day) Order 1991 (S.I. 1991 No. 685) brought the amendments made by ss.128, 130 and 132 and s.162(2) relating to the repeals of the Countryside Act 1968 and the Wildlife and Countryside Act 1981 into force on April 1, 1991. It also appointed April 1, 1991 as the day for the discharge of the respective functions of the Countryside Council for Wales and the Countryside Commission and the Nature Conservancy Council for England and the Nature Conservancy Council for Scotland. The Nature Conservancy Council was accordingly dissolved on December 21, 1991 by the Nature Conservancy Council (Dissolution) Order 1991 (S.I. 1991 No. 2923).

New Councils for England, Scotland and Wales

Creation and constitution of new Councils

128.—(1) There shall be [two] councils, to be called the Nature Conservancy Council for England, [...] and the Countryside Council for Wales (in this Part referred to as "the Councils").

(2) The Councils shall have the following membership, that is to say—

(a) the Nature Conservancy Council for England shall have not less than 10 nor more than 14 members;

(b) [...]; and

(c) the Countryside Council for Wales shall have not less than 8 nor more than 12 members;

and those members shall be appointed by the Secretary of State.

(3) The Secretary of State may by order amend paragraph (a), (b) or (c) of subsection (2) above so as to substitute for the number for the time being specified as the maximum membership of a Council such other number as he thinks appropriate.

(4) The Councils shall establish a committee to be called the Joint Nature Conservation Committee (in this Part referred to as "the joint committee").

(5) Schedules 6 and 7 to this Act shall have effect with respect to the constitution and proceedings of the Councils and of the joint committee and related matters.

DEFINITIONS
"the Councils": subs. (1).
"the joint committee": subs. (4).

AMENDMENTS
Subsection (1) was amended by the Natural Heritage (Scotland) Act 1991, Sched. 2 and Sched. 11. Subsection (2) was amended by the Natural Heritage (Scotland) Act 1991, Sched. 11.

GENERAL NOTE
The Councils: This section created three new Councils in England, Scotland and Wales to take over nature conservation functions from the NCC. The functions of the Nature Conservancy Council for Scotland were integrated with those of the Countryside Commission for Scotland within a new body, Scottish Natural Heritage, which was established by the Natural Heritage (Scotland) Act 1991. The amendments to the section reflect this and by virtue of s.4(1) and (2) of the Natural Heritage (Scotland) Act 1991, with the exception of subss. (4) and (5) (see below), the section no longer applies to Scotland. Members of the Councils are appointed by the Secretary of State (subs. (3)). Sched. 6 contains the detailed provisions as to constitution and membership, remuneration of members, staff, committees, reports and accounts, and similar practical matters.

The NCC for England is known as English Nature.

The first Chairman of the NCC for England is the Earl of Cranbrook. For Scotland the first chairman was Mr Magnus Magnusson who subsequently became Chairman of the Scottish Natural Heritage and for Wales Mr Michael Griffith.

The Joint Nature Conservation Committee: By subs. (4) the Councils are under a duty to establish a committee to be called the Joint Nature Conservation Committee. Detailed provisions as to the constitution of that Committee are contained in Sched. 7. Paragraphs 2–4 of the Schedule deal with the membership, which consists of a chairman appointed by the Secretary of State, three members appointed by the Secretary of State, the Chairman and one member of each Council, the chairman of the Countryside Commission, plus two non-voting members appointed by the Development of the Environment for Northern Ireland.

The statutory remit of the Joint Committee does not extend to countryside matters, but the Government sees the Committee as being in a position to take account of countryside interests by reason of its membership.

As to proposals for staffing and resourcing the Joint Committee, see *Hansard*, H.L. Vol. 522, col. 896.

Subss. (4) and (5): the joint committee
These subss. continue to apply to Scotland by virtue of s.4(2) of the Natural Heritage (Scotland) Act 1991 and all references to "the Councils" in these subss. include a reference to Scottish Natural Heritage.

Grants by Secretary of State to new Councils

129.—(1) The Secretary of State may with the approval of the Treasury make to the Councils grants of such amounts as the Secretary of State thinks fit.

(2) A grant under this section may be made subject to such conditions (including in particular conditions as to the use of the money for purposes of the joint committee) as the Secretary of State may with the approval of the Treasury think fit.

DEFINITIONS
"the Councils": s.128(1).
"the joint committee": s.128(4).

Countryside matters

Countryside functions of Welsh Council

130.—(1) The Countryside Council for Wales shall, in place of the Commission established under section 1 of the National Parks and Access to the Countryside Act 1949 (so far as concerns Wales), have such of the functions under the Acts amended by Schedule 8 to this Act (which relates to countryside matters) as are assigned to them in accordance with the amendments effected by that Schedule.

(2) The Countryside Council for Wales shall discharge those functions—

(a) for the conservation and enhancement of natural beauty in Wales and of the natural beauty and amenity of the countryside in Wales, both in the areas designated under the National Parks and Access to the Countryside Act 1949 as National Parks or as areas of outstanding natural beauty and elsewhere;

(b) for encouraging the provision or improvement, for persons resorting to the countryside in Wales, of facilities for the enjoyment thereof and for the enjoyment of the opportunities for open-air recreation and the study of nature afforded thereby;

and shall have regard to the social and economic interests of rural areas in Wales.

(3) The reference in subsection (2) above to the conservation of the natural beauty of the countryside includes the conservation of its flora, fauna and geological and physiographical features.

(4) The Countryside Council for Wales and the Countryside Commission shall discharge their respective functions under those Acts (as amended by Schedule 8) on and after a day to be appointed by an order made by the Secretary of State.

GENERAL NOTE

This section makes special arrangements for countryside matters in Wales. The Countryside Council for Wales is to exercise functions not only of the NCC but also of the Countryside Commission so far as concern Wales. The relevant functions are those set out at Sched. 8, which also makes the amendments to the relevant provisions necessary to substitute the name of the Countryside Council for Wales. The transfer of functions is effective on a day to be appointed by the Secretary of State (subs. (4)). The Environmental Protection Act 1990 (Commencement No. 6 and Appointed Day) Order 1991 (S.I. 1991 No. 685) appointed April 1, 1991 as the day for the transfer of functions.

Subsection (2) contains provisions as to the purposes for which the Welsh Council shall exercise its functions and the matters to which it shall have regard. The subsection as originally introduced by the Government on amendment at Lords' Report Stage qualified the reference to National Parks with the word "particularly", corresponding to the relevant wording in the National Parks and Access to the Countryside Act 1949, s.1. The word "particularly" was dropped at Third Reading stage and amendments have been made to the 1949 Act to achieve consistency: see Sched. 8, para. 1(2).

The Welsh Council has issued a "Statement of Policy" (1991). The Statement sets out the functions and responsibilities of the Council. The Council is responsible for undertaking in Wales the previously separate functions of the Countryside Commission in relation to conservation of the natural beauty of the countryside and its public enjoyment, and of the Nature Conservancy Council in relation to the conservation of nature. The Statement highlights the Council's duty to ensure that an appropriate balance is maintained between these functions in accordance with its statutory obligations. Much of the effectiveness of this work depends upon good relationships with organisations in both the public and private sector and with voluntary organisations both national and international.

The Council is expected to develop policies based upon research that it has carried out, commissioned or supported, on all matters affecting its function and to advise Ministers, local authorities and other organisations accordingly. It is also its function to participate fully in the development of policies falling under the Statutory Joint Nature Conservancy Council, that is, policies with a U.K. or international element. The Statement points out that the Council must not lose sight of economic or social considerations when formulating its policies, paying particular regard to the needs of agriculture, forestry and rural areas. Accordingly, the Council will encourage those social and economic activities that conserve or enhance the natural beauty of the countryside. The Council is responsible for the dissemination of information about conservation and public enjoyment of the countryside in Wales and education to increase public awareness. Within Wales, the council has the authority, with the approval of the Secretary of State, to designate areas as National Parks, areas of outstanding beauty, etc. and to maintain and manage designated sites, providing advice on management matters and financial support when appropriate. Another function is to develop a comprehensive Welsh language policy.

It is anticipated by the Council that more use will be made of the powers to grant aid to organisations wishing to acquire land for conservation or recreational purposes rather than acquire extensive areas itself as was the case under the Nature Conservancy Council.

Nature conservation in Great Britain

Nature conservation functions: preliminary

131.—(1) For the purposes of nature conservation, and fostering the understanding thereof, the Councils shall, in place of the Nature Conservancy Council established under the Nature Conservancy Council Act 1973, have the functions conferred on them by sections 132 to 134 below (which are in this Part referred to as "nature conservation functions").

(2) It shall be the duty of the Councils in discharging their nature conservation functions to take appropriate account of actual or possible ecological changes.

(3) The Councils shall discharge their nature conservation functions on and after a day to be appointed by an order made by the Secretary of State.

(4) The Secretary of State may give the Councils, or any of them, directions of a general or specific character with regard to the discharge of any of their nature conservation functions other than those conferred on them by section 132(1)(a) below.

(5) Any reference in this section to the Councils includes a reference to the joint committee and, accordingly, directions under subsection (4) above may be given to the joint committee as respects any of the functions dischargeable by them (other than under section 133(2)(a)).

(6) In this Part "nature conservation" means the conservation of flora, fauna or geological or physiographical features.

DEFINITIONS
"the Councils": s.128(1).
"the joint committee": s.128(4).
"nature conservation": subs. (6).
"nature conservation functions": subs. (1).

GENERAL NOTE
This section confers upon the new Councils the "nature conservation functions" referred to in ss.132 and 133 as from a date to be appointed by the Secretary of State (subs. (3)). The Environmental Protection Act 1990 (Commencement No. 6 Appointed Day) Order 1991 S.I. No. 685 appoints April 1, 1991 as the relevant day. The functions are conferred for "the purposes of nature conservation" (defined in subs. (6) as the conservation of flora, fauna or geological or physiographical features) and the Councils and Joint Council are under a statutory duty by subs. (2) to "take appropriate account of actual or possible ecological changes" in exercising their functions.

By subs. (4), except in relation to the functions conferred by s.132(1)(a), the Councils can be subject to directions of the Secretary of State as to the discharge of their functions. By virtue of s.4(3) of the Natural Heritage (Scotland) Act 1991, this section only applies to Scotland in so far as it relates to the joint committee.

Habitats Directive
Functions under ss.131–134 are to be exercised so as to secure compliance with the requirements of the Habitats Directive 92/43/EEC (O.J. L206/7, 22.7.92). This requirement is imposed by the Conservation (Natural Habitats, &c.) Regulations 1994 (S.I. 1994 No. 2716), reg. 3(2).

General functions of the Councils

132.—(1) The Councils shall each have the following functions, namely—
   (a) such of the functions previously discharged by the Nature Conservancy Council under the Acts amended by Schedule 9 to this Act as

are assigned to them in accordance with the amendments effected by that Schedule;

(b) the establishment, maintenance and management of nature reserves (within the meaning of section 15 of the National Parks and Access to the Countryside Act 1949) in their area;

(c) the provision of advice for the Secretary of State or any other Minister on the development and implementation of policies for or affecting nature conservation in their area;

(d) the provision of advice and the dissemination of knowledge to any persons about nature conservation in their area or about matters arising from the discharge of their functions under this section or section 134 below;

(e) the commissioning or support (where by financial means or otherwise) of research which in their opinion is relevant to any of their functions under this section or section 134 below,

and the Councils shall, in discharging their functions under this section, have regard to any advice given to them by the joint committee under section 133(3) below.

(2) The Councils shall each have power—

(a) to accept any gift or contribution made to them for the purposes of any of the functions conferred on them by subsection (1) above or section 134 below and, subject to the terms of the gift or contribution, to apply it to those purposes;

(b) to initiate and carry out such research directly related to those functions as it is appropriate that they should carry out instead of commissioning or supporting other persons under paragraph (e) of that subsection;

and they may do all such other things as are incidental or conducive to those functions including (without prejudice to the generality of this provision) making charges and holding land or any interest in or right over land.

(3) Nothing in this section [or in the Natural Heritage (Scotland) Act 1991 (in so far as it relates to the nature conservation functions of Scottish Natural Heritage)] shall be taken as preventing any of the Councils—

(a) if consulted by another of the Councils about a matter relating to the functions of that other Council, from giving that other Council any advice or information which they are able to give; or

(b) from giving advice or information to the joint committee about any matter relating to any of the functions conferred by section 133(2) and (3) below.

DEFINITIONS
   "the Councils": s.128(1).
   "the joint committee": s.128(4).
   "nature conservation": s.131(6).

AMENDMENTS
Subsection (3) was amended by the Natural Heritage (Scotland) Act 1991, Sched. 3, para. 10(5).

GENERAL NOTE
This section states the general functions of the Councils. As well as the functions previously discharged by the NCC under the provisions set out in Sched. 9 (which also makes the necessary consequential amendments), the functions include: advice to the Secretary of State or any other Minister (subs. (1)(c)); the provision of advice and the dissemination of knowledge generally (subs. (1)(d)); the commissioning or support of research (subs. (1)(e)); the acceptance of gifts (subs. (2)(a)); direct research activities (subs. (2)(b)); and the provision of advice and information to another of the Councils or to the Joint Committee (subs. (3)). With the exception of subs. (3), in which all references to "the Councils" in that subs. include a reference to Scottish

Natural Heritage: Natural Heritage (Scotland) Act 1991, ss.4(1) and (2), this section no longer applies to Scotland.

Sched. 9: substantive amendments
Schedule 9 in the main consists simply of consequential amendments. However, para. 4(2) of the Schedule makes an important substantive amendment to s.15(2) of the Countryside Act 1968 (dealing with agreements for the management of sites of special scientific interest or SSSIs) by (a) deleting the reference to "in the national interest"; and (b) making it clear that agreements may be entered into with owners of land adjacent to the SSSI.

This second amendment is particularly important, since, as was pointed out by Lord Cranbrook (*Hansard*, H.L. Vol. 520, col. 2224), operations on land adjoining SSSIs can frequently affect the conservation value of the SSSI itself.

It was also suggested by Lord Cranbrook that an amendment should be made to clarify that the power to enter management agreement extends to owners and occupiers with a lesser interest in land, such as crofters or commoners. The Government, however, took the view that this was already clearly the case (*Hansard*, H.L. Vol. 522, col. 973).

Schedule 9, para. 11(9) makes a further unobtrusive but substantive amendment to correct defective working in s.29 of the Wildlife and Countryside Act 1981. It makes it clear that the owner or occupier of land subject to a nature conservation order under s.29 must *after the making of the Order*, give notice of any intention to carry out a potentially damaging operation (*Hansard*, H.L. Vol. 522, cols. 2232–3).

The Government also in the course of debate on Pt. VII clarified the position as to its views on the scope of existing powers to support positive conservation works in the wider countryside outside SSSIs, the Government's view being that grant schemes to that effect are already permissible under existing legislation (*Hansard*, H.L. Vol. 522, col. 981). It should be noted that the Natural Heritage (Scotland) Act 1991 effects certain repeals in Sched. 9. Subject to those repeals the amendments made by Sched. 9 continue to extend to Scotland subject to the proviso that references to Scottish Natural Heritage are substituted for all references to the Nature Conservancy Council for Scotland: Natural Heritage (Scotland) Act 1991, s.4(5) and (10).

Habitats Directive
Functions under ss.131–134 are to be exercised so as to secure compliance with the requirements of the Habitats Directive 92/43/EEC (O.J. No. L206/7, 22.7.92). This requirement is imposed by the Conservation (Natural Habitats, &c.) Regulations 1994 (S.I. 1994 No. 2716), reg. 3(2).

Special functions of Councils

133.—(1) The Councils shall jointly have the following functions which may, however, be discharged only through the joint committee; and in this section the functions so dischargeable are referred to as "special functions".
(2) The special functions of the Council are—
  (a) such of the functions previously discharged by the Nature Conservancy Council under the Wildlife and Countryside Act 1981 as are assigned to the Councils jointly as special functions in accordance with the amendments to that Act effected by Schedule 9 to this Act;
  (b) the provision of advice for the Secretary of State or any other Minister on the development and implementation of policies for or affecting nature conservation for Great Britain as a whole or nature conservation outside Great Britain;
  (c) the provision of advice and the dissemination of knowledge to any persons about nature conservation for Great Britain as a whole or nature conservation outside Great Britain;
  (d) the establishment of common standards throughout Great Britain for the monitoring of nature conservation and for research into nature conservation and the analysis of the resulting information;
  (e) the commissioning or support (whether by financial means or otherwise) of research which in the opinion of the joint committee is relevant to any matter mentioned in paragraphs (a) to (d) above;
and section 132(2) above shall apply to the special functions as it applies to the functions conferred by subsection (1) of that section.
(3) The joint committee may give advice or information to any of the

Councils on any matter arising in connection with the functions of that Council under section 132 above [or, as the case may be, the nature conservation functions of Scottish Natural Heritage] which, in the opinion of the committee, concerns nature conservation for Great Britain as a whole or nature conservation outside Great Britain.

(4) For the purposes of this section, references to nature conservation for Great Britain as a whole are references to—

(a) any nature conservation matter of national or international importance or which otherwise affect the interests of Great Britain as a whole; or

(b) any nature conservation matter which arises throughout Great Britain and raises issues common to England, Scotland and Wales,

and it is immaterial for the purposes of paragraph (a) above that a matter arises only in relation to England, to Scotland or to Wales.

(5) The Secretary of State may, as respects any matters arising in connection with—

(a) any special function of the Councils, or

(b) the function of the joint committee under subsection (3) above,

give directions to any of the Councils requiring that Council (instead of the joint committee) to discharge that function in relation to that matter.

DEFINITIONS
  "the Councils": s.128(1).
  "the joint committee": s.128(4).
  "nature conservation": s.131(6).
  "special functions": subs. (1).

AMENDMENT
Subsection (3) was amended by the Natural Heritage (Scotland) Act 1991, s.4(4)(b).

GENERAL NOTE
This important section provides the demarcation line between the functions exercisable by each of the Councils independently and those "special functions" that may only be discharged jointly through the Joint Committee. These "special functions" are listed at subs. (2) and include: the provision of advice to Ministers on policies for nature conservation in Great Britain as a whole or nature conservation outside Great Britain; the dissemination of knowledge and the giving of general advice on such matters; the commissioning or support of research on such matters; and the establishment of common standards for monitoring, research and analysis.

Under subs. (3) the Joint Committee may give advice to the Councils on any matter which, in the opinion of the Joint Committee, concerns nature conservation for Great Britain as a whole or nature conservation outside Great Britain. Subsection (4) defines "nature conservation for Great Britain as a whole" by reference to (a) matters of national or international importance, or which otherwise affect the interests of Great Britain as a whole whether arising in England, Scotland or Wales; and (b) matters arising throughout Great Britain and raising issues common to England, Scotland and Wales.

Presumably the first of these categories would include the designation or conservation of sites which are of national or international importance, whether or not designated as such by E.C. or international law. The second category is intended to enable data, for example on nationally or internationally important species or habitats, to be collected and analysed in a form which meets the requirements of the Government, Joint Committee and, where relevant, the European Community or other international bodies. It will also enable the scientific and research standards of the new Councils to be monitored by the Joint Committee.

Concern was expressed by the Carver Committee on how possible disputes between the Councils and the Joint Committee as to whether a matter fell within the Council's special functions should be resolved. The Government's view expressed in its response to the Carver Committee is that such issues are, in the last analysis, matters of interpretation for the courts and so the views of the Joint Committee cannot be conclusive, though the reference on the opinion of the Joint Committee in subs. (3) inevitably introduces a considerable element of subjectivity.

By s.132(1) the Councils must have regard to any advice given by the Joint Committee under s.133(3).

It should be noted that this section continues to apply to Scotland and that all references to "the Councils" should be read as including a reference to Scottish Natural Heritage: Natural Heritage (Scotland) Act 1991, s.4(1) and (4). In discharging its nature conservation functions, Scottish Natural Heritage must have regard to any advice given to it by the joint committee under subs. (3): Natural Heritage (Scotland) Act 1991, s.4(4).

Habitats Directive
Functions under ss.131–134 are to be exercised so as to secure compliance with the requirements of the Habitats Directive 92/43/EEC (O.J. No. L206/7, 22.7.92). This requirement is imposed by the Conservation (Natural Habitats, &c.) Regulations 1994 (S.I. 1994 No. 2716), reg. 3(2).

Grants and loans by the Councils

134.—(1) The Councils may each, with the consent of or in accordance with a general authorisation given by the Secretary of State, give financial assistance by way of grant or loan (or partly in one way and partly in the other) to any person in respect of expenditure incurred or to be incurred by him in doing anything which in their opinion is conducive to nature conservation or fostering the understanding of nature conservation.

(2) No consent or general authorisation shall be given by the Secretary of State under subsection (1) above without the approval of the Treasury.

(3) On making a grant or loan a Council may impose such conditions as they think fit, including (in the case of a grant) conditions for repayment in specified circumstances.

(4) The Councils shall exercise their powers under subsection (3) above so as to ensure that any person receiving a grant or loan under this section in respect of premises to which the public are to be admitted (on payment or otherwise) shall, in the means of access both to and within the premises, and in the parking facilities and sanitary conveniences to be available (if any), make provision, so far as it is in the circumstances both practicable and reasonable, for the needs of members of the public visiting the premises who are disabled.

DEFINITIONS
　"the Councils": s.128(1).
　"nature conservation": s.131(6).

GENERAL NOTE
This section gives power to the Councils to provide financial assistance by grant or loan to any person incurring, or proposing to incur, expenditure on any activity which in their opinion is conducive to nature conservation or the understanding of it. It retains for the new Councils the enlarged powers of grants and loans given to the NCC by s.38 of the Wildlife and Countryside Act 1981 and follows closely the drafting of that section. This section no longer extends to Scotland: Natural Heritage (Scotland) Act 1991, s.4(1).

Habitats Directive
Functions under ss.131–134 are to be exercised so as to secure compliance with the requirements of the Habitats Directive 92/43/EEC (O.J. No. L206/7, 22.7.92). This requirement is imposed by the Conservation (Natural Habitats, &c.) Regulations 1994 (S.I. 1994 No. 2716), reg. 3(2).

Transfer of property, rights and liabilities to new Councils

Schemes for the transfer of property etc. of the Nature Conservancy Council

135.—(1) The Nature Conservancy Council shall make one or more schemes ("transfer schemes") for the division of all their property, rights and liabilities (other than rights and liabilities under the contracts of employment of their staff and in respect of the provision of pensions, allowances or gratuities) between the Councils.

(2) On the date appointed to a transfer scheme, the property, rights and

liabilities of the Nature Conservancy Council which are the subject of the scheme shall, by virtue of this subsection, become property, rights and liabilities of the Council to which they are allocated by the Scheme.

(3) Part I of Schedule 10 to this Act shall have effect in relation to transfer schemes under this section.

(4) The rights and liabilities of the Nature Conservancy Council in respect of the provision of pensions, allowances and gratuities for or in respect of their members and employees or their former members or employees shall, on the date appointed under section 131(3) above, by virtue of this subsection, become rights and liabilities of the Secretary of State.

DEFINITION
"transfer schemes": subs. (1).

GENERAL NOTE
The NCC is placed under a duty by this section to draw up a scheme or schemes for the division and transfer of the NCC's property, rights and liabilities as between the Councils.

Subsection (2) has the effect of vesting such property, rights and liabilities in the new Councils in accordance with the transfer schemes. Schedule 10, Pt. I makes detailed provision for the scheme-making procedure and as to the contents of schemes.

Matters of employment and pension rights cannot be dealt with by such schemes, and the rights and liabilities of the NCC in relation to such matters become rights and liabilities of the Secretary of State by virtue of subs. (4). This section no longer extends to Scotland: Natural Heritage (Scotland) Act 1991, s.4(1).

Transfer to Welsh Council of certain property etc. of Countryside Commission

136.—(1) The Countryside Commission shall make one or more schemes ("transfer schemes") for allocating to the Countryside Council for Wales so much of their property, rights and liabilities (other than rights and liabilities under the contracts of employment of their staff) as the Commission consider appropriate having regard to the countryside functions conferred on the Council by section 130 above.

(2) On the date appointed by a transfer scheme, the property, rights and liabilities of the Countryside Commission which are the subject of the scheme shall, by virtue of this subsection, become property, rights and liabilities of the Countryside Council for Wales.

(3) Part II of Schedule 10 to this Act shall have effect in relation to transfer schemes under this section.

DEFINITION
"transfer schemes": subs. (1).

GENERAL NOTE
This section contains equivalent provisions to s.135 in relation to the property, rights and liabilities of the Countryside Commission to be transferred to the Countryside Council for Wales (see s.130). Sched. 10, Pt. II contains the detailed provisions on the necessary schemes of transfer.

Employment by new Councils of staff of existing bodies

Offers of employment to employees of Nature Conservancy Council and certain employees of Countryside Commission

137.—(1) Any person who immediately before the date appointed under section 131(3) above is employed by the Nature Conservancy Council shall be entitled to receive an offer of employment from one of the Councils (to be determined in accordance with proposals made by the Nature Conservancy Council).

(2) Subsection (1) above does not apply to a person whose contract of

employment with the Nature Conservancy Council terminates on the day immediately preceding the date appointed under section 131(3) above.

(3) The Countryside Council for Wales shall also make an offer of employment to any person who—

(a) is, immediately before the date appointed under section 130(4) above, employed by the Countryside Commission; and

(b) is a person the Commission has proposed should receive such an offer.

(4) Part III of Schedule 10 to this Act shall have effect with respect to the offers and proposals under this section.

<small>DEFINITION

"the Councils": s.128(1).

GENERAL NOTE

This section ensures that all staff employed by the NCC immediately before the appointed day (see s.131(3)) are entitled to receive an offer of employment from one of the new Councils. The terms of the offers are to be determined in accordance with proposals made by the NCC under Sched. 10, Pt. III (para. 10). The Secretary of State may approve the proposals submitted or substitute his own proposals, in each case after consultation with the new Councils (Sched. 10, para. 11).

The terms offered must be such that, taken as a whole, they are not less favourable to the person to whom the offer is made than the terms on which he is employed at the date of the offer (Sched. 10, para. 14(3)). Any dispute as to whether the offer complies with this requirement is to be referred to an industrial tribunal (Sched. 10, para. 17(1)).

Offers may not be revoked for a period of three months (Sched. 10, para. 14(4)) and unreasonable refusal of an offer results in loss of redundancy rights (Sched. 10, para. 16). Where an offer is accepted, continuity of employment is preserved (Sched. 10, para. 15).

Equivalent provisions apply to employees of the Countryside Commission in relation to any person to whom the Commission proposes an offer of employment with the Countryside Council for Wales should be made (subs. (3)).

This section no longer extends to Scotland Natural Heritage (Scotland) Act 1991, s.4(1).</small>

Dissolution of Nature Conservancy Council

Winding up and dissolution of Nature Conservancy Council

138.—(1) On the date appointed under section 131(3) above the chairman and other members of the Nature Conservancy Council shall cease to hold office and after that date—

(a) the Council shall consist only of a chairman appointed by the Secretary of State and such one or more other persons as may be so appointed; and

(b) the Council shall have only the following functions, namely—

(i) anything which falls to be done by the Council under any transfer scheme under section 135 above;

(ii) the preparation of such accounts and reports as the Secretary of State may direct;

and such other functions as are necessary for winding up their affairs.

(2) The Secretary of State may, by order, after consultation with the Nature Conservancy Council and the Councils, dissolve the Nature Conservancy Council on a day specified in the order as soon as he is satisfied that nothing remains to be done by that Council.

(3) The Secretary of State may pay to persons who cease to hold office by virtue of subsection (1) above such sums by way of compensation for loss of office, or loss or diminution of pension rights as the Secretary of State may, with the approval of the Treasury, determine.

<small>DEFINITION

"the Councils": s.128(1).</small>

GENERAL NOTE
This section provides for the winding up and ultimate dissolution of the NCC. Provision is made for fulfilment of residual functions of transfer, accounting and reporting. The NCC was dissolved by an order under subs. (2) as from December 21, 1991: The Nature Conservancy Council (Dissolution) Order 1991 (S.I. 1991 No. 2923). This section no longer extends to Scotland: Natural Heritage (Scotland) Act 1991, s.4(1).

Transitional provisions and savings

Transitional provisions and savings

139. Schedule 11 of this Act (which contains transitional provisions and savings relating to this Part) shall have effect.

GENERAL NOTE
This section applies the detailed transitional provisions of Sched. 11. These provisions deal with continuity of functions and construction of documents.
Paragraph 5 of the Schedule deals with existing designated areas of outstanding natural beauty and long-distance routes which straddle the English and Welsh border. The English and Welsh parts of such AONBs are to be treated as distinct AONBs, whereas long-distance routes continue to be single routes for the purposes of Pt. IV of the National Parks and Access to the Countryside Act 1949, but with the relevant Council exercising their functions over their relevant part. The relevant Councils may only exercise their respective functions in relation to their part of the area or route after consultation with the other Council concerned, and arrangements may be made for joint exercise of functions (para. 5(4)). Similarly, by para. 11, nature reserves or SSSIs which straddle the English-Welsh border are to be treated as distinct reserves or sites, but the new Councils concerned may only exercise their functions in consultation with each other or jointly by arrangement (para. 11(3)).
Only para. 12 of Sched. 11 continues to apply to Scotland and references therein to a new council in relation to Scotland must be construed as references to Scottish Natural Heritage: Natural Heritage (Scotland) Act 1991, s.4(8).

PART VIII

MISCELLANEOUS

GENERAL NOTE
Part VIII contains a number of miscellaneous provisions of varying importance. The most significant are:
(1) power to restrict the importation, use, supply or storage of substances or articles for the purpose of avoiding pollution, or harm to man, animals or plants (s.140);
(2) power to restrict the importation or exportation of waste for the purpose of preventing pollution or harm to human health or for conserving facilities or resources for dealing with waste (s.141);
(3) powers to make provision for the obtaining of information about substances with potential to cause pollution or harm to human health (s.142);
(4) provision (now repealed) for public registers of potentially contaminated land (s.143);
(5) amendments of the legislation of control of hazardous substances (s.144 and Sched. 13);
(6) increase of maximum penalties in respect of water pollution offences (s.145);
(7) amendments on legislation as to marine deposits (s.146) and creation of public registers as to such deposits and marine incineration (s.147);
(8) amendments of the provisions as to oil pollution offences from ships (s.148);
(9) provisions for the control of stray dogs (ss.149–151);
(10) provision as to banning the burning of straw, stubble and other crop residues (s.152).

Other controls on substances, articles or waste

Power to prohibit or restrict the importation, use, supply or storage of injurious substances or articles

140.—(1) The Secretary of State may by regulations prohibit or restrict—
(a) the importation into and the landing and unloading in the United Kingdom,

  (b) the use for any purpose,
  (c) the supply for any purpose, and
  (d) the storage,
of any specified substance or article if he considers it appropriate to do so for
the purpose of preventing the substance or article from causing pollution of
the environment or harm to human health or to the health of animals or
plants.

  (2) Any such prohibition or restriction may apply—
    (a) in all, or only in specified, areas;
    (b) in all, or only in specified, circumstances or if conditions imposed by
        the regulations are not complied with; and
    (c) to all, or only to specified descriptions of, persons.

  (3) Regulations under this section may—
    (a) confer on the Secretary of State power to direct that any substance
        or article whose use, supply or storage is prohibited or restricted is
        to be treated as waste or controlled waste of any description and in
        relation to any such substance or article—
        (i) to apply, with or without modification, specified provisions of
            Part II; or
        (ii) to direct that it be disposed of or treated in accordance with the
            direction;
    (b) confer on the Secretary of State power, where a substance or article
        has been imported, landed or unloaded in contravention of a
        prohibition or restriction imposed under subsection (1)(a) above,
        to require that the substance or article be disposed of or treated in
        or removed from the United Kingdom;
    (c) confer powers corresponding to those conferred by section 17
        above on persons authorised for any purpose of the regulations by
        the Secretary of State or any local or other authority; and
    (d) include such other incidental and supplemental, and such tran-
        sitional provisions, as the Secretary of State considers appropriate.

  (4) The Secretary of State may, by regulations under this section, direct
that, for the purposes of any power conferred on him under subsection
(3)(b) above, any prohibition or restriction on the importation into or the
landing and unloading in the United Kingdom imposed—
    (a) by or under any Community instrument, or
    (b) by or under any enactment,
shall be treated as imposed under subsection (1)(a) above and any power
conferred on him under subsection (3)(b) above shall be exercisable
accordingly.

  (5) The Secretary of State may by order establish a committee to give him
advice in relation to the exercise of the power to make regulations under this
section and Schedule 12 to this Act shall have effect in relation to it.

  (6) Subject to subsection (7) below, it shall be the duty of the Secretary of
State before he makes any regulations under this section other than
regulations under subsection (4) above—
    (a) to consult the committee constituted under subsection (5) above
        about the proposed regulations;
    (b) having consulted the committee, to publish in the London Gazette
        and, if the regulations apply in Scotland or Northern Ireland, the
        Edinburgh Gazette or, as the case may be, Belfast Gazette and in
        any other publication which he considers appropriate, a notice
        indicating the effect of the proposed regulations and specifying—
        (i) the date on which it is proposed that the regulations will come
            into force;
        (ii) a place where a draft of the proposed regulations may be
            inspected free of charge by members of the public during office
            hours; and

(iii) a period of not less than 14 days, beginning with the date on which the notice is first published, during which representations in writing may be made to the Secretary of State about the proposed regulations; and

(c) to consider any representations which are made to him in accordance with the notice.

(7) The Secretary of State may make regulations under this section in relation to any substance or article without observing the requirements of subsection (6) above where it appears to him that there is an imminent risk, if those requirements are observed, that serious pollution of the environment will be caused.

(8) The Secretary of State may, after performing the duty imposed on him by subsection (6) above with respect to any proposed regulations, make the regulations either—

(a) in the form of the draft mentioned in subsection (6)(b) above, or

(b) in that form with such modifications as he considers appropriate;

but the Secretary of State shall not make any regulations incorporating modifications unless he is of opinion that it is appropriate for the requirements of subsection (6) above to be disregarded.

(9) Regulations under this section may provide that a person who contravenes or fails to comply with a specified provision of the regulations or causes or permits another person to contravene or fail to comply with a specified provision of the regulations commits an offence and may prescribe the maximum penalty for the offence.

(10) No offence under the regulations shall be made punishable with imprisonment for more than two years or punishable on summary conviction with a fine exceeding level 5 on the standard scale (if not calculated on a daily basis) or, in the case of a continuing offence, exceeding one-tenth of the level on the standard scale specified as the maximum penalty for the original offence.

(11) In this section—

"the environment" means the air, water and land, or any of those media, and the medium of air includes the air within buildings and the air within other natural or man-made structures above or below ground;

"specified" means specified in the regulations; and

"substance" means any natural or artificial substance, whether in solid or liquid form or in the form of a gas or vapour and it includes mixtures of substances.

DEFINITIONS
"the environment": subs. (11).
"specified": subs. (11).
"substance": subs. (11).

COMMENCEMENT
January 1, 1991, (s.164(2)).

GENERAL NOTE
This section replaces and expands the powers previously contained in s.100 of the Control of Pollution Act 1974, which empowered the Secretary of State to prohibit or restrict the importation, exportation, use and supply of hazardous substances. The new powers are wider than s.100 in a number of respects. "Articles" are covered as well as "substances", there is an express power to require re-exportation, storage may now be restricted or prohibited, and use "for any purpose" may now be controlled (as opposed to use "in connection with any trade or business or manufacturing process" under the 1974 Act, s.100(1)(b)).

Four statutory instruments have been made under this section.

The Environmental Protection (Controls on Injurious Substances) Regulations 1992 (S.I. 1992 No. 31) have been made under these powers to control the supply or use of preparations or waste with a specified content of PCB or PCT; the supply and use of certain lead paint; and the supply and use of mercury compounds.

The Environmental Protection (Controls on Injurious Substances) (No. 2) Regulations 1992 (S.I. 1992 No. 1583) have been made prohibiting the marketing and use of Ugilec 141 as from June 18, 1994, and Ugilec 121 and DBBT as from July 31, 1992.

The Environmental Protection (Controls on Injurious Substances) Regulations 1993 (S.I. 1993 No. 1) have been made to prohibit the marketing and use of PCPs, with a few specific exemptions.

The Environmental Protection (Non-Refillable Refrigerant Containers) Regulations 1994 (S.I. 1994 No. 199) impose, subject to exceptions for certain purposes, prohibitions on importation, supply and storage of non-refillable containers holding certain CFCs and HCFCs for use as refrigerants in air-conditioning and refrigeration machinery.

A further statutory instrument is to be made under this section, primarily to implement Council Regulation (EEC) No. 3093/94 on substances that deplete the ozone layer, but also to amend S.I. 1994 No. 199 above in certain respects: draft Environmental Protection (Controls on Substances that Deplete the Ozone Layer) Regulations [1996] (October 10, 1995 draft available as at the end of 1995). Council Regulations are directly applicable within Member States, but a number of procedural matters are to be addressed by the regulations: designation of a competent authority (the Secretary of State), the application of enforcement powers and criminal sanctions, etc.

Subs. (3)
This subsection gives some important ancillary powers including the power to direct that relevant substances or articles be treated as controlled waste and so subjected to the regime of Pt. II of the Act. There is also the power to direct how substances or articles landed in breach of a prohibition or restriction are to be dealt with, whether by treatment or disposal within the U.K. or by re-exportation.

Subs. (5): advisory committee
The Secretary of State is given express power to constitute an advisory committee which must then be consulted by him in exercising his powers under the section (subs. (6)). Sched. 12 contains provisions as to membership, terms of office, facilities and remuneration. The Secretary of State established the Advisory Committee on July 25, 1991 by the Advisory Committee on Hazardous Substances Order 1991 (S.I. 1991 No. 1487) and specified the terms of office of its Members by the Advisory Committee on Hazardous Substances (Terms of Office) Regulations 1991 (S.I. 1991 No. 1488).

Territorial extent
The section applies to imports and exports to and from England, Scotland and Wales and imports to Northern Ireland (s.164(4)).

Power to prohibit or restrict the importation or exportation of waste

141.—(1) The Secretary of State may, for the purpose of preventing any risk of pollution of the environment or of harm to human health arising from waste being imported or exported or of conserving the facilities or resources for dealing with waste, make regulations prohibiting or restricting, or providing for the prohibition or restriction of—

(a) the importation into and the landing and unloading in the United Kingdom, or

(b) the exportation, or the loading for exportation, from the United Kingdom,

of waste of any description.

(2) Regulations under this section may make different provision for different descriptions of waste or waste of any description in different circumstances.

(3) Regulations under this section may, as respects any description of waste, confer or impose on waste regulation authorities or any of them such functions in relation to the importation of waste as appear to be appropriate to the Secretary of State, subject to such limitations and conditions as are specified in the regulations.

(4) Regulations under this section may confer or impose on waste regulation authorities or any of them functions of enforcing any of the regulations on behalf of the Secretary of State whether or not the functions fall within subsection (3) above.

(5) Regulations under this section may—

(a) as respects functions conferred or imposed on waste regulation authorities—

    (i) make them exercisable in relation to individual consignments or consignments in a series by the same person but not in relation to consignments or descriptions of consignments generally; and

    (ii) [...]

(b) impose or provide for the imposition of prohibitions either absolutely or only if conditions or procedures prescribed in or under the regulations are not complied with;

(c) impose duties to be complied with before, on or after any importation or exportation of waste by persons who are, or are to be, consignors, consignees, carriers or holders of the waste or any waste derived from it;

(d) confer powers corresponding to those conferred by section 69(3) above;

(e) provide for appeals to the Secretary of State from determinations made by authorities under the regulations;

(f) provide for the keeping by the Secretary of State, waste regulation authorities and waste collection authorities of public registers of information relating to the importation and exportation of waste and for the transmission of such information between any of those persons;

(g) create offences, subject to the limitation that no offence shall be punishable with imprisonment for more than two years or punishable on summary conviction with imprisonment for more than six months or a fine exceeding level 5 on the standard scale (if not calculated on a daily basis) or, in the case of a continuing offence, exceeding one-tenth of the level on the standard scale specified as the maximum penalty for the original offence.

(6) In this section—

"the environment" means land, water and air or any of them;

"harm" includes offence to any of man's senses;

"waste", "waste collection authority", and "waste regulation authority" have the same meaning as in Part II; and

"the United Kingdom" includes its territorial sea.

(7) In the application of this section to Northern Ireland and the territorial sea of the United Kingdom adjacent to Northern Ireland "waste regulation authority" means a district council established under the Local Government Act (Northern Ireland) 1972.

DEFINITIONS

"the environment": subs. (6).
"harm": subs. (6).
"the United Kingdom": subs. (6).
"waste": s.75(2) and (3).
"waste collection authority": s.30(3).
"waste regulation authority": s.30(1).

COMMENCEMENT
January 1, 1991 (s.164(2)).

AMENDMENT
Subsection (5)(a)(ii) was revoked by the Environment Act 1995, Sched. 24.

GENERAL NOTE
This section contains a new power to control imports and exports of waste by way of regulations. The provisions no doubt stem, to some degree, from public concern as to the importation of waste for incineration or treatment within the U.K. The Second Report of HM Inspectorate of Pollution (August 1990) contains information on waste imports for the period 1988/89 (para. 5.20 *ff*). In the relevant period it is estimated that some 52,000 tonnes of special waste were imported into England and Wales, the majority going to plants in Pontypool, Manchester and the West Midlands. No special waste was exported during the period.

However, as the HMIP report points out, to put the matter in context, only about 3 per cent of special waste disposed of in the U.K. was imported, a figure scarcely justifying the description applied by some environmental groups and M.P.s of the "dustbin of Europe" (para. 5.22). The HMIP Report also refers to two incidents involving proposals for the landing of imported waste, which "caused considerable public anxiety and took up a significant amount of the Inspectorate's time." These were the "Karin B" incident and a proposal to import two million tonnes of household waste from the USA for landfill in a site in Cornwall. Since the reporting period for the HMIP Report, there have been further similar incidents which have received media coverage.

The relevant regulations under subs. (1) may be made for the following purposes:
  (a) preventing any risk of pollution of the environment or of harm to human health. It appears this could cover, for example, the import of waste of unknown composition or characteristics so that safe treatment or handling could not be assured, or the export of waste to countries with no facilities for dealing with it safely. Such exports are intended to be avoided by the Basel Convention on *The Control of Transboundary Movements of Hazardous Wastes and their Disposal* (Cm. 984), to which the U.K. is a signatory. The Government's general stance is in favour of national self-sufficiency in waste disposal facilities (see Cm. 1200, *This Common Inheritance*, paras. 14.60–14.62);
  (b) conserving the facilities or resources for dealing with waste. In particular the Government's policy is that waste should not be imported to Britain for direct landfill (Cm. 1200, para. 14.64); and see also HMIP Second Report, August 1990, para. 47, and the Report of the House of Commons Environment Committee, Session 1988–89, Second Report, *Toxic Waste* (February 1989, para. 255).

Enforcement of any regulations made will, by subs. (4), fall to waste regulation authorities. The regulations may include provision as to public registers of information as to the importation and exportation of waste (subs. (5)(f)).

UK Policy on Imports and Exports of Waste
A draft U.K. Waste Management Plan on Imports and Export of Waste to be made under the Transfrontier Shipment of Waste Regulations 1994 (S.I. 1994 No. 1137), reg. 11, was issued for consultation in February 1995. The Plan is to implement the requirement in the Waste Framework Directive 91/156/EEC article 7, that Member States prepare waste management plans. One significant factor determining the content of the Plan is the E.C. Regulation (EEC) No. 259/93 on the supervision and control of shipments of waste within, into and out of the E.C.; another is the 1989 Basal Convention on the control of transboundary movements of hazardous wastes and their disposal and subsequent important Decisions taken by the parties to that Convention, including the U.K.

Territorial extent
The section applies to England, Scotland, Wales and Northern Ireland (s.164(4)).

Powers to obtain information about potentially hazardous substances

142.—(1) The Secretary of State may, for the purposes of assessing their potential for causing pollution of the environment or harm to human health, by regulations make provision for and in connection with the obtaining of relevant information relating to substances which may be specified by him by order for the purposes of this section.

(2) The Secretary of State shall not make an order under subsection (1) above specifying any substance—
  (a) which was first supplied in any member State on or after September 18, 1981; or
  (b) in so far as it is a regulated substance for the purposes of any relevant enactment.

(3) The Secretary of State shall not make an order under subsection (1)

above specifying any substance without consulting the committee established under section 140(5) except where it appears to him that information about the substance needs to be obtained urgently under this section.

(4) Regulations under this section may—

(a) prescribe the descriptions of relevant information which are to be furnished under this section in relation to specified substances;

(b) impose requirements on manufacturers, importers or suppliers generally to furnish information prescribed under paragraph (a) above;

(c) provide for the imposition of requirements on manufacturers, importers or suppliers generally to furnish relevant information relating to products or articles containing specified substances in relation to which information has been furnished in pursuance of paragraph (b) above;

(d) provide for the imposition of requirements on particular manufacturers, importers or suppliers to furnish further information relating to specified substances in relation to which information has been furnished in pursuance of paragraph (b) above;

(e) provide for the imposition of requirements on particular manufacturers or importers to carry out tests of specified substances and to furnish information of the results of the tests;

(f) authorise persons to comply with requirements to furnish information imposed on them by or under the regulations by means of representative persons or bodies;

(g) impose restrictions on the disclosure of information obtained under this section and provide for determining what information is, and what information is not, to be treated as furnished in confidence;

(h) create offences, subject to the limitation that no offence shall be punishable with imprisonment or punishable on summary conviction with a fine exceeding level 5 on the standard scale;

(i) make any public authority designated by the regulations responsible for the enforcement of the regulations to such extent as may be specified in the regulations;

(j) include such other incidental and supplemental, and such transitional, provisions as the Secretary of State considers appropriate.

(5) The Secretary of State shall have regard, in imposing or providing for the imposition of any requirement under subsection (4)(b), (c), (d) or (e) above, to the cost likely to be involved in complying with the requirement.

(6) In this section—

"the environment" means the air, water and land or any of them;

"relevant information", in relation to substances, products or articles, means information relating to their properties, production, distribution, importation or use or intended use and, in relation to products or articles, to their disposal as waste;

"substance" means any natural or artificial substance, whether in solid or liquid form or in the form of a gas or vapour and it includes mixtures of substances.

(7) The enactments which are relevant for the purposes of subsection (2)(b) above are the following—

the Explosive Substances Act 1875;

[the Radioactive Substances Act 1993];

Parts II, III and VIII of the Medicines Act 1968;

Part IV of the Agriculture Act 1970;

the Misuse of Drugs Act 1971;

Part III of the Food and Environment Protection Act 1985; and

the Food Safety Act 1990;

and a substance is a regulated substance for the purposes of any such enactment in so far as any prohibition, restriction or requirement is imposed in relation to it by or under the enactment for the purposes of that enactment.

DEFINITIONS
"the environment": subs. (6).
"relevant information": subs. (6).
"substance": subs. (6).

COMMENCEMENT
January 1, 1991 (s.164(2)).

AMENDMENTS
The words in square brackets in subs. (7) were substituted by the Radioactive Substances Act 1993. Previously the reference had been to the Radioactive Substances Act 1960, which is now consolidated into the 1993 Act.

GENERAL NOTE
This provision enables the Secretary of State to make regulations to require manufacturers, importers, or suppliers of specified substances, natural or artificial, to provide information on those substances. The intention is to use such information to evaluate possible hazards to human health or to the environment caused by the use, storage or disposal of the substance. Information may also be required under the regulations as to products or articles containing such substances (subs. (4)(c)).

By subs. (2) no substance first supplied in any European Community member state on or after September 18, 1981 may be specified, nor may any substance regulated under the other enactments listed in subs. (7). The definitive list of substances on the EEC market before September 18, 1981, is set out at O.J. C146A, June 15, 1990. "New" substances outside that list are subject to the testing and notification requirements of the so-called "Sixth Amendment" Directive 79/831/EEC and related Directives (Directive amending the Sixth Time Directive 67/548/EEC on the approximation of the laws, regulations and administrative provisions relating to the classification, packaging and labelling of dangerous substances; O.J. L259, October 15, 1979). Implementation of this Directive is by means of the Notification of New Substances Regulations 1982 No. 1496.

Section 142 is therefore to be seen in conjunction with this legislation.

Consultation
Except in an emergency the exercise of the order-making powers must, by subs. (3), be the subject of consultation with any advisory committee established in relation to hazardous substances under s.140(5).

Content of regulations
Subsection (4) deals with the content of regulations made under the section. As well as furnishing information (under subs. (4)(a)–(d)), manufacturers or importers (but not suppliers) can be required to carry out tests on specified substances and furnish the resulting information. In these cases, the Secretary of State must, in formulating the requirements, have regard to the likely costs of compliance (subs. (5)).

Territorial extent
The section applies fully to England, Scotland and Wales and applies to Northern Ireland in respect of importation only (s.164(4)).

Public registers of land which may be contaminated.

143. [...]

[Section 143, which provided for the establishment of public registers of land which may be contaminated, was revoked by the Environment Act 1995, Sched. 24. However, for a discussion of the part which s.143 played, without ever coming into force, in the evolution of Government policy on contaminated land, see the general introductory note to Pt. IIA of this Act.]

Amendments of hazardous substances legislation

144. Schedule 13 to this Act (which contains miscellaneous amendments to the legislation relating to hazardous substances) shall have effect.

COMMENCEMENT
January 1, 1992 in so far as the section relates to Sched. 13, Pt. I (Sched. 13, Pt. II relates only to Scotland): S.I. 1991 No. 2829. The remainder comes into force on a day to be appointed.

GENERAL NOTE
This section was inserted by amendment at Committee stage in the Lords. Sched. 13 of the Act contains various amendments to the Planning (Hazardous Substances) Act 1990 and to the equivalent Scottish legislation. The Parliamentary Under-Secretary of State for the Environment (Lord Hesketh) in moving the amendment, described it as being to rectify shortcomings in the legislation controlling the location of hazardous substances, and to enable "this important new control system, which is not yet in force, to be introduced on a much more satisfactory basis than would be possible under existing provisions." Lord Hesketh summarised the main effects of the amendments as follows (*Hansard*, Vol. 520, col. 2267, July 5, 1990):

"The legislation concerns the storage and use of substances which could present major hazards to people in the surrounding area. Hazardous substances consent will be required where named substances are present at or above specified amounts. There are transitional provisions designed to give existing users of hazardous substances an entitlement to a deemed consent in respect of their existing operations. The intention was that these deemed consents would relate to the situation in the 12-month period preceding the introduction of the new controls.

After considering representations from industry, we have concluded that the standard conditions which would attach to all these deemed consents under the existing legislation are effectively unworkable. They would mean that a substance would have to be kept and used in the same place and manner as it was immediately before the new controls came into force. This would contradict the objective of basing deemed consents on activity in the whole of the 12 months prior to the commencement date. Indeed, a substance used regularly during these 12 months may not even be present immediately before the commencement date. Therefore, paragraph 4 of Part I of the new Schedule deletes the two offending conditions and enables revised conditions to be prescribed in regulations.

This is the most crucial defect. But there are other shortcomings in the legislation which we should like to remedy. These concern the position of statutory undertakers, arrangements for charging fees for applications, and technical points relating to conditions and compensation. Similar amendments are made in Part II to the equivalent Scottish provisions."

Territorial extent
The section does not apply to Northern Ireland (s.164(4)).

Penalties for offences of polluting controlled waters etc.

145.—(1) In section 107(6) of the Water Act 1989 (penalties for offences of polluting controlled waters or contravening consent conditions), in paragraph (a), for the words "the statutory maximum" there shall be substituted "£20,000".

(2) In sections 31(7)(a), 31A(2)(c)(i) and 32(7)(a) of the Control of Pollution Act 1974 (corresponding penalties for Scotland), for the words "the statutory maximum" there shall be substituted "£20,000".

COMMENCEMENT
January 1, 1991 (s.164(2)).

GENERAL NOTE
This section raises the maximum fines on summary conviction for water pollution offences in relation to controlled waters in England and Wales (now consolidated into the Water Resources Act 1991) and Scotland from £2,000 to £20,000.

Territorial extent
The section does not apply to Northern Ireland (s.164(4)).

Pollution at sea

Deposits of substances and articles in the sea, etc.

146.—(1) Part II of the Food and Environment Protection Act 1985 (under which licences are required for deposits by British vessels etc. at sea anywhere or by foreign vessels etc. in United Kingdom waters or, in certain circumstances, within British fishery limits) shall be amended as follows.

(2) In section 5 (licences for depositing at sea)—

(a) in paragraph (a), after the words "United Kingdom waters" there shall be inserted the words "or United Kingdom controlled waters";

(b) paragraphs (c) and (d) shall be omitted;

(c) in paragraph (e)—

(i) in sub-paragraph (i), after the words "United Kingdom waters" there shall be inserted the words "or United Kingdom controlled waters" and at the end there shall be inserted the word "or"; and

(ii) sub-paragraph (iii) shall be omitted.

(3) In section 6 (licences for incineration at sea), in subsection (1)(a)—

(a) in sub-paragraph (i), after the words "United Kingdom waters" there shall be inserted the words "or United Kingdom controlled waters" and at the end there shall be inserted the word "or"; and

(b) sub-paragraph (iii) shall be omitted.

(4) In section 9(5) (Convention State defence to offence of acting without or in contravention of a licence), in paragraph (b), for the word "waters" there shall be substituted the words "controlled waters (and not within United Kingdom waters)".

(5) In section 11 (powers of officers)—

(a) in subsection (2)(b), for the words "British fishery limits" there shall be substituted the words "United Kingdom waters or United Kingdom controlled waters;"; and

(b) in subsection (3)(a), for the words "British fishery limits" there shall be substituted the words "United Kingdom waters or United Kingdom controlled waters;".

(6) In section 21 (penalties for offences)—

(a) in subsection (2), for the words "2(4) and 9(1)" there shall be substituted the words "and 2(4)"; and

(b) after that subsection, there shall be inserted the following subsection—

"(2A) A person guilty of an offence under section 9(1) shall be liable—

(a) on summary conviction, to a fine of an amount not exceeding £50,000; and

(b) on conviction on indictment, to a fine or to imprisonment for a term not exceeding two years or to both."

(7) In section 24(1) (definitions) at the end of the definition of "United Kingdom waters" there shall be inserted the words "and 'United Kingdom controlled waters' means any part of the sea within the limits of an area designated under section 1(7) of the Continental Shelf Act 1964."

(8) In Schedule 2 (powers in relation to vessels, aircraft, etc. for the purposes of Part I or Part II or both Parts of the Act), in paragraph 3(3) (removal to United Kingdom), after the words "Part I" there shall be inserted the words "or II."

COMMENCEMENT

January 1, 1991 (s. 164(2)).

GENERAL NOTE

The main effect of this section is to widen the scope of the prohibition on deposits at sea and incineration at sea in the absence of a licence granted under Pt. II of the Food and Environmental Protection Act 1985. Under FEPA this prohibition applied to British vessels anywhere in the world (s.5(b)), to foreign vessels loaded in Britain within British fishery limits (s.5(c)(i)) and to other foreign vessels within U.K. 12-mile territorial waters (s.5(a)). The Parliamentary secretary to the Ministry of Agriculture Fisheries and Food, Mr David Curry, described the objects of the section as follows in the Commons Committee stage:

"The clause is disappointingly devoid of conspiracy. It has virtually nothing to do with the issue discussed by the hon. Gentleman. Its purpose is to plug a gap in our existing ability to control dumping at sea. At present we control the fisheries limits of our vessels in international waters, but we cannot control a foreign vessel that loads abroad and dumps outside our territorial waters. If it dumps at 11¾ miles, we can control it, but if it dumps at 12 miles 100 yards, we cannot. So it can dump whatever it wants and we can do nothing.
  The clause aims to give us enforcement measures to control dumping by foreign vessels. It extends United Kingdom control to all vessels inside the continental shelf. A change is necessary, which is why that measure is riding piggy back upon this Bill. It can do so because we have agreed with states that share coastal waters on the location of the continental shelf. We could not do that in the past, but we can now take the powers offered by international convention. We are entitled to plug that gap under the E.C. convention. We shall probably not be in a position to issue licences. We have not taken this path in order to do that but to get to grips with people who dump waste illegally in waters that we control. That is the sole purpose of the amendment ... We made it clear that we would cease dumping except in the case of toxic substances and where there was no other safe alternative. We have taken a precautionary approach. A hundred licences were issued a decade ago, only 20 in 1987 and nine now. Five of those will go this year, leaving four. By the end of 1992, all will have disappeared, except those mentioned by the hon. Gentleman. They will also go in a matter of months—there will be no indefinite extension of those licences. Large quantities of waste cannot be stored on land, as that would be environmentally dangerous." (31st sitting, March 15, 1990, col. 1280).

The amendments contained in the section have the effect of extending the prohibition on unlicensed dumping and incineration for foreign vessels loaded in foreign ports from the 12-mile limit out to any U.K. controlled waters, *i.e.* any part of the sea within limits designated under the Continental Shelf Act 1964 (subs. (7)). Continental Shelf limits accord with the limits laid down by international law for jurisdiction for the purposes of sea deposits. The distinction between foreign vessels loaded in the U.K. and those loaded elsewhere is ended, so that foreign vessels loaded in the U.K. are also subject to the Continental Shelf limits. For policy on waste disposal at sea generally, see the White Paper of September 1990, *This Common Inheritance* (Cm. 1200), para. 12.35.

Subs. (2)
This makes the relevant jurisdictional changes for the deposit of articles from foreign vessels. A single limit (U.K.-controlled waters, as defined above) is created for the scuttling of vessels.

Subs. (3)
This subsection makes the relevant jurisdictional changes for incineration at sea. A licence is needed for incineration on British vessels anywhere in the world and for other vessels within the U.K. Continental Shelf limits.

Subs. (4)
This removes the Convention state defence to a charge of unlicensed incineration or deposit in cases where the operation takes place within U.K.-controlled (*i.e.* Continental Shelf) waters. Thus all deposits within such waters now require a licence.

Subs. (5)
This extends the relevant powers of enforcement to the new jurisdictional limits.

Subs. (6)
This subsection increases the maximum fine on summary conviction for unlicensed deposits from £2,000 to £50,000.

Subs. (8)
This extends the powers of enforcement officers under Pt. II of the 1985 Act to allow them to order a vessel to be taken to the nearest convenient port, or to take the vessel to port themselves.

Territorial extent
The section extends to Northern Ireland (s.164(4)).

Public registers relating to deposits in the sea and incineration at sea

147. In Part II of the Food and Environment Protection Act 1985, for section 14 (registers of licences) there shall be substituted the following section—

"Duty of licensing authority to keep public registers of information

14.—(1) It shall be the duty of each licensing authority, as respects licences for which it is the licensing authority, to maintain, in accordance with regulations, a register containing prescribed particulars of or relating to—
(a) applications for licences made to that authority;
(b) the licences issued by that authority;
(c) variations of licences effected by that authority;
(d) revocations of licences effected by that authority;
(e) convictions for any offences under section 9 above;
(f) information obtained or furnished in pursuance of section 8(3), (4) or (5) above;
(g) the occasions on which either of the Ministers has carried out any operation under section 10 above; and
(h) such other matters relating to operations for which licences are needed under this Part of this Act as may be prescribed.
(2) No information shall be included in any register which, in the opinion of either of the Ministers, is such that its disclosure on the register—
(a) would be contrary to the interests of national security, or
(b) would prejudice to an unreasonable degree some person's commercial interests.
(3) Information excluded from a register by virtue of subsection (2)(b) above shall be treated as ceasing to prejudice a person's commercial interests at the expiry of the period of four years beginning with the date on which the Minister made his decision under that subsection; but, on the application of any person to whom it relates, the Minister shall decide whether the information should be included or continue to be excluded from the register.
(4) Where information of any description is excluded from a register by virtue of subsection (2)(b) above, a statement shall be entered in the register indicating the existence of information of that description.
(5) It shall be the duty of each licensing authority—
(a) to secure that the register maintained by the authority under this section is available, at all reasonable times, for inspection by the public free of charge; and
(b) to afford to members of the public facilities for obtaining copies of entries, on payment of reasonably charges.
(6) Registers under this section may be kept in any form.
(7) In this section "prescribed" means prescribed in regulations.
(8) Either of the Ministers may exercise any power to make regulations under this section and any such power shall be exercisable by statutory instrument, subject to annulment in pursuance of a resolution of either House of Parliament."

GENERAL NOTE
This is another provision introduced by amendment at Lords' Committee stage. The object is simply to make the same provision for public registers in relation to licensing activities under Pt.

II of the Food and Environment Protection Act 1985 (dumping and incineration at sea) as appear in Pt. I of the 1990 Act. The same exclusions as to national security and commercial confidentiality apply.

Territorial extent
The section applies to Northern Ireland (s.164(4)).

COMMENCEMENT
May 31, 1991 (S.I. 1991 No. 1319).

Oil pollution from ships

148.—[Section 148, and Sched. 14 to which it gave effect, made provision in relation to oil pollution from ships. Both were repealed by the Merchant Shipping Act 1995, s.314, and consolidated into that Act as follows: s.148 into part of ss.128(3), 144 and 145 of that Act, and paras. 1–4 of Sched. 14 into ss.144–146. The repeal of Sched. 14 is "except so far as the amendments [which it makes to the Prevention of Oil Pollution Act 1971] relate to offences under section 2(1) of [the 1971 Act]."

Control of Dogs

Seizure of stray dogs

149.—(1) Every local authority shall appoint an officer (under whatever title the authority may determine) for the purpose of discharging the functions imposed or conferred by this section for dealing with stray dogs found in the area of the authority.

(2) The officer may delegate the discharge of his functions to another person but he shall remain responsible for securing that the functions are properly discharged.

(3) Where the officer has reason to believe that any dog found in a public place or on any other land or premises is a stray dog, he shall (if practicable) seize the dog and detain it, but, where he finds it on land or premises which is not a public place, only with the consent of the owner or occupier of the land or premises.

(4) Where any dog seized under this section wears a collar having inscribed thereon or attached thereto the address of any person, or the owner of the dog is known, the officer shall serve on the person whose address is given on the collar, or on the owner, a notice in writing stating that the dog has been seized and where it is being kept and stating that the dog will be liable to be disposed of if it is not claimed within seven clear days after the service of the notice and the amounts for which he would be liable under subsection (5) below are not paid.

(5) A person claiming to be the owner of a dog seized under this section shall not be entitled to have the dog returned to him unless he pays all the expenses incurred by reason of its detention and such further amount as is for the time being prescribed.

(6) Where any dog seized under this section has been detained for seven clear days after the seizure or, where a notice has been served under subsection (4) above, the service of the notice and the owner has not claimed the dog and paid the amounts due under subsection (5) above the officer may dispose of the dog—
  (a) by selling it or giving it to a person who will, in his opinion, care properly for the dog;
  (b) by selling it or giving it to an establishment for the reception of stray dogs; or
  (c) by destroying it in a manner to cause as little pain as possible;

but no dog seized under this section shall be sold or given for the purposes of vivisection.

(7) Where a dog is disposed of under subsection (6)(a) or (b) above to a person acting in good faith, the ownership of the dog shall be vested in the recipient.

(8) The officer shall keep a register containing the prescribed particulars of or relating to dogs seized under this section and the register shall be available, at all reasonable times, for inspection by the public free of charge.

(9) The officer shall cause any dog detained under this section to be properly fed and maintained.

(10) Notwithstanding anything in this section, the officer may cause a dog detained under this section to be destroyed before the expiration of the period mentioned in subsection (6) above where he is of the opinion that this should be done to avoid suffering.

(11) In this section—

"local authority", in relation to England and Wales, means a district council, a London borough council, the Common Council of the City of London or the Council of the Isles of Scilly and, in relation to Scotland, means [a council constituted under section 2 of the Local Government etc. (Scotland) Act 1994];

"officer" means an officer appointed under subsection (1) above;

"prescribed" means prescribed in regulations made by the Secretary of State; and

"public place" means—

  (i) as respects England and Wales, any highway and any other place to which the public are entitled or permitted to have access;

  (ii) as respects Scotland, any road (within the meaning of the Roads (Scotland) Act 1984) and any other place to which the public are entitled or permitted to have access;

and, for the purposes of section 160 below in its application to this section, the proper address of the owner of a dog which wears a collar includes the address given on the collar.

DEFINITION
See subs. (11).

COMMENCEMENT
April 1, 1992 (S.I. 1992 No. 266).

AMENDMENTS
The definition of "local authority" in subs. (11) was amended by the Local Government (Wales) Act 1994, Sched. 9, para. 17 and by the Local Government etc. (Scotland) Act 1994, Sched. 13, para. 167(17).

GENERAL NOTE
The problem of uncontrolled dogs was recognised by the Government, both in the Consultation Paper, *Action on Dogs: the Government's Proposals for Legislation* (DoE/Welsh Office, August 1989) and in the subsequent Consultative Paper of the Home Office, Scottish Office, Welsh Office and DoE, *The Control of Dogs* (June 1990). The first paper identified three main problems: (1) the numbers of stray dogs; (2) the high incidence of dog fouling in public places; and (3) an increase in the number of reports of attacks by dangerous dogs, which Lord Mancroft in debate somewhat unfortunately described as "large and rather unpleasant dogs biting small and almost as unpleasant children" (*Hansard*, H.L. Vol. 520, col. 2278).

The problem of fouling was considered at length in relation to the provisions of Part IV of the Act on litter in public places. The third problem, dangerous dogs, is to some extent addressed by the greater powers and penalties introduced by the Dangerous Dogs Act 1989. The second consultation paper rejected the creation of a dog registration scheme and canvassed a package of other measures including a new offence of allowing a dog to be dangerously out of control, additional powers of control by the courts, a ban on the keeping or ownership of certain breeds of dog, an offence of allowing a dog to stray (coining the memorable phrase "latch-key dogs" in the process) a fixed penalty scheme for failure to ensure a dog wears a collar and identification tag in a public place, and a review of by-laws and by-law-making powers.

Section 149, together with ss.150 and 151, is an attempt to tackle the problem of stray dogs. The provisions represent a defeat for proponents of a scheme for the compulsory registration of dogs. Such a scheme was tabled on a Commons amendment and defeated by 12 votes. A similar amendment was put forward in the House of Lords by Lord Stanley of Alderley and was carried. Lord Stanley's amendment caused the Government considerable difficulty in the closing stages of the Bill (see General Note to the Act) but was ultimately defeated and replaced by the Government's package of measures now contained in ss.149–151. The Government's view was that a dog registration scheme would be "an expensive and bureaucratic diversion from the need to act decisively against the actual problems" (*Hansard*, H.C. Vol. 178, col. 795). On the other hand, Dame Janet Fookes, the principal proponent of registration in the Commons, was able to point to the support of the RSPCA and other relevant agencies for a registration scheme and the lack of technical means for the implementation of the Government's package of measures (*Hansard*, H.C. Vol. 178, col. 804).

Section 149 places a duty on English district, London borough councils, Welsh county or county borough councils and Scottish councils to appoint an officer for the purpose of discharging the functions under the section for dealing with stray dogs. Those functions are as follows:

(1) the seizure and detention (if practicable) of dogs which appear to be strays (subs. (3));
(2) notification of the owner, if known, or of the person whose name and address appears on the dog's collar, if any (subs. (4));
(3) the owner may claim the dog within seven clear days of notification on payment of expenses and a sum prescribed by regulations (subss. (4) and (5));
(4) if not claimed, the dog may be disposed of by sale or gift, either to a person who will care properly for it or to a stray dogs' home, or by destroying it (subss. (4) and (6));
(5) keeping a public register of dogs seized (subs. (8));
(6) properly feeding and maintaining dogs detained after seizure (subs. (9));
(7) destroying any detained dog where necessary to avoid suffering (subs. (10)).

Subsection (5): prescribed amount
Under the Environmental Protection (Stray Dogs) Regulations 1992 (S.I. 1992 No. 288), the Secretary of State prescribed £25 as the amount of to be paid by a person claiming to be the owner of a seized dog. It prescribes particulars to be contained in a register of seized dogs; *i.e.*, its details, particulars of seizure such as time and place and date; and if disposed of, details of the disposal. Finally the regulations prescribe the procedure to be followed where a dog is found by a member of the public who wishes to keep it.

Territorial extent
The section does not apply to Northern Ireland (s.164(4)), where a dog licensing scheme is already in place.

Delivery of stray dogs to police or local authority officer

150.—(1) Any person (in this section referred to as "the finder") who takes possession of a stray dog shall forthwith either—
   (a) return the dog to its owner; or
   (b) take the dog—
      (i) to the officer of the local authority for the area in which the dog was found; or
      (ii) to the police station which is nearest to the place where the dog was found;
and shall inform the officer of the local authority or the police officer in charge of the police station, as the case may be, where the dog was found.

(2) Where a dog has been taken under subsection (1) above to the officer of a local authority, then—
   (a) if the finder desires to keep the dog, he shall inform the officer of this fact and shall furnish his name and address and the officer shall, having complied with the procedure (if any) prescribed under subsection (6) below, allow the finder to remove the dog;

(b) if the finder does not desire to keep the dog, the officer shall, unless he has reason to believe it is not a stray, treat it as if it had been seized by him under section 149 above.

(3) Where the finder of a dog keeps the dog by virtue of this section he must keep it for not less than one month.

(4) In Scotland a person who keeps a dog by virtue of this section for a period of two months without its being claimed by the person who has right to it shall at the end of that period become the owner of the dog.

(5) If the finder of a dog fails to comply with the requirements of subsection (1) or (3) above he shall be liable on summary conviction to a fine not exceeding level 2 on the standard scale.

(6) The Secretary of State may, by regulations, prescribe the procedure to be followed under subsection (2)(a) above.

(7) In this section "local authority" and "officer" have the same meaning as in section 149 above.

DEFINITIONS
"the finder": subs. (1).
"local authority": s.149(11).
"officer": s.149(11).

COMMENCEMENT
April 1, 1992 (S.I. 1992 No. 266).

GENERAL NOTE
As a second strand of the Government's package of measures on stray dogs (see is someone who takes possession of a stray dog, and the obligation is to return the dog to its owner, or to take it to the relevant officer of the local authority or to the nearest police station. Failure to do so is an offence.

The finder may indicate to the officer of the authority that he desires to keep the dog and may, following a prescribed procedure, be allowed to do so (subs. (2)(a)). Otherwise the dog is treated as a stray seized under s.149.

Consequential amendments are made by Sched. 15, para. 3, in order to harmonise the similar procedures as to delivery of stray dogs to the police in s.4 of the Dogs Act 1906.

Territorial extent
The section does not apply to Northern Ireland (s.164(4)).

Enforcement of orders about collars and tags for dogs

151.—(1) Section 13 of the Animal Health Act 1981 (orders for control, etc. of dogs) shall be amended by the insertion, after subsection (2), of the following subsections—

"(3) An order under subsection (2)(a) above may include provision for the execution and enforcement of the order by the officers of local authorities (and not by the police force for any area).

(4) In subsection (3) above "local authority" and "officer" have the same meaning as in section 149 of the Environmental Protection Act 1990."

(2) In section 50(1) of that Act (meaning of "local authority") at the end there shall be inserted the words "and to section 13(3) above."

(3) In section 60(1) of that Act (enforcement), at the end, there shall be inserted the words "but subject, in the case of orders under section 13, to any provision made under subsection (3) of that section".

COMMENCEMENT
February 14, 1992 (partially); April 1, 1992 (the remainder): S.I. 1992 No. 266.

GENERAL NOTE
This section amends s.13 of the Animal Health Act 1981 to allow orders made under s.13(2)(a) to be executed and enforced by the local authority officers appointed under s.149 of the Act,

rather than by the police. The orders in question are for prescribing and regulating the wearing of collars by dogs, while in highways or "places of public resort", giving the name and address of the owner.

Straw and stubble burning

Burning of straw and stubble etc.

152.—(1) The appropriate Minister may by regulations prohibit or restrict the burning of crop residues on agricultural land by persons engaged in agriculture and he may (by the same or other regulations) provide exemptions from any prohibition or restriction so imposed.

(2) Regulations providing an exemption from any prohibition or restriction may make the exemption applicable—

(a) in all, or only in specified, areas;

(b) to all, or only to specified, crop residues; or

(c) in all, or only in specified, circumstances.

(3) Any power to make regulations under this section includes power—

(a) to make different provision for different areas or circumstances;

(b) where burning of a crop residue is restricted, to impose requirements to be complied with before or after the burning;

(c) to create offences subject to the limitation that no offence shall be made punishable otherwise than on summary conviction and the fine prescribed for the offence shall not exceed level 5 on the standard scale; and

(d) to make such incidental, supplemental and transitional provision as the appropriate Minister consider appropriate.

(4) Where it appears to the appropriate Minister appropriate to do so in consequence of any regulations made under the foregoing provisions of this section, the appropriate Minister may, by order, repeal any byelaws of local authorities dealing with the burning of crop residues on agricultural land.

(5) In this section—

"agriculture" and "agricultural land" have, as respects England or as respects Wales, the same meaning as in the Agriculture Act 1947 and, as respects Scotland, the same meaning as in the Agriculture (Scotland) Act 1948;

"crop residue" means straw or stubble or any other crop residue;

"the appropriate Minister" means the Minister of Agriculture, Fisheries and Food or the Secretary of State or both of them.

DEFINITIONS
See subs. (5).

COMMENCEMENT
July 10, 1991 (S.I. 1991 No. 1577).

GENERAL NOTE
This section gives power to make regulations prohibiting or restricting the burning of stubble or other crop residues by farmers. The public nuisance caused by the practice of stubble-burning and the resulting smoke and ash had for some years been a cause of public discontent, and was referred to as a potentially serious problem by the Royal Commission on Environmental Pollution in its Tenth Report, *Tackling Pollution: Experience and Prospects*, Cm. 9149 (1984, paras. 2.7–2.11). The Royal Commission called for immediate legislation banning the practice, to take effect in five years' time, and for greater priority to be given to research and development on alternative uses for straw.

The Government's response to the problem hitherto had been a mixture of urging voluntary restraint by farmers and the use of local authority bye-laws. However, the inadequacy of such a regime to prevent major public nuisance and, in some cases, danger to highway users, was becoming increasingly apparent.

Very wide discretion is given to the Secretary of State to frame the controls by reference to different areas and circumstances (subs. (3)). Exemptions may be made applicable to specified areas, crop residues or circumstances. The Government's intention expressed in debates in both Houses, is that such exemptions will be rigidly confined. In the Commons, the Parliamentary Secretary to the Minister of Agriculture, Fisheries and Food said:

> "Hon. Members will be interested in the exemptions that we envisage, which are of two sorts. First, exemptions of certain crop residues will be permanent. Secondly, some exemptions will be temporary and apply in particular circumstances.
>
> A candidate for the first sort—this is not yet definitive—would be linseed straw and straw used to protect horticultural crops such as strawberries, carrots and potatoes. Exceptional circumstances might involve a waterlogged field where it is difficult to use normal equipment. We have no intention to exempt heavy land as such, but we are aware of the difficulties trying to follow cereals with oilseed rape crop, especially in very wet or very dry years.
>
> We shall examine the matter carefully, but it will be difficult to monitor and control any general exemption of this sort. We are considering the special circumstances and problems that may demand special provision. I wish to make it clear that fruit pruning, clipping and heather are not crop residues and are not covered by the clause.
>
> The permanent exemptions will permit burning subject only to the regulations that replace the byelaw. They will not be subject to any special application or permit, but be under broad general law. They will be specified from the outset. However, the exceptional cases would involve farmers or farmers' organisations applying to the Minister who would introduce a statutory instrument which would determine the area to be exempt. It could be as small as a parish or as large as several counties, depending on circumstances. Details of exemption relating to a specific crop will be set out. The Ministry will publicise applications by press release to the local paper and I give an undertaking that we shall not grant exemptions until a clear opportunity for other interested parties to comment had been given." (H.C. Standing Committee H, 31st sitting, March 15, 1990, cols. 1288–9.)

Similarly in the Lords, Baroness Trumpington gave the following assurances (*Hansard*, Vol. 520, col. 2311):

> "I can assure the noble Lord, Lord McIntosh of Haringey, and this Committee that when we receive applications for exemptions to the ban, where there is evidence of genuine need, we shall take steps to ensure that everyone with an interest is made aware of the position. We have it in mind to issue a press release. This will give organisations such as the National Society for Clean Air and any others an opportunity to make representations, and their views will be considered when Ministers decide whether to grant exemptions. The noble Lord will, I hope, recognise that there will be a degree of urgency, but there will be no secrets in our decision-making.
>
> I can also assure the noble Lord that it is our firm intention only to allow exemptions where there is no practicable alternative method of disposal. Our guiding principle will always be the practicability of alternatives, not their costs."

The intention of the Government is to apply a general prohibition from the 1993 harvest onwards. The Crop Residues (Restrictions on Burning) (No. 2) Regulations 1991 (S.I. 1991 No.1590) were made under these powers.

On the scheme coming into force, all existing local authority bye-laws will have to be repealed under subs. (4). By Sched. 15, para. 21 (when in force), the relevant bye-law making power under the Criminal Justice Act 1982, s.43 will be repealed.

Territorial extent
The section does not apply to Northern Ireland (s.164(4)).

Subsection (1): regulations
Under the Crop Residues (Restriction of Burning) (No. 2) Regulations 1991 (S.I. 1991 No. 1590), the Minister with effect from July 12, 1991, restricted the burning of straw from cereal, field beans, linseed, oilseed rape and peas. The regulations also created an offence of burning in contravention of the Regulations. The (No. 2) regulations were necessary because the original regulations were made before the section came into force and were therefore void.

Environmental expenditure

Financial assistance for environmental purposes

153.—(1) The Secretary of State may, with the consent of the Treasury, give financial assistance to, or for the purposes of, any of the following—

(a) the United Nations Environment Programme;
(b) the European Environmental Bureau;
(c) the chemicals programme of the Organisation for Economic Co-operation and Development;
(d) the joint inter-Governmental panel on Climate Change of the United Nations Environment Programme and the World Meteorological Organisation;
(e) the International Union for the Conservation of Nature and Natural Resources;
(f) the Convention on International Trade in Endangered Species of Wild Fauna and Flora;
(g) the Convention on Wetlands of International Importance Especially as Waterfowl Habitat;
(h) the Convention on Long-range Transboundary Air Pollution and any protocol to that Convention;
(i) the Convention and Protocol for the Protection of the Ozone Layer;
(j) the Convention on the Conservation of Migratory Species of Wild Animals;
(k) the Groundwork Foundation and Trusts;
(l) the environmental protection technology scheme for research and development in the United Kingdom in relation to such technology;
(m) the programme known as the special grants programme so far as it relates to the protection, improvement or better understanding of the environment of, or of any part of, Great Britain;
[(n) the Royal Society for the Encouragement of Arts, Manufactures and Commerce so far as its activities relate to the protection, improvement or better understanding of the environment;]
[(o) UK 2000 Scotland;]
[(p) the programme known as the Environment Wales programme so far as it relates to the protection, improvement or better understanding of the environment of, or of any part of, Wales;]
[(q) the grant programme known as the Environmental Action Fund;
(r) the programmes or schemes of the United Nations Habitat and Human Settlements Foundation;
(s) the programmes or schemes of the International Federation for Housing and Planning so far as they relate to the protection, improvement or better understanding of the environment;
(t) the programmes or schemes of the INTA.AIVN—International Urban Development Association so far as they relate to the protection, improvement or better understanding of the environment;
(u) the scheme known as the Darwin Initiative for the Survival of Species that provides support for the conservation and sustainable use of biological resources and habitats and for the furtherance of the aims of the Convention on Biological Diversity.]
[(v) the programme known as the Promotion of Positive Environmental Management in Industry Programme.]
[(w) any national or international architectural award scheme or competition scheme relating to the protection, improvement, or better understanding of the environment;
(x) the National Forest Company;]
[(y) the Energy Saving Trust;]
[(z) the Convention on Biological Diversity;
(aa) the United Nations Framework Convention on Climate Change;]
[(bb) the programme administered by the National Radiological Protection Board for the measurement of radon in premises in England.]
(2) Financial assistance may be given in respect of particular activities or

generally in respect of all or some part of the activities carried on or supported by the recipient.

(3) Financial assistance shall be given in such form and on such terms as the Secretary of State may think fit and, in particular, assistance may be given by making grants (whether or not repayable), loans or guarantees to, or by incurring expenditure, or providing services, staff or equipment for the benefit of, the recipient.

(4) The Secretary of State may, by order, vary subsection (1) above by adding to or deleting from it any description of organisation, scheme, programme or international agreement whose purposes relate to the protection, improvement or better understanding of the environment.

(5) Subject to any Order made after the passing of this Act by virtue of subsection (1)(a) of section 3 of the Northern Ireland Constitution Act 1973, the environmental protection technology scheme for research and development in the United Kingdom in relation to such technology shall not be a transferred matter for the purposes of that Act but shall for the purposes of subsection (2) of that section be treated as specified in Schedule 3 to that Act.

COMMENCEMENT
January 1, 1991 (s.164(2)).

AMENDMENTS
Additions to subs. (1) have been made as follows:
(n) by S.I. 1991 No. 682; (o) by S.I. 1991 No. 1179 (s.118); (p) by S.I. 1992 No. 654; (q)–(u) by S.I. 1993 No. 1062; (v) by S.I. 1993 No. 1518; (w) and (x) by S.I. 1995 No. 150; (y) by S.I. 1995 No. 554; (z) and (aa) by S.I. 1995 No. 1085; and (bb) by S.I. 1995 No. 3099.

GENERAL NOTE
This section expressly authorises the Secretaries of State for the Environment, Wales and Scotland, with Treasury consent, to give financial assistance to a wide range of international environmental programmes and initiatives. Many of the payments are already made under the general authority provided by the annual Appropriation Act, but this practice was criticised by the House of Commons Environment Committee and the DoE undertook to take specified legislative powers at the earliest opportunity.

The list of recipients may be widened or narrowed by orders made under subs. (4). Further detail on research and other initiatives funded by the Government is given throughout the White Paper, *This Common Inheritance* (Cm. 1200, September 25, 1990).

Subs. (5)
This enables the Government's environmental protection technology (EPT) scheme to be treated as a reserved item under the Northern Ireland constitution, thus allowing grants under the scheme to continue to be paid to organisations working in this field in Northern Ireland.

Territorial extent
The section applies to Northern Ireland with the exception of paras. (k) and (m) of subs. (1) (s.164(4)).

The Groundwork Foundation: superannuation

154. Employment with the Groundwork Foundation shall be and shall be deemed always to have been included among the kinds of employment to which a superannuation scheme under section 1 of the Superannuation Act 1972 can apply, and accordingly in Schedule 1 to that Act (in which those kinds of employment are listed) the words "Groundwork Foundation" shall be inserted after the words "Gaming Board for Great Britain."

COMMENCEMENT
January 1, 1991 (s.164(2)).

This section allows employees of the Groundwork Foundation to remain in the Principal Civil Service Pension Scheme. The Foundation was set up by the Countryside Commission in 1985 with staff seconded from the Commission. On April 1, 1988 the Foundation's Staff became employees of the Foundation when the DoE took over the Foundation's core funding. At that time an undertaking was given by the DoE to obtain statutory cover under the PCSP Scheme as soon as possible.

Territorial extent
The section does not apply to Northern Ireland (s.164(4)).

Remuneration of chairman of Inland Waterways Amenity Advisory Council

155. In section 110 of the Transport Act 1968 (Inland Waterways Amenity Advisory Council) at the end there shall be inserted—

"(7) The Secretary of State may, with the consent of the Treasury, pay the chairman of the Council out of money provided by Parliament such remuneration as the Secretary of State may determine; and where the chairman is in receipt of such remuneration he shall not be paid any allowance under subsection (6) of this section in respect of loss of remunerative time."

COMMENCEMENT
January 1, 1991 (s.164(2)).

GENERAL NOTE
The section allows the Secretary of State, with Treasury consent, to remunerate the Chairman of the Inland Waterways Amenity Advisory Council. The Council was constituted by s.110 of the Transport Act 1968, which provided for remuneration of expenses by the British Waterways Board, but not for allowances in respect of loss of remunerative time.

Territorial extent
The section does not apply to Northern Ireland (s.164(4)).

PART IX

GENERAL

Power to give effect to Community and other international obligations etc.

156.—(1) The Secretary of State may by regulations provide that the provisions to which this section applies shall have effect with such modifications as may be prescribed for the purpose of enabling Her Majesty's Government in the United Kingdom—
  (a) to give effect to any Community obligation or exercise any related right; or
  (b) to give effect to any obligation or exercise any related right under any international agreement to which the United Kingdom is for the time being a party.
(2) This section applies to the following provisions of this Act—
  (a) Part I;
  (b) Part II;
  (c) Part VI; and
  (d) in Part VIII, sections 140, 141 or 142;
and the provisions of the [Radioactive Substances Act 1993].
(3) In this section—
  "modifications" includes additions, alterations and omissions;
  "prescribed" means prescribed in regulations under this section; and

"related right," in relation to an obligation, includes any derogation or other right to make more onerous provisions available in respect of that obligation.

(4) This section, in its application to Northern Ireland, has effect subject to the following modification, that is to say—

(a) in its application in relation to Part VI and sections 140, 141, and 142, the reference to Her Majesty's Government in the United Kingdom includes a reference to Her Majesty's Government in Northern Ireland; and

(b) in its application in relation to the Radioactive Substances Act 1960, the reference to the Secretary of State shall be construed as a reference to the Department of the Environment for Northern Ireland and the reference to Her Majesty's Government in the United Kingdom shall be construed as a reference to Her Majesty's Government in Northern Ireland;

and regulations under it made by that Department shall be a statutory rule for the purposes of the Statutory Rules (Northern Ireland) Order 1979 and shall be subject to negative resolution within the meaning of section 41(6) of the Interpretation Act (Northern Ireland) 1954.

DEFINITIONS
See subs. (3).

COMMENCEMENT
April 1, 1991 (S.I. 1991 No. 1042).

AMENDMENTS
The words in square brackets in subs. (2) were substituted by the Radioactive Substances Act 1993, replacing reference to the Radioactive Substances Act 1960, which is now consolidated into the 1993 Act.

GENERAL NOTE
This section gives a general power to the Secretary of State to amend various parts of the Act and the whole of the Radioactive Substances Act 1993 by regulations in order (a) to give effect to any European Community obligation or exercise any "related right"; and (b) to give effect to any obligation under an international agreement to which the U.K. is a party, or to exercise any "related right".

In each case, by subs. (3), "related right" includes making any derogation from E.C. or international obligations or the exercise of any right to make more onerous provisions at domestic level.

Territorial extent
The section applies to Northern Ireland with modifications (subs. (4)) in so far as it relates to Pt. VI, ss.140–142 and the Radioactive Substances Act 1960.

Offences by bodies corporate

157.—(1) Where an offence under any provision of this Act committed by a body corporate is proved to have been committed with the consent or connivance of, or to have been attributable to any neglect on the part of, any director, manager, secretary or other similar officer of the body corporate or a person who was purporting to act in any such capacity, he as well as the body corporate shall be guilty of that offence and shall be liable to be proceeded against and punished accordingly.

(2) Where the affairs of a body corporate are managed by its members, subsection (1) above shall apply in relation to the acts or defaults of a member in connection with his functions of management as if he were a director of the body corporate.

COMMENCEMENT
January 1, 1991 (s.164(2)).

GENERAL NOTE
By the Waste Management Licensing Regulations 1994 (S.I. 1994 No. 1056) reg. 20(6), this section applies in relation to an offence under that regulation as it applies in relation to an offence under the Act.

Consent. "It would seem that where a director consents to the commission of an offence by his company, he is well aware of what is going on and agrees to it" (*Huckerby v. Elliott* [1970] All E.R. 189, 194, Ashworth J.).

Connivance. This term implies acquiescence in a course of conduct reasonably likely to lead to the commission of the offence. "Where he [the director] connives at the offence committed by the company he is equally well aware of what is going on but his agreement is tacit, not actively encouraging what happens but letting it continue and saying nothing about it": *Huckerby v. Elliott* (*ibid.*). See also Glanville Williams, *Criminal Law: the General Part*, para. 284, describing connivance in the criminal law context as requiring "knowledge (including wilful blindness) plus negligent failure to prevent".

Neglect. This term implies "failure to perform a duty which the person knows or ought to know": *Hughes, Re* [1943] 2 All E.R. 269. A director's duty is not absolute and some act or omission constituting neglect must be shown: *Huckerby v. Elliott* (*ibid.*). As to director's duties, see *City Equitable Fire Insurance Co., Re* [1925] Ch. 407 and as to duties of persons responsible for health and safety policy matters see *Armour v. Skeen* [1977] I.L.L.R. 310. Duties may in certain circumstances be properly delegated: "a director may delegate, but each case is one of fact and of the circumstances of the case" (*Hirschler v. Birch* (1987) 151 J.P. 396, and see *City Equitable Fire Insurance Co., Re* (*ibid.*)).

Director, manager, secretary or other similar officer. See *Armour v. Skeen* (*ibid.*) (held to include a senior officer of a Scottish Regional Council).

Or a person purporting to act in any such capacity. This term will cover directors or officers whose appointment is irregular or defective: see, *e.g. Dean v. Hiesler* [1942] 2 All E.R. 340.
   The case of *R. v. Boal* [1992] 3 All E.R. 177, provides some authority on the meaning of the word "manager" in a directors and officers liability provision under the Fire Precautions Act 1971 which is phrased in virtually identical terms to s.157 of the EPA. The Court of Appeal held that the intention of the provision was to fix with criminal liability only those who are in a position of real authority and who were responsible for putting proper procedures into place. In this case, the defendant, an assistant general manager of a bookshop who was placed in charge of the shop whilst the general manager was away on a week's holiday, was found not to be a manager for the purposes of this provision. The Divisional Court has recently applied the decision in *R. v. Boal* to a waste management case involving a disposal site manager. In *Woodhouse v. Walsall MBC* [1994] Env.L.R. 30, the manager of a waste disposal site was convicted together with the company of an offence under the Control of Pollution Act 1974. The Divisional Court held that although the manager had considerable powers and responsibilities nevertheless he did not have the power and responsibility to decide corporate policy and strategy. The crucial issue (which is clearly a matter of fact and degree) is therefore whether a defendant has the power and responsibility to decide corporate policy and strategy. In many cases it would thus appear to be difficult to convict a manager below board level.

Territorial extent
The section does not extend to Northern Ireland (s.164(4)).

Offences under Parts I, II, IV, VI, etc. due to fault of others

158. Where the commission by any person of an offence under Part I, II, IV, or VI, or section 140, 141 or 142 above is due to the act or default of some other person, that other person may be charged with and convicted of the offence by virtue of this section whether or not proceedings for the offence are taken against the first-mentioned person.

COMMENCEMENT
April 1, 1991 (S.I. 1991 No. 1042).

GENERAL NOTE
This section allows persons whose acts or defaults result in the commission of certain offences by other persons to be charged and convicted of the offence, whether or not proceedings are taken against the person committing the offence. The section could be used, for example, to prosecute employees whose acts cause offences on the part of their employer or a waste producer who deliberately misdescribed waste so as to cause a waste contractor to commit an offence under Pt. II of the Act.

Territorial extent
The section applies to Northern Ireland in so far as it relates to Pt. VI and ss.140–142 (s.164(4)).

Application to Crown

159.—(1) Subject to the provisions of this section, the provisions of this Act and of regulations and orders made under it shall bind the Crown.

(2) No contravention by the Crown of any provision of this Act or of any regulations or order made under it shall make the Crown criminally liable; but the High Court or, in Scotland, the Court of Session may, on the application of any public or local authority charged with enforcing that provision, declare unlawful any act or omission of the Crown which constitutes such a contravention.

(3) Notwithstanding anything in subsection (2) above, the provisions of this Act and of regulations and orders made under it shall apply to persons in the public service of the Crown as they apply to other persons.

(4) If the Secretary of State certifies that it appears to him, as respects any Crown premises and any powers of entry exercisable in relation to them specified in the certificate that it is requisite or expedient that, in the interests of national security, the powers should not be exercisable in relation to the premises, those powers shall not be exercisable in relation to those premises; and in this subsection "Crown premises" means premises held or used by or on behalf of the Crown.

(5) Nothing in this section shall be taken as in any way affecting Her Majesty in her private capacity; and this subsection shall be construed as if section 38(3) of the Crown Proceedings Act 1947 (interpretation of references in that Act to Her Majesty in her private capacity) were contained in this Act.

(6) References in this section to regulations or orders are references to regulations or orders made by statutory instrument.

(7) For the purposes of this section in its application to Part II and Part IV the authority charged with enforcing the provisions of those Parts in its area is—

(a) in the case of Part II, any waste regulation authority, and
(b) in the case of Part IV, any principal litter authority.

DEFINITION
"Crown premises": subs. (4).

COMMENCEMENT
January 1, 1991 (S.I. 1990 No. 2635).

GENERAL NOTE
Crown premises, notably hospital incinerators, have been subject to much criticism in the past for failure to observe proper environmental standards whilst subject to the doctrine of Crown immunity. This important section provides that the Act and all regulations made under it bind the Crown. The only exception is that powers of entry may be removed in relation to Crown premises in the interests of national security by subs. (4).

Also, the Crown cannot be criminally liable under the legislation. Instead, subs. (2) provides a means by which the relevant enforcing authority may obtain a declaration that the Crown is in contravention of the Act from the High Court or Court of Session.

Territorial extent
The section does not extend to Northern Ireland (s.164(4)).

Service of notices

160.—(1) Any notice required or authorised by or under this Act to be served on or given to an inspector may be served or given by delivering it to him or by leaving it at, or sending it by post to, his office.

(2) Any such notice required or authorised to be served on or given to a person other than an inspector may be served or given by delivering it to him, or by leaving it at his proper address, or by sending it by post to him at that address.

(3) Any such notice may—

(a) in the case of a body corporate, be served on or given to the secretary or clerk of that body;

(b) in the case of a partnership, be served on or given to a partner or a person having the control or management of the partnership business.

(4) For the purposes of this section and of section 7 of the Interpretation Act 1978 (service of documents by post) in its application to this section, the proper address of any person on or to whom any such notice is to be served or given shall be his last known address, except that—

(a) in the case of a body corporate or their secretary or clerk, it shall be the address of the registered or principal office of that body;

(b) in the case of a partnership or person having the control or the management of the partnership business, it shall be the principal office of the partnership;

and for the purposes of this subsection the principal office of a company registered outside the United Kingdom or of a partnership carrying on business outside the United Kingdom shall be their principal office within the United Kingdom.

(5) If the person to be served with or given any such notice has specified an address in the United Kingdom other than his proper address within the meaning of subsection (4) above as the one at which he or someone on his behalf will accept notices of the same description as that notice, that address shall also be treated for the purposes of this section and section 7 of the Interpretation Act 1978 as his proper address.

(6) The preceding provisions of this section shall apply to the sending or giving of a document as they apply to the giving of a notice.

COMMENCEMENT
January 1, 1991 (s.164(2)).

GENERAL NOTE
Reg. 1(7) of the Waste Management Licensing Regulations 1994 (S.I. 1994 No. 1056), as inserted by reg. 3(2) of S.I. 1995 No. 288, provides that the service or giving of any notice and the sending or giving of any document under the 1994 Regulations is governed by this section.

Subs. (4): principal office
The "principal" office of a body corporate or partnership is where its general superintendence and management is carried out: *Davies v. British Geon Ltd* [1956] 3 All E.R. 389 (C.A.).

Territorial extent
This section does not apply to Northern Ireland (s.164(4)).

Regulations, orders and directions

161.—(1) Any power of the Secretary of State or the Minister of Agriculture, Fisheries and Food under this Act to make regulations or orders shall be exercisable by statutory instrument; but this subsection does not apply to orders under section 72 above or paragraph 4 of Schedule 3.

(2) A statutory instrument containing regulations under this Act shall be subject to annulment in pursuance of a resolution of either House of Parliament.

(3) Except in the cases specified in subsection (4) below, a statutory instrument containing an order under this Act shall be subject to annulment in pursuance of a resolution of either House of Parliament.

(4) Subsection (3) above does not apply to [a statutory instrument—
  (a) which contains an order under s.78M(4) above, or
  (b) by reason only that it contains] an order under section 130(4), 131(3) or 138(2) above or section 164(3) below.

(5) Any power conferred by this Act to give a direction shall include power to vary or revoke the direction.

(6) Any direction given under this Act shall be in writing.

COMMENCEMENT
January 1, 1991 (s.164(2)).

AMENDMENTS
Subsection (4) was amended by the Environment Act 1995, Sched. 22, para. 92. Section 78M(4), to which subs. (4) as amended refers, allows the Secretary of State by order to increase the maximum fine payable upon non-compliance with a contaminated land remediation notice under that Part of the Act, where the land in question is industrial, trade or business premises.

GENERAL NOTE

Territorial extent
The section does not apply to Northern Ireland (s.164(4)).

Consequential and minor amendments and repeals

162.—(1) The enactments specified in Schedule 15 to this Act shall have effect subject to the amendments specified in that Schedule.

(2) The enactments specified in Schedule 16 are hereby repealed subject to section 77 above, Schedule 11 to this Act and any provision made by way of a note in Schedule 16.

(3) The repeal of section 124 of the Civic Government (Scotland) Act 1982 shall not affect a compulsory purchase order made for the purposes of that section under the Local Government (Scotland) Act 1973 before the coming into force of the repeal and such compulsory purchase order may be proceeded with and shall have effect as if the said section 124 had not been repealed.

(4) The Secretary of State may by order repeal or amend any provision of any local Act passed before this Act (including an Act confirming a provisional order) or of any order or other instrument made under an Act so passed if it appears to him that the provisions is inconsistent with, or has become unnecessary or requires alteration in consequence of, any provision of this Act or corresponds to any provision repealed by this Act.

(5) Any regulations made under section 100 of the Control of Pollution Act 1974 shall have effect after the repeal of that section by subsection (2) above as if made under section 140 of this Act.

COMMENCEMENT
Subsection (1) (partially) by s.164(2). Subsection (1) (partially) on January 14, 1991; S.I. 1991 No. 96. Subsection (1) (partially) on April 1, 1991; S.I. 1991 No. 1042. Subsection (1) (partially) on May 31, 1991; S.I. 1991 No. 1319. Subsection (1) (partially) on April 1, 1992; S.I. 1991 No. 2829. Subsection (1) (partially) on April 1, 1992; S.I. 1992 No. 266. Subsection (1) (partially) on February 18, 1993; S.I. 1993 No. 274. Subsection (2) (partially) by s.164(2). Subsection (2) (partially) on January 1, 1991; S.I. 1990 No. 2565. Subsection (2) (partially) on January 1, 1991; S.I. 1990 No. 2635. Subsection (2) (partially) on April 1, 1991; S.I. 1991 No. 685. Subsection (2) (partially) on April 1, 1991; S.I. 1991 No. 1042. Subsection (2) (partially) on May 31, 1991; S.I. 1991 No. 1319. Subsection (2) (partially) on January 1, 1992; S.I. 1991 No. 2829. Subsection (2) (partially) on April 1, 1992; S.I. 1991 No. 2829. Subsection (2) (partially) on April 1, 1992; S.I. 1992 No. 266. Subsection (2) (partially) on February 18, 1993 and May 1, 1993; S.I. 1993 No. 274. Subsection (2) (partially) on December 1, 1994 or later in certain circumstances; S.I. 1994 No. 2854. Subsection (3) on April 1, 1992; S.I. 1992 No. 266. Subsection (4): not yet in force. Subsection (5) by s.164(2).

GENERAL NOTE
Section 162 introduces Sched. 15, which makes amendments to various Acts. Many of these amendments are of a consequential nature only. Others are intended to clarify the relationship between controls introduced by the Act and other systems of control, for example:

    (a) the exclusion of the Alkali, & c. Works Regulation Act 1906 in relation to processes prescribed under Pt. I of the 1990 Act (para. 2). When a number of processes were removed from Pt. I control with effect from December 1, 1994 (or later in certain circumstances) by S.I. 1994 No. 1271 as amended by S.I. 1994 No. 1329, s.162(2) was also brought into force to the extent necessary to repeal the 1906 Act insofar as it related to such descriptions of process: S.I. 1994 No. 2854. If this had not bee⌐ 'one, those processes would have reverted to control under the 1906 Act, contrary ' the deregulatory intent behind removing them from Pt. I control;

    (b) the exclusion of s.5 of the Health and Safety at Work, etc. Act 1974 (general duty in relation to harmful emissions into the air from prescribed premises) in relation to prescribed processes (para. 14);

    (c) the exclusion of control by the Secretary of State (now exercised in any event by the Environment Agency) over trade effluent discharges to sewers under Pt. IV, Chapter III of the Water Industry Act 1991 in relation to trade effluent produced in prescribed processes designated for central control (para. 28); and

    (d) the exclusion of pollution controls under Pt. III of the Water Resources Act 1991 in relation to discharges from authorised prescribed processes designated for central control (para. 30).

One important substantive amendment (para. 10) relates to the provisions of the Transport Act 1968 on goods vehicle operators' licences. A further ground for suspension or revocation of such licences under s.69 is given, namely conviction of the holder of the licence or of a servant or agent of his (apparently, whether or not acting in the course of employment) of a range of waste-related offences. These include the illegal deposit of waste under the Act or the Control of Pollution Act 1974 and the transport of controlled waste with a view to profit without registration under the Control of Pollution (Amendment) Act 1989. This represents a useful extension of powers for use against persons fly-tipping or dealing with wastes in a similarly irresponsible manner.

Territorial extent
The section does not extend to Northern Ireland (s.164(4)).

Financial provisions

163.—(1) There shall be paid out of money provided by Parliament—

    (a) any administrative or other expenses incurred by any Minister of the Crown in consequence of the provisions of this Act; and

    (b) any increase attributable to this Act in the sums payable out of money so provided under any other Act.

(2) Any fees or other sums received by any Minister of the Crown by virtue of any provisions of this Act shall be paid into the Consolidated Fund.

COMMENCEMENT
January 1, 1991, (s.164(2)).

Territorial extent
The section does not extend to Northern Ireland (s.164(4)).

Short title, commencement and extent

164.—(1) This Act may be cited as the Environmental Protection Act 1990.

(2) The following provisions of the Act shall come into force at the end of the period of two months beginning with the day on which it is passed, namely—

> sections 79 to 85;
> section 97;
> section 99;
> section 105 in so far as it relates to paragraphs 7, 13, 14 and 15 of Schedule 5;
> section 140;
> section 141;
> section 142;
> section 145;
> section 146;
> section 148;
> section 153;
> section 154;
> section 155;
> section 157;
> section 160;
> section 161;
> section 162(1) in so far as it relates to paragraphs 4, 5, 7, 8, 9, 18, 22, 24 and 31(4)(b) of Schedule 15; but, in the case of paragraph 22, in so far only as that paragraph inserts a paragraph (m) into section 7(4) of the Act of 1984;
> section 162(2) in so far as it relates to Part III of Schedule 16 and, in Part IX of that Schedule, the repeal of section 100 of the Control of Pollution Act 1974;
> section 162(5);
> section 163.

(3) The remainder of this Act (except this section) shall come into force on such day as the Secretary of State may by order appoint and different days may be appointed for different provisions or different purposes.

(4) Only the following provisions of this Act (together with this section) extend to Northern Ireland, namely—

> section 3(5) to (8);
> section 62(2)(e) in so far as it relates to importation;
> Part V;
> Part VI in so far as it relates to importation and, without that restriction, section 127(2) in so far as it relates to the continental shelf;
> section 140 in so far as it relates to importation;
> section 141;
> section 142 in so far as it relates to importation;
> section 146;
> section 147;
> section 148;
> section 153 except subsection (1)(k) and (m);
> section 156 in so far as it relates to Part VI and sections 140, 141 and 142

in so far as they extend to Northern Ireland and in so far as it relates to the Radioactive Substances Act 1960;

section 158 in so far as it relates to Part VI and sections 140, 141 and 142 in so far as they extend to Northern Ireland.

(5) Where any enactment amended or repealed by this Act extends to any part of the United Kingdom, the amendment or repeal extends to that part, subject, however, to any express provision in Schedule 15 or 16.

GENERAL NOTE

Apart from the listed provisions in subs. (2) which come into force after two months, the remainder of the Act comes into force on an appointed day or appointed days.

Where the Government has given an indication of the proposed timetable for implementation, this is referred to in the notes to the relevant Part or section. The information is also given in composite form in the General Note to the Act.

Section 6   SCHEDULE 1

AUTHORISATION FOR PROCESSES: SUPPLEMENTARY PROVISIONS

PART I

GRANT OF AUTHORISATIONS

Applications for authorisations

1.—(1) An application to the enforcing authority for an authorisation must contain such information, and be made in such manner, as may be prescribed in regulations made by the Secretary of State.

(2) An application to the enforcing authority for an authorisation must also, unless regulations made by the Secretary of State exempt applications of that class, be advertised in such manner as may be prescribed in regulations so made.

(3) The enforcing authority may, by notice in writing to the applicant, require him to furnish such further information specified in the notice, within the period so specified, as the authority may require for the purpose of determining the application.

(4) If a person fails to furnish any information required under sub-paragraph (3) above within the period specified thereunder the enforcing authority may refuse to proceed with the application.

(5) Regulations under this paragraph may make different provision for different classes of applications.

Determination of applications

2.—(1) Subject to sub-paragraph (2) below, the enforcing authority shall give notice of any application for an authorisation, enclosing a copy of the application, to the persons who are prescribed or directed to be consulted under this paragraph and shall do so within the specified period for notification.

(2) The Secretary of State may, by regulations, exempt any class of application from the requirements of this paragraph or exclude any class of information contained in applications for authorisations from those requirements, in all cases or as respects specified classes only of persons to be consulted.

(3) Any representations made by the persons so consulted within the period allowed shall be considered by the enforcing authority in determining the application.

(4) For the purposes of sub-paragraph (1) above—

(a) persons are prescribed to be consulted on any description of application for an authorisation if they are persons specified for the purposes of applications of that description in regulations made by the Secretary of State;

(b) persons are directed to be consulted on any particular application if the Secretary of State specifies them in a direction given to the enforcing authority;

and the "specified period for notification" is the period specified in the regulations or in the direction.

(5) Any representations made by any other persons within the period allowed shall also be considered by the enforcing authority in determining the application.

(6) Subject to sub-paragraph (7) below, the period allowed for making representation is—

(a) in the case of persons prescribed or directed to be consulted, the period of 28 days beginning with the date on which notice of the application was given under sub-paragraph (1) above, and

(b) in the case of other persons, the period of 28 days beginning with the date on which the making of the application was advertised in pursuance of paragraph 1(2) above.

(7) The Secretary of State may, by order, substitute for the period for the time being specified in sub-paragraph (6)(a) or (b) above, such other period as he considers appropriate.

3.—(1) The Secretary of State may give directions to the enforcing authority requiring that any particular application or any class of applications for an authorisation shall be transmitted to him for determination pending a further direction under sub-paragraph (5) below.

(2) The enforcing authority shall inform the applicant of the fact that his application is being transmitted to the Secretary of State.

(3) Where an application for an authorisation is referred to him under sub-paragraph (1) above the Secretary of State may—

(a) cause a local inquiry to be held in relation to the application; or

(b) afford the applicant and the authority concerned an opportunity of appearing before and being heard by a person appointed by the Secretary of State;

and he shall exercise one of the powers under this sub-paragraph in any case where, in the manner prescribed by regulations made by the Secretary of State, a request is made to be heard with respect to the application by the applicant or the [... enforcing authority] concerned.

(4) Subsections (2) to (5) of section 250 of the Local Government Act 1972 (supplementary provisions about local inquiries under that section) or, in relation to Scotland, subsections (2) to (8) of section 210 of the Local Government (Scotland) Act 1973 (which make similar provision) shall, without prejudice to the generality of subsection (1) of either of those sections, apply to inquiries in pursuance of sub-paragraph (3) above as they apply to inquiries in pursuance of either of those sections and, in relation to England and Wales, as if the reference to a local authority in subsection (4) of the said section 250 included a reference to the enforcing authority.

(5) The Secretary of State shall, on determining any application transferred to him under this paragraph, give to the enforcing authority such a direction as he thinks fit as to whether it is to grant the application and, if so, as to the conditions that are to be attached to the authorisation.

4. The Secretary of State may give the enforcing authority a direction with respect to any particular application or any class of applications for an authorisation requiring the authority not to determine or not to proceed with the application or applications of that class until the expiry of any such period as may be specified in the direction, or until directed by the Secretary of State that they may do so, as the case may be.

5.—(1) Except in a case where an application has been referred to the Secretary of State under paragraph 3 above and subject to sub-paragraphs (3) below, the enforcing authority shall determine an application for an authorisation within the period of four months beginning with the day on which it received the application or within such longer period as may be agreed with the applicant.

(2) If the enforcing authority fails to determine an application for an authorisation within the period allowed by or under this paragraph the application shall, if the applicant notifies the authority in writing that he treats the failure as such, be deemed to have been refused at the end of that period.

(3) The Secretary of State may, by order, substitute for the period for the time being specified in sub-paragraph (1) above such other period as he considers appropriate and different periods may be substituted for different classes of application.

PART II

VARIATION OF AUTHORISATION

Variations by the enforcing authority

6.—(1) [Except as provided by sub-paragraph (1A) below;] the requirements of this paragraph apply where an enforcing authority has decided to vary an authorisation under section 10 and is of the opinion that any action to be taken by the holder of the authorisation in consequence of the variation will involve a substantial change in the manner in which the process is being carried on.

[(1A) The requirements of this paragraph shall not apply in relation to any variations of an authorisation which an enforcing authority has decided to make in consequence of representations made in accordance with this paragraph and which are specified by way of variation of a variation notice by a further notice under section 10(3A) of this Act.]

(2) Subject to sub-paragraph (3) below, the enforcing authority shall give notice of the action to be taken by the holder of the authorisation to the persons who are prescribed or directed to be consulted under this paragraph and shall do so within the specified period for notification; and the holder shall advertise the action in the manner prescribed in regulations made by the Secretary of State.

(3) The Secretary of State may, by regulations, exempt any class of variation from all or any of the requirements of this paragraph or exclude any class of information relating to action to be taken by holders of authorisations from all or any of those requirements, in all cases or as respects specified classes only of persons to be consulted.

(4) Any representations made by the persons so consulted within the period allowed shall be considered by the enforcing authority in taking its decision.

(5) For the purposes of sub-paragraph (2) above—
  (a) persons are prescribed to be consulted on any description of variation if they are persons specified for the purposes of variations of that description in regulations made by the Secretary of State;
  (b) persons are directed to be consulted on any particular variation if the Secretary of State specifies them in a direction given to the enforcing authority;
and the "specified period for notification" is the period specified in the regulations or in the direction.

(6) Any representations made by any other persons within the period allowed shall also be considered by the enforcing authority in taking its decision.

(7) Subject to sub-paragraphs (8) below, the period allowed for making representations is—
  (a) in the case of persons prescribed or directed to be consulted, the period of 28 days beginning with the date on which notice was given under sub-paragraph (2) above, and
  (b) in the case of other persons, the period of 28 days beginning with the date of the advertisement under sub-paragraph (2) above.

(8) The Secretary of State may, by order, substitute for the period for the time being specified in sub-paragraph (7)(a) or (b) above, such other period as he considers appropriate.

Applications for variation

7.—(1) The requirements of this paragraph apply where an application is made to an enforcing authority under section 11(4) for the variation of an authorisation.

(2) Subject to sub-paragraph (3) below, the enforcing authority shall give notice of any such application for a variation of an authorisation, enclosing a copy of the application, to the persons who are prescribed or directed to be consulted under this paragraph and shall do so within the specified period for notification; and the holder of the authorisation shall advertise the application in the manner prescribed in regulations made by the Secretary of State.

(3) The Secretary of State may, by regulations, exempt any class of application from all or any of the requirements of this paragraph or exclude any class of information furnished with applications for variations of authorisation from all or any of those requirements, in all cases or as respects specified classes only of persons to be consulted.

(4) Any representations made by the persons so consulted within the period allowed shall be considered by the enforcing authority in determining the application.

(5) For the purposes of sub-paragraph (2) above—
  (a) persons are prescribed to be consulted on any description of application for a variation if they are persons specified for the purposes of applications of that description in regulations made by the Secretary of State;
  (b) persons are directed to be consulted on any particular application if the Secretary of State specifies them in a direction given to the enforcing authority;
and the "specified period for notification" is the period specified in the regulations or in the direction.

(6) Any representation made by any other persons within the period allowed shall also be considered by the enforcing authority in determining the application.

(7) Subject to sub-paragraph (8) below, the period allowed for making representations is—
  (a) in the case of persons prescribed or directed to be consulted, the period of 28 days beginning with the date on which notice of the application was given under sub-paragraph (2) above; and
  (b) in the case of other persons, the period of 28 days beginning with the date on which the making of the application was advertised in pursuance of sub-paragraph (2) above.

(8) The Secretary of State may, by order, substitute for the period for the time being specified in sub-paragraph (7)(a) or (b) above, such other period as he considers appropriate.

[Call in of applications for variation

8.—(1) The Secretary of State may give directions to the enforcing authority requiring that any particular application or any class of applications for the variation of an authorisation shall be transmitted to him for determination pending a further direction under sub-paragraph (5) below.

(2) The enforcing authority shall inform the applicant of the fact that his application is being transmitted to the Secretary of State.

(3) Where an application for the variation of an authorisation is referred to him under sub-paragraph (1) above the Secretary of State may
  (a) cause a local inquiry to be held in relation to the application; or
  (b) afford the applicant and the authority concerned an opportunity of appearing before and being heard by a person appointed by the Secretary of State;
and he shall exercise one of the powers under this sub-paragraph in any case where, in the manner prescribed by regulations made by the Secretary of State, a request is made to be heard with respect to the application by the applicant or the enforcing authority concerned.

(4) Subsections (2) to (5) of section 250 of the Local Government Act 1972 (supplementary provisions about local inquiries under that section) or, in relation to Scotland, subsections (2) to (8) of section 210 of the Local Government (Scotland) Act 1973 (which make similar provision) shall, without prejudice to the generality of subsection (1) of either of those sections, apply to local inquiries or other hearings in pursuance of sub-paragraph (3) above as they apply to inquiries in pursuance of either of those sections and, in relation to England and Wales, as if the reference to a local authority in subsection (4) of the said section 250 included a reference to the enforcing authority.

(5) The Secretary of State shall, on determining any application transferred to him under this paragraph, give to the enforcing authority such a direction as he thinks fit as to whether it is to grant the application and, if so, as to the conditions that are to be attached to the authorisation by means of the variation notice.

9. The Secretary of State may give the enforcing authority a direction with respect to any particular application or any class of applications for the variation of an authorisation requiring the authority not to determine or not to proceed with the application or applications of that class until the expiry of any such period as may be specified in the direction, or until directed by the Secretary of State that they may do so, as the case may be.

10.—(1) Except in a case where an application for the variation of an authorisation has been referred to the Secretary of State under paragraph 8 above and subject to sub-paragraph (3) below, the enforcing authority shall determine an application for the variation of an authorisation within the period of four months beginning with the day on which it received the application or within such longer period as may be agreed with the applicant.

(2) If the enforcing authority fails to determine an application for the variation of an authorisation within the period allowed by or under this paragraph the application shall, if the applicant notifies the authority in writing that he treats the failure as such, be deemed to have been refused at the end of that period.

(3) The Secretary of State may, by order, substitute for the period for the time being specified in sub-paragraph (1) above such other period as he considers appropriate and different periods may be substituted for different classes of application.]

Section 32   SCHEDULE 2

WASTE DISPOSAL AUTHORITIES AND COMPANIES

PART I

TRANSITION TO COMPANIES

Preliminary

1. In this Part of this Schedule—
  "authority" means an existing disposal authority as defined in section 32(1);
  "company" means a waste disposal contractor formed under the Companies Act 1985 by a waste disposal authority as mentioned in section 30(5);
  "direction" means a direction under section 32(2);
  "joint company" means a company in which more than one authority holds securities;

"securities," in relation to a company included shares, debentures, bonds or other securities of the company, whether or not constituting a charge on the assets of the company; and

"the vesting date" means the date on which property, rights and liabilities vest in a company by virtue of a transfer scheme under paragraph 6 below.

Notice of direction

2.—(1) The Secretary of State, before giving any directions to any authority or constituent authority, shall give notice of his intention to do so to that authority.

(2) A notice under this paragraph shall give a general indication of the provisions to be included in the direction, indicating in particular whether the proposed direction will require the formation of one or more than one company and the authority or authorities who are to form or control the company or companies and whether any existing disposal authority will be abolished.

(3) A notice under this paragraph shall state that the authority to whom it is given is entitled, within a period specified in the notice, to make to the Secretary of State applications or representations with respect to the proposed direction under paragraph 3 below.

Applications for exemption from and representations about directions

3.—(1) An authority which has been given notice under paragraph 2 above of a proposed direction may, within the period specified in the notice, make to the Secretary of State either an application under sub-paragraph (2) below or representations under sub-paragraph (3) below.

(2) An authority may, under this sub-paragraph, apply to the Secretary of State requesting him not to make a direction in its case on the ground that the authority falls within any of paragraphs (a), (b), (c) or (d) of section 32(3).

(3) An authority may, under this sub-paragraph, make representations to the Secretary of State requesting him to make, in the direction, other provision than that proposed in the notice.

(4) It shall be the duty of the Secretary of State to consider any application duly made under sub-paragraph (2) above and to notify the authority of his decision.

(5) It shall be the duty of the Secretary of State to consider any representations duly made under sub-paragraph (3) above before he gives a direction.

Directions

4.—(1) A direction may require the authority or authorities to whom it is given to form or participate in forming one or more than one company or to form or participate in forming one or more than one joint company and it shall specify the date before which the company or companies is or are to be formed.

(2) Where a direction is to require a joint company to be formed the direction may be given to such of the authorities as the Secretary of State considers appropriate (the "representative authority").

(3) Where a direction is given to an authority as the representative authority it shall be the duty of that representative authority to consult the other authorities concerned before forming a company in accordance with the direction.

(4) The Secretary of State may exercise his powers to vary or revoke a direction and give a further direction at any time before the vesting date, whether before or after a company has been formed in accordance with the direction or previous direction, as the case may be.

Formation and status of companies

5.—(1) An authority which has been directed to form a company shall do so by forming it under the Companies Act 1985 as a company which—

(a) is limited by shares, and

(b) is a wholly-owned subsidiary of the authority or authorities forming it;

and it shall do so before such date as the Secretary of State specifies in the direction.

(2) The authority shall so exercise its control of the company as to secure that, at some time before the vesting date, the conditions specified in section 68(6)(a) to (h) of the Local Government and Housing Act 1989 (conditions for "arm's length companies") apply in relation to the company and shall, at some time before the vesting date, resolve that the company shall be an arm's length company for the purposes of Part V of that Act.

(3) In this paragraph "wholly-owned subsidiary", in relation to a company and an authority, is to be construed in accordance with section 736 of the Companies Act 1985.

Transfer schemes

6.—(1) Where an authority has formed a company or companies in pursuance of a direction, the authority shall, before such date as the Secretary of State may specify in a direction given to the authority under this sub-paragraph, submit to the Secretary of State a scheme providing for the transfer to the company or companies of any property, rights or liabilities of that or that and any other authority, or of any subsidiary of its or theirs, which appear to be appropriate to transfer as representing the relevant part of the undertaking of that authority or of that authority and the other authorities.

(2) In preparing a scheme in pursuance of sub-paragraph (1) above the authority shall take into account any advice given by the Secretary of State as to the provisions he regards as appropriate for inclusion in the scheme (and in particular any advice as to the description of property, rights and liabilities which it is in his view appropriate to transfer to the company).

(3) A scheme under this paragraph shall not come into force until it is has been approved by the Secretary of State and the date on which it is to come into force shall be such date as the Secretary of State may, either in giving his approval or subsequently, specify in writing to the authority; and the Secretary of State may approve a scheme either without modifications or with such modifications as he thinks fit after consulting the authority who submitted the scheme.

(4) If it appears to the Secretary of State that a scheme submitted under sub-paragraph (1) above does not accord with any advice given by him, he may do one or other of the following things, as he thinks fit, namely—

(a) approve the scheme under sub-paragraph (3) above with modifications; or

(b) after consulting the authority who submitted the scheme, substitute for it a scheme of his own, to come into force on such date as may be specified in the scheme.

(5) In the case of a scheme for the transfer to a company or joint company of the relevant part of the undertaking of two or more authorities, the representative authority shall consult the other authority or authorities before submitting the scheme under sub-paragraph (1) above; and the Secretary of State shall not approve the scheme (whether with or without modifications), or substitute a scheme of his own unless—

(a) he has given that other authority or (as the case may be) those other authorities an opportunity of making, within such time as he may allow for the purpose, written representations with respect to the scheme; and

(b) he has considered any such representations made to him within that time.

(6) The Secretary of State shall not specify the date on which the scheme is to come into force without consulting the authority which submitted the scheme and, where the scheme was submitted by a representative authority, the other authorities concerned.

(7) On the coming into force of a scheme under this paragraph the property, rights and liabilities affected by the scheme shall be transferred and vest in accordance with the scheme.

(8) As a consequence of the vesting by virtue of the scheme of property, rights and liabilities of an authority in a company, that company shall issue to the authority such securities of the company as are specified in the transfer scheme.

Transfer schemes: opportunity provisions

7. A scheme under paragraph 6 above may define the property, rights and liabilities to be transferred by the scheme—

(a) by specifying the property, rights and liabilities in question; or

(b) by referring to all the property, rights and liabilities comprised in any specified part of the undertaking or undertakings to be transferred; or

(c) partly in one way and partly in the other;

and may make such supplemental, incidental and consequential provision as the authority making the scheme considers appropriate.

8.—(1) The provisions of this paragraph apply to the transfer to a company of the property, rights and liabilities representing the relevant part of an authority's undertakings.

(2) Any property, rights or liabilities held or subsisting partly for the purpose of the relevant part of the authority's undertaking and partly for the purpose of another part shall, where the nature of the property, rights or liabilities permits, be divided or apportioned between the authority and the company in such proportions as may be appropriate; and where any estate or interest in land falls to be so divided, any rent payable under a lease in respect of that estate or interest, and any rent charged on that estate or interest, shall be correspondingly apportioned or divided so that the one part is payable in respect of, or charged on, only one part of the estate or interest and the other part is payable in respect of, or charged on, only the other part of the estate or interest.

(3) Any property, rights or liabilities held or subsisting as mentioned in sub-paragraph (2) above the nature of which does not permit their division or apportionment as so mentioned shall be transferred to the company or retained by the authority according to which of them appear at the vesting date likely to make use of the property, or, as the case may be, to be affected by the right or liability, to the greater extent, subject to such arrangements for the protection of the other of them as may be agreed between them.

(4) It shall be the duty of the authority and the company, before or after the vesting date, so far as practicable to enter into such written agreements, and to execute such other instruments as are necessary or expedient to identify or define the property, rights and liabilities transferred to the company or retained by the authority and as will—

(a) afford to the authority and the company as against one another such rights and safeguards as they may require for the proper discharge of the authority's functions and the proper carrying on of the company's undertaking; and

(b) make, as from such date (not being earlier than the vesting date) as may be specified in that agreement or instrument, such clarifications and modifications of the division of the authority's undertaking as will best serve the proper discharge of the authority's functions and the proper carrying on of the company's undertaking.

(5) Any such agreement shall provide so far as it is expedient—

(a) for the granting of leases and for the creation of other liabilities and rights over land whether amounting in law to interests in land or not, and whether involving the surrender of any existing interest or the creation of a new interest or not;

(b) for the granting of indemnities in connection with the severance of leases and other matters;

(c) for responsibility for complying with any statutory requirements as respects matters to be registered and any licences, authorisations or permissions which need to be obtained.

(6) If the authority or the company represents to the Secretary of State, or if it appears to him without such a representation, that it is unlikely in the case of any matter on which agreement is required under sub-paragraph (4) above that such agreement will be reached, the Secretary of State may, whether before or after the vesting date, give a direction determining the manner in which the property, rights or liabilities in question are to be divided between the authority and the company, and may include in the direction any provision which might have been included in an agreement under that sub-paragraph; and any property, rights or liabilities required by the direction to be transferred to the company shall be regarded as having been transferred to, and by virtue of the transfer scheme vested in, the company accordingly.

Tax and company provisions

9.—(1) Any shares in a company which are issued as a consequence of the vesting by a transfer scheme of property, rights and liabilities in the company shall—

(a) be issued as fully paid; and

(b) treated for the purposes of the application of the Companies Act 1985 in relation to that company as if they had been paid up by virtue of the payment to the company of their nominal value in cash.

(2) For the purposes of Chapter I of Part II of the Capital Allowances Act 1990 (capital allowance in respect of machinery and plant) property which is vested in a company by virtue of a transfer scheme shall be treated as if—

(a) it had been acquired by the company on the transfer date for the purposes for which it is used by the company on and after that date; and

(b) capital expenditure of an amount equal to the price which the property would have fetched if sold in the open market had been incurred on that date by the company on the acquisition of the property for the purposes mentioned in paragraph (a) above.

Benefit of certain planning permission

10.—(1) This paragraph applies in relation to planning permission deemed to have been granted to the authority under Regulation 4 of the Town and Country Planning General Regulations 1976 (deemed planning permission for development by local authorities) which subsists at the vesting date.

(2) Any planning permission to which this paragraph applies which authorises the use of land by the authority for the treatment, keeping or disposal of waste shall, on the transfer of the land to the company by the scheme, enure for the benefit of the land.

Right to production of documents of title

11. Where on any transfer by virtue of a transfer scheme the authority is entitled to retain possession of any documents relating to the title to, or to the management of, any land or other property transferred to the company, the authority shall be deemed to have given to the company an acknowledgement in writing of the right of the company to production of that document and to delivery of copies thereof; and, in England and Wales, section 64 of the Law of Property Act 1925 shall have effect accordingly, and on the basis that the acknowledgement did not contain any such expression of contrary intention as is mentioned in that section.

Proof of title by certificate

12.—(1) A joint certificate by or on behalf of the authority and the company that any property specified in the certificate, or any such interest in or right over any such property as may be specified in the certificate, is by virtue of the transfer scheme for the time being vested in the authority or in the company shall be conclusive evidence for all purposes of that fact.

(2) If on the expiration of one month after a request from the authority or the company for the preparation of such a joint certificate the authority and the company have failed to agree on the terms of the certificate, they shall refer the matter to the Secretary of State and issue the certificate in such terms as the Secretary of State may direct.

Construction of agreements

13. Where any of the rights or liabilities transferred by a transfer scheme are rights or liabilities under an agreement to which the authority was a party immediately before the vesting date, whether in writing or not, and whether or not of such a nature that rights and liabilities thereunder could be assigned by the authority, that agreement shall have effect on and after the vesting date as if—
  (a) the company had been a party to the agreement; and
  (b) for any reference (however worded and whether express or implied) to the authority there were substituted a reference, as respects anything falling to be done on or after the vesting date, to the company; and
  (c) any reference (however worded and whether express or implied) to any officer or servant of the authority were, as respects anything falling to be done on or after the vesting date, a reference to such person as the company may appoint or, in default of appointment, to the officer or servant of the company who corresponds as nearly as may be to that officer or servant of the authority; and
  (d) where the agreement refers to property, rights or liabilities which fall to be apportioned or divided between the authority and the company, as if the agreement constituted two separate agreements separately enforceable by and against the authority and the company respectively as regards the part of the property, rights and liabilities retained by the authority or, as the case may be, the part of the property, rights and liabilities vesting in the company and not as regards the other part;
and sub-paragraph (d) above shall apply in particular to the covenants, stipulations and conditions of any lease by or to the authority.

14. Without prejudice to the generality of the provisions of paragraph 13 above, the company and any other persons shall, as from the vesting date, have the same rights, powers and remedies (and in particular the same rights and powers as to the taking or resisting of legal proceedings or the making or resisting of applications to any authority) for ascertaining, perfecting or enforcing any right or liability transferred to and vested in the company by a transfer scheme as he would have had if that right or liability had at all times been a right or liability of the company, and any legal proceedings or applications to any authority pending on the vesting date by or against the authority, in so far as they relate to any property, right or liability transferred to the company by the scheme, or to any agreement to any such property, right or liability, shall be continued by or against the company to the exclusion of the authority.

Third parties affected by vesting provisions

15.—(1) Without prejudice to the provisions of paragraphs 13 and 14 above, any transaction effected between the authority and the company in pursuance of paragraph 8(4) above or of a direction under paragraph 8(6) above shall be binding on all other persons, and notwithstanding that it would, apart from this sub-paragraph, have required the consent or concurrence of any other person.

(2) It shall be the duty of the authority and the company, if they effect any transaction in pursuance of paragraph 8(4) above or of a direction under paragraph 8(6) above, to notify any person who has rights or liabilities which thereby become enforceable as to part by or against the authority and as to part by or against the company; and if such a person applies to the Secretary of State and satisfies him that the transaction operated unfairly against him the Secretary of State may give such directions to the authority and the company as appear to him to be appropriate for varying the transaction.

(3) If in consequence of a transfer by a transfer scheme or of anything done in pursuance of paragraphs 8 to 14 above the rights or liabilities of any person other than the authority which were enforceable against or by the authority become enforceable as to part against or by the authority and as to part against or by the company, and the value of any property or interest of that person is thereby diminished, such compensation as may be just shall be paid to that person by the authority, the company or both, and any dispute as to whether and if so how much

compensation is payable, or as to the person by whom it shall be paid, shall be referred to, and determined by, the Lands Tribunal.

Transfer of staff

16.—(1) The Transfer of Undertakings (Protection of Employment) Regulations 1981 shall apply in relation to the relevant employees of an authority in accordance with sub-paragraph (2) below.

(2) For the purposes of the application of those regulations in relation to any of the relevant employees of an authority, the relevant part of the undertaking of the authority shall (whether or not it would otherwise be so regarded) be regarded—

(a) as a part of an undertaking within the meaning of those regulations which is transferred from the authority to the company on the vesting date, and

(b) as being so transferred by a transfer to which those regulations apply and which is completed on that date.

(3) Where a person is, in pursuance of section 32, to cease to be employed by an authority and to become employed by a company, none of the agreed redundancy procedures applicable to persons employed by waste disposal authorities shall apply to him.

(4) For the purposes of this paragraph persons are "relevant employees" of an authority if they are to become, in pursuance of section 32, employees of a company to which the relevant part of the undertaking of the authority is to be transferred.

Information for purposes of transfer scheme

17.—(1) The Secretary of State may, by directions, prescribe descriptions of information which are to be furnished for purposes connected with the transfer by authorities to companies of the relevant part of the undertakings of authorities.

(2) It shall be the duty of [...] a waste disposal authority, on being requested to do so by a written notice served on it by the Secretary of State, to furnish to the Secretary of State such information of a description prescribed under sub-paragraph (1) above as may be specified in the notice.

PART II

PROVISIONS REGULATING WASTE DISPOSAL AUTHORITIES AND COMPANIES

Terms of waste disposal contracts

18. A waste disposal authority shall, in determining the terms and conditions of any contract which the authority proposes to enter into for the keeping, treatment or disposal of waste, so frame the terms and conditions as to avoid undue discrimination in favour of one description of waste disposal contractor as against other descriptions of waste disposal contractors.

19.—(1) A waste disposal authority shall have regard to the desirability of including in any contract which the authority proposes to enter into for the keeping, treatment or disposal of waste terms or conditions designed to—

(a) minimise pollution of the environment or harm to human health due to the disposal or treatment of the waste under the contract; and

(b) maximise the recycling of waste under the contract.

(2) A waste disposal authority shall be entitled—

(a) to invite tenders for any such contract, and

(b) to accept or refuse to accept any tender for such a contract and accordingly to enter or not to enter into a contract,

by reference to acceptance or refusal of acceptance by persons tendering for the contract of any terms or conditions included in the draft contract in pursuance of sub-paragraph (1) above.

Procedure for putting waste disposal contracts out to tender

20.—(1) A waste disposal authority which proposes to enter into a contract for the keeping, treatment or disposal of controlled waste shall comply with the following requirements before making the contract and if it does not any contract which is made shall be void.

(2) The authority shall publish, in at least two publications circulating among waste disposal contractors, a notice containing—

(a) a brief description of the contract work;

(b) a statement that during a specified period any person may inspect a detailed specification of the contract work free of charge at a specified place and time;

(c) a statement that during that period any person will be supplied with a copy of the detailed specification on request and on payment of the specified charge;

(d) a statement that any person who wishes to submit a tender for the contract must notify the authority of his wish within a specified period; and

(e) a statement that the authority intend to invite tenders for the contract, in accordance with sub-paragraph (4) below.

(3) The authority shall—

(a) ensure that the periods, place and time and the charge specified in the notice are such as are reasonable;

(b) make the detailed specification available for inspection in accordance with the notice; and

(c) make copies of the detailed specification available for supply in accordance with the notice.

(4) If any persons notified the authority, in accordance with the notice, of their wish to submit tenders for the contract, the authority shall—

(a) if more than four persons did so, invite at least four of them to tender for the contract;

(b) if less than four persons did so, invite each of them to tender for the contract.

(5) In this paragraph—

"the contract work", in relation to a contract for the keeping, treatment or disposal of waste, means the work comprising the services involved in the keeping, treatment or disposal of the waste under the contract; and

"specified" means specified in the notice under sub-paragraph (2) above.

21. A waste disposal authority, in taking any of the following decisions, namely—

(a) who to invite to tender for the contract under paragraph 20(4)(a) above, and

(b) who to enter into the contract with,

shall disregard the fact that any waste disposal contractor tendering for the contract is, or is not, controlled by the authority.

Variation of waste disposal contracts

22. Where a waste disposal authority has entered into a contract with a waste disposal contractor under the authority's control, paragraph 18 above shall, with the necessary modifications, apply on any proposed variation of the contract during the subsistence of that control in relation to the terms and conditions that would result from the variation as it applies to the original contract.

Avoidance of restrictions on transfer of securities of companies

23.—(1) Subject to sub-paragraph (3) below, any provision to which this paragraph applies shall be void in so far as it operates—

(a) to preclude the holder of any securities of a waste disposal contractor from disposing of those securities; or

(b) to require the holder of any such securities to dispose, or offer to dispose, of those securities to particular persons or to particular classes of persons; or

(c) to preclude the holder of any securities from disposing of those securities except—

(i) at a particular time or at particular times; or

(ii) on the fulfilment of particular conditions or in other particular circumstances.

(2) This paragraph applies to any provision relating to any securities of a waste disposal contractor which is controlled by a waste disposal authority or to which the authority has transferred the relevant part of its undertaking and contained in—

(a) the memorandum or articles of association of the company or any other instrument purporting to regulate to any extent the respective rights and liabilities of the members of the company;

(b) any resolution of the company; or

(c) any instrument issued by the company and embodying terms and conditions on which any such securities are to be held by persons for the time being holding them.

(3) No provision shall be void by reason of its operating as mentioned in sub-paragraph (1) above if the Secretary of State has given his approval in writing to that provision.

[Sections 44A and 44B   SCHEDULE 2A

OBJECTIVES FOR THE PURPOSES OF THE NATIONAL WASTE STRATEGY

1. Ensuring that waste is recovered or disposed of without endangering human health and without using processes or methods which could harm the environment and, in particular, without—

    (a) risk to water, air, soil, plants or animals;

    (b) causing nuisance through noise or odours; or

    (c) adversely affecting the countryside or places of special interest.

2. Establishing an integrated and adequate network of waste disposal installations, taking account of the best available technology not involving excessive costs.

3. Ensuring that the network referred to in paragraph 2 above enables—

    (a) the European Community as a whole to become self-sufficient in waste disposal, and the Member States individually to move towards that aim, taking into account geographical circumstances or the need for specialised installations for certain types of waste; and

    (b) waste to be disposed of in one of the nearest appropriate installations, by means of the most appropriate methods and technologies in order to ensure a high level of protection for the environment and public health.

4. Encouraging the prevention or reduction of waste production and its harmfulness, in particular by—

    (a) the development of clean technologies more sparing in their use of natural resources;

    (b) the technical development and marketing of products designed so as to make no contribution or to make the smallest possible contribution, by the nature of their manufacture, use or final disposal, to increasing the amount of harmfulness of waste and pollution hazards; and

    (c) the development of appropriate techniques for the final disposal of dangerous substances contained in waste destined for recovery.

5. Encouraging—

    (a) the recovery of waste by means of recycling, reuse or reclamation or any other process with a view to extracting secondary raw materials; and

    (b) the use of waste as a source of energy.]

* This Schedule was inserted by the Environment Act 1995, s.92(2) and Sched. 12.

[Section 75   SCHEDULE 2B

CATEGORIES OF WASTE

1. Production or consumption residues not otherwise specified below.

2. Off-specification products.

3. Products whose date for appropriate use has expired.

4. Materials spilled, lost or having undergone other mishap, including any materials, equipment, etc, contaminated as a result of the mishap.

5. Materials contaminated or soiled as a result of planned actions (*e.g.* residues from cleaning operations, packing materials, containers, etc.).

6. Unusable parts (*e.g.* reject batteries, exhausted catalysts, etc.).

7. Substances which no longer perform satisfactorily (*e.g.* contaminated acids, contaminated solvents, exhausted tempering salts, etc.).

8. Residues of industrial processes (*e.g.* slags, still bottoms, etc.).

9. Residues from pollution abatement processes (*e.g.* scrubber sludges, baghouse dusts, spent filters, etc.).

10. Machining or finishing residues (*e.g.* lathe turnings, mill scales, etc.).

11. Residues from raw materials extraction and processing (*e.g.* mining residues, oil field slops, etc.).

12. Adulterated materials (*e.g.* oils contaminated with PCBs, etc.).

13. Any materials, substances or products whose use has been banned by law.

14. Products for which the holder has no further use (*e.g.* agricultural, household, office, commercial and shop discards, etc.).

15. Contaminated materials, substances or products resulting from remedial action with respect to land.

16. Any materials, substances or products which are not contained in the above categories.]

* This Schedule was inserted by the Environment Act 1995, Sched. 22, para. 95.

Section 81   SCHEDULE 3

STATUTORY NUISANCES: SUPPLEMENTARY PROVISIONS

Appeals to magistrates' court

1.—(1) This paragraph applies in relation to appeals under section 80(3) against an abatement notice to a magistrates' court.

(2) An appeal to which this paragraph applies shall be by way of complaint for an order and the Magistrates' Courts Act 1980 shall apply to the proceedings.

(3) An appeal against any decision of a magistrates' court in pursuance of an appeal to which this paragraph applies shall lie to the Crown Court at the instance of any party to the proceedings in which the decision was given.

(4) The Secretary of State may make regulations as to appeals to which this paragraph applies and the regulations may in particular—

(a) include provisions comparable to those in section 290 of the Public Health Act 1936 (appeals against notices requiring the execution of works);

(b) prescribe the cases in which an abatement notice is, or is not, to be suspended until the appeal is decided, or until some other stage in the proceedings;

(c) prescribe the cases in which the decision on appeal may in some respects be less favourable to the appellant than the decision from which he is appealing;

(d) prescribe the cases in which the appellant may claim that an abatement notice should have been served on some other person and prescribe the procedure to be followed in those cases.

[Appeals to Sheriff

1A.—(1) This paragraph applies in relation to appeals to the sheriff under section 80(3) against an abatement notice.

(2) An appeal to which this paragraph applies shall be by way of a summary application.

(3) The Secretary of State may make regulations as to appeals to which this paragraph applies and the regulations may in particular include or prescribe any of the matters referred to in sub-paragraphs (4)(a) to (d) of paragraph 1 above.]

Powers of entry etc.

2.—(1) Subject to sub-paragraph (2) below, any person authorised by a local authority may, on production (if so required) of his authority, enter any premises at any reasonable time—

(a) for the purpose of ascertaining whether or not a statutory nuisance exists; or

(b) for the purpose of taking any action, or executing any work, authorised or required by Part III.

(2) Admission by virtue of sub-paragraph (1) above to any premises used wholly or mainly for residential purposes shall not except in an emergency be demanded as of right unless 24 hours notice of the intended entry has been given to the occupier.

(3) If it is shown to the satisfaction of a justice of the peace on sworn information in writing—

(a) that admission to any premises has been refused, or that refusal is apprehended, or that the premises are unoccupied or the occupier is temporarily absent, or that the case is one of emergency, or that an application for admission would defeat the object of the entry; and

(b) that there is reasonable ground for entry into the premises for the purpose for which entry is required,

the justice may by warrant under his hand authorise the local authority by any authorised person to enter the premises, if need be by force.

(4) An authorised person entering any premises by virtue of sub-paragraph (1) or a warrant under sub-paragraph (3) above may—

(a) take with him such other person and such equipment as may be necessary;

(b) carry out such inspections, measurements and tests as he considers necessary for the discharge of any of the local authority's functions under Part III; and

(c) take away such samples or articles as he considers necessary for that purpose.

(5) On leaving any unoccupied premises which he has entered by virtue of sub-paragraph (1) above or a warrant under sub-paragraph (3) above the authorised person shall leave them as effectually secured against trespassers as he found them.

(6) A warrant issued in pursuance of sub-paragraph (3) above shall continue in force until the purpose for which the entry is required has been satisfied.

(7) Any reference in this paragraph to an emergency is a reference to a case where the person requiring entry has reasonable cause to believe that circumstances exist which are likely to endanger life or health and that immediate entry is necessary to verify the existence of those circumstances or to ascertain their cause and to effect a remedy.

[(8) In the application of this paragraph to Scotland, a reference to a justice of the peace or to a justice includes a reference to the sheriff.]

[2A.—(1) Any person authorised by a local authority may on production (if so required) of his authority—

  (a) enter or open a vehicle, machinery or equipment, if necessary by force, or
  (b) remove a vehicle, machinery or equipment from a street [or, in Scotland, road] to a secure place,

for the purpose of taking any action, or executing any work, authorised by or required under Part III in relation to a statutory nuisance within section 79(1)(ga) above caused by noise emitted from or caused by the vehicle, machinery or equipment.

(2) On leaving any unattended vehicle, machinery or equipment that he has entered or opened under sub-paragraph (1) above, the authorised person shall (subject to sub-paragraph (3) below) leave it secured against interference or theft in such manner and as effectually as he found it.

(3) If the authorised person is unable to comply with sub-paragraph (2) above, he shall for the purpose of securing the unattended vehicle, machinery or equipment either—

  (a) immobilise it by such means as he considers expedient, or
  (b) remove it from the street to a secure place.

(4) In carrying out any function under sub-paragraph (1), (2) or (3) above, the authorised person shall not cause more damage than is necessary.

(5) Before a vehicle, machinery or equipment is entered, opened or removed under sub-paragraph (1) above, the local authority shall notify the police of the intention to take action under that sub-paragraph.

(6) After a vehicle, machinery or equipment has been removed under sub-paragraph (1) or (3) above, the local authority shall notify the police of its removal and current location.

(7) Notification under sub-paragraph (5) or (6) above may be given to the police at any station in the local authority's area or, in the case of the Temples, at any police station of the City of London Police.

(8) For the purposes of section 81(4) above, any expenses reasonably incurred by a local authority under sub-paragraph (2) or (3) above shall be treated as incurred by the authority under section 81(3) above in abating or preventing the recurrence of the statutory nuisance in question.]

Offences relating to entry

3.—(1) A person who wilfully obstructs any person acting in the exercise of any powers conferred by paragraph 2 [or 2A] above shall be liable, on summary conviction, to a fine not exceeding level 3 on the standard scale.

(2) If a person discloses any information relating to any trade secret obtained in the exercise of any powers conferred by paragraph 2 above he shall, unless the disclosure was made in the performance of his duty or with the consent of the person having the right to disclose the information, be liable, on summary conviction, to a fine not exceeding level 5 on the standard scale.

Default powers

4.—(1) This paragraph applies to the following function of a local authority, that is to say its duty under section 79 to cause its area to be inspected to detect any statutory nuisance which ought to be dealt with under section 80 [or sections 80 and 80A] and its powers under paragraph 2 [or 2A] above.

(2) If the Secretary of State is satisfied that any local authority has failed, in any respect, to discharge the function to which this paragraph applies which it ought to have discharged, he may make an order declaring the authority to be in default.

(3) An order made under sub-paragraph (2) above which declares an authority to be in default may, for the purpose of remedying the default, direct the authority ("the defaulting authority") to perform the function specified in the order and may specify the manner in which and the time or times within which the function is to be performed by the authority.

(4) If the defaulting authority fails to comply with any direction contained in such an order the

Secretary of State may, instead of enforcing the order by mandamus, make an order transferring to himself the function of the authority specified in the order.

(5) Where the function of a defaulting authority is transferred under sub-paragraph (4) above, the amount of any expenses which the Secretary of State certifies were incurred by him in performing the function shall on demand be paid to him by the defaulting authority.

(6) Any expenses required to be paid by a defaulting authority under sub-paragraph (5) above shall be defrayed by the authority in like manner, and shall be debited to the like account, as if the function had not been transferred and the expenses had been incurred by the authority in performing them.

(7) The Secretary of State may by order vary or revoke any order previously made by him under this paragraph.

(8) Any order under this paragraph may include such incidental, supplemental and transitional provisions as the Secretary of State considers appropriate.

[(9) This paragraph does not apply to Scotland.]

Protection from personal liability

5. Nothing done by, or by a member of, a local authority or by any officer of or other person authorised by a local authority shall, if done in good faith for the purpose of executing Part III, subject them or any of them personally to any action, liability, claim or demand whatsoever (other than any liability under section 19 or 20 of the Local Government Finance Act 1982 (powers of district auditor and court)).

Statement of right of appeal in notices

6. Where an appeal against a notice served by a local authority lies to a magistrates' court [or, in Scotland, the sheriff,] by virtue of section 80, it shall be the duty of the authority to include in such a notice a statement indicating that such an appeal lies as aforesaid and specifying the time within which it must be brought.

Section 99   SCHEDULE 4

ABANDONED SHOPPING AND LUGGAGE TROLLEYS

Application

1.—(1) Subject to sub-paragraph (2) below, this Schedule applies where any shopping or luggage trolley is found by an authorised officer of the local authority on any land in the open air and appears to him to be abandoned.

(2) This Schedule does not apply in relation to a shopping or luggage trolley found on the following descriptions of land, that is to say—
  (a) land in which the owner of the trolley has a legal estate or, in Scotland, of which the owner of the trolley is the owner or occupier;
  (b) where an off-street parking place affords facilities to the customers of shops for leaving there shopping trolleys used by them, land on which those facilities are afforded;
  (c) where any other place designated by the local authority for the purposes of this Schedule affords like facilities, land on which those facilities are afforded; and
  (d) as respects luggage trolleys, land which is used for the purposes of their undertaking by persons authorised by an enactment to carry on any railway, light railway, tramway or road transport undertaking or by a relevant airport operator (within the meaning of Part V of the Airports Act 1986).

Power to seize and remove trolleys

2.—(1) Where this Schedule applies in relation to a shopping or luggage trolley, the local authority may, subject to sub-paragraph (2) below,—
  (a) seize the trolley; and
  (b) remove it to such place under its control as the authority thinks fit.

(2) When a shopping or luggage trolley is found on any land appearing to the authorised officer to be occupied by any person, the trolley shall not be removed without the consent of that person unless—
  (a) the local authority has served on that person a notice stating that the authority proposes to remove the trolley; and

(b) no notice objecting to its removal is served by that person on the local authority within the period of 14 days beginning with the day on which the local authority served the notice of the proposed removal on him.

Retention, return and disposal of trolleys

3.—(1) Subject to the following sub-paragraphs, the local authority, as respects any shopping or luggage trolley it has seized and removed,—

(a) shall keep the trolley for a period of six weeks; and

(b) may sell or otherwise dispose of the trolley at any time after the end of that period.

(2) The local authority shall, as respects any trolley it has seized or removed, as soon as reasonably practicable (but not later than 14 days) after its removal, serve on the person (if any) who appears to the authority to be the owner of the trolley a notice stating—

(a) that the authority has removed the trolley and is keeping it;

(b) that place where it is being kept; and

(c) that, if it is not claimed, the authority may dispose of it.

(3) Subject to sub-paragraph (4) below, if, within the period mentioned in sub-paragraph (1)(a) above, any person claims to be the owner of a shopping or luggage trolley being kept by the authority under that sub-paragraph, the local authority shall, if it appears that the claimant is the owner, deliver the trolley to him.

(4) A person claiming to be the owner of a shopping or luggage trolley shall not be entitled to have the trolley delivered to him unless he pays the local authority, on demand, such charge as the authority requires.

(5) No shopping or luggage trolley shall be disposed of by the local authority unless (where it has not been claimed) the authority has made reasonable enquiries to ascertain who owns it.

Charges

4.—(1) The local authority, in fixing the charge to be paid under paragraph 3 above by the claimant of a shopping or luggage trolley, shall secure that the charges so payable by claimants shall be such as are sufficient, taking one financial year with another, to cover the cost of removing, storing and disposing of such trolleys under this Schedule.

(2) The local authority may agree with persons who own shopping or luggage trolleys and make them available for use in its area a scheme for the collection by them of trolleys they make available for use; and where such an agreement is in force with any person, no charge may be demanded under paragraph 3 above by the local authority in respect of any trolley within the scheme in relation to which the provisions of the scheme are complied with.

Definitions

5. In this Schedule—

"luggage trolley" means a trolley provided by a person carrying on an undertaking mentioned in paragraph 1(2)(d) above to travellers for use by them for carrying their luggage to, from or within the premises used for the purposes of his undertaking, not being a trolley which is power-assisted; and

"shopping-trolley", means a trolley provided by the owner of a shop to customers for use by them for carrying goods purchased at the shop, not being a trolley which is power-assisted.

Section 105   SCHEDULE 5

FURTHER AMENDMENTS OF THE RADIOACTIVE SUBSTANCES ACT 1960

[*Schedule 5 was repealed by the Radioactive Substances Act 1993*]

Section 128   SCHEDULE 6

THE NATURE CONSERVANCY COUNCIL FOR ENGLAND AND THE COUNTRYSIDE COUNCIL FOR WALES: CONSTITUTION

Preliminary

1. In this Part of this Schedule any reference to the council is a reference to each of the Councils established by section 128 of this Act.

Constitution and membership

2. The council shall be a body corporate.

3.—(1) The council shall not be regarded as the servant or agent of the Crown, or as enjoying any status, immunity or privilege of the Crown; and the council's property shall not be regarded as property of, or property held on behalf of, the Crown.

(2) Sub-paragraph (1) above has effect subject to paragraph 18 below.

4.—(1) The Secretary of State shall appoint one of the members of the council to be chairman of the council and may appoint a member to be deputy chairman.

(2) The chairman, deputy chairman and other members of the council shall hold and vacate office in accordance with the terms of their appointment.

(3) A member of the council may, by notice in writing addressed to the Secretary of State, resign his membership, and the chairman and deputy chairman of the council may by such a notice resign their office as such without resigning their membership.

5. A member of the council who ceases to be a member or ceases to be chairman or deputy chairman of the council shall be eligible for reappointment.

6. The Secretary of State may remove a member of the council from membership if he has—
   (a) become bankrupt or made an arrangement with his creditors or, in Scotland, had his estate sequestrated or made a trust deed for behoof of his creditors or a composition contract; or
   (b) been absent from meeting of the council for a period longer than six consecutive months without the permission of the council;

or if he is, in the opinion of the Secretary of State unable or unfit to discharge the functions of a member.

Remuneration and allowances for members of council

7.—(1) The council shall—
   (a) pay to their members such remuneration and allowances (if any); and
   (b) as regards any member or former member in whose case the Secretary of State may so determine, pay such pension, allowance or gratuity to or in respect of him, or make such payments towards the provision of such pension, allowance or gratuity,

as the Secretary of State may with the approval of the Treasury determine.

(2) If a person ceases to be a member of the council, and it appears to the Secretary of State that there are special circumstances which make it right that he should receive compensation, the Secretary of State may require the council to pay to that person a sum of such amount as the Secretary of State may with the approval of the Treasury determine.

Staff

8.—(1) There shall be a chief officer of the council.

(2) The first appointment of a chief officer shall be made by the Secretary of State after consultation with the chairman of the council (if there is a person holding that office when the appointment is made); and the council shall, with the approval of the Secretary of State, make the subsequent appointments.

9. The council may appoint such number of other employees as they may, with the approval of the Secretary of State given with the consent of the Treasury, determine.

10. The council shall pay to the chief officer and their other employees such remuneration and allowances as the council may, with the approval of the Secretary of State given with the consent of the Treasury, determine.

11. The council shall, in the case of such of their employees or former employees as they may, with the approval of the Secretary of State given with the consent of the Treasury, determine—
   (a) pay such pensions, allowances or gratuities to or in respect of those employees,
   (b) make such payments towards provision of such pensions, allowances or gratuities, or
   (c) provide and maintain such schemes (whether contributory or not) for the payment of such pensions, allowances or gratuities,

as they may, with the approval of the Secretary of State given with the consent of the Treasury, determine.

Proceedings

12.—(1) The council may regulate their own procedure (including making provision in relation to quorum).

(2) The proceedings of the council and any committee of the council shall not be invalidated by any vacancy amongst their members or by any defect in the appointment of any such member.

Delegation of powers

13.—(1) Anything authorised or required by or under any enactment to be done by the council may be done by any committee of theirs which, or by any member or employee of the council who, is authorised (generally or specially) for the purpose by the council.

(2) Nothing in sub-paragraph (1) above shall prevent the council from doing anything that a committee, member or employee has been authorised to do.

Committees

14.—(1) The council may appoint persons who are not members of the council to be members of any committee established by the council (in addition to any members of the council).

(2) The council shall pay to a person so appointed such remuneration and allowances (if any) as the Secretary of State may with the approval of the Treasury determine.

(3) The council may regulate the procedure of any committee of theirs.

Documents

15.—(1) This paragraph applies in England and Wales only.

(2) The application of the seal of the council shall be authenticated by the signature of any member or employee of the council who is authorised (generally or specially) for the purpose by the council.

(3) Any document purporting to be an instrument made or issued by the council and to be duly executed under the seal of the council, or to be signed or executed by a person authorised for the purpose by the council, shall be received in evidence and treated, without further proof, as being so made or issued unless the contrary is shown.

16. [...]. [Paragraph 16 was repealed by the Natural Heritage (Scotland) Act 1991.]

Public records

17. In Schedule 1 to the Public Records Act 1958 (definition of public records), in Part II of the Table at the end of paragraph 3 (organisations whose records are public records) there shall be inserted in the appropriate places entries relating to the Countryside Council for Wales and the Nature Conservancy Council for England.

Land

18.—(1) For the purposes of the application of any enactment or rule of law to land an interest in which belongs to the council, and which is managed as a nature reserve, the council shall be deemed to be a Government department; and any other land occupied by them shall be deemed, for the purpose of any rate on property, to be property occupied by or on behalf of the Crown for public purposes.

(2) In sub-paragraph (1) above "interest" and "land" have the meanings assigned to them by section 114 of the National Parks and Access to the Countryside Act 1949.

Reports, accounts etc.

19. The council shall—

(a) furnish the Secretary of State with such returns, accounts and other information with respect to their property and activities or proposed activities as he may from time to time require;

(b) afford to the Secretary of State facilities for the verification of information so furnished; and

(c) for the purpose of such verification, permit any person authorised in that behalf by the Secretary of State to inspect and make copies of the council's accounts, books, documents or papers and give that person such explanation of anything he is entitled to inspect as he may reasonably require.

20. The council shall—

(a) as soon as possible after the March 31 following the date appointed under section 131(3) of this Act make to the Secretary of State a report on the exercise and performance of their functions down to that date, and

(b) make a similar report to him as to each period of 12 months thereafter as soon as possible after its end;

and a copy of each such report shall be laid before each House of Parliament by the Secretary of State.

(2) Without prejudice to the generality of sub-paragraph (1) above, the report of the Countryside Council for Wales for any year shall include statement of the action taken by the

Council to promote the enjoyment of the countryside by members of the public who are disabled.

21.—(1) The council shall keep proper accounts and other records, and shall prepare for each financial year a statement of account in such form as the Secretary of State with the approval of the Treasury may direct and submit those statements of account to the Secretary of State at such time as he may with the approval of the Treasury direct.

(2) The Secretary of State shall, on or before November 30 in any year, transmit to the Comptroller and Auditor General the statements of account of the council for the financial year last ended.

(3) The Comptroller and Auditor General shall examine and certify the statements of account transmitted to him under this paragraph, and lay copies of them together with his report thereon before each House of Parliament.

(4) In this paragraph "financial year" means the period beginning with the day appointed under section 131(3) of this Act and ending with the March 31 following that date and each period of 12 months thereafter.

Superannuation Act 1965 (c.74)

22. In paragraph 7 of section 39(1) of the Superannuation Act 1965 (public offices)—
   (a) there shall be inserted in the appropriate place the following entry—

     "The Countryside Council for Wales.";

   (b) for the entry relating to the Nature Conservancy Council there shall be substituted the following entries—

     "The Nature Conservancy Council for England.
     [Scottish Natural Heritage]."

Parliamentary Commissioner Act 1967 (c.13)

23. In Schedule 2 to the Parliamentary Act 1967 (departments and authorities subject to investigation)—
   (a) after the entry for the [Scottish Natural Heritage] there shall be inserted the following entry—

     "Countryside Council for Wales.";

   (b) for the entry relating to the Nature Conservancy Council there shall be substituted the following entries—

     "Nature Conservancy Council for England.
     [Scottish Natural Heritage]."

House of Commons Disqualification Act 1975 (c.24)

24. In Part III of Schedule 1 to the House of Commons Disqualification Act 1975 (other disqualifying offices), for the entry relating to members of the Nature Conservancy Council in receipt of remuneration there shall be substituted—
     "Any member of the Nature Conservancy Council for England, [Scottish Natural Heritage] or the Countryside Council for Wales in receipt of remuneration."

Inheritance Tax Act 1984 (c.51)

25. In Schedule 3 to the Inheritance Tax Act 1984 (gifts for national purpose), for the entry relating to the Nature Conservancy Council there shall be substituted the following entries—

     "Nature Conservancy Council for England.
     [Scottish Natural Heritage].
     Countryside Council for Wales."

SCHEDULE 7

Section 128

THE JOINT NATURE CONSERVATION COMMITTEE

Preliminary

1. In this Schedule—
     "chairman" means (except in paragraph 2(1) below) the chairman of the committee;

"the committee" means the Joint Nature Conservation Committee; and
"council" means a council established by section 128(1) of this Act.

Membership

2.—(1) The committee shall consist of 11 voting members, namely—
 (a) a chairman appointed by the Secretary of State;
 (b) three members appointed by the Secretary of State;
 (c) the chairman of each council and one other member of each council appointed by that council; and
 (d) the chairman of the Countryside Commission;
and two non-voting members appointed by the Department of the Environment for Northern Ireland.

(2) The committee may appoint any voting member to be deputy chairman.

(3) The chairman and the three members appointed by the Secretary of State shall be persons who are not members of any of the councils and shall hold and vacate office in accordance with the terms of their appointments.

4.—(1) The three members appointed by the Secretary of State shall be persons appearing to the Secretary of State to have experience in or scientific knowledge of nature conservation; and the Secretary of State shall, in determining who to appoint, have regard to any recommendations made to him by the chairman.

(2) Before appointing such a member the Secretary of State shall consult the chairman and such persons having scientific knowledge of nature conservation as the Secretary of State considers appropriate.

Remuneration and allowances for members

5.—(1) The council shall—
 (a) pay to the chairman such remuneration and allowances; and
 (b) pay such pension, allowance or gratuity to or in respect of the chairman or make such payments towards the provision of such pension, allowance or gratuity;
as the Secretary of State may with the approval of the Treasury determine.

(2) If a person ceases to be chairman and it appears to the Secretary of State that there are special circumstances which make it right that he should receive compensation, the Secretary of State may require the councils to pay to that person a sum of such amount as the Secretary of State may with the approval of the Treasury determine.

6. The councils shall pay to the three members appointed by the Secretary of State, and to the non-voting members, such remuneration and allowances as the Secretary of State may with the approval of the Treasury determine.

Staff etc. and expenses

7.—(1) The councils shall provide the committee with such staff, accommodation and other facilities, and such financial resources, as the councils, after consultation with the committee, consider appropriate for the proper discharge of the functions conferred by section 133(2) and (3) of this Act.

(2) The expenses of the committee shall be defrayed by the councils in such proportions as the councils may agree.

(3) In default of agreement between the councils as to any question arising under sub-paragraph (1) or (2) above the Secretary of State shall determine that question.

Proceedings

8.—(1) The committee may regulate their own procedure (including making provision in relation to the quorum of voting members).

(2) The proceedings of the committee shall not be invalidated by any vacancy amongst their members or defect in the appointment of any member.

Delegation of functions

9.—(1) Anything authorised or required to be done by the committee may be done by any member of the committee, by any council or by any employee of a council who is authorised (generally or specially) for the purpose by the committee.

(2) Nothing in sub-paragraph (1) above shall prevent the committee from doing anything that another person has been authorised to do.

Annual reports

10.—(1) The committee shall—

(a) as soon as possible after March 31 following the date appointed under section 131(1) of this Act make to the Secretary of State a report on their activities down to that date; and

(b) make a similar report to him as to each period of 12 months thereafter as soon as possible after its end;

and a copy of each such report shall be laid before each House of Parliament by the Secretary of State.

(2) The Committee shall, at the same time as they make a report under sub-paragraph (1) above, send a copy of it to each of the councils.

Section 130   SCHEDULE 8

AMENDMENT OF ENACTMENTS RELATING TO COUNTRYSIDE MATTERS

National Parks and Access to the Countryside Act 1949 (c.97)

1.—(1) The National Parks and Access to the Country Act 1949 shall be amended as follows.

(2) For section 1 (the Countryside Commission) there shall be substituted the following section—

"The Countryside Commission and the Countryside Council for Wales

1.—(1) There shall be a Countryside Commission which shall exercise functions in relation to England for the purposes specified in subsection (2) below; and the Countryside Council for Wales (established by section 128 of the Environmental Protection Act 1990) shall exercise corresponding functions in relation to Wales for the corresponding purposes specified in section 130(2) of the Environmental Protection Act 1990.

(2) The purposes for which the functions of the Commission are exercisable are—

(a) the preservation and enhancement of natural beauty in England, both in the areas designated under this Act as National Parks or as areas of outstanding natural beauty and elsewhere;

(b) encouraging the provision or improvement, for persons resorting to National Parks, or facilities for the enjoyment thereof and for the enjoyment of the opportunities for open-air recreation and the study of nature afforded thereby."

(3) In section 3 (power of Minister to give directions), in subsection (1) after the word "Commission" in the first place it occurs there shall be inserted the words "or to the Council" and after that word in the second place it occurs there shall be inserted the words "or Council".

(4) Before section 5 (National Parks) there shall be inserted the following section—

"Application of Part II of this Act in Wales

4A.—(1) The provisions of this Part of this Act shall, subject to the next following subsection, apply to land in Wales as they apply to land in England.

(2) Where a provision of this Part of this Act confers a function on the Countryside Commission as respects England (or areas of any description in England), the Countryside Council for Wales shall have the corresponding function as respects Wales (or areas of a similar description in Wales)."

(5) In sections 5(2) and 6(1) the words "and Wales" shall be omitted.

(6) Before section 51 (long-distance routes) there shall be inserted the following section—

"Application of Part IV of this Act in Wales

50A.—(1) The provisions of this Part of this Act shall, subject to the next following subsection, apply to land in Wales as they apply to land in England.

(2) Where a provision of this Part of this Act confers a function on the Countryside Commission as respects England (or land of any description in England), the Countryside Council for Wales shall have the corresponding function as respects Wales (or land of a similar description in Wales)."

(7) In section 51(1) the words "or Wales" shall be omitted.

(8) In sections 62(1) and 64(5) (consultation requirements as to land in National Parts), after the word "Commission" there shall be inserted the words "(where the Part in England) or the Council (where the Part in Wales)".

(9) In section 65 (access orders), in subsection (5), after the word "Park" in both places in which it occurs, there shall be inserted the words "in England" and after that subsection there shall be inserted the following subsection—

"(5A) The preceding subsection shall apply in relation to National Parks in Wales, and the Council, as it applies in relation to National Parks in England, and the Commission."

(10) In section 85 (general advisory duties)—
    (a) for the words "the duties of the Commission" there shall be substituted the words "their respective duties";
    (b) after the word "Commission", in the second place in which it occurs, there shall be inserted the words "and the Council";
    (c) in paragraph (b), after the word "Commission" there shall be inserted the words ", or, as the case may be, to the Minister and the Council,"; and
    (d) in paragraph (c), after the word "Commission" there shall be inserted the words "(as respects England) or to the Council (as respects Wales)".

(11) After section 86 (information services provided by Commission regarding National Parks) there shall be inserted the following section—

"Information services to be provided by Council
    86A. The provisions of section 86 of this Act shall apply to the Council in relation to National Parks and other land in Wales as they apply to the Commission in relation to National Parks and other land in England."

(12) In section 87 (designation of areas of outstanding natural beauty)—
    (a) in subsection (1), after the word "Commission" there shall be inserted the words ", or as the case may be, the Council,";
    (b) after that subsection there shall be inserted the following subsection—

        "(1A) The following provisions shall apply to the Council in relation to land in Wales as they apply to the Commission in relation to land in England."

(13) […]

(14) In section 90(4) (consultation before making certain byelaws) after the word "Commission" there shall be inserted the words "as regards land in England) or the Council (as regards land in Wales)".

(15) In section 91(1) (consultation before making certain byelaws) after the word "Commission" there shall be inserted the words "(as regards land or waterways in England) or the Council (as regards land or waterways in Wales)".

(16) In section 114 (interpretation), after the definition of "area of outstanding natural beauty" there shall be inserted the following definitions—
    "the Commission" means the Commission established by section one of this Act;
    "the Council" means the "Countryside Council for Wales;".

(17) In the first Schedule (procedure for certain orders), in paragraph 2(5), after the word "Commission" where it first appears there shall be inserted the words ", the Council" and after that word in the second place it appears there shall be inserted the word ", Council".

The Countryside Act 1968 (c.41)

2.—(1) The Countryside Act 1968 shall be amended as follows.
(2) In section 1 (additional general functions)—
    (a) for subsection (1) there shall be inserted the following subsections—

        "(1) The National Parks Commission shall in future be known as the 'Countryside Commission' and shall exercise functions in relation to England.
        (1A) The functions of the Countryside Commission (in this Act referred to as 'the Commission') in England and the corresponding functions of the Countryside Council for Wales (in this Act referred to as 'the Council') in Wales shall be enlarged in accordance with this Act.";
    (b) in subsection (2)—
        (i) after the word "recreation" there shall be inserted the words "and the study of nature"; and
        (ii) at the end, there shall be inserted the words "; and the purposes for which the functions of the Council in Wales are to be exercised are the corresponding purposes specified in section 130(2) of the Environmental Protection Act 1990.";
    (c) in subsection (3) for the word "shall" there shall be substituted the words "and the Council shall each".
(3) In section 2 (new functions)—
    (a) in subsection (1), for the word "shall" where it first appears there shall be substituted the words "and the Council shall each" and after the word "Commission" in the second and third place it appears there shall be inserted the words "or Council";

  (b) in subsections (2) and (3), after the word "Commission" where it first appears there shall be inserted the words "and the Council" and after that word in the second place it appears there shall be inserted the words "or Council";

  (c) in subsection (4), after the word "Commission" where it first appears there shall be inserted the words "and the Council" and after that word in the second and third place it appears there shall be inserted the words "or Council";

  (d) in subsection (5), after the word "Commission" where it first appears there shall be inserted the words "or to the Council" and after that word in the second place it appears there shall be inserted the words "or, as the case may be, the Council";

  (e) in subsection (5)(b), after the word "Commission" in each place it appears there shall be inserted the words "or Council";

  (f) in subsection (6) after the word "Commission" there shall be inserted the words "and the Council";

  (g) in subsections (7), (8) and (9), after the word "Commission" where it first appears there shall be inserted the words "and the Council" and after that word in the second place it appears there shall be inserted the words "or Council".

(4) In section 4 (experimental projects or schemes)—

  (a) in subsection (1), after the word "Commission" where it first appears there shall be inserted the words "and the Council" and after that word in the second place it appears there shall be inserted the words "or Council";

  (b) in subsection (3) after the word "Commission" there shall be inserted the words "or, as the case may be, the Council";

  (c) in subsection (4) after the word "Commission" there shall be inserted the words "or Council";

  (d) in subsection (5) after the word "Commission" where it first appears there shall be inserted the words "or by the Council" and after that word in the second place it appears there shall be inserted the words "or Council";

  (e) in subsection (6), after the word "Commission" where it first appears there shall be inserted the words "or of the Council" and after that word in the second place it appears there shall be inserted the words "or Council".

(5) In section 8 (sailing, boating and fishing in country parks), in subsection (5) after the word "Commission" there shall be inserted the words "(if the works are in England) or the Council (if the works are in Wales)".

(6) In section 12 (facilities in or near National Parks)—

  (a) in subsection (1) after the word "Commission" where it first appears there shall be inserted the words "or, as the case may be, the Council" and after that word in the second place it appears there shall be inserted the words "or the Council";

  (b) in subsection (5) after the word "Commission" there shall be inserted the words "(if the National Park in England) or the Council (if the National Parks is in Wales)".

(7) In section 13 (control of boats etc. in National Parks) in subsection (4), after the word "Commission" there shall be inserted the words "(if the National Park is in England) or the Council (if the National Park is in Wales)".

(8) In section 13 (provision of facilities by Forestry Commissioners), in subsection (5) for the word "shall" there shall be inserted the words "and the Countryside Council for Wales shall each".

(9) In section 38 (avoidance of pollution) after the words "the Commission" there shall be inserted the words ", the Council".

(10) In section 41 (byelaws etc.)—

  (a) in subsection (2), for the word "may" there shall be substituted the words "and the Council may each";

  (b) in subsection (5), after the word "Commission" there shall be inserted the words "(as respects a park or area in England) or the Council (as respects a part or area in Wales)";

  (c) in subsection (8), for the words "were a local authority" there shall be substituted the words "and the Council were local authorities";

  (d) in subsection (9), for the words "or the Commission" there shall be substituted the words ", the Commission or the Council".

(11) In section 45 (agreements with landowners), in subsection (1) after the word "Commission" there shall be inserted the words ", the Council".

(12) In section 46 (application of general provisions of 1949 Act), in subsection (2), at the end there shall be inserted "and any reference to the Nature Conservancy Council, so far as referring to the Countryside Council for Wales for purposes connected with their nature

conservation functions (within the meaning of section 131 of the Environmental Protection Act 1990) shall include a reference to that Council for purposes connected with their countryside functions (whether conferred by this Act, the Act of 1949 or otherwise)".

(13) In section 49 (interpretation), after the definition of "bridleway" there shall be inserted the following definitions—

" 'the Commission' means the Countryside Commission;
'the Council' means the Countryside Council for Wales;"

3. [...]

Local Government Act 1974 (c.7)

4. [...] In section 9 of that Act (grants and loans by the Countryside Commission)—
   (a) in subsection (1), for the word "may" there shall be substituted the words "and the Countryside Council for Wales may each" and after the word "Commission" in the second place it appears there shall be inserted the words "or, as the case may be, the Council";
   (b) in subsection (2), after the word "Commission" there shall be inserted the word "or the Countryside Council for Wales";
   (c) in subsection (3), for the words "Countryside Commission's power" there shall be substituted the words "the power of the Countryside Commission and of the Countryside Council for Wales" and after the word "Commission" in the second place it appears there shall be inserted the words "or to the Council".

Highways Act 1980 (c.66)

5.—(1) The Highways Act 1980 shall be amended as follows.

(2) In section 105A (environmental assessment for highway projects) in subsection (6)(a), after the word "land" there shall be inserted the words "in England" and, at the end, there shall be inserted the words "or the Countryside Council for Wales, if it relates to land in Wales falling within that paragraph of that subsection".

(3) In section 120 (orders for extinguishment or diversion of public paths), in subsection (2)(c), at the end there shall be inserted the words "(if the National Park is in England) or the Countryside Council for Wales (if the National Park is in Wales)".

Wildlife and Countryside Act 1981 (c.69)

6.—(1) The Wildlife and Countryside Act 1981 shall be amended as follows.

(2) In section 34 (limestone pavement orders), in subsection (6) in the definition of "the Commission", the words "and Wales" shall be omitted.

(3) In section 43 (maps of National Parks showing certain areas of moor or heath), in subsection (1A) the words "by the Countryside Commission" shall be omitted and—
   (a) in subsection (1B) for the word "shall" there shall be substituted the words "and the Countryside Council for Wales shall each" and for the word "may" there shall be substituted "the Commission and the Council may each";
   (b) in subsection (1C), after the word "Commission" there shall be inserted the words "or, as the case may be, the Council".

(4) Section 45 (power to vary orders designating National Parks) shall be subsection (1) of that section and, in that subsection, after the word "Park" in the first place it appears there shall be inserted the word "in England"; and at the end there shall be inserted, as subsection (2) of that section, the following words—

"(2) Subsection (1) shall apply to the Countryside Council for Wales, in relation to any National Park in Wales, as it applies to the Countryside Commission in relation to any National Park in England."

(5) In section 47(2) (power of Secretary of State to give grants) after the word "Commission" there shall be inserted the words "or the Countryside Council for Wales".

(6) In section 49 (extension of power to appoint wardens), in subsection (1)(b), after the word "authority" in the second place it appears there shall be inserted the words ", the Countryside Council for Wales", and, in subsection (4), after the word "Commission" in both places it appears there shall be inserted the words "or the Countryside Council for Wales".

The Road Traffic Regulation Act 1984 (c.27)

7. In section 22 of the Road Traffic Regulation Act 1984 (traffic regulation orders in special areas), in subsection (1)(a)(iv), after the word "Commission" there shall be inserted the words "or the Countryside Council for Wales" and, in subsection (4), for the words from "or" in the

first place it appears to "may", in the second place it appears, there shall be substituted ", the Countryside Council for Wales and the Countryside Commission for Scotland may each".

The Water Act 1989 (c.15)

8. In section 152 of the Water Act 1989 (restrictions on disposal of land) in subsection (5)(c)(i), after the word "Commission" there shall be inserted the words "(as respects land in England) or the Countryside Council for Wales (as respects land in Wales)"; and, in subsection (5)(d), after the word "Commission", where it first appears there shall be inserted the words "or the Countryside Council for Wales" and at the end there shall be inserted the words "or that Council".

Section 132   SCHEDULE 9

AMENDMENT OF ENACTMENTS CONFERRING NATURE CONSERVANCY FUNCTIONS

National Parks and Access to the Countryside Act 1949 (c.97)

1.—(1) The National Parks and Access to the Countryside Act 1949 shall be amended as follows.
(2) After section 15 there shall be inserted the following section—

"Meaning of 'Nature Conservancy Council'
15A. In this Part of this Act references to 'the Nature Conservancy Council' are references—
(a) in relation to land in England, to the Nature Conservancy Council for England;
(b) in relation to land in Scotland, to [Scottish Natural Heritage]; and
(c) in relation to land in Wales, to the Countryside Council for Wales."
(3) [...] [Subparagraph (3) was repealed by the Natural Heritage (Scotland) Act 1991.]
(4) In section 103 (general provisions as to acquisition of land)—
(a) in subsection (1), after the words "the Nature Conservancy Council" there shall be inserted the words "(as defined in section 15A of this Act)"; and
(b) [...] [subparagraph (4)(b) was repealed by the Natural Heritage (Scotland) Act 1991.]
(5) In section 106 (supplementary provisions as to bye-laws), in subsection (1), after the words "the Nature Conservancy Council" there shall be inserted the words "(as defined in section 15A of this Act)".

Deer (Scotland) Act 1959 (c.40)

2. [...] [Paragraph 2 was repealed by the Natural Heritage (Scotland) Act 1991.]

Deer Act 1963 (c.36)

3. In section 11 of the Deer Act 1963 (power to grant licences), after subsection (2) there shall be inserted—

"(3) In this section 'the Nature Conservancy Council' means in relation to the doing of an act in Wales, the Countryside Council for Wales and in relation to the doing of an act in England, the Nature Conservancy Council for England."

Countryside Act 1968 (c.41)

4.—(1) The Countryside Act 1968 shall be amended as follows.
(2) In section 15 (areas of special scientific interest)—
(a) in subsection (2), the words "in the national interest" shall be omitted and, after the words "any such land" there shall be inserted the words "(or of any adjacent land)"; and
(b) after subsection (6) there shall be inserted the following subsection—

"(6A) In this section references to 'the Nature Conservancy Council' or 'the Council' are references to the Nature Conservancy Council for England, [Scottish Natural Heritage] or the Council, according as the land in question is in England, Scotland or Wales."

(3) In section 37 (protection for interests in countryside) for the words "Nature Conservancy

Council" there shall be substituted the words ", the Council, the Nature Conservancy Council for England and [Scottish Natural Heritage]".

Conservation of Seals Act 1970 (c.30)

5. In section 10 of the Conservation of Seals Act 1970 (power to grant licences), after subsection (4) there shall be inserted the following subsection—

"(5) In this section a reference to 'the Nature Conservancy Council' is a reference to the Nature Conservancy Council for England, [Scottish Natural Heritage] or the Countryside Council for Wales, according as the area in question is in or is in waters adjacent to England, Scotland or Wales."

Badgers Act 1973 (c.57)

6. [...] [The Badgers Act 1973 was repealed by the Protection of Badgers Act 1992].

Import of Live Fish (Scotland) Act 1978 (c.35)

7. [...] [Paragraph 7 was repealed by the Natural Heritage (Scotland) Act 1991.]

Import of Live Fish (England and Wales) Act 1980 (c.27)

8. In section 1 of the Import of Live Fish (England and Wales) Act 1980 (power to limit imports), in subsection (2) after the word "Council" there shall be inserted the words "for England, the Countryside Councils for Wales".

Highways Act 1980 (c.66)

9. In section 105A of the Highways Act 1980 (environmental assessment of highway projects), for subsection (6)(c) there shall be substituted the following paragraph—
    (c) the Nature Conservancy Council for England or the Countryside Council for Wales, if it relates to land in England or, as the case may be, in Wales, falling within paragraph (c)."

Animal Health Act 1981 (c.22)

10.—(1) The Animal Health Act 1981 shall be amended as follows.
(2) In section 21 (destruction of wildlife on infection)—
    (a) in subsection (3), after the word "Council" there shall be inserted the words "for the area to which it will apply";
    (b) in subsection (9), after the definition of "animals" there shall be inserted the following definition—

        " 'Nature Conservancy Council' means the Nature Conservancy Council for England, [Scottish Natural Heritage] or the Countryside Council for Wales."

(3) In section 22 (powers of entry for s.21), in subsection (7)(a) for the words from "the Nature Conservancy" to "1973", there shall be substituted the words "a Nature Conservancy Council under section 132 of the Environmental Protection Act 1990".

Wildlife and Countryside Act 1981 (c.69)

11.—(1) The Wildlife and Countryside Act 1981 shall be amended as follows.
(2) In section 10(5) (consultation with Council required before taking or killing a bat) after the word "Council" there shall be inserted the words "for the area in which the house is situated or, as the case may be, the act is to take place".
(3) In section 15(2) (endangered species) for the word "Council" there shall be substituted the word "Councils".
(4) In section 16 (power to grant licences)—
    (a) in subsection (9)(a) and (9)(c), before the word "Nature" there shall be inserted the word "relevant";
    (b) in subsection (10)(a), for the words "the Nature Conservancy Council" there shall be substituted the words "each of the Nature Conservancy Councils" and, after the word "exercise" there shall be inserted the words "in the area of that Council";
    (c) in subsection (10)(b), before the word "Council" there shall be inserted the word "relevant Nature Conservancy"; and

(d) after subsection (10) there shall be inserted the following subsection—

"(11) For the purposes of this section a reference to a relevant Nature Conservancy Council is a reference to the Nature Conservancy Council for the area in which it is proposed to carry on the activity requiring a licence."

(5) In section 22(3) (power of Secretary of State to amend Schedules 5 or 8 to Act) for the words "to him by the Nature Conservancy Council" there shall be substituted the words "jointly to him by the Nature Conservancy Councils", and at the end of that subsection there shall be inserted the words—

"and the functions of the Nature Conservancy Councils under this subsection shall be special functions of the Council for the purposes of section 133 of the Environmental Protection Act 1990."

(6) In section 24 (functions of Nature Conservancy Council)—

(a) in subsection (1), for the word "Council" there shall be substituted the words "Councils, acting jointly", for the words "the passing of this Act" there shall be substituted the words "October 30, 1991" and at the end there shall be inserted the words—

"and the functions of the Nature Conservancy Councils under this subsection shall be special functions of the Councils for the purposes of section 133 of the Environmental Protection Act 1990";

(b) in subsection (2), for the words from "the Council" to the end there shall be substituted the words "to that advice being given.";

(c) for subsection (3) there shall be substituted the following subsection—

"(3) The Secretary of State shall lay before each House of Parliament a copy of any advice so given and the statements accompanying it."; and

(d) in subsection (4), for the word "Council" there shall be substituted the words "Nature Conservancy Councils".

(7) In section 27 (interpretation of Part I)—

(a) in subsection (1), in the definition of authorised person, for the words "the Nature Conservancy Council" there shall be substituted the words "any of the Nature Conservancy Councils"; and

(b) after subsection (3) there shall be inserted the following subsection—

"(3A) Any reference in this Part to the Nature Conservancy Councils is a reference to the Nature Conservancy Council for England, [Scottish Natural Heritage] and the Countryside Council for Wales."

(8) In Part II (nature conservation etc.), before section 28 there shall be inserted the following section—

"Construction of references to Nature Conservancy Council

27A. In this Part references to 'the Nature Conservancy Council' are, unless the contrary intention appears, references—

(a) in relation to land in, or land covered by waters adjacent to, England, to the Nature Conservancy Council for England;

(b) in relation to land in, or land covered by waters adjacent to, Scotland, to [Scottish Natural Heritage]; and

(c) in relation to land in, or land covered by waters adjacent to, Wales, to the Countryside Council for Wales;

and references to 'the Council' shall be construed accordingly."

(9) In section 29 (special protection for certain area of special scientific interest), in subsection (4)(a), for the words "commencement date" there shall be substituted the words "making of the order".

(10) In section 29 (special protection for certain areas of special scientific interest), in subsection (4)(a), after the word "Council" there shall be inserted the word "written".

(11) In section 29 (protection for areas of special scientific interest), in subsection (11), for the words "paragraph 17 of Schedule 3 to the Nature Conservancy Council Act 1973" there shall be substituted the words "paragraph 20 of Schedule 6 to the Environmental Protection Act 1990".

(12) In section 33 (Ministerial guidance) in subsection (1) for the word "Council" there shall be substituted the word "Councils".

(13) In section 52 (interpretation of Part II), in subsection (1) at the end there shall be inserted the following words—

" 'the Nature Conservancy Councils' means the Nature Conservancy Council for England, [Scottish Natural Heritage] and the Countryside Council for Wales;
and references to 'the Nature Conservancy Council' shall be construed in accordance with section 27A."

Roads (Scotland) Acts 1984 (c.54)

12. [...] [Paragraph 12 was repealed by the Natural Heritage (Scotland) Act 1991.]

Agriculture Act 1986 (c.49)

13. In section 18 of the Agriculture Act 1986 (environmentally sensitive areas), in subsection (2)—

   (a) in paragraph (a) after the word "Council" there shall be inserted the words "for England";
   (b) in paragraph (b) for the words "Countryside Commission and the Nature Conservancy Council" there shall be substituted the words "Countryside Council for Wales";
   (c) [...] [subparagraph (c) was repealed by the Natural Heritage (Scotland) Act 1991.]

Channel Tunnel Act 1987 (c.53)

14. In paragraph 5 of Schedule 2, and in paragraph 17 of Schedule 3, to the Channel Tunnel Act 1987, after the words "Nature Conservancy Council" there shall be inserted the words "for England".

Norfolk and Suffolk Broads Act 1988 (c.4)

15. The Norfolk and Suffolk Broads Act 1988, for each reference to the Nature Conservancy Council there shall be substituted a reference to the Nature Conservancy Council for England.

Electricity Act 1989 (c.29)

16. In Schedule 9 to the Electricity Act 1989 (preservation of amenity)—

   (a) in paragraph 2(2) for the words from "the Nature" to "Wales", where it first appears, there shall be substituted the words "and—
      (a) where the activities which he is authorised by his licence to carry on include activities in England, the Nature Conservancy Council for England and the Historic Buildings and Monuments Commission for England; and
      (b) where those activities include activities in Wales, the Countryside Council for Wales and"; and
   (b) [...] [Subparagraph (b) was repealed by the Natural Heritage (Scotland) Act 1991.]

Water Act 1989 (c.15)

17.—(1) The Water Act 1989 shall be amended as follows:
(2) In section 9 (environmental duties)—

   (a) in subsection (1) after the words "Conservancy Council" there shall be inserted the words "for England or the Countryside Council for Wales" and after the word "land" where it first appears there shall be inserted the words "in England or (as the case may be) in Wales";
   (b) in subsection (4), after the word "Council" there shall be inserted the words "in question".

(3) In section 10 (codes of practice), in subsection (4) after the words "Conservancy Council" there shall be inserted the words "for England, the Countryside Council for Wales".
(4) In section 152 (restriction on disposals of land), in subsection (5)(c)(i) after the word "interest" there shall be inserted the words "in England" and after the word "Council" there shall be inserted the words "for England".

TRANSFER SCHEME AND STAFF OF EXISTING COUNCILS

PART I

TRANSFER SCHEMES: NATURE CONSERVANCY COUNCIL

Making and approval of schemes

1.—(1) Before such date or dates as the Secretary of State may direct, the Nature Conservancy Council shall make, and submit to the Secretary of State for his approval, their transfer scheme or scheme under section 135 of this Act (in this Part of this Schedule referred to as a "transfer scheme").

(2) A transfer scheme shall not take effect unless approved by the Secretary of State, who may modify such a scheme before approving it.

(3) The Secretary of State may make a transfer scheme himself if—

(a) he decides not to approve a scheme which has been submitted to him before the due date (with or without modifications); or

(b) no scheme is submitted to him for approval before the due date;

but nothing in this sub-paragraph shall prevent the Secretary of State from approving any scheme which may be submitted to him after the due date.

(4) A scheme made by the Secretary of State shall be treated for all purposes as having been made by the Council and approved by him.

Modification of schemes

2.—(1) If at any time after a transfer scheme has come into force the Secretary of State considers it appropriate to do so, having consulted any of the Councils established by section 128 of this Act (in this Schedule referred to as "the new Councils") which may be affected, he may by order provide that the scheme shall for all purposes be deemed to have come into force with such modifications as may be specified in the order.

(2) An order under sub-paragraph (1) above may make, with effect from the coming into force of the scheme, such provision as could have been made by the scheme and in connection with giving effect to that provision from that time may contain such supplemental, consequential and transitional provision as the Secretary of State considers appropriate.

Provision of information to Secretary of State

3. It shall be the duty of the Nature Conservancy Council and the new Councils to provide the Secretary of State with all such information and other assistance as he may reasonably require for the purposes of or in connection with the exercise of any power conferred on him by paragraphs 1 and 2 above.

Contents of schemes

4. A transfer scheme may—

(a) define the property, rights and liabilities to be allocated to a particular new Council by specifying or describing them or by referring to all the property, right and liabilities comprised in a specified part of the undertaking of the Nature Conservancy Council (or partly in one way and partly in the other);

(b) create in favour of a new Council—

(i) an interest in or right over property transferred in accordance with the scheme (or any earlier scheme) to another new Council;

(ii) new rights and liabilities as between that Council and the others;

(c) provide that any rights or liabilities specified or described in the scheme shall, or shall to any extent, be enforceable either by or against each of the new Councils or by or against any two of the new Councils which are so specified;

(d) require a new Council to enter into written agreements with, or execute other instruments in favour of, another new Council;

and a scheme may make such supplemental, incidental and consequential provision as the Nature Conservancy Council considers appropriate (including provision as to the order in which transfers or transactions are to be regarded as having occurred).

5. For the avoidance of doubt property, rights and liabilities of the Nature Conservancy Council may be allocated to a new Council notwithstanding—

    (a) that they would not, or would not without the consent or concurrence of another person, otherwise be capable of being transferred or assigned;

    (b) that, in the case of foreign property, steps must be taken by the Council to secure its effective vesting under the relevant foreign law.

PART II

TRANSFER SCHEMES: THE COUNTRYSIDE COMMISSION

Making and approval of schemes

6.—(1) Before such date or dates as the Secretary of State may direct, the Countryside Commission shall make, and submit to the Secretary of State for his approval, their transfer scheme or schemes under section 136 of this Act (in this Part of this Schedule referred to as a "transfer scheme").

(2) A transfer scheme shall not take effect unless approved by the Secretary of State, who may modify such a scheme before approving it.

(3) The Secretary of State may make a transfer scheme himself if—

    (a) he decides not to approve a scheme which has been submitted to him before the due date (with or without modifications); or

    (b) no scheme is submitted to him for approval before the due date;

but nothing in this sub-paragraph shall prevent the Secretary of State from approving any scheme which may be submitted to him after the due date.

(4) A scheme made by the Secretary of State shall be treated for all purposes as having been made by the Countryside Commission and approved by him.

Modification of schemes

7.—(1) If at any time after a transfer scheme has come into force the Secretary of State considers it appropriate to do so, having consulted the Countryside Council for Wales and the Countryside Commission, he may by order provide that the scheme shall for all purposes be deemed to have come into force with such modifications as may be specified in the order.

(2) An order under sub-paragraph (1) above may make, with effect from the coming into force of scheme, such provision as could have been made by the scheme and in connection with giving effect to that provision from that time may contain such supplemental, consequential and transitional provision as the Secretary of State considers appropriate.

Provision of information to Secretary of State

8. It shall be the duty of the Countryside Council for Wales and the Countryside Commission to provide the Secretary of State with all such information and other assistance as he may reasonably require for the purposes of or in connection with the exercise of any power conferred on him by paragraphs 6 and 7 above.

Contents of scheme

9.—(1) A transfer scheme may—

    (a) define the property, rights and liabilities to be allocated to the Countryside Council for Wales by specifying or describing them or by referring to all the property, rights and liabilities comprised in a specified part of the undertaking of the Countryside Commission (or partly in one way and partly in the other);

    (b) create in favour of the Countryside Commission an interest in or right over property transferred in accordance with the scheme (or any earlier scheme) to the Countryside Council for Wales;

    (c) require the Countryside Council for Wales to enter into written agreements with, or execute other instruments in favour of, the Countryside Commission;

and a scheme may make such supplemental, incidental and consequential provision as the Countryside Commission consider appropriate (including provision as to the order in which transfers or transactions are to be regarded as having occurred).

(2) Paragraph 5 above shall apply to transfer schemes under section 136 of this Act.

PART III

EMPLOYMENT OF STAFF OF EXISTING BODIES

Proposals for staff of Nature Conservancy Council

10. Not later than such date or dates as the Secretary of State may determine, the Nature Conservancy Council shall prepare and submit to the Secretary of State for approval proposals that would secure that an offer is made by one of the new Councils to each person who will be entitled to receive an offer under section 137 of this Act.

11.—(1) The Secretary of State may, after consultation with the new Councils—

(a) approve the proposals submitted to him under paragraph 10 above or modify the proposals before approving them;

(b) if he decides not to approve the proposals or if the Nature Conservancy Council fail to submit the proposals by the due date, make his own proposals;

and any proposals made by the Secretary of State shall be treated for all purposes as if they were made by the Council and approved by him.

(2) It shall be the duty of the Nature Conservancy Council and the new Councils to provide the Secretary of State with all such information and other assistance as he may reasonably require for the purposes of or in connection with the exercise of any power conferred on him by this paragraph.

Proposals for certain staff of the Countryside Commission

12. Not later than such date or dates as the Secretary of State may determine, the Countryside Commission shall prepare and submit to the Secretary of State for approval proposals as to which of their employees are to receive offers of employment from the Countryside Council for Wales under section 137 of this Act.

13.—(1) The Secretary of State may, after consultation with the Countryside Council for Wales—

(a) approve the proposals submitted to him under paragraph 12 above or modify the proposals before approving them;

(b) if he decides not to approve the proposals or if the Countryside Commission fail to submit the proposals by the due date, make his own proposals;

and any proposals made by the Secretary of State shall be treated for all purposes as if they were made by the Commission and approved by him.

(2) It shall be the duty of the Countryside Commission and the Countryside Council for Wales to provide the Secretary of State with all such information and other assistance as he may reasonably require for the purposes of or in connection with the exercise of any power conferred on him by this paragraph.

Offers of employment

14.—(1) Each new Council shall, before such date as the Secretary of State may direct, make offers of employment in accordance with this paragraph to those persons allocated to that Council by the proposals under paragraph 10 above as approved by the Secretary of State.

(2) The Countryside Council for Wales shall, before such date as the Secretary of State may direct, make offers of employment in accordance with this paragraph to those persons who are the subject of proposals under paragraph 12 above as approved by the Secretary of State.

(3) The terms of employment to be offered shall be such that they are, taken as a whole, not less favourable to the person to whom the offer is made than the terms on which he is employed on the date on which the offer is made.

(4) An offer under this paragraph shall not be revocable during the period of three months commencing with the date on which it is made.

Continuity of employment, redundancy etc.

15. Where a person becomes an employee of a new Council in consequence of an offer made under paragraph 14(1) or (2) above, then, for the purposes of the Employment Protection (Consolidation) Act 1978, his period of employment with the Nature Conservancy Council, or as the case may be, the Countryside Commission shall count as a period of employment by the new Council and the change of employment shall not break the continuity of the period of employment.

16. Where an offer is made to a person in pursuance of paragraph 14(1) or (2) above, none of the redundancy procedures applicable to such a person shall apply to him; and where that

person ceases to be employed by the Nature Conservancy Council or, as the case may be, the Countryside Commission—

    (a) on becoming employed by a new Council, or

    (b) having unreasonably refused an offer,

Part VI of the Employment Protection (Consolidation) Act 1978 shall not apply to him and he shall not be treated for the purposes of any superannuation or other pension scheme as having been retired on redundancy.

Disputes

17.—(1) Any dispute as to whether an offer under paragraph 14(1) or (2) above complies with sub-paragraph (3) of that paragraph shall be referred to and determined by an industrial tribunal.

(2) An industrial tribunal shall not consider a complaint referred to it under sub-paragraph (1) above unless the complaint is presented to the tribunal before the end of the period of three months beginning with the date of the offer or, where the tribunal is satisfied that it was not reasonably practicable for that to be done, within such further period as the tribunal considers reasonable.

(3) Subject to sub-paragraph (4) below, there shall be no appeal from the decision of an industrial tribunal under this paragraph.

(4) An appeal to the Employment Appeal Tribunal may be made only on a point of law arising from a decision of, or in proceedings before, an industrial tribunal under this paragraph.

Section 139   SCHEDULE 11

TRANSITIONAL PROVISIONS AND SAVINGS FOR PART VII

PART I

COUNTRYSIDE FUNCTIONS

Preliminary

1. In this Part of this Schedule—

    "the appointed day" means the day appointed under section 130(4) of this Act;

    "the Commission" means the Countryside Commission;

    "the Council" means the Countryside Council for Wales;

    "relevant" in relation to anything done by or in relation to the Commission before the appointed day, means anything which, if it were to be done on or after the appointed day, would be done by or in relation to the Council or, as the case may be, by or in relation to both the Commission (so far as concerning England) and the Council (so far as concerning Wales).

Continuity of exercise of functions

2.—(1) Any relevant thing done by or in relation to the Commission before the appointed day shall, so far as is required for continuing its effect on and after that date, have effect as if done by or in relation to the Council or, as the case may be, by or in relation to both the Council and the Commission.

(2) Any relevant thing which, immediately before the appointed day, is in the process of being done by or in relation to the Commission may be continued by or in relation to the Council or, as the case may be, by or in relation to both the Council and the Commission.

Construction of references to the Countryside Commission

3.—(1) This paragraph applies to any provision of any agreement, or of any instrument or other document, subsisting immediately before the appointed day which refers (in whatever terms) to the Commission and does so (or is to be construed as doing so) in relation to, or to things being done in or in connection with, Wales.

(2) Any provision to which this paragraph applies shall, subject to sub-paragraphs (3) and (4) below, have effect on and after the appointed day with the substitution for, or the inclusion in, any reference to the Commission of a reference to the Council, according as the reference concerns Wales only or concerns both England and Wales.

(3) Any provision to which this paragraph applies which refers in general terms to members of or to persons employed by or agents of the Commission shall have effect on and after the appointed day with the substitution for, or the inclusion in, any such reference of a reference to

members of or persons employed by or agents of the Council, according as the reference concerns Wales only or concerns both England and Wales.

(4) Any provision to which this paragraph applies which refers to a member or employee of the Commission shall have effect on and after the appointed day with the substitution for, or the inclusion in, any such reference of—

(a) a reference to such person as the Council may appoint, or

(b) in default of appointment, to the member or employee of the Council who corresponds as nearly as may be to the member or employee in question,

according as the reference concerns Wales only or concerns both England and Wales.

4.—(1) This paragraph applies to any provision of a local Act passed, or subordinate legislation made, before the appointed day which refers (in whatever terms) to the Commission and relates to, or to things being done in or in connection with, Wales.

(2) The Secretary of State may by order make such consequential modifications of any provision to which this paragraph applies as appear to him to be necessary or expedient.

(3) Subject to any exercise of the power conferred by sub-paragraph (2) above, any provision to which this paragraph applies shall have effect on and after the appointed day with the substitution for, or inclusion in, any reference to the Commission of a reference to the Council, according as the reference concerns Wales only or concerns both England and Wales.

Existing areas of outstanding natural beauty and long distance routes

5.—(1) This paragraph applies to—

(a) any area of land which immediately before the appointed day is an area of outstanding natural beauty designated under section 87 of the 1949 Act of which part is in England and part is in Wales (referred to as "the two parts" of such an area); and

(b) any long distance route under Part IV of that Act of which some parts are in England and other parts in Wales.

(2) On and after the appointed day the two parts of an area to which this paragraph applies shall be treated as if each were a distinct area of outstanding natural beauty; and accordingly, so far as may be necessary for the purpose of applying paragraphs 2 and 3 above, anything done by or in relation to the Commission in relation to both parts of that area shall be treated as having been done in relation to the part in Wales by or in relation to the Council.

(3) On and after the appointed day any route to which this paragraph applies shall not cease, by virtue of this Part of this Act, to be a single route for the purposes of Part IV of the 1949 Act; but any function which before that day is exercisable by or in relation to the Commission shall, on and after that day be exercisable by or in relation to the Commission (so far as concerns parts of the route in England) and by or in relation to the Council (so far as concerns parts of the route in Wales).

(4) On or after the appointed day the Commission and the Council shall each exercise any function of theirs in relation to an area or route to which this paragraph applies only after consultation with the other; and the Commission and the Council may make arrangements for discharging any of their functions in relation to such an area or route jointly.

PART II

NATURE CONSERVATION FUNCTIONS

Preliminary

6. In this Part of this Schedule—

"appointed day" means the date appointed under section 131(3) of this Act;

"appropriate new council" shall be construed in accordance with paragraph 7 below; and

"new council" means a council established by section 128(1) of this Act.

7.—(1) In this Part of this Schedule a reference to "the appropriate new council" is, in relation to or to things done in connection with property, rights or liabilities of the Nature Conservancy Council which are transferred by section 135(2) of this Act to a new council, a reference to that new council.

(2) Subject to sub-paragraph (1) above, a reference in this Part of this Schedule to "the appropriate new council" is, in relation to anything else done before the appointed day by or in

relation to the Nature Conservancy Council in the exercise of or in connection with any function of theirs (other than a function corresponding to a special function of the new councils)—

    (a) a reference to the new council by whom the nature conservation function corresponding to that function is exercisable on and after that date; or

    (b) where the thing done relates to a matter affecting the area of more than one new council, a reference to each new council by whom the nature conservation function corresponding to that function is exercisable on and after that date;

and in relation to anything done in the exercise of or in connection with any function of the Nature Conservancy Council corresponding to a special function of the new councils a reference to "the appropriate new council" is a reference to the joint committee or, where directions under section 133(5) of this Act have been given, the new council by whom the corresponding special function is dischargeable (on behalf of the new councils) on and after that day.

(3) Any question arising under this paragraph as to which new council is the appropriate new council in relation to any particular function of the Nature Conservancy Council may be determined by a direction given by the Secretary of State.

Continuity of exercise of functions

8.—(1) Anything done (or deemed by any enactment to have been done) by or in relation to the Nature Conservancy Council before the appointed day shall, so far as is required for continuing its effect on and after that date, have effect as if done by or in relation to the appropriate new council.

(2) Anything which immediately before the appointed day is in the process of being done by or in relation to the Nature Conservancy Council may be continued by or in relation to the appropriate new council as if it had been done by or in relation to that council.

Construction of references to the Nature Conservancy Council

9.—(1) This paragraph applies to any agreement, any instrument and any other document subsisting immediately before the appointed day which refers (in whatever terms) to the Nature Conservancy Council, other than a scheme provided by that Council under paragraph 12 of Schedule 3 to the Nature Conservancy Council Act 1973.

(2) Any agreement, instrument or other document to which this paragraph applies shall have effect on and after the appointed day with the substitution—

    (a) for any reference to the Nature Conservancy Council of a reference to the appropriate new council;

    (b) for any reference in general terms to members of or to persons employed by or agents of the Nature Conservancy Council of a reference to members of or persons employed by or agents of the appropriate new council; and

    (c) for any reference to a member or officer of the Nature Conservancy Council of a reference to such person as the appropriate new council may appoint or, in default of appointment, to the member or employee of that council who corresponds as nearly as may be to the member or officer in question.

10.—(1) This paragraph applies to any provision of a local Act passed, or subordinate legislation made, before the appointed day which refers (in whatever terms) to the Nature Conservancy Council.

(2) The Secretary of State may by order make such consequential modifications of any provision to which this paragraph applies as appear to him to be necessary or expedient.

(3) Subject to any exercise of the power conferred by sub-paragraph (2) above, any provision to which this paragraph applies shall have effect on and after the appointed day with the substitution for each reference to the Nature Conservancy Council of a reference to such one or more of the new councils as may be appropriate, according as the provision relates to, or to things being done in or in connection with, England, Scotland or Wales.

Pensions for Nature Conservancy Council staff

11.—(1) The repeal by this Act of paragraph 12 of Schedule 3 to the Nature Conservancy Council Act 1973 shall not affect the operation on and after the appointed day of any scheme provided by the Nature Conservancy Council for the payment to or in respect of its officers of pensions, allowances or gratuities.

(2) Any such scheme shall have effect on and after the appointed day with the substitution for any reference to the Nature Conservancy Council of a reference to the Secretary of State.

Existing nature reserves and areas of special scientific interest

12.—(1) This paragraph applies to any land which, immediately before the appointed day is—

(a) a nature reserve (within the meaning of Part III of the 1949 Act) which is managed by, or under an agreement entered into with, the Nature Conservancy Council or which is the subject of a declaration under section 35 of the 1981 Act; or

(b) an area of special scientific interest which has been notified by the Nature Conservancy Council under section 28(1) of the 1981 Act or is treated by section 28(13) of that Act as having been notified under section 28(1)(a) of that Act or is an area to which an order unless section 29(1) of that Act relates;

and of which part is in England and part is in Wales or, as the case may be, part is in England and part is in Scotland (referred to as "the two parts" of such a reserve or area).

(2) On and after the appointed day, the two parts of any reserve or area to which this paragraph applies shall be treated as if each were a distinct nature reserve or area of special scientific interest; and accordingly, so far as may be necessary for the purpose of applying paragraphs 8 and 9 above, anything done by or in relation to the Nature Conservancy Council affecting both parts of that reserve or area shall be treated as having been done by or in relation to each of the two parts separately.

(3) On and after the appointed day the new council exercising functions as respects either part of a reserve or area to which this paragraph applies shall exercise those functions only after consultation with the new council exercising functions as respects the other part; and those councils may make arrangements for discharging any of those functions jointly.

PART III

SUPPLEMENTARY

13. Paragraphs 3, 4, 5, 8, 9, 10 and 12 above are without prejudice to any provision made by or under this Part of this Act in relation to any particular functions, property, rights or liabilities; and, in particular, nothing in this Schedule applies in relation to contracts of employment made by the Countryside Commission or the Nature Conservancy Council.

14. The Secretary of State may, in relation to any particular functions of the Countryside Commission or the Nature Conservancy Council, by order exclude, or modify or supplement any provision of this Schedule or make such other transitional provision as he may think necessary or expedient.

15. In this Schedule "the 1949 Act" means the National Parks and Access to the Countryside Act 1949 and "the 1981 Act" means the Wildlife and Countryside Act 1981.

Sections 140 and 142   SCHEDULE 12

INJURIOUS OR HAZARDOUS SUBSTANCES: ADVISORY COMMITTEE

1. The Secretary of State shall appoint the members of the committee, and shall appoint one of those members to be chairman.

2. The committee shall include persons who appear to the Secretary of State to be representative of—

(a) persons engaged in carrying on industrial or commercial undertakings;

(b) persons having scientific knowledge of matters concerning pollution of the environment;

(c) bodies concerned with the protection or improvement of the environment; and

(d) bodies concerned with the protection of persons using substances or articles subject to regulation under section 140 or 142 of this Act.

3. The Secretary of State may make provision by regulations with respect to the terms on which members of the committee are to hold and vacate office, including the terms on which any person appointed as chairman is to hold and vacate office as chairman.

4. The Secretary of State shall provide the committee with such services and other facilities as appear to him to be necessary or expedient for the proper performance of the committee's functions.

5. The Secretary of State may pay to the members of the committee such remuneration (if

any) and such allowances as may be determined by the Secretary of State with the consent of the Treasury.

SCHEDULE 13

AMENDMENTS OF HAZARDOUS SUBSTANCES LEGISLATION

PART I

ENGLAND AND WALES

1. The Planning (Hazardous Substances) Act 1990 shall be amended as provided in this Part of this Schedule.

2.—(1) Section 2 (appropriate Minister to be hazardous substances authority for land used or to be used by statutory undertakers) shall be omitted.

(2) In section 7(3), for the words from "means" to "with" in the third place it occurs there shall be substituted the words "means consultations with the Health and Safety Executive and with".

(3) In section 10(2), for the words from the beginning to "3" there shall be substituted the words "A hazardous substances authority".

(4) In section 28(1)—

(a) in paragraph (a), for the words following the word "consent" there shall be substituted the words "made to that authority;

(aa) to applications under section 17(1) made to that authority;"; and

(b) after paragraph (d), there shall be inserted the following words—

"; and every such register shall also contain such information as may be prescribed as to the manner in which applications for hazardous substances consent have been dealt with."

(5) In section 29, in subsection (3) and (4), for the words "appropriate body" there shall be substituted the words "Health and Safety Executive".

(6) In section 38(5) for the words "1 to 3" there shall be substituted "1, 3".

(7) In section 39(1), in the definition of "hazardous substances authority", for the word "to", in the second place it occurs, there shall be inserted the word "and".

3. In section 7(1)(a) (applications for consent), after the word "applications" there shall be inserted the words "under this Act".

4. In section 11 (deemed hazardous substances consent in transitional cases)—

(a) in subsection (2) for the words "immediately before the relevant date" there shall be substituted the words "while it was so present"; and

(b) in subsection (7), in paragraph (a), at the beginning there shall be inserted the words "to the condition that" and, for paragraphs (b) and (c), there shall be substituted the words ", and

(b) to such other conditions (if any) as are prescribed for the purposes of this section and are applicable in the case of that consent."

5. In section 12 (deemed consent: government authorisation), at the end there shall be added the following subsection—

"(6) A government department or the Secretary of State shall, as respects any hazardous substances consent deemed to be granted by virtue of directions under this section, send to the hazardous substances authority concerned any such information as appears to be required by them for the purposes of a register under section 28."

6. In section 13 (applications for hazardous substances consent in place of subsisting consent subject to conditions), subsection (7) shall be omitted.

7. In section 22 (validity of decisions as to applications), in subsection (4), for the words "1971 Act" there shall be substituted the words "principal Act."

8. In section 25(1)(c) (provisions of principal Act capable of application to hazardous substances contravention notices), after "184," there shall be inserted "186,".

9. Before section 27 there shall be inserted the following section—

"Fees for consent applications

26A.—(1) Provision may be made by regulations for the payment of a fee of the prescribed amount to a hazardous substances authority in respect of an application for, or for the continuation of, hazardous substances consent.

(2) Regulations under this section may provide for the payment to the Secretary of State of a fee of the prescribed amount in respect of any application which is, by virtue of regulations under section 25, deemed to have been made for hazardous substances consent.

(3) Regulations under this section may provide—

(a) for the transfer of prescribed fees received by a hazardous substances authority in respect of any application which is referred to the Secretary of State under section 20;

(b) for the remission of refunding of a prescribed fee (in whole or in part) in prescribed circumstances or in pursuance of a direction given by the Secretary of State;

and the regulations may make different provision for different areas or for different cases or descriptions of cases."

10. In section 303(6) of the Town and Country Planning Act 1990 (meaning of "Planning Acts" for purposes of fees chargeable under that section), at the end there shall be inserted the words "or the Planning (Hazardous Substances) Act 1990").

PART II

SCOTLAND

11.—(1) The Town and Country Planning (Scotland) Act 1972 shall be amended as provided in this paragraph.

(2) Section 56B (appropriate Minister to be planning authority in respect of hazardous substances in relation to land used or to be used by statutory undertakers) shall be omitted.

(3) In section 56D(1)(a) (applications for consent, after the word "applications" there shall be inserted the words "under this Act".

(4) In section 56D(5) for the words from "means" to "with" in the third place it occurs there shall be substituted the words "means consultations with the Health and Safety Executive and with".

(5) After section 56D there shall be inserted the following section—

"Fees

56DA.—(1) The Secretary of State may by regulations make provision for fees of the prescribed amount in respect of applications for, or for the continuation of, hazardous substances consent—

(a) made to an urban development corporation under section 56A(2) above to be paid to the corporation;

(b) referred to him under section 32 above as having effect by virtue of section 56F below to be paid to him;

(c) deemed to have been made to him under section 85(7) below by virtue of regulations made under section 97B(10) below to be paid to him.

(2) Regulations made under this section may provide for—

(a) the transfer to the Secretary of State of any fee received by a planning authority in respect of an application referred to in paragraph (b) or (c) of subsection (1) above;

(b) the remission of refunding of a prescribed fee (in whole or in part) in prescribed circumstances or in pursuance of a direction given by him;

and the regulations may make different provision for different areas or for different cases or descriptions of cases."

(6) In section 56E(5) for the words "a planning authority other than the appropriate Minister" there shall be substituted the word "they".

(7) In section 56G (deemed consent: government authorisation), at the end there shall be added the following subsection—

"(5) A government department or the Secretary of State shall, as respects any hazardous substances consent deemed to be granted by virtue of directions under this section, send to the planning authority concerned any such information as appears to be required by them for the purposes of a register under section 56N."

(8) In section 56H (applications for hazardous substances consent in place of subsisting consent subject to conditions) subsection (5) shall be omitted.

(9) In section 56N(1)—

(a) in paragraph (a), for the words following the word "consent" there shall be substituted the words "made to that authority;

(aa) to applications under section 56K(2) above made to that authority;" and

(b) after paragraph (d), there shall be inserted the following words—

", and every such register shall also contain such information as may be prescribed as to the manner in which applications for hazardous substances consent have been dealt with."

(10) In section 56O, in subsections (2) and (3), for the words "appropriate body" there shall be substituted the words "Health and Safety Executive".

(11) In section 97B(10)(c) (hazardous substances contravention notices), after "89A" there shall be inserted "and 166".

12.—(1) Section 38 of the Housing and Planning Act 1986 (transitional provisions) shall be amended as provided in this paragraph.

(2) In subsection (4), for the words "immediately before the commencement date" there shall be substituted the words "while it was so present".

(3) In subsection (9)—

(a) for the words "subject to the conditions that—(a)" there shall be substituted the words "subject to—

(a) the condition that";

(b) for paragraphs (b) and (c) there shall be substituted—

"(b) such other conditions (if any) as are prescribed, by statutory instrument subject to annulment in pursuance of a resolution of either House of Parliament, for the purposes of this section and are applicable in the case of that consent."

13. In section 87 of the Local Government, Planning and Land Act 1980 (fees for planning applications etc.), at the end there shall be inserted the following subsection—

"(9) Without prejudice to the generality of subsection (1) above the reference in that subsection to an application for any consent includes, in relation to a planning authority in Scotland, an application under section 56K(2) of the Town and Country Planning (Scotland) Act 1972 for the continuation of hazardous substances consent."

Section 148   SCHEDULE 14

[Schedule 14 was repealed by the Merchant Shipping Act 1995 save to the extent provided therein—see the note to s.148].

Section 162   SCHEDULE 15

CONSEQUENTIAL AND MINOR AMENDMENTS OF ENACTMENTS

Statutory nuisances: Scotland

1. In section 3 of the Public Health (Scotland) Act 1897 at the end there shall be added the following paragraph—

"The word 'ratepayer' means a person who either is liable to pay any of the community charges or community water charges imposed under the Abolition of Domestic Rates Etc. (Scotland) Act 1987 (or would be so liable but for any enactment or anything provided or done under any enactment) or is a non-domestic ratepayer."

Exclusion of Alkali Works Act for prescribed processes

2. In the Alkali, &c. Works Regulation Act 1906 there shall be inserted, after section 2, the following section—

"Relation to Environmental Protection Act 1990, Part I

2A.—(1) The preceding provisions of this Part of this Act shall not apply to any process which is a prescribed process as from the date which is the determination date for that process.

(2) The 'determination date' for a prescribed process is—

(a) in the case of a process for which an authorisation is granted, the date on which the enforcing authority grants it, whether in pursuance of the application or, on an appeal, of a direction to grant it;

(b) in the case of a process for which an authorisation is refused, the date of the refusal or, on an appeal, of the affirmation of the refusal.

(3) In this section 'authorisation', 'enforcing authority' and 'prescribed process' have the meaning given in section 1 of the Environmental Protection Act 1990 and the reference to an appeal is a reference to an appeal under section 15 of that Act.".

and, immediately before section 25, as section 24A, a section in the same terms as the section 2A inserted after section 2.

Stray dogs

3.—(1) The following provisions of the Dogs Act 1906 shall be amended as follows.

(2) The amendments made to section 3 by section 39(2) of the Local Government Act 1988 and section 128(1)(a) of the Civic Government (Scotland) Act 1982 shall cease to have effect.

(3) In section 4—

(a) subsection (1) shall be omitted;

(b) in subsection (2), for the words "so taken to a police station" there shall be substituted the words "taken to a police station in pursuance of section 150(1) of the Environmental Protection Act 1990";

(c) in subsection (2)(a), for the words from "his name and address' to "other" there shall be substituted the words "this fact and shall furnish his name and address and the police officer shall, having complied with the procedure (if any) prescribed under subsection (5) below, allow the finder to remove the dog";

(d) in subsection (3), for the words from "fails" to "section" there shall be substituted the words "removes the dog but fails to keep it for at least one month,"; and

(e) after subsection (3) or, as respects Scotland, subsection (4) there shall be inserted as subsection (4) or subsection (5) the following subsection—

"( ) The Secretary of State may, by regulations made by statutory instrument, prescribe the procedure to be followed under subsection (2)(a) above and any instrument containing regulations under this subsection shall be subject to annulment in pursuance of a resolution of either House of Parliament."

Statutory nuisances

4.—(1) The following provisions of the Public Health Act 1936 (matters deemed statutory nuisances) shall be amended as follows.

(2) In section 141, for the words "Part III of this Act" there shall be substituted the words "Part III of the Environmental Protection Act 1990".

(3) In section 259(1), for the words "Part III of this Act" there shall be substituted the words "Part III of the Environmental Protection Act 1990".

(4) In section 268—

(a) in subsection (1), for the words "Part III" there shall be substituted the words "Part III of the Environmental Protection Act 1990 and Parts";

(b) in subsection (2), for the words "the said Part III" there shall be substituted the words "Part III of the Environmental Protection Act 1990"; and

(c) in subsection (3), for the words "Part III of this Act" there shall be substituted the words "Part III of the Environmental Protection Act 1990".

5.—(1) Section 151 of the Mines and Quarries Act 1954 (matters deemed statutory nuisances) shall be amended as follows.

(2) In subsection (2), for the words "Part III of the Public Health Act 1936" there shall be substituted the words "Part III of the Environmental Protection Act 1990".

(3) In subsection (3), for the words "Part III of the Public Health Act 1936" there shall be substituted the words "Part III of the Environmental Protection Act 1990".

[...]

Exclusion of Clean Air Act 1956 for prescribed processes

6. [...] [Paragraph 6 was repealed by the Clean Air Act 1993.]

Statutory nuisances

7. [...] [Paragraph 7 was repealed by the Clean Air Act 1993.]

8. The Radioactive Substances Act 1960 shall be amended by the insertion in Part I of Schedule 1 (exclusion of other controls) at the end, of the following paragraph—

"9. Part III of the Environmental Protection Act 1990."

9. In section 1(1)(g) of the Hovercraft Act 1968 (power to exclude noise nuisance proceedings), after the word "1974" there shall be inserted the words "or Part III of the Environmental Protection Act 1990".

Goods vehicle operators' licences: pollution offences

10.—(1) The following provisions of the Transport Act 1968 shall be amended as follows.

(2) [...] [Subparagraph (2) was repealed by the Goods Vehicles (Licensing of Operators) Act 1995, Sched. 8.]

(3) In section 108(1) (statutory nuisance proceedings in relation to waterways), for the words "said Act of 1936" there shall be substituted the words "Environmental Protection Act 1990".

National Park Wardens

11. In section 42 of the Countryside Act 1968 (National Park Wardens), in subsection (4)(a), for the words "section 1 of the Litter Act 1983" there shall be substituted the words "section 87 of the Environmental Protection Act 1990".

Exclusion of Clean Air Act 1968 for prescribed processes

12. [...] [Paragraph 12 was repealed by the Clean Air Act 1993.]

Sale of electricity: Scotland

13. In section 170A(3) of the Local Government (Scotland) Act 1973 (restriction on sale of electricity by local authority) after the word "prescribed," there shall be inserted the words "or in cases where it is produced from waste,".

Workplace emissions into the air

14. Section 5 of the Health and Safety at Work etc. Act 1974 (general duty in relation to harmful emissions into the air from prescribed premises) shall be amended by the insertion—
    (a) in subsection (1), at the beginning, of the words "Subject to subsection (5) below,"; and
    (b) after subsection (4), of the following subsections—

"(5) The foregoing provisions of this section shall not apply in relation to any process which is a prescribed process as from the date which is the determination date for that process.

(6) For the purposes of subsection (5) above, the 'determination date' for a prescribed process is—
    (a) in the case of a process for which an authorisation is granted, the date on which the enforcing authority grants it, whether in pursuance of the application or, on an appeal, of a direction to grant it;
    (b) in the case of a process for which an authorisation is refused, the date of the refusal or, on an appeal, of the affirmation of the refusal.

(7) In subsections (5) and (6) above 'authorisation', 'enforcing authority' and 'prescribed process' have the meaning given in section 1 of the Environmental Protection Act 1990 and the reference to an appeal is a reference to an appeal under section 15 of that Act."

Water, noise and atmospheric pollution

15.—(1) The following provisions of the Control of Pollution Act 1974 shall be amended as follows.

(2) In section 30D, after the words "and 1965" there shall be inserted the words "and of the Environmental Protection Act 1990".

(3) In section 61(9), at the end, there shall be inserted the words "(in relation to Scotland) or section 82 of the Environmental Protection Act 1990 (in relation to England and Wales)".

(4) In section 65(8), at the end, there shall be inserted the words "(in relation to Scotland) or section 82 of the Environmental Protection Act 1990 (in relation to England and Wales)".

(5) In section 74(2), after paragraph (b), there shall be inserted the following:

"; or

(c) under section 80(4) of the Environmental Protection Act 1990,".

[Subparagraphs 15(6) to 15(9) were repealed by the Clean Air Act 1993.]
(6)–(9) […]

Exclusion of Part II of Control of Pollution Act 1974 for radioactive substances: Scotland

17. For subsection (6) of section 56 of the Control of Pollution Act 1974 (interpretation of Part II) there shall be substituted the following subsection—

"(6) Except as provided by regulations made under this subsection, nothing in this Part of this Act applies to radioactive waste within the meaning of the [Radioactive Substances Act 1993]; but regulations may—

(a) provide for prescribed provisions of this Part of this Act to have effect with such modifications as the Secretary of State considers appropriate for the purposes of dealing with such radioactive waste;

(b) make such modifications of the [Radioactive Substances Act 1993] and any other Act as the Secretary of State considers appropriate in connection with regulations made under paragraph (a) above."

Statutory nuisances

18. In Section 33(2) of the Land Drainage Act 1976 (restriction on deposit of spoil), for the words "Part III of the Public Health Act 1936" there shall be substituted the words "Part III of the Environmental Protection Act 1990".

Refuse Disposal: Scotland

19.—(1) Section 1 of the Refuse Disposal (Amenity) Act 1978 (provision by waste disposal authorities of places, etc., for disposal of refuse) shall be amended in relation to Scotland as follows.

(2) In subsection (1) at the end there shall be inserted the words "and to dispose of refuse so deposited".

(3) In subsection (6) for the words from "mandamus" to the end of the subsection there shall be substituted the words "by proceedings under section 45 of the Court of Session Act 1988".

(4) In subsection (7) the definition of "local authority" and the word "and" which follows it shall be omitted.

Street cleansing: Scotland

20. In section 25 of the Local Government and Planning (Scotland) Act 1982, for subsection (3) there shall be substituted—

"(3) In subsection (2) above 'cleansing' means such cleansing as appears to the islands or as the case may be district council to be necessary in the interests of public health or safety or of the amenities of their area but does not include operations for the removal of snow or ice and 'relevant land' means any land, in the open air, to which members of the public have access and which is not comprehended in a public road within the meaning of the Roads (Scotland) Act 1984."

Byelaws relating to straw or stubble burning

21. Section 43 of the Criminal Justice Act 1982 (creation by byelaws of offences relating to burning of straw or stubble) shall cease to have effect.

Functions assignable to London port health authority

22. In section 7(4) of the Public Health (Control of Disease) Act 1984 (enactments functions under which are assignable to London port health authority), after the paragraph (k) inserted by paragraph 23 of Schedule 6 to the Building Act 1984, there shall be inserted the following paragraphs—

"(l) Part I of the Environmental Protection Act 1990;
(m) Part III of the Environmental Protection Act 1990;".

Street cleaning, etc.: restriction of traffic

23. Section 14 of the Road Traffic Regulation Act 1984 (temporary prohibition or restriction of traffic) shall be amended as follows.

(2) In section 14, after subsection (3) there shall be inserted the following subsection—

"(3A) Subject to the following provisions of this section and to sections 15 and 16 of this Act, a highway or roads authority may also make an order under subsection (1) or issue a notice under subsection (3) above where the authority is satisfied (or as the case may be) where it appears to the authority that traffic on the highway or road should be restricted or prohibited for the purpose of enabling the duty imposed by subsection (1)(a) or (2) of section 89 of the Environmental Protection Act 1990 (litter clearing and cleaning) to be discharged."

Statutory nuisance

24. In section 76(1)(b) and (4)(a) of the Building Act 1984, for the words "sections 93 to 96 of the Public Health Act 1936" there shall be substituted the words "section 80 of the Environmental Protection Act 1990".

Registers of deposits etc. at sea: Northern Ireland Assembly control of regulations

25. In section 25(3) of the Food and Environment Protection Act 1985, after paragraph (a)(ii) there shall be inserted the following sub-paragraph—

"(iii) in section 14(8), for the words from 'and any such power' onwards there shall be substituted the words 'and any such regulations shall be subject to negative resolution within the meaning of section 41(6) of the Interpretation Act (Northern Ireland) 1954; and'."

Constitution of authorities for waste disposal

26. In section 10 of the Local Government Act 1985 (joint arrangements for waste disposal functions), in subsection (4), for the words "Part I of the Control of Pollution Act 1974" there shall be substituted the words "Part II of the Environmental Protection Act 1990".

Meaning of household waste: competition

27. In Schedule 1 to the Local Government Act 1988 (competition: collection of household waste), paragraph 1 shall be amended as follows—

(a) in sub-paragraph (1), the words "In the application of this Part to England and Wales," shall be omitted;

(b) in sub-paragraph (2)(a), for the words "section 12 of the Control of Pollution Act 1974" there shall be substituted the words "section 45 of the Environmental Protection Act 1990";

(c) in sub-paragraph (3), for the words "section 30(4) of the Control of Pollution Act 1974" there shall be substituted the words "section 75(8) of the Environmental Protection Act 1990"; and

(d) sub-paragraph (4) shall be omitted.

Exclusion of Water Act 1989 controls of exercise of trade effluent function in case of prescribed processes

28.—(1) Section 74 of the Water Act 1989 (control by Secretary of State of exercise of trade effluent functions in certain cases) shall be amended as follows.

(2) In subsection (1), after the word "shall" there shall be inserted the words "subject to subsection (3) below".

(3) After subsection (2), there shall be inserted the following subsections—

"(3) The provisions of Schedule 9 shall not apply in relation to any trade effluent produced or to be produced in any process which is a prescribed process designated for central control as from the date which is the determination date for that process.

(4) The 'determination date' for a prescribed process is—

(a) in the case of a process for which an authorisation is granted, the date on which the enforcing authority grants it, whether in pursuance of the application or, on an appeal, of a direction to grant it;

(b) in the case of a process for which an authorisation is refused, the date of the refusal or, on an appeal, of the affirmation of the refusal.

(5) In this section, 'authorisation', 'enforcing authority' and 'prescribed process' have the meaning given in section 1 of the Environmental Protection Act 1990 and the references to designation for central control and an appeal are references respectively to designation under section 4 and an appeal under section 15 of that Act."

Exclusion of Part III of Water Act 1989 for discharges from prescribed processes

29.—(1) Section 108 of the Water Act 1989 (no pollution offence where discharge authorised) shall be amended as follows.

(2) In subsection (1)—

(a) after paragraph (a), there shall be inserted the following paragraph—

"(aa)   an authorisation for a prescribed process designated for central control granted under Part I of the Environmental Protection Act 1990;";

(b) in paragraph (b), at the beginning, there shall be inserted the words "a waste management licence or".

(3) In subsection (9) the word "and" shall be omitted and at the end, there shall be inserted the words "; 'waste management licence' means such a licence granted under Part II of the Environmental Protection Act 1990".

Contents of registers of National Rivers Authority

30. In section 117(1) of the Water Act 1989 (registers for purposes of pollution control) at the end, there shall be inserted the following paragraph—

"(f) any matter about which particulars are required to be kept in any register under section 20 of the Environmental Protection Act 1990 (particulars about authorisations for prescribed processes, etc.) by the chief inspector under Part I of that Act."

Carriers of controlled waste

31.—(1) The Control of Pollution (Amendment) Act 1989 shall be amended as follows.

(2) In the following provisions, for the words "disposal authority" and "disposal authorities" there shall be substituted the words "regulation authority" and "regulation authorities" respectively, that is to say, in sections 1(4)(a), 2(1), (2)(b) and (e), (3)(a) and (e) and (4)(a), (b) and (c), 3(1), (2) and (6), 4(1), (3), (4), (5) and (8)(b) and (c), 5(1) and (4)(a), 6(1), [...], (3), (5), [...], (7)(a) and (c), (8) and (9) and 7(1), (2), (3)(a) and (8).

(3) In section 6(1) (offences justifying seizure of vehicles), in paragraph (a)(i)—

(a) after "1974" there shall be inserted the words "or section 33 of the Environmental Protection Act 1990"; and

(b) after the word "unlicensed" there shall be inserted the words "deposit, treatment or".

(4) In section 7 (enforcement)—

(a) in subsection (1), for the words from "91" to "information)" there shall be substituted the words "68(3), (4) and (5), 69, 70 and 71 of the Environmental Protection Act 1990 (powers of entry, of dealing with imminent pollution and to obtain information)";

(b) in subsection (2), paragraph (b) shall be omitted; and

(c) [...]

(5) In section 9(1)—

(a) in the definition of "controlled waste"—

(i) for the words ", subject to subsection (2) below," there shall be substituted the words ", at any time,"; and

(ii) for the words "in Part I of the Control of Pollution Act 1974" there shall be substituted the words "for the purposes of Part II of the Environmental Protection Act 1990";

(b) the definition of "disposal authority" shall be omitted; and

(c) [...]

(6) Section 9(2) shall be omitted.

      SCHEDULE 16

REPEALS

PART I

ENACTMENTS RELATING TO PROCESSES

Chapter	Short title	Extent of repeal
1906 c. 14.	Alkali, &c. Works Regulation Act 1906.	The whole Act so far as unrepealed.
1956 c. 52.	Clean Air Act 1956.	Section 17(4). In section 29(1), in the proviso, paragraph (a). In section 31(1), the words from "(other" to "1906)". Schedule 2.
1968 c. 62.	Clean Air Act 1968.	Section 11.
1972 c. 70.	Local Government Act 1972.	In section 180(3), paragraph (b).
1973 c. 65.	Local Government (Scotland) Act 1973.	In section 142(2), paragraph (b).
1974 c. 37.	Health and Safety at Work etc. Act 1974.	Section 1(1)(d) and the word "and" preceding it. Section 5.
1974 c. 40.	Control of Pollution Act 1974.	In section 76(4), the words "or work subject to the Alkali Act". In section 78(1), the words "or work subject to the Alkali Act". In section 79(4), the words "or work subject to the Alkali Act". In section 80(3), the words "or work subject to the Alkali Act". In section 84(1), the definition of "a work subject to the Alkali Act". In section 103(1)(a), the words "Alkali Act or the". In section 105(1), the definition of "the Alkali Act".
1990 c. 43.	Environmental Protection Act 1990.	In section 79(10), the words following "Part I".

Note: The repeal of the Alkali, &c. Works Regulation Act 1906 does not extend to Northern Ireland.

PART II

ENACTMENTS RELATING TO WASTE ON LAND

Chapter	Short title	Extent of repeal
1974 c. 40.	Control of Pollution Act 1974.	Sections 1 to 21. Sections 27 to 30.
1978 c. 3.	Refuse Disposal (Amenity) Act 1978.	Section 1.
1982 c. 45.	Civic Government (Scotland) Act 1982.	Sections 124 and 125 and in section 126, subsections (1) and (3).
1988 c. 9.	Local Government Act 1988.	In Schedule 1, in paragraph 1, in sub-paragraph (1) the words "in the application of this Part to England and Wales," and sub-paragraph (4).

Chapter	Short title	Extent of repeal
1989 c. 14.	Control of Pollution (Amendment) Act 1989.	In section 7(2), paragraph (b) and the word "and" preceding it. In section 9, in subsection (1), the definition of "disposal authority" and subsection (2).
1989 c. 15.	Water Act 1989.	In Schedule 25, in paragraph 48, sub-paragraphs (1) to (6).
1989 c. 29.	Electricity Act 1989.	In Schedule 16, paragraph 18.
1990 c. 43.	Environmental Protection Act 1990.	In section 34(3)(b), the words following "below". Section 36(8).

Note: The repeal in the Refuse Disposal (Amenity) Act 1978 does not extend to Scotland.

PART III

ENACTMENTS RELATING TO STATUTORY NUISANCES

Chapter	Short title	Extent of repeal
1936 c. 49.	Public Health Act 1936.	Sections 91 to 100. Sections 107 and 108. Sections 109 and 110. In section 267(4), "III".
1956 c. 52.	Clean Air Act 1956.	Section 16. In section 30(1), the words from "or a nuisance" to "existed".
1960 c. 34.	Radioactive Substances Act 1960.	In Schedule 1— (a) In paragraph 3, the words "and ninety-two"; (b) in paragraph 3, the words "subsection (2) of section one hundred and eight"; and (c) in paragraph 8, the words "and sixteen".
1961 c. 64.	Public Health Act 1961.	Section 72.
1963 c. 33.	London Government Act 1963.	In Schedule 11, in Part I, paragraph 20.
1963 c. 41.	Offices, Shops and Railway Premises Act 1963.	Section 76(3).
1969 c. 25.	Public Health (Recurring Nuisances) Act 1969.	The whole Act.
1972 c. 70.	Local Government Act 1972.	In section 180(3), paragraph (j). In Schedule 14— (a) in paragraph 4, the words "107(1) and (2), 108"; (b) paragraph 11; and (c) paragraph 12.
1974 c. 40.	Control of Pollution Act 1974.	In section 57, paragraph (a). Sections 58 and 59. In section 69, in subsection (1), paragraph (a) and, in paragraph (c), the words "section 59(2) or", and in subsection (3) the words "section 59(6) or" and paragraph (i). In Schedule 2, paragraphs 11 and 12.
1982 c. 30.	Local Government (Miscellaneous Provisions) Act 1982.	Section 26(1) and (2).
1989 c. 17.	Control of Smoke Pollution Act 1989.	Section 1.
1990 c. 8.	Town and Country Planning Act 1990.	In Schedule 17, paragraph 1.

Note: The repeals in the Clean Air Act 1956, the Control of Pollution Act 1974 and the Control of Smoke Pollution Act 1989 do not extend to Scotland.

PART IV

ENACTMENTS RELATING TO LITTER

Chapter	Short title	Extent of repeal
1974 c. 40.	Control of Pollution Act 1974.	Section 22(1) and (2).
1982 c. 43.	Local Government and Planning (Scotland) Act 1982.	Section 25(1).
1983 c. 35.	Litter Act 1983.	Sections 1 and 2. Section 12(1).
1986 c. ii.	Berkshire Act 1986.	Section 13.
1987 c. xi.	Exeter City Council Act 1987.	Section 24.
1988 c. viii.	City of Westminster Act 1988.	The whole Act.
1990 c. vii.	London Local Authorities Act 1990.	Section 43.

PART V

ENACTMENTS RELATING TO RADIOACTIVE SUBSTANCES

Chapter	Short title	Extent of repeal
1960 c. 34.	Radioactive Substances Act 1960.	Section 2(1). In section 4, subsection (1) and in subsection (2) the word "further". Section 7(3)(a). Section 8(1)(a). In section 12, subsection (1), in subsection (2)(b) the words "of waste" and, at the end "and", and in subsection (3)(b) the words "subsection (1) or". In section 19(1) the definition of "the Minister". Section 21(4). In Schedule 1, paragraphs 9 and 11.

PART VI

ENACTMENTS RELATING TO NATURE CONSERVATION AND COUNTRYSIDE MATTERS

Chapter	Short title	Extent of repeal
1968 c. 41.	Countryside Act 1968.	In section 15(2), the words "in the national interest". Section 19. In section 46(2), the words "and (2)".
1973 c. 54.	Nature Conservancy Council Act 1973.	In section 1, subsections (1), (2) and (4) to (8). Sections 2 and 4. In Schedule 1, paragraphs 6, 10 and 12. In Schedule 3, Parts I and II.
1981 c. 69.	Wildlife and Countryside Act 1981.	In section 34(6) the words "and Wales". Section 38. In section 43(1A) the words "by the Countryside Commission". In Schedule 13, paragraph 5.

PART VII

ENACTMENTS RELATING TO DEPOSITS AT SEA

Chapter	Short title	Extent of repeal
1972 c. 52.	Town and Country Planning (Scotland) Act 1972.	In section 56A(1), the words "and to section 56B below". Section 56B. In section 56E(2)(e) and 56K(5)(b), the words "or Health and Safety Commission". In section 56F(1), the words "and (3)". Section 56F(3). Section 56H(5). In section 56J(5), the words from "other" to "applies". In section 56M(3), the words "Subject to subsection (4) below,". Section 56M(4). In section 56N, in subsection (1)(b), the words from "or" to "would be" and subsection (2). In section 56O, the definition of "the appropriate body" and the word "and" immediately following.
1986 c. 63.	Housing and Planning Act 1986.	In Part II of Schedule 7, in paragraph 8 the word "56B,".
1989 c. 29.	Electricity Act 1989.	In Schedule 17, paragraph 37(1)(b).
1990 c. 10.	Planning (Hazardous Substances) Act 1990.	In section 1, the words "2 or". Section 2. Section 3(6). In section 9(2)(e) and 18(2)(b), the words "or Health and Safety Commission". In section 11(7), the words "to the conditions that". Section 13(7). In section 15(1), the words from "other" to applies)". Section 20(6). Section 21(7). Section 27(4). In section 28(1), the words "authority who are a" and the words "by virtue of section 1 or 3". In section 28(1)(b), the words "or but for section 2 would be". Section 28(2). In section 29(6), the definition of "the appropriate body" and the word "and" immediately following that definition. In section 30(1), the words "by virtue of section 1 or 3". Section 33. In section 38(2), the words "(being a local planning authority)". In section 39(2), the entries for "the 1971 Act", "the appropriate Minister" and "operational land". In section 39(4), the words "2," and "and his undertaking a statutory undertaking".

Chapter	Short title	Extent of repeal
1990 c. 11.	Planning (Consequential Provisions) Act 1990.	In section 39(5), the word "2,", in the first place it occurs and the words following "undertaker" in the second place it occurs. In section 39(6), the words "and their undertakings statutory undertakings". Section 39(7) and (8). In Schedule 2, paragraph 82(2).

PART VIII

ENACTMENTS RELATING TO DEPOSITS AT SEA

Chapter	Short title	Extent of repeal
1985 c. 48.	Food and Environment Protection Act 1985.	Section 5(c), (d) and (e)(iii). Section 6(1)(a)(iii). Schedule 4.

PART IX

MISCELLANEOUS ENACTMENTS

Chapter	Short title	Extent of repeal
1906 c. 32.	Dogs Act 1906.	Section 4(1).
1974 c. 40.	Control of Pollution Act 1974.	Section 100.
1982 c. 45.	Civic Government (Scotland) Act 1982.	Section 128(1).
1982 c. 48.	Criminal Justice Act 1982.	Section 43.
1988 c. 9.	Local Government Act 1988.	Section 39(2) and (4).
1988 c. 33.	Criminal Justice Act 1988.	Section 58.

ENVIRONMENT ACT 1995

(1995 c. 25)

CHAPTER III

MISCELLANEOUS, GENERAL AND SUPPLEMENTAL PROVISIONS RELATING TO THE NEW AGENCIES

Additional general powers and duties

Charging schemes

Incidental power to impose charges

General financial provisions

Information

Supplemental provisions

PART II

CONTAMINATED LAND AND ABANDONED MINES

An Act to provide for the establishment of a body corporate to be known as the Environment Agency and a body corporate to be known as the Scottish

Environment Protection Agency; to provide for the transfer of functions, property, rights and liabilities to those bodies and for the conferring of other functions on them; to make provision with respect to contaminated land and abandoned mines; to make further provision in relation to National Parks; to make further provision for the control of pollution, the conservation of natural resources and the conservation or enhancement of the environment; to make provision for imposing obligations on certain persons in respect of certain products or materials; to make provision in relation to fisheries; to make provision for certain enactments to bind the Crown; to make provision with respect to the application of certain enactments in relation to the Isles of Scilly; and for connected purposes.

[19th July 1995]

GENERAL NOTE AND INTRODUCTION TO THE ACT

During the passage of the Environmental Protection Act 1990, the Government indicated that the 1990 Act could not be regarded as its "last word" on the environment: see *Hansard*, H.C. Vol. 165, col. 33. How true that was. The Environment Act 1995 is the product of a further five years' evolution of Government policy, including some notable changes of direction. In the five years between the Environmental Protection Act 1990 and the 1995 Act, environmental law and policy have been the subject of continuous, and in some cases concentrated, attention. At the most general level, the Government's environmental policy document, *This Common Inheritance* (Cm. 1200, September 1990) has been kept under review by regular reports monitoring progress in implementation and adding further objectives. In January 1994 the Government published four key strategy documents (Cm. 2426–2429) relating to obligations under the UNCED (Rio) Conference dealing with sustainable development, climate change, biodiversity, and sustainable forestry. At the same time the Government appointed an advisory panel on sustainable development, which was also the subject of an important report by the House of Lords Committee on the subject: Session 1994–1995, H.L. Paper 72, Vols I and II, June 21, 1995.

More specifically, considerable problems have been encountered in the implementation of Part II of the 1990 Act dealing with waste, and in particular the consistency of that legislation with EC law in terms of scope and general objectives. The result of such deliberations can be seen in various changes made by the 1995 Act. In these and other respects, thinking has moved on considerably since 1990. Such changes are referred to in the relevant context in the 1995 Act and its modifications to the 1990 Act.

Like the Environmental Protection Act 1990, the 1995 Act is heterogeneous in content, opportunity having been taken to include various new provisions or refinements of existing law which had for some time been under consideration. However, the heart, and origin, of the Act lies in Part I which establishes two new bodies, the Environment Agency and the Scottish Environmental Protection Agency. These bodies will assume key functions of environmental protection and resource management from existing authorities, and will be under a variety of general and specific duties; some of which have aroused considerable interest and controversy. Whilst the 1995 Act is still far from the goal of complete and effective integration of the environment with other areas of policy and regulation—or even full integration within the field of environmental protection—it represents a significant step in that direction. It includes, at s.4(3), the first statutory mention of the concept and objective of sustainable development, although it should be noted that since 1991 Scottish Natural Heritage has been under a duty in regard to "sustainability" which is in some respects comparable: see the General Note to s.31.

Part II of the 1995 Act deals with what has proven for the Government to be an extremely thorny topic, that of contaminated land. The proposal contained in s.143 of the Environmental Protection Act 1990, for registers of land subject to past or present contaminative uses, proved to be unacceptable and has been replaced by a scheme for identifying and securing the remediation of actually contaminated land. The new provisions are modelled—though with numerous refinements and complexities—on the traditional scheme for abating statutory nuisances. Not surprisingly, the creation of law which might potentially have both strict and retrospective effect, as well as applying to the detriment of current landowners and lenders, aroused much concern. The result was that the provisions of Part II were heavily amended in both Houses, allaying at least partially the concerns of the relevant interests. Part II also contains provisions to deal with what has, over the years since 1990, been a recurrent concern: that of water pollution emanating from abandoned mines.

Parts III and IV of the 1995 Act deal with the diverse but important issues of national parks and air quality. Part III (the provisions of which are not reproduced here) amends existing legislation on national parks (in particular the National Parks and Access to the Countryside Act 1949) to provide for the creation of new National Park Authorities which will become the local planning authorities for the parks. The 1995 Act also modifies the statutory purposes of national parks—an issue which aroused strong feelings and much debate in the House of Lords. Problems with air quality in the UK's towns and cities have become increasingly high-profile and acute since 1990, and Part IV of the Act attempts to address what may be a very intractable problem by way of creating a national air quality strategy and imposing new duties on local authorities.

Part V (Miscellaneous, General and Supplemental Provisions) is indeed miscellaneous in content. It contains provisions on waste, the review of mineral planning permissions, protection of hedgerows, drainage, fisheries, water pollution and statutory nuisance.

As with the 1990 Act, to appreciate fully the new provisions, it is helpful to be aware of the underlying evolution of policy. Reference is accordingly made in the notes and annotations to the relevant consultation papers, ministerial statements and similar material. Some of the provisions also relate to current or proposed EC measures, particularly in the field of packaging waste recovery.

In conclusion, what is not in the 1995 Act is perhaps equally important as what is contained. The Secretary of State for the Environment, in moving the Second Reading of the Bill in the Commons, saw the Bill as the latest in a long line of Bills to protect the UK environment, but also to be seen in the context of "... a new century and a new millennium, in which sustainable development will be the watchword of well-being for all our people. The Bill puts in place a key instrument for preserving and enhancing the quality of life for the British people as we enter a new era" (*Hansard*, H.C. Vol. 258, col. 48).

In giving the Labour Party's response, Mr Frank Dobson, MP acknowledged that many of the Bill's proposals were in line with Labour Party policy and were welcomed as such. However, he went on to criticise what he saw as missed opportunities:

> "The Bill could have placed on all Government Departments and public bodies a general duty to further the protection and enhancement of the environment; it does not. It could have enshrined in law the precautionary principle that could be applied to new materials and processes; it does not ... The Bill proposes no action to tackle noise pollution. The Government have not taken the opportunity provided by the establishment of the new Agencies to end the present confusion over responsibility, which is holding back an integrated effort to reduce marine pollution, especially in the North and Irish seas. In short, the Bill is welcome in general, but it falls short of what is needed if the environment is to be given proper priority as we approach the 21st century" (*Hansard*, H.C. Vol. 258, cols. 49–50).

The Act is ambitious in what it sets out to achieve, and its success or failure may ultimately depend on the resources made available to those charged with duties and functions under it. In many respects, however, the success or failure of environmental policy will depend on the willingness of an often misleadingly educated public to modify its behaviour. It is perhaps therefore to be regretted that Mr Matthew Taylor, MP (Truro) did not succeed in his objective of inserting a provision on environmental claims into the Bill. He pointed out that too many misleading, meaningless and unsubstantiated environmental claims are made for products. In particular, he gave the example of a make of sock promoted as "ozone friendly", with a label bearing the following rubric:

> "Helps prevent foot odour which is probably a major cause of the destruction of the ozone layer" (*Hansard*, H.C. Vol. 258, col. 66).

EC and International Law
The underlying international and EC law was vital to the understanding of the 1990 Act and its operation in practice. If anything, the importance of such law has increased over the intervening five years. Implementation of the 1992 UN Convention on Climate Change has been a major preoccupation both within the UK and European Community, and likewise the 1987 Montreal Protocol on Substances that Deplete the Ozone Layer and the 1989 Basel Convention on the Transboundary Movement of Hazardous Wastes and their Disposal.

Similarly, many aspects of EC environmental policy have generated activity, some of which is reflected in the UK legislation, and some of which may in due course necessitate further legislative changes. Of particular relevance to the Environment Act 1995 are the various directives dealing with air quality (Part IV), the waste framework directives 75/442/EEC and 91/156/EEC, the packaging waste directive 94/62/EC and the proposed landfill directive (COM(93)275 final; political agreement June 1994) (Part V). The proposed directive on integrated pollution prevention and control (COM(93)423 final; amended COM(95)88 final; political agreement June 1995) may result in changes of approach under Part I of the 1990 Act.

The importance of EC law is shown by the various provisions in the 1990 and 1995 Acts which make provision for its implementation. Examples in the 1990 Act include s.7(2)(b) relating to the conditions of authorisation for prescribed processes, and s.156, giving a general power to make regulations. Similarly under the 1995 Act, reference may be made to ss.80(2) and 87(1) referring to the national air quality strategy, ss.44A(10) and 44B(9) of the 1990 Act (as inserted by s.92 of the 1995 Act) dealing with the national waste strategy, and ss.93(2) and 94(2) dealing with producer responsibility for re-use, recovery and recycling.

As well as such overt references to EC measures, the doctrine of indirect effect or sympathetic interpretation will ensure that the legislation receives a purposive construction so as to ensure compliance with the relevant EC legislation: see the Occasional Paper in the Sweet & Maxwell *Environmental Law Bulletin* No. 8 (September/October 1994).

COMMENCEMENT

The following provisions of the Environment Act 1995 have been brought into force by commencement orders up to and including S.I. 1995 No. 2765 or by s.125(2) and (3) of the Act.

Provision	Date of Commencement	S.I. No.
Section 1	28.7.1995	1995/1983
Section 3(2) to (8)	28.7.1995	
Section 4	28.7.1995	
Section 7	28.7.1995	
Section 9	28.7.1995	
Section 12	28.7.1995	
Section 20	12.10.1995	1995/2649
Section 21	12.10.1995	
Section 22	12.10.1995	
Section 23	12.10.1995	
Section 30	12.10.1995	
Section 31	12.10.1995	
Section 32	12.10.1995	
Section 36	12.10.1995	
Section 37(1), (2) and (9)	28.7.1995	1995/1983
Sections 38 to 40	28.7.1995	
Section 41 (partially)	21.9.1995	
Section 42	21.9.1995	
Sections 43 to 52	28.7.1995	
Section 56	28.7.1995	
Section 57 (partially)	21.9.1995	
Section 58 (partially)	21.9.1995	
Section 59 (partially)	12.10.1995	1995/2649
Section 61	19.9.1995	s.125(2)
Section 62	19.9.1995	s.125(2)
Section 63 and all but paragraph 7(2) of Schedule 7	19.9.1995	s.125(2)
Section 64	19.9.1995	s.125(2)
Section 65	19.9.1995	s.125(2)
Section 66	19.9.1995	s.125(2)
Section 67	19.9.1995	s.125(2)
Section 68	19.9.1995	s.125(2)
Section 69	19.9.1995	s.125(2)
Section 70	19.9.1995	s.125(2)
Section 71	19.9.1995	s.125(2)
Section 72	19.9.1995	s.125(2)
Section 73	19.9.1995	s.125(2)
Section 74	19.7.1995	s.125(3)
Section 75	19.9.1995	s.125(2)
Section 76	19.9.1995	s.125(2)
Section 77	19.9.1995	s.125(2)
Section 79	19.9.1995	s.125(2)
Sections 93 to 95	21.9.1995	1995/1983
Section 96(1) and 96(4) to (6) (partially)	1.11.1995	1995/2765
Section 96(2)	1.11.1995	1995/2765
Sections 97 to 103	21.9.1995	

Provision	Date of Commencement	S.I. No.
Section 105 (partially) and paragraphs 25 and 26(1) of Schedule 15	21.9.1995	
Section 105 (partially) and paragraphs 13, 14(1) and (4), 17, 20 and 26(2) of Schedule 15	1.1.1999	
Section 116 (partially) and paragraphs 2(1) to (3) of Schedule 21	21.9.1995	
Section 120(1) (partially) and paragraphs 4, 31, 42, 213(1), (2)(b) and (3) and 223(1) (c) of Schedule 22	28.7.1995	
Section 120(1) (partially) and paragraphs 15, 29(1) and (22) (partially), 51(1) to (3) and (5) and 53	12.10.1995	1995/2649
Section 120(1) (partially) and paragraphs 37(1) and (4), 38, 39, 76(1) and (3), 80(1) and (2), 82(1) and (5) (partially), 133(1), 137 to 139, 147, 153, 162 (partially), 182, 187(1) and 192 of Schedule 22	21.9.1995	19951983
Section 120(2) (partially) and paragraphs 14(5), (6) and (8) (partially) of Schedule 23	1.1.1999	
Section 120(3) (partially) and the repeals in Schedule 24 in relation to sections 68, 69(5), 126(6) and 129(4) of the Water Resources Act 1991	21.9.1995	
Section 120(3) (partially) and the repeals in Schedule 24 in relation to sections 30 and 41(1) of the Salmon and Freshwater Fisheries Act 1975	1.1.1999	
Section 120(3) (partially) and the repeal in Schedule 24 in relation to section 105 of the Town and Country Planning Act 1990	1.11.1995	1995/2765
Section 120(4) to (6)	28.7.1995	
Sections 121 to 124	28.7.1995	

PART I

THE ENVIRONMENT AGENCY AND THE SCOTTISH ENVIRONMENT PROTECTION AGENCY

INTRODUCTION TO PART I
Part I of the Act fulfils a longstanding Government commitment to create a unified environmental regulatory body for England and Wales, and an equivalent for Scotland.

As will no doubt be appreciated, such a major reorganisation does not come about overnight nor without decisions being taken on a large number of significant and often hotly disputed issues. This introduction looks first at the policy background to, and evolution of the proposals, from the first announcement of a Government commitment to establish such agencies to the publication of the first full Environment Bill in December 1994. It then examines briefly some of the key issues: the functions transferred to the Environment Agency and Scottish Environment Protection Agency ("the Agency" and "SEPA"), those functions which were *not* transferred, new functions given to them, their statutory functions, aims and objectives, the question of the agencies' regional and managerial structure, and finally the implications of the agencies for public access to environmental information.

Policy Background: Environmental integration and a "One-Stop Shop"?
The establishment of unified environmental agencies had for some time been advocated by both business interests and environmentalists as well as by distinguished bodies such as the House of Commons Environment Committee, and this is considered more fully below in the separate contexts north and south of the border.

A business might previously have had to deal on environmental matters (to take the example of England) with:—

— HM Inspectorate of Pollution (HMIP)
— The National Rivers Authority (NRA)
— the county council as waste regulation authority and mineral planning authority
— the district council for air pollution control and statutory nuisance, as local planning authority and in relation to hazardous substance control
— the Health and Safety Executive in relation to major accident hazards, genetically modified organisms, the carriage of dangerous goods and general health and safety (and possibly also the HSE's Inspectorates such as its Nuclear Installations Inspectorate)
— the Ministry of Agriculture, Fisheries and Food in relation to disposal at sea, and
— the local statutory water and sewerage undertaker in relation to discharges to sewer.

A Scottish business might also be required to deal with a similar range of environmental regulators, albeit different ones.

Although numerous provisions seek to define the relationships between these various regimes, not all overlap is avoided and these provisions themselves can be complex.

The number of bodies with which a business may have to deal on environmental matters is reduced by the establishment of the agencies, although there may still be several because of the range of functions *not* transferred to the agencies (see below), and there is no change in the number of consents, authorisations and licences which a business may require.

However, the Government has indicated that the "Establishment of the Agency [and by implication, one would assume, SEPA] offers an advance towards single permitting ... In the medium term the Government would review in the light of experience whether the legislation might be amended to achieve greater integration": Advisory Committee on Business and the Environment (ACBE) Fifth Progress Report to and Response From the President of the Board of Trade and the Secretary of State for the Environment (July 1995).

Environmentalists saw the creation of unified agencies as a key step not only in the direction of the effective integration of different strands of environmental policy, but also towards the integration of environmental concerns into general Government policy: perceived as a pre-condition for the attainment of sustainable development.

The extent to which the agencies, as established by the Act, are viewed as likely to fulfil the aspirations of industry and environmentalists is considered below in the discussion of the evolution of the Environment Bill in the course of its passage through Parliament and in the discussion of functions which were not transferred.

The bringing together of staff from various disciplines in a single organisation offers the potential for more effective integration of a range of pollution control (and, especially in the case of the Agency, non-pollution control) functions. This might occur through the combining of staff with expertise in different areas into multi-disciplinary teams replacing the previous network of formal and informal consultation processes. Indeed, given the range of matters to which the Agency and SEPA are to have regard in carrying out their functions (see below), the alternative would presumably be daunting in the extreme to ordinary Agency/SEPA officers.

Policy Background—England and Wales
The Earl of Cranbrook's attempt in 1990 to introduce an integrated system of environmental regulation is noted in the Introduction to the 1990 Act (above). This attempt failed in the face of Government opposition, yet in July 1991 the Prime Minister John Major announced a firm Government intention to do just that. As the House of Commons Environment Select Committee noted at the time: "In just two years, the government's policy had shifted from outright rejection of the notion of such an agency to enthusiastic acceptance": First Report, Session 1991/92 (H.C. Pap 55). For an analysis of the political issues and choices which the Government sought to address in developing its plans for the Environment Agency see N. Carter and P. Lowe, *Environmental Politics and Administrative Reform, Political Quarterly,* 1994, pp. 263–274, which cites this Select Committee remark.

The following table lists many of the announcements and publications which chart the development of Government policy on the Agency since the first indication that it was under active consideration.

Statement or document	Issue
This Common Inheritance (HMSO, 1990, Cm.1200)	Government considering possible "umbrella" organisation to oversee the pollution control work of the NRA and HMIP
Speech by Prime Minister John Major, July 8, 1991	"I can announce today that we plan to set up an Environment Agency. This will bring together HMIP, and related functions of the NRA, to create a new agency for environmental protection and enhancement"
Improving Environmental Quality: the Government Proposals for a new, independent Environment Agency (DoE, MAFF Welsh Office, October 1991, DoE News Release 589, October 3, 1991	Set out four options: — Agency to take over waste regulation and HMIP's non-water functions; HMIP's water functions to be taken over by NRA; — Agency to be an "umbrella body" to co-ordinate NRA and HMIP; — Agency to take over waste regulation, NRA, HMIP — Agency to take over waste regulation, NRA (water pollution only), HMIP NB: Government "minded" also to transfer the Drinking Water Inspectorate
Statement by Environment Secretary Michael Heseltine (*The Independent*, October 4, 1991)	Agency to be a "one-stop shop" for environmental regulation
H.C. Written Answer (*Hansard*, H.C. July 8, 1992)	Government decided to transfer NRA, HMIP and Waste Regulation, but not the DWI, to the Agency
H.C. Written Answers *Hansard*, H.C. July 15, 1992, C857-8W and February 23, 1993, c527W)	Government states that legislation to establish the Agency/SEPA to be introduced at the earliest opportunity.
Queen's Speech, November 18, 1993	"Paving Bill" to enable preparatory work for establishment of the Agency/SEPA to be introduced into Parliament in 1993/4 session: "[A Bill] will be introduced to take forward Environmental Agency planning".
Statement to Parliament by Parliamentary Under Secretary of State for Wales, (*Hansard*, H.C., cols.1195–6, November 30, 1994)	"The Government propose that the Environment Agency should be established as an England and Wales organisation": no separate Welsh Agency.
Options for the Geographical and Managerial Structure of the proposed Environment Agency (Touche Ross report to DoE, June 1994, deposited paper ns 348)	Five options proposed: Options A–E Model D is closest to what has ultimately been decided: see below for outline of the options
DoE News Release 440, July 20, 1994	Paving Bill cancelled as no longer necessary in view of progress already made towards establishing the Agency/SEPA Intention to produce main Bill in draft by October 1994, establish Agency during 1995 and transfer function at beginning of 1996/7 financial year indicated. Intention to establish environment Agency Advisory Committee (EAAC) indicated Touche ross report published.

Statement or document	Issue
Draft Environment Agencies Bill (Deposited Paper 486) published, October 13, 1994 (DoE News 576)	A draft of the part of the Bill dealing with establishing the Agency published together with a draft Management Statement for the Agency (appended to the News Release).
DoE News Release 650, November 18, 1994	Amendments to clause 7 published (appended to News Release), in response to concern over absence of duty to "further" conservation; EAAC (the "shadow Board" of the Agency) established and its membership announced.
Environment Bill (H.L. Bill to 1994/95), December 1, 1994 (subsequent versions of the Bill not listed have)	Bill published and enters House of Lords
Draft Guidance to Agency: January 17, 1995, DoE News Release 010	"Draft outline showing the scope of guidance Ministers intend to give to the Environment Agency on its Contribution to sustainable development" under Clause 4 of the Bills published (appended to News Release).
Draft Guidance to Agency: April 21, 1995, DoE News Release 202.	Full draft of the guidance under clause 4 issued by DoE, MAFF and Welsh Office
Environment Agency Update No. 5 (September 1995)	Regional structure of the Agency announced: See below.

One influential body which has commented on the issue of a unified environmental regulator a number of times is the House of Commons Environment Select Committee. In February 1989 it recommended the establishment of an Environmental Protection Agency or Commission, to which much of the Department of the Environment's work, at least in the area of waste management policy, would be transferred: Second Report, Session 1988–89, *Toxic Waste*, 22I, p. xvi. The Committee scrutinised the Government's proposals for an agency in its First Report of House of Commons Session 1991–92, The Government's Proposals for an Environment Agency (551–III) (to which the Government responded in November 1992: the Committee's First Special Report of Session 1992–93 (256). More recently, the Committee took evidence on the first draft of what became Part I of the 1995 Act: Session 1994–95, *Environment Bill: Hearings on the Draft Environment Agencies Bill* (40 I–iii), from which no report has been forthcoming.

Policy Background—Scotland
Until the establishment of SEPA by virtue of this Act environmental protection in Scotland was the responsibility of several bodies. Water pollution control functions were performed by river purification authorities (consisting of the seven river purification boards and three islands councils); integrated pollution control functions were performed by Her Majesty's Industrial Pollution Inspectorate (HMIPI) and river purification authorities in their respective capacities; radioactive substances control functions were performed by HMIPI; while district and islands councils performed waste regulation functions in their capacity as waste regulation authorities and air pollution control functions in their capacity as enforcing authorities for Part B processes by virtue of Part I of the Environmental Protection Act 1990 and the Environmental Protection (Prescribed Processes and Substances) Regulations 1991. It should be noted that in Scotland the Environmental Protection Act 1990 did not provide as in England and Wales for the separation of local authority waste regulation and disposal functions; hence the potential for conflict remained.

Although a more integrated approach to pollution control was seen as desirable, for example, in the Government White Paper *This Common Inheritance*, Cm. 1200, 1990 the fragmented nature of the existing Scottish regulatory system posed problems for developing such an approach and also posed problems for business given the lack of a one-door approach to environmental licensing.

It was against this background that proposals for a Scottish Environment Protection Agency were developed. The following table lists many of the announcements and publications which chart the development of Government policy on SEPA since the first indication that it was under active consideration.

Statement or document	Issue
Statement by Secretary of State for Scotland (September 23, 1991)	Announcement that a Scottish Environment Protection Agency was to be established
H.C. Written Answer *Hansard*, H.C., Vol. 196, col. 406w, October 21, 1991	Government confirms proposal to establish SEPA, that primary legislation would be needed for this and indicates that consultation paper on SEPA's functions will be issued
Improving Scotland's Environment The Way Forward (Scottish Office, January 1992)	Scottish Office presents case for SEPA: — present fragmented system of pollution control lacks benefit of integrated approach which a single agency could offer — industry would benefit from a one-door approach to environmental regulation Three key principles should underpin proposals for reform: — need to remove potential for overlap and conflict between different regulatory agencies — operational and regulatory responsibilities should be separated and — effective pollution control requires centralised expertise which a unified agency could offer. Accordingly proposed that SEPA should take over all the functions of HMIPI; the Hazardous Waste Inspectorate; the river purification authorities; and the functions of local authorities as waste regulation authorities and air pollution control enforcing authorities under Part I of the 1990 Act.
H.C. Written Answer *Hansard*, H.C. Vol. 219, cols. 713–4w, February 25, 1993	Government announces: — major proposals in *Improving Scotland's Environment* would not be altered, but that in the light of consultation there may be scope for delegating responsibility to regional committees and that further work would be commissioned on SEPA's regional structure; and — that legislation to establish SEPA would be established at the earliest opportunity.
Scottish Environment Protection Agency Consultancy Report (KPMG Management Consultancy, March 1993)	Four options for SEPA's regional structure proposed. Option 3 proposing three or four regional boards exercising limited executive boards recommended.
Queen's Speech, November 18, 1993	Announcement of "Paving Bill" to enable preparatory work for establishment of the Agency/SEPA to be introduced into Parliament in 1993/4 session.
DoE News Release 440, July 20, 1994	Paving Bill cancelled as no longer necessary in view of progress already made towards establishing the Agency/SEPA. Intention to produce main Bill in draft by October 1994, establish the Agency/SEPA during 1995 and transfer functions to the Agency/SEPA at beginning of financial year 1996/97.
Draft Environment Agencies Bill (Deposited Paper 486) published, October 13, 1994	A draft of the part of the Bill dealing with establishing the Agency/SEPA published together with a draft Management Statement for SEPA.

Statement or document	Issue
Environment Bill (H.L. Bill to 1994/5), December 1, 1994 (subsequent versions of the Bill not listed here)	Bill published and enters House of Lords.
H.C. Written Answer *Hansard*, H.C. Vol. 258, col. 218w, April 19, 1995	Secretary of State announces that he intends to appoint Professor William Turmeau as Chairman of SEPA.
Draft Guidance to SEPA (Scottish Office Environment Department, May 1995)	"Draft Guidance to the Scottish Environment Protection Agency under Clause 29 of the Environment Bill". Guidance on SEPA's aims and objectives, contribution to sustainable development and costs and benefits.
SEPA Newsletter No. 4 August 1995	Appointment of SEPA's Chief Executive announced.
Scottish Office Press Release (October 5, 1995)	Secretary of State announces appointment of remaining SEPA board members.
Scottish Office Environment Department Circular 19/1995 (October 12, 1995)	"Environment Act 1995: Transfer of Property, Rights and Liabilities from District and Islands Councils to the Scottish Environment Protection Agency". Guidance for local authorities.
Scottish Office Press Release (October 27, 1995)	Announcement of SEPA's headquarters and that three Regional Boards are being established.
Revised Draft Guidance to SEPA (Scottish Office Agriculture, Environment and Fisheries Department, November 1995)	"The Scottish Environment Protection Agency and Sustainable Development" including Statutory Guidance under s.31 of the Environment Act on SEPA's aims and objectives and its contribution towards achieving sustainable development.

It should also be noted that the transfer of local authority functions to SEPA is proceeding against the background of local government reorganisation in Scotland. Briefly, the Local Government etc. (Scotland) Act 1994 provides for the replacement of the existing two-tier structure of local government in Scotland consisting of regional and district councils together with the three islands councils by a system of 32 unitary authorities.

The Government indicated in Parliament that having local government reorganisation and the establishment of SEPA proceeding in tandem was deliberate and that:

> "There is a great advantage in transferring local authority functions to SEPA at the same time as local government is to be reorganised. The transfer can be taken into account by the new unitary authorities and they can be given a fresh start with their full new range of responsibilities" (*per* the Earl of Lindsay *Hansard*, H.L. Vol. 560, col. 1423).

The functions of the new agencies
The discussion which follows examines first the existing functions which the Act transfers to the Agency/SEPA, both the common features and the notable differences, then the new functions bestowed upon the two agencies, and finally the other functions which might have been transferred to the Agency/SEPA, as in some cases the Government was urged to do, but which were not.

Functions transferred: Common features
The main functions transferred to the agencies relate to water pollution and management (although the discussion below should be noted in relation to water management), integrated pollution control, radioactive substances control and waste regulation (see general notes to ss.2 and 21).

It should be noted that the staff and resources of the existing bodies are transferred along with the relevant functions (see general notes to ss.3 and 22).

It should also be noted that even where the agencies take over existing functions, the legislative position will have changed following the transfer, for three reasons:—

— the Act makes a number of amendments to existing legislation, such as the introduction by paragraph 162 of Schedule 22 of "works notices" in relation to water pollution;
— the agencies have aims, objectives and duties, such as the Environment Agency's principal aim of contributing to the achievement of sustainable development (s.4), which differ from those of the bodies previously responsible for exercising those functions; and
— the powers of entry, etc., granted to the bodies whose functions have been taken over by the agencies varied from body to body. In relation to given legislative provisions, therefore, the powers of the relevant agency (see ss.108–9) may differ from those which were previously applicable.

Functions transferred and differences between the Agencies
There are two principal differences between the Agency and SEPA in terms of functions transferred. Firstly, the functions of local authorities in their capacity as enforcing authorities for air pollution control for Part B processes under Part I of the 1990 Act are transferred to SEPA in Scotland but not to the Agency, and there was never any likelihood of such a transfer being effected in England and Wales. This gave rise to considerable concern in Parliament both on the grounds that it might lead to an inconsistent approach to air pollution control as between England and Wales on the one hand and Scotland on the other and because of the perceived removal of this function from local accountable control which it was argued was more appropriate. This issue is considered in more detail in relation to SEPA in the general note to s.21: for debate on a proposed amendment which would have required the Agency to "work together with local authorities", see H.C. Standing Committee B, 3rd sitting, May 2, 1995, cols. 8–24. It should also be noted that the transfer of local authority waste regulation functions also gave rise to similar concerns and opposition both north and south of the border: see, for example, a discussion paper *Protecting the Future—the Environment Agency and its relationship with local government in England and Wales—a new approach* published by the Association of County Councils, Association of District Councils and Association of Metropolitan Authorities; see also *Hansard*, H.L. Vol. 562, cols. 1016–1018; H.C. Standing Committee B, 3rd sitting, May 2, 1995, cols. 80–89 (in which both English and Scottish concerns were raised, and the fear of a loss of integration at a local level between regulatory and planning controls over waste activities was expressed). The Government response, and reasons for effecting the transfer in the face of such opposition could, said the then Minister for the Environment and Countryside, Mr Robert Atkins, be summed up "in three words: integration, consistency and expertise": H.C. Standing Committee B, 2nd sitting, May 2, 1995, col. 76.

The second principal difference is that the functions of RPAs have never been as broad as those of the NRA and hence SEPA's functions are not as broad as those of the Agency. For example, RPAs had very limited powers to control water abstraction for irrigation purposes under Part II of the Natural Heritage (Scotland) Act 1991, they had no flood defence powers nor had they catchment management powers, all of which were enjoyed by the NRA, and indeed, which constituted the workload of the majority of NRA staff. This is primarily the reason why SEPA is essentially a pollution control body in contrast to the Agency, which has integrated environmental management functions relating, for example, to water resources management and flood defence in addition to its pollution control functions.

Proposals were made in Parliament for giving SEPA (i) the Scottish local authorities' flood defence powers (see *e.g.* Lord Ewing of Kirkford, *Hansard*, H.L. Vol. 560, cols. 553–554; Lord Carmichael of Kelvingrove, *Hansard*, H.L. Vol. 560, col. 1185; (ii) a new integrated catchment management function for river systems in Scotland (Lord Carmichael of Kelvingrove, *Hansard*, H.L. Vol. 560, col. 1209; see also Sam Galbraith (Standing Committee B, May 16, 1995, col. 249); and (iii) a new comprehensive water abstraction control function (per Lord Carmichael of Kelvingrove, *Hansard*, H.L. Vol. 560, cols. 1217–1219, Archie Kirkwood, *Hansard* H.C. Vol. 262, col. 920–1).

These proposals were all rejected by the Government on the basis (i) that river purification authorities had never exercised flood defence powers (see note on functions not transferred below); and (ii) that the pressures on the water environment were not the same as those in England and Wales and did not therefore justify giving these powers to SEPA:

"Scotland's geography is very different from that south of the Border. Its rivers are relatively short and fast flowing with nothing comparable to the long meandering rivers such as the Thames, the Severn, the Ouse and Bristol Avon. In addition, 95 per cent. of Scotland's public water supplies come from upland sources whereas that is true for only one-third of water supplies in England. The other two-thirds in England come from abstraction lower down the river or from groundwater sources.

These factors, combined with Scotland's relatively lower density of population and comparative lack of heavy industry, mean that the scale of potential pollution is less. As

Scotland's river flow is greater, the result is that the effects of any pollution incidents are mitigated. Against this background there is less of a need for comprehensive controls of the kind which have been adopted in England and Wales." (per the Earl of Lindsay, *Hansard*, H.L. vol. 560, col. 1210; see also Viscount Ullswater, Minister of State, Department of the Environment, *Hansard*, H.L. Vol. 560, col. 558; and Sir Hector Monro, the then Parliamentary Under-Secretary of State for Scotland, Standing Committee B, May 16, 1995 cols. 250–252)

However, the Government accepted that in specific locations and at specific times there were temporary pressures and that there was accordingly a need for selective abstraction controls and re-affirmed the Secretary of State's announcement made on November 1, 1994 that they intended to introduce such controls in separate legislation in the light of the European Commission's action programme on groundwater, on which proposals were due by mid-1995. The timing of the European action programme meant that it was not practical to include such provisions in the Act. Furthermore, the Government indicated that it envisaged further public consultation on the proposed charging arrangements before any scheme was introduced. (per the Earl of Lindsay *Hansard* Vol. 560, cols. 1220–1221; Sir Hector Monro, Standing Committee B, May 16, 1995, col. 251; Mr Robert Atkins, Minister for the Environment and Countryside, *Hansard*, H.C. Vol. 262, col. 922).

The Government also acknowledged that the existing arrangements relating to catchment management in Scotland could be improved. This would be achieved by the integration of pollution control functions in SEPA and by the establishment of memoranda of understanding between SEPA and other public bodies which impinged on its work, for example, the Health and Safety Executive or Scottish Natural Heritage (per the Earl of Lindsay *Hansard*, H.L. Vol. 560, cols. 1210–1211).

Although there were no concerted campaigns during the passage of the Bill to exclude the NRA's non-pollution control functions from transfer to the Agency, concern was expressed about the transfer specifically of its navigation authority functions (see H.C. Standing Committee B, 3rd sitting, May 2, 1995, cols. 103–105; *Hansard*, H.L. Vol. 560, cols. 630–633 and Vol. 561, cols. 1610–1612, *per* Lord McNair. These concerns were twofold: that such transfer would perpetuate an arbitrary division of responsibilities whereby the NRA (now the Agency) has responsibility for navigation on one third of the inland waterways in England and Wales, whilst the British Waterways Board has responsibility for navigation on the remainder: that navigation had a low priority within the NRA and was likely to have even lower priority within the Agency, and that the transfer would make meaningless the recent Government consultation on a number of options for restructuring the allocation of navigation responsibilities: Sir Paul Beresford, Parliamentary Under-Secretary of State for the Environment, assured the Commons Committee that "no decisions will be taken until the consultation is completed" (col. 104).

New Functions
A number of functions to be exercised by the agencies are new. Some of these are considered in the annotations to the relevant sections in Part I of the Act. Some new functions, however, are created not by Part I but as a part of new legislation in the Act. These include:—

— *Contaminated Land (section 57 of the Act)*
    Powers to give guidance to local authorities as enforcing authorities, and a role as enforcing authorities themselves in relation to the so called "special sites". These are sites designated as such in accordance with the procedures inserted by s.57 into the 1990 Act as its ss.78C and 78D. Land is required to be so designated if it meets a description to be prescribed by regulations to be made under those provisions.

— *Air Quality (Part IV of the Act)*
    The role of statutory consultee when the Secretary of State:
    (i) prepares a national air quality strategy for Great Britain; and
    (ii) makes regulations in relation to the implementation of the air quality strategy and international obligations regarding air quality, and generally in relation to the assessment and management of air quality. In Scotland SEPA also has reserve powers, which in England and Wales are held by the Secretary of State, to assess whether and in what areas air quality standards or objectives are not being met and, in certain circumstances, to give directions to local authorities.

— *Waste Strategy (section 92 of the Act)*
    As with the air quality strategy, the Environment Agency is a statutory consultee for the Secretary of State's National Waste Strategy for England and Wales. The Agency is to carry out a national survey of waste arisings, on which the strategy will be based. In Scotland SEPA itself is charged with preparing the waste strategy.

— *Producer Responsibility (sections 93 and 94 of the Act)*
    A significant role for the agencies is anticipated by the Act in connection with producer

responsibility for waste and for other materials which may be used, recovered or recycled. The Act provides for regulations to be made imposing producer responsibility obligations. Agency and SEPA duties of compliance monitoring, enforcement and guidance in relation to such obligations appear to be envisaged, and certainly form the basis on which consultation has been conducted on the introduction of producer responsibility for packaging waste.
— *Nuclear Installations* (paras. 7–9 of Sched. 22 to the Act)
The Agency or SEPA must be consulted by the Health & Safety Executive before it grants or revokes a nuclear site licence and also before it places a condition on or varies such a licence where such condition or variation relates to or affects the creation, accumulation or disposal of radioactive waste.

Functions not transferred—Features Common to the Agency and SEPA
Air pollution control, unlike in Scotland, is retained by local authorities in England and Wales, and this is considered more fully in the general note to s.21.
   A number of other functions which were not transferred to the agencies were mooted for transfer in various quarters, both within and outside Parliament. Some of these functions and notable advocates of their transfer are noted here:—
— A monitoring and co-ordinating role for marine pollution, marine disposal of wastes and radionuclide monitoring (currently the responsibility of the Ministry of Agriculture, Fisheries and Food ("MAFF" in England and Wales and the Scottish Office in Scotland); advocated for transfer by the Worldwide Fund for Nature ("WWF") in its Memorandum to the House of Commons Select Committee's Hearings on the draft Environment Agencies Bill (H.C. Pap. 40 I–iii; Appx 8));
— Pesticide registration and enforcement (currently the Pesticide Safety Directorate and Welsh Office/MAFF in England and Wales and the Scottish Office in Scotland; transfer advocated by the Labour Party: for this and the references below to Labour Party policy, see its policy document *In Trust for Tomorrow*, and *the Surveyor*, December 8, 1994, p. 14); and
— Policy on coastal protection (currently Welsh Office/MAFF/Scottish Office; transfer advocated by the Labour Party: see also H.C. Standing Committee B, 3rd sitting, May 2, 1995, cols. 94–99. Relatedly, *Hansard*, H.C., Vol. 258, cols. 77–78 may be noted, where Mr Gareth Wardell urges that the Crown Estates' function of licensing aggregate dredging, which can affect Agency coastal protection/flood defence schemes, be transferred);
— Drinking water standards regulation (currently the Drinking Water Inspectorate in England and Wales and the Secretary of State in Scotland; transfer advocated by the Labour Party; see also H.C. Standing Committee B, 3rd sitting, May 2, 1995, cols. 89–94).
— The authorisation and regulation of nuclear installation operation, bringing this together with radioactive substance control (currently the Nuclear Installations Inspectorate both south and north of the border: transfer advocated by the Labour Party).
— The role of consenting and regulatory authority in relation to the contained use and deliberate release of genetically modified organisms ("GMOs", currently the responsibility of the Secretary of State; transfer advocated by Mrs Anne Campbell, whose speech in support of a proposed amendment to this effect, citing GMO research on agricultural crops, prompted the Chairman of the Commons Standing Committee, Mrs Gwyneth Dunwoody, to remark that "the hon. Lady ... has put me off tomatoes for life": H.C. Standing Committee B, 3rd sitting, May 2, 1995, cols. 99–103. During that debate the then Parliamentary Under-Secretary of State for the Environment, Sir Paul Beresford, commented that "we think that once the divisions of responsibility between the Department and the agency for work on genetically modified organisms can be clearly identified, clause 36 [s.38 of the Act] ... could be used to transfer at least some of the Secretary of State's functions in this regard to the agency" (col. 102)).
— A supervisory and guidance role on the effective implementation of environmental impact assessment procedures for those operations regulated by it (currently DoE responsibility in England and Wales and Scottish Office responsibility in Scotland; advocated by the WWF).
— In the House of Lords, amendments proposed the transfer to a separate Welsh Environment Agency of the functions of the Countryside Commission for Wales: *Hansard*, H.L. Vol. 560, col. 587.

Functions not transferred—Scotland
Many environmental protection functions are not transferred to SEPA by the Act which raises doubts about the extent to which the administration of environmental protection has truly become integrated.

Local authority functions
The new Scottish local authorities established by virtue of the Local Government etc. (Scotland) Act 1994 have inherited the functions of the former district and islands councils by virtue of the Clean Air Act 1993 and in relation to statutory nuisance by virtue of the Public Health (Scotland) Act 1897 which are replaced by the extension of Part III of the Environmental Protection Act 1990 to Scotland by virtue of s.107 and Sched. 17 to this Act.

The new Scottish local authorities have also inherited the functions of the former regional and islands councils in relation to flood defence under the Flood Prevention (Scotland) Act 1961 and coast protection under the Coast Protection Act 1949. Former regional and islands council functions in relation to water supply and provision of sewerage, which they exercised by virtue of the Sewerage (Scotland) Act 1968 and the Water (Scotland) Act 1980, have been transferred to three new public non-departmental water authorities by virtue of Part II of the Local Government etc. (Scotland) Act 1994: the North, East and West of Scotland Water Authorities.

Functions, aims and objectives
The Agency and SEPA both operate within a complex web of aims, objectives, purposes, powers, duties and other functions. Some of those are to be found in the 1995 Act, of which some are transferred from other legislation and extended to cover regulatory regimes to which they had not previously applied (for the Agency, notably the Water Resources Act 1991: see ss.6–8), and others are new or extended in scope (notably ss.4, 5, 31, 33 and 39: see also the note on new functions established by the Act, above). Of course, separate legislation (such as the 1990 Act) contains the main regulatory regimes for which the agencies are responsible, and that legislation may contain its own purposes and objectives. Of the new functions, those which prompted the most debate in Parliament were the agencies' objectives (which debate led to the introduction of a "principal aim" for the Agency, but not for SEPA: see ss.4 and 31), and the duty imposed on them to have regard to costs and benefits in certain cases (see s.39).

The range of duties on the Agency and SEPA is so wide that, if they were all couched in absolute terms there would be a real possibility of their being incompatible in particular circumstances: accordingly some are couched in terms such as "to have regard to" specified matters (see ss.7 and 32; the term is considered further at the end of this discussion of aims and objectives) or "to such extent as it considers desirable, to promote ... " *e.g.* (s.6, s.34(2)). Similarly, some duties are expressed to be subject to others (subs. 7(2) is subject to subs. 7(1), of which subs. (1)(a) is in turn subject to s.4). Wide discretion is thus granted to the Agency and to SEPA as to the weight to be given to such matters, and in practice, therefore, only their ignoring the matters in question in a given instance is likely to enable a decision to be successfully challenged in the courts.

"Functions" includes powers and duties (s.124(1)). Generally, one discharges one's duties through the exercise of one's powers, although powers may be exercised where there is no duty to act. It may be that particular functions are to be exercised for a particular purpose (see ss.5 and 33) or so as to obtain a specific objective or set of objectives. The imposition of statutory objectives in the context of specific functions is increasingly prevalent in United Kingdom environmental law, primarily through the requirement to implement EC legislation containing such objectives. A good example is the Waste Framework Directive (as amended by Directive 91/156/EEC), which led to the Waste Management Licensing Regulations 1994 (S.I. 1994 No.1056, see Appendix 3), Sched. 4, imposing "relevant objectives" on a range of bodies including the waste regulation authorities whose functions are to be taken on by the Agency and SEPA. The same objectives appear again in relation to the waste strategies (s.92) in the production of which the Agency and SEPA will play major parts. Such objectives also feature, for example, in EC water pollution legislation, and the statutory requirement that they be attained significantly limits the discretion available to the Agency and SEPA in the exercise of their powers.

Overlaid onto these functions are the general aims and objectives of the agencies themselves, provided by ss.4 and 31. The context of these is to be provided by guidance to which the agencies must have regard (although the note to s.4 suggests that, as regards the Agency's principal aim, the role of the guidance is more significant than this, and accordingly that aim is qualified by being "subject to and in accordance with" other provisions with which it might otherwise have conflicted). Once again, whilst the agencies cannot disregard such guidance, they have discretion as to how much weight to accord it in given circumstances: the term "have regard to" is considered further below.

Finally there is the duty to have regard to costs and benefits, so far as is reasonable, in the exercise, non-exercise and manner of exercise of the agencies' powers (s.39; again, this duty is heavily qualified: see especially s.39(2)). It will be noted that this duty applies only to the exercise of the agencies' *powers*, not to the fulfilment of their duties. This, and the way in which it is qualified, restricts the significance of the s.39 duty, and an example of it as applicable only in the exercise of *discretionary powers* in fulfilment of a duty (in that case the setting of discharge consent conditions) was given by the Government in Parliament: see the general note to s.39. A particularly limiting factor will, it is submitted, prove to be the (frequently EC-driven) statutory objectives to be attained, noted above. Where one must exercise one's duties so as to *ensure* that waste is disposed of "without risk to water, air, soil, plants and animals [and] without adversely affecting the countryside or places of special interest" (these are two of the Waste framework Directive objectives), then the scope for taking into account costs and benefits, and (as in the case of the Agency) for pursuing one's principal aim are significantly constrained.

The s.39 duty remains important, however: where, for example, the Agency or SEPA is considering the service of a works notice for water pollution (introduced by Sched. 22: see note to s.120), it is submitted that it will in most cases have to take into account costs and benefits in determining whether or not to serve the notice and what requirements to impose. As this is a pollution control function, the s.5/s.33 duty will be relevant (prevention or minimisation of pollution); but in determining what, in the circumstances, constitutes the "minimising" of pollution, costs and benefits will be a consideration.

" … have regard to … "
As the above comments illustrate, the Agency and SEPA have a range of duties to "have regard to" guidance. Case law on the term is therefore worth consideration, since the meaning given to the term by Courts will play a large part in determining the scope for challenging the actions of the Agency/SEPA where such duties are relevant. Planning and housing law are both fruitful areas for such judicial decisions. For example a requirement to have regard to a Code of Guidance issued by the Secretary of State is imposed on housing authorities in relation to homelessness law. In that area of law it is clear that ignoring the guidance will result in a decision being unlawful as, for example, occurred in *Kelly v. Monklands District Council* 1986 S.L.T. 169 where a housing authority ignored provisions in the Scottish Code in relation to their assessment that a 17 year-old girl was not vulnerable. However, it is also clear from case law that as long as regard is had to the guidance it is possible to depart from it as, for example, in *Mazzaccherini v. Argyll and Bute District Council* 1987 S.C.L.R. 475 where Lord Jauncey held that while a housing authority had to have regard to the Code of Guidance it could depart from it and added, "if a housing authority considers that in a particular case the circumstances do not merit the rigid application of a part of the Code I do not consider they could be faulted at law or said to have acted unreasonably" (see also *DeFalco v. Crawley Borough Council* [1980] Q.B. 460). However, in the planning case *Pye (J.A.) (Oxford) Estates Ltd v. Wychavon District Council and the Secretary of State for the Environment* [1982] JPL 575 it was held that a body departing from guidance provided by a ministerial circular must justify such a departure by giving sound and clear reasons. Where there is a conflict between the wording of the Act and the guidance, it is the terms of the Act which must be followed (see also: *London Borough of Tower Hamlets v. Secretary of State for the Environment* (1993) 25 H.L.R. 524 (C.A.)). Once final guidance is issued regard must be had to the current edition of such guidance, see *e.g. R. v. Slough Borough Council, ex p. Casey*, May 28, 1993, unreported in which the decision of a housing authority was quashed after regard was had to an old edition of the Code of Guidance produced for housing authorities in relation to the homelessness legislation.

Regional and Managerial Structure—England and Wales
In July 1994, the Government published a report it had commissioned from Touche Ross: *Options for the Geographical and Managerial Structure of the Proposed Environment Agency.* The report set out for consultation five Models A–E: unsurprisingly, it will be noted that each of the NRA, HMIP and the waste regulation authorities were proponents of options that significantly reflected their own existing structures:
  — **Model A** Initially proposed by the WRAs. The NRA, HMIP and waste organisations would continue to run in parallel but there would be a new regional and national structure for waste. Integration would be achieved through joint input in planning and policy at national level and sub-regional co-operation.
  — **Model B** Initially proposed by HMIP. Operation and regulation would be separated. One large HQ would have three "field" directorates (Regulation, Flood Defence and

River Basin Management) and an Environmental Quality Directorate for policy and planning. Multi-media regulatory teams would work to regional managers with support centres of excellence. Seven regions would be based on local authority boundaries, even for water management.
— **Model C** The "NRA" model; based on river catchment boundaries. A small head office would have one policy making directorate and a single field/operations directorate. Co-located staff at regional level would work in multi-media teams and multi-disciplinary managers, with shared support services.
— **Model D** Separation of regulation and operations; regulation based on local authority boundaries and operation on river catchment areas. HMIP, NRA and waste staff would be co-located at regional level but would work in separate teams, with a more integrated approach being aimed at long-term.
— **Model E** Separate operation and regulation but brought together at Head Office level. Multi-skilled industry-facing (not media-facing) teams supported by technical specialists. River catchment boundaries.

HMIP at the time had seven regions, the NRA eight and the nine voluntary waste regulation committees in England represented the closest waste regulation came to formal regional structures. Neither the number of regions, nor their boundaries, corresponded with the NRA boundaries based on river catchment areas and waste regulation boundaries on local authority (primarily County Council) boundaries.

The issues of principle at stake were primarily:
— The difference of opinion between the NRA and HMIP over the desirability of separating operational (*e.g.* water management) and regulatory functions: the NRA saw the two as mutually supportive in terms of shared knowledge and expertise, and also as a cost effective way of structuring the Agency, and their division as inappropriate. The NRA itself had no such structural divide. HMIP saw the issue as the avoidance of conflicts of interest which might arise when an organisation is "self-policing". See further Viscount Mills, *Hansard*, H.L., Vol. 559, col. 1451.
— The NRA's desire to retain boundaries based on environmental rather than political considerations, to further integrated river catchment managements.
— The local accountability and public access argument that the public and business are familiar with and already have to deal with local authority boundaries; and
— The "business facing Agency"/"one stop shop" argument that to operate one set of boundaries for water management and another for pollution control would mean that some members of the public and businesses would, where boundaries differed, find themselves having to deal with different Agency regions on different matters.

In the event, the third of those arguments lost out as a compromise solution has been adopted to reconcile as far as possible the first two positions: *Environment Agency Update No. 5*, September 1995. Water Management boundaries are to remain based on the NRA's river catchment areas, but pollution (including water pollution) control functions are to be organised on the basis of political (*i.e.* local authority) boundaries. These will principally be county council boundaries, but district council boundaries will be used in places where that gives a better "match" with the water management boundaries.

Regional and Managerial Structure: Scotland
Improving Scotland's Environment sought views on local participation (paras. 20–22) and envisaged that "SEPA might set up a regional advisory committee structure in order to provide for local involvement and participation" (para. 20). The consultation paper appeared to envisage that these committees would be purely advisory and that they would not exercise any delegated executive functions (para. 21). However, as a result of misgivings expressed about this approach in the consultation exercise, the Secretary of State announced that he believed that there was scope for delegating responsibilities to regional staff without prejudicing SEPA's overall control and that he intended to commission further work on this issue (*Hansard*, H.C. Vol. 219, cols. 713–4w). Subsequently management consultants KPMG were commissioned to produce a report on possible regional structures for SEPA and recommended the establishment of three or four regional boards. Their report, *Scottish Environment Protection Agency: Consultancy Report*, (March 1993) considered four options:

1. Minimum change. SEPA itself would continue to operate along the lines of existing bodies. The regional structure would involve seven local boards based on the existing river purification board structure. There would be strong local authority representation on these boards which would exercise major executive powers.
2. Reduced number of regional boards with full executive powers. This option envisaged a clearer break from present arrangements with SEPA having a regional structure of three or four boards although these would retain full executive powers.

3. Reduced number of regional boards with delegated authority. This would involve the same number of regional boards as in option 2 above but their executive powers would be more limited and would be delegated by the main SEPA board.

4. Regional advisory committees. This option involved regional committees with a consultative role and no executive powers which would be exercised by the main SEPA board. This was in line with the Government's original proposals in *Improving Scotland's Environment: The Way Forward*, paras. 20–21.

These four options were evaluated on the basis of the following criteria developed by KPMG Management Consulting: ability to plan and set policy centrally and deliver services locally; organisational effectiveness; independence and professionalism; and sensitivity to local needs.

KPMG argued that the first option would fail to change the status quo and that there would still be the potential for regional inconsistencies hindering SEPA's development as a cohesive agency committed to an integrated approach to pollution control. In relation to the second option they considered that having regional boards with full executive powers could not be reconciled with the concept of a unified agency. They also rejected the fourth option on the basis that an agency with such a structure would be too centralised, remote and unresponsive to local sensitivities. Their preferred option was the third option:

> "It gives the main board of the agency the authority to ensure that policy is applied consistently and rigorously throughout the agency, but it allows for the delegation of some decisions to a local level, where appropriate. It therefore strikes a balance between the need for an effective, unified organisation, and the requirement for an agency which is responsive to local needs" (Executive Summary).

In relation to the remote rural areas, in particular the Orkney Islands, Shetland Islands and Western Isles, KPMG also recommended that the main SEPA boards should be empowered "to enter into contractual arrangements with third parties for the delivery of services, where this does not involve a conflict between regulatory and operational responsibilities" (ibid.).

KPMG's recommended option has been adopted as the appropriate model in the 1995 Act which provides that SEPA must establish Regional Boards with the approval of the Secretary of State who is also to issue guidance to assist SEPA in appointing members to such Boards (Sched. 6, para. 16). Each Board is to be chaired by a member of the main SEPA Board and is to have executive functions delegated to it by the main Board with the approval of the Secretary of State (Sched. 6, para. 16). It should be noted that in contrast in England and Wales, the Agency's Regional Advisory Committees will not have executive functions delegated to them. The 1995 Act does not, however, specify the number of Boards to be established and the Government stressed that this was a matter for SEPA (*per* Sir Hector Monro, Standing Committee B, May 16, 1995, col. 235). On October 27, 1995 it was announced that SEPA was establishing three Regional Boards for the North, East and West of Scotland (Scottish Office Press Release, October 27, 1995). These Boards will be based in Dingwall, Riccarton near Edinburgh and East Kilbride respectively (ibid.). It was also announced that SEPA's headquarters is to be at Stirling (ibid.).

The 1995 Act provides that SEPA must establish regional boards with the approval of the Secretary of State for Scotland who is also to issue guidance to assist SEPA in appointing members to these regional boards (Sched. 6 para. 16). Each Board is to be chaired by a member of SEPA. However, unlike the Regional Advisory Committees which the Agency must establish in England and Wales, the Scottish Regional Boards are to have executive functions delegated to them.

Issues of accountability raised by these provisions are discussed in the note to s.20 and Sched. 6.

The Agencies and Access to Information
An increasingly important function of environmental regulatory bodies is the provision of information for the public by means of statutory registers or under the Environmental Information Regulations 1992. (S.I. 1992 No. 3240) ("the 1992 Regulations").

The Agency and SEPA are to hold the statutory registers previously held by a variety of regulatory bodies in relation to functions transferred to the agencies. The statutory registers transferred to the Agency are as follows:

Information on register	Statute and regulator
Integrated Pollution Control Part A processes	Environmental Protection Act 1990, s.20 (HMIP)
Prescribed Works	Alkali etc. Works Regulation Act 1906, s.9; Control of Industrial Air Pollution (Registration of Works) Regulations 1989 (S.I. 1989 No. 318) (HMIP)
Radioactive substances registrations and authorisations	Radioactive Substances Act 1993, s.39 (HMIP)
Water Quality Objectives, discharge consents to controlled waters and sampling results	Water Resources Act 1991, s.190; Control of Pollution (Registers) Regulations 1989 (S.I. 1989 No. 1160) (NRA)
Water abstraction and impounding licences	1991 Act, s.189 (NRA)
Waste management licenses	1990 Act, s.64 (waste regulation authority)
Registration of waste carriers	Control of Pollution (Amendment) Act 1989, s.2; Controlled Waste (Registration of Carriers and Seizure of Vehicles) Regulations 1991, reg. 3 (S.I. 1991 No. 1624) (waste regulation authority)
Registration of activities exempt from waste management licensing	Waste Management Licensing Regulations 1994 (S.I. 1994 No. 1056), reg. 18 (waste regulation authority)
Registration of brokers of controlled waste	1994 Regulations, reg. 20 and Sched. 5 (waste regulation authority)

The statutory registers which will be transferred to SEPA are as follows:

Information on register	Statute and regulator
Integrated Pollution Control Part A processes	1990 Act, s.20 (HMIPI and RPAs)
Prescribed works	Alkali etc. Works Regulation Act 1906, s.9; Control of Industrial Air Pollution (Registration of Works) Regulations 1989 (S.I. 1989 No. 318) (HMIPI)
Radioactive substances registrations and authorisations	Radioactive Substances Act 1993, s.39 (HMIPI)
Air Pollution Control Part B processes	1990 Act, s.20 (District and islands councils)
Water Quality Objectives, discharge consents to controlled waters and sampling results	Control of Pollution Act 1974, s.41; Control of Pollution (Registers) (Scotland) Regulations 1993 (S.I. 1993 No. 1155) (RPAs)
Waste management licenses	1990 Act, s.64 (Waste regulation authority)
Registration of waste carriers	Control of Pollution (Amendment) Act 1989, s.2; Controlled Waste (Registration of Carriers and Seizure of Vehicles) Regulations 1991, reg. 3 (S.I. 1991 No. 1624) (Waste regulation authority)
Registration of activities exempt from waste management licensing	Waste Management Licensing Regulations 1994 (S.I. 1994 No. 1056), reg. 18 (Waste regulation authority)
Registration of brokers of controlled waste	Waste Management Licensing Regulations 1994 (S.I. 1994 No. 1056), reg. 20, Sched. 5 (Waste regulation authority)

Both agencies also inherit responsibility for the non-statutory Chemical Releases Inventory. Aside from their statutory duties in relation to registers the Agency and SEPA are also clearly subject to the 1992 Regulations (see, *e.g.* Viscount Ullswater, Minister of State, *Hansard*, H.L. Vol. 560, col. 792 and the Earl of Lindsay *Hansard*, H.L. Vol. 560, cols. 1198–1199) and the Directive on Freedom of Access to Information on the Environment (90/313/EEC) which they implement. Although the 1992 Regulations provide a general right of access to environmental information, there are several grounds on which refusal to supply information is legitimate (regs. 3(3) and 4). This explains why in s.30 which relates to record keeping by SEPA and s.37(5) which empowers the Agency/SEPA to carry out research, they are given a discretion to provide access to records or the results of research to the public. They may withhold information where one of the grounds for refusal to disclose information under the 1992 Regulations applies but, it is submitted, they cannot do so in any other circumstances.

As to the rejection by the Government of the suggestion that the Agency/SEPA should be obliged to make their meetings public, see the note to s.1 and Sched. 1.

The Government appear committed to a culture of openness in the agencies:

> "The Government are keen to ensure maximum openness in the affairs of SEPA, without compromising its ability to discharge its functions effectively" (*per* the Earl of Lindsay *Hansard*, H.L. Vol. 560 col. 1198).

The draft Agency management statement (December 1995) states that "the Agency should meet the standards of openness and transparency expected of public bodies. It should publish its own Code on openness. The Code should be drawn up in consultation with the Department, and should reflect the principles of the Government's Code of Practice on Access to Government Information" (para. 6.1).

The Government have indicated in relation to SEPA at least that "minutes of its meetings will be available to the public through the Environmental Information Regulations 1992." (*ibid.*, see also Sir Hector Monro, the then Parliamentary Under-Secretary of State for Scotland, Standing Committee B, May 16, 1995 col. 248). This commitment may also be seen in the agencies' respective draft management statements.

Certain advantages may accrue to members of the public from this concentration of registers and information. Firstly, administrative practices and photocopying charges should be standardised:

> "One of the potential benefits of SEPA is consistency of procedures and I would hope for a standard photocopying charge, not fluctuations depending on which local office is involved." (*per* the Earl of Lindsay, *Hansard* H.L. Vol. 561, col. 1698)

This will clearly benefit the public since previous administrative practices and charging regimes varied significantly between the various bodies responsible for keeping statutory registers. For examples of diverse administrative practices in respect of IPC registers, see *Integrated Pollution Control: The First Three Years* (ENDS, 1994, para. 13.1) and in respect of LAAPC registers in Scotland, see *Come Clean! Public Access to Information about Local Authority Air Pollution Control* (Scottish Consumer Council & Friends of the Earth Scotland, 1993).

Concerns have, however, been expressed about the agencies' powers to charge for providing copies or extracts and, in certain instances (*e.g.* s.30) to charge for the provision of inspection facilities. The fear is that the agencies will seek to maximise their income and hence in effect deny access to information to many members of the public.

Secondly, the Government argued that the accessibility of the registers would also improve:

> "One immediate and tangible benefit of the establishment of SEPA will be in relation to the greater ease of access to its public registers. For the first time, those registers will be available for inspection at single points of contact, greatly improving the existing arrangements where the registers are dispersed across a number of authorities". (*per e.g.* the Earl of Lindsay *Hansard*, H.L. Vol. 560, col. 1198)

This statement, however, overlooks the fact that having registers at single points of contact may actually be disadvantageous to the public as the point of contact concerned may be much less accessible than a local authority based register. It is not yet clear how far such a person will have to travel to inspect the registers after the agencies are established or what information will actually be held by regional offices. To an extent the 1992 Regulations will assist in overcoming problems of accessibility as they may be used to obtain information by letter or even by telephone. *Integrated Pollution Control: The First Three Years* (ENDS, 1994) identified accessibility of HMIP registers held by the then three regional headquarters as somewhat problematic (paras. 13.1–13.2). These registers were subsequently devolved to seven new regional sites. Furthermore it is not clear that the lack of a central register which would benefit those with a legitimate interest in the wider national impact of IPC, which was identified as a serious problem by that study, is to be rectified with the advent of the agencies.

In cases where a person wished to challenge the refusal of one of the agencies to disclose information or the level of its charge for inspection facilities or copies, it should be noted that the only remedies available would be judicial review or recourse to the Parliamentary Ombudsman. Formerly in relation to information held by local authorities, recourse could have been had to the Local Government Ombudsman. With the transfer to the agencies of various local authority functions and information associated therewith, this remedy will no longer be available to aggrieved persons who will require to seek redress from the Parliamentary Ombudsman. However, the Government indicated in their White Paper, *Open Government* (Cm. 2290, July 1993) that they would consider establishing a tribunal to hear disputes relating to access to health and safety and environmental information (para. 6.16). Subsequently, a commitment has been made to legislate for such a tribunal: see [1995] 243 ENDS Report at p. 32.

ABBREVIATIONS

ACBE: Advisory Committee on Business and the Environment
Agency, the: the Environment Agency
BATNEEC: Best Available Techniques Not Entailing Excessive Cost
BPEO: Best Practicable Environmental Option
CPRE: Council for the Protection of Rural England
DOE: Department of the Environment
DWI: Drinking Water Inspectorate
Edwards Report: Report of the National Parks Review Committee, 1990, Fit for the Future
EAAC: Environment Agency Advisory Committee
EPAC: Environment Protection Advisory Committee
HMIP: Her Majesty's Inspectorate of Pollution
HMIPI: Her Majesty's Industrial Pollution Inspectorate
IPC: Integrated Pollution Control
LAPC: Local Air Pollution Control
LAAPC: Local Authority Air Pollution Control
MAFF: Ministry of Agriculture, Fisheries and Food
NRA: National Rivers Authority
RPA: River Purification Authority
RPB: River Purification Board
SEPA: Scottish Environment Protection Agency
WRA: Waste Regulation Authority
WWF: Worldwide Fund for Nature
1906 Act: Alkali etc., Works Regulation Act 1906
1949 Act: National Parks and Access to the Countryside Act 1949
1974 Act: Control of Pollution Act 1974
1981 Act: Wildlife and Countryside Act 1981
1990 Act: Environmental Protection Act 1990
1991 Act: Water Resources Act 1991
1992 Regulations: Environmental Information Regulations 1992 (S.I. 1992 No. 3240)
1994 Regulations: Waste Management Licensing Regulations 1994 (S.I. 1994 No. 1056)

CHAPTER I

THE ENVIRONMENT AGENCY

Establishment of the Agency

The Environment Agency

1.—(1) There shall be a body corporate to be known as the Environment Agency or, in Welsh, Asiantaeth yr Amgylchedd (in this Act referred to as "the Agency"), for the purpose of carrying out the functions transferred or assigned to it by or under this Act.

(2) The Agency shall consist of not less than eight nor more than fifteen members of whom—

    (a) three shall be appointed by the Minister; and

    (b) the others shall be appointed by the Secretary of State.

(3) The Secretary of State shall designate—

    (a) one of the members as the chairman of the Agency, and

    (b) another of them as the deputy chairman of the Agency.

(4) In appointing a person to be a member of the Agency, the Secretary of State or, as the case may be, the Minister shall have regard to the desirability of appointing a person who has experience of, and has shown capacity in, some matter relevant to the functions of the Agency.

(5) Subject to the provisions of section 38 below, the Agency shall not be regarded—

    (a) as the servant or agent of the Crown, or as enjoying any status, immunity or privilege of the Crown; or

    (b) by virtue of any connection with the Crown, as exempt from any tax, duty, rate, levy or other charge whatsoever, whether general or local;

and the Agency's property shall not be regarded as property of, or property held on behalf of, the Crown.

(6) The provisions of Schedule 1 to this Act shall have effect with respect to the Agency.

DEFINITIONS
"the Agency": s.124(1).
"functions": s.124(1).
"the Minister": s.56(1).

COMMENCEMENT
July 28, 1995 (S.I. 1995 No. 1983).

GENERAL NOTE
This section provides for the establishment of the Environment Agency and gives effect to Schedule I which deals with the constitution of the Agency. The constituent elements of the Agency and the background to their establishment are discussed in the General Note to this Part of the Act, and the functions transferred to it are considered in the note to s.2 below. It should be noted that if the Agency were to carry out other functions it would be acting *ultra vires*, and that as non-departmental public body, the Agency is accountable to Parliament through the Secretary of State for the Environment.

Subs. (1): Body Corporate
By subs. (1), the Agency is a body corporate. One implication of this is in relation to officers' liability. Were the Agency itself to commit any one of a range of offences (including, in the environmental sphere, any offence under the Environmental Protection Act 1990 and the Water Resources Act 1991), then individual criminal liability for its officers might follow.

    Typical wording can be found in s.157 of the 1990 Act. In such provisions liability can accrue not only to officers, but to members where the affairs of the body corporate are managed by its members. In a limited liability company, the shareholders are the members of the company, but it will be noted from subs. (2) below that the members of the Agency are the members of its Board. Whilst it is not possible for the Agency as enforcing authority to prosecute itself, and unlikely that the Agency would prosecute one of its officers or members under such provisions, most environmental legislation does not rule out the possibility of private prosecution. It is therefore possible in principle for the Agency to be prosecuted for offences for which it is the statutory enforcing authority, and officers' liability under such provisions could in principle follow.

Subs. (2): Appointments
Subs. (2) provides for the appointment of the members of the Agency—effectively its Board—of whom there are to be between 8 and 15. At least three are to be appointed by the Minister of Agriculture, Fisheries and food; the remainder by the Secretary of State, who also

designates the chairman and deputy chairman (subs. (3)) on August 8 1995, the Secretary of State appointed
- Lord De Ramsey as Chairman (a Cambridgeshire farmer and former President of the Country Landowners Association, President of the Association of Drainage Authorities and former Chairman of the Cambridge Water Company);
- Peter Burnham (previously associated with Coopers & Lybrand, the HMIP Advisory Committee and English Heritage);
- Imtiaz Farookhi (Leicester City Council);
- Nigel Haigh (Institute of European Environment Policy and the Green Alliance);
- Christopher Hampson (Yorkshire Electricity, HMIP Advisory Committee, A former Chairman of CBI Environment Committee);
- John Harman (Kirklees Council, Association of Metropolitan Authorities);
- Karen Morgan (NRA, University of West England, formerly ICI);
- Joan Wykes (NRA, London Borough of Bromley, formerly London Waste Regulation Committee, GLC and Thames Water Authority);
- Ed Gallagher (Chief Executive of Agency and formerly of NRA, formerly Amersham International and Black & Decker);
- Professor Ronald Edwards (appointee of Secretary of State for Wales; formerly NRA and its Welsh Regional Advisory Committee, formerly Welsh Water, Natural Environment Research Council and National Parks Review Panel).

The Minister of Agriculture Fisheries and Food made three appointments:
- Sir Richard George (Weetabix, Food and Drink Federation, Institute of Food Research);
- John Norris (NRA, Essex farmer, Country Landowners Association, Crown Estate Commissioner, involvement in flood defence and land drainage);
- Dr. Anne Powell (NRA fisheries, WWF, Agenda 21 Steering Group for Oxfordshire, Inland Waterways Amenity Advisory Council).

Of these, Lord de Ramsey (as chairman,) Peter Burnham, Imtiaz Farookhi, Nigel Haigh, Christopher Hampson, John Harman and John Norris had previously been members of the Environment Agency Advisory Committee appointed on November 18, 1994 (DoE News Release 650) and charged with setting up the Agency. It was anticipated by the Government that the Environment Agency Advisory Committee, which advised the Government on the establishment of the Agency and was chaired by Lord de Ramsey, would form the nucleus of the Agency's Board, and so it proved.

Subs. (4) indicates that the desirability of an appointee having experience relevant to the Agency's functions is something to which the Secretary of State and minister must have regard in making appointments. Given the wide range of functions to be exercised by the Agency, and indeed of its aims and objectives in discharging those functions, it appears likely that it would be extremely difficult in practice to challenge an appointment on this basis.

Other appointments

A number of members of Agency staff were appointed between June and September 1995 including the Chief Executive Ed Gallagher, six Directors (three, like Mr Gallagher, from the NRA: one from HMIP) of Environmental Strategy, Water Management, Finance, Pollution Prevention and Control, Operations and Personnel, and eight Regional General Managers (seven of whom are from the NRA, the other from HMIP). The regions are Anglian Midlands, North East, North West, Southern, South West, Thames and Welsh.

Crown Immunity

Subs. (5) provides that the Agency does not have Crown privilege, immunity or exemption from taxation. Section 38 qualifies this position. Under that section, the Agency and any Minister of the Crown may into an agreement authorising the Agency or any of its employees to exercise a ministerial function. In such a case, by s.38(5), where the Agency's acts or omissions are in, or in connection with, the exercise or purported exercise by the Agency of a ministerial function pursuant to such an agreement, those acts and omissions are to be treated as the acts or omissions of the Minister of the Crown in question. It should be noted that, even in such circumstances, the immunity provided by s.38 is not total and in particular (s.38(6)) does not extend to criminal proceedings in respect of such act or omission.

Schedule 1—Constitution of the Agency

Subs. (6) gives effect to Schedule 1, which contains a number of provisions relating to the constitution of the Environment Agency.

These provisions fall under the following headings:

Membership; chairman and deputy chairman; remuneration, pensions etc.; staff; proceedings of the Agency; delegation of powers; members' interests; vacancies and defective appointments; minutes; application of seal and proof of instruments; documents served etc. by or on the Agency; and interpretation. Certain of these provisions are outlined below.

Schedule 1—membership, chairman and deputy chairman
Paras. 1 and 2 of Sched. 1 provide for the resignation or removal from office, and reappointment, of members appointed to the Agency under subs. (2) above, and of the chairman and deputy chairman designated under subs. (3) above. By sub-para. (1)(3) and the definition of "appropriate Minister" in para. 12 (which, should be noted, differs from the definition of that term provided by s.56(1) for the purposes of Part I of the Act), a member of the Agency may only be removed from office by the person who appointed him—that is, the Secretary of State, or the Minister of Agriculture, Fisheries and Food, as appropriate. Ceasing to be a member of the Agency automatically terminates an individual's office as chairman or deputy chairman.

Schedule 1—staff, remuneration and pensions
By para. 4, the Agency has absolute discretion in the appointment of officers and employees, save that the Secretary of State's consent is required to the appointment of the chief executive.
Remuneration and pension arrangements for each member are determined by the person who appointed that member: para. 3. For other officers and employees, the Agency may determine its provisions for their pensions, allowances and gratuities (this does not appear to cover remuneration, but does include compensation for loss of employment or diminution of emoluments), subject to the approval of the Secretary of State to the setting of those pensions, allowances and gratuities: para. 4. The Agency's discretion is presumably also restricted by the provisions in para. 3 regarding the transfer to the Agency of rights or liabilities under existing contracts of employment.

Schedule 1—proceedings
Subject to the subsequent provisions of Sched. 1, and to the obligation in s.106 of the Water Resources Act 1991 to carry out its flood defence functions through committees, para. 5 allows the Agency to regulate its own procedure, including quorum. ss.14–19 of and Scheds. 4 and 5 to the Environment Act modify the 1991 Act's provisions in relation to flood defence committees.
During debates on SEPA's proceedings, concern was expressed that its meetings would not be open to the public unlike local authority meetings (*e.g. per* Sam Galbraith Standing Committee B, May 2, 1995, col. 59). However, the Government's view is that it is not appropriate to compel SEPA or the Agency to have meetings in public since it is a national body and opening its meetings "would inhibit the informal development of its strategic thinking ahead of wider exposure to the public. Unlike local authorities, for whom such access is part of their accountability to local electorates, the agencies will be responsible to Ministers who are accountable to Parliament" (per Sir Paul Beresford, Parliamentary Under-Secretary of State for the Environment, Standing Committee B, May 2, 1995, cols. 62–63).

Schedule 1—delegation of powers
Para. 6 (again subject to s.106 of the 1991 Act) provides that anything authorised or required to be done by the Agency may be done the member, officer, employee, committee or sub-committee authorised (whether generally or specially) by the Agency to do so. This administrative provision is distinct from those in ss.108 and 109 of the Environment Act which provide that the Agency (*i.e.* any employee, etc., authorised to do so pursuant to this paragraph) may also authorise any suitable person (not necessarily an employee, etc.) to exercise a range of powers including entry and seizure, contained in those sections.

Schedule 1—Members' interests
Para. 7 provides, subject to relieving provisions where para. 7 would impede the transaction of business, that a member of the Agency who is "in any way directly or indirectly interested" in any matter brought up for consideration of a meeting of the Agency or any of its committees or sub-committees must disclose that interest and not take part in any deliberation or decision taken with respect to that matter. What would constitute sufficient disclosure is outlined.
The provision applied whether or not the interested member attends the meeting and, by sub-para. (3), the interest may be declared by way of a written notice read and considered at the meeting. It would appear that the provision applies even where the member is not a member of the committee or sub-committee considering the matter.

Schedule 1—documents served etc. by or on the Agency
Notices require or authorised to be served by or on the Agency must be in writing. Any notice or other document may be signed on behalf of the Agency by any member, officer or employee

who is authorise (generally or specially) by the Agency to do so. Documents purporting to be made, issued, executed or signed on its behalf by the Agency or by a duly authorised person on its behalf shall be received in evidence as being so made, issued, executed or signed unless the contrary is shown. This evidential provision is potentially of importance in a case where a party seeks to challenge the authority of someone who has acted purportedly with the authority of the Agency.

As to service of documents generally, see s.123.

Transfer of functions, property etc. to the Agency

Transfer of functions to the Agency

2.—(1) On the transfer date there shall by virtue of this section be transferred to the Agency—

  (a) the functions of the National Rivers Authority, that is to say—

      (i) its functions under or by virtue of Part II (water resources management) of the Water Resources Act 1991 (in this Part referred to as "the 1991 Act");

      (ii) its functions under or by virtue of Part III of that Act (control of pollution of water resources);

      (iii) its functions under or by virtue of Part IV of that Act (flood defence) and the Land Drainage Act 1991 and the functions transferred to the Authority by virtue of section 136(8) of the Water Act 1989 and paragraph 1(3) of Schedule 15 to that Act (transfer of land drainage functions under local statutory provisions and subordinate legislation);

      (iv) its functions under or by virtue of Part VII of the 1991 Act (land and works powers);

      (v) its functions under or by virtue of the Diseases of Fish Act 1937, the Sea Fisheries Regulation Act 1966, the Salmon and Freshwater Fisheries Act 1975, Part V of the 1991 Act or any other enactment relating to fisheries;

      (vi) the functions as a navigation authority, harbour authority or conservancy authority which were transferred to the Authority by virtue of Chapter V of Part III of the Water Act 1989 or paragraph 23(3) of Schedule 13 to that Act or which have been transferred to the Authority by any order or agreement under Schedule 2 to the 1991 Act;

      (vii) its functions under Schedule 2 to the 1991 Act;

      (viii) the functions assigned to the Authority by or under any other enactment, apart from this Act;

  (b) the functions of waste regulation authorities, that is to say, the functions conferred or imposed on them by or under—

      (i) the Control of Pollution (Amendment) Act 1989, or

      (ii) Part II of the Environmental Protection Act 1990 (in this Part referred to as "the 1990 Act"),

or assigned to them by or under any other enactment, apart from this Act;

  (c) the functions of disposal authorities under or by virtue of the waste regulation provisions of the Control of Pollution Act 1974;

  (d) the functions of the chief inspector for England and Wales constituted under section 16(3) of the 1990 Act, that is to say, the functions conferred or imposed on him by or under Part I of that Act or assigned to him by or under any other enactment, apart from this Act;

  (e) the functions of the chief inspector for England and Wales appointed under section 4(2)(a) of the Radioactive Substances Act

1993, that is to say, the functions conferred or imposed on him by or under that Act or assigned to him by or under any other enactment, apart from this Act;
  (f) the functions conferred or imposed by or under the Alkali, &c, Works Regulation Act 1906 (in this section referred to as "the 1906 Act") on the chief, or any other, inspector (within the meaning of that Act), so far as exercisable in relation to England and Wales;
  (g) so far as exercisable in relation to England and Wales, the functions in relation to improvement notices and prohibition notices under Part I of the Health and Safety at Work etc. Act 1974 (in this section referred to as "the 1974 Act") of inspectors appointed under section 19 of that Act by the Secretary of State in his capacity as the enforcing authority responsible in relation to England and Wales for the enforcement of the 1906 Act and section 5 of the 1974 Act; and
  (h) the functions of the Secretary of State specified in subsection (2) below.
(2) The functions of the Secretary of State mentioned in subsection (1)(h) above are the following, that is to say—
  (a) so far as exercisable in relation to England and Wales, his functions under section 30(1) of the Radioactive Substances Act 1993 (power to dispose of radioactive waste);
  (b) his functions under Chapter III of Part IV of the Water Industry Act 1991 in relation to special category effluent, within the meaning of that Chapter, other than any function of making regulations or of making orders under section 139 of that Act;
  (c) so far as exercisable in relation to England and Wales, the functions conferred or imposed on him by virtue of his being, for the purposes of Part I of the 1974 Act, the authority which is by any of the relevant statutory provisions made responsible for the enforcement of the 1906 Act and section 5 of the 1974 Act;
  (d) so far as exercisable in relation to England and Wales, his functions under, or under regulations made by virtue of, section 9 of the 1906 Act (registration of works), other than any functions of his as an appellate authority or any function of making regulations;
  (e) so far as exercisable in relation to England and Wales, his functions under regulations 7(1) and 8(2) of, and paragraph 2(2)(c) of Schedule 2 to, the Sludge (Use in Agriculture) Regulations 1989 (which relate to the provision of information and the testing of soil).
(3) The National Rivers Authority and the London Waste Regulation Authority are hereby abolished.

Definitions
  "the 1906 Act": subs. (1)(f).
  "the 1974 Act ": subs. (1)(g).
  "the 1990 Act": s.56(1).
  "the 1991 Act": s.56(1).
  "the Agency": s.124(1).
  "conservancy authority": s.56(1).
  "disposal authority": s.56(1).
  "functions": s.124(1).
  "harbour authority": s.56(1).
  "navigation authority": s.56(1).
  "transfer date": s.56(1).
  "waste regulation authority": s.56(1).

Commencement
April 1, 1996 (S.I. 1996 No. 186).

GENERAL NOTE
This section transfers from existing persons or bodies to the Agency established by Section 1, a range of functions (summarised below) previously exercised by those persons or bodies (subss. (1) and (2)). The transfer took place on April 1, 1996. Sched. 22 to the Act makes a large number of consequential amendments to other enactments, substituting references to the Agency for references to the persons or bodies it replaces, and para. 223 of that Schedule has the same effect in relation to subordinate and local legislation.

National Rivers Authority and Waste Regulation Authorities
Two of these bodies (the National Rivers Authority and the London Waste Regulation Authority) are consequently abolished by subs. (3), since all of their functions have been transferred. By s.30(1) of the 1990 Act the waste regulation authorities outside London were the Greater Manchester Waste Disposal Authority, Merseyside Waste Disposal Authority and elsewhere in England the county or metropolitan district councils; in Wales they are district councils. All of these bodies of course, retain other functions and are not, therefore, abolished.
    Reference in s.2(1)(c) to disposal authorities is to the Greater Manchester and Merseyside Waste Disposal Authorities in their waste regulation capacities.

HM Inspectorate of Pollution and the Secretary of State
Although HMIP could easily be thought of as a body similar in kind to the NRA, it is not. In fact, its functions are the functions of the chief inspector or other inspectors as individuals, or delegated functions of the Secretary of State: this is reflected in the wording of subs. 2(1)(d)–(g) and subs. 2(2). It should be noted that the Secretary of State's power to make regulations under the Water Industry Act 1991 and the Alkali, etc., Works Regulation Act 1906 and his appellate function under the latter Act are excluded from the transfer of his functions under those two Acts: subs. 2(2)(b) and (d).

Functions transferred
The main functions transferred to the Agency are summarised here in simplified form. Reference should be made to the statutes in question for the detail of the duties and for consequential and administrative duties. It should be noted that powers are usually exercisable only in certain circumstances and/or for the carrying out of certain functions.

Subs. (1)(a)—NRA's functions
All of the NRA's functions are transferred, as follows:—

Subs. (1)(a)(I)
Water resources management (Water Resources Act 1991, Part II).

Pt II, Ch. 1—general water resource management
The general water resource management duty (s.19) is now found in s.6(2) of the Act.
    Duty so far as reasonably practicable to enter into arrangements with water undertakers for securing the proper management or operation of such waters, etc., as the Agency considers appropriate for the undertakers to carry out their functions (s.20).
    Power (duty where directed by Secretary of State) to submit to him a draft statement containing provisions determining the minimum acceptable flow, level or volume of specified inland waters (ss. 21–23).

Pt II, Ch. 2—abstraction and impoundment licensing
— Role as licensing and enforcement authority for water abstraction and for water impoundment (*i.e.* dams, weirs, etc.) (ss.24–25)
    NB—Para. 20 of Sched. 23 to the 1995 Act makes transitional provision regarding such licences
— emergency power to restrict quantities of water used for irrigation spraying under abstraction licence (s.57);
    — duty in some cases to pay compensation where licence varied/revoked (possible indemnity from Secretary of State).
— Potential action for breach of statutory duty against NRA (now Agency) by person with a protected right (s.60).
— Right to challenge certain decisions of the Secretary of State (s.69).

Pt. III, Ch. 3—drought orders
— Power to apply to Secretary of State for ordinary or emergency drought orders (s.73) and to exercise powers granted thereby
— Duty to pay compensation for certain acts carried out under drought orders (s.79).

— Power to prosecute for breach of drought order provision (s.80).
— *NB*—Paras. 139–141 of Sched. 22 to the 1995 Act modify these provisions.

Subs. (1)(a)(ii)—control of pollution of water resources—Water Resources Act 1991, Pt. III
NB—The Secretary of State has the power to modify the water pollution provisions of the 1991 Act so as to give effect to European Community or international obligations (s.102). See also s.40 of the Environment Act 1995.

Pt. III Ch. 1—water quality objectives
— Duty to exercise its powers in relation to water pollution, so as to ensure, so far as practicable, that water quality objectives established by Secretary of State are achieved at all times (s.84).
— Duty to monitor water pollution and to consult with Scottish counterparts, for the purposes of carrying out its water pollution functions (s.84).
— Power to request review of any such water quality objectives (s.83).

Pt. III, Ch. 2—enforcement of water pollution law
— Power to prosecute for causing or knowingly permitting water pollution (s.85).
— Power to prohibit by notice certain discharges to water (s.86) and to prosecute for breach of such prohibition (s.85).
— Role as consenting authority in relation to applications for consent to discharge to controlled waters (s.88).
      NB: Para. 21 of Sched. 23 of the 1995 Act makes transitional provision regarding such consents.
— Power to consent, subject to conditions, to the removal of deposits from inland freshwaters, or the cutting or uprooting of vegetation in or near such waters, and power to prosecute such actions where carried out without, or in breach of such consent (s.90).

Pt. III, Ch. 3—pollution control and prevention powers
— Power (where provided for in regulations) to require any person who has custody or control of poisonous, noxious or polluting matter, to carry out works, or take precautions or other steps, to prevent or control entry of that matter into controlled waters (s.92).
— Role (where provided for in regulations) as consenting and enforcing authority in relation to *water protection zones* (s.93).
— Role as enforcing authority for *nitrate sensitive areas* (s.94).

Subs. (1)(a)(iii)—Flood defence (Water Resources Act 1991 Pt. IV Land Drainage Act 1991, Water Act 1989)
NB—The general flood defence supervision duty is now found in s.6(4) of the 1995 Act.
— Duty to have due regard to the interests of sea and other fisheries in exercising its flood defence powers (s.105(3));
— Duty to carry out surveys of the areas in which it has flood defence functions (s.105(2));
— Duty to carry out its flood defence functions under the Water Resources Act 1991 and the Land Drainage Act 1991 through regional flood defence committees (s.106). The flood defence committees continued or established under the Water Resources Act 1991 are replaced by committees established under ss.14–19 of the 1995 Act, but s.15(2) provides for transitional continuity of membership of the old and new committees.
— In relation to main rivers, the functions of drainage boards in relation to other watercourses (s.107), including:—
      — the functions of the NRA (now the Agency) which under the Land Drainage Act 1991 are exercisable by it concurrently with an internal drainage board;
      — any rights, powers, duties, obligations and liabilities of any drainage body transferred to it by a transfer scheme under s.108 Water Resources Act 1991;
      — power to give or withhold consent to the erection of certain structures in, under, over or designed to contain or divert a main river. (s.109);
      — power to alter or pull down such works and recover costs (s.109);
      — power to make arrangements with a navigation or conservancy authority for the transfer of functions and property to the NRA (now the Agency) or for the carrying out of works by it (s.111);
      — functions as a drainage board (Land Drainage Act 1991).

The amendments to drainage legislation made by ss.100 and 101 of the 1995 Act will be noted.

Subs. (1)(a)(iv)—land and works powers (Water Resources Act 1991. Pt. VII)
— Power (compulsorily or otherwise) to purchase or lease land or interests in land (ss.154–6, 168).
— Power to carry out or arrange for works, lay and maintain pipes, drains etc. (ss.156, 158–161), to recover costs (s.161) and to prosecute for or consent to interference with such works (s.176).
— Power to serve a works notice requiring anti-pollution works to be carried out and to prosecute for failure to do so (ss.161–161D, of which ss.161A–D have been inserted by the 1995 Act).
— Power to enter premises or authorise entry for enforcement purposes, carry out tests, take away samples, carry out experimental borings or other works and install monitoring apparatus (ss.169–172): but once the Agency's powers exercisable under s.108 of the 1995 Act in relation to its pollution control functions come into force, the s.169 powers are to be exercisable only for the purposes of its other functions: 1995 Act, Sched. 22, para. 165. The 1995 Act, Sched. 22, para. 166 restricts s.172 powers to exercise for the purpose of non-pollution control functions only.

Subs. (1)(a)(v)—Fisheries (Water Resources Act 1991, Pt. V, etc.)

Water Resources Act 1991
            NB: Each of the Secretary of State and the Minister of Agriculture, Fisheries and Food has the power to modify the NRA (now the Agency)'s fisheries functions under any enactment so as to give effect to EU or international obligations (s.116). See also s.40 of the 1995 Act.
— The general fisheries duty of the NRA (s.114) is now found in s.6(6) of the 1995 Act.
— Role as consultee in relation to the making of ministerial fisheries orders (s.115).

Sea Fisheries Regulation Act 1966
— pursuant to order, the powers of a local fisheries committee (s.18);
— power to appoint a representative to such a committee (s.2);
— fisheries byelaws enforcement where appointed (s.19)

Diseases of Fish Act 1937
— functions in relation to infected waters

Salmon and Freshwater Fisheries Act 1975
— bye-law making function (Sched. 3);
— enforcement function under the 1975 Act or for the protection of fisheries in any area (Sched. 3);

Salmon Act 1986
— enforcement function (s.32)
The amendments to fisheries legislation made by ss.102–105 of and Sched. 15 to the 1995 Act will be noted.

Subs. (1)(a)(vi): navigation, harbour or conservancy authority
The NRA inherited under the Water Act 1989 the functions that water authorities exercised under a variety of local Acts, and these functions are transferred to the Agency: their nature varies accordingly to the local Act in question.

Subs. (1)(a)(vii)—Navigation, harbour and conservancy functions

(Water Resources Act 1991, Sched. 2)
— Power to apply for an order transferring to it functions or property of a navigation, harbour or conservancy authority (see s.221(1) Water Resources Act 1991 for definitions of those authorities), or, with ministerial consent, to agree such transfer with the authority in question (para. 1).

Subs. (1)(a)(viii)—other functions assigned to NRA under any other enactment
Of particular note are:
— Role as statutory consultee under a range of legislation, including the planning process. The NRA's *Policy and Practice for the Protection of Groundwater* (1992) contains at

page 13 a useful list of its functions as consultee in relation especially to groundwater protection.
— Power (or duty if so directed) to agree exemption from charges due from abstraction licence holder in certain circumstances (ss.127–130 Water Resources Act 1991).
— The surviving information functions in Pt. VIII of the Water Resources Act 1991, in relation to registers, maps and the obtainment and provision of information (ss.188–208 Water Resources Act 1991).
— The power to make and enforce byelaws, and the duty to pay compensation in respect of certain fisheries byelaws (ss.210–212 Water Resources Act 1991).

Subs. (1)(b)—waste regulation
— the licensing of waste management activities, including inspections, compliance monitoring and enforcement (Part II, Environmental Protection Act 1990);
— the assessment of site completion, power to accept the transfer and surrender of site licences and the issue of completion certificates (1990 Act, ss.39 and 40);
— the registration of licensing exemptions (Waste Management Licensing Regulations 1994, reg. 18);
— the inspection of sites used for the recovery of scrap metal etc. which are registered as exempt from waste management licensing (1994 Regulations, regs. 17 and 18; Waste Management Licensing (Amendment etc.) Regulations 1995 (S.I. 1995 No. 288, reg. 20);
— the registration and regulation of waste carriers and brokers (Control of Pollution (Amendment) Act 1989, s.2; Controlled Waste (Registration of Carriers and Seizure of Vehicles) Regulations 1991; 1994 Regulations, reg. 20);
— functions in connection with the duty of care for waste (1990 Act, s.34);
— the regulation of the transfrontier shipment of waste including enforcement (Transfrontier Shipment of Waste Regulations 1994);
— enforcement action against unlicensed waste management (1990 Act, s.33);
— collecting fees and charges in respect of waste management licensing, the registration of carriers and brokers and the transfrontier shipment of waste;
— the provision of waste management advice and information, including the maintenance of public registers (1990 Act, Part II; Waste Management Licensing Regulations 1994; Control of Pollution (Amendment) Act 1989);
— the production of the Waste Disposal Plan (1990 Act, s.50; superseded by the waste strategy provisions of the 1995 Act, s.92: see the general note to that section);
— acting as statutory consultees in relation to proposals for development adjacent to landfill sites and former landfill sites.

Subs. (1)(c): waste regulation: residual COPA functions
By s.30(1) of the Control of Pollution Act 1974 ("COPA"), waste regulation functions for the purposes of that Act are as follows:—
— functions relating to disposal licences (ss.3–11);
— the removal of waste deposited in breach of licensing provisions (s.16);
— the giving of directions in relation to special waste, where provided for by regulations (under s.17 (s.17(1)(a)); and
— the supervision of activities authorised by such special waste regulations, recovery of cost and expenses and functions in relation to appeals against disposal authority decisions under those regulations (s.17(2)(b)–(d)).
This subsection transfers to the Agency all local authority functions in their capacity as waste disposal authorities under Part I of COPA. They include the old waste disposal licensing provisions which were only replaced when the new waste management licensing regime under Part II of the 1990 Act was brought into force on June 1, 1994. These functions have been transferred to the Agency as there may still be actions pending under the old legislation. Therefore, the importance of these transferred functions will become progressively less important with the passage of time and will become redundant when the last action under COPA is dealt with. The special waste controls in COPA, and the Control of Pollution (Special Waste) Regulations 1980 which were made under it, are far from being residual functions and run alongside the 1990 Act provisions. However, it is anticipated that by the time waste regulation is transferred the 1980 Regulations will have been supplanted by new regulations implementing the EC Hazardous Waste Directive 91/689/EEC: draft Special Waste Regulations 1995, to be made under the 1990 Act s.62.

Subss. 1(d)–(g): the Chief Inspector's functions
All of the functions of HMIP are transferred to the Agency as follows:

Subs. (1)(d): IPC
This subsection transfers to the Agency all HMIP functions as enforcing authority for processes prescribed under Part A of Sched. 1 to the Environmental Protection (Prescribed Processes and Substances) Regulations 1991 (S.I. 1991 No. 472 as amended, see Appendix 1) for integrated pollution control (IPC) by virtue of Part I of the 1990 Act.

Subs. (1)(e): radioactive substances
This subsection transfers to the Agency all HMIP functions under the Radioactive Substances Act 1993:
— the registration of the keeping and use of radioactive material on premises and the registration of mobile radioactive apparatus 1993 Act, ss.7 and 10)
— the authorisation of the disposal or accumulation of radioactive waste (1993 Act, s.16)
— the enforcement of controls over radioactive substances (1993 Act, ss.6, 9, 13–14, 17, 21–22, and 32)
— the maintenance of registers of registrations and authorisations (1993 Act, s.39).

Subss. (f) and (g): pre-1990 Act controls
These subsections transfer to the Agency all functions conferred on or delegated to HMIP by virtue of the Alkali etc. Works Regulations Act 1906 and Part I of the Health and Safety at Work, etc. Act 1974. The significance of these transferred functions will cease when the last process registered under the 1906 Act is authorised under Part I of the 1990 Act (see subs. (1)(d) above) and when the last action under the old legislation has been concluded.
— the registration of prescribed works (Alkali etc. Works Regulation Act 1906, s.9; Control of Industrial Air Pollution (Registration of Works) Regulations 1989 (S.I. 1989 No. 318))
— enforcement of 1906 Act controls by means of prohibition and improvement notices (Health and Safety at Work etc. Act 1974)
— maintenance of a register of prescribed works registrations (1906 Act, s.9; 1989 Regulations).

Subss. (1)(h) and (2)—the Secretary of State's functions
The following functions of the Secretary of State are transferred to the Agency:

(2)(a): radioactive substances
His power in England and Wales to dispose of radioactive waste where he is satisfied that it is likely for any reason that it will be unlawfully disposed of (Radioactive Substances Act 1993, s.30(1));

(2)(b): special category effluent
His supervisory and enforcement roles under the Water Industry Act 1991 in relation to the discharge of "special category effluent" to sewers, including:
— having questions relating to such effluent referred to him by sewerage undertakers prior to their giving consent to such discharges to sewer (s.120);
— reviewing agreements and consents for such discharges (ss.127, 130–131);
— being the determinant of appeals in relation to applications for consent to make such discharges (s.123);
— power to prosecute for breach of the legislation relating to special category effluent.

(2)(c) and (d): miscellaneous 1906 Act functions
— his enforcement role under the 1906 Act and s.5 of the Health and Safety at Work, etc., Act 1974. This role, although not his appellate function which is not transferred, was in practice delegated to HMIP.

(2)(e): sludge (Use in Agriculture) Regulations 1989 (S.I. 1989 No. 1263) functions
— inspection of a sludge producer's register;
— as recipient of certain information which sludge producers are required to supply;
— requesting a sludge producer to check the soil of agricultural land; and
— as enforcing authority for breach of the regulations (see further the note to s.37(1)(a), in which Viscount Ullswater's comments in Parliament in this connection are cited).

Transfer of property, rights and liabilities to the Agency

3.—(1) On the transfer date—
(a) the property, rights and liabilities—
(i) of the National Rivers Authority, and

(ii) of the London Waste Regulation Authority,

shall, by virtue of this paragraph, be transferred to and vested in the Agency;

  (b) any property, rights or liabilities which are the subject of—

      (i) a scheme made under the following provisions of this section by the Secretary of State, or

      (ii) a scheme made under those provisions by a body which is a waste regulation authority and approved (with or without modifications) under those provisions by the Secretary of State,

shall be transferred to and vested in the Agency by and in accordance with the scheme.

(2) The Secretary of State may, before the transfer date, make a scheme for the transfer to the Agency of such of—

  (a) his property, rights and liabilities, or

  (b) the property, rights and liabilities of any of the inspectors or chief inspectors mentioned in subsection (1) of section 2 above,

as appear to the Secretary of State appropriate to be so transferred in consequence of the transfer of any functions to the Agency by virtue of any of paragraphs (d) to (h) of that subsection.

(3) It shall be the duty of every body which is a waste regulation authority, other than the London Waste Regulation Authority—

  (a) to make a scheme, after consultation with the Agency, for the transfer to the Agency of such of the body's property, rights and liabilities as appear to the body appropriate to be so transferred in consequence of the transfer of any functions to the Agency by virtue of section 2(1)(b) or (c) above; and

  (b) to submit that scheme to the Secretary of State for his approval before such date as he may direct.

(4) Any body preparing a scheme in pursuance of subsection (3) above shall take into account any guidance given by the Secretary of State as to the provisions which he regards as appropriate for inclusion in the scheme.

(5) Where a scheme under subsection (3) above is submitted to the Secretary of State, he may—

  (a) approve the scheme;

  (b) approve the scheme subject to such modifications as he considers appropriate; or

  (c) reject the scheme;

but the power conferred on the Secretary of State by paragraph (b) above shall only be exercisable after consultation with the body which submitted the scheme to him and with the Agency.

(6) The Secretary of State may, in the case of any body which is required to make a scheme under subsection (3) above, himself make a scheme for the transfer to the Agency of such of the body's property, rights or liabilities as appear to him appropriate to be so transferred in consequence of the transfer of any functions to the Agency by virtue of section 2(1)(b) or (c) above, if—

  (a) the body fails to submit a scheme under subsection (3) above to him for approval before the due date; or

  (b) the Secretary of State rejects a scheme under that subsection submitted to him by that body;

but nothing in this subsection shall prevent the Secretary of State from approving any scheme which may be submitted to him after the due date.

(7) The Secretary of State may, at any time before the transfer date, modify any scheme made or approved by him under this section but only after consultation with the Agency and, in the case of a scheme which was approved by him (with or without modifications), after consultation with the body which submitted the scheme to him for approval.

(8) Schedule 2 to this Act shall have effect in relation to transfers by or under this section.

D<small>EFINITIONS</small>
"the Agency": s.124(1).
"functions": s.124(1).
"transfer date": s.56(1).
"waste regulation authority": s.56(1).

C<small>OMMENCEMENT</small>
Subss. 3(2)–(8): July 28, 1995 (S.I. 1995 No. 1983).
Subs. 3(1) came into force on April 1, 1996 (S.I. 1996 No. 186).

G<small>ENERAL</small> N<small>OTE</small>
This section, and Sched. 2 to which it gives effect (subs. (8)), deal with the transfer of property, rights and liabilities to the Agency. Department of the Environment Circular 15/95 *Transfer of Property, Rights and Liabilities from Waste Regulation Authorities to the Environment Agency* (August 29, 1995, ISBN 0 11 753170 7) gives guidance to waste regulation authorities in England: separate guidance is to be given by the Welsh Office to Welsh waste regulation authorities.

Property, rights and liabilities: These terms are not defined, but details of what they include are given in paras. 2 and 3 of Sched. 3. These paragraphs are summarised below in the discussion of Sched. 3, but of particular importance is the transfer to the Agency of the employers' rights and liabilities under certain contracts of employment: para. 3.

The Transfer Date: The key date, on which all transfers to the Agency of property, rights and liabilities take effect, is "the transfer date". The Secretary of State, by order under s.56(1), set April 1, 1996 as the transfer date: S.I. 1996 No. 234).
On the transfer date, by subs. (1) all property, rights and liabilities of the NRA and London Waste Regulation Authority (which bodies, when subs. 2(3) comes into force are abolished) are transferred to and vested in the Agency, as are such other property, rights and liabilities as are subject to a scheme made under this section.

Schemes of Transfer: Two kinds of scheme of transfer are provided for by s.3. Subss. 2(1)(d)–(h) transfer the various functions of the Secretary of State and of inspectors and chief inspectors to the Agency. Before the transfer date the Secretary of State may make a scheme for the transfer to the Agency of such of his and their property, rights and liabilities as appears to him to be appropriate in consequence of the transfer of those functions: subs. (2).
Subss. 2(1)(b) and (c) transfer waste regulation functions of waste regulation authorities (including the Greater Manchester Waste Regulation Authority and Merseyside Waste Regulation) Authority, which are disposal authorities with waste regulation functions) to the Agency. Each of these bodies is placed under a duty to make a scheme for the transfer to the Agency of such of its property, rights and liabilities as appear to it (after consultation with the Agency, and (subs. (4)) taking into account any guidance from the Secretary of State, including Circular 15/95) to be appropriate to be transferred in consequence of the transfer to the Agency of those functions: subs. (3). (It will be noted that these bodies are under a duty to make a scheme, whereas the Secretary of State is merely empowered to do so by subs. (2)). Circular 15/95 includes, at Annex B, a Model Transfer Scheme which is divided into Supporting Information and the Scheme itself which in turn divides into:
— rights and liabilities in respect of contracts of employment;
— property and rights and liability in respect of property;
— rights and liabilities under contracts for services to be provided to or by the authority;
— interests, right and liabilities to be created between the authority and the Agency; and
— a provision that all other (unspecified) minor items of property which the authority was accustomed to use in discharging its waste regulation functions shall transfer to the Agency.
Notably, Circular 15/95 speculates as to the descriptions of "special site" which are to be designated by the Secretary of State for the purposes of the contaminated land provisions inserted in the Environmental Protection Act 1990 by s.57 of the 1995 Act:

"at this stage the Department considers the following types of former landfill sites might be prescribed as 'special sites': sites which are designated as active gas-producing sites; sites which are generating leachate containing red list substances; and sites which were formerly licensed for the deposit of special wastes". (para. A15).

The significance of this in the present context is that responsibility for special sites rests with the Agency by reason of its relevant expertise. It is therefore suggested in the Model Transfer Scheme that the names of employees "who have been spending a significant proportion of their time carrying out functions on behalf of a district with respect to sites of [the] type described "or advising districts in this regard, be included where the authority considers that it would be appropriate for their contracts of employment to transfer to the Agency (Model Transfer Scheme, para. I.5)

Each body's scheme must be submitted to the Secretary of State by such date as he may direct, although he may nonetheless approve a scheme received after that date: subss. (3) and (6). Circular 15/95 indicated that for waste regulation authorities in England "the Secretary of State is directing [them] to submit their transfer schemes for approval no later than Friday December 1, 1995" (para. 3).

The Secretary of State may approve or reject the scheme, or (following consultation with the body in question and with the Agency) may approve it with modifications: subs. (5). Where he rejects it, or it is received after the date directed, he may himself make a scheme in relation to the transfer of that body's property, rights and liabilities: subs (6). Even once he has made or approved a scheme, he may modify it prior to the transfer date provided that he has consulted the Agency and (if the scheme had been approved rather than made by him) with the body in question: subs. (7).

Schedule 2: Subs. (8) gives effect to Sched. 2, which deals with transfers of property, rights and liabilities to the Agency. The Schedule falls into three parts, covering property and contracts of employment, the content of transfer schemes, and general provisions relating to transfers (whether or not pursuant to transfer schemes).

Schedule 2, Part I—Property, etc. and Contracts of Employments
By para. 2, property, rights and liabilities transferred include the following:—
— Those which would not otherwise be capable of being so transferred;
— Any (if specified in the relevant scheme of transfer) which are required between the making of the scheme and the transfer date;
— Property wherever in the world it is situated; and
— Rights and liabilities under enactments or the law of any country or territory (including the United Kingdom and any part of it).
By para. 3, employers' rights and liabilities under the contracts of employment of "qualifying employees" are transferred to the Agency. Criteria are set out which must be met for a person to be a qualifying employee. The person must be employed (either by the Civil Service or by a waste regulation authority) for the purposes of, or in connection with, functions which are being transferred to the Agency. In addition, that person's transfer into the employment of the Agency must be considered necessary or expedient by the Secretary of State (in the case of a civil servant) or (in the case of a waste regulation authority employee) by the waste regulation authority in question. Para. 3 goes on to make transitional provisions for the transfer of such contracts of employment, and for the termination of the employment of any qualifying employee who objects to becoming employed by the Agency.

In Parliament, Mr Robert Atkins, Minister for the Environment and Countryside, confirmed that

"the agency will, through secondary legislation, be designated as an administering authority for the local government pension scheme. That will allow all eligible employees to join the scheme, but we do not need the Bill to so designate the agency. The usual procedure of an amendment to the relevant statutory instrument, which will be subject to consultation with relevant parties, will be sufficient" (*Hansard*, HC, Vol. 262, col. 1027)

He went on to indicate that

"the agency will inherit a wide variety of terms and conditions of employment. It will undoubtedly wish to draw up systems of pay, grading, terms and conditions which are more consistent than those it inherits, but the legislation should not prevent the agency from adopting variations to take account of factors such as the job market" (col. 1027).

Schedule 2, Part II—Transfer Schemes
Transfer schemes may describe the property, etc., being transferred either inclusively or specifically or partly in one way and partly in the other: para. 4.

Where appropriate, the property need not be transferred outright: an interest in or right over it may be created in favour of the Agency, or it could be transferred subject to the creation of such right or interest in favour of the transferor. Equally, new rights and liabilities between the two parties may be created: para. 5.

Incidental, supplemental and consequential provisions may be made in transfer schemes, including provision for arbitration in the event of subsequent dispute between the parties as to the effect of the scheme in question: para. 6.

After a transfer scheme has come into force, the Secretary of State may by statutory instrument make an order modifying it, having first consulted with the Agency and, where the transferor under the scheme is a waste regulation authority, with that authority: para. 7. The order may make consequential, supplemental or transitional provisions. The statutory instrument may be annulled by a resolution of either House of Parliament.

Since the exercise by the Agency and the Secretary of State of their functions in relation to transfer schemes is to a significant degree dependent on information from HMIP and waste regulation authorities, it is the duty of the Chief Inspector and the waste regulation authorities to provide such information and assistance as they reasonably require: para. 8.

Schedule 2, Part III—General provisions regarding transfers: consideration, continuity, remedies and foreign property
Consideration may be provided by the Agency under a transfer scheme in relation to new rights, liabilities or interests created by the scheme, but no consideration may be provided in relation to the transfer (whether or not under a transfer scheme) of existing rights, liabilities or interests: para. 9.

To ensure that all relevant rights, liabilities and property is transferred (by a transfer scheme or otherwise) para. 10 provides that subject to contrary provision in a transfer scheme, all references to the transferor in agreements (written or otherwise) or documents are from the transfer date to be references to the Agency, and all agreements or transactions made by or affecting the transferor are to be treated as made by or affecting the Agency. Thus in particular all rights, powers and remedies existing in relation to the rights and liabilities in question are transferred to the Agency: para. 11.

Where legal proceedings in relation to any rights, liabilities and property which is being transferred would be subject to foreign law, both the transferor and the Agency are to ensure that their vesting in the Agency is effective under that foreign law. Until that point, such right and property, are to be held for the benefit of the Agency and such liabilities discharged by the transferor on behalf of the Agency: para. 12.

Principal aim and objectives of the Agency

4.—(1) It shall be the principal aim of the Agency (subject to and in accordance with the provisions of this Act or any other enactment and taking into account any likely costs) in discharging its functions so to protect or enhance the environment, taken as a whole, as to make the contribution towards attaining the objective of achieving sustainable development mentioned in subsection (3) below.

(2) The Ministers shall from time to time give guidance to the Agency with respect to objectives which they consider it appropriate for the Agency to pursue in the discharge of its functions.

(3) The guidance given under subsection (2) above must include guidance with respect to the contribution which, having regard to the Agency's responsibilities and resources, the Ministers consider it appropriate for the Agency to make, by the discharge of its functions, towards attaining the objective of achieving sustainable development.

(4) In discharging its functions, the Agency shall have regard to guidance given under this section.

(5) The power to give guidance to the Agency under this section shall only be exercisable after consultation with the Agency and such other bodies or persons as the Ministers consider it appropriate to consult in relation to the guidance in question.

(6) A draft of any guidance proposed to be given under this section shall be laid before each House of Parliament and the guidance shall not be given until after the period of 40 days beginning with the day on which the draft was so laid or, if the draft is laid on different days, the later of the two days.

(7) If, within the period mentioned in subsection (6) above, either House resolves that the guidance, the draft of which was laid before it, should not be given, the Ministers shall not give that guidance.

(8) In reckoning any period of 40 days for the purposes of subsection (6) or (7) above, no account shall be taken of any time during which Parliament is dissolved or prorogued or during which both Houses are adjourned for more than four days.

(9) The Ministers shall arrange for any guidance given under this section to be published in such manner as they consider appropriate.

DEFINITIONS
"the Agency": s.124(1).
"costs": s.56(1).
"environment": s.56(1).
"functions": s.124(1).
"the Ministers": s.56(1).

COMMENCEMENT
July 28, 1995 (S.I. 1995 No. 1983)

GENERAL NOTE

Background
This section started life, in the draft Environment Agencies Bill published by the Department of the Environment in October 1994, containing only provision for the Secretary of State and Minister of Agriculture, Fisheries and Food to give guidance to the Agency as to the appropriate objectives for it to pursue in carrying out its functions: such guidance would have to include guidance as to the appropriate contribution for the Agency to make towards the attainment of sustainable development, and the Agency would have to have regard to such guidance. At the Bill's Second Reading in the Lords, Viscount Ullswater, Minister of State for the Environment, described this as "the inclusion for the first time in English law of a duty in relation to sustainable development" (*Hansard*, H.L. Vol. 559, col. 1462).

These provisions raised significant concern (expressed, for instance, in the House of Lords by Lord Crickhowell and Viscount Mills (*Hansard*, H.L. Vol. 560, col. 1776, and Vol. 559, col. 1450)) at the scope of discretion left to the Government to determine the Agency's objectives and thus its approach to its functions, following enactment of the Act.

The Government therefore introduced, at the Lords Report Stage, amendments (equivalent to what are now subss. (1), (5) and (9)) introducing the Agency's principal aim and the obligation on the Government to consult before issuing such guidance and publish it once issued.

By the time the Bill entered the House of Commons on March 21, 1995, the Government had added further amendments (now subss. (6) to (8)). These provide the further safeguards, typically afforded in relation to statutory instruments, of Parliamentary scrutiny and an opportunity for either House to resolve within 40 days that the guidance should not be given.

The principal aim: subs. (1)
The principal aim relates to the Agency's contribution to the attainment of the objective of sustainable development. In moving the amendment to introduce the principal aim, Viscount Ullswater said that it:

> "seeks to meet the desire expressed by a number of noble Lords in Committee for a strategic purpose for the agency to be included on the face of the Bill. It incorporates within Clause 4 a new principal aim [which] is not to overrule the specific purpose of the various enactments under which the agency operates" (*Hansard*, H.L. Vol. 561, cols. 1620–1621).

What is meant by sustainable development, and the contribution considered appropriate for the Agency to make to its attainment, are discussed below in the note to subs. (3).

However, several points may be noted in relation to the principal aim:

— *Status of the principal aim*
The principal aim only applies "subject to and in accordance with the provisions of this Act or any other enactment". It can thus be seen as applicable only where the Agency has discretion in the exercise of its statutory duties, powers and other functions. The principal aim would appear for the same reason to be subject to any statutory purpose or objective specified for a given function. Thus, the principal aim may only be pursued in relation, for example, to the Agency's pollution control duties within the context of the statutory purpose for which powers are required by s.5 to be exercised.

Such discretion clearly exists where the duty in question is to "have regard to" or "take account of" a consideration (see, for example, s.7(1)(c) and, in relation to the national air quality strategy, s.81(1). See the General Introduction to this Part of the Act for a discussion of the term "have regard to". One can have regard to a consideration and in appropriate circumstances can properly act contrary to that consideration. It is likely, moreover, that even where the duty in question is "to further" a consideration, there will in practice be scope for discretion in the manner of exercise of one's powers in order to comply with that duty. In the exercise of discretion by the Agency its principal aim (and indeed its other objectives where relevant) would be applicable.

The significance of the word "principal" would, then, appear to be confined to the situation where the Agency is deciding whether to act so as to further its principal aim or another objective, but in the circumstances cannot act so as to further both. In that situation, the principal aim ought to prevail. Even this, however, could be disputed since the principal aim is subject to other provisions of the Act and its duty to have regard to guidance on its other objectives are other such provisions. It is submitted that to suggest that the principal aim is subject (by implication) to its subsidiary objectives leads to absurdity. The choice of the term "principal aim" is perhaps curious, however, in that the Agency has no other "aims" characterised as such: the others are "objectives".

It should be noted that, in contrast to the Agency, SEPA lacks a principal aim. For a discussion of SEPA's aims and objectives see the note to s.31.

— *Importance of guidance*
The principal aim is entirely dependent on guidance: if none were in force, the Agency's principal aim would be devoid of content. The role of such guidance is considered further below.

— *Nature of Agency's contribution*
The principal aim is not simply "so to discharge its functions as to make" the appropriate contribution to such development. Rather, the Agency must make that contribution through the protection and enhancement of the environment.

— *"Any likely costs"*
However, the Agency must take into account "any likely costs": this includes the likely costs to any person and to the environment (s.56(1)). It will be noted that, unless the principal aim is considered not itself to be a form of objective, the controversial "costs and benefits" duty imposed on both agencies by s.39 would appear not to apply to the Agency's pursuit of its principal aim, as that duty is expressed not to affect the pursuit of any statutory Agency objectives (s.39(2)). Thus, without the costs provision in this section, the Agency would not have had an explicit duty on the face of the Act to take account of costs in pursuing its principal aim. As Viscount Ullswater put it, in the absence of a statutory definition or judicial interpretation of "sustainable development", "the inclusion of the reference to costs is therefore intended to ensure that the principal aim includes explicit recognition of both sides of the equation to reduce the risk of challenge in the courts from anyone who might seek to argue that sustainable development is to be interpreted exclusively in environmental terms" (*Hansard*, H.L. Vol. 561, col. 1628). The relationship between the principal aim and the s.39 duty is considered further in the note to subs. (3).

— *"Environment"*
The definition of the environment as "all or any of the following media: land, water and the air" (taken from s.1(2) of the Environmental Protection Act 1990) does not include man or any other organisms which are or might be dependent on the environment.

As regards the aquatic environment, the principal aim will, together with other Agency objectives, determine what (under s.6(1)(b)) the Agency considers desirable in terms of the conservation of flora and fauna which are dependent on that environment.

As regards flora and fauna which are dependent on the non-aquatic (*i.e.* air and land) environment, the Agency's explicit concern in relation to the exercise of its functions generally appears to be restricted to those which are of special interest or natural beauty (s.7(1)(a)–(c)), excluded as they are from the principal aim.

Nevertheless, it is submitted that the notions of a cost to an environmental medium and the protection and enhancement of the environment can ultimately only be understood in terms of harm and benefit to organisms or ecosystems in or dependent on that medium.

— *"Taken as a whole"*
The principal aim relates to the conservation and enhancement of the environment "taken as a whole". In Parliament Viscount Ullswater, for the Government, explained this term as follows:

"we mean by that an integrated analysis of all the environmental media of air, land and water and the judgments should be taken in the round and be based on overall factors and should not be preoccupied by the minutiae of the detail" (*Hansard*, H.L. Vol. 561, col. 1630).

Were the phrase ever to be considered by a court to be ambiguous or obscure, then this explanation may be admissible in court to clarify the meaning of the term.

— *Role of guidance on the principal aim*
By subs. (4), the Agency need only "have regard to" guidance given to it under subs. (3). That is, the considerations in the guidance must influence its decision-making processes but it can, where other considerations are of sufficient importance, act contrary to the guidance: see further the General Introduction to this Part.

The implications of this for the Agency's principal aim are unclear. The principal aim is worded in such a way that its content is actually to be found in the relevant parts of the guidance (some of which relates not to the principal aim but to the Agency's other objectives). Yet if this is so, and subs. (4) is taken to indicate the status of the guidance in relation to the Agency, it follows that the Agency may by virtue of subs. (4) in appropriate circumstances act contrary to its own principal aim. The principal aim is, as is noted above, already subject to the other statutory provisions affecting the Agency.

This difficulty may be resolved by taking the view that, insofar as such guidance is expressed to relate to the Agency's contribution to sustainable development, the Agency is obliged (subject to the qualifications in the language of the principal aim which are considered above) to act in accordance with that guidance rather than merely to have regard to it, since it is the Agency's principal aim to do so.

Guidance on objectives and principal aim: subss. (2) and (3)
On October 13, 1994, the Government published a draft Management Statement for the Agency (revised December 1995). This non-statutory document contained a number of proposed main objectives for the Agency.

Similar main objectives appeared in section 2 of the draft *Outline of Scope of Guidance to the Environment Agency under Clause 4 of the Environment Bill*, which was published on January 17, 1995 (DoE News Release 010) in order to assist the House of Lords in its consideration of clause 4—a number of their Lordships had requested sight of such a draft.

On April 21, 1995 (revised December 1995) the Government issued a full draft of its proposed guidance, which was predominantly non-statutory but included at Appx. 1 draft statutory guidance under s.4. This contained at Appx. 1, para. 9, a revised set of proposed objectives:

(a) to adopt, across all its functions, an integrated approach to environment protection and enhancement which considers impacts of substances and activities on all environmental media and on natural resources;

(b) to work with all relevant sectors of society, including regulated organisations, to develop approaches which deliver environmental requirements and goals without imposing excessive costs (in relation to benefits gained) on regulated organisations or society as a whole;

(c) to adopt clear and effective procedures for serving its customers, including by developing single points of contact through which regulated organisations can deal with the Agency;

(d) to operate to high professional standards, based on sound science information and analysis of the environment and of processes which affect it;

(e) to organize its activities in ways which reflect good environment practice and provide value for money for those who pay its charges and taxpayers as a whole;

(f) to provide clear and readily available advice and information on its work;

(g) to develop a close and responsive relationship with the public, local authorities and other representatives of local communities and regulated organisations.

The key parts of the draft guidance are Chapters 3, 4 and 5 setting out the principles of sustainable development, the contribution which the Environment Agency is to make towards achieving sustainable development, and issues of costs and benefits (the draft guidance on costs and benefits is reproduced in full in the note to s.39). Although these are non-statutory the principles are reflected in the more condensed draft statutory guidance at Appx. 1. The guidance stresses that sustainable development does not mean having less economic development "on the contrary, a healthy economy is better able to generate the resources to meet people's needs, and new investment and environmental improvement often go hand in hand Nor does it mean that every aspect of the present environment should be preserved at all costs. What it requires is that decisions throughout society are taken with proper regard to environmental impact" (para. 3.3). Para. 3.8 of the draft contains one of the first explicit comments on the importance of natural environmental capital to be found in Government policy. The guidance points out that natural capital consists of both renewable and non-renewable resources and that the challenge of sustainable development is to find ways of enhancing total wealth while using common natural resources prudently, so that renewable resources can be conserved and non-renewable used at a rate which considers the needs of future generations. In this, the guidance points out that it is especially important to consider whether there is a risk of irreversible environmental effects and, if so, how significant they may be.

The guidance points out that the Government must take the broadest view of the action the United Kingdom needs to achieve sustainable development, domestically and globally, and that the Agency cannot itself achieve sustainable development but will have a crucial role to play in operating a regulatory framework so as to ensure that the development which it regulates is sustainable. The draft statutory guidance in Appx. 1, para. 11, indicates that it would be "appropriate" for the Agency to act (in summary) as follows:

— take a holistic approach to the protection and enhancement of the environment;

— take a long term perspective in considering sustainable development, seeking to take properly into account longer term implications and effects, particularly those which appear likely to be irreversible or reversible only at high cost over a long time scale, or which would raise issues of inter-generational equity;

— maintaining bio-diversity as an essential element of sustainable development, paying particular attention to its statutory obligations with respect to conservation;

— recognising, within the areas for which the Agency is responsible, the great scope for reconciling the needs of the environment to the needs of development through the adoption of improved technologies and management techniques by regulated organis-ations, discharging its functions where possible in partnership with business, including the encouragement of adoption of plans and management techniques such as BS7750 and the EU eco-management and audit regulation; and promoting environmental initiatives, high standards and high levels of understanding and knowledge of the best pollution prevention and minimisation techniques;

— recognising that the achievement of sustainable development will involve contributions from many different organisations and individuals and the desirability of maximising the value of the Agency's contribution to those wider developments, striving to develop close and responsible relationships with the public, local communities, regulated organisations, non-governmental organisations and local government; and

— recognising the importance of the availability of high quality information and advice on the environment, striving within the areas of its responsibility to become a recognised centre of knowledge and expertise and to provide and promulgate clear and readily available advice and information on its work and on best environmental practice.

On the issue of costs and benefits, the guidance suggests that the Agency should concern itself primarily with the costs and benefits of its actions for society as a whole, the effects on welfare of people and business, changes in the use of resources and impacts on the environment. The Agency should take into account the views of the Government's chief medical officer, impacts on individual companies and industry sectors and the distribution of costs and benefits across the economy. The Agency should develop practical procedures to ensure it meets the requirements of the duty to have regard to costs and benefits. Such procedures should include advice to staff on relevant techniques for assessing costs and benefits; on those cases where the Agency's discretion is limited by obligations arising from other duties, requirements or objectives; and on identification of circumstances in which detailed consideration of costs and benefits might be unreasonable.

In developing practical procedures, the Agency should ensure consistency with principles to be set out in new Government guidance on risk assessment and existing guidance on economic and policy appraisal. The way in which the Agency reaches its judgement should involve due rigour in all cases, but be proportionate to the implications in the circumstances of the particular case. Costs and benefits which are unquantifiable or which cannot readily be given monetary values should also be considered.

Status of guidance: subs (4)
The Agency is required to have regard to guidance given under subs. (2). This is the usual requirement in relation to guidance, and allows the Agency in appropriate circumstances to act contrary to the guidance, having had due regard to it. See the final paragraph of the note to subs. (1) above, however, as to the status of such of the guidance as it relates to the principal aim.

Unusually and by contrast, it will be noted that the enforcing authorities, including the Agency, for the contaminated land provisions in s.57, are required to "act in accordance with" some of the guidance provided for in that section.

Consultation: subs. (5)
It is submitted that the duties on the Ministers and the Agency under s.7 in relation to the formulation and consideration of proposals in relation to the Agency's functions can be argued to apply to the process of consultation required in relation to guidance issued under subs. (2).

Both Houses of Parliament will have the power to prevent any proposed guidance under subs. (2) from being issued, but as with statutory instruments they may not amend the proposed guidance.

Publication: subs. (9)
The draft Guidance states that "the final text of this document will be published".

General functions with respect to pollution control

5.—(1) The Agency's pollution control powers shall be exercisable for the purpose of preventing or minimising, or remedying or mitigating the effects of, pollution of the environment.

(2) The Agency shall, for the purpose—
    (a) of facilitating the carrying out of its pollution control functions, or
    (b) of enabling it to form an opinion of the general state of pollution of the environment,
compile information relating to such pollution (whether the information is acquired by the Agency carrying out observations or is obtained in any other way).

(3) If required by either of the Ministers to do so, the Agency shall—
    (a) carry out assessments (whether generally or for such particular purpose as may be specified in the requirement) of the effect, or likely effect, on the environment of existing or potential levels of pollution of the environment and report its findings to that Minister; or
    (b) prepare and send to that Minister a report identifying—
        (i) the options which the Agency considers to be available for preventing or minimising, or remedying or mitigating the effects of, pollution of the environment, whether generally or in cases or circumstances specified in the requirement; and
        (ii) the costs and benefits of such options as are identified by the Agency pursuant to sub-paragraph (i) above.

(4) The Agency shall follow developments in technology and techniques for preventing or minimising, or remedying or mitigating the effects of, pollution of the environment.

(5) In this section, "pollution control powers" and "pollution control functions", in relation to the Agency, mean respectively its powers or its functions under or by virtue of the following enactments, that is to say—
    (a) the Alkali, &c, Works Regulation Act 1906;
    (b) Part I of the Health and Safety at Work etc. Act 1974;
    (c) Part I of the Control of Pollution Act 1974;
    (d) the Control of Pollution (Amendment) Act 1989;
    (e) Parts I, II and IIA of the 1990 Act (integrated pollution control etc., waste on land and contaminated land);

(f) Chapter III of Part IV of the Water Industry Act 1991 (special category effluent);
(g) Part III and sections 161 to 161D of the 1991 Act (control of pollution of water resources);
(h) the Radioactive Substances Act 1993;
(j) regulations made by virtue of section 2(2) of the European Communities Act 1972, to the extent that the regulations relate to pollution.

<small>DEFINITIONS</small>
"the Agency": s.124(1).
"costs": s.56(1).
"environment": s.56(1).
"the Ministers": s.56(1).
"pollution control functions": subs. (5).
"pollution control powers": subs. (5).

<small>COMMENCEMENT</small>
Subss. (2) and (5) came into force on February 1, 1996, and the remainder on April 1, 1996 (S.I. 1996 No. 186).

<small>GENERAL NOTE</small>
This section introduces a distinction between the Agency's pollution control and non-pollution powers and functions, and makes general provision in relation to its pollution control functions. The same distinction is also employed in s.7 and (in relation to the national air quality strategy) in s.81(1). It is discussed further in the note to s.7. Pollution control powers and functions are defined here and in those sections by reference to a list of Agency functions: subs. (5).

Purpose: subs. (1)
By subs. (1) the Agency's pollution control powers are exercisable for the purpose of preventing or minimising pollution of the environment or remedying or mitigating its effects.
    The key term "pollution of the environment" is undefined: however, the term is defined in the Environmental Protection Act 1990 for the purposes of both Part I and Part II of that Act (in ss.1(3) and 29(3) respectively), and it is submitted that for the application of this subsection to the purposes of the Agency's pollution control functions under both of those Parts (IPC and waste regulation respectively), those definitions should apply. Each defines the term by reference to harm to human health or the health of living organisms.

IPC
The Agency inherits (by virtue of para. 46 of Sched. 22 to the 1995 Act) the similar duty imposed by s.4(2) EPA 1990 on HMIP in relation to its functions under Part I of that Act. The position is thus that the Agency's IPC pollution control functions are all exercisable for the purpose of preventing or minimising pollution of the environment, and such of those functions as are powers (rather than, for instance, duties) are additionally exercisable for the purpose of remedying or mitigating the effects of such pollution.

Waste Regulation
Authorities under both Parts I and II of the Environmental Protection Act 1990 (IPC and waste regulation, as far as the Agency is concerned) must discharge their functions under those Parts so as to fulfil the "relevant objectives" as defined in Sched. 4, Para. 2 to the Waste Management Licensing Regulations 1994 (S.I. 1994 No. 1056).
    Waste regulation authorities had no duty under Part II EPA comparable to that imposed on HMIP under Part I. As noted above, Part II of the 1990 Act contains a definition of "pollution of the environment".

Water Pollution
The NRA had no comparable duty in relation to its pollution control functions, although it has a power to serve works notices requiring, *inter alia*, the remedying or mitigation of any water pollution and to carry out such works itself: ss.161–161D Water Resources Act 1991 and nowhere in the legislation containing those functions is a definition of pollution of the environment to be found. Courts may look to the definitions in Parts I and II of the 1990 Act for guidance as to the interpretation of the term, although there is case law (see, for instance, *R. v.*

Dovermoss Limited [1995] Env.L.R. 258 (C.A.); *NRA v. Eggar U.K. Ltd.* Newcastle Upon Tyne Crown Court, June 15–17, 1992 (unreported) in the water pollution context as to the meaning of "polluting matter" in s.85(1) of the Water Resources Act 1991).

Radioactive Substances Control
There is no comparable duty on the regulator under the Radioactive Substances Act 1993 and no reference to pollution of the environment. Authorisations under that Act may be granted simply subject to such conditions or limitations as HMIP or the Minister "think fit".

Research and information: subss. (2)–(4)
An integrated approach to environmental protection requires accurate information on the often complex relationship between impacts on the different environmental media.
　Accordingly, the Agency has specific research and information duties in relation to environmental pollution:—
　　— to compile information on it (subs. (2))
　　— to carry out assessments (where required to do so) on its effect on the environment (subs. (3)(a))
　　— to report (where required to do so) on the available options for tackling it and its effects (subs. (3)(b)); and,
　　— to follow developments in technology and techniques for tackling it and its effects (subs. (4)). A similar duty had previously been placed on HMIP and local authorities in relation to developments in technology and techniques for preventing or reducing pollution from prescribed processes under Part I of the 1990 Act (s.4(9)). Now of course, a significantly wider range of technologies and techniques is required to be followed. The word "techniques", as contrasted with technology, is worthy of note: matters such as operator training and management systems are included as with the term in its "BATNEEC" context (Part I of the 1990 Act). The Government's draft Guidance to the Agency under s.4, discussed in the note to subss. 4(2) and (3), states that it should encourage knowledge and understanding, particularly in regulated organisations, of best available techniques not entailing excessive costs for the prevention and minimisation of pollution, including the efficient use of resources, such as energy, and the minimisation of waste (Appx. 1, para. 11(iv)(e)) adding that the Agency should "strive within its area of responsibility to become a recognised centre of knowledge and expertise, and to provide and promulgate clear and readily accessible advice and information on its work and on best environmental practice" (para. 11(vi)).
It will be noted that the subs. (2) duty is not only to facilitate the exercise of the Agency's pollution control functions, but also for enabling the Agency to form an opinion on the general state of environment pollution: it is in part on the basis of this opinion that the Agency's consultative role, in particular on policy matters such as the national air quality and waste strategies, can be anticipated to be exercised.

General provisions with respect to water

　6.—(1) It shall be the duty of the Agency, to such extent as it considers desirable, generally to promote—
　　(a) the conservation and enhancement of the natural beauty and amenity of inland and coastal waters and of land associated with such waters;
　　(b) the conservation of flora and fauna which are dependent on an aquatic environment; and
　　(c) the use of such waters and land for recreational purposes;
and it shall be the duty of the Agency, in determining what steps to take in performance of the duty imposed by virtue of paragraph (c) above, to take into account the needs of persons who are chronically sick or disabled.
　This subsection is without prejudice to the duties of the Agency under section 7 below.
　(2) It shall be the duty of the Agency to take all such action as it may from time to time consider, in accordance with any directions given under section 40 below, to be necessary or expedient for the purpose—
　　(a) of conserving, redistributing or otherwise augmenting water resources in England and Wales; and

(b) of securing the proper use of water resources in England and Wales; but nothing in this subsection shall be construed as relieving any water undertaker of the obligation to develop water resources for the purpose of performing any duty imposed on it by virtue of section 37 of the Water Industry Act 1991 (general duty to maintain water supply system).

(3) The provisions of the 1991 Act relating to the functions of the Agency under Chapter II of Part II of that Act and the related water resources provisions so far as they relate to other functions of the Agency shall not apply to so much of any inland waters as—

    (a) are part of the River Tweed;

    (b) are part of the River Esk or River Sark at a point where either of the banks of the river is in Scotland; or

    (c) are part of any tributary stream of the River Esk or the River Sark at a point where either of the banks of the tributary stream is in Scotland.

(4) Subject to section 106 of the 1991 Act (obligation to carry out flood defence functions through committees), the Agency shall in relation to England and Wales exercise a general supervision over all matters relating to flood defence.

(5) The Agency's flood defence functions shall extend to the territorial sea adjacent to England and Wales in so far as—

    (a) the area of any regional flood defence committee includes any area of that territorial sea; or

    (b) section 165(2) or (3) of the 1991 Act (drainage works for the purpose of defence against sea water or tidal water, and works etc. to secure an adequate outfall for a main river) provides for the exercise of any power in the territorial sea.

(6) It shall be the duty of the Agency to maintain, improve and develop salmon fisheries, trout fisheries, freshwater fisheries and eel fisheries.

(7) The area in respect of which the Agency shall carry out its functions relating to fisheries shall be the whole of England and Wales, together with—

    (a) such part of the territorial sea adjacent to England and Wales as extends for six miles from the baselines from which the breadth of that sea is measured,

    (b) in the case of—

        (i) the Diseases of Fish Act 1937,

        (ii) the Salmon and Freshwater Fisheries Act 1975,

        (iii) Part V of the 1991 Act (general control of fisheries), and

        (iv) subsection (6) above,

    so much of the River Esk, with its banks and tributary streams up to their source, as is situated in Scotland, and

    (c) in the case of sections 31 to 34 and 36(2) of the Salmon and Freshwater Fisheries Act 1975 as applied by section 39(1B) of that Act, so much of the catchment area of the River Esk as is situated in Scotland,

but, in the case of the enactments specified in paragraph (b) above, excluding the River Tweed.

(8) In this section—

    "miles" means international nautical miles of 1,852 metres;

    "the related water resources provisions" has the same meaning as it has in the 1991 Act;

    "the River Tweed" means "the river" within the meaning of the Tweed Fisheries Amendment Act 1859 as amended by byelaws.

DEFINITIONS
  "the 1991 Act": s.56(1).
  "the Agency": s.124(1).

"functions": s.124(1).
"miles": subs. (8).
"the related water resources provisions": subs. (8).
"the River Tweed": subs. (8).

COMMENCEMENT
April 1, 1996 (S.I. 1996 No. 186).

GENERAL NOTE
This section imposes on the Agency a range of duties in relation to its water functions, and defines the geographical extent of certain of those functions.
    The duties are all modelled on duties imposed on the NRA by provisions in the Water Resources Act 1991 which this section replaces, as follows:—
    — subs. (1) replaces s.2(2) of the 1991 Act (environmental and recreational)
    — subs. (2) replaces s.19 of the 1991 Act (water resource management)
    — subs. (4) replaces s.105(1) of the 1991 Act (flood defence)
    — subs. (6) replaces s.114 of the 1991 Act (fisheries)
The other subsections, (3), (5) and (7) relate to the geographical extent of the Agency's functions in relation respectively to water resource management, flood defence and fisheries. They replace subss. (4), (5) and (6) respectively of s.2 of the 1991 Act.

Environmental and recreational duties: subs. (1)
These duties, as under the 1991 Act, are without prejudice to the Agency's other duties under what is now s.7 of the 1995 Act. The duties require action from the Agency only to such extent as it considers desirable. In exercising such discretion, the Agency's objectives and principal aim under s.4 will apply. So will the relevant duties under s.7 in so far as its exercise involves the formulation or consideration of proposals for the promotion of the matters specified in this subs.
    The subs. (1)(c) duty, relating to the recreational use of inland and coastal waters, should be read in conjunction with the duty in subs. 7(4) which relates to the recreational use of water or associated land over which the Agency has rights of use.
    The term "chronically sick or disabled" is not defined in the Act. One source of definition which might be of some use in construing the term is the Chronically Sick and Disabled Persons Act 1970, which provides for the welfare of such persons. Section 28 of the Act provides for the terms, *inter alia*, "chronically sick" and "disabled" to be defined by statutory instrument, but the Secretary of State has not exercised that power. The Agency has a duty (which subs. 7(5) also imposes in relation to its duty under subs. 7(4)) to take account of the needs of persons who fit that description in determining the steps it should take in the performance of its duty generally to promote, to the extent which it considers desirable, the use of water for recreational purposes.
    Two aspects of the draft guidance to the Agency on its aims and objectives (revised December 1995, see note to s.4) 1995—see the General Note to Pt I of this Act) would appear particularly relevant to this duty:
    — the Agency's objective of developing a close and responsive relationship with the public and local communities (Appx. 1, para. 9 (vii)); and
    — the non-statutory guidance that the Agency should take into account the distribution as well as the absolute level of costs and benefits: "some options open to the Agency may impose particularly heavy costs on particular groups of people or companies or on certain parts of the environment" (para. 5.6(d)).
Taken together, these suggest that the Agency should seek to learn from sick and disabled people themselves, and from people working with them, what their needs are in terms of access and facilities and what costs would be imposed on them by the different options available to the Agency, before the Agency reaches its view on the desirable extent to which it should promote such recreational use.
    It will be noted that the subs. (1)(b) duty relates only to the aquatic environment. There is no comparable duty elsewhere in relation to flora and fauna dependent on other environments: the duties in subss. 7(1)–(3) below relate only to the formulation and consideration of proposals.

Subs. (2): Water resources management
Subs. (2) imposes a general water management duty on the Agency, subject to the strategic responsibility which still rests with the duty on the water undertakers under the Water Industry Act 1991, s.37, to maintain the water supply system by developing an efficient and economical system of water supply for premises in their area. The subsection gives the Agency considerable discretion, subject only to the requirement to act in accordance with directions of the Secretary

of State, in relation to the wide-ranging subject matter of its duty to conserve, redistribute or otherwise augment water resources (subs. (2)(a)) and secure their proper use (subs. (2)(b)). As a transitional arrangement, para. 2 of Sched. 23 to the Act provides that any directions given to the NRA for the purposes of s.19 of the Water Resources Act 1991 (which this subsection replaces) have effect after the transfer date (April 1, 1996) as directions given to the Agency by this subsection.

Subss. (4) and (5)): Flood defence
The NRA's flood defence functions are transferred to the Agency by subsection 2(1)(iii) and are summarised in the Note to that subsection. Subs. (5) specifies the geographical extent of the Agency's flood defence functions, and subs. (4) places the Agency under a general supervision duty in relation to all matters relating to flood defence. This duty is in addition to its other, more specific flood defence functions, and by the Water Resources Act 1991, s.106, it and all of those other functions are to be carried out through regional flood defence committees. Such committees are now provided for by ss.14–19 of, and Schedule 5 to, this Act.
The amendments to land drainage legislation made by ss.100 and 101 of this Act will be noted.

Subss. (6) and (7): Fisheries
The NRA's fisheries functions under a number of Acts are transferred to the Agency by subs. 2(1)(v) and are summarised in the note to that subsection. Subs. 6(7) defines the geographical extent of those functions and subs. (6) adds the transfer to the Agency of the NRA's duty to maintain, improve and develop a range of fisheries. The amendments to fisheries legislation made by ss.102–105 of and Sched. 15 to this Act will be noted, although not all of them relate directly to Agency functions.
It should be noted that, by subs. 105(3) of the Water Resources Act 1991, the Agency has a duty in the exercise of its flood defence functions (see Note to subs. (4)) to have due regard to the interests of fisheries, including sea fisheries.
Subs. (7)(c) was introduced as a Government amendment during the Bill's Third Reading in the Commons. Sir Hector Monro, the then Parliamentary Under-Secretary of State for Scotland, in moving the amendment, said that:

> "[The mouth of the Tweed is in England, and most of the river is in Scotland, but the Tweed Commissioners look after the whole river. With the Border Esk, however, which runs into the Solway, the mouth is in England and the rest of the river is in Scotland, but there has been a difficulty.
> "The Bailiffs who are the responsibility of the National Rivers Authority and are managing the river have not been able to take all the action they have wanted to take when operating in Scotland. When Scottish poachers are running, the bailiffs have had to stop once they have left the river. If we pass the amendment, the bailiffs could follow them up the banks to their motor cars and take appropriate action.
> "This will be a helpful opportunity to improve the policing of the river … " (*Hansard*, H.C. Vol. 262, col. 940). See also *Hansard*, H.L. Vol. 565, col. 1476 *per* the Earl of Lindsay.

The provisions of para.19 of Sched. 15 should be noted in this regard.

General environmental and recreational duties

7.—(1) It shall be the duty of each of the Ministers and of the Agency, in formulating or considering—
  (a) any proposals relating to any functions of the Agency other than its pollution control functions, so far as may be consistent—
      (i) with the purposes of any enactment relating to the functions of the Agency,
      (ii) in the case of each of the Ministers, with the objective of achieving sustainable development,
      (iii) in the case of the Agency, with any guidance under section 4 above,
      (iv) in the case of the Secretary of State, with his duties under section 2 of the Water Industry Act 1991,
    so to exercise any power conferred on him or it with respect to the proposals as to further the conservation and enhancement of natural beauty and the conservation of flora, fauna and geological or physiographical features of special interest;

    (b) any proposals relating to pollution control functions of the Agency, to have regard to the desirability of conserving and enhancing natural beauty and of conserving flora, fauna and geological or physiographical features of special interest;

    (c) any proposal relating to any functions of the Agency—

        (i) to have regard to the desirability of protecting and conserving buildings, sites and objects of archaeological, architectural, engineering or historic interest;

        (ii) to take into account any effect which the proposals would have on the beauty or amenity of any rural or urban area or on any such flora, fauna, features, buildings, sites or objects; and

        (iii) to have regard to any effect which the proposals would have on the economic and social well-being of local communities in rural areas.

(2) Subject to subsection (1) above, it shall be the duty of each of the Ministers and of the Agency, in formulating or considering any proposals relating to any functions of the Agency—

    (a) to have regard to the desirability of preserving for the public any freedom of access to areas of woodland, mountains, moor, heath, down, cliff or foreshore and other places of natural beauty;

    (b) to have regard to the desirability of maintaining the availability to the public of any facility for visiting or inspecting any building, site or object of archaeological, architectural, engineering or historic interest; and

    (c) to take into account any effect which the proposals would have on any such freedom of access or on the availability of any such facility.

(3) Subsections (1) and (2) above shall apply so as to impose duties on the Agency in relation to—

    (a) any proposals relating to the functions of a water undertaker or sewerage undertaker,

    (b) any proposals relating to the management, by the company holding an appointment as such an undertaker, of any land for the time being held by that company for any purpose whatever (whether or not connected with the carrying out of the functions of a water undertaker or sewerage undertaker), and

    (c) any proposal which by virtue of section 156(7) of the Water Industry Act 1991 (disposals of protected land) falls to be treated for the purposes of section 3 of that Act as a proposal relating to the functions of a water undertaker or sewerage undertaker,

as they apply in relation to proposals relating to the Agency's own functions, other than its pollution control functions.

(4) Subject to obtaining the consent of any navigation authority, harbour authority or conservancy authority before doing anything which causes obstruction of, or other interference with, navigation which is subject to the control of that authority, it shall be the duty of the Agency to take such steps as are—

    (a) reasonably practicable, and

    (b) consistent with the purposes of the enactments relating to the functions of the Agency,

for securing, so long as the Agency has rights to the use of water or land associated with water, that those rights are exercised so as to ensure that the water or land is made available for recreational purposes and is so made available in the best manner.

(5) It shall be the duty of the Agency, in determining what steps to take in performance of any duty imposed by virtue of subsection (4) above, to take into account the needs of persons who are chronically sick or disabled.

(6) Nothing in this section, the following provisions of this Act or the 1991 Act shall require recreational facilities made available by the Agency to be made available free of charge.

(7) In this section—

"building" includes structure;

"pollution control functions", in relation to the Agency, has the same meaning as in section 5 above.

DEFINITIONS

"the Agency": s.124(1).
"building": subs. (7).
"conservancy authority": s.56(1).
"functions": s.124(1).
"harbour authority": s.56(1).
"the Ministers": s.56(1).
"navigation authority": s.56(1).
"pollution control functions": subs. (7) and s.5(5).

COMMENCEMENT

April 1, 1996 (S.I. 1996 No. 186).

GENERAL NOTE

This section falls into two halves. Subss. (1)–(3) impose duties on the Agency and the Ministers concerned in relation to certain policy functions, and subss. (4)–(6) impose a duty on the Agency in relation to public recreational access to water.

Subss. (1)–(3): Consideration of proposals

These subsections impose on the Agency, the Secretary of State and the Minister of Agriculture, Fisheries and Food duties in relation specifically to their functions of formulating or considering proposals relating to the functions of the Agency.

Background

The duties in this section are closely aligned to the duties which sewerage undertakers have by virtue of s.3 of the Water Industry Act 1991, and are modelled, in modified form, on the duties imposed on the NRA and the same Ministers by s.16 of the Water Resources Act 1991 (which these provisions replace). Those s.16 duties were in turn modelled on those previously imposed on water authorities by the Water Act 1973 and the Wildlife & Countryside Act 1973/1981.

It should be noted however, that the duties do not apply solely to the Agency's water functions but to all of its functions which meet the description of formulating or considering proposals.

There are four main differences between this section and its Water Resources Act 1991 predecessor, other than the fact that references to the Agency replace references to the NRA:—

— *Subss. (1)(a) and (b)*

The former subs. 16(1)(a) of the 1991 Act imposed a duty on the Ministers and the NRA (subject to consistency with other enactments relating to NRA functions and, in the case of the Secretary of State, his duties under s.2 of the Water Industry Act 1991), to exercise any power conferred on them with respect to the proposals so as to further the conservation and enhancement of natural beauty and the conservation of flora, fauna and geological or physiographical features of special interest.

This duty now exists only where the proposals concern the Agency's non-pollution control functions: subs.(1)(a). Where the proposals concern the Agency's pollution control functions, the weaker duty to "have regard to the desirability of" such conservation and enhancement applies: subs. (1)(b).

The original draft Environment Agencies Bill (October 1994) contained the weaker, subs. (1)(b) duty for all Agency functions. The Financial Times commented that environmental groups were "universal in their condemnation" of what they saw as a weakening of the Agency's duty compared to the NRA's duty: "Lobbyists force change", November 19, 1994, p6. On November 18, 1994, the Secretary of State announced that the Bill had been amended to apply the stronger duty in relation to the Agency's non-pollution control functions: DoE News Release 650.

The fact that the weaker duty applies in relation to its pollution control functions apparently reflects the Government's view that it is conceptually flawed for a regulatory body on the one hand to have duties in relation to the licensing or authorisation of polluting activities (as the Agency does, in relation both to IPC and discharge to controlled waters), which will inevitably in some cases adversely affect environmental and recreational conservation and enhancement which, on the other hand, it has a duty to further. See for example H.C. Standing Committee B, 6th Sitting, May 11, 1995, cols. 196–198 *per* Mr Robert Atkins, Minister for the Environment and Countryside; *Hansard* H.L. Vol 560, cols. 805–806, *per* Viscount Ullswater, Minister of State, Department of the Environment.

It might with some justification be argued, however, that the qualifications applied by subss. (1)(a)(i) and (iii) would be adequate to reconcile this perceived conflict.

To provide further comfort to those who remained concerned about the new formulation, the Government assured the Commons Committee considering the Bill that "if the agency faciled against reasonable expectations to do what was right and reasonable to further conservation, we would not hesitate to use our powers to ensure that it did more": H.C. Standing Committee B, 9th Sitting, May 18, 1995, col. 285 *per* Mr Robert Atkins, Minister for the Environment and Countryside. These powers would include in particular the power to give directions to the Agency/SEPA under s.40 of the Act.

It will be noted that s.5 employs a distinction between pollution control and non pollution control powers (as opposed to the broader term "functions" used here).

— *Subs. (1)(a)*
Whilst this subsection, as indicated above, contains a duty couched in similar terms to its s.16 predecessor, the duty is subject to two new qualifications: subss. (1)(a)(ii) and (iii). These introduce a ministerial objective of achieving sustainable development, and make the Agency's duty subject to guidance it receives under s.4 relating to its objectives and its principal aim of making an appropriate contribution to the attainment of sustainable development. Sustainable development is defined nowhere in the Act (or indeed in English law) but its meaning is considered in the draft of the s.4 guidance which is discussed in the note to s.4. Interestingly, the Scottish Office's draft guidance to SEPA does contain a definition of the term: see the note to s.31.

— *Subs. (1)(c)(i)*
This duty equates to that in s.16(1)(b) of the Water Resources Act 1991, save that the word "engineering" has been inserted, (see the note to subs. 32(2). As regards the introduction of this term in relation to SEPA's equivalent duty, creating a duty to have regard, in formulating or considering proposals relating to any Agency functions, to the desirability of protecting and conserving buildings, sites and objects of engineering interest.

— *Subs. (1)(c)(iii)*
This creates a new duty to have regard, in relation to any such proposals, to any effect which they would have on the economic and social well-being of local communities in rural areas. This duty is significantly different from the equivalent duty imposed by subs.32(1)(d) on SEPA and the Secretary of State in relation to Scotland.

It should be noted that in subss. 7(1)(c)(ii) and (iii) and in subs. 7(2)(c) the phrase "effect which the proposal would have" (as opposed to "might have") is used. This suggests that a degree of certainty that the effect would follow is necessary in order for any duty to have regard to it or take it into account to exist.

Examples of functions of formulating or considering proposals are those of the Agency, Secretary of State and Minister in s.2 of the Water Resources Act 1991 in relation to the proposals for the revocation or variation of water abstraction or impoundment licences and their s.82(4) Water Resources Act 1991 functions in relation to the proposals for the establishment of statutory water quality objectives.

However, the key term "proposals" is undefined both in the 1995 Act and the Water Resources Act 1991. Thus, insofar as the Agency's role as statutory consultee, for example in relation to "special site" designation (s.78C(3) of the Environmental Protection Act 1990, inserted by s.57 of the 1995 Act), the national air quality strategy (s.80(6)(a) of the 1995 Act) or national waste strategy (s.92(1), inserting s.44A(5)(a) into the 1990 Act), can be construed as involving the consideration of proposals, then the duties in this section would appear to apply to such considerations.

Similarly, the Secretary of State's role in formulating those proposals, or indeed in preparing consultation papers, and the Agency's role in considering licence applications, could be argued to fall within this section. Indeed, that a wide reading of the term "proposals" was intended by the Government might be inferred from the remarks at the Bill's Second Reading in the

Commons by the Minister for the Environment and Countryside, Mr Robert Atkins: "Clause 7 [s.7] provides a specific duty on the agency to take account of conservation in exercising its function under integrated pollution control, for example, and waste management licensing for the first time ... Although the conservation considerations are ... relevant to the issue of water discharge consents, they do not override all other considerations": *Hansard*, H.C. Vol. 258, col. 117.

The duties in subs. (1) are expressed by subs. (2) to take priority over the duties in subs. (2). The latter duties are worded identically to those imposed on the Ministers and the NRA by s.16(2) of the Water Resources Act 1991.

Subss. (4)–(6): Recreational access to water
These subsections impose a duty on the Agency, which duty is qualified by requirements of reasonable practicability and consistency with certain other enactments, and is subject to obtaining the consent of the appropriate authority where navigation will be interfered with or obstructed. The duty (which closely parallels that imposed on water and sewerage undertakers by s.3(5) of the Water Industry Act 1991) is to ensure that water, or land associated with water, over which the Agency has rights of use, are made available in the best manner for recreational purposes (subs. (4)), taking into account the needs of chronically sick or disabled people (subs. (5)), but not necessarily free of charge (subs. (6)). The word "best" is potentially a very strong requirement, but it is qualified by the notion of reasonable practicability. As regards the term "chronically sick or disabled", the related duty in relation to the recreational use of inland and coastal waters imposed by s.6(1), and for a discussion of the implications of its parallel provision regarding chronically sick and disabled people, see the note to s.6.

In formulating or considering proposals relating to Agency functions, the Ministers and the Agency must (subject to certain qualifications) act so as to further, or have regard to the desirability of, or take account any effect on specified environmental or recreational matters.

Environmental duties with respect to sites of special interest

8.—(1) Where the Nature Conservancy Council for England or the Countryside Council for Wales is of the opinion that any area of land in England or, as the case may be, in Wales—

    (a) is of special interest by reason of its flora, fauna or geological or physiographical features, and

    (b) may at any time be affected by schemes, works, operations or activities of the Agency or by an authorisation given by the Agency,

that Council shall notify the fact that the land is of special interest for that reason to the Agency.

(2) Where a National Park authority or the Broads Authority is of the opinion that any area of land in a National Park or in the Broads—

    (a) is land in relation to which the matters for the purposes of which sections 6(1) and 7 above (other than section 7(1)(c)(iii) above) have effect are of particular importance, and

    (b) may at any time be affected by schemes, works, operations or activities of the Agency or by an authorisation given by the Agency,

the National Park authority or Broads Authority shall notify the Agency of the fact that the land is such land, and of the reasons why those matters are of particular importance in relation to the land.

(3) Where the Agency has received a notification under subsection (1) or (2) above with respect to any land, it shall consult the notifying body before carrying out or authorising any works, operations or activities which appear to the Agency to be likely—

    (a) to destroy or damage any of the flora, fauna, or geological or physiographical features by reason of which the land is of special interest; or

    (b) significantly to prejudice anything the importance of which is one of the reasons why the matters mentioned in subsection (2) above are of particular importance in relation to that land.

(4) Subsection (3) above shall not apply in relation to anything done in an emergency where particulars of what is done and of the emergency are notified to the Nature Conservancy Council for England, the Countryside

Council for Wales, the National Park authority in question or, as the case may be, the Broads Authority as soon as practicable after that thing is done.

(5) In this section—

"authorisation" includes any consent or licence;

"the Broads" has the same meaning as in the Norfolk and Suffolk, Broads Act 1988; and

"National Park authority", subject to subsection (6) below, means a National Park authority established under section 63 below which has become the local planning authority for the National Park in question.

(6) As respects any period before a National Park authority established under section 63 below in relation to a National Park becomes the local planning authority for that National Park, any reference in subsections (1) to (4) above to a National Park authority shall be taken as a reference to the National Park Committee or joint or special planning board for that National Park.

DEFINITIONS
"the Agency": s.124(1).
"authorisation": subs. (5).
"the Broads": subs. (5).
"National Park authority": subss. (5) and (6) and s.63(1).

COMMENCEMENT
April 1, 1996 (S.I. 1996 No. 186).

GENERAL NOTE
This section confers on the Agency duties modelled on those originally conferred on the NRA by s.17 of the Water Resources Act 1991, which it replaces.

It adds to the general environmental and recreational duties imposed on the Agency by ss.6(1) and 7 the extra requirement, where land falls into the categories identified in subss. (1)(a) and (2)(a), to consult with specified bodies (except in emergency: subs. (4)) before undertaking or authorising potentially damaging operations and works: subs. (3). As to the Government's view of what might constitute an "emergency", the commentary on the equivalent provision for Scotland (s.35(5)), should be noted.

Section 7(1)(c)(iii), alone in ss.6(1) and 7, is a new Agency duty not transferred to it in identical or modified form from the NRA. It relates to economic and social well-being rather than to environmental or recreational matters. It is thus expressly excluded from subs. (2)(a).

Transitional provision is made by subs. (6) for the period prior to the establishment of a National Park authority: until then its predecessor local planning authority is the notifier and consultee in its stead.

Codes of practices with respect to environmental and recreational duties

9.—(1) Each of the Ministers shall have power by order to approve any code of practice issued (whether by him or by another person) for the purpose of—

(a) giving practical guidance to the Agency with respect to any of the matters for the purposes of which sections 6(1), 7 and 8 above have effect, and

(b) promoting what appear to him to be desirable practices by the Agency with respect to those matters,

and may at any time by such an order approve a modification of such a code or withdraw his approval of such a code or modification.

(2) In discharging its duties under section 6(1), 7 or 8 above, the Agency shall have regard to any code of practice, and any modifications of a code of practice, for the time being approved under this section.

(3) Neither of the Ministers shall make an order under this section unless he has first consulted—

(a) the Agency;
(b) the Countryside Commission, the Nature Conservancy Council for England and the Countryside Council for Wales;
(c) the Historic Buildings and Monuments Commission for England;
(d) the Sports Council and the Sports Council for Wales; and
(e) such other persons as he considers it appropriate to consult.

(4) The power of each of the Ministers to make an order under this section shall be exercisable by statutory instrument; and any statutory instrument containing such an order shall be subject to annulment in pursuance of a resolution of either House of Parliament.

DEFINITIONS
"the Agency": s.124(1).
"the Ministers": s.56(1).
"modification": s.124(1).

COMMENCEMENT
April 1, 1996 (S.I. 1996 No. 186).

GENERAL NOTE
This section parallels s.18 of the Water Resources Act 1991, which it replaces. It gives to each of the Secretary of State and the Minister of Agriculture, Fisheries and Food the power to give and withdraw, by statutory instrument (subs. (4)), statutory approval to any code of practice which promotes desirable Agency practices in relation to specified environmental or recreational functions: subs. (1). Codes of practice which are approved under this section provide a mechanism for translating the Agency's general environmental and recreational duties into more specific requirements. Under its predecessor section of the 1991 Act, only one code of practice was approved, by the Water and Sewerage (Conservation, Access and Recreation) (Code of Practice) Order 1989 (S.I. 1989 No. 1152). Since the NRA's functions have been transferred to the Agency, this Code is applicable to the Agency's exercise of the relevant functions.

The Code states that the functions of the NRA and internal drainage boards and their management of their resources can affect in many ways the conservation of the environment, the preservation of public access to the countryside, and the provision of facilities for sport and other forms of recreation. In the process there are bound to be conflicting environmental, operational and recreational considerations which can rarely be reconciled by decisions taken solely in relation to individual projects. Consistent, cost-effective reconciliation is likely to be achieved through the preparation of land use and management plans, particularly for sites which are likely to be subject to competing uses and pressures. In carrying out these functions the NRA should ensure that channels for liaison and consultation with appropriate organisations and individuals are established and open at all times so that action can proceed speedily in appropriate cases. In relation to the NRA's functions of issuing abstraction and discharge licences, the Code advises that where it proposes granting licences for abstraction which would affect a site of special scientific interest, a scheduled ancient monument or a site of importance for conservation, it should consult the appropriate conservation bodies. Similarly, the NRA should be alert to circumstances in which steps to upgrade standards of effluent quality are required to avoid impact on sites of scientific interest, or other sites of importance to conservation. In particular where an SSSI is sustaining damage as a consequence of nutrient enrichment, to which sewage disposal is making a significant contribution, it should consider suitable remedial action.

Subs. (2): Status of approved codes
The requirement in subs. (2) is new. Section 18 of the 1991 Act expressly provided that breach of a code which was approved under it did not of itself constitute a contravention of any of the conservation duties now found, as regards the Agency, in ss.6(1), 7 and 8. The new position is that, in carrying out those duties, the Agency must "have regard to" such an approved code. See the General Introduction to this Part of the Act for a discussion of this term.

The 1991 Act provisions also stated that breach of such a code would not have given rise to any civil or criminal liability on the part of the NRA, but this protection has been removed, and no comparable provision appears in relation to the Agency anywhere in the Act. In principle, therefore, an action for breach of statutory duty could, if the general criteria for such an action were met, be brought against the Agency as a result of a failure on its part to have regard to the code, although a breach of the code would not of itself amount to a breach of statutory duty.

Subs. (3): Consultation
The Ministers must consult a number of bodies, including the Agency, before making an order under this section. In what is now subs. (3)(e), specific reference to consultation of sewerage and water undertakers has been removed. This latter change does not appear to be significant in practice: such undertakers may still, of course, be considered appropriate to consult and could before have been considered inappropriate to consult notwithstanding the specific reference to them.

Incidental functions of the Agency

10.—(1) This section has effect—
  (a) for the purposes of section 37(1) below, as it applies in relation to the Agency; and
  (b) for the construction of any other enactment which, by reference to the functions of the Agency, confers any power on or in relation to the Agency;
and any reference in this section to "the relevant purposes" is a reference to the purposes described in paragraphs (a) and (b) above.

(2) For the relevant purposes, the functions of the Agency shall be taken to include the protection against pollution of—
  (a) any waters, whether on the surface or underground, which belong to the Agency or any water undertaker or from which the Agency or any water undertaker is authorised to take water;
  (b) without prejudice to paragraph (a) above, any reservoir which belongs to or is operated by the Agency or any water undertaker or which the Agency or any water undertaker is proposing to acquire or construct for the purpose of being so operated; and
  (c) any underground strata from which the Agency or any water undertaker is for the time being authorised to abstract water in pursuance of a licence under Chapter II of Part II of the 1991 Act (abstraction and impounding).

(3) For the relevant purposes, the functions of the Agency shall be taken to include joining with or acting on behalf of one or more relevant undertakers for the purpose of carrying out any works or acquiring any land which at least one of the undertakers with which it joins, or on whose behalf it acts, is authorised to carry out or acquire for the purposes of—
  (a) any function of that undertaker under any enactment; or
  (b) any function which is taken to be a function of that undertaker for the purposes to which section 217 of the Water Industry Act 1991 applies.

(4) For the relevant purposes, the functions of the Agency shall be taken to include the provision of supplies of water in bulk, whether or not such supplies are provided for the purposes of, or in connection with, the carrying out of any other function of the Agency.

(5) For the relevant purposes, the functions of the Agency shall be taken to include the provision of houses and other buildings for the use of persons employed by the Agency and the provision of recreation grounds for persons so employed.

(6) In this section—
  "relevant undertaker" means a water undertaker or sewerage undertaker; and
  "supply of water in bulk" means a supply of water for distribution by a water undertaker taking the supply.

DEFINITIONS
 "the 1991 Act": s.56(1).
 "the Agency": s.124(1).
 "functions": s.124(1).
 "the relevant purposes": subs. (1).
 "relevant undertaker": subs. (6).
 "supply of water in bulk": subs. (6).

COMMENCEMENT
April 1, 1996 (S.I. 1996 No. 186).

GENERAL NOTE
This section confers on the Agency incidental functions modelled on those conferred on the National Rivers Authority by s.3 of the Water Resources Act 1991, which it replaces.
 The Agency's functions, conferred on it by statute, include powers and duties to act in certain ways. A number of statutory provisions confer additional powers to facilitate the Agency's carrying out of these functions. As a residual provision, s.37(1) of the Act confers on the Agency very widely worded incidental general powers, including the power to do anything which in its opinion will facilitate the carrying out of its functions.
 This section extends the range of functions for the purposes of which the Agency may exercise those powers, to include the functions listed in subss. (2)–(5). Because of their origin in the 1991 Act, the functions primarily relate to water: they are the protection against pollution of certain waters, reservoirs and underground strata, (subs. (2)), the carrying out of works with or on behalf of water or sewerage undertakers (subs. (3)), the provision of supplies of water in bulk (subs. (4)), and the provision of housing and recreation grounds for Agency employees (subs. 5)). These correspond to subss. (2), (4), (5) and (6) respectively of s.3 of the 1991 Act. Subs. 3(3) of the 1991 Act, which conferred the function of furthering research into matters relating to the functions of the NRA or of water or sewerage undertakers, will not apply to the Agency as it does not appear in this section.
 As an example of the effect of this section, subs. (5) provides that the functions of the Agency shall be taken to include the provision of housing for Agency employees: this allows the s.37(1)(b) power to acquire land to be exercised for that purpose.

Advisory committees

Advisory committee for Wales

 11.—(1) The Secretary of State shall establish and maintain a committee for advising him with respect to matters affecting, or otherwise connected with, the carrying out in Wales of the Agency's functions.
 (2) The committee shall consist of such persons as may from time to time be appointed by the Secretary of State.
 (3) The committee shall meet at least once a year.
 (4) The Secretary of State may pay to the members of the committee such sums by way of reimbursement (whether in whole or in part) for loss of remuneration, for travelling expenses and for other out-of-pocket expenses as he may determine.

DEFINITIONS
 "the Agency": s.124(1).
 "functions": s.124(1).

COMMENCEMENT
April 1, 1996 (S.I. 1996 No. 186).

GENERAL NOTE
Sections 11–13 provide for various advisory committees.

Advisory Committee for Wales
This section provides for an advisory committee to meet at least once a year (subs. (3)) and advise the Secretary of State on the carrying out in Wales of the Agency's functions. Reference in this section to the Secretary of State is to the Secretary of State for Wales. This Committee is to be distinguished from the Environmental Protection Advisory Committee for Wales, established under s.12, which advises the Agency rather than the Secretary of State.

Background

The committee established by this section is to carry out a similar role to that previously carried out in relation to the NRA's functions in Wales by a committee under s.6 of the 1991 Act, which this section replaces.

As the Environment Bill passed through Parliament, the argument that there should be a separate Agency for Wales, as there is for Scotland, was raised on more than one occasion. In the debate in the House of Lords on an amendment to this effect tabled by Lord Prys-Davies (*Hansard*, H.L. Vol. 560, cols. 585–605), two former Secretaries of State for Wales, Lord Cledwyn of Penthos and Lord Crickhowell disagreed on the question. The former argued that a separate Welsh Agency could be combined sensibly with the Countryside Council for Wales and that environmental protection in Wales is "the duty and privilege of the Welsh people and, therefore, of a Welsh agency."

The latter opposed the amendment primarily on two grounds:

First, that "the rivers of Wales do not, as they do on the whole rather conveniently in the Scottish context, flow along and apart from the national boundary. They happen to cross the boundary" (*Hansard*, H.L. Vol. 560, col. 592). Therefore integrated management, in his view, requires one Agency.

Secondly, to duplicate the specialist skill and expertise developed by the NRA and other constituent elements of the Agency "would be a shocking waste of resources" (col. 593).

In the same debate (col. 603), Viscount Ullswater, Minister of State, Department of the Environment, set the committee envisaged by this section into the context of other provisions. He indicated that the Secretary of State for Wales

> "... will be responsible for setting the policy framework within which the environment Agency will discharge its functions in Wales and the Agency will report to him on its operations in Wales. There will also be arrangements for Welsh Office Ministers to have an input into the policy and the corporate planning processes of the agency, and these will be defined in a memorandum of understanding between the agency and the Welsh Office. My noble friend will be responsible also for the appointment of one member to the agency board [The first appointee was Professor Ronald Edwards: see the Note to s.1] and the Welsh interests will be further protected by the existence of the Advisory Committee for Wales. [*i.e.* the Committee established by this section.] That committee will advise my right honourable friend on the issues relating to the agency's activities in the principality and inform his input into the agency's corporate planning process.
>
> There will be an environment protection advisory committee for the Welsh region [see s.12(6) below] which will advise the agency itself on the specific needs of Wales and matters of particular relevance to its operations in Wales. The chairman of that committee will be appointed by my right honourable friend the Secretary of State for Wales, he will also approve the membership scheme prepared by the agency for its Welsh region and in doing so will ensure that its composition reflects a representative balance of interests. [s.12(2)]. The N.R.A. was set up on an England and Wales basis and the arrangements for the authority to take the needs of Wales fully into account have been very successful."

Viscount Ullswater could have added that by s.13(5) there is to be a regional fisheries advisory committee for a region consisting wholly or mainly of, or of most of Wales.

Environment protection advisory committees

12.—(1) It shall be the duty of the Agency—
  (a) to establish and maintain advisory committees, to be known as Environment Protection Advisory Committees, for the different regions of England and Wales;
  (b) to consult the advisory committee for any region as to any proposals of the Agency relating generally to the manner in which the Agency carries out its functions in that region; and
  (c) to consider any representations made to it by the advisory committee for any region (whether in response to consultation under paragraph (b) above or otherwise) as to the manner in which the Agency carries out its functions in that region.

(2) The advisory committee for any region shall consist of—
  (a) a chairman appointed by the Secretary of State; and
  (b) such other members as the Agency may appoint in accordance with the provisions of the approved membership scheme for that region.

(3) In appointing the chairman of any advisory committee, the Secretary of State shall have regard to the desirability of appointing a person who has experience of, and has shown capacity in, some matter relevant to the functions of the committee.

(4) The members of advisory committees appointed by virtue of subsection (2)(b) above—

(a) must not be members of the Agency; but
(b) must be persons who appear to the Agency to have a significant interest in matters likely to be affected by the manner in which the Agency carries out any of its functions in the region of the advisory committee in question.

(5) The duty imposed by subsection (1)(a) above to establish and maintain advisory committees is a duty to establish and maintain an advisory committee for each area which the Agency considers it appropriate for the time being to regard as a region of England and Wales for the purposes of this section.

(6) It shall be the duty of the Agency, in determining the regions for which advisory committees are established and maintained under this section, to ensure that one of those regions consists wholly or mainly of, or of most of, Wales.

(7) For the purposes of this section, functions of the Agency which are carried out in any area of Scotland, or of the territorial sea, which is adjacent to any region for which an advisory committee is maintained, shall be regarded as carried out in that region.

(8) Schedule 3 to this Act shall have effect with respect to advisory committees.

(9) In this section—

"advisory committee" means an advisory committee under this section;
"approved membership scheme" means a scheme, as in force for the time being, prepared by the Agency and approved (with or without modification) by the Secretary of State under Schedule 3 to this Act which makes provision with respect to the membership of the advisory committee for a region.

DEFINITIONS
"advisory committee": subs. (9).
"the Agency": s.124(1).
"approved membership scheme": subs. (9).
"functions": s.124(1).

COMMENCEMENT
April 1, 1996 (S.I. 1996 No. 186).

GENERAL NOTE
Sections 11–13 provide for various advisory committees.

This section provides for the establishment of regional Environment Protection Advisory Committees (EPACs) to advise the Agency on the exercise of its functions, and gives effect to Sched. 3 which makes provision in relation to such EPACs. It is closely modelled on existing provisions in s.7 of the Water Resources Act 1991 (which this section replaces) for regional rivers advisory committees to advise the NRA on the exercise of its functions in the various regions, but the EPACs will advise in relation to all Agency functions.

Waste regulation authorities, which prior to the advent of the Agency have been local authorities, have been advised by non-statutory regional advisory bodies such as the South East Waste Regulation Advisory Committee. There has been no such arrangement on a regional basis, statutory or otherwise, in relation to the exercise by HMIP of its functions.

Subss. (1)–(2): EPACs
EPACs are to be established and consulted by the Agency, and any representations made to the Agency by an EPAC in relation to the exercise of the Agency's functions in the region in question must be considered by the Agency (subs. (1)). However, unlike the previous provisions in s.7 of the 1991 Act, under which the NRA had sole discretion over the

appointment of a committee's members and chairman, the Secretary of state appoints the chairman in accordance with subs. (3) and the Agency's scheme for appointing the other members requires the Secretary of State's approval.

It may be noted that the proposals put to EPACs by the Agency would appear to be proposals to which the duties in s.7 apply.

Subss. (3) and (4): Committee Members
No member of the Agency may also be a member of an EPAC. Members must appear to the Agency to have a significant interest in the relevant matters (in s.7 of the 1991 Act the element of significance was absent), and the Secretary of State must have regard, in appointing the chairman, to the desirability of his having experience and capacity in such matters.

Subss. (5) and (6): Regions
The Agency must appoint an EPAC for each area which it considers to be a region, and one such region must consist wholly or mainly of Wales, or be most of Wales.

Viscount Ullswater's description in Parliament of the specific provisions for Wales, such as subs. (6), is quoted in the Note to s.11. In particular, for the Wales EPAC, references in subss. (2) and (3) to the Secretary of State are references to the Secretary of State for Wales.

Schedule 3
Para. 2 of Sched. 3 makes it the duty of the Agency to prepare a Membership Scheme for each region and submit it to the Secretary of State for approval: each such scheme must identify bodies and persons with a significant interest in the Agency's functions and activities in the region in question, and must provide for the EPAC to reflect those interests. The Government has indicated that "experience of business will be an important contribution for the Agency to take into account": Advisory Committee on Business and the Environment (ACBE), Fifth Progress Report (July 1995).

Para. 3 requires the Agency to publish its proposed scheme when it is submitted to the Secretary of State for approval, so that people may make representations to the Secretary of State. The Agency must also submit a statement of the Agency's justification of the scheme and supporting evidence; however, it need not publish these.

The Secretary of State may approve the scheme, reject it or approve it in modified form: para. 3(4). When the scheme is approved, the Agency must publicise it to interested parties: para. 3(5).

The Agency may (and, if so directed, must) vary the scheme in accordance with the same procedures as apply to the original preparation of a scheme: para. 4.

Before actually appointing a member, the Agency must consult at least the bodies and persons identified in the scheme under para. 2(2) as having a significant interest: para. 5.

Provision is made for EPAC proceedings to be valid notwithstanding a number of specified problems para. 6), and for remuneration of various kinds to the chairman and members of an EPAC (para. 7).

Regional and local fisheries advisory committees

13.—(1) It shall be the duty of the Agency—
> (a) to establish and maintain advisory committees of persons who are not members of the Agency but appear to it to be interested in salmon fisheries, trout fisheries, freshwater fisheries or eel fisheries in the different parts of the controlled area; and
> (b) to consult those committees as to the manner in which the Agency is to perform its duty under section 6(6) above.

(2) If the Agency, with the consent of the Ministers, so determines, it shall also be under a duty to consult those committees, or such of them as may be specified or described in the determination, as to—
> (a) the manner in which it is to perform its duties under or by virtue of such of the enactments relating to recreation, conservation or navigation as may be the subject of the determination, or
> (b) such matters relating to recreation, conservation or navigation as may be the subject of the determination.

(3) Where, by virtue of subsection (2) above, the Agency is under a duty to consult those committees or any of them, there may be included among the members of the committees in question persons who are not members of the Agency but who appear to it to be interested in matters—

(a) likely to be affected by the manner in which it performs the duties to which the determination in question relates, or

(b) which are the subject of the determination,

if the Ministers consent to the inclusion of persons of that description.

(4) The duty to establish and maintain advisory committees imposed by subsection (1) above is a duty to establish and maintain—

(a) a regional advisory committee for each such region of the controlled area as the Agency considers it appropriate for the time being to regard as a region of that area for the purposes of this section; and

(b) such local advisory committees as the Agency considers necessary to represent—

(i) the interests referred to in subsection (1)(a) above, and

(ii) where persons may be appointed members of those committees by virtue of subsection (3) above by reference to any such interests as are mentioned in that subsection, the interests in question,

in the different parts of each such region.

(5) It shall be the duty of the Agency in determining the regions for which regional advisory committees are established and maintained under this section to ensure that one of those regions consists (apart from territorial waters) wholly or mainly of, or of most of, Wales.

(6) In addition to any members appointed under the foregoing provisions of this section, there shall, in the case of each regional advisory committee established and maintained under this section, also be a chairman appointed—

(a) by the Secretary of State, in the case of the committee established and maintained for the region described in subsection (5) above; or

(b) by the Minister, in any other case.

(7) There shall be paid by the Agency—

(a) to the chairman of any regional or local advisory committee established and maintained under this section such remuneration and such travelling and other allowances; and

(b) to any other members of that committee such sums by way of reimbursement (whether in whole or in part) for loss of remuneration, for travelling expenses or for any other out-of-pocket expenses,

as may be determined by one of the Ministers.

(8) In this section "the controlled area" means the area specified in section 6(7) above in respect of which the Agency carries out functions under section 6(6) above and Part V of the 1991 Act.

DEFINITIONS

"the Agency": s.124(1).
"controlled area": subs. (8).
"the Minister": s.56(1).
"the Ministers": s.56(1).

COMMENCEMENT
April 1, 1996 (S.I. 1996 No. 186).

GENERAL NOTE
Sections 11–13 provide for various advisory committees.

This section requires the Agency to establish and consult regional and (where considered necessary—subs. (4)(b)) local *fisheries advisory committees*. The section is modelled on s.8 of the Water Resources Act 1991 which established such committees for the NRA, but modifies those provisions in three ways:

— The duty is to consult regional and local (*i.e.*, sub-regional) committees not only (as previously) in relation to the Agency's fisheries duties (subs. (1)(b)) but also, if it so

determines and if the Ministers consent, in relation to the exercise of its recreation, conservation or navigation functions (subs. (2)).
— The chairman of the Welsh committee required by subs. (5) is to be appointed by the Secretary of State for Wales, and the Minister of Agriculture, Fisheries and Food appoints the chairman of the other committees including, it would seem, local committees established in Wales: subs. (6). Previously the chairman for every committee, like the members, had been an NRA appointee.
— Remuneration of chairmen and members of the Committees, whilst still determined by the Ministers, no longer requires Treasury consent: s.7.

The functions of these committees other than as consultees under subss. (1) and (2) are not precisely spelt out. In practice the predecessor committees established under s.8 Water Resources Act often exercised considerable delegated powers, such as setting fishing licence charges and promoting bye-laws. Whether this will continue, and even (as a result of subs. (2)) be extended beyond fisheries matters to recreation, conservation or navigation matters, remains to be seen.

Subss. (2) and (3): Matters other than fisheries
The formal nature of the process by which the Agency may consult the committees on matters other than its exercise of its fisheries duties should be noted:
— the Agency must make a formal determination to do so, which the Ministers must both approve: subs. (2);
— Although the Agency is under no duty to make a determination, once a determination is made, the Agency has a duty to consult in accordance with it.
— the determination must specify which of the committees which have been established are to be consulted, and on what: (subs. (2)). Consultation with different committees on different matters does not appear to be ruled out, nor does the making of more than one concurrent determination relating to different committees or matters.
— the subject matter of the determination, and therefore of the consultation, is not limited to the performance of the Agency's duties, but may include other matters: subs. (2)(b). This appears to create the curious situation where the Agency may consult with fisheries committees more widely in relation to navigation, recreation or conservation than it can (under subs. (1)(b)) in relation to fisheries.
— Membership of committees which, by virtue of a determination, the Agency must consult on non-fisheries matters, may (but need not) include persons who are interested in those matters: subs. (3). This contrasts with the requirement, in subs. (1)(a), that the committees must comprise persons interested in fisheries.

Subs. (5): Wales
The Agency's discretion to determine the areas which, for the purposes of this section, it considers appropriate for the time being to consider as a region (subs. (4)(a)) is constrained by subs. (5): one such region must consist (apart from territorial waters) wholly or mainly of, or of most of, Wales.

Flood defence committees

Regional flood defence committees

14.—(1) There shall be committees, known as regional flood defence committees, for the purpose of carrying out the functions which fall to be carried out by such committees by virtue of this Act and the 1991 Act.

(2) Subject to Schedule 4 to this Act (which makes provision for the alteration of the boundaries of and the amalgamation of the areas of regional flood defence committees)—

    (a) there shall be a regional flood defence committee for each of the areas for which there was an old committee immediately before the transfer date; but

    (b) where under section 165(2) or (3) of the 1991 Act any function of the Agency falls to be carried out at a place beyond the seaward boundaries of the area of any regional flood defence committee, that place shall be assumed for the purposes of this Act and the 1991 Act to be within the area of the regional flood defence committee to whose area the area of sea where that place is situated is adjacent.

(3) The Agency shall maintain a principal office for the area of each regional flood defence committee.

(4) In this section "old committee" means a regional flood defence committee for the purposes of section 9 of the 1991 Act.

DEFINITIONS
"the 1991 Act": s.56(1).
"the Agency": s.124(1).
"function": s.124(1).
"old committee": subs. (9).
"regional flood defence committee": subs. (1).

COMMENCEMENT
April 1, 1996 (S.I. 1996 No. 186).

GENERAL NOTE

Flood defence and regional flood defence committees (ss.14–19)
Sections 14 to 19, and Sched. 5, all deal with flood defence committees.

Section 14 establishes regional flood defence committees, s.15 determines their composition and s.16 provides a mechanism for changing their composition. Section 14 also gives effect to Sched. 4, which makes provisions in relation to the boundaries of regional flood defence committees.

Section 17 allows a regional flood defence committee to prepare and submit to the Agency a local flood defence scheme for any district within its region, establishing and determining the functions of a local flood defence committee for that district. Section 18 determines the composition of such local committees.

Section 19 gives effect to Sched. 5, which makes provisions in relation to the membership and proceedings of both regional and local flood defence committees.

The NRA's flood defence functions and its general supervision duty in relation to all matters relating to flood defence are all transferred to the Agency by this Act (by subss. 2(1)(iii) and 6(4)—see subs. 6(5) for the geographical extent of these functions and the General Note to subs. 2(1)(iii) for a summary of them).

Section 106 of the Water Resources Act 1991 requires the Agency to arrange for all of its functions relating to flood defence under that Act and the Land Drainage Act 1991 to be carried out by regional flood defence committees.

These committees have semi-autonomous powers and quasi-independent status from the Agency, but at the same time essentially act as its agent in carrying out its flood defence functions subject to its general supervision.

The Agency may only go beyond its general supervisory relationship with such committees, and give them directions as to the carrying out of their functions, where their manner of doing so appears to the Agency likely materially to affect its management of water for non-flood defence purposes (s.106(3) Water Resources Act 1991). A committee must comply with such a direction.

Regional and local flood defence committees are thus very different from the various advisory committees provided for by ss.11–13 above, in that they are executive bodies. The provisions of ss.14–19 reflect this. In particular they give a significant role to local authorities, both in the determination of the composition of regional and local flood defence committees (subss. 15(3)(b), 16(7), 18(4)(c) and 18(5)) and as consultees in the preparation of local flood defence schemes which create local flood defence committees (subs. 17(4)(a)). Also, Sched. 4 contains tight procedural safeguards on the amalgamation of regions.

Section 14: Regional Flood Defence Committees
The Water Resources Act 1991 provided (subs. 9(1)) that there would continue to be the regional flood defence committees which were established under previous legislation. This section takes a different approach: on the transfer date which the Secretary of State will determine by order, new regional flood defence committees are to replace the existing ones (subs. (2)).

Although Sched. 4 provides a procedure for the amalgamation of regions and the alteration of their boundaries, which is summarised in the Note to s.19 below, without such procedures being undertaken regions and boundaries are to be the same as previously.

As previously (subs. 9(2) of the 1991 Act), the area of a regional flood defence committee includes any place which is adjacent to it but is beyond its seaward boundaries, if the Agency has to exercise its functions under subss. 165(2) or (3) of the 1991 Act in that place. Subs. 165(2) and (3) of that Act give the Agency power to carry out drainage works for defence against sea or tidal water and to carry out works to secure an adequate outfall for a main river.

The requirement that the Agency shall maintain a principal office for each committee region is carried over from s.9(3) of the 1991 Act: subs. 9(3).

Composition of regional flood defence committees

15.—(1) Subject to subsection (2) below, a regional flood defence committee shall consist of the following, none of whom shall be a member of the Agency, that is to say—

    (a) a chairman and a number of other members appointed by the relevant Minister;

    (b) two members appointed by the Agency;

    (c) a number of members appointed by or on behalf of the constituent councils.

(2) Any person who immediately before the transfer date is, by virtue of his appointment—

    (a) by a Minister of the Crown,

    (b) by or on behalf of any council, or

    (c) by the National Rivers Authority,

the chairman or a member of an old committee which, by virtue of section 14 above, is replaced by a new committee shall be treated, on and after that date, for the remainder of the period for which he would, under the terms of his appointment, have held office in relation to the old committee, as if he had been appointed as the chairman or, as the case may be, a member of the new committee, and on the same terms, by that Minister or, as the case may be, by or on behalf of that council or, in the case of a person appointed by the National Rivers Authority, by the Agency.

(3) Subject to section 16 below and to any order under Schedule 4 to this Act amalgamating the areas of any two or more regional flood defence committees—

    (a) the total number of members of a new committee for any area shall be the same as the total number of members of the old committee for that area immediately before the transfer date;

    (b) the number of members to be appointed to a new committee for any area by or on behalf of each of the constituent councils or, as the case may be, jointly by or on behalf of more than one of them shall be the same as the number of members of the old committee for that area which fell to be so appointed immediately before the transfer date.

(4) In any case where—

    (a) the appointment of one or more members of a regional flood defence committee is (by virtue of subsection (3) above or an order under section 16(5) below), to be made jointly by more than one constituent council, and

    (b) the councils by whom that appointment is to be made are unable to agree on an appointment,

the member or members in question shall be appointed by the relevant Minister on behalf of those councils.

(5) In appointing a person to be the chairman or a member of a regional flood defence committee under subsection (1)(a) or (c) or (4) above the relevant Minister or, as the case may be, a constituent council shall have regard to the desirability of appointing a person who has experience of, and has shown capacity in, some matter relevant to the functions of the committee.

(6) The councils of every county, county borough, metropolitan district or London borough any part of which is in the area of a regional flood defence committee shall be the constituent councils for the regional flood defence committee for that area, and the Common Council of the City of London

shall be a constituent council for the regional flood defence committee for any area which comprises any part of the City.

(7) In this section—
"old committee" has the same meaning as in section 14 above;
"new committee" means a regional flood defence committee established under section 14 above;
"the relevant Minister"—
  (a) in relation to the regional flood defence committee for an area the whole or the greater part of which is in Wales, means the Secretary of State; and
  (b) in relation to any other regional flood defence committee, means the Minister.

DEFINITIONS
"the Agency": s.124(1).
"constitutional council": subs. (6).
"functions": s.124(1).
"the Minister": s.56(1).
"new committee": subs. (7).
"old committee": subs. (7) and s.14(4).
"regional flood defence committee" s.14(1).
"relevant Minister": subs. (7).
"transfer date": s.56(1).

COMMENCEMENT
April 1, 1996 (S.I. 1996 No. 186).

GENERAL NOTE
This section determines the membership of the regional flood defence committees established under s.14.

As a transitional arrangement, the members and chairman of each old committee are to be treated as being the members and chairman of its replacement committee, on the same terms, and as appointees of the same body or person, as before: subs. (2).

Subject to these transitional provisions,
  — the Agency appoints two members: subs. (1)(b);
  — each local authority in the region (see subs. (6)) appoints the same number of members (in some cases jointly with other local authorities) as it did before: subss. (1)(c) and (3)(b); and
  — The Minister of Agriculture, Fisheries and Food (or in Wales, the Secretary of State) appoints the chairman, the balance of the members and any member whose appointment could not be agreed on by local authorities who were to have jointly appointed him subss. (1)(a) and (4).
However, s.16 and Sched. 4 provide procedures, respectively, for altering the number of members of a committee and amalgamating two or more regions (with a possible consequent effect on the membership of the committee for the resulting region).

The Minister or Secretary of State, as the case may be, and the local authorities, must have regard, in making their appointments, to the desirability of appointing persons with relevant capacity and experience. The discretion (subs. (5)) which this allows them is considerable and identical to that granted by subs. 1(4) in relation to the appointment of members of the Agency itself. (See the general note to that section). Notably, subs. (5) does not place the Agency under the same duty with regard to its appointments to the committees.

Schedule 4
Section 14 gives effect to Sched. 4, which allows the Minister of Agriculture, Fisheries and Food (or in Wales, the Secretary of State) by order to alter the boundaries of any regional flood defence committee's area or to amalgamate two or more such areas. Where such a change is made, the order making it may (but need not) make supplemental, consequential and transitional provisions: para. 1(3).

Where the change is the amalgamation of regions, provision may (but again, need not) be made regarding the number of members of the committee for the amalgamated region and their appointors): para. 1(4). Such provisions are subject to the subss. 16(7) and (8) provisions that the number of local council appointees must exceed by one the number of other appointees but that individual local councils may have their right to appoint, or to solely appoint, members withdrawn. It appears that where no express provision is made regarding membership of the flood defence committee for an amalgamated region, the committees for the predecessor regions are themselves simply amalgamated.

Before the Order
Alteration or amalgamation must be by order made by the Minister (or, in Wales, the Secretary of State) by statutory instrument (para. 1(1)), after:
— consulting persons he considers it appropriate to consult: para. 2(1);
— publishing a notice stating his intention and its general effect: para. 2(2);
— making a draft of the proposed order available both generally (para. 2(2)) and to every person considered to have relevant statutory functions: para. 2(3);
— considering objections made within the time specified in the published notice and, if he thinks fit, holding a public inquiry: para. 3(1); and
— modifying the order, if he thinks fit, in the light of such objections and inquiry: para. 3(2)—note the restriction on modification in para. 3(3).

Making the order
When the order is made, he must serve notice of that fact on any person who was entitled to receive notice of the original draft order, duly objected to the draft order and has not withdrawn that objection: para. 4(1). Any such person then has 28 days within which to object by notice to the order (para. 4(3)), and, if even one such objection is made and not withdrawn, then the order is subject to special Parliamentary procedure: para. 4(4). If there is no such person, or if there is such a person and they do not object to the order in its final form, it has effect at the end of the 28 days: para. 4(2).

Once the order is made
If an order is made without the special Parliamentary procedure being triggered then it can be annulled by a resolution of either House of Parliament: para. 4(4).
   Notice that the order has been made must be published, after the 28 day period if such is necessary under para. 4(2), and must state if it is to be subject to special Parliamentary procedure: para. 5. The validity of a Sched. 4 order may not be questioned in legal proceedings (para. 6(4)) unless it is questioned (by application to the High Court) within 6 weeks of such notice being published (para. 6(1)); on such application the order may be quashed either generally or in so far as it affects the applicant: para. 6(2).

Change of composition of regional flood defence committee

   16.—(1) The Agency may, in accordance with the following provisions of this section, from time to time make a determination varying the total number of members of a regional flood defence committee.
   (2) The Agency shall submit any determination under subsection (1) above to the relevant Minister.
   (3) For the purposes of this section—
     (a) the total number of members of a regional flood defence committee shall not be less than eleven; and
     (b) any determination by the Agency under subsection (1) above that a regional flood defence committee should consist of more than seventeen members shall be provisional and shall take effect only if the relevant Minister makes an order under subsection (4) below.
   (4) If the Agency submits a provisional determination to the relevant Minister with respect to any regional flood defence committee and he considers that the committee should consist of more than seventeen members, he may by order made by statutory instrument—
     (a) confirm it; or
     (b) substitute for the number of members determined by the Agency some other number not less than seventeen.
   (5) Subject to the following provisions of this section, whenever—
     (a) the total number of members of a regional flood defence committee is varied under this section, or
     (b) the relevant Minister considers it necessary or expedient to make an order under this subsection,

the relevant Minister shall by order made by statutory instrument specify the number of members to be appointed to the committee by each of the constituent councils.

(6) An order under subsection (5) above shall relate—

    (a) where paragraph (a) of that subsection applies, to times after the coming into force of the variation; and

    (b) where paragraph (b) of that subsection applies, to such times as are specified in the order.

(7) An order under subsection (5) above shall be so framed that the total number of members appointed under section 15(1)(a) and (b) above is one less than the number of those appointed by or on behalf of constituent councils.

(8) For the purpose of determining for the purposes of subsection (5) above the number of persons to be appointed to a regional flood defence committee by or on behalf of each constituent council, the relevant Minister—

    (a) if he considers it to be inappropriate that that council should appoint a member of the committee, or

    (b) if he considers that one or more members should be appointed jointly by that council and one or more other constituent councils,

may include provision to that effect in the order.

(9) In this section—

    "member", in relation to a regional flood defence committee, includes the chairman of the committee;

    "the relevant Minister" has the same meaning as in section 15 above.

DEFINITIONS
"the Agency": s.124(1).
"constituent council": s.15(6).
"member": subs. (9).
"regional flood defence committee": s.14(1).
"relevant Minister": subs. (9) and s.15(7).

COMMENCEMENT
April 1, 1996 (S.I. 1996 No. 186).

GENERAL NOTE
This section, which is in all key respects identical to s.11 of the Water Resources Act 1991 which it replaces, provides

    — a procedure for the Agency to vary the number of members of a regional flood defence committee; and

    — a procedure for the relevant Minister (the Minister of Agriculture, Fisheries and Food or, in Wales, the Secretary of State), whether or not as a result of such a variation in the number of members, to vary the composition of such a committee.

The Agency may vary the number of members by making a determination to this effect and submitting it to the relevant minister (subss. (1) and (2)). The number of members must always be at least 11, and, if the determination would make the number of members more than 17, then it is provisional until the relevant Minister confirms or varies it by order made by statutory instrument: subss (3) and (4).

Since all members are appointed by someone, a change in the number of members requires provision to be made deciding the composition of the committee in terms of who is whose appointee. In such circumstances, or tin the absence of such a determination by the Agency) where the relevant Minister considers it necessary or expedient, the relevant Minister must make such provision by order made by statutory instrument: subs. (5). In so doing, he may if appropriate remove an individual local authority's right to appoint, or solely (as opposed to jointly) to appoint, a committee member (subs. (8)), and he must ensure that local authority appointees outnumber by one the other members of the committee: subs. (7).

Local flood defence schemes and local flood defence committees

17.—(1) A scheme, known as a local flood defence scheme, may be made by the Agency, in accordance with the following provisions of this section—

(a) for the creation in the area of a regional flood defence committee of one or more districts, to be known as local flood defence districts; and

(b) for the constitution, membership, functions and procedure of a committee for each such district, to be known as the local flood defence committee for that district.

(2) Any local flood defence scheme which was made under the 1991 Act or continued in force by virtue of paragraph 14(1) of Schedule 2 to the Water Consolidation (Consequential Provisions) Act 1991 and which, immediately before the transfer date, is in force in relation to the area of a regional flood defence committee, shall on and after that date have effect, and may be amended or revoked, as if it were a local flood defence scheme made under this section in relation to that area; and, accordingly, subject to any such amendment or revocation—

(a) any local flood defence district created by that scheme and in being immediately before that date shall be treated, on and after that date, as a local flood defence district created by a scheme under this section in relation to the area of that regional flood defence committee; and

(b) any local flood defence committee created by that scheme for any such district and in being immediately before that date shall be treated, on and after that date, as the local flood defence committee for that district.

(3) A regional flood defence committee may at any time submit to the Agency—

(a) a local flood defence scheme for any part of their area for which there is then no such scheme in force; or

(b) a scheme varying a local flood defence scheme or revoking such a scheme and, if the committee think fit, replacing it with another such scheme;

and references in the following provisions of this section and in section 18 below to local flood defence schemes are references to schemes under either of paragraphs (a) and (b) above.

(4) Before submitting a scheme to the Agency under subsection (3) above, a regional flood defence committee shall consult—

(a) every local authority any part of whose area will fall within the area to which the scheme is proposed to relate; and

(b) such organisations representative of persons interested in flood defence (within the meaning of Part IV of the 1991 Act) or agriculture as the regional flood defence committee consider to be appropriate.

(5) It shall be the duty of the Agency to send any scheme submitted to it under subsection (3) above to one of the Ministers.

(6) A local flood defence scheme may define a local flood defence district—

(a) by reference to the districts which were local land drainage districts immediately before 1st September 1989;

(b) by reference to the area of the regional flood defence committee in which that district is situated;

(c) by reference to a map;

or partly by one of those means and partly by another or others.

(7) A local flood defence scheme may contain incidental, consequential and supplementary provisions.

(8) Either of the Ministers may approve a local flood defence scheme with or without modifications; and any scheme approved under this subsection shall come into force on a date fixed by the Minister approving it.

DEFINITIONS
"the 1991 Act": s.56(1).
"the Agency": s.124(1).
"local authority": s.56(1).
"local flood defence committee": subs. (1).
"local flood defence district": subs. (1).
"local flood defence scheme": subs. (1).
"the Ministers": s.56(1).
"regional flood defence committee": s.14(1).
"transfer date": s.56(1).

COMMENCEMENT
April 1, 1996 (S.I. 1996 No. 186).

GENERAL NOTE
This section, which is closely modelled on s.12 of the Water Resources Act 1991 which it replaces, provides for local flood defence committees for areas within regions, which are in addition to the regional flood defence committees established under s.14.

The procedure is triggered by a regional flood defence committee submitting to the Agency under subs. (3) a local flood defence scheme (or a proposed variation or revocation or replacement of such a scheme) which:

— defines as a district an area within its region, by reference to one or more of the criteria set out in subs. (6), but apparently not otherwise;
— establishes a local flood defence committee for that district (subs. (1)(a)); and
— establishes functions, constitution, membership and procedure for that local flood defence committee (regarding which, the provisions of Sched. 5 in relation to membership and proceedings apply).

The regional flood defence committee must, before submitting such a scheme, consult local authorities for the district in question and such organisations representing interested persons as it considers appropriate: subs. (4).

On receiving the scheme, the Agency must send it to "one of the Ministers" (subs. (5)) for approval and the fixing of a date for entry into force under subs. (8).

The term "one of the Ministers", used instead of the term "the relevant Minister" which is employed elsewhere in ss. 14–19, appears to give the Agency the option in England to send such a scheme to the Secretary of State rather than to the Minister of Agriculture, Fisheries and Food since "the Ministers" is a defined term including the Secretary of State.

Subs. (2) makes transitional provision under which any local flood defence district and committee existing prior to the transfer date (April 1, 1996) is treated as a local flood defence district and committee under this section.

Composition of local flood defence committees

18.—(1) Subject to subsections (2) and (3) below, a local flood defence scheme shall provide that any local flood defence committee to which it relates shall consist of not less than eleven and not more than fifteen members.

(2) A regional flood defence committee may include in a local flood defence scheme which they submit to the Agency a recommendation that a committee to which the scheme relates should consist of a number of members greater than fifteen; and a scheme so submitted shall be taken to provide for the number of members of a committee if it contains a recommendation under this subsection relating to that committee.

(3) The power conferred on each of the Ministers by section 17(8) above shall include power to direct that a committee to which a recommendation under subsection (2) above relates shall consist either of the recommended number of members or of some other number of members greater than fifteen.

(4) A local flood defence committee shall consist of—

(a) a chairman appointed from among their own members by the regional flood defence committee;

(b) other members appointed by that committee; and
(c) members appointed, in accordance with and subject to the terms of the local flood defence scheme, by or on behalf of constituent councils.

(5) The number of members appointed to a local flood defence committee by or on behalf of constituent councils shall be one more than the total number of members appointed by the regional flood defence committee.

(6) In appointing a person to be a member of a local flood defence committee, the regional flood defence committee shall have regard to the desirability of appointing a person who has experience of, and has shown capacity in, some matter relevant to the functions of the committee to which he is appointed.

(7) Any person who, immediately before the transfer date is, by virtue of an appointment by an old regional committee or by or on behalf of any council, the chairman or a member of a local flood defence committee which is continued in force by virtue of section 17(2) above shall be treated, on and after that date, for the remainder of the period for which he would, under the terms of his appointment, have held office in relation to the local flood defence committee—

(a) as if he had been appointed as such under this section by the regional flood defence committee or, as the case may be, by or on behalf of that council; and
(b) in the case of the chairman, as if he were a member of the regional flood defence committee.

(8) The councils of every county, county borough, metropolitan district or London borough any part of which is in a local flood defence district shall be the constituent councils for the local flood defence committee for that district, and the Common Council of the City of London shall be a constituent council for the local flood defence committee of any local flood defence district which comprises any part of the City.

(9) In this section "old regional committee" means a regional flood defence committee for the purposes of section 9 of the 1991 Act.

<small>Definitions
"the 1991 Act": s.56(1).
"the Agency": s.124(1).
"constituent councils": subs. (8).
"functions" s.124(1).
"local flood defence committee": s.17(1).
"local flood defence scheme": s.17(1).
"the Ministers": s.56(1).
"old regional committee": subs. (9).
"regional flood defence committee": s.14(1).
"transfer date": s.56(1).

Commencement
April 1, 1996 (S.I. 1996 No. 186).

General Note
This section, which is closely modelled on s.13 of the Water Resources Act 1991 which it replaces, provides for the determination of the composition of the local flood defence committees established by s.17.

In a transitional provision which builds on that in s.17(2) the chairman and members of any local flood defence committee existing at the transfer date are to be treated for the remainder of their appointment as if appointed under this section, by whoever originally appointed them.

Subject to those provisions, there are to be between 11 and 15 members of such a local committee (subs. (1)), unless a Minister directs otherwise on the basis of a recommendation in the scheme submitted by the regional flood defence committee that there should be more than 15 members: subs. (3).

Members are appointed either by the regional flood defence committee (including the</small>

chairman, who must be a member of that regional committee) or, in accordance with the scheme, by the local authorities for the district in question: subs. (4). Local authority appointees must outnumber by one the regional committee appointees: subs. (5). The regional flood defence committee must, in appointing members of a local committee, have regard to the desirability of the appointees' having relevant experience and capacity: subs. (6). This provision mirrors that in s.15(5) in relation to appointments to regional flood defence committees, and as there the implication is that wide discretion may be exercised in making appointments. However, unlike in s.15(5), local authorities are not also under this duty in making their appointments.

Membership and proceedings of flood defence committees

19. Schedule 5 to this Act shall have effect in relation to regional flood defence committees and local flood defence committees.

DEFINITIONS
"local flood defence committee": s.17(1).
"regional flood defence committee": s.14(1).

COMMENCEMENT
April 1, 1996 (S.I. 1996 No. 186).

GENERAL NOTE
This section gives effect to Schedule 5, which makes provision in relation to the membership and proceedings of both regional and local flood defence committees.

Membership of flood defence committees—Sched. 5, Pt. I
Members hold office according to their terms of appointment and, in most cases, do so for four years from the start of June after their appointment: para. 1.
   A member may also be a member of the local authority which appoints him to the committee (para. 2), just as there is nothing in s.18 barring a regional flood defence committee from appointing its own members to a local committee.
   However, he may not be a paid Agency officer (para. 3, which also details other grounds for disqualification including bankruptcy and certain criminal convictions). Extended absence from committee meetings without approved cause is one of the disqualifying events listed in para. 4 which result in a member's office becoming vacant.
   Para. 7 provides for casual vacancies to be filled, and para. 9 allows local authorities to nominate deputies to attend and vote at committee meetings in place of their appointees.
   Para. 10 provides for the payment, as determined by the relevant Minister, of remuneration, allowances, pension and compensation in appropriate circumstances, to any present or past chairman and of allowances to other members.

Proceedings of Flood Defence Committees—Sched. 5, Pt. II
A flood defence committee, or two or more jointly, may appoint sub-committees and determine the number, terms of appointment and identity of the members of such sub-committees, save that anyone disqualified from committee membership cannot be a sub-committee member: para. 11.
   A flood defence committee or sub-committee may delegate the carrying out of its functions to one or more other committees or sub-committees, acting jointly or alone, or to an Agency officer. It may also carry out its functions jointly with another committee: para. 12. However, s. 106 of the Water Resources Act 1991, which requires the Agency to delegate the carrying out of its functions to regional committees, restricts the scope of delegation back to the Agency: para. 12(1).
   Having delegated functions under s.17 to a local committee, a regional committee may not then arrange under para. 12 for the carrying out by itself or anyone else of those functions (para. 12(6)) but in contrast may do so in relation to functions it has delegated under para. 12.
   A flood defence committee may, with the approval of the relevant Minister, make rules regulating its own proceedings, and the Agency may not regulate committee proceedings: para. 13. However, as regards declarations of interest, committee members are bound by ss.94–98 of the Local Government Act 1972, as modified to suit committee circumstances by para. 14.
   Provision is also made for the authentication of documents given, made or issued by such a committee and for the proof and validity of its proceedings: paras. 15 and 16. In particular, an Agency official whom a committee has authorised by resolution to sign on its behalf may do so.

CHAPTER II

THE SCOTTISH ENVIRONMENT PROTECTION AGENCY

Establishment of SEPA

The Scottish Environment Protection Agency

20.—(1) There shall be a body to be known as the Scottish Environment Protection Agency (in this Act referred to as "SEPA"), for the purpose of carrying out the functions transferred or assigned to it by or under this Act.

(2) Schedule 6 to this Act shall have effect with respect to SEPA.

DEFINITIONS
"functions": s.124(1).
"SEPA": s.124(1).

COMMENCEMENT
April 1, 1996 (S.I. 1996 No. 186).

GENERAL NOTE
This section provides for the establishment of SEPA and gives effect to Schedule 6 which deals in detail with the constitution and proceedings of SEPA. It should be noted that references to the Secretary of State throughout Chapter II and Sched. 6 are references to the Secretary of State for Scotland.

Subs. (1)
SEPA exists for the purpose of carrying out the functions transferred or assigned to it by the Act. If SEPA were to carry out any other functions, it would he acting *ultra vires*.

Subs. (2)
This subsection gives effect to Schedule 6 which makes detailed provision regarding the composition, constitution and proceedings of SEPA. These are considered below.

Status
SEPA is given the status of a body corporate. The implications of this are similar to those outlined in the equivalent note on s.1(1) in relation to the Agency. However, although a private prosecution of SEPA or its officers is a possibility in Scotland as in England and Wales, it is submitted that such a private prosecution is extremely unlikely to occur in practice given that the consent of the Lord Advocate is required for initiating a private prosecution in Scotland (Renton & Brown *Criminal Procedure* 5th ed., 1983, 4–04; *Robertson v. H.M.A.* (1892) 3 White 230). Such consent is unlikely to be forthcoming and while the refusal of the Lord Advocate to give consent is reviewable (*J & P Coats Ltd. v. Brown* (1909) 6 Adam 19; *X v. Sweeney* 1982 J.C. 70), such a review is, it is submitted, unlikely to succeed.

It should also be noted that as a non-departmental public body, SEPA is accountable to Parliament through the Secretary of State.

Para. 2 provides that SEPA does not have Crown privilege, immunity or exemption from taxation. See also the note to s.1(5).

Membership, Chairman and deputy-chairman
There was considerable debate in Parliament relating to the composition of SEPA (see *e.g.* *Hansard*, H.L. Vol. 560, cols. 1188–1192). Fears that there would be a loss of accountability by having all SEPA's members appointed by the Secretary of State led to amendments being proposed which would require all its members to be local councillors appointed by the Convention of Scottish Local Authorities (per Lord Carmichael of Kelvingrove, *Hansard*, H.L. Vol. 560, col. 1188). This amendment was rejected by the Government which argued that members "would be appointed for their personal qualities and, most important, those appointments would not be made simply because their status is that of a councillor" and that "It would be very difficult for this non-departmental public body to be accountable to the Secretary

of State and through him to Parliament, if he was not responsible for appointing the members of that body" (*per* the Earl of Lindsay, *Hansard*, H.L. Vol. 560, cols. 1191–1192). In fact, no fewer than four councillors have been appointed to the 12 strong board (see below).

Schedule 6, paras. 3–8 make provision in relation to the membership, chairman and deputy-chairman of SEPA. Para. 3 provides for the appointment of members of SEPA of whom there are to be between 8 and 12. The Secretary of State is responsible for all the appointments and also has the power to alter the maximum/minimum membership of SEPA by statutory instrument using the negative resolution procedure (para. 6). The Secretary of State is also required to appoint a chairman and deputy chairman of SEPA from amongst the members who have been appointed under para. 3 (para. 8). On April 19, 1995 it was announced by the Secretary of State that Professor William Turmeau, recently retired Principal and Vice-Chancellor of Napier University, would be appointed as the first Chairman of SEPA (*Hansard*, H.C. vol. 258, col. 218w). In addition the Secretary of State appointed the following Board members on October 5, 1995:

— Councillor Basil Baird (Councillor for Eastwood District Council and the new East Renfrewshire Council; Member of Clyde River Purification Board; farmer)
— Alexander Buchan (Vice-Chairman, North East River Purification Board; farmer and Vice-Chairman, NFU Area Executive; former President of the Royal Northern Agricultural Society
— Brian Fitzgerald (Vice-Chairman of CBI Scotland and Chairman CBI Scotland Environment Committee; civil engineer; formerly director John Laing Construction Ltd)
— Graeme Gordon OBE (Vice-Chairman, Solway River Purification Board; Convenor of the Scottish Landowners Federation; Managing Director/Owner, Kenmure Fisheries; member, Advisory Committee, Institute of Agriculture, University of Stirling)
— David Hughes Hallett FRICS (Director of the Scottish Wildlife Trust; chartered surveyor; former Chairman of the Royal Institute of Chartered Surveyors in Scotland; former Director of the Scottish Landowners Federation)
— Professor Cliff Johnston (Head of Heriot-Watt University's Institute of Offshore Engineering Group)
— Councillor Cormick McChord (Vice-Convenor and Leader of Central Regional Council and Leader of the new Stirling Council; represents the Convention of Scottish Local Authorities ("COSLA") on the UK Central Local Government Environment Forum and the Local Agenda 21 Steering Committee).
— Cameron McLatchie (Chairman & Chief Executive of British Polythene Industries; non-executive director, Motherwell Bridge Holdings Ltd.; member of Advisory Group on Sustainable Development; formerly member, United Kingdom Advisory Committee on Business and the Environment)
— Councillor Alison Magee (Convenor, Sutherland District Council, and the new Highland Council; vice-chairman, non-aligned group, COSLA)
— Councillor Jennifer Shaw JP (Councillor, Moray District Council, and on the new Moray Council; member North-East River Purification Board)
Alasdair Paton, who has been appointed as SEPA's Chief Executive, is also a Board member, bringing the total number of Board members to 12.

In appointing members the Secretary of State is required to have regard to the desirability of appointing persons with knowledge or experience in a matter relevant to SEPA's functions (para. 4). It should be noted that this provision differs from the equivalent English provision (s.1(4)) which requires an appointee to have some experience of and to have shown some capacity in, a matter relevant to the functions of the Agency. In contrast Scottish appointees need not have shown any capacity in a matter relevant to SEPA's functions. It would appear, therefore, that the requisite standard for appointment to the Agency in England is slightly higher than the standard applicable in Scotland. Furthermore, it is most unlikely that an appointment could be challenged given the breadth of SEPA's functions. See also the note to s.1(4). It should also be noted that the Scottish Office has indicated on the membership application form that before appointing a person as a member of SEPA, the Secretary of State must be satisfied that the person has no interests likely to be prejudicial to performance as a member.

Para. 5 provides for the tenure of office, resignation and reappointment of the members of SEPA appointed under para. 3. The initial term of appointment has been fixed at four years (Scottish Office Press Release October 5, 1995). Furthermore, the membership application form also indicates that members are not normally to be more than 67 years old at the date of their appointment. Ceasing to be a member of SEPA automatically terminates an individual's office as chairman or deputy chairman (para. 8(3)).

The Secretary of State may remove a member from office on the grounds (a) of being absent from SEPA's meetings for more than 3 months without permission; (b) that he has been adjudged bankrupt etc.; or (c) that he is unable or unfit to carry out his functions (para. 7).

Remuneration, pensions and staff
Remuneration and pension arrangements for members of SEPA are determined by the Secretary of State (para. 9). He announced on April 19, 1995 that the Chairman's salary would initially be £36,000 *per annum* (*Hansard*, H.C. Vol. 258, col. 218w) and subsequently he has determined that members are to be paid £5,000 per year plus expenses (Scottish Office Press Release October 5, 1995). In relation to its staff SEPA must determine their remuneration and pension arrangements subject to the approval of the Secretary of State (para. 12(1)).

Like the Agency, SEPA has absolute discretion in the appointment of staff (para. 11) except in the case of its first chief officer who is to be appointed by the Secretary of State following consultation with the person appointed as Chairman (para. 10(2)). Subsequent chief officers are to be appointed by SEPA with the approval of the Secretary of State (*ibid.*) On August 17, 1995 the Earl of Lindsay, Minister for the Environment at the Scottish Office appointed Alasdair Paton (Director and Chief Engineer of the Engineering, Water and Waste Directorate, Scottish Office Environment Department) as SEPA's Chief Executive. A number of other SEPA staff have since been appointed including a Director of Corporate Services, a Director of Environmental Strategy and three Regional Directors (SEPA Bulletin, Issue 10, November 7, 1995).

Proceedings
SEPA may regulate its own procedure, including the quorum for its meetings and meetings of its committees (para. 13). None of these meetings will be open to the public: see the note to s.1 (under *Schedule 1—proceedings*).

Committee
SEPA may establish committees and appoint persons who are not members to these committees subject to the proviso that at least one member of each committee must be a member of SEPA (para. 14(1)). The Secretary of State is to determine what remuneration is to be paid by SEPA to any such persons appointed (para. 14(2)).

Delegation of powers
SEPA may by para. 15 delegate anything which it is authorised or required to do to any committee, member or employee who is authorised by SEPA for that purpose.

Regional Boards
The question of SEPA's accountability at local level occupied much time in Parliament as several of the functions being transferred to it were previously subject to local accountable control. These functions were those previously performed by local authorities (air pollution control under Part I of the 1990 Act and waste regulation) and those performed by river purification authorities. In contrast to the NRA in England and Wales, RPAs were accountable at a local level as they comprised the three islands councils and the RPBs whose boards consisted of 50 per cent Secretary of State appointees and 50 per cent local authority appointees (by virtue of s.135A of the Local Government (Scotland) Act 1973, added by s.27 and Sched. 10, para. 6 of the Natural Heritage (Scotland) Act 1991).

The Government acknowledged this concern in its consultation paper on SEPA, *Improving Scotland's Environment. The Way Forward* where it was stated that "[T]he Government therefore envisage that SEPA might set up a regional advisory committee structure in order to provide for local involvement and participation" (para. 20). In the light of misgivings expressed by respondents in the consultation process, the Government indicated that rather than simply having regional advisory committees there might be scope for delegating certain executive responsibility to regional bodies (*Hansard*, H.C. cols. 713–4w, February 25, 1993). This resulted in KPMG Management Consulting being commissioned to report on this issue. In their *Scottish Environment Protection Agency Consultancy Report* (March, 1993) they argued for the creation of three or four regional boards with delegated executive functions. In Parliament, various attempts were made to force the Government to reserve places on regional boards for elected councillors (*e.g. per* Lord Ewing of Kirkford, *Hansard*, H.L. Vol. 560, col. 581). Although the Government rejected such moves, they explained that they would be "keen to secure the services of effective board members from all sources. We certainly envisage elected councillors playing a full part on the regional boards" (*per* Viscount Ullswater, *Hansard*, H.L. Vol. 560, col. 583; see also the Earl of Lindsay, *Hansard*, H.L. Vol. 560, col. 1192 and Sir Hector Monro Standing Committee B col. 235 May 16, 1995).

The Government accepted KPMG's recommendations. Accordingly the 1995 Act provides that SEPA must establish regional boards although the number of boards to be established is not specified (para. 16(1)). Subject to the approval of the Secretary of State, SEPA is to determine the functions which the regional boards are to discharge and the areas which they are to cover (para. 16(1)). SEPA will appoint the chairman of each regional board from amongst its own members (para. 16(2)). SEPA must comply with guidance issued by the Secretary of State in relation to such issues as the number of members regional boards are to have, their qualifications and experience (para. 16(3)).

SEPA's regional boards are notable in that they are not simply advisory bodies but will exercise such powers as may be delegated by SEPA's Board. In this respect they differ significantly from the Regional Advisory Committees which are to be established in Wales and the English regions by the Agency. It is for this reason that, in contrast to the position in respect of Regional Advisory Committees in England and Wales, the Government is

"not minded to require SEPA to provide for open access to meetings at regional level, as the regional boards will exercise delegated powers on behalf of the main SEPA board, so the same considerations will apply to the regional boards as to the main board" (Sir Paul Beresford Standing Committee B, col. 68, May 2, 1995).

The regional boards may delegate their powers either to a member of the board in question or to an employee of SEPA authorised for that purpose.

On October 27, 1995 it was announced that SEPA was establishing three Regional Boards for the North, East and West of Scotland (see also the Introduction to Part I under *Regional and Managerial Structure: Scotland*). These Boards are based upon river purification board catchment areas with the North Regional Board incorporating the Highland and North East RPB areas, the East Regional Board the Forth, Tay and Tweed RPB areas and the West Regional Board the Clyde and Solway RPB areas.

Members' interests
Paragraph 17 makes provision in relation to members' interests. See also note to s.1 and Sched. 1, para. 7.

Minutes
Paragraph 18 makes provision in relation to minutes. The Government has indicated that it hopes that SEPA will make its minutes available to any member of the public who requests them under the Environmental Information Regulations 1992 (*e.g. per* the Earl of Lindsay *Hansard*, H.L. Vol. 560, col. 1198). See also introductory note to Part I under heading, *The Agencies and access to information* above.

Transfer of functions, property etc. to SEPA

Transfer of functions to SEPA

21.—(1) On the transfer date there shall by virtue of this section be transferred to SEPA—
  (a) the functions of river purification authorities, that is to say—
     (i) their functions with respect to water resources under or by virtue of Part III of the Rivers (Prevention of Pollution) (Scotland) Act 1951 (in this Part referred to as "the 1951 Act") and Part II of the Natural Heritage (Scotland) Act 1991;
    (ii) their functions with respect to water pollution under or by virtue of Part III of the 1951 Act, the Rivers (Prevention of Pollution) (Scotland) Act 1965 and Part II of the Control of Pollution Act 1974;
    (iii) their functions as enforcing authority, in relation to releases of substances into the environment, under or by virtue of Part I of the 1990 Act;
    (iv) their functions with respect to flood warning systems under or by virtue of Part VI of the Agriculture Act 1970; and
    (v) the functions assigned to them by or under any other enactment apart from this Act;
  (b) the functions of waste regulation authorities, that is to say, the functions conferred or imposed on them by or under—

     (i) the Control of Pollution (Amendment) Act 1989; or
     (ii) Part II of the 1990 Act,
    or assigned to them by or under any other enactment apart from this Act;
  (c) the functions of disposal authorities under or by virtue of sections 3 to 10, 16, 17(1)(a) and 17(2)(b) to (d) of the Control of Pollution Act 1974;
  (d) the functions of the chief inspector for Scotland constituted under section 16(3) of the 1990 Act, that is to say, the functions conferred or imposed on him by or under Part I of that Act or assigned to him by or under any other enactment apart from this Act;
  (e) the functions of the chief inspector for Scotland appointed under section 4(2)(b) of the Radioactive Substances Act 1993, that is to say, the functions conferred or imposed on him by or under that Act or assigned to him by or under any other enactment apart from this Act;
  (f) the functions conferred or imposed by or under the Alkali, &c, Works Regulation Act 1906 (in this section referred to as "the 1906 Act") on the chief, or any other, inspector (within the meaning of that Act), so far as exercisable in relation to Scotland;
  (g) so far as exercisable in relation to Scotland, the functions in relation to improvement notices and prohibition notices under Part I of the Health and Safety at Work etc. Act 1974 (in this section referred to as "the 1974 Act") of inspectors appointed under section 19 of that Act by the Secretary of State in his capacity as enforcing authority responsible in relation to Scotland for the enforcement of the 1906 Act and section 5 of the 1974 Act;
  (h) the functions of local authorities as enforcing authority, in relation to releases of substances into the air, under or by virtue of Part I of the 1990 Act; and
  (i) the functions of the Secretary of State specified in subsection (2) below.

(2) The functions of the Secretary of State mentioned in subsection (1)(i) above are, so far as exercisable in relation to Scotland—
  (a) the functions conferred or imposed on him by virtue of his being, for the purposes of Part I of the 1974 Act, the authority which is by any of the relevant statutory provisions made responsible for the enforcement of the 1906 Act and section 5 of the 1974 Act;
  (b) his functions under, or under regulations made by virtue of, section 9 of the 1906 Act (registration of works), other than any functions of his as an appellate authority or any function of making regulations;
  (c) his functions under section 19 of the Clean Air Act 1993 with respect to the creation of smoke control areas by local authorities; and
  (d) his functions under section 30(1) of the Radioactive Substances Act 1993 (power to dispose of radioactive waste).

(3) River purification boards shall be dissolved on the transfer date.

DEFINITIONS
"disposal authority": s.56(1); s.30(2) of the 1974 Act.
"the environment": s.56(1); s.1(2) of the 1990 Act.
"functions": s.124(1).
"local authority": s.56(1)–(2).
"river purification authority": s.56(1); s.17(2) of the Rivers (Prevention of Pollution) (Scotland) Act 1951.
"river purification board": s.56(1); s.135 of the Local Government (Scotland) Act 1973.
"SEPA": s.124(1).
"transfer date": s.56(1).
"waste regulation authority": s.56(1); s.30(1)(g) of the 1990 Act.

Commencement
April 1, 1996 (S.I. 1996 No. 186).

GENERAL NOTE
This section provides for the transfer of various functions from existing Scottish environmental
regulatory bodies to SEPA which is established by s.20.

River purification boards
River purification boards are consequently dissolved by subs. (3) since all of their functions are
transferred by subs. (1).

Her Majesty's Industrial Pollution Inspectorate
Although HMIPI could be thought of as a body similar to a river purification board, it is not. Its
functions are the functions of the chief inspector or other inspectors as individuals, or delegated
functions of the Secretary of State: this is reflected in the wording of s.21(1)(d)–(g) and subs. (2).
It should be noted that the Secretary of State's power to make regulations under the Alkali etc.
Works Regulation Act 1906 and his appellate function thereunder are excluded from the
transfer of his functions under that Act: subs. (2)(b).

Functions transferred
All the functions of river purification authorities, HMIPI together with the functions of local
authorities in their capacities as waste regulation authorities and enforcing authorities for air
pollution control for Part B processes under Part I of the 1990 Act and certain functions of the
Secretary of State are transferred by subss. (1) and (2). The functions transferred are identified
in the section by reference to the statutes in which they are set out. The main functions
transferred to SEPA are summarised below in simplified form. Reference should be made to
the statutes in question for the detail of the functions transferred.

River Purification Authority functions

Subs. (1)(a)(i)–(v)
All of the functions of RPAs are transferred to SEPA as follows:

Subs. (1)(a)(i)
This subsection transfers to SEPA all RPA water resources management functions including:
— the promotion of the cleanliness of rivers, other inland waters or tidal waters and the
conservation of water resources (s.17, Rivers (Prevention of Pollution (Scotland) Act
1951))
— powers to survey, gauge and keep records of flow or volume of water bodies and rainfall
(s.18, Rivers (Prevention of Pollution (Scotland) Act 1951) and the power to take
samples of water or of effluent (s.19, Rivers (Prevention of Pollution (Scotland) Act
1951))
— the power to control water abstraction for irrigation purposes (Part II (ss.15–19) and
Sched. 5 to Natural Heritage (Scotland) Act 1991))
The functions transferred to SEPA in this respect are less broad than those transferred to the
Agency and this reflects the fact that RPAs enjoyed a less extensive role than the NRA. For
example, in contrast to the NRA, RPAs had very limited powers in relation to water
abstraction. Attempts in Parliament to secure for SEPA broader powers in this regard are
discussed above in the Introductory Note to Part I under *Functions transferred and differences
between the Agencies.*

Subs. (1)(a)(ii)
This subs. transfers to SEPA all general RPA water pollution functions (excluding IPC
functions which are transferred by subs. (1)(a)(iii)) including:
— the duty to ensure that specified water quality objectives are achieved (Control of
Pollution Act 1974, s.30D(1))
— the duty to consent discharges of trade and sewage effluent. (s.34 of the 1974 Act) and to
keep consents under review (s.37 of the 1974 Act)
— the duty to monitor pollution in controlled waters (s.30D(2) of the 1974 Act)
— the duty to maintain registers of consents for public inspection. (s.41 of the 1974 Act;
the Control of Pollution (Registers) (Scotland) Regulations 1993 S.I. 1993 No. 1155)

— the power to enforce water pollution controls (ss.31–32; s.37 of the 1974 Act).
— the power to carry out preventive or remedial anti-pollution works and operations (s.46 of the 1974 Act)

It should be noted that the statutory provisions contained in Part II of the Control of Pollution Act 1974 (as amended by Sched. 23 to the Water Act 1989) which govern water pollution controls in Scotland are substantially amended by s.106 and Sched. 16 to this Act. These amendments include the replacement of the general water pollution offence sections (ss.31–32) by a new s.30F (see the note to s.30F in Sched. 16); the introduction of a new s.30G providing for a system of prohibitions in relation to certain discharges (see the note to s.30G in Sched. 16); the introduction of new ss.46A–46D providing for works notices which may require persons to carry out preventive or remedial anti-pollution works or operations (see the note to s.120, Sched. 22, paras. 29(22) and 162); and the introduction of new ss.49A–B providing for encorcement notices in relation to contraventions of consent conditions (see the note to s.120, Sched. 22, paras. 29(26) and 142). For the text of Part II of the 1974 act as amended by this Act, see Appendix 4).

Subs. (1)(a)(iii)
This subs. transfers to SEPA all RPA integrated pollution control (IPC) functions as enforcing authorities for processes prescribed under Part A of Sched. 1 to the Environmental Protection (Prescribed Processes and Substances) Regulations 1991 by virtue of Part I of the 1990 Act. In Scotland it should be noted that RPAs were the enforcing authority for IPC in cases where there were emissions to water only or to water and land only by virtue of s.5 of the 1990 Act and the Environmental Protection (Determination of Enforcing Authority etc.) (Scotland) Regulations 1992 (S.1.1992 No. 530). HMIPI were the enforcing authority in all other instances.

Subs. (1)(a)(iv)
This subs. transfers to SEPA all RPA flood warning functions under Part VI of the Agriculture Act 1970 (as amended). Despite attempts in Parliament to extend SEPA's role in this respect, flood defence functions in Scotland which are governed by the Flood Prevention (Scotland) Act 1961 are not transferred to SEPA and remain with local authorities.

Subs. (1)(a)(v)
These functions include the role of RPA's as consultees in certain cases under the planning legislation: Town and Country Planning (General Development Procedure) (Scotland) Order 1992, art. 15(1)(h).

Local authority functions: subs. 1(b), (c) and (h)

Subs. (1)(b)—waste regulation
This subsection transfers to SEPA all local authority functions in their capacity as waste regulation authorities under the Control of Pollution (Amendment) Act 1989 and the Part II of the 1990 Act, including:

— the registration of carriers of controlled waste (Control of Pollution (Amendment) Act 1989, s.2; Controlled Waste (Registration of Carriers and Seizure of Vehicles) Regulations 1991 (S.I. 1991 No. 1624));
— the licensing of sites and plant for the disposal, treatment and storage of controlled waste (1990 Act, ss.35–36; Waste Management Licensing Regulations 1994 (S.I. 1994 No. 1056));
— the registration of sites and plant exempt from waste management licensing requirements (Waste Management Licensing Regulations 1994, reg. 18);
— the inspection of sites used for the recovery of scrap metal etc., which are registered as exempt from waste management licensing (1994 Regulations, regs. 17 and 18; Waste Management Licensing (Amendment etc.) Regulations 1995 (S.I. 1995 No. 288));
— the supervision and enforcement of waste law including the suspension and revocation of licences and the prosecution of offenders of waste facilities (1990 Act, ss.33; 37–38; and 42);
— functions in connection with the duty of care for waste (1990 Act, s.34; Environmental Protection (Duty of Care) Regulations 1991 (S.I. 1991, No. 2839));
— the regulation of the transfrontier shipment of waste including enforcement (Transfrontier Shipment of Waste Regulations 1994 (S.I. 1994 No. 1137));
— the registration of waste brokers (Waste Management Licensing Regulations 1994, reg. 20, Sched. 5);

— the power to accept the transfer and surrender of waste management licences (1990 Act, ss.39–40);
— the maintenance of registers of waste carrier registration, waste management licences, exemption from waste management licensing registration and waste broker registration (1990 Act, s.64; Waste Management Licensing Regulations 1994);
— the production of the Waste Disposal Plan (1990 Act, s.50; superseded by the waste strategy provisions of s.44B inserted by the 1995 Act, s.92: see the general note to ss.44A and 44B); and
— acting as statutory consultees in relation to proposals for development adjacent to landfill sites and former landfill sites (Town and Country Planning (General Development Procedure) (Scotland) Order 1992, art. 15(1)(1)).

Whereas in England and Wales, Part II of the 1990 Act brought about the division of waste regulatory and operational functions by requiring local authorities to set up arm's length local authority waste disposal companies or engage private waste contractors, similar changes were not introduced in Scotland where both regulatory and operational functions remained within district and islands councils. The potential for conflict which this arrangement might cause was identified in the Government's consultation paper on SEPA, *Improving Scotland's Environment: The Way Forward*, (para. 13) and was one of the key principles underlying the proposal to reform existing regulatory arrangements.

However, there was considerable criticism of the transfer of waste regulation functions to SEPA in Parliament on the grounds firstly, that waste was essentially a local problem and, secondly, that there presently existed perfectly satisfactory local accountable control over these functions (per Lord Carmichael of Kelvingrove *Hansard*, H.L. Vol. 560, col. 1188; see also Sam Galbraith—Standing Committee B, 2 May 1995 cols. 83–84)). The Government reiterated that the removal of the potential for conflict arising from the dual responsibility of district and islands councils for waste regulation and waste disposal was a key benefit which the transfer of WRA functions to SEPA would bring about along with the wider benefits which integration of these functions with other pollution control functions would secure (*per* Earl of Lindsay, *Hansard* H.L. Vol. 560, col. 1192; see also Sir Hector Monro, the then Parliamentary Under-Secretary of State for Scotland, H.C. Standing Committee, May 2, 1995, cols. 84–85).

Subs. (1)(c): waste regulation: residual functions under the 1974 Act

By s.30(1) of the Control of Pollution Act 1974 ("the 1974 Act"), waste regulation functions for the purposes of that Act are as follows:
— functions relating to disposal licences (ss.3–11);
— the removal of waste deposited in breach of licensing provisions (s.16);
— the giving of directions in relation to special waste, where provided for by regulations under s.17 (s.17(1)(a)); and
— the supervision of activities authorised by such special waste regulations, recovery of cost and expenses and functions in relation to appeals against disposal authority decisions under such regulations (s.17(2) (b)–(d)).

This subsection transfers to SEPA all local authority functions in their capacity as waste disposal authorities under Part I of the 1974 Act. They include the old waste disposal licensing functions which were only replaced when the new waste management licensing regime under Part II of the 1990 Act was brought into force on May 1, 1994. These functions have been transferred to SEPA as there may still be actions pending under the old legislation. Therefore, the importance of these transferred functions will become progressively less important with the passage of time and will become redundant when the last action under the 1974 Act is dealt with. The special waste controls in the 1974 Act, and the Control of Pollution (Special Waste) Regulations 1980 which were made under it, are far from being residual functions and run alongside the 1990 Act provisions. However, it is anticipated that soon after waste regulation is transferred the 1980 Regulations will have been supplanted by new regulations implementing the EC Hazardous Waste Directive 91/689/EEC.

Subs. (1)(h): Air Pollution Control

This subsection transfers to SEPA all local authority functions in their capacity as enforcing authorities for processes prescribed under Part B of Sched. 1 to the Environmental Protection (Prescribed Processes and Substances) Regulations 1991 for air pollution control by virtue of Part I of the 1990 Act. In England and Wales this function has not been transferred to the Agency and remains with local authorities.

The transfer of these functions to SEPA provoked considerable debate in Parliament. It was argued that it appeared inconsistent as this function was not being transferred to the Agency in

England and Wales and might therefore lead to differing approaches to air pollution control within Great Britain (see, for example, Lord Williams of Elvel, *Hansard*, H.L. Vol. 560, cols. 1194–1195). It was also argued that this function was being transferred from local accountable control which could respond quickly to an incident to a centralised, less accountable and less responsive control (see *e.g.* Archie Kirkwood, *Hansard*, H.C. Vol. 262, cols. 936–7).

However, the Government explained that the reasons for transferring this function to SEPA in Scotland were (1) that there were comparatively few Part B processes in Scotland in contrast to England and Wales and, of those, most were located in a very small number of local authority areas in the central belt with many local authorities having little or no experience of Part B processes at all even after taking into account local government reorganisation; and (2) that given that SEPA was being established with all the facilities and back-up which that entailed it made little sense to leave the 25–30 local authority staff who worked on air pollution dispersed throughout the country as the pooling resources would bring real benefits (*e.g. per* the Earl of Lindsay *Hansard*, H.L. Vol. 560, col. 1193 and Sir Hector Monro, Standing Committee B May 16, 1995 col. 240).

Subs. (1)(d)–(g): HMIPI functions
All of the functions of HMIPI are transferred to SEPA as follows:

Subs. (1)(d): Integrated pollution control
This subsection transfers to SEPA all HMIPI functions as enforcing authority for processes prescribed under Part A of Sched. 1 to the Environmental Protection (Prescribed Processes and Substances) Regulations 1991 (see Appendix 1) for integrated pollution control by virtue of Part I of the 1990 Act. In Scotland it should be noted that HMIPI was the enforcing authority for IPC in all cases except where there were emissions to water only or to water and land only in which case the relevant RPA was the enforcing authority by virtue of s.5 of the 1990 Act and the Environmental Protection (Determination of Enforcing Authority etc.) (Scotland) Regulations 1992 (S.I. 1992 No. 530)

Subs. (1)(e): Radioactive Substances
This subsection transfers to SEPA all HMIPI functions under the Radioactive Substances Act 1993 including:
— the registration of the keeping and use of radioactive material on premises and the registration of mobile radioactive apparatus (1993 Act, ss.7 and 10);
— the authorisation of the disposal or accumulation of radioactive waste (1993 Act, s.16);
— the enforcement of controls over radioactive substances (1993 Act, ss.6, 9, 13–14, 17, 21–22, and 32); and
— the maintenance of registers of registrations and authorisations (1993 Act, s.39).

Subs. (1)(f)–(g): pre-1990 Act controls
These subsections transfer to SEPA all functions conferred on or delegated to HMIPI by virtue of the Alkali etc. Works Regulation Act 1906 and Part I of the Health and Safety at Work etc. Act 1974, including:
— the registration of prescribed works (Alkali etc. Works Regulation Act 1906, s.9; Control of Industrial Air Pollution (Registration of Works) Regulations 1989 (S.I. 1989 No. 318));
— enforcement of 1906 Act controls by means of prohibition and improvement notices (Health and Safety at Work etc. Act 1974); and
— maintenance of a register of prescribed works registrations (1906 Act, s.9; 1989 Regulations).
The functions in subss. (1)(f)–(g) have been transferred to SEPA since they continue to apply to certain existing industrial processes which are not yet subject to Part I of the 1990 Act. For example, applications for Chapter 6 processes must be made by January 31, 1996 (Sched. 3, para. 18 to the Environmental Protection (Prescribed Processes & Substances) Regulations 1991). There may also still be actions pending under the old legislation. However, the significance of these transferred functions will progressively diminish with the passage of time and will cease when the last process registered under the 1906 Act is authorised under Part I of the 1990 Act and when the last action under the old legislation has been concluded.

Subs. (1)(i) & subs. (2) Functions of the Secretary of State
The miscellaneous functions specified in subs. (2) which have been exercised by the Secretary of State are transferred to SEPA by subs. (1)(i). These functions include his powers:

— to enforce controls under the Alkali etc. Works Regulation Act 1906 and s.5 of the Health and Safety at Work etc. Act 1974 (Health and Safety at Work etc. Act 1974, s.33). It should be noted that this role had been delegated to HMIPI.

Note that certain other miscellaneous functions are also transferred:

— in relation to the registration of works under the 1906 Act, although these do not include his appellate function;

— to require local authorities to declare smoke control areas (Clean Air Act 1993, s.19); and

— to dispose of radioactive waste on any premises where he is satisfied that it is unlikely for any reason that it will be lawfully disposed of (Radioactive Substances Act 1993, s.30).

Transfer of property, rights and liabilities to SEPA

22.—(1) On the transfer date—

(a) the property, rights and liabilities of every river purification board shall, by virtue of this paragraph, be transferred to and vested in SEPA;

(b) any property, rights and liabilities which are the subject of a scheme under this section—

(i) made by the Secretary of State; or

(ii) made by a local authority and approved by the Secretary of State,

shall be transferred to and vested in SEPA by and in accordance with the scheme.

(2) The Secretary of State may, before the transfer date, make a scheme for the transfer to SEPA of such of—

(a) his property, rights and liabilities; or

(b) the property, rights and liabilities of any of the inspectors or chief inspectors mentioned in subsection (1) of section 21 above,

as appear to the Secretary of State appropriate to be so transferred in consequence of the transfer of any functions to SEPA by virtue of that subsection.

(3) It shall be the duty of every local authority to make a scheme, after consultation with SEPA, for the transfer to SEPA of—

(a) such of the authority's property and rights as are held by it for the purposes of its functions as—

(i) a waste regulation authority;

(ii) a disposal authority under or by virtue of the provisions mentioned in section 21(1)(c) above;

(iii) enforcing authority, in relation to releases of substances into the air, by virtue of Part I of the 1990 Act; and

(iv) in the case of an islands council, a river purification authority; and

(b) such of its liabilities as are liabilities to which it is subject by virtue of its being an authority mentioned in paragraph (a)(i) to (iv) above,

and to submit that scheme to the Secretary of State for his approval before such date as he may direct.

(4) Any local authority preparing a scheme in pursuance of subsection (3) above shall take into account any guidance given by the Secretary of State as to the provisions which he regards as appropriate for inclusion in the scheme.

(5) Where a scheme under subsection (3) above is submitted to the Secretary of State, he may—

(a) approve the scheme;

(b) approve the scheme subject to such modifications as he considers appropriate; or

(c) reject the scheme;
but the power conferred on the Secretary of State by paragraph (b) above shall be exercisable only after consultation with the local authority which submitted the scheme to him and with SEPA.

(6) The Secretary of State may, in the case of any local authority which is required to make a scheme under subsection (3) above, himself make a scheme for the transfer to SEPA of such of the body's property, rights or liabilities as are mentioned in paragraph (a) or (b) of that subsection, if—

    (a) the authority fails to submit a scheme under that subsection to him for his approval before the due date; or

    (b) the Secretary of State rejects a scheme under that subsection submitted to him by the authority;

but nothing in this subsection shall prevent the Secretary of State from approving any scheme which may be submitted to him after the due date.

(7) Where the Secretary of State makes a transfer scheme under subsection (6) above, he may recover his reasonable expenses in doing so, or such proportion of those expenses as he thinks fit, from the local authority in question by such means as appear to him to be appropriate including, without prejudice to that generality, setting off the expenses payable by the local authority against revenue support grant or non-domestic rate income payable by the Secretary of State to the local authority under paragraph 3 of Schedule 12 to the Local Government Finance Act 1992.

(8) The Secretary of State may, at any time before the transfer date, modify any scheme made or approved by him under this section but only after consultation with SEPA and, in the case of a scheme which was approved by him (with or without modifications), after consultation with the local authority which submitted the scheme to him for approval.

(9) Schedule 2 to this Act shall have effect in relation to transfers by or under this section.

DEFINITIONS
"disposal authority": s.56(1); s.30(2) of the 1974 Act.
"enforcing authority": s.1(8) of the 1990 Act.
"functions": s.124(1).
"local authority": s.56(1)–(2).
"modifications": s.124(1).
"river purification authority": s.56(1); s.17(2) of the Rivers (Prevention of Pollution) (Scotland) Act 1951.
"river purification board": s.56(1); s.135 of the Local Government (Scotland) Act 1973.
"transfer date": s.56(1).
"SEPA": s.124(1).
"waste regulation authority": s.56(1).

COMMENCEMENT
October 12, 1995 (S.I. 1995 No. 2649).

GENERAL NOTE
This section and Schedule 2 to which it gives effect (subs. (9)), deal with the transfer of property, rights and liabilities from existing bodies to SEPA. The provisions mirror those in relation to the Agency. See also the note to s.3, Scottish Office Environment Department Circular 19/95, *Transfer of Property, Rights and Liabilities from District and Islands Councils to the Scottish Environment Protection Agency* (October 12, 1995) provides guidance to local authorities on their duties under this section in respect of these transfers. Circular 19/95 was produced following consultation with COSLA, UNISON and the Local Government Staff Commission on draft guidance.

Property, rights and liabilities
These terms are not further defined but details of what they include are given in paras. 2 and 3 of Sched. 2.

The Transfer Date
The date on which all transfers of property, rights and liabilities from existing bodies to SEPA take effect is the "transfer date". The Secretary of State appointed April 1, 1996 as the transfer date. April 1, 1996 was also appointed as the transfer date in England and Wales.

On the transfer date, by subs. (1) all the property, rights and liabilities of every river purification board (which bodies, when s.21(3) came into force were dissolved) were transferred to and vested in SEPA, as were such other property, rights and liabilities as were subject to a scheme made under this section by the Secretary of State or by a local authority and approved by the Secretary of State. See also the note to s.3.

Schemes of Transfer
Two kinds of transfer schemes are provided for by s.22. First, s.21(1)(d)–(g) and (i) transfer functions of the inspectors, the chief inspector (HMIPI) and the Secretary of State to SEPA. Subs. (2) provides that before the transfer date the Secretary of State may make a scheme of such of his and their property, rights and liabilities as appear to him appropriate in consequence of the transfer of those functions.

Secondly, s.21(1)(b)–(c) and (h) transfer the local authority functions as waste regulation authorities, disposal authorities and as enforcing authorities in relation to air pollution control by virtue of Part I of the Environmental Protection Act 1990 and, in the case of islands councils, as river purification authorities to SEPA.

Subs. (3) provides that every local authority is placed under a duty to make a scheme for the transfer to SEPA of such of its property, rights and liabilities as are held by it or, to which it is subject, in relation to its transferred functions. This must be done after consultation with SEPA and taking into account any guidance issued by the Secretary of State under subs. (4) including Circular 19/95. This Circular includes, at Annex B, a Model Transfer Scheme which is divided into two sections: I—Supporting Information; and II—Scheme. The Scheme is further divided into rights and liabilities under the following heads: contracts of employment; property (including land and buildings, vehicles, equipment, intellectual property and records); rights and liabilities under contracts for the provision of services to or by the council; and interests, rights and liabilities to be created between the Council and SEPA.

The Circular also indicates that the Scheme should include all other minor items of property which the Council is accustomed to use in the discharge of any of its functions which are to be transferred to SEPA and are not specified fully elsewhere in the Scheme.

Circular 19/95 indicates that where waste regulation authority staff within a council have been working on the monitoring or control of closed landfill sites which will not come under the control of SEPA they should not be included in a transfer scheme (para. A19). However, where they have been engaged in spending a significant proportion of their work in performing an advisory role in relation to contaminated land and closed landfills, the Circular indicates that councils may consider it appropriate for them to transfer to SEPA since their advisory role may be seen as analogous to the advisory, guidance giving role which SEPA will have in relation to contaminated land (paras. A20–A21). Each local authority must submit its scheme to the Secretary of State for his approval by such date as he may direct, although he may nonetheless approve a scheme received after that date: subs. (3) and (6). Circular 19/95 indicates that the Secretary of State directed all district and islands councils to submit their transfer schemes for approval no later than Friday, December 15, 1995 (para. 3).

Subs. (5)
The Secretary of State has considerable discretion on receipt of a scheme. He may approve it (with or without modifications) or reject it. However, the Secretary of State may only exercise the power to approve the scheme subject to modifications after consultation with the local authority which submitted the scheme and with SEPA.

Subs. (6)
This subsection provides the Secretary of State with default powers enabling him to make a scheme which he may exercise (a) where no scheme is submitted by a local authority by the due date or (b) where he has rejected a scheme which has been submitted. However, he may also approve a scheme submitted after the due date.

Subs. (7)
This subsection applies where the Secretary of State has exercised his default powers under subs. (6) to make a scheme and enables him to recover his reasonable expenses or such

proportion of those expenses as he thinks fit from the local authority in question. The method of recovery may include setting off his expenses against revenue support grant or non-domestic rate income payable by the Secretary of State to the local authority.

Functions of staff commission

23. The functions of the staff commission established under section 12 of the Local Government etc. (Scotland) Act 1994 shall include—
  (a) considering and keeping under review the arrangements for the transfer to SEPA, in consequence of this Act or of any scheme made under it, of staff employed by local authorities;
  (b) considering such staffing problems arising out of, consequential on or connected with any provision of, or scheme made under, this Act as may be referred to them by the Secretary of State or by any local authority;
  (c) advising the Secretary of State as to the steps necessary to safeguard the interests of the staff referred to in paragraph (a) above.

DEFINITIONS
"local authority": s.56(1)–(2).
"SEPA": s.124(1).

COMMENCEMENT
October 12, 1995 (S.I. 1995 No. 2649).

GENERAL NOTE
The remit of the staff commission provided for by s.12 of the Local Government etc. (Scotland) Act 1994 in connection with local government reorganisation in Scotland is extended by this section to cover issues arising out of the transfer of staff to SEPA (s.23(a)–(b)) and advising the Secretary of State on steps necessary to safeguard the interests of staff being transferred to SEPA (s.23(c)) given that local government reorganisation is proceeding in tandem with the establishment of SEPA and because not only WRA functions but also local air pollution control functions are being transferred to SEPA. The Government have assured Parliament that "… staff who transfer to SEPA will have protection under TUPE or equivalent provisions …" (Viscount Ullswater, Minister of State, Department of the Environment, *Hansard*, H.L. Vol. 560, col. 624). See also Circular 19/95, *Transfer of Property, Rights and Liabilities from District and Islands Councils to the Scottish Environment Protection Agency* (October 12, 1995, para. 7).
    It should be noted that the staff commission was established by order on November 25, 1994 (see the Local Government Staff Commission (Scotland) Order 1994 (S.1. 1994 No. 2958)).

Other functions etc. of SEPA

Consultation with respect to drainage works

24.—(1) Subject to subsection (2) below, any person proposing to carry out drainage works shall—
  (a) before commencing such works, consult SEPA as to precautions to be taken to prevent pollution to controlled waters as a result of the works; and
  (b) in carrying out such works, take account of SEPA's views.
    (2) The Secretary of State may, by regulations made by statutory instrument subject to annulment in pursuance of a resolution of either House of Parliament, prescribe types of drainage works in relation to which subsection (1) above shall not apply.
    (3) In this section, "drainage works" has the same meaning as in the Land Drainage (Scotland) Act 1958 and "controlled waters" has the same meaning as in the Control of Pollution Act 1974.

DEFINITIONS
"controlled waters": subs. (3); s.30A of the 1974 Act.
"drainage works": subs. (3); s.18(1) of the Land Drainage (Scotland) Act 1958.
"SEPA": s.124(1).

Commencement
April 1, 1996 (S.I. 1996 No. 186).

GENERAL NOTE

This section provides SEPA with a new function which requires persons proposing to undertake drainage works to consult with SEPA subject to certain exceptions which are to be prescribed in regulations which the Secretary of State is empowered to make (subs. (2)). The Government explained that their intention was "to place on a statutory footing the consultation which is currently required as a condition of the payment of grant for drainage works from the Forestry Commission and the Scottish Office, and to extend the consultation requirement to other significant drainage works" (*per* the Earl of Lindsay, *Hansard*, H.L. Vol. 560, col. 1216).

Concern was expressed that there is no criminal penalty attached to this section for failure to consult with SEPA before undertaking drainage works (see *e.g.* Sam Galbraith, Standing Committee B, May 16, 1995 col. 241) However, interdict may be available to SEPA in the absence of a prescribed statutory remedy (see also note to s.37) and, if the works in question resulted in pollution of controlled waters, a charge of causing or knowingly permitting pollution of controlled waters could be brought under the new s.30F of the Control of Pollution Act 1974 (which replaces s.31 of the 1974 Act) introduced by this Act.

Subs. (1)

Consultation is restricted to precautions to be taken to prevent pollution of controlled waters. The rather limited scope of consultation appears, for example, to exclude precautions to prevent any environmental damage and flooding. Concern was expressed about this at Report Stage in the House of Lords (*per* Lord Carmichael of Kelvingrove, *Hansard*, H.L. Vol. 560, col. 1692). However, the Government stated that they considered that any amendment which would widen the range of precautions to be included in the consultation would considerably extend SEPA's interest beyond its normal span of responsibilities, *i.e.* pollution prevention and control:

> "There is one very clear reason why it would make sense for SEPA to be consulted as to the precautions to prevent pollution resulting from drainage works. If pollution was to result from the carrying on of such works, SEPA might have to prepare a case for the procurator fiscal. The agency would have no corresponding role if the drainage works were alleged to have caused other environmental damage" (*per* the Earl of Lindsay, *Hansard*, H.L. Vol. 560, cols. 1692–1693).

Subs. (2)

The Secretary of State is empowered to prescribe exceptions to the duty to consult by means of regulations using the negative resolution procedure which gives Parliament some degree of oversight in that it may reject the proposed regulations although it cannot amend them.

The Government envisaged that regulations made under this subs. would prescribe minor drainage works such as tile drains and repairs to existing drains where the risk of pollution was so low as to make the need to consult unwarranted and promised wide consultation among interested parties (see *e.g.* the Earl of Lindsay *Hansard*, H.L. Vol. 560, col. 1216; see also Sir Hector Monro, the then Parliamentary Under-Secretary of State for Scotland, Standing Committee B, May 16, 1995, col. 242).

Assessing flood risk

25.—(1) Without prejudice to section 92 of the Agriculture Act 1970 (provision of flood warning systems), SEPA shall have the function of assessing, as far as it considers it appropriate, the risk of flooding in any area of Scotland.

(2) If requested by a planning authority to do so, SEPA shall, on the basis of such information as it holds with respect to the risk of flooding in any part of the authority's area, provide the authority with advice as to such risk.

DEFINITIONS

"planning authority": s.172(1) of the Local Government (Scotland) Act 1973.
"SEPA": s.124(1).

COMMENCEMENT
April 1, 1996 (S.I. 1996 No. 186).

GENERAL NOTE

This section provides SEPA with another new function. Recent flooding in various parts of Scotland gave rise to considerable parliamentary debate regarding SEPA's role in relation to flooding (see also the Introductory Note to Part I under *Functions transferred and differences between the Agencies*). Responsibility for functions in relation to flooding has in the past been split between river purification authorities and local authorities. Part VI of the Agriculture Act 1970 empowered river purification authorities to provide and operate flood warning systems within their areas. However, responsibility for flood defence works under the Flood Prevention (Scotland) Act 1961 lay with regional and islands councils. Although the 1995 Act transfers RPA responsibility for flood warning systems to SEPA by s.21(1)(a)(iv) and Sched. 22 para. 14 which makes the necessary consequential amendments, flood defence powers will remain with local authorities although they were transferred to the new unitary authorities established by the local Government etc. (Scotland) Act 1994 on April 1, 1996. The Government did not consider that it was appropriate to transfer flood prevention and defence powers to SEPA as

"We believe that the lead in all planning matters must be unambiguous. Local authorities already have all the powers they need to tackle flooding and to take any precautionary measures against the threat of flooding. Local authorities must retain unambiguously that responsibility to prevent flooding. Similarly, with its undoubted role in planning, we believe that it is much better that an elected council makes the final decision as to where development can or cannot take place, having taken all factors into account" (*per* the Earl of Lindsay *Hansard*, H.L. Vol. 565, col. 1482).

This section is intended to complement those existing provisions by imposing on SEPA a new duty to assess the risk of flooding in any area of Scotland. A planning authority will also be able to request SEPA to provide it with advice on the risk of flooding anywhere within its area. This provision was introduced to "ensure that councils can take well-informed decisions on flooding matters which will reflect local concerns and the general public interest" (*per* the Earl of Lindsay, *Hansard*, H.L. Vol. 565, col. 1481).

Subs. (1)

SEPA's duty assess flood risk in any area of Scotland is limited to the extent that any assessment it makes is only to the extent that it considers appropriate.

Subs. (2)

SEPA is placed under a duty to advise any planning authority which requests advice as to flood risk within any part of the authority's area. The Government explained that

"Local authorities must give flood prevention a high priority if SEPA's advice is that flooding is a serious risk. . . . SEPA will give advice to the planning authority before it gives approval. It is important to realise that, if SEPA's advice is that the area in question is dangerous, and if the planning authority still wants to go ahead, the application must go to the Secretary of State, and, if necessary, he will call it in." (Sir Hector Monro, the then Parliamentary Under-Secretary of State for Scotland, *Hansard*, H.C. Vol. 262, cols. 948–949)

It should also be noted that the Government have produced a National Planning Policy Guideline, *NPPG 7 "Planning and Flooding"* (Scottish Office Environment Department, September 1995) which provides that the susceptibility of land to flooding is a material consideration in determining a planning application even if flooding is not mentioned in the current development plan (para. 60). It is in the context of preparing development plans and determining planning applications that planning authorities should request SEPA to provide advice on the risk of flooding (paras. 13 and 60).

Power of SEPA to purchase land compulsorily

26.—(1) The Secretary of State may authorise SEPA, for the purpose of any of its functions, to purchase land compulsorily.

(2) The Acquisition of Land (Authorisation Procedure) (Scotland) Act 1947 shall apply in relation to the compulsory purchase of land under this section as if this section had been in force immediately before the commencement of that Act and, in relation to such purchase of land, SEPA shall be treated as if it were a local authority within the meaning of that Act.

DEFINITIONS
   "functions": s.124(1).
   "SEPA": s.124(1).

COMMENCEMENT
April 1, 1996 (S.I. 1996 No. 186).

GENERAL NOTE

This section re-enacts the existing power of the Secretary of State to authorise compulsory purchase by river purification authorities under s.9 of the Rivers (Prevention of Pollution) (Scotland) Act 1951. Despite this considerable concern was expressed in Parliament regarding the potential for misuse of these powers and amendments were proposed to provide additional safeguards for landowners on their use (*Hansard*, H.L. Vol. 560, cols. 1221–1222; Vol. 561, cols. 1694–1697; H.L. Vol. 562, cols. 1029–1031).

In particular, it was pointed out that additional safeguards involving the use of a special parliamentary procedure (provided in the Statutory Orders (Special Procedure) Acts 1945 and 1965) had been placed on similar powers in s.5(4) of the Natural Heritage (Scotland) Act 1991 in relation to Scottish Natural Heritage (SNH). However, the Government argued that greater safeguards were necessary in the case of SNH as the power to purchase land compulsorily was potentially a powerful tool in the hands of a nature conservation body whereas the purchase of land was not a normal means of preventing or controlling pollution (*per* the Earl of Lindsay, *Hansard*, H.L. Vol. 561, col. 1696 and Vol. 562, col. 1031). Accordingly, the Government argued that additional safeguards were unnecessary and that the Secretary of State's role would provide "a safety net against any unreasonable use of such powers" (*per* the Earl of Lindsay *Hansard*, H.L. Vol. 560, col. 1223). Moreover, it was pointed out that the compulsory purchase powers in the 1951 Act had never in fact been used (*per* the Earl of Lindsay, *Hansard*, H.L. Vol. 561, col. 1696). Use of the powers would be authorised by the Secretary of State as a last resort "in relation to specific land required by the agency to discharge its functions effectively only in circumstances where other locations were unsuitable and where it was not possible for a reasonable agreement between SEPA and the landowner to be reached" (*per* the Earl of Lindsay *Hansard*, H.L. Vol. 561, col. 1696). The powers are further limited by being exercisable only for the purpose of any of SEPA's functions (subs. (1)).

Land

Since there is no definition of land in the Act, it would appear that the definition of land in the Interpretation Act 1978 is applicable. Therefore, land includes, for example, a right over land and also land covered by water.

Power of SEPA to obtain information about land

27.—(1) Where, with a view to performing a function conferred on it by any enactment, SEPA considers that it ought to have information connected with any land, it may serve on one or more of the persons mentioned in subsection (2) below a notice—

(a) specifying the land, the function and the enactment; and

(b) requiring the recipient of the notice to furnish to SEPA, within such period of not less than 14 days from the date of service of the notice as is specified in the notice—

(i) the nature of his interest in the land; and

(ii) the name and address of each person whom he believes is, as respects the land, a person mentioned in subsection (2) below.

(2) The persons referred to in subsection (1) above are—

(a) the occupier of the land;

(b) any person—

(i) who has an interest in the land as owner, creditor in a heritable security or lessee; or

(ii) who directly or indirectly receives rent for the land; and

(c) any person who, in pursuance of an agreement between himself and a person interested in the land, is authorised to manage the land or to arrange for the letting of it.

(3) A person who—

(a) fails to comply with the requirements of a notice served on him in pursuance of subsection (1) above; or

(b) in furnishing any information in compliance with such a notice makes a statement which he knows to be false in a material particular or recklessly makes a statement which is false in a material particular,

shall be guilty of an offence and liable on summary conviction to a fine not exceeding level 5 on the standard scale.

DEFINITIONS
    "functions": s.124(1).
    "notice": s.124(1).
    "SEPA": s.124(1).

COMMENCEMENT
April 1, 1996 (S.I. 1996 No. 186).

GENERAL NOTE
This section empowers SEPA to obtain information regarding the persons who have an interest in a particular piece of land. The Government explained that "The power is needed by the agencies in order to enable them to carry out their pollution control and prevention functions" (*per* the Earl of Lindsay, *Hansard*, H.L. Vol 565, col. 1484) which can hardly be said to shed much light on the need for this power. However, the need for the power was clearly illustrated in *R v. Dovermoss Ltd.* [1995] Env. L.R. 258 (C.A.), a prosecution under s.85 of the Water Resources Act 1991 in Wales, in which the appellants succeeded on appeal in having their conviction quashed as they established that the prosecution had not proved that they owned or occupied the farm at which the pollution had occurred or carried on the farming enterprise there. It should be noted that similar provision is made for England and Wales by virtue of Sched. 22, para. 33 to the Act which amends the Local Government (Miscellaneous Provisions) Act 1976 to enable the Agency to exercise similar powers.

Subs. (1)
The notice must comply with the procedural requirements in subs. (1)(a) and may only be served on a person specified in subs. (2). The information which may be sought is also limited to that detailed in subs. (1)(b).

Subs. (3)
Failure to comply with the requirements of a notice, or to knowingly or recklessly make a statement which is false in a material particular, is made a criminal offence with a maximum penalty not exceeding level 5, presently £5,000.

Power of SEPA to promote or oppose private legislation

28.—(1) SEPA may, where it is satisfied that it is expedient to do so—
    (a) with the consent of the Secretary of State, petition for the issue of a provisional order under the Private Legislation Procedure (Scotland) Act 1936; or
    (b) oppose any private legislation in Parliament.
(2) An application for the consent mentioned in paragraph (a) of subsection (1) above shall be accompanied by a concise summary of the purposes of the order petitioned for.
(3) In paragraph (b) of subsection (1) above, "private legislation in Parliament" includes—
    (a) a provisional order and a Confirmation Bill relating to such an order; and
    (b) any local or personal Bill.

DEFINITIONS
    "private legislation in Parliament": subs. (3).
    "SEPA": s.124(1).

COMMENCEMENT
April 1, 1996 (S.I. 1996 No. 186).

GENERAL NOTE
SEPA is empowered by this section to promote private legislation with the consent of the Secretary of State under the Private Legislation Procedure (Scotland) Act 1936 or to oppose such legislation.

Procedure relating to making of byelaws

29. The following provisions of the Local Government (Scotland) Act 1973—
    (a) section 202 (procedure etc. for byelaws);
    (b) section 202C (revocation of byelaws);
    (c) section 204 (evidence of byelaws),
shall apply in relation to SEPA as they apply in relation to a local authority, provided that in the application of the said section 202 to SEPA for subsection (13) there shall be substituted—

"(13) The Scottish Environment Protection Agency shall send a copy of any byelaws made by it to the proper officer of the local authority for any area to the whole or any part of which the byelaws will apply.".

DEFINITIONS
"local authority": s.56(1)–(2).
"SEPA": s.124(1).

COMMENCEMENT
April 1, 1996 (S.I. 1996 No. 186).

GENERAL NOTE
Certain provisions of the Local Government (Scotland) Act 1973 relating to byelaws are extended by this section to include SEPA which is empowered thereunder to make byelaws as though it were a local authority.

Records held by SEPA

30.—(1) Subject to subsection (3) below—
    (a) this section applies to all records (in whatever form or medium)—
        (i) transferred to and vested in SEPA by or under section 22 above;
        (ii) created or acquired by it in the exercise of any of its functions; or
        (iii) otherwise in its keeping;
    (b) SEPA shall ensure that the records, other than such as are mentioned in paragraph (c) below, are preserved and managed in accordance with such arrangements as it, after consulting the Keeper of the Records of Scotland, shall put into effect;
    (c) records which in SEPA's opinion are not worthy of preservation may be disposed of by it;
    (d) SEPA may from time to time revise the arrangements mentioned in paragraph (b) above but before making any material change to those arrangements shall consult the Keeper; and
    (e) SEPA—
        (i) shall secure that the Keeper has, at all reasonable hours, unrestricted access to the records preserved by it;
        (ii) may afford members of the public, free of charge or on payment of reasonable charges, facilities for inspecting and for obtaining copies or extracts from those records.

(2) Nothing in subsection (1)(e)(ii) above permits infringement of copyright or contravention of conditions subject to which records are in SEPA's keeping.

(3) Insofar as any provision of any enactment, being a provision which relates to records of a specific kind, is (but for this subsection) inconsistent

with subsection (1) above, that subsection is subject to the provision in question.

DEFINITIONS
"functions": s.124(1).
"records": s.124(1).
"SEPA": s.124(1).

COMMENCEMENT
April 1, 1996 (S.I. 1996 No. 186).

GENERAL NOTE
This section provides for record keeping and disposal by SEPA and makes provision for access to records held by SEPA. It should be noted that these provisions are distinct from statutory requirements to keep registers in relation to SEPA's various pollution control functions.

The provisions relating to public access to records held by SEPA proved to be highly controversial in Parliament. This is because subs. (1)(e)(ii) gives SEPA discretion in deciding whether to allow members of the public access to its records and whether to provide inspection facilities and copies free of charge or on payment of a reasonable sum.

Firstly, it was argued in Parliament that SEPA should be placed under a duty to provide access to its records rather than merely having a power to provide such access (*e.g. per* Lord Carmichael of Kelvingrove *Hansard*, H.L. Vol. 561, col. 1697). However, the Government pointed out that SEPA's discretion in this respect was limited as it was subject to the Environmental Information Regulations 1992 (S.I. 1992 No. 3240) (*per* the Earl of Lindsay *Hansard*, H.L. Vol. 560, cols. 1198–1199), and that refusal to afford access would only be possible on the basis of exemptions provided for in those Regulations (*per* the Earl of Lindsay, *Hansard*, H.L. Vol. 561, col. 1697).

Secondly, concern was also expressed about the power given to SEPA to set "reasonable" charges for inspection facilities or for obtaining copies of records. The Government justification for this discretion was that "If the inconvenience and staff time involved appears disproportionate to the value of the data on the record, then it is surely right that SEPA should have some discretion" (*per* the Earl of Lindsay, *Hansard*, H.L. Vol. 561, col. 1698). As to the interpretation of "reasonable", the Earl of Lindsay explained "I recognise the concern that can arise about the interpretation which may be placed on the 'reasonableness' of photocopying charges. The establishment of a single, national agency should assist in this respect. I also believe that it is right in principle that SEPA should be able to set reasonable charges which recover the costs it incurs in providing copies of documents. But I agree that it should not seek to debar access through inflated charges" (*Hansard*, H.L. Vol. 560, col. 1198). It should be noted that in the past photocopying charges imposed by local authorities for copies from the statutory air pollution control register under Part I of the Environmental Protection Act 1990 have in some cases been as high as £5 per page which may be sufficient to debar access (see: *Come Clean! Public Access to information about local authority air pollution control* (Scottish Consumer Council & Friends of the Earth Scotland, 1993)).

Reference should also be made to the Introductory Note to Part I under the heading *The Agencies and access to information*.

Subs. (1)
SEPA must consult the Keeper of the Records of Scotland prior to making arrangements for preserving and managing records (subs. (1)(b)) except in the case of records which, in SEPA's opinion, are not worthy of preservation and which may accordingly be disposed of (subs. (1)(c)). Although record keeping arrangements may be revised, SEPA must consult with the Keeper before any material change is made (subs. (1)(d)). A *material* change would clearly not include minor changes but nonetheless what constituted a *material change* is likely to be very largely a matter of fact and degree as planning law illustrates: *e.g. East Barnet U.D.C. v. British Transport Commission* [1963] 1 W.L.R. 247; and *Braddon v. Secretary of State for the Environment* [1977] J.P.L. 450.

Although SEPA has a discretion as regards public access to records (subs. (1)(e)(ii)), it is under a duty to ensure that the Keeper has unrestricted access to its records at all reasonable hours (subs. (1)(e)(i)).

Subs. (3)
Where any provision in any other enactment is inconsistent with subs. (1), the provision in question is to prevail over subs. (1). This is of considerable significance in the context of the

relationship between subs. (1)(c) and the Environmental Information Regulations 1992 (S.I. 1992 No. 3240). There appears to be potential for conflict between subs. (1)(c) and those Regulations as SEPA has discretion in determining which records are worthy of preservation. It may be that in exercising that discretion SEPA disposes of records which contain information relating to the environment in terms of the Regulations and which are not subject to any of the exemptions set out in the Regulations. The disposal of such records would be unlawful, although clearly no legal action could recover them. If a person were aware that such records had existed, it presumably would be possible to raise an action of proving the tenor in the Court of Session to attempt to ascertain details of the contents of the records disposed of.

General powers and duties

Guidance on sustainable development and other aims and objectives

31.—(1) The Secretary of State shall from time to time give guidance to SEPA with respect to aims and objectives which he considers it appropriate for SEPA to pursue in the performance of its functions.

(2) The guidance given under subsection (1) above must include guidance with respect to the contribution which, having regard to SEPA's responsibilities and resources, the Secretary of State considers it appropriate for SEPA to make, by the performance of its functions, towards attaining the objective of achieving sustainable development.

(3) In performing its functions, SEPA shall have regard to guidance given under this section.

(4) The power to give guidance to SEPA under this section shall be exercisable only after consultation with SEPA and such other bodies or persons as the Secretary of State considers it appropriate to consult in relation to the guidance in question.

(5) A draft of any guidance proposed to be given under this section shall be laid before each House of Parliament and the guidance shall not be given until after the period of 40 days beginning with the day on which the draft was so laid or, if the draft is laid on different days, the later of the two days.

(6) If, within the period mentioned in subsection (5) above, either House resolves that the guidance, the draft of which was laid before it, should not be given, the Secretary of State shall not give that guidance.

(7) In reckoning any period of 40 days for the purposes of subsection (5) or (6) above, no account shall be taken of any time during which Parliament is dissolved or prorogued or during which both Houses are adjourned for more than four days.

(8) The Secretary of State shall arrange for any guidance given under this section to be published in such manner as he considers appropriate.

DEFINITIONS
 "functions": s.124(1).
 "SEPA": s.124(1).

COMMENCEMENT
October 12, 1995 (S.I. 1995 No. 2649).

GENERAL NOTE
Unlike the Agency, SEPA has no principal aim. The Secretary of State is under a duty to give SEPA guidance on the aims and objectives he considers it appropriate for SEPA to pursue (subs. (1)). However, this guidance must include guidance on the contribution SEPA is to make to the objective of achieving sustainable development (subs. (2)). In the original Environment Bill, wording identical to s.31(1)–(3) was used in relation to the Agency in the then cl.4. Concerns were expressed in Parliament that the agencies had no specified statutory aims and objectives particularly in relation to sustainable development (see *e.g. Hansard*, H.L. Vol. 559, col. 1450; Vol. 560, col. 1776). However, the Government argued that specifying a statutory purpose for the agencies related to sustainable development was not appropriate, firstly, as it was "dangerous to seek to overspecify on the face of the Bill the full contents of the guidance. A long list might appear exhaustive but not cover all issues on which, in future, the Ministers might need to give guidance to the Agency to SEPA" and that specification in detail might lead to the

wrong emphasis being given to certain aspects of sustainable development (*per* Viscount Ullswater, Minister of State, Department of the Environment, *Hansard*, H.L. Vol. 560, cols. 574–575). Secondly, they argued that the agencies, could not on their own achieve sustainable development (*per* Viscount Ullswater *Hansard*, H.L. Vol. 560, col. 575).

Although a principal aim was subsequently introduced for the Agency in s.4, no similar provision was made for SEPA. The Government's reasons for refusing to introduce a parallel principal aim for SEPA were essentially the same as those given by Viscount Ullswater above (see *e.g.* Robert Atkins, M.P., Minister for the Environment and Countryside, Standing Committee B, April 27, 1995, col. 32) although they also explained:

> "Given the fact that SEPA would already have a more defined focus on the prevention and control of pollution than the Environment Agency for England and Wales, which would have wider functions, the Government are not convinced that it is necessary for SEPA to have a principal aim set out in legislation" (*per* the Earl of Lindsay *Hansard*, H.L. Vol. 561, col. 1689).

SEPA's narrower focus essentially arises from the fact that the functions transferred to it from the RPAs do not include the wide ranging functions in relation to water resources management and flood defence which the NRA enjoyed in England and Wales. It is, however, noteworthy that SEPA's sister agency, Scottish Natural Heritage (SNH) which deals, *inter alia*, with nature conservation matters, is required to have regard to the desirability of ensuring that anything done in relation to natural heritage "is undertaken in a manner which is sustainable" (Natural Heritage (Scotland) Act 1991, s.1(1)).

There was also debate on whether SEPA should be given a statutory aim to protect or enhance the environment in discharging its functions along lines similar to the aim given to the Agency in s.4 (*e.g. per.* Lord Carmichael of Kelvingrove *Hansard*, H.L. Vol. 560, col. 1687). The Government again rejected such suggestions and explained

> "In practice, an aim of this type in a management statement or guidance can sit more comfortably alongside any duties of the agency which could in other circumstances have led to conflict with the aim. However, if that non-statutory duty were to be enshrined in the Bill as a duty, . . . , there would be no obvious way of establishing a hierarchy of action" (*per* the Earl of Lindsay *Hansard*, H.L. Vol. 560, col. 1689).

This explanation leaves something to be desired since the Government were prepared to give such a principal aim to the Agency: the implications of that aim are considered in the general note to s.4.

Subs. (1)–(2)

Guidance on aims and objectives
On October 13, 1994, the Government published a draft *Management Statement* for SEPA. This non-statutory document contained a number of proposed main objectives for SEPA. On May 3, 1995 the Government issued a preliminary draft of the proposed guidance: *Draft Guidance to the Scottish Environment Protection Agency under Clause 29 of the Environment Bill*. Revised draft guidance, *The Scottish Environment Protection Agency and Sustainable Development* (November 1995), was issued for consultation on December 12, 1995. It is divided into statutory and non-statutory sections. The statutory guidance on SEPA's aims and objectives and its contribution towards achieving sustainable development to which SEPA must have regard by virtue of subs. (3) is contained in Appendix I while the remainder of the guidance on the principles of sustainable development and costs and benefits is non-statutory. Although SEPA is not obliged to have regard to non-statutory guidance such guidance will still be of considerable significance in, for example, appeals to the Secretary of State where all relevant matters whether statutory or not would be considered. However, it is not always apparent why certain provisions have been omitted from the statutory section of the guidance as, for example, in the case of the guidance on SEPA's contribution to sustainable development (see further below).

The revised draft guidance indicates that the Government's main purpose in creating SEPA was

> "to enable existing functions to be exercised in such a way as to bring greater benefit both to the environment and to those who are being regulated" (Appendix I, para. 4).

SEPA's principal aim is to be:

> "to deliver well-managed integrated environmental protection, not only as an end in itself but as a contribution to the Government's goal of sustainable development" (Appendix I, para. 6).

SEPA's principal aim is subject to the provisions of the Environment Act 1995, any other enactment under which SEPA will operate and the requirement to take into account costs (App. I, para. 7) and is therefore only applicable where SEPA has some discretion in the exercise of its functions and even then SEPA must only have regard to it. See also the note to s.4. As regards objectives, the guidance provides that SEPA should:

"(i) adopt, across all its functions, an integrated approach to environmental protection and enhancement which considers impacts of substances and activities on all environmental media and on natural resources;

(ii) work with all relevant sectors of society, including regulated organisations, to develop approaches which deliver environmental requirements and goals without imposing excessive costs (in relation to benefits gained) on regulated organisations or society as a whole;

(iii) adopt clear and effective procedures for serving its customers, including by developing single points of contact through which regulated organisations can deal with the Agency [sic];

(iv) operate to high professional standards, based on sound science, information and analysis of the environment and of processes which affect it;

(v) organise its activities in ways which reflect good environmental and management practice and provide value for money for those who pay its charges and taxpayers as a whole;

(vi) provide clear and readily available advice and information on its work; and

(vii) develop a close and responsive relationship with the public, local authorities and other representatives of local communities and regulated organisations" (App. I, para. 8).

Principles of Sustainable Development
The non-statutory part of the revised draft guidance outlines the principles of sustainable development and provides the definition of sustainable development adopted by the World Commission on Environment and Development in 1987:

"Development that meets the needs to the present without compromising the ability of future generations to meet their own needs" (para. 4.1)

However, it does not attempt to define the phrase further. What it does do is to refer to the *UK Strategy on Sustainable Development* (Cm.2426, 1994) which emphasises both the need for economic development and the importance of caring for the environment (para. 2.1). The specific principles which the guidance indicates are of especial relevance to SEPA are as follows:

— using the best scientific information available;

— the precautionary principle on which action should be based when damage to the environment is both uncertain and significant;

— the "polluter pays" principle which "requires that, when production processes threaten or cause damage to the environment, the cost of necessary environmental measures should be borne by the producer, and not by society at large, giving incentives to reduce the pollution";

— the wise use of natural environmental capital which involves finding ways of enhancing total wealth while using common natural resources in prudent ways which consider the interests of future generations and whether there is a risk of irreversible environmental effects and, if so, how significant they may be;

— the carrying capacity of habitats and ecosystems which involves the consideration the ability of a habitat to support a particular species or the capacity of the environmental to absorb pollution or waste; and

— the interests of future generations which should be allowed for when judgments are being made about whether environmental costs have to be accepted as the price of economic development or not. (paras. 2.3–2.9)

SEPA's Contribution
The statutory section of the guidance (App. I, para. 9) indicates that SEPA should (i) take a holistic approach to **the protection and enhancement of the environment** and accordingly carry out its functions so as to take account of the cross media impacts of pollutants; (ii) take a **long term perspective** taking into account longer term implications and effects; (iii) pay particular attention to its statutory conservation obligations since maintaining **biodiversity** is an essential element of sustainable development; (iv) where possible discharge its regulatory functions in **partnership with business** in ways which maximise the scope for cost-effective investment in **improved technologies and management techniques** and, in general, SEPA should seek "(a) to establish clear and stable policy parameters, so that regulated organisations can plan for the

future; (b) to encourage regulated organisations to adopt plans and management techniques—such as those envisaged in BS7750 and the EU Eco-Management and Audit Scheme—to enable them to meet the policy parameters at (a) above and to seek innovative ways of meeting environmental objectives. In doing so it should bear in mind that different approaches may be appropriate for large and small businesses; (c) to encourage regulated organisations fully to exploit the potential for environmental initiatives to result in cost savings, thus enhancing their own and the UK's competitive position; (d) to encourage regulated organisations to adopt high environmental standards where cost-effective, for example, by co-operating with business organisations such as the Advisory Committee on Business and the Environment and the CBI to promote voluntary initiatives; and (e) to encourage knowledge and understanding, particularly in regulated organisations, of best available techniques not entailing excessive costs for the prevention and minimisation of pollution, including the efficient use of resources, such as energy, and the minimisation of waste"; (v) since achieving sustainable development will involve contributions from many different groups in society, SEPA should strive to develop **close and responsive relationships** with the different groups and to work in partnership with them; (vi) SEPA should strive to become a recognised centre of knowledge and expertise and to provide clear and readily accessible advice and information on its work and on best environmental practice since **high quality information and advice** is an important element in advancing sustainable development strategies.

The non-statutory section of the revised draft guidance points out that SEPA cannot by itself achieve sustainable development but that it is expected to make "a significant contribution" to it in relation to its functions which are designed to ensure environmental protection (para. 3.1). SEPA is encouraged (paras. 3.1 and 3.3)

— to seek to integrate environmental requirements with the need for economic and social development to allow improvements in the overall quality of life; and

— to consider the distinct characteristics of Scotland's environment and economy in performing its functions which may mean that national standards need to be tempered by sensitivity to local circumstances given Scotland's diverse natural environment, its remote rural communities and extremes of population density except where significant global effects would suggest otherwise. It is unclear why this latter provision has not been included in the statutory guidance as it would seem to be of considerable importance.

Costs and benefits
The non-statutory section of the guidance also discusses the issue of costs and benefits which SEPA must take into account in certain circumstances under s.39 (see also note to s.39). The guidance explains the purpose of this duty as follows:

"The Secretary of State considers that as SEPA is a body with powers to make decisions with significant impacts on individuals, organisations and the environment, it should take account of all types of costs and benefits when making such decisions. This will not only ensure that financial and other considerations are taken into account, but also that environmental considerations are given the central role that is necessary for sustainable development" (para. 4.2).

The restrictions on the scope of the duty are noted whereby it does not apply where it would be unreasonable and that it does not affect SEPA's mandatory obligations to discharge specific duties, comply with requirements or pursue objectives (paras. 4.1 and 4.2). It is made clear that the duty is to apply where SEPA is exercising discretion either in considering whether or not to take action and the manner in which action should be taken (para. 4.4). While all costs and benefits should be taken into account, there is no need for precise quantification especially where such quantification is inherently difficult as, for example, in relation to likely environmental costs and benefits such as the value of a forest (para. 4.5). In assessing costs and benefits the guidance suggests that SEPA may consider it appropriate to consider principles, procedures and techniques, particularly risk assessment and economic and policy appraisal, the precautionary principle, reliance on sound science, the likely impact on the carrying capacity of the environment and on natural environmental capital and longer term implications and effects (para. 4.6). It is stressed that such analyses should take proper account of long-term environmental benefits as well as immediate financial costs (ibid.)

SEPA should concern itself primarily with the costs and benefits of its actions for society as a whole, the effects on the welfare of people and business, changes in the use of resources and impacts on the environment (para. 4.6(vi)). SEPA should take into account the views of the chief medical officer, impacts on individual companies and industry sectors and the distribution of costs and benefits across the economy (ibid.). The guidance urges SEPA to develop practical procedures to ensure that it meets the requirements of the duty to take into account costs and benefits where appropriate. Such procedures should include advice to staff on relevant techniques for assessing costs and benefits; circumstances where SEPAs discretion is limited by obligations arising from other duties, requirements and objectives; and on the extent to which consideration of costs and benefits might be unreasonable (para. 4.7).

It would appear to be sensible to ensure that such procedures are similar to those developed by the Agency so that there is consistency throughout Great Britain in the application of this duty.

Subs. (3)

Shall have regard to

SEPA is required to "have regard to" the guidance given under subs. (1). The phrase "have regard to" is considered in the Introductory note to this Part of the Act.

It is submitted that it may not be easy to establish as an evidential point that SEPA has failed to have regard to the guidance issued under s.31(1). Also the fact that the guidance is likely to be couched in very general terms will also not assist those who wish to challenge SEPA on the basis that it did not have regard to the guidance.

It should be noted that SEPA is not under a duty to "have regard to" any non-statutory guidance, although such guidance will clearly still be of considerable importance in, for example, appeals to the Secretary of State where all relevant matters whether statutory or not would require to be considered.

Subss. (4)–(7)

The original Environment Bill contained no provisions for consultation or Parliamentary scrutiny of the guidance issued by the Secretary of State. There was considerable criticism of this omission in Parliament especially regarding the degree of control over SEPA which the original provisions gave to the Secretary of State (see *e.g.* the Earl of Kintore *Hansard*, H.L. Vol. 560, col. 1687). To allay such criticism the Government introduced provisions requiring the Secretary of State to consult with SEPA itself and such other bodies as he considered appropriate before issuing guidance. Furthermore some degree of parliamentary scrutiny has also been provided for as the guidance is to be laid before Parliament under the negative resolution procedure, which enables either House of Parliament to reject the guidance although it may not be amended.

Subs. (8)

No provision was originally made for publication of the guidance issued by the Secretary of State. This subs. is designed to rectify that.

General environmental and recreational duties

32.—(1) It shall be the duty of the Secretary of State and of SEPA, in formulating or considering any proposals relating to any functions of SEPA—

   (a) to have regard to the desirability of conserving and enhancing the natural heritage of Scotland;

   (b) to have regard to the desirability of protecting and conserving buildings, sites and objects of archaeological, architectural, engineering or historic interest;

   (c) to take into account any effect which the proposals would have on the natural heritage of Scotland or on any such buildings, sites or objects; and

   (d) to have regard to the social and economic needs of any area or description of area of Scotland and, in particular, to such needs of rural areas.

(2) Subject to subsection (1) above, it shall be the duty of the Secretary of State and of SEPA, in formulating or considering any proposals relating to any functions of SEPA—

   (a) to have regard to the desirability of preserving for the public any freedom of access (including access for recreational purposes) to areas of forest, woodland, mountains, moor, bog, cliff, foreshore, loch or reservoir and other places of natural beauty;

(b) to have regard to the desirability of maintaining the availability to the public of any facility for visiting or inspecting any building, site or object of archaeological, architectural, engineering or historic interest; and

(c) to take into account any effect which the proposals would have on any such freedom of access or on the availability of any such facility.

(3) In this section—

"building" includes structure; and

"the natural heritage of Scotland" has the same meaning as in section 1(3) of the Natural Heritage (Scotland) Act 1991.

DEFINITIONS
"building": subs. (3).
"functions": s.124(1).
"natural heritage": subs. (3); s.1(3) of the NHSA 1991.
"SEPA": s.124(1).

COMMENCEMENT
October 12, 1995 (S.I. 1995 No. 2649).

GENERAL NOTE
This section imposes on the Secretary of State and SEPA a duty either to have regard to or take account of certain environmental and recreational matters. It should be noted that the duty only applies where the Secretary of State or SEPA is formulating or considering proposals in relation to any of SEPA's functions. However, the term "proposals" is not defined. (See note to s.7.) It arguably includes any proposal by the Secretary of State to issue guidance under s.31(1).

The duties imposed in subs. (2) are subject to those in subs. (1) which means that those in subs. (1) must be given priority. It is left to the discretion of the Secretary of State and SEPA to determine how much weight such considerations should be given in the case of a particular proposal, which means that it is only if SEPA completely ignores a relevant issue that its decisions could be challenged in the courts. In exercising its discretion, SEPA must have regard to the guidance issued under s.31(1). In legal terms the duties, which may prompt the development of appropriate Memoranda of Understanding, do serve a useful purpose in ensuring that the matters listed are always going to be relevant considerations, which must at least be addressed by the Secretary of State and SEPA in formulating or considering any proposals, and in giving some standing to bodies representing the listed interests to make representations both to the Secretary of State and to SEPA and, ultimately, to the courts. The statutory requirement to have regard to such matters will also influence the policy-making of SEPA.

No distinction is drawn in the section between pollution control and non-pollution control functions as is the case in the equivalent provision for England and Wales, s.7. This is because SEPA's functions are largely pollution control functions and it has a much narrower focus than the Agency with regard, for example, to conserving water resources.

The lack of a stronger duty to promote or further the conservation and enhancement of the natural heritage of Scotland was severely criticised both in parliamentary debates and outwith Parliament. In England and Wales, a stronger duty does apply in s.7(1) but only in relation to the Agency's non-pollution control functions. The Government's rationale for not imposing the stronger duty on SEPA is as follows:

> "The Bill recognises that matters such as nature conservation are important, and SEPA should, where appropriate, take account of them. However, a duty to further nature conservation could distort the exercise of SEPA's pollution control functions, and its pollution prevention and control functions lie at the heart of its very existence. Few pollution control licences could be issued if SEPA were required to ensure that the levels of pollution they permitted furthered nature conservation. Unlike the provisions for the Environment Agency for England and Wales, there is no need to make a distinction in the Scottish provisions between SEPA's pollution control and other functions. The more limited scope of the Scottish agency means that it will not have functions for which a duty to 'further' would be appropriate." (*per* the Earl of Lindsay *Hansard*, H.L. Vol. 560, col. 1220).

This is certainly a logical approach in the light of SEPA's focus on pollution control functions. Furthermore, Scottish Natural Heritage, is much better placed than SEPA to further the conservation and enhancement of Scotland's natural heritage as it is given the aim:

"(a) to secure the conservation and enhancement of; and
(b) to foster understanding and facilitate the enjoyment of, the natural heritage of Scotland, ..." (Natural Heritage (Scotland) Act 1991, s.1(1)).

Subs. (1)–(2)
No equivalent duties were imposed on the bodies whose functions are transferred by the Act to SEPA. However, duties similar to subss. (1)(b), (2)(a) and (b) are imposed on the Secretary of State and the new Scottish water authorities by virtue of s.65 of the Local Government etc. (Scotland) Act 1994 which substitutes a new s.1 for the existing s.1 of the Water (Scotland) Act 1980. The new water authorities are, however, under a stronger duty to further conservation by virtue of s.1(2)(b) of the amended Water (Scotland) Act 1980. SEPA should have regard to the guidance issued under s.31(1) in the discharge of these duties which involve considerable discretion.

Subs. (1)(b)
The word *engineering* did not appear in the original provision in the Environment Bill and was included after it was pointed out in Parliament (*per e.g.* Lord Howie of Troon *Hansard*, H.L. Vol. 560, cols. 1224–1225) that the existing wording would not cover buildings, objects or sites such as the Forth Railway Bridge or the Glenfinnan Viaduct on the West Highland railway line which, Lord Howie of Troon argued, could not properly be said to be of architectural or historic interest but were of engineering interest.

Subs. (1)(d)
The wording of this subs. is significantly different from its approximate equivalent in the legislation for England and Wales s.7(1)(c)(iii) which provides that it shall be the duty of the Ministers and the Agency "to have regard to any effect which the proposals would have on the economic and social well-being of local communities in rural areas". However, the scope of the Scottish provision is considerably wider in that the duty extends to having regard to social and economic effects in any area of Scotland not just in rural areas, although regard should be had to their needs in particular.

Subs. (3)
The definition of building includes structure in order for it to include, for example, viaducts, bridges and tunnels, none of which could otherwise be said with confidence to be "buildings".

General duties with respect to pollution control

33.—(1) SEPA's pollution control powers shall be exercisable for the purpose of preventing or minimising, or remedying or mitigating the effects of, pollution of the environment.

(2) SEPA shall, for the purpose—

(a) of facilitating the carrying out of its pollution control functions; or
(b) of enabling it to form an opinion of the general state of pollution of the environment,

compile information relating to such pollution (whether the information is acquired by SEPA carrying out observations or is obtained in any other way).

(3) If required by the Secretary of State to do so, SEPA shall—

(a) carry out assessments (whether generally or for such particular purpose as may be specified in the requirement) of the effect, or likely effect, on the environment of existing or potential levels of pollution of the environment and report its findings to the Secretary of State; or
(b) prepare and send to the Secretary of State a report identifying—
  (i) the options which SEPA considers to be available for preventing or minimising, or remedying or mitigating the effects of, pollution of the environment, whether generally or in cases or circumstances specified in the requirement; and
  (ii) the costs and benefits of such options as are identified by SEPA pursuant to sub-paragraph (i) above.

(4) SEPA shall follow developments in technology and techniques for

preventing or minimising, or remedying or mitigating the effects of, pollution of the environment.

(5) In this section, "pollution control powers" and "pollution control functions" in relation to SEPA, mean respectively its powers or its functions under or by virtue of—

(a) the Alkali, &c. Works Regulation Act 1906;
(b) Part III of the 1951 Act, the Rivers (Prevention of Pollution) (Scotland) Act 1965 and Parts I, IA and II of the Control of Pollution Act 1974;
(c) Part I of the Health and Safety at Work etc. Act 1974;
(d) the Control of Pollution (Amendment) Act 1989;
(e) Parts I, II and IIA of the 1990 Act;
(f) section 19 of the Clean Air Act 1993;
(g) the Radioactive Substances Act 1993; and
(h) regulations made by virtue of section 2(2) of the European Communities Act 1972, to the extent that the regulations relate to pollution.

DEFINITIONS
"costs": s.56(1).
"the environment": s.56(1); s.1(2) of the 1990 Act.
"pollution control powers": subs. (5).
"pollution control functions": subs. (5).
"SEPA": s.124(1).

COMMENCEMENT
April 1, 1996 (S.I. 1996 No. 186).

GENERAL NOTE
This section provides a single statutory purpose for all SEPA's pollution control functions which are listed by the statutes in which they are contained in subs. (5). Of the pollution control functions transferred to SEPA, only those functions in relation to integrated pollution control and air pollution were exercisable for a similar purpose under s.4(2)–(3) of the Environmental Protection Act 1990. For example s.4(2) read as follows:

"Those functions ... shall be exercisable for the purpose of preventing or minimising pollution of the environment due to the release of substances into any environmental medium."

Neither waste regulation functions nor radioactive substances control functions nor general water pollution control functions were exercisable for a similar purpose although it should be noted that the Waste Management Licensing Regulations 1994 provide that waste regulation authorities must discharge their functions under both Parts I and II of the 1990 Act so as to fulfil the "relevant objectives": Sched. 4, paras. 2 and 4, 1994 Regulations and that RPAs may exercise their powers to carry out preventive or remedial works under ss.46 and their power to serve works notice 46A for a similar purpose.

The key term *pollution of the environment* is not defined in subs. (1). However, definitions may be found in s.1(3) and s.29(3) of the Environmental Protection Act 1990. The former definition applies in the case of IPC and LAPC functions and the latter in the case of waste regulation functions and it is submitted that those definitions would apply in relation to those particular functions of SEPA. There may, however, be an argument that since the wording of s.33(1) is drawn from Part I of the 1990 Act which deals with IPC and LAPC and since SEPA will be integrating pollution control functions to a greater degree at least in administrative terms, the definition in s.1(3) is to be preferred for wider application across all SEPA's pollution control functions. Certainly, there is no definition of *pollution of the environment* which could be drawn from Scots water pollution legislation under the Control of Pollution Act 1974. There is, however, some case law on the definition of *polluting matter* as discussed in the note to s.5.

The circumstances in which a legal challenge for breach of this statutory duty by SEPA are probably fairly limited and might include, for example, malicious use of pollution control powers against a company; although it is hard to envisage such a situation occurring in practice.

Subs. (2)–(3)
The revised draft guidance to SEPA notes that the Government is currently undertaking work on sustainable development indicators (para. 5). The duties to compile information and carry out specified assessments for the Secretary of State in subs. (2) and (3), which are new functions, should have an important role in that context. These duties will also be of importance in relation (i) to SEPA's duty to prepare a national waste strategy for Scotland (see note to s.92) (ii) in its consultative role in relation to the new national air quality strategy under s.80(6) and (iii) in relation to the duty of Member States under Art. 7 of Directive 90/313/EEC on the freedom of access to information on the environment to provide general information to the public on the state of the environment by such means as the periodic publication of descriptive reports.

It should also be noted that an integrated approach to environmental protection requires accurate information on the often complex relationship between impacts on the different environmental media. See also the note to s.5(2)–(4).

Subs. (4)
A similar duty was imposed on HMIPI and river purification authorities in relation to integrated pollution control and local authorities in relation to air pollution control under the Environmental Protection Act 1990:

> "It shall be the duty of the chief inspector or, in Scotland, of the chief inspector and river purification authorities to follow developments in technology and techniques for preventing or reducing pollution of the environment due to releases of substances from prescribed processes; and the local enforcing authorities shall follow such of those development as concern releases into the air of substances from prescribed processes designated for local control." (s.4(9)).

This duty is now applied across the whole field of pollution control functions, so that it would also now apply, for example, to developments in landfill technology or waste disposal techniques in relation to radioactive substances. The duty is very important in relation to the concept of best available techniques not entailing excessive cost.

General duties with respect to water

34.—(1) It shall be the duty of SEPA—
    (a) to promote the cleanliness of—
        (i) rivers, other inland waters and ground waters in Scotland; and
        (ii) the tidal waters of Scotland; and
    (b) to conserve so far as practicable the water resources of Scotland.
(2) Without prejudice to section 32 above, it shall be the duty of SEPA, to such extent as it considers desirable, generally to promote—
    (a) the conservation and enhancement of the natural beauty and amenity of inland and coastal waters and of land associated with such waters; and
    (b) the conservation of flora and fauna which are dependent on an aquatic environment.
(3) Subsection (1) above is without prejudice to section 1 of the Water (Scotland) Act 1980 (general duties of Secretary of State and water authorities as respects water resources and supplies).
(4) In subsection (1) above, "tidal waters" means any part of the sea or the tidal part of any river, watercourse or inland water (whether natural or artificial) and includes the waters of any enclosed dock which adjoins tidal waters.

DEFINITIONS
    "tidal waters": subs. (4).
    "SEPA": s.124(1).

COMMENCEMENT
April 1, 1996 (S.I. 1996 No. 186).

GENERAL NOTE
This section includes a re-enactment of the duties imposed on river purification authorities by s.17 of the Rivers (Prevention of Pollution) (Scotland) Act 1951 as amended and significantly extends that duty to ground waters. Cleanliness is not defined. Given the limited functions

SEPA will have in relation to the conservation of water resources in Scotland, particularly as it lacks powers to control abstraction except in the case of abstraction for irrigation purposes by virtue of Part II of the Natural Heritage (Scotland) Act 1991, it is unlikely that SEPA will be able in discharging the duty in subs. (1)(b) to make a significant contribution to conserving water resources in Scotland on its own. The Secretary of State and the new Scottish water authorities established by the Local Government etc. (Scotland) Act 1994 have a conservation duty in relation to water resources in Scotland by virtue of s.1 of the Water (Scotland) Act 1980 as substituted by s.65 of the Local Government etc. (Scotland) Act 1994 and will have a much more significant contribution to make in this regard than SEPA, given their much more extensive role in this context. Their duties are unaffected by the duty imposed on SEPA (subs. (3)). Consultation, and perhaps even Memoranda of Understanding, between SEPA and the new water authorities may be required in order for SEPA effectively to discharge its duties under subs. (1).

The Environment Bill as originally drafted provided that the duty now contained in s.34(1) was to be "in accordance with any directions under section 33 [now s.40] below", *i.e.* in accordance with any directions made by the Secretary of State. However, this latter part of the provision was removed by the Government in recognition of their intention to leave day-to-day operational matters with SEPA (*per* the Earl of Lindsay *Hansard*, H.L. Vol. 562, cols. 1032–1033) following concerns expressed in the House of Lords regarding meddling by the Secretary of State in SEPA's day-to-day operations (see *e.g.* the Earl of Dundonald *Hansard*, H.L. Vol. 562, col. 1033).

Subs. (2)

The extent to which SEPA discharges this duty to promote conservation of specified waters is left to its discretion although in discharging this duty it should have regard to any guidance issued under s.31(1). The effective discharge of SEPA's duty may require a Memorandum of Understanding with Scottish Natural Heritage.

Environmental duties as respects Natural Heritage Areas and sites of special interest

35.—(1) Where an area of land—

(a) has been designated, under section 6(2) of the Natural Heritage (Scotland) Act 1991 (in this section referred to as "the 1991 Act") as a Natural Heritage Area; or

(b) is, in the opinion of Scottish Natural Heritage (in this section referred to as "SNH"), of special interest by reason of its flora, fauna or geological or physiographical features,

and SNH consider that it may at any time be affected by schemes, works, operations or activities of SEPA or by an authorisation given by SEPA, SNH shall give notice to SEPA in accordance with subsection (2) below.

(2) A notice under subsection (1) above shall specify—

(a) in the case of an area of land mentioned in paragraph (a) of that subsection, SNH's reasons for considering that the area is of outstanding value to the natural heritage of Scotland; and

(b) in the case of an area of land mentioned in paragraph (b) of that subsection, SNH's reasons for holding the opinion there mentioned.

(3) Where SNH has given notice under subsection (1) above in respect of an area of land and—

(a) in the case of an area of land mentioned in paragraph (a) of that subsection, the designation is cancelled or varied under section 6(7) of the 1991 Act; or

(b) in the case of an area of land mentioned in paragraph (b) of that subsection, SNH ceases to be of the opinion there mentioned,

SNH shall forthwith notify SEPA of that fact.

(4) Where SEPA has received notice under subsection (1) above with respect to any area of land, it shall (unless SNH has given notice under subsection (3) above with respect to the land) consult SNH before carrying

out or authorising any schemes, works, operations or activities which appear to SEPA to be likely—

    (a) in the case of an area of land mentioned in subsection (1)(a), significantly to prejudice the value of the land, or any part of it, as a Natural Heritage Area; and

    (b) in the case of an area of land mentioned in subsection (1)(b), to destroy or damage any of the flora or fauna or features by reason of which SNH formed the opinion there mentioned.

(5) Subsection (4) above shall not apply in relation to anything done in an emergency if particulars of what is done and of the emergency are notified by SEPA to SNH as soon as practicable after the thing is done.

(6) In this section, "authorisation" includes any consent, licence or permission.

(7) Any expression used in this section and in Part I of the 1991 Act and not defined in this Act shall be construed in accordance with that Part.

DEFINITIONS

    "authorisation": subs. (6).
    "land": s.22(1) of the NHSA 1991.
    "natural heritage": s.1(3) of the NHSA 1991.
    "Natural Heritage Area": s.6 of the NHSA 1991.
    "notice": s.124(1).
    "SEPA": s.124(1).

COMMENCEMENT

April 1, 1996 (S.I. 1996 No. 186).

GENERAL NOTE

The Natural Heritage (Scotland) Act 1991 merged the Countryside Commission for Scotland and the Nature Conservancy Council for Scotland into a single body called Scottish Natural Heritage (SNH). SNH performs all the functions of its predecessors as well as having powers to provide for access in the countryside. The Natural Heritage (Scotland) Act 1991 also gives SNH the power to designate land as a Natural Heritage Area, in order to assist in the care of natural heritage which is defined by s.1(3) thereof as including "the flora and fauna of Scotland, its geological and physiographical features, its natural beauty and amenity". Natural heritage is a concept designed to draw together the areas of responsibility of SNH's predecessors and reflects the integrated approach which SNH was intended to take.

This section requires SNH to notify (subs. (2)) SEPA of Natural Heritage Areas (subs. (1)(a) and sites of special interest (subs. (1)(b)) which SNH considers may be affected by schemes, works, operations or activities of SEPA or by authorisations granted by SEPA and SNH must give its reasons for holding this opinion (subs. (2)). The Government explained why they had introduced the requirement that SNH should provide reasons for its opinion:

> "I believe that it is appropriate for SNH to be additionally obliged to make the reasons for its considerations known to SEPA. SEPA must, except in an emergency, consult SNH where it appears likely to SEPA that its actions may affect such land. Knowing why SNH thought that the land might be so affected in the first place would, I suggest, help SEPA meet that obligation" (*per* the Earl of Lindsay *Hansard*, H.L. Vol. 560, col. 1229).

Where SEPA has been so notified by SNH it must consult SNH before carrying out or authorising any schemes, works, operations or activities or granting any authorisations which appear likely to give rise to the circumstances specified in subs. (4)(a) and (b). There is an exception to this requirement in the case of an emergency. A proposal to restrict definition of emergency to "danger to life or health" was opposed by the Government on the grounds that it would fetter SEPA's discretion to an unreasonable extent:

> "For example, it does not seem to cover an emergency which may cause serious environmental harm. Much would depend on how 'life' was interpreted. Contamination of soil may not directly threaten life but it could well constitute an emergency. We should be prepared to trust SEPA to discharge its statutory functions to protect the environment when it believes it is imperative to do so urgently." (*per* the Earl of Lindsay *Hansard*, H.L. Vol. 560, col. 1229).

Codes of practice with respect to environmental and recreational duties

36.—(1) The Secretary of State shall have power by order to approve any code of practice issued (whether by him or by another person) for the purpose of—

(a) giving practical guidance to SEPA with respect to any of the matters for the purposes of which sections 32, 34(2) and 35 above have effect; and

(b) promoting what appear to him to be desirable practices by SEPA with respect to those matters,

and may at any time by such an order approve a modification of such a code or withdraw his approval of such a code or modification.

(2) In discharging its duties under section 32, 34(2) or 35 above, SEPA shall have regard to any code of practice, and any modifications of a code of practice, for the time being approved under this section.

(3) The Secretary of State shall not make an order under this section unless he has first consulted—

(a) SEPA;

(b) Scottish Natural Heritage;

(c) Scottish Enterprise;

(d) Highlands and Islands Enterprise;

(e) the East of Scotland Water Authority;

(f) the West of Scotland Water Authority;

(g) the North of Scotland Water Authority; and

(h) such other persons as he considers it appropriate to consult.

(4) The power of the Secretary of State to make an order under this section shall be exercisable by statutory instrument; and any statutory instrument containing such an order shall be subject to annulment in pursuance of a resolution of either House of Parliament.

DEFINITIONS
"modifications": s.124(1).
"SEPA": s.124(1).

COMMENCEMENT
October 12, 1995 (S.I. 1995 No. 2649).

GENERAL NOTE
This section is modelled to an extent upon s.51 of the Control of Pollution Act 1974 (as amended by Sched. 23 to the Water Act 1989) which makes provision for the Secretary of State to approve codes of practice giving practical guidance to persons engaged in agriculture with respect to activities that might affect controlled waters and promoting desirable practices by such persons for avoiding or minimising water pollution. However, this section applies to codes of practice issued to SEPA giving guidance on the discharge of its environmental and recreational duties under s.32, s.34(2) and s.35. The Codes of Practice will provide SEPA with more detailed guidance on how they should discharge these duties.

Interestingly s.51(2) of the 1974 Act provides that a contravention of a Code of Practice would not of itself give rise to any criminal or civil liability: that is not the case here. See further the note to s.9(2).

Subs. (2)

Shall have regard to
SEPA is not bound by the codes of practice, and may depart from them. However, they must be considered and a failure to do so would render any action by SEPA in the discharge of its duties under s.32, s.34(2) or s.35 unlawful. See also the discussion of this term in the Introductory note to this Part of the Act.

SEPA must only have regard to any Codes of Practice which are for the time being approved under s.36. This means that it need not have regard to any draft code issued for consultation but not yet approved under this section.

Subs. (3)
Concern was expressed in Parliament that all the consultees specified were "quangos" and it was argued that if there was to be any accountability the list of consultees should include democratically elected councillors (*per* Lord Carmichael of Kelvingrove *Hansard*, H.L. Vol. 560, cols. 1233–1234). Although the Government declined to extend the list to include councillors (*per* the Earl of Lindsay *Hansard*, H.L. Vol. 560, cols. 1234) it is difficult to envisage a situation in which the Secretary of State would not consult the appropriate councillors in relation to any proposed Code of Practice under s.36(3)(h).

It should be noted that the list of statutory consultees is more extensive than that appearing in the equivalent provision for England and Wales, s.9 references to sewerage and water undertakers were removed during the passage of the Bill through Parliament. However, in Scotland, the three new water authorities are listed as statutory consultees and Scottish Enterprise and Highlands and Islands Enterprise also appear on the list. Interestingly, however, the Historic Buildings and Monuments Commission, the Sports Council and the Sports Council for Wales are included in the list of statutory consultees in s.9 but, neither Historic Scotland nor the Scottish Sports Council are listed as consultees in s.36. The omission of these bodies from the list of consultees was explained for the Government by the Earl of Lindsay:

"I agree ... that it is important that the views of Historic Scotland are fed into the process of approving a code of practice. But as that body is an executive agency of the Scottish Office, a requirement on the Secretary of State to consult Historic Scotland is tantamount to a requirement to consult himself.
As SEPA will not have the range of responsibilities of the Environment Agency, I do not believe the Scottish Sports Council has a strong enough interest in the activities of SEPA to justify its specific and automatic inclusion" (*Hansard*, H.L. Vol. 560, col. 1234).

CHAPTER III

MISCELLANEOUS, GENERAL AND SUPPLEMENTAL PROVISIONS RELATING TO THE NEW AGENCIES

Additional general powers and duties

Incidental general functions

37.—(1) Each new Agency (that is to say, in this Part, the Agency or SEPA)—
　　(a) may do anything which, in its opinion, is calculated to facilitate, or is conducive or incidental to, the carrying out of its functions; and
　　(b) without prejudice to the generality of that power, may, for the purposes of, or in connection with, the carrying out of those functions, acquire and dispose of land and other property and carry out such engineering or building operations as it considers appropriate;
and the Agency may institute criminal proceedings in England and Wales.

(2) It shall be the duty of each new Agency to provide the Secretary of State or the Minister with such advice and assistance as he may request.

(3) Subject to subsection (4) below, each new Agency may provide for any person, whether in or outside the United Kingdom, advice or assistance, including training facilities, as respects any matter in which that new Agency has skill or experience.

(4) Without prejudice to any power of either new Agency apart from subsection (3) above to provide advice or assistance of the kind mentioned in that subsection, the power conferred by that subsection shall not be exercised in a case where the person for whom the advice or assistance is provided is outside the United Kingdom, except with the consent in writing of the appropriate Minister which consent may be given subject to such conditions as the Minister giving it thinks fit.

(5) Each new Agency—

(a) shall make arrangements for the carrying out of research and related activities (whether by itself or by others) in respect of matters to which its functions relate; and

(b) may make the results of any such research or related activities available to any person in return for payment of such fee as it considers appropriate.

(6) Subsection (5) above shall not be taken as preventing a new Agency from making the results of any research available to the public free of charge whenever it considers it appropriate to do so.

(7) Each new Agency may by agreement with any person charge that person a fee in respect of work done, or services or facilities provided, as a result of a request made by him for advice or assistance, whether of a general or specific character, in connection with any matter involving or relating to environmental licences.

(8) Subsection (7) above—

(a) is without prejudice to the generality of the powers of either new Agency to make charges; but

(b) is subject to any such express provision with respect to charging by the new Agency in question as is contained in the other provisions of this Part or in any other enactment.

(9) In this section "engineering or building operations", without prejudice to the generality of that expression, includes—

(a) the construction, alteration, improvement, maintenance or demolition of any building or structure or of any reservoir, watercourse, dam, weir, well, borehole or other works; and

(b) the installation, modification or removal of any machinery or apparatus.

DEFINITIONS:
"the Agency": s.124(1).
"appropriate Minister": s.56(1).
"engineering or building operations": subs. (9).
"environmental licence": s.56(1).
"functions": s.124(1).
"the Minister": s.56(1).
"new Agency": s.56(1).
"SEPA": s.124(1).

COMMENCEMENT
Subss. (1), (2) and (9): July 28, 1995 (S.I. 1995 No. 1983). The remainder came into force on April 1, 1996 (S.I. 1996 No. 186).

GENERAL NOTE
This section provides, for each of the Agency and SEPA:
— additional powers (subss. (1), (3), (5)(b), (6) and (7)); and
— additional duties (subs. (2) and (5)(a)) which are considered incidental to the carrying out of its functions.
In relation to the Agency it should be noted that its "functions" referred to in subss. (1)(a) and (b) are expressed by s.10 to include the functions set out in that section. See the General Note to that section.

Subs. (1): General incidental powers
This subsection is modelled on the provisions of s.4(1) of the Water Resources Act 1991 in relation to the NRA.
  Each agency is given extremely wide incidental powers to do anything which, in its opinion, will facilitate or is conducive or incidental to the carrying out of its functions (subs. (1)(a)). The opinion of the agency in question is the test: thus it would be extremely difficult for any action which could reasonably (in the wide *Wednesbury* sense of reasonableness employed in judicial review cases) be said to so relate to its functions to be challenged. This avoids the need for a lengthy list of incidental powers, although for the avoidance of doubt the power to carry out the activities most likely to involve large commitments of an agency's resources are expressly

included by subss. (1)(b) and (9). Subsection (7) gives the Agency/SEPA the power to charge for the provision of services or facilities in connection with advice or assistance on any matter relating to environmental licences. Subsection (1) would in any event appear wide enough to allow such charging for services not covered by subs. (7), provided that in the opinion of the agency in question those services relate to its functions in the way required by the subsection. It will also be noted that the power provided by s.43 to charge for services and facilities provided in the course of carrying out its functions is expressly without prejudice to the generality of the Agency/SEPA's powers by virtue of this subsection.

Criminal Proceedings: the Agency
The Agency may institute criminal proceedings in England and Wales, as could its predecessor bodies. Section 54 provides additionally that anyone authorised by the Agency to prosecute on its behalf before a magistrates' court may do so even though they are not a solicitor or barrister: see the note to that section.

Criminal Proceedings: SEPA
Although the Agency may institute criminal proceedings, SEPA may not do so. In Scotland, environmental regulatory bodies have not in the past been able to bring their own prosecutions. They must report incidents to the Procurator Fiscal who will decide whether or not to institute criminal proceedings. Thus, whereas in England and Wales, there is only one level of discretion operating in the decision whether or not to prosecute, in Scotland there are two levels. The regulator must decide whether or not the matter is serious enough to be reported to the Procurator Fiscal and the Procurator Fiscal will then decide whether or not to prosecute. This system has recently been subject to considerable criticism from various quarters (see *e.g.* Scottish River Purification Boards' Association, Annual Report 1994–95; Friends of the Earth Scotland, *Watered Down—Why the Law is Failing to protect Scotland's Water*, 1994). It is alleged that Procurators Fiscal are not specialists in environmental law and are unfamiliar with it; that they do not take environmental crime as seriously as "traditional" crime, and that this is adversely affecting the enforcement of environmental law. Criticism has also been levelled at environmental regulators for not preparing cases adequately. However, the 1995 Act does not enable SEPA to bring its own prosecutions. It should, however, be noted that SEPA is apparently to have its own legal staff to prepare cases for the Procurator Fiscal (*Improving Scotland's Environment, The Way Forward*, 1992, para. 17) and that the Crown Office did improve its liaison arrangements with SEPA's predecessors and is instituting training for Procurators Fiscal and is issuing guidance to them on the prosecution of environmental offences: (*Herald*, October 6, 1995; Crown Office Environmental Criminal Law Handbook). The establishment of SEPA should certainly bring benefits with respect to the prosecution of environmental offences as the Crown Office and the Procurator Fiscal service will now have to deal with one organisation only rather than a whole range of RPAs and local authorities together with HMIPI. Standardised reporting procedures and a more consistent enforcement policy should become possible across Scotland.

Subs. (1): Injunctions
The NRA supported an amendment to subs. (1) to the effect that the Agency "may institute and appear in any legal proceedings in England and Wales": NRA Media Briefing "Environment Bill—Lords Committee Stage, January 17, 1995". Its argument was that the Agency needs "a clear specific power to institute and appear in not only criminal but also civil proceedings".

The prime significance of such a power is that it enables a regulator to apply for an injunction to prevent action which criminal sanctions are failing or likely to fail to deter. An injunction can be a particularly powerful remedy because it is backed by the threat of imprisonment or sequestration of assets for contempt of court, but with two exceptions the Attorney's-General's leave is required to bring an injunction for the purpose of restraining a criminal action, where the legislation under consideration contains no express provision allowing the authority to take civil proceedings. One exception is where one's own interest in property is affected by the act in question and one is a member of a specific class of persons whom the legislation in question was intended to protect. Neither the Agency nor SEPA is likely to be in this situation. The second exception is provided by s.222 of the Local Government Act 1972 for local authorities, provided that they consider it "expedient for the promotion or protection of the interests of the inhabitants of their area".

The Agency's waste regulation authority predecessors, benefitting from the Local Government Act provision, have in some cases succeeded in obtaining injunctions which have led to imprisonment for contempt of court through the continued breach of waste legislation: *Lancashire County Council and Blackpool Borough Council v. Owen Baguley* (unreported) is a good example. In that case, the waste regulation authority and planning authority are understood to have obtained High Court orders for imprisonment of the defendant, first (on December 15, 1992) for three months, and subsequently (on November 11, 1994) for seven periods totalling five years and seven months but running concurrently (the seven periods included five of 12 months each).

It is submitted, however, that notwithstanding the lack of the specific provision sought by the NRA, it is probable that the Agency and SEPA do have the ability, by virtue of subs. (1)(a), to seek and obtain injunctions in appropriate cases to secure compliance. This certainly appears to be the Government's understanding of the provision. Arguing that an amendment which would simply have inserted the words "and civil" after "criminal" in subs. (1)(a), and was thus similar in effect to that supported by the NRA was unnecessary, Viscount Ullswater, Minister of State, Department of the Environment, suggested in Parliament that "so far as civil proceedings are concerned the agency will be able to take any civil proceedings which in its opinion are calculated to facilitate or are conducive or incidental to the carrying out of its functions by virtue of Clause 35 [now s.37(1)(a)]" (*Hansard*, H.L., Vol. 562, col. 1035). He contrasted this situation with that for criminal proceedings ("it is necessary to give the agency express power to take criminal proceedings since it is to be a prosecuting authority under the legislation in respect of which it has functions") and gave the example of the agency's functions under the Sludge (Use in Agriculture) Regulations 1989:

> "The agency's functions under these regulations are limited, for example, to inspecting the sludge producer's register and being provided with information, but it is wished that the agency be the prosecuting authority for any breach in the regulations. It could not be said in this case that prosecuting would facilitate or be conducive or incidental to the specific functions given to the agency by the regulations and thus fall within [what became s.37(1)(a)]; therefore an express provision is required on the face of the Bill" (col. 1035).

Since subs. (1)(a) and s.4(1) of the Water Resources Act 1991 are worded identically for present purposes, and the NRA's understanding of that provision appears to be that it may not have served to authorise the seeking of an injunction for these purposes without the Attorney-General's consent, this explanation is particularly valuable. It may, in appropriate circumstances, be admissible in court to inform the interpretation of subs. (1)(a).

Subs. (1): SEPA: Interdicts
The position with regard to the ability of regulatory agencies in Scotland to obtain interdicts to restrain criminal action is less clear than in England and Wales. In *Buckhaven and Methil Magistrates v. Wemyss Coal Company Limited* 1932 S.C. 201, a case involving an attempt to obtain an interdict to prevent the dumping of colliery waste on the foreshore in circumstances in which the burgh had a statutory duty to prevent the deposit of rubbish under the Burgh Police (Scotland) Act 1892 which was reinforced with criminal sanctions against offending waste tippers, the then Lord President held:

> "It has long been settled in Scotland that a statutory body which is set up to enforce a system of statutory regulations, or to establish and enforce a system of bye-laws of its own, has no power to resort to the common law process of interdict for the purpose of enforcing such regulations or bye-laws, when the statute provides penalties for their breach and authorises recovery of such penalties" (*ibid.*, at p. 211. See also *Kelso Magistrates v. Alexander* 1939 S.C. 78).

Although this would appear to settle matters, nonetheless there are conflicting authorities, *e.g. Watney v. Menzies* (1898) 6 S.L.T. 189; and *National Dock Labour Board v. Sheppard Group* 1989 S.L.T. 661). Furthermore, the principle in *Buckhaven and Methil Magistrates* has been modified in relation to local authorities in subsequent legislation, which provides that local authorities may institute legal proceedings where they "consider it expedient for the promotion or protection of the interests of the inhabitants of their area" (Local Government (Scotland) Act 1973, s.189). However, this provision did not apply to river purification boards. Nonetheless, it should also be noted that in practice river purification boards have obtained interdict or interim interdict against persons who have been committing ongoing water pollution offences: *e.g. Forth River Purification Board v. Adam Robertson, The Scotsman,* December 7, 1990. In that case the defender had been previously convicted for water pollution offences under the 1974 Act and despite subsequent warnings had continued to pollute a river. An interim interdict was granted, apparently on the basis of nuisance rather than to prevent an ongoing breach of the criminal law under COPA (see Scott-Robinson), *The Law of Interdict* (2nd ed., Butterworths, 1994, pp. 50 and 222).

In the light of *Buckhaven and Methil Magistrates* it remains unclear whether in the absence of express statutory language, the wording of s.37(1)(a) is sufficient to give SEPA the power to seek an interdict in circumstances where a statutory interdict is not otherwise expressly available despite the views of Viscount Ullswater discussed above which, it should be noted, referred expressly to the Agency alone. It is possible, however, that where the offence constituted a nuisance as in *Adam Robertson* (above) an interdict or at least an interim interdict may be available.

Availability of statutory injunctions or interdicts
To an extent whether or not this general provision allows the Agency to obtain an injunction in England and Wales, and SEPA an interdict in Scotland, is becoming of less importance as the tendency appears increasingly to be to make provision for such a power expressly in the context of various statutory regimes. The 1995 Act itself amends existing legislation to include further such express provisions. To the extent that such express provisions exist, the importance of s.37(1)(a) in this context is reduced. Such provisions generally relate to circumstances of non-compliance with an extant licence, consent or notice although there are Agency licensing regimes which do not contain such provisions (*e.g.* water abstraction licensing), and the circumstance where a person is operating without the benefit of a licence at all, to which such express provisions do act in general apply, may be of particular concern to a regulator. Given the view expressed by Viscount Ullswater, quoted above, as to the effect of s.37(1)(a), this may seem unnecessary, and it is conceivable that the existence of such express provisions in such cases may be taken by a court to cast doubt on whether s.37(1)(a) is indeed capable of being construed so as to permit civil proceedings where they are absent. For the regimes for which the Agency/SEPA are to be regulatory authorities, the position is as follows:—

IPC (and, for SEPA, LAPC)
The Agency/SEPA have an express power to apply to the High Court or, in Scotland, any court of competent jurisdiction for the purpose of securing compliance with a prohibition or enforcement notice where it is of the opinion that criminal proceedings for a breach of such a notice would afford an ineffectual remedy (s.24 of the 1990 Act). This effectively gives the Agency/SEPA standing to apply for an injunction (or, in Scotland, an interdict), but is of course no guarantee that they will succeed in obtaining one.

However, where the criminal act is the operation of a prescribed process without any authorisation at all, neither prohibition nor enforcement notices may be served, so s.24 does not assist the enforcing authority in that situation.

Waste regulation
The 1990 Act (as amended by the 1995 Act: see paras. 72(2) and 76(7) of Sched. 22) provides an equivalent power in the context of waste regulation, where:
— the breach is a failure to comply with requirements imposed under s.38(9) of the 1990 Act in the context of the suspension of a waste management licence, and the Agency/SEPA considers that proceedings under s.38(10) or (11) would be ineffectual: s.38(13); or
— the breach is a failure to comply with requirements imposed under s.42(5)(a) of the 1990 Act in the context of breach of licence condition, and the Agency/SEPA considers that suspension or revocation of the licence would be ineffectual: s.42(6A).
Prior to the transfer to the Agency/SEPA of waste regulation, the power to take civil proceedings was available by virtue of s.222 of the Local Government Act 1972 or, in Scotland, s.189 of the Local Government (Scotland) Act 1973. It will be noted that provisions equivalent to ss.38(13) and 42(6A) have not been inserted in relation to other waste offences, such as breach of s.33(1)(c). For these, it would appear that the Agency/SEPA will have to rely on the general subs. (1)(a) power.

Contaminated land
In relation to "special sites", the Agency/SEPA are enforcing authorities under Part IIA of the 1990 Act, as inserted by the 1995 Act. They may take civil proceedings where they are of the opinion that proceedings under s.78M for non-compliance with a remediation notice would be an ineffectual remedy: s.78M(5).

Water pollution
This Act inserts new ss.90A and 90B into the Water Resources Act 1991, and ss.49A and 49B into the Control of Pollution Act 1974, providing for the service by the Agency/SEPA of enforcement notices for contravention of conditions of consents to discharge to controlled waters: paras. 29(26) and 142 of Sched. 22. Section 90B(4) permits the Agency to take civil proceedings where proceedings under subsection 90B(3) for breach of an enforcement notice would in the opinion of the Agency afford an ineffectual remedy for such breach. Section 49B(4) is of identical effect for SEPA.

Where a consent has not been applied for, however, or where it is another licence such as a drought permit or abstraction or impoundment licence whose conditions are being breached, it appears that the agencies will have to rely on the general subs. (1)(a) power.

Schedule 22 also introduces works notices for the remediation of actual or likely water pollution (ss.161A–161D of the 1991 Act and ss.46A–46D of the 1974 Act), and similar provision for civil action is made where such notices are not complied with: paras. 29(22) and 162 of Sched. 22.

Radioactive Substances Act 1993
Where a person fails to comply with a prohibition or enforcement notice served in relation to a registration or authorisation under the 1993 Act, the 1995 Act inserts a provision for the Agency/SEPA to take civil proceedings where it considers that criminal proceedings would be ineffectual to remedy the breach: s.32(3), inserted by para. 219 of Sched. 22.

Subss. (3) and (4): Advice and assistance
The Agency/SEPA are given a range of powers in relation to research and advice.

The benefits which the Agency/SEPA should bring in terms of the pooling, sharing and development of knowledge and expertise which staff in their constituent bodies already possessed in a range of fields have been widely emphasised.

This anticipated role is reflected in their duties to compile information on pollution, assess and report on its effects and follow developments in technologies and techniques for its abatement (ss.5(2)–(4) and 33(2)–(4)). It can also be seen in their roles in relation to contaminated land "special sites" (s.57), the national air quality strategies (ss.80(6)(a) and 87(7)(a)) and the national waste strategies (ss.44A(5)(a) and (6) and 44B of the Environmental Protection Act 1990, as inserted into that Act by s.92(1) of this Act).

Note also SEPA's lead role (held by the Secretary of State in England and Wales) in relation to air quality review and assessment in Scotland, and in particular its power to give directions to local authorities where it considers that developments in science and technology have rendered their actions inappropriate (s.85(2) and (3)(d)).

Each of the Agency and SEPA is placed under a specific duty to provide the Secretary of State or the Minister of Agriculture, Fisheries and Food with such advice and assistance as he may request: subs. (2). These Ministers can thus call on such advice and assistance without resort to directions under s.40.

In addition to these statutory roles, each agency may provide any person with advice, assistance or training: subs. (3). In this regard, it is notable that the Government's draft Guidance to the Agency on its objectives (April 1995, discussed in the General Note to s.4(2) and (3)) indicates that the Agency "should strive within the areas of its responsibility to become a recognised centre of knowledge and expertise and to provide and promulgate clear and readily available advice and information on its work and on best environmental practice" (para. 5.7). The revised draft guidance to SEPA contains a virtually identical provision (App. 1, para. 9(vi)). The equivalent provision relating to the NRA, which this subsection replaces (s.4(2) of the Water Resources Act 1991), referred only to persons outside the United Kingdom; that the Agency/SEPA may provide such advice to persons within the United Kingdom is made clear.

It would appear possible for the Agency/SEPA to find itself in the potentially embarrassing position of serving a notice such as a contaminated land remediation notice (in relation to a "special site") or a water pollution works notice, and then charging for advice as to how best the remediation might be carried out so as to comply with the notice.

This is more likely the more the Agency/SEPA succeeds in establishing itself as a recognised centre of expertise on the remediation techniques involved, since it will already have at least a threefold commercial advantage over its "competitors":

— the Agency/SEPA is in the best position to know what will satisfy it that the notice has been complied with, where there is any scope for differing interpretations of its terms;
— the Agency/SEPA is already familiar with the site, having investigated it sufficiently to allow the requirements in the notice to be determined; and
— the Agency/SEPA is "on the spot" and already in contact with the recipient of the notice: indeed, where the notice is a remediation notice or (depending on the content of the regulations to be made under s.161A(5)(a) of the Water Resources Act 1991 or, in Scotland, s.46(5)(a) of the Control of Pollution Act 1974) a works notice, the Agency/SEPA has already consulted with the recipient over what might be done by way of remediation.

Indeed, depending on the point at which "consultation" becomes "advice", it may be that the potential conflict between the Agency/SEPA's roles of enforcing authority and commercial supplier of technical advice could emerge even prior to the service of the notice.

A further potential conflict would manifest itself if the awkward situation arose where commercially-given Agency/SEPA advice proved to be less than adequate. If remediation was carried out in accordance with that advice, then the Agency/SEPA would have a commercial interest in nevertheless declining to serve a further notice or otherwise pursue the matter, since to do so would be to expose itself to possible legal action for negligence or breach of contract.

It should be noted that subs. (3) makes no reference to charging for the advice or assistance to which it refers, and the Agency/SEPA are not under any obligation to charge for it, merely empowered to do so (*e.g.* by subs. (1)(a)). However, it may be that budgetary constraints will encourage them to charge for such services and even to compete actively to supply them. It is in the latter circumstance, should it arise, that the potential for conflict—or at least, for perceived conflict—would be greatest.

Subsection (4) places a restriction on the agencies' ability to provide such advice, etc. Written ministerial consent is required where the advice etc. is being provided to any person outside the United Kingdom, and such consent may be subject to conditions. Four points may be noted in relation to this provision:

— the same restriction previously existed in relation to advice etc. to persons outside the United Kingdom by the NRA (s.4(3) of the Water Resources Act 1991), but an additional restriction imposed by that section of the 1991 Act in such a case (that Treasury approval he required where capital expenditure of the guaranteeing of a liability by the NRA was involved) is not imposed on the agencies;

— the restriction is, as it is seen by Nigel Haigh, an Agency board member, intended to ensure that the Agency (and presumably SEPA) concentrates on issues affecting the United Kingdom (*Guardian*, September 6, 1995, Society p. 5). However, it has been criticised as "an intolerable restriction [which] needs to be challenged if British environmental expertise is to play its full role in the development of European policy" (P. Lowe, H. Talbot and S. Ward in *Ecos*, [September, 1995]);

— the consent requirement would appear to apply to advice etc. provided to United Kingdom citizens and residents who happen to be abroad, whilst not applying to advice, etc., given in relation to non-United Kingdom environmental matters to any person who happens to be within the United Kingdom at the time; and

— the consent requirement applies only where advice, etc., is given under the subs. (3) power, and is without prejudice to other Agency or SEPA powers. It could be argued, therefore, that advice, etc. may be given to persons outside the United Kingdom by virtue of the wide power contained in subs. (1)(a), provided that in the opinion of the agency in question the provision of such advice, etc. will facilitate, or is conducive or incidental to the carrying out of its functions.

Subss. (5) and (6): Research
The Agency and SEPA must each carry out or commission relevant research and related activities (subs. (5)(a)). This duty supports the s.5(4)/s.33(4) duty to follow developments in pollution control technology and techniques. To whom the results are made available, and at what price, is left to their discretion (subs. (5)(b)), and they may make such results publicly available free of charge: subs. (6). It is submitted that the discretion granted in these provisions is subject to the Environmental Information Regulations 1992 and the E.U. directive on freedom of access to environmental information (90/313/EEC) which they implement, and that therefore any decision by the Agency/SEPA to refuse access to documents relating to such research would require to be supported by reference to an exemption provided by that legislation.

Subss. (7) and (8): Charging for services in connection with environmental licences
The Agency/SEPA may by agreement charge for advice and assistance provided on request in connection with the range of consents, licences and authorisations which are granted and administered by them.

Such charges are separate from charging schemes in relation to such environmental licences which are provided for by ss.41 and 42 and are discussed in the note to s.41. However, the Agency/SEPA's constituent bodies have often provided such advice and assistance free of charge, for example in the course of discussions prior to an application being made. Since environmental licence charging schemes have typically been based on fixed fees, this situation is capable of being seen as violating the "polluter pays" principle, since less time-consuming businesses, paying the same fee as equivalent but more time-consuming ones, are effectively subsidising them even assuming that the charging scheme recovers overall regulatory costs.

Charges levied under subs. (7), and outside the charging scheme, may therefore be seen as a step towards remedying this situation. For further discussion of this issue, see the notes to ss.41 and 42.

By subs. (8), subs. (7) does not restrict any other charging powers of the Agency/SEPA (under ss.41–43 and s.37(1)), and any statutory provision made in relation to Agency/SEPA charges (for example, a charging scheme under s.41) takes precedence over subs. (7) so the Agency/SEPA may not charge separately or on a different basis for any services or facilities expressly covered by another charging provision.

Delegation of functions by Ministers, etc., to the new Agencies

38.—(1) Agreements may be made between—
　(a) any Minister of the Crown, and
　(b) a new Agency,
authorising the new Agency (or any of its employees) to exercise on behalf of that Minister, with or without payment, any eligible function of his.

(2) An agreement under subsection (1) above shall not authorise the new Agency (or any of its employees) to exercise on behalf of a Minister of the Crown any function which consists of a power to make regulations or other instruments of a legislative character or a power to fix fees or charges.

(3) An agreement under this section may provide for any eligible function to which it relates to be exercisable by the new Agency in question (or any of its employees)—
　(a) either wholly or to such extent as may be specified in the agreement;
　(b) either generally or in such cases or areas as may be so specified; or
　(c) either unconditionally or subject to the fulfilment of such conditions as may be so specified.

(4) Subsection (5) below applies where, by virtue of an agreement under this section, a new Agency (or any of its employees) is authorised to exercise any function of a Minister of the Crown.

(5) Subject to subsection (6) below, anything done or omitted to be done by the new Agency (or an employee of the new Agency) in, or in connection with, the exercise or purported exercise of the function shall be treated for all purposes as done or omitted to be done by that Minister in his capacity as such.

(6) Subsection (5) above shall not apply—
　(a) for the purposes of so much of any agreement made between that Minister and the new Agency as relates to the exercise of the function; or
　(b) for the purposes of any criminal proceedings brought in respect of anything done or omitted to be done as mentioned in that subsection.

(7) An agreement under this section shall not prevent a Minister of the Crown exercising any function to which the agreement relates.

(8) Where a Minister of the Crown has power to include, in any arrangements which he makes in relation to the performance by him of an eligible function, provision for the making of payments to him—
　(a) by other parties to the arrangements, or
　(b) by persons who use any facilities or services provided by him pursuant to the arrangements or in relation to whom the function is otherwise exercisable,
he may include in any such arrangements provision for the making of such payments to him or a new Agency in cases where the new Agency (or any of its employees) acts on his behalf by virtue of an agreement under this section.

(9) The power conferred on a Minister of the Crown by subsection (1) above is in addition to any other power by virtue of which functions of his may be exercised by other persons on his behalf.

(10) In this section—
　　"eligible function" means any function of a Minister of the Crown which the Secretary of State, having regard to the functions conferred or imposed upon the new Agency in question under or by virtue of this Act or any other enactment, considers can appropriately be

exercised by that new Agency (or any of its employees) on behalf of that Minister;
"Minister of the Crown" has the same meaning as in the Ministers of the Crown Act 1975.

DEFINITIONS
"eligible function": subs. (10).
"functions": s.124(1).
"Minister of the Crown": subs. (10).
"new Agency": s.56(1).

COMMENCEMENT
July 28, 1995 (S.I. 1995 No. 1983).

GENERAL NOTE
This section provides considerable scope for the Government to delegate ministerial functions to either agency by agreement with that agency. When this section, then clause 36, was introduced into the Bill, one commentator suggested that "early candidates for transfer from the DoE are aspects of chemicals control and the provision of technical guidance on waste and contaminated land. The Ministry of Agriculture, Fisheries and Food's (or, in Scotland, the Scottish Office's) responsibilities in relation to the dumping of waste at sea, effluent pipelines and radioactive discharges are also understood to be candidates for transfer": *ENDS Report* 238, November 1994, pp. 20–21. In Commons Standing Committee, the then Parliamentary Under-Secretary of State for the Environment, Sir Paul Beresford, indicated that "at least some of the Secretary of State's functions" under Pt. VI of the 1990 Act in relation to genetically modified organisms could be transferred to the Environment Agency under this section": H.C. Standing Committee B, 3rd sitting, May 2, 1995, col. 102.

Such an agreement may be made between any Minister of the Crown and either of the Agency/SEPA (subs. (1)) and may provide for payment to the Agency/SEPA by that Minister (subs. (1)) or by any other person who would otherwise be required to make payment to that Minister in connection with the delegated function: subs. (8). It may transfer all or only part of a function, conditionally or unconditionally: subs. (3).

However, there are two important restrictions on a Minister's right to enter into such an agreement:—

— only a function which the Secretary of State considers can appropriately be exercised by the agency in question, given that agency's existing functions, may be delegated under this section: subss. (1) and (10); and

— no legislative power or power to fix fees or charges may be delegated under this section: subs. (2).

Further, the Minister in question retains the power to exercise the delegated function himself: subs. (7). Sir Paul Beresford indicated on behalf of the Government in Committee that:

"Except in the case of consequential criminal proceedings [see below], the Minister has responsibility for ultimately ensuring that the function is exercised or performed satisfactorily and is, of course, therefore accountable to Parliament. [Subsection] (7) ensures that the Minister will have sufficient power to exercise those delegated functions should it be exceptionally necessary" (H.C. Standing Committee B, 8th Sitting, col. 256, May 16, 1995).

Ministers of the Crown have, as a rule, Crown immunity from criminal or civil liability in respect of actions or omissions in their ministerial capacity. Neither of the agencies has such Crown immunity (s.1(5)(a) and Sched. 6, para. 2), but subs. (5) provides that any act or omission by the Agency/SEPA or its employees in connection with the exercise or (importantly) the purported exercise of a function delegated under this section is deemed to be the act or omission of the delegating Minister. This effectively confers Crown immunity in relation to such acts or omissions, but it is qualified by subs. (6)(b) so that the Agency/SEPA have no such immunity from criminal liability.

Subsection (5) alone would also, without subs. (6)(a), have the unpalatable effect of removing any Agency/SEPA responsibility to the delegating Minister for failing to carry out the delegated functions, by providing that agency's failure to do so was in fact an omission by that Minister. Subsection (6)(a) therefore qualifies subs. (5) so that it does not apply for the purposes of the agreement between the parties.

General duty of the new Agencies to have regard to costs and benefits in exercising powers

39.—(1) Each new Agency—
(a) in considering whether or not to exercise any power conferred upon it by or under any enactment, or
(b) in deciding the manner in which to exercise any such power,
shall, unless and to the extent that it is unreasonable for it to do so in view of the nature or purpose of the power or in the circumstances of the particular case, take into account the likely costs and benefits of the exercise or non-exercise of the power or its exercise in the manner in question.

(2) The duty imposed upon a new Agency by subsection (1) above does not affect its obligation, nevertheless, to discharge any duties, comply with any requirements, or pursue any objectives, imposed upon or given to it otherwise than under this section.

DEFINITIONS
"costs": s.56(1).
"new Agency": s.56(1).

COMMENCEMENT
July 28, 1995 (S.1. 1995 No. 1983)

GENERAL NOTE
This section places both the Agency and SEPA, in certain circumstances, under a duty to take into account the likely costs and benefits of their exercise and non-exercise of their statutory powers.

Of all the provisions in the Act, this section has been among the most controversial. None of the Agency/SEPA's predecessors, and whilst it was welcomed by many in industry and elsewhere (notably the Director General of Water Services: see OFWAT News Release 27/94, December 12, 1994) no other U.K. environmental regulators, had been placed under a duty couched in these terms, and on its publication it was reported to have alarmed environmentalists, who feared that it would leave "any aggrieved industry open to challenge the agency in the courts if benefits could not be shown to outweigh costs—an almost impossible task": *The Guardian*, p. 10, "Lobbyists attack environment agency plans", October 14, 1994.

The provision also provoked concern in Parliament that the potential for such challenges might lead to excessive bureaucracy within the agencies and might conflict with or undermine their conservation and pollution prevention functions), (see generally the eighth and ninth sittings of H.C. Standing Committee B (May 16 and 18, 1995) when the clause was discussed), which prompted the then Minister for the Environment and Countryside, Robert Atkins, to give the following example of its application in relation to discharge consents:

"My hon. Friend ... asked about the relationship of clause 37 [s.39] to the conservation duties in clause 7 [s.7]. The two clauses do not conflict. The requirement to consider costs and benefits does not override obligations to conservation. However, it rightly requires that in deciding how far to pursue discretionary programmes the agency should take costs and benefits into account. My hon. Friend mentioned Bassenthwaite Lake. If, in pursuing conservation there, the agency wanted to impose discharge requirements beyond those necessary to reach water quality targets, it would need to consider the costs and benefits. ... However, it would not be prevented from pursuing conservation programmes simply because it could not demonstrate that benefits exceeded costs": H.C. Standing Committee B, 9th sitting, May 18, 1995, cols. 284–285.

Mr Atkins went on to indicate that, "on the strength of our legal advice, [legal opinions obtained by the CPRE and Greenpeace] gravely overstate the danger that new agencies will become bogged down in judicial review as a result of clause 37" (col. 285).

The relationship between this duty and the agencies' other functions is considered further in the Introductory Note to this Part of the Act under *Functions, aims and objectives*.

The Government's draft Guidance to the Environment Agency under the Environment Bill on its contribution to sustainable development (April 1995, revised December 1995) (Chapter 4 of the Scottish Office's draft Guidance to SEPA (May 1995, revised December 1995) is essentially identical) considers this section in Chapter 5. This, it should be noted, is a draft of non-statutory guidance, but it is worth quoting in full:

"Chapter V

Costs and Benefits

Scope of the duty

5.1 Section 4 of the Environment Act requires the Agency to take into account any likely costs in achieving its principal aim (set out at paragraph 2.4 above). Section 39 places the Agency under a duty when it considers whether or how to exercise any power to take into account the likely costs and benefits of its action or inaction. Costs are defined in section 56(1) as including costs to any person (which also means organizations) and to the environment. This duty:

(i) does not apply if it would be unreasonable in the circumstances of a particular case. Or there might be cases where it would be unreasonable for the duty to apply to the full extent.

(ii) does not affect the Agency's mandatory obligations to discharge specific duties, comply with requirements or pursue objectives. Legal requirements (such as water quality objectives) remain unaffected by the duty; they must still be observed. But the general duty with regard to costs and benefits will apply whenever there is more than one way of achieving the legal requirements, and if the Agency retains discretion as to how they should be achieved.

Purpose of the duty

5.2 These provisions recognise that sustainable development involves reconciling the need for economic development with that for protecting and enhancing the environment. Ministers consider that as the Agency is a body with powers to make decisions with significant impacts on individuals, organizations and the environment, it should take account of all types of costs and benefits when making such decisions. This will not only ensure that financial and other considerations are taken into account, but also that environmental considerations are given the central role that is necessary for sustainable development. But the duty does not apply in cases where it would be unreasonable nor can it be used to override other statutory requirements.

Principle of application

5.3 The principle behind section 39 is that generally in appropriate circumstances— whether in individual cases or in guiding the Agency's policy-making and executive functions—the Agency should take account of all types of likely costs and benefits, including the environmental impact of a project and the compliance and any other economic costs and benefits. Sometimes this may involve environmental assessment. This is already a statutory requirement in many cases and may also be appropriate in others. While it cannot of itself make decisions, environmental appraisal can when properly applied highlight new options such as remediation. It can also reduce the extent of uncertainty confronting decision makers and improve the quality of the decision making process and inform public debate.

Selection of options

5.4 In discharging its duty, the Agency will need to decide what are the relevant options to consider, for example:

(i) whether or not to take actions, and

(ii) the various options, including the appropriate levels of any controls, for achieving a given environmental outcome.

Quantification

5.5 Whilst the Agency should take into account all likely costs and benefits, Ministers consider that it does not follow that all need to be precisely quantified. For example:

(i) where the Agency has no discretion about the outcome it may only be the differences in likely costs and benefits between the particular options that are relevant

(ii) the Agency may be able to take account of clear and appropriate precedent, for example for the granting of individual fishing licences or certain types of discharge consents

(iii) many likely costs and benefits, particularly in relation to the environment, are inherently difficult to quantify, especially in monetary terms: for example, the possible health effects of exposure to very low levels of pollutants, the value of a forest, the visual impacts of development or global warming. Judgments will therefore sometimes need to be made.

Methodologies and procedures

5.6 When assessing likely costs and benefits in the circumstances of the case, the Agency may consider it appropriate to consider the following:
  (i) principles, procedures and techniques—in particular, risk assessment, and economic and policy appraisal[1]—for giving proper consideration to non-market impacts including those on the environment
  (ii) the precautionary principle
  (iii) reliance on sound science
  (iv) the likely impact on the carrying capacity of the environment, and on natural environmental capital
  (v) the likely longer-term implications and effects, having particular regard to those which appear likely to be irreversible or reversible only at high cost and over a long time-scale. In the Ministers' view, such analyses should take proper account of long-term environmental benefits as well as immediate financial costs.
  (vi) the likely costs and benefits of its actions for society as a whole, including the effects on the welfare of people and business, impacts on the environment and changes in the use of resources (labour, capital and natural resources). In so doing the Agency may be guided where appropriate by:
    (a) the views of the Government's Chief Medical Officers, the Health and Safety Executive and Commission and other interested bodies as to the effects on human health
    (b) evidence within the UK and internationally about proven and likely impacts on the environment
    (c) the impacts on the economy and on all affected business sectors and individual companies, and
    (d) the distribution of costs and benefits across the economy. For example, some options open to the Agency may impose particularly heavy costs on particular groups of people or companies or on certain parts of the environment.

Internal guidance

5.7 The Agency should develop and make available practical procedures to ensure that it meets the requirements of the duty having regard to this guidance. Such procedures should be set out in a document which provides internal advice for staff and is made available to others so as to promote public understanding of the principles it adopts. It should include advice to staff on:
  (i) relevant techniques for assessing costs and benefits
  (ii) where the Agency's discretion is limited by obligations arising from other duties, requirements and objectives, and
  (iii) the extent to which detailed consideration of costs and benefits might be unreasonable in particular circumstances."

The question of where the duty in this section fits into the array of duties, powers, aims, objectives and purposes to which the two agencies are subject is discussed in the Introductory Note to Part I of the Act under *Functions, aims and objectives* but a number of points may be noted:
  (a) *Comparison with cost-benefit analysis*
     The duty, where it applies, is only to take into account likely costs and benefits: it is neither a requirement for a cost-benefit analysis of a kind which would demonstrate

---

[1] A useful guidance is contained in
A Guide to Risk Assessment and Risk Management for Environmental Protection HMSO 1995
Economic Appraisal in Central Government: A Technical Guide for Departments, HM Treasury 1991
Policy Appraisal and the Environment: A Guide for Government Departments, Department of the Environment HMSO 1991
Environmental Appraisal in Government Departments, Department of the Environment HMSO 1994
Checking the Cost to Business: A Guide to Compliance Cost Assessment, Department of Trade and Industry 1992
Policy Appraisal and Health, Department of Health (in preparation)

costs outweighing benefits or vice versa (and once again, the statement by Mr Atkins quoted above may be admissible were a court to consider that the provision might have this effect and is ambiguous or obscure), nor a requirement to act in accordance with the conclusions yielded by a consideration of likely costs and benefits. Paragraph 5.5 of the revised draft Guidance to the Agency, quoted above, confirms this (see also para. 4.5 of the revised draft Guidance to SEPA).

(b) *Circumstances where the duty applies*
The duty only applies "unless and to the extent that it is unreasonable for it to do so in view of the nature or purpose of the power or in the circumstances of the particular case" (subs. (1)).

(c) *Duty subject to other duties, requirements and objectives*
The duty is subject to the agencies' respective obligations to discharge their duties, comply with requirements and pursue objectives imposed on them. It thus operates only where the agencies' duties and objectives may be fulfilled equally well in different ways and there thus remains a discretion as to how to do so. The relationship of the duty with these other matters is considered in the Introduction to this Part of the Act, under the heading *Functions, Aims and Objectives.*

(d) *"Costs and benefits"*
"Costs" are defined by s.56(1) to include costs to the environment as well as to any person; this definition was added during the passage of the Environment Bill to allay concerns that a court might otherwise have taken the contrary view. "Benefits" is not a defined term but it appears beyond doubt, particularly in view of paras. 5.3 and 5.5(iii) of the revised draft Guidance, that the Government expects the Agency and SEPA to treat the term as including benefits to the environment as well as to any person (see also paras. 4.3 and 4.5(iii) of the revised draft Guidance to SEPA).

(e) *Geographical extent of costs and benefits*
It would appear that costs and benefits to the environment outside the U.K. are to be taken into account under s.39 but the position is less clear regarding costs and benefits to persons outside the United Kingdom.
The definition of "the environment" at s.56(1) does not geographically restrict the scope of the term to the United Kingdom environment. Equally, the Government's draft Guidance to the Agency referred to above indicates that, "In the present age, [environmental] concerns have broadened beyond people's immediate environment to global issues, such as the protection of the stratospheric ozone layer and the world's climate" (para. 3.4), and that the Agency's judgements "should make a proper allowance for the interests of *future generations* and for the pressures that society places upon the *global environment*" (para. 3.9—emphasis in the original text). It may also be noted that a number of E.U. and international United Kingdom obligations are to be implemented by the agencies, which contain references to the "environment" in contexts which clearly envisage the term having international scope. The proposed Directive on Integrated Pollution Prevention and Control, on which political agreement was reached by the Council of Environment Ministers in June, 1995, is an example (see article 8.1).
Equally important is the question whether costs and benefits to any person includes persons outside the United Kingdom. The answer to this question would determine whether, and the extent to which, the agencies are allowed (or indeed required) by s.39, where it applies, to give any weight to the United Kingdom's competitive advantage. No geographical limitation to the term is set by the Act, and in the draft of its Guidance to the Agency under s.4 the Government indicates that it "has to take the broadest view of the action the U.K. needs to take to achieve sustainable development, domestically and globally": para. 4.1. Thus it would appear that references in the draft Guidance's discussion of costs and benefits to "impacts on the economy and on all affected business sectors and individual companies" (para. 5.6(c)) are to companies and sectors wherever located, and no ground is provided on which to justify giving a greater weight to impacts on U.K. persons and businesses than to those on persons and businesses elsewhere. Although para. 4.6(vi)(c) of the revised draft Guidance to SEPA is identical to para. 5.6(c) of the revised draft Guidance to the Agency, interestingly the foregoing conclusion does not apply north of the border since the revised draft Guidance to SEPA no longer contains a provision equivalent to para. 4.1 of the revised draft Guidance to the Agency mentioned above. However, it should be noted that there is reference in the statutory part of the draft Guidance to both agencies encouraging regulated organisations to enhance "their own and the UK's

competitive position" (Appx. 1, para. 11(iv)(c); revised draft Guidance to SEPA, Appx. 1, para. 9(iv)(c)).

(f) *Challenges under section 39*

It is noted above that there has been concern in some quarters that the Agency/SEPA may face numerous challenges under this section. The duty is sufficiently hedged in with qualifications that it may prove difficult for a judicial review application to succeed in practice. In addition, where the relevant statute provides an appeal mechanism in relation to the action or omission complained of, then the appropriate means of challenge is an appeal under those provisions.

Ministerial directions to the new Agencies

40.—(1) The appropriate Minister may give a new Agency directions of a general or specific character with respect to the carrying out of any of its functions.

(2) The appropriate Minister may give a new Agency such directions of a general or specific character as he considers appropriate for the implementation of—

    (a) any obligations of the United Kingdom under the Community Treaties, or

    (b) any international agreement to which the United Kingdom is for the time being a party.

(3) Any direction under subsection (2) above shall be published in such manner as the Minister giving it considers appropriate for the purpose of bringing the matters to which it relates to the attention of persons likely to be affected by them; and—

    (a) copies of the direction shall be made available to the public; and

    (b) notice shall be given—

        (i) in the case of a direction given to the Agency, in the London Gazette, or

        (ii) in the case of a direction given to SEPA, in the Edinburgh Gazette,

    of the giving of the direction and of where a copy of the direction may be obtained.

(4) The provisions of subsection (3) above shall have effect in relation to any direction given to a new Agency under an enactment other than subsection (2) above for the implementation of—

    (a) any obligations of the United Kingdom under the Community Treaties, or

    (b) any international agreement to which the United Kingdom is for the time being a party,

as those provisions have effect in relation to a direction given under subsection (2) above.

(5) In determining—

    (a) any appeal against, or reference or review of, a decision of a new Agency, or

    (b) any application transmitted from a new Agency,

the body or person making the determination shall be bound by any direction given under this section or any other enactment by a Minister of the Crown to the new Agency to the same extent as the new Agency.

(6) Any power to give a direction under this section shall be exercisable, except in an emergency, only after consultation with the new Agency concerned.

(7) Any power of the appropriate Minister to give directions to a new Agency otherwise than by virtue of this section shall be without prejudice to any power to give directions conferred by this section.

(8) It is the duty of a new Agency to comply with any direction which is

given to that new Agency by a Minister of the Crown under this section or any other enactment.

<small>DEFINITIONS</small>
"appropriate Minister": s.56(1).
"functions": s.124(1).
"new Agency": s.56(1).
"notice": s.124(1).

<small>COMMENCEMENT</small>
July 28, 1995 (S.I. 1995 No. 1983)

<small>GENERAL NOTE</small>
This section (which should be read together with s.122) allows the Secretary of State (and additionally, in the case of the Agency, the Minister of Agriculture, Fisheries and Food) to exercise considerable control over any activity of the agencies by giving them directions as to the carrying out of their functions (subs. (1)), with which the agency concerned must comply (subs. (8)). Subsection (8) also requires the agencies to comply with any directions given to them by other Ministers of the Crown by virtue of other legislation.

Directions under other legislation
A range of other legislation provides for directions to be given to the Agency/SEPA: see, for instance, the Environmental Protection Act 1990 where directions may require specified conditions to be included or not included in IPC authorisations (s.7(3)) and waste management licences (s.35(7)), or may govern enforcement measures under IPC (ss.12(5), 13(3) and 14(4)) and waste management licensing (ss.37(3), 38(7) and 42(8)) (see the General Notes to Pts. I and II of the 1990 Act for a fuller account). Sections 44(A)(6) and 44(B) of the 1990 Act, as inserted by s.92 of this Act, also provide for directions to be given to the Agency and SEPA in relation to their respective national waste strategies, see also s.207 of the Water Resources Act 1991, which allows for directions to be given to the Agency on grounds of civil emergency or national security. Such other powers to give directions to the agencies do not restrict the power to give directions which is established under this section: subs. (7). The draft Guidance issued to the Agency under s.4 contains at Annex B a list of directions issued to HMIP and the NRA, which are as follows:—

Date of issue	Direction	Purpose
1/4/91	The Large Combustion Plant (New Plant) Directions 1991	To give effect to E.C. Directive 88/609/EEC
1/11/91	The Municipal Waste-Incineration Directions 1991	To give effect to E.C. Directive 89/369/EEC and 89/429/EEC
28/3/94	The Environmental Protection (Titanium Dioxide) Direction 1994	To give effect to E.C. Directive 92/112/EEC
10/10/89	Security Measures (National Rivers Authority) Direction 1989	To give effect to section 170(1) of the Water Act 1989 (superseded by s.207(1) of the Water Resources Act 1991) on directions in the interests of national security
5/5/92	National Rivers Authority (Bathing Water) Directions 1992	To give effect to Council Directive 76/160/EEC concerning the quality of bathing water and to S.I. 1991 No. 1597 Bathing Waters (Classification) Regulations 1991
27/1/92	National Rivers Authority (Nitrate Pollution) (Council Directive 91/676/EEC) Directions 1992	To give effect to Council Directive 91/676/EEC concerning the protection of waters against pollution caused by nitrates from agricultural sources

Date of issue	Direction	Purpose
13/7/92	Directions to the National Rivers Authority under s.5 of the Water Resources Act 1991 and relating to Council Directive 80/68/EEC on the protection of groundwater	To give effect to Council Directive 80/68/EEC on the protection of groundwater against pollution caused by certain dangerous substances

It may be noted that the revised draft Guidance to SEPA does not contain such a list.
This list is not to be included in the final form of that Guidance. Since then, there has been one set of directions issued:— On June 23, 1995, the Large Combustion Plant (New Plant) Directions 1995 were issued to HMIP to replace the 1991 Directions of the same name listed in the table, and to give effect to amendments to the 1988 Directive by Directive 94/66/E.C.

Procedure
It is important in practice which provision is relied upon in giving a direction, where it may be that several alternative provisions could have been relied upon, because different procedures may be involved. Directions given under this section may be made only after consultation with the agency concerned, unless in emergency (subs. (6)), and directions given so as to implement E.C. or international obligations whether or not they are given under this section, must be published: subss. (3) and (4).

Appeals and transmissions
The role of directions in appeals against Agency/SEPA decisions or called-in applications is notable: subs (5). Whoever hears an appeal—generally an inspector (or, in Scotland, a reporter) appointed by the Secretary of State—is bound by any relevant direction to the Agency/SEPA concerned just as that agency is. Since directions are often given in order to implement E.C. or international obligations, this provision affords the Government a degree of control which can ensure that such obligations are complied with.

Previous directions
Directions given to the NRA for the purposes of s.19 of the Water Resources Act 1991 have effect after the transfer date as directions to the Agency under s.6(2) of this Act (Sched. 23, para. 2).
More generally, any direction given to a predecessor of either of the Agency/SEPA, in relation to a function which has been transferred to one of them, has effect after the transfer date as if given to the Agency/SEPA: (s.55(4)(d)).
This section should be read in conjunction with s.122 which makes general provision in relation to directions given to any person or body under this Act and makes specific provision for the circumstance where a direction given to either of the agencies to give effect to E.C. obligations is varied or revoked by virtue of that section.
The Agency/SEPA's annual reports must set out any directions given to them under this section (s.52(2)). This provision is important as directions which do not implement E.C. or international obligations are not covered by subss. (3) and (4) and therefore need not be published at the time they are given, although there is nothing in the legislation which bars the Agency/SEPA from publishing the direction at the time.

Charging schemes

Power to make schemes imposing charges

    41.—(1) Subject to the following provisions of this section and section 42 below—

    (a) in the case of any particular licence under Chapter II of Part II of the 1991 Act (abstraction and impounding), the Agency may require the payment to it of such charges as may from time to time be prescribed;

    (b) in relation to other environmental licences, there shall be charged by and paid to a new Agency such charges as may from time to time be prescribed; and

(c) as a means of recovering costs incurred by it in performing functions conferred by regulations under section 62 of the 1990 Act (dangerous or intractable waste) each of the new Agencies may require the payment to it of such charges as may from time to time be prescribed;

and in this section "prescribed" means specified in, or determined under, a scheme (in this section referred to as a "charging scheme") made under this section by the new Agency in question.

(2) As respects environmental licences, charges may be prescribed in respect of—

(a) the grant or variation of an environmental licence, or any application for, or for a variation of, such a licence;

(b) the subsistence of an environmental licence;

(c) the transfer (where permitted) of an environmental licence to another person, or any application for such a transfer;

(d) the renewal (where permitted) of an environmental licence, or any application for such a renewal;

(e) the surrender (where permitted) of an environmental licence, or any application for such a surrender; or

(f) any application for the revocation (where permitted) of an environmental licence.

(3) A charging scheme may, for the purposes of subsection (2)(b) above, impose—

(a) a single charge in respect of the whole of any relevant licensed period;

(b) separate charges in respect of different parts of any such period; or

(c) both such a single charge and such separate charges;

and in this subsection "relevant licensed period" means the period during which an environmental licence is in force or such part of that period as may be prescribed.

(4) Without prejudice to subsection (7)(a) below, a charging scheme may, as respects environmental licences, provide for different charges to be payable according to—

(a) the description of environmental licence in question;

(b) the description of authorised activity in question;

(c) the scale on which the authorised activity in question is carried on;

(d) the description or amount of the substance to which the authorised activity in question relates;

(e) the number of different authorised activities carried on by the same person.

(5) A charging scheme—

(a) shall specify, in relation to any charge prescribed by the scheme, the description of person who is liable to pay the charge; and

(b) may provide that it shall be a condition of an environmental licence of any particular description that any charge prescribed by a charging scheme in relation to an environmental licence of that description is paid in accordance with the scheme.

(6) Without prejudice to subsection (5)(b) above, if it appears to a new Agency that any charges due and payable to it in respect of the subsistence of an environmental licence have not been paid, it may, in accordance with the appropriate procedure, suspend or revoke the environmental licence to the extent that it authorises the carrying on of an authorised activity.

(7) A charging scheme may—

(a) make different provision for different cases, including different provision in relation to different persons, circumstances or localities;

(b) provide for the times at which, and the manner in which, the charges prescribed by the scheme are to be paid;

(c) revoke or amend any previous charging scheme;

(d) contain supplemental, incidental, consequential or transitional provision for the purposes of the scheme.

(8) If and to the extent that a charging scheme relates to licences under Chapter II of Part II of the 1991 Act (abstraction and impounding), the scheme shall have effect subject to any provision made by or under sections 125 to 130 of that Act (exemption from charges, imposition of special charges for spray irrigation, and charges in respect of abstraction from waters of the British Waterways Board).

(9) A new Agency shall not make a charging scheme unless the provisions of the scheme have been approved by the Secretary of State under section 42 below.

(10) In this section—

"the appropriate procedure" means such procedure as may be specified or described in regulations made for the purpose by the Secretary of State;

"authorised activity" means any activity to which an environmental licence relates.

(11) Any power to make regulations under this section shall be exercisable by statutory instrument; and a statutory instrument containing any such regulations shall be subject to annulment pursuant to a resolution of either House of Parliament.

DEFINITIONS
"the 1990 Act": s.56(1)
"the 1991 Act": s.56(1)
"the Agency": s.124(1)
"appropriate procedure": subs. (10)
"authorised activity": subs. (10)
"charging scheme": subs. (1)
"environmental licence": s.56(1)
"new Agency": s.56(1)
"prescribed": subs. (1)
"relevant licensed period" subs. (3)

COMMENCEMENT
February 1, 1996 in so far as this section confers power on the Secretary of State to make regulations and makes provision in relation to the exercise of that power; the remainder came into force on April 1, 1996 (S.I. 1996 No. 186).

GENERAL NOTE
This section provides for each of the Agency/SEPA to make charging schemes for its range of licensing activities (subss. (1)(a) and (b)) and for the recovery of costs incurred by them under regulations made under s.62 of the Environmental Protection Act 1990: subs. (1)(c). The range of environmental licences, as they are termed in this Act, to which this section applies is listed in s.56(1). The most recent of them is the registration of exempt scrap metal recovery and motor vehicle dismantling activities which have been added to Sched. 3 to the Waste Management Licensing Regulations 1994 by S.I. 1995 No. 288, for which, unlike the other Sched. 3 exemptions, a registration fee is payable.

The particular regulations in the legislators' minds in respect of s.62 of the 1990 Act are presumably the draft Special Waste Regulations on which the 1995 consultation had closed by the time this Act received Royal Assent. The consultation draft of these regulations introduced, among other things, charges for the waste regulators' involvement in the consignment note procedure for special waste, and in part for this reason, para. 80(1) and (2) of Sched. 22 to the Act, which have the same commencement date as this subsection amend s.62 of the 1990 Act to extend the range of supervisory activities for which costs may be recovered in relation to special waste.

Procedure for making charging schemes
The fact that charging schemes are made by the agencies themselves rather than by the Secretary of State is a departure from the previous position for both Parts I and II of the 1990 Act (IPC and waste regulation) and for Radioactive Substances Act 1993 registration and

licensing, although charging schemes for the other principal licensing regimes in England and Wales—abstraction licensing and discharge consenting—have until the advent of the Agency been exercised by the NRA under ss.123 and 131 of the Water Resources Act 1991. In Scotland, charging schemes in relation to discharge consents have been made by the river purification authorities under s.53 of the Control of Pollution Act 1974.

Just as with the NRA under the 1991 Act, there are significant procedural checks on the agencies' freedom in relation to the making of charging schemes:
— a draft must be published (s.42(1));
— the proposed scheme must be approved, and may be modified, by the Secretary of State (subs. (9));
— such approval in turn requires the consent of the Treasury (s.42(7));
— the additional consent of the Minister of Agriculture, Fisheries and Food is required by the Agency where the scheme relates to authorisations for the disposal of radioactive waste (s.42(7));
— the charging scheme must be made by statutory instrument which may be annulled by a resolution of Either House of Parliament (subs. (11)).

Content of Charging Schemes
The agencies enjoy a wide discretion as to the focus and charging structure of a charging scheme, although this is subject to the procedural checks listed above, and in particular:
— water abstraction and impoundment licence charges are subject to the British Waterways Board's statutory exemptions (subs. (8)); and
— in approving a scheme, the Secretary of State must have regard to a cost recovery criterion (s.42(2) and (3)), the policy background to which is discussed in the General Note to that section.
The flexibility in this regard which is provided by subss. (4) and (7)(a) reflects a significant point of principle.

Charging structures based on a fixed fee will inevitably approximate only crudely to the widely differing burdens placed on a regulator by different applications, even of the same description — an application for a waste management licence to operate a landfill site, for example, can involve lengthy and complex negotiations on the question of adequate financial provision for the purposes of s.74(3)(c) of the Environmental Protection Act 1990, whereas an application for a waste management licence for a waste transfer station is unlikely to do so. Similarly, IPC fees and charges have been levied at fixed rates on the grant or variation of an authorisation and there is a fixed annual subsistence charge. These fees and charges only crudely reflect the amount of regulators' time taken by the kind of activity concerned (to take the example of IPC again, the annual subsistence charge is levied per component of the process authorised, which reflects only to a degree the complexity of the process). HMIP and HMIPI/ the relevant RPA in particular can spend a great deal of time discussing and advising on particular authorisation applications, even before the application is made.

It has been suggested that this situation fails to accord with the "polluter pays" principle: see for example the Interim Report by Her Majesty's Inspectorate of Pollution Advisory Committee (February 13, 1995, available from Department of Environment), which recommended that "HMIP develop a method of classifying customers which will both apportion costs more fairly and reward those firms which by their own actions, reduce the work required by HMIP" (para. 12). HMIP's consultation paper on its 1995/96 charging scheme for IPC (January 1995) also raised this issue, with the comment that "HMIP encourages operators to discuss their approach to making an application before it falls due, and this has proved a valuable process. It does, however, involve a substantial cost to HMIP [and] Ministers may conclude that it should more properly be borne by the polluter than by the tax-payer". This approach was not in fact pursued in the 1995/96 charging scheme for IPC. It may be noted that the "polluter pays" principle was itself questioned in the House of Lords: Baroness Hamwee commented that "we shall have a body that will be vulnerable to control by the polluters themselves. In other words, they will become the paymasters in a sense": *Hansard*, H.L. Vol. 559, col. 1454.

Subsection (7)(a), and the provisions of subs. (4) which can be seen as examples of the kind of provision allowed by subs. (7)(a), allow the Agency/SEPA to tackle this issue. So too does s.37(7), which operates outside the charging scheme system.

The Agency/SEPA may charge for unsuccessful or withdrawn, as well as for successful applications for the grant, variation, transfer, renewal, surrender or revocation of an environmental licence (subs. (2)). They may charge a subsistence fee, and this may be a one-off charge for the whole period of the licence combined with, or in place of a periodic (for example, annual) fee (subss.(2)(b) and (3)).

Subss. (5) and (6): Payment under charging schemes
The only statutory requirement as regards the content of a charging scheme is that it must specify who is liable to pay the charges it imposes (subs. (5)(a)). It may in addition make payment of charges prescribed by it a condition of any licence to which those charges relate (subs. (5)(b)), and both agencies have the power to revoke or suspend any licence where such a payment condition, relating to a subsistence fee, is breached (subs. (6)). This revocation or suspension power is, however, subject to such procedures as may be prescribed in regulations (subss. (6) and (10)).

Previous charging schemes and transitional arrangements
The Agency/SEPA take over existing charging schemes in relation to transferred functions from their predecessors as from the transfer date:
— fees and charges paid to a predecessor of one of the agencies have effect as if paid to that agency: s.55(3) and (4)(g); and
— such a charging scheme takes effect as if made under this section: Sched. 23, para. 4);
— Circular 15/95, discussed in the note to s.3 (or in relation to Scotland, Circular 19/95, discussed in the note to s.22), gives guidance that "the general approach to payments and receipts is that there should be a clean cut-off at April 1, 1996, with [waste regulation] authorities responsible for payments and receipts arising before that date and the Agency for those after" (para. 19). It goes on to give an example of the application of these principles to payments and receipts in respect of waste regulation fees and charges: para. 20(a).
The main relevant charging schemes at the time of writing are as follows:—
1. *The HMIP Integrated Pollution Control Fees and Charges Scheme (England and Wales) Revised 1995* and the *Integrated Pollution Control Fees and Charges (Scotland) Scheme 1995* (which were made under s.8(2) of the 1990 Act and came into operation on April 1, 1995).
2. *The Radioactive Substances Authorisations and Registrations Fees and Charges Scheme (England and Wales) Revised 1995* and the *Radioactive Substances Act 1993 Fees and Charges (Scotland) Scheme 1995* (which were made under s.43 of the Radioactive Substances Act 1993 and came into force on April 1, 1995).
3. *The Waste Management Licensing (Fees and Charges) Scheme 1995* (which was made under s.41 of the 1990 Act, came into force on September 1, 1995 and applies throughout England, Wales and Scotland).
4. *The National Rivers Authority Applications and Discharges Charges Scheme* (which was made under s.131 of the Water Resources Act 1991 and has effect from April 1, 1994 to March 31, 1999, with the figures specified revised for each subsequent year from April 1) and *Schemes for Charges for Applications for Consent to Discharge* made under s.53 of the Control of Pollution Act 1974 by each of the river purification authorities in Scotland and which came into force on January 1, 1992.
5. *The National Rivers Authority Scheme of Abstraction Charges* (which was made under s.123 of the Water Resources Act 1991 and came into force on April 1, 1993, with the figures specified revised for each subsequent year beginning April 1, and relates to applications and licences for the abstraction and impoundment of water in England and Wales).
6. *The Local Authority Air Pollution Control Fees and Charges (Scotland) Scheme 1995* (as revised) (which was made under s.8(2) of the 1990 Act, came into force on April 1, 1995 and is included here as a result of the transfer of LAPC functions to SEPA in Scotland but not to the Agency in England and Wales.

Approval of charging schemes

42.—(1) Before submitting a proposed charging scheme to the Secretary of State for his approval, a new Agency shall, in such manner as it considers appropriate for bringing it to the attention of persons likely to be affected by the scheme, publish a notice—
(a) setting out its proposals; and
(b) specifying the period within which representations or objections with respect to the proposals may be made to the Secretary of State.
(2) Where any proposed charging scheme has been submitted to the Secretary of State for his approval, he shall, in determining whether or not to approve the scheme or to approve it subject to modifications,—
(a) consider any representations or objections duly made to him and not withdrawn; and

(b) have regard to the matter specified in subsection (3) below.

(3) The matter mentioned in subsection (2)(b) above is the desirability of ensuring that, in the case of each of the descriptions of environmental licence specified in the paragraphs of the definition of that expression in section 56 below, the amounts recovered by the new Agency in question by way of charges prescribed by charging schemes are the amounts which, taking one year with another, need to be recovered by that new Agency to meet such of the costs and expenses (whether of a revenue or capital nature)—

    (a) which it incurs in carrying out its functions,

    (b) in the case of environmental licences which are authorisations under section 13(1) of the Radioactive Substances Act 1993—

        (i) which the Minister incurs in carrying out his functions under or in consequence of that Act, and

        (ii) which the Secretary of State incurs under that Act in carrying out in relation to Scotland or Wales such of his functions under or in consequence of that Act as are exercised by the Minister in relation to England,

as the Secretary of State may consider it appropriate to attribute to the carrying out of those functions in relation to activities to which environmental licences of the description in question relate.

(4) Without prejudice to the generality of the expression "costs and expenses", in determining for the purposes of subsection (3) above the amounts of the costs and expenses which the Secretary of State considers it appropriate to attribute to the carrying out of a new Agency's or the Minister's or the Secretary of State's functions in relation to the activities to which environmental licences of any particular description relate, the Secretary of State—

    (a) shall take into account any determination of the new Agency's financial duties under section 44 below; and

    (b) may include amounts in respect of the depreciation of, and the provision of a return on, such assets as are held by the new Agency, the Minister or the Secretary of State, as the case may be, for purposes connected with the carrying out of the functions in question.

(5) If and to the extent that a charging scheme relates to any licence under Chapter II of Part II of the 1991 Act (abstraction and impounding), the Secretary of State may consider it appropriate to attribute to the carrying out of the Agency's functions in relation to activities to which such a licence relates any costs and expenses incurred by the Agency in carrying out any of its functions under Part II of that Act or under section 6(2) above.

(6) Subsection (5) above is without prejudice to what costs and expenses the Secretary of State may consider it appropriate to attribute to the carrying out of any functions of a new Agency, the Minister or the Secretary of State in relation to activities to which environmental licences of any particular description relate.

(7) The consent of the Treasury shall be required for the giving of approval to a charging scheme and, if and to the extent that the scheme relates to authorisations by the Agency under section 13 of the Radioactive Substances Act 1993 (disposal of radioactive waste), the consent of the Minister shall also be required.

(8) It shall be the duty of a new Agency to take such steps as it considers appropriate for bringing the provisions of any charging scheme made by it which is for the time being in force to the attention of persons likely to be affected by them.

(9) If and to the extent that any sums recovered by a new Agency by way of charges prescribed by charging schemes may fairly be regarded as so recovered for the purpose of recovering the amount required to meet (whether in whole or in part)—

(a) such of the costs and expenses incurred by the Secretary of State as fall within subsection (3) above, or

(b) such of the costs and expenses incurred by the Minister as fall within that subsection,

those sums shall be paid by that new Agency to the Secretary of State or, as the case may be, to the Minister.

(10) For the purposes of subsection (9) above, any question as to the extent to which any sums may fairly be regarded as recovered for the purpose of recovering the amount required to meet the costs and expenses falling within paragraph (a) or paragraph (b) of that subsection shall be determined—

(a) in the case of costs and expenses falling within paragraph (a) of that subsection, by the Secretary of State; and

(b) in the case of costs and expenses falling within paragraph (b) of that subsection, by the Secretary of State and the Minister.

(11) In this section "charging scheme" has the same meaning as in section 41 above.

DEFINITIONS
"the 1991 Act": s.56(1)
"the Agency": s.124(1)
"charging scheme": s.41(1)
"environmental licence": s.56(1)
"functions": s.124(1)
"the Minister": s.56(1)
"modifications": s.124(1)
"new Agency": s.56(1)
"notice": s.124(1)

COMMENCEMENT
September 21, 1995 (S.I. 1995 No. 1983).

GENERAL NOTE
This section makes further provisions in relation to the charging schemes provided for by s.41. The procedural constraints on the making of such schemes are noted in the General Note to that section.

Secretary of State's approval of schemes
The requirement (s.41(9)) for the Secretary of State to approve a s.41 charging scheme does not give him complete discretion in deciding whether to give or withhold such approval. He must first consider any representations or objections made to him within the required period following the publication by the agency in question of the proposed scheme: subs. (2)(a).

Cost recovery
In addition, the Secretary of State must have regard to the desirability of ensuring that the regulatory costs and expenses associated with the particular licensing regime under consideration will be recovered by the scheme: subs. (3). The statutory position in relation to cost recovery varied between the different regimes now covered by this provision: in relation to IPC, for example, the Secretary of State was under a duty "so far as practicable [to] secure" that costs were recovered: subs. 8(6) of the Environmental Protection Act 1990.

At the other extreme, waste management licensing charging schemes had no legislative link with cost recovery (s.41 of the 1990 Act), although the Government's intention that regulatory costs should be covered was made clear by the Earl of Arran on behalf of the Government during Parliamentary debate on what was to become the 1990 Act (*Hansard*, H.L. Vol. 522, col. 335). Notwithstanding this, there has been criticism of the level of fees and charges set by the 1995/96 fees and charges scheme for waste management licensing: it has been suggested by the National Association of Waste Regulation officers that the levels set will not permit full cost recovery (*ENDS Report* 247, August 1995, p.32). The same article also suggests that waste regulation authorities have not attributed the full overheads of waste regulation work to the function, thus concealing overheads which the Agency/SEPA will have to bear. If true, this can be expected to exacerbate any shortfall. This provision aims to minimise the amount of cross-subsidisation between different functions within an agency and must inevitably involve the apportionment between different functions of the costs of shared facilities and assets. This exercise may include the imputation of depreciation of or return on assets (subs. (4)(b)) so that as far as possible the real value of an asset is reflected in this consideration by the Secretary of State.

In the special case of water abstraction or impoundment licences, a charging scheme may, if the Secretary of State considers it appropriate, treat the Agency's water resource management costs and expenses generally as attributable to its licensing activities: subs. (5).

Overall cost recovery is only one aspect of the application of the "polluter pays" principle. Others are the equitable apportionment of overall cost recovery among different businesses, which is considered in the note to s.41, and the issue of charging for advice and assistance, in particular at the pre-application stage, which is considered there and in the note to s.37. The cost recovery provisions limit the scope for other charging options, such as incentive charging (on which Agency Chief Executive Ed Gallagher is reported to be keen: *ENDS Report* [1995] 249, p. 6).

Incidental power to impose charges

Incidental power of the new Agencies to impose charges

43. Without prejudice to the generality of its powers by virtue of section 37(1)(a) above and subject to any such express provision with respect to charging by a new Agency as is contained in the preceding provisions of this Chapter or any other enactment, each new Agency shall have power to fix and recover charges for services and facilities provided in the course of carrying out its functions.

DEFINITIONS
"functions": s.124(1)
"new Agency": s.56(1)

COMMENCEMENT
July 28, 1995 (S.I. 1995 No. 1983).

GENERAL NOTE
This section permits the Agency/SEPA to charge for services and facilities provided in the course of carrying out their functions. It is expressed not to be taken as limiting in any way the agencies' general incidental power to do whatever they consider conducive to the exercise of their functions: s.37(1)(a). This section contains none of the procedural constraints imposed by ss.41 and 42 on the setting of charging schemes, and it is therefore expressed to be subject to the express provision for such schemes in those sections and any other enactment. Otherwise the agencies could have used this section to bypass those constraints.

It would appear that where the services and facilities are provided in connection with environmental licences, this section is also subject to s.37(7). The implication of this would appear to be that even where charges have been fixed under this section, different charges may in the context of an environmental licence be agreed and charged for services and facilities.

General financial provisions

General financial duties

44.—(1) The appropriate Ministers may—
  (a) after consultation with a new Agency, and
  (b) with the approval of the Treasury,
determine the financial duties of that new Agency; and different determinations may be made for different functions and activities of the new Agency.

(2) The appropriate Ministers shall give a new Agency notice of every determination of its financial duties under this section, and such a determination may—
  (a) relate to a period beginning before, on, or after, the date on which it is made;
  (b) contain supplemental provisions; and
  (c) be varied by a subsequent determination.

(3) The appropriate Minister may, after consultation with the Treasury

and a new Agency, give a direction to that new Agency requiring it to pay to him an amount equal to the whole or such part as may be specified in the direction of any sum, or any sum of a description, so specified which is or has been received by that new Agency.

(4) Where it appears to the appropriate Minister that a new Agency has a surplus, whether on capital or revenue account, he may, after consultation with the Treasury and the new Agency, direct the new Agency to pay to him such amount not exceeding the amount of that surplus as may be specified in the direction.

(5) In the case of the Agency—

(a) subsection (1) above is subject to section 118 of the 1991 Act (special duties with respect to flood defence revenue);

(b) subsection (3) above is subject to sections 118(1)(a) and 119(1) of the 1991 Act (special duties with respect to flood defence revenue and funds raised for fishery purposes under local enactments); and

(c) subsection (4) above is subject to sections 118(1)(b) and 119(2) of the 1991 Act (which provide for flood defence revenue and certain funds raised under local enactments to be disregarded in determining whether there is a surplus).

DEFINITIONS
"the 1991 Act": s.56(1).
"appropriate Minister": s.56(1).
"appropriate Ministers": s.56(1).
"functions": s.124(1).
"new Agency": s.56(1).

COMMENCEMENT
July 28, 1995 (S.I. 1995 No. 1983).

GENERAL NOTE
This section is closely modelled on s.117 of the Water Resources Act 1991 which imposed financial duties on the NRA.

A general purpose of the section is to enable the Government to ensure that the agencies do not accumulate surplus payments or funds without them being claimed from the agency in question for central funds. Both agencies have the power to buy and sell property, for example, which could lead to capital gains, and it is possible that charging schemes may in a given year more than cover regulatory costs. The Agency in particular, with its water management functions in relation especially to flood defence might find itself in receipt of such payments or surpluses.

The section essentially contains two mechanisms, the first relating to financial duties and the second to surpluses held or received by the Agency/SEPA.

Financial duties
Subsections (1) and (2) provide a procedure for the Secretary of State (acting jointly, as regards the Agency, with the Minister of Agriculture, Fisheries and Food) to determine and notify to the agencies their respective financial duties. Such a determination must be taken into account by the Secretary of State when seeking to ensure that the Agency/SEPA's charging schemes are set so as to recover costs: s.42(2).

Surpluses
The section also contains an extremely widely phrased power for the Secretary of State to direct the Agency/SEPA to pay to him an amount equal to or less than the amount of a payment which it has received (subs. (3)) or a surplus it possesses (subs. (4)). In relation to the Agency, the Minister of Agriculture, Fisheries and Food also has this power. In introducing subsection (3) as an amendment, the then Parliamentary Under-Secretary of State for the Environment, Sir Paul Beresford, explained that it "will enable the return to the Consolidated Fund of receipts, other than surpluses [see subs. (4)], which, in line with the normal rules of Government accounting, ought to be returned to the Exchequer" H.C. Standing Committee B, 9th sitting, May 18, 1995, col. 296.

Much of the Agency's funding for the exercise of its flood defence functions will, as was the case for the NRA before it, be raised through levies on local authorities and for specific localflood defence purposes, and the effect of subs. (5) is to prevent such funds becoming subject to the provisions of this section.

Accounts and records

45.—(1) Each new Agency shall—

(a) keep proper accounts and proper accounting records; and

(b) prepare in respect of each accounting year a statement of accounts giving a true and fair view of the state of affairs and the income and expenditure of the new Agency.

(2) Every statement of accounts prepared by a new Agency in accordance with this section shall comply with any requirement which the appropriate Ministers have, with the consent of the Treasury, notified in writing to the new Agency and which relates to any of the following matters, namely—

(a) the information to be contained in the statement;

(b) the manner in which that information is to be presented;

(c) the methods and principles according to which the statement is to be prepared.

(3) In this section—

"accounting records", in the case of a new Agency, includes all books, papers and other records of the new Agency relating to, or to matters dealt with in, the accounts required to be kept by virtue of this section;

"accounting year", subject to subsection (4) below, means, in relation to a new Agency, a financial year.

(4) If the Secretary of State so directs in relation to any accounting year of either new Agency, that accounting year shall end with such date other than the next 31st March as may be specified in the direction; and, where the Secretary of State has given such a direction, the following accounting year shall begin with the day after the date so specified and, subject to any further direction under this subsection, shall end with the next 31st March.

DEFINITIONS

"accounting records": subs. (3).

"accounting year": subs. (3).

"appropriate Ministers": s.56(1).

"financial year": s.124(1).

"new Agency": s.56(1).

COMMENCEMENT

July 28, 1995 (S.I. 1995 No. 1983)

GENERAL NOTE

This section, which is closely modelled on s.121 of the Water Resources Act 1991 in relation to the NRA, requires each of the Agency/SEPA to keep proper accounts and accounting records giving a true and fair view of its income and expenditure (subs. (1)), and to do so in accordance with such requirements as are notified to it under subs. (2) and for such financial year as it is directed under subs. (4) to use.

Neither HMIP, HMIPI nor waste regulation authorities were previously under such a duty, although waste regulation authorities were all under a duty to publish an annual report containing some very limited financial information (s.67 of the Environmental Protection Act 1990—see s.52 of this Act). The NRA's latest Annual Report and Accounts is its sixth for the financial year ending March 31, 1995 (ISBN 1 873160 25 9).

Audit

46.—(1) The accounts of each new Agency shall be audited by an auditor appointed for each accounting year by the Secretary of State.

(2) A person shall not be qualified for appointment under subsection (1) above unless—

(a) he is eligible for appointment as a company auditor under Part II of the Companies Act 1989; and

(b) he would not be ineligible for appointment as company auditor of the new Agency in question by virtue of section 27 of that Act (ineligibility on ground of lack of independence), if that new Agency were a body to which section 384 of the Companies Act 1985 (duty to appoint auditor) applies.

(3) A copy of—

(a) any accounts of a new Agency which are audited under subsection (1) above, and

(b) the report made on those accounts by the auditor,

shall be sent to each of the appropriate Ministers as soon as reasonably practicable after the report is received by the new Agency; and the Secretary of State shall lay before each House of Parliament a copy of those accounts and that report.

(4) The Comptroller and Auditor General—

(a) shall be entitled to inspect the contents of all accounts and accounting records of a new Agency; and

(b) may report to the House of Commons the results of any inspection carried out by him under paragraph (a) above;

and section 6 of the National Audit Act 1983 (examinations of economy, efficiency and effectiveness) accordingly applies to each new Agency.

(5) In this section—

"accounting records" has the same meaning as in section 45 above;

"accounting year" has the same meaning as in section 45 above;

"accounts", in relation to the Agency, includes any statement under section 45 above.

DEFINITIONS
"accounting records": subs. (5).
"accounting year": subs. (5).
"accounts": subs. (5).
"appropriate Ministers": s.56(1).
"new Agency": s.56(1).

COMMENCEMENT
July 28, 1995 (S.I. 1995 No. 1983)

GENERAL NOTE
This section, which is modelled on s.122 of the Water Resources Act 1991 in relation to the NRA, regulates the auditing of the accounts required to be prepared under s.45.

Grants to the new Agencies

47. The appropriate Minister may, with the approval of the Treasury, make to a new Agency grants of such amounts, and on such terms, as he thinks fit.

DEFINITIONS
"appropriate Minister": s.56(1).
"new Agency": s.56(1).

COMMENCEMENT
July 28, 1995 (S.I. 1995 No. 1983)

GENERAL NOTE
Sections 41–43 deal with the Agency/SEPA's specific powers to raise funds through charging schemes which are generally intended to recover from regulated businesses the costs of regulating them.

Sections 47–50 make provision for other ways in which the agencies may raise funds: through grants or loans from the Government (ss.47 and 49 respectively) and by borrowing (s.48), with or without the backing of Government guarantees (s.50).

Grants under this section require Treasury approval.

Borrowing powers

48.—(1) Each new Agency shall be entitled to borrow in accordance with the following provisions of this section, but not otherwise.

(2) Subject to subsection (5) below, each new Agency may—
  (a) with the consent of the appropriate Minister, and
  (b) with the approval of the Treasury,
borrow temporarily in sterling, by way of overdraft or otherwise, from persons other than the appropriate Ministers, such sums as it may require for meeting its obligations and carrying out its functions.

(3) Subject to subsection (5) below, each new Agency may borrow from the appropriate Minister, by way of temporary loan or otherwise, such sums in sterling as it may require for meeting its obligations and carrying out its functions.

(4) Any consent under subsection (2)(a) above may be granted subject to conditions.

(5) The aggregate amount outstanding in respect of the principal of sums borrowed under this section by a new Agency shall not at any time exceed—
  (a) in the case of the Agency, £100 million or such greater sum, not exceeding £160 million, as the Ministers may by order specify; or
  (b) in the case of SEPA, £5 million or such greater sum, not exceeding £10 million, as the Secretary of State may by order specify.

(6) The power to make an order under subsection (5) above shall be exercisable by statutory instrument; but no order shall be made under that subsection unless a draft of the order has been laid before, and approved by a resolution of, the House of Commons.

DEFINITIONS
  "the Agency": s.124(1).
  "appropriate Minister": s.56(1).
  "appropriate Ministers": s.56(1).
  "functions": s.124(1).
  "new Agency": s.56(1).
  "SEPA": s.124(1).

COMMENCEMENT
July 28, 1995 (S.I. 1995 No. 1983)

GENERAL NOTE
In addition to charging schemes (ss.41–43) and Government grants (s.47), the Agency/SEPA have the power under this section to borrow sums which borrowing may in some circumstances be backed by a Government guarantee: s.50.
  The power is circumscribed in a number of ways:
  • borrowing may only be for the purposes of meeting the obligations of the agency in question and carrying out its functions: subss. (2) and (3);
  • where borrowing is from Ministers, Treasury approval is required (s.49(1)) and the terms of the loan are governed by s.49;
  • where borrowing is from someone other than the appropriate Ministers, Ministerial consent and Treasury approval is required (subs. (2)) and such consent may be conditional (subs. (4)); and
  • the aggregate sum borrowed at any one time is restricted to £100 million for the Agency and £5 million for SEPA, unless a Ministerial order made by statutory instrument and expressly approved by the House of Commons raises those sums to not more than £160 million and £10 million respectively subss. (5) and (6)).
The Environment Bill as originally drafted fixed SEPA's borrowing limits as between £2 and £5 million. These were amended in Standing Committee to between £5 and £10 million (*per* Sir Hector Monro, Standing Committee B, May 18, 1995, col. 297). The reason for SEPA's significantly smaller borrowing limits is related to the fact that since SEPA lacks flood defence powers in contrast to the Agency it is unlikely to be undertaking any major capital works (see *e.g.* the Earl of Lindsay *Hansard*, H.L. Vol. 560, col. 1414).

The insertion in respect of England and Wales of ss.161A–161D into the Water Resources Act 1991, and the equivalent provisions for Scotland into the Control of Pollution Act 1974 as ss.46A–46D, are notable in this context. They provide for the Agency/SEPA to serve "works notices" requiring remedial works to be carried out where pollution of controlled waters has occurred or is likely to occur. Previously, the regulators only had at their disposal in such circumstances a power to carry out such works themselves and then seek to recover its costs from the polluter, always an uncertain exercise. It is understood that this constrained their ability to secure remediation in such circumstances, in part because of the limits on the their ability to raise funds for the carrying out of such works. The new provisions, by reducing one source of possible pressure on Agency/SEPA funding, may make the borrowing limits in this section less problematical than they might otherwise have been.

Government loans to the new Agencies

49.—(1) The appropriate Minister may, with the approval of the Treasury, lend to a new Agency any sums which it has power to borrow under section 48(3) above.

(2) Any loan made under this section by one of the appropriate Ministers shall be repaid to him at such times and by such methods, and interest on the loan shall be paid to him at such rates and at such times, as that Minister may with the approval of the Treasury from time to time determine.

(3) If in any financial year any of the appropriate Ministers lends any sums to a new Agency under this section, he shall—

(a) prepare in respect of that financial year an account of the sums so lent by him; and

(b) send that account to the Comptroller and Auditor General before the end of September in the following financial year;

and the form of the account and the manner of preparing it shall be such as the Treasury may direct.

(4) The Comptroller and Auditor General shall examine, certify and report on each account sent to him under this section and shall lay copies of it and of his report before each House of Parliament.

(5) The Treasury may issue to any of the appropriate Ministers—

(a) out of the National Loans Fund, or

(b) out of money provided by Parliament,

such sums as are necessary to enable him to make loans to a new Agency under this section; and any sums received by a Minister of the Crown in pursuance of subsection (2) above shall be paid into the National Loans Fund or, as the case may be, the Consolidated Fund.

DEFINITIONS
"appropriate Minister": s.56(1).
"appropriate Ministers": s.56(1).
"financial year": s.124(1).
"new Agency": s.56(1).

COMMENCEMENT
July 28, 1995 (S.I. 1995 No. 1983).

GENERAL NOTE
Where sums authorised to be borrowed by the Agency/SEPA under s.48 are borrowed from the Government, Treasury approval is required both for the loan (subs. (1)) and for its terms (subs. (2)).

The action of the Minister concerned in making the loan is subject to reporting and Parliamentary scrutiny requirements (subs. (3) and (4)), and subs. (5) allows for the origin of the funds to be the Treasury, as will often be the case.

Government guarantees of a new Agency's borrowing

50.—(1) The appropriate Minister may, with the consent of the Treasury, guarantee, in such manner and on such conditions as he may think fit, the repayment of the principal of, the payment of interest on, and the discharge of any other financial obligation in connection with, any sum which a new Agency borrows from any person.

(2) A Minister who gives a guarantee under this section shall forthwith lay a statement of the guarantee before each House of Parliament.

(3) Where any sum is paid out for fulfilling a guarantee under this section, the Minister who gave the guarantee shall, as soon as reasonably practicable after the end of each financial year (beginning with that in which the sum is paid out and ending with that in which all liability in respect of the principal of the sum and in respect of interest on it is finally discharged), lay before each House of Parliament a statement relating to that sum.

(4) If any sums are paid out in fulfilment of a guarantee under this section, the new Agency which borrowed the sum by reference to which the guarantee was given shall make to the Minister who gave the guarantee, at such times and in such manner as he may from time to time direct,—
  (a) payments of such amounts as he may so direct in or towards repayment of the sums so paid out; and
  (b) payments of interest, at such rate as he may so direct, on what is outstanding for the time being in respect of sums so paid out;
and the consent of the Treasury shall be required for the giving of a direction under this subsection.

DEFINITIONS
"appropriate Minister": s.56(1).
"financial year": s.124(1).
"new Agency": s.56(1).

COMMENCEMENT
July 28, 1995 (S.I. 1995 No. 1983).

GENERAL NOTE
Section 48 allows the Agency/SEPA to borrow, and s.49 provides for the case where that borrowing is from the Government. An alternative, where private sector funds might not otherwise be forthcoming, is provided by this section: a Government guarantee of the financial obligations of the Agency/SEPA in question under the loans subs. (1).

A statement of the guarantee must be laid before each House of Parliament (subs. (2)) and, where the guarantee is called upon so that the Minister concerned has to pay out any sum,
  — he must lay a statement about this sum before each House of Parliament (subs. (3)); and
  — the agency in question must repay him on such terms as, with the consent of the Treasury, he may direct (subs. (4)).

Information

Provision of information by the new Agencies

51.—(1) A new Agency shall furnish the appropriate Minister with all such information as he may reasonably require relating to—
  (a) the new Agency's property;
  (b) the carrying out and proposed carrying out of its functions; and
  (c) its responsibilities generally.

(2) Information required under this section shall be furnished in such form and manner, and be accompanied or supplemented by such explanations, as the appropriate Minister may reasonably require.

(3) The information which a new Agency may be required to furnish to the appropriate Minister under this section shall include information which, although it is not in the possession of the new Agency or would not otherwise come into the possession of the new Agency, is information which it is reasonable to require the new Agency to obtain.

(4) A requirement for the purposes of this section shall be contained in a direction which—

(a) may describe the information to be furnished in such manner as the Minister giving the direction considers appropriate; and

(b) may require the information to be furnished on a particular occasion, in particular circumstances or from time to time.

(5) For the purposes of this section a new Agency shall—

(a) permit any person authorised for the purpose by the appropriate Minister to inspect and make copies of the contents of any accounts or other records of the new Agency; and

(b) give such explanation of them as that person or the appropriate Minister may reasonably require.

DEFINITIONS
"the appropriate Minister": s.56(1).
"functions": s.124(1).
"new Agency": s.56(1).
"records": s.124(1).

COMMENCEMENT
July 28, 1995 (S.I. 1995 No. 1983).

GENERAL NOTE
Section 45 provides for each agency to publish accounts and s.52 requires them each to publish an annual report; this section can he seen as plugging the gaps in such information by providing that the Secretary of State (or, additionally, in the case of the Agency the Minister of Agriculture Fisheries and Food) may direct the agencies to furnish him with information on its property, activities and responsibilities (subs. (1)). Such information need not be in the possession of the agency in question (subs. (3)).

The section also allows these Ministers to authorise a person to inspect and copy agency records and have them explained to that person (subs. (5)).

Annual report

52.—(1) As soon as reasonably practicable after the end of each financial year, each new Agency shall prepare a report on its activities during that year and shall send a copy of that report to each of the appropriate Ministers.

(2) Every such report shall set out any directions under section 40 above which have been given to the new Agency in question during the year to which the report relates, other than directions given under subsection (1) of that section which are identified to that new Agency in writing by the appropriate Minister as being directions the disclosure of which would, in his opinion, be contrary to the interests of national security.

(3) The Secretary of State shall lay a copy of every such report before each House of Parliament and shall arrange for copies of every such report to be published in such manner as he considers appropriate.

(4) A new Agency's annual report shall be in such form and contain such information as may be specified in any direction given to the new Agency by the appropriate Ministers.

DEFINITIONS
"appropriate Ministers": s.56(1).
"financial year": s.124(1).
"new Agency": s.56(1).

COMMENCEMENT
July 28, 1995 (S.I. 1995 No. 1983).

GENERAL NOTE
This section requires the Agency/SEPA to prepare an annual report and submit it to the Secretary of State (and also, in the case of the Agency, to the Minister of Agriculture, Fisheries and Food): subs. (1). There is a separate obligation on each of them to prepare and publish accounts: s.45.

The form and content of such annual report may be specified in a direction given to the agency in question (subs. (4)), and also (except in the case of certain directions which may be excluded by the appropriate Minister on national security grounds). The report must list directions received during the period of the report: subs. (2). Otherwise there are no restrictions on the form or content of the annual report.

It is the responsibility of the Secretary of State to publish the report and place it before Parliament: subs. 3.

Previous provisions: England and Wales
This section is similar to s.187 of the Water Resources Act 1991 which placed a duty on the NRA to produce an annual report but is less prescriptive than the equivalent provision for waste regulation authorities (s.67 of the Environmental Protection Act 1990) which it supersedes. It remains to be seen whether directions under subs. (4) will replicate the list of matters to be included in an annual report under s.67(2) of the 1990 Act:

    (a) modifications, grants, revocations, etc., of waste management licences;
    (b) exercise of certain powers;
    (c) implementation of its own waste recycling plan;
    (d) number and description of prosecutions brought; and
    (e) costs incurred and sums received in the course of waste regulation.

Previous provisions: Scotland
Prior to the advent of SEPA, under s.16 of the Rivers (Prevention of Pollution) (Scotland) Act 1951, river purification boards were under a duty to produce annual reports for the Secretary of State, which were also published. In contrast, there were no reporting duties laid on HMIPI. Nevertheless, HMIPI produced two reports, the first covering the period 1987–88 which was published in 1990 and the second, covering the period April 1988 and March 1992, was published in 1994. Given the time lag between the publication of these reports and the period they cover, they cannot be said to be particularly useful. For example, at the time of the transfer date, HMIPI had not yet published a report on the implementation of IPC in Scotland. The duty on SEPA to produce an annual report is therefore welcome and will assist in making its operations more accessible to the public. In relation to reporting requirements, the Government explained in Parliament that:

> "The situation in Scotland is somewhat different. The Scottish Office does not compile and publish environmental information on this scale. Because of that, the Government intends SEPA to publish an annual report on the state of the environment. My right honourable friend the Secretary of State for Scotland will use his powers under Clause 49(4) [s.52(4)] to require SEPA to publish as an annexe to its annual report a state of the environment report. That will be based on SEPA's duty to compile such information under Clause 31(2) [33(2)]." (*per* Viscount Ullswater *Hansard*, H.L. Vol. 560, col. 1418.)

Transitional arrangements
The first report of one of the agencies may include a report on the activities of one or more of its predecessor bodies, and SEPA must as soon as reasonably practicable after the transfer date prepare a report on the activities of river purification boards and waste regulation authorities (para. 5 of Sched. 23 to the 1995 Act).

Supplemental provisions

Inquiries and other hearings

53.—(1) Without prejudice to any other provision of this Act or any other enactment by virtue of which an inquiry or other hearing is authorised or required to be held, the appropriate Minister may cause an inquiry or other hearing to be held if it appears to him expedient to do so—

    (a) in connection with any of the functions of a new Agency; or
    (b) in connection with any of his functions in relation to a new Agency.

(2) Subsections (2) to (5) of section 250 of the Local Government Act 1972 (which contain supplementary provisions with respect to local inquiries held in pursuance of that section) shall apply to inquiries or other hearings under this section or any other enactment—

    (a) in connection with any of the functions of the Agency, or
    (b) in connection with any functions of the Secretary of State or the Minister in relation to the Agency,

as they apply to inquiries under that section, but taking the reference in subsection (4) of that section to a local authority as including a reference to the Agency.

(3) The provisions of subsections (2) to (8) of section 210 of the Local Government (Scotland) Act 1973 (which relate to the holding of local inquiries) shall apply to inquiries or other hearings held under this section or any other enactment—

(a) in connection with any of the functions of SEPA, or

(b) in connection with any functions of the Secretary of State in relation to SEPA,

as they apply to inquiries held under that section.

DEFINITIONS
"the Agency": s.124(1).
"appropriate Minister": s.56(1).
"functions": s.124(1).
"the Minister": s.56(1).
"new Agency": s.56(1).
"SEPA": s.124(1).

COMMENCEMENT
April 1, 1996 (S.I. 1996 No. 186).

GENERAL NOTE
This section gives the Secretary of State (and additionally in respect of the Agency, the Minister of Agriculture, Fisheries and Food) a wide power to cause a public inquiry or other hearing to be held, in connection with any Agency/SEPA function or any function of his own in relation to either of them.

This power is expressed to be without prejudice to other provisions which may allow for such inquiries or hearings: these will generally relate to appeals against Agency/SEPA acts or omissions. Thus, for example, it does not override the appeals procedure in relation to IPC which is found in s.15 of the Environmental Protection Act 1990.

This section is not the only provision in the 1995 Act with a bearing on the conduct of inquiries: s.114 gives the Secretary of State the power in specified circumstances to delegate his appellate function or refer matters involved in appeals, and Sched. 22 contains amendments to certain provisions in relaxation to appeals and inquiries.

Subs. (3)
This subsection applies the provisions of s.210(2)–(8) of the Local Government (Scotland) Act 1973 to the holding of inquiries or other hearings in connection with any functions of SEPA and the Secretary of State in relation to SEPA.

Appearance in legal proceedings

54. In England and Wales, a person who is authorised by the Agency to prosecute on its behalf in proceedings before a magistrates' court shall be entitled to prosecute in any such proceedings although not of counsel or a solicitor.

DEFINITION
"the Agency": s.124(1).

COMMENCEMENT
April 1, 1996 (S.I. 1996 No. 186).

GENERAL NOTE
This important section, which builds upon the provision in s.37(1) that the Agency may institute legal proceedings, and which accordingly applies only to the Agency, allows its enforcing officers to prosecute cases which they have worked on, even if they are not legally qualified, thus avoiding duplication of time spent familiarising a legally qualified advocate with the matter. It will be noted that the right does not extend beyond the level of the magistrates' court, however, it is in such a court that almost all Agency enforcement actions will commence.

It should be noted also that this section does not provide a "blanket" right of audience for authorised Agency personnel before a magistrates' court. It applies only to prosecutions and not, therefore, to other matters such as appeals before magistrates' courts against remediation notices under the contaminated land provisions inserted into the 1990 Act by s.57 of this Act.

Scotland
Since SEPA cannot institute criminal proceedings, this section does not apply to Scotland. See also the note to s.37.

Continuity of exercise of functions: the new Agencies

55.—(1) The abolition of—
  (a) the National Rivers Authority,
  (b) the London Waste Regulation Authority, or
  (c) a river purification board,
shall not affect the validity of anything done by that Authority or board before the transfer date.

(2) Anything which, at the transfer date, is in the process of being done by or in relation to a transferor in the exercise of, or in connection with, any of the transferred functions may be continued by or in relation to the transferee.

(3) Anything done by or in relation to a transferor before the transfer date in the exercise of, or otherwise in connection with, any of the transferred functions, shall, so far as is required for continuing its effect on and after that date, have effect as if done by or in relation to the transferee.

(4) Subsection (3) above applies in particular to—
  (a) any decision, determination, declaration, designation, agreement or instrument made by a transferor;
  (b) any regulations or byelaws made by a transferor;
  (c) any licence, permission, consent, approval, authorisation, exemption, dispensation or relaxation granted by or to a transferor;
  (d) any notice, direction or certificate given by or to a transferor;
  (e) any application, request, proposal or objection made by or to a transferor;
  (f) any condition or requirement imposed by or on a transferor;
  (g) any fee or charge paid by or to a transferor;
  (h) any appeal allowed by or in favour of or against a transferor;
  (j) any proceedings instituted by or against a transferor.

(5) Any reference in the foregoing provisions of this section to anything done by or in relation to a transferor includes a reference to anything which, by virtue of any enactment, is treated as having been done by or in relation to that transferor.

(6) Any reference to a transferor in any document constituting or relating to anything to which the foregoing provisions of this section apply shall, so far as is required for giving effect to those provisions, be construed as a reference to the transferee.

(7) The foregoing provisions of this section—
  (a) are without prejudice to any provision made by this Act in relation to any particular functions; and
  (b) shall not be construed as continuing in force any contract of employment made by a transferor;
and the Secretary of State may, in relation to any particular functions, by order exclude, modify or supplement any of the foregoing provisions of this section or make such other transitional provisions as he thinks necessary or expedient.

(8) Where, by virtue of any provision of Schedule 15 to this Act, the Minister is the transferor in the case of any functions, he shall have the same powers under subsection (7) above in relation to those functions as the Secretary of State.

(9) The power to make an order under subsection (7) above shall be

exercisable by statutory instrument; and any statutory instrument containing such an order shall be subject to annulment pursuant to a resolution of either House of Parliament.

(10) In this section—

"the transferee", in the case of any transferred functions, means the new Agency whose functions they become by virtue of any provision made by or under this Act;

"transferred functions" means any functions which, by virtue of any provision made by or under this Act, become functions of a new Agency; and

"transferor" means any body or person any or all of whose functions become, by virtue of any provision made by or under this Act, functions of a new Agency.

COMMENCEMENT
Subsections (7)–(10) came into force on February 1, 1996; the remainder came into force on April 1, 1996 (S.I. 1996 No. 186).

GENERAL NOTE
This section provides for continuity between the Agency/SEPA and their predecessors on the transfer from those bodies or persons to the Agency/SEPA of some or all of their functions.

In particular licences, conditions and legal proceedings granted, imposed or commenced by a transferor take effect following the transfer date as if done by the relevant agency: subs. (4). It should be noted that the list at subs. (4)) is an inclusive one.

The Secretary of State may modify the extent of this section's otherwise very comprehensive continuity provisions: subs. (7). Schedule 15 transfers to the Agency a number of fisheries functions. Mostly these are transferred from the NRA but several functions of the Minister of Agriculture, Fisheries and Food under the Salmon and Freshwater Fisheries Act 1975 are also transferred. Where this is the case, he rather than the Secretary of State may modify the continuity provision in this section: subs. (8).

To an extent this section duplicates provisions such as those made under s.3 (or, in Scotland, under s.22) in relation to transfers and schemes of transfer of property, rights and liabilities, and it is expressed by subs. (7) to be without prejudice to such other provisions.

Interpretation of Part I

56.—(1) In this Part of this Act, except where the context otherwise requires—

"the 1951 Act" means the Rivers (Prevention of Pollution) (Scotland) Act 1951;

"the 1990 Act" means the Environmental Protection Act 1990;

"the 1991 Act" means the Water Resources Act 1991;

"the appropriate Minister"—

(a) in the case of the Agency, means the Secretary of State or the Minister; and

(b) in the case of SEPA, means the Secretary of State;

"the appropriate Ministers"—

(a) in the case of the Agency, means the Secretary of State and the Minister; and

    (b) in the case of SEPA, means the Secretary of State;
"conservancy authority" has the meaning given by section 221(1) of the
    1991 Act;
"costs" includes—
    (a) costs to any person; and
    (b) costs to the environment;
"disposal authority"—
    (a) in the application of this Part in relation to the Agency, has the
        same meaning as it has in Part I of the Control of Pollution Act
        1974 by virtue of section 30(1) of that Act; and
    (b) in the application of this Part in relation to SEPA, has the
        meaning assigned to it by section 30(2) of that Act;
"the environment" has the same meaning as in Part I of the 1990 Act;
"environmental licence", in the application of this Part in relation to the
    Agency, means any of the following—
    (a) registration of a person as a carrier of controlled waste under
        section 2 of the Control of Pollution (Amendment) Act 1989,
    (b) an authorisation under Part I of the 1990 Act, other than any
        such authorisation granted by a local enforcing authority,
    (c) a waste management licence under Part II of that Act,
    (d) a licence under Chapter II of Part II of the 1991 Act,
    (e) a consent for the purposes of section 88(1)(a), 89(4)(a) or 90 of
        that Act,
    (f) registration under the Radioactive Substances Act 1993,
    (g) an authorisation under that Act,
    (h) registration of a person as a broker of controlled waste under
        the Waste Management Licensing Regulations 1994,
    (j) registration in respect of an activity falling within paragraph
        45(1) or (2) of Schedule 3 to those Regulations,
    so far as having effect in relation to England and Wales;
"environmental licence", in the application of this Part in relation to
    SEPA, means any of the following—
    (a) a consent under Part II of the Control of Pollution Act 1974,
    (b) registration of a person as a carrier of controlled waste under
        section 2 of the Control of Pollution (Amendment) Act 1989,
    (c) an authorisation under Part I of the 1990 Act,
    (d) a waste management licence under Part II of that Act,
    (e) a licence under section 17 of the Natural Heritage (Scotland)
        Act 1991,
    (f) registration under the Radioactive Substances Act 1993,
    (g) an authorisation under that Act,
    (h) registration of a person as a broker of controlled waste under
        the Waste Management Licensing Regulations 1994,
    (j) registration in respect of an activity falling within paragraph
        45(1) or (2) of Schedule 3 to those Regulations,
    so far as having effect in relation to Scotland;
"flood defence functions", in relation to the Agency, has the same
    meaning as in the 1991 Act;
"harbour authority" has the meaning given by section 221(1) of the 1991
    Act;
"local authority", in the application of this Part in relation to SEPA,
    means a district or islands council in Scotland;
"the Minister" means the Minister of Agriculture, Fisheries and Food;
"the Ministers" means the Secretary of State and the Minister;
"navigation authority, has the meaning given by section 221(1) of the
    1991 Act;

"new Agency" means the Agency or SEPA;

"river purification authority" means a river purification authority within the meaning of the 1951 Act;

"river purification board" means a river purification board established by virtue of section 135 of the Local Government (Scotland) Act 1973;

"the transfer date" means such date as the Secretary of State may by order made by statutory instrument appoint as the transfer date for the purposes of this Part; and different dates may be appointed for the purposes of this Part—

    (i) as it applies for or in connection with transfers under or by virtue of Chapter I above, and

    (ii) as it applies for or in connection with transfers under or by virtue of Chapter II above;

"waste regulation authority"—

    (a) in the application of this Part in relation to the Agency, means any authority in England or Wales which, by virtue of section 30(1) of the 1990 Act, is a waste regulation authority for the purposes of Part II of that Act; and

    (b) in the application of this Part in relation to SEPA, means any council which, by virtue of section 30(1)(g) of the 1990 Act, is a waste regulation authority for the purposes of Part II of that Act.

(2) In relation to any time on or after 1st April 1996—

    (a) subsection (1) above shall have effect as if, in the definition of "local authority", for the words "district or islands council in Scotland" there were substituted the words "council constituted under section 2 of the Local Government etc. (Scotland) Act 1994"; and

    (b) in section 22(3)(a)(iv) above the reference to an islands council shall be construed as a reference to a council mentioned in section 3(1) of the Local Government etc. (Scotland) Act 1994.

(3) Where by virtue of any provision of this Part any function of a Minister of the Crown is exercisable concurrently by different Ministers, that function shall also be exercisable jointly by any two or more of those Ministers.

DEFINITIONS
"the Agency": s.124(1).
"functions": s.124(1).
"SEPA": s.124(1).

COMMENCEMENT
July 28, 1995 (S.I. 1995 No. 1983).

GENERAL NOTE

"the appropriate Minister"
Note the distinction between this term and the one immediately following, and the provision in relation to this term that any function exercisable concurrently by Ministers is also exercisable jointly: subs. (3).

    Although it is a constitutional principle that the office of Secretary of State is indivisible, nevertheless in practice, as regards Scotland and Wales, the Secretary of State will be the Secretary of State for Scotland or Wales respectively.

"Conservancy authority"
Section 22(1) of the Water Resources Act 1991 defines this term to mean "any person who has a duty or power under any enactment to conserve, maintain or improve the navigation of a tidal water and is not a navigation authority or harbour authority". For the meaning of these last two kinds of authority, see below.

"Costs"
For a consideration of the geographical extent of this term and the undefined "benefits", see the General Note to s.39.

"Disposal authority"
By subss. 2(1)(c) and 21(1)(c) of the 1995 Act only the functions of waste disposal authorities under or by virtue of the *waste regulation* provisions of the Control of Pollution Act 1974 are transferred to the Agency: for the purposes of such provisions:

England and Wales
Section 30(1) of the 1974 Act defines disposal authorities for the purposes of those waste regulation functions as:
— the London Waste Regulation Authority
— the Greater Manchester Waste Disposal Authority
— in all other local authority areas in England, the council of the county or metropolitan district; and
— in Wales, the council of the district.
Scotland
In Scotland "disposal authority" means a district or islands council. However, from April 1, 1996 when local government reorganisation under the Local Government etc. (Scotland) Act 1994 took effect, "disposal authority" means a council established under the 1994 Act.

"The environment"
This term is defined for the purposes of Part I of the Environmental Protection Act 1990 by s.1(2) of that Act as consisting of "all, or any, of the following media, namely, the air, water and land; and the medium of air includes the air within buildings and the air within other natural or man-made structures above or below ground".

For a consideration of the geographical extent of this term in the context of costs and benefits to the environment, see the General Note to section 39.

The term "pollution of the environment" is not defined. For a consideration of the meaning of that term, see the General Note to section 5.

"Environmental licence"
This term is defined for each of the two agencies by reference to a specific range of registrations, consents, licences and authorisations, which exist under regimes the regulation of which has been transferred to the agency in question. It should be noted that in the case of the Agency there are consent functions which are not on this list. An example is its function of consenting, subject to conditions, to the erection of structures in, over or under main rivers (s.109 of the Water Resources Act 1991).

The Government has indicated that it is its medium term aim to move towards a system whereby each agency issues a single environmental licence to any business which at present needs a number of environmental licences from it in respect of its activities on one site. See further the introduction to this Part of the Act.

It may not be immediately clear what activities are governed by certain of the environmental licences listed here. For example, in relation to the Agency, para.
  (b) refers to IPC authorisation;
  (d) refers to water abstraction and impoundment;
  (e) refers to discharging to controlled waters;
  (f) and (g) refer to registration as a person holding a radioactive substance and authorisation to do so;
  (j) refers to scrap metal activities and the dismantling of motor vehicles, the registration requirements for which are more onerous than for other activities exempted from waste management licensing by Schedule 3 to the 1994 Regulations.

In relation to SEPA, para.
  (a) refers to discharging to controlled water;
  (c) refers to IPC and LAPC authorisation;
  (e) refers to water abstraction for irrigation purposes;
  (f) refers to registration as a person holding a radioactive substance; and
  (j) refers to scrap metal activities and the dismantling of motor vehicles as in para. (j) in relation to the Agency.

"Flood defence functions"
The definition of this term in the 1991 Act is printed in the Encyclopedia as substituted by para. 175(7) of Sched. 22 to the 1995 Act, and the reader is referred to that para.

"Harbour authority"
Section 221(1) of the Water Resources Act defines this term in two different ways:
— in relation to the flood defence provisions of that Act (that is, those provisions cited above in the definition of "flood defence provisions"), it is defined by reference to the Merchant Shipping Act 1894, which is now consolidated into the Merchant Shipping Act 1995 and defines it as "includ[ing] all persons entrusted with the function of constructing, improving, managing, regulating, maintaining or lighting a harbour": s.313(1).
— otherwise, it is defined as a person who is a harbour authority within the meaning of the Prevention of Oil Pollution Act 1971 but who is not a navigation authority (see below). The 1971 Act definition reads: "a person or body or persons empowered by an enactment to make charges in respect of vessels entering a harbour in the United Kingdom or using facilities therein": s.8(2).

"Local authority"
This definition applies to Scotland only. Prior to April 1, 1996 this meant a district or islands council. However, from that date when local government reorganisation took effect in Scotland, the meaning changed to a council constituted under the Local Government etc. (Scotland) Act 1994: s.56(2).

"Navigation authority"
This term is defined by s.221(1) of the Water Resources Act 1991 to mean "any person who has a duty or power under any enactment to work, maintain, conserve, improve or control any canal or other inland navigation, navigable river, estuary, harbour or dock".

"River purification authority"
Section 17(2) of the Rivers (Prevention of Pollution) (Scotland) Act 1951 as substituted by Sched. 16, para. 5 of the Local Government (Scotland) Act 1973 provides that RPAs are "river purification boards established under section 135 of the Local Government (Scotland) Act 1973 and islands councils".

"River purification board"
River Purification Boards were originally established under the Rivers (Prevention of Pollution) (Scotland) Act 1951. However, the recently dissolved boards were established under sections 135 and 135A of the Local Government (Scotland) Act 1973. By s.135 of the 1973 Act, each board could have a membership of up to three times the number of local authority districts wholly or partly within its area. Section 135 also provided for one third of the board to be appointed by regional councils within its area, one third by district councils within its area and one third by the Secretary of State to represent interests such as agriculture, fisheries and industry. However, s.135A of the 1973 Act which was inserted by s.27 and Sched 10, para. 6 of the Natural Heritage (Scotland) Act 1991, gave the Secretary of State the power to vary the size of the boards and to appoint up to half the members with regional and district councils being restricted to one quarter each. At the time of the transfer date there were seven RPBs: Tweed, Solway, Clyde, Forth, Tay, North-East and Highland.

"Waste regulation authority"
By s.30(1) of the 1990 Act, prior to the transfer date waste regulation authorities in England and Wales were: county councils for English non-metropolitan counties; district councils, the Greater Manchester Waste Disposal Authority or the Merseyside Waste Disposal Authority as appropriate for English metropolitan counties; the London Waste Regulation Authority for Greater London; and district councils in Wales. Waste regulation authorities in Scotland were islands or district councils prior to the transfer date. However, on the transfer date these functions were transferred to the Agency/SEPA.

Subs. (2): "Local authority"
The new definition which took effect on April 1, 1996 reflects the reorganisation of local government in Scotland under the Local Government etc. (Scotland) Act 1994, whereby unitary authorities were set up in place of regional and district councils.

PART II

CONTAMINATED LAND AND ABANDONED MINES

[Section 57 establishes a new regime for contaminated land. It does so by inserting a new Part IIA (sections 78A–78YC) into the Environmental Protection Act 1990, and it is to be found, together with commentary, in that Act].

Abandoned mines: England and Wales

Background

Part II, through ss.58–60, brings about significant changes in the law relating to water pollution from abandoned mines in Great Britain, including the removal as from December 31, 1999 of an important defence against the criminal charge of having knowingly permitted water pollution, and the introduction of notification procedures on abandonment.

The problem of water pollution from abandoned mines has worsened in recent years with the demise of much of the coal and other mining industries. Some 200 km of waters are affected by abandoned coal mines in England and Wales together with 400 km of waters affected by abandoned metal mines (*Abandoned Mines and the Water Environment*, NRA, March 1994, p. 1). In Scotland 134 km of surface waters were affected by discharges from abandoned coal mines (*per* Mr Sam Galbraith MP, Standing Committee B, May 23, 1995, col. 411). No figures appear to be available for the length of rivers polluted by abandoned metal mines in Scotland. When a mine is abandoned the cessation of pumping operations may result in the mine filling up with water which becomes contaminated by reason of its lengthy residence time underground. Commonly the water reacts with oxidised iron pyrite to form a ferruginous compound which is highly acidic. This contaminated water may then break out of old shafts or adits and cause tremendous damage to aquatic life. Notable examples include the water pollution from the Wheal Jane tin mine in Cornwall (see (1991) 195 ENDS Report 8) and from the Dalquharran Colliery in Ayrshire which resulted in the death of all fish along a 16 km stretch of the Water of Girvan, an important salmon river, the threatened closure of a factory employing 500 people which abstracted water from the river and the corrosion of ships' hulls in Girvan Harbour (see (1993) 57 Mineral Planning 25). Much concern has also focused on the possible cessation of pumping operations and the likely effects thereof in the now closed Durham coalfield (see (1993) 223 ENDS Report 11; and *e.g. Hansard*, H.C. Vol. 258, cols. 57–58) although pumping operations there are presently being continued.

Under s.85 of the Water Resources Act 1991 and, in Scotland, in s.30F (substituted for the offence provisions in s.31 by s.106 and Sched. 16 to the 1995 Act) of the Control of Pollution Act 1974 (the 1974 Act), although it is an offence for a person to "cause or knowingly permit any poisonous, noxious or polluting matter or any solid waste matter to enter any controlled waters", there is a specific defence available to any person who *permits* water pollution from abandoned mines, contained in s.89(3) of the 1991 Act and s.30J(3) (substituted for s.31(2) by s.106 and Sched. 16 to the 1995 Act) of the 1974 Act. No definition of abandoned mines is given in this legislation although in the 1974 Act, the definition of "mine" is the same as in the Mines and Quarries Act 1954.

An exemption is also available for any person permitting water pollution from abandoned mines in the case of statutory cost recovery actions under s.161 of the 1991 Act and, in Scotland, s.46 of the 1974 Act for preventive or remedial works undertaken by the Agency/SEPA. Hence, while it is possible for the Agency/SEPA to carry out preventive or remedial works where a person has permitted water pollution from an abandoned mine, they may not recover the costs of doing so.

The rationale for the defence and exemption has been that they are needed to protect innocent landowers or occupiers who may be aware of old mineshafts or adits on their land which are discharging polluted water or who may have polluted water from abandoned mines on another person's land crossing their land and entering controlled waters. During the Parliamentary passage of the Coal Industry Act 1994 the Government explained that:

> "The legislation [the 1991 Act and, in Scotland, the 1974 Act] is there in that form because when the Bill was introduced and the Act debated it was felt to be unreasonable to place an absolute obligation in respect of environmental damage on a landowner who may never have been responsible for mining at all and who may have bought the land without being aware that it was undermined" (*per* the Minister for Energy, *Hansard*, H.C. Vol. 240, col. 297).

Since the defence and exemption apply only to a person who permits water pollution from an abandoned mine, it is possible (1) for a person to be prosecuted for causing or for knowingly permitting water pollution from an *active* mine; (2) for a person to be prosecuted for *causing* pollution from abandoned mines; and (3) for the water pollution regulator (now the Agency/SEPA) to recover costs from a person who has caused such pollution in relation to preventive or remedial anti-pollution works which the regulator has undertaken (see generally, Poustie, *The demise of coal and causing water pollution* [1994] 6 ELM 95). The 1995 Act introduces the further possibility (4) that the Agency/SEPA may serve a works notice, by inserting ss.46A to 46D into the 1974 Act (Scotland) and ss.161A to 161D into the 1991 Act (England and Wales). However, there are considerable difficulties in establishing that a person has *caused* water pollution from an abandoned mine. The act of switching off the pumps is not in itself regarded as the cause of the pollution but rather the whole sequence of events involving the sinking of the mine, the carrying on of pumping operations and the cessation of pumping operations is regarded as the cause. This view of causation was adopted by the High Court of Justiciary in Scotland in the only successful prosecution for an abandoned mine causing pollution: *Lockhart v. NCB* 1981 S.L.T. 161 at p. 172 (see also NRA, *Abandoned Mines and the Water Environment*, March 1994, p. 37). This view of causation essentially appears to be concerned with creation of the latent risk of pollution. The person who created the risk of pollution will be liable for *causing* the pollution. This has major implications for the privatised coal industry. Since, in the case of existing mines, the new private operators did not create any of the pollution risks which they inherited from British Coal, they cannot be held liable for pollution on the abandonment of a mine if any of those risks subsequently result in water pollution, as the Coal Industry Act 1994 did not transfer liability for such risks to them. They would only be liable for pollution resulting from such risks if liability had been transferred to them as part of the transfer of British Coal's undertaking. The only other occasions on which the new operators could be held liable for *causing* pollution is where it results from a latent risk of pollution which they themselves created, for example by sinking new mines or by driving new roads and opening up new coal faces in their existing mines.

The causal link between a person and a pollution incident may be broken by intervening factors such as natural forces, the act of a third party or an Act of God (*Lockhart v. NCB* 1981 S.L.T. 161 at p. 171). Thus, where the real cause of the pollution was created by someone or something else (*e.g.* another mine operator or extreme weather conditions) then the alleged offender will escape conviction. This was illustrated by the case *R. v. British Coal Corp.*, Cardiff Crown Court, December 2, 1993, 227 (1993) ENDS Report 44, a private prosecution brought by the Anglers Co-operative Association. In that case British Coal were prosecuted for causing pollution by switching off the pumps at a colliery which resulted in severe water pollution of a river. However, it was established that the water became contaminated in old mine workings adjacent to the British Coal workings for which British Coal had never had any responsibility and escaped from old adits into the river. It was also established in the trial that, as a result of these old workings, the pollution would have occurred in any event regardless of British Coal's pumping operations and, in fact, but for those operations, would have occurred many years earlier. The trial judge instructed the jury to acquit British Coal since the cessation of pumping had allowed what he described as natural forces to operate again and that that was the real cause of the pollution. It would arguably have been more correct to say that the pollution was actually caused by the act of a third party, *i.e.* the pre-nationalisation mine operators who had sunk and operated the old workings in which the water actually became contaminated. Since current mine operators will often be working in seams where there are adjacent old mineworkings, in many cases it will be difficult to establish that a person *caused* the water pollution.

Given these difficulties with establishing *causation* and the demise of deep mining, the pressure for reform of the law to withdraw the statutory protections in respect of *permitting* pollution has been considerable. The passage of the Coal Industry Act 1994 through Parliament saw attempts to bring about legislative amendments in relation to water pollution from abandoned mines and to impose on the new Coal Authority a duty to deal with water pollution from abandoned mines. The Government resisted these proposals although they indicated that they expected the Coal Authority to go beyond the minimum standards of environmental responsibility set by its legal duties (*per* Lord Strathclyde, *Hansard*, H.L. Vol. 554, col. 541). This "expectation", however, does not amount even to a commitment and is not enforceable or legally binding. Furthermore, it may be that this expectation cannot be met by the Coal Authority if it lacks sufficient resources.

The problem of water pollution from abandoned mines has been under consideration for some time as the Commission on Energy and the Environment report, *Coal and the Environment*, (HMSO, 1081) illustrates. However, more recently a considerable number of reports have also focused on this issue and how to deal with it, for example, *A Clear Future for Waters in the Forth Catchment* (Forth River Purification Board, 1993), *Abandoned Mines and the Water Environment*, (NRA, March 1994) which recommended, *inter alia*, clarification of the definition of abandoned mine, *Sixteenth Report: Freshwater Quality* (Royal Commission on Environmental Pollution, Cm. 1966, June 1992), and the *Government Response to the Sixteenth*

Report of the Royal Commission on Environmental Pollution (DoE, January 1995). The Government's consultation papers on contaminated land, *Paying for Our Past* (DoE, March 1994) and *Contaminated Land Clean-up and Control* (Scottish Office, March 1994) also acknowledged the unique exemptions under water pollution legislation from criminal liability and recommended that the justification for those special exemptions should be reassessed in the light of the emerging conclusions of the review. The results of that consultation exercise (*Framework for Contaminated Land* (DoE, November 1994); *Contaminated Land Clean-up and Control: Outcome of Review* (Scottish Office, November 1994)) indicated that proposals for legislative amendments to withdraw the defence and exemption in relation to permitting water pollution from abandoned mines and to impose a duty on mine operators to give six months' prior notice of a proposed abandonment would be introduced.

A small step forward in dealing with the problem was also made when the NRA entered into a Memorandum of Understanding with British Coal (November 18, 1993) which provided, *inter alia*, for regular meetings of the two parties and for two weeks' notice of cessation of pumping operations to be given to the NRA (see *Abandoned Mines and the Water Environment*, NRA, March 1994, Appendix 2). The NRA subsequently entered into a similar Memorandum of Understanding with RJB Mining PLC (dated August 10, 1995). In Scotland, Forth River Purification Board entered into an agreement (made on April 21, 1995) with the British Coal Corporation and the Coal Authority which requires British Coal to notify the Board of cessation of pumping, and British Coal and the Coal Authority to carry out a specified monitoring and pumping programme. The agreement relates to the protection of the water environment from possible long-term pollution from the connected workings of the Frances Colliery (mothballed in 1984) and the Michael Colliery (where coal production ceased in 1967 but pumping operations have continued) in Fife (*per* Sir Hector Monro, Standing Committee B, May 23, 1995, cols. 411–412). At the time of writing pumping operations had recently ceased at both collieries.

Since the law of contract in Scotland differs from that in England and Wales, in that there is no requirement for consideration and therefore unilateral obligations are enforceable, it appears to be the case that the Scottish agreement would be enforceable at the instance of SEPA in the Scottish courts by way of interdict to prevent the breach of its terms or specific implement to require performance of the positive obligations contained in it, provided that the obligations contained therein are sufficiently clear and precise.

It was against this background that the provisions in Part II of the 1995 Act in relation to abandoned mines were introduced.

The scheme of the provisions
The new provisions contained in ss.58–60 impose a new duty on mine operators to give the appropriate agency six months' notice of any proposed abandonment, introduce a definition of "abandonment" in respect of mines for the purposes of that notification duty and, in relation to England and Wales only, withdraw the defence and exemption contained in s.89(3) and s.161 of the Water Resources Act 1991, but only after December 31, 1999. In relation to Scotland only, the 1995 Act does withdraw the defence and exemption in relation to permitting pollution from abandoned mines, but this is done in Sched. 16, which introduces a new s.30J(3)–(6) (in relation to the defence) and in Sched. 22 which introduces a new s.46(3) and (3A) into the 1974 Act (in relation to the cost recovery exemption).

Although these changes to the law were broadly welcomed in Parliament the delayed withdrawal of the defence and exemption to the end of 1999 was severely criticised, for example, on the ground that it enabled current mine operators to abandon their mines before that date and escape liability for permitting any water pollution from them once they had closed (*e.g. Hansard*, H.L. Vol. 560, cols. 1481–1483; *Hansard*, H.C. Vol. 258, col. 52; Standing Committee B, May 23, 1995, cols. 414–415). In the Government's note on the financial effects of the original Bill (p. xiii) it was stated that:

> "Since these proposals are coming forward in parallel with the privatisation of the coal industry, there could be some adverse effect on proceeds to the Government. Accordingly, the removal of the statutory protections is being timed to reduce any possible effect."

The impression given by these comments is that the delay in the changes was solely to benefit the privatisation of the industry and that they showed "a blatant disregard for the environment and the likely pollution problems caused by the abandonment of mines" (*per* Lord Mason of Barnsley, *Hansard*, H.L. Vol. 560, col. 1482). Amendments were accordingly proposed at Report stage to bring forward the date of withdrawal of the defence and the exemption to January 1, 1996 (*e.g. per* Baroness Hilton of Eggardon, *Hansard*, H.L. Vol. 560, cols. 1481–1482). However, the Government rejected such an amendment, explaining:

> "Our decision to remove the defence and exemption was taken in the knowledge that that

would be a step of great significance not just as a means of improving the quality of discharges from mines abandoned in the future, but with the practical and financial implications for the current owners and operators of mines.

The effect on revenue from coal privatisation was only one of a number of issues considered in deciding that the statutory protection would be lifted at the end of 1999. The Government wanted to allow all mine owners time to adapt to the change. In addition, the agency will have powers to clean up or prevent pollution if it considers that necessary under the Water Resources Act 1991.

The measures in Clause 55 [s.58], which define abandonment and require mine operators to notify the agency six months before abandoning a mine, will take effect from the transfer date. [That is, the date of the transfer of water pollution regulation to the Agency/SEPA: April 1, 1996]. They are designed to work as a precursor to the removal of the defence and exemption. However, we have taken the view that it would be right to allow those involved a period until the end of 1999 in which to adjust to the proposed changes in the existing regulatory regime because of the obvious practical and financial implications" (*per* Viscount Ullswater, *Hansard*, H.L. Vol. 560, col. 1484).

In contrast to the position in England and Wales, the defence only became available to Scottish mine operators with the coming into force of the 1974 Act in the mid-1980s, since it was not provided for in the Rivers (Prevention of Pollution) (Scotland) Act 1951. As a result, insofar as the Government's concern was to ease the transition from a long-standing statutory protection, this concern has less force in Scotland than south of the border.

It may also be of significance that the major coal supply contracts inherited by RJB and Mining (Scotland) Ltd for the supply of the principal generators, National Power plc, PowerGen plc and Scottish Power plc all expire in 1998 (see DTI, *The Energy Report: Markets in Transition*, HMSO 1994, ch. 4.24, p. 54). If these contracts are not renewed or are renewed in a much reduced form, the 1999 date might allow the private mine operators to abandoned many of the remaining coal mines before the withdrawal of the defence and the exemption, although clearly they would be under an obligation in ss.58–59 to notify the appropriate agency of a proposed abandonment.

There were also attempts to make the Coal Authority (established by the Coal Industry Act 1994) liable for pollution from abandoned mines (*per* Baroness Hilton of Eggardon, *Hansard*, H.L. Vol. 560, col. 1479 and *per* Ms Joan Ruddock MP, *Hansard*, H.C. Vol. 262, cols. 761–776). Although the Coal Authority does have responsibility for *all* abandoned mines by virtue of the operation of s.7(3) of the Coal Industry Act 1994, the Government nevertheless rejected this proposal. They argued that:

> "Outright removal of the defence and exemption as proposed in the amendment would require the Coal Authority to seek discharge consents for all discharges regardless of the degree of pollution, and to comply with them. That would not be justified in many cases and would place a heavy burden on the public purse. ... We believe it would be wrong to withdraw suddenly those statutory protections which apply now to all abandoned coal mines for which the Coal Authority has responsibility. The Government have already said that they would expect the Coal Authority to go beyond the minimum standards of environmental responsibility which are set by its legal duties and to seek the best environmental result which can be secured by the use of the resources that are available to it. We must accept that the Coal Authority, like all public bodies, has limited financial resources" (*per* Viscount Ullswater, *Hansard*, H.L. Vol. 560, col. 1480; see also *Hansard*, H.L. Vol. 562, col. 226).

There remain uncertainties about the role of the Coal Authority in relation to abandoned mines. Under the Coal Industry Act 1994, the Coal Authority has a duty, so far as practicable, to ensure that mine operators "are able to finance both the proper carrying on of the coal mining operations that they are authorised to carry on and the discharge of liabilities arising from the carrying on of those operations" (s.2(1) of the Coal Industry Act 1994). In this licensing role the Coal Authority may impose such conditions as it thinks fit (s.28(1) of the 1994 Act) which clearly could include conditions relating to water pollution issues. However, in relation to mines which have already been abandoned the position is less clear. Furthermore, by virtue of s.29(1) of the 1994 Act, the Coal Authority may also impose conditions to provide for security for the performance of obligations imposed by other conditions of the licence. Such security could include a requirement for bonds for potential environmental liabilities. As the owner of already abandoned mines, the Coal Authority benefits from the statutory protections afforded by water pollution legislation until after December 31, 1999 when it will lose those protections. However, the Coal Authority itself appears unsure of the extent of its potential liabilities with respect to abandoned mines, with conflicting statements being made by senior officials. While Neville Washington, Chief Executive of the Coal Authority explained "The Coal Authority is not responsible for water that emerges from pits" (*Newcastle Evening Chronicle*, April 26, 1995). Albert Schofield, Director of Contracts, interviewed on the "Report Back" programme broadcast on BBC Radio Nottingham indicated that the Bill was not clear in assigning responsibility for minewater pollution from abandoned mines to the Coal Authority. However, on several occasions during the passage of the 1995 Act through Parliament the Government reiterated its pledge that the Coal Authority would continue pumping where necessary (*e.g. per* Robert Atkins, *Hansard*, H.C. Vol. 262, col. 776) and would not limit itself to minimum standards of environmental responsibility (col. 774).

Concerns were also expressed by Lord Crickhowell (*Hansard*, H.L. Vol. 562, cols. 148–149) in relation to the abandonment of metalliferous mines and the applicability of Directive 76/464/EEC on pollution caused by certain dangerous substances discharged into the aquatic environment (1976 OJ L129/23) and Directive 80/68/EEC on the protection of groundwater against pollution caused by certain dangerous substances (1980 OJ L20/43). However, although the Government recognised these concerns, significantly they failed to address them to any extent at all (*Hansard*, H.L. Vol. 562, col. 152). It is clear that whereas the Coal Authority has responsibility for abandoned coal mines, no similar authority has responsibility for abandoned metalliferous mines. Furthermore, Lord Crickhowell went on to suggest that by not withdrawing the defence and exemption for permitting water pollution from abandoned mines until December 31, 1999 the UK may be in non-compliance with the provisions of Directives 76/464/EEC and 80/68/EEC (cols. 148–149).

Relationship of new abandoned mines provisions and contaminated land provisions

Section 78A(2) of the new Part IIA of the 1990 Act defines contaminated land as "any land which appears to the local authority in whose area it is situated to be in such a condition, by reason of substances in, on or under the land, that ... (b) pollution of controlled waters is being, or is likely to be, caused". This would appear to encompass the issue of water pollution from abandoned mines. Furthermore, since s.91B of the Water Resources Act 1991 and, in relation to Scotland, s.30Z of the 1974 Act provide that the appropriate agency must inform the relevant local authority of any proposed abandonment when it receives notice of the same from a mine operator where it considers that in consequence of the abandonment or proposed abandonment any land has or is likely to become contaminated land, there is a clear intention to give local authorities a role in the remediation of contamination resulting from water pollution from abandoned mines using their new contaminated land powers.

However, at Report Stage in the House of Lords, Lord Williams of Elvel (*Hansard*, H.L. Vol. 562, cols. 144–145) attempted to ensure that abandoned mines would be treated as contaminated land between the date of the Royal Assent and the withdrawal of the defence and exemption in water pollution legislation since the Bill as originally drafted did not restrict the application of the contaminated land provisions in the case of permitting water pollution from abandoned mines. The Government responded that:

> "It was no part of the Government's intention that the current clause, establishing the contaminated land powers, would have the effect of removing the existing defence and exemption which apply in the circumstances. However, that appears to have been the inadvertent result of the existing provisions in the Bill and the Government will be bringing forward an amendment at a later date to rectify this" (*per* Viscount Ullswater, *Hansard*, H.L. Vol. 562, col. 151).

The Government duly moved swiftly to close this loophole and introduced the provision which is now s.78J(3) of the 1990 Act (see the note to that section in the 1990 Act) which limits the application of the contaminated land provisions in cases where a person is permitting water pollution from abandoned mines until December 31, 1999 so that those provisions are consistent with the delay in the withdrawal of the defence/exemption in the abandoned mines provisions. However, it would still be possible for a local authority to use the contaminated land provisions where a person has caused water pollution and indeed where a person has knowingly permitted contamination in terms of the first limb of the s.78A(2) test (see also General Notes to ss.78A and 78J(3) of the 1990 Act.

58. After Chapter II of Part III of the Water Resources Act 1991 (pollution offences) there shall be inserted—

"CHAPTER IIA

ABANDONED MINES

Introductory

91A.—(1) For the purposes of this Chapter, "abandonment", in relation to a mine,—
- (a) subject to paragraph (b) below, includes—
  - (i) the discontinuance of any or all of the operations for the removal of water from the mine;
  - (ii) the cessation of working of any relevant seam, vein or vein-system;
  - (iii) the cessation of use of any shaft or outlet of the mine;
  - (iv) in the case of a mine in which activities other than mining activities are carried on (whether or not mining activities are also carried on in the mine)—
    - (A) the discontinuance of some or all of those other activities in the mine; and
    - (B) any substantial change in the operations for the removal of water from the mine; but
- (b) does not include—
  - (i) any disclaimer under section 178 or 315 of the Insolvency Act 1986 (power of liquidator, or trustee of a bankrupt's estate, to disclaim onerous property) by the official receiver acting in a compulsory capacity; or
  - (ii) the abandonment of any rights, interests or liabilities by the Accountant in Bankruptcy acting as permanent or interim trustee in a sequestration (within the meaning of the Bankruptcy (Scotland) Act 1985);

and cognate expressions shall be construed accordingly.

(2) In this Chapter, except where the context otherwise requires—

"the 1954 Act" means the Mines and Quarries Act 1954;

"acting in a compulsory capacity", in the case of the official receiver, means acting as—
- (a) liquidator of a company;
- (b) receiver or manager of a bankrupt's estate, pursuant to section 287 of the Insolvency Act 1986;
- (c) trustee of a bankrupt's estate;
- (d) liquidator of an insolvent partnership;
- (e) trustee of an insolvent partnership;
- (f) trustee, or receiver or manager, of the insolvent estate of a deceased person;

"mine" has the same meaning as in the 1954 Act;

"the official receiver" has the same meaning as it has in the Insolvency Act 1986 by virtue of section 399(1) of that Act;

"prescribed" means prescribed in regulations;

"regulations" means regulations made by the Secretary of State;

"relevant seam, vein or vein-system", in the case of any mine, means any seam, vein or vein-system for the purpose of, or in connection with, whose working any excavation constituting or comprised in the mine was made.

DEFINITIONS

"1954 Act": subs. (2).

"acting in a compulsory capacity": subs. (2).

"mine": subs. (2); s.180(1) of the Mines and Quarries Act 1954.

"official receiver": subs. (2); s.399(1) of the Insolvency Act 1986.

"prescribed": subs. (2).

"regulations": subs. (2).
"relevant seam, vein or vein-sytem": subs. (2).

COMMENCEMENT
This section will be brought into force by a commencement order made under s.125(3) of the 1995 Act.

GENERAL NOTE
This section provides a definition of "abandonment" in relation to mines for the purposes of the new Chapter IIA of the Water Resources Act 1991 which it also introduces. This was one of the changes which the NRA wished to see brought about in its report, *Abandoned Mines and the Water Environment* (March 1994), pp. 38 and 42.

The definition of abandonment provided by subs. (1) must be read together with the definition of mine which is that appearing in s.180(1) of the Mines and Quarries Act 1954 (subs. (2)):

> "... an excavation or system of excavations, including all such excavations to which a common system of ventilation is provided, made for the purpose of, or in connection with, the getting, wholly or substantially by means involving the employment of persons below ground, of minerals (whether in their natural state or in solution or suspension) or products of minerals."

This definition is elaborated upon in s.180(3):

> "there shall be deemed to form part of a mine so much of the surface (including buildings, structures and works thereon) surrounding or adjacent to the shafts or outlets of the mine as is occupied together with the mine for the purpose of, or in connection with, the working of the mine, the treatment, preparation for sale, consumption or use, storage or removal from the mine of the minerals or products thereof gotten from the mine or the removal from the mine of the refuse thereof ...";

by s.182(2) which provides that:

> "For the purposes of this Act mine workings having a common system or ventilation, or any part of a system of ventilation in common, shall be deemed to form part of the same mine";

and by s.183(1) which provides:

> "For the purposes of this Act an excavation or system of excavations made for training purposes shall be deemed to be a mine, and the use for those purposes of any premises which are a mine as defined by subsection (1) of section one hundred and eighty of this Act ... shall be deemed, for the purposes of this Act, to constitute the working of the mine ...".

It is thus clear that the definition of a mine includes, for example, the surface buildings, a number of mineworkings which share a common system of ventilation and a mine used for training purposes.

Subs. (1)
The definition of abandonment provided is not exhaustive but is very wide. A variety of physical indicators are used to define abandonment. Importantly, it is abundantly clear that abandonment of a mine includes abandonment of part of a mine. The combination of this definition and the duty contained in the new s.91B to give six months' prior notice to the Agency of any proposed abandonment should provide the Agency with very valuable information and may enable any likely pollution problems to be dealt with at an early stage. It should be noted that the definition of abandonment does not apply beyond the boundaries of Chapter IIA of the Water Resources Act 1991. This means it is only applicable in relation to the notification duty in the new s.91B of the 1991 Act. In the original Bill this clause did apply the definition of abandonment to the whole Act. However, the definition was restricted by a Government amendment at Standing Committee stage in the House of Commons (Standing Committee B, May 23, 1995, col. 389). The defence in s.89(3) of the 1991 Act to permitting water pollution from an abandoned mine is amended to include an abandoned part of a mine by s.60. See the note to s.60.

The non-exhaustive definition of abandonment in subs. (1) appears to be broken into two groupings: subs. (1)(a)(i) to (iii) which may be regarded as covering examples of mining activities and subs. (1)(a)(iv) which covers non-mining activities.

Paragraph (a)(i). This provision clearly encompasses the cessation of pumping and drainage operations in a mine. As originally drafted it did not include the words "any or all of the". However, the Government moved amendments at the Standing Committee Stage to extend the scope of the provision:

> "We wanted to ensure that acts of abandonment that affected large parts of a mine would be notifiable even when the mine continued to be worked—that is possible through changes in the mine–water pumping regime. We did not want it to be necessary for operators to notify cessation of working in small parts of a mine when that would have no implication for water pollution" (Mr Robert Atkins, Standing Committee B, May 23, 1995, col. 390).

As the provision now stands it includes partial cessation of these activities in addition to total cessation. However, it is not clear that the words of the statute actually have the effect which the Government intended since they did not have the *de minimis* exception to which Mr Atkins referred. They appear to refer to the discontinuation of any pumping or drainage operations without qualification.

Paragraph (a)(ii). This would encompass the common situation where a mine has several working seams and the work on a particular seam or vein in a mine ceased presumably even if pumping operations were continued in that seam or elsewhere in the mine.

Paragraph (a)(iii). The cessation of use of any shaft or outlet of the mine will count as abandonment. Shaft means a shaft the top of which is, or is intended to be, at the surface (see s.182(1) of the Mines and Quarries Act 1954. Although outlet is not defined in the Mines and Quarries Act 1954, it is clear, *e.g.* from s.30(2) thereof that an outlet may be one through which it is not possible to walk. Outlets may often be used for drainage or ventilation purposes.

Paragraph (a)(iv). This provision deals with situations where mining activities have ceased at a mine but non-mining activities are being carried on. Mining activities are not defined in the Act. However, in the light of the definition of mine in the Mines and Quarries Act 1954 (see above) it would appear that a mine which was being used only for ventilation or training purposes is still a mine in which mining activities are being carried on. It is further submitted that a mine which is used solely for pumping water from mineworkings which are still in use from another mine or a mine which has been "mothballed" (*i.e.* which is maintained on a care and maintenance basis only) is still a mine in which mining activities are being carried on. Further assistance on what constitutes a mining activity, in relation to coal mines at least, may be found in the Coal Industry Act 1994 which includes a definition of coal-mining operations in s.65(1). While an operation is not necessarily synonymous with an activity, the definition still provides useful guidance. Coal-mining operations include:

> "(a) searching for coal and boring for it,
> (b) winning, working and getting it (whether underground or in the course of opencast operations),
> (c) bringing underground coal to the surface, treating coal and rendering it saleable,
> (d) treating coal in the strata for the purpose of winning any product of coal and winning, working or getting any product of coal resulting from such treatment, and
> (e) depositing spoil from any activities carried on in the course of any coal-mining operations and draining coal mines,
> and an operation carried on in relation to minerals other than coal is a coal-mining operation in so far as it is carried on in relation to those minerals as part of, or as ancillary to, operations carried on in relation to coal."

Furthermore, although this definition applies to coal-mining operations, it is of some relevance in terms of what constitutes a mining operation or activity more generally.

It is likely that the provision in subs. (1)(a)(iv) is targetted at the following types of situation: (i) where part of or all of a mine ceases to be used for mining but remains open to facilitate salvage of equipment; (ii) where a mine has become a museum; or (iii) where a mine is being used, for example, for the disposal of waste unconnected with mining. If a mine is being used in such a way and some or all of those activities are discontinued and there is any substantial change in pumping or drainage operations then that will constitute abandonment. A substantial change is one which is considerable: *Granada Theatres v. Freehold Investment (Leytonstone)* [1958] 1 W.L.R. 845; *Palser v. Grinling*; *Property Holding Co. v. Mischeff* [1948] A.C. 291.

There was considerable uncertainty as to the scope of the definition in subs. (1) in Parliament (*per* Mr William O'Brien MP, Standing Committee B, May 23, 1995, cols. 390–391 and *per* Mr Tipping MP, col. 394) particularly in relation to mines where coal production and pumping had ceased but salvage works or surface activities such as coal storage, stocking and removal were still continuing. However, the Government argued:

"If activities other than mining activities are being carried on in the mine, there is no act of abandonment. If mining, pumping and storage activities have ceased, the mine is considered to be abandoned for the purposes of these provisions" (*per* Mr Robert Atkin, Standing Committee B, May 23, 1995, col. 393).

It is submitted that this explanation is not very helpful. The implication of the definition in subs. (1) is in fact that there may be several acts of abandonment at the same mine. For example, work on a particular seam could cease while work elsewhere continued; thereafter, work on all remaining seams could cease although pumping operations continued. Finally, pumping operations could cease. Each of these occurrences would in itself count as an abandonment in terms of the new statutory definition and hence require advance notification. That this is anticipated is apparent from the wording of the new s.89(3B) and (3C) of the 1991 Act. Hence Mr Atkin's statement that "If activities other than mining activities are being carried on in the mine, there is no act of abandonment" is somewhat misleading. In fact there may well have been several acts of abandonment up to that point.

Paragraph (b). This paragraph makes provision for certain exceptions in relation to the official receiver and the Accountant in Bankruptcy. These are designed to deal with the fact that abandonment sometimes accompanies the insolvency of the operator and to provide protection for the official receiver and the Accountant in Bankruptcy (see also note to s.91B(5) below).

Mine operators to give the Agency six months' notice of any proposed abandonment

91B.—(1) If, in the case of any mine, there is to be an abandonment at any time after the expiration of the initial period, it shall be the duty of the operator of the mine to give notice of the proposed abandonment to the Agency at least six months before the abandonment takes effect.

(2) A notice under subsection (1) above shall contain such information (if any) as is prescribed for the purpose, which may include information about the operator's opinion as to any consequences of the abandonment.

(3) A person who fails to give the notice required by subsection (1) above shall be guilty of an offence and liable—

(a) on summary conviction, to a fine not exceeding the statutory maximum;

(b) on conviction on indictment, to a fine.

(4) A person shall not be guilty of an offence under subsection (3) above if—

(a) the abandonment happens in an emergency in order to avoid danger to life or health; and

(b) notice of the abandonment, containing such information as may be prescribed, is given as soon as reasonably practicable after the abandonment has happened.

(5) Where the operator of a mine is—

(a) the official receiver acting in a compulsory capacity, or

(b) the Accountant in Bankruptcy acting as permanent or interim trustee in a sequestration (within the meaning of the Bankruptcy (Scotland) Act 1985),

he shall not be guilty of an offence under subsection (3) above by reason of any failure to give the notice required by subsection (1) above if, as soon as reasonably practicable (whether before or after the abandonment), he gives to the Agency notice of the abandonment or proposed abandonment, containing such information as may be prescribed.

(6) Where a person gives notice under subsection (1), (4)(b) or (5) above, he shall publish prescribed particulars of, or relating to, the notice in one or more local newspapers circulating in the locality where the mine is situated.

(7) Where the Agency—

(a) receives notice under this section or otherwise learns of an abandonment or proposed abandonment in the case of any mine, and

(b) considers that, in consequence of the abandonment or proposed abandonment taking effect, any land has or is likely to become contaminated land, within the meaning of Part IIA of the Environmental Protection Act 1990,

it shall be the duty of the Agency to inform the local authority in whose area that land is situated of the abandonment or proposed abandonment.

(8) In this section—

"the initial period" means the period of six months beginning with the day on which subsection (1) above comes into force;

"local authority" means—

(a) any unitary authority;

(b) any district council, so far as it is not a unitary authority;

(c) the Common Council of the City of London and, as respects the Temples, the Sub-Treasurer of the Inner Temple and the Under-Treasurer of the Middle Temple respectively;

"unitary authority" means—

(a) the council of a county, so far as it is the council of an area for which there are no district councils;

(b) the council of any district comprised in an area for which there is no county council;

(c) the council of a London borough;

(d) the council of a county borough in Wales."

DEFINITIONS

"abandonment": s.91A(1) of the Water Resources Act 1991.

"acting in a compulsory capacity": s.91A(2) of the Water Resources Act 1991.

"initial period": subs. (8).

"local authority": subs. (8).

"mine": s.91A(2) of the Water Resources Act 1991; s.180 of the 1954 Act.

"notice": s.221(1) of the Water Resources Act 1991.

"official receiver": s.91A(2) of the Water Resources Act 1991; s.399(1) of the Insolvency Act 1986.

"prescribed": s.91A(2) of the Water Resources Act 1991.

"unitary authority": subs. (8).

COMMENCEMENT

September 21, 1995 insofar as this section confers power on the Secretary of State to make regulations (S.I. 1995 No. 1983). The remainder will be brought into force by a commencement order made under s.125(3) of the 1995 Act.

GENERAL NOTE

This section imposes a new duty on mine operators to give six months' prior notice of a proposed abandonment to the Agency. Notification of abandonment of mines has been a legislative requirement since the Mines Inspection and Regulation Act 1870 although the requirement was to notify a Mines' Inspector within two months after the abandonment. However this requirement and its successors have had little, if anything, to do with the environmental consequences of the abandonment of a mine. The rationale for this new measure is simple and was explained by the Government at Committee Stage in the House of Lords:

"It is sensible that mineowners should give notice to the agency of their intention to abandon a mine so that proper steps can be taken to prevent minewater pollution in future" (*per* Viscount Ullswater, *Hansard*, H.L. Vol. 559, col. 1465).

Given the wide definition of "abandonment" in the new s.91A of the Water Resources Act 1991, the imposition of this duty on mine operators should provide the Agency with considerably more information than the NRA had access to in relation to proposed abandonments, especially abandonments of parts of mines. This should put the Agency in a better position to plan or advise on or undertake anti-pollution measures. Since the definition of abandonment in s.91A(1) also clearly encompasses several abandonments at the same mine, it may be prudent for an operator who intends to cease production and close a mine to give notification to the Agency at the same time (*i.e.* at least six months prior to the first of the proposed abandonments) that a series of abandonments are to take place, *e.g.* (1) cessation of working of seams which will be followed by salvage, *i.e.* a non-mining activity; (2) cessation of salvage activities and total cessation of pumping operations.

It should also be noted that these provisions for prior notification to the Agency on abandonment supplement lease conditions requiring notification to the Coal Authority, imposed by it on the operators of coal mines. (See further the Coal Authority's Model Underground Mine Lease, Sched. 7, para. 4.2.) The Government explained:

> "Under those arrangements, the mine operator has to give the Coal Authority six months' notice of any proposed abandonment and a report on the consequences, except in the case of real emergency.
>
> As regards the consequences for the water environment, the report is to be based on consultation with the appropriate regulator, the agencies or the present bodies. The operator then has to take all steps necessary to ensure that the mine can be returned to the authority in a satisfactory condition; that is, a condition which does not expose the authority to future liability. If necessary, the operator would have to make an appropriate payment to the authority for any continuing cost before he could relinquish the lease" (*per* Viscount Ullswater, *Hansard*, H.L. Vol. 562, col. 152).

In the case of metalliferous mines there is no similar licensing system, although it is submitted that, in relation to new metal mines at least, the planning authority could impose conditions in relation to aftercare of the site which might to a limited extent include certain anti-pollution measures insofar as they related to land use.

Subs. (1)
The duty on mine operators to give notice only applies in relation to an abandonment after the expiry of the initial period, *i.e.* the period of six months after the subsection comes into force. The implications of this are that mine operators are free to abandon mines within the initial period but that if they are proposing to abandon at any time after the expiry of that period they would require to give at least six months' notice. Therefore, if a mine operator wished to abandon a mine on the day following the expiry of the initial period he would be required to give notice on the day following the start of the initial period.

Operator of the mine
This phrase is not defined in the Act. However, the person who is conducting mining operations may be regarded as the operator. In relation to coal mines, the Coal Industry Act 1994 definition of coal-mining operations is set out above in the General Note to s.91A(1)(a)(iv). Thus, in relation to a coal mine, the operator of such a mine is likely to be the person carrying on such operations in the mine. In relation to other mines, the 1994 Act provides a good indication of the sorts of operations which the operator of the mine is carrying on.

In the case of coal mines, it may be possible to narrow the scope of the term "mine operator" still further as the operator will usually be the person licensed to carry on coal-mining operations, *i.e.* the licensed operator under Pt. II of the Coal Industry Act 1994 (as defined in s.65(1) of that Act). However, it should be noted that the definition of coal-mining operations given in s.65(1) is wider than the definition of coal-mining operations which require to be licensed under Pt. II (s.25) and hence the operator of the mine may not always be the licensed operator in terms of the Coal Industry Act 1994. It should also be noted that even in the case of a licensed coal mine, it may be that the operator of the mine for the purposes of Chap. IIA of the 1991 Act is not the licensed operator at all. The reason for this is that it is possible for a licensed operator to subcontract the work at a mine to another person: Model Underground Operating Licence, clause 12. In such a situation, it may be that it should be the contractor who notifies the Agency and not necessarily the licensed operator. If the Agency wished to prosecute a person in such a situation for failing to comply with the notification requirement it might be well advised to prosecute both the licensed operator and the contractor.

Subs. (2)
The Secretary of State may make regulations prescribing the information (if any) which must be contained in a notice. No regulations have yet been made. Little guidance is given by the subsection as to the possible scope of the information which may be required except that it may include information about the operator's opinion on the consequences of any abandonment which will be of considerable importance. There may be practical limitations on the information which may be required. For example, although a mine operator may be able to indicate that mining activities involving working the seams of a mine will cease on a particular date, he may be in no position to notify the Agency of the identity of the contractors who will subsequently

carry out salvage work and may not yet be in a position to indicate how long salvage operations will take.

Subs. (3)
The maximum penalty on summary conviction is presently a fine of £5,000.

Subs. (4)
No offence is committed in the limited emergency circumstances provided by this subsection.

Subs. (5)
A defence is also available to the official receiver acting in a compulsory capacity and the Accountant in Bankruptcy acting as permanent or interim trustee in a sequestration (within the meaning of the Bankruptcy (Scotland) Act 1985) if he gives notice of the abandonment or proposed abandonment as soon as reasonably practicable. This defence is designed to deal with the fact that abandonment sometimes accompanies the insolvency of the operator. While private sector insolvency practitioners may refuse to act, neither the official receiver nor the Accountant in Bankruptcy may do so. If this defence were not available, they could be compelled to continue some mining operations when there were no assets in the company to fund this, or face prosecution for the criminal offence of failure to notify. These provisions are therefore designed to provide protection to the official receiver and the Accountant in Bankruptcy so that even if the physical factors denoting abandonment apply, nevertheless no offence is committed by the official receiver or Accountant in Bankruptcy when he abandons a mine or part of a mine without giving six months' notice providing he notifies the agency as soon as possible (*per* Earl Ferrers, *Hansard*, H.L. Vol. 565, col. 1521).

Subs. (6)
This subsection lays down publicity requirements which apply in all cases where notice is given under subs. (1). Hence, even when an operator ceases working a seam, then notice will be required. The Government initially took the view that this was "an unnecessary bureaucratic burden on industry" (Mr Robert Atkins, Standing Committee B, May 23, 1995, col. 397), although having considered the matter further they brought forward their own amendment (*per* Earl Ferrers, *Hansard*, H.L. Vol. 565, cols. 1520–1521) laying down publicity requirements. No offence appears to be committed by an operator if he fails to comply with these publicity requirements.

Subs. (7)
This subsection provides a link between the abandoned mines provisions and the new contaminated land provisions. The Agency is under a duty to inform the relevant local authority where it receives a notice of abandonment or proposed abandonment and as a consequence thereof any land has or is likely to become contaminated in terms of the definition of contaminated land in Pt. IIA of the 1990 Act. Insofar as it is not prevented from doing so by s.78J(3), the local authority must then serve a remediation notice if the appropriate tests of contamination in s.78A are met.

Abandoned mines: Scotland

59. After Part I of the Control of Pollution Act 1974 (waste on land) there shall be inserted—

"PART IA

ABANDONED MINES

Introductory

    30Y.—(1) For the purposes of this Part, "abandonment", in relation to a mine,—
        (a) subject to paragraph (b) below, includes—
            (i) the discontinuance of any or all of the operations for the removal of water from the mine;
            (ii) the cessation of working of any relevant seam, vein or vein-system;
            (iii) the cessation of use of any shaft or outlet of the mine;

(iv) in the case of a mine in which activities other than mining activities are carried on (whether or not mining activities are also carried on in the mine)—

    (A) the discontinuance of some or all of those other activities in the mine; and

        (B) any substantial change in the operations for the removal of water from the mine; but

(b) does not include—

    (i) the abandonment of any rights, interests or liabilities by the Accountant in Bankruptcy acting as permanent or interim trustee in a sequestration (within the meaning of the Bankruptcy (Scotland) Act 1985); or

    (ii) any disclaimer under section 178 or 315 of the Insolvency Act 1986 (power of liquidator, or trustee of bankrupt's estate, to disclaim onerous property) by the official receiver acting in a compulsory capacity;

and cognate expressions shall be construed accordingly.

(2) In this Part, except where the context otherwise requires—

"acting in a compulsory capacity", in the case of the official receiver, means acting as—

(a) liquidator of a company;

(b) receiver or manager of a bankrupt's estate, pursuant to section 287 of the Insolvency Act 1986;

(c) trustee of a bankrupt's estate;

(d) liquidator of an insolvent partnership;

(e) trustee of an insolvent partnership;

(f) trustee, or receiver or manager, of the insolvent estate of a deceased person;

"the official receiver" has the same meaning as it has in the Insolvency Act 1986 by virtue of section 399(1) of that Act;

"relevant seam, vein or vein-system", in the case of any mine, means any seam, vein or vein-system for the purpose of, or in connection with, whose working any excavation constituting or comprised in the mine was made.

(3) This Part extends only to Scotland.

DEFINITIONS
"acting in a compulsory capacity": subs. (2).
"mine": s.105(1) of the 1974 Act; s.180(1) of the 1954 Act.
"official receiver": subs. (2); s.399(1) of the Insolvency Act 1986.
"relevant seam, vein or vein-system": subs. (2).

COMMENCEMENT
This section will be brought into force by a commencement order made under s.125(3) of the 1995 Act.

GENERAL NOTE
This section makes identical provision for Scotland relating to the definition of abandonment. See the General Note to s.91A of the 1991 Act above. References to the relevant sections of the Control of Pollution Act 1974 should be substituted for references to the provisions of the 1991 Act in that note. This section and s.30Z which follows are inserted into the 1974 Act out of sequence. Section 59 of the 1995 Act inserts them as Part IA, after s.30 (the final section of Part I of the 1974 Act), and therefore before ss.30A–30J (ss.30F–30J are inserted by Sched. 16 to the 1995 Act).

Mine operators to give SEPA six months' notice of any proposed abandonment

30Z.—(1) If, in the case of any mine, there is to be an abandonment at any time after the expiration of the initial period, it shall be the duty of the operator of the mine to give notice of the proposed abandonment to SEPA at least six months before the abandonment takes effect.

(2) A notice under subsection (1) above shall contain such information (if any) as is prescribed for the purpose, which may include information about the operator's opinion as to any consequences of the abandonment.

(3) A person who fails to give the notice required by subsection (1) above shall be guilty of an offence and liable—

    (a) on summary conviction, to a fine not exceeding the statutory maximum;

    (b) on conviction on indictment, to a fine.

(4) A person shall not be guilty of an offence under subsection (3) above if—

    (a) the abandonment happens in an emergency in order to avoid danger to life or health; and

    (b) notice of the abandonment, containing such information as may be prescribed, is given as soon as reasonably practicable after the abandonment has happened.

(5) Where the operator of a mine is—

    (a) the Accountant in Bankruptcy acting as permanent or interim trustee in a sequestration (within the meaning of the Bankruptcy (Scotland) Act 1985); or

    (b) the official receiver acting in a compulsory capacity,

he shall not be guilty of an offence under subsection (3) above by reason of any failure to give the notice required by subsection (1) above if, as soon as is reasonably practicable (whether before or after the abandonment), he gives to SEPA notice of the abandonment or proposed abandonment, containing such information as may be prescribed.

(6) Where a person gives notice under subsection (1), (4)(b) or (5) above, he shall publish prescribed particulars of, or relating to, the notice in one or more local newspapers circulating in the locality where the mine is situated.

(7) Where SEPA—

    (a) receives notice under this section or otherwise learns of an abandonment or proposed abandonment in the case of any mine, and

    (b) considers that, in consequence of the abandonment or proposed abandonment taking effect, any land has or is likely to become contaminated land, within the meaning of Part IIA of the Environmental Protection Act 1990,

it shall be the duty of SEPA to inform the local authority in whose area that land is situated of the abandonment or proposed abandonment.

(8) In this section—

    "the initial period" means the period of six months beginning with the day on which subsection (1) above comes into force;

    "local authority" means a council constituted under section 2 of the Local Government etc. (Scotland) Act 1994."

DEFINITIONS

"abandonment": s.30Y(1) of the 1974 Act.
"acting in a compulsory capacity": s.30Y(2) of the 1974 Act.
"initial period": subs. (8).
"local authority": subs. (8).
"mine": s.105(1) of the 1974 Act; s.180(1) of the 1954 Act.
"notice": s.105(1) of the 1974 Act.
"official receiver": s.30Y(2) of the 1974 Act; s.399(1) of the Insolvency Act 1986.
"prescribed": s.105(1) of the 1974 Act.

"regulations": s.105(1) of the 1974 Act.

COMMENCEMENT
This section will be brought into force by a commencement order made under s.125(3).

GENERAL NOTE
This section is the Scottish equivalent of s.91B of the Water Resources Act. See also General Note to s.91B of the 1991 Act above.

Amendments to sections 89 and 161 of the Water Resources Act 1991

60.—(1) In section 89 of the Water Resources Act 1991 (defences) in subsection (3) (person not to be guilty of an offence under section 85 by reason only of permitting water from an abandoned mine to enter controlled waters) after the words "an abandoned mine" there shall be inserted the words "or an abandoned; part of a mine".

(2) After that subsection there shall be inserted—

"(3A) Subsection (3) above shall not apply to the owner or former operator of any mine or part of a mine if the mine or part in question became abandoned after 31st December 1999.

(3B) In determining for the purposes of subsection (3A) above whether a mine or part of a mine became abandoned before, on or after 31st December 1999 in a case where the mine or part has become abandoned on two or more occasions, of which—

(a) at least one falls on or before that date, and

(b) at least one falls after that date,

the mine or part shall be regarded as becoming abandoned after that date (but without prejudice to the operation of subsection (3) above in relation to that mine or part at, or in relation to, any time before the first of those occasions which falls after that date).

(3C) Where, immediately before a part of a mine becomes abandoned, that part is the only part of the mine not falling to be regarded as abandoned for the time being, the abandonment of that part shall not be regarded for the purposes of subsection (3A) or (3B) above as constituting the abandonment of the mine, but only of that part of it."

(3) In section 161 of that Act (anti-pollution works and operations) in subsection (1), after paragraph (b) there shall be inserted the words—

"and, in either case, the Agency shall be entitled to carry out investigations for the purpose of establishing the source of the matter and the identity of the person who has caused or knowingly permitted it to be present in controlled waters or at a place from which it was likely, in the opinion of the Agency, to enter controlled waters."

(4) In subsection (3) of that section (Agency entitled to recover expenses of works or operations from the person responsible for the pollution) for the words "or operations" there shall be substituted the words "operations or investigations".

(5) In subsection (4) of that section (exception for expenses of works or operations in respect of water from an abandoned mine)—

(a) for the words "or operations" there shall be substituted the words "operations or investigations"; and

(b) after the words "an abandoned mine" there shall be inserted the words "or an abandoned part of a mine".

(6) After that subsection there shall be inserted—

"(4A) Subsection (4) above shall not apply to the owner or former operator of any mine or part of a mine if the mine or part in question became abandoned after 31st December 1999.

(4B) Subsections (3B) and (3C) of section 89 above shall apply in relation to subsections (4) and (4A) above as they apply in relation to subsections (3) and (3A) of that section."

(7) In subsection (6) of that section (definitions), after the definition of "controlled waters" there shall be inserted—
"to clear 'expenses' includes costs;".

DEFINITIONS
"abandonment": s.91A(1) of the Water Resources Act 1991.
"controlled waters": s.104 of the Water Resources Act 1991.
"expenses": subs. (7).
"mine": s.91A(2) of the Water Resources Act 1991; s.180 of the Mines and Quarries Act 1954.

COMMENCEMENT
October 12, 1995 insofar as this section confers power on the Secretary of State to make regulations (S.I. 1995 No. 2649). The remainder will be brought into force by a commencement order made under s.125(3) of the 1995 Act.

GENERAL NOTE
This section, which applies only to England and Wales, amends, by subss. (1) and (2), s.89 of the Water Resources Act 1991, removing the defence to a charge of permitting water pollution from an abandoned mine after December 31, 1999 insofar as it is available to the owner and former operator of an abandoned mine; and by subss. (3) to (6) amends s.161 of the Water Resources Act 1991 enabling the Agency to recover the costs of preventive or remedial works undertaken, from the owner or former operator of an abandoned mine who permitted pollution of controlled waters or who permitted pollution to be at a place where it was likely to enter controlled waters after December 31, 1999. The equivalent Scottish legislative changes may be found in Sched. 16, para. 2 which introduces a new s.30J(3) to (6) which removes the defence after December 31, 1999 and in Sched. 22, para. 21(e) which introduces a new s.46(3A) of the 1974 Act which removes the cost recovery exemption from the same date.

Subs. (1)
The defence in s.89(3) of the Water Resources Act 1991 is amended to include permitting water pollution from "an abandoned part of a mine". This will have the effect of widening the ambit of the defence since it is not clear at present whether the current definition of abandoned mine includes part of an abandoned mine. Although this widening of the scope of the defence is only temporary it is clearly a retrograde step as at present, where a mine is only partially abandoned, it could be argued that a prosecution for permitting water pollution from a mine might succeed on the basis that partial abandonment is not currently part of the definition of abandonment. However, it is understandable in the light of the new definition of abandonment in s.58. Although that definition does not apply in Chap. II as is made clear by the words "For the purposes of this Chapter [*i.e.* IIA of the 1991 Act], 'abandonment', in relation to a mine ... includes...", an awkward situation might otherwise have arisen whereby under ss.91A and B an operator might have to give notice that he was discontinuing some pumping operations in his mine which would constitute abandonment in terms of s.91A(1)(a)(i) but could still be prosecuted for permitting water pollution from a mine since the defence in s.89(3) did not originally refer to permitting water pollution from an abandoned part of a mine. The addition of the words "or part of an abandoned mine" to s.89(3) ensures that such a situation could not arise.
Schedule 16, para. 2 makes identical provision for Scotland inserting a new s.30J(3) and (4) into the 1974 Act.

Subs. (2)
The subsection inserts new s.89(3A) to (3C) into the Water Resources Act 1991. Section 89(3) of the Water Resources Act 1991 provides:

"A person shall not be guilty of an offence under section 85 by reason only of his permitting water from an abandoned mine to enter controlled waters."

New s.89(3A) provides for the removal of that defence from December 31, 1999 but it should be noted that the defence will not be withdrawn from every person after that date. It is only withdrawn from the owner or former operator of the abandoned mine. Thus, landowners who never operated an abandoned mine on their property, yet are aware of water pollution issuing from it, will be liable along with the former operator after December 31, 1999.
Concerns regarding the extension of liability to innocent landowners and occupiers were expressed in Parliament (*e.g. per* Lord Stanley of Alderley, *Hansard*, H.L. Vol. 562, cols.

231–232; and cols. 1057–1058). Lord Stanley of Alderley managed to force an amendment at Third Reading in the House of Lords (Vol. 562, cols. 1057–1058) which limited the scope of persons from whom the defence is withdrawn from December 31, 1999. As originally drafted the clause had provided for the defence being withdrawn from every person. However, Lord Stanley's amendment which was subsequently accepted by the Government provides protection for an innocent landowner or occupier who is aware of polluted water from an abandoned mine located on someone else's land coming on to his land and entering controlled waters. Formerly the Government's intention had been to remove the defence from such innocent occupiers.

However, the Government were not prepared to accept an amendment preserving the defence for innocent landowners on whose land an abandoned mine was actually situated:

> "An offence would be committed only if a person had caused or knowingly permitted the pollution of controlled waters. This is a strong test and there would be no liability for truly innocent landowners. To be liable a landowner would have to know about the discharge and it would have to be within his or her power to do something to prevent it. ... The knowledge of an ability to prevent the pollution occurring is required to satisfy "knowingly permitted". That would be a difficult test to meet where there was pollution of an aquifer deep underground. The owner of the surface land would be unlikely to know about it or be able to prevent such pollution" (*per* Viscount Ullswater, *Hansard*, H.L. Vol. 562, cols. 237–238).

Furthermore, given that the Government's intention is to bring into force the notification of abandonment provisions "immediately", the Agency will be aware of who the operator is and should be equipped with the appropriate information to tackle any possible pollution problems (*per* Viscount Ullswater, *Hansard*, H.L. Vol. 562, col. 1060). In the light of such assurances it seems very unlikely that the Agency would wish to proceed against an innocent landowner since it should have details of the former operator.

The provisions in s.89(3B) and (3C) are designed to ensure that mines or parts of mines abandoned before the end of 1999, and so benefiting from the existing statutory protections, will not lose those protections if another part of the mine or an adjoining mine, possibly under separate ownership, is abandoned after that date (Mr Robert Atkins, Standing Committee B, May 23, 1995, col. 412).

The new s.89(3B) provides assistance in determining whether a mine which has undergone a number of abandonments partial or otherwise was abandoned before, on or after December 31, 1999. Thus, a mine or part of a mine is considered to have been abandoned after December 31, 1999 where it has been abandoned on two or more occasions and at least one of those occasions falls on or before that date and at least one after that date. However, the wording in brackets ensures that the statutory defence continues to apply up to the first abandonment which occurs after December 31, 1999. The implication of this is that although a mine is abandoned several times and at least one of those occasions occurs before December 31, 1999 and another after that date, and although the mine will be regarded as being abandoned after that date, nonetheless the defence will be available in relation to any potential criminal liability which arose as a result of any abandonment of the mine before December 31, 1999.

The new s.89(3C) covers the type of situation where a mine has been largely abandoned and the final part of the mine is about to be abandoned. It provides that the abandonment of that final part of the mine must not be regarded for the purposes of subss. (3A) and (3B) as the abandonment of the whole mine but only that final part which is actually abandoned. This provision is presumably designed to limit the potential liability of an operator who has abandoned most parts of a mine by December 31, 1999 and abandons the final part of the mine after that date. Although being the final abandonment of the mine, that abandonment will only be regarded as the abandonment of that part of the mine and hence liability will only arise in respect of water pollution which is permitted from that abandonment. In practice it may be extremely difficult to distinguish between water pollution which is being permitted from that final part of the abandoned mine and that being permitted from other parts of the mine which were abandoned earlier.

Schedule 16, para. 2 makes identical provision for Scotland inserting a new s.30J(5)–(6) of the 1974 Act (see also General Note to Sched. 16 below).

Subss. (3) and (4)

Subsection (3) amends s.161(1) of the Water Resources Act 1991 in order to provide the Agency with a valuable new power to carry out investigations to ascertain the source of the polluting matter and the identity of the person who caused or knowingly permitted it to be present in controlled waters or to reach a place from which it was likely, to enter controlled waters. Since the Agency is given this power in addition to its power to undertake preventive or remedial anti-pollution works or operations, it is also given the power by subs. (4), which amends s.161(3) of the 1991 Act, to recover expenses from the person responsible for the pollution for investigations as well as the anti-pollution works or operations.

Schedule 22, para. 21(b) and (c) makes equivalent provision for Scotland by inserting a new s.46(1A) into the 1974 Act and making the appropriate amendment to s.46(2) of the 1974 Act.

Subs. (5)

The exception for recovery of expenses for preventive or remedial anti-pollution works or operations in relation to permitting water pollution from abandoned mines is extended to include (a) investigations given the amendments in subss. (3) and (4), and (b) an abandoned part of a mine in addition to an abandoned mine in the light of the new definition of abandonment which includes partial abandonment (see General Note to s.91A of the 1991 Act as inserted by s.58, above).

Schedule 22, para. 21(d) makes equivalent provision for Scotland by making the appropriate amendments to the 1974 Act, s.46(3)(b).

Subs. (6)

This subsection, which inserts a new s.161(4A) and (4B) to the Water Resources Act 1991 removes the expense recovery exception after December 31, 1999. It also applies the provisions in s.89(3B) and (3C) to the removal of the cost recovery exemption in s.161(4A) and (4B) in the same way as they apply to the withdrawal of the defence in s.89(3) and (3A) of the 1991 Act.

Schedule 22, para. 21(e) makes equivalent provision for Scotland by inserting new s.46(3A) and (3B) into the 1974 Act (see also the General Note to Sched. 22, para. 21).

Subs. (7)

This subsection inserts a definition of expenses into s.161(6) of the Water Resources Act 1991 to clarify that expenses includes costs.

PART III

NATIONAL PARKS

[*Not reproduced here*]

PART IV

AIR QUALITY

GENERAL NOTE

Part IV of the Act contains new provisions aimed at addressing the seemingly intractable problems of national and local air quality. Attention has focused sharply in recent years on poor air quality in many urban areas, with the attendant loss of amenity and potentially serious health implications. By way of example, it was reported in *The Times* on June 23, 1994, that an incident of traffic which generated winter smog in London over four days in December 1991, was estimated to have led to about 155 deaths. Nitrogen dioxide and black smoke reached particularly high levels over that period. In January 1992, it was reported that the Government was threatened with EC action in relation to sulphur dioxide and particulate levels in Sunderland, following a complaint by a local resident which led to the issue of a reasoned opinion by the European Commission: *The Surveyor*, January 23, 1992.

Whereas the problem which prompted the Clean Air Act of 1956 (now consolidated in the Clean Air Act 1993) was that of smoke, dust and grit from domestic hearths and industrial furnaces, the most widely perceived cause of urban air quality problems in the 1990s is that of vehicle emissions, a problem recognised only in the 1970s, and then regarded as an area where expenditure on control was unlikely to be cost effective (see Eric Ashby and Mary Anderson, *The Politics of Clean Air* (Clarendon Press, Oxford, 1981, p.143)). The most recent problem encountered is that of photochemical smog arising from processes such as the oxidation of the nitrous oxides arising from vehicle engine combustion, resulting in increases in ozone levels and the formation of potentially harmful compounds. Somewhat paradoxically, the cleaner air resulting from the Clean Air legislation has contributed to this problem, since sunlight provides suitable conditions for photo-oxidation processes: see Peter Brimblecombe, *The Big Smoke* (Routledge, London, 1988).

It remains to be seen whether the provisions of Part IV will be as effective in improving air quality as the 1956 Act.

Policy Background

A considerable amount of factual material on the current problems of air quality in Britain can be found in two reports of House of Commons Committees. In October 1994 the Commons Transport Committee published its report on *Transport-related Air Pollution in London* (Session 1993–94, Sixth Report, H.C. 506—I and II). The Committee was persuaded by the evidence that the quality of air in London was deteriorating and that, in relation to the possible link between air pollution and ill-health, a precautionary approach was justified. The Commons Environment Committee reported in April 1995 on *Volatile Organic Compounds* (Session 1994–5, First Report, H.C.39—I and II). This report called for further work in monitoring VOCs and further research into their possible health impacts. Again, a precautionary approach was supported.

Another extremely important review of the problems of air quality caused by vehicle emissions is provided by the Eighteenth Report of the Royal Commission on Environment Pollution, *Transport and the Environment*, published in October 1994 (Cm.2674). The Report unequivocally stated that emissions from road vehicles are the major source of outdoor exposure to air pollution and proposed two specific targets:

1. to achieve full compliance by the year 2005 with World Health Organisation guidelines for transport-related pollutants; and
2. to establish in appropriate areas by 2005 local air quality standards based on the critical levels required to protect sensitive eco-systems.

One of the recommendations of the Commission was that local authorities be given new duties to assess ambient air quality, the sources of air pollution in their area, and the risk of pollutant concentrations exceeding threshold levels to be set by the Government; they should also have the duty to draw up and implement an air quality management plan, if necessary to prevent any thresholds from being breached (para. 14.23). As will be seen, these proposals are very similar to the system created by Part IV of the Act. The Commission recommended that the Government should set thresholds for the major pollutants at levels enabling action to be taken to prevent air quality from deteriorating to a dangerous level. Such pollutants include carbon monoxide, nitrogen dioxide and $PM10$, *i.e.* particles with a diameter of less than $10\mu m$ (10 millionths of a metre).

The Government's progress towards legislation on air quality should be seen against this background. Significant developments include the following:–

1. The publication in November 1992 of a draft "UK VOC Strategy Document", detailing the Government's proposed strategy for reducing VOC emissions by 30 per cent by 1999, so as to meet the United Kingdom's obligations under the UNECE protocol on VOC emissions signed in 1991.
2. The publication in November 1993 of proposals entitled *The Future of Air Quality Monitoring Networks in the UK*, setting out ways in which local and national monitoring can be encouraged by better harmonisation and co-ordination.
3. In January 1994 the Government published a comprehensive paper setting out its strategy for reducing emissions of VOCs and consequent formation of ground-level ozone.
4. The announcement by the Secretary of State for the Environment, on February 23, 1994, of new action for the improvement of local air quality, comprising three main elements: development of a new set of health related air quality standards, better management of air quality at local level, and a review of the scope for tightening vehicle emission limits from the year 2000.
5. This announcement was followed by a discussion paper, *Improving Air Quality*, in April 1994. This paper stressed the Government's belief that progress must be based on an effects-based approach, complemented by source-based controls, and that traditional regulation and control methods were unlikely to be sufficient of themselves. Sections III–V of the paper dealt with the issue of air quality standards and local air quality management. This contemplated a framework based on a strategic approach dealing with all sources and deploying a variety of measures in a concerted way.
6. The series of reports by the Government's independent Expert Panel on Air Quality Standards (EPAQS) recommending the establishment of air quality standards for a range of pollutants in the UK. To date there have been six EPAQS reports, on benzene (February 1994), ozone (May 1994), 1, 3-butadiene (December 1994), carbon monoxide (December 1994), sulphur dioxide (September 1995) and particles (November 1995: in the same month the Government published a combined response (entitled *Health Effects of Particles*) to the particles report and to a separate report, *Non-Biological Particles and Health*, by the Committee on the Medical Effects of Air Pollutants).
7. The announcement in January 1995 of a wide package of proposals intended to improve air quality in towns and cities: *Improving Air Quality: Meeting the Challenge*. This expanded upon the 1994 consultation paper in identifying three main areas:

namely a new framework of national air quality standards and targets, local air quality management areas, and air pollution and transport.
8. New measures to reduce urban air pollution from vehicles were announced by the Department of Transport in February 1995: Press Release 53. These include the expediting of tougher MOT standards and stricter enforcement against drivers and vehicle operators.
9. During the Lords Committee Stage of the Environment Bill, the Minister, Viscount Ullswater, announced in response to an amendment proposing the insertion of a clause on air quality management, that the Government would bring forward their own proposals at the Commons stage: *Hansard* H.L. Vol. 561, col. 318.

Overview of the Legislation
The scheme of Part IV may be summarised as follows:
1. The Secretary of State is required to prepare and publish a statement, referred to as the national air quality strategy, and containing policies with respect to the assessment or management of the quality of air: s.80.
2. The Environment Agency/SEPA must have regard to the national air quality strategy in discharging its own pollution control functions: s.81. For SEPA these functions include the role of enforcing authority under the air pollution control regime, exercised in England and Wales by local authorities, and the reserve power to establish smoke control areas under s.19 of the Clean Air Act 1993 which is held by the Secretary of State in England and Wales.
3. Wide powers to make regulations are conferred by s.87, which may include prescribing air quality standards, prescribing objectives for restricting levels of particular substances in air, conferring new powers and duties on local authorities, prohibiting or restricting activities or the access of vehicles to prescribed areas, and prescribing measures to be taken by local authorities or others in ensuring the attainment of air quality standards or objectives.
4. Every local authority (at district level) is under a duty to cause reviews to be conducted of current and likely future air quality within its area: s.82. The review should include an assessment of whether air quality standards and objectives are being or are likely to be achieved; the authority should also identify any parts of its areas where standards are objectives are not likely to be achieved within the relevant period.
5. Areas identified in this way are to be designated by the local authority as air quality management areas: s.83. Where an order designating such an area comes into force a further assessment must be made of air quality in the area and the respects in which the relevant standards or objectives are not likely to be achieved. This must be followed by a written report and action plan, with a timescale, for the exercise by the authority of any powers exercisable by it, to achieve the relevant objectives and standards: s.84. Here it should be noted that Scottish local authorities have fewer functions exercisable in this regard than their counterparts in England and Wales. This is a consequence of the transfer to SEPA by s.21(1)(h) of the Act of the role as enforcing authority in relation to the air pollution control regime, a role retained by local authorities in England and Wales.
6. Local authorities are placed under no express statutory duty to implement such an action plan. However, the Secretary of State in England and Wales and SEPA in Scotland have wide reserve powers in the event of default or non-attainment by local authorities: s.85. The Secretary of State may also issue guidance to local authorities: s.88.
7. County councils in England may make recommendations and proposals to district councils with respect to reviews, assessments and action plans, and in relation to the exercise by the county council of powers available to it: s.86. A procedure for reference to the Secretary of State is provided to resolve any disagreement between county and district as to the contents of proposed action plans: s.84(5).
8. Sched. 11 contains various supplementary provisions relating to consultation by local authorities in carrying out their functions, joint exercise of local authority functions, exchange of information with county councils, public access to information about air quality, and the creation of fixed penalty offences by regulations made under Part IV.

National air quality strategy

80.—(1) The Secretary of State shall as soon as possible prepare and publish a statement (in this Part referred to as "the strategy") containing policies with respect to the assessment or management of the quality of air.

(2) The strategy may also contain policies for implementing—
  (a) obligations of the United Kingdom under the Community Treaties, or
  (b) international agreements to which the United Kingdom is for the time being a party,
so far as relating to the quality of air.

(3) The strategy shall consist of or include—
  (a) a statement which relates to the whole of Great Britain; or
  (b) two or more statements which between them relate to every part of Great Britain.

(4) The Secretary of State—
  (a) shall keep under review his policies with respect to the quality of air; and
  (b) may from time to time modify the strategy.

(5) Without prejudice to the generality of what may be included in the strategy, the strategy must include statements with respect to—
  (a) standards relating to the quality of air;
  (b) objectives for the restriction of the levels at which particular substances are present in the air; and
  (c) measures which are to be taken by local authorities and other persons for the purpose of achieving those objectives.

(6) In preparing the strategy or any modification of it, the Secretary of State shall consult—
  (a) the appropriate new Agency;
  (b) such bodies or persons appearing to him to be representative of the interests of local government as he may consider appropriate;
  (c) such bodies or persons appearing to him to be representative of the interests of industry as he may consider appropriate; and
  (d) such other bodies or persons as he may consider appropriate.

(7) Before publishing the strategy or any modification of it, the Secretary of State—
  (a) shall publish a draft of the proposed strategy or modification, together with notice of a date before which, and an address at which, representations may be made to him concerning the draft so published; and
  (b) shall take into account any such representations which are duly made and not withdrawn.

DEFINITIONS
"the appropriate new Agency": s.91(1).
"modification": s.124(1).
"notice": s.124(1).
"the strategy": subs. (1).

COMMENCEMENT
February 1, 1996 (S.I. 1996 No. 186).

GENERAL NOTE
This section requires the preparation of a national air quality strategy taking the form of a statement or statements of policies. There may be a single statement relating to the whole of Great Britain, or a number of statements giving such coverage (subs. (3)).

Content of Strategy
As a minimum, the strategy must include statements with respect to the three matters set out at subs. (5), which equate to a number of the matters which may be dealt with by regulations made under s.87. The strategy may also contain policies for implementing obligations of the UK under EC law, or under international agreements, Relevant directives and agreements imposing such

obligations include the following (references are to paragraph numbers in *The Encyclopedia of Environmental Law*, Sweet & Maxwell):

International Agreements
    1985 Vienna Convention for Protection of the Ozone Layer (B17–001)
    1987 Montreal Protocol on Substances that Deplete the Ozone Layer (B17–026)

E.C. Measures
    1980 Directive on air quality limit values and guide values for sulphur dioxide and suspended particulates 80/779/EEC (C80/5–001)
    1982 Directive on limit value for lead in air 82/884/EEC (C82/4–001)
    1985 Directive on air quality standards for nitrogen dioxide 82/203/EEC (C85/1–001)
    1991 Regulation on substances that deplete the ozone layer 91/594/EEC (C91/6–001)
    1992 Directive on air pollution by ozone 92/72/EEC (C91/1b–001)
    1994 Proposed directive on ambient air quality assessment and management COM(94)109 final, O.J. No. C216/4, 6.8.94, on which a Common Position was reached by the Council of Environment Ministers in June 1995.
    1994 Proposed Council decision establishing a reciprocal exchange of information and data from networks and individual stations measuring ambient air pollution within the Member States COM (94) 345 Final, O.J. No. C281/9, 7.10.94, on which a Common Position was agreed by the Council of Environment Ministers in October 1995.

Implementation of Strategy
The strategy will be implemented by:
    (a) regulations made under s.87;
    (b) guidance issued by the Secretary of State under s.88;
    (c) the exercise of pollution control functions by the Agency/SEPA (s.81); and
    (d) the powers and duties conferred on local authorities by ss.82–84.

Functions of the new Agencies

81.—(1) In discharging its pollution control functions, each new Agency shall have regard to the strategy.

(2) In this section "pollution control functions", in relation to a new Agency, means—
    (a) in the case of the Agency, the functions conferred on it by or under the enactments specified in section 5(5) above; or
    (b) in the case of SEPA, the functions conferred on it by or under the enactments specified in section 33(5) above.

DEFINITIONS
    "the Agency": s.124(1).
    "air quality objectives": s.91(1).
    "air quality standards": s.91(1).
    "functions": s.124(1).
    "local authority": s.91(1).
    "pollution control functions": subs. (2).
    "the relevant period": s.91(1).
    "SEPA": s.124(1).

COMMENCEMENT
This section comes into force on a day to be appointed (s.125(3)).

GENERAL NOTE
This section requires the Agency and SEPA to have regard to the national air quality strategy in the exercise of their pollution control functions, which are different as between England and Wales and Scotland. Those functions have wider application than air quality, relating as they do to other environmental media and to waste disposal and recovery. The most obvious functions relating to air are those under Part I of the Environmental Protection Act 1990 (integrated pollution control). In relation to Scotland, those powers include the functions exercised by local authorities in relation to air pollution control under Part I of the 1990 Act: see note to s.21.

It may also be noted that an amendment by Sched. 22, para. 36 of this Act to the Road Traffic Regulation Act 1984 requires local authorities to have regard to the national air quality strategy, so far as practicable, in exercising their functions under the 1984 Act.

Local authority reviews

82.—(1) Every local authority shall from time to time cause a review to be conducted of the quality for the time being, and the likely future quality within the relevant period, of air within the authority's area.

(2) Where a local authority causes a review under subsection (1) above to be conducted, it shall also cause an assessment to be made of whether air quality standards and objectives are being achieved, or are likely to be achieved within the relevant period, within the authority's area.

(3) If, on an assessment under subsection (2) above, it appears that any air quality standards or objectives are not being achieved, or are not likely within the relevant period to be achieved, within the local authority's area, the local authority shall identify any parts of its area in which it appears that those standards or objectives are not likely to be achieved within the relevant period.

DEFINITIONS
  "air quality objectives": s.91(1).
  "air quality standards": s.91(1).
  "local authority": s.91(1).
  "the relevant period": s.91(1).

COMMENCEMENT
This section comes into force on a day to be appointed (s.125(3)).

GENERAL NOTE
This section requires local authorities to carry out reviews of the quality of air within their area, and its likely future quality within the relevant period (to be prescribed). The review should relate to any air quality standards or objectives prescribed by regulations, in that the authority should assess whether such standards or objectives are being achieved, or are likely to be achieved within the relevant period. This in turn leads to the identification of those areas where this is not the case (subs. (3)) which in its turn will trigger the obligation under s.83 to designate air quality management areas.

  The Government's consultation paper, *Air Quality: Meeting the Challenge* suggests that the new duty to review air quality ought not to be more onerous than the appraisal required in connection with development planning under Planning Policy Guidance Note 12: nonetheless it should be carried out regularly and systematically. The Government intends to expand the national database of air quality information, and to improve the arrangements for local authority access to it. It is also the Government's intention to develop guidance on when central data should be supplemented by further work, and to develop good practice guidance.

County Councils
In England county councils may make recommendations to their districts with respect to the review and assessment, and such recommendations must be taken into account: s.86(2).

Procedural Issues
Schedule 11 contains a number of relevant requirements relating to air quality reviews. These include consultation (para. 1) exchange of information with county councils (para. 2), joint exercise of functions with other local authorities (para. 3), and public access to the results (para. 4).

Designation of air quality management areas

83.—(1) Where, as a result of an air quality review, it appears that any air quality standards or objectives are not being achieved, or are not likely within the relevant period to be achieved, within the area of a local authority, the local authority shall by order designate as an air quality management area (in this Part referred to as a "designated area") any part of its area in which it appears that those standards or objectives are not being achieved, or are not likely to be achieved within the relevant period.

(2) An order under this section may, as a result of a subsequent air quality review,—

(a) be varied by a subsequent order; or

(b) be revoked by such an order, if it appears on that subsequent air quality review that the air quality standards and objectives are being achieved, and are likely throughout the relevant period to be achieved, within the designated area.

DEFINITIONS
"air quality objectives": s.91(1).
"air quality review": s.91(1).
"air quality standards": s.91(1).
"designated area": subs. (1).
"local authority": s.91(1).
"the relevant period": s.91(1).

COMMENCEMENT
This section comes into force on a day to be appointed (s.125(3)).

GENERAL NOTE
This section follows logically from s.82 and requires local authorities to make orders designating as "air quality management areas" those areas identified on review where air quality standards or objectives are not, and are not likely to be, complied with. The consequence of such designation is that the local authority then falls under further duties by virtue of s.84. If the problems of non-compliance are successfully addressed, then the order may be revoked under s.83(2)(b), or may be varied under s.83(2)(a).

Procedure
The section should be read in conjunction with the requirements of Sched. 11, *e.g.* as to consultation. Provision may also be made in regulations under s.87 as to designation orders under s.83, or in circumstances falling outside s.83: s.87(2)(f)–(h).

Smoke Control Areas
In *Air Quality: Meeting the Challenge* the Government indicated that apart from Northern Ireland, where around 80 per cent of homes rely on coal for heating, there were no plans to implement any further controls on domestic fuels. Existing Smoke Control Areas under the Clean Air Act will remain in force, but the procedure for declaring any further Smoke Control Areas will be brought within the general framework of Part IV of the Act.

Duties of local authorities in relation to designated areas

84.—(1) Where an order under section 83 above comes into operation, the local authority which made the order shall, for the purpose of supplementing such information as it has in relation to the designated area in question, cause an assessment to be made of—

(a) the quality for the time being, and the likely future quality within the relevant period, of air within the designated area to which the order relates; and

(b) the respects (if any) in which it appears that air quality standards or objectives are not being achieved, or are not likely within the relevant period to be achieved, within that designated area.

(2) A local authority which is required by subsection (1) above to cause an assessment to be made shall also be under a duty—

(a) to prepare, before the expiration of the period of twelve months beginning with the coming into operation of the order mentioned in that subsection, a report of the results of that assessment; and

(b) to prepare, in accordance with the following provisions of this Part, a written plan (in this Part referred to as an "action plan") for the exercise by the authority, in pursuit of the achievement of air quality standards and objectives in the designated area, of any powers exercisable by the authority.

(3) An action plan shall include a statement of the time or times by or within which the local authority in question proposes to implement each of the proposed measures comprised in the plan.

(4) A local authority may from time to time revise an action plan.

(5) This subsection applies in any case where the local authority preparing an action plan or a revision of an action plan is the council of a district in England which is comprised in an area for which there is a county council; and if, in a case where this subsection applies, the county council disagrees with the authority about the contents of the proposed action plan or revision of the action plan—

    (a) either of them may refer the matter to the Secretary of State;

    (b) on any such reference the Secretary of State may confirm the authority's proposed action plan or revision of the action plan, with or without modifications (whether or not proposed by the county council) or reject it and, if he rejects it, he may also exercise any powers of his under section 85 below; and

    (c) the authority shall not finally determine the content of the action plan, or the revision of the action plan, except in accordance with his decision on the reference or in pursuance of directions under section 85 below.

DEFINITIONS

"action plan": subs. (2).
"air quality objectives": s.91(1).
"air quality standards": s.91(1).
"designated area": s.83(1).
"local authority": s.91(1).
"modifications": s.124(1).
"the relevant period": s.91(1).

COMMENCEMENT

This section comes into force on a day to be appointed (s.125(3)).

GENERAL NOTE

This section imposes various duties on local authorities in relation to air quality management areas designated by order under s.83. The requirements are essentially:

    (1) to supplement existing information by an assessment of current and likely future air quality within the area and the respects in which it appears that air quality standards or objectives are not being met (subs. (1));

    (2) to prepare, within 12 months of the designating order coming into effect, a report of the results of that assessment (subs. (2)(a)); and

    (3) to prepare an action plan (subs. (2)(b)) as to which, see below.

The Government's intention is that local authorities will be able to bid for central funding to support the preparation of the assessment: *Improving Air Quality: Meeting the Challenge*, p.18. The system is to be phased in, following consultation with local authority associations and taking account of local government reorganisation; however, it is intended that reviews should be completed within two years.

Action Plans

The action plan must be in writing, and relates to the use of any powers exercisable by the authority in pursuit of achieving air quality standards and objectives: subs. (2)(b). It must include a timetable by which the measures referred to in the plan are proposed to be completed: subs. (3).

    The reference is to "any" powers exercisable; the authority must therefore consider all powers available to it, in terms of the possible contribution their exercise may make to fulfilment of the plan. Such powers will include those relating to air pollution control under Part I of the Environmental Protection Act 1990 (except in Scotland where these powers are transferred to SEPA), statutory nuisance powers, (smoke control powers under the Clean Air Act 1993), land-use planning powers under the Town and Country Planning Act 1990, or, in Scotland, under the Town and Country Planning (Scotland) Act 1972, and road traffic regulation powers. The Government's strategy document, *Improving Air Quality: Meeting the Challenge*, indicates that whilst traffic is the greatest single source of many pollutants, other sources (*e.g.* domestic and industrial) should not be overlooked. Part V of that paper is devoted exclusively to an action programme for air pollution and transport.

Local authorities are placed under no statutory duty to implement action plans, although clearly they would be under considerable political pressure to do so and the reserve powers exercisable under s.85 are capable of placing them under such a duty.

County Councils
Under Sched. 11, para. 2, English county and district councils are to cooperate in sharing relevant information. In the course of preparation of the action plan, the county council (if any) must submit to the district its proposals for the exercise of any powers exercisable by the county council, *e.g.* highway powers: ss. 86(3) and (4). Such proposals must then be included in the action plan: s.86(5). Where the County and district disagree about the content of the action plan, either may refer the issue to the Secretary of State for determination under s.85(5).

Reserve powers of the Secretary of State or SEPA

85.—(1) In this section, "the appropriate authority" means—
    (a) in relation to England and Wales, the Secretary of State; and
    (b) in relation to Scotland, SEPA acting with the approval of the Secretary of State.
(2) The appropriate authority may conduct or make, or cause to be conducted or made,—
    (a) a review of the quality for the time being, and the likely future quality within the relevant period, of air within the area of any local authority;
    (b) an assessment of whether air quality standards and objectives are being achieved, or are likely to be achieved within the relevant period, within the area of a local authority;
    (c) an identification of any parts of the area of a local authority in which it appears that those standards or objectives are not likely to be achieved within the relevant period; or
    (d) an assessment of the respects (if any) in which it appears that air quality standards or objectives are not being achieved, or are not likely within the relevant period to be achieved, within the area of a local authority or within a designated area.
(3) If it appears to the appropriate authority—
    (a) that air quality standards or objectives are not being achieved, or are not likely within the relevant period to be achieved, within the area of a local authority,
    (b) that a local authority has failed to discharge any duty imposed on it under or by virtue of this Part,
    (c) that the actions, or proposed actions, of a local authority in purported compliance with the provisions of this Part are inappropriate in all the circumstances of the case, or
    (d) that developments in science or technology, or material changes in circumstances, have rendered inappropriate the actions or proposed actions of a local authority in pursuance of this Part,
the appropriate authority may give directions to the local authority requiring it to take such steps as may be specified in the directions.
(4) Without prejudice to the generality of subsection (3) above, directions under that subsection may, in particular, require a local authority—
    (a) to cause an air quality review to be conducted under section 82 above in accordance with the directions;
    (b) to cause an air quality review under section 82 above to be conducted afresh, whether in whole or in part, or to be so conducted with such differences as may be specified or described in the directions;

(c) to make an order under section 83 above designating as an air quality management area an area specified in, or determined in accordance with, the directions;

(d) to revoke, or modify in accordance with the directions, any order under that section;

(e) to prepare in accordance with the directions an action plan for a designated area;

(f) to modify, in accordance with the directions, any action plan prepared by the authority; or

(g) to implement, in accordance with the directions, any measures in an action plan.

(5) The Secretary of State shall also have power to give directions to local authorities requiring them to take such steps specified in the directions as he considers appropriate for the implementation of—

(a) any obligations of the United Kingdom under the Community Treaties, or

(b) any international agreement to which the United Kingdom is for the time being a party,

so far as relating to the quality of air.

(6) Any direction given under this section shall be published in such manner as the body or person giving it considers appropriate for the purpose of bringing the matters to which it relates to the attention of persons likely to be affected by them; and—

(a) copies of the direction shall be made available to the public; and

(b) notice shall be given—

(i) in the case of a direction given to a local authority in England and Wales, in the London Gazette, or

(ii) in the case of a direction given to a local authority in Scotland, in the Edinburgh Gazette,

of the giving of the direction and of where a copy of the direction may be obtained.

(7) It is the duty of a local authority to comply with any direction given to it under or by virtue of this Part.

DEFINITIONS
"action plan": s.84(2).
"air quality objectives": s.91(1).
"air quality review": s.91(1).
"air quality standards": s.91(1).
"the appropriate authority": subs. (1).
"designated area": s.83(1).
"local authority" s.91(1).
"modify": s.124(1).
"notice": s.124(1).
"the relevant period": s.91(1).
"SEPA": s.124(1).

COMMENCEMENT
This section comes into force on a day to be appointed (s.125(3)).

GENERAL NOTE
This section contains wide reserve powers exercisable by the Secretary of State in England and Wales or, in Scotland, by SEPA with the approval of the Secretary of State. The reserve powers include the carrying out of reviews and assessments of air quality (subs.(2)) and the giving of directions to local authorities in cases of failure to achieve air quality standards or objectives (subs. (3)(a)), default or inappropriate actions by local authorities (subs. (3)(b) and (c)), changes in science or technology or in general circumstances which render the authority's actions inappropriate (subs. (3)(d)), or to comply with E.C. or international obligations (subs.

(5)). The local authority is under a duty to comply with directions: subs. (7). Perhaps most importantly, the direction may require the local authority to implement any measures in an action plan: subs. (4)(g). Power to give directions to English county councils is contained in subs. 86(6)–(10).

SEPA would appear to have been given these reserve powers for the same reason as was given for the allocation to it of responsibility to draw up the Scottish national waste strategy (see general note to s.92). The explanation there was that SEPA, unlike the Scottish Office, has the specialist staff required to carry out the function.

Functions of county councils for areas for which there are district councils

86.—(1) This section applies in any case where a district in England for which there is a district council is comprised in an area for which there is a county council; and in this paragraph—
  (a) any reference to the county council is a reference to the council of that area; and
  (b) any reference to a district council is a reference to the council of a district comprised in that area.

(2) The county council may make recommendations to a district council with respect to the carrying out of—
  (a) any particular air quality review,
  (b) any particular assessment under section 82 or 84 above, or
  (c) the preparation of any particular action plan or revision of an action plan,
and the district council shall take into account any such recommendations.

(3) Where a district council is preparing an action plan, the county council shall, within the relevant period, submit to the district council proposals for the exercise (so far as relating to the designated area) by the county council, in pursuit of the achievement of air quality standards and objectives, of any powers exercisable by the county council.

(4) Where the county council submits proposals to a district council in pursuance of subsection (3) above, it shall also submit a statement of the time or times by or within which it proposes to implement each of the proposals.

(5) An action plan shall include a statement of—
  (a) any proposals submitted pursuant to subsection (3) above; and
  (b) any time or times set out in the statement submitted pursuant to subsection (4) above.

(6) If it appears to the Secretary of State—
  (a) that air quality standards or objectives are not being achieved, or are not likely within the relevant period to be achieved, within the area of a district council,
  (b) that the county council has failed to discharge any duty imposed on it under or by virtue of this Part,
  (c) that the actions, or proposed actions, of the county council in purported compliance with the provisions of this Part are inappropriate in all the circumstances of the case, or
  (d) that developments in science or technology, or material changes in circumstances, have rendered inappropriate the actions or proposed actions of the county council in pursuance of this Part,
the Secretary of State may give directions to the county council requiring it to take such steps as may be specified in the directions.

(7) Without prejudice to the generality of subsection (6) above, directions under that subsection may, in particular, require the county council—
  (a) to submit, in accordance with the directions, proposals pursuant to subsection (3) above or a statement pursuant to subsection (4) above;

(b) to modify, in accordance with the directions, any proposals or statement submitted by the county council pursuant to subsection (3) or (4) above;

(c) to submit any proposals or statement so modified to the district council in question pursuant to subsection (3) or (4) above; or

(d) to implement, in accordance with the directions, any measures included in an action plan.

(8) The Secretary of State shall also have power to give directions to county councils for areas for which there are district councils requiring them to take such steps specified in the directions as he considers appropriate for the implementation of—

(a) any obligations of the United Kingdom under the Community Treaties, or

(b) any international agreement to which the United Kingdom is for the time being a party,

so far as relating to the quality of air.

(9) Any direction given under this section shall be published in such manner as the Secretary of State considers appropriate for the purpose of bringing the matters to which it relates to the attention of persons likely to be affected by them; and—

(a) copies of the direction shall be made available to the public; and

(b) notice of the giving of the direction, and of where a copy of the direction may be obtained, shall be given in the London Gazette.

(10) It is the duty of a county council for an area for which there are district councils to comply with any direction given to it under or by virtue of this Part.

DEFINITIONS
"action plan": s.84(2).
"air quality objectives": s.91(1).
"air quality review": s.91(1).
"air quality standards": s.91(1).
"designated area": s.83(1).
"notice": s.124(1).
"the relevant period": s.91(1).

COMMENCEMENT
This section comes into force on a day to be appointed (s.125(3)).

GENERAL NOTE
This section applies in those areas of England where there are county councils. It allows counties to make recommendations to districts with regard to air quality reviews, assessments and action plans, and such recommendations are to be taken into account: subs. (2).

Subsections (3)–(5) provide a mechanism by which the proposed exercise of county council powers is to be incorporated into action plans, and subss. (6)–(10) provide a means to secure the cooperation and action of county councils by directions given by the Secretary of State.

Regulations for the purposes of Part IV

87.—(1) Regulations may make provision—

(a) for, or in connection with, implementing the strategy;

(b) for, or in connection with, implementing—

(i) obligations of the United Kingdom under the Community Treaties, or

(ii) international agreements to which the United Kingdom is for the time being a party,

so far as relating to the quality of air; or

(c) otherwise with respect to the assessment or management of the quality of air.

(2) Without prejudice to the generality of subsection (1) above, regulations under that subsection may make provision—

    (a) prescribing standards relating to the quality of air;

    (b) prescribing objectives for the restriction of the levels at which particular substances are present in the air;

    (c) conferring powers or imposing duties on local authorities;

    (d) for or in connection with—

        (i) authorising local authorities (whether by agreements or otherwise) to exercise any functions of a Minister of the Crown on his behalf;

        (ii) directing that functions of a Minister of the Crown shall be exercisable concurrently with local authorities; or

        (iii) transferring functions of a Minister of the Crown to local authorities;

    (e) prohibiting or restricting, or for or in connection with prohibiting or restricting,—

        (i) the carrying on of prescribed activities, or

        (ii) the access of prescribed vehicles or mobile equipment to prescribed areas,

    whether generally or in prescribed circumstances;

    (f) for or in connection with the designation of air quality management areas by orders made by local authorities in such cases or circumstances not falling within section 83 above as may be prescribed;

    (g) for the application, with or without modifications, of any provisions of this Part in relation to areas designated by virtue of paragraph (f) above or in relation to orders made by virtue of that paragraph;

    (h) with respect to—

        (i) air quality reviews;

        (ii) assessments under this Part;

        (iii) orders designating air quality management areas; or

        (iv) action plans;

    (j) prescribing measures which are to be adopted by local authorities (whether in action plans or otherwise) or other persons in pursuance of the achievement of air quality standards or objectives;

    (k) for or in connection with the communication to the public of information relating to quality for the time being, or likely future quality, of the air;

    (l) for or in connection with the obtaining by local authorities from any person of information which is reasonably necessary for the discharge of functions conferred or imposed on them under or by virtue of this Part;

    (m) for or in connection with the recovery by a local authority from prescribed persons in prescribed circumstances, and in such manner as may be prescribed, of costs incurred by the authority in discharging functions conferred or imposed on the authority under or by virtue of this Part;

    (n) for a person who contravenes, or fails to comply with, any prescribed provision of the regulations to be guilty of an offence and liable on summary conviction to a fine not exceeding level 5 on the standard scale or such lower level on that scale as may be prescribed in relation to the offence;

    (o) for or in connection with arrangements under which a person may discharge any liability to conviction for a prescribed offence by payment of a penalty of a prescribed amount;

    (p) for or in connection with appeals against determinations or decisions made, notices given or served, or other things done under or by virtue of the regulations.

(3) Without prejudice to the generality of paragraph (h) of subsection (2) above, the provision that may be made by virtue of that paragraph includes provision for or in connection with any of the following, that is to say—

    (a) the scope or form of a review or assessment;

    (b) the scope, content or form of an action plan;

    (c) the time at which, period within which, or manner in which a review or assessment is to be carried out or an action plan is to be prepared;

    (d) the methods to be employed—

        (i) in carrying out reviews or assessments; or

        (ii) in monitoring the effectiveness of action plans;

    (e) the factors to be taken into account in preparing action plans;

    (f) the actions which must be taken by local authorities or other persons in consequence of reviews, assessments or action plans;

    (g) requirements for consultation;

    (h) the treatment of representations or objections duly made;

    (j) the publication of, or the making available to the public of, or of copies of,—

        (i) the results, or reports of the results, of reviews or assessments; or

        (ii) orders or action plans;

    (k) requirements for—

        (i) copies of any such reports, orders or action plans, or

        (ii) prescribed information, in such form as may be prescribed, relating to reviews or assessments,

    to be sent to the Secretary of State or to the appropriate new Agency.

(4) In determining—

    (a) any appeal against, or reference or review of, a decision of a local authority under or by virtue of regulations under this Part, or

    (b) any application transmitted from a local authority under or by virtue of any such regulations,

the body or person making the determination shall be bound by any direction given by a Minister of the Crown or SEPA to the local authority to the same extent as the local authority.

(5) The provisions of any regulations under this Part may include—

    (a) provision for anything that may be prescribed by the regulations to be determined under the regulations and for anything falling to be so determined to be determined by such persons, in accordance with such procedure and by reference to such matters, and to the opinion of such persons, as may be prescribed;

    (b) different provision for different cases, including different provision in relation to different persons, circumstances, areas or localities; and

    (c) such supplemental, consequential, incidental or transitional provision (including provision amending any enactment or any instrument made under any enactment) as the Secretary of State considers appropriate.

(6) Nothing in regulations under this Part shall authorise any person other than a constable in uniform to stop a vehicle on any road.

(7) Before making any regulations under this Part, the Secretary of State shall consult—

    (a) the appropriate new Agency;

    (b) such bodies or persons appearing to him to be representative of the interests of local government as he may consider appropriate;

    (c) such bodies or persons appearing to him to be representative of the interests of industry as he may consider appropriate; and

    (d) such other bodies or persons as he may consider appropriate.

(8) Any power conferred by this Part to make regulations shall be

exercisable by statutory instrument; and no statutory instrument containing regulations under this Part shall be made unless a draft of the instrument has been laid before, and approved by a resolution of, each House of Parliament.

(9) If, apart from this subsection, the draft of an instrument containing regulations under this Part would be treated for the purposes of the Standing Orders of either House of Parliament as a hybrid instrument, it shall proceed in that House as if it were not such an instrument.

DEFINITIONS
"action plan": s.84(2).
"air quality objectives": s.91(1).
"air quality review": s.91(1).
"air quality standards": s.91(1).
"the appropriate new Agency": s.91(1).
"functions": s.124(1).
"local authority": s.91(1).
"notice": s.124(1).
"prescribed": s.91(1).
"regulations": s.91(1).
"the strategy": s.80(1).

COMMENCEMENT
February 1, 1996 (S.I. 1996 No. 186).

GENERAL NOTE
This section provides the power to make regulations for the general purposes specified in subs. (1), *i.e.* implementation of the national strategy, implementation of Community obligations and international agreements, and generally with respect to the assessment and management of air quality. It should also be noted that the Act amends the Road Traffic Regulation Act 1984 so as to allow traffic regulation orders made under the 1984 Act to be made for any of these three purposes: Sched. 22, para. 36.

The specific matters which may be covered are listed at subs. (2). These matters include the prescribing of air quality standards and objectives (see below). They also include issues of manner and form as to the exercise of local authority functions under Part IV (subss. (2)(f)–(l) and (3)), the prohibition or restriction of prescribed activities or vehicular access (subss. (2)(e) and (6)), appeals (subss. (2)(p) and (4) and the creation of offences, including fixed penalty offences (subss. (2)(a) and (o) and Sched. 11, para. 5).

Air Quality Standards
Air quality standards already exist for certain substances, as required by E.C. law: the Air Quality Standards Regulations 1989 No. 317 (sulphur dioxide, suspended particulates, lead and nitrogen dioxide). Essentially these Regulations impose an obligation on the Secretary of State to take any necessary measures to ensure that the relevant E.C. limit values are not exceeded.

Part 2 of the Government's policy document, *Improving Air Quality: Meeting the Challenge*, suggests two main levels of air quality standards as "anchor points". One will be a guideline figure, essentially a long-term goal, representing a level at which the pollutant had been rendered harmless or where no significant further benefit could be obtained by reasonable expenditure. This would be achieved by measures such as cost effective progressive introduction of new technology. The second standard would be a trigger level, denoting cases where air quality is so poor that an immediate response would be justified to prevent serious damage. In terms of the scope of standards, the Government has concluded that the following pollutants should be covered: ozone, benzene, 1,3-butadiene, sulphur dioxide, carbon monoxide, nitrogen dioxide, particulates, polycyclic aromatic hydrocarbons (PAHs), and lead. Further information on each of these pollutants is given in Part 3 of *Improving Air Quality: Meeting the Challenge*. In setting the standards, the Government is advised by the independent Expert Panel on Air Quality Standards (EPAQS). As noted in the *Policy Background* to this Part, this body has already made recommendations for or has reported on benzene, ozone, 1,3-butadiene, carbon monoxide, sulphur dioxide and particles.

Guidance for the purposes of Part IV

88.—(1) The Secretary of State may issue guidance to local authorities with respect to, or in connection with, the exercise of any of the powers conferred, or the discharge of any of the duties imposed, on those authorities by or under this Part.

(2) A local authority, in carrying out any of its functions under or by virtue of this Part, shall have regard to any guidance issued by the Secretary of State under this Part.

(3) This section shall apply in relation to county councils for areas for which there are district councils as it applies in relation to local authorities.

DEFINITIONS
"functions": s.124(1).
"local authorities": s.91(1).

COMMENCEMENT
February 1, 1996 (S.I. 1996 No. 186).

GENERAL NOTE
This section allows the Secretary of State to issue guidance to local authorities (including, where applicable, English county councils) in relation to the carrying out of duties and the exercise of functions under Part IV. The local authority must have regard to such guidance.

Application of Part IV to the Isles of Scilly

89.—(1) Subject to the provisions of any order under this section, this Part, other than section 80, shall not apply in relation to the Isles of Scilly.

(2) The Secretary of State may, after consultation with the Council of the Isles of Scilly, by order provide for the application of any provisions of this Part (other than section 80) to the Isles of Scilly; and any such order may provide for the application of those provisions to those Isles with such modifications as may be specified in the order.

(3) An order under this section may—

  (a) make different provision for different cases, including different provision in relation to different persons, circumstances or localities; and

  (b) contain such supplemental, consequential and transitional provision as the Secretary of State considers appropriate, including provision saving provision repealed by or under any enactment.

(4) The power of the Secretary of State to make an order under this section shall be exercisable by statutory instrument; and a statutory instrument containing such an order shall be subject to annulment in pursuance of a resolution of either House of Parliament.

DEFINITION
"modifications": s.124(1).

COMMENCEMENT
February 1, 1996 (S.I. 1996 No. 186).

Supplemental provisions

90. Schedule 11 to this Act shall have effect.

COMMENCEMENT
This section comes into force on a day to be appointed (s.125(3)).

GENERAL NOTE
Schedule 11 deals with the following matters:

  (a) Consultation by local authorities in the course of carrying out functions of review, assessment and action plan preparation: para. 1.

  (b) Mutual exchange of information between district and county councils in England: para. 2.

  (c) The joint exercise of functions by two or more local authorities under direction from the Secretary of State or SEPA: para. 3.

(d) The provision to the public of copies of the various documents produced under Part IV: para. 4.
(e) Express authority for the creation of fixed penalty offences by regulations under s.87: para. 5.

Joint exercise of functions
In relation to the joint exercise of functions, Government Offices for the Regions will be expected to consider and consult on the need for joint arrangements in areas such as conurbations, metropolitan areas and estuaries: *Improving Air Quality: Meeting the Challenge,* p.19.

Interpretation of Part IV

91.—(1) In this Part—
"action plan" shall be construed in accordance with section 84(2)(b) above;
"air quality objectives" means objectives prescribed by virtue of section 87(2)(b) above;
"air quality review" means a review under section 82 or 85 above;
"air quality standards" means standards prescribed by virtue of section 87(2)(a) above;
"the appropriate new Agency" means—
    (a) in relation to England and Wales, the Agency;
    (b) in relation to Scotland, SEPA;
"designated area" has the meaning given by section 83(1) above;
"local authority", in relation to England and Wales, means—
    (a) any unitary authority,
    (b) any district council, so far as it is not a unitary authority,
    (c) the Common Council of the City of London and, as respects the Temples, the Sub-Treasurer of the Inner Temple and the Under-Treasurer of the Middle Temple respectively,
and, in relation to Scotland, means a council for an area constituted under section 2 of the Local Government etc. (Scotland) Act 1994;
"new Agency" means the Agency or SEPA;
"prescribed" means prescribed, or of a description prescribed, by or under regulations;
"regulations" means regulations made by the Secretary of State;
"the relevant period", in the case of any provision of this Part, means such period as may be prescribed for the purposes of that provision;
"the strategy" has the meaning given by section 80(1) above;
"unitary authority" means—
    (a) the council of a county, so far as it is the council of an area for which there are no district councils;
    (b) the council of any district comprised in an area for which there is no county council;
    (c) the council of a London borough;
    (d) the council of a county borough in Wales.
(2) Any reference in this Part to it appearing that any air quality standards or objectives are not likely within the relevant period to be achieved includes a reference to it appearing that those standards or objectives are likely within that period not to be achieved.

DEFINITIONS
"the Agency": s.124(1).
"SEPA": s.124(1).

COMMENCEMENT
February 1, 1996 (S.I. 1996 No. 186).

Subs. (2)
Possibly from abundance of caution, this subsection makes it clear that references to it appearing that air quality standards or objectives are not likely to be achieved include the more pessimistic assessment that they are likely not to be achieved.

PART V

MISCELLANEOUS, GENERAL AND SUPPLEMENTAL PROVISIONS

Waste

[Section 92 (together with Sched. 2 to which it gives effect) inserts new sections 44A and 44B and a new Schedule 2A into the Environmental Protection Act 1990, relating to national waste strategies for England and Wales and for Scotland. See the general note to those sections.]

Producer responsibility general

93.—(1) For the purpose of promoting or securing an increase in the re-use, recovery or recycling of products or materials, the Secretary of State may by regulations make provision for imposing producer responsibility obligations on such persons, and in respect of such products or materials, as may be prescribed.

(2) The power of the Secretary of State to make regulations shall be exercisable only after consultation with bodies or persons appearing to him to be representative of bodies or persons whose interests are, or are likely to be, substantially affected by the regulations which he proposes to make.

(3) Except in the case of regulations for the implementation of—

(a) any obligations of the United Kingdom under the Community Treaties, or

(b) any international agreement to which the United Kingdom is for the time being a party,

the power to make regulations shall be exercisable only where the Secretary of State, after such consultation as is required by subsection (2) above, is satisfied as to the matters specified in subsection (6) below.

(4) The powers conferred by subsection (1) above shall also be exercisable, in a case falling within paragraph (a) or (b) of subsection (3) above, for the purpose of sustaining at least a minimum level of (rather than promoting or securing an increase in) re-use, recovery or recycling of products or materials.

(5) In making regulations by virtue of paragraph (a) or (b) of subsection (3) above, the Secretary of State shall have regard to the matters specified in subsection (6) below; and in its application in relation to the power conferred by, virtue of subsection (4) above, subsection (6) below shall have effect as if—

(a) any reference to an increase in the re-use, recovery or recycling of products or materials were a reference to the sustaining of at least a minimum level of re-use, recovery or recycling of the products or materials in question, and

(b) any reference to the production of environmental or economic benefits included a reference to the sustaining of at least a minimum level of any such existing benefits,

and any reference in this section or section 94 below to securing or achieving any such benefits shall accordingly include a reference to sustaining at least a minimum level of any such existing benefits.

(6) The matters mentioned in subsections (3) and (5) above are—

(a) that the proposed exercise of the power would be likely to result in an increase in the re-use, recovery or recycling of the products or materials in question;

(b) that any such increase would produce environmental or economic benefits;

(c) that those benefits are significant as against the likely costs resulting from the imposition of the proposed producer responsibility obligation;

(d) that the burdens imposed on businesses by the regulations are the minimum necessary to secure those benefits; and

(e) that those burdens are imposed on persons most able to make a contribution to the achievement of the relevant targets—

    (i) having regard to the desirability of acting fairly between persons who manufacture, process, distribute or supply products or materials; and

    (ii) taking account of the need to ensure that the proposed producer responsibility obligation is so framed as to be effective in achieving the purposes for which it is to be imposed;

but nothing in sub-paragraph (i) of paragraph (e) above shall be taken to prevent regulations imposing a producer responsibility obligation on any class or description of person to the exclusion of any others.

(7) The Secretary of State shall have a duty to exercise the power to make regulations in the manner which he considers best calculated to secure that the exercise does not have the effect of restricting, distorting or preventing competition or, if it is likely to have any such effect, that the effect is no greater than is necessary for achieving the environmental or economic benefits mentioned in subsection (6) above.

(8) In this section—

"prescribed" means prescribed in regulations;

"product" and "material" include a reference to any product or material (as the case may be) at a time when it becomes, or has become, waste;

"producer responsibility obligation" means the steps which are required to be taken by relevant persons of the classes or descriptions to which the regulations in question apply in order to secure attainment of the targets specified or described in the regulations;

"recovery", in relation to products or materials, includes—

    (a) composting, or any other form of transformation by biological processes, of products or materials; or

    (b) the obtaining, by any means, of energy from products or materials;

"regulations" means regulations under this section;

"relevant persons", in the case of any regulations or any producer responsibility obligation, means persons of the class or description to which the producer responsibility obligation imposed by the regulations applies;

"relevant targets" means the targets specified or described in the regulations imposing the producer responsibility obligation in question;

and regulations may prescribe, in relation to prescribed products or materials, activities, or the activities, which are to be regarded for the purposes of this section and sections 94 and 95 below or any regulations as re-use, recovery or recycling of those products or materials.

(9) The power to make regulations shall be exercisable by statutory instrument.

(10) Subject to the following provisions of this section, a statutory instrument containing regulations shall not be made unless a draft of the instrument has been laid before and approved by a resolution of each House of Parliament.

(11) Subsection (10) above shall not apply to a statutory instrument by reason only that it contains regulations varying any relevant targets.

(12) A statutory instrument which, by virtue of subsection (11) above, is not subject to any requirement that a draft of the instrument be laid before and approved by a resolution of each House of Parliament shall be subject to annulment in pursuance of a resolution of either House of Parliament.

DEFINITIONS
"material": subs. (8).
"prescribed": subs. (8).
"producer responsibility obligation": subs. (8).
"product": subs. (8).
"recovery": subs. (8).
"regulations": subs. (8).
"relevant persons": subs. (8).
"relevant targets": subs. (8).

COMMENCEMENT
September 21, 1995 (S.I. 1995 No. 1983).

GENERAL NOTE
Sections 93–95 provide for regulations to be made, following consultation, imposing "producer responsibility" obligations on such persons as the regulations prescribe (ss.93 and 94), and make provision in relation to the offences of contravening requirements of the regulations (s.95).

Policy background
Even more than is often the case with framework or "enabling" legislation, the significance of many of the producer responsibility provisions is difficult to appreciate without an understanding of the policy background: the E.C. priority waste streams project and Directive on Packaging and Packaging Waste, developing Government thinking on its waste strategy (see the general note to ss.44A and 44B of the Environmental Protection Act 1990, inserted by s.92 of this Act), and the Government's "producer responsibility challenge" to industry. Much, though far from all, of this background relates to developments in connection with packaging and packaging waste.

Priority waste streams
As part of its Fourth Action Programme on the Environment (O.J. C328, 7.12. 1987), in the late 1980s and early 1990s the European Commission singled out a number of "priority waste streams" for special attention, with a view to the identification of the specific problems and opportunities they present and the development of an EU policy response which might include legislation. The Commission established a Priority Waste Streams Programme which involved a number of Working Groups comprised of representatives from Member States, and each Working Group was allocated a waste stream for consideration. Included in the remit of each Working Group was to make recommendations as to the appropriate policy response. The priority waste streams were chlorinated solvents, used tyres, healthcare waste, end of life vehicles, construction and demolition waste, and waste electrical and electronic equipment. Packaging and packaging waste was not included in the programme because plans were already underway for a directive on such waste.

The Producer Responsibility Challenge
In part in response to this development at EC level, and in particular to the submission by the European Commission in 1992 of a proposal for a Directive on Packaging and Packaging Waste (O.J. No. C263/1, 12.10.1992), which was ultimately adopted as Directive 94/62/EC in December 1994 (O.J. No. L365/10, 31.12.94), on July 27, 1993 the DoE and Department of Trade and Industry launched the Government's "producer responsibility challenge" to the businesses involved in the "packaging chain". The "packaging chain" consists of the raw material producers, the businesses which convert such materials into packaging ("converters"), those which place goods into the packaging ("packer/fillers"), those who wholesale or retail such goods and those businesses, and arguably private consumers, in whose hands the packaging becomes waste. It also includes those who import raw materials for use in packaging or import packaging or packaged goods. The challenge was to make voluntary, industry-led arrangements to meet a recovery target of 50–70 per cent recovery of packaging waste by the year 2000 (DoE News Release 519, DTI P/93/442).

Later that year, six other industrial sectors were issued with the challenge (DTI Press

Releases P/93/658 and P/93/745): newspapers, automotive batteries, consumer batteries, electrical and electronic goods, tyres and end of life motor vehicles.

The "match" between priority waste streams and producer responsibility sectors is not total: batteries, like packaging waste, were dealt with by way of a directive at EC level (in the case of batteries, Directive 91/157/EEC, O.J. L78/38, 26.3.91), and it will be noted that there are EC priority waste streams, such as "healthcare waste", for which no United Kingdom producer responsibility challenge has yet been issued. None of the Working Group recommendations have as yet prompted the European Commission to formally propose a directive on the waste stream concerned, although the Commission is understood to be planning a proposal for a directive on end of life motor vehicles—contrary to the recommendations of that Working Group.

Whilst packaging waste leads the way, both the Priority Waste Streams Programme and the series of producer responsibility challenges might ultimately lead to producer responsibility legislation of the kind provided for in ss.93–95.

"Free riders" and the need for legislation
The initial aim behind the producer responsibility challenges was to avoid the use of legislation to achieve recycling and recovery of waste and other improvements in industry's management of its wastes and the wastes from its products. However, as the Government noted in its draft Waste Strategy for England and Wales (January 1995) "In some cases, the relevant business groups have asked for legislative underpinning to deter "free riders" who seek to avoid involvement in a business-led scheme" (para. 2.94). This pressure culminated in the announcement in October 1994 that the Government would legislate to support industry-led schemes for packaging waste, which legislation would be "minimum required to provide an effective deterrent to "free-riders" (DoE News Release 579).

Packaging and Packaging Waste
The Packaging and Packaging Waste Directive 94/62/EC was adopted in December 1994 (O.J. No. L365/10, 31.12.94). It contains a number of requirements, including those for the establishment of packaging/packaging waste return, collection and recovery systems (Article 7), a "daughter" directive on the uniform marking of packaging (Article 8), the content of packaging (Articles 9 and 11), and the establishment of databases on packaging and packaging waste and dissemination to consumers of information on their role in its recovery and recycling (Articles 12 and 13). However, the provisions on which the producer responsibility initiative focuses are those in Article 6 which require Member States to meet the following targets by June 30, 2001:
— recovery of 50–65 per cent (by weight) of all packaging waste;
— within this target, 25–45 per cent (by weight) of all packaging waste to be recycled;
— within this target, 15 per cent (by weight) of each material type (*e.g.* glass, plastic) to be recycled.

Given impetus by the Packaging and Packaging Waste Directive, as noted above the producer responsibility initiative has progressed significantly further for this waste stream than for the others, and once it was conceded that underpinning legislation for it was required (DoE News Release 579), then the inclusion of such legislation in the 1995 Act became inevitable. Packaging and packaging waste is to be the first subject of regulations under the provisions. Indeed, the form taken by the provisions in the Act was undoubtedly influenced by the ongoing debate between the Government and various business and industry bodies in the packaging chain, since this debate informed Government thinking on the kinds of industry-led scheme which are workable, enforceable and, where necessary (as in the case of packaging waste), are demonstrably capable of implementing the United Kingdom's EC obligations.

One key industry organisation has been the Producer Responsibility Group (PRG), which produced a Plan entitled "*Real Value From Packaging Waste*", first in consultation draft form in February 1994 and then in final form in November that year. The PRG Plan envisaged the setting up of an industry body, funded by a levy from companies in the packaging chain, to procure the collection and recycling or recovery of packaging waste on behalf of the packaging chain. It entitled this future body "VALPAK", and envisaged the possibility of VALPAK and perhaps other competing bodies being approved by Government or the Environment Agency/SEPA to carry out these tasks. The requirement for approval was considered necessary since the payment of a levy to VALPAK would serve to discharge a packaging chain company's statutory producer responsibility obligations under the anticipated underpinning legislation.

On the crucial question of where in the packaging chain the producer responsibility and consequent levy obligation should be placed, PRG commissioned a report by Sir Sydney

Lipworth QC which, entitled *"Packaging Levy Report on Point of Funding"*, was published in July 1994. The report envisaged what it called a "modified converter levy", under which the levy would be placed on those who convert raw material into packaging ("converters") or who import packaging, subject to provisions for the burden of the levy to be passed on instead to "packer/fillers" of packaging and/or retailers and wholesalers of packaged goods. The final version of the PRG Plan endorsed this approach for the medium- to long-term.

The PRG Plan proposed achievement of a 58 per cent recovery rate for packaging waste by the year 2000, estimated that an annual levy of £100 million would be required, and envisaged the establishment of five "Material Organisations" (for aluminium, glass, packaging paper, plastics and steel) which would be represented on the VALPAK Board to ensure co-ordination of efforts.

Having produced its Plan, the PRG disbanded, to give way to a body entitled V-WRAG, or VALPAK Working Representative Advisory Group, to continue dialogue with the Government and produce a prospectus for the establishment of VALPAK.

In May 1995 the DoE, DTI, Welsh and Scottish Offices issued a consultation paper, *Producer Responsibility for Packaging Waste*, which sought views on options for the form of legal obligation on individual businesses needed to underpin collaborative industry schemes and ensure that recovery and recycling of packaging waste reaches national and international targets. The paper was concerned specifically with the scope and nature of the legal obligation to be placed on individual businesses, to be contained in regulations made under ss.93–95.

In the paper the Government indicated eight tests which it proposed to bear in mind in formulating its approach to legislation. These were:

— the need to be confident that the targets set by the EC Packaging Waste Directive can be met;

— the practicality, cost effectiveness, and potential benefits as against the likely cost (taking into account environmental and economic considerations) and fairness of the available options;

— the desirability of minimising regulatory burdens on business;

— the desirability of business choice in the manner in which the obligation is satisfied;

— compatibility of the available options with existing EC and domestic law, *e.g.* to ensure that they do not create a barrier to trade with other Member States;

— the need to take account of competition policy, *e.g.* to ensure that regulations do not have the effect of distorting competition unnecessarily;

— the desirability of business freedom and flexibility and of minimising the public sector role; and

— the desirability of targeting as closely as possible those responsible for determining the content, nature and amount of packaging used for a particular product.

Various chapters of the paper covered the different possible schemes which had at that point been put forward.

The various schemes were entitled Single-point, Omni-point, Multi-point and Equi-point. Their differences can be characterised as relating to the extent to which they spread the obligation along the packaging chain, and thus the extent to which they relied upon market forces to spread the cost burden along the chain, and to the form which the obligation would take. The Equi-point option proposed two sets of targets relating to own use packaging/packaging waste arising on the premises of any business in the chain (this being the easiest form of packaging waste to deal with) and, separately, household packaging waste. In working up the various options, some forms of "supplementary legal obligation" were proposed by supporters of various options.

In the paper the Government urged the proponents of different approaches to build a consensus behind the best option, and the paper indicated that in order to be considered at the close of the exercise any new proposal not described in whole or in part of the paper must receive a wide circulation to interested parties and trade associations, in sufficient time for them to consider the proposal fully and comment on it before the end of the consultation period.

One subsequent proposal was put forward, by V-WRAG, entitled *Shared Producer Responsibility*. This option appears to have excited widespread interest within the industry, and accordingly a supplementary consultation paper was issued in August 1995 by the DoE containing it as a seventh option. However, the version circulated by the DoE was acknowledged to have been "supplemented and amended by Government" to indicate how it would enable the Government to implement the Directive. One key aspect of the option as originally formulated was excluded by the DoE from the consultation paper version. This was its employment of a "duty of care" on businesses (modelled on that in the Environmental Protection Act 1990, s.34) in relation to packaging which becomes waste in the hands of consumers, rather than an obligation which could be related in some way to a "target" for the recycling or recovery of a particular quantity of packaging waste.

Debate and discussion continued, culminating in the announcement on December 15, 1995, that a consensus had been reached by industry representatives on the form of obligation to be imposed (DoE New Release 639). The principles agreed involved a staged approach with legal obligations upon businesses operating outside what s.94(6) terms an "exemption scheme" allocated (having taken into account of imports and exports) primarily to retailers and to packer fillers, who would be responsible for 45 per cent, and 35 per cent respectively of the target imposed in respect of a given weight of material passing through their hands. Raw material producers (5½ per cent) and converters (14½ per cent) would bear the remainder of the obligation. Companies joining an exemption scheme would be charged a turnover-related annual membership fee as well as complying with the conditions of membership. The Secretary of State commented that "Government will now need to consider and decide on the best form of legal obligation, taking account of all relevant considerations", no doubt including the industry consensus which Government had been seeking, before producing draft regulations which were awaited at the time of writing.

Subss. (1)–(7): increasing or maintaining re-use, recovery or recycling levels
The elaborate provisions of subss. (1)–(7) may perhaps be best understood if the distinction is drawn at the outset between two circumstances in which regulations may be made under s.93. The first circumstance is where the regulations are to implement E.C. or international obligations, and the second is where they are not, and are thus a solely domestic initiative.

In the first circumstance, it may be that levels or rates of recycling, etc., once achieved, need only to be maintained (rather than increased), or perhaps could even be allowed to fall as long as a minimum level was maintained, in order to implement the obligation. The provisions therefore allow for that possibility: subs. (4) (*per* Viscount Ullswater, *Hansard*, H.L. Vol. 561, col. 355). In the other circumstance, however, it is assumed that the Government (if it is legislating at all) will wish to promote an increase in such levels, so regulations may only be made for this reason: subs. (1).

The extent to which the Secretary of State may act on considerations which the Government considers important in this context is also affected by the EC/international dimension. Thus, where the regulations are a domestic initiative, the Secretary of State must (after the consultation required by subs. (2)) be "satisfied" as to the subs. (6) list of likely benefits and burdens of the regulations (subs. (3)). By contrast, where an EC/international obligation is being implemented, he need only "have regard to" that list, which as before must in that circumstance be read to include maintaining a minimum level of recycling, etc., or of economic or environmental benefits, as well as promoting their increase: subs. (5).

The obligation to consult (subs. (2)) applies in either circumstance, although unusually the requirement is only to consult bodies representative of those who are, or are likely to be, "substantially affected" by the proposed regulations.

The Secretary of State's duty in relation to competition in making the regulations should be noted: subs. (7).

Subs. (6): matters to be considered
The Secretary of State must be satisfied (subs. (3)), or, where an EC/international obligation is being implemented, must have regard to (subs. (5)) the matters listed in subs. (6). These are that the regulations will not only (a) have the intended outcome but will (b) as a result lead to environmental or economic benefits; that the benefits are (c) significant as against the likely costs; and that the burdens imposed are (d) the minimum necessary and (e) fairly and efficiently placed. Such a concern for fairness is expressly disbarred, however, from preventing an uneven imposition of the producer responsibility burden. This is reinforced by subs. 94(7).

Subs. (8): "product" and "material"
These terms allow extremely wide scope for the subject matter of producer responsibility regulations. They are defined inclusively: they include waste products and materials. It follows that they may well include products and materials which are not waste, and there is good reason for this. One purpose of the regulations might be to promote their re-use (subs. (1)), and where something is re-used it is the Government's view that in many cases it does not become "waste" as statutorily defined (s.75(2) of the 1990 Act as inserted by the 1995 Act, Sched. 22, para. 88 and interpreted by DoE/Welsh Office Circular 11/94: although that definition is not applicable to s.93, the Government would no doubt wish to avoid introducing a different definition for those purposes, and in any event this may lead to complexities where the provisions are to be used to implement EC legislation which employs the definition which s.75(2) implements). Thus there are difficulties with the notion of re-using waste, which are avoided by the provisions as drafted.

Subs. (8): "re-use", "recovery" and "recycling"
"Recovery" is also defined inclusively. This definition was introduced by the Government at the Commons Committee stage, and its wording was queried by Mr Tipping. He expressed the view that "one could have a fire and get energy from it, but it would still be waste if one did not apply the result" (H.C. Standing Committee B, 13th Sitting, June 6, 1995, col. 556). The suggestion appeared to be that any form of decomposition or burning could be brought within the definition by the wording. Whether this is the case turns in part on the meaning of "obtaining" in part (b) of the definition: one could argue that simply to release energy is not to obtain it since it is not released in usable form, in which case Mr Tipping's concern would be unfounded.

It is not clear precisely how the wording might fit with the definition of recovery in EC legislation which the provisions might be employed to implement. The wording does not map neatly onto the definitions of "recovery", "recycling", "energy recovery" and "organic recycling" in the Packaging and Packaging Waste Directive, nor onto the list of recovery operations set out at Annex II B to the Waste Framework Directive 75/442/EEC as amended by Directive 91/156/EEC (O.J. L78/32, 26.3.91). However, this definition should be read together with the concluding clause of this subsection, which provides that regulations may stipulate what will constitute the re-use, recovery or recycling of given products or materials. Thus the appropriate EC definitions, where applicable, may be employed.

Subss. (9)–(12): Parliamentary procedures
Regulations under s.93, imposing or (by implication) modifying, removing or replacing producer responsibility obligations, must be made by statutory instrument and approved by both Houses of Parliament (the "affirmative resolution" procedure): subss. (9) and (10).

However, where such a statutory instrument only varies any targets by reference to which producer responsibility obligations are determined, it is subject only to the "negative resolution" procedure whereby no such approval is required but both Houses have an opportunity to annul it: subss. (11) and (12).

An amendment to remove subss. (11) and (12) was moved at the Commons Committee stage by Mr Bennett, who argued that "if something is important enough to be done in the first instance using … the affirmative method—the same considerations should apply if it is to be altered" (H.C. Standing Committee B, 13th Sitting, June 6, 1995, col. 556). The amendment was rejected by Mr Atkins on behalf of the Government on the grounds that "we may need to make changes to targets at short notice and perhaps respond quickly to problems such as fluctuations in market prices" (col. 556).

Producer responsibility supplementary provisions

94.—(1) Without prejudice to the generality of section 93 above, regulations may, in particular, make provision for or with respect to—

   (a) the classes or descriptions of person to whom the producer responsibility obligation imposed by the regulations applies;

   (b) the classes or descriptions of products or materials in respect of which the obligation applies;

   (c) the targets which are to be achieved with respect to the proportion (whether by weight, volume or otherwise) of the products or materials in question which are to be re-used, recovered or recycled, whether generally or in any prescribed way;

   (d) particulars of the obligation imposed by the regulations;

   (e) the registration of persons who are subject to a producer responsibility obligation and who are not members of registered exemption schemes, the imposition of requirements in connection with such registration, the variation of such requirements, the making of applications for such registration, the period for which any such registration is to remain in force and the cancellation of any such registration;

   (f) the approval, or withdrawal of approval, of exemption schemes by the Secretary of State;

   (g) the imposition of requirements on persons who are not members of registered exemption schemes to furnish certificates of compliance to the appropriate Agency;

   (h) the approval of persons by the appropriate Agency for the purpose of issuing certificates of compliance;

(j) the registration of exemption schemes, the imposition of conditions in connection with such registration, the variation of such conditions, the making of applications for such registration and the period for which any such registration is to remain in force;

(k) the requirements which must be fulfilled, and the criteria which must be met, before an exemption scheme may be registered;

(l) the powers of the appropriate Agency in relation to applications received by it for registration of exemption schemes;

(m) the cancellation of the registration of an exemption scheme;

(n) competition scrutiny of registered exemption schemes or of exemption schemes in whose case applications for registration have been received by the appropriate Agency;

(o) the exclusion or modification of any provision of the Restrictive Trade Practices Acts 1976 and 1977 in relation to exemption schemes or in relation to agreements where at least one of the parties is an operator of an exemption scheme;

(p) the fees, or the method of determining the fees, which are to be paid to the appropriate Agency—

    (i) in respect of the approval of persons for the purpose of issuing certificates of compliance;

    (ii) on the making of an application for registration of an exemption scheme;

    (iii) in respect of the subsistence of the registration of that scheme;

    (iv) on submission to the appropriate Agency of a certificate of compliance;

    (v) on the making of an application for, or for the renewal of, registration of a person required to register under the regulations;

    (vi) in respect of the renewal of the registration of that person;

(q) appeals against the refusal of registration, the imposition of conditions in connection with registration, or the cancellation of the registration, of any exemption scheme;

(r) the procedure on any such appeal;

(s) cases, or classes of case,—

    (i) in which an exemption scheme is, or is not, to be treated as registered, or

    (ii) in which a person is, or is not, to be treated as a member of a registered exemption scheme,

pending the determination or withdrawal of an appeal, and otherwise with respect to the position of persons and exemption schemes pending such determination or withdrawal;

(t) the imposition on the appropriate Agency of a duty to monitor compliance with any of the obligations imposed by the regulations;

(u) the imposition on prescribed persons of duties to maintain records, and furnish to the Secretary of State or to the appropriate Agency returns, in such form as may be prescribed of such information as may be prescribed for any purposes of, or for any purposes connected with, or related to, sections 93 to 95 of this Act or any regulations;

(w) the imposition on the appropriate Agency of a duty to maintain, and make available for inspection by the public, a register containing prescribed information relating to registered exemption schemes or persons required to register under the regulations;

(y) the powers of entry and inspection which are exercisable by a new Agency for the purposes of its functions under the regulations;

(ya) the conferring on prescribed persons of power to require, for the purposes of or otherwise in connection with competition scrutiny, the provision by any person of any information which he has, or

which he may at any future time acquire, relating to any exemption
scheme or to any acts or omissions of an operator of such a scheme
or of any person dealing with such an operator.

(2) If it appears to the Secretary of State—

  (a) that any action proposed to be taken by the operator of a registered
exemption scheme would be incompatible with—

    (i) any obligations of the United Kingdom under the Community
Treaties, or

    (ii) any international agreement to which the United Kingdom is
for the time being a party, or

  (b) that any action which the operator of such a scheme has power to
take is required for the purpose of implementing any such
obligations or agreement,

he may direct that operator not to take or, as the case may be, to take the
action in question.

(3) Regulations may make provision as to which of the new Agencies is the
appropriate Agency for the purposes of any function conferred or imposed
by or under this section or section 93 above, or for the purposes of the
exercise of that function in relation to the whole or a prescribed part of Great
Britain, and may make provision for things done or omitted to be done by
either new Agency in relation to any part of Great Britain to be treated for
prescribed purposes as done or omitted to be done by the other of them in
relation to some other part of Great Britain.

(4) Persons issuing certificates of compliance shall act in accordance with
guidance issued for the purpose by the appropriate Agency, which may
include guidance as to matters which are, or are not, to be treated as
evidence of compliance or as evidence of non-compliance.

(5) In making any provision in relation to fees, regard shall be had to the
desirability of securing that the fees received by each new Agency under the
regulations are sufficient to meet the costs and expenses incurred by that
Agency in the performance of its functions under the regulations.

(6) In this section—

"the appropriate Agency", subject to regulations made by virtue of
subsection (3) above, means—

  (a) in relation to England and Wales, the Agency;

  (b) in relation to Scotland, SEPA;

"certificate of compliance" means a certificate issued by a person
approved for the purpose by the appropriate Agency to the effect
that that person is satisfied that the person in respect of whom the
certificate is issued is complying with any producer responsibility
obligation to which he is subject;

"competition scrutiny", in the case of any scheme, means scrutiny of the
scheme for the purpose of enabling the Secretary of State to satisfy
himself—

  (i) whether or not the scheme has or is likely to have the effect of
restricting, distorting or preventing competition or, if it
appears to him that the scheme has or is likely to have any such
effect, that the effect is or is likely to be no greater than is
necessary for achieving the environmental or economic benefits mentioned in section 93(6) above; or

  (ii) whether or not the scheme leads or is likely to lead to an abuse
of market power;

"exemption scheme" means a scheme which is (or, if it were to be
registered in accordance with the regulations, would be) a scheme
whose members for the time being are, by virtue of the regulations
and their membership of that scheme, exempt from the requirement to comply with the producer responsibility obligation
imposed by the regulations;

"new Agency" means the Agency or SEPA;
"operator", in relation to an exemption scheme, includes any person
    responsible for establishing, maintaining or managing the scheme;
"registered exemption scheme" means an exemption scheme which is
    registered pursuant to regulations;
and expressions used in this section and in section 93 above have the same
meaning in this section as they have in that section.

(7) Regulations—

  (a) may make different provision for different cases;

  (b) without prejudice to the generality of paragraph (a) above, may
impose different producer responsibility obligations in respect of
different classes or descriptions of products or materials and for
different classes or descriptions of person or exemption scheme;

  (c) may include incidental, consequential, supplemental or transitional
provision.

(8) Any direction under this section—

  (a) may include such incidental, consequential, supplemental or transitional provision as the Secretary of State considers necessary or
expedient; and

  (b) shall, on the application of the Secretary of State, be enforceable by
injunction or, in Scotland, by interdict or by an order for specific
performance under section 45 of the Court of Session Act 1988.

DEFINITIONS
"the appropriate Agency": subs. (6).
"certificate of compliance": subs. (6).
"competition scrutiny": subs. (6).
"exemption scheme": subs. (6).
"functions": s.124(1).
"materials": s.93(8).
"modification": s.124(1).
"new Agency": subs. (6).
"operator": subs. (6).
"prescribed": s.93(8).
"producer responsibility obligation": s.93(8).
"product": s.93(8).
"records": s.124(1).
"recovery": s.93(8).
"registered exemption scheme": subs. (6).
"regulations": s.93(8).

COMMENCEMENT
September 21, 1995 (S.I. 1995 No. 1983).

GENERAL NOTE
This section makes supplementary provisions in relation to the producer responsibility
provisions contained in s.93. It identifies some twenty three different matters which might be
addressed by regulations made under s.93 (subs. (1)(a)–(ya)), although it should be noted that
the list is expressed to be without prejudice to the generality of s.93. Thus it appears that Mr
Clifton-Brown may have been incorrect in suggesting that "an opportunity will be lost" if the
Government rejected his proposed amendment to include in the list the possibility that
regulations might make provision for the imposition of a duty of care and issuing of a related
Code of Practice (H.C. Standing Committee B, 13th Sitting, June 6 1995, cols. 557–558). The
amendment, which the Government rejected, was clearly related to the V-WRAG *Shared
Producer Responsibility* proposal discussed in the *Policy Background* to s.93.

Subss. (1) and (7): Content of regulations
The extensive list of possible considerations which regulations might address is in most cases
self-explanatory, although a few comments may be made. The considerable flexibility at the
Government's disposal in making regulations is reinforced by subs. (7) which, for example
would expressly allow a "single point" option for packaging waste to be adopted.

Subs. (1)(a)–(d): targets. materials. obligations and classes of person
The opening items on the list are the key issues which, in relation to packaging and packaging waste, were addressed by the different options in the consultation paper discussed in the note to s.93.

Subs. (1)(e)–(o): individual and collective routes to compliance
One Government concern apparent from the consultation paper on packaging and packaging waste is that an individual route to compliance should be available. They did not consider it appropriate to require businesses to group together or join schemes, and thus regulations may provide for targets for the registration of, and a certificate of compliance for, individual businesses (paras. (e) and (g)).
At the same time, they recognised that what many businesses needed was the ability to discharge their obligations by joining, or paying a levy to, a collective scheme which would undertake (to oversimplify) to meet a business' target on its behalf. In those circumstances, it may be appropriate for the obligation to transfer to the collective scheme and the business to be exempt from its obligation. Hence the term "exemption scheme" (paras. (e)–(g), (j)–(q), (s)): however, the Government's view is that only suitable collective schemes may have this role, and they should be registered: hence "registered exemption scheme".
The need to ensure that collective schemes are not hampered by inappropriate competition laws yet are prevented from acting anti-competitively is also acknowledged (paras. (n) and (o)).

Subs. (1)(g), (h), (l), (n), (p), (t)–(y) and subs. (4): the Agency/SEPA
A substantial role is envisaged for the Environment Agency and SEPA, some of which may be taking at least some of their staff into hitherto uncharted waters: aside from their role in compliance monitoring and the registration of exemption schemes, they may be approving and (subs. (4)) giving guidance to persons who are to issue certificates of compliance (effectively delegating compliance monitoring) (para. (h)) and perhaps exercising competition scrutiny (para. (n)). Extended powers of entry and inspection are catered for (para. (y)).

Subs. (1)(t)–(ya): records and compliance monitoring
One concern evidenced by the Government was that it must be able to monitor compliance and to demonstrate the same to the European Commission to show that EC obligations had been implemented, as required for example by Article 17 of the Packaging and Packaging Waste Directive (see the Earl of Lindsay's remarks in the House of Lords: Hansard, H.L. Vol. 562, col. 1563). Another was that any collective schemes should not operate as cartels or otherwise anti-competitively. These provisions suggest that regulations will address those concerns, although the Earl of Lindsay added that "we shall, of course, take the necessary steps to ensure that commercial confidentiality is maintained" (*ibid.*).

Subss. (2) and (8): Directions and EC and international obligations
Subsection (2) allows considerable scope for the Secretary of State to act outside the regulations so as to implement EC or international obligations, to the extent of issuing directions to private individuals (operators of collective schemes). Such directions may be enforced by way of injunction or (in Scotland) interdict or an order for specific performance in the Court of Session: subs. (8)(b).

Subs. (3): Great Britain
It is clearly considered possible that a simple geographical divide between the spheres of activity of the Agency and SEPA may not be appropriate. One example of this might be where a given business operates both in England or Wales and in Scotland. Normally Agency/SEPA functions (such as licensing) relate to businesses on a site by site basis, so a business which operates both north and south of the border neither causes nor is caused a problem, but where compliance is an issue for the corporate entity as a whole, that may not be the case.

Producer responsibility offences

95.—(1) Regulations may make provision for a person who contravenes a prescribed requirement of the regulations to be guilty of an offence and liable—
    (a) on summary conviction, to a fine not exceeding the statutory maximum;
    (b) on conviction on indictment, to a fine.
(2) Where an offence under any provision of the regulations committed by a body corporate is proved to have been committed with the consent or

connivance of, or to have been attributable to any neglect on the part of, any director, manager, secretary or other similar officer of the body corporate or a person who was purporting to act in any such capacity, he as well as the body corporate shall be guilty of that offence and shall be liable to be proceeded against and punished accordingly.

(3) Where the affairs of a body corporate are managed by its members, subsection (2) above shall apply in relation to the acts or defaults of a member in connection with his functions of management as if he were a director of the body corporate.

(4) Where the commission by any person of an offence under the regulations is due to the act or default of some other person, that other person may be charged with and convicted of the offence by virtue of this section whether or not proceedings for the offence are taken against the first-mentioned person.

(5) Expressions used in this section and in section 93 or 94 above have the same meaning in this section as they have in that section.

DEFINITIONS
"functions": s.124(1).
"prescribed": s.93(8).
"regulations": s.93(8).

COMMENCEMENT
September 21, 1995 (S.I. 1995 No. 1983).

GENERAL NOTE
With ss.93 and 94 having provided for regulations to impose producer responsibility obligations, s.95 makes provision for offences where such obligations are not complied with.

The regulations may provide for contravention to be punishable on summary conviction with the maximum fine available (presently £5,000) and, on conviction on indictment, with an unlimited fine (subs. (1)). The standard environmental legislation provisions for officers' and members' criminal liability are included (subss. (2) and (3), as is the common provision that, where one person causes another to contravene the regulations, both or either may be convicted of the offence (subs. (4)). This last provision is potentially very significant in the light of one frequently expressed concern in the public debate over the form and content of the anticipated producer responsibility obligations for packaging and packaging waste. This was that one person's compliance may be dependent on the conduct of another, since most companies do not have the capacity themselves to recycle or otherwise recover, or indeed to collect, packaging waste. The spectre of a company holding another to "ransom" over its fear of criminal liability was also raised. This provision does not necessarily protect a company in that unfortunate position. It does, however, allow it to point out to the miscreant that it may be rendering itself criminally liable, and it gives the enforcing authority the power to prosecute the miscreant instead of the innocent company.

[*Sections 96–99 are not reproduced here*]

Drainage

Meaning of "drainage" in certain enactments

100.—(1) In the definition of "drainage" in section 113(1) of the Water Resources Act 1991, after paragraph (c) there shall be added the words
"and
    (d) the carrying on, for any purpose, of any other practice which involves management of the level of water in a watercourse;".
(2) For the definition of "drainage" in section 72(1) of the Land Drainage Act 1991 there shall be substituted—
"drainage" includes—
    (a) defence against water (including sea water);
    (b) irrigation, other than spray irrigation;
    (c) warping; and
    (d) the carrying on, for any purpose, of any other practice which involves management of the level of water in a watercourse;".

COMMENCEMENT
September 21, 1995 (S.I. 1995 No. 1983).

GENERAL NOTE
This section widens the meaning of "drainage" in Part IV in the Water Resources Act 1991 and in the Land Drainage Act 1991, to clarify that they include the management of watercourse water levels. These Acts (together with sections 6 and 14–19 of the 1995 Act) govern land drainage (or "flood defence", as the Water Resources Act terms it) in England and Wales: the Water Resources Act deals with the role of the Environment Agency (previously the NRA) and its flood defence committees, whilst the Land Drainage Act deals with internal drainage boards. The definitions in the two Acts remain identical with each other.
   In debate at the Lords Committee stage, in rejecting an amendment which would have deleted the words "other than spray irrigation" from subs. (1)(b) of the amended Land Drainage Act definition proposed by the clause, Earl Howe provided the following explanation both of the amended definitions and of the retention in them of the spray irrigation exclusions:

"Although in the past [internal drainage boards] concentrated on drainage matters, over the years there has been a change of emphasis, and indeed the purpose of [s.100] is to clarify that drainage bodies can undertake water level management, for example for conservation purposes. I recognise that there are also arguments for changing the definition so as to include spray irrigation but, on the other hand, it would be important to ensure that any such change did not have unforeseen adverse repercussions on the water abstraction provisions in Part II of the Water Resources Act 1991, which will continue in force, in particular Section 29, which deals with the right to abstract for drainage purposes. We do not think it would be appropriate to extend the exemption from restrictions on abstraction, which drainage operations enjoy, to cover spray irrigation". (*Hansard*, H.L. Vol. 561, col. 607.)

Grants in connection with drainage works

101.—(1) In section 147 of the Water Resources Act 1991 (grants for drainage works) in subsection (4), after the words "expenditure properly incurred by it with a view to" there shall be inserted "(a)" and at the end of that subsection there shall be added—
   "(b) enabling it to determine in any particular case whether drainage works, or drainage works of any particular description, should or should not be carried out;
   (c) obtaining or organising information, including information about natural processes affecting the coastline, to enable it to formulate or develop its plans with respect to the defence against sea water of any part of the coastline; or
   (d) obtaining, at any time after the carrying out of drainage works, information with respect to—
      (i) the quality or effectiveness, or the effect on the environment, of those works; or
      (ii) any matter of a financial nature relating to those works.
   (4A) Paragraphs (b) to (d) of subsection (4) above are without prejudice to any power—
      (a) to make any grant under subsection (1) or (4)(a) above, or
      (b) to impose any condition under subsection (2) above,
   which could be made or imposed apart from those paragraphs."

(2) In section 59 of the Land Drainage Act 1991 (grants to drainage bodies) in subsection (4), after the words "expenditure properly incurred by them with a view to" there shall be inserted "(a)" and at the end of that subsection there shall be added—
   "(b) enabling them to determine in any particular case whether drainage works, or drainage works of any particular description, should or should not be carried out;
   (c) obtaining or organising information, including information about natural processes affecting the coastline, to enable them

to formulate or develop their plans with respect to the defence against sea water of any part of the coastline; or

(d) obtaining, at any time after the carrying out of drainage works, information with respect to—

(i) the quality or effectiveness, or the effect on the environment, of those works; or

(ii) any matter of a financial nature relating to those works.

(4A) Paragraphs (b) to (d) of subsection (4) above are without prejudice to any power—

(a) to make any grant under subsection (1) or (4)(a) above, or

(b) to impose any condition under subsection (2) above,

which could be made or imposed apart from those paragraphs."

COMMENCEMENT
September 21, 1995 (S.l. 1995 No. 1983).

GENERAL NOTE
This section, like s.100, widens the scope of the drainage provisions in the Water Resources Act (WRA) 1991 and the Land Drainage Act (LDA) 1991. The provisions in question provide for grants for drainage purposes to be made by the Minister of Agriculture, Fisheries and Food, or in Wales, the Secretary of State, to the NRA (now the Environment Agency: see s.2 of the 1995 Act) in the case of s.147 of the WRA and to internal drainage boards in the case of s.59 of the LDA. The amendments allow grants to be made not only as previously for drainage works themselves but also for research and investigation work to underpin coastal defence plans, to determine whether works are appropriate, and to assesses such works following their completion.

It will be noted that the new ss.147(4A) and 59(4A) in each case ensure that the new grounds for grants are additional to the existing grounds and not to be read as in any way limiting their scope; equally, however, those subsections provide that grants made on the new grounds may be subject to conditions in the same way as grants made on the previous grounds.

Fisheries

Sea fisheries

102.—(1) The Sea Fisheries Regulation Act 1966 shall be amended in accordance with the following provisions of this section.

(2) In section 2 (constitution of local fisheries committees) in subsection (2) (which includes provision for the members appointed by the Minister to be persons acquainted with the needs and opinions of the fishing interests of that district) after the words "of that district" there shall be added the words "or as being persons having knowledge of, or expertise in, marine environmental matters".

(3) After that subsection there shall be inserted—

"(2A) In addition to the members appointed as mentioned in subsection (1) above, a local fisheries committee may appoint such number of persons with knowledge of or expertise in marine environmental matters as it thinks fit as further members of the committee for those occasions on which it is considering any proposed byelaw under section 5 below by virtue of section 5A below, or any proposed amendment or revocation of such a byelaw."

(4) At the end of that section there shall be added—

"(7) In this section "marine environmental matters" means—

(a) the conservation or enhancement of the natural beauty or amenity of marine or coastal areas (including their geological or physiographical features) or of any features of archaeological or historic interest in such areas; or

(b) the conservation of flora or fauna which are dependent on, or associated with, a marine or coastal environment."

(5) After section 5 (byelaws for regulation etc of sea fisheries) there shall be inserted—

"Byelaws under section 5 for marine environmental purposes

5A.—(1) Any power to make byelaws conferred by section 5 above may be exercised for marine environmental purposes.

(2) The power to make byelaws under section 5 above by virtue of this section is in addition to, and not in derogation from, the power to make byelaws under that section otherwise than by virtue of this section.

(3) Byelaws under section 5 above by virtue of this section shall be submitted for confirmation under section 7 below—

(a) in the case of a byelaw which is to have effect in England, only after consultation with the Nature Conservancy Council for England;

(b) in the case of a byelaw which is to have effect in Wales, only after consultation with the Countryside Council for Wales.

(4) In this section "marine environmental purposes" means the purposes—

(a) of conserving or enhancing the natural beauty or amenity of marine or coastal areas (including their geological or physiographical features) or of any features of archaeological or historic interest in such areas; or

(b) of conserving flora or fauna which are dependent on, or associated with, a marine or coastal environment."

(6) In section 8 (power of Minister to revoke byelaws if it appears necessary or desirable for the maintenance or improvement of fisheries) after the words "maintenance or improvement of fisheries" there shall be inserted the words "or for marine environmental purposes, within the meaning of section 5A above,".

COMMENCEMENT
September 21, 1995 (S.I. 1995 No. 1983).

GENERAL NOTE
Sections 102 and 103 both introduce the notion of 'marine environmental purposes" (as defined) into a range of legislation dealing with fisheries byelaws and orders.

Section 102 amends the Sea Fisheries Regulation Act 1966 to add "marine environmental purposes" (defined in the new s.5A(4) of the 1966 Act) to the list of purposes for which a local sea fisheries committee for a sea fisheries district may make byelaws. The changes accord with Government proposals on which it consulted in August 1994. It will be noted that the new s.5A(3) requires the committee to consult the relevant statutory conservation body before submitting for confirmation a byelaw made for the new purposes.

Provision is made for the membership of such committees to include persons with knowledge of marine environmental matters when the proposal of such a byelaw is being considered: amended s.2(2) and new s.2(2A) of the 1966 Act.

Other marine or aquatic environmental conservation powers

103.—(1) After section 5 of the Sea Fish (Conservation) Act 1967 (power to restrict fishing for sea fish) there shall be inserted—

"Powers to restrict fishing for environmental purposes

"**5A.**—(1) Any power to make an order under section 5 above may be exercised for marine environmental purposes.

(2) The power to make an order under section 5 above by virtue of this section is in addition to, and not in derogation from, the power to

make an order under that section otherwise than by virtue of this section.

(3) In this section "marine environmental purposes" means the purposes—

    (a) of conserving or enhancing the natural beauty or amenity of marine or coastal areas (including their geological or physiographical features) or of any features of archaeological or historic interest in such areas; or

    (b) of conserving flora or fauna which are dependent on, or associated with, a marine or coastal environment."

(2) After section 2 of the Inshore Fishing (Scotland) Act 1984 there shall be inserted—

"Powers to restrict fishing, or to prohibit the carriage of specified types of net, for marine environmental purposes

"**2A.**—(1) Any power to make an order under section 1 or 2 above may be exercised for marine environmental purposes.

(2) The power to make an order under section 1 or 2 above by virtue of this section is in addition to, and not in derogation from, the power to make an order under that section otherwise than by virtue of this section.

(3) In this section "marine environmental purposes" means the purposes—

    (a) of conserving or enhancing the natural beauty or amenity of marine or coastal areas (including their geological or physiographical features) or of any features of archaeological or historic interest in such areas; or

    (b) of conserving flora or fauna which are dependent on, or associated with, a marine or coastal environment."

(3) In Schedule 25 to the Water Resources Act 1991 (byelaw making powers) after paragraph 6 (byelaws for purposes of fisheries functions) there shall be inserted—

"Fisheries byelaws for marine or aquatic environmental purposes

6A.—(1) Any power to make byelaws conferred by paragraph 6 above may be exercised for marine or aquatic environmental purposes.

(2) The power to make byelaws under paragraph 6 above by virtue of this paragraph is in addition to, and not in derogation from, the power to make byelaws under that paragraph otherwise than by virtue of this paragraph.

(3) In this paragraph "marine or aquatic environmental purposes" means—

    (a) the conservation or enhancement of the natural beauty or amenity of marine or coastal, or aquatic or waterside, areas (including their geological or physiographical features) or of any features of archaeological or historic interest in such areas; or

    (b) the conservation of flora or fauna which are dependent on, or associated with, a marine or coastal, or aquatic or waterside, environment."

COMMENCEMENT
September 21, 1995 (S.I. 1995 No. 1983).

GENERAL NOTE
Section 103, which is parallel in some respects to s.102, amends three pieces of fisheries legislation.

The first is the Sea Fish (Conservation) Act 1967. "Marine environmental purposes" (as defined in the new s.5A(3) of the 1967 Act) are added to the purposes for which an order restricting fishing in England and Wales may be made under s.5 of that Act.

Parallel provision is made in relation to Scotland by an amendment of the Inshore Fishing (Scotland) Act 1984. It will be noted that the scope of the orders which can be made under the latter Act is wider than under the amended 1967 Act provision, since it encompasses restrictions on the carriage of specified types of net.

The third amendment, to the Water Resources Act 1991, is broader in scope in that it adds "marine *or aquatic* environmental purposes" (as defined in the new para. 6 of Sched. 25 of the 1991 Act) to the purposes for which the Environment Agency (previously the NRA) may make fisheries byelaws. The wider scope reflects the fact that the NRA regulates inland freshwaters as well as marine and coastal waters.

Fixed penalty system for certain fisheries offences

104.—(1) After section 37 of the Salmon and Freshwater Fisheries Act 1975 there shall be inserted—

"Fixed penalty notices for certain offences

"**37A.**—(1) Where on any occasion a water bailiff or other officer of the Agency finds a person who he has reason to believe is committing, or has on that occasion committed, a fixed penalty offence, he may give to that person a notice (in this section referred to as a "fixed penalty notice") offering him the opportunity of discharging any liability to conviction for that offence by payment of a fixed penalty.

(2) Where a person is given a fixed penalty notice in respect of a fixed penalty offence—

    (a) no proceedings shall be instituted for that offence before the expiration of the period for paying the fixed penalty; and

    (b) he shall not be convicted of that offence if the fixed penalty is paid before the expiration of that period.

(3) The Agency may extend the period for paying the fixed penalty in any particular case if it considers it appropriate to do so in all the circumstances of the case.

(4) If, in any particular case, the Agency considers that a fixed penalty notice which has been given ought not to have been given, it may give to the person to whom the fixed penalty notice was given a notice withdrawing the fixed penalty notice; and where notice under this subsection is given—

    (a) the Agency shall repay any amount which has been paid by way of fixed penalty in pursuance of the fixed penalty notice; and

    (b) no proceedings shall be instituted or continued against that person for the offence in question.

(5) The amount by which the sums received by the Agency by way of fixed penalties exceed the sums repaid by it under subsection (4)(a) above shall be paid into the Consolidated Fund.

(6) In any proceedings, a certificate purporting to be signed by or on behalf of the Chief Executive of the Agency and stating either—

    (a) that payment of a fixed penalty was, or (as the case may be) was not, received by the Agency on or before a date specified in the certificate, or

    (b) that an envelope containing an amount sent by post in payment of a fixed penalty was marked as posted on a date specified in the certificate,

shall be received as evidence of the matters so stated and shall be treated, without further proof, as being so signed unless the contrary is shown.

(7) A fixed penalty notice shall give such reasonable particulars of the

circumstances alleged to constitute the fixed penalty offence to which the notice relates as are necessary for giving reasonable information of the offence and shall state—

    (a) the monetary amount of the fixed penalty which may be paid;
    (b) the person to whom and the address at which—
        (i) the fixed penalty may be paid, and
        (ii) any correspondence relating to the fixed penalty notice may be sent;
    (c) the method or methods by which payment of the fixed penalty may be made;
    (d) the period for paying the fixed penalty;
    (e) the consequences of the fixed penalty not being paid before the expiration of that period.

(8) A fixed penalty notice may also contain such other information relating to or for the purpose of facilitating, the administration of the fixed penalty system as the Agency considers necessary or desirable.

(9) Regulations may—

    (a) make provision with respect to the giving of fixed penalty notices, including, in particular, provision with respect to—
        (i) the methods by which,
        (ii) the officers, servants or agents by, to or on whom, and
        (iii) the places at which,
    fixed penalty notices may be given by, or served on behalf of, a water bailiff or other officer of the Agency;
    (b) prescribe the method or methods by which fixed penalties may be paid;
    (c) make provision for or with respect to the issue of prescribed documents to persons to whom fixed penalty notices are or have been given.

(10) In this section—

"fixed penalty" means a penalty of such amount as may be prescribed (whether by being specified in, or made calculable under, regulations);

"fixed penalty offence" means, subject to subsection (11) below, any offence—

    (a) under this Act,
    (b) under the Salmon Act 1986,
    (c) under or by virtue of regulations or orders made under section 115, 116 or 142 of the Water Resources Act 1991, or
    (d) under section 211(3) of that Act, so far as relating to byelaws made by virtue of paragraph 6 of Schedule 25 to that Act,

which is for the time being prescribed for the purpose;

"the fixed penalty system" means the system implementing this section and regulations made under it;

"the Ministers" means the Secretary of State and the Minister;

"notice" means notice in writing;

"the period for paying", in relation to any fixed penalty, means such period as may be prescribed for the purpose;

"prescribed" means prescribed by regulations;

"regulations" means regulations made under this section by the Ministers.

(11) The provision that may be made by regulations prescribing fixed penalty offences includes provision for an offence to be a fixed penalty offence—

    (a) only if it is committed in such circumstances or manner as may be prescribed; or

(b) except if it is committed in such circumstances or manner as may be prescribed.

(12) Regulations may provide for any offence which is a fixed penalty offence to cease to be such an offence.

(13) An offence which, in consequence of regulations made by virtue of subsection (12) above, has ceased to be a fixed penalty offence shall be eligible to be prescribed as such an offence again.

(14) Regulations may—

(a) make different provision in relation to different cases or classes of case; or

(b) provide for such exceptions, limitations and conditions, or make such incidental, supplemental, consequential or transitional provision, as the Ministers consider necessary or expedient.

(15) Any power to make regulations under this section shall be exercisable by statutory instrument made by the Ministers; and a statutory instrument containing any such regulations shall be subject to annulment pursuant to a resolution of either House of Parliament."

(2) In section 35 of that Act (which, among other things, creates an offence of failing to state one's name and address when required to do so under that section) in subsection (1) (water bailiffs and constables), for the words from "A water bailiff" to "any constable" there shall be substituted the words "A water bailiff or other officer of the Agency, or any constable,".

(3) After that subsection there shall be inserted—

"(1A) Without prejudice to subsection (1) above, a water bailiff or other officer of the Agency who on any occasion finds a person who he has reason to believe is committing, or has on that occasion committed, a fixed penalty offence, within the meaning of section 37A below, may require that person to state his name and address."

(4) In section 41(1) of that Act (definitions), before the definition of "authorised officer" there shall be inserted—

""the Agency" means the Environment Agency;".

COMMENCEMENT
April 1, 1996 (S.I. 1996 No. 186).

GENERAL NOTE
This section provides for regulations to designate as fixed penalty offences a range of fisheries offences under certain provisions of the Salmon and Freshwater Fisheries Act 1975, Salmon Act 1986 and Water Resources Act 1991 (see new s.37A(10) of the 1975 Act).

A fixed penalty notice system for such offences is introduced and an amendment to s.35 of the 1975 Act by subs. (3) enables Environment Agency officers to obtain the name and address of a person whom they have reason to believe is committing or has committed such an offence.

Minor and consequential amendments relating to fisheries

105. Schedule 15 to this Act (which makes minor and consequential amendments relating to fisheries) shall have effect.

COMMENCEMENT
On the following dates in so far as this section gives effect to the following paras. of Sched. 15:

September 21, 1995 for paras. 25 and 26(1); and January 1, 1999 for paras. 13, 14(1) and (4), 17, 20 and 26(2) (S.I. 1995 No. 1983). February 1, 1996 for paras. 3 and 5(1) of that Schedule; and April 1, 1996 for paras. 1, 2, 4, 5(2) and (3), 6 to 12, 14(2) and (3), 15, 16, 18, 19 and 21 to 24 (S.I. 1996 No. 186). The remainder comes into force on a day to be appointed (s.125(3)).

GENERAL NOTE
This section gives effect to Sched. 15, which makes a number of minor and consequential amendments to fisheries legislation. The majority of these fall into five categories:

— substitutions of references to the Environment Agency for references to the NRA as from the date of transfer of fisheries functions to the Agency (especially para. 2);

— the transfer of certain Ministerial functions under the Salmon and Freshwater Fisheries Act 1975 to the Agency and the removal of certain requirements under that Act for Ministerial consent to Agency (previously NRA) actions (paras. 7–16);

— provision for Ministerial Orders amending or revoking previous subordinate legislation so as to facilitate the coming into force of the provisions of the Act (paras. 3 and 5);

— the amendment of Salmon and Freshwater Fisheries Act 1975 provisions relating to the use of gratings in fish farms and elsewhere, substituting provisions relating to the use of "screens", which term is defined to include gratings (paras. 13–17); and

— the extension of the geographical scope of certain enforcement powers of Agency officers and water bailiffs (para. 19; see also s.6(7)).

In Parliament, the Earl of Lindsay explained the fourth of these sets of amendments as follows:

"the … amendments … have two main purposes—to prevent salmon and migrating trout from becoming trapped in fish farm intakes and outfalls and to prevent farmed fish from escaping into the wild". Replacement of s.14 of the Act "extends the requirements to fit gratings (now referred to as 'screens') to fish farms and provides that these must be capable of preventing the ingress of wild fish and the escape of farmed fish. It also removes the requirement for minis- terial approval. Instead, more general requirements similar to those enshrined in recent Scottish legislation will apply to the placing and nature of screens and will allow for the use of devices other than gratings to prevent the passage of fish" *Hansard* H.L. Vol. 565, cols. 1476 and 1477.

New provisions for Scotland

Control of pollution of water in Scotland

106. Schedule 16 to this Act (which amends the Control of Pollution Act 1974 as respects the control of pollution of rivers and coastal waters in Scotland) shall have effect.

COMMENCEMENT
April 1, 1996 (S.I. 1996 No. 186).

GENERAL NOTE
This section gives effect to Sched. 16 which makes considerable changes to Pt. II of the 1974 Act which contains the principal provisions relating to water pollution control in Scotland. The effect of these changes is to bring Scottish water pollution legislation broadly in line with the provisions of the Water Resources Act 1991, although certain differences remain. These are noted in the General Note to Sched. 16. The new ss.30F–J which Sched. 16 inserts into the 1974 Act are modelled closely on ss.85–89 of the 1991 Act. These provisions replace the main water pollution offence provisions which were contained in ss.31 and 32 of the 1974 Act (s.30F), together with the available statutory defences (ss.30H–J) and they also introduce a system for controlling certain discharges by prohibition notices (s.30G). Fuller details are provided in the General Notes to Sched. 16 itself.

It should also be noted that considerable additional amendments are made to Scottish water pollution legislation by other provisions of the 1995 Act: s.59, s.120 and Sched. 22, para. 29. Section 59 introduces a new definition of abandonment in relation to mines (see the General Notes to ss.58 and 59), while Sched. 22(21) makes the necessary amendments to withdraw the cost recovery exemption in relation to water pollution from abandoned mines from after December 31, 1999 (see the General Note to s.60), Sched. 22, para. 29(22) introduces notices known as "works notices" whereby SEPA may require certain persons to undertake anti-pollution works (see the General Note to s.120) and Sched. 22, para. 29(26) which introduces notices known as "enforcement notices" whereby SEPA may require a consent holder to remedy any contravention of a consent condition (see the General Note to s.120). The scattered arrangement of these amendments is hardly satisfactory from a Scottish perspective. A full text of Parts IA and II of the 1974 Act is provided in Appendix 4.

Statutory nuisances: Scotland

107. Schedule 17 to this Act (which makes provision with respect to statutory nuisances in Scotland) shall have effect.

COMMENCEMENT
April 1, 1996 (S.I. 1996 No. 186).

GENERAL NOTE

Part III of the 1990 Act which established a comprehensive set of controls for statutory nuisances in England and Wales did not originally extend to Scotland where, as a result, the existing controls contained in the Public Health (Scotland) Act 1897 (the 1897 Act) and Pt. III of the 1974 Act (in relation to noise nuisances) continued to apply. However, in August 1994 the Scottish Office Environment Department issued a consultation paper: *The Extension of Part III of the Environmental Protection Act 1990 to Scotland: A Consultation Paper.*

Although this paper noted that advantages had been perceived in retaining a separate framework of statutory nuisance law in Scotland at the time of the passage of the 1990 Act through Parliament, it nevertheless pointed out that experience of the more streamlined system provided by Pt. III of the 1990 Act in England and Wales had highlighted deficiencies in the Scottish system. The paper also noted that the removal of some processes from Pt. I control under the 1990 Act by virtue of the Environmental Protection (Prescribed Processes and Substances) (Amendment) Regulations 1994 (S.I. 1994 No. 1271) necessitated an alternative form of control which Pt. III of the 1990 Act was capable of providing whereas the Scottish provisions in the 1897 Act were perceived as less robust, particularly in the light of the lower penalties available under the 1897 Act.

A further reason for seeking to overhaul the system of statutory nuisance in Scotland was that the operation of the 1897 and 1990 Acts created a potential for double jeopardy. Whereas in England and Wales, s.79(10) of the 1990 Act provides that a local authority cannot take action against a nuisance caused by the operation of a process subject to Pt. I control without the consent of the Secretary of State, the 1897 Act had no such provision. This meant that a local authority could take action against a nuisance caused by a Pt. I process under the 1897 Act even if the process operator was complying with all his authorisation conditions under Pt. I of the 1990 Act. The Government argued that the extension of Pt. III of the 1990 Act to Scotland would remove this double jeopardy altogether.

The Government also indicated that the extension of Pt. III to Scotland would replace the provisions of the Clean Air Act 1993 which provide for smoke to be treated as a nuisance, and the noise provisions of the 1974 Act. They argued that this would broaden the scope of nuisance control in Scotland.

Finally, the paper noted that the extension of Pt. III to Scotland would provide for redress by individuals which hitherto had been lacking in relation to nuisances under the 1987 Act. It should, however, be noted that, under the 1897 Act, where a local authority failed in their duty as regards nuisances, 10 council tax payers who resided in the district could give written notice to the authority of the alleged neglect of duty, and if the authority did nothing within 14 days to remedy the nuisance, they could petition the sheriff who could enforce the abatement of the nuisance at the expense of the local authority (1897 Act, s.146). Alternatively, the procurator fiscal might, with the approval of the Lord Advocate, institute proceedings to compel the authority to carry out their duty (1897 Act, s.148). In relation to noise nuisances the 1974 Act provided for individual remedies for affected occupiers. Part III of the 1990 Act, however, provides for enforcement of the statutory nuisance provisions by any aggrieved person (s.82(1)). Accordingly, the Government announced in *Contaminated Land Clean-up and Control: Outcome of Review* (November 24, 1994) that Pt. III of the 1990 Act was to be extended to Scotland, replacing the relevant provisions of the 1897 and 1974 Acts (see also *Hansard,* H.C. Vol. 250, col. 196w and *ibid.,* cols. 347–348w).

This section gives effect to Sched. 17 which extends Pt. III of the 1990 Act to Scotland. The necessary repeals of the statutory nuisance provisions in the 1897 Act and Pt. III of the 1974 Act are affected by Sched. 24. Accordingly, English and Welsh case law on statutory nuisance will become relevant for Scotland also.

Enforcement of the statutory nuisance provisions in s.82 of the 1990 Act by an aggrieved person in Scotland is to be by way of summary application to the Sheriff (s.82(1) as amended by Sched. 17, para. 6). See the Sheriff Court Summary Application Rules 1993 (S.I. 1993 No. 3240).

Powers of entry

Powers of enforcing authorities and persons authorised by them

108.—(1) A person who appears suitable to an enforcing authority may be authorised in writing by that authority to exercise, in accordance with the terms of the authorisation, any of the powers specified in subsection (4) below for the purpose—

    (a) of determining whether any provision of the pollution control enactments in the case of that authority is being, or has been, complied with;

    (b) of exercising or performing one or more of the pollution control functions of that authority; or

    (c) of determining whether and, if so, how such a function should be exercised or performed.

(2) A person who appears suitable to the Agency or SEPA may be authorised in writing by the Agency or, as the case may be, SEPA to exercise, in accordance with the terms of the authorisation, any of the powers specified in subsection (4) below for the purpose of enabling the Agency or, as the case may be, SEPA to carry out any assessment or prepare any report which the Agency or, as the case may be, SEPA is required to carry out or prepare under section 5(3) or 33(3) above.

(3) Subsection (2) above only applies where the Minister who required the assessment to be carried out, or the report to be prepared, has, whether at the time of making the requirement or at any later time, notified the Agency or, as the case may be, SEPA that the assessment or report appears to him to relate to an incident or possible incident involving or having the potential to involve—

    (a) serious pollution of the environment,

    (b) serious harm to human health, or

    (c) danger to life or health.

(4) The powers which a person may be authorised to exercise under subsection (1) or (2) above are—

    (a) to enter at any reasonable time (or, in an emergency, at any time and, if need be, by force) any premises which he has reason to believe it is necessary for him to enter;

    (b) on entering any premises by virtue of paragraph (a) above, to take with him—

        (i) any other person duly authorised by the enforcing authority and, if the authorised person has reasonable cause to apprehend any serious obstruction in the execution of his duty, a constable; and

        (ii) any equipment or materials required for any purpose for which the power of entry is being exercised;

    (c) to make such examination and investigation as may in any circumstances be necessary;

    (d) as regards any premises which he has power to enter, to direct that those premises or any part of them, or anything in them, shall be left undisturbed (whether generally or in particular respects) for so long as is reasonably necessary for the purpose of any examination or investigation under paragraph (c) above;

    (e) to take such measurements and photographs and make such recordings as he considers necessary for the purpose of any examination or investigation under paragraph (c) above;

    (f) to take samples, or cause samples to be taken, of any articles or substances found in or on any premises which he has power to enter, and of the air, water or land in, on, or in the vicinity of, the premises;

    (g) in the case of any article or substance found in or on any premises which he has power to enter, being an article or substance which appears to him to have caused or to be likely to cause pollution of the environment or harm to human health, to cause it to be dismantled or subjected to any process or test (but not so as to damage or destroy it, unless that is necessary);

(h) in the case of any such article or substance as is mentioned in paragraph (g) above, to take possession of it and detain it for so long as is necessary for all or any of the following purposes, namely—

  (i) to examine it, or cause it to be examined, and to do, or cause to be done, to it anything which he has power to do under that paragraph;

  (ii) to ensure that it is not tampered with before examination of it is completed;

  (iii) to ensure that it is available for use as evidence in any proceedings for an offence under the pollution control enactments in the case of the enforcing authority under whose authorisation he acts or in any other proceedings relating to a variation notice, enforcement notice or prohibition notice under those enactments;

(j) to require any person whom he has reasonable cause to believe to be able to give any information relevant to any examination or investigation under paragraph (c) above to answer (in the absence of persons other than a person nominated by that person to be present and any persons whom the authorised person may allow to be present) such questions as the authorised person thinks fit to ask and to sign a declaration of the truth of his answers;

(k) to require the production of, or where the information is recorded in computerised form, the furnishing of extracts from, any records—

  (i) which are required to be kept under the pollution control enactments for the enforcing authority under whose authorisation he acts, or

  (ii) which it is necessary for him to see for the purposes of an examination or investigation under paragraph (c) above,

and to inspect and take copies of, or of any entry in, the records;

(l) to require any person to afford him such facilities and assistance with respect to any matters or things within that person's control or in relation to which that person has responsibilities as are necessary to enable the authorised person to exercise any of the powers conferred on him by this section;

(m) any other power for—

  (i) a purpose falling within any paragraph of subsection (1) above, or

  (ii) any such purpose as is mentioned in subsection (2) above,

which is conferred by regulations made by the Secretary of State.

(5) The powers which by virtue of subsections (1) and (4) above are conferred in relation to any premises for the purpose of enabling an enforcing authority to determine whether any provision of the pollution control enactments in the case of that authority is being, or has been, complied with shall include power, in order to obtain the information on which that determination may be made,—

(a) to carry out experimental borings or other works on those premises; and

(b) to install, keep or maintain monitoring and other apparatus there.

(6) Except in an emergency, in any case where it is proposed to enter any premises used for residential purposes, or to take heavy equipment on to any premises which are to be entered, any entry by virtue of this section shall only be effected—

(a) after the expiration of at least seven days' notice of the proposed entry given to a person who appears to the authorised person in question to be in occupation of the premises in question, and

(b) either—

      (i) with the consent of a person who is in occupation of those premises; or

     (ii) under the authority of a warrant by virtue of Schedule 18 to this Act.

(7) Except in an emergency, where an authorised person proposes to enter any premises and—

    (a) entry has been refused and he apprehends on reasonable grounds that the use of force may be necessary to effect entry, or

    (b) he apprehends on reasonable grounds that entry is likely to be refused and that the use of force may be necessary to effect entry,

any entry on to those premises by virtue of this section shall only be effected under the authority of a warrant by virtue of Schedule 18 to this Act.

(8) In relation to any premises belonging to or used for the purposes of the United Kingdom Atomic Energy Authority, subsections (1) to (4) above shall have effect subject to section 6(3) of the Atomic Energy Authority Act 1954 (which restricts entry to such premises where they have been declared to be prohibited places for the purposes of the Official Secrets Act 1911).

(9) The Secretary of State may by regulations make provision as to the procedure to be followed in connection with the taking of, and the dealing with, samples under subsection (4)(f) above.

(10) Where an authorised person proposes to exercise the power conferred by subsection (4)(g) above in the case of an article or substance found on any premises, he shall, if so requested by a person who at the time is present on and has responsibilities in relation to those premises, cause anything which is to be done by virtue of that power to be done in the presence of that person.

(11) Before exercising the power conferred by subsection (4)(g) above in the case of any article or substance, an authorised person shall consult—

    (a) such persons having duties on the premises where the article or substance is to be dismantled or subjected to the process or test, and

    (b) such other persons,

as appear to him appropriate for the purpose of ascertaining what dangers, if any, there may be in doing anything which he proposes to do or cause to be done under the power.

(12) No answer given by a person in pursuance of a requirement imposed under subsection (4)(j) above shall be admissible in evidence in England and Wales against that person in any proceedings, or in Scotland against that person in any criminal proceedings.

(13) Nothing in this section shall be taken to compel the production by any person of a document of which he would on grounds of legal professional privilege be entitled to withhold production on an order for discovery in an action in the High Court or, in relation to Scotland, on an order for the production of documents in an action in the Court of Session.

(14) Schedule 18 to this Act shall have effect with respect to the powers of entry and related powers which are conferred by this section.

(15) In this section—

    "authorised person" means a person authorised under subsection (1) or (2) above;

    "emergency" means a case in which it appears to the authorised person in question—

      (a) that there is an immediate risk of serious pollution of the environment or serious harm to human health, or

      (b) that circumstances exist which are likely to endanger life or health,

    and that immediate entry to any premises is necessary to verify the existence of that risk or those circumstances or to ascertain the cause of that risk or those circumstances or to effect a remedy;

    "enforcing authority" means—

 (a) the Secretary of State;
 (b) the Agency;
 (c) SEPA; or
 (d) a local enforcing authority;
"local enforcing authority" means—
 (a) a local enforcing authority, within the meaning of Part I of the
      Environmental Protection Act 1990;
 (b) a local authority, within the meaning of Part IIA of that Act, in
      its capacity as an enforcing authority for the purposes of that
      Part;
 (c) a local authority for the purposes of Part IV of this Act or
      regulations under that Part;
"mobile plant" means plant which is designed to move or to be moved
      whether on roads or otherwise;
"pollution control enactments", in relation to an enforcing authority,
      means the enactments and instruments relating to the pollution
      control functions of that authority;
"pollution control functions", in relation to the Agency or SEPA,
      means the functions conferred or imposed on it by or under—
 (a) the Alkali, &c, Works Regulation Act 1906;
 (b) Part III of the Rivers (Prevention of Pollution) (Scotland) Act
      1951;
 (c) the Rivers (Prevention of Pollution) (Scotland) Act 1965;
 (d) Part I of the Health and Safety at Work etc. Act 1974;
 (e) Parts I, IA and II of the Control of Pollution Act 1974;
 (f) the Control of Pollution (Amendment) Act 1989;
 (g) Parts I, II and IIA of the Environmental Protection Act 1990
      (integrated pollution control, waste on land and contaminated
      land);
 (h) Chapter III of Part IV of the Water Industry Act 1991 (special
      category effluent);
 (j) Part III and sections 161 to 161D of the Water Resources Act
      1991;
 (k) section 19 of the Clean Air Act 1993;
 (l) the Radioactive Substances Act 1993;
 (m) regulations made by virtue of section 2(2) of the European
      Communities Act 1972, to the extent that the regulations
      relate to pollution;
"pollution control functions", in relation to a local enforcing authority,
      means the functions conferred or imposed on, or transferred to,
      that authority—
 (a) by or under Part I or IIA of the Environmental Protection Act
      1990;
 (b) by or under regulations made by virtue of Part IV of this Act;
      or
 (c) by or under regulations made by virtue of section 2(2) of the
      European Communities Act 1972, to the extent that the
      regulations relate to pollution;
"pollution control functions", in relation to the Secretary of State,
      means any functions which are conferred or imposed upon him by
      or under any enactment or instrument and which relate to the
      control of pollution;
"premises" includes any land, vehicle, vessel or mobile plant.
  (16) Any power to make regulations under this section shall be exercisable
by statutory instrument; and a statutory instrument containing any such
regulations shall be subject to annulment pursuant to a resolution of either
House of Parliament.

"the Agency": s.124(1).
"authorised person": subs. (15).
"emergency": subs. (15).
"enforcing authority": subs. (15).
"functions": s.124(1).
"local enforcing authority": subs. (15).
"mobile plant": subs. (15).
"notice": s.124(1).
"pollution control enactments": subs. (15).
"pollution control functions": subs. (15).
"premises": subs. (15).
"records": s.124(1).
"SEPA": s.124(1).

COMMENCEMENT
April 1, 1996 (S.I. 1996 No. 186).

GENERAL NOTE
This section is of great practical importance in that it provides a comprehensive set of powers of entry and investigation which apply to all enforcing authorities exercising pollution control functions at central and local level. The authorities to which the powers apply are defined at subs. (15) and are the Secretary of State, the Environment Agency, SEPA and local authorities. Existing statutory powers of entry (*e.g.* those relating to Parts I and II of the Environmental Protection Act 1990) cease to have effect: see Sched. 22, paras. 55, 85 and 86.

The pollution control functions of the Agency and SEPA are as listed at paras. (a)–(m) in subs. (15) and are comprehensive (with the exception of SEPA's local air pollution control functions which are listed under the pollution control functions of local enforcing authorities discussed below). The pollution control functions of local enforcing authorities are also listed at subs. (15) and cover local air pollution control under Part I of the 1990 Act, contaminated land functions under Part IIA of that Act (as inserted), regulations under Part IV of the 1995 Act relating to air quality, and any pollution control regulations made under s.2(2) of the European Communities Act 1972. Notably, the functions of local authorities in relation to statutory nuisance under Part III of the 1990 Act, noise under the Control of Pollution Act 1974, and air pollution under the Clean Air Act 1993 are not included. In the case of the Secretary of State, those functions are any conferred on him which relate to the control of pollution.

Extensions to the geographical scope of Agency officers' powers in relation to the enforcement of certain fisheries provisions in the catchment area of the River Esk should be noted: s.6(7) and Sched. 15, para. 19.

Subs. (1): Authorisation to exercise powers
The enforcing authorities (see above) may under this subsection authorise in writing the exercise of the relevant powers by any suitable person, for three purposes. Those purposes are:
   (a) determining whether pollution control law is being or has been complied with, *e.g.* compliance monitoring and investigation of possible offences;
   (b) exercising or performing one of the pollution control functions of the authority, *e.g.* supervision of licensed activities; and
   (c) determining whether and, if so, how such a function should be performed.
The terms of this subsection and of the written authorisation are important, since they will affect the validity of the exercise of the relevant powers, and may affect the admissibility of evidence gained as a result of such exercise. The enforcing authority will therefore need to be sure that each pollution control officer is authorised in writing and that when acting they do so within the terms of their authorisation. The authorisation may relate to all the pollution control powers vested in the authority, or to specified powers, *e.g.* waste regulation. If the authorisation is limited in such a way—which would seem inadvisable from the point of view of the authority—then the individual's powers will be limited, to continue the example, to waste regulatory functions.

Even when authorised, the exercise of the powers must not only be within the ambit of subs. (4), but must also be for one of the three purposes listed in subs. (1). The designated officer ought therefore to be prepared to state what his purpose was in exercising the powers. By Sched. 18, para. 3, the designated person must produce evidence of his designation and other authority before exercising the power. By para. 6(4) a designated person shall not be liable in civil or criminal proceedings for anything done in the purported exercise of a relevant power if the court is satisfied the act was done in good faith and on reasonable grounds.

Information obtained by exercise of powers
Information obtained in consequence of the exercise of the relevant powers, whether with or without consent, is admissible in evidence against any person: Sched. 18, para. 4.

Subss. (2) and (3): Assessments and reports
Subsection (2) confers an additional power on the Agency/SEPA to authorise persons to exercise the powers listed at subs. (4) for the purpose of enabling the preparation of assessments and reports on the actual or likely effects of existing or potential levels of pollution, on the options available for control and clean-up, and on the respective costs and benefits. The Agency/SEPA will only be under a duty to carry out such an assessment where required to do so by the Secretary of State or Minister, and will then only have the ability to authorise the exercise of the powers where notified by the Secretary of State/Minister that the assessment relates to an incident or possible incident involving the serious consequences set out at subs. (3). The powers are not available in relation to the Agency/SEPA's general duty to follow developments in technology and techniques under ss.5(4) and 33(4).

Subs. (4): Powers
This is the vital subsection which lists the powers available, which a person may be authorised to exercise. There is no reason why a person could not be authorised to exercise some but not all of those powers, though to avoid complications, the authority will presumably wish to authorise the exercise of all or any of the powers. The conditions for the exercise of the powers are phrased in various terms, and close attention needs to be paid to the wording in each case. The powers may be grouped as follows:
Entry: Paragraphs (a) and (b) together provide a power of entry based upon whether the authorised officer has reason to believe that it is necessary for him to enter the premises. Whilst it is not stated expressly, it is submitted that the necessity to enter the premises must relate to the statutory purposes set out at subs. (1) (see below). Case law on wording in the field of police powers of entry suggests that the authorised officer must not only have reason to believe it necessary to enter, but must actually have that belief: *R. v. Banks* [1916] 2 K.B. 621; *R. v. Harrison* [19381 3 All E.R. 134; *Nakkuda Ali v. Jayaratwe* [1951] A.C. 66 (P.C.); *Chapman v. DPP* (1988) 89 Cr.App.Rep. 190. It is submitted that there must be reasonable grounds on which the belief is based, such that a reasonable person could hold that belief: see *e.g. McArdle v. Egan* (1933) 150 L.T. 412; *IRC v. Rossminster Ltd* [1980] A.C. 952, [1980] 1 All E.R. 80.
The power is substantially wider in cases of emergency, where it can be exercised at any time (whether reasonable or not) and by force if necessary. "Emergency" is defined at subs. (15). The power is extended by para. (b) to other authorised persons and to necessary equipment and materials, as well as to police presence if there is a reasonable cause to apprehend serious obstruction (which may be an offence under s.110(1)).
The provisions need to be read with subss. (6)–(8). Entry is restricted by subs. (6) in the case of residential premises, or where heavy equipment is to be taken onto the premises: unless the situation is one of emergency, entry may only be effected after seven days' notice to the apparent occupier, and then either with the occupier's consent or under a warrant.
Forcible entry may be effected where there is an emergency (subs. (1)), but in other cases by subs. (7) a warrant will be necessary if entry has been or is likely to be refused. In the case of premises belonging to or used for the purposes of the U.K. Atomic Energy Authority entry may be restricted under subs. (8). Entry to Crown Premises generally may be subject to restriction on grounds of national security under s.115(5).
Schedule 18 is also relevant to powers of entry. Paragraph 2 deals with the issue of warrants in cases where entry is refused or refusal is anticipated, where the premises are unoccupied, where the occupier is temporarily absent and the case is one of urgency or where application for admission would defeat the object of the proposed entry. Paragraph 5 imposes a duty in the case of entry on unoccupied premises, or where the occupier is temporarily absent, to leave the premises secured as effectively as they were initially. Paragraph 6 provides for the payment of full compensation for loss or damage sustained by reason of entry or failure to leave the premises secure.

Examination and inspection
The power to examine and investigate is a very general one, simply related to what may in any circumstances be necessary: para. (c). In relation to premises which have been or may be

entered under para. (a) a direction may be given (not necessarily in writing) that the premises or anything in them shall be left undisturbed for so long as is reasonably necessary for examination or investigation: para. (d).

Measurements, photographs and recordings
This useful power, contained in para. (e), is related to examination and investigation, in that the authorised person must consider it necessary for such purposes.

Samples
Under para. (f) samples may be taken of articles or substances on the premises entered, and of the air, water or land in, on or in the vicinity of premises which the authorised person has power to enter. Where samples are taken outside the premises, there may in practical terms be no need to enter, but it appears that there must still be power to do so. Regulations on sampling procedures may be made under subs. (9).

Subsection (5) is also relevant to sampling. It enables the authorised person to carry out experimental borings or other works (*e.g.* to obtain soil or groundwater samples) and to install and keep monitoring or other apparatus on the premises. This power is ancillary to the purpose of determining whether environmental legislation is being complied with (subs. (1)(a)) and is exercisable only in that context. This may give rise to difficulty in the case of investigation for contaminated land under Pt. IIA of the 1990 Act as inserted by this Act, which may well require "experimental borings" to be carried out. Such investigation is for the purpose of determining whether the land is contaminated, not whether environmental law is being complied with. This in turn raises the question of the relationship of subs. (5) to subs. (4)(f), and whether the soil or groundwater samples could be obtained under the latter provision. The s.108(4)(m) provision for regulations to extend the list of powers in subs. (4) may need to be called upon to resolve such difficulties.

Possession, testing and destruction of articles and substances
By paras. (g) and (h) there is power to dismantle and test articles or substances which appear to the authorised person to have caused or be likely to cause pollution (including power to damage or destroy them if necessary), or to take possession of such an article or substance and detain it for the purposes set out in para. (h). Those purposes include ensuring it is not tampered with, and for evidence in subsequent criminal or enforcement proceedings. The article or substance must be found in or on premises which the authorised person has power to enter. By subs. (10) any person present on the premises and having responsibilities in relation to them may require that they be present during the exercise of the power under para. (g).

Before exercising the powers under para. (g), the procedure set out at subs. (11) must be followed: the authorised person must consult such persons having duties on the premises, and such other persons, as seem appropriate, to ascertain the possible hazards involved in taking the proposed action. The power of detention under para. (h) applies for so long as detention is necessary for the three purposes (i)–(iii) set out in the paragraph. It is likely that the power to take possession of the article or substance may only be exercised by the authorised person and not by any person accompanying him: *R. v. Central Criminal Court and British Railways Board. ex p. A.J.D. Holdings Ltd, Royle and Stanley Ltd.* [1992] Crim. L.R. 669. If possession is taken of the article or substance unlawfully or following unlawful entry, then it is doubtful whether it can lawfully be retained even if required as evidence: see *R. v. Chief Constable of Lancashire, ex p. Parker & McGrath* [1993] 2 All E.R. 56.

Information requests
Paragraph (j) allows any person who with reasonable cause is believed to have relevant information to be required to answer questions and to sign a declaration as to the truth of the answers. The authority may require the interview to be conducted in private, except for the presence of a person nominated by the person under questioning, and any other person who the authority may allow to be present.

Failure to comply with the request is an offence under s.110(1)(a), but no answer given will be admissible against the person giving it in any proceedings in England and Wales, or in criminal proceedings in Scotland: subs. (12).

Production of records
The authorised person may under para. (k) require the production of records. Two types of records are covered: those required to be kept under a pollution control enactment (*e.g.*

monitoring data required by an authorisation condition) or those which it is necessary for the authorised person to see for the purposes of his powers of examination and investigation. Computer records and any other records kept otherwise than in a document are within the provision: s.124(1). The term "record" may give rise to difficulties of interpretation in this context. There is some authority to suggest that the term extends only to primary sources of information: *R. v. Tirado* (1974) 59 Cr. App. R. 50. If so, it might not cover reports, files of correspondence, memoranda or consignment notes which are secondary rather than primary sources: see *R. v. Gwilliam* [1968] 1 W.L.R. 1839 (files of correspondence). Documents which are a digest or analysis of primary or original sources of information may not constitute a record: see *R. v. Schering Chemicals Ltd.* [1983] 1 W.L.R. 143. On the other hand, notes of a meeting or a report might be said to constitute a record of that meeting or of events referred to in the report, and at least one case suggests a wider interpretation of the term: see *R. v. Jones (Benjamin)* [1978] 1 W.L.R. 195. Matters of opinion may be distinguished from records: see *Savings and Investment Bank v. Gasco Investments (Netherlands) B.V.* [1984] 1 W.L.R. 271 (report of inspector).

Documents covered by legal professional privilege cannot be required to be disclosed: see subs. (13) below.

The power to require production of records does not include the power to remove them: *Barge v. British Gas Corporation* (1983) 81 L.G.R. 53. However para. (k) does give the right to take copies. If copying facilities are not available at the premises on which the records are held, the authorised person may have difficulties in legitimately taking copies where the para. (l) power does not assist.

Other facilities and assistance
Any person may be required to afford the authorised person with facilities or assistance necessary to enable the exercise of the statutory powers, so far as those things are within their control or they have responsibility for them: para. (l). This might include, for example, the use of equipment or office or changing facilities.

Subs. (13): privilege
Nothing in s.108 can compel the production of documents protected by legal professional privilege. This exemption would cover communications between clients and legal professional advisors, whether independent or "in-house". It would not cover communications with other professional advisors, such as engineers or chemists nor would it cover the giving of legal advice by other professionals such as accountants in the course of their work. It is doubtful if businesses could obtain protection for their documents simply by depositing them with their legal advisors. The matter protected by privilege must have formed part of the substance of the seeking or giving of legal advice and not have a completely independent origin: *R. v. Peterborough Justices, ex p. Hicks* [1977] 1 W.L.R. 1371; *R. v. King* [1983] 1 All E.R. 929. However, privilege would attach to documents which were fairly referable to a contemplated relationship: *Minter v. Priest* [1930] A.C. 558. Furthermore, documents "are privileged, although they may not relate to any suit depending or contemplated or apprehended": *McCowan v. Wright* (1852) 15 D. 229 *per* Lord Wood at p. 237. Attendance notes recording meetings or advice between legal advisors and clients would also be privileged (*Balabel v. Air India* [1988] Ch. 317) but not notes simply recording meetings or conversations between opposing parties or their legal advisors (*Parry v. News Group Newspapers* [1990] New L.J. 1791). Nor is legal professional privilege conferred simply by marking a document "without prejudice". A legal advisor's professional duty need not be confined to giving advice on matters of law or on the construction of documents. It may extend to the commercial wisdom of entering into a particular transaction in respect of which legal advice is also sought: *Nederlandse Reassurantie Group Holding N.V. v. Bacon & Woodrow* [1995] 1 All E.R. 976.

Subs. (14): Sched. 18
Schedule 18 contains supplementary provisions dealing with the procedure for the issue of warrants required under the section. The detailed grounds for the issue of warrants are set out at para. 2.

Paragraph 3 requires an authorised person to produce evidence of their authority before exercising a statutory power under s.108, and to produce evidence of their warrant if acting under one. As to the production of warrants, see *R. v. Chief Constable of Lancashire, ex p. Parker* [1993] 2 All E.R. 56 and in respect of the position in Scotland: Stoddart, *Criminal Warrants* (Butterworths, 1991), 3.14; and Alison, *Practice of the Criminal Law of Scotland* (1833), 117.

By para. 4 evidence obtained in the exercise of the powers, whether with or without consent, is admissible in evidence against any person, subject to the special limitation provided by subs. (12) relating to self-incrimination.

Relevance of Police and Criminal Evidence Act Codes of Practice
Various matters dealt with in section 108 are regulated in England and Wales by the Codes of Practice issued under ss.60 and 66 of the Police and Criminal Evidence Act 1984, *i.e.* powers of search and questioning. By s.67(9) of the 1984 Act, persons other than police officers who are charged with the duty of investigating offences or charging offenders shall in the discharge of that duty have regard to the relevant provisions of any such Code. The Codes may therefore apply to routine inspections to establish compliance with legislation, as well as to the investigation of specific infractions: *Dudley Metropolitan County Council v. Debenhams plc, The Times,* August 19, 1994. Since the purposes for which the statutory pollution control powers are provided include, but are not confined to, establishing compliance with legislation, it will be a question of fact as to whether the officer in question was, at the relevant time, discharging the duty of investigating offences as opposed to some other duty, *e.g.* the exercise of licensing functions.

Power to deal with cause of imminent danger of serious pollution, etc.

109.—(1) Where, in the case of any article or substance found by him on any premises which he has power to enter, an authorised person has reasonable cause to believe that, in the circumstances in which he finds it, the article or substance is a cause of imminent danger of serious pollution of the environment or serious harm to human health, he may seize it and cause it to be rendered harmless (whether by destruction or otherwise).

(2) As soon as may be after any article or substance has been seized and rendered harmless under this section, the authorised person shall prepare and sign a written report giving particulars of the circumstances in which the article or substance was seized and so dealt with by him, and shall—

    (a) give a signed copy of the report to a responsible person at the premises where the article or substance was found by him; and

    (b) unless that person is the owner of the article or substance, also serve a signed copy of the report on the owner;

and if, where paragraph (b) above applies, the authorised person cannot after reasonable inquiry ascertain the name or address of the owner, the copy may be served on him by giving it to the person to whom a copy was given under paragraph (a) above.

(3) In this section, "authorised person" has the same meaning as in section 108 above.

D<small>EFINITION</small>
"authorised person": s.108(15).

C<small>OMMENCEMENT</small>
April 1, 1996 (S.I. 1996 No. 186).

G<small>ENERAL</small> N<small>OTE</small>
This section provides a power to seize articles or substances found on premises which there is power to enter under s.108. The authorised person must have reasonable cause to believe the article or substance to be a cause of imminent danger in the circumstances in which it is found. As to the words "reasonable cause to believe", see note to s.108. Subsection (2) requires a written report of the circumstances of seizure to be prepared.

    The section must be read alongside s.108(4)(g) and (h) which also gives power to take possession of substances and articles, but for the purposes of investigation, examination, testing and evidence. The purpose of s.109 is to render harmless a source of imminent danger. It will be important for the pollution control officer who intends to remove substances or articles or to interfere with them in some other way to be clear as to which provision he is acting under, since the procedural requirements of the two sections are quite different.

Offences

110.—(1) It is an offence for a person intentionally to obstruct an authorised person in the exercise or performance of his powers or duties.

(2) It is an offence for a person, without reasonable excuse,—

   (a) to fail to comply with any requirement imposed under section 108 above;

   (b) to fail or refuse to provide facilities or assistance or any information or to permit any inspection reasonably required by an authorised person in the execution of his powers or duties under or by virtue of that section; or

   (c) to prevent any other person from appearing before an authorised person, or answering any question to which an authorised person may require an answer, pursuant to subsection (4) of that section.

(3) It is an offence for a person falsely to pretend to be an authorised person.

(4) A person guilty of an offence under subsection (1) above shall be liable—

   (a) in the case of an offence of obstructing an authorised person in the execution of his powers under section 109 above—

     (i) on summary conviction, to a fine not exceeding the statutory maximum;

     (ii) on conviction on indictment, to a fine or to imprisonment for a term not exceeding two years, or to both;

   (b) in any other case, on summary conviction, to a fine not exceeding level 5 on the standard scale.

(5) A person guilty of an offence under subsection (2) or (3) above shall be liable on summary conviction to a fine not exceeding level 5 on the standard scale.

(6) In this section—

"authorised person" means a person authorised under section 108 above and includes a person designated under paragraph 2 of Schedule 18 to this Act;

"powers and duties" includes powers or duties exercisable by virtue of a warrant under Schedule 18 to this Act.

DEFINITIONS
"authorised person": subs. (6).
"powers and duties": subs. (6).

COMMENCEMENT
April 1, 1996 (S.I. 1996 No. 186).

GENERAL NOTE
This section creates a number of separate offences relating to the exercise of powers under ss.108 and 109. These are:

   (1) Intentional obstruction of an authorised person in the exercise of his powers or duties: subs. (1). Obstruction need not include physical violence and may involve anything which makes the exercise of the powers more difficult: *Hinchcliffe v. Sheldon* [1955] 1 W.L.R. 1207. Giving a warning to someone may therefore constitute obstruction: *Green v. Moore* [1982] Q.B. 1044. It should be noted that in Scotland the offence has been construed much more narrowly and it has been held that there must be a physical element to obstruction: *Curlett v. McKechnie* 1938 J.C. 176 *per* Lord Fleming at p. 179 (making false statements to the police not obstruction). This position was modified to some extent by *Skeen v. Shaw* 1979 S.L.T. (Notes) 58 where it was held that the addition of the word "hinder" to the statutory definition of the offence in s.41 of the Police (Scotland) Act 1967 reduced any necessary physical element to a minimum and hence that standing in front of officers and shouting at them constituted the offence

although no physical contact had occurred. Given that the word "hinder" does not appear in s.110 of the 1995 Act, it is likely that the Scottish courts would require the presence of a physical element for there to be obstruction. However, in order to be an offence the obstruction must be intentional, *i.e.* done with the intention of obstructing: *Willmott v. Atack* [1977] Q.B. 498. If the act was done intentionally it will be immaterial that the person doing the act did not appreciate that it constituted obstruction at law, or that it was not aimed primarily at the person obstructed: see, *e.g. Green v. Moore* [1982] Q.B. 1044; *Hills v. Ellis* [1983] Q.B. 680; *Lewis v. Cox* [1984] 3 All E.R. 672. However, it would appear to be necessary for the accused to know that the person he was obstructing was indeed an authorised person. *Ostler v. Elliott* [1980] Crim. L.R. 584 indicates that the requirement of wilfulness in the offence of "wilful obstruction" under s.51 of the Police Act 1967 could provide a defence for a person who honestly and reasonably believed that the police officers were robbers. The position is the same in Scotland: *Annan v. Tait* 1981 S.C.C.R. 326 (accused acquitted where he did not realise that he was struggling with plain-clothes police officers). The authorised person must also be acting in the exercise or performance of his powers. Where this is not the case it would appear to be common ground both south and north of the border that obstruction would not be unlawful: *Pedro v. Diss* [1981] 2 All E.R. 59; *Twycross v. Farrell* 1973 S.L.T. (Notes) 85; *Wither v. Reid* 1979 S.L.T. 192; *Stocks v. Hamilton* 1991 S.C.C.R. 190.

(2) Failure to comply with any requirement under s.108 without reasonable excuse: subs. (2)(a). What is a reasonable excuse will depend on the circumstances of each case, but the standard will be objective in that the excuse must be capable of being regarded as reasonable, in the sense of being consistent with a reasonable standard of conduct: *Pascoe v. Nominal Defendant (Queensland) (No. 2)* [1964] Qd.R. 373. The fact that the defendant did not know that he was obliged to comply with the requirement may not of itself constitute a reasonable excuse: *Greenwich London Borough Council v. Millcroft Construction Ltd* [1986] 85 L.G.R. 66; 150 J.P. 645. Complete lack of comprehension of what was being required may however be an excuse: *Beck v. Sager* [1979] Crim.L.R. 257.

(3) Failure, without reasonable excuse, to provide facilities or assistance which are reasonably required: subs. (2)(b).

(4) Without reasonable excuse, preventing any other person from appearing before an authorised person or answering any question: subs. 2(c).

(5) Impersonating an authorised person: subs. (3).

Penalties
Most of the offences under the section are punishable on summary conviction only. However, the obstruction of an authorised person acting under s.109 in relation to a substance or article which is a cause of imminent danger is punishable on indictment by an unlimited fine and up to two years imprisonment: subs. (4)(a).

Evidence

Evidence in connection with certain pollution offences

111.—(1) The following provisions (which restrict the admissibility in evidence of information obtained from samples) shall cease to have effect—
　(a) section 19(2) to (2B) of the Rivers (Prevention of Pollution) (Scotland) Act 1951;
　(b) section 49 of the Sewerage (Scotland) Act 1968;
　(c) section 171(4) and (5) of the Water Industry Act 1991; and
　(d) section 209(1), (2) and (4) of the Water Resources Act 1991.

(2) Information provided or obtained pursuant to or by virtue of a condition of a relevant licence (including information so provided or obtained, or recorded, by means of any apparatus) shall be admissible in evidence in any proceedings, whether against the person subject to the condition or any other person.

(3) For the purposes of subsection (2) above, apparatus shall be presumed in any proceedings to register or record accurately, unless the contrary is shown or the relevant licence otherwise provides.

(4) Where—
(a) by virtue of a condition of a relevant licence, an entry is required to be made in any record as to the observance of any condition of the relevant licence, and
(b) the entry has not been made,
that fact shall be admissible in any proceedings as evidence that that condition has not been observed.

(5) In this section—
"apparatus" includes any meter or other device for measuring, assessing, determining, recording or enabling to be recorded, the volume, temperature, radioactivity, rate, nature, origin, composition or effect of any substance, flow, discharge, emission, deposit or abstraction;
"condition of a relevant licence" includes any requirement to which a person is subject under, by virtue of or in consequence of a relevant licence;
"environmental licence" has the same meaning as it has in Part I above as it applies in relation to the Agency or SEPA, as the case may be;
"relevant licence" means—
(a) any environmental licence;
(b) any consent under Part II of the Sewerage (Scotland) Act 1968 to make discharges of trade effluent;
(c) any agreement under section 37 of that Act with respect to, or to any matter connected with, the reception, treatment or disposal of such effluent;
(d) any consent under Chapter III of Part IV of the Water Industry Act 1991 to make discharges of special category effluent; or
(e) any agreement under section 129 of that Act with respect to, or to any matter connected with, the reception or disposal of such effluent.

(6) In section 25 of the Environmental Protection Act, after subsection (2) (which makes similar provision to subsection (4) above) there shall be inserted—

"(3) Subsection (2) above shall not have effect in relation to any entry required to be made in any record by virtue of a condition of a relevant licence, within the meaning of section 111 of the Environment Act 1995 (which makes corresponding provision in relation to such licences)."

DEFINITIONS
"the Agency": s.124(1).
"apparatus": subs. (5).
"condition of a relevant licence": subs. (5).
"environmental licence": subs. (5).
"SEPA": s.124(1).

COMMENCEMENT
April 1, 1996 (S.I. 1996 No. 186).

GENERAL NOTE
This section deals with the issue of evidence in relation to pollution offences, and makes some important changes to existing law.

Subs. (1): removal of tripartite sampling requirement
This subsection removes the time honoured requirement relating to evidence of samples in various water pollution offences that the sample on being taken should be divided into three parts, one for the authority, the second to be given to the occupier of the relevant premises, and the third to be retained for future analysis. This procedure was seen as becoming increasingly inconvenient, incompatible with automated sampling methods, and had given rise to some difficult issues of interpretation. See *Attorney-General's Reference (No. 2 of 1994), The Times,*

August 4, 1994; *R. v. CPC (U.K.) Ltd, The Times*, August 4, 1994. For an article on the issue, see Albert Mumma [1993] J.E.L. Vol. 5, No. 2, p. 191.

It should be noted that, in relation to Scotland, the removal of the requirement for tripartite sampling does not affect the need for corroboration of the material facts.

Subs. (2)
This subsection deals with information obtained pursuant to or by virtue of a condition of an environmental licence and makes it clear that such information is admissible if obtained by means of apparatus. Consent conditions, for example on discharge consents, may require self-monitoring and the making of returns: see, *e.g.* Sched. 10, para. 2(4) of the Water Resources Act 1991. Advances in technology mean that much environmental monitoring is carried out on a continuous basis by various types of device: many environmental licences will contain conditions requiring the licensee to carry out such monitoring. Similarly, the enforcing authorities themselves make use of such devices, which will sometimes operate on a remote sensing basis to generate data elsewhere.

It should be noted that the subsection applies only to information provided or obtained pursuant to or by virtue of a licence condition. This leaves some doubt over the position of information produced by apparatus in other circumstances: for example apparatus maintained by the enforcing authority on other land, or apparatus used by environmental groups. It is submitted that such information would be admissible in evidence, but would not benefit from the presumption contained in subs. (3), as to which see below.

Subs. (3)
Apparatus which produces information falling within subs. (2) is presumed by this subsection to have registered or recorded accurately, unless the contrary is shown, or the licence pursuant to which the information is obtained provides otherwise.

Subs. (4)
Under this subsection, which is similar in effect to s.25(2) of the 1990 Act, where a licence condition requires compliance with other conditions to be recorded, the absence of any such record is admissible as evidence that that condition has not been observed.

There is, however, one problem of interpretation raised by the new provision. Under s.25(2) of the 1990 Act it was clear that the condition in question was that in respect of which observance was required to be recorded: in subs. (4) the final reference to "that condition" could be taken to refer either to the condition requiring the entry to be made, or the condition the observance of which is required to be recorded. It is submitted that the second interpretation is correct.

Subs. (5)
Apparatus. The definition is not exhaustive and could clearly include automatic samplers.

Offences

Amendment of certain offences relating to false or misleading statements or false entries

112. Schedule 19 to this Act shall have effect.

COMMENCEMENT
April 1, 1996 (S.I. 1996 No. 186).

GENERAL NOTE
Schedule 19 creates various offences relating to false or misleading statements made in the course of applications, or in response to requests for information made by authorities, or false records. The offences are created in relation to the existing legislation referred to in the Schedule, which hitherto have lacked such sanctions or (like s.44 of the 1990 Act) have phrased the offence in different terms. The essentials of the offences are the making of a statement which is known to be false or misleading in a material particular, or recklessly making a statement which is false or misleading in a material particular.

Disclosure of information

113.—(1) Notwithstanding any prohibition or restriction imposed by or under any enactment or rule of law, information of any description may be disclosed—

(a) by a new Agency to a Minister of the Crown, the other new Agency or a local enforcing authority,

(b) by a Minister of the Crown to a new Agency, another Minister of the Crown or a local enforcing authority, or

(c) by a local enforcing authority to a Minister of the Crown, a new Agency or another local enforcing authority,

for the purpose of facilitating the carrying out by either of the new Agencies of any of its functions, by any such Minister of any of his environmental functions or by any local enforcing authority of any of its relevant functions; and no person shall be subject to any civil or criminal liability in consequence of any disclosure made by virtue of this subsection.

(2) Nothing in this section shall authorise the disclosure to a local enforcing authority by a new Agency or another local enforcing authority of information—

(a) disclosure of which would, in the opinion of a Minister of the Crown, be contrary to the interests of national security; or

(b) which was obtained under or by virtue of the Statistics of Trade Act 1947 and which was disclosed to a new Agency or any of its officers by the Secretary of State.

(3) No information disclosed to any person under or by virtue of this section shall be disclosed by that person to any other person otherwise than in accordance with the provisions of this section, or any provision of any other enactment which authorises or requires the disclosure, if that information is information—

(a) which relates to a trade secret of any person or which otherwise is or might be commercially confidential in relation to any person; or

(b) whose disclosure otherwise than under or by virtue of this section would, in the opinion of a Minister of the Crown, be contrary to the interests of national security.

(4) Any authorisation by or under this section of the disclosure of information by or to any person shall also be taken to authorise the disclosure of that information by or, as the case may be, to any officer of his who is authorised by him to make the disclosure or, as the case may be, to receive the information.

(5) In this section—

"new Agency" means the Agency or SEPA;

"the environment" has the same meaning as in Part I of the Environmental Protection Act 1990;

"environmental functions", in relation to a Minister of the Crown, means any function of that Minister, whether conferred or imposed under or by virtue of any enactment or otherwise, relating to the environment; and

"local enforcing authority" means—

(a) any local authority within the meaning of Part IIA of the Environmental Protection Act 1990, and the "relevant functions" of such an authority are its functions under or by virtue of that Part;

(b) any local authority within the meaning of Part IV of this Act, and the "relevant functions" of such an authority are its functions under or by virtue of that Part;

(c) in relation to England, any county council for an area for which there are district councils, and the "relevant functions" of such a county council are its functions under or by virtue of Part IV of this Act; or

(d) in relation to England and Wales, any local enforcing authority within the meaning of section 1(7) of the Environmental Protection Act 1990, and the "relevant functions" of such an authority are its functions under or by virtue of Part I of that Act.

DEFINITIONS
"the Agency": s.124(1).
"the environment": subs. (5).
"environmental functions": subs. (5).
"functions": s.124(1).
"local enforcing authority": subs. (5).
"relevant functions": subs. (5).
"SEPA": s.124(1).

COMMENCEMENT
April 1, 1996 (S.I. 1996 No. 186).

GENERAL NOTE
This section gives a general power of mutual disclosure of information between Ministers, the new agencies and local authorities for the purpose of facilitating the carrying out of their relevant environmental functions. Immunity against civil or criminal liability is given in respect of such disclosure. The power is potentially important: the Environment Agency in the course of its functions may, for example, obtain information relevant to the identification by a local enforcing authority of contaminated land. Power to disclose information extends to officers of the relevant bodies who are authorised to make the disclosure or to receive the information: subs. (4). However, restrictions are imposed by subs. (2) in relation to the disclosure of certain information to local enforcing authorities.

Subsection (3) is important as it deals with the treatment of information disclosed under the section. The further disclosure of that information is restricted where the information relates to a trade secret, is commercially confidential in nature, or affects national security. In those cases the information may only be further disclosed in accordance with the provisions of s.113 (*i.e.* under subs. (1)) or in accordance with any other provision which authorises or requires its disclosure. Such provisions will include those relating to the placing of information on public registers and to requests for information under the Environmental Information Regulations 1992 (S.I. 1992 No. 3240). Those provisions themselves contain inbuilt restrictions on the disclosure of information which is commercially confidential or affects national security.

The power to disclose information contained in subs. (1) is overriding in nature, in that it applies notwithstanding any statutory prohibition or restriction, or any rule of law (*e.g.* confidentiality). The general principle is that information obtained pursuant to statutory powers can only be disclosed by the recipient to such persons and for such purposes as are envisaged by the statute conferring those powers: *Marcel v. Commissioner of Police of the Metropolis* [1992] 1 W.L.R. 50; *Hoechst U.K. Ltd v. Chemiculture Ltd* [19931 F.S.R. 270. That principle of confidentiality will be overridden in cases to which s.113 applies but, it is submitted, will continue to apply to disclosure outside the scope of the section (subject to any statutory rights of access to information).

Subs. (5): "the environment"
In Part I of the 1990 Act, the "environment" is defined as "consist[ing] of all, or any, of the following media, namely, the air, water and land; and the medium of air includes the air within buildings and the air within other natural or man-made structures above or below ground": s.1(2). Although subs. (11) of that section of the 1990 Act provides rules for the determination of whether a "release" is a release into land or water, the term "land" is not defined and therefore the definition in Sched. 1 to the Interpretation Act 1978 is applicable: "land" includes buildings and other structures, land covered with water, and any estate, interest, easement, servitude or right in or over land.

Power of Secretary of State to delegate his functions of determining, or to refer matters involved in, appeals

114.—(1) The Secretary of State may—
   (a) appoint any person to exercise on his behalf, with or without payment, any function to which this paragraph applies; or
   (b) refer any item to which this paragraph applies to such person as the Secretary of State may appoint for the purpose, with or without payment.

(2) The functions to which paragraph (a) of subsection (1) above applies are any of the Secretary of State's functions of determining—
   (a) an appeal under—
      (i) section 31A(2)(b), 42B(5), 46C or 49B of the Control of Pollution Act 1974,
      (ii) section 4 of the Control of Pollution (Amendment) Act 1989,
      (iii) section 15, 22(5), 43, 62(3)(c), 66(5), 78L or 78T of the Environmental Protection Act 1990,
      (iv) paragraph 2 or paragraph 3(3) of Schedule 6 to the Natural Heritage (Scotland) Act 1991,
      (v) section 43, 91, 92, 96, 161C or 191B(5) of the Water Resources Act 1991,
      (vi) section 26 of the Radioactive Substances Act 1993 against any decision of, or notice served by, SEPA,
      (vii) paragraph 6 of Schedule 5 to the Waste Management Licensing Regulations 1994,
      or any matter involved in such an appeal;
   (b) the questions, or any of the questions, which fall to be determined by the Secretary of State under section 39(1) or section 49(4) of the Control of Pollution Act 1974.

(3) The items to which paragraph (b) of subsection (1) above applies are—
   (a) any matter involved in an appeal falling within subsection (2)(a) above;
   (b) any of the questions which fall to be determined by the Secretary of State under section 39(1) or section 49(4) of the Control of Pollution Act 1974.

(4) Schedule 20 to this Act shall have effect with respect to appointments under subsection (1)(a) above.

DEFINITION
   "function": s.124(1).

COMMENCEMENT
April 1, 1996 (S.I. 1996 No. 186).

GENERAL NOTE
This section, together with Sched. 20, provides a general power for the Secretary of State to delegate to any appointed person his appellate functions under the relevant environmental legislation. The appointed person has basically the same powers as the Secretary of State in relation to the appeal (Sched. 20, para. 3). Provision is made for hearings and the holding of local inquiries: para. 4. Either party is entitled as of right to a hearing, but a local inquiry may be held whether or not a party to the appeal requests it. No local inquiry may be held in relation to appeals on commercial confidentiality: para. 4(3). The appointed person is bound by any direction given to the Agency/SEPA when determining any appeal from a decision of that body: s.40(5).

Crown application

Application of this Act to the Crown

115.—(1) Subject to the provisions of this section, this Act shall bind the Crown.

(2) Part III of this Act and any amendments, repeals and revocations made by other provisions of this Act (other than those made by Schedule 21, which shall bind the Crown) bind the Crown to the extent that the enactments to which they relate bind the Crown.

(3) No contravention by the Crown of any provision made by or under this Act shall make the Crown criminally liable; but the High Court or, in Scotland, the Court of Session may, on the application of the Agency or, in Scotland, SEPA, declare unlawful any act or omission of the Crown which constitutes such a contravention.

(4) Notwithstanding anything in subsection (3) above, any provision made by or under this Act shall apply to persons in the public service of the Crown as it applies to other persons.

(5) If the Secretary of State certifies that it appears to him, as respects any Crown premises and any powers of entry exercisable in relation to them specified in the certificate, that it is requisite or expedient that, in the interests of national security, the powers should not be exercisable in relation, to those premises, those powers shall not be exercisable in relation to those premises; and in this subsection "Crown premises" means premises held or used by or on behalf of the Crown.

(6) Nothing in this section shall be taken as in any way affecting Her Majesty in her private capacity; and this subsection shall be construed as if section 38(3) of the Crown Proceedings Act 1947 (interpretation of references to Her Majesty in her private capacity) were contained in this Act.

DEFINITIONS
  "the Agency": s.124(1).
  "Crown premises": subs. (5).
  "SEPA": s.124(1).

COMMENCEMENT
April 1, 1996 (S.I. 1995 No. 2950 and S.I. 1996 No. 186).

GENERAL NOTE
The general principle is that the 1995 Act binds the Crown (as is the case with the Environmental Protection Act 1990). The main exceptions are that contravention does not render the Crown criminally liable (though its acts may be declared unlawful), and the certification procedure for exclusion of powers of entry to Crown premises on national security grounds: subss. (3) and (5). Application for a declaration (or, in Scotland, a declarator) of unlawfulness in relation to contravention by the Crown may only be made by the Agency or SEPA.

Application of certain other enactments to the Crown

116. Schedule 21 to this Act shall have effect.

COMMENCEMENT
September 21, 1995 in so far as this section gives effect to paras. 2(1)–(3) of Sched. 21 (S.I. 1995 No. 1983). The remainder comes into force on a day to be appointed (s.125(3)).

GENERAL NOTE
Schedule 21 ensures consistency on the issue of Crown application by inserting a provision in the same terms as s.115 into the Water Industry Act 1991, the Water Resources Act 1991 (with various modifications in relation to land drainage), the Sewerage (Scotland) Act 1968, the Control of Pollution Act 1974, the Water (Scotland) Act 1980, and the Local Government etc. (Scotland) Act 1994.

Isles of Scilly

Application of this Act to the Isles of Scilly

117.—(1) Subject to sections 77, 80 and 89 above and the provisions of any order under this section or section 89 above, nothing in this Act shall require or authorise any function, duty or power to be carried out, performed or exercised in relation to the Isles of Scilly by the Agency; and references in the other provisions of this Act (apart from Part III) to England and Wales shall not include references to those Isles.

(2) The Secretary of State may, after consultation with the Council of the Isles of Scilly, by order make provision with respect to the carrying out in those Isles of functions (other than functions under or by virtue of Part III or IV of this Act) falling to be carried out in relation to other parts of England and Wales by the Agency.

(3) Without prejudice to the generality of the power conferred by subsection (2) above, an order under this section may apply any provision of this Act (other than a provision contained in Part III or IV) in relation to the Isles of Scilly with or without modifications.

(4) An order under this section may—

    (a) make different provision for different cases, including different provision in relation to different persons, circumstances or localities; and

    (b) contain such supplemental, consequential and transitional provision as the Secretary of State considers appropriate, including provision saving provision repealed by or under any enactment.

(5) The power of the Secretary of State to make an order under this section shall be exercisable by statutory instrument; and a statutory instrument containing such an order shall be subject to annulment in pursuance of a resolution of either House of Parliament.

DEFINITIONS
"the Agency": s.124(1).
"functions": s.124(1).
"modifications": s.124(1).

COMMENCEMENT
February 1, 1996 (S.I. 1996 No. 186).

GENERAL NOTE
This section deals with the application of the Act to the Isles of Scilly. The general principle is that the Act does not extend to the Isles of Scilly (save for the provisions on national parks and air quality, as to which specific provision is made) but that it may be applied, with or without modifications, by order.

Application of certain other enactments to the Isles of Scilly

118.—(1) After section 10 of the Control of Pollution (Amendment) Act 1989 there shall be inserted—

"Application to the Isles of Scilly

10A.—(1) Subject to the provisions of any order under this section, this Act shall not apply in relation to the Isles of Scilly.

(2) The Secretary of State may, after consultation with the Council of the Isles of Scilly, by order provide for the application of any provisions of this Act to the Isles of Scilly; and any such order may provide for the application of those provisions to those Isles with such modifications as may be specified in the order.

(3) An order under this section may—

(a) make different provision for different cases, including different provision in relation to different persons, circumstances or localities; and

(b) contain such supplemental, consequential and transitional provision as the Secretary of State considers appropriate, including provision saving provision repealed by or under any enactment.

(4) The power of the Secretary of State to make an order under this section shall be exercisable by statutory instrument; and a statutory instrument containing such an order shall be subject to annulment in pursuance of a resolution of either House of Parliament."

(2) In section 11 of that Act, subsection (3) (which provides for section 107 of the Control of Pollution Act 1974 to have effect in relation to the application and modification of that Act to the Isles of Scilly) shall cease to have effect.

(3) For section 76 of the Environmental Protection Act 1990 (which provides for Part II of that Act to have effect in its application to the Isles of Scilly with modifications specified by order) there shall be substituted—

"Application to the Isles of Scilly

76.—(1) Subject to the provisions of any order under this section, this Part shall not apply in relation to the Isles of Scilly.

(2) The Secretary of State may, after consultation with the Council of the Isles of Scilly, by order provide for the application of any provisions of this Part to the Isles of Scilly; and any such order may provide for the application of those provisions to those Isles with such modifications as may be specified in the order.

(3) An order under this section may—

(a) make different provision for different cases, including different provision in relation to different persons, circumstances or localities; and

(b) contain such supplemental, consequential and transitional provision as the Secretary of State considers appropriate, including provision saving provision repealed by or under any enactment."

(4) For section 222 of the Water Industry Act 1991 (application to Isles of Scilly) there shall be substituted—

"Application to the Isles of Scilly

222.—(1) Subject to the provisions of any order under this section, this Act shall not apply in relation to the Isles of Scilly.

(2) The Secretary of State may, after consultation with the Council of the Isles of Scilly, by order provide for the application of any provisions of this Act to the Isles of Scilly; and any such order may provide for the application of those provisions to those Isles with such modifications as may be specified in the order.

(3) An order under this section may—

(a) make different provision for different cases, including different provision in relation to different persons, circumstances or localities; and

(b) contain such supplemental, consequential and transitional provision as the Secretary of State considers appropriate, including provision saving provision repealed by or under any enactment.

(4) The power of the Secretary of State to make an order under this section shall be exercisable by statutory instrument subject to annulment in pursuance of a resolution of either House of Parliament."

(5) For section 224 of the Water Resources Act 1991 (application to Isles of Scilly) there shall be substituted—

"Application to the Isles of Scilly

224.—(1) Subject to the provisions of any order under this section, this Act shall not apply in relation to the Isles of Scilly.

(2) The Secretary of State may, after consultation with the Council of the Isles of Scilly, by order provide for the application of any provisions of this Act to the Isles of Scilly; and any such order may provide for the application of those provisions to those Isles with such modifications as may be specified in the order.

(3) An order under this section may—

(a) make different provision for different cases, including different provision in relation to different persons, circumstances or localities; and

(b) contain such supplemental, consequential and transitional provision as the Secretary of State considers appropriate, including provision saving provision repealed by or under any enactment.

(4) The power of the Secretary of State to make an order under this section shall be exercisable by statutory instrument subject to annulment in pursuance of a resolution of either House of Parliament."

(6) For section 75 of the Land Drainage Act 1991 (application to the Isles of Scilly) there shall be substituted—

"Application to the Isles of Scilly

75.—(1) Subject to the provisions of any order under this section, this Act shall not apply in relation to the Isles of Scilly.

(2) The Secretary of State may, after consultation with the Council of the Isles of Scilly, by order provide for the application of any provisions of this Act to the Isles of Scilly; and any such order may provide for the application of those provisions to those Isles with such modifications as may be specified in the order.

(3) An order under this section may—

(a) make different provision for different cases, including different provision in relation to different persons, circumstances or localities; and

(b) contain such supplemental, consequential and transitional provision as the Secretary of State considers appropriate, including provision saving provision repealed by or under any enactment.

(4) The power of the Secretary of State to make an order under this section shall be exercisable by statutory instrument subject to annulment in pursuance of a resolution of either House of Parliament."

COMMENCEMENT

Subsections (1) to (3) and (6), and (in so far as they confer power to make an order or make provision in relation to the exercise of that power) subss. (4) and (5): February 1, 1996. The remainder of this section comes into force on a day to be appointed (s.125(3)).

GENERAL NOTE

Similar provision as in s.117 on application to the Isles of Scilly is made in relation to the other Acts referred to in this section.

Miscellaneous and supplemental

Stamp duty

119.—(1) No transfer effected by Part I of this Act shall give rise to any liability to stamp duty.

(2) Stamp duty shall not be chargeable—
    (a) on any transfer scheme; or
    (b) on any instrument or agreement which is certified to the Commissioners of Inland Revenue by the Secretary of State as made in pursuance of a transfer scheme.

(3) No transfer scheme, and no instrument which is certified as mentioned in subsection (2)(b) above, shall be taken to be duly stamped unless—
    (a) it has, in accordance with section 12 of the Stamp Act 1891, been stamped with a particular stamp denoting that it is not chargeable with that duty or that it is duly stamped; or
    (b) it is stamped with the duty to which it would be liable, apart from this section.

(4) In this section "transfer scheme" means a scheme made or approved by the Secretary of State under section 3 or 22 above for the transfer of property, rights or liabilities to the Agency or to SEPA.

DEFINITIONS
"the Agency": s.124(1).
"SEPA": s.124(1).
"transfer scheme": subs. (4).

COMMENCEMENT
February 1, 1996 (S.I. 1996 No. 186).

Minor and consequential amendments, transitional and transitory provisions, savings and repeals

120.—(1) The enactments mentioned in Schedule 22 to this Act shall have effect with the amendments there specified (being minor amendments and amendments consequential on provisions of this Act); and, without prejudice to any power conferred by any other provision of this Act, the Secretary of State and the Minister shall each have power by regulations to make such additional consequential amendments—
    (a) of public general enactments passed before, or in the same Session as, this Act, and
    (b) of subordinate legislation made before the passing of this Act,
as he considers necessary or expedient by reason of the coming into force of any provision of this Act.

(2) The transitional provisions, transitory provisions and savings contained in Schedule 23 to this Act shall have effect; but those provisions are without prejudice to sections 16 and 17 of the Interpretation Act 1978 (effect of repeals).

(3) The enactments mentioned in Schedule 24 to this Act (which include some that are spent or no longer of practical utility) are hereby repealed to the extent specified in the third column of that Schedule.

(4) The power to make regulations under subsection (1) above shall be exercisable by statutory instrument; and a statutory instrument containing any such regulations shall be subject to annulment in pursuance of a resolution of either House of Parliament.

(5) The power to make regulations under subsection (1) above includes power to make such incidental, supplemental, consequential and transitional provision as the Secretary of State or the Minister thinks necessary or expedient.

(6) In this section—
"the Minister" means the Minister of Agriculture, Fisheries and Food;
"subordinate legislation" has the same meaning as in the Interpretation
    Act 1978.

DEFINITIONS
"the Minister": subs. (6).
"subordinate legislation": subs. (6).

COMMENCEMENT
Subsection (1) (partially) on July 28, 1995, (partially) on September 21, 1995 (S.I. 1995 No. 1983), (partially) on October 12, 1995 (S.I. 1995 No. 2649), (partially) on February 1, 1996 and (partially) on April 1, 1996 (S.I. 1996 No. 186). Subsection (2) (partially) on January 1, 1999 (S.I. 1995 No. 1983) and (partially) on April 1, 1996 (S.I. 1996 No. 186). Subsection (3) (partially) on September 21, 1995 and (partially) on January 1, 1999 (S.I. 1995 No. 1983). Subsection (3) (partially) on November 1, 1995 (S.I. 1995 No. 2765), (partially) on February 1, 1996 and (partially) on April 1, 1996 (S.I. 1996 No. 186). Subsections (4)–(6): July 28, 1995 (S.I. 1995 No. 1983).
    Section 125(3) makes separate provision for the commencement on July 19, 1995 of part of Sched. 22.

GENERAL NOTE
This section deals with amendments, transitional provisions and savings (in respect of which s.125(3) should be noted) and repeals. Whilst the amendments in Sched. 22 are referred to as minor and consequential, this is by no means the case with all of them: some effect significant substantive changes to existing law.

Subs. (6): "subordinate legislation"
The Interpretation Act 1978, s.21(1), defines subordinate legislation as "Orders in Council, orders, rules, regulations, schemes, warrants, byelaws and other instruments made or to be made under any Act".

Sched. 22—amendments
Many of the amendments in the Schedule are consequential, for example those inserting references to the Agency or SEPA, in place of those to the existing enforcement agencies. Some however are worthy of note:

Para. 29(15): appeals against revocation or modification notices. A new s.39(5A)–(5C) is added to COPA 1974 providing that where there is an appeal under s.39(1)(b) against such a notice on the grounds that it is unreasonable, the notice shall not take effect while the reference is pending unless this is necessary in SEPA's opinion for the purposes set out in s.39(5B). Where SEPA is of the opinion that the notice must take effect while the reference is pending, the consent holder or former consent holder may challenge the reasonableness of such a decision by application to the Secretary of State (s.39(5C)). If the Secretary of State determines that SEPA acted unreasonably the notice will not take effect until the original reference is finally determined and the applicant will also be entitled to recover compensation from SEPA for any loss suffered as a result of the notice taking effect while the original reference was still pending.

Paras. 29(22) and 162: works notices in respect of anti-pollution operations. New provisions are inserted into the Control of Pollution Act 1974 and the Water Resources Act 1991 (ss.46A–46D and 161A–161D respectively). These allow SEPA/the Agency, where it appears that poisonous, noxious or polluting matter or solid waste matter is likely to enter controlled waters, or to be or to have been present in such waters, to serve a "works notice" on any person who caused or knowingly permitted the matter to be present in controlled waters, or to be present at a place from which it is likely to enter such waters. The notice may require that person to carry out preventive, remedial or restorative works within specified periods. Provision is made for appeals against notices, for the granting of rights of entry necessary to comply with such notices, and offences and other remedies in relation to non-compliance. The new procedure provides a more effective remedy than existing law (s.46 of the 1974 Act and s.161 of the 1991 Act) under which the relevant authority could take clean-up action itself and then recover its reasonable costs from the polluter. Those powers are now only exercisable where it is considered necessary to act forthwith, or where after reasonable inquiry no person has been found on whom a works notice would be served: paras. 29(21)(b) and 161(3).

Paras. 29(26) and 142: enforcement notices on discharge consents. New provisions (ss.49A and

B of the Control of Pollution Act 1974 and 90B of the Water Resources Act 1991) create a new remedy in relation to breach or likely breach of consents for discharge to controlled waters. Instead of simply prosecuting for contravention of the consent conditions, the Agency/SEPA may serve a notice specifying the steps to be taken to remedy the contravention or to remedy the matters making it likely that the contravention will occur. Failure to comply with any requirement imposed by the notice is an offence, and provision is made for appeals against notices. Again, this will no doubt be a welcome power to regulators, particularly in a case where there is regular non-compliance with conditions and prosecution may not necessarily result in the necessary expenditure being made to achieve compliance.

Para. 36: road traffic regulation powers and air quality. The Road Traffic Regulation Act 1984 is amended to make it clear (if indeed it was previously in doubt) that traffic regulation orders may be made for purposes relating to air quality.

Para. 51: variation notices under Pt. 1 of the 1990 Act. Provision is made for an enforcing authority which has issued a notice varying the conditions of an authorisation to serve a further notice varying the variation notice (new s.10(3A)). Previously the only course would be to withdraw the first variation notice and issue a new one.

Para. 67: compensation for rights granted pursuant to waste management licence. Section 35(4) of the 1990 Act provided for the grant to the holder of a waste management licence by third parties of rights necessary in order to comply with licence conditions. New s.35A (inserted by para. 67) confers a statutory right of compensation on such third parties.

Para. 68: waste licence applications. Express provision is made for a waste regulation authority refusing to proceed with the licence application because of the failure of the applicant to provide information reasonably required by the authority.

Para. 69: consultation before grant of waste licences. Where a waste regulation authority (now the Agency/SEPA) proposes to impose conditions under s.35(4) of the 1990 Act which would require a third party to concur in granting rights (see para. 67 above) the authority is required by new s.36A to follow a consultation procedure with the owner and occupier of affected land, and to consider representations made by them. A similar consultation procedure is applied to the variation of licence conditions (s.37A as inserted by para. 71) and to the requirements imposed where a licence is suspended (s.38(9B) as inserted by para. 72).

Para. 72: rights granted pursuant to requirements imposed on suspension of waste licence. Where a waste licence is suspended, the waste regulation authority (now the Agency/SEPA) may impose requirements pursuant to s.38(9) of the 1990 Act (subject now to the consultation procedure introduced by this para. : see note to para. 69 above). As regards third parties, the new s.39(9A) inserted by para. 72 brings the position regarding such requirements into line with that regarding licence conditions (s.35(4) of the 1990 Act): any third party consent needed for such requirements to be complied with shall be granted. New s.35A (inserted by para 67) confers a statutory right of compensation on such third parties.

Para. 76: notice requiring compliance with waste licence conditions. Section 42 of the 1990 Act provides for the revocation or suspension of a waste licence where the holder has been required to, and has failed to, remedy non-compliance with a licence condition. Paragraph 76 amends s.42(5) so that *likely* (as opposed to actual) non-compliance may be the subject of such a requirement. Also, requirements must now take the form of a notice which, rather than merely requiring compliance, specifies the matters constituting the non-compliance and the steps to be taken.

Para. 78: waste disposal plans. Section 50 of the 1990 Act, dealing with waste disposal plans of waste regulation authorities, ceases to have effect.

Para. 79: closed landfills. Section 61 of the 1990 Act, dealing with closed landfills, ceases to have effect (never having been implemented). The provision is of course replaced by the new powers and duties relating to contaminated land introduced by Pt. II.

Paras. 88 and 95: definition of waste. Section 75 of the 1990 Act is replaced by a new definition of waste, following the definition of the E.C. waste framework directive 75/442/EEC as amended by 91/156/EEC: new Sched. 2B is inserted into the 1990 Act for that purpose. The changes insert into primary legislation the definition contained in the Waste Management Licensing Regulations 1994. The presumption contained in s.75(3) of the 1990 Act (that anything discarded is waste unless the contrary is proved) is revoked.

Para. 91: section 143 registers. This provision, on registers of land which may be subject to contamination, ceases to have effect, never having been implemented. See, generally, the note to Part IIA of the 1990 Act.

Para. 102: promotion of the efficient use of water (England and Wales). A new section 93A is inserted into the Water Industry Act 1991, imposing a duty on each water undertaker to promote the efficient use of water by its customers. The Director General of Water Services is given power to impose requirements on water undertakers in pursuance of that duty: s.93B. However, neither the duty nor any such requirements may authorise or require the imposition of any requirement on customers of the undertaker: ss.93A(3) and 93B(6).

Para. 103: provision of public sewers (England and Wales). An alternative to the procedure for requisitioning public sewers is provided by new s.101A of the Water Industry Act 1991. Water undertakers are placed under a duty to provide public sewers to serve domestic premises in certain circumstances, in particular that the lack of drainage by sewer is giving rise, or is likely to give rise, to such adverse effects on the environment or on amenity that provision is appropriate The matters to be considered in making that decision include the number of dwellings involved, the cost of provision, and the geology of the locality.

Paras. 105–113: special category effluent (England and Wales). Some changes are made to the provisions in the Water Industry Act dealing with special category effluent. Failure by a sewerage undertaker to refer applications or agreements involving special category effluent to the Agency is made an offence: ss.120(9) and 130(7). New powers are given to the Agency to require information for the purpose of its functions in relation to special category effluent: s.135A.

Para. 140: drought permits (England and Wales). A new section of the Water Resources Act 1991 (s.79A) provides a means whereby, in cases of serious water shortage caused by exceptional lack of rain, the Agency may issue drought permits authorising water undertakers to take water from any source specified in the permit for a limited period.

Para. 143: enforcement notices (England and Wales). A new enforcement notice procedure is introduced in a new s.90B of the Water Resources Act 1991, applicable to the contravention of conditions of discharge consents and consents under s..89(4)(a) and 90(1) or (2) of the 1991 Act.

Para. 183: discharge consents (England and Wales). A new Sched. 10 is substituted in the Water Resources Act 1991 dealing with the procedure for applications for discharge consent The new provisions on the transfer of consents, and the introduction of criminal penalties for failure to notify the Agency of such transfers (para. 11) should particularly be noted, as should the resulting transitional provisions in Sched. 23, para. 21 whereby any person benefiting from a discharge consent which existed on April 1, 1996 who fails to notify the Agency by October 1. 1996 that he proposes to rely on it after October 1, 1996, loses the benefit of it.

An unresolved issue: the exclusivity or inclusivity of discharge consents. One matter raised but not resolved during the passage of the Act was the construction of discharge consents under the Water Resources Act 1991 (and, by implication, under the Control of Pollution Act 1974 in Scotland) and in particular whether the consent provides a defence in relation to substances not mentioned (either by way of permission or prohibition) in the consent. The legal position on this issue was thrown into doubt by the House of Lords decision in *NRA v. Yorkshire Water Services Ltd* [1995] 1 All E.R. 225 and by legal opinions obtained by the NRA. The undesirable nature of the uncertainty was referred to by the Chairman of the NRA, Lord Crickhowell, in debate: see *Hansard*, H.L., Vol. 561, col. 680. Various options for amendment of the Water Resources Act were put forward to make it clear that a consent should not be taken as authorising the discharge of substances (or at least poisonous noxious or polluting substances) other than those referred to specifically: see *e.g. Hansard*, H.L., Vol. 561, col. 680. The Government rejected such amendments on the basis that retrospective legislation was not the right way of dealing with technical problems affecting large numbers of consents (possibly the vast majority of the 110,000 estimated extant consents) granted over many years in various forms: *Hansard*, H.L., Vol. 561, cols. 681–683. On this issue see D. McGillivray, *Discharge Consents and the Unforeseen* [1995] Water Law 101.

Para. 193: spray irrigation (England and Wales). Power is given, by a new s.61F of the Water Resources Act 1991, for internal drainage boards and local authorities to operate drainage works under their control so as to manage the level of water in a watercourse for the purpose of facilitating spray irrigation.

Sched. 23—Transitional Provisions and Savings. This Schedule contains various transitional and saving provisions, ensuring the continuance in effect of any directions given to the NRA under s.15 of the Water Resources Act 1991, any statutory charging scheme, and similar matters.

Local statutory provisions: consequential amendments, etc.

121.—(1) If it appears to the Secretary of State or the Minister to be appropriate to do so—
(a) for the purposes of, or in consequence of, the coming into force of any enactment contained in this Act; or
(b) in consequence of the effect or operation at any time after the transfer date of any such enactment or of anything done under any such enactment,
he may by order repeal, amend or re-enact (with or without modifications) any local statutory provision, including, in the case of an order by virtue of paragraph (b) above, a provision amended by virtue of paragraph (a) above.
(2) An order made by the Secretary of State or the Minister under subsection (1) above may—
(a) make provision applying generally in relation to local statutory provisions of a description specified in the order;
(b) make different provision for different cases, including different provision in relation to different persons, circumstances or localities;
(c) contain such supplemental, consequential and transitional provision as the Secretary of State or, as the case may be, the Minister considers appropriate; and
(d) in the case of an order made after the transfer date, require provision contained in the order to be treated as if it came into force on that date.
(3) The power under this section to repeal or amend a local statutory provision shall include power to modify the effect in relation to any local statutory provision of any provision of Schedule 23 to this Act.
(4) Nothing in any order under this section may abrogate or curtail the effect of so much of any local statutory provision as confers any right of way or confers on or preserves for the public—
(a) any right of enjoyment of air, exercise or recreation on land; or
(b) any right of access to land for the purposes of exercise or recreation.
(5) The power to make an order under subsection (1) above shall be exercisable by statutory instrument subject to annulment in pursuance of a resolution of either House of Parliament.
(6) The power to make an order under subsection (1) above shall be without prejudice to any power conferred by any other provision of this Act.
(7) In this section—
"local statutory provision" means—
(a) a provision of a local Act (including an Act confirming a provisional order);
(b) a provision of so much of any public general Act as has effect with respect to a particular area, with respect to particular

persons or works or with respect to particular provisions falling within any paragraph of this definition;

(c) a provision of an instrument made under any provision falling within paragraph (a) or (b) above; or

(d) a provision of any other instrument which is in the nature of a local enactment;

"the Minister" means the Minister of Agriculture, Fisheries and Food;

"the transfer date" has the same meaning as in Part I of this Act.

DEFINITIONS
"local statutory provision": subs. (7).
"the Minister": subs. (7).
"modifications": s.124(1).
"the transfer date": s.56(1).

COMMENCEMENT
July 28, 1995 (S.I. 1995 No. 1983)

GENERAL NOTE
This section gives a wide power for the Secretary of State to repeal, amend or re-enact any local statutes. The power is constrained by subs. (4) in that such changes may not restrict or curtail the rights of access, recreation and enjoyment referred to there.

Directions

122.—(1) Any direction given under this Act shall be in writing.

(2) Any power conferred by this Act to give a direction shall include power to vary or revoke the direction.

(3) Subsections (4) and (5) below apply to any direction given—

(a) to the Agency or SEPA under any provision of this Act or any other enactment, or

(b) to any other body or person under any provision of this Act,

being a direction to any extent so given for the purpose of implementing any obligations of the United Kingdom under the Community Treaties.

(4) A direction to which this subsection applies shall not be varied or revoked unless, notwithstanding the variation or revocation, the obligations mentioned in subsection (3) above, as they have effect for the time being, continue to be implemented, whether by directions or any other instrument or by any enactment.

(5) Any variation or revocation of a direction to which this subsection applies shall be published in such manner as the Minister giving it considers appropriate for the purpose of bringing the matters to which it relates to the attention of persons likely to be affected by them; and—

(a) copies of the variation or revocation shall be made available to the public; and

(b) notice of the variation or revocation, and of where a copy of the variation or revocation may be obtained, shall be given—

(i) if the direction has effect in England and Wales, in the London Gazette;

(ii) if the direction has effect in Scotland, in the Edinburgh Gazette.

DEFINITIONS
"the Agency": s.124(1).
"notice": s.124(1).
"SEPA": s.124(1).

COMMENCEMENT
July 28, 1995 (S.I. 1995 No. 1983).

GENERAL NOTE
This section makes provision as to the various directions which may be given under the Act. All directions must be in writing. Restrictions apply to the variation or revocation of any direction which is given for the purpose of implementing obligations of the U.K. under E.C. law.

Service of documents

123.—(1) Without prejudice to paragraph 17(2)(d) of Schedule 7 to this Act, any notice required or authorised by or under this Act to be served (whether the expression "serve" or the expression "give" or "send" or any other expression is used) on any person may be served by delivering it to him, or by leaving it at his proper address, or by sending it by post to him at that address.

(2) Any such notice may—
    (a) in the case of a body corporate, be served on the secretary or clerk of that body;
    (b) in the case of a partnership, be served on a partner or a person having the control or management of the partnership business.

(3) For the purposes of this section and of section 7 of the Interpretation Act 1978 (service of documents by post) in its application to this section, the proper address of any person on whom any such notice is to be served shall be his last known address, except that—
    (a) in the case of a body corporate or their secretary or clerk, it shall be the address of the registered or principal office of that body;
    (b) in the case of a partnership or person having the control or the management of the partnership business, it shall be the principal office of the partnership;
and for the purposes of this subsection the principal office of a company registered outside the United Kingdom or of a partnership carrying on business outside the United Kingdom shall be their principal office within the United Kingdom.

(4) If the person to be served with any such notice has specified an address in the United Kingdom other than his proper address within the meaning of subsection (3) above as the one at which he or someone on his behalf will accept notices of the same description as that notice, that address shall also be treated for the purposes of this section and section 7 of the Interpretation Act 1978 as his proper address.

(5) Where under any provision of this Act any notice is required to be served on a person who is, or appears to be, in occupation of any premises then—
    (a) if the name or address of such a person cannot after reasonable inquiry be ascertained, or
    (b) if the premises appear to be or are unoccupied,
that notice may be served either by leaving it in the hands of a person who is or appears to be resident or employed on the premises or by leaving it conspicuously affixed to some building or object on the premises.

(6) This section shall not apply to any notice in relation to the service of which provision is made by rules of court.

(7) The preceding provisions of this section shall apply to the service of a document as they apply to the service of a notice.

(8) In this section—
"premises" includes any land, vehicle, vessel or mobile plant;
"serve" shall be construed in accordance with subsection (1) above.

DEFINITIONS
  "the Agency": s.124(1).
  "notice": s.124(1).
  "premises": subs. (8).
  "SEPA": s.124(1).
  "serve": subs. (8).

COMMENCEMENT
July 18, 1995 (S.I. 1995 No. 1983).

GENERAL NOTE
This section makes provision as to the service of notices under the Act. Para. 17(2)(d) of Sched. 7, which is referred to in subs. (1), relates only to National Park authorities, and applies ss.231–234 of the Local Government Act 1972 (service and authentication of documents). The provisions of s.123 apply to documents as well as notices: subs. (7).

Subss. (3)–(6): address for service

Detailed provision is made in subss. (3)–(5) as to the proper address for service of notices and other documents under the Act. It will be noted, however, that any rules of court relating to the service of such notices take precedence over subs. (3)–(5). So, for example, insofar as s.37(1)(a) authorises the Agency to take civil proceedings in the High Court, then the Rules of the Supreme Court and case law on the address for service and on proof of service under those rules will apply (*e.g. Berry v. Farrow* [1914] 1 K.B. 632: "address" includes both domestic and business address; *A/S Catherineholm v. Norequipment Trading Ltd* [1972] 2 Q.B. 314: proof of service by post; *Cooper v. Scott-Farnell* [1969] 1 All E.R. 178 (C.A.): defendant's temporary absence does not affect validity of service). Similar considerations apply in relation to Scotland.

The "principal" office of a body corporate or partnership (subs. (3)(a) and (b)) is where its general superintendence and management is carried out: *Davies v. British Geon Ltd* [1956] 3 All E.R. 389 (C.A.).

General interpretation

124.—(1) In this Act, except in so far as the context otherwise requires—
"the Agency" means the Environment Agency;
"financial year" means a period of twelve months ending with 31st March;
"functions" includes powers and duties;
"modifications" includes additions, alterations and omissions and cognate expressions shall be construed accordingly;
"notice" means notice in writing;
"records", without prejudice to the generality of the expression, includes computer records and any other records kept otherwise than in a document;
"SEPA" means the Scottish Environment Protection Agency.

(2) The amendment by this Act of any provision contained in subordinate legislation shall not be taken to have prejudiced any power to make further subordinate legislation amending or revoking that provision.

(3) In subsection (2) above, "subordinate legislation" has the same meaning as in the Interpretation Act 1978.

COMMENCEMENT
July 28, 1995 (S.I. 1995 No. 1983).

Short title, commencement, extent, etc.

125.—(1) This Act may be cited as the Environment Act 1995.

(2) Part III of this Act, except for section 78, paragraph 7(2) of Schedule 7 and Schedule 10, shall come into force at the end of the period of two months beginning with the day on which this Act is passed.

(3) Except as provided in subsection (2) above and except for this section, section 74 above and paragraphs 76(8)(a) and 135 of Schedule 22 to this Act (which come into force on the passing of this Act) and the repeal of sub-paragraph (1) of paragraph 22 of Schedule 10 to this Act (which comes into force in accordance with sub-paragraph (7) of that paragraph) this Act shall come into force on such day as the Secretary of State may specify by

order made by statutory instrument; and different days may be so specified for different provisions or for different purposes of the same provision.

(4) Without prejudice to the provisions of Schedule 23 to this Act, an order under subsection (3) above may make such transitional provisions and savings as appear to the Secretary of State necessary or expedient in connection with any provision brought into force by the order.

(5) The power conferred by subsection (4) above includes power to modify any enactment contained in this or any other Act.

(6) An Order in Council under paragraph 1(1)(b) of Schedule 1 to the Northern Ireland Act 1974 (legislation for Northern Ireland in the interim period) which states that it is made only for purposes corresponding to those of section 98 of this Act—

    (a) shall not be subject to paragraph 1(4) and (5) of that Schedule (affirmative resolution of both Houses of Parliament); but

    (b) shall be subject to annulment in pursuance of a resolution of either House of Parliament.

(7) Except for this section and any amendment or repeal by this Act of any provision contained in—

    (a) the Parliamentary Commissioner Act 1967,

    (b) the Sea Fish (Conservation) Act 1967,

    (c) the House of Commons Disqualification Act 1975, or

    (d) the Northern Ireland Assembly Disqualification Act 1975,

this Act shall not extend to Northern Ireland.

(8) Part III of this Act, and Schedule 24 to this Act so far as relating to that Part, extends to England and Wales only.

(9) Section 106 of, and Schedule 16 to, this Act extend to Scotland only.

(10) Subject to the foregoing provisions of this section and to any express provision made by this Act to the contrary, any amendment, repeal or revocation made by this Act shall have the same extent as the enactment or instrument to which it relates.

COMMENCEMENT

With a few specified exceptions, the Act's provisions come into force on such date as the Secretary of State may specify by statutory instrument. To date there have been five commencement orders: S.I. 1995 No. 1983, S.I. 1995 No. 2649 (S.199) (affecting Scotland only), S.I. 1995 No. 2765, S.I. 1995 No. 2950 and S.I. 1996 No. 186. See the General Introduction to the Act for a table of sections in force.

The provisions on national parks (Pt. III) in general come into force two months from the passage of the Act (subs. (2)). A handful of provisions came into force immediately (subs. (3)).

Territorial extent

The Act does not (save in the cases specified) extend to Northern Ireland: subs. (7). The provisions on national parks (Pt. III) do not extend to Scotland: subs. (8). Section 106 and Sched. 16 (which amend the law on water pollution in Scotland) extend to Scotland only. Further provision as to territorial extent is made by individual sections of the Act.

SCHEDULES

SCHEDULE 1

THE ENVIRONMENT AGENCY

Membership

1.—(1) Subject to the following provisions of this paragraph, a member shall hold and vacate office in accordance with the terms of his appointment and shall, on ceasing to be a member, be eligible for re-appointment.

(2) A member may at any time resign his office by giving notice to the appropriate Minister.

(3) The appropriate Minister may remove a member from that office if he is satisfied—
  (a) that the member has been absent from meetings of the Agency for a period of more than three months without the permission of the Agency;
  (b) that the member has been adjudged bankrupt, that his estate has been sequestrated or that he has made a composition or arrangement with or granted a trust deed for, his creditors; or
  (c) that the member is unable or unfit to carry out the functions of a member.

Chairman and deputy chairman

2. The chairman or deputy chairman of the Agency shall hold office as such unless and until—
  (a) he resigns that office by giving notice to the Secretary of State, or
  (b) he ceases to be a member,
and shall, on ceasing to be the chairman or deputy chairman, be eligible for further designation as such in accordance with section 1(3) of this Act at any time when he is a member.

Remuneration, pensions, etc.

3.—(1) The Agency shall pay to its members such remuneration, and such travelling and other allowances, as may be determined by the appropriate Minister.
  (2) The Agency shall, if so required by the appropriate Minister,—
  (a) pay such pension, allowances or gratuities as may be determined by that Minister to or in respect of a person who is or has been a member;
  (b) make such payments as may be determined by that Minister towards provision for the payment of a pension, allowances or gratuities to or in respect of a person who is or has been a member; or
  (c) provide and maintain such schemes (whether contributory or not) as may be determined by that Minister for the payment of pensions, allowances or gratuities to or in respect of persons who are or have been members.
  (3) If, when any member ceases to hold office, the appropriate Minister determines that there are special circumstances which make it right that that member should receive compensation, the Agency shall pay to him a sum by way of compensation of such amount as may be so determined.

Staff

4.—(1) The Agency may appoint such officers and employees as it may determine.
  (2) No member or other person shall be appointed by the Agency to act as chief executive of the Agency unless the Secretary of State has consented to the appointment of that person.
  (3) The Agency may—
  (a) pay such pensions, allowances or gratuities to or in respect of any persons who are or have been its officers or employees as it may, with the approval of the Secretary of State, determine;
  (b) make such payments as it may so determine towards provision for the payment of pensions, allowances or gratuities to or in respect of any such persons;
  (c) provide and maintain such schemes as it may so determine (whether contributory or not) for the payment of pensions, allowances or gratuities to or in respect of any such persons.
  (4) Any reference in sub-paragraph (3) above to pensions, allowances or gratuities to or in respect of any such persons as are mentioned in that sub-paragraph includes a reference to pensions, allowances or gratuities by way of compensation to or in respect of any of the Agency's officers or employees who suffer loss of office or employment or loss or diminution of emoluments.

Proceedings of the Agency

5. Subject to the following provisions of this Schedule and to section 106 of the 1991 Act (obligation to carry out flood defence functions through committees), the Agency may regulate its own procedure (including quorum).

Delegation of powers

6. Subject to section 106 of the 1991 Act, anything authorised or required by or under any enactment to be done by the Agency may be done—
  (a) by any member, officer or employee of the Agency who has been authorised for the purpose, whether generally or specially, by the Agency; or
  (b) by any committee or sub-committee of the Agency which has been so authorised.

Members' interests

7.—(1) A member who is in any way directly or indirectly interested in any matter that is brought up for consideration at a meeting of the Agency shall disclose the nature of his interest to the meeting; and, where such a disclosure is made—

  (a) the disclosure shall be recorded in the minutes of the meeting; and

  (b) the member shall not take any part in any deliberation or decision of the Agency, or of any of its committees or sub-committees, with respect to that matter.

(2) For the purposes of sub-paragraph (1) above, a general notification given at a meeting of the Agency by a member to the effect that he—

  (a) is a member of a specified company or firm, and

  (b) is to be regarded as interested in any matter involving that company or firm,

shall be regarded as a sufficient disclosure of his interest in relation to any such matter.

(3) A member need not attend in person at a meeting of the Agency in order to make a disclosure which he is required to make under this paragraph if he takes reasonable steps to secure that the disclosure is made by a notice which is read and considered at the meeting.

(4) The Secretary of State may, subject to such conditions as he considers appropriate, remove any disability imposed by virtue of this paragraph in any case where the number of members of the Agency disabled by virtue of this paragraph at any one time would be so great a proportion of the whole as to impede the transaction of business.

(5) The power of the Secretary of State under sub-paragraph (4) above includes power to remove, either indefinitely or for any period, a disability which would otherwise attach to any member, or members of any description, by reason of such interests, and in respect of such matters, as may be specified or described by the Secretary of State.

(6) Nothing in this paragraph precludes any member from taking part in the consideration or discussion of, or voting on, any question whether an application should be made to the Secretary of State for the exercise of the power conferred by sub-paragraph (4) above.

(7) Any reference in this paragraph to a meeting of the Agency includes a reference to a meeting of any committee or sub-committee of the Agency.

Vacancies and defective appointments

8. The validity of any proceedings of the Agency shall not be affected by a vacancy amongst the members or by a defect in the appointment of a member.

Minutes

9.—(1) Minutes shall be kept of proceedings of the Agency, of its committees and of its sub-committees.

(2) Minutes of any such proceedings shall be evidence of those proceedings if they are signed by a person purporting to have acted as chairman of the proceedings to which the minutes relate or of any subsequent proceedings in the course of which the minutes were approved as a correct record.

(3) Where minutes of any such proceedings have been signed as mentioned in sub-paragraph (2) above, those proceedings shall, unless the contrary is shown, be deemed to have been validly convened and constituted.

Application of seal and proof of instruments

10.—(1) The application of the seal of the Agency shall be authenticated by the signature of any member, officer or employee of the Agency who has been authorised for the purpose, whether generally or specially, by the Agency.

(2) In this paragraph the reference to the signature of a person includes a reference to a facsimile of a signature by whatever process reproduced; and, in paragraph 11 below, the word "signed" shall be construed accordingly.

Documents served etc. by or on the Agency

11.—(1) Any document which the Agency is authorised or required by or under any enactment to serve, make or issue may be signed on behalf of the Agency by any member, officer or employee of the Agency who has been authorised for the purpose, whether generally or specially, by the Agency.

(2) Every document purporting to be an instrument made or issued by or on behalf of the Agency and to be duly executed under the seal of the Agency, or to be signed or executed by a person authorised by the Agency for the purpose, shall be received in evidence and be treated, without further proof, as being so made or issued unless the contrary is shown.

(3) Any notice which is required or authorised, by or under any provision of any other Act, to be given, served or issued by, to or on the Agency shall be in writing.

Interpretation

12. In this Schedule—
"the appropriate Minister", in relation to any person who is or has been a member, means the Minister or the Secretary of State, according to whether that person was appointed as a member by the Minister or by the Secretary of State; and
"member", except where the context otherwise requires, means any member of the Agency (including the chairman and deputy chairman).

SCHEDULE 2

TRANSFERS OF PROPERTY ETC: SUPPLEMENTAL PROVISIONS

PART I

INTRODUCTORY

Interpretation

1. In this Schedule—
"the chief inspector"—
    (a) in the application of this Schedule in relation to transfers by or under section 3 of this Act, means any of the inspectors or chief inspectors mentioned in section 2(1) of this Act;
    (b) in the application of this Schedule in relation to transfers by or under section 22 of this Act, means any of the inspectors or chief inspectors mentioned in section 21(1) of this Act;
and any reference to the chief inspector for England and Wales or the chief inspector for Scotland shall be construed accordingly;
"the relevant new Agency" means—
    (a) in the application of this Schedule in relation to transfers by or under section 3 of this Act, the Agency; and
    (b) in the application of this Schedule in relation to transfers by or under section 22 of this Act, SEPA;
"transfer scheme" means a scheme under section 3 or 22 of this Act;
"the transferor", in relation to transfers by or under section 3 of this Act, means—
    (a) in the case of any transfer by section 3(1)(a) of this Act, the National Rivers Authority or the London Waste Regulation Authority, as the case may be; or
    (b) in the case of any transfer scheme, or any transfer by transfer scheme—
        (i) the Secretary of State,
        (ii) the chief inspector, or
        (iii) any waste regulation authority,
(as the case may be) from whom any property, rights or liabilities are, or are to be, transferred by that scheme;
"the transferor", in relation to transfers by or under section 22 of this Act, means—
    (a) in the case of any transfer by section 22(1)(a) of this Act, the river purification board in question; or
    (b) in the case of any transfer scheme, or any transfer by transfer scheme—
        (i) the Secretary of State;
        (ii) the chief inspector; or
        (iii) any local authority,
(as the case may be) from whom any property, rights or liabilities are or are to be, transferred by that scheme; and, as respects any such local authority which is a district or islands council, includes, in relation to any time on or after 1st April 1996, the council for any local government area named in column 1 of Schedule 1 to the Local Government etc. (Scotland) Act 1994 which is wholly or partly conterminous with the area of that council.

The property etc. which may be transferred

2.—(1) The property, rights and liabilities which are transferred by, or may be transferred by transfer scheme under, section 3 or 22 of this Act include—

(a) property, rights and liabilities that would not otherwise be capable of being transferred or assigned by the transferor;

(b) in the case of a transfer scheme, such property, rights and liabilities to which the transferor may become entitled or subject after the making of the scheme and before the transfer date as may be specified in the scheme;

(c) property situated anywhere in the United Kingdom or elsewhere;

(d) rights and liabilities under enactments;

(e) rights and liabilities under the law of any part of the United Kingdom or of any country or territory outside the United Kingdom.

(2) The transfers authorised by paragraph (a) of sub-paragraph (1) above include transfers which, by virtue of that paragraph, are to take effect as if there were no such contravention, liability or interference with any interest or right as there would be, in the case of a transfer or assignment otherwise than by or under section 3 or 22 of this Act, by reason of any provision having effect (whether under any enactment or agreement or otherwise) in relation to the terms on which the transferor is entitled or subject to the property, right or liability in question.

(3) This paragraph is subject to paragraph 3 below.

Contracts of employment

3.—(1) The rights and liabilities that may be transferred by and in accordance with a transfer scheme include (subject to the following provisions of this paragraph) any rights or liabilities of the employer under the contract of employment of any person—

(a) who is employed—
  (i) in the civil service of the State;
  (ii) by a body which is a waste regulation authority in England or Wales; or
  (iii) by a local authority in Scotland;

(b) who appears to the appropriate authority to be employed for the purposes of, or otherwise in connection with, functions which are by virtue of this Act to become functions of a new Agency; and

(c) whom the appropriate authority considers it necessary or expedient to transfer into the employment of that new Agency;

and in the following provisions of this paragraph any reference to a "qualifying employee" is a reference to such a person.

(2) A transfer scheme which provides for the transfer of rights or liabilities under the contracts of employment of qualifying employees must identify those employees—

(a) by specifying them;

(b) by referring to persons of a description specified in the scheme (with or without exceptions); or

(c) partly in the one way and partly in the other.

(3) A transfer scheme shall not operate to transfer rights or liabilities under so much of a contract of employment as relates to an occupational pension scheme, other than any provisions of such a pension scheme which do not relate to benefits for old age, invalidity or survivors.

(4) Where a transfer scheme provides for the transfer of rights or liabilities under the contract of employment of a qualifying employee—

(a) all the employer's rights, powers, duties and liabilities under or in connection with the contract of employment shall be transferred to the relevant new Agency on the transfer date by and in accordance with the scheme, and

(b) anything done by or in relation to the employer in respect of the qualifying employee before the transfer date shall be treated on and after that date as done by or in relation to the relevant new Agency,

except in a case where objection is made by the qualifying employee as mentioned in sub-paragraph (8)(b) below.

(5) Sub-paragraphs (6) and (7) below shall have effect in any case where rights or liabilities under the contract of employment of a qualifying employee are transferred by and in accordance with a transfer scheme.

(6) In a case falling within sub-paragraph (5) above—

(a) the transfer shall be regarded for the purposes of section 84 of the Employment Protection (Consolidation) Act 1978 (renewal of contract or re-engagement) as a renewal of the qualifying employee's contract of employment, or a re-engagement of the qualifying employee, falling within subsection (1) of that section; and

(b) the qualifying employee shall accordingly not be regarded as having been dismissed by virtue of the transfer.

(7) In a case falling within sub-paragraph (5) above, for the purposes of Schedule 13 to the Employment Protection (Consolidation) Act 1978 (ascertainment of the length of an employee's period of employment and whether that employment is continuous)—

  (a) so much of the qualifying employee's period of continuous employment as ends with the day preceding the transfer date shall be treated on and after that date as a period of employment with the relevant new Agency; and

  (b) the continuity of the period of employment of the qualifying employee shall be treated as not having been broken by the transfer.

(8) Sub-paragraph (9) below shall have effect in any case where—

  (a) a transfer scheme contains provision for the transfer of rights or liabilities under the contract of employment of a qualifying employee, but

  (b) the qualifying employee informs the appropriate authority or the relevant new Agency that he objects to becoming employed by that new Agency.

(9) In a case falling within sub-paragraph (8) above—

  (a) the transfer scheme—

    (i) shall not operate to transfer any rights, powers, duties or liabilities under or in connection with the contract of employment; but

    (ii) shall operate so as to terminate that contract on the day preceding the transfer date; and

  (b) the qualifying employee shall not, by virtue of that termination, be treated for any purpose as having been dismissed.

(10) In this paragraph—

"the appropriate authority" means—

  (a) in the case of a person employed in the civil service of the State, the Secretary of State;

  (b) in the case of a transfer scheme under section 3 of this Act and a person employed by a body which is a waste regulation authority, that body;

  (c) in the case of a transfer scheme under section 22 of this Act and a person employed by a local authority, that authority;

"occupational pension scheme" has the meaning given by section 1 of the Pension Schemes Act 1993.

(11) This paragraph shall apply in relation to any qualifying employee as if, as respects any time before the transfer date,—

  (a) any reference to a person's contract of employment included a reference to his employment in the civil service of the State or to the terms of that employment, as the case may require; and

  (b) any reference to the dismissal of a person included a reference to the termination of his employment in that service.

PART II

TRANSFER SCHEMES

Description of the property etc. to be transferred by scheme

4. A transfer scheme may define the property, rights and liabilities to be transferred by the scheme—

  (a) by specifying or describing the property, rights and liabilities in question;

  (b) by referring to all (or all but so much as may be excepted) of the property, rights and liabilities comprised in a specified part of the undertaking of the transferor; or

  (c) partly in the one way and partly in the other.

Division of property etc. to be transferred by scheme: creation of new rights and interests

5.—(1) For the purpose of making any division of property, rights or liabilities which it is considered appropriate to make in connection with the transfer of property, rights and liabilities by and in accordance with a transfer scheme, any such scheme may—

  (a) create in favour of the transferor an interest in, or right over, any property transferred by the scheme;

  (b) create in favour of the relevant new Agency an interest in, or right over, any property retained by the transferor;

  (c) create new rights and liabilities as between the relevant new Agency and the transferor; or

  (d) in connection with any provision made by virtue of paragraph (a), (b) or (c) above, make incidental provision as to the interests, rights and liabilities of persons other than the transferor and the relevant new Agency with respect to the subject-matter of the transfer scheme;

657

and references in the other provisions of Part I of this Act to the transfer of property, rights or liabilities (so far as relating to transfers by and in accordance with transfer schemes) shall accordingly be construed as including references to the creation of any interest, right or liability by virtue of paragraph (a), (b) or (c) above or the making of provision by virtue of paragraph (d) above.

(2) The provision that may be made by virtue of paragraph (c) of sub-paragraph (1) above includes—

   (a) provision for treating any person who is entitled by virtue of a transfer scheme to possession of a document as having given another person an acknowledgement in writing of the right of that other person to the production of the document and to delivery of copies of it; and

   (b) in the case of a transfer scheme under section 3 of this Act, provision applying section 64 of the Law of Property Act 1925 (production and safe custody of documents) in relation to any case in relation to which provision falling within paragraph (a) above has effect.

Transfer schemes: incidental, supplemental and consequential provision

6.—(1) A transfer scheme may make such incidental, supplemental and consequential provision—

   (a) as the Secretary of State considers appropriate, in the case of a scheme made by him,

   (b) as a body which is a waste regulation authority considers appropriate, in the case of a scheme made by that body under section 3 of this Act, or

   (c) as a local authority considers appropriate, in the case of a scheme made by that authority under section 22 of this Act.

(2) Without prejudice to the generality of sub-paragraph (1) above, a transfer scheme may provide—

   (a) that disputes as to the effect of the scheme between the transferor and the relevant new Agency are to be referred to such arbitration as may be specified in or determined under the transfer scheme;

   (b) that determinations on such arbitrations and certificates given jointly by the transferor and the relevant new Agency as to the effect of the scheme as between them are to be conclusive for all purposes.

Modification of transfer schemes

7.—(1) If at any time after a transfer scheme has come into force the Secretary of State considers it appropriate to do so, he may by order provide that the scheme shall for all purposes be deemed to have come into force with such modifications as may be specified in the order.

(2) An order under sub-paragraph (1) above—

   (a) may make, with effect from the coming into force of the transfer scheme in question, such provision as could have been made by the scheme; and

   (b) in connection with giving effect to that provision from that time, may contain such supplemental, consequential or transitional provision as the Secretary of State considers appropriate.

(3) The Secretary of State shall not make an order under sub-paragraph (1) above except after consultation with—

   (a) the relevant new Agency; and

   (b) if the transfer scheme in question is—

      (i) a scheme under section 3 of this Act which transferred property, rights or liabilities of a waste regulation authority, or

      (ii) a scheme under section 22 of this Act which transferred property, rights or liabilities of a local authority,

   the body which was the transferor in the case of that scheme.

(4) The power to make an order under sub-paragraph (1) above shall be exercisable by statutory instrument; and a statutory instrument containing any such order shall be subject to annulment in pursuance of a resolution of either House of Parliament.

Provision of information and assistance to the Secretary of State and the new Agencies in connection with transfer schemes

8.—(1) It shall be the duty of each of the following, that is to say—

   (a) the chief inspector for England and Wales,

   (b) any body which is a waste regulation authority in England or Wales, and

   (c) any officer of such a body,

to provide the Secretary of State or the Agency with such information or assistance as the

Secretary of State or, as the case may be, the Agency may reasonably require for the purposes of, or in connection with, the exercise of any powers of the Secretary of State or the Agency in relation to transfer schemes.

(2) It shall be the duty of each of the following, that is to say—

(a) the chief inspector for Scotland,

(b) any local authority, and

(c) any officer of a local authority,

to provide the Secretary of State or SEPA with such information or assistance as the Secretary of State or, as the case may be, SEPA may reasonably require for the purposes of, or in connection with, the exercise of any powers of the Secretary of State or SEPA in relation to transfer schemes.

PART III

GENERAL PROVISIONS WITH RESPECT TO TRANSFERS BY OR UNDER SECTION 3 OR 22

Consideration

9. No consideration shall be provided in respect of the transfer of any property, rights or liabilities by or under section 3 or 22 of this Act; but—

(a) a transfer scheme may contain provision for consideration to be provided by the relevant new Agency in respect of the creation of interests, rights or liabilities by means of the transfer scheme; and

(b) any such provision shall be enforceable in the same way as if the interests, rights or liabilities had been created, and (if the case so requires) had been capable of being created, by agreement between the parties.

Continuity

10.—(1) This paragraph applies in relation to—

(a) any transfer of property, rights or liabilities by section 3 or 22 of this Act; or

(b) subject to any provision to the contrary in the transfer scheme in question, any transfer of property, rights or liabilities by a transfer scheme.

(2) Where this paragraph applies in relation to a transfer, then, so far as may be necessary for the purposes of, or in connection with, the transfer—

(a) any agreements made, transactions effected or other things done by or in relation to the transferor shall be treated as made, effected or done by or in relation to the relevant new Agency;

(b) references (whether express or implied and, if express, however worded) to the transferor in any agreement (whether in writing or not) or in any deed, bond, instrument or other document relating to the property, rights or liabilities transferred shall, as respects anything falling to be done on or after the transfer date, have effect as references to the relevant new Agency.

Remedies

11.—(1) Without prejudice to the generality of paragraph 10 above, a new Agency and any other person shall, as from the transfer date, have the same rights, powers and remedies (and, in particular, the same rights and powers as to the taking or resisting of legal proceedings or the making or resisting of applications to any authority) for ascertaining, perfecting or enforcing any right or liability transferred to that new Agency by or under this Act as that new Agency or that person would have had if that right or liability had at all times been a right or liability of that new Agency.

(2) Without prejudice to the generality of paragraph 10 above, any legal proceedings or applications to any authority pending immediately before the transfer date by or against a transferor, in so far as they relate to any property, right or liability transferred to the relevant new Agency by or under this Act or to any agreement relating to any such property, right or liability, shall be continued by or against the relevant new Agency to the exclusion of the transferor.

Perfection of vesting of foreign property, rights and liabilities

12.—(1) This paragraph applies in the case of any transfer by or under section 3 or 22 of this Act of any foreign property, rights or liabilities.

(2) It shall be the duty of the transferor and the relevant new Agency to take, as and when that new Agency considers it appropriate, all such steps as may be requisite to secure that the vesting in that new Agency by, or by transfer scheme under, section 3 or 22 of this Act of any foreign property, right or liability is effective under the relevant foreign law.

(3) Until the vesting in the relevant new Agency by, or by transfer scheme under, section 3 or 22 of this Act of any foreign property, right or liability is effective under the relevant foreign law, it shall be the duty of the transferor to hold that property or right for the benefit of, or to discharge that liability on behalf of, the relevant new Agency.

(4) Nothing in sub-paragraphs (2) and (3) above shall be taken as prejudicing the effect under the law of any part of the United Kingdom of the vesting in the relevant new Agency by, or by transfer scheme under, section 3 or 22 of this Act of any foreign property, right or liability.

(5) The transferor shall have all such powers as may be requisite for the performance of his duty under this paragraph, but it shall be the duty of the relevant new Agency to act on behalf of the transferor (so far as possible) in performing the duty imposed on the transferor by this paragraph.

(6) References in this paragraph to any foreign property, right or liability are references to any property, right or liability as respects which any issue arising in any proceedings would have been determined (in accordance with the rules of private international law) by reference to the law of a country or territory outside the United Kingdom.

(7) Duties imposed on the transferor or the relevant new Agency by this paragraph shall be enforceable in the same way as if the duties were imposed by a contract between the transferor and that new Agency.

(8) Any expenses reasonably incurred by the transferor under this paragraph shall be met by the relevant new Agency.

SCHEDULE 3

ENVIRONMENT PROTECTION ADVISORY COMMITTEES

Introductory

1.—(1) In this Schedule, "scheme" means a scheme prepared under this Schedule.

(2) Subject to sub-paragraph (1) above, expressions used in this Schedule and in section 12 of this Act have the same meaning in this Schedule as they have in that section.

Duty of Agency to prepare and submit schemes for each region

2.—(1) It shall be the duty of the Agency, in accordance with such guidance as may be given for the purpose by the Secretary of State,—

    (a) to prepare, in respect of each region, a scheme with respect to the appointment of persons as members of the advisory committee for that region; and

    (b) to submit that scheme to the Secretary of State for his approval before such date as may be specified in the guidance.

(2) Every scheme shall—

    (a) specify descriptions of bodies which, or persons who, appear to the Agency likely to have a significant interest in matters likely to be affected by the manner in which it carries out its functions in the region to which the scheme relates;

    (b) indicate how the membership of the advisory committee is to reflect the different descriptions of bodies or persons so specified;

    (c) specify or describe bodies which, and persons whom, the Agency proposes to consult in connection with appointments of persons as members of the advisory committee; and

    (d) make provision with respect to such other matters as the Agency considers relevant to the membership of the advisory committee.

Approval of schemes

3.—(1) A scheme shall not come into force unless it has been approved by the Secretary of State or until such date as he may specify for the purpose in giving his approval.

(2) Where the Agency submits a scheme to the Secretary of State for his approval, it shall also submit to him—

    (a) a statement of the Agency's reasons for considering that the scheme is one which it is appropriate for him to approve; and

    (b) such information in support of those reasons as it considers necessary.

(3) On submitting a scheme to the Secretary of State for his approval, the Agency shall publish the scheme, in such manner as it considers appropriate for bringing it to the attention of

persons likely to be interested in it, together with a notice specifying the period within which representations or objections with respect to the scheme may be made to the Secretary of State.

(4) Where a scheme has been submitted to the Secretary of State for his approval, it shall be the duty of the Secretary of State, in determining whether to—

(a) approve the scheme,

(b) reject the scheme, or

(c) approve the scheme subject to modifications,

to consider any representations or objections made to him within the period specified pursuant to sub-paragraph (3) above and not withdrawn.

(5) Where the Secretary of State approves a scheme, with or without modifications, it shall be the duty of the Agency to take such steps as it considers appropriate for bringing the scheme as so approved to the attention of persons whom it considers likely to be interested in it.

Replacement and variation of approved membership schemes

4.—(1) The Agency may from time to time, and if required to do so by the Secretary of State shall,—

(a) prepare in accordance with paragraph 2 above a fresh scheme with respect to the appointment of persons as members of the advisory committee for any particular region; and

(b) submit that scheme to the Secretary of State for his approval;

and paragraph 3 above shall have effect accordingly in relation to any such scheme.

(2) An approved membership scheme may from time to time be varied by the Agency with the approval of the Secretary of State.

(3) The provisions of paragraph 3 above shall have effect in relation to any variation of an approved membership scheme as they have effect in relation to a scheme.

Appointment of members

5.—(1) Before appointing a person to be a member of an advisory committee, the Agency—

(a) shall consult such of the associates for that advisory committee as it considers appropriate in the particular case; and

(b) may, if it considers it appropriate to do so, also consult bodies or persons who are not associates for that advisory committee.

(2) In this paragraph, "associates", in the case of any advisory committee, means those bodies and persons specified or described in the approved membership scheme for that advisory committee pursuant to paragraph 2(2)(c) above.

Vacancies, defective appointments etc.

6. The validity of any proceedings of an advisory committee shall not be affected by—

(a) any vacancy amongst the members;

(b) any defect in the appointment of a member; or

(c) any temporary breach of the terms of the approved membership scheme for the advisory committee.

Remuneration and allowances

7.—(1) The Agency shall pay to the chairman of an advisory committee such remuneration, and such travelling and other allowances, as the Secretary of State may determine.

(2) The Agency shall pay to the members of an advisory committee other than the chairman such sums by way of reimbursement (whether in whole or in part) for loss of remuneration, for travelling expenses and for other out-of-pocket expenses as the Secretary of State may determine.

SCHEDULE 4

BOUNDARIES OF REGIONAL FLOOD DEFENCE AREAS

Power to make order

1.—(1) The relevant Minister may by order made by statutory instrument—

(a) alter the boundaries of the area of any regional flood defence committee; or

(b) provide for the amalgamation of any two or more such areas.

(2) Where an order under this Schedule makes provision by reference to anything shown on a main river map, that map shall be conclusive evidence for the purposes of the order of what is shown on the map.

(3) The power to make an order under this Schedule shall include power to make such supplemental, consequential and transitional provision as the relevant Minister considers appropriate.

(4) In the case of an order under this Schedule amalgamating the areas of any two or more regional flood defence committees, the provision made by virtue of sub-paragraph (3) above may include provision determining—

(a) the total number of members of the amalgamated committee; and

(b) the total number of such members to be appointed by the constituent councils of that committee;

and subsections (7) and (8) of section 16 of this Act shall apply in relation to so much of an order under this Schedule as is made by virtue of this sub-paragraph as they apply in relation to an order under subsection (5) of that section.

(5) In this paragraph and the following paragraphs of this Schedule "the relevant Minister"—

(a) in relation to any alteration of the boundaries of an area where the whole or any part of that area is in Wales, means the Ministers;

(b) in relation to the amalgamation of any two or more areas where the whole or any part of any one of those areas is in Wales, means the Ministers; and

(c) in any other case, means the Minister.

(6) In this paragraph—

"main river" means a main river within the meaning of Part IV of the 1991 Act; and

"main river map" has, subject to section 194 of the 1991 Act, the meaning given by section 193(2) of that Act.

Consultation and notice of intention to make order

2.—(1) Before making an order under this Schedule, the relevant Minister shall—

(a) consult such persons or representative bodies as he considers it appropriate to consult at that stage;

(b) prepare a draft order;

(c) publish a notice complying with sub-paragraph (2) below in the London Gazette and in such other manner as he considers appropriate for bringing the draft order to the attention of persons likely to be affected by it if it is made.

(2) A notice for the purposes of sub-paragraph (1)(c) above with respect to a draft order shall—

(a) state the relevant Minister's intention to make the order and its general effect;

(b) specify the places where copies of the draft order and of any map to which it refers may be inspected by any person free of charge at all reasonable times during the period of twenty-eight days beginning with the date on which the notice is first published otherwise than in the London Gazette; and

(c) state that any person may within that period by notice in writing to the relevant Minister object to the making of the order.

(3) The relevant Minister shall also cause copies of the notice and of the draft order to be served on every person carrying out functions under any enactment who appears to him to be concerned.

Objections to draft order and making of order

3.—(1) Before making an order under this Schedule, the relevant Minister—

(a) shall consider any representations or objections which are duly made with respect to the draft order and are not withdrawn; and

(b) may, if he thinks fit, cause a local inquiry to be held with respect to any such representations or objections.

(2) Where notice of a draft order has been published and given in accordance with paragraph 2 above and any representations or objections considered under sub-paragraph (1) above, the relevant Minister may make the order either in the terms of the draft or in those terms as modified in such manner as he thinks fit, or may decide not to make the order.

(3) The relevant Minister shall not make a modification of a draft order in so far as the modification is such as to include in the area of any regional flood defence committee any tidal waters which, if the order had been made in the form of the draft, would have been outside the area of every regional flood defence committee.

Procedure for making of order

4.—(1) Where the relevant Minister makes an order under this Schedule, he shall serve notice of the making of the order on every person (if any) who—

(a) is a person on whom notice is required to have been served under paragraph 2(3) above; and

(b) has duly made an objection to the making of the order that has not been withdrawn.

(2) Where a notice is required to be served under sub-paragraph (1) above with respect to any order, the order shall not have effect before the end of a period of twenty-eight days from the date of service of the last notice served under that sub-paragraph.

(3) If before an order takes effect under sub-paragraph (2) above—

(a) any person who has been served with a notice under sub-paragraph (1) above with respect to that order serves notice objecting to the order on the Minister (or, in the case of an order made jointly by the Ministers, on either of them), and

(b) the objection is not withdrawn,

the order shall be subject to special parliamentary procedure.

(4) A statutory instrument containing an order under this Schedule which is not subject to special parliamentary procedure under sub-paragraph (3) above shall be subject to annulment in pursuance of a resolution of either House of Parliament.

Notice after making of order

5.—(1) Subject to sub-paragraph (2) below, after making an order under this Schedule, the relevant Minister shall publish in the London Gazette, and in such other manner as he considers appropriate for bringing the order to the attention of persons likely to be affected by it, a notice—

(a) stating that the order has been made; and

(b) naming the places where a copy of the order may be inspected at all reasonable times.

(2) In the case of an order to which sub-paragraph (2) of paragraph 4 above applies, the notice—

(a) shall not be published until the end of the period of twenty-eight days referred to in that sub-paragraph; and

(b) shall state whether or not the order is to be subject to special parliamentary procedure.

Questioning of order in courts

6.—(1) Subject to sub-paragraph (3) below, if any person desires to question the validity of an order under this Schedule on the ground—

(a) that it is not within the powers of this Schedule, or

(b) that any requirement of this Schedule has not been complied with,

he may, within six weeks after the date of the first publication of the notice required by paragraph 5 above, make an application for the purpose to the High Court.

(2) On an application under this paragraph the High Court, if satisfied—

(a) that the order is not within the powers of this Schedule, or

(b) that the interests of the applicant have been substantially prejudiced by a failure to comply with any of the requirements of this Schedule,

may quash the order either generally or in so far as it affects the applicant.

(3) Sub-paragraph (1) above—

(a) shall not apply to any order which is confirmed by Act of Parliament under section 6 of the Statutory Orders (Special Procedure) Act 1945; and

(b) shall have effect in relation to any other order which is subject to special parliamentary procedure by virtue of the provisions of this Schedule as if the reference to the date of the first publication of the notice required by paragraph 5 above were a reference to the date on which the order becomes operative under that Act of 1945.

(4) Except as provided by this paragraph the validity of an order under this Schedule shall not, either before or after the order has been made, be questioned in any legal proceedings whatsoever.

SCHEDULE 5

MEMBERSHIP AND PROCEEDINGS OF REGIONAL AND LOCAL FLOOD DEFENCE COMMITTEES

PART I

MEMBERSHIP OF FLOOD DEFENCE COMMITTEES

Terms of membership

1.—(1) Members of a flood defence committee (that is to say a regional flood defence committee or a local flood defence committee), other than those appointed by or on behalf of one or more constituent councils, shall hold and vacate office in accordance with the terms of their appointment.

(2) The first members of a local flood defence committee appointed by or on behalf of any one or more constituent councils—

(a) shall come into office on the day on which the committee comes into existence or, in the case of a member who is for any reason appointed after that day, on the day on which the appointment is made; and

(b) subject to the following provisions of this Schedule, shall hold office until the end of May in such year as may be specified for the purposes of this paragraph in the scheme establishing the committee.

(3) Any members of a flood defence committee appointed by or on behalf of any one or more constituent councils who are not members to whom sub-paragraph (2) above applies—

(a) shall come into office at the beginning of the June next following the day on which they are appointed; and

(b) subject to the following provisions of this Schedule, shall hold office for a term of four years.

(4) If for any reason any such member as is mentioned in sub-paragraph (3) above is appointed on or after the day on which he ought to have come into office, he shall—

(a) come into office on the day on which he is appointed; and

(b) subject to the following provisions of this Schedule, hold office for the remainder of the term.

(5) References in this paragraph and the following provisions of this Schedule to a member of a flood defence committee include references to the chairman of such a committee.

Membership of constituent council as qualification for membership of committee

2.—(1) Members of a flood defence committee appointed by or on behalf of any one or more constituent councils may be members of that council, or one of those councils, or other persons.

(2) Any member of a flood defence committee appointed by or on behalf of a constituent council who at the time of his appointment was a member of that council shall, if he ceases to be a member of that council, also cease to be a member of the committee with whichever is the earlier of the following—

(a) the end of the period of three months beginning with the date when he ceases to be a member of the council; and

(b) the appointment of another person in his place.

(3) For the purposes of sub-paragraph (2) above a member of a council shall not be deemed to have ceased to be a member of the council by reason of retirement if he has been re-elected a member of the council not later than the date of his retirement.

Disqualification for membership of committee

3.—(1) Subject to the following provisions of this paragraph, a person shall be disqualified for appointment as a member of a flood defence committee if he—

(a) is a paid officer of the Agency; or

(b) is a person who has been adjudged bankrupt, or whose estate has been sequestrated or who has made a composition or arrangement with, or granted a trust deed for, his creditors; or

(c) within the period of five years before the day of his appointment, has been convicted, in the United Kingdom, the Channel Islands or the Isle of Man, of any offence and has had passed on him a sentence of imprisonment (whether suspended or not) for a period of not less than three months without the option of a fine; or

(d) is disqualified for being elected or for being a member of a local authority under Part III of the Local Government Finance Act 1982 (accounts and audit) or Part III of the Representation of the People Act 1983 (legal proceedings).

(2) Where a person is disqualified under sub-paragraph (1) above by reason of having been adjudged bankrupt, the disqualification shall cease—

(a) unless the bankruptcy order made against that person is previously annulled, on his discharge from bankruptcy; and

(b) if the bankruptcy order is so annulled, on the date of the annulment.

(3) Where a person is disqualified under sub-paragraph (1) above by reason of having had his estate sequestrated, the disqualification shall cease—

(a) unless the sequestration is recalled or reduced, on the person's discharge under section 54 of the Bankruptcy (Scotland) Act 1985; and

(b) if the sequestration is recalled or reduced, on the date of the recall or reduction.

(4) Where a person is disqualified under sub-paragraph (1) above by reason of his having

made a composition or arrangement with, or having granted a trust deed for, his creditors, the disqualification shall cease—

    (a) if he pays his debts in full, on the date on which the payment is completed; and

    (b) in any other case, at the end of five years from the date on which the terms of the deed of composition or arrangement, or of the trust deed, are fulfilled.

(5) For the purposes of sub-paragraph (1)(c) above the date of the conviction shall be taken to be—

    (a) the ordinary date on which the period allowed for making an appeal or application with respect to the conviction expires; or

    (b) if such an appeal or application is made, the date on which it is finally disposed of or abandoned or fails by reason of non-prosecution.

(6) Section 92 of the Local Government Act 1972 (proceedings for disqualification) shall apply in relation to disqualification under this paragraph for appointment as a member of a flood defence committee as it applies in relation to disqualification for acting as a member of a local authority.

Vacation of office by disqualifying event

4.—(1) The office of a member of a flood defence committee shall become vacant upon the fulfilment of any of the following conditions, that is to say—

    (a) the person holding that office is adjudged bankrupt, is a person whose estate is sequestrated or makes a composition or arrangement with, or grants a trust deed for, his creditors;

    (b) that person is convicted, in the United Kingdom, the Channel Islands or the Isle of Man, of any offence and has passed on him a sentence of imprisonment (whether suspended or not) for a period of not less than three months without the option of a fine;

    (c) that person is disqualified for being elected or for being a member of a local authority under Part III of the Local Government Finance Act 1982 (accounts and audit) or Part III of the Representation of the People Act 1983 (legal proceedings); or

    (d) that person has, for a period of six consecutive months been absent from meetings of the committee, otherwise than by reason of illness or some other cause approved during the period by the committee.

(2) For the purposes of sub-paragraph (1)(d) above, the attendance of a member of a flood defence committee—

    (a) at a meeting of any sub-committee of the committee of which he is a member, or

    (b) at any joint committee to which he has been appointed by that committee,

shall be treated as attendance at a meeting of the committee.

Resignation of office by members of regional committee

5.—(1) The chairman of a regional flood defence committee may resign his office at any time by giving notice to the chairman of the Agency and to one of the Ministers.

(2) Any other member of such a committee may resign his office at any time by giving notice to the chairman of the committee and also, if he was appointed by one of the Ministers, to that Minister.

Resignation of office by members of local committee

6.—(1) The chairman of a local flood defence committee may resign his office at any time by giving notice to the chairman of the regional flood defence committee.

(2) Any other member of a local flood defence committee may resign his office at any time by giving notice to the chairman of that local flood defence committee.

Appointments to fill casual vacancies

7.—(1) Where, for any reason whatsoever, the office of a member of a flood defence committee becomes vacant before the end of his term of office, the vacancy—

    (a) shall, if the unexpired portion of the term of office of the vacating member is six months or more, be filled by the appointment of a new member; and

    (b) may be so filled in any other case.

(2) A person appointed by virtue of sub-paragraph (1) above to fill a casual vacancy shall hold office for so long only as the former member would have held office.

Eligibility of previous members for re-appointment

8. Subject to the provisions of this Schedule, a member of a flood defence committee shall be eligible for reappointment.

Appointment of deputies

9.—(1) Subject to the following provisions of this paragraph, a person nominated by one or more constituent councils may act as deputy for a member of a flood defence committee appointed by or on behalf of that council or those councils and may, accordingly, attend and vote at a meeting of the committee, instead of that member.

(2) A person nominated under sub-paragraph (1) above as deputy for a member of a flood defence committee may, by virtue of that nomination, attend and vote at a meeting of a sub-committee of that committee which—

　　(a) has been appointed by that committee under Part II of this Schedule; and

　　(b) is a committee to which the member for whom he is a deputy belongs.

(3) A person acting as deputy for a member of a flood defence committee shall be treated for the purposes for which he is nominated as a member of that committee.

(4) A person shall not act as deputy for a member of a flood defence committee unless his nomination has been notified to such officer of the Agency as is appointed to receive such nominations.

(5) A nomination under this paragraph shall be in writing and may apply either to a particular meeting or to all meetings during a stated period or until the nomination is revoked.

(6) A person shall not act as deputy for more than one member of a flood defence committee.

(7) Nothing in this paragraph shall entitle a person to attend and vote at a meeting of a local flood defence committee by reason of his nomination as deputy for a member of a regional flood defence committee.

Payments to past and present chairmen and to members

10.—(1) The Agency shall pay to any person who is a chairman of a flood defence committee such remuneration and allowances as may be determined by the relevant Minister.

(2) If the relevant Minister so determines in the case of any person who is or has been chairman of a flood defence committee, the Agency shall pay or make arrangements for the payment of a pension in relation to that person in accordance with the determination.

(3) If a person ceases to be chairman of a flood defence committee and it appears to the relevant Minister that there are special circumstances which make it right that that person should receive compensation in respect of his ceasing to be chairman, the relevant Minister may require the Agency to pay to that person a sum of such amount as that Minister may determine.

(4) The Agency may pay to any person who is a member of a flood defence committee such allowances as may be determined by the relevant Minister.

(5) In this paragraph—

"pension", in relation to any person, means a pension (whether contributory or not) of any kind payable to or in respect of him, and includes an allowance, gratuity or lump sum so payable and a return of contributions with or without interest or any other addition; and

"the relevant Minister"—

　　(a) in relation to the regional flood defence committee for an area the whole or the greater part of which is in Wales and in relation to any local flood defence committee for any district comprised in the area of such a regional flood defence committee, means the Secretary of State; and

　　(b) in relation to any other flood defence committee, means the Minister.

PART II

PROCEEDINGS OF FLOOD DEFENCE COMMITTEES

Appointment of sub-committees, joint sub-committees etc.

11.—(1) For the purpose of carrying out any functions in pursuance of arrangements under paragraph 12 below—

　　(a) a flood defence committee may appoint a sub-committee of the committee;

　　(b) two or more regional or two or more local flood defence committees may appoint a joint sub-committee of those committees;

(c) any sub-committee may appoint one or more committees of that sub-committee ("under sub-committees").

(2) The number of members of any sub-committee and their terms of office shall be fixed by the appointing committee or committees or, in the case of an under sub-committee, by the appointing sub-committee.

(3) A sub-committee appointed under this paragraph may include persons who are not members of the appointing committee or committees or, in the case of an under sub-committee, the committee or committees of whom they are an under sub-committee; but at least two thirds of the members appointed to any such sub-committee shall be members of that committee or those committees, as the case may be.

(4) A person who is disqualified for being a member of a flood defence committee shall be disqualified also for being a member of a sub-committee or under sub-committee appointed under this paragraph.

Delegation of functions to sub-committees etc.

12.—(1) Subject to section 106 of the 1991 Act and to any other express provision contained in any enactment, a flood defence committee may arrange for the carrying out of any of their functions—

(a) by a sub-committee, or an under sub-committee of the committee or an officer of the Agency; or

(b) by any other regional or, as the case may be, local flood defence committee;

and two or more regional or two or more local flood defence committees may arrange to carry out any of their functions jointly or may arrange for the carrying out of any of their functions by a joint sub-committee of theirs.

(2) Where by virtue of this paragraph any functions of a flood defence committee or of two or more such committees may be carried out by a sub-committee, then, unless the committee or committees otherwise direct, the sub-committee may arrange for the carrying out of any of those functions by an under sub-committee or by an officer of the Agency.

(3) Where by virtue of this paragraph any functions of a flood defence committee or of two or more such committees may be carried out by an under sub-committee, then, unless the committee or committees or the sub-committee otherwise direct, the under sub-committee may arrange for the carrying out of any of those functions by an officer of the Agency.

(4) Any arrangements made by a flood defence committee under this paragraph for the carrying out of any function shall not prevent the committee from discharging their functions themselves.

(5) References in the preceding provisions of this paragraph to the carrying out of any functions of a flood defence committee include references to the doing of anything which is calculated to facilitate, or is conducive or incidental to, the carrying out of any of those functions.

(6) A regional flood defence committee shall not, under this paragraph, make arrangements for the carrying out in a local flood defence district of any functions which fall to be carried out there by the local flood defence committee.

Rules of procedure

13.—(1) A flood defence committee may, with the approval of the relevant Minister, make rules for regulating the proceedings of the committee.

(2) Nothing in section 6(4) of this Act or section 105 or 106 of the 1991 Act shall entitle the Agency to make any arrangements or give any directions for regulating the proceedings of any flood defence committee.

(3) In this paragraph "the relevant Minister" has the same meaning as in paragraph 10 above.

Declarations of interest etc.

14.—(1) Subject to the following provisions of this paragraph, the provisions of sections 94 to 98 of the Local Government Act 1972 (pecuniary interests of members of local authorities) shall apply in relation to members of a flood defence committee as those provisions apply in relation to members of local authorities.

(2) In their application by virtue of this paragraph those provisions shall have effect in accordance with the following provisions—

(a) for references to meetings of the local authority there shall be substituted references to meetings of the committee;

(b) in section 94(4), for the reference to provision being made by standing orders of a local authority there shall be substituted a reference to provisions being made by directions of the committee;

(c) in section 96, for references to the proper officer of the local authority there shall be substituted a reference to an officer of the Agency appointed for the purposes of this paragraph; and

(d) section 97 shall apply as it applies to a local authority other than a parish or community council.

(3) Subject to sub-paragraph (4) below, a member of a flood defence committee shall be disqualified, for so long as he remains such a member and for twelve months after he ceases to be such a member, for appointment to any paid office by the Agency or any regional flood defence committee.

(4) Sub-paragraph (3) above shall not disqualify any person for appointment to the office of chairman of a local flood defence committee.

Authentication of documents

15.—(1) Any notice or other document which a flood defence committee are required or authorised to give, make or issue by or under any enactment may be signed on behalf of the committee by any member of the committee or any officer of the Agency who is generally or specifically authorised for that purpose by a resolution of the committee.

(2) Any document purporting to bear the signature of a person expressed to be authorised as mentioned in sub-paragraph (1) above shall be deemed, unless the contrary is shown, to be duly given, made or issued by authority of the committee.

(3) In this paragraph "signature" includes a facsimile of a signature by whatever process reproduced.

Proof and validity of proceedings

16.—(1) A minute of the proceedings of a meeting of a flood defence committee, purporting to be signed at that or the next ensuing meeting by—
- (a) the chairman of the meeting to the proceedings of which the minute relates, or
- (b) by the chairman of the next ensuing meeting,

shall be evidence of the proceedings and shall be received in evidence without further proof.

(2) Where a minute has been signed as mentioned in sub-paragraph (1) above in respect of a meeting of a committee or sub-committee, then, unless the contrary is shown—
- (a) the meeting shall be deemed to have been duly convened and held;
- (b) all the proceedings had at any such meeting shall be deemed to have been duly had; and
- (c) that committee or sub-committee shall be deemed to have been duly constituted and have had power to deal with the matters referred to in the minute.

(3) The validity of any proceedings of a flood defence committee shall not be affected by any vacancy among the members of the committee or by any defect in the appointment of such a member.

SCHEDULE 6

THE SCOTTISH ENVIRONMENT PROTECTION AGENCY

Status

1. SEPA shall be a body corporate with a common seal.
2. Subject to section 38 of this Act, SEPA shall not—
- (a) be regarded as a servant or agent of the Crown;
- (b) have any status, immunity or privilege of the Crown;
- (c) by virtue of its connection with the Crown, be exempt from any tax, duty, rate, levy or other charge whatsoever whether general or local,

and its property shall not be regarded as property of, or held on behalf of, the Crown.

Membership

3. SEPA shall consist of not less than eight, nor more than twelve, members appointed by the Secretary of State.

4. In making appointments under paragraph 3 above, the Secretary of State shall have regard to the desirability of appointing persons who have knowledge or experience in some matter relevant to the functions of SEPA.

5. Subject to paragraphs 7 and 8 below, each member—

(a) shall hold and vacate office in accordance with the terms of his appointment;

(b) may, by giving notice to the Secretary of State, resign his office; and

(c) after ceasing to hold office shall be eligible for reappointment as a member.

6. The Secretary of State may, by order made by statutory instrument subject to annulment in pursuance of a resolution of either House of Parliament, amend paragraph 3 above so as to substitute for the numbers for the time being specified as, respectively, the minimum and maximum membership such other numbers as he thinks fit.

7. The Secretary of State may remove a member from office if he is satisfied that the member—

(a) has been absent from meetings of SEPA for a period longer than three months without the permission of SEPA; or

(b) has been adjudged bankrupt, has made an arrangement with his creditors, has had his estate sequestrated or has granted a trust deed for his creditors or a composition contract; or

(c) is unable or unfit to carry out the functions of a member.

Chairman and deputy chairman

8.—(1) The Secretary of State shall appoint one of the members of SEPA to be chairman and another of those members to be deputy chairman.

(2) The chairman and deputy chairman shall hold and vacate office in terms of their appointments.

(3) A member who is chairman or deputy chairman may resign his office by giving notice to the Secretary of State; but if the chairman or deputy chairman ceases to be a member (whether or not on giving notice under paragraph 5(b) above) he shall cease to be chairman or, as the case may be, deputy chairman.

(4) A person who ceases to be chairman or deputy chairman shall be eligible for reappointment as such under sub-paragraph (1) above at any time when he is a member.

Remuneration, pensions, etc.

9.—(1) SEPA shall—

(a) pay to its members such remuneration and such travelling and other allowances (if any); and

(b) as regards any member or former member in whose case the Secretary of State may so determine—

(i) pay such pension, allowance or gratuity to or in respect of him;

(ii) make such payments towards the provision of such pension, allowance or gratuity; or

(iii) provide and maintain such schemes (whether contributory or not) for the payment of pensions, allowances or gratuities,

as the Secretary of State may determine.

(2) If a person ceases to be a member, and it appears to the Secretary of State that there are special circumstances which make it right that he should receive compensation, the Secretary of State may require SEPA to pay to that person a sum of such amount as the Secretary of State may determine.

Staff

10.—(1) There shall be a chief officer of SEPA.

(2) The Secretary of State shall, after consultation with the chairman or person designated to be chairman (if there is a person holding or designated to hold that office), make the first appointment of chief officer on such terms and conditions as he may determine; and thereafter SEPA may, with the approval of the Secretary of State, make subsequent appointments to that office on such terms and conditions as it may with such approval determine.

11. SEPA may appoint such other employees as it thinks fit.

12.—(1) SEPA shall, in the case of such of its employees or former employees as it may, with the approval of the Secretary of State, determine—

(a) pay such pensions, allowances or gratuities to or in respect of those employees;

(b) make such payments towards provision of such pensions, allowances or gratuities; or

(c) provide and maintain such schemes (whether contributory or not) for the payment of such pensions, allowances or gratuities,

as it may, with the approval of the Secretary of State, determine.

(2) References in sub-paragraph (1) above to pensions, allowances or gratuities in respect of employees of SEPA include references to pensions allowances or gratuities by way of compensation to or in respect of any such employee who suffers loss of office or employment.

Proceedings

13.—(1) SEPA may regulate its own procedure and that of any committee established by it (including making provision in relation to the quorum for its meetings and the meetings of any such committee).

(2) The proceedings of SEPA and of any committee established by it shall not be invalidated by any vacancy amongst its members or the members of such committee or by any defect in the appointment of such member.

Committees

14.—(1) SEPA may appoint persons who are not members of it to be members of any committee established by it, but at least one member of any such committee shall be a member of SEPA.

(2) SEPA shall pay to a person so appointed such remuneration and allowances (if any) as the Secretary of State may determine.

(3) Any committee established by SEPA shall comply with any directions given to them by it.

Delegation of powers

15.—(1) Anything authorised or required by or under any enactment to be done by SEPA may be done by any of its committees which, or by any of its members or employees who, is authorised (generally or specifically) for the purpose by SEPA.

(2) Nothing in sub-paragraph (1) above shall prevent SEPA from doing anything that a committee, member or employee has been authorised or required to do.

Regional Boards

16.—(1) Without prejudice to the generality of its power to establish committees, SEPA shall establish committees (to be known as "Regional Boards") for the purposes of discharging in relation to such areas as it may, with the approval of the Secretary of State, determine, such of its functions as it may, with such approval, determine.

(2) A Regional Board shall have a chairman who shall be a member of SEPA and appointed to that office by SEPA.

(3) It shall be the duty of SEPA to comply with such guidance as the Secretary of State may from time to time give as to—
  (a) the number of persons to be appointed to a Regional Board;
  (b) the qualifications and experience which persons (other than members of SEPA) should have to be eligible for appointment to a Regional Board;
  (c) the descriptions of bodies which, or persons who, have a significant interest in matters likely to be affected by the discharge by a Regional Board of its functions; and
  (d) how the membership of a Regional Board is to reflect the different descriptions of bodies or persons referred to in paragraph (c) above.

(4) Anything authorised or required to be done by a Regional Board by virtue of sub-paragraph (1) above may be done by any member of the Board, or by any employee of SEPA, who is authorised (generally or specifically) for the purpose by the Board.

(5) Nothing in sub-paragraph (4) above shall prevent a Regional Board doing anything that a member or employee has been authorised or required to do.

Members' interests

17.—(1) A member who is in any way directly or indirectly interested in any matter that is brought up for consideration at a meeting of SEPA shall disclose the nature of his interest to the meeting; and, where such a disclosure is made—
  (a) the disclosure shall be recorded in the minutes of the meeting; and
  (b) the member shall not take any part in any deliberation or decision of SEPA or of any of its committees with respect to that matter.

(2) For the purposes of sub-paragraph (1) above, a general notification given at a meeting of SEPA by a member to the effect that he—
  (a) is a member of a specified company or firm, and
  (b) is to be regarded as interested in any matter involving that company or firm,
shall be regarded as a sufficient disclosure of his interest in relation to any such matter.

(3) A member need not attend in person at a meeting of SEPA in order to make a disclosure

which he is required to make under this paragraph if he takes reasonable steps to secure that the disclosure is made by a notice which is read and considered at the meeting.

(4) The Secretary of State may, subject to such conditions as he considers appropriate, remove any disability imposed by virtue of this paragraph in any case where the number of members of SEPA disabled by virtue of this paragraph at any one time would be so great a proportion of the whole as to impede the transaction of business.

(5) The power of the Secretary of State under sub-paragraph (4) above includes power to remove, either indefinitely or for any period, a disability which would otherwise attach to any member, or members of any description, by reason of such interests, and in respect of such matters, as may be specified or described by the Secretary of State.

(6) Nothing in this paragraph precludes any member from taking part in the consideration or discussion of, or voting on, any question whether an application should be made to the Secretary of State for the exercise of the power conferred by sub-paragraph (4) above.

(7) In this paragraph—
    (a) any reference to a meeting of SEPA includes a reference to a meeting of any of SEPA's committees; and
    (b) any reference to a member includes a reference to a person who is not a member of SEPA but who is a member of any such committee.

Minutes

18.—(1) Minutes shall be kept of proceedings of SEPA and of its committees.

(2) Minutes of any such proceedings shall be evidence of those proceedings if they are signed by a person purporting to have acted as chairman of the proceedings to which the minutes relate or of any subsequent proceedings in the course of which the minutes were approved as a correct record.

(3) Where minutes of any such proceedings have been signed as mentioned in sub-paragraph (2) above, those proceedings shall, unless the contrary is shown, be deemed to have been validly convened and constituted.

[*Schedules 7 to 10 are not reproduced here*]

SCHEDULE 11

AIR QUALITY: SUPPLEMENTAL PROVISIONS

Consultation requirements

1.—(1) A local authority in carrying out its functions in relation to—
    (a) any air quality review,
    (b) any assessment under section 82 or 84 of this Act, or
    (c) the preparation of an action plan or any revision of an action plan,
shall consult such other persons as fall within sub-paragraph (2) below.

(2) Those persons are—
    (a) the Secretary of State;
    (b) the appropriate new Agency;
    (c) in England and Wales, the highway authority for any highway in the area to which the review or, as the case may be, the action plan or revision relates;
    (d) every local authority whose area is contiguous to the authority's area;
    (e) any county council in England whose area consists of or includes the whole or any part of the authority's area;
    (f) any National Park authority for a National Park whose area consists of or includes the whole or any part of the authority's area;
    (g) such public authorities exercising functions in, or in the vicinity of, the authority's area as the authority may consider appropriate;
    (h) such bodies appearing to the authority to be representative of persons with business interests in the area to which the review or action plan in question relates as the authority may consider appropriate;
    (j) such other bodies or persons as the authority considers appropriate.

(3) In this paragraph "National Park authority", subject to sub-paragraph (4) below, means a National Park authority established under section 63 of this Act which has become the local planning authority for the National Park in question.

(4) As respects any period before a National Park authority established under section 63 of this Act in relation to a National Park becomes the local planning authority for that National

Park, any reference in sub-paragraph (2) above to a National Park authority shall be taken as a reference to the National Park Committee or joint or special planning board for that National Park.

Exchange of information with county councils in England

2.—(1) This paragraph applies in any case where a district in England for which there is a district council is comprised in an area for which there is a county council; and in this paragraph—
    (a) any reference to the county council is a reference to the council of that area; and
    (b) any reference to a district council is a reference to the council of a district comprised in that area.

(2) It shall be the duty of the county council to provide a district council with all such information as is reasonably requested by the district council for purposes connected with the carrying out of its functions under or by virtue of this Part.

(3) It shall be the duty of a district council to provide the county council with all such information as is reasonably requested by the county council for purposes connected with the carrying out of any of its functions relating to the assessment or management of the quality of air.

(4) Information provided to a district council or county council under sub-paragraph (2) or (3) above shall be provided in such form and in such manner and at such times as the district council or, as the case may be, the county council may reasonably require.

(5) A council which provides information under sub-paragraph (2) or (3) above shall be entitled to recover the reasonable cost of doing so from the council which requested the information.

(6) The information which a council may be required to provide under this paragraph shall include information which, although it is not in the possession of the council or would not otherwise come into the possession of the council, is information which it is reasonable to require the council to obtain.

Joint exercise of local authority functions

3.—(1) The appropriate authority may give directions to any two or more local authorities requiring them to exercise the powers conferred by—
    (a) section 101(5) of the Local Government Act 1972 (power of two or more local authorities to discharge functions jointly), or
    (b) section 56(5) of the Local Government (Scotland) Act 1973 (which makes similar provision for Scotland),
in relation to functions under or by virtue of this Part in accordance with the directions.

(2) The appropriate authority may give directions to a local authority requiring it—
    (a) not to exercise those powers, or
    (b) not to exercise those powers in a manner specified in the directions,
in relation to functions under or by virtue of this Part.

(3) Where two or more local authorities have exercised those powers in relation to functions under or by virtue of this Part, the appropriate authority may give them directions requiring them to revoke, or modify in accordance with the directions, the arrangements which they have made.

(4) In this paragraph, "the appropriate authority" means—
    (a) in relation to England and Wales, the Secretary of State; and
    (b) in relation to Scotland, SEPA acting with the approval of the Secretary of State.

Public access to information about air quality

4.—(1) It shall be the duty of every local authority—
    (a) to secure that there is available at all reasonable times for inspection by the public free of charge a copy of each of the documents specified in sub-paragraph (2) below; and
    (b) to afford to members of the public facilities for obtaining copies of those documents on payment of a reasonable charge.

(2) The documents mentioned in sub-paragraph (1)(a) above are—
    (a) a report of the results of any air quality review which the authority has caused to be conducted;
    (b) a report of the results of any assessment which the authority has caused to be made under section 82 or 84 of this Act;

(c) any order made by the authority under section 83 of this Act;
(d) any action plan prepared by the authority;
(e) any proposals or statements submitted to the authority pursuant to subsection (3) or (4) of section 86 of this Act;
(f) any directions given to the authority under this Part;
(g) in a case where section 86 of this Act applies, any directions given to the county council under this Part.

Fixed penalty offences

5.—(1) Without prejudice to the generality of paragraph (o) of subsection (2) of section 87 of this Act, regulations may, in particular, make provision—

(a) for the qualifications, appointment or authorisation of persons who are to issue fixed penalty notices;
(b) for the offences in connection with which, the cases or circumstances in which, the time or period at or within which, or the manner in which fixed penalty notices may be issued;
(c) prohibiting the institution, before the expiration of the period for paying the fixed penalty, of proceedings against a person for an offence in connection with which a fixed penalty notice has been issued;
(d) prohibiting the conviction of a person for an offence in connection with which a fixed penalty notice has been issued if the fixed penalty is paid before the expiration of the period for paying it;
(e) entitling, in prescribed cases, a person to whom a fixed penalty notice is issued to give, within a prescribed period, notice requesting a hearing in respect of the offence to which the fixed penalty notice relates;
(f) for the amount of the fixed penalty to be increased by a prescribed amount in any case where the person liable to pay the fixed penalty fails to pay it before the expiration of the period for paying it, without having given notice requesting a hearing in respect of the offence to which the fixed penalty notice relates;
(g) for or in connection with the recovery of an unpaid fixed penalty as a fine or as a civil debt or as if it were a sum payable under a county court order;
(h) for or in connection with execution or other enforcement in respect of an unpaid fixed penalty by prescribed persons;
(j) for a fixed penalty notice, and any prescribed proceedings or other prescribed steps taken by reference to the notice, to be rendered void in prescribed cases where a person makes a prescribed statutory declaration, and for the consequences of any notice, proceedings or other steps being so rendered void (including extension of any time limit for instituting criminal proceedings);
(k) for or in connection with the extension, in prescribed cases or circumstances, by a prescribed person of the period for paying a fixed penalty;
(l) for or in connection with the withdrawal, in prescribed circumstances, of a fixed penalty notice, including—
  (i) repayment of any amount paid by way of fixed penalty in pursuance of a fixed penalty notice which is withdrawn; and
  (ii) prohibition of the institution or continuation of proceedings for the offence in connection with which the withdrawn notice was issued;
(m) for or in connection with the disposition of sums received by way of fixed penalty;
(n) for a certificate purporting to be signed by or on behalf of a prescribed person and stating either—
  (i) that payment of a fixed penalty was, or (as the case may be) was not, received on or before a date specified in the certificate, or
  (ii) that an envelope containing an amount sent by post in payment of a fixed penalty was marked as posted on a date specified in the certificate,
  to be received as evidence of the matters so stated and to be treated without further proof, as being so signed unless the contrary is shown;
(o) requiring a fixed penalty notice to give such reasonable particulars of the circumstances alleged to constitute the fixed penalty offence to which the notice relates as are necessary for giving reasonable information of the offence and to state—
  (i) the monetary amount of the fixed penalty which may be paid;
  (ii) the person to whom, and the address at which, the fixed penalty may be paid and any correspondence relating to the fixed penalty notice may be sent;

   (iii) the method or methods by which payment of the fixed penalty may be made;
   (iv) the period for paying the fixed penalty;
   (v) the consequences of the fixed penalty not being paid before the expiration of that period;
  (p) similar to any provision made by section 79 of the Road Traffic Offenders Act 1988 (statements by constables in fixed penalty cases);
  (q) for presuming, in any proceedings, that any document of a prescribed description purporting to have been signed by a person to whom a fixed penalty notice has been issued has been signed by that person;
  (r) requiring or authorising a fixed penalty notice to contain prescribed information relating to, or for the purpose of facilitating, the administration of the fixed penalty system;
  (s) with respect to the giving of fixed penalty notices, including, in particular, provision with respect to—
   (i) the methods by which,
   (ii) the officers, servants or agents by, to or on whom, and
   (iii) the places at which,
  fixed penalty notices may be given by, or served on behalf of, a prescribed person;
  (t) prescribing the method or methods by which fixed penalties may be paid;
  (u) for or with respect to the issue of prescribed documents to persons to whom fixed penalty notices are or have been given;
  (w) for a fixed penalty notice to be treated for prescribed purposes as if it were an information or summons or any other document of a prescribed description.

(2) The provision that may be made by regulations prescribing fixed penalty offences includes provision for an offence to be a fixed penalty offence—

  (a) only if it is committed in such circumstances or manner as may be prescribed; or
  (b) except if it is committed in such circumstances or manner as may be prescribed.

(3) Regulations may provide for any offence which is a fixed penalty offence to cease to be such an offence.

(4) An offence which, in consequence of regulations made by virtue of sub-paragraph (3) above, has ceased to be a fixed penalty offence shall be eligible to be prescribed as such an offence again.

(5) Regulations may make provision for such exceptions, limitations and conditions as the Secretary of State considers necessary or expedient.

(6) In this paragraph—

"fixed penalty" means a penalty of such amount as may be prescribed (whether by being specified in, or made calculable under, regulations);

"fixed penalty notice" means a notice offering a person an opportunity to discharge any liability to conviction for a fixed penalty offence by payment of a penalty of a prescribed amount;

"fixed penalty offence" means, subject to sub-paragraph (2) above, any offence (whether under or by virtue of this Part or any other enactment) which is for the time being prescribed as a fixed penalty offence;

"the fixed penalty system" means the system implementing regulations made under or by virtue of paragraph (o) of subsection (2) of section 87 of this Act;

"the period for paying", in relation to any fixed penalty, means such period as may be prescribed for the purpose;

"regulations" means regulations under or by virtue of paragraph (o) of subsection (2) of section 87 of this Act.

SCHEDULE 12

[*This Schedule inserts Schedule 2a into the Environmental Protection Act 1990, and is reproduced there*].

[*Schedules 13 and 14 are not reproduced here.*]

SCHEDULE 15

MINOR AND CONSEQUENTIAL AMENDMENTS RELATING TO FISHERIES

Interpretation

1. In this Schedule—
  "local statutory provision" means—

(a) a provision of a local Act (including an Act confirming a provisional order);

(b) a provision of so much of any public general Act as has effect with respect to particular persons or works or with respect to particular provisions falling within any paragraph of this definition;

(c) a provision of an instrument made under any provision falling within paragraph (a) or (b) above;

(d) a provision of any other instrument which is in the nature of a local enactment;

"the Minister" means the Minister of Agriculture, Fisheries and Food;

"subordinate legislation" has the same meaning as in the Interpretation Act 1978;

"the transfer date" has the same meaning as in Part I of this Act.

General modifications of references to the National Rivers Authority

2.—(1) Subject to—

(a) the following provisions of this Schedule,

(b) the provisions of sections 102 to 104 of this Act, and

(c) any repeal made by this Act,

any provision to which this paragraph applies which contains, or falls to be construed as containing, a reference (however framed and whether or not in relation to an area) to the National Rivers Authority shall have effect on and after the transfer date as if that reference were a reference to the Agency.

(2) Sub-paragraph (1) above is subject to paragraph 1(2)(a) of Schedule 17 to the Water Act 1989 (references in certain local statutory provisions or subordinate legislation to the area of a particular water authority to have effect as references to the area which, immediately before the transfer date within the meaning of that Act, was the area of that authority for the purposes of their functions relating to fisheries).

(3) Subject as mentioned in sub-paragraph (1) above, any provision to which this paragraph applies which contains, or falls to be construed as containing, a reference (however framed) to the whole area in relation to which the National Rivers Authority carries out its functions in relation to fisheries shall have effect on and after the transfer date as if that reference were a reference to the whole area in relation to which the Agency carries out its functions relating to fisheries.

(4) The provisions to which this paragraph applies are the provisions of—

(a) the Sea Fisheries Regulation Act 1966;

(b) the Salmon and Freshwater Fisheries Act 1975; and

(c) any local statutory provision or subordinate legislation which is in force immediately before the transfer date and—

(i) relates to the carrying out by the National Rivers Authority of any function relating to fisheries; or

(ii) in the case of subordinate legislation, was made by virtue of any provision to which this paragraph applies or under the Diseases of Fish Act 1937.

(5) The modifications made by this paragraph shall be subject to any power by subordinate legislation to revoke or amend any provision to which this paragraph applies; and, accordingly, any such power, including the powers conferred by section 121 of this Act and paragraph 3 below, shall be exercisable so as to exclude the operation of this paragraph in relation to the provisions in relation to which the power is conferred.

Power to amend subordinate legislation etc.

3.—(1) If it appears to the Minister or the Secretary of State to be appropriate to do so for the purposes of, or in consequence of, the coming into force of any provision of this Schedule, he may by order revoke or amend any subordinate legislation.

(2) An order under this paragraph may—

(a) make different provision for different cases, including different provision in relation to different persons, circumstances or localities; and

(b) contain such supplemental, consequential and transitional provision as the Minister or the Secretary of State considers appropriate.

(3) The power conferred by virtue of this paragraph in relation to subordinate legislation made under any enactment shall be without prejudice to any other power to revoke or amend subordinate legislation made under that enactment, but—

(a) no requirement imposed with respect to the exercise of any such other power shall apply in relation to any revocation or amendment of that legislation by an order under this paragraph; and

(b) the power to make an order under this paragraph shall be exercisable (instead of in accordance with any such requirement) by statutory instrument subject to annulment in pursuance of a resolution of either House of Parliament.

The Diseases of Fish Act 1937

4.—(1) Subject to sub-paragraph (2) below, in the Diseases of Fish Act 1937—

(a) any reference which to any extent is, or falls to be construed as, a reference to the National Rivers Authority shall have effect, in relation to the area which by virtue of section 6(7) of this Act is the area in relation to which the Agency carries out functions under that Act, as a reference to the Agency; and

(b) references to an area (including references which fall to be construed as references to the area which by virtue of subsection (6) of section 2 of the Water Resources Act 1991 is the area in relation to which the National Rivers Authority carries out functions under the said Act of 1937), in relation to the Agency, shall have effect as references to the area described in paragraph (a) above.

(2) In section 8(3) of the said Act of 1937 (offences in relation to the Esk) for the words "National Rivers Authority" there shall be substituted the words "Environment Agency".

(3) Nothing in this paragraph or in that Act shall authorise the Agency to take legal proceedings in Scotland in respect of any offence.

The Sea Fisheries Regulation Act 1966

5.—(1) The provisions of section 1 of the Sea Fisheries Regulation Act 1966 (establishment of fisheries committees) which provide that an order under that section modifying a previous such order is to be made only on such an application and after such consultation as is mentioned in that section shall not apply to an order under that section which contains a statement that the only provision made by the order is provision which appears to the Minister making the order to be appropriate in consequence of any of the provisions of this Act.

(2) In section 2(2) of that Act (constitution of local fisheries committee) for the words "the National Rivers Authority" there shall be substituted the words "the Environment Agency".

(3) In section 18(3) of that Act (provision where a water authority or harbour authority have the powers of a local fisheries committee) for the words "National Rivers Authority)" there shall be substituted the words "Environment Agency)".

The Sea Fish (Conservation) Act 1967

6. In section 18(1) of the Sea Fish (Conservation) Act 1967 (enforcement of orders relating to salmon and migratory trout)—

(a) for the words "subsection (6) of section 2 of the Water Resources Act 1991" there shall be substituted the words "subsection (7) of section 6 of the Environment Act 1995"; and

(b) for the words "the National Rivers Authority" there shall be substituted the words "the Environment Agency".

The Salmon and Freshwater Fisheries Act 1975

7. In section 5 of the Salmon and Freshwater Fisheries Act 1975 (prohibition of use of explosives, poisons, electrical devices etc) in subsection (2), the words following paragraph (b) (which require Ministerial approval for the giving of permission to use noxious substances) shall be omitted.

8. In section 6(3) of that Act (definition of "unauthorised fixed engine") in paragraph (d) for the words "the National Rivers Authority" there shall be substituted the words "the Agency".

9. In section 8(2) of that Act (fishing mill dams to have attached to them fish passes of form and dimensions approved by the Minister) for the words "the Minister" there shall be inserted the words "the Agency".

10. In section 9(1) of that Act (owner or occupier of certain dams or other obstructions to make fish passes of form and dimensions approved by the Minister) for the words "the Minister" there shall be substituted the words "the Agency".

11.—(1) In section 10 of that Act, in subsection (1) (power of the National Rivers Authority, with the written consent of the Minister, to construct and maintain fish passes of form and dimensions approved by the Minister)—

(a) the words "with the written consent of the Minister," shall be omitted; and

(b) for the words "as the Minister may approve" there shall be substituted the words "as it may determine".

(2) In subsection (2) of that section (power of the National Rivers Authority, with the consent of the Minister, to alter etc. fish passes and free gaps) the words "with the written consent of the Minister," shall be omitted.

12.—(1) In section 11 of that Act (Minister's consents and approvals for fish passes) for subsection (1) there shall be substituted—

"(1) Any approval given by the Agency to or in relation to a fish pass may, if in giving it the Agency indicates that fact, be provisional until the Agency notifies the applicant for approval that the pass is functioning to its satisfaction.

(1A) The applicant for any such approval—

(a) shall be liable to meet any costs incurred (whether by him or by the Agency or any other person) for the purposes of, or otherwise in connection with, the performance of the Agency's function of determining for the purposes of subsection (1) above whether or not the fish pass in question is functioning to its satisfaction; and

(b) shall provide the Agency with such information or assistance as it may require for the purpose of performing that function."

(2) In subsection (2) of that section (Minister's power to revoke approval or consent while still provisional)—

(a) for the words "or consent is provisional, the Minister" there shall be substituted the words "is provisional, the Agency"; and

(b) for the words from "his intention" onwards there shall be substituted the words "its intention to do so, revoke the approval".

(3) In subsection (3) of that section (Minister's power, when revoking provisional approval, to extend period for making fish pass)—

(a) for the words "the Minister" there shall be substituted the words "the Agency"; and

(b) for the word "he" there shall be substituted the word "it".

(4) In subsection (4) of that section (Minister's power to approve and certify fish pass if he is of the opinion that it is efficient)—

(a) for the words "The Minister" there shall be substituted the words "The Agency"; and

(b) for the word "he" there shall be substituted the word "it".

(5) In subsection (5) of that section (fish passes approved by the Minister deemed to be in conformity with the Act) for the words "the Minister" there shall be substituted the words "the Agency".

13. For section 14 of that Act (gratings) there shall be substituted—

"**14.**—(1) This section applies in any case where—

(a) by means of any conduit or artificial channel, water is diverted from waters frequented by salmon or migratory trout; and

(b) any of the water so diverted is used for the purposes of a water or canal undertaking or for the purposes of any mill or fish farm;

and in this section "the responsible person" means the owner of the water or canal undertaking or (as the case may be) the occupier of the mill or the owner or occupier of the fish farm.

(2) Where this section applies, the responsible person shall unless an exemption from the obligation is granted by the Agency, ensure (at his own cost) that there is placed and maintained at the entrance of, or within, the conduit or channel a screen which—

(a) subject to subsection (4) below, prevents the descent of the salmon or migratory trout; and

(b) in a case where any of the water diverted is used for the purposes of a fish farm, prevents the egress of farmed fish from the fish farm by way of the conduit or channel.

(3) Where this section applies, the responsible person shall also, unless an exemption from the obligation is granted by the Agency, ensure (at his own cost) that there is placed and maintained across any outfall of the conduit or channel a screen which—

(a) prevents salmon or migratory trout from entering the outfall; and

(b) in a case where any of the water diverted is used for the purposes of a fish farm, prevents the egress of farmed fish from the fish farm by way of the outfall.

(4) Where a screen is placed within any conduit or channel pursuant to subsection (2) above, the responsible person shall ensure that a continuous by-wash is provided

immediately upstream of the screen, by means of which salmon or migratory trout may return by as direct a route as practicable to the waters from which they entered the conduit or channel (and accordingly nothing in subsection (2) or (3) above applies in relation to a by-wash provided for the purposes of this subsection).

(5) Any screen placed, or by-wash provided, in pursuance of this section shall be so constructed and located as to ensure, so far as reasonably practicable, that salmon or migratory trout are not injured or damaged by it.

(6) No such screen shall be so placed as to interfere with the passage of boats on any navigable canal.

(7) Any exemption under subsection (2) or (3) above may be granted subject to conditions.

(8) If any person who is required to do so by this section fails to ensure that a screen is placed or maintained, or that a by-wash is provided, in accordance with the provisions of this section, he shall be guilty of an offence.

(9) In any proceedings for an offence under subsection (8) above, it shall, subject to subsection (10) below, be a defence for the person charged to prove that he took all reasonable precautions and exercised all due diligence to avoid the commission of the offence by himself or a person under his control.

(10) If in any case the defence provided by subsection (9) above involves the allegation that the commission of the offence was due to an act or default of another person, or to reliance on information supplied by another person, the person charged shall not, without leave of the court, be entitled to rely on that defence unless—

    (a) at least seven clear days before the hearing, and

    (b) where he has previously appeared before a court in connection with the alleged offence, within one month of his first such appearance,

he has served on the prosecutor a notice in writing giving such information identifying or assisting in the identification of that other person as was then in his possession.

(11) Any reference in subsection (10) above to appearing before a court includes a reference to being brought before a court.

(12) The obligations imposed by subsections (2) to (6) above, except so far as relating to farmed fish, shall not be in force during such period (if any) in each year as may be prescribed by byelaw.

(13) The obligations imposed by subsections (2) to (6) above on the occupier of a mill shall apply only where the conduit or channel was constructed on or after 18th July 1923.

(14) Any reference in this section to ensuring that a screen is placed and maintained includes, in a case where the screen takes the form of apparatus the operation of which prevents the passage of fish of the descriptions in question, a reference to ensuring that the apparatus is kept in continuous operation.

(15) In this section 'by-wash' means a passage through which water flows."

14.—(1) In section 15 of that Act (power of National Rivers Authority, with the consent of the Minister, to use gratings etc. to limit movements of salmon and trout) for the word "grating" or "gratings", wherever occurring (including in the side-note), there shall be substituted respectively the word "screen" or "screens".

(2) In subsection (1) of that section (placing of gratings, deepening of channels etc.) the words "with the written consent of the Minister" shall be omitted.

(3) In subsection (3) of that section (use of such means as the Minister may approve for preventing ingress)—

    (a) the words "with the written consent of the Minister" shall be omitted; and

    (b) for the words "as the Minister may approve" there shall be substituted the words "as in its opinion are necessary".

(4) At the end of that section there shall be added—

    "(5) In this section "open", in relation to a screen which consists of apparatus, includes the doing of anything which interrupts, or otherwise interferes with, the operation of the apparatus."

15. In section 17 of that Act (restrictions on taking salmon or trout above or below an obstruction etc.) in subsection (3) (section not to be enforced, in cases where the fish pass is approved by the Minister, until compensation has been paid) for the words "approved by the Minister" there shall be substituted—

    "(a) approved by the Agency, or

    (b) constructed and maintained by the Agency in accordance with section 10(1) above,".

16. In section 18 of that Act (provisions supplementary to Part II) for subsection (2) (notice of application for Ministerial consent to the doing of certain acts to be given to the owner and occupier of the dam etc. in question) there shall be substituted—

"(2) The Agency shall not—
(a) construct, abolish or alter any fish pass, or abolish or alter any free gap, in pursuance of section 10 above, or
(b) do any work under section 15 above,

unless reasonable notice of its intention to do so (specifying the section in question) has been served on the owner and occupier of the dam, fish pass or free gap, watercourse, mill race, cut, leat, conduit or other channel, with a plan and specification of the proposed work; and the Agency shall take into consideration any objections by the owner or occupier, before doing the proposed work."

17. In section 30 of that Act, the paragraph defining "fish farm" (which is superseded by amendments made by this Schedule) shall be omitted.

18.—(1) In section 35 of that Act (power to require production of fishing licences) in subsection (3), for the words "the National Rivers Authority" there shall be substituted the words "the Agency".

(2) For subsection (4) of that section (definition of "the appropriate office of the National Rivers Authority") there shall be substituted—

"(4) In subsection (3) above, "the appropriate office of the Agency" means—
(a) in a case where the person requiring the production of the licence or other authority specifies a particular office of the Agency for its production, that office; and
(b) in any other case, any office of the Agency;

and for the purposes of that subsection where a licence or other authority which any person has been required to produce is sent by post to an office of the Agency that licence or other authority shall be treated as produced by that person at that office."

19. After subsection (1A) of section 39 of that Act (application of Act to River Esk in Scotland) there shall be inserted—

"(1B) Sections 31 to 34 and 36(2) of this Act shall, subject to the modifications set out in subsection (1C) below, apply throughout the catchment area of the River Esk in Scotland but a water bailiff shall exercise his powers under those sections as so applied only in relation to an offence—
(a) against this Act;
(b) against section 1 of the Salmon and Freshwater Fisheries (Protection) (Scotland) Act 1951; or
(c) which is deemed to be an offence under this Act by virtue of section 211 (6) of the Water Resources Act 1991,

which he has reasonable cause to suspect has been committed in a place to which this Act applies by virtue of subsection (1)(b) above.

(1C) The modifications referred to in subsection (1B) above are—
(a) references in sections 31 to 34 of this Act to "this Act" shall be construed as including references to section 1 of the Salmon and Freshwater Fisheries (Protection) (Scotland) Act 1951 (as applied to the River Esk by section 21 of that Act); and
(b) in section 33—
(i) references to a justice of the peace shall be construed as including references to a sheriff; and
(ii) in subsection (2), the reference to an information on oath shall be construed as including a reference to evidence on oath.".

20. In section 41(1) of that Act (general definitions) the following definitions shall be inserted at the appropriate places, that is to say—
(a) ""fish farm" has the same meaning as in the Diseases of Fish Act 1937;"; and
(b) ""screen" means a grating or other device which, or any apparatus the operation of which, prevents—
(a) the passage of salmon or migratory trout, and
(b) if the screen is required in connection with a fish farm, the passage of any fish farmed at that fish farm,

or any combination of devices or apparatus which, taken together, achieve that result;";

and the definition of "grating" shall be omitted.

21. In subsection (3) of section 43 of that Act (extent of Act to Scotland), after the words "(1A)" there shall be inserted the words ", (1B), (1C)".

22. In paragraph 1 of Schedule 1 to that Act (close seasons and close times) for the words "the National Rivers Authority" there shall be substituted the words "the Agency".

The Diseases of Fish Act 1983

23. In section 9(1)(d) of the Diseases of Fish Act 1983 (disclosure of information for the purpose of enabling the National Rivers Authority to carry out any of its functions) for the words "the National Rivers Authority" there shall be substituted the words "the Environment Agency".

The Salmon Act 1986

24. In section 37(3) of the Salmon Act 1986 (byelaws requiring consent of the National Rivers Authority) for the words "the National Rivers Authority has" there shall be substituted the words "the Environment Agency has".

The Water Resources Act 1991

25. In section 115 of the Water Resources Act 1991, in subsection (1) (power by order to make provision in relation to an area defined by the order for the modification, in relation to the fisheries in that area, of the enactments specified in the paragraphs of that subsection) for paragraph (b) there shall be substituted—

"(b) of section 142 or 156 below or paragraph 6 or 7 of Schedule 25 to this Act; or"

26.—(1) In paragraph 6 of Schedule 25 to that Act (powers to make byelaws in relation to any part or parts of the area in relation to which the National Rivers Authority carries out its functions in relation to fisheries under Part V of that Act) in sub-paragraphs (1) to (5) for the words "in relation to any part or parts", in each place where they occur, there shall be substituted the words "in relation to the whole or any part or parts".

(2) In sub-paragraph (3)(c) of that paragraph (byelaws for the purpose of determining for the purposes of the Salmon and Freshwater Fisheries Act 1975 the period of the year during which gratings need not be maintained) for the word "gratings" there shall be substituted the word "screens".

SCHEDULE 16

POLLUTION OF RIVERS AND COASTAL WATERS IN SCOTLAND: AMENDMENT OF THE CONTROL OF POLLUTION ACT 1974

1. The Control of Pollution Act 1974, as it has effect in Scotland, shall be amended in accordance with the following paragraphs.

2. After section 30E there shall be inserted the following sections—

"Control of entry of polluting matter and effluents into water

Pollution offences

30F.—(1) A person contravenes this section if he causes or knowingly permits any poisonous, noxious or polluting matter or any solid waste matter to enter any controlled waters.

(2) A person contravenes this section if he causes or knowingly permits any matter, other than trade effluent or sewage effluent, to enter controlled waters by being discharged from a sewer or from a drain in contravention of a prohibition imposed under section 30G below.

(3) A person contravenes this section if he causes or knowingly permits any trade effluent or sewage effluent to be discharged—

(a) into any controlled waters; or

(b) from land in Scotland, through a pipe, into the sea outside the seaward limits of controlled waters.

(4) A person contravenes this section if he causes or knowingly permits any trade effluent or sewage effluent to be discharged, in contravention of any prohibition imposed under section 30G below, from a building or from any plant—

(a) on to or into any land; or

(b) into any waters of a loch or pond which are not inland waters.

(5) A person contravenes this section if he causes or knowingly permits any matter whatever to enter any inland waters so as to tend (either directly or in combination with other matter which he or another person causes or permits to enter those waters) to impede

the proper flow of the waters in a manner leading, or likely to lead, to a substantial aggravation of—
(a) pollution due to other causes; or
(b) the consequences of such pollution.
(6) Subject to the following provisions of this Part, a person who contravenes this section shall be guilty of an offence and liable—
(a) on summary conviction, to imprisonment for a term not exceeding three months or to a fine not exceeding £20,000 or to both;
(b) on conviction on indictment, to imprisonment for a term not exceeding two years or to a fine or to both.

DEFINITIONS
"controlled waters": s.30A(1) of the 1974 Act.
"drain": s.56(1) of the 1974 Act; s.59(1) of the Sewerage (Scotland) Act 1968.
"effluent": s.56(1) of the 1974 Act.
"inland waters": s.30A(1) of the 1974 Act.
"sewage effluent": s.56(1) of the 1974 Act.
"sewer": s.56(1) of the 1974 Act; s.59(1) of the Sewerage (Scotland) Act 1968.
"trade effluent": s.56(1) of the 1974 Act.

GENERAL NOTE

This section replaces the water pollution offence provisions formerly contained in the 1974 Act, ss.31 and 32, bringing together in a single section the various offences although it should be noted that the new provisions differ in certain ways from the previous provisions as noted below. The relevant subsections of s.31 and all of s.32 are accordingly repealed (para. 3). Subsection (1) replaces the offences previously contained in s.31(1)(a) and (c); subs. (3) those previously contained in s.32(1)(a)(i) and (ii); and subs. (5) those previously contained in s.31(1)(b). This provision together with s.30I provides the basis for the system of regulation by means of consents.
One significant difference from the previous regime is that certain discharges will no longer necessarily constitute offences in themselves (subss. (2) and (4)) unless they also contravene a prohibition notice imposed under s.30G (see also the general note to s.30G). Such discharges were previously offences under s.32(1)(a)(iii), s.32(1)(b) and s.32(1)(c) unless they were made under a consent.
However, it should be noted that if a discharge takes place in terms of s.30F(2) or (4) and it contained poisonous, noxious or polluting matter which subsequently entered controlled waters, that would constitute an offence under s.30F(1): *NRA v. Egger UK Ltd.*, Newcastle Upon Tyne Crown Court, June 15–17, 1992, unreported.
Furthermore, although this section is largely based on s.85 of the Water Resources Act, it differs in an important respect from that provision. Whereas s.85(6) of the 1991 Act makes it an offence to contravene the conditions of a consent (which includes a failure to comply, see s.221 of the 1991 Act) in addition to the other offences in s.85, no similar provision is found in s.30F. This may prove problematic since the contravention of certain consent conditions may not give rise to a discharge in terms of this section since they may be designed to prevent discharges, e.g. a condition requiring the installation of standby pumps. Although an enforcement notice could be served under the new s.49A (inserted by Sched. 22, para. 29(26)) where such a condition was contravened an appeal mechanism is available under the new s.49B which may make enforcement by such means a somewhat lengthy process even though the appeal does not suspend the operation of the notice. The provision of an offence of contravening a consent condition as provided for in the 1991 Act might have been more useful to ensure compliance in such a situation.

Causing or knowingly permitting. The courts in Scotland have indicated that Scots law on the interpretation of this phrase is the same as south of the border: *Lockhart v. National Coal Board* 1981 S.L.T. 161. There are two distinct offences: *Mcleod v. Buchanan* [1940] 2 All E.R. 179; *Alphacell v. Woodward* [1972] A.C. 824.

Causing. A charge of causing pollution does not require proof of *mens rea* or negligence and should be given a commonsense meaning: *Alphacell; Lockhart.* Causing also involves an active operation or chain of operations the inevitable result of which is the polluting incident: *Alphacell; Lockhart; NRA v. Yorkshire Water Services Ltd.* [1994] 3 W.L.R. 1202, (H.L.). More than one person may be held to have caused the same event: *Attorney General's Reference (No. 1) of 1994* [1995] 2 All E.R. 1007. The chain causal link between the person charged and the polluting incident may be broken by intervening factors such as the act of a third party (e.g. a trespasser as in *Impress (Worcester) Ltd. v. Rees* [1971] 2 All E.R. 357; and *NRA v. Wright Engineering Ltd.* [1994] Env.L.R. 186), natural forces (*Southern Water Authority v. Pegrum* [1989] Crim.L.R. 442; *R. v. British Coal Corporation*, Cardiff Crown Court, December 2, 1993, unreported) or an Act of God (*Southern Water Authority v. Pegrum*): see generally *Alphacell*; and *Lockhart. Although it is unlikely that passivity will be sufficient to found a case of causing pollution (Price v. Cromack* [1975] 1 W.L.R. 988; *Wychavon District Council v. NRA* [1993] 1 W.L.R. 125), it should be noted that the House of Lords in *NRA v. Yorkshire Water Services Ltd.* indicated *obiter* that those cases should not be regarded as having established a general principle that a positive act is required to establish causation.

Knowingly permitting. Two elements are required to establish *knowingly permitting*: (1) knowledge of the polluting act and (2) giving leave for the polluting act or failure to take steps to prevent or terminate the pollution (*Berton v. Alliance Economic Investment Co. Ltd.* [1992] 1 K.B. 742 (C.A.) at 759); see also *Carmichael v. L.A.W. Mining Ltd.*, 1995 Env.L.B. 9–10. Although passively standing by may not amount to causing pollution it may amount to knowingly permitting polluting: *Price v. Cromack* [1975] 1 W.L.R. 988. Where there is no evidence that a person charged with knowingly permitting pollution could have prevented the pollution, it will not be possible to establish the charge: *Schulmans Incorporated Ltd. v. NRA* [1993] Env.L.R. D1.

Poisonous, noxious or polluting matter. There is no statutory definition of this phrase. However, case law indicates that *polluting* matter need only be potentially polluting or harmful: *NRA v. Egger UK Ltd.*, Newcastle Upon Tyne Crown Court, June 15–17, 1992, unreported; *R. v. Dovermoss Ltd.*, [1995] Env.L.R. 258 (C.A.).

Solid waste matter. There is no statutory definition of this phrase although it is likely to include litter. An offence is committed under s.30F(1) regardless of whether the matter is poisonous, noxious or polluting.

Subss. (2) and (4)
Under subs. (2) a discharge of matter, other than trade effluent or sewage effluent from a sewer or drain which enters controlled waters will now generally not necessarily constitute an offence unless the discharge is subject to a prohibition notice imposed under s.30G. Such matter would include rainwater run-off from a site. However, where the discharge is also poisonous, noxious or polluting an offence would be committed under s.30F(1): *NRA v. Egger UK Ltd.*
   Similarly, under subs. (4) the discharge of any trade or sewage effluent from any building or plant on to or into land or any waters which are not inland waters will now generally not necessarily constitute an offence unless a prohibition notice has been imposed under s.30G. This would include, for example, discharges to soakaways. However, where such a discharge is poisonous, noxious or polluting enters ground waters or surface waters which are controlled waters an offence would be committed under s.30F(1).

Prohibition of certain discharges by notice or regulations
   30G.—(1) For the purposes of section 30F above a discharge of any effluent or other matter is, in relation to any person, in contravention of a prohibition imposed under this section if, subject to the following provisions of this section—
      (a) SEPA has given that person notice prohibiting him from making or, as the case may be, continuing the discharge; or
      (b) SEPA has given that person notice prohibiting him from making or, as the case may be, continuing the discharge unless specified conditions are observed, and those conditions are not observed.
   (2) For the purposes of section 30F above a discharge of any effluent or other matter is also in contravention of a prohibition imposed under this section if the effluent or matter discharged—
      (a) contains a prescribed substance or a prescribed concentration of such a substance; or
      (b) derives from a prescribed process or from a process involving the use of prescribed substances or the use of such substances in quantities which exceed the prescribed amounts.
   (3) Nothing in subsection (1) above shall authorise the giving of a notice for the purposes of that subsection in respect of discharges from a vessel; and nothing in any regulations made by virtue of subsection (2) above shall require any discharge from a vessel to be treated as a discharge in contravention of a prohibition imposed under this section.
   (4) A notice given for the purposes of subsection (1) above shall expire at such time as may be specified in the notice.

(5) The time specified for the purposes of subsection (4) above shall not be before the end of the period of three months beginning with the day on which the notice is given, except in a case where SEPA is satisfied that there is an emergency which requires the prohibition in question to come into force at such time before the end of that period as may be so specified.

(6) Where, in the case of such a notice for the purposes of subsection (1) above as (but for this subsection) would expire at a time at or after the end of the said period of three months, an application is made before that time for a consent in pursuance of section 34 of this Act in respect of the discharge to which the notice relates, that notice shall be deemed not to expire until the result of the application becomes final—

(a) on the grant or withdrawal of the application;

(b) on the expiration, without the bringing of an appeal with respect to the decision on the application, of any period prescribed by virtue of section 39(2) below as the period within which any such appeal must be brought; or

(c) on the withdrawal or determination of any such appeal.

DEFINITIONS
"effluent" s.56(1) of the 1974 Act.
"notice": s.105(1) of the 1974 Act.
"prescribed": s.105(1) of the 1974 Act.
"regulations": s.105(1) of the 1974 Act.
"SEPA": s.105(1) of the 1974 Act.
"substance": s.56(1) of the 1974 Act.
"vessel": s.105(1) of the 1974 Act.

GENERAL NOTE
This section which is modelled on s.86 of the 1991 Act provides for the use of prohibition notices by SEPA in relation to discharges (1) of any matter other than trade or sewage effluent from a sewer or drain which enter controlled waters (s.30F(2)) and (2) of trade or sewage effluent from a building or any plant on to or into land or into any surface waters which are not controlled waters (s.30F(4)). SEPA may serve a prohibition notice to prohibit a person making a discharge or from continuing a discharge (subs. (1)(a)); or to prohibit a person making or continuing such a discharge unless specified conditions are observed (subs. (1)(b)). There is also a standing prohibition contained in subs. (2) (see note below) which does not require service of a prohibition notice. A prohibition notice may also be served on a roads authority in relation to discharges from drains which it is obliged or entitled to keep open (s.30J(8)).

Although apparently designed to strengthen controls over surface water discharges, the section has a deregulatory effect since such discharges would previously have required a consent and its effects may therefore not be wholly satisfactory. For example, a person installing a septic tank with a discharge to a soakaway would fall into the ambit of these provisions (s.30F(4)(a)). Previously, such a person would have been required to apply to a river purification authority for a consent before making any discharge under s.32(1)(a)(iii). In this way unsatisfactory installations might have been dealt with prior to construction. However, unless SEPA is notified before such a discharge commences, this provision only permits SEPA to deal with such discharges after the installation of the septic tank and soakaway. This may make it much harder for SEPA to rectify defective installations where they have already been constructed. For the prohibition notice system to work effectively, SEPA will need to be informed of planned discharges by means of notification through the planning systems, *e.g.* under the Town and Country Planning (General Permitted Development) (Scotland) Order 1992, which provide for river purification authorities (and hence SEPA) to be consulted *inter alia* where the development consists of the carrying out of building or other operations (other than *e.g.* the laying of sewers or building of septic tanks and cesspools for dwellings of less than 10 people) or the use of the land for the retention, treatment or disposal of sewage, trade waste or effluent.

Subs. (2)
There is a standing prohibition where the discharge contains prescribed substances or a prescribed concentration of such substance or derives from a prescribed process. Hence it will always be an offence where this subsection is contravened regardless of whether a notice has been served.

Subs. (3)
Prohibition notices under subs. (1) and the standing prohibition under subs. (2) do not apply to discharges from vessels. However, any discharge from a vessel which resulted in poisonous,

noxious or polluting matter or solid waste entering controlled waters would constitute an offence under s.30F(1).

Subss. (4)–(6)

A prohibition notice will not normally take effect until the end of three months beginning with the day on which notice is given unless SEPA is satisfied that there is an emergency when the notice may take effect immediately: subss. (4)–(5). The use of the present tense, *there is an emergency*, may have the effect of restricting the use of prohibition notices in cases of anticipated discharges.

Where a person applies for a consent during the period before the notice takes effect, the notice will not take effect until the result of the application and any appeal arising out of the application becomes final (subs. (6)).

Discharges into and from sewers etc.

30H.—(1) For the purposes of section 30F above where—

(a) any sewage effluent is discharged as mentioned in subsection (3) or (4) of that section from any sewer or works—

   (i) vested in a sewerage authority; or

   (ii) vested in a person other than a sewerage authority and forming (or forming part of) a system provided by him such as is mentioned in section 98(1)(b) of the Local Government etc. (Scotland) Act 1994; and

(b) the authority or, as the case may be, the person did not cause or knowingly permit the discharge but was bound (either unconditionally or subject to conditions which were observed) to receive into the sewer or works matter included in the discharge,

the authority or person shall be deemed to have caused the discharge.

(2) A sewerage authority shall not be guilty of an offence under section 30F of this Act by reason only of the fact that a discharge from a sewer or works vested in the authority contravenes conditions of a consent relating to the discharge if—

(a) the contravention is attributable to a discharge which another person caused or permitted to be made into the sewer or works; and

(b) the authority either was not bound to receive the discharge into the sewer or works or was bound to receive it there subject to conditions but the conditions were not observed; and

(c) the authority could not reasonably have been expected to prevent the discharge into the sewer or works;

and a person shall not be guilty of such an offence in consequence of a discharge which he caused or permitted to be made into a sewer or works vested in a sewerage authority if the authority was bound to receive the discharge there either unconditionally or subject to conditions which were observed.

(3) A person in whom any such sewer or works as is described in subsection (1)(a)(ii) above is vested (such person being in this subsection referred to as a "relevant person") shall not be guilty of an offence under section 30F of this Act by reason only of the fact that a discharge from the sewer or works contravenes conditions of a consent relating to the discharge if—

(a) the contravention is attributable to a discharge which another person caused or permitted to be made into the sewer or works; and

(b) the relevant person either was not bound to receive the discharge into the sewer or works or was bound to receive it there subject to conditions but the conditions were not observed; and

(c) the relevant person could not reasonably have been expected to prevent the discharge into the sewer or works;

and another person shall not be guilty of such an offence in consequence of a discharge which he caused or permitted to be made into a sewer or works vested in a relevant person if the relevant person was bound to receive the discharge there either unconditionally or subject to conditions which were observed.

DEFINITIONS

"effluent": s.56(1) of the 1974 Act.

"sewage effluent": s.56(1) of the 1974 Act.

"sewer": s.56(1) of the 1974 Act; s.59(1) of the Sewerage (Scotland) Act 1968.

"sewerage authority": s.56(1) of the 1974 Act; s.62 of the Local Government etc. (Scotland) Act 1994.

GENERAL NOTE
This section which is modelled on s.87 of the 1991 Act deems the sewerage authority or private sector undertaking under a Build, Own, Operate (B.O.O.) scheme (see below) to have caused the discharge for the purposes of any offence under s.30F where it has been discharged from any sewer or works vested in them; and although they did not cause or knowingly permit the discharge, they were bound to receive it (subs. (1)).

However, a defence is provided for authorities by subs. (2) and for B.O.O. private sector undertakings by subs. (3) whereby if they contravene the conditions of their discharge consent in circumstances where the contravention (a) is attributable to a discharge into the sewer or works by another person; (b) the authority or person was not bound to receive it or was bound to receive it but the conditions to which it was subject were not observed and (c) the authority or person could not reasonably have been expected to prevent the discharge, they will not be guilty of an offence. For the application of this defence, see: *NRA v. Yorkshire Water Services Ltd.* [1994] 3 W.L.R. 1202 (H.L.) which involved an unconsented discharge by an unknown party into the sewers of the defendants. The discharge could not be prevented from passing through the defendants' works and into controlled waters. Although the defendants were deemed to have caused the polluting discharge, the equivalent provision in the Water Resources Act 1991 in England and Wales, s.87(2) provided them with a defence to a charge of causing poisonous, noxious or polluting matter to enter controlled waters.

Furthermore, persons who discharge effluent into a sewer or works will not be guilty of a s.30F offence if the authority or B.O.O. private sector undertaking was bound to receive it unconditionally or subject to conditions which were observed (subss. (2) and (3)).

Vested in a person other than a sewerage authority (subs. (1)(a)(ii)/relevant person (subs. (3)). This refers to a private sector undertaking providing water and sewerage services for one of the new Scottish water and sewerage authorities established by the Local Government etc. (Scotland) Act 1994 in return for money under a B.O.O. scheme by virtue of the Private Finance Initiative (P.F.I.) (see: *Breaking New Ground: towards a new partnership between the public and private sectors (1993)*).

Defence to principal offences in respect of authorised discharges

30I.—(1) Subject to the following provisions of this section, a person shall not be guilty of an offence under section 30F above in respect of the entry of any matter into any waters or any discharge if the entry occurs or the discharge is made under and in accordance with, or as a result of, any act or omission under and in accordance with—

(a) a consent in pursuance of section 34 of this Act or under Chapter II of Part III of the Water Resources Act 1991 (which makes corresponding provision for England and Wales);

(b) an authorisation for a prescribed process designated for central control granted under Part I of the Environmental Protection Act 1990;

(c) a waste management or disposal licence;

(d) a licence granted under Part II of the Food and Environment Protection Act 1985;

(e) section 33 of the Water (Scotland) Act 1980 (temporary discharge by authorities in connection with the construction of works);

(f) any provision of a local Act or statutory order which expressly confers power to discharge effluent into water; or

(g) any prescribed enactment.

(2) Nothing in any disposal licence shall be treated for the purposes of subsection (1) above as authorising—

(a) any such entry or discharge as is mentioned in subsections (2) to (4) of section 30F above; or

(b) any act or omission so far as it results in any such entry or discharge.

(3) In this section—

"disposal licence" means a licence issued in pursuance of section 5 of this Act;

"local Act" includes enactments in a public general Act which amend a local Act;

"statutory order" means an order, byelaw, scheme or award made under an Act of Parliament, including an order or scheme confirmed by Parliament or brought into operation in accordance with special parliamentary procedure; and

"waste management licence" means such a licence granted under Part II of the Environmental Protection Act 1990.

DEFINITIONS
"disposal licence": subs.(3); s.5 of the 1974 Act.
"effluent": s.56(1) of the 1974 Act.

"local Act": subs. (3).
"prescribed": s.105(1) of the 1974 Act.
"statutory order": subs. (3).
"waste management licence": subs. (3).

GENERAL NOTE
This section provides for defences to the offences in s.30F where the discharge is authorised by various environmental licences or by Local Act, statutory order or prescribed enactment. For an example of a waste management licence providing a defence under the equivalent English and Welsh legislation, see *NRA v. Coal Products Ltd.* [1993] 227 ENDS Report at p. 45.

Other defences to principal offences
    30J.—(1) A person shall not be guilty of an offence under section 30F above in respect of the entry of any matter into any waters or any discharge if—
        (a) the entry is caused or permitted, or the discharge is made, in an emergency in order to avoid danger to life or health;
        (b) that person takes all such steps as are reasonably practicable in the circumstances for minimising the extent of the entry or discharge and of its polluting effects; and
        (c) particulars of the entry or discharge are furnished to SEPA as soon as reasonably practicable after the entry occurs.
    (2) A person shall not be guilty of an offence under section 30F above by reason of his causing or permitting any discharge of trade or sewage effluent from a vessel.
    (3) A person shall not be guilty of an offence under section 30F above by reason only of his permitting water from an abandoned mine or an abandoned part of a mine to enter controlled waters.
    (4) Subsection (3) above shall not apply to the owner or former operator of any mine or part of a mine if the mine or part in question became abandoned after 31st December 1999.
    (5) In determining for the purposes of subsection (4) above whether a mine or part of a mine became abandoned before, on or after 31st December 1999 in a case where the mine or part has become abandoned on two or more occasions, of which—
        (a) at least one falls on or before that date, and
        (b) at least one falls after that date,
the mine or part shall be regarded as becoming abandoned after that date (but without prejudice to the operation of subsection (3) above in relation to that mine or part at, or in relation to, any time before the first of those occasions which falls after that date).
    (6) Where, immediately before a part of a mine becomes abandoned, that part is the only part of the mine not falling to be regarded as abandoned for the time being, the abandonment of that part shall not be regarded for the purposes of subsection (4) or (5) above as constituting the abandonment of the mine, but only of that part of it.
    (7) A person shall not, otherwise than in respect of the entry of any poisonous, noxious or polluting matter into any controlled waters, be guilty of an offence under section 30F above by reason of his depositing the solid refuse of a mine or quarry on any land so that it falls or is carried into inland waters if—
        (a) he deposits the refuse on the land with the consent of SEPA;
        (b) no other site for the deposit is reasonably practicable; and
        (c) he takes all reasonably practicable steps to prevent the refuse from entering those inland waters.
    (8) A roads authority obliged or entitled to keep open a drain by virtue of section 31 of the Roads (Scotland) Act 1984 shall not be guilty of an offence under section 30F above by reason of its causing or permitting any discharge to be made from a drain kept open by virtue of that section unless the discharge is made in contravention of a prohibition imposed under section 30G above."

DEFINITIONS
"controlled waters": s.30A(1) of the 1974 Act.
"drain": s.56(1) of the 1974 Act; s.59(1) of the Sewerage (Scotland) Act 1968.
"effluent": s.56(1) of the 1974 Act.
"inland waters": s.30A(1) of the 1974 Act.
"mine": s.105(1) of the 1974 Act; s.180(1) of the Mines and Quarries Act 1954.
"quarry": s.105(1) of the 1974 Act; s.180(2) of the Mines and Quarries Act 1954.
"roads authority": s.105(1) of the 1974 Act; s.151(1) of the Roads (Scotland) Act 1984.
"SEPA": s.105(1) of the 1974 Act.
"sewage effluent": s.56(1) of the 1974 Act.
"trade effluent": s.56(1) of the 1974 Act.
"vessel": s.105(1) of the 1974 Act.

General Note
This section provides various other defences to the offences in s.30F. These include an emergency defence (subs. (1)), the defence to permitting water pollution from an abandoned mine or part of a mine which will be withdrawn after December 31, 1999 (see the General Notes to ss.58–60) (subss. (3)–(6)); and a defence in specified circumstances for persons depositing the solid refuse of a mine or quarry so that it falls or is carried into inland waters (subs. (7)). A roads authority will also not be guilty of any offence in relation to a discharge made from any drain which it is obliged or entitled to keep open unless the discharge is made in contravention of a prohibition notice imposed under s.30G.

3. Sections 31(1), (2), (3), (7) and (10) (offences relating to pollution of rivers and coastal waters) and 32 (control of discharges of trade and effluent etc. into rivers and coastal waters etc.) shall cease to have effect.

4. In section 31 (8) (maximum penalties) for the words "paragraphs (a) and (b) of the preceding subsection" there shall be substituted the words "section 30F(6) above".

5. In section 31B(4)(d) (nitrate sensitive areas: maximum penalties) for the words "subsection (7) of section 31 above" there shall be substituted the words "subsection (6) of section 30F above".

6. In section 34(3) (consents for discharges of trade and effluent) for the words "section 32(1)" there shall be substituted the words "section 30F(2) to (4)".

7. In section 39(1)(a) (appeals to the Secretary of State) for the words "section 31(3)" there shall be substituted the words "section 30J(4)".

8. In section 56(1) (interpretation etc. of Part II) the following definitions shall be inserted in the appropriate places—
" 'drain' has the same meaning as in the Sewerage (Scotland) Act 1968;"; and
" 'sewer' has the same meaning as in the Sewerage (Scotland) Act 1968;".

9. In section 87(3) (time-bar in relation to legal proceedings)—
(a) the words from the beginning to "offence; and" shall cease to have effect;
(b) for the words "section 23 of the Summary Jurisdiction (Scotland) Act 1954" there shall be substituted the words "section 331 of the Criminal Procedure (Scotland) Act 1975";
(c) for the words "such offence" there shall be substituted the words "offence under section 30F of this Act or regulations or byelaws made in pursuance of section 31 of this Act"; and
(d) for the words "subsection (2) of section 23 of the said Act of 1954" there shall be substituted the words "subsection (3) of section 331 of the said Act of 1975";
(e) the words "in its application to Scotland" shall cease to have effect.

Commencement
April 1, 1996 (S.I. 1996 No. 186).

General Note
See also the General Note to s.106.

SCHEDULE 17

STATUTORY NUISANCES: SCOTLAND

Amendments of the Environmental Protection Act 1990

1. The Environmental Protection Act 1990 shall be amended in accordance with the provisions of paragraphs 2 to 7 of this Schedule.

2. In section 79 (statutory nuisances etc.)—
(a) in subsection (1)(ga) after the word "street" there shall be inserted the words "or in Scotland, road";
(b) in subsection (7)—
(i) in the definition of "local authority", before the word "outside" in paragraph (b) there shall be inserted "in England and Wales", the word "and" after paragraph (b) shall cease to have effect, and after paragraph (c) there shall be inserted "and (d) in Scotland, a district or islands council or a council constituted under section 2 of the Local Government etc. (Scotland) Act 1994;";
(ii) in the definition of "premises" after the word "and" where it second occurs there shall be inserted the words ", in relation to England and Wales,";
(iii) at the appropriate place there shall be inserted—
" "road" has the same meaning as in Part IV of the New Roads and Street Works Act 1991;";

(c) in subsection (8)—
  (i) after the words "port health district" where they first occur there shall be inserted the words "or in Scotland where by an order under section 172 of the Public Health (Scotland) Act 1897 a port local authority or a joint port local authority has been constituted for the whole or part of a port,";
  (ii) after the words "port health authority" where they second occur there shall be inserted the words ", port local authority or joint port local authority, as the case may be";
(d) in subsection (10) after the words "or (e)" there shall be inserted "and, in relation to Scotland, paragraph (g) or (ga),";
(e) in subsection (11) after the words "subsection (12) and" there shall be inserted the words ", in relation to England and Wales,".

3. In section 80 (summary proceedings) in subsection (3) after the words "magistrate's court" there shall be inserted the words "or in Scotland, the sheriff";

4. In section 81 (supplementary provisions)—
(a) in subsection (2) after the words "magistrate's court" there shall be inserted the words "or in Scotland, the sheriff";
(b) in subsection (3) after the word "offence" there shall be inserted the words "or, in Scotland, whether or not proceedings have been taken for an offence,";
(c) in subsection (4) after the word "court" where it first occurs there shall be inserted the word "or sheriff" and after the words "court consider" there shall be inserted the words "or sheriff considers";
(d) in subsection (5) after the words "High Court" there shall be inserted the words "or, in Scotland, in any court of competent jurisdiction,".

5. In section 81A at the end, as subsection (10), and in section 81B at the end, as subsection (6), there shall be added—
  "( ) This section does not apply to Scotland.".

6. In section 82 (proceedings by persons aggrieved)—
(a) in subsection (1) after the word "complaint" there shall be inserted the words "or, in Scotland, the sheriff may act under this section on a summary application,";
(b) in subsection (2)—
  (i) after the words "magistrate's court" there shall be inserted the words "or, in Scotland, the sheriff";
  (ii) after the word "street" there shall be inserted the words "or, in Scotland, road";
  (iii) after the words "the court" there shall be inserted the words "or the sheriff";
  (iv) in paragraph (a) after the word "defendant" there shall be inserted the words "or, in Scotland, defender";
  (v) in paragraph (b) after the word "defendant" there shall be inserted the words "or defender";
  (vi) after the word "and" where it third occurs there shall be inserted the words ", in England and Wales,";
(c) in subsection (3), after the words "magistrate's court" there shall be inserted the words "or the sheriff" and after the words "of the court" in both places where they occur there shall be inserted the words "or of the sheriff";
(d) in subsection (11), after the words "magistrate's court" there shall be inserted the words "or the sheriff";
(e) in subsection (12) after the word "complaint" there shall be inserted the words "or summary application", after the words "the court" in both places where they occur there shall be inserted the words "or the sheriff" and for the words "defendant (or defendants" there shall be substituted the words "defendant or defender (or defendants or defenders";
(f) in subsection (13), after the words "magistrate's court" there shall be inserted the words "or to the sheriff" and after the words "the court" in both place where they occur there shall be inserted the words "or the sheriff".

7. In Schedule 3 (statutory nuisance; supplementary provisions)—
(a) after paragraph 1 there shall be inserted—

"Appeals to Sheriff

1A.—(1) This paragraph applies in relation to appeals to the sheriff under section 80(3) against an abatement notice.
  (2) An appeal to which this paragraph applies shall be by way of a summary application.
  (3) The Secretary of State may make regulations as to appeals to which this paragraph applies and the regulations may in particular include or prescribe any of the matters referred to in sub-paragraphs (4)(a) to (d) of paragraph 1 above.";

(b) in paragraph 2 at the end there shall be added—

"(8) In the application of this paragraph to Scotland, a reference to a justice of the peace or to a justice includes a reference to the sheriff.";

(c) in paragraph 2A(1)(b) after the word "street" there shall be inserted the words "or, in Scotland, road";

(d) in paragraph 4 at the end there shall be added—

"(9) This paragraph does not apply to Scotland.";

(e) in paragraph 6 after the words "magistrate's court" there shall be inserted the words "or, in Scotland, the sheriff".

Amendments of the Radioactive Substances Act 1993

8. In the Radioactive Substances Act 1993, in Part II of Schedule 3—

(a) in paragraph 12, for the words "Sections 16 and 17" there shall be substituted the words "Section 16";

(b) at the end there shall be added—

"17A. Part III of the Environmental Protection Act 1990.".

GENERAL NOTE
See General Note to s.107, above.

SCHEDULE 18

SUPPLEMENTAL PROVISIONS WITH RESPECT TO POWERS OF ENTRY

Interpretation

1.—(1) In this Schedule—
"designated person" means an authorised person, within the meaning of section 108 of this Act and includes a person designated by virtue of paragraph 2 below;
"relevant power" means a power conferred by section 108 of this Act, including a power exercisable by virtue of a warrant under this Schedule.

(2) Expressions used in this Schedule and in section 108 of this Act have the same meaning in this Schedule as they have in that section.

Issue of warrants

2.—(1) If it is shown to the satisfaction of a justice of the peace or, in Scotland, the sheriff or a justice of the peace, on sworn information in writing—

(a) that there are reasonable grounds for the exercise in relation to any premises of a relevant power; and

(b) that one or more of the conditions specified in sub-paragraph (2) below is fulfilled in relation to those premises,

the justice or sheriff may by warrant authorise an enforcing authority to designate a person who shall be authorised to exercise the power in relation to those premises, in accordance with the warrant and, if need be, by force.

(2) The conditions mentioned in sub-paragraph (1)(b) above are—

(a) that the exercise of the power in relation to the premises has been refused;

(b) that such a refusal is reasonably apprehended;

(c) that the premises are unoccupied;

(d) that the occupier is temporarily absent from the premises and the case is one of urgency; or

(e) that an application for admission to the premises would defeat the object of the proposed entry.

(3) In a case where subsection (6) of section 108 of this Act applies, a justice of the peace or sheriff shall not issue a warrant under this Schedule by virtue only of being satisfied that the exercise of a power in relation to any premises has been refused, or that a refusal is reasonably apprehended, unless he is also satisfied that the notice required by that subsection has been given and that the period of that notice has expired.

(4) Every warrant under this Schedule shall continue in force until the purposes for which the warrant was issued have been fulfilled.

Manner of exercise of powers

3. A person designated as the person who may exercise a relevant power shall produce evidence of his designation and other authority before he exercises the power.

Information obtained to be admissible in evidence

4.—(1) Subject to section 108(12) of this Act, information obtained in consequence of the exercise of a relevant power, with or without the consent of any person, shall be admissible in evidence against that or any other person.

(2) Without prejudice to the generality of sub-paragraph (1) above, information obtained by means of monitoring or other apparatus installed on any premises in the exercise of a relevant power, with or without the consent of any person in occupation of the premises, shall be admissible in evidence in any proceedings against that or any other person.

Duty to secure premises

5. A person who, in the exercise of a relevant power enters on any premises which are unoccupied or whose occupier is temporarily absent shall leave the premises as effectually secured against trespassers as he found them.

Compensation

6.—(1) Where any person exercises any power conferred by section 108(4)(a) or (b) or (5) of this Act, it shall be the duty of the enforcing authority under whose authorisation he acts to make full compensation to any person who has sustained loss or damage by reason of—
  (a) the exercise by the designated person of that power; or
  (b) the performance of, or failure of the designated person to perform, the duty imposed by paragraph 5 above.

(2) Compensation shall not be payable by virtue of sub-paragraph (1) above in respect of any loss or damage if the loss or damage—
  (a) is attributable to the default of the person who sustained it; or
  (b) is loss or damage in respect of which compensation is payable by virtue of any other provision of the pollution control enactments.

(3) Any dispute as to a person's entitlement to compensation under this paragraph, or as to the amount of any such compensation, shall be referred to the arbitration of a single arbitrator or, in Scotland, arbiter appointed by agreement between the enforcing authority in question and the person who claims to have sustained the loss or damage or, in default of agreement, by the Secretary of State.

(4) A designated person shall not be liable in any civil or criminal proceedings for anything done in the purported exercise of any relevant power if the court is satisfied that the act was done in good faith and that there were reasonable grounds for doing it.

SCHEDULE 19

OFFENCES RELATING TO FALSE OR MISLEADING STATEMENTS OR FALSE ENTRIES

The Control of Pollution Act 1974

1.—(1) The Control of Pollution Act 1974 shall be amended in accordance with the following provisions of this paragraph.

(2) For subsection (5) of section 34 (offences relating to consents for discharge of effluent etc) there shall be substituted—

"(5) A person who, in an application for consent in pursuance of this section, makes any statement which he knows to be false or misleading in a material particular or recklessly makes any statement which is false or misleading in a material particular shall be guilty of an offence and shall be liable—
  (a) on summary conviction, to a fine not exceeding the statutory maximum;
  (b) on conviction on indictment, to a fine or to imprisonment for a term not exceeding two years, or to both.".

(3) For subsection (3) of section 93 (offences relating to power of authorities to obtain information) there shall be substituted—

"(3) A person who—
  (a) fails without reasonable excuse to comply with the requirements of a notice served on him in pursuance of this section; or

(b) in furnishing any information in compliance with such a notice, makes any statement which he knows to be false or misleading in a material particular or recklessly makes any statement which is false or misleading in a material particular,

shall be guilty of an offence.

(3A) A person guilty of an offence under this section shall be liable—

  (a) on summary conviction, to a fine not exceeding the statutory maximum; or
  (b) on conviction on indictment, to a fine or to imprisonment for a term not exceeding two years, or to both.".

The Water (Scotland) Act 1980

2.—(1) The Water (Scotland) Act 1980 shall be amended in accordance with the following provisions of this paragraph.

(2) In section 93 (obtaining of information as to underground water) after subsection (7) there shall be inserted—

  "(8) Any person who in keeping a journal under subsection (1) or in furnishing information under subsection (2) or (3) makes any statement which he knows to be false or misleading in a material particular or recklessly makes any statement which is false or misleading in a material particular shall be guilty of an offence and shall be liable—

  (a) on summary conviction, to a fine not exceeding the statutory maximum;
  (b) on conviction on indictment, to a fine or to imprisonment for a term not exceeding two years, or to both.".

(3) In section 94 (false information) after the word "Act" there shall be inserted the words "(other than by or under section 93)".

The Control of Pollution (Amendment) Act 1989

3. In section 7(3)(b) of the Control of Pollution (Amendment) Act 1989 (offences of making false statements), after the word "false" in each place where it occurs there shall be inserted the words "or misleading".

The Environmental Protection Act 1990

4.—(1) For section 44 of the Environmental Protection Act 1990 (offences of making false statements) there shall be substituted—

"Offences of making false or misleading statements or false entries

  44.—(1) A person who—

  (a) in purported compliance with a requirement to furnish any information imposed by or under any provision of this Part, or
  (b) for the purpose of obtaining for himself or another any grant of a licence, any modification of the conditions of a licence, any acceptance of the surrender of a licence or any transfer of a licence,

makes a statement which he knows to be false or misleading in a material particular, or recklessly makes any statement which is false or misleading in a material particular, commits an offence.

  (2) A person who intentionally makes a false entry in any record required to be kept by virtue of a licence commits an offence.

  (3) A person who commits an offence under this section shall be liable—

  (a) on summary conviction, to a fine not exceeding the statutory maximum;
  (b) on conviction on indictment, to a fine or to imprisonment for a term not exceeding two years, or to both."

(2) In section 71(3) of that Act, paragraph (b) (offence of making false or misleading statements) shall cease to have effect.

The Water Resources Act 1991

5.—(1) Section 206 of the Water Resources Act 1991 (making of false statements etc.) shall be amended in accordance with the following provisions of this paragraph.

(2) For subsection (1), there shall be substituted—

  "(1) If, in furnishing any information or making any application under or for the purposes of any provision of this Act, any person makes a statement which he knows to be false or misleading in a material particular, or recklessly makes any statement which is false or misleading in a material particular, he shall be guilty of an offence under this section."

(3) Subsection (2) (which is superseded by the amendment made by sub-paragraph (2) above) shall be omitted.

(4) After subsection (3) (offences relating to the use of meters in connection with licences under Chapter II of Part II) there shall be inserted—

"(3A) If a person intentionally makes a false entry in any record required to be kept by virtue of a licence under Chapter II of Part II of this Act, or a consent under Chapter II of Part III of this Act, he shall be guilty of an offence under this section."

(5) For subsections (5) to (7) (which require consent to the prosecution of certain offences and provide different penalties for different offences) there shall be substituted—

"(5) A person who is guilty of an offence under this section shall be liable—
   (a) on summary conviction, to a fine not exceeding the statutory maximum;
   (b) on conviction on indictment, to a fine or to imprisonment for a term not exceeding two years, or to both."

The Radioactive Substances Act 1993

6. After section 34 of the Radioactive Substances Act 1993 (offences relating to disclosure of information about trade secrets etc.) there shall be inserted—

"Offences of making false or misleading statements or false entries
   34A.—(1) Any person who—
   (a) for the purpose of obtaining for himself or another any registration under section 7 or 10, any authorisation under section 13 or 14 or any variation of such an authorisation under section 17, or
   (b) in purported compliance with a requirement to furnish information imposed under section 31(1)(d),
makes a statement which he knows to be false or misleading in a material particular, or recklessly makes a statement which is false or misleading in a material particular, shall be guilty of an offence.

(2) Any person who intentionally makes a false entry in any record—
   (a) which is required to be kept by virtue of a registration under section 7 or 10 or an authorisation under section 13 or 14, or
   (b) which is kept in purported compliance with a condition which must be complied with if a person is to have the benefit of an exemption under section 8, 11 or 15,
shall be guilty of an offence.

(3) A person guilty of an offence under this section shall be liable—
   (a) on summary conviction, to a fine not exceeding the statutory maximum;
   (b) on conviction on indictment, to a fine or to imprisonment for a term not exceeding two years, or to both."

SCHEDULE 20

DELEGATION OF APPELLATE FUNCTIONS OF THE SECRETARY OF STATE

Interpretation

1. In this Schedule—
   "appointed person" means a person appointed under section 114(1)(a) of this Act; and
   "appointment", in the case of any appointed person, means appointment under section 114(1)(a) of this Act.

Appointments

2. An appointment under section 114(1)(a) of this Act must be in writing and—
   (a) may relate to any particular appeal, matters or questions specified in the appointment or to appeals, matters or questions of a description so specified;
   (b) may provide for any function to which it relates to be exercisable by the appointed person either unconditionally or subject to the fulfilment of such conditions as may be specified in the appointment; and
   (c) may, by notice in writing given to the appointed person, be revoked at any time by the Secretary of State in respect of any appeal, matter or question which has not been determined by the appointed person before that time.

Powers of appointed person

3. Subject to the provisions of this Schedule, an appointed person shall, in relation to any appeal, matter or question to which his appointment relates, have the same powers and duties as the Secretary of State, other than—

(a) any function of making regulations;

(b) any function of holding an inquiry or other hearing or of causing an inquiry or other hearing to be held; or

(c) any function of appointing a person for the purpose—

  (i) of enabling persons to appear before and be heard by the person so appointed; or

  (ii) of referring any question or matter to that person.

Holding of local inquiries and other hearings by appointed persons

4.—(1) If either of the parties to an appeal, matter or question expresses a wish to appear before and be heard by the appointed person, the appointed person shall give both of them an opportunity of appearing and being heard.

(2) Whether or not a party to an appeal, matter or question has asked for an opportunity to appear and be heard, the appointed person—

(a) may hold a local inquiry or other hearing in connection with the appeal, matter or question, and

(b) shall, if the Secretary of State so directs, hold a local inquiry in connection with the appeal, matter or question,

but this sub-paragraph is subject to sub-paragraph (3) below.

(3) No local inquiry shall be held by virtue of this Schedule in connection with an appeal under—

(a) section 42B(5) of the Control of Pollution Act 1974,

(b) section 22(5), 66(5) or 78T(3) of the Environmental Protection Act 1990, or

(c) section 191B(5) of the Water Resources Act 1991,

(appeals against decisions that information is not commercially confidential), or any matter involved in such an appeal, and any hearing held by virtue of this Schedule in connection with any such appeal or matter must be held in private.

(4) Where an appointed person holds a local inquiry or other hearing by virtue of this Schedule, an assessor may be appointed by the Secretary of State to sit with the appointed person at the inquiry or hearing and advise him on any matters arising, notwithstanding that the appointed person is to determine the appeal, matter or question.

(5) Subject to paragraph 5 below, the costs of a local inquiry held under this Schedule shall be defrayed by the Secretary of State.

Local inquiries under this Schedule: evidence and costs

5.—(1) In relation to England and Wales, subsections (2) to (5) of section 250 of the Local Government Act 1972 (local inquiries: evidence and costs) shall apply to local inquiries or other hearings held under this Schedule by an appointed person as they apply to inquiries caused to be held under that section by a Minister, but with the following modifications, that is to say—

(a) with the substitution in subsection (2) (evidence) for the reference to the person appointed to hold the inquiry of a reference to the appointed person;

(b) with the substitution in subsection (4) (recovery of costs of holding the inquiry) for the references to the Minister causing the inquiry to be held of references to the Secretary of State;

(c) taking the reference in that subsection to a local authority as including the Agency; and

(d) with the substitution in subsection (5) (orders as to the costs of the parties) for the reference to the Minister causing the inquiry to be held of a reference to the appointed person or the Secretary of State.

(2) In relation to Scotland, subsections (3) to (8) of section 210 of the Local Government (Scotland) Act 1973 (which relate to the costs of and holding of local inquiries) shall apply to local inquiries or other hearings held under this Schedule as they apply to inquiries held under that section, but with the following modifications, that is to say—

(a) with the substitution in subsection (3) (notice of inquiry) for the reference to the person appointed to hold the inquiry of a reference to the appointed person;

(b) with the substitution in subsection (4) (evidence) for the reference to the person appointed to hold the inquiry and, in paragraph (b), the reference to the person holding the inquiry of references to the appointed person;

(c) with the substitution in subsection (6) (expenses of witnesses etc.) for the references to the Minister causing the inquiry to be held of a reference to the appointed person or the Secretary of State;

(d) with the substitution in subsection (7) (expenses) for the references to the Minister of references to the appointed person or the Secretary of State;
(e) with the substitution in subsection (7A) (recovery of entire administrative expense)—
    (i) for the first reference to the Minister of a reference to the appointed person or the Secretary of State;
    (ii) in paragraph (a), for the reference to the Minister of a reference to the Secretary of State; and
    (iii) in paragraph (b), for the reference to the Minister holding the inquiry of a reference to the Secretary of State;
(f) with the substitution in subsection (7B) (power to prescribe daily amount)—
    (i) for the first reference to the Minister of a reference to the Secretary of State;
    (ii) in paragraphs (a) and (c), for the references to the person appointed to hold the inquiry of references to the appointed person; and
    (iii) in paragraph (d), for the reference to the Minister of a reference to the appointed person or the Secretary of State; and
(g) with the substitution in subsection (8) (certification of expenses) for the reference to the Minister, the reference to him and the reference to the Crown of references to the appointed person or the Secretary of State.

Revocation of appointments and making of new appointments

6.—(1) Where under paragraph 2(c) above the appointment of the appointed person is revoked in respect of any appeal, matter or question, the Secretary of State shall, unless he proposes to determine the appeal, matter or question himself, appoint another person under section 114(1)(a) of this Act to determine the appeal, matter or question instead.

(2) Where such a new appointment is made, the consideration of the appeal, matter or question, or any hearing in connection with it, shall be begun afresh.

(3) Nothing in sub-paragraph (2) above shall require any person to be given an opportunity of making fresh representations or modifying or withdrawing any representations already made.

Certain acts and omissions of appointed person to be treated as those of the Secretary of State

7.—(1) Anything done or omitted to be done by an appointed person in, or in connection with, the exercise or purported exercise of any function to which the appointment relates shall be treated for all purposes as done or omitted to be done by the Secretary of State in his capacity as such.

(2) Sub-paragraph (1) above shall not apply—
(a) for the purposes of so much of any contract made between the Secretary of State and the appointed person as relates to the exercise of the function; or
(b) for the purposes of any criminal proceedings brought in respect of anything done or omitted to be done as mentioned in that sub-paragraph.

SCHEDULE 21

APPLICATION OF CERTAIN ENACTMENTS TO THE CROWN

PART I

ENACTMENTS RELATING TO ENGLAND AND WALES

The Water Industry Act 1991

1.—(1) For section 221 of the Water Industry Act 1991 (Crown application) there shall be substituted—

"Crown application
    221.—(1) Subject to the provisions of this section, this Act shall bind the Crown.

    (2) No contravention by the Crown of any provision made by or under this Act shall make the Crown criminally liable; but the High Court may, on the application of the Environment Agency, a water undertaker or a sewerage undertaker, declare unlawful any act or omission of the Crown which constitutes such a contravention.

    (3) Notwithstanding anything in subsection (2) above, any provision made by or under this Act shall apply to persons in the public service of the Crown as it applies to other persons.

    (4) If the Secretary of State certifies that it appears to him, as respects any Crown

premises and any powers of entry exercisable in relation to them specified in the certificate, that it is requisite or expedient that, in the interests of national security, the powers should not be exercisable in relation to those premises, those powers shall not be exercisable in relation to those premises.

(5) Nothing in this section shall be taken as in any way affecting Her Majesty in her private capacity; and this subsection shall be construed as if section 38(3) of the Crown Proceedings Act 1947 (interpretation of references to Her Majesty in her private capacity) were contained in this Act.

(6) Subject to subsections (4) and (5) above, the powers conferred by sections 155, 159, 161(2) and 167 above shall be exercisable in relation to land in which there is a Crown or Duchy interest only with the consent of the appropriate authority.

(7) In this section—

"the appropriate authority" has the same meaning as it has in Part XIII of the Town and Country Planning Act 1990 by virtue of section 293(2) of that Act;

"Crown or Duchy interest" means an interest which belongs to Her Majesty in right of the Crown or of the Duchy of Lancaster, or to the Duchy of Cornwall, or belonging to a government department or held in trust for Her Majesty for the purposes of a government department;

"Crown premises" means premises held by or on behalf of the Crown.

(8) The provisions of subsection (3) of section 293 of the Town and Country Planning Act 1990 (questions relating to Crown application) as to the determination of questions shall apply for the purposes of this section."

The Water Resources Act 1991

2.—(1) The Water Resources Act 1991 shall be amended in accordance with the following provisions of this paragraph.

(2) In section 115 (fisheries orders) in subsection (7) (orders affecting Crown or Duchy property) in paragraph (a), after the words "an order under this section" there shall be inserted the words "making provision, by virtue of subsection (1)(b) above, for the modification of section 156 below in relation to fisheries in an area".

(3) In section 142 (orders providing for the imposition and collection of fisheries contributions), in subsection (2) (which applies, in relation to orders under that section, the provisions of subsections (2) to (9) of section 115 of that Act) for the words "(2) to (9)" there shall be substituted the words "(2) to (6)".

(4) For section 222 (Crown application) there shall be substituted—

"Crown application

222.—(1) Subject to the provisions of this section, this Act binds the Crown.

(2) No contravention by the Crown of any provision made by or under this Act shall make the Crown criminally liable; but the High Court may, on the application of the Agency, declare unlawful any act or omission of the Crown which constitutes such a contravention.

(3) Notwithstanding anything in subsection (2) above, the provisions of this Act shall apply to persons in the public service of the Crown as they apply to other persons.

(4) If the Secretary of State certifies that it appears to him, as respects any Crown premises and any powers of entry exercisable in relation to them specified in the certificate, that it is requisite or expedient that, in the interests of national security, the powers should not be exercisable in relation to those premises, those powers shall not be exercisable in relation to those premises.

(5) Subject to subsection (4) above, the powers conferred by sections 154, 156, 160, 162(3) and 168 above shall be exercisable in relation to land in which there is a Crown or Duchy interest only with the consent of the appropriate authority.

(6) Nothing in this section shall be taken as in any way affecting Her Majesty in her private capacity; and this subsection shall be construed as if section 38(3) of the Crown Proceedings Act 1947 (interpretation of references to Her Majesty in her private capacity) were contained in this Act.

(7) Nothing in this Act, as read with the other provisions of this section, shall be construed as conferring any power of levying drainage charges in respect of lands below the high-water mark of ordinary spring tides.

(8) Section 74 of the Land Drainage Act 1991 (Crown application), so far as it relates to land in which there is a Crown or Duchy interest, shall apply in relation to the flood defence provisions of this Act as it applies in relation to that Act; but nothing in this subsection shall affect any power conferred by this Act for the purposes both of the Agency's functions under those provisions and of other functions of the Agency.

(9) In this section—

"the appropriate authority" has the same meaning as it has in Part XIII of the Town and Country Planning Act 1990 by virtue of section 293(2) of that Act;

"Crown or Duchy interest" means an interest which belongs to Her Majesty in right of the Crown or of the Duchy of Lancaster, or to the Duchy of Cornwall, or belonging to a government department or held in trust for Her Majesty for the purposes of a government department;

"Crown premises" means premises held by or on behalf of the Crown.

(10) The provisions of subsection (3) of section 293 of the Town and Country Planning Act 1990 (questions relating to Crown application) as to the determination of questions shall apply for the purposes of this section."

PART II

ENACTMENTS RELATING TO SCOTLAND

The Sewerage (Scotland) Act 1968

3. For section 55 of the Sewerage (Scotland) Act 1968 (Crown application) there shall be substituted—

"Application of Act to Crown
55.—(1) Subject to the provisions of this section, this Act shall bind the Crown.

(2) No contravention by the Crown of any provision made by or under this Act shall make the Crown criminally liable; but the Court of Session may, on the application of a sewerage authority, declare unlawful any act or omission of the Crown which constitutes such a contravention.

(3) Notwithstanding anything in subsection (2) above, any provision made by or under this Act shall apply to persons in the public service of the Crown as it applies to other persons.

(4) If the Secretary of State certifies that it appears to him, as respects any Crown premises and any powers of entry exercisable in relation to them specified in the certificate, that it is requisite or expedient that, in the interests of national security, the powers should not be exercisable in relation to those premises, those powers shall not be exercisable in relation to those premises.

(5) Nothing in this section shall be taken as in any way affecting Her Majesty in her private capacity.

(6) In this section "Crown premises" means premises held by or on behalf of the Crown.".

The Control of Pollution Act 1974

4. For subsection (3) of section 105 of the Control of Pollution Act 1974 (application to Crown) as it has effect in relation to Scotland, there shall be substituted the following subsections—

"(3) Subject to subsections (3A) to (3D) below, this Act shall bind the Crown.

(3A) No contravention by the Crown of any provision made by or under this Act shall make the Crown criminally liable; but the Court of Session may, on the application of—

(a) the Scottish Environment Protection Agency; or

(b) any other public or local authority charged with enforcing that provision,

declare unlawful any act or omission of the Crown which constitutes such a contravention.

(3B) Notwithstanding anything in subsection (3A) above, any provision made by or under this Act shall apply to persons in the public service of the Crown as it applies to other persons.

(3C) If the Secretary of State certifies that it appears to him, as respects any Crown premises and any powers of entry exercisable in relation to them specified in the certificate, that it is requisite or expedient that, in the interests of national security, the powers should not be exercisable in relation to those premises, those powers shall not be exercisable in relation to those premises; and in this subsection "Crown premises" means premises held or used by or on behalf of the Crown.

(3D) Nothing in this section shall be taken as in any way affecting Her Majesty in her private capacity."

The Water (Scotland) Act 1980

5. After section 110 of the Water (Scotland) Act 1980 there shall be inserted—

"Application of Act to Crown
    110A.—(1) Subject to the provisions of this section, this Act shall bind the Crown.
    (2) No contravention by the Crown of any provision made by or under this Act shall make the Crown criminally liable; but the Court of Session may, on the application of a water authority, declare unlawful any act or omission of the Crown which constitutes such a contravention.
    (3) Notwithstanding anything in subsection (2) above, any provision made by or under this Act shall apply to persons in the public service of the Crown as it applies to other persons.
    (4) If the Secretary of State certifies that it appears to him, as respects any Crown premises and any powers of entry exercisable in relation to them specified in the certificate, that it is requisite or expedient that, in the interests of national security, the powers should not be exercisable in relation to those premises, those powers shall not be exercisable in relation to those premises.
    (5) Nothing in this section shall be taken as in any way affecting Her Majesty in her private capacity.
    (6) Subject to subsections (4) and (5) above, the powers conferred by sections 16 to 18 above shall be exercisable in relation to land in which there is a Crown interest only with the consent of the appropriate authority.
    (7) In this section—
        "the appropriate authority" has the same meaning as it has in section 253(7) of the Town and Country Planning (Scotland) Act 1972;
        "Crown interest" means an interest belonging to Her Majesty in right of the Crown, or belonging to a government department or held in trust for Her Majesty for the purposes of a government department;
        "Crown premises" means premises held by or on behalf of the Crown.
    (8) The provisions of subsection (7) of section 253 of the Town and Country Planning (Scotland) Act 1972 (questions relating to Crown application) as to the determination of questions shall apply for the purposes of this section.".

The Local Government etc. (Scotland) Act 1994

6. After section 125 of the Local Government etc. (Scotland) Act 1994 there shall be inserted—

"Application of Part II to Crown
    125A.—(1) Subject to the provisions of this section, this Part of this Act shall bind the Crown.
    (2) No contravention by the Crown of any provision made by or under this Part of this Act shall make the Crown criminally liable; but the Court of Session may, on the application of a new water and sewerage authority, declare unlawful any act or omission of the Crown which constitutes such a contravention.
    (3) Notwithstanding anything in subsection (2) above, any provision made by or under this Part of this Act shall apply to persons in the public service of the Crown as it applies to other persons.
    (4) Nothing in this section shall be taken as in any way affecting Her Majesty in her private capacity.
    (5) Subject to subsection (4) above, the powers conferred by section 99 above shall be exercisable in relation to land in which there is a Crown interest only with the consent of the appropriate authority.
    (6) In this section—
        "the appropriate authority" has the same meaning as it has in section 253(7) of the Town and Country Planning (Scotland) Act 1972;
        "Crown interest" means an interest belonging to Her Majesty in right of the Crown, or belonging to a government department or held in trust for Her Majesty for the purposes of a government department;
        "Crown premises" means premises held by or on behalf of the Crown.
    (7) The provisions of subsection (7) of section 253 of the Town and Country Planning (Scotland) Act 1972 (questions relating to Crown application) as to the determination of questions shall apply for the purposes of this section.".

SCHEDULE 22*

MINOR AND CONSEQUENTIAL AMENDMENTS

The Alkali, &c., Works Regulation Act 1906

1.—(1) The Alkali, &c, Works Regulation Act 1906 shall be amended in accordance with the following provisions of this paragraph.

(2) In section 1(1) (alkali work to be carried on so as to secure that the condensation of hydrochloric acid gas, to the satisfaction of the chief inspector, falls below certain levels) for the words "the chief inspector" there shall be substituted the words "the appropriate Agency".

(3) In section 2(1) (no objection to be taken by an inspector to certain discharges) for the words "an inspector" there shall be substituted the words "the appropriate Agency".

(4) In section 9—
    (a) in subsection (5) (condition of issue of certificate on first registration that the work is furnished with such appliances as appear to the chief inspector or, on appeal, the Secretary of State to be necessary for certain purposes) for the words "the chief inspector" there shall be substituted the words "the appropriate Agency";
    (b) the proviso to that subsection (power of Secretary of State to dispense with certain requirements) shall cease to have effect; and
    (c) in subsection (7) (notice of certain changes to be sent to the Secretary of State) for the words which are to be construed as a reference to the Secretary of State, there shall be substituted the words "the appropriate Agency".

(5) In section 22(1) (power of Secretary of State, after inquiring into a complaint, to direct proceedings to be taken by an inspector) for the words "an inspector" there shall be substituted the words "the appropriate Agency".

(6) In section 23(2) (damages not recoverable under the section from a person with a certificate of compliance from the chief inspector) for the words "the chief inspector" there shall be substituted the words "the appropriate Agency".

(7) Section 25 (basis on which the chief inspector may determine questions) shall cease to have effect.

(8) In section 27(1) (interpretation of terms)—
    (a) after the definition of the expression "alkali works" there shall be inserted—
       "The expression "the appropriate Agency" means—
           (a) in relation to England and Wales, the Environment Agency; and
           (b) in relation to Scotland, the Scottish Environment Protection Agency:";
       and
    (b) the definitions of the expressions "chief inspector" and "inspector" shall be omitted.

(9) In paragraph (b) of section 28 (application to Scotland)—
    (a) the words "other than offences under subsection four of section twelve of this Act",
    (b) in sub-paragraph (ii) (prosecution not to be instituted without consent) the words from "without the consent" to "direct, nor", and
    (c) sub-paragraph (iii) (person taking proceedings presumed to be inspector),
shall cease to have effect.

The Statistics of Trade Act 1947

2. In the Statistics of Trade Act 1947, after section 9 (restrictions on disclosure of information) there shall be inserted—

"Exceptions from section 9

   9A.—(1) Nothing in section nine of this Act shall prevent or penalise the disclosure by the Secretary of State of information obtained under this Act—
    (a) to the Environment Agency or the Scottish Environment Protection Agency; or
    (b) to an officer of either of those Agencies authorised by that Agency to receive the information.

(2) A person to whom information is disclosed in pursuance of the last foregoing subsection shall not use the information for any purpose other than the purposes of any functions of the Agency in question."

The Rivers (Prevention of Pollution) (Scotland) Act 1951

3.—(1) The Rivers (Prevention of Pollution) (Scotland) Act 1951 shall be amended in accordance with the following provisions of this paragraph.

---

*Authors' note: some principal amendments made by Schedule 22 are discussed in the General Note to s.120.

(2) Part II (river purification boards) (so far as unrepealed) and section 17 (duties of river purification authorities) shall cease to have effect.

(3) In section 18 (provision and obtaining of information)—

    (a) in subsection (1) (power to obtain information)—

        (i) for the word "them" in each place where it occurs there shall be substituted the word "it";

        (ii) for the words "a river purification authority" there shall be substituted the words "SEPA"; and

        (iii) the words "of their area", "in their area" (where first occurring) and "in their area or any part thereof" shall cease to have effect;

    (b) in subsection (2) (Secretary of State's power to give directions) for the words "any river purification authority" and "the authority" there shall be substituted the words "SEPA", and for the word "them" there shall be substituted the word "it"; and

    (c) in subsection (3) (duty to provide reasonable facilities for inspection of records)—

        (i) for the words "Every river purification authority" and "the river purification authority" there shall be substituted the words "SEPA";

        (ii) for the word "them" there shall be substituted the word "it"; and

        (iii) the words "in their area" and the words from "whose" to "authority" where it next occurs shall cease to have effect; and

    (d) in subsection (6) (interpretation of "stream") for the words "the river purification authority's" there shall be substituted the words "SEPA's".

(4) In section 19 (power to take samples of effluents)—

    (a) in subsection (1) (power to obtain and take away samples of water from any stream or effluent)—

        (i) for the words "A river purification authority" there shall be substituted the words "SEPA"; and

        (ii) the words "in the area of the authority" shall cease to have effect; and

    (b) in subsection (3) (interpretation of "stream") for the words "the river purification authority's" there shall be substituted the words "SEPA's".

(5) In section 35 (interpretation)—

    (a) the definitions of "river purification authority", "river purification board" and "river purification board area" shall cease to have effect; and

    (b) there shall be inserted at the appropriate place—

        " "SEPA" means the Scottish Environment Protection Agency;".

The Public Records Act 1958

4. In the First Schedule to the Public Records Act 1958 (definition of public records) in Part II of the Table at the end of paragraph 3 (organisations whose records are public records) there shall be inserted at the appropriate place the entry—

    "The Environment Agency.".

The Opencast Coal Act 1958

5.—(1) In section 7(8) of the Opencast Coal Act 1958 (definitions etc. for the purposes of section 7) in paragraph (i) of the definition of "statutory water undertakers" for the words "National Rivers Authority" there shall be substituted the words "Environment Agency".

(2) In section 52(3) of that Act (general application to Scotland) for the words "a river purification authority within the meaning of the Rivers (Prevention of Pollution) (Scotland) Act 1951" there shall be substituted the words "the Scottish Environment Protection Agency".

The Rivers (Prevention of Pollution) (Scotland) Act 1965

6. In section 10 of the Rivers (Prevention of Pollution) (Scotland) Act 1965 (samples of effluent)—

    (a) in subsection (2)—

        (i) for the words "A river purification authority" there shall be substituted the words "the Scottish Environment Protection Agency (in this section referred to as "SEPA")"; and

        (ii) for the words "the river purification authority's" there shall be substituted the words "SEPA's"; and

    (b) in subsections (3) to (5), for the words "the river purification authority", in each place where they occur, and "Every river purification authority" there shall be substituted the words "SEPA".

The Nuclear Installations Act 1965

7.—(1) In section 3 of the Nuclear Installations Act 1965, after subsection (1) (grant of nuclear site licences) there shall be inserted—

"(1A) The Health and Safety Executive shall consult the appropriate Agency before granting a nuclear site licence in respect of a site in Great Britain."

(2) In subsection (3) of that section (consultation with certain bodies), in paragraph (b), the words "the National Rivers Authority," shall cease to have effect.

(3) After subsection (6) of that section (variation of nuclear site licences) there shall be inserted—

"(6A) The Health and Safety Executive shall consult the appropriate Agency before varying a nuclear site licence in respect of a site in Great Britain, if the variation relates to or affects the creation, accumulation or disposal of radioactive waste, within the meaning of the Radioactive Substances Act 1993."

8. In section 4 of that Act (attachment of conditions to licences) after subsection (3) there shall be inserted—

"(3A) The Health and Safety Executive shall consult the appropriate Agency—
(a) before attaching any condition to a nuclear site licence in respect of a site in Great Britain, or
(b) before varying or revoking any condition attached to such a nuclear site licence,
if the condition relates to or affects the creation, accumulation or disposal of radioactive waste, within the meaning of the Radioactive Substances Act 1993."

9. In section 5 of that Act (revocation and surrender of licences) after subsection (1) there shall be inserted—

"(1A) The Health and Safety Executive shall consult the appropriate Agency before revoking a nuclear site licence in respect of a site in Great Britain."

10. In section 26 (interpretation) in subsection (1), there shall be inserted at the appropriate place—
" "the appropriate Agency" means—
(a) in the case of a site in England or Wales, the Environment Agency;
(b) in the case of a site in Scotland, the Scottish Environment Protection Agency;".

The Parliamentary Commissioner Act 1967

11. In Schedule 2 to the Parliamentary Commissioner Act 1967 (departments and authorities subject to investigation)—
(a) there shall be inserted at the appropriate places the entries—
(i) "Environment Agency"; and
(ii) "Scottish Environment Protection Agency";
(b) after note 1, there shall be inserted—
"1A. The reference to the Environment Agency is a reference to that Agency in relation to all its functions other than its flood defence functions, within the meaning of the Water Resources Act 1991."; and
(c) there shall be omitted—
(i) the entry relating to the National Rivers Authority; and
(ii) the note 9 inserted by paragraph 11 of Schedule 1 to the Water Act 1989 (which relates to that Authority).

The Sewerage (Scotland) Act 1968

12.—(1) In section 38(3) of the Sewerage (Scotland) Act 1968 (duty of Secretary of State to consult on proposed extension of Part II to non-trade effluents)—
(a) after the word "consult" where it first occurs there shall be inserted the words "the Scottish Environment Protection Agency and"; and
(b) the words "river purification authorities," shall cease to have effect.
(2) In section 59(1) of that Act (interpretation) the definition of "river purification authority" shall cease to have effect.

The Local Authorities (Goods and Services) Act 1970

13. The Local Authorities (Goods and Services) Act 1970 (supply of goods and services by local authorities to public bodies) shall have effect as if the Agency and SEPA were each both a

local authority and a public body for the purposes of that Act other than section 2(2) (accounting requirements in relation to local authority agreements entered into in pursuance of section 1).

The Agriculture Act 1970

14.—(1) The Agriculture Act 1970 shall be amended in accordance with the following provisions of this paragraph.

(2) In section 92(1) (provision of flood warning systems)—

(a) for the words from the beginning to "may" where it first occurs there shall be substituted the words "The Scottish Environment Protection Agency may";

(b) the words "for their area" and "both within (and in the case of a river purification board) outwith, that area," shall cease to have effect;

(c) in sub-paragraph (i) of the proviso—

(i) for the words "a river purification board" there shall be substituted the words "the Scottish Environment Protection Agency";

(ii) for the word "them" there shall be substituted the word "it"; and

(iii) for the words "that board" there shall be substituted the words "the Agency"; and

(d) in sub-paragraph (ia) of the proviso for the words following "exercise" to "shall" there shall be substituted the words ", the Agency shall".

(3) In section 92(2)—

(a) in paragraph (a)(iii) for the words "the authority providing the system" there shall be substituted the words "the Scottish Environment Protection Agency";

(b) paragraph (c) (definition of "river purification board") shall cease to have effect.

(4) In section 94 (co-operation with other persons as regards flood warning systems)—

(a) in subsection (1) for the words following "warning system" to "may" where it first occurs there shall be substituted the words "the Scottish Environment Protection Agency may" and for the words following "belonging to the" to "for" there shall be substituted the words "Agency for";

(b) in subsection (2) for the words from the beginning to "may" and for the words following "apparatus of" there shall be substituted the words "The Agency may" and " the Agency" respectively.

(5) In section 98 (extent of Part VI)—

(a) for the words from the beginning to "England" there shall be substituted the words "The Scottish Environment Protection Agency";

(b) for the words "section 92(1)(b)" there shall be substituted the words "section 92(1)"; and

(c) for the words "the National Rivers Authority" there shall be substituted the words "the Environment Agency".

The Prevention of Oil Pollution Act 1971

15.—(1) The Prevention of Oil Pollution Act 1971 shall be amended in accordance with the following provisions of this paragraph.

(2) After section 11 (duty to report discharge of oil into waters of harbours) there shall be inserted—

"Certain provisions not to apply where a discharge or escape is authorised under Part I of the Environmental Protection Act 1990

11A.—(1) The provisions of sections 2(1) and (2A), 3(1) and 11(1) of this Act shall not apply to any discharge which is made under, and the provisions of section 11(1) of this Act shall not apply to any escape which is authorised by, an authorisation granted under Part I of the Environmental Protection Act 1990.

(2) This section does not extend to Northern Ireland."

(3) In section 25(1) (power to extend certain provisions of the Act to the Isle of Man etc.), after the words "other than section 3" there shall be inserted the word ", 11A".

The Town and Country Planning (Scotland) Act 1972

16. In Schedule 7 to the Town and Country Planning (Scotland) Act 1972 (determination of certain appeals by persons appointed by the Secretary of State), in paragraph 2, after sub-paragraph (f) there shall be inserted—

"(g) in relation to appeals under paragraphs 6(11) and (12) and 11(1) of Schedule 13 and paragraph 9(1) of Schedule 14 to the Environment Act 1995, paragraph 6 of Schedule 10A to this Act.".

The Local Government Act 1972

17. In section 223 of the Local Government Act 1972 (which includes provision for authorised members or officers of the National Rivers Authority to conduct certain magistrates' court proceedings on its behalf) in subsection (2)—
    (a) after the words "joint authority" there shall be inserted the word "and"; and
    (b) the words "and the National Rivers Authority" shall cease to have effect.

The Local Government Act 1974

18. In section 25(1) of the Local Government Act 1974 (authorities subject to investigation by Local Commissioners), for paragraph (d) there shall be substituted—

    "(d) in relation to the flood defence functions of the Environment Agency, within the meaning of the Water Resources Act 1991, the Environment Agency and any regional flood defence committee."

The Control of Pollution Act 1974

19.—(1) Section 5 of the Control of Pollution Act 1974 (licences to dispose of waste) shall be amended in accordance with the following provisions of this paragraph.
    (2) In subsection (3) (duty of recipient of application for licence where planning permission is in force)—
    (a) for the words "Where a disposal authority receives an application" there shall be substituted the words "Where an application has been received"; and
    (b) for the words "the authority", where first occurring, there shall be substituted the words "the appropriate Agency" and, where secondly occurring, there shall be substituted the words "that Agency".
    (3) In subsection (4) (duty of disposal authority to refer to National Rivers Authority etc proposals to issue licences)—
    (a) for the words "a disposal authority" there shall be substituted the words "the appropriate Agency";
    (b) for the words "the authority" there shall be substituted the words "that Agency";
    (c) for paragraph (a), there shall be substituted—
      "(a) to refer the proposal to any collection authority whose area includes any part of the relevant land; and";
    (d) in paragraph (b), for the words "the disposal authority", in both places where they occur, there shall be substituted the words "that Agency"; and
    (e) the words following paragraph (b) (reference of proposal to Secretary of State in certain cases) shall cease to have effect.
    (4) Subsection (5) (separate provision for Scotland) shall cease to have effect.
20.—(1) Section 6 of that Act (provisions supplementary to section 5) shall be amended in accordance with the following provisions of this paragraph.
    (2) In subsection (2) (conditions which may be included in disposal licences)—
    (a) for the words "the disposal authority which issues it" there shall be substituted the words "the appropriate Agency"; and
    (b) for the words "the authority" there shall be substituted the words "that Agency".
    (3) In subsection (3) (offence of contravening a licence condition without reasonable excuse) for the words "the disposal authority which issued the licence" there shall be substituted the words "the Environment Agency".
    (4) In subsection (4) (duty of each disposal authority to maintain registers etc)—
    (a) for the words "each disposal authority" there shall be substituted the words "the Environment Agency and of SEPA";
    (b) for paragraph (a) there shall be substituted—
      "(a) to maintain a register containing copies of all disposal licences which are for the time being in force in respect of land in England and Wales or, as the case may be, Scotland;" and
    (c) in paragraph (c), for the words "the authority" there shall be substituted the words "that Agency".
    (5) In subsection (5) (applications deemed to be refused if not granted within two months of receipt)—
    (a) for the words "a disposal authority receives an application duly made to it for a disposal licence" there shall be substituted the words "a duly made application for a disposal licence was received";

(b) for the words "the authority", in the first two places where they occur, there shall be substituted the words "the appropriate Agency"; and

(c) for the words "the authority", wherever else occurring, there shall be substituted the words "that Agency".

21.—(1) Section 7 of that Act (variation of conditions and revocation of licences) shall be amended in accordance with the following provisions of this paragraph.

(2) In subsection (1) (modification of conditions of disposal licences issued by disposal authorities)—

(a) the words "issued by a disposal authority" shall be omitted; and

(b) for the words "the authority", where first occurring, there shall be substituted the words "the appropriate Agency" and, wherever else occurring, there shall be substituted the words "that Agency".

(3) In subsection (2) (application of section 5(4))—

(a) the words "or, in relation to Scotland, subsection (5)" shall cease to have effect; and

(b) for paragraphs (a) and (b) there shall be substituted—

"(a) the Environment Agency or SEPA, as the case may be, may postpone the reference in pursuance of the said subsection (4) so far as it considers that by reason of an emergency it is appropriate to do so; and

(b) the Environment Agency or SEPA, as the case may be, may disregard any collection authority for the purposes of the preceding provisions of this subsection in relation to a modification which, in the opinion of that Agency, will not affect that authority."

(4) In subsection (4) (revocation of disposal licences issued by disposal authorities)—

(a) the words "issued by a disposal authority" shall be omitted;

(b) for the words "the authority", where first occurring, there shall be substituted the words "the appropriate Agency" and, in the other place where they occur, there shall be substituted the words "that Agency".

22.—(1) Section 8 of that Act (transfer and relinquishment of licences) shall be amended in accordance with the following provisions of this paragraph.

(2) In subsection (1) (transfer of licences)—

(a) for the words "the authority which issued the licence" there shall be substituted the words "the appropriate Agency"; and

(b) for the words "the authority", in both places where they occur, there shall be substituted the words "that Agency".

(3) In subsection (4) (cancellation of licences)—

(a) for the words "the authority which issued it" there shall be substituted the words "the appropriate Agency"; and

(b) for the words "the authority", in the other place where they occur, there shall be substituted the words "that Agency".

23.—(1) Section 9 of that Act (supervision of licensed activities) shall be amended in accordance with the following provisions of this paragraph.

(2) In subsection (1) (duties of the authority which issued the licence) for the words "the authority which issued the licence" there shall be substituted the words "the appropriate Agency".

(3) In subsection (2) (powers of entry of authorised officers to carry out works in an emergency)—

(a) for the words "a disposal authority" there shall be substituted the words "the Environment Agency or SEPA, as the case may be,"; and

(b) for the words "the authority", wherever occurring, there shall be substituted the words "that Agency".

(4) In subsection (3) (recovery of certain expenditure from licence holders)—

(a) for the words "a disposal authority" there shall be substituted the words "the Environment Agency or SEPA"; and

(b) for the words "the authority" there shall be substituted the word "it".

(5) In subsection (4) (breach of conditions of licences)—

(a) for the words "a disposal authority" there shall be substituted the words "the appropriate Agency";

(b) the words "issued by the authority" shall be omitted; and

(c) for the words "the authority", wherever else occurring, there shall be substituted the words "that Agency".

24.—(1) Section 10 of that Act (appeals to Secretary of State from decisions with respect to licences) shall be amended in accordance with the following provisions of this paragraph.

(2) In subsection (1) (duty of disposal authority concerned to implement Secretary of State's determination) for the words "the disposal authority concerned" there shall be substituted the words "the appropriate Agency".

(3) In subsection (3) (cases where the decision under appeal is effective pending the determination of the appeal)—

(a) for the words "to a decision of a disposal authority" there shall be substituted the words "if the decision in question is a decision";

(b) for the words "in the opinion of the authority" there shall be substituted the words "in the opinion of the body making the decision in question";

(c) for the words "the authority acted" there shall be substituted the words "that body acted"; and

(d) in paragraph (b), for the words "the authority" there shall be substituted the words "the appropriate Agency".

25. In section 11 of that Act (special provision for land occupied by disposal authorities: resolutions etc) subsections (1) to (11) shall cease to have effect.

26.—(1) Section 16 of that Act (removal of waste deposited in breach of licensing provisions) shall be amended in accordance with the following provisions of this paragraph.

(2) In subsection (1) (power of disposal or collection authority to serve notice on occupier of land in its area) for the words from "in the area" to "the authority may" there shall be substituted the words "in contravention of section 3(1) of this Act, any authority to which this section applies may".

(3) After subsection (7) there shall be added—

"(8) The authorities to which this section applies are—

(a) the appropriate Agency;

(b) any collection authority in whose area the land mentioned in subsection (1) above is situated."

27. In section 30 of that Act (interpretation of Part I) in subsection (1)—

(a) the following definition shall be inserted at the appropriate place—

" "the appropriate Agency" means—

(a) in relation to England and Wales, the Environment Agency;

(b) in relation to Scotland, SEPA;";

(b) for the definition of "waste" there shall be substituted—

" "waste" has the same meaning as it has in Part II of the Environmental Protection Act 1990 by virtue of section 75(2) of that Act;"; and

(c) the words from "and for the purposes" to the end (which provide a presumption that anything discarded is waste unless the contrary is proved) shall cease to have effect.

28. In section 62(2)(a) of that Act (exceptions to restrictions on the operation of loudspeakers in streets), as it has effect in relation to England and Wales, for the words "National Rivers Authority" there shall be substituted the words "Environment Agency".

29.—(1) The Control of Pollution Act 1974, as it has effect in relation to Scotland, shall be amended in accordance with the following provisions of this paragraph.

(2) Subject to the amendments made by the following provisions of this paragraph, for the words "a river purification authority", "the river purification authority", "river purification authority", "river purification authorities", "the river purification authorities", "each river purification authority" and "any river purification authority", in each place where they occur in the undernoted provisions, there shall be substituted the words "SEPA"—

section 30A(2)(a) and (3);

section 30C(1);

section 30D;

section 31(4)(d) and (6);

section 31 A(2);

section 33(1);

sections 34 to 39;

section 41;

sections 46 to 51;

section 96(3); and

Schedule 1A.

(3) In section 30A(2)(a) (Secretary of State to deposit maps showing freshwater limits of every relevant river or watercourse) the words "in the area of that authority" shall cease to have effect.

(4) In section 30C (water quality objectives)—

(a) in subsection (1) (Secretary of State to establish water quality objectives), the words "within the area of that authority" shall cease to have effect;

(b) in subsection (3)(b) (Secretary of State to review water quality objectives) for the words "the river purification authority on which that notice has been served" there shall be substituted the words "SEPA";

(c) in subsection (4) (Secretary of State to give notice and consider representations when reviewing water quality objectives—
  (i) the words "in the area of a river purification authority" shall cease to have effect; and
  (ii) in paragraph (a) for the words "that authority" there shall be substituted the words "SEPA";

(d) in subsection (5)(b) (form of notice to be given by the Secretary of State when varying water quality objectives) for the words "the authority" there shall be substituted the words "SEPA"; and

(e) in subsection (6) (Secretary of State to serve further notice where water quality objectives remain unchanged)—
  (i) the words "in the area of a river purification authority" shall cease to have effect; and
  (ii) for the words "that authority" there shall be substituted the words "SEPA".

(5) In section 30E (consultation and collaboration)—
  (a) for the word "their" there shall be substituted the word "its";
  (b) for the words "river purification authorities" there shall be substituted the words "SEPA"; and
  (c) for the words "National Rivers Authority" there shall be substituted the words "Environment Agency".

(6) In section 31 (control of pollution of rivers and coastal waters etc.)—
  (a) in subsection (4)(b) (Secretary of State power to restrict or prohibit prescribed activities in designated areas) for the words "the river purification authority in whose area the place is situated" there shall be substituted the words "SEPA"; and
  (b) in subsection (6) (power to make byelaws to prohibit or regulate prescribed activities)—
    (i) for the words "the authority" there shall be substituted the word "it"; and
    (ii) the words "in its area" shall cease to have effect.

(7) Section 31D (powers of entry in relation to agreements under section 31B) shall cease to have effect.

(8) In section 33(1) (power to make byelaws regulating or prohibiting sanitary appliances on vessels)—
  (a) for the words "the authority" where they first occur there shall be substituted the word "it"; and
  (b) the words "in the area of the authority" shall cease to have effect.

(9) In section 34 (consents for discharges of trade and sewage effluent etc.)—
  (a) for the words "the authority" and "the authority's" in each place where they occur (other than the last reference in subsection (2)) there shall be substituted the words "SEPA" and "SEPA's" respectively;
  (b) in subsection (2) (disposal of application)—
    (i) for the words "a river purification authority to which an application for consent is" there shall be substituted the words "SEPA, in relation to an application for consent";
    (ii) for the word "three" there shall be substituted the word "four"; and
    (iii) for the words "the authority shall be deemed to have refused the consent" there shall be substituted the words "the applicant may treat the consent applied for as having been refused"; and
  (c) in subsection (3) (consent not to relate to discharges which occurred prior to consent) the words "in its area" shall cease to have effect.

(10) In the following provisions, for the words "an authority", "any authority", "the authority", "the authorities" and "the relevant river purification authority" in each place where they occur there shall be substituted the words "SEPA"—
  sections 35 to 39;
  section 41;
  sections 46 to 49; and
  Schedule 1A, paragraph 2.

(11) In section 36 (provisions supplementary to sections 34 and 35)—

(a) in subsection (1), after the word "shall" there shall be inserted the words ", subject to subsections (2A) and (2B) below,";

(b) after subsection (2) there shall be inserted the following subsections—

"(2A) A person who proposes to make, or has made, an application to SEPA for consent in pursuance of section 34 of this Act may apply to the Secretary of State within a prescribed period for a certificate providing that subsection (1) above shall not apply to that application.

(2B) If the Secretary of State is satisfied that—

(a) it would be contrary to the interests of national security; or

(b) it would prejudice to an unreasonable degree the commercial interests of any person,

not to issue a certificate applied for under subsection (2A) above, he may issue the certificate and, if he does so, subsection (1) above shall not apply to the application specified in the certificate."; and

(c) in subsection (6), for the word "three" there shall be substituted the word "four".

(12) In section 37(1) (revocation of consents and alteration and imposition of conditions), for the words from the beginning to "consent" in the second place where it occurs there shall be substituted the words "SEPA may from time to time review any consent given in pursuance of section 34 of this Act".

(13) In section 38 (restriction as to variation and revocation of consent and of previous variation), in each of subsections (1) and (2), for the word "two" there shall be substituted the word "four".

(14) After section 38 there shall be inserted—

"General review of consents

38A.—(1) If it appears appropriate to the Secretary of State to do so he may at any time direct SEPA to review—

(a) the consents given under section 34 of this Act; or

(b) any description of such consents,

and the conditions (if any) to which those consents are subject.

(2) A direction given by virtue of subsection (1) above—

(a) shall specify the purpose for which; and

(b) may specify the manner in which,

the review is to be conducted.

(3) After carrying out the review, SEPA shall submit to the Secretary of State its proposals (if any) for—

(a) the modification of the conditions of any consent reviewed pursuant to the direction; or

(b) in the case of any such consent which is unconditional, subjecting the consent to conditions.

(4) Where the Secretary of State has received any proposals under subsection (3) above in relation to any consent he may, if it appears appropriate to him to do so, direct SEPA, in relation to that consent—

(a) to make modifications of the conditions of the consent; or

(b) in the case of an unconditional consent, to subject the consent to conditions.

(5) A direction given by virtue of subsection (4) above may direct SEPA to do, in relation to any such consent, only—

(a) any such thing as SEPA has proposed should be done in relation to that consent; or

(b) any such thing with such modifications as appear to the Secretary of State to be appropriate.".

(15) In section 39 (appeals to Secretary of State)—

(a) in subsection (1), in each of paragraphs (b) and (c), for the words "the preceding section" there shall be substituted the words "section 38 of this Act";

(b) in subsection (5), for the words "terms and period as are" there shall be substituted the words "period as is";

(c) after that subsection there shall be inserted the following subsections—

"(5A) Subject to subsection (5B) below, where a question is referred to the Secretary of State in pursuance of subsection (1)(b) above, the revocation of the consent or, as the case may be, the modification of the conditions of the consent or the provision that the consent (having been unconditional) shall be subject to conditions, shall not take effect while the reference is pending.

(5B) Subsection (5A) above shall not apply to a reference where the notice effecting the revocation, modification or provision in question includes a statement that in the opinion of SEPA it is necessary for the purpose of preventing or, where that is not practicable, minimising—

(a) the entry into controlled waters of any poisonous, noxious or polluting matter or any solid waste matter, or

(b) harm to human health,

that that subsection should not apply.

(5C) Where the reference falls within subsection (5B) above, if, on the application of the holder or former holder of the consent, the Secretary of State (or other person determining the question referred) determines that SEPA acted unreasonably in excluding the application of subsection (5A) above, then—

(a) if the reference is still pending at the end of the day on which that determination is made, subsection (5A) above shall apply to the reference from the end of that day; and

(b) the holder or former holder of the consent shall be entitled to recover compensation from SEPA in respect of any loss suffered by him in consequence of the exclusion of the application of that subsection;

and any dispute as to a person's entitlement to such compensation or as to the amount of it shall be determined by a single arbiter appointed, in default of agreement between the parties concerned, by the Secretary of State on the application of any of the parties."; and

(d) at the end there shall be added—

"(7) This section is subject to section 114 of the Environment Act 1995 (delegation or reference of appeals).

(8) In this section "the holder", in relation to a consent, is the person who has the consent."

(16) Section 40(4) (transitional provisions relating to consents) shall cease to have effect.

(17) In section 41(1) (maintenance of registers)—

(a) after the words "prescribed particulars of" there shall be inserted the words "or relating to";

(b) the following provisions shall cease to have effect—

(i) in paragraph (c) (information contained in registers) the words "(except section 40(4))";

(ii) in paragraph (d) (duty to maintain registers of samples of effluent), sub-paragraph (ii); and

(iii) paragraph (e) (duty to register certain notices);

(c) there shall be added at the end the following paragraphs—

"(f) enforcement notices served under section 49A of this Act;

(g) directions given by the Secretary of State in relation to SEPA's functions under this Part of this Act;

(h) convictions, for offences under this Part of this Act, of persons who have the benefit of consents under section 34 of this Act;

(j) information obtained or furnished in pursuance of conditions of such consents;

(k) works notices under section 46A of this Act;

(l) appeals under section 46C of this Act;

(m) convictions for offences under section 46D of this Act; and

(n) such other matters relating to the quality of water as may be prescribed."

(18) In section 41(2) (registers to be available for inspection by, and facilities for obtaining copies of entries to be afforded to, the public), after paragraph (b) there shall be added the words—

"and, for the purposes of this subsection, places may be prescribed at which any such registers or facilities as are mentioned in paragraph (a) or (b) above are to be available or afforded to the public in pursuance of the paragraph in question."

(19) At the end of section 41 there shall be added the following subsection—

"(3) The Secretary of State may give SEPA directions requiring the removal from any register maintained by it under this section of any specified information which is not prescribed for inclusion under subsection (1) of this section or which, by virtue of section 42A or 42B of this Act, ought to have been excluded from the registers."

(20) For section 42, there shall be substituted the following sections—

"Exclusion from registers of information affecting national security

42A.—(1) No information shall be included in a register kept or maintained by SEPA under section 41 of this Act if and so long as, in the opinion of the Secretary of State, the inclusion in such a register of that information, or information of that description, would be contrary to the interests of national security.

(2) The Secretary of State may, for the purposes of securing the exclusion from registers of information to which subsection (1) of this section applies, give SEPA directions—

(a) specifying information, or descriptions of information, to be excluded from their registers; or

(b) specifying descriptions of information to be referred to the Secretary of State for his determination;

and no information to be referred to the Secretary of State in pursuance of paragraph (b) of this subsection shall be included in any such register until the Secretary of State determines that it should be so included.

(3) SEPA shall notify the Secretary of State of any information it excludes from a register in pursuance of directions under subsection (2) of this section.

(4) A person may, as respects any information which appears to him to be information to which subsection (1) of this section may apply, give a notice to the Secretary of State specifying the information and indicating its apparent nature; and, if he does so—

(a) he shall notify SEPA that he has done so; and

(b) no information so notified to the Secretary of State shall be included in any such register until the Secretary of State has determined that it should be so included.

Exclusion from registers of certain confidential information

42B.—(1) No information relating to the affairs of any individual or business shall, without the consent of that individual or the person for the time being carrying on that business, be included in a register kept or maintained by SEPA under section 41 of this Act, if and so long as the information—

(a) is, in relation to him, commercially confidential; and

(b) is not required to be included in the register in pursuance of directions under subsection (7) of this section;

but information is not commercially confidential for the purposes of this section unless it is determined under this section to be so by SEPA, or, on appeal, by the Secretary of State.

(2) Where information is furnished to SEPA for the purpose of—

(a) an application for a consent under section 34 of this Act;

(b) complying with any condition of such a consent; or

(c) complying with a notice under section 93 of this Act,

then, if the person furnishing it applies to SEPA to have the information excluded from any register kept or maintained by SEPA under section 41 of this Act, on the ground that it is commercially confidential (as regards himself or another person), SEPA shall determine whether the information is or is not commercially confidential.

(3) A determination under subsection (2) of this section must be made within the period of fourteen days beginning with the date of the application and if SEPA fails to make a determination within that period it shall be treated as having determined that the information is commercially confidential.

(4) Where it appears to SEPA that any information (other than information furnished in circumstances within subsection (2) of this section) which has been obtained by SEPA under or by virtue of any provision of any enactment might be commercially confidential, SEPA shall—

(a) give to the person to whom or whose business it relates notice that that information is required to be included in a register kept or maintained by SEPA under section 41 of this Act, unless excluded under this section; and

(b) give him a reasonable opportunity—

(i) of objecting to the inclusion of the information on the ground that it is commercially confidential; and

(ii) of making representations to SEPA for the purpose of justifying any such objection;

and, if any representations are made, SEPA shall, having taken the representations into account, determine whether the information is or is not commercially confidential.

(5) Where, under subsection (2) or (4) of this section, SEPA determines that information is not commercially confidential—

(a) the information shall not be entered on the register until the end of the period of twenty-one days beginning with the date on which the determination is notified to the person concerned; and

(b) that person may appeal to the Secretary of State against the decision;

and, where an appeal is brought in respect of any information, the information shall not be entered on the register pending the final determination or withdrawal of the appeal.

(6) Subsections (2), (4) and (7) of section 49B of this Act shall apply in relation to appeals under subsection (5) of this section; but

(a) subsection (4) of that section shall have effect for the purposes of this subsection with the substitution for the words from ("which may" onwards of the words "(which must be held in private)"; and

(b) subsection (5) of this section is subject to section 114 of the Environment Act 1995 (delegation or reference of appeals etc.).

(7) The Secretary of State may give SEPA directions as to specified information, or descriptions of information, which the public interest requires to be included in registers kept or maintained by SEPA under section 41 of this Act notwithstanding that the information may be commercially confidential.

(8) Information excluded from a register shall be treated as ceasing to be commercially confidential for the purposes of this section at the expiry of the period of four years beginning with the date of the determination by virtue of which it was excluded; but the person who furnished it may apply to SEPA for the information to remain excluded from the register on the ground that it is still commercially confidential and SEPA shall determine whether or not that is the case.

(9) Subsections (5) and (6) of this section shall apply in relation to a determination under subsection (8) of this section as they apply in relation to a determination under subsection (2) or (4) of this section.

(10) The Secretary of State may prescribe the substitution (whether in all cases or in such classes or descriptions of case as may be prescribed) for the period for the time being specified in subsection (3) above of such other period as he considers appropriate.

(11) Information is, for the purposes of any determination under this section, commercially confidential, in relation to any individual or person, if its being contained in register would prejudice to an unreasonable degree the commercial interests of that individual or person."

(21) In section 46 (operations to remedy or forestall pollution of water)—

(a) in subsection (1)—

(i) at the beginning there shall be inserted the words "Subject to subsection (1B) below,"; and

(ii) the words "in its area" where they first occur and "in its area or elsewhere" shall cease to have effect;

(b) after subsection (1) there shall be inserted—

"(1A) In either case mentioned in subsection (1) of this section, SEPA shall be entitled to carry out investigations for the purpose of establishing the source of the matter and the identity of the person who has caused or knowingly permitted it to be present in controlled waters or at a place from which it was likely, in the opinion of SEPA, to enter controlled waters.

(1B) Without prejudice to the power of SEPA to carry out investigations under subsection (1A) above, the power conferred by subsection (1) above to carry out operations shall be exercisable only in a case where—

(a) SEPA considers it necessary to carry out forthwith any operations falling within paragraph (a) or (b) of subsection (1) above; or

(b) it appears to SEPA, after reasonable inquiry, that no person can be found on whom to serve a works notice under section 46A of this Act.";

(c) in subsection (2) after the words "any operations" there shall be inserted the words "or investigations";

(d) in subsection (3)(b)—

(i) after the words "any operations" there shall be inserted the words "or investigations"; and

(ii) after the words "an abandoned mine" there shall be inserted the words "or an abandoned part of a mine"; and

(e) after subsection (3) there shall be inserted—

"(3A) Subsection (3)(b) of this section shall not apply to the owner or former operator of any mine or part of a mine if the mine or part in question became abandoned after 31st December 1999.

(3B) Subsections (5) and (6) of section 30J above shall apply in relation to subsections (3) and (3A) above as they apply in relation to subsections (3) and (4) of that section.".

(22) After section 46 there shall be inserted the following sections—

"Notices requiring persons to carry out anti-pollution operations

46A.—(1) Subject to the following provisions of this section, where it appears to SEPA that any poisonous, noxious or polluting matter or any solid waste matter is likely to enter, or to be or to have been present in, any controlled waters, SEPA shall be entitled to serve a works notice on any person who, as the case may be,—

    (a) caused or knowingly permitted the matter in question to be present at the place from which it is likely, in the opinion of SEPA, to enter any controlled waters; or

    (b) caused or knowingly permitted the matter in question to be present in any controlled waters.

(2) For the purposes of this section, a "works notice" is a notice requiring the person on whom it is served to carry out such of the following operations as may be specified in the notice, that is to say—

    (a) in a case where the matter in question appears likely to enter any controlled waters, operations for the purpose of preventing it from doing so; or

    (b) in a case where the matter appears to be or to have been present in any controlled waters, operations for the purpose—

        (i) of removing or disposing of the matter;

        (ii) of remedying or mitigating any pollution caused by its presence in the waters; or

        (iii) so far as it is reasonably practicable to do so, of restoring the waters, including any flora and fauna dependent on the aquatic environment of the waters, to their state immediately before the matter became present in the waters.

(3) A works notice—

    (a) must specify the periods within which the person on whom it is served is required to do each of the things specified in the notice; and

    (b) is without prejudice to the powers of SEPA by virtue of section 46(1B)(a) of this Act.

(4) Before serving a works notice on any person, SEPA shall reasonably endeavour to consult that person concerning the operations which are to be specified in the notice.

(5) The Secretary of State may by regulations make provision for or in connection with—

    (a) the form or content of works notices;

    (b) requirements for consultation, before the service of a works notice, with persons other than the person on whom that notice is to be served;

    (c) steps to be taken for the purposes of any consultation required under subsection (4) above or regulations made by virtue of paragraph (b) above; and

    (d) any other steps of a procedural nature which are to be taken in connection with, or in consequence of, the service of a works notice.

(6) A works notice shall not be regarded as invalid, or as invalidly served, by reason only of any failure to comply with the requirements of subsection (4) above or of regulations made by virtue of paragraph (b) of subsection (5) above.

(7) Nothing in subsection (1) above shall entitle SEPA to require the carrying out of any operations which would impede or prevent the making of any discharge in pursuance of a consent given by SEPA by virtue of section 34 of this Act.

(8) No works notice shall be served on any person requiring him to carry out any operations in respect of water from an abandoned mine or an abandoned part of a mine which that person permitted to reach such a place as is mentioned in subsection (1)(a) above or to enter any controlled waters.

(9) Subsection (8) above shall not apply to the owner or former operator of any mine or part of a mine if the mine or part in question became abandoned after 31st December 1999.

(10) Subsections (5) and (6) of section 30J of this Act shall apply in relation to subsections (8) and (9) above as they apply in relation to subsections (3) and (4) of that section.

(11) Where SEPA—

    (a) carries out any such investigations as are mentioned in section 46(1A) of this Act, and

    (b) serves a works notice on a person in connection with the matter to which the investigations relate,

it shall (unless the notice is quashed or withdrawn) be entitled to recover the costs or expenses reasonably incurred in carrying out those investigations from that person.

(12) The Secretary of State may, if he thinks fit in relation to any person, give directions to SEPA as to whether or how it should exercise its powers under this section.

Grant of, and compensation for, rights of entry etc.

46B.—(1) A works notice may require a person to carry out operations in relation to any land or waters notwithstanding that he is not entitled to carry out those operations.

(2) Any person whose consent is required before any operations required by a works notice may be carried out shall grant, or join in granting, such rights in relation to any land or waters as will enable the person on whom the works notice is served to comply with any requirements imposed by the works notice.

(3) Before serving a works notice, SEPA shall reasonably endeavour to consult every person who appears to it—

(a) to be the owner or occupier of any relevant land, and

(b) to be a person who might be required by subsection (2) above to grant, or join in granting, any rights,

concerning the rights which that person may be so required to grant.

(4) A works notice shall not be regarded as invalid, or as invalidly served, by reason only of any failure to comply with the requirements of subsection (3) above.

(5) A person who grants, or joins in granting, any rights pursuant to subsection (2) above shall be entitled, on making an application within such period as may be prescribed and in such manner as may be prescribed to such person as may be prescribed, to be paid by the person on whom the works notice in question is served compensation of such amount as may be determined in such manner as may be prescribed.

(6) Without prejudice to the generality of the regulations that may be made by virtue of subsection (5) above, regulations by virtue of that subsection may make such provision in relation to compensation under this section as may be made by regulations by virtue of subsection (4) of section 35A of the Environmental Protection Act 1990 in relation to compensation under that section.

(7) In this section—

"relevant land" means—

(a) any land or waters in relation to which the works notice in question requires, or may require, operations to be carried out; or

(b) any land adjoining or adjacent to that land or those waters;

"works notice" means a works notice under section 46A of this Act.

Appeals against works notices

46C.—(1) A person on whom a works notice is served may, within the period of twenty-one days beginning with the day on which the notice is served, appeal against the notice to the Secretary of State.

(2) On any appeal under this section the Secretary of State—

(a) shall quash the notice, if he is satisfied that there is a material defect in the notice; but

(b) subject to that, may confirm the notice, with or without modification, or quash it.

(3) The Secretary of State may by regulations make provision with respect to—

(a) the grounds on which appeals under this section may be made; or

(b) the procedure on any such appeal.

(4) Regulations under subsection (3) above may (among other things)—

(a) include provisions comparable to those in section 290 of the Public Health Act 1936 (appeals against notices requiring the execution of works);

(b) prescribe the cases in which a works notice is, or is not, to be suspended until the appeal is decided, or until some other stage in the proceedings;

(c) prescribe the cases in which the decision on an appeal may in some respects be less favourable to the appellant than the works notice against which he is appealing;

(d) prescribe the cases in which the appellant may claim that a works notice should have been served on some other person and prescribe the procedure to be followed in those cases;

(e) make provision as respects—

(i) the particulars to be included in the notice of appeal;

(ii) the persons on whom notice of appeal is to be served and the particulars, if any, which are to accompany the notice; or

(iii) the abandonment of an appeal.

(5) In this section "works notice" means a works notice under section 46A of this Act.

(6) This section is subject to section 114 of the Environment Act 1995 (delegation or reference of appeals).

Consequences of not complying with a works notice

46D.—(1) If a person on whom SEPA serves a works notice fails to comply with any of the requirements of the notice, he shall be guilty of an offence.

(2) A person who commits an offence under subsection (1) above shall be liable—

   (a) on summary conviction, to imprisonment for a term not exceeding three months or to a fine not exceeding £20,000 or to both;

   (b) on conviction on indictment, to imprisonment for a term not exceeding two years or to a fine or to both.

(3) If a person on whom a works notice has been served fails to comply with any of the requirements of the notice, SEPA may do what that person was required to do and may recover from him any costs or expenses reasonably incurred by SEPA in doing it.

(4) If SEPA is of the opinion that proceedings for an offence under subsection (1) above would afford an ineffectual remedy against a person who has failed to comply with the requirements of a works notice, SEPA may take proceedings in any court of competent jurisdiction for the purpose of securing compliance with the notice.

(5) In this section "works notice" means a works notice under section 46A of this Act.".

(23) In section 47 (duty to deal with waste from vessels etc.)—

   (a) in subsection (1) (duty), the words "in its area" shall cease to have effect; and

   (b) in subsection (2) (provision of facilities), the words "in the authority's area" shall cease to have effect.

(24) In section 48(1) (power to exclude unregistered vessels from rivers etc.) the words "in its area" shall cease to have effect.

(25) In section 49 (deposit and vegetation in rivers etc.) at the end there shall be added—

"(5) This section is subject to section 114 of the Environment Act 1995 (delegation or reference of appeals)."

(26) After that section there shall be inserted—

"Enforcement notices as respects discharge consents

49A.—(1) If SEPA is of the opinion that the holder of a relevant consent is contravening any condition of the consent, or is likely to contravene any such condition, it may serve on him a notice (an "enforcement notice").

(2) An enforcement notice shall—

   (a) state that SEPA is of the said opinion;

   (b) specify the matters constituting the contravention or the matters making it likely that the contravention will arise;

   (c) specify the steps that must be taken to remedy the contravention or, as the case may be, to remedy the matters making it likely that the contravention will arise; and

   (d) specify the period within which those steps must be taken.

(3) Any person who fails to comply with any requirement imposed by an enforcement notice shall be guilty of an offence and liable—

   (a) on summary conviction, to imprisonment for a term not exceeding three months or to a fine not exceeding £20,000 or to both;

   (b) on conviction on indictment, to imprisonment for a term not exceeding two years or to a fine or to both.

(4) If SEPA is of the opinion that proceedings for an offence under subsection (3) above would afford an ineffectual remedy against a person who has failed to comply with the requirements of an enforcement notice, SEPA may take proceedings in any court of competent jurisdiction for the purpose of securing compliance with the notice.

(5) The Secretary of State may, if he thinks fit in relation to any person, give to SEPA directions as to whether it should exercise its powers under this section and as to the steps which must be taken.

(6) In this section—

"relevant consent" means a consent for the purposes of section 30J(7)(a), 34 or 49(1) of this Act; and

"the holder", in relation to a relevant consent, is the person who has the consent in question.

Appeals against enforcement notices

49B.—(1) A person upon whom an enforcement notice has been served under section 49A of this Act may appeal to the Secretary of State.

(2) This section is subject to section 114 of the Environment Act 1995 (delegation or reference of appeals etc.).

(3) An appeal under this section shall, if and to the extent a requirement to do so is prescribed, be advertised in the manner prescribed.

(4) If either party to the appeal so requests or the Secretary of State so decides, an appeal shall be or continue in the form of a hearing (which may, if the person hearing the appeal so decides, be held, or held to any extent, in private).

(5) On the determination of an appeal under this section, the Secretary of State may either quash or affirm the enforcement notice and, if he affirms it, may do so either in its original form or with such modifications as he may in the circumstances think fit.

(6) The bringing of an appeal under this section shall not have the effect of suspending the operation of the notice appealed against.

(7) The period within which and the manner in which appeals under this section are to be brought and the manner in which they are to be considered shall be as prescribed.".

(27) In section 50 (investigation of water pollution problems arising from closures of mines) the words "in its area" shall cease to have effect.

(28) Sections 53 (charges in respect of consents to certain discharges in Scotland), 54 (directions to the river purification authority), 55 (discharges by islands councils) and 56(4) (meaning of the area of a river purification authority) shall cease to have effect.

(29) In section 56(1) (interpretation of Part II), the following definition shall be inserted in the appropriate place in alphabetical order—

" "operations" includes works;".

(30) In section 90(3) (establishment charges etc. in relation to Scotland), for the words from "a river" to the end there shall be substituted the words "SEPA".

(31) Section 91(5)(a) (application of that section to Scotland) shall cease to have effect.

(32) In section 96(3) (local inquiries) the words from "but as if" to the end shall cease to have effect.

(33) In section 98 (interpretation of Part V), for paragraph (b) of the definition of "relevant authority" there shall be substituted—

"(b) in Scotland—
  (i) as respects sections 91 and 92, a council constituted under section 2 of the Local Government etc. (Scotland) Act 1994; and
  (ii) as respects this Part other than those sections, the Secretary of State, SEPA or a council constituted under section 2 of the Local Government etc. (Scotland) Act 1994.".

(34) In section 104(1) (orders and regulations) the words "59" shall cease to have effect.

(35) In section 105 (interpretation etc.—general) there shall be inserted in the appropriate place—

" "SEPA" means the Scottish Environment Protection Agency;".

The Health and Safety at Work etc. Act 1974

30.—(1) The Health and Safety at Work etc. Act 1974 (in this paragraph referred to as "the 1974 Act") shall have effect in accordance with the following provisions of this paragraph.

(2) The appropriate new Agency shall, in consequence of the transfer effected by virtue of section 2(2)(c) or, as the case may be, 21(2)(a) of this Act, be regarded for the purposes of Part I of the 1974 Act as the authority which is, by any of the relevant statutory provisions, made responsible in relation to England and Wales or, as the case may be, Scotland for the enforcement of the relevant enactments (and, accordingly, as the enforcing authority in relation to those enactments).

(3) Neither the Agency nor SEPA shall have power to appoint inspectors under section 19 of the 1974 Act.

(4) Sections 21 to 23 (improvement notices and prohibition notices) shall have effect in any case where the relevant statutory provision in question is any of the relevant enactments as if references in those sections to an inspector were references to the appropriate new Agency.

(5) Section 27 (obtaining of information by the Commission etc.) shall have effect in relation to the appropriate new Agency, in its relevant capacity, as it has effect in relation to the Health and Safety Commission (and not as it has effect in relation to an enforcing authority), except that the consent of the Secretary of State shall not be required to the service by the appropriate new Agency of a notice under subsection (1) of that section; and, accordingly, where that section has effect by virtue of this sub-paragraph—

(a) any reference in that section to the Commission shall be construed as a reference to the appropriate new Agency;
(b) any reference to an enforcing authority shall be disregarded; and

(c) in subsection (3) of that section, the words from "and also" onwards shall be disregarded.

(6) In section 28 (restrictions on disclosure of information)—

(a) in paragraph (a) of subsection (3) (exception for disclosure of information to certain bodies) after the words "the Executive," there shall be inserted the words "the Environment Agency, the Scottish Environment Protection Agency,";

(b) in paragraph (c)(ii) of that subsection (exception for disclosure to officers of certain bodies) as it applies to England and Wales—

(i) the words "of the National Rivers Authority or", and

(ii) the word "Authority," (where next occurring),

shall be omitted;

(c) for paragraph (c)(ii) of that subsection as it applies to Scotland there shall be substituted—

"(ii) an officer of a water undertaker, sewerage undertaker, sewerage authority or water authority who is authorised by that authority to receive it;";

(d) paragraph (c)(iii) of that subsection (exception for disclosure to officers of river purification boards) shall cease to have effect;

(e) in subsection (4) (references to certain bodies to include references to officers or inspectors), after the words "the Executive" (in the first place where they occur) there shall be inserted the words "the Environment Agency, the Scottish Environment Protection Agency,";

(f) in subsection (5) (information disclosed in pursuance of subsection (3) not to be used by recipient except for specified purposes)—

(i) in paragraph (a) (use for a purpose of the Executive etc.) after the words "of the Executive or" there shall be inserted the words "of the Environment Agency or of the Scottish Environment Protection Agency or";

(ii) in paragraph (b) as it applies to England and Wales (use for the purposes of certain bodies of information given to officers of those bodies), the words "the National Rivers Authority" shall be omitted;

(iii) in the said paragraph (b) as it applies to Scotland, for the words from the beginning to "in connection" there shall be substituted the words "in the case of information given to an officer of a body which is a local authority, a water undertaker, a sewerage undertaker, a sewerage authority or a water authority the purposes of the body in connection".

(7) In section 38 (restriction on institution of proceedings in England and Wales) after the words "except by an inspector or" there shall be inserted the words "the Environment Agency or".

(8) In this paragraph—

"the appropriate new Agency" means—

(a) in relation to England and Wales, the Agency; and

(b) in relation to Scotland, SEPA;

"relevant capacity", in relation to the appropriate new Agency, means its capacity as the enforcing authority, for the purposes of Part I of the 1974 Act, which is responsible in relation to England and Wales or, as the case may be, Scotland for the enforcement of the relevant enactments;

"the relevant enactments" means the Alkali, &c, Works Regulation Act 1906 and section 5 of the 1974 Act;

"the relevant statutory provisions" has the same meaning as in Part I of the 1974 Act.

The House of Commons Disqualification Act 1975 and the Northern Ireland Assembly Disqualification Act 1975

31. In Part II of Schedule I to the House of Commons Disqualification Act 1975 (bodies of which all members are disqualified for membership of the House of Commons) the following entries shall be inserted at the appropriate places—

(a) "The Environment Agency.";

(b) "The Scottish Environment Protection Agency.";

and the like insertions shall be made in Part II of Schedule 1 to the Northern Ireland Assembly Disqualification Act 1975 (bodies of which all members are disqualified for membership of the Northern Ireland Assembly).

The Local Government (Scotland) Act 1975

32.—(1) The Local Government (Scotland) Act 1975 shall be amended in accordance with the following provisions.

(2) In section 16 (borrowing and lending by local authorities and certain other bodies)—
    (a) after the words "local authorities" there shall be inserted the word "and";
    (b) the words "and river purification boards" shall cease to have effect.
(3) In Schedule 3 (further provision relating to borrowing and lending by local authorities and certain other bodies) in paragraph 28—
    (a) in sub-paragraph (1)—
        (i) after the word "money" there shall be inserted the word "and";
        (ii) the words "or a river purification board," shall cease to have effect;
    (b) in sub-paragraph (2) for sub-paragraph (a) there shall be substituted—
    "(a) a joint board; and".

The Local Government (Miscellaneous Provisions) Act 1976

33. In section 44 of the Local Government (Miscellaneous Provisions) Act 1976 (interpretation of Part I of that Act) after subsection (1A) (certain provisions of that Act, including section 16 (obtaining information about land), to have effect as if the Broads Authority were a local authority) there shall be inserted—

"(1B) Section 16 of this Act shall have effect as if the Environment Agency were a local authority.".

The Water (Scotland) Act 1980

34.—(1) The Water (Scotland) Act 1980 shall be amended in accordance with the following provisions of this paragraph.
(2) In section 31(1) (consultation where limits of water supply adjoin any part of England) for paragraph (b) there shall be substituted—
    "(b) the Scottish Environment Protection Agency."
(3) In section 33(3)(a) (notice of temporary discharge of water into watercourses)—
    (a) sub-paragraph (ii) and the preceding "and" shall cease to have effect; and
    (b) at the end of the paragraph there shall be inserted—
    "and
        (ii) to the Scottish Environment Protection Agency.".
(4) In section 109(1) (interpretation) the definitions of "river purification authority" and "river purification board" shall cease to have effect.
(5) In Schedule 1—
    (a) in paragraph 2(ii) for the words following "section 17(2)" to the end there shall be substituted the words "on the Scottish Environment Protection Agency";
    (b) in paragraph 11(ii) the words "and any river purification authority" shall cease to have effect and at the end there shall be added the words "and on the Scottish Environment Protection Agency";
    (c) in paragraph 19 for the words following "any fishery district" to the words "any public undertakers" there shall be substituted the words "any navigation authority exercising jurisdiction in relation to any watercourse from which water is proposed to be taken under the rights to be acquired, the Scottish Environment Protection Agency and any public undertakers".

The Criminal Justice (Scotland) Act 1980

35. In Schedule 1 to the Criminal Justice (Scotland) Act 1980 (sufficiency of evidence by certificate in certain routine matters) in the entry relating to the Control of Pollution Act 1974—
    (a) for the words from "Section 31(1)" to "such waters etc.)" there shall be substituted the words "Section 30F (pollution offences)"; and
    (b) for the words "a river purification authority (within the meaning of that Act)" there shall be substituted the words "the Scottish Environment Protection Agency".

The Road Traffic Regulation Act 1984

36.—(1) In section 1 of the Road Traffic Regulation Act 1984 (traffic regulation orders outside Greater London) in subsection (1), after paragraph (f) (which allows a traffic regulation order to be made for preserving or improving the amenities of the area through which the road runs) there shall be added "or
    (g) for any of the purposes specified in paragraphs (a) to (c) of subsection (1) of section 87 of the Environment Act 1995 (air quality).".
(2) In section 6 of that Act (orders similar to traffic regulation orders in Greater London) in

subsection (1)(b) (which allows orders in Greater London to be made for equivalent purposes to those in section 1(1)(a) to (f) of that Act) for the words "(a) to (f)" there shall be substituted the words "(a) to (g)".

(3) In section 122(2) of that Act (matters to which, so far as practicable, regard is to be had by local authorities in exercising their functions under the Act) after paragraph (b) there shall be inserted—

"(bb) the strategy prepared under section 80 of the Environment Act 1995 (national air quality strategy);".

The Control of Pollution (Amendment) Act 1989

37.—(1) The Control of Pollution (Amendment) Act 1989 shall be amended in accordance with the following provisions of this paragraph.

(2) In section 2 (registration of carriers)—
   (a) in subsection (3), without prejudice to the power of regulation authorities to impose a charge in respect of their consideration of any such application, paragraph (e) (power to require them to impose such charges) shall cease to have effect; and
   (b) after that subsection there shall be added—

"(3A) Without prejudice to the generality of paragraphs (b) and (d) of subsection (3) above—
   (a) the power to prescribe a form under paragraph (b) of that subsection includes power to require an application to be made on any form of any description supplied for the purpose by the regulation authority to which the application is to be made; and
   (b) the power to impose requirements with respect to information under paragraph (d) of that subsection includes power to make provision requiring an application to be accompanied by such information as may reasonably be required by the regulation authority to which it is to be made."

(3) In section 4 (appeals to the Secretary of State against refusal of registration etc.) after subsection (8) there shall be added—

"(9) This section is subject to section 114 of the Environment Act 1995 (delegation or reference of appeals etc.)."

(4) In section 6 (seizure and disposal of vehicles used for illegal waste disposal) for subsection (6) there shall be substituted—

"(6) Regulations under this section shall not authorise a regulation authority to sell or destroy any property or to deposit any property at any place unless—
   (a) the following conditions are satisfied, that is to say—
      (i) the authority have published such notice, and taken such other steps (if any), as may be prescribed for informing persons who may be entitled to the property that it has been seized and is available to be claimed; and
      (ii) the prescribed period has expired without any obligation arising under the regulations for the regulation authority to return the property to any person; or
   (b) the condition of the property requires it to be disposed of without delay."

(5) In section 7 (further enforcement provisions) in subsection (1) (which applies certain provisions of the Environmental Protection Act 1990) for the words "sections 68(3), (4) and (5), 69, 70 and 71" there shall be substituted the words "section 71".

(6) Subsection (2) of that section (disclosure of information between certain authorities) shall cease to have effect.

(7) Subsection (8) of that section (which applies section 72 of the 1990 Act) shall cease to have effect.

(8) In section 9, for the definition of "regulation authority" there shall be substituted—
"regulation authority" means—
      (a) in relation to England and Wales, the Environment Agency; and
      (b) in relation to Scotland, the Scottish Environment Protection Agency;
   and any reference to the area of a regulation authority shall accordingly be construed as a reference to any area in England and Wales or, as the case may be, in Scotland;".

The Electricity Act 1989

38.—(1) Section 3 of the Electricity Act 1989 (general duties of the Secretary of State and the Director General of Electricity Supply when exercising certain functions) shall be amended in accordance with the following provisions of this paragraph.

(2) In subsection (1)(c) (duty, subject to subsection (2), to promote competition), for the words "subsection (2)" there shall be substituted the words "subsections (2) and (2A)".

(3) After subsection (2) (duties as regards the supply of electricity in Scotland in certain cases) there shall be inserted—

"(2A) If an order under section 32(1) below requires a public electricity supplier to make, or produce evidence showing that he has made, arrangements or additional arrangements which will secure the result mentioned in subsection (2B) below, the order, so far as relating to any such requirement, may be made for the purpose of, or for purposes which include, promoting the supply to any premises of—
(a) heat produced in association with electricity, or
(b) steam produced from, or air or water heated by, such heat.

(2B) The result referred to in subsection (2A) above is that, for a period specified in the order, there will be available to the public electricity supplier—
(a) from combined heat and power stations; or
(b) from combined heat and power stations of any particular description,
an aggregate amount of generating capacity which is not less than that specified in relation to him in the order.

(2C) In subsection (2B) above, "combined heat and power station" has the meaning given by section 32(8) below.".

(4) In subsection (3) (further duties), for the words "and (2)" there shall be substituted the words ", (2) and (2A)".

39.—(1) Section 32 of that Act (electricity from non-fossil fuel sources) shall be amended in accordance with the following provisions of this paragraph.

(2) After subsection (2) (result to be secured by arrangements made pursuant to an order under subsection (1)) there shall be inserted—

"(2A) For the purposes of this section—
(a) combined heat and power stations generally; and
(b) combined heat and power stations of any particular description,
are to be taken as being particular descriptions of non-fossil fuel generating stations.

(2B) A particular description of combined heat and power stations may be described by reference to, or by reference to matters which include—
(a) the heat or, as the case may be, the steam or heated air or water to be supplied from the station to any premises;
(b) any premises to which any such heat, steam or heated air or water is to be supplied (including, without prejudice to the generality of the foregoing, the use to which any such premises are put);
(c) the means or method by which any such heat, steam or heated air or water is to be supplied to any premises (including, without prejudice to the generality of the foregoing, any system or network of supply or distribution); or
(d) the arrangements (including financial or contractual arrangements) under which any such heat, steam or heated air or water is to be supplied to any premises.

(2C) Subsections (2A) and (2B) above are without prejudice to—
(a) the generality of subsection (2)(b) above, or
(b) section 111(2) below;
and subsection (2B) above is without prejudice to the generality of subsection (2A)(b) above.".

(3) In subsection (8) (interpretation), after the definition of "coal products" there shall be inserted—

"combined heat and power station" means a non-fossil fuel generating station which is (or may be) operated for purposes including the supply to any premises of—
(a) heat produced in association with electricity, or
(b) steam produced from, or air or water heated by, such heat;".

40. In Schedule 4 to that Act (other powers etc. of licence holders) in paragraph 4(1)(b) (power for certain bodies to execute works involving alterations of electric lines or plant) for the words "National Rivers Authority" there shall be substituted the words "Environment Agency".

41. In Schedule 5 to that Act (water rights) in paragraph 8(b) for the words "river purification authority within whose area the watercourse or loch affected is situated" there shall be substituted the words "Scottish Environment Protection Agency".

The Town and Country Planning Act 1990

42. In section 2 of the Town and Country Planning Act 1990 (joint planning boards for National Parks and other areas) after subsection (6) there shall be inserted—

"(6A) Section 241 of the Local Government Act 1972 shall be taken to authorise the application to a joint planning board, subject to any necessary modifications, of any provisions of Part III (accounts and audit) of the Local Government Finance Act 1982 (as well as of any provisions of the Local Government Act 1972) by such an order as is mentioned in subsection (6) above."

43. In Schedule 5 to that Act (conditions relating to mineral working) in paragraph 4 (consultations) after sub-paragraph (4) there shall be inserted—

"(4A) Without prejudice to the application of this paragraph in relation to consultation with the Forestry Commission, where the Minister is consulted pursuant to any provision of this paragraph—
(a) he is not required to inspect any land or to express a view on any matter or question; and
(b) he is not precluded from responding in general terms or otherwise in terms which are not specific to the land in question.".

44. In Schedule 6 to that Act (determination of certain appeals by person appointed by the Secretary of State) in paragraph 1(1) (power, in respect of appeals under certain provisions, to prescribe classes of appeals to be determined by an appointed person instead of by the Secretary of State), after "208," there shall be inserted "and paragraphs 6(11) and (12) and 11(1) of Schedule 13 and paragraph 9(1) of Schedule 14 to the Environment Act 1995,".

The Environmental Protection Act 1990

45.—(1) Section 1 of the Environmental Protection Act 1990 (interpretation of Part I) shall be amended in accordance with the following provisions of this paragraph.

(2) In subsection (7) (definition of "enforcing authority" in relation to England and Wales), for the words "the chief inspector or the local authority by whom" there shall be substituted the words "the Environment Agency or the local authority by which".

(3) For subsection (8) (definition of "enforcing authority" in relation to Scotland) there shall be substituted—

"(8) In relation to Scotland, references to the "enforcing authority" and a "local enforcing authority" are references to the Scottish Environment Protection Agency (in this Part referred to as "SEPA")."

(4) After subsection (13) there shall be added—

"(14) In this Part "the appropriate Agency" means—
(a) in relation to England and Wales, the Environment Agency; and
(b) in relation to Scotland, SEPA."

46.—(1) Section 4 of that Act (determination of authority by whom functions are exercisable) shall be amended in accordance with the following provisions of this paragraph.

(2) In subsection (2) (functions of the chief inspector etc in relation to prescribed processes designated for central control) for the words "the chief inspector appointed for England and Wales by the Secretary of State under section 16 below and, in relation to Scotland, of the chief inspector so appointed for Scotland or of the river purification authority, as determined under regulations made under section 5(1) below" there shall be substituted the words "the appropriate Agency".

(3) In subsection (3) (discharge of functions designated for local control) for paragraphs (a) and (b) there shall be substituted—

"(a) in the case of a prescribed process carried on (or to be carried on) by means of a mobile plant, where the person carrying on the process has his principal place of business—
(i) in England and Wales, the local authority in whose area that place of business is;
(ii) in Scotland, SEPA;
(b) in any other cases, where the prescribed processes are (or are to be) carried on—
(i) in England and Wales, the local authority in whose area they are (or are to be) carried on;
(ii) in Scotland, SEPA;".

(4) In subsection (4) (directions transferring functions to the chief inspector) for the words "the chief inspector" there shall be substituted the words "the Environment Agency".

(5) After that subsection there shall be inserted—

"(4A) In England and Wales, a local authority, in exercising the functions conferred or imposed on it under this Part by virtue of subsection (3) above, shall have regard to the strategy for the time being published pursuant to section 80 of the Environment Act 1995."

(6) In subsection (5) (effect of such a transfer)—
  (a) for the words "the chief inspector" there shall be substituted the words "the Environment Agency"; and
  (b) for the word "him" there shall be substituted the words "that Agency".

(7) In subsection (8) (giving or withdrawal of directions)—
  (a) for the words "the chief inspector" in each place where they occur there shall be substituted the words "the Environment Agency"; and
  (b) the words "or, as the case may be, in the Edinburgh Gazette", in each place where they occur, shall be omitted.

(8) After subsection (8) there shall be inserted—

"(8A) The requirements of sub-paragraph (ii) of paragraph (a) or, as the case may be, of paragraph (b) of subsection (8) above shall not apply in any case where, in the opinion of the Secretary of State, the publication of notice in accordance with that sub-paragraph would be contrary to the interests of national security.

(8B) Subsections (4) to (8A) above shall not apply to Scotland."

(9) For subsection (9) (which, among other things, imposed a duty on the chief inspector etc. to follow developments in technology etc and which is partly superseded by this Act) there shall be substituted—

"(9) It shall be the duty of local authorities to follow such developments in technology and techniques for preventing or reducing pollution of the environment due to releases of substances from prescribed processes as concern releases into the air of substances from prescribed processes designated for local control."

(10) In subsection (10) (duty of chief inspector etc to give effect to directions) for the words "the chief inspector, river purification authorities" there shall be substituted the words "the Environment Agency, SEPA".

(11) In subsection (11) (meaning of "local authority")—
  (a) at the beginning of paragraph (b) there shall be inserted the words "in England and Wales," and
  (b) paragraph (c) and the word "and" immediately preceding it shall cease to have effect.

47. Section 5 of that Act (further provision for Scotland as to discharge and scope of functions) shall cease to have effect.

48. In section 6 of that Act, in subsection (2) (fee payable on application for authorisation) after the words "shall be accompanied by" there shall be inserted—

"(a) in a case where, by virtue of section 41 of the Environment Act 1995, a charge prescribed by a charging scheme under that section is required to be paid to the appropriate Agency in respect of the application, the charge so prescribed; or
  (b) in any other case,".

49.—(1) In section 7 of that Act (conditions of authorisations) in subsection (9) the words from "and, in relation to Scotland," to the end of the subsection shall be omitted.

(2) At the end of subsection (12) of that section (definition of "relevant enactments" for the purposes of subsection (2)) there shall be added "; and
  (g) section 87 of the Environment Act 1995.".

50.—(1) Section 8 of that Act (fees and charges for authorisations) shall be amended in accordance with the following provisions of this paragraph.

(2) In subsection (1) (payments to be charged by, or paid to, the enforcing authority in accordance with schemes), for the words "enforcing authority" there shall be substituted the words "local enforcing authority".

(3) Subsection (4) (separate schemes for different descriptions of enforcing authority) shall cease to have effect.

(4) In subsection (7) (meaning of "relevant expenditure attributable to authorisations")—
  (a) for the words "enforcing authorities" there shall be substituted the words "local enforcing authorities"; and
  (b) the words from "together with the expenditure incurred by the National Rivers Authority" onwards shall be omitted.

(5) In subsection (8) (power to revoke authorisation for non-payment of charge), for the words "enforcing authority" there shall be substituted the words "local enforcing authority.

(6) Subsection (9) (payments by the Secretary of State to the National Rivers Authority) shall cease to have effect.

(7) For subsections (10) and (11) (special provision as respects Scotland) there shall be substituted—

"(10) The foregoing provisions of this section shall not apply to Scotland."

51.—(1) Section 10 of that Act (variation of authorisations by enforcing authority) shall be amended in accordance with the following provisions of this paragraph.

(2) In subsection (3) (which provides for the variation specified in a variation notice to take effect on the date so specified unless the notice is withdrawn) after the words "unless the notice is withdrawn" there shall be inserted the words "or is varied under subsection (3A) below".

(3) After that subsection there shall be inserted—

"(3A) An enforcing authority which has served a variation notice may vary that notice by serving on the holder of the authorisation in question a further notice—
    (a) specifying the variations which the enforcing authority has decided to make to the variation notice; and
    (b) specifying the date or dates on which the variations specified in the variation notice, as varied by the further notice, are to take effect;
and any reference in this Part to a variation notice, or to a variation notice served under subsection (2) above, includes a reference to such a notice as varied by a further notice served under this subsection."

(4) In subsection (4) of that section, for paragraph (b) (requirement to pay the fee prescribed under section 8 of that Act) there shall be substituted—

"(b) require the holder to pay, within such period as may be specified in the notice,—
    (i) in a case where the enforcing authority is the Environment Agency or SEPA, the charge (if any) prescribed for the purpose by a charging scheme under section 41 of the Environment Act 1995; or
    (ii) in any other case, the fee (if any) prescribed by a scheme under section 8 above."

(5) In subsection (8) of that section, in the definition of "vary", after the word "vary" there shall be inserted "(a)" and after the words "any of them;" there shall be added the words "and
    (b) in relation to a variation notice, means adding to, or varying or rescinding the notice or any of its contents;".

52. In section 11 of that Act (application by holders of authorisations for variation of conditions etc.) for subsection (9) (fees) there shall be substituted—

"(9) Any application to the enforcing authority under this section shall be accompanied—
    (a) in a case where the enforcing authority is the Environment Agency or SEPA, by the charge (if any) prescribed for the purpose by a charging scheme under section 41 of the Environment Act 1995; or
    (b) in any other case, by the fee (if any) prescribed by a scheme under section 8 above."

53. At the end of section 13 of that Act (enforcement notices) there shall be added—

"(4) The enforcing authority may, as respects any enforcement notice it has issued to any person, by notice in writing served on that person, withdraw the notice."

54.—(1) Section 15 of that Act (appeals against certain authorisations and notices) shall be amended in accordance with the following provisions of this paragraph.

(2) In subsection (2) (appeals against variation notices, enforcement notices or prohibition notices to the Secretary of State) after the words "to the Secretary of State" there shall be added the words "(except where the notice implements a direction of his)."

(3) For subsection (3) (reference of matters involved in appeals under that section to, and determination of such appeals by, persons appointed by the Secretary of State) there shall be substituted—

"(3) This section is subject to section 114 of the Environment Act 1995 (delegation or reference of appeals etc.)."

(4) For subsection (5) (hearings) there shall be substituted—

"(5) Before determining an appeal under this section, the Secretary of State may, if he thinks fit—

(a) cause the appeal to take or continue in the form of a hearing (which may, if the person hearing the appeal so decides, be held, or held to any extent, in private); or

(b) cause a local inquiry to be held;

and the Secretary of State shall act as mentioned in paragraph (a) or (b) above if a request is made by either party to the appeal to be heard with respect to the appeal."

(5) In subsection (10) (regulations about appeals) after paragraph (b) there shall be added—

"and any such regulations may make different provision for different cases or different circumstances."

55. Sections 16 to 18 of that Act (appointment of inspectors, powers of inspectors and others and power to deal with cause of imminent danger of serious harm) shall cease to have effect.

56. In section 19 of that Act (obtaining of information from persons and authorities) in subsection (2) (power of specified authorities by notice in writing to require provision of information)—

(a) for paragraphs (c) and (d) (the chief inspector and river purification authorities) there shall be substituted—

"(c) the Environment Agency, and

(d) SEPA,"; and

(b) after the words "service of the notice" there shall be inserted the words ", or at such time,".

57.—(1) Section 20 of that Act (public registers of information) shall be amended in accordance with the following provisions of this paragraph.

(2) In subsection (2) (local registers also to contain prescribed particulars of relevance to the area which are contained in central registers) after the word "authority", where it first occurs, there shall be inserted the words "in England and Wales" and for the words "the chief inspector or river purification authority", in each place where they occur, there shall be substituted the words "the Environment Agency".

(3) Subsection (3) (registers in Scotland) shall cease to have effect.

(4) In subsection (4) (port health authorities) after the word "authority" where it first occurs there shall be inserted the words "in England and Wales" and for the words "the chief inspector" there shall be substituted the words "the Environment Agency".

(5) In subsection (7) (registers to be available for inspection by, and facilities for obtaining copies of entries to be afforded to, the public) after paragraph (b) there shall be added the words—

"and, for the purposes of this subsection, places may be prescribed by the Secretary of State at which any such registers or facilities as are mentioned in paragraph (a) or (b) above are to be available or afforded to the public in pursuance of the paragraph in question."

(6) Subsection (9) (duty to furnish the National Rivers Authority with information for purposes of its register) shall cease to have effect.

58.—(1) Section 22 of that Act (exclusion from registers of certain confidential information) shall be amended in accordance with the following provisions of this paragraph.

(2) In subsection (5) (information not to be entered on the register until expiration of certain time limits)—

(a) in paragraph (a), for the words "on the register" there shall be substituted the words "in the register"; and

(b) in the words following paragraph (b), for the words from "on the register" onwards there shall be substituted the words "in the register until the end of the period of seven days following the day on which the appeal is finally determined or withdrawn".

(3) For subsection (6) (which applies subsections (3), (5) and (10) of section 15 in relation to appeals to the Secretary of State against decisions that information is not commercially confidential) there shall be substituted—

"(6) Subsections (5) and (10) of section 15 above shall apply in relation to an appeal under subsection (5) above as they apply in relation to an appeal under that section, but—

(a) subsection (5) of that section shall have effect for the purposes of this subsection with the substitution for the words from "(which may" onwards of the words "(which must be held in private)"; and

(b) subsection (5) above is subject to section 114 of the Environment Act 1995 (delegation or reference of appeals etc.)."

59.—(1) Section 23 of that Act (offences) shall be amended in accordance with the following provisions of this paragraph.

(2) In subsection (I) (offences) paragraphs (d) to (f) and (k) shall cease to have effect.

(3) In subsection (2)(a) (which provides for a fine not exceeding £20,000 on summary conviction of any offence under section 23(1)(a), (c) or (l)) after the words "£20,000" there shall be inserted the words "or to imprisonment for a term not exceeding three months, or to both".

(4) Subsection (4) (punishment for offences under paragraph (d), (e), (f) or (k) of subsection (1)) shall cease to have effect.

(5) Subsection (5) (right of inspector to prosecute before a magistrates' court if authorised to do so by the Secretary of State) shall cease to have effect.

60.—(1) In section 27 of that Act (power of chief inspector etc. to remedy harm) in subsection (1), for the words "the chief inspector or, in Scotland, a river purification authority" there shall be substituted the words "the appropriate Agency".

(2) In subsection (2) of that section (powers not to be exercised without the Secretary of State's written approval) for the words from "The chief inspector" to "their" there shall be substituted the words "The Environment Agency or SEPA, as the case may be, shall not exercise its".

61.—(1) In section 28 of that Act, in subsection (1) (which includes provision that the enforcing authority shall notify the waste regulation authority if a process involves final disposal of controlled waste by deposit in or on land) the words from "but the enforcing authority shall notify" onwards shall cease to have effect.

(2) Subsections (3) and (4) of that section (which involve liaison between the enforcing authority and the National Rivers Authority) shall cease to have effect.

62.—(1) Section 30 of that Act (authorities for purposes of Part II) shall be amended in accordance with the following provisions of this paragraph.

(2) For subsection (1) (waste regulation authorities) there shall be substituted—

> "(1) Any reference in this Part to a waste regulation authority—
> (a) in relation to England and Wales, is a reference to the Environment Agency; and
> (b) in relation to Scotland, is a reference to the Scottish Environment Protection Agency;
> and any reference in this Part to the area of a waste regulation authority shall accordingly be taken as a reference to the area over which the Environment Agency or the Scottish Environment Protection Agency, as the case may be, exercises its functions or, in the case of any particular function, the function in question."

(3) In subsection (4) of that section (construction of references to authorities constituted as particular descriptions of authority and provision for the section to be subject to orders under section 10 of the Local Government Act 1985 establishing authorities for certain purposes)—
 (a) the words "or regulation", and
 (b) the words from "establishing authorities" onwards,
shall cease to have effect.

(4) Subsections (6) (definition of "river purification authority"), (7) and (8) (which relate to authorities which are both waste disposal and waste regulation authorities) shall cease to have effect.

63. Section 31 of that Act (power to create regional authorities for purposes of waste regulation) shall cease to have effect.

64. In section 33 of that Act (prohibition on unauthorised or harmful deposit, treatment or disposal etc of waste) in subsection (7) (defences) for paragraph (c) there shall be substituted—
> "(c) that the acts alleged to constitute the contravention were done in an emergency in order to avoid danger to human health in a case where—
> (i) he took all such steps as were reasonably practicable in the circumstances for minimising pollution of the environment and harm to human health; and
> (ii) particulars of the acts were furnished to the waste regulation authority as soon as reasonably practicable after they were done."

65. In section 34 of that Act (duty of care etc as respects waste), after subsection (3) (which specifies the persons who are authorised persons for the purposes of subsection (1)(c)) there shall be inserted—

> "(3A) The Secretary of State may by regulations amend subsection (3) above so as to add, whether generally or in such circumstances as may be prescribed in the regulations, any person specified in the regulations, or any description of person so specified, to the persons who are authorised persons for the purposes of subsection (1)(c) above."

66.—(1) Section 35 of that Act (waste management licences: general) shall be amended in accordance with the following provisions of this paragraph.

(2) After subsection (7) there shall be inserted—

"(7A) In any case where—
(a) an entry is required under this section to be made in any record as to the observance of any condition of a licence, and
(b) the entry has not been made,
that fact shall be admissible as evidence that that condition has not been observed.

(7B) Any person who—
(a) intentionally makes a false entry in any record required to be kept under any condition of a licence, or
(b) with intent to deceive, forges or uses a licence or makes or has in his possession a document so closely resembling a licence as to be likely to deceive,
shall be guilty of an offence.

(7C) A person guilty of an offence under subsection (7B) above shall be liable—
(a) on summary conviction, to a fine not exceeding the statutory maximum;
(b) on conviction on indictment, to a fine or to imprisonment for a term not exceeding two years, or to both."

67. After section 35 of that Act there shall be inserted—

"Compensation where rights granted pursuant to section 35(4) or 38(9A)

35A.—(1) This section applies in any case where—
(a) the holder of a licence is required—
(i) by the conditions of the licence; or
(ii) by a requirement imposed under section 38(9) below,
to carry out any works or do any other thing which he is not entitled to carry out or do;
(b) a person whose consent would be required has, pursuant to the requirements of section 35(4) above or 38(9A) below, granted, or joined in granting, to the holder of the licence any rights in relation to any land; and
(c) those rights, or those rights together with other rights, are such as will enable the holder of the licence to comply with any requirements imposed on him by the licence or, as the case may be, under section 38(9) below.

(2) In a case where this section applies, any person who has granted, or joined in granting, the rights in question shall be entitled to be paid compensation under this section by the holder of the licence.

(3) The Secretary of State shall by regulations provide for the descriptions of loss and damage for which compensation is payable under this section.

(4) The Secretary of State may by regulations—
(a) provide for the basis on which any amount to be paid by way of compensation under this section is to be assessed;
(b) without prejudice to the generality of subsection (3) and paragraph (a) above, provide for compensation under this section to be payable in respect of—
(i) any effect of any rights being granted, or
(ii) any consequence of the exercise of any rights which have been granted;
(c) provide for the times at which any entitlement to compensation under this section is to arise or at which any such compensation is to become payable;
(d) provide for the persons or bodies by whom, and the manner in which, any dispute—
(i) as to whether any, and (if so) how much and when, compensation under this section is payable; or
(ii) as to the person to or by whom it shall be paid,
is to be determined;
(e) provide for when or how applications may be made for compensation under this section;
(f) without prejudice to the generality of paragraph (d) above, provide for when or how applications may be made for the determination of any such disputes as are mentioned in that paragraph;
(g) without prejudice to the generality of paragraphs (e) and (f) above, prescribe the form in which any such applications as are mentioned in those paragraphs are to be made;
(h) make provision similar to any provision made by paragraph 8 of Schedule 19 to the Water Resources Act 1991;
(j) make different provision for different cases, including different provision in relation to different persons or circumstances;

(k) include such incidental, supplemental, consequential or transitional provision as the Secretary of State considers appropriate.".

68.—(1) Section 36 of that Act (grant of licences) shall be amended in accordance with the following provisions of this paragraph.

(2) In subsection (1) (making of applications) for the words following paragraph (b) there shall be substituted—

"and shall be made on a form provided for the purpose by the waste regulation authority and accompanied by such information as that authority reasonably requires and the charge prescribed for the purpose by a charging scheme under section 41 of the Environment Act 1995.

(1A) Where an applicant for a licence fails to provide the waste regulation authority with any information required under subsection (1) above, the authority may refuse to proceed with the application, or refuse to proceed with it until the information is provided."

(3) In subsection (4) (reference of proposals to, and consideration of representations made by, other bodies)—
  (a) in paragraph (a), for the words "the National Rivers Authority" there shall be substituted the words "the appropriate planning authority", and
  (b) in paragraph (b), for the word "Authority" there shall be substituted the word "authority".

(4) Subsections (5) (reference by National Rivers Authority to the Secretary of State) and (6) (which makes provision for Scotland in place of subsection (4)) shall cease to have effect.

(5) After subsection (9) (application deemed to be rejected if not granted or refused within four months from being received) there shall be inserted—

"(9A) Subsection (9) above—
  (a) shall not have effect in any case where, by virtue of subsection (1A) above, the waste regulation authority refuses to proceed with the application in question, and
  (b) shall have effect in any case where, by virtue of subsection (1A) above, the waste regulation authority refuses to proceed with it until the required information is provided, with the substitution for the period of four months there mentioned of the period of four months beginning with the date on which the authority received the information."

(6) For subsection (10) (period of 21 days allowed for bodies to make representations) there shall be substituted—

"(10) The period allowed to the appropriate planning authority, the Health and Safety Executive or the appropriate nature conservancy body for the making of representations under subsection (4) or (7) above about a proposal is the period of twenty-eight days beginning with the day on which the proposal is received by the waste regulation authority or such longer period as the waste regulation authority, the appropriate planning authority, the Executive or the body, as the case may be, agree in writing.

(11) In this section—
  "the appropriate planning authority" means—
    (a) where the relevant land is situated in the area of a London borough council, that London borough council;
    (b) where the relevant land is situated in the City of London the Common Council of the City of London;
    (c) where the relevant land is situated in a non-metropolitan county in England, the council of that county;
    (d) where the relevant land is situated in a National Park or the Broads, the National Park authority for that National Park or, as the case may be, the Broads Authority;
    (e) where the relevant land is situated elsewhere in England or Wales, the council of the district or, in Wales, the county or county borough, in which the land is situated;
    (f) where the relevant land is situated in Scotland, the council constituted under section 2 of the Local Government etc. (Scotland) Act 1994 for the area in which the land is situated;
  "the Broads" has the same meaning as in the Norfolk and Suffolk Broads Act 1988;
  "National Park authority", subject to subsection (12) below, means a National Park

authority established under section 63 of the Environment Act 1995 which has become the local planning authority for the National Park in question;
"the relevant land" means—
    (a) in relation to a site licence, the land to which the licence relates; and
    (b) in relation to a mobile plant licence, the principal place of business of the operator of the plant to which the licence relates.

(12) As respects any period before a National Park authority established under section 63 of the Environment Act 1995 in relation to a National Park becomes the local planning authority for that National Park, any reference in this section to a National Park authority shall be taken as a reference to the National Park Committee or joint or special planning board for that National Park.

(13) The Secretary of State may by regulations amend the definition of "appropriate planning authority" in subsection (11) above.

(14) This section shall have effect subject to section 36A below."

69. After section 36 of that Act there shall be inserted—

Consultation before the grant of certain licences

36A.—(1) This section applies where an application for a licence has been duly made to a waste regulation authority, and the authority proposes to issue a licence subject (by virtue of section 35(4) above) to any condition which might require the holder of the licence to—
    (a) carry out any works, or
    (b) do any other thing,
which he might not be entitled to carry out or do.

(2) Before issuing the licence, the waste regulation authority shall serve on every person appearing to the authority to be a person falling within subsection (3) below a notice which complies with the requirements set out in subsection (4) below.

(3) A person falls within this subsection if—
    (a) he is the owner, lessee or occupier of any land; and
    (b) that land is land in relation to which it is likely that, as a consequence of the licence being issued subject to the condition in question, rights will have to be granted by virtue of section 35(4) above to the holder of the licence.

(4) A notice served under subsection (2) above shall—
    (a) set out the condition in question;
    (b) indicate the nature of the works or other things which that condition might require the holder of the licence to carry out or do; and
    (c) specify the date by which, and the manner in which, any representations relating to the condition or its possible effects are to be made to the waste regulation authority by the person on whom the notice is served.

(5) The date which, pursuant to subsection (4)(c) above, is specified in a notice shall be a date not earlier than the date on which expires the period—
    (a) beginning with the date on which the notice is served, and
    (b) of such length as may be prescribed in regulations made by the Secretary of State.

(6) Before the waste regulation authority issues the licence it must, subject to subsection (7) below, consider any representations made in relation to the condition in question, or its possible effects, by any person on whom a notice has been served under subsection (2) above.

(7) Subsection (6) above does not require the waste regulation authority to consider any representations made by a person after the date specified in the notice served on him under subsection (2) above as the date by which his representations in relation to the condition or its possible effects are to be made.

(8) In subsection (3) above—
"owner", in relation to any land in England and Wales, means the person who—
    (a) is for the time being receiving the rack–rent of the land, whether on his own account or as agent or trustee for another person; or
    (b) would receive the rack-rent if the land were let at a rack-rent,
    but does not include a mortgagee not in possession; and
"owner", in relation to any land in Scotland, means a person (other than a creditor in a heritable security not in possession of the security subjects) for the time being entitled to receive or who would, if the land were let, be entitled to receive, the rents of the land in connection with which the word is used and includes a trustee, factor, guardian or curator and in the case of public or municipal land includes the persons to whom the management of the land is entrusted.".

70.—(1) In section 37 of that Act (variation of licences) in subsection (1)(b) (which requires an application to be accompanied by the prescribed fee) for the words "the prescribed fee payable under section 41 below," there shall be substituted the words "the charge prescribed for the purpose by a charging scheme under section 41 of the Environment Act 1995,".

(2) In subsection (5) of that section (which applies certain provisions of section 36) the words "(5), (6)," and "(8)" shall be omitted.

(3) After subsection (6) of that section (cases where an application for modification is deemed to have been rejected) there shall be added—

"(7) This section shall have effect subject to section 37A below."

71. After section 37 of that Act there shall be inserted—

"Consultation before certain variations

37A.—(1) This section applies where—

(a) a waste regulation authority proposes to modify a licence under section 37(1) or (2)(a) above; and

(b) the licence, if modified as proposed, would be subject to a relevant new condition.

(2) For the purposes of this section, a "relevant new condition" is any condition by virtue of which the holder of the licence might be required to carry out any works or do any other thing—

(a) which he might not be entitled to carry out or do, and

(b) which he could not be required to carry out or do by virtue of the conditions to which, prior to the modification, the licence is subject.

(3) Before modifying the licence, the waste regulation authority shall serve on every person appearing to the authority to be a person falling within subsection (4) below a notice which complies with the requirements set out in subsection (5) below.

(4) A person falls within this subsection if—

(a) he is the owner, lessee or occupier of any land; and

(b) that land is land in relation to which it is likely that, as a consequence of the licence being modified so as to be subject to the relevant new condition in question, rights will have to be granted by virtue of section 35(4) above to the holder of the licence.

(5) A notice served under subsection (3) above shall—

(a) set out the relevant new condition in question;

(b) indicate the nature of the works or other things which that condition might require the holder of the licence to carry out or do but which he could not be required to carry out or do by virtue of the conditions (if any) to which, prior to the modification, the licence is subject; and

(c) specify the date by which, and the manner in which any representations relating to the condition or its possible effects are to be made to the waste regulation authority by the person on whom the notice is served.

(6) The date which, pursuant to subsection (5)(c) above, is specified in a notice shall be a date not earlier than the date on which expires the period—

(a) beginning with the date on which the notice is served, and

(b) of such length as may be prescribed in regulations made by the Secretary of State.

(7) Before the waste regulation authority issues the licence it must, subject to subsection (8) below, consider any representations made in relation to the condition in question, or its possible effects, by any person on whom a notice has been served under subsection (3) above.

(8) Subsection (7) above does not require the waste regulation authority to consider any representations made by a person after the date specified in the notice served on him under subsection (3) above as the date by which his representations in relation to the condition or its possible effects are to be made.

(9) A waste regulation authority may postpone the service of any notice or the consideration of any representations required under the foregoing provisions of this section so far as the authority considers that by reason of an emergency it is appropriate to do so.

(10) In subsection (3) above, "owner" has the same meaning as it has in subsection (3) of section 36A above by virtue of subsection (8) of that section.".

72.—(1) In section 38 of that Act (revocation and suspension of licences) after subsection (9) (power to require certain measures to be taken where licence suspended) there shall be inserted—

"(9A) A requirement imposed under subsection (9) above may require the holder of a licence to carry out works or do other things notwithstanding that he is not entitled to carry out the works or do the thing and any person whose consent would be required shall grant, or join in granting, the holder of the licence such rights in relation to the land as will enable the holder of the licence to comply with any requirements imposed on him under that subsection.

(9B) Subsections (2) to (8) of section 36A above shall, with the necessary modifications, apply where the authority proposes to impose a requirement under subsection (9) above which may require the holder of a licence to carry out any such works or do any such thing as is mentioned in subsection (9A) above as they apply where the authority proposes to issue a licence subject to any such condition as is mentioned in subsection (1) of that section, but as if—

(a) the reference in subsection (3) of that section to section 35(4) above were a reference to subsection (9A) above; and

(b) any reference in those subsections—

(i) to the condition, or the condition in question, were a reference to the requirement; and

(ii) to issuing a licence were a reference to serving a notice, under subsection (12) below, effecting the requirement.

(9C) The authority may postpone the service of any notice or the consideration of any representations required under section 36A above, as applied by subsection (9B) above, so far as the authority considers that by reason of an emergency it is appropriate to do so."

(2) After subsection (12) of that section (revocations and suspensions etc. to be effected by service of notice) there shall be added—

"(13) If a waste regulation authority is of the opinion that proceedings for an offence under subsection (10) or (11) above would afford an ineffectual remedy against a person who has failed to comply with any requirement imposed under subsection (9) above, the authority may take proceedings in the High Court or, in Scotland, in any court of competent jurisdiction for the purpose of securing compliance with the requirement."

73.—(1) Section 39 of that Act (surrender of licences) shall be amended in accordance with the following provisions of this paragraph.

(2) In subsection (3) (application for surrender of a site licence) for the words from "in such form" onwards there shall be substituted the words "on a form provided by the authority for the purpose, giving such information and accompanied by such evidence as the authority reasonably requires and accompanied by the charge prescribed for the purpose by a charging scheme under section 41 of the Environment Act 1995."

(3) In subsection (7) (consideration of representations before accepting surrender of a licence)—

(a) for the words "the National Rivers Authority" and "the Authority" there shall be substituted the words "the appropriate planning authority"; and

(b) the words following paragraph (b) shall cease to have effect.

(4) Subsection (8) (which makes provision for Scotland in place of subsection (7)) shall cease to have effect.

(5) In subsection (11) (meaning of "the allowed period") for the words "subsections (7) and (8) above" there shall be substituted the words "subsection (7) above".

(6) After subsection (11) there shall be added—

"(12) In this section—

"the appropriate planning authority" means—

(a) where the relevant land is situated in the area of a London borough council, that London borough council;

(b) where the relevant land is situated in the City of London, the Common Council of the City of London;

(c) where the relevant land is situated in a non-metropolitan county in England, the council of that county;

(d) where the relevant land is situated in a National Park or the Broads, the National Park authority for that National Park or, as the case may be, the Broads Authority;

(e) where the relevant land is situated elsewhere in England or Wales, the council of the district or, in Wales, the county or county borough, in which the land is situated;

(f) where the relevant land is situated in Scotland, the council constituted under section 2 of the Local Government etc. (Scotland) Act 1994 for the area in which the land is situated;

"the Broads" has the same meaning as in the Norfolk and Suffolk Broads Act 1988;

"National Park authority", subject to subsection (13) below, means a National Park authority established under section 63 of the Environment Act 1995 which has become the local planning authority for the National Park in question;

"the relevant land", in the case of any site licence, means the land to which the licence relates.

(13) As respects any period before a National Park authority established under section 63 of the Environment Act 1995 in relation to a National Park becomes the local planning authority for that National Park, any reference in this section to a National Park authority shall be taken as a reference to the National Park Committee or joint or special planning board for that National Park.

(14) The Secretary of State may by regulations amend the definition of "appropriate planning authority" in subsection (12) above."

74. In section 40 of that Act (transfer of licences) in subsection (3) (mode of making application for transfer of licence) for the words from "in such form" to "section 41 below" there shall be substituted the words "on a form provided by the authority for the purpose, accompanied by such information as the authority may reasonably require, the charge prescribed for the purpose by a charging scheme under section 41 of the Environment Act 1995".

75. Section 41 of that Act (fees and charges for licences) shall cease to have effect.

76.—(1) Section 42 of that Act (supervision of licensed activities) shall be amended in accordance with the following provisions of this paragraph.

(2) Subsection (2) (consultation with the National Rivers Authority etc) shall cease to have effect.

(3) In subsection (4) (recovery of expenditure from the holder or, if it has been surrendered, the former holder of a licence) for the words "the holder of the licence or, if the licence has been surrendered, from the former holder of it" there shall be substituted the words "the holder, or (as the case may be) the former holder, of the licence".

(4) In subsection (5) (powers where it appears that a condition of a licence is not being complied with) after the words "is not being complied with" there shall be inserted the words "or is likely not to be complied with,".

(5) For paragraph (a) of that subsection there shall be substituted—

"(a) serve on the holder of the licence a notice—
(i) stating that the authority is of the opinion that a condition of the licence is not being complied with or, as the case may be, is likely not to be complied with;
(ii) specifying the matters which constitute the non-compliance or, as the case may be, which make the anticipated non-compliance likely;
(iii) specifying the steps which must be taken to remedy the non-compliance or, as the case may be, to prevent the anticipated non-compliance from occurring; and
(iv) specifying the period within which those steps must be taken; and".

(6) In paragraph (b) of that subsection (powers which become exercisable on non-compliance) for the words "has not complied with the condition within that time," there shall be substituted the words "has not taken the steps specified in the notice within the period so specified,".

(7) After subsection (6) (power to revoke or suspend a licence) there shall be inserted—

"(6A) If a waste regulation authority is of the opinion that revocation or suspension of the licence, whether entirely or to any extent, under subsection (6) above would afford an ineffectual remedy against a person who has failed to comply with any requirement imposed under subsection (5)(a) above, the authority may take proceedings in the High Court or, in Scotland, in any court of competent jurisdiction for the purpose of securing compliance with the requirement."

(8) In subsection (7) (application of certain provisions of section 38 to revocation or suspension of a licence)—
(a) for the words from "subsections (5)" to "38" there shall be substituted the words "subsections (5) and (12) or, as the case may be, subsections (8) to (12) of section 38"; and
(b) the words from "and the power" onwards shall cease to have effect.

77. In section 43 of that Act, in subsection (2), paragraphs (a) and (b) (reference of matters involved in appeals under that section to, and determination of such appeals by, persons appointed by the Secretary of State) shall cease to have effect and after that section there shall be inserted—

"(2A) This section is subject to section 114 of the Environment Act 1995 (delegation or reference of appeals etc)."

78. Section 50 of that Act (waste disposal plans of waste regulation authorities) shall cease to have effect.
79. Section 61 of that Act (duty of waste regulation authorities as respects closed landfills) shall cease to have effect.
80.—(1) Section 62 of that Act (special provision with respect to certain dangerous and intractable waste) shall be amended in accordance with the following provisions of this paragraph.
(2) In subsection (3), for paragraph (a) (regulations providing for the supervision of certain activities and the recovery of the costs from persons carrying on the activities) there shall be substituted—

"(a) for the supervision by waste regulation authorities—
(i) of activities authorised by virtue of the regulations or of activities by virtue of carrying on which persons are subject to provisions of the regulations, or
(ii) of persons who carry on activities authorised by virtue of the regulations or who are subject to provisions of the regulations,
and for the recovery from persons falling within sub-paragraph (ii) above of the costs incurred by waste regulation authorities in performing functions conferred upon those authorities by the regulations;".

(3) After that subsection (which also includes provision for regulations to provide for appeals to the Secretary of State) there shall be added—

"(3A) This section is subject to section 114 of the Environment Act 1995 (delegation or reference of appeals etc.)."

81. In section 63 of that Act (waste other than controlled waste) for subsection (2) (offences relating to the deposit of waste which is not controlled waste but which, if it were such waste, would be special waste) there shall be substituted—

"(2) A person who deposits, or knowingly causes or knowingly permits the deposit of, any waste—
(a) which is not controlled waste, but
(b) which, if it were controlled waste, would be special waste,
in a case where he would be guilty of an offence under section 33 above if the waste were special waste and any waste management licence were not in force, shall, subject to subsection (3) below, be guilty of that offence and punishable as if the waste were special waste."

82.—(1) Section 64 of that Act (public registers) shall be amended in accordance with the following provisions of this paragraph.
(2) After subsection (2) there shall be inserted—

"(2A) The Secretary of State may give to a waste regulation authority directions requiring the removal from any register of its of any specified information not prescribed for inclusion under subsection (1) above or which, by virtue of section 65 or 66 below, ought to be excluded from the register."

(3) In subsection (4) (duty of waste collection authorities in England to maintain registers)—
(a) after the word "England" there shall be inserted the words "or Wales"; and
(b) the words "which is not a waste regulation authority" shall be omitted.
(4) For subsection (5) (waste regulation authorities in England to furnish information to waste collection authorities) there shall be substituted—

"(5) The waste regulation authority in relation to England and Wales shall furnish any waste collection authorities in its area with the particulars necessary to enable them to discharge their duty under subsection (4) above."

(5) In subsection (6) (registers to be available for inspection by, and facilities for obtaining copies of entries to be afforded to, the public)—
(a) after the words "waste collection authority" there shall be inserted "(a)";
(b) after the words "hours and" there shall be inserted "(b)"; and
(c) after the paragraph (b) so formed, there shall be added the words—
"and, for the purposes of this subsection, places may be prescribed by the Secretary of State at which any such registers or facilities as are mentioned in paragraph (a) or (b)

above are to be available or afforded to the public in pursuance of the paragraph in question."

83.—(1) In section 66 of that Act (exclusion from registers of certain confidential information) in subsection (5) (information not to be entered on the register until expiration of certain time limits) in the words following paragraph (b), for the words from "pending" onwards there shall be substituted the words "until the end of the period of seven days following the day on which the appeal is finally determined or withdrawn".

(2) For subsection (6) (which applies section 43(2) and (8) to appeals to the Secretary of State against decisions that information is not commercially confidential) there shall be substituted—

"(6) Subsections (2) and (8) of section 43 above shall apply in relation to appeals under subsection (5) above as they apply in relation to appeals under that section; but

(a) subsection (2)(c) of that section shall have effect for the purposes of this subsection with the substitution for the words from "(which may" onwards of the words "(which must be held in private)"; and

(b) subsection (5) above is subject to section 114 of the Environment Act 1995 (delegation or reference of appeals etc.)."

84. Section 67 of that Act (annual reports of waste regulation authorities) shall cease to have effect.

85. Sections 68 to 70 of that Act (functions of the Secretary of State and appointment etc. of inspectors, powers of entry and power to deal with cause of imminent danger of serious pollution) shall cease to have effect.

86.—(1) In section 71 of that Act (obtaining of information from persons and authorities) subsection (1) (which is superseded by this Act) shall cease to have effect.

(2) In subsection (2) of that section (power by notice to require a person to furnish information within such period as may be specified in the notice) after the words "service of the notice" there shall be inserted the words ", or at such time,".

87. Section 72 of that Act (default powers of the Secretary of State) shall cease to have effect.

88.—(1) Section 75 of that Act (meaning of "waste" etc.) shall be amended in accordance with the following provisions of this paragraph.

(2) For subsection (2) (definition of "waste") there shall be substituted—

"(2) "Waste" means any substance or object in the categories set out in Schedule 2B to this Act which the holder discards or intends or is required to discard; and for the purposes of this definition—

"holder" means the producer of the waste or the person who is in possession of it; and

"producer" means any person whose activities produce waste or any person who carries out pre-processing, mixing or other operations resulting in a change in the nature or composition of this waste."

(3) Subsection (3) (presumption that anything discarded is waste unless the contrary is proved) shall cease to have effect.

(4) After subsection (9) there shall be added—

"(10) Schedule 2B to this Act (which reproduces Annex I to the Waste Directive) shall have effect.

(11) Subsection (2) above is substituted, and Schedule 2B to this Act is inserted, for the purpose of assigning to "waste" in this Part the meaning which it has in the Waste Directive by virtue of paragraphs (a) to (c) of Article 1 of, and Annex I to, that Directive, and those provisions shall be construed accordingly.

(12) In this section "the Waste Directive" means the directive of the Council of the European Communities, dated 15th July 1975, on waste, as amended by—

(a) the directive of that Council, dated 18th March 1991, amending directive 75/442/EEC on waste; and

(b) the directive of that Council, dated 23rd December 1991, standardising and rationalising reports on the implementation of certain Directives relating to the environment."

89.—(1) Section 79 of that Act (statutory nuisances) shall be amended in accordance with the following provisions of this paragraph.

(2) In subsection (1) (the paragraphs of which specify, subject to subsections (2) to (6A), the matters which constitute statutory nuisances) for the words "Subject to subsections (2) to (6A) below" there shall be substituted the words "Subject to subsections (1A) to (6A) below".

(3) After that subsection there shall be inserted—

"(1A) No matter shall constitute a statutory nuisance to the extent that it consists of, or is caused by, any land being in a contaminated state.

(1B) Land is in a "contaminated state" for the purposes of subsection (1A) above if, and only if, it is in such a condition, by reason of substances in, on or under the land, that—
(a) harm is being caused or there is a possibility of harm being caused; or
(b) pollution of controlled waters is being, or is likely to be, caused;
and in this subsection "harm", "pollution of controlled waters" and "substance" have the same meaning as in Part IIA of this Act.".

90. In section 141 of that Act (power to prohibit or restrict the importation or exportation of waste) subsection (5)(a)(ii) (power of Secretary of State by direction to make functions of certain authorities exercisable instead by him) shall cease to have effect.

91. Section 143 of that Act (public registers of land which may be contaminated) shall cease to have effect.

92. In section 161 of that Act (regulations and orders) in subsection (4) (which specifies the orders under that Act which are not subject to negative resolution procedure under subsection (3)) after the words "does not apply to" there shall be inserted the words "a statutory instrument—
(a) which contains an order under section 78M(4) above, or
(b) by reason only that it contains".

93.—(1) Schedule 1 to that Act (authorisations for processes: supplementary provisions) shall be amended in accordance with the following provisions of this paragraph.

(2) In Part I (grant of authorisations) in paragraph 3(3) (local inquiry or hearing to be held where request to be heard made by the applicant or the local enforcing authority) for the words "the local enforcing authority" there shall be substituted the words "the enforcing authority".

(3) In Part II (variation of authorisations) in paragraph 6, at the beginning of sub-paragraph (1) there shall be inserted the words "Except as provided by sub-paragraph (1A) below,".

(4) After that sub-paragraph there shall be inserted—

"(1A) The requirements of this paragraph shall not apply in relation to any variations of an authorisation which an enforcing authority has decided to make in consequence of representations made in accordance with this paragraph and which are specified by way of variation of a variation notice by a further notice under section 10(3A) of this Act."

(5) After paragraph 7 (applications for variation) there shall be inserted—

"Call in of applications for variation

8.—(1) The Secretary of State may give directions to the enforcing authority requiring that any particular application or any class of applications for the variation of an authorisation shall be transmitted to him for determination pending a further direction under sub-paragraph (5) below.

(2) The enforcing authority shall inform the applicant of the fact that his application is being transmitted to the Secretary of State.

(3) Where an application for the variation of an authorisation is referred to him under sub-paragraph (1) above the Secretary of State may—
(a) cause a local inquiry to be held in relation to the application; or
(b) afford the applicant and the authority concerned an opportunity of appearing before and being heard by a person appointed by the Secretary of State;
and he shall exercise one of the powers under this sub-paragraph in any case where, in the manner prescribed by regulations made by the Secretary of State, a request is made to be heard with respect to the application by the applicant or the enforcing authority concerned.

(4) Subsections (2) to (5) of section 250 of the Local Government Act 1972 (supplementary provisions about local inquiries under that section) or, in relation to Scotland, subsections (2) to (8) of section 210 of the Local Government (Scotland) Act 1973 (which make similar provision) shall, without prejudice to the generality of subsection (1) of either of those sections, apply to local inquiries or other hearings in pursuance of sub-paragraph (3) above as they apply to inquiries in pursuance of either of those sections and, in relation to England and Wales, as if the reference to a local authority in subsection (4) of the said section 250 included a reference to the enforcing authority.

(5) The Secretary of State shall, on determining any application transferred to him under this paragraph, give to the enforcing authority such a direction as he thinks fit as to whether it is to grant the application and, if so, as to the conditions that are to be attached to the authorisation by means of the variation notice.

9. The Secretary of State may give the enforcing authority a direction with respect to any

particular application or any class of applications for the variation of an authorisation requiring the authority not to determine or not to proceed with the application or applications of that class until the expiry of any such period as may be specified in the direction, or until directed by the Secretary of State that they may do so, as the case may be.

10.—(1) Except in a case where an application for the variation of an authorisation has been referred to the Secretary of State under paragraph 8 above and subject to sub-paragraph (3) below, the enforcing authority shall determine an application for the variation of an authorisation within the period of four months beginning with the day on which it received the application or within such longer period as may be agreed with the applicant.

(2) If the enforcing authority fails to determine an application for the variation of an authorisation within the period allowed by or under this paragraph the application shall, if the applicant notifies the authority in writing that he treats the failure as such, be deemed to have been refused at the end of that period.

(3) The Secretary of State may, by order, substitute for the period for the time being specified in sub-paragraph (1) above such other period as he considers appropriate and different periods may be substituted for different classes of application."

94. In Schedule 2 to that Act (waste disposal authorities and companies) in paragraph 17(2) (which requires a waste regulation authority or waste disposal authority to furnish information on request to the Secretary of State) the words "a waste regulation authority or" shall cease to have effect.

95. After Schedule 2A to that Act there shall be inserted—

"SCHEDULE 2B

CATEGORIES OF WASTE

1. Production or consumption residues not otherwise specified below.
2. Off-specification products.
3. Products whose date for appropriate use has expired.
4. Materials spilled, lost or having undergone other mishap, including any materials, equipment, etc, contaminated as a result of the mishap.
5. Materials contaminated or soiled as a result of planned actions (e.g. residues from cleaning operations, packing materials, containers, etc.).
6. Unusable parts (e.g. reject batteries, exhausted catalysts, etc.).
7. Substances which no longer perform satisfactorily (e.g. contaminated acids, contaminated solvents, exhausted tempering salts, etc.).
8. Residues of industrial processes (e.g. slags, still bottoms, etc.).
9. Residues from pollution abatement processes (e.g. scrubber sludges, baghouse dusts, spent filters, etc.).
10. Machining or finishing residues (e.g. lathe turnings, mill scales, etc.).
11. Residues from raw materials extraction and processing (e.g. mining residues, oil field slops, etc.).
12. Adulterated materials (e.g. oils contaminated with PCBs, etc.).
13. Any materials, substances or products whose use has been banned by law.
14. Products for which the holder has no further use (e.g. agricultural, household, office, commercial and shop discards, etc.).
15. Contaminated materials, substances or products resulting from remedial action with respect to land.
16. Any materials, substances or products which are not contained in the above categories."

The Natural Heritage (Scotland) Act 1991

96.—(1) The Natural Heritage (Scotland) Act 1991 shall be amended in accordance with the following provisions of this paragraph.

(2) In section 15—
(a) in subsection (2) for the words "a river purification authority, acting in pursuance of their duties under section 17(1) of the Rivers (Prevention of Pollution) (Scotland) Act 1951" there shall be substituted the words "SEPA acting in pursuance of its duties under section 34(1) of the Environment Act 1995";
(b) in subsection (3) for the words "said Act of" and "a river purification authority" where they first occur there shall be substituted the words "Rivers (Prevention of Pollution

(Scotland) Act" and "SEPA" respectively and the words "and a river purification authority of whom such a requirement is made shall make such an application" shall cease to have effect;
(c) for subsection (5) there shall be substituted—

"(5) A control area shall comprise an area or areas shown in a map or plan contained in the order."

(3) In section 17—
(a) in subsection (1) for the words "A river purification authority" there shall be substituted the words "SEPA";
(b) in subsection (3) for the words "A river purification authority", "their" in both places where it occurs, "they" and "the authority" there shall be substituted the words "SEPA", "its", "it" and "SEPA" respectively.
(4) In section 18—
(a) in subsection (1) for the words "a river purification authority" and "they" there shall be substituted the words "SEPA" and "it" respectively;
(b) in subsection (2) for the words "the river purification authority decide" there shall be substituted the words "SEPA decides";
(c) in subsection (3) for the words "a river purification authority" and "the authority" there shall be substituted the words "SEPA" and "it" respectively;
(d) in subsection (4) for the words "the river purification authority declare" there shall be substituted the words "SEPA declares";
(e) in subsection (5) for the words "A river purification authority" and "them" there shall be substituted the words "SEPA" and "it" respectively.
(5) In section 24—
(a) in subsection (1)—
(i) for the words "a river purification authority" there shall be substituted the words "SEPA"; and
(ii) in paragraph (a), after the word "on" there shall be inserted the words "SEPA or"; and
(b) in subsection (9)—
(i) for the words "a river purification authority or" there shall be substituted the words "SEPA or a"; and
(ii) in paragraph (a), after the word "by" where it second occurs there shall be inserted the words "SEPA or".
(6) After section 26 there shall be inserted—

"Meaning of SEPA
26A. In this Act "SEPA" means the Scottish Environment Protection Agency."

(7) In Schedule 5—
(a) in paragraph 1 for the words "the river purification authority concerned consider" there shall be substituted the words "SEPA considers";
(b) in paragraph 2 for the words "the river purification authority concerned" there shall be substituted the words "SEPA" and the words "in their area and" shall cease to have effect;
(c) in paragraph 3 for the words "the river purification authority" and "their" wherever they occur there shall be substituted the words "SEPA" and "its" respectively;
(d) in paragraphs 4 and 9 for the words "the river purification authority" wherever they occur there shall be substituted the words "SEPA".
(8) In Schedule 6—
(a) in paragraph 1—
(i) in sub-paragraph (1) for the words "the river purification authority" there shall be substituted the words "SEPA";
(ii) in sub-paragraph (2) for the words "A river purification authority", "them", "the authority" and "their" there shall be substituted respectively the words "SEPA", "it", "it" and "its" respectively;
(iii) in sub-paragraph (3) for the words "the river purification authority" there shall be substituted the words "SEPA";
(iv) in sub-paragraph (4) for the words "the river purification authority", "the authority fail" and "their" there shall be substituted the words "SEPA", "it fails" and "its" respectively;
(v) sub-paragraph (5) shall cease to have effect;
(vi) in sub-paragraph (6) for the words "the river purification authority to whom the application has been made" there shall be substituted the words "SEPA";

(b) in paragraph 2—
    (i) in sub-paragraph (1) for the words "the river purification authority" wherever they occur there shall be substituted the words "SEPA";
    (ii) in sub-paragraphs (3) and (4) for the words "the river purification authority" wherever they occur there shall be substituted the words "SEPA";
    (iii) at the end there shall be added—

"(6) This paragraph is subject to section 114 of the Environment Act 1995 (delegation or reference of appeals etc).";

(c) in paragraph 3—
    (i) in sub-paragraph (1) for the words "A river purification authority" there shall be substituted the words "SEPA";
    (ii) in sub-paragraph (2) for the words "A river purification authority" and "they are" there shall be substituted the words "SEPA" and "it is" respectively;
    (iii) in sub-paragraph (4) for the words "the river purification authority" there shall be substituted the words "SEPA";
    (iv) in sub-paragraph (5) for the words "the river purification authority" and "them" there shall be substituted the words "SEPA" and "it" respectively;
    (v) in sub-paragraph (6) for the words "the authority fail to intimate their" and "the river purification authority" there shall be substituted the words "SEPA fails to intimate its" and "SEPA" respectively;
(d) in paragraph 4 for the words "A river purification authority" and "them" there shall be substituted the words "SEPA" and "it" respectively;
(e) in paragraph 5(2) for the words "the river purification authority" there shall be substituted the words "SEPA".
(9) In Schedule 8, in paragraph 1—
  (a) for sub-paragraph (1) there shall be substituted—

"(1) Before making an application for a drought order, the applicant shall consult—
    (a) SEPA, in a case where notice of the application is required to be served on it under this paragraph; and
    (b) any district salmon fishery board on whom notice of the application is required to be served under this paragraph.";

  (b) in sub-paragraph (3), in the second column of the Table, in the fourth entry (relating to orders concerning the taking of water from a source or the discharge of water to a place), in paragraph (a) the words ", river purification authority" shall cease to have effect and at the end there shall be added—
    "(c) SEPA";
  (c) in sub-paragraph (3), in the second column of the Table, in the fifth entry (relating to orders which authorise the execution of any works) for the words "every river purification authority and" there shall be substituted the words "SEPA and every".

The Water Industry Act 1991

97. In section 3 of the Water Industry Act 1991 (general environmental and recreational duties) in subsection (4) (which imposes duties on the Director and relevant undertakers in relation to proposals relating to functions of the National Rivers Authority etc) for the words "the NRA", in each place where they occur, there shall be substituted the words "the Environment Agency".

98. In section 5 of that Act (codes of practice with respect to environmental duties) in subsection (4), in paragraph (a) (which requires consultation with the National Rivers Authority) for the words "the NRA" there shall be substituted the words "the Environment Agency".

99. In section 40 of that Act (bulk supplies of water) in subsection (5) (which requires the Director to consult the National Rivers Authority before making an order) for the words "the NRA" there shall be substituted the words "the Environment Agency".

100. In section 40A of that Act (variation and termination of bulk supply agreements) in subsection (3) (which requires the Director to consult the National Rivers authority before making an order) for the words "the NRA" there shall be substituted the words "the Environment Agency".

101.—(1) In section 71 of that Act (waste from water resources) in subsection (6) (power of court to authorise the National Rivers Authority to take steps to execute an order) for the words "the NRA" there shall be substituted—
  (a) where it first occurs, the words "the Environment Agency"; and
  (b) where it next occurs, the words "the Agency".

(2) In subsection (7) (powers of entry etc of persons designated by the National Rivers Authority) for the words "the NRA" in each place where it occurs there shall be substituted the words "the Environment Agency".

102. After section 93 of that Act (interpretation of Part III) there shall be inserted—

"PART IIIA

PROMOTION OF THE EFFICIENT USE OF WATER

Duty to promote the efficient use of water

93A.—(1) It shall be the duty of every water undertaker to promote the efficient use of water by its customers.

(2) The duty of a water undertaker under this section shall be enforceable under section 18 above—

(a) by the Secretary of State; or

(b) with the consent of or in accordance with a general authorisation given by the Secretary of State, by the Director.

(3) Nothing in this Part shall have effect to authorise or require a water undertaker to impose any requirement on any of its customers or potential customers.

Power of Director to impose requirements on water undertakers

93B.—(1) The Director may require a water undertaker, in its performance of its duty under section 93A above, to—

(a) take any such action; or

(b) achieve any such overall standards of performance,

as he may specify in the document imposing the requirement.

(2) Where the Director, in the document imposing a requirement on a water undertaker under subsection (1) above, stipulates that any contravention of the requirement by the undertaker will be a breach of its duty under section 93A above, any contravention of that requirement by the undertaker shall be a breach of that duty.

(3) Without prejudice to the generality of subsection (1) above, a requirement under that subsection may—

(a) require a water undertaker to make available to its customers or potential customers such facilities as may be specified in the document imposing the requirement;

(b) require a water undertaker to provide or make available to its customers or potential customers such information as may be specified in the document imposing the requirement, and may specify the form in which, the times at which or the frequency with which any such information is to be provided or made available.

(4) In exercising his powers under this section in relation to any water undertaker the Director shall have regard to the extent to which water resources are available to that undertaker.

(5) Before imposing any requirement on a water undertaker under subsection (1) above the Director shall consult that undertaker.

(6) Nothing in this section authorises the Director to impose any requirement on a water undertaker which has or may have the effect of authorising or requiring that undertaker to impose any requirement on any of its customers or potential customers.

Publicity of requirements imposed under section 93B

93C.—(1) Where, under section 93B(1) above, the Director imposes any requirement on a water undertaker, the Director may arrange for that requirement to be publicised in any such manner as he may consider appropriate for the purpose of bringing it to the attention of that undertaker's customers.

(2) Without prejudice to the generality of subsection (1) above, the Director may arrange for such publicising of the requirement as is mentioned in that subsection by—

(a) himself publicising the requirement or causing it to be publicised; or

(b) directing the undertaker to inform or arrange to inform its customers of the requirement.

Information as to compliance with requirements under section 93B

93D.—(1) Where a water undertaker is subject to any requirement imposed under section 93B(1) above, the Director may arrange for there to be given to the customers of that undertaker at any such times or with such frequency, and in any such manner, as he may consider appropriate, such information about the level of performance achieved by the undertaker in relation to that requirement as appears to the Director to be expedient to be given to those customers.

(2) Without prejudice to the generality of subsection (1) above, the Director may arrange for such giving of information as is mentioned in that subsection by—

(a) himself disseminating the information or causing it to be disseminated; or

(b) directing the undertaker to give or arrange to give the information to its customers.

(3) At such times and in such form or manner as the Director may direct, a water undertaker shall provide the Director with such information as may be specified in the direction in connection with the undertaker's performance in relation to any requirement imposed upon the undertaker under section 93B(1) above.

(4) A water undertaker who fails without reasonable excuse to do anything required of him by virtue of subsection (3) above shall be guilty of an offence and liable on summary conviction to a fine not exceeding level 5 on the standard scale.".

103. After section 101 of that Act (which provides for the determination of certain details in relation to requisitioned sewers) there shall be inserted—

"Provision of public sewers otherwise than by requisition

Further duty to provide sewers

101A.—(1) Without prejudice to section 98 above, it shall be the duty of a sewerage undertaker to provide a public sewer to be used for the drainage for domestic sewerage purposes of premises in a particular locality in its area if the conditions specified in subsection (2) below are satisfied.

(2) The conditions mentioned in subsection (1) above are—

(a) that the premises in question, or any of those premises, are premises on which there are buildings each of which, with the exception of any shed, glasshouse or other outbuilding appurtenant to a dwelling and not designed or occupied as living accommodation, is a building erected before, or whose erection was substantially completed by, 20th June 1995;

(b) that the drains or sewers used for the drainage for domestic sewerage purposes of the premises in question do not, either directly or through an intermediate drain or sewer, connect with a public sewer; and

(c) that the drainage of any of the premises in question in respect of which the condition specified in paragraph (a) above is satisfied is giving, or is likely to give, rise to such adverse effects to the environment or amenity that it is appropriate, having regard to any guidance issued under this section by the Secretary of State and all other relevant considerations, to provide a public sewer for the drainage for domestic sewerage purposes of the premises in question.

(3) Without prejudice to the generality of subsection (2)(c) above, regard shall be had to the following considerations, so far as relevant, in determining whether it is appropriate for any sewer to be provided by virtue of this section—

(a) the geology of the locality in question or of any other locality;

(b) the number of premises, being premises on which there are buildings, which might reasonably be expected to be drained by means of that sewer;

(c) the costs of providing that sewer;

(d) the nature and extent of any adverse effects to the environment or amenity arising, or likely to arise, as a result of the premises or, as the case may be, the locality in question not being drained by means of a public sewer; and

(e) the extent to which it is practicable for those effects to be over- come otherwise than by the provision (whether by virtue of this section or otherwise) of public sewers, and the costs of so overcoming those effects.

(4) Guidance issued by the Secretary of State under this section may—

(a) relate to how regard is to be had to the considerations mentioned in paragraphs (a) to (e) of subsection (3) above;

(b) relate to any other matter which the Secretary of State considers may be a relevant consideration in any case and to how regard is to be had to any such matter;

(c) set out considerations, other than those mentioned in paragraphs (a) to (e) of subsection (3) above, to which (so far as relevant) regard shall be had in determining whether it is appropriate for any sewer to be provided by virtue of this section;

(d) relate to how regard is to be had to any such consideration as is mentioned in paragraph (c) above;

(e) without prejudice to paragraphs (a) to (d) above, relate to how a sewerage undertaker is to discharge its functions under this section.

(5) Before issuing guidance under this section the Secretary of State shall consult—

(a) the Environment Agency;

(b) the Director; and

(c) such other bodies or persons as he considers appropriate;

and the Secretary of State shall arrange for any guidance issued by him under this section to be published in such manner as he considers appropriate.

(6) Subject to the following provisions of this section, the duty of a sewerage undertaker by virtue of subsection (1) above shall be enforceable under section 18 above—

(a) by the Secretary of State; or

(b) with the consent of or in accordance with a general authorisation given by the Secretary of State, by the Director.

(7) Any dispute between a sewerage undertaker and an owner or occupier of any premises in its area as to—

(a) whether the undertaker is under a duty by virtue of subsection (1) above to provide a public sewer to be used for any such drainage of those premises as is mentioned in that subsection;

(b) the domestic sewerage purposes for which any such sewer should be provided; or

(c) the time by which any such duty of the undertaker should be performed,

shall be determined by the Environment Agency, and may be referred to the Environment Agency for determination by either of the parties to the dispute.

(8) The Environment Agency—

(a) shall notify the parties of the reasons for its decision on any dispute referred to it under subsection (7) above; and

(b) may make any such recommendations, or give any such guidance, relating to or in connection with the drainage of the premises or locality in question as it considers appropriate.

(9) The decision of the Environment Agency on any dispute referred to it under subsection (7) above shall be final.

(10) A sewerage undertaker shall only be taken to be in breach of its duty under subsection (1) above where, and to the extent that, it has accepted, or the Environment Agency has determined under this section, that it is under such a duty and where any time accepted by it, or determined by the Environment Agency under this section, as the time by which the duty is to that extent to be performed has passed.".

104. In section 110A of that Act (new connections with public sewers) in subsection (6) (which requires the Director to consult the National Rivers Authority before making an order) for the words "the NRA" there shall be substituted the words "the Environment Agency".

105.—(1) Section 120 of that Act (application for the discharge of special category effluent) shall be amended in accordance with the following provisions of this paragraph.

(2) In subsection (1) (sewerage undertakers to refer certain questions to the Secretary of State) for the words "the Secretary of State" there shall be substituted the words "the Environment Agency".

(3) In subsection (4) (undertaker not to give consent etc until Secretary of State gives notice of his determination of the questions) for the words "the Secretary of State" there shall be substituted the words "the Environment Agency".

(4) For subsections (7) and (8) (enforcement by Secretary of State) there shall be substituted—

"(9) If a sewerage undertaker fails, within the period provided by subsection (2) above, to refer to the Environment Agency any question which he is required by subsection (1) above to refer to the Agency, the undertaker shall be guilty of an offence and liable—

(a) on summary conviction, to a fine not exceeding the statutory maximum;

(b) on conviction on indictment, to a fine.

(10) If the Environment Agency becomes aware of any such failure as is mentioned in subsection (9) above, the Agency may—

(a) if a consent under this Chapter to make discharges of any special category effluent has been granted on the application in question, exercise its powers of review under section 127 or 131 below, notwithstanding anything in subsection (2) of the section in question; or

(b) in any other case, proceed as if the reference required by this section had been made."

106. In section 123 of that Act (appeals with respect to the discharge of special category effluent) for the words "the Secretary of State" or "the Secretary of State's", wherever

occurring, there shall be substituted respectively the words "the Environment Agency" or "the Environment Agency's".

107. In section 127 of that Act (review by the Secretary of State of consents relating to special category effluent) for the words "the Secretary of State" or "the Secretary of State's", wherever occurring, there shall be substituted respectively the words "the Environment Agency" or "the Environment Agency's".

108.—(1) Section 130 of that Act (reference to the Secretary of State of agreements relating to special category effluent) shall be amended in accordance with the following provisions of this paragraph.

(2) For the words "the Secretary of State", wherever occurring, there shall be substituted the words "the Environment Agency".

(3) For subsections (5) and (6) (enforcement by Secretary of State) there shall be substituted—

"(7) If a sewerage undertaker fails, before giving any consent or entering into any agreement with respect to any such operations as are mentioned in paragraph (a) of subsection (1) above, to refer to the Environment Agency any question which he is required by that subsection to refer to the Agency, the undertaker shall be guilty of an offence and liable—
(a) on summary conviction, to a fine not exceeding the statutory maximum;
(b) on conviction on indictment, to a fine.
(8) If the Environment Agency becomes aware—
(a) that a sewerage undertaker and the owner or occupier of any trade premises are proposing to enter into any such agreement as is mentioned in subsection (1) above, and
(b) that the sewerage undertaker has not referred to the Agency any question which it is required to refer to the Agency by that subsection,
the Agency may proceed as if the reference required by that subsection had been made.
(9) If the Environment Agency becomes aware that any consent has been given or agreement entered into with respect to any such operations as are mentioned in paragraph (a) of subsection (1) above without the sewerage undertaker in question having referred to the Environment Agency any question which he is required by that subsection to refer to the Agency, the Agency may exercise its powers of review under section 127 above or, as the case may be, section 131 below, notwithstanding anything in subsection (2) of the section in question."

109. In section 131 of that Act (review by the Secretary of State of agreements relating to special category effluent) for the words "the Secretary of State" or "the Secretary of State's", wherever occurring, there shall be substituted respectively the words "the Environment Agency" or "the Environment Agency's".

110.—(1) Section 132 of that Act (powers and procedure on references and reviews) shall be amended in accordance with the following provisions of this paragraph.

(2) For the words "the Secretary of State", wherever occurring, there shall be substituted the words "the Environment Agency".

(3) In subsection (2)(b) of that section (duty of the Secretary of State to consider representations or objections duly made to him) for the words "him" and "he" there shall be substituted the words "the Agency".

(4) In subsection (6) of that section (section 121(1) and (2) not to restrict power to impose conditions under subsection (4)(b)) for the word "he" there shall be substituted the words "the Agency".

(5) Subsection (7) (powers of entry) shall cease to have effect.

111. In section 133 of that Act (effect of determination on reference or review) for subsection (4) (duties of sewerage undertaker to be enforceable under section 18 by the Secretary of State) there shall be substituted—

"(5) A sewerage undertaker which fails to perform its duty under subsection (1) above shall be guilty of an offence and liable—
(a) on summary conviction, to a fine not exceeding the statutory maximum;
(b) on conviction on indictment, to a fine.
(6) The Environment Agency may, for the purpose of securing compliance with the provisions of a notice under section 132 above, by serving notice on the sewerage undertaker in question and on the person specified in section 132(2)(a)(ii) above, vary or revoke—

(a) any consent given under this Chapter to make discharges of any special category effluent, or

(b) any agreement under section 129 above."

112. In section 134 of that Act (compensation in respect of determinations made for the protection of public health etc.)—

(a) for the words "the Secretary of State" or "the Secretary of State's", wherever occurring, there shall be substituted respectively the words "the Environment Agency" or "the Environment Agency's"; and

(b) in subsection (2)(b) for the word "him" there shall be substituted the words "the Agency".

113. After section 135 there shall be inserted—

"Power of the Environment Agency to acquire information for the purpose of its functions in relation to special category effluent

135A.—(1) For the purpose of the discharge of its functions under this Chapter, the Environment Agency may, by notice in writing served on any person, require that person to furnish such information specified in the notice as that Agency reasonably considers it needs, in such form and within such period following service of the notice, or at such time, as is so specified.

(2) A person who—

(a) fails, without reasonable excuse, to comply with a requirement imposed under subsection (1) above, or

(b) in furnishing any information in compliance with such a requirement, makes any statement which he knows to be false or misleading in a material particular, or recklessly makes a statement which is false or misleading in a material particular,

shall be guilty of an offence.

(3) A person guilty of an offence under subsection (2) above shall be liable—

(a) on summary conviction, to a fine not exceeding the statutory maximum;

(b) on conviction on indictment, to a fine or to imprisonment for a term not exceeding two years, or to both."

114.—(1) Section 142 of that Act (powers of undertakers to charge) shall be amended in accordance with the following provisions of this paragraph.

(2) In subsection (2) (manner in which charging powers to be exercised) for the words "subsection (3)" there shall be substituted the words "subsections (3) and (3A)".

(3) After subsection (3) (restriction on charging by agreement for trade effluent functions) there shall be inserted—

"(3A) The power of a sewerage undertaker to charge, by virtue of subsection (1) above, for any services provided in the course of carrying out its duty under section 101A(1) above shall be exercisable only by or in accordance with a charges scheme under section 143 below."

115. In section 143 of that Act (charges schemes) after subsection (3) (charges which may be imposed in certain cases) there shall be inserted—

"(3A) A sewerage undertaker is under a duty to ensure that any charges scheme made by the undertaker, so far as having effect to recover the undertaker's costs of providing a sewer by virtue of its duty under section 101A(1) above, causes those costs to be borne by the undertaker's customers generally; and a sewerage undertaker's duty under this subsection shall be enforceable under section 18 above—

(a) by the Secretary of State; or

(b) with the consent of or in accordance with a general authorisation given by the Secretary of State, by the Director."

116. Section 151 of that Act shall cease to have effect.

117. In section 161 of that Act (power to deal with foul water and pollution) in subsections (3) and (4) for the words "the NRA", wherever occurring, there shall be substituted the words "the Environment Agency".

118. In section 166 of that Act (consents for certain discharges under section 165) in subsection (1) (which requires the consent of the National Rivers Authority to certain discharges) for the words "the NRA" there shall be substituted the words "the Environment Agency".

119. In section 184 of that Act (power of certain undertakers to alter public sewers etc) in subsection (1) for the words "NRA", in each place where it occurs there shall be substituted the words "Environment Agency".

120. In section 202 of that Act (duties of undertakers to furnish the Secretary of State with information) in subsection (6) (which defines the expression "the other consolidation Acts") for the words "the NRA" there shall be substituted the words "the Environment Agency".

121.—(1) In section 206 of that Act (restriction on disclosure of information) in subsection (2) (information furnished under section 196 or 204) the words "196 or" shall cease to have effect.

(2) In subsection (3)(a) of that section (exception for disclosure of information for purposes of functions under certain enactments)—

(a) for the words "the NRA" there shall be substituted the words "the Environment Agency, the Scottish Environment Protection Agency"; and

(b) for the words "or the Water Act 1989" there shall be substituted the words ", the Water Act 1989, Part I or IIA of the Environmental Protection Act 1990 or the Environment Act 1995".

(3) In subsection (4), in paragraph (a) (which provides that nothing in subsection (1) shall limit the matters which may be included in reports made by specified bodies under specified enactments)—

(a) for the words "the NRA" there shall be substituted the words "the Environment Agency, the Scottish Environment Protection Agency"; and

(b) for the words "or of the Water Resources Act 1991" there shall be substituted the words ", Part I or IIA of the Environmental Protection Act 1990, the Water Resources Act 1991 or the Environment Act 1995".

122. In section 209 of that Act (civil liability of undertakers for escapes of water etc.) in subsection (3) (exceptions for loss sustained by other public undertakers) for the words "the NRA" there shall be substituted the words "the Environment Agency".

123. In section 215 of that Act (local inquiries) in subsection (3) (application of section 250(4) of the Local Government Act 1972 in relation to the National Rivers Authority) for the words "the NRA", in each place where they occur, there shall be substituted the words "the Environment Agency".

124. In section 217 of that Act (construction of provisions conferring powers by reference to undertakers' functions) for the words "NRA", wherever occurring, there shall be substituted the words "Environment Agency".

125. In section 219 of that Act (general interpretation) in subsection (1)—

(a) the definition of "the NRA" shall be omitted; and

(b) subject to that, for the words "the NRA", wherever occurring, there shall be substituted the words "the Environment Agency".

126. In Schedule 11 to that Act (orders conferring compulsory works powers) in paragraph 1(3) (persons on whom copy notices are to be served) in paragraph (a), for the words "the NRA" there shall be substituted the words "the Environment Agency".

127. In Schedule 13 to that Act (protective provisions in respect of certain undertakers) in paragraph 1, in sub-paragraphs (2) and (5)(a), for the words "the NRA", wherever occurring, there shall be substituted the words "the Environment Agency".

The Water Resources Act 1991

128. Subject to the other provisions of this Act, in the Water Resources Act 1991, for the word "Authority" or "Authority's", wherever occurring, other than in section 119(1), there shall be substituted respectively the word "Agency" or "Agency's".

129. Sections 1 to 14 of that Act (the National Rivers Authority and committees with functions in relation to that Authority) shall cease to have effect.

130. In section 15 of that Act (general duties with respect to the water industry), in subsection (2)(a) (provisions conferring powers in the exercise of which the Ministers are to take into account the duties imposed on the Agency by subsection (1)) after the words "by virtue of" there shall be inserted the words "the 1995 Act,".

131. Sections 16 to 19 of that Act (which relate to the environmental and recreational duties of the National Rivers Authority and the general management of resources by that Authority) shall cease to have effect.

132. In section 20 of that Act (water resources management schemes) in subsection (1) of that section (duty to enter into arrangements with water undertakers for the management or operation of certain waters etc.) for the words "section 19(1) above" there shall be substituted the words "section 6(2) of the 1995 Act".

133.—(1) In section 21 of that Act (minimum acceptable flows) in subsection (3), at the end of paragraph (f) (consultation with person authorised by a licence under Part I of the Electricity Act 1989 to generate electricity) there shall be added the words "who has a right to abstract water from those waters".

(2) In subsection (4)(b) of that section (which refers to certain enactments which are repealed, but whose effect is reproduced, by this Act) for the words "sections 2(2), 16 and 17 above" there shall be substituted the words "sections 6(1), 7 and 8 of the 1995 Act".

134. In section 43 of that Act (appeals to the Secretary of State from decisions with respect to licences) after subsection (1) there shall be inserted—

"(1A) This section is subject to section 114 of the 1995 Act (delegation or reference of appeals etc)."

135.—(1) In section 50 of that Act, in subsection (1) (power to make regulations, in relation to cases to which section 49 applies, for conferring succession rights to abstraction licences where a person becomes the occupier of part of the relevant land) for the words "cases to which section 49 above applies" there shall be substituted the words "cases in which the holder of a licence under this Chapter to abstract water ("the prior holder") is the occupier of the whole or part of the land specified in the licence as the land on which water abstracted in pursuance of the licence is to be used ("the relevant land")".

(2) That section shall have effect, and be taken always to have had effect, as if it had originally been enacted with the amendment made by sub-paragraph (1) above.

136. Section 58 (revocation of licence for non-payment of charges) shall cease to have effect.

137. Section 68 of that Act (power by order to establish a tribunal to which certain appeals and references shall lie) shall cease to have effect.

138. Section 69(5) of that Act (which refers to the tribunal established under section 68) shall cease to have effect.

139.—(1) Section 73 of that Act (power to make ordinary and emergency drought orders) shall be amended in accordance with the following provisions of this paragraph.

(2) In subsection (1) (power to make ordinary drought orders) for the words from the beginning to "then" there shall be substituted the words—

"(1) If the Secretary of State is satisfied that, by reason of an exceptional shortage of rain, there exists or is threatened—
  (a) a serious deficiency of supplies of water in any area, or
  (b) such a deficiency in the flow or level of water in any inland waters as to pose a serious threat to any of the flora or fauna which are dependent on those waters,
then,".

(3) In subsection (3) (power to make drought order not to be exercisable except where an application is made by the National Rivers Authority or a water undertaker)—
  (a) for the words "except where" there shall be substituted the word "unless"; and
  (b) at the beginning of paragraph (b) (water undertakers) there shall be inserted the words "except in the case of an ordinary drought order by virtue of subsection (1)(b) above,".

140. After section 79 of that Act (compensation and charges where drought order made) there shall be inserted—

"Drought permits
79A.—(1) If the Agency is satisfied that, by reason of an exceptional shortage of rain, a serious deficiency of supplies of water in any area exists or is threatened then, subject to the following provisions of this section, it may, upon the application of a water undertaker which supplies water to premises in that area, issue to that undertaker a drought permit making such provision authorised by this section as appears to the Agency to be expedient with a view to meeting the deficiency.

(2) A drought permit may contain any of the following provisions, that is to say—
  (a) provision authorising the water undertaker to which it is issued to take water from any source specified in the permit subject to any conditions or restrictions so specified;
  (b) provision suspending or modifying, subject to any conditions specified in the permit, any restriction or obligation to which that undertaker is subject as respects the taking of water from any source.

(3) A drought permit shall specify—
  (a) the day on which it comes into force; and
  (b) the period for which, subject to subsections (4) and (5) below, any authorisation given, or suspension or modification effected, by the permit is to have effect.

(4) Subject to subsection (5) below, the period for which—

(a) an authorisation given by a drought permit, or

(b) a suspension or modification effected by such a permit,

has effect shall expire before the end of the period of six months beginning with the day on which the permit comes into force.

(5) At any time before the expiration of the period for which such an authorisation, suspension or modification has effect the Agency may, by giving notice to the water undertaker to which the permit in question was issued, extend that period, but not so as to extend it beyond the end of the period of one year beginning with the day on which the permit came into force.

(6) A drought permit which—

(a) authorises the taking of water from a source from which water is supplied to an inland navigation; or

(b) suspends or modifies—

    (i) a restriction as respects the taking of water from a source from which water is supplied to an inland navigation; or

    (ii) an obligation to discharge compensation water into a canal or into any river or stream which forms part of, or from which water is supplied to, an inland navigation,

shall not be issued without the consent of every navigation authority exercising functions over any or all of the parts of the canal or inland navigation in question which are affected by the permit.

(7) Schedule 8 to this Act shall have effect with respect to the procedure on an application for a drought permit as it has effect with respect to the procedure on an application for a drought order, but with the following modifications, that is to say—

(a) with the substitution for any reference to a drought order of a reference to a drought permit;

(b) with the substitution for any reference to the Secretary of State of a reference to the Agency;

(c) with the omission of the reference to the Agency in the Table in paragraph 1;

(d) with the insertion, in paragraph 1(3)(c), of a requirement that the notice in question shall specify the address at which any objections are to be made to the Agency; and

(e) with the omission—

    (i) of paragraph 2(1)(a) and the word "either" immediately preceding it, and

    (ii) of paragraph 2(6).

(8) For the purposes of sections 125 to 129 below any water authorised by a drought permit to be abstracted from a source of supply shall be treated as if it had been authorised to be so abstracted by a licence granted under Chapter II of this Part, whether the water undertaker to which the permit is issued is the holder of such a licence or not.

(9) Section 79 above and Schedule 9 to this Act shall apply in relation to drought permits and their issue as they apply in relation to ordinary drought orders and their making.

(10) A drought permit may—

(a) make different provision for different cases, including different provision in relation to different persons, circumstances or localities; and

(b) contain such supplemental, consequential and transitional provisions as the Agency considers appropriate.

(11) In this section—

"compensation water" has the same meaning as in section 77 above;

"drought permit" means a drought permit under this section;

"inland navigation" has the same meaning as in section 77 above."

141. In section 80 of that Act (offences against drought orders)—

(a) in subsection (1)(a) (taking or using water otherwise than in accordance with any condition or restriction imposed by or under a drought order) for the words "so imposed" there shall be substituted the words "imposed by or under any drought order or by any drought permit";

(b) in subsection (2)(a) (failure to construct or maintain measuring apparatus required by any drought order) after the words "by any drought order" there shall be inserted the words "or drought permit"; and

(c) in subsection (2)(b) (failure to allow person authorised by or under any such order to inspect etc. apparatus or records) after the words "by or under any such order" there shall be inserted the words "or by virtue of any such permit".

142. After section 90 of that Act (offences in connection with deposits and vegetation in rivers) there shall be inserted—

"Consents for the purposes of sections 88 to 90

Applications for consent under section 89 or 90

90A.—(1) Any application for a consent for the purposes of section 89(4)(a) or 90(1) or (2) above—

(a) must be made on a form provided for the purpose by the Agency, and

(b) must be advertised in such manner as may be required by regulations made by the Secretary of State,

except that paragraph (b) above shall not have effect in the case of an application of any class or description specified in the regulations as being exempt from the requirements of that paragraph.

(2) The applicant for such a consent must, at the time when he makes his application, provide the Agency—

(a) with all such information as it reasonably requires; and

(b) with all such information as may be prescribed for the purpose by the Secretary of State.

(3) The information required by subsection (2) above must be provided either on, or together with, the form mentioned in subsection (1) above.

(4) The Agency may give the applicant notice requiring him to provide it with all such further information of any description specified in the notice as it may require for the purpose of determining the application.

(5) If the applicant fails to provide the Agency with any information required under subsection (4) above, the Agency may refuse to proceed with the application or refuse to proceed with it until the information is provided.

Enforcement notices

90B.—(1) If the Agency is of the opinion that the holder of a relevant consent is contravening any condition of the consent, or is likely to contravene any such condition, the Agency may serve on him a notice (an "enforcement notice").

(2) An enforcement notice shall—

(a) state that the Agency is of the said opinion;

(b) specify the matters constituting the contravention or the matters making it likely that the contravention will arise;

(c) specify the steps that must be taken to remedy the contravention or, as the case may be, to remedy the matters making it likely that the contravention will arise; and

(d) specify the period within which those steps must be taken.

(3) Any person who fails to comply with any requirement imposed by an enforcement notice shall be guilty of an offence and liable—

(a) on summary conviction, to imprisonment for a term not exceeding three months or to a fine not exceeding £20,000 or to both;

(b) on conviction on indictment, to imprisonment for a term not exceeding two years or to a fine or to both.

(4) If the Agency is of the opinion that proceedings for an offence under subsection (3) above would afford an ineffectual remedy against a person who has failed to comply with the requirements of an enforcement notice, the Agency may take proceedings in the High Court for the purpose of securing compliance with the notice.

(5) The Secretary of State may, if he thinks fit in relation to any person, give to the Agency directions as to whether the Agency should exercise its powers under this section and as to the steps which must be taken.

(6) In this section—

"relevant consent" means—

(a) a consent for the purposes of section 89(4)(a) or 90(1) or (2) above; or

(b) a discharge consent, within the meaning of section 91 below; and

"the holder", in relation to a relevant consent, is the person who has the consent in question."

143.—(1) In section 91 of that Act (appeals in respect of consents under Chapter II of Part III of that Act), in subsection (1) (which specifies the decisions which are subject to appeal)—

(a) in paragraph (d) (which refers to paragraph 7(1) or (2) of Schedule 10) for the words "7(1)" there shall be substituted the words "8(1)"; and

(b) at the end there shall be added—

"(g) has refused a person a variation of any such consent as is mentioned in paragraphs (a) to (f) above or, in allowing any such variation, has made the consent subject to conditions; or

(h) has served an enforcement notice on any person."

(2) In subsection (2) of that section (persons who may appeal)—
  (a) after the words "who applied for the consent" there shall be inserted the words "or variation"; and
  (b) after the words "would be authorised by the consent" there shall be inserted the words ", or the person on whom the enforcement notice was served,".
(3) For subsections (3) to (7) of that section there shall be substituted—

"(2A) This section is subject to section 114 of the 1995 Act (delegation or reference of appeals etc.).

(2B) An appeal under this section shall, if and to the extent required by regulations under subsection (2K) below, be advertised in such manner as may be prescribed by regulations under that subsection.

(2C) If either party to the appeal so requests or the Secretary of State so decides, an appeal shall be or continue in the form of a hearing (which may, if the person hearing the appeal so decides, be held, or held to any extent, in private).

(2D) On determining an appeal brought by virtue of any of paragraphs (a) to (g) of subsection (1) above against a decision of the Agency, the Secretary of State—
  (a) may affirm the decision;
  (b) where the decision was a refusal to grant a consent or a variation of a consent, may direct the Agency to grant the consent or to vary the consent, as the case may be;
  (c) where the decision was as to the conditions of a consent, may quash all or any of those conditions;
  (d) where the decision was to revoke a consent, may quash the decision;
  (e) where the decision relates to a period specified for the purposes of paragraph 8(1) or (2) of Schedule 10 to this Act, may modify any provisions specifying that period;
and where he exercises any of the powers in paragraphs (b), (c) or (d) above, he may give directions as to the conditions to which the consent is to be subject.

(2E) On the determination of an appeal brought by virtue of paragraph (h) of subsection (1) above, the Secretary of State may either quash or affirm the enforcement notice and, if he affirms it, may do so either in its original form or with such modifications as he may in the circumstances think fit.

(2F) Subject to subsection (2G) below, where an appeal is brought by virtue of subsection (1)(c) above against a decision—
  (a) to revoke a discharge consent,
  (b) to modify the conditions of any such consent, or
  (c) to provide that any such consent which was unconditional shall be subject to conditions,
the revocation, modification or provision shall not take effect pending the final determination or the withdrawal of the appeal.

(2G) Subsection (2F) above shall not apply to a decision in the case of which the notice effecting the revocation, modification or provision in question includes a statement that in the opinion of the Agency it is necessary for the purpose of preventing or, where that is not practicable, minimising—
  (a) the entry into controlled waters of any poisonous, noxious or polluting matter or any solid waste matter, or
  (b) harm to human health,
that that subsection should not apply.

(2H) Where the decision under appeal is one falling within subsection (2G) above, if, on the application of the holder or former holder of the consent, the Secretary of State or other person determining the appeal determines that the Agency acted unreasonably in excluding the application of subsection (2F) above, then—
  (a) if the appeal is still pending at the end of the day on which the determination is made, subsection (2F) above shall apply to the decision from the end of that day; and
  (b) the holder or former holder of the consent shall be entitled to recover compensation from the Agency in respect of any loss suffered by him in consequence of the exclusion of the application of that subsection;
and any dispute as to a person's entitlement to such compensation or as to the amount of it shall be determined by arbitration.

(2J) Where an appeal is brought under this section against an enforcement notice, the bringing of the appeal shall not have the effect of suspending the operation of the notice.

(2K) Provision may be made by the Secretary of State by regulations with respect to appeals under this section and in particular—

(a) as to the period within which and the manner in which appeals are to be brought; and

(b) as to the manner in which appeals are to be considered."

(4) In subsection (8) of that section (which refers to paragraph 5 of Schedule 10) for the word "5" there shall be substituted the word "6".

144. In section 92 of that Act (requirements to take precautions against pollution) after subsection (2) (which includes provision for regulations to provide for appeals to the Secretary of State) there shall be added—

"(3) This section is subject to section 114 of the 1995 Act (delegation or reference of appeals etc)."

145. In section 96 of that Act (regulations with respect to consents required by virtue of section 93 etc, including provision with respect to appeals) after subsection (3) there shall be added—

"(4) This section is subject to section 114 of the 1995 Act (delegation or reference of appeals etc)."

146. Section 105(1) of that Act (National Rivers Authority to exercise general supervision over matters relating to flood defence) shall cease to have effect.

147.—(1) In section 110 of that Act (applications for consents and approvals under section 109) in subsection (1) (which confers power to charge an application fee of £50 or such other sum as may be specified by order made by the Ministers) for the words "specified by order made by the Ministers" there shall be substituted the word "prescribed".

(2) In subsection (4)(b) of that section (which provides for questions as to unreasonable withholding of any consent or approval to be referred to the Ministers or the Secretary of State if the parties cannot agree on an arbitrator) for the words "the Ministers" there shall be substituted the words "the Minister".

(3) After subsection (5) of that section there shall be inserted—

"(6) In subsection (1) above "prescribed" means specified in, or determined in accordance with, an order made by the Ministers; and any such order may make different provision for different cases, including different provision in relation to different persons, circumstances or localities."

148. Section 114 (general fisheries duty of the National Rivers Authority) shall cease to have effect.

149. Section 117 (general financial duties of the National Rivers Authority) shall cease to have effect.

150.—(1) Section 118 of that Act (special duties with respect to flood defence revenue) shall be amended in accordance with the following provisions of this paragraph.

(2) In subsection (1)(b) (such revenue to be disregarded in determining the amount of any surplus for the purposes of section 117(3)) for the words "section 117(3) above" there shall be substituted the words "section 44(4) of the 1995 Act".

(3) In subsection (2)(b) (flood defence revenue to include revenue raised by general drainage charges under sections 134 to 136) for the words "to 136" there shall be substituted the words "and 135".

151.—(1) In section 119 of that Act (duties with respect to certain funds raised under local enactments) for subsection (1) (duty of the National Rivers Authority, in respect of funds created for fishery purposes under local enactments, not to use those funds except for the purposes for which they could have been used if the Water Resources Act 1963 had not been passed) there shall be substituted—

"(1) Where the Agency holds any funds, or any interest in any funds, which immediately before the transfer date the National Rivers Authority, by virtue of this subsection as originally enacted, was not permitted to use except for particular purposes, those funds or that interest shall not be used except for the purposes for which they could be used by virtue of this subsection as originally enacted.

(1A) For the purposes of subsection (1) above, "the transfer date" has the same meaning as in Part I of the 1995 Act."

(2) In subsection (2) of that section (certain funds raised under local enactments to be disregarded in determining the amount of any surplus for the purposes of section 117(3)) for the words "section 117(3) above" there shall be substituted the words "section 44(3) of the 1995 Act".

152. Sections 121 to 124 of that Act (accounts of the Authority, audit and schemes imposing water resources charges) shall cease to have effect.

153. Sections 126(6) and 129(4) of that Act (each of which applies section 68) shall cease to have effect.

154. Sections 131 and 132 of that Act (schemes of charges in connection with control of pollution) shall cease to have effect.

155. Section 146 of that Act (revenue grants by the Secretary of State to the National Rivers Authority) shall cease to have effect.

156. Sections 150 to 153 of that Act (grants for national security purposes, borrowing powers of the National Rivers Authority, loans to the Authority, and Treasury guarantees of the Authority's borrowing) shall cease to have effect.

157. In section 154 of that Act (compulsory purchase etc.) in subsection (6), for the words "(including section 4 above) or otherwise" there shall be substituted the words "or otherwise (including section 37 of the 1995 Act (incidental general powers of the Agency))".

158. In section 156 of that Act (acquisition of land etc for fisheries purposes) for the words "Without prejudice to section 4 above", in each place where they occur, there shall be substituted the words "Without prejudice to section 37 of the 1995 Act (incidental general powers of the Agency)".

159. In section 157 of that Act (restriction on disposals of compulsorily acquired land) for subsection (6) (meaning of "compulsorily acquired land") there shall be substituted—

"(6) In this section "compulsorily acquired land", in relation to the Agency, means any land of the Agency which—
 (a) was acquired by the Agency compulsorily under the provisions of section 154 above or of an order under section 168 below;
 (b) was acquired by the Agency at a time when it was authorised under those provisions to acquire the land compulsorily;
 (c) being land which has been transferred to the Agency from the Authority by section 3 of the 1995 Act, was acquired by the Authority—
   (i) compulsorily, under the provisions of section 154 above or of an order under section 168 below or under the provisions of section 151 of the Water Act 1989 or of an order under section 155 of that Act; or
   (ii) at a time when it was authorised under those provisions to acquire the land compulsorily;
 (d) being land—
   (i) which has been so transferred, and
   (ii) which was transferred to the Authority in accordance with a scheme under Schedule 2 to the Water Act 1989,
   was acquired by a predecessor of the Authority compulsorily under so much of any enactment in force at any time before 1st September 1989 as conferred powers of compulsory acquisition; or
 (e) being land transferred as mentioned in sub-paragraphs (i) and (ii) of paragraph (d) above, was acquired by such a predecessor at a time when it was authorised to acquire the land by virtue of any such powers as are mentioned in that paragraph."

160. In section 158 of that Act (works agreements for water resources purposes) in subsection (1) (which is expressed to be without prejudice to the generality of the powers conferred by section 4) for the words "section 4 above" there shall be substituted the words "section 37 of the 1995 Act (incidental general powers of the Agency)".

161.—(1) Section 161 of that Act (anti-pollution works and operations) shall be amended in accordance with the following provisions of this paragraph.

(2) In subsection (1) (power, subject to subsection (2), to carry out works and operations etc.) for the words "Subject to subsection (2) below," there shall be substituted the words "Subject to subsections (1A) and (2) below,".

(3) After that subsection there shall be inserted—

"(1A) Without prejudice to the power of the Agency to carry out investigations under subsection (1) above, the power conferred by that subsection to carry out works and operations shall only be exercisable in a case where—
 (a) the Agency considers it necessary to carry out forthwith any works or operations falling within paragraph (a) or (b) of that subsection; or
 (b) it appears to the Agency, after reasonable inquiry, that no person can be found on whom to serve a works notice under section 161A below."

162. After that section there shall be inserted—

"Notices requiring persons to carry out anti-pollution works and operations

161A.—(1) Subject to the following provisions of this section, where it appears to the Agency that any poisonous, noxious or polluting matter or any solid waste matter is likely to enter, or to be or to have been present in, any controlled waters, the Agency shall be entitled to serve a works notice on any person who, as the case may be,—

(a) caused or knowingly permitted the matter in question to be present at the place from which it is likely, in the opinion of the Agency, to enter any controlled waters; or

(b) caused or knowingly permitted the matter in question to be present in any controlled waters.

(2) For the purposes of this section, a "works notice" is a notice requiring the person on whom it is served to carry out such of the following works or operations as may be specified in the notice, that is to say—

(a) in a case where the matter in question appears likely to enter any controlled waters, works or operations for the purpose of preventing it from doing so; or

(b) in a case where the matter appears to be or to have been present in any controlled waters, works or operations for the purpose—

(i) of removing or disposing of the matter;

(ii) of remedying or mitigating any pollution caused by its presence in the waters; or

(iii) so far as it is reasonably practicable to do so, of restoring the waters, including any flora and fauna dependent on the aquatic environment of the waters, to their state immediately before the matter became present in the waters.

(3) A works notice—

(a) must specify the periods within which the person on whom it is served is required to do each of the things specified in the notice; and

(b) is without prejudice to the powers of the Agency by virtue of section 161(1A)(a) above.

(4) Before serving a works notice on any person, the Agency shall reasonably endeavour to consult that person concerning the works or operations which are to be specified in the notice.

(5) The Secretary of State may by regulations make provision for or in connection with—

(a) the form or content of works notices;

(b) requirements for consultation, before the service of a works notice, with persons other than the person on whom that notice is to be served;

(c) steps to be taken for the purposes of any consultation required under subsection (4) above or regulations made by virtue of paragraph (b) above; or

(d) any other steps of a procedural nature which are to be taken in connection with, or in consequence of, the service of a works notice.

(6) A works notice shall not be regarded as invalid, or as invalidly served, by reason only of any failure to comply with the requirements of subsection (4) above or of regulations made by virtue of paragraph (b) of subsection (5) above.

(7) Nothing in subsection (1) above shall entitle the Agency to require the carrying out of any works or operations which would impede or prevent the making of any discharge in pursuance of a consent given under Chapter II of Part III of this Act.

(8) No works notice shall be served on any person requiring him to carry out any works or operations in respect of water from an abandoned mine or an abandoned part of a mine which that person permitted to reach such a place as is mentioned in subsection (1)(a) above or to enter any controlled waters.

(9) Subsection (8) above shall not apply to the owner or former operator of any mine or part of a mine if the mine or part in question became abandoned after 31st December 1999.

(10) Subsections (3B) and (3C) of section 89 above shall apply in relation to subsections (8) and (9) above as they apply in relation to subsections (3) and (3A) of that section.

(11) Where the Agency—

(a) carries out any such investigations as are mentioned in section 161(1) above, and

(b) serves a works notice on a person in connection with the matter to which the investigations relate,

it shall (unless the notice is quashed or withdrawn) be entitled to recover the costs or expenses reasonably incurred in carrying out those investigations from that person.

(12) The Secretary of State may, if he thinks fit in relation to any person, give directions to the Agency as to whether or how it should exercise its powers under this section.

(13) In this section—

"controlled waters" has the same meaning as in Part III of this Act;

"mine" has the same meaning as in the Mines and Quarries Act 1954.

Grant of, and compensation for, rights of entry etc.

161B.—(1) A works notice may require a person to carry out works or operations in relation to any land or waters notwithstanding that he is not entitled to carry out those works or operations.

(2) Any person whose consent is required before any works or operations required by a works notice may be carried out shall grant, or join in granting, such rights in relation to any land or waters as will enable the person on whom the works notice is served to comply with any requirements imposed by the works notice.

(3) Before serving a works notice, the Agency shall reasonably endeavour to consult every person who appears to it—

(a) to be the owner or occupier of any relevant land, and

(b) to be a person who might be required by subsection (2) above to grant, or join in granting, any rights,

concerning the rights which that person may be so required to grant.

(4) A works notice shall not be regarded as invalid, or as invalidly served, by reason only of any failure to comply with the requirements of subsection (3) above.

(5) A person who grants, or joins in granting, any rights pursuant to subsection (2) above shall be entitled, on making an application within such period as may be prescribed and in such manner as may be prescribed to such person as may be prescribed, to be paid by the person on whom the works notice in question is served compensation of such amount as may be determined in such manner as may be prescribed.

(6) Without prejudice to the generality of the regulations that may be made by virtue of subsection (5) above, regulations by virtue of that subsection may make such provision in relation to compensation under this section as may be made by regulations by virtue of subsection (4) of section 35A of the Environmental Protection Act 1990 in relation to compensation under that section.

(7) In this section—

"prescribed" means prescribed in regulations made by the Secretary of State;

"relevant land" means—

(a) any land or waters in relation to which the works notice in question requires, or may require, works or operations to be carried out; or

(b) any land adjoining or adjacent to that land or those waters;

"works notice" means a works notice under section 161A above.

Appeals against works notices

161C.—(1) A person on whom a works notice is served may, within the period of twenty-one days beginning with the day on which the notice is served, appeal against the notice to the Secretary of State.

(2) On any appeal under this section the Secretary of State—

(a) shall quash the notice, if he is satisfied that there is a material defect in the notice; but

(b) subject to that, may confirm the notice, with or without modification, or quash it.

(3) The Secretary of State may by regulations make provision with respect to—

(a) the grounds on which appeals under this section may be made; or

(b) the procedure on any such appeal.

(4) Regulations under subsection (3) above may (among other things)—

(a) include provisions comparable to those in section 290 of the Public Health Act 1936 (appeals against notices requiring the execution of works);

(b) prescribe the cases in which a works notice is, or is not to be suspended until the appeal is decided, or until some other stage in the proceedings;

(c) prescribe the cases in which the decision on an appeal may in some respects be less favourable to the appellant than the works notice against which he is appealing;

(d) prescribe the cases in which the appellant may claim that a works notice should have been served on some other person and prescribe the procedure to be followed in those cases;

(e) make provision as respects—

(i) the particulars to be included in the notice of appeal;

(ii) the persons on whom notice of appeal is to be served and the particulars, if any, which are to accompany the notice; or

(iii) the abandonment of an appeal.

(5) In this section "works notice" means a works notice under section 161A above.

(6) This section is subject to section 114 of the 1995 Act (delegation or reference of appeals).

Consequences of not complying with a works notice

161D.—(1) If a person on whom the Agency serves a works notice fails to comply with any of the requirements of the notice, he shall be guilty of an offence.

(2) A person who commits an offence under subsection (1) above shall be liable—

(a) on summary conviction, to imprisonment for a term not exceeding three months or to a fine not exceeding £20,000 or to both;

(b) on conviction on indictment to imprisonment for a term not exceeding two years or to a fine or to both.

(3) If a person on whom a works notice has been served fails to comply with any of the requirements of the notice, the Agency may do what that person was required to do and may recover from him any costs or expenses reasonably incurred by the Agency in doing it.

(4) If the Agency is of the opinion that proceedings for an offence under subsection (1) above would afford an ineffectual remedy against a person who has failed to comply with the requirements of a works notice, the Agency may take proceedings in the High Court for the purpose of securing compliance with the notice.

(5) In this section "works notice" means a works notice under section 161A above."

163. In section 162 of that Act (other powers to deal with foul water or pollution) in subsection (1) (which refers to section 161 of that Act) for the words "section 161" there shall be substituted the words "sections 161 to 161D".

164. In section 166 of that Act (power to carry out works for purposes of flood warning system) in subsection (1) (which is expressed to be without prejudice to the Agency's other powers by virtue of section 4) for the words "section 4 above" there shall be substituted the words "section 37 of the 1995 Act (incidental general powers of the Agency)".

165. In section 169 of that Act (powers of entry for enforcement purposes) at the beginning of subsection (3) there shall be inserted the words "Subject to subsection (4) below," and after that subsection there shall be added—

"(4) The powers conferred by this section shall not have effect for the purposes of any of the Agency's pollution control functions, within the meaning of section 108 of the 1995 Act."

166. In section 172 of that Act (powers of entry for other purposes) at the beginning of subsection (3) there shall be inserted the words "Subject to subsection (3A) below," and after that subsection there shall be added—

"(3A) The powers conferred by this section shall not have effect for the purposes of any of the Agency's pollution control functions, within the meaning of section 108 of the 1995 Act."

167. In section 174 of that Act (impersonation of persons exercising powers of entry) in subsection (1) (which creates a summary offence punishable by a fine not exceeding level 4) for the words from "liable, on summary conviction," onwards there shall be substituted the words "liable—

(a) on summary conviction, to a fine not exceeding the statutory maximum;

(b) on conviction on indictment, to a fine or to imprisonment for a term not exceeding two years, or to both."

168. Section 187 of that Act (annual report of the Authority) shall cease to have effect.

169.—(1) Section 190 of that Act (pollution control register) shall be amended in accordance with the following provisions of this paragraph.

(2) In subsection (1) (which requires a register to be kept containing prescribed particulars of the items there specified) after the words "prescribed particulars of" there shall be inserted the words "or relating to".

(3) Paragraph (d) of that subsection (which relates to certificates under paragraph 1(7) of Schedule 10) shall be omitted.

(4) Paragraph (f) of that subsection, and the word "and" immediately preceding it, shall be omitted and at the end of that subsection there shall be added—

"(g) applications made to the Agency for the variation of discharge consents;

(h) enforcement notices served under section 90B above;

(j) revocations, under paragraph 7 of Schedule 10 to this Act, of discharge consents;

(k) appeals under section 91 above;

(l) directions given by the Secretary of State in relation to the Agency's functions under the water pollution provisions of this Act;

(m) convictions, for offences under Part III of this Act, of persons who have the benefit of discharge consents;

(n) information obtained or furnished in pursuance of conditions of discharge consents;

(o) works notices under section 161A above;

(p) appeals under section 161C above;

(q) convictions for offences under section 161D above;

(r) such other matters relating to the quality of water or the pollution of water as may be prescribed by the Secretary of State.

(1A) Where information of any description is excluded from any register by virtue of section 191B below, a statement shall be entered in the register indicating the existence of information of that description."

(5) In subsection (2) (registers to be available for inspection by, and facilities for obtaining copies of entries to be afforded to, the public) after paragraph (b) there shall be added the words—

"and, for the purposes of this subsection, places may be prescribed by the Secretary of State at which any such registers or facilities as are mentioned in paragraph (a) or (b) above are to be available or afforded to the public in pursuance of the paragraph in question."

(6) After subsection (3) there shall be added—

"(4) The Secretary of State may give to the Agency directions requiring the removal from any register maintained by it under this section of any specified information which is not prescribed for inclusion under subsection (1) above or which, by virtue of section 191A or 191B below, ought to have been excluded from the register.

(5) In this section "discharge consent" has the same meaning as in section 91 above."

170. After section 191 of that Act (register for the purposes of works discharges) there shall be inserted—

"Exclusion from registers of information affecting national security

191A.—(1) No information shall be included in a register kept or maintained by the Agency under any provision of this Act if and so long as, in the opinion of the Secretary of State, the inclusion in such a register of that information, or information of that description, would be contrary to the interests of national security.

(2) The Secretary of State may, for the purpose of securing the exclusion from registers of information to which subsection (1) above applies, give to the Agency directions—

(a) specifying information, or descriptions of information, to be excluded from their registers; or

(b) specifying descriptions of information to be referred to the Secretary of State for his determination;

and no information referred to the Secretary of State in pursuance of paragraph (b) above shall be included in any such register until the Secretary of State determines that it should be so included.

(3) The Agency shall notify the Secretary of State of any information it excludes from a register in pursuance of directions under subsection (2) above.

(4) A person may, as respects any information which appears to him to be information to which subsection (1) above may apply, give a notice to the Secretary of State specifying the information and indicating its apparent nature; and, if he does so—

(a) he shall notify the Agency that he has done so; and

(b) no information so notified to the Secretary of State shall be included in any such register until the Secretary of State has determined that it should be so included.

Exclusion from registers of certain confidential information

191B.—(1) No information relating to the affairs of any individual or business shall, without the consent of that individual or the person for the time being carrying on that business, be included in a register kept or maintained by the Agency under any provision of this Act, if and so long as the information—

(a) is, in relation to him, commercially confidential; and

(b) is not required to be included in the register in pursuance of directions under subsection (7) below;

but information is not commercially confidential for the purposes of this section unless it is determined under this section to be so by the Agency or, on appeal, by the Secretary of State.

(2) Where information is furnished to the Agency for the purpose of—

(a) an application for a discharge consent or for the variation of a discharge consent,

(b) complying with any condition of a discharge consent, or

(c) complying with a notice under section 202 below,

then, if the person furnishing it applies to the Agency to have the information excluded from any register kept or maintained by the Agency under any provision of this Act, on the ground that it is commercially confidential (as regards himself or another person), the Agency shall determine whether the information is or is not commercially confidential.

(3) A determination under subsection (2) above must be made within the period of fourteen days beginning with the date of the application and if the Agency fails to make a determination within that period it shall be treated as having determined that the information is commercially confidential.

(4) Where it appears to the Agency that any information (other than information furnished in circumstances within subsection (2) above) which has been obtained by the Agency under or by virtue of any provision of any enactment might be commercially confidential, the Agency shall—

(a) give to the person to whom or whose business it relates notice that that information is required to be included in a register kept or maintained by the Agency under any provision of this Act, unless excluded under this section; and

(b) give him a reasonable opportunity—

(i) of objecting to the inclusion of the information on the ground that it is commercially confidential; and

(ii) of making representations to the Agency for the purpose of justifying any such objection;

and, if any representations are made, the Agency shall, having taken the representations into account, determine whether the information is or is not commercially confidential.

(5) Where, under subsection (2) or (4) above, the Agency determines that information is not commercially confidential—

(a) the information shall not be entered on the register until the end of the period of twenty-one days beginning with the date on which the determination is notified to the person concerned; and

(b) that person may appeal to the Secretary of State against the decision;

and, where an appeal is brought in respect of any information, the information shall not be entered on the register until the end of the period of seven days following the day on which the appeal is finally determined or withdrawn.

(6) Subsections (2A), (2C) and (2K) of section 91 above shall apply in relation to appeals under subsection (5) above; but—

(a) subsection (2C) of that section shall have effect for the purposes of this subsection with the substitution for the words from "(which may" onwards of the words "(which must be held in private)"; and

(b) subsection (5) above is subject to section 114 of the 1995 Act (delegation or reference of appeals etc.).

(7) The Secretary of State may give to the Agency directions as to specified information, or descriptions of information, which the public interest requires to be included in registers kept or maintained by the Agency under any provision of this Act notwithstanding that the information may be commercially confidential.

(8) Information excluded from a register shall be treated as ceasing to be commercially confidential for the purposes of this section at the expiry of the period of four years beginning with the date of the determination by virtue of which it was excluded; but the person who furnished it may apply to the Agency for the information to remain excluded from the register on the ground that it is still commercially confidential and the Agency shall determine whether or not that is the case.

(9) Subsections (5) and (6) above shall apply in relation to a determination under subsection (8) above as they apply in relation to a determination under subsection (2) or (4) above.

(10) The Secretary of State may by regulations substitute (whether in all cases or in such classes or descriptions of case as may be specified in the regulations) for the period for the time being specified in subsection (3) above such other period as he considers appropriate.

(11) Information is, for the purposes of any determination under this section, commercially confidential, in relation to any individual or person, if its being contained in the register would prejudice to an unreasonable degree the commercial interests of that individual or person.

(12) In this section "discharge consent" has the same meaning as in section 91 above."

171. Section 196 of that Act (provision of information by the Authority to Ministers) shall cease to have effect.

172.—(1) In section 202 of that Act (information and assistance required in connection with the control of pollution) in subsection (4) (which creates a summary offence punishable by a fine not exceeding level 5 on the standard scale) for the words from "liable, on summary conviction," onwards there shall be substituted the words "liable—

(a) on summary conviction, to a fine not exceeding the statutory maximum;

(b) on conviction on indictment, to a fine or to imprisonment for a term not exceeding two years, or to both."

(2) Subsection (5) of that section (which is superseded in consequence of the amendment made by sub-paragraph (1) above) shall cease to have effect.

173.—(1) Section 204 of that Act (restriction on disclosure of information with respect to any particular business) shall be amended in accordance with the following provisions of this paragraph.

(2) In subsection (2)(a) (exception for disclosure of information for purposes of functions under certain enactments)—

(a) for the words "the Authority" there shall be substituted the words "the Agency, the Scottish Environment Protection Agency"; and

(b) for the words "or the Water Act 1989" there shall be substituted the words ", the Water Act 1989, Part I or IIA of the Environmental Protection Act 1990 or the 1995 Act".

(3) In subsection (3), in paragraph (a) (which provides that nothing in subsection (1) shall limit the matters which may be included in reports made by specified bodies under specified enactments)—

(a) after sub-paragraph (i), there shall be inserted—

"(ia) the Scottish Environment Protection Agency;"; and

(b) for the words "or that Act of 1991" there shall be substituted the words ", Part I or IIA of the Environmental Protection Act 1990, that Act of 1991 or the 1995 Act".

(4) In paragraph (b) of that subsection, after the words "that Act" there shall be inserted the words "of 1991".

174. Sections 213 to 215 of that Act (local inquiries) shall cease to have effect.

175. Section 218 of that Act (no judicial disqualification by virtue of liability to pay charges to the Authority) shall cease to have effect.

176. In section 219 of that Act (powers to make regulations)—

(a) in subsection (2), the words "Subject to subsection (3) below,", and

(b) subsection (3) (which restricts certain powers to make regulations),

shall cease to have effect.

177.—(1) Section 221 (1) of that Act (general interpretation) shall be amended in accordance with the following provisions of this paragraph.

(2) Before the definition of "abstraction" there shall be inserted—

"the 1995 Act" means the Environment Act 1995;".

(3) After the definition of "accessories" there shall be inserted—

" "the Agency" means the Environment Agency;".

(4) The definition of "the Authority" shall be omitted.

(5) The definition of "constituent council" shall be omitted.

(6) After the definition of "enactment" there shall be inserted—

"enforcement notice" has the meaning given by section 90B above;".

(7) For the definition of "flood defence functions" there shall be substituted—

" "flood defence functions", in relation to the Agency, means—

(a) its functions with respect to flood defence and land drainage by virtue of Part IV of this Act, the Land Drainage Act 1991 and section 6 of the 1995 Act;

(b) those functions transferred to the Agency by section 2(1)(a)(iii) of the 1995 Act which were previously transferred to the Authority by virtue of section 136(8) of the Water Act 1989 and paragraph 1(3) of Schedule 15 to that Act (transfer of land drainage functions under local statutory provisions and subordinate legislation); and

(c) any other functions of the Agency under any of the flood defence provisions of this Act;".

(8) For the definition of "flood defence provisions" there shall be substituted—

"flood defence provisions", in relation to this Act, means—

(a) any of the following provisions of this Act, that is to say—

(i) Part IV;

      (ii) sections 133 to 141 (including Schedule 15), 143, 147 to 149, 155, 165 to 167, 180, 193, 194 and paragraph 5 of Schedule 25;

    (b) any of the following provisions of the 1995 Act, that is to say—

      (i) section 6(4) (general supervision of flood defence);

      (ii) section 53 (inquiries and other hearings); and

      (iii) Schedule 5 (membership and proceedings of regional and local flood defence committees); and

    (c) any other provision of this Act or the 1995 Act so far as it relates to a provision falling within paragraph (a) or (b) above;".

(9) For the definition of "the related water resources provisions" there shall be substituted—

" "the related water resources provisions", in relation to Chapter II of Part II of this Act, means—

    (a) the following provisions of this Act, that is to say, the provisions—

      (i) of sections 21 to 23 (including Schedule 5);

      (ii) of sections 120, 125 to 130, 158, 189, 199 to 201, 206(3), 209(3), 211(1) and 216; and

      (iii) of paragraph 1 of Schedule 25; and

    (b) the following provisions of the 1995 Act, that is to say, the provisions—

      (i) of sections 41 and 42 (charging schemes) as they have effect by virtue of subsection (1)(a) of section 41 (licences under Chapter II of Part II of this Act); and

      (ii) of subsections (1) and (2) of section 53 (inquiries and other hearings);".

(10) In the definition of "water pollution provisions"—

    (a) in paragraph (b)—

      (i) after the words "161" there shall be inserted the words "to 161D"; and

      (ii) for the words "203 and 213(2) above" there shall be substituted the words "and 203"; and

    (b) after paragraph (c), there shall be added the words—

"and the following provisions of the 1995 Act, that is to say, the provisions of subsections (1) and (2) of section 53."

178. Schedule 1 to that Act (the National Rivers Authority) shall cease to have effect.

179. Schedules 3 and 4 to that Act (boundaries of regional flood defence areas and membership and proceedings of regional and local flood defence committees) shall cease to have effect.

180. In Schedule 5 to that Act (procedure relating to statements on minimum acceptable flow) in paragraph 2(3)(g) (copy of notice to be served on person authorised by a licence under Part I of the Electricity Act 1989 to generate electricity) after the words "to generate electricity" there shall be added the words "who has a right to abstract water from any such waters or related inland waters".

181. In Schedule 6 to that Act (orders providing for exemption from restrictions on abstraction) in paragraph 1(4)(h) (copy of notice to be served on person authorised by a licence under Part I of the Electricity Act 1989 to generate electricity) after the words "to generate electricity" there shall be added the words "who has a right to abstract water from any such source of supply or related inland waters".

182. In Schedule 10 to that Act (discharge consents) after paragraph 7 (restriction on variation and revocation of consent and previous variation) there shall be added—

"General review of consents

8.—(1) If it appears appropriate to the Secretary of State to do so he may at any time direct the Authority to review—

    (a) the consents given under paragraphs 2 and 5 above, or

    (b) any description of such consents,

and the conditions (if any) to which those consents are subject.

(2) A direction given by virtue of sub-paragraph (1) above—

    (a) shall specify the purpose for which, and

    (b) may specify the manner in which,

the review is to be conducted.

(3) After carrying out a review pursuant to a direction given by virtue of sub-paragraph (1) above, the Authority shall submit to the Secretary of State its proposals (if any) for—

    (a) the modification of the conditions of any consent reviewed pursuant to the direction, or

    (b) in the case of any unconditional consent reviewed pursuant to the direction, subjecting the consent to conditions.

(4) Where the Secretary of State has received any proposals from the Authority under

sub-paragraph (3) above in relation to any consent he may, if it appears appropriate to him to do so, direct the Authority to do, in relation to that consent, anything mentioned in paragraph 6(2)(b) or (c) above.

(5) A direction given by virtue of sub-paragraph (4) above may only direct the Authority to do, in relation to any consent,—

(a) any such thing as the Authority has proposed should be done in relation to that consent, or

(b) any such thing with such modifications as appear to the Secretary of State to be appropriate."

183. For that Schedule there shall be substituted—

"SCHEDULE 10

DISCHARGE CONSENTS

Application for consent

1.—(1) An application for a consent, for the purposes of section 88(1)(a) of this Act, for any discharges—

(a) shall be made to the Agency on a form provided for the purpose by the Agency; and

(b) must be advertised by or on behalf of the applicant in such manner as may be required by regulations made by the Secretary of State.

(2) Regulations made by the Secretary of State may make provision for enabling the Agency to direct or determine that any such advertising of an application as is required under sub-paragraph (1)(b) above may, in any case, be dispensed with if, in that case, it appears to the Agency to be appropriate for that advertising to be dispensed with.

(3) The applicant for such a consent must provide to the Agency, either on, or together with, the form mentioned in sub-paragraph (1) above—

(a) such information as the Agency may reasonably require; and

(b) such information as may be prescribed for the purpose by the Secretary of State;

but, subject to paragraph 3(3) below and without prejudice to the effect (if any) of any other contravention of the requirements of this Schedule in relation to an application under this paragraph, a failure to provide information in pursuance of this sub-paragraph shall not invalidate an application.

(4) The Agency may give the applicant notice requiring him to provide it with such further information of any description specified in the notice as it may require for the purpose of determining the application.

(5) An application made in accordance with this paragraph which relates to proposed discharges at two or more places may be treated by the Agency as separate applications for consents for discharges at each of those places.

Consultation in connection with applications

2.—(1) Subject to sub-paragraph (2) below, the Agency shall give notice of any application under paragraph 1 above, together with a copy of the application, to the persons who are prescribed or directed to be consulted under this paragraph and shall do so within the specified period for notification.

(2) The Secretary of State may, by regulations, exempt any class of application from the requirements of this paragraph or exclude any class of information contained in applications from those requirements, in all cases or as respects specified classes only of persons to be consulted.

(3) Any representations made by the persons so consulted within the period allowed shall be considered by the Agency in determining the application.

(4) For the purposes of sub-paragraph (1) above—

(a) persons are prescribed to be consulted on any description of application if they are persons specified for the purposes of applications of that description in regulations made by the Secretary of State;

(b) persons are directed to be consulted on any particular application if the Secretary of State specifies them in a direction given to the Agency;

and the "specified period for notification" is the period specified in the regulations or in the direction.

(5) Any representations made by any other persons within the period allowed shall also be considered by the Agency in determining the application.

(6) Subject to sub-paragraph (7) below, the period allowed for making representations is—

(a) in the case of persons prescribed or directed to be consulted, the period of six weeks beginning with the date on which notice of the application was given under sub-paragraph (1) above, and

(b) in the case of other persons, the period of six weeks beginning with the date on which the making of the application was advertised in pursuance of paragraph 1(1)(b) above.

(7) The Secretary of State may, by regulations, substitute for any period for the time being specified in sub-paragraph (6)(a) or (b) above, such other period as he considers appropriate.

Consideration and determination of applications

3.—(1) On an application under paragraph 1 above the Agency shall be under a duty, if the requirements—
   (a) of that paragraph, and
   (b) of any regulations made under paragraph 1 or 2 above or of any directions under paragraph 2 above,
are complied with, to consider whether to give the consent applied for, either unconditionally or subject to conditions, or to refuse it.

(2) Subject to the following provisions of this Schedule, on an application made in accordance with paragraph 1 above, the applicant may treat the consent applied for as having been refused if it is not given within the period of four months beginning with the day on which the application is received or within such longer period as may be agreed in writing between the Agency and the applicant.

(3) Where any person, having made an application to the Agency for a consent, has failed to comply with his obligation under paragraph 1(3) or (4) above to provide information to the Agency, the Agency may refuse to proceed with the application, or refuse to proceed with it until the information is provided.

(4) The conditions subject to which a consent may be given under this paragraph shall be such conditions as the Agency may think fit and, in particular, may include conditions—
   (a) as to the places at which the discharges to which the consent relates may be made and as to the design and construction of any outlets for the discharges;
   (b) as to the nature, origin, composition, temperature, volume and rate of the discharges and as to the periods during which the discharges may be made;
   (c) as to the steps to be taken, in relation to the discharges or by way of subjecting any substance likely to affect the description of matter discharged to treatment or any other process, for minimising the polluting effects of the discharges on any controlled waters;
   (d) as to the provision of facilities for taking samples of the matter discharged and, in particular, as to the provision, maintenance and use of manholes, inspection chambers, observation wells and boreholes in connection with the discharges;
   (e) as to the provision, maintenance and testing of meters for measuring or recording the volume and rate of the discharges and apparatus for determining the nature, composition and temperature of the discharges;
   (f) as to the keeping of records of the nature, origin, composition, temperature, volume and rate of the discharges and, in particular, of records of readings of meters and other recording apparatus provided in accordance with any other condition attached to the consent; and
   (g) as to the making of returns and the giving of other information to the Authority about the nature, origin, composition, temperature, volume and rate of the discharges;
and it is hereby declared that a consent may be given under this paragraph subject to different conditions in respect of different periods.

(5) The Secretary of State may, by regulations, substitute for any period for the time being specified in sub-paragraph (2) above, such other period as he considers appropriate.

4. The Secretary of State may give the Agency a direction with respect to any particular application, or any description of applications, for consent under paragraph 1 above requiring the Agency not to determine or not to proceed with the application or applications of that description until the expiry of any such period as may be specified in the direction, or until directed by the Secretary of State that it may do so, as the case may be.

Reference to Secretary of State of certain applications for consent

5.—(1) The Secretary of State may, either in consequence of representations or objections made to him or otherwise, direct the Agency to transmit to him for determination such applications for consent under paragraph 1 above as are specified in the direction or are of a description so specified.

(2) Where a direction is given to the Agency under this paragraph, the Agency shall comply with the direction and inform every applicant to whose application the direction relates of the transmission of his application to the Secretary of State.

(3) Paragraphs 1(1) and 2 above shall have effect in relation to an application transmitted to the Secretary of State under this paragraph with such modifications as may be prescribed.

(4) Where an application is transmitted to the Secretary of State under this paragraph, the Secretary of State may at any time after the application is transmitted and before it is granted or refused—

　(a) cause a local inquiry to be held with respect to the application; or

　(b) afford the applicant and the Agency an opportunity of appearing before, and being heard by, a person appointed by the Secretary of State for the purpose.

(5) The Secretary of State shall exercise his power under sub-paragraph (4) above in any case where a request to be heard with respect to the application is made to him in the prescribed manner by the applicant or by the Agency.

(6) It shall be the duty of the Secretary of State, if the requirements of this paragraph and of any regulations made under it are complied with, to determine an application for consent transmitted to him by the Agency under this paragraph by directing the Agency to refuse its consent or to give its consent under paragraph 3 above (either unconditionally or subject to such conditions as are specified in the direction).

(7) Without prejudice to any of the preceding provisions of this paragraph, the Secretary of State may by regulations make provision for the purposes of, and in connection with, the consideration and disposal by him of applications transmitted to him under this paragraph.

Consents without applications

6.—(1) If it appears to the Agency—

　(a) that a person has caused or permitted effluent or other matter to be discharged in contravention—

　　(i) of the obligation imposed by virtue of section 85(3) of this Act; or

　　(ii) of any prohibition imposed under section 86 of this Act; and

　(b) that a similar contravention by that person is likely,

the Agency may, if it thinks fit, serve on him an instrument in writing giving its consent, subject to any conditions specified in the instrument, for discharges of a description so specified.

(2) A consent given under this paragraph shall not relate to any discharge which occurred before the instrument containing the consent was served on the recipient of the instrument.

(3) Sub-paragraph (4) of paragraph 3 above shall have effect in relation to a consent given under this paragraph as it has effect in relation to a consent given under that paragraph.

(4) Where a consent has been given under this paragraph, the Agency shall publish notice of the consent in such manner as may be prescribed by the Secretary of State and send copies of the instrument containing the consent to such bodies or persons as may be so prescribed.

(5) It shall be the duty of the Agency to consider any representations or objections with respect to a consent under this paragraph as are made to it in such manner, and within such period, as may be prescribed by the Secretary of State and have not been withdrawn.

(6) Where notice of a consent is published by the Agency under sub-paragraph (4) above, the Agency shall be entitled to recover the expenses of publication from the person on whom the instrument containing the consent was served.

Revocation of consents and alteration and imposition of conditions

7.—(1) The Agency may from time to time review any consent given under paragraph 3 or 6 above and the conditions (if any) to which the consent is subject.

(2) Subject to such restrictions on the exercise of the power conferred by this sub-paragraph as are imposed under paragraph 8 below, where the Agency has reviewed a consent under this paragraph, it may by a notice served on the person making a discharge in pursuance of the consent—

(a) revoke the consent;

(b) make modifications of the conditions of the consent; or

(c) in the case of an unconditional consent, provide that it shall be subject to such conditions as may be specified in the notice.

(3) If on a review under sub-paragraph (1) above it appears to the Agency that no discharge has been made in pursuance of the consent to which the review relates at any time during the preceding twelve months, the Agency may revoke the consent by a notice served on the holder of the consent.

(4) If it appears to the Secretary of State appropriate to do so—

(a) for the purpose of enabling Her Majesty's Government in the United Kingdom to give effect to any Community obligation or to any international agreement to which the United Kingdom is for the time being a party;

(b) for the protection of public health or of flora and fauna dependent on an aquatic environment; or

(c) in consequence of any representations or objections made to him or otherwise,

he may, subject to such restrictions on the exercise of the power conferred by virtue of paragraph (c) above as are imposed under paragraph 8 below, at any time direct the Agency, in relation to a consent given under paragraph 3 or 6 above, to do anything mentioned in sub-paragraph (2)(a) to (c) above.

(5) The Agency shall be liable to pay compensation to any person in respect of any loss or damage sustained by that person as a result of the Agency's compliance with a direction given in relation to any consent by virtue of sub-paragraph (4)(b) above if—

(a) in complying with that direction the Agency does anything which, apart from that direction, it would be precluded from doing by a restriction imposed under paragraph 8 below; and

(b) the direction is not shown to have been given in consequence of—

(i) a change of circumstances which could not reasonably have been foreseen at the beginning of the period to which the restriction relates; or

(ii) consideration by the Secretary of State of material information which was not reasonably available to the Agency at the beginning of that period.

(6) For the purposes of sub-paragraph (5) above information is material, in relation to a consent, if it relates to any discharge made or to be made by virtue of the consent, to the interaction of any such discharge with any other discharge or to the combined effect of the matter discharged and any other matter.

Restriction on variation and revocation of consent and previous variation

8.—(1) Each instrument signifying the consent of the Agency under paragraph 3 or 6 above shall specify a period during which no notice by virtue of paragraph 7(2) or (4)(c) above shall be served in respect of the consent except, in the case of a notice doing anything mentioned in paragraph 7(2)(b) or (c), with the agreement of the holder of the consent.

(2) Each notice served by the Agency by virtue of paragraph 7(2) or (4)(c) above (except a notice which only revokes a consent) shall specify a period during which a subsequent such notice which alters the effect of the first-mentioned notice shall not be served except, in the case of a notice doing anything mentioned in paragraph 7(2)(b) or (c) above, with the agreement of the holder of the consent.

(3) The period specified under sub-paragraph (1) or (2) above in relation to any consent shall not, unless the person who proposes to make or makes discharges in pursuance of the consent otherwise agrees, be less than the period of four years beginning—

(a) in the case of a period specified under sub-paragraph (1) above, with the day on which the consent takes effect; and

(b) in the case of a period specified under sub-paragraph (2) above with the day on which the notice specifying that period is served.

(4) A restriction imposed under sub-paragraph (1) or (2) above shall not prevent the service by the Agency of a notice by virtue of paragraph 7(2) or (4)(c) above in respect of a consent given under paragraph 6 above if—

(a) the notice is served not more than three months after the beginning of the period prescribed under paragraph 6(5) above for the making of representations and objections with respect to the consent; and

(b) the Agency or, as the case may be, the Secretary of State considers, in consequence of any representations or objections received by it or him within that period, that it is appropriate for the notice to be served.

(5) A restriction imposed under sub-paragraph (1) or (2) above shall not prevent the service by the Agency of a notice by virtue of paragraph 7(2)(b) or (c) or (4)(c) above in respect of a consent given under paragraph 6 above if the holder has applied for a variation under paragraph 10 below.

General review of consents

9.—(1) If it appears appropriate to the Secretary of State to do so he may at any time direct the Agency to review—
(a) the consents given under paragraph 3 or 6 above, or
(b) any description of such consents,
and the conditions (if any) to which those consents are subject.
(2) A direction given by virtue of sub-paragraph (1) above—
(a) shall specify the purpose for which, and
(b) may specify the manner in which,
the review is to be conducted.
(3) After carrying out a review pursuant to a direction given by virtue of sub-paragraph (1) above, the Agency shall submit to the Secretary of State its proposals (if any) for—
(a) the modification of the conditions of any consent reviewed pursuant to the direction, or
(b) in the case of any unconditional consent reviewed pursuant to the direction, subjecting the consent to conditions.
(4) Where the Secretary of State has received any proposals from the Agency under sub-paragraph (3) above in relation to any consent he may, if it appears appropriate to him to do so, direct the Agency to do, in relation to that consent, anything mentioned in paragraph 7(2)(b) or (c) above.
(5) A direction given by virtue of sub-paragraph (4) above may only direct the Agency to do, in relation to any consent,—
(a) any such thing as the Agency has proposed should be done in relation to that consent, or
(b) any such thing with such modifications as appear to the Secretary of State to be appropriate.

Applications for variation

10.—(1) The holder of a consent under paragraph 3 or 6 above may apply to the Agency, on a form provided for the purpose by the Agency, for the variation of the consent.
(2) The provisions of paragraphs 1 to 5 above shall apply (with the necessary modifications) to applications under sub-paragraph (1) above, and to the variation of consents in pursuance of such applications, as they apply to applications for, and the grant of, consents.

Transfer of consents

11.—(1) A consent under paragraph 3 or 6 above may be transferred by the holder to a person who proposes to carry on the discharges in place of the holder.
(2) On the death of the holder of a consent under paragraph 3 or 6 above, the consent shall, subject to sub-paragraph (4) below, be regarded as property forming part of the deceased's personal estate, whether or not it would be so regarded apart from this sub-paragraph, and shall accordingly vest in his personal representatives.
(3) If a bankruptcy order is made against the holder of a consent under paragraph 3 or 6 above, the consent shall, subject to sub-paragraph (4) below, be regarded for the purposes of any of the Second Group of Parts of the Insolvency Act 1986 (insolvency of individuals; bankruptcy), as property forming part of the bankrupt's estate, whether or not it would be so regarded apart from this sub-paragraph, and shall accordingly vest as such in the trustee in bankruptcy.
(4) Notwithstanding anything in the foregoing provisions of this paragraph, a consent under paragraph 3 or 6 above (and the obligations arising out of, or incidental to, such a consent) shall not be capable of being disclaimed.
(5) A consent under paragraph 3 or 6 above which is transferred to, or which vests in, a person under this section shall have effect on and after the date of the transfer or vesting as if it had been granted to that person under paragraph 3 or 6 above, subject to the same conditions as were attached to it immediately before that date.
(6) Where a consent under paragraph 3 or 6 above is transferred under sub-paragraph (1) above, the person from whom it is transferred shall give notice of that fact to the Agency

not later than the end of the period of twenty-one days beginning with the date of the transfer.

(7) Where a consent under paragraph 3 or 6 above vests in any person as mentioned in sub-paragraph (2) or (3) above, that person shall give notice of that fact to the Agency not later than the end of the period of fifteen months beginning with the date of the vesting.

(8) If—

(a) a consent under paragraph 3 or 6 above vests in any person as mentioned in sub-paragraph (2) or (3) above, but

(b) that person fails to give the notice required by sub-paragraph (7) above within the period there mentioned,

the consent, to the extent that it permits the making of any discharges, shall cease to have effect.

(9) A person who fails to give a notice which he is required by sub-paragraph (6) or (7) above to give shall be guilty of an offence and liable—

(a) on summary conviction, to a fine not exceeding the statutory maximum;

(b) on conviction on indictment, to a fine or to imprisonment for a term not exceeding two years, or to both."

184. In Schedule 11 to that Act (water protection zone orders) in paragraph 4 (which is expressed to be without prejudice to section 213 of that Act) for the words "section 213 of this Act" there shall be substituted the words "section 53 of the 1995 Act (inquiries and other hearings)".

185. In Schedule 12 to that Act (nitrate sensitive area orders) in paragraph 6 (which is expressed to be without prejudice to section 213 of that Act) for the words "section 213 of this Act" there shall be substituted the words "section 53 of the 1995 Act (inquiries and other hearings)".

186. In Schedule 13 to that Act (transitional water pollution provisions) in paragraph 4 (discharge consents on application of undertakers etc.)—

(a) in sub-paragraph (2), in paragraphs (a) and (b) (which contain references to paragraph 4 of Schedule 10) for the word "4", in each place where it occurs, there shall be substituted the word "5";

(b) in sub-paragraph (3) (which contains references to various provisions of Schedule 10) for the words "paragraphs 1(4) to (6) and 2(1) or, as the case may be, paragraph 4(3)" there shall be substituted the words "paragraph 1(1), apart from paragraph (a), paragraph 2 or, as the case may be, paragraph 5(3)"; and

(c) in sub-paragraph (4)(a) (which contains a reference to paragraph 2(5) of Schedule 10) for the words "2(5)" there shall be substituted the words "3(4)".

187.—(1) In Schedule 15 to that Act (supplemental provisions with respect to drainage charges) in paragraphs 4(3) and 9(4) (which specify the penalty for certain offences of failing, and after conviction continuing, without reasonable excuse, to comply with notices) after the words "he continues without reasonable excuse" there shall be inserted the words "to fail".

(2) In paragraph 12(2) of that Schedule (which is expressed to be without prejudice to powers by virtue of section 4 or paragraph 5 of Schedule 1) for the words "section 4 of this Act and paragraph 5 of Schedule 1 to this Act" there shall be substituted the words "section 37 of, and paragraph 6 of Schedule 1 to, the 1995 Act".

188. In Schedule 20 to that Act (supplemental provisions with respect to powers of entry) in paragraph 7 (which creates an offence of obstruction, punishable on summary conviction by a fine not exceeding level 3) for the words from "liable, on summary conviction," onwards there shall be substituted the words "liable—

(a) on summary conviction, to a fine not exceeding the statutory maximum;

(b) on conviction on indictment, to a fine or to imprisonment for a term not exceeding two years, or to both."

189. In Schedule 22 to that Act (protection for particular undertakings) in paragraph 5 (protection for telecommunication systems) for the words "section 4(1) of this Act)" there shall be substituted the words "section 37 of the 1995 Act)".

190. In Schedule 25 to that Act (byelaw-making powers) in paragraph 1(1) for the words "paragraphs (a), (c) and (d) of section 2(1) of this Act" there shall be substituted the words "sub-paragraphs (i), (iii) and (v) of section 2(1)(a) of the 1995 Act".

The Land Drainage Act 1991

191. In the Land Drainage Act 1991, for the words "NRA", wherever occurring, there shall be substituted the word "Agency".

192.—(1) In section 23 of that Act (prohibition on obstructions etc. in watercourses) in subsection (2) (which confers power to charge an application fee of £50 or such other sum as may be specified by order made by the Ministers) for the words "specified by order made by the Ministers" there shall be substituted the word "prescribed".

(2) After subsection (7) of that section there shall be inserted—

"(7A) In subsection (2) above "prescribed" means specified in, or determined in accordance with, an order made by the Ministers; and any such order may make different provision for different cases, including different provision in relation to different persons, circumstances or localities."

193. At the beginning of Part V of that Act (miscellaneous and supplemental provisions) there shall be inserted—

"Spray irrigation

Powers of internal drainage boards and local authorities to facilitate spray irrigation
    61F.—(1) Any internal drainage board or local authority may, with the consent of the Agency, operate any drainage works under the control of the board or authority so as to manage the level of water in a watercourse for the purpose of facilitating spray irrigation.

(2) Subsection (1) above is without prejudice to—
  (a) the powers of an internal drainage board or local authority in relation to drainage; or
  (b) any requirement—
     (i) for any other consent of the Agency or any other person; or
     (ii) for any licence, approval, authorisation or other permission or registration."

194.—(1) In section 72 of that Act, in subsection (1) (general definitions) there shall be inserted at the appropriate place—
  " "the Agency" means the Environment Agency;".

(2) In that subsection, the definition of "the NRA" shall be omitted.

The Clean Air Act 1993

195. In section 2 of the Clean Air Act 1993 (emission of dark smoke from industrial or trade premises) in subsection (5) (which creates a summary offence punishable with a fine not exceeding level 5 on the standard scale) for the words "level 5 on the standard scale" there shall be substituted the words "£20,000".

196.—(1) Section 19 of that Act (power to require creation of smoke control areas by local authorities) as it applies to Scotland shall be amended in accordance with the following provisions of this paragraph.

(2) In subsection (1)—
  (a) for the words "Secretary of State" there shall be substituted the words "Scottish Environment Protection Agency (in this section referred to as "the Agency")"; and
  (b) for the words "he", "him" and "his" there shall be substituted respectively "the Agency", "it" and "its".

(3) In subsections (2), (3), (4)(a) and (6), for the words "Secretary of State" there shall be substituted the words "Agency".

(4) In subsection (3), for the word "him" there shall be substituted the word "it".

(5) In subsection (4), before the words "the Secretary of State" in the second place where they occur there shall be inserted the words "the Agency, with the consent of".

197. In section 59 of that Act (local inquiries) in subsection (1)—
  (a) for the words "a local inquiry" there shall be substituted the words "an inquiry"; and
  (b) for the words "such an inquiry" there shall be substituted the words "an inquiry";
and for the side-note to that section there shall accordingly be substituted "Inquiries.".

198. In section 60(7)(b) of that Act as it applies to Scotland for the words "the Secretary of State" and "Secretary of State's" there shall be substituted the words "SEPA" and "SEPA's" respectively.

199. In section 63(1)(c) of that Act as it applies to Scotland for the words "sections 19(4) and" there shall be substituted the words "section".

The Radioactive Substances Act 1993

200. Subject to the other provisions of this Act, in the Radioactive Substances Act 1993, for the words "chief inspector" or "chief inspector's", wherever occurring, there shall be substituted respectively the words "appropriate Agency" or "appropriate Agency's".

201. Sections 4 and 5 of that Act (appointment of inspectors and chief inspectors) shall cease to have effect.

202.—(1) In section 7 of that Act (registration of users of radioactive material) in subsection

(1)(c) (application to be accompanied by prescribed fee), for the words "prescribed fee" there shall be substituted the words "charge prescribed for the purpose by a charging scheme under section 41 of the Environment Act 1995".

(2) In subsection (7) of that section (chief inspector to have regard exclusively to amount and character of radioactive waste), for the word "him" there shall be substituted the word "it".

203. In section 8 of that Act (exemptions from registration under section 7), in subsection (2) (power of chief inspector to impose conditions) for the word "he" there shall be substituted the word "it".

204.—(1) In section 10 of that Act (registration of mobile radioactive apparatus) in subsection (1)(c) (application to be accompanied by prescribed fee), for the words "prescribed fee" there shall be substituted the words "charge prescribed for the purpose by a charging scheme under section 41 of the Environment Act 1995".

(2) In each of subsections (3) and (5)(b) of that section (duty to supply copy of application, and to send copy of certificate, to local authority) for the word "him" there shall be substituted the words "the appropriate Agency".

205.—(1) Section 16 of that Act (authorisations) shall be amended in accordance with the following provisions of this paragraph.

(2) In subsection (2) (power to grant authorisations to be exercisable by the chief inspector) the words "Subject to subsection (3)" shall be omitted.

(3) Subsection (3) (power to grant authorisations in England, Wales and Northern Ireland) shall be omitted.

(4) In subsection (4) (application to be accompanied by prescribed fee), for the words "prescribed fee" there shall be substituted the words "charge prescribed for the purpose by a charging scheme under section 41 of the Environment Act 1995".

(5) After subsection (4) there shall be inserted—

"(4A) Without prejudice to subsection (5), on any application for an authorisation under section 13(1) in respect of the disposal of radioactive waste on or from any premises situated on a nuclear site in any part of Great Britain, the appropriate Agency—

(a) shall consult the relevant Minister and the Health and Safety Executive before deciding whether to grant an authorisation on that application and, if so, subject to what limitations or conditions, and

(b) shall consult the relevant Minister concerning the terms of the authorisation, for which purpose that Agency shall, before granting any authorisation on that application, send that Minister a copy of any authorisation which it proposes so to grant."

(6) In subsection (5) (consultation by chief inspector and, where the premises are in England, Wales or Northern Ireland, the appropriate Minister with local authorities etc.)—

(a) for the words from "and, where" to "shall each" there shall be substituted the word "shall"; and

(b) for the word "him", in each place where it occurs, there shall be substituted the words "that Agency".

(7) In subsection (7) (applications, other than those to which subsection (3) applies, deemed to be refused if not determined within prescribed period) for the words "(other than an application to which subsection (3) applies)" there shall be substituted the words "(other than an application for an authorisation under section 13(1) in respect of the disposal of radioactive waste on or from any premises situated on a nuclear site in any part of Great Britain)".

(8) In subsection (8)(b) (conditions or limitations subject to which authorisations may be granted) for the words from "or, as" to "think" there shall be substituted the word "thinks".

(9) In subsection (10) of that section (fixing of date from which authorisation is to have effect)—

(a) the words from "or, as" to "appropriate Minister" shall cease to have effect; and

(b) for the words "him or them" and "his or their" there shall be substituted respectively the words "it" and "its".

(10) After that subsection there shall be inserted—

"(11) In this section, "the relevant Minister" means—

(a) in relation to premises in England, the Minister of Agriculture, Fisheries and Food, and

(b) in relation to premises in Wales or Scotland, the Secretary of State."

206.—(1) In section 17 of that Act, after subsection (2) (variation of authorisations) there shall be inserted—

"(2A) On any proposal to vary an authorisation granted under section 13(1) in respect of the disposal of radioactive waste on or from any premises situated on a nuclear site in any part of Great Britain, the appropriate Agency—

    (a) shall consult the relevant Minister and the Health and Safety Executive before deciding whether to vary the authorisation and, if so, whether by attaching, revoking or varying any limitations or conditions or by attaching further limitations or conditions, and

    (b) shall consult the relevant Minister concerning the terms of any variation, for which purpose that Agency shall, before varying the authorisation, send that Minister a copy of any variations which it proposes to make."

(2) Subsection (4) of that section (adaptations for authorisations granted by the chief inspector and the appropriate Minister) shall cease to have effect.

(3) At the end of that section there shall be added—

    "(5) In this section, "the relevant Minister" has the same meaning as in section 16 above."

207.—(1) In section 18 of that Act (functions of public and local authorities in relation to authorisations under section 13) in subsection (1)—

    (a) the words from "(or, in a case" to "that Minister)", and

    (b) the words "or the appropriate Minister, as the case may be,",

shall cease to have effect.

(2) In subsection (2)(b) of that section (special precautions taken with the approval of the chief inspector etc.) the words from "(or, where" to "that Minister)" shall cease to have effect.

208. In section 20 of that Act (retention and production of site or disposal records) subsection (3) (adaptation where powers exercisable by chief inspector and appropriate Minister) shall cease to have effect.

209.—(1) In section 21 of that Act (enforcement notices) in subsection (1) (power of chief inspector to serve such a notice) for the word "he" there shall be substituted the word "it".

(2) Subsection (3) of that section (adaptation in case of authorisations granted by the chief inspector and the appropriate Minister) shall cease to have effect.

(3) In subsection (4) of that section (copies of notices to be sent to certain public or local authorities) the words from "or, where" to "that Minister" shall cease to have effect.

210.—(1) In section 22 of that Act (prohibition notices) in subsection (1) (power of chief inspector to serve such a notice) for the word "he" there shall be substituted the word "it".

(2) Subsection (5) of that section (adaptation in case of authorisations granted by the chief inspector and the appropriate Minister) shall cease to have effect.

(3) In subsection (6) of that section (copies of notices to be sent to certain public or local authorities) the words from "or, where" to "that Minister" shall cease to have effect.

(4) In subsection (7) of that section (withdrawal of notices)—

    (a) the words from "or, where" to "that Minister" shall cease to have effect; and

    (b) for the word "he", in each place where it occurs, there shall be substituted the words "that Agency".

211.—(1) In section 23 of that Act (powers of Secretary of State to give directions to the chief inspector)—

    (a) in subsections (1) and (3) for the word "him" there shall be substituted the word "it"; and

    (b) in subsection (2) for the word "his" there shall be substituted the word "its".

(2) After subsection (4) of that section there shall be inserted—

    "(4A) In the application of this section in relation to authorisations, and applications for authorisations, under section 13 in respect of premises situated on a nuclear site in England, references to the Secretary of State shall have effect as references to the Secretary of State and the Minister of Agriculture, Fisheries and Food."

212.—(1) In section 24 of that Act (power of Secretary of State to require certain applications to be determined by him) in subsections (1) and (4), for the word "him", in each place where it occurs, there shall be substituted the word "it".

(2) After subsection (4) of that section there shall be inserted—

    "(4A) In the application of this section in relation to authorisations, and applications for authorisations, under section 13 in respect of premises situated on a nuclear site in England, references to the Secretary of State shall have effect as references to the Secretary of State and the Minister of Agriculture, Fisheries and Food."

213.—(1) In section 25 of that Act (power of Secretary of State to restrict knowledge of applications etc.) in subsection (1) (applications under section 7 to 10 etc.), after the words "knowledge of" there shall be inserted the words "such information as may be specified or described in the directions, being information contained in or relating to—".

(2) In subsection (2) of that section (applications under section 13 or 14 etc.)—

(a) the words from "or, in a case" to "Food," and "or their" shall cease to have effect; and

(b) after the words "knowledge of" there shall be inserted the words "such information as may be specified or described in the directions, being information contained in or relating to—".

(3) In subsection (3) of that section (copies of certain applications etc. which are the subject of a direction not to be sent to local or public authorities)—

(a) after the words "send a copy of" there shall be inserted the words "so much of"; and

(b) after the words "as the case may be" there shall be inserted the words "as contains the information specified or described in the directions—".

(4) After that subsection there shall be inserted—

"(3A) No direction under this section shall affect—

(a) any power or duty of the Agency to which it is given to consult the relevant Minister; or

(b) the information which is to be sent by that Agency to that Minister."

(5) At the end of that section there shall be added—

"(5) In this section "the relevant Minister" has the same meaning as in section 16 above."

214.—(1) Section 26 of that Act (appeals) shall be amended in accordance with the following provisions of this paragraph.

(2) Subsection (3)(a) (appeal not to lie in relation to authorisations subject to section 16(3)) shall cease to have effect.

(3) In subsection (4) (appeals in respect of enforcement or prohibition notices) the words "England, Wales or" shall be omitted.

(4) After subsection (5) there shall be inserted—

"(5A) In the application of this section in relation to authorisations, and applications for authorisations, under section 13 in respect of premises situated on a nuclear site in England, references in subsection (1) to (3) to the Secretary of State shall have effect as references to the Secretary of State and the Minister of Agriculture, Fisheries and Food."

215.—(1) Section 27 of that Act (procedure on appeals under section 26) shall be amended in accordance with the following provisions of this paragraph.

(2) In subsection (1) (power of Secretary of State to refer appeal to appointed person) after the word "26" there shall be inserted the words ", other than an appeal against any decision of, or notice served by, SEPA,".

(3) After that subsection there shall be inserted—

"(1A) As respects an appeal against any decision of, or notice served by, SEPA, this section is subject to section 114 of the Environment Act 1995 (delegation or reference of appeals)."

(4) After subsection (7) there shall be inserted—

"(7A) In the application of this section in relation to authorisations, and applications for authorisations, under section 13 in respect of premises situated on a nuclear site in England, references in subsections (1) to (6) to the Secretary of State shall have effect as references to the Secretary of State and the Minister of Agriculture, Fisheries and Food."

216. Section 28 of that Act (representations in relation to authorisations and notices where appropriate Minister is concerned) shall cease to have effect.

217.—(1) Section 30 of that Act (power of Secretary of State to dispose of radioactive waste) shall be amended in accordance with the following provisions of this paragraph.

(2) In subsection (1) (which confers the power)—

(a) for the words "the Secretary of State", in the first place where they occur, there shall be substituted the words "the appropriate Agency";

(b) for those words, wherever else occurring, there shall be substituted the words "that Agency"; and

(c) for the word "his" there shall be substituted the word "its".

(3) In subsection (3) (application of certain definitions of "owner") for the words "Secretary of State" there shall be substituted the words "Environment Agency".

(4) In subsection (4) (adaptations for Scotland) for the words "the Secretary of State" there shall be substituted the words "SEPA".

218. Section 31 of that Act (rights of entry and inspection) shall cease to have effect.

219. In section 32 of that Act (offences relating to registration or authorisation, including the offence of failure to comply with the requirements of an enforcement or prohibition notice under section 21 or 22 of the Act) after subsection (2) there shall be added—

"(3) If the appropriate Agency is of the opinion that proceedings for an offence under subsection (1)(d) would afford an ineffectual remedy against a person who has failed to comply with the requirements of a notice served on him under section 21 or 22, that Agency may take proceedings in the High Court or, in Scotland, in any court of competent jurisdiction, for the purpose of securing compliance with the notice."

220. In section 34(1) of that Act (which, with certain exceptions, makes it an offence to disclose certain trade secrets) after paragraph (b) (no offence where disclosure made in accordance with directions) there shall be inserted—
"(bb) under or by virtue of section 113 of the Environment Act 1995, or".

221. Section 35 of that Act (obstruction of inspectors or other persons) shall cease to have effect.

222. In section 38 of that Act (restriction on prosecution) in subsection (1) (provision for England and Wales) for paragraph (b) there shall be substituted—
"(b) by the Environment Agency, or".

223.—(1) In section 39 of that Act (public access to documents and records) in subsection (1) (duties of chief inspector)—

    (a) for the word "him", in each place where it occurs, there shall be substituted the word "it";

    (b) for the word "he" there shall be substituted the words "the appropriate Agency"; and

    (c) for the words "applications or certificates" there shall be substituted the word "information".

(2) In subsection (2), the words "or, as the case may be, the appropriate Minister and the chief inspector," shall cease to have effect.

224. In section 40 of that Act (radioactivity to be disregarded for purposes of certain statutory provisions) in subsection (2)(b)(ii), after the words "imposed by the statutory provision on" there shall be inserted the words "the Environment Agency or SEPA or on".

225. Section 42(5) of that Act (which precludes, in the interests of national security, the exercise of certain powers of entry in relation to Crown premises and which is superseded by provisions of this Act) shall cease to have effect.

226. Section 43 of that Act (which relates to fees and charges and which is superseded by provisions of this Act) shall cease to have effect.

227.—(1) Subsection (1) of section 47 of that Act (general definitions) shall be amended in accordance with the following provisions of this paragraph.

(2) There shall be inserted at the appropriate place—
" "the appropriate Agency" means—
    (a) in relation to England and Wales, the Environment Agency; and
    (b) in relation to Scotland, SEPA;".

(3) In the definition of "the appropriate Minister", paragraphs (a) and (b) shall cease to have effect.

(4) In the definition of "the chief inspector", paragraphs (a) and (b) shall cease to have effect.

(5) In the definition of "prescribed", the words from "or, in relation to fees" onwards shall cease to have effect.

(6) In the definition of "relevant water body"—

    (a) in paragraph (a), the words "the National Rivers Authority", and

    (b) in paragraph (b), the words "a river purification authority within the meaning of the Rivers (Prevention of Pollution) (Scotland) Act 1951",
shall be omitted.

(7) There shall be inserted at the appropriate place—
" "SEPA" means the Scottish Environment Protection Agency;".

228. In section 48 of that Act (index of defined expressions) in the Table—

    (a) the following entries shall be inserted at the appropriate place—

        (i) "the appropriate Agency   section 47(1)";

        (ii) "SEPA   section 47(1)";

    (b) the entry relating to the chief inspector shall be omitted.

229. Schedule 2 to that Act (exercise of rights of entry and inspection) shall cease to have effect.

230.—(1) In Schedule 3 to that Act (enactments, other than local enactments, to which s.40 applies) in paragraph 9 (which specifies certain provisions in the Water Resources Act 1991) for the words "203 and 213" there shall be substituted the words "and 203".

(2) For paragraph 16 of that Schedule there shall be substituted—

"16. Sections 30A, 30B, 30D, 30F, 30G, 30H(1), 31(4), (5), (8) and (9), 31A, 34 to 42B, 46 to 46D and 56(1) to (3) of the Control of Pollution Act 1974."

The Local Government (Wales) Act 1994

231. In Schedule 9 to the Local Government (Wales) Act 1994 (which makes provision for the transfer to the new principal councils in Wales of functions in relation to public health and related matters), in paragraph 17(2) (which amends the definitions of waste regulation and disposal authorities for the purposes of Part II of the Environmental Protection Act 1990) for the words "each of subsections (1)(f) and (2)(f)" there shall be substituted the words "subsection (2)(f)"

The Local Government etc. (Scotland) Act 1994

232.—(1) In section 2(2) of the Local Government etc. (Scotland) Act 1994 (constitution of councils) after the words "this Act" there shall be inserted the words "and of the Environment Act 1995".

(2) In Schedule 13 to that Act (minor and consequential amendments) in paragraph 75(27) (which amends certain provisions of the Sewerage (Scotland) Act 1968) for the words from the beginning to "premises)" there shall be substituted the words "In section 53 (notices to be in writing)".

Subordinate legislation and local statutory provisions

233.—(1) In any subordinate legislation or local statutory provisions, for any reference (however framed) to the National Rivers Authority, and for any reference which falls to be construed as such a reference, there shall be substituted a reference to the Agency.

(2) In any subordinate legislation, for any reference (however framed) to a relevant inspector, and for any reference which falls to be construed as such a reference, there shall be substituted a reference to the appropriate Agency.

(3) The provisions of this paragraph are subject to the other provisions of this Act and to any provision made under or by virtue of this Act.

(4) In this paragraph—
"the appropriate Agency" means—
 (a) in relation to England and Wales, the Agency;
 (b) in relation to Scotland, SEPA;
"local statutory provision" means—
  (a) a provision of a local Act (including an Act confirming a provisional order);
  (b) a provision of so much of any public general Act as has effect with respect to particular persons or works or with respect to particular provisions falling within any paragraph of this definition;
  (c) a provision of an instrument made under any provision falling within paragraph (a) or (b) above;
  (d) a provision of any other instrument which is in the nature of a local enactment;
"relevant inspector" means—
   (i) the chief inspector for England and Wales constituted under section 16(3) of the Environmental Protection Act 1990;
   (ii) the chief inspector for Scotland constituted under section 16(3) of that Act;
   (iii) the chief inspector for England and Wales appointed under section 4(2)(a) of the Radioactive Substances Act 1993;
   (iv) the chief inspector for Scotland appointed under section 4(2)(b) of that Act;
   (v) the chief, or any other, inspector, within the meaning of the Alkali, &c, Works Regulation Act 1906;
   (vi) an inspector appointed under section 19 of the Health and Safety at Work etc. Act 1974 by the Secretary of State in his capacity as the enforcing authority responsible for the enforcement of the Alkali, &c, Works Regulation Act 1906 or section 5 of the said Act of 1974;
"subordinate legislation" has the same meaning as in the Interpretation Act 1978.

GENERAL NOTE
Some principal amendments made by Sched. 22, are discussed in the General Note to s.120.

SCHEDULE 23

TRANSITIONAL AND TRANSITORY PROVISIONS AND SAVINGS

PART I

GENERAL TRANSITIONAL PROVISIONS AND SAVINGS

Interpretation of Part I

1. In this Part of this Schedule, the "transfer date" has the same meaning as in Part I of this Act.

Directions

2. Any directions given to the National Rivers Authority for the purposes of section 19 of the Water Resources Act 1991 shall have effect on and after the transfer date as directions given to the Agency for the purposes of section 6(2) of this Act.

Regional and local fisheries advisory committees

3. If and so long as the Agency requires, on and after the transfer date any advisory committee established and maintained before the transfer date by the National Rivers Authority under section 8(1) of the Water Resources Act 1991 shall be treated as if—
   (a) it had been established by the Agency,
   (b) the area by reference to which that committee was established had been determined by the Agency, and
   (c) in the case of a regional advisory committee, the chairman of that committee had been appointed,
in accordance with section 13 of this Act.

Charging schemes

4.—(1) Without prejudice to section 55 of this Act, any charging scheme—
   (a) which relates to any transferred functions,
   (b) which was made before the transfer date, and
   (c) which is in force immediately before that date or would (apart from this Act) have come into force at any time after that date,
shall, subject to the provisions of section 41 of this Act, have effect on and after the transfer date, with any necessary modifications, and for the remainder of the period for which the charging scheme would have been in force apart from any repeal made by this Act, as a scheme made under that section by the transferee in accordance with section 42 of this Act.

(2) Any costs or expenses incurred before the transfer date by any person in carrying out functions transferred to a new Agency by or under this Act may be treated for the purposes of subsections (3) and (4) of section 42 of this Act as costs or expenses incurred by that new Agency in carrying out those functions.

(3) In this paragraph—
   "charging scheme" means a scheme specifying, or providing for the determination of, any fees or charges;
   "new Agency" means the Agency or SEPA;
   "transferred functions" means any functions which, by virtue of any provision made by or under this Act, become functions of a new Agency and "the transferee" means the new Agency whose functions they so become.

Preparation of reports

5.—(1) The first report prepared by the Agency under section 52 of this Act may, to the extent that it relates to functions transferred to the Agency from any other body or person include a report on the exercise and performance of those functions by the transferor during the period between the end of the last year in respect of which the transferor prepared a report and the transfer date.

(2) SEPA shall, as soon as reasonably practicable after the transfer date, prepare a report on—
   (a) the exercise and performance of the functions of each river purification board during the period between the end of the last year in respect of which the board sent a report to the Secretary of State under section 16 of the Rivers (Prevention of Pollution) (Scotland) Act 1951 and the transfer date; and

(b) the exercise and performance of the functions of each waste regulation authority during the period between the end of the last financial year in respect of which the authority prepared and published a report under section 67 of the Environmental Protection Act 1990 and the transfer date.

(3) Subsections (3) and (4) of section 52 of this Act shall apply to a report prepared under sub-paragraph (2) above as they apply to a report prepared under that section.

Preparation of accounts

6. Notwithstanding the repeal by this Act of subsection (9) of section 135 of the Local Government (Scotland) Act 1973 (application to river purification board of certain provisions of that Act), the provisions applied to a river purification board by virtue of that section shall, as respects the period between the end of the last financial year in respect of which accounts have been made up by the board and the transfer date, continue to apply in relation to the board; but anything which shall or may be done or enjoyed, or any access, inspection or copying which shall or may be allowed, under or by virtue of any of those provisions or of section 118 of that Act (financial returns) by, or by an officer of, the board shall, or as the case may be may, after the transfer date, be done, enjoyed or allowed by, or by an officer of, SEPA in place of the board or of an officer of the board.

Membership of Welsh National Park authorities

7.—(1) Where a body corporate constituted as a Welsh National Park planning board becomes, or has become, the National Park authority in relation to the National Park in question by virtue of an order under section 63 of this Act made by virtue of section 64(1) of this Act, paragraph 2 of Schedule 7 to this Act shall, in its application in relation to that National Park authority at any time before 31st March 1997, have effect with the following modifications.

(2) In sub-paragraph (5)—
(a) in paragraph (a), after the word "council" there shall be inserted the words "or, if earlier, until the council which appointed him as a local authority member of that authority is excluded from the councils by whom such members of that authority are to be appointed"; and
(b) in paragraph (b), after the word "cessation" there shall be inserted the words "or exclusion".

(3) In sub-paragraph (6), after the words "Sub-paragraph (5)(a) above" there shall be inserted the words ", so far as relating to cessation of membership of a council,".

(4) In this paragraph, "Welsh National Park planning board" means a National Park planning board, as defined in section 64 of this Act, for the area of a National Park in Wales.

The Alkali, &c., Works Regulation Act 1906

8. Any dispensation which was granted under the proviso to subsection (5) of section 9 of the Alkali, &c, Works Regulation Act 1906 before the transfer date and which would, apart from this Act, have been in force on that date shall have effect on and after that date notwithstanding the repeal of that proviso by this Act.

The Public Records Act 1958

9.—(1) Such of the administrative and departmental records (in whatever form or medium) of a transferor as are transferred to and vested in the Agency by or under section 3 of this Act shall be treated for the purposes of the Public Records Act 1958 as administrative or departmental records of the Agency.

(2) In this paragraph, "transferor" means any body or person any or all of whose administrative and departmental records are transferred to and vested in the Agency by or under section 3 of this Act.

The Parliamentary Commissioner Act 1967

10.—(1) Nothing in this Act shall prevent the completion on or after the transfer date of any investigation begun before that date under the Parliamentary Commissioner Act 1967 in pursuance of a complaint made in relation to the National Rivers Authority.

(2) Nothing in this Act shall prevent the making on or after the transfer date of a complaint under that Act in respect of any action which was taken by or on behalf of the National Rivers Authority before that date.

(3) Notwithstanding the amendment of that Act by paragraph 11 of Schedule 22 to this Act, the provisions of that Act shall have effect on and after the transfer date in relation to any complaint to which sub-paragraph (1) or (2) above applies and to its investigation as they would

have had effect before that date; but, in relation to any such complaint, the Agency shall on and after that date stand in the place of the National Rivers Authority for the purposes of this paragraph.

The Local Government Act 1974

11.—(1) Where for any year, a Rate Support Grant Report under section 60 of the Local Government, Planning and Land Act 1980, or a supplementary report under section 61 of that Act, has effect to determine the amount of supplementary grants to be paid under section 7 of the Local Government Act 1974 to the council of a county or county borough in Wales, and at any time—
  (a) after that report or, as the case may be, that supplementary report is approved by a resolution of the House of Commons, but
  (b) not later than the end of that year,
a body corporate constituted as a National Park planning board for a National Park the whole or any part of which is included in that county or county borough becomes the National Park authority for that National Park by virtue of section 64 of this Act, those supplementary grants shall, subject to the provisions of any, or any further, such supplementary report, continue to be paid for that year notwithstanding that that body corporate has ceased to be a National Park planning board.
  (2) In this paragraph—
  "National Park planning board" has the meaning given by section 64(9) of this Act; and
  "year" means a period of 12 months beginning with 1st April.
12.—(1) Nothing in this Act shall prevent the completion on or after the transfer date by a Local Commissioner of any investigation which he began to conduct before that date and which is an investigation under Part III of the Local Government Act 1974 in pursuance of a complaint made in relation to the National Rivers Authority.
  (2) Nothing in this Act shall prevent the making on or after the transfer date of a complaint under Part III of that Act in respect of any action which was taken by or on behalf of the National Rivers Authority before that date.
  (3) Notwithstanding the amendment of Part III of that Act by paragraph 18 of Schedule 22 to this Act, the provisions of that Part shall have effect on and after the transfer date in relation to any complaint to which sub-paragraph (1) or (2) above applies and to its investigation as they would have had effect before that date; but, in relation to any such complaint, the Agency shall on and after that date stand in the place of the National Rivers Authority for the purposes of this paragraph.

The Control of Pollution Act 1974

13. As respects England and Wales, any resolution passed in pursuance of section 11 of the Control of Pollution Act 1974 (special provision for land occupied by disposal authorities: resolutions etc.) which is in force immediately before the day on which the repeals in that section made by this Act come into force shall have effect on and after that day as if it were a waste management licence granted by the Environment Agency under Part II of the Environmental Protection Act 1990 subject to the conditions specified in the resolution pursuant to subsection (3)(e) of that section.

The Salmon and Freshwater Fisheries Act 1975

14.—(1) Any approval or certificate given under or by virtue of section 8(2), 9(1) or 11(4) of the Salmon and Freshwater Fisheries Act 1975 by a Minister of the Crown before the transfer date shall, so far as is required for continuing its effect on and after that date, have effect as if given by the Agency.
  (2) Any application for the grant of an approval or certificate by a Minister of the Crown under or by virtue of any of the provisions specified in sub-paragraph (1) above which, at the transfer date, is in the process of being determined shall on and after that date be treated as having been made to the Agency.
  (3) Any notice given by a Minister of the Crown under section 11(2) of that Act before the transfer date shall, so far as is required for continuing its effect on and after that date, have effect as if given by the Agency.
  (4) Any extension of a period granted by a Minister of the Crown under section 11(3) of that Act before the transfer date shall, so far as is required for continuing its effect on and after that date, have effect as if granted by the Agency.
  (5) Without prejudice to section 16 or 17 of the Interpretation Act 1978, any exemption granted under subsection (1) or (2) of section 14 of the Salmon and Freshwater Fisheries Act 1975 which is in force immediately before the substitution date shall have effect on and after

that date as an exemption granted by the Agency under subsection (2) or, as the case may be, subsection (3) of section 14 of that Act as substituted by paragraph 13 of Schedule 15 to this Act.

(6) Any grating constructed and placed in a manner and position approved under section 14(3) of that Act as it had effect before the substitution date (including a grating so constructed and placed at any time as a replacement for a grating so constructed and placed) shall, if—

    (a) the approval was in force immediately before the substitution date, and

    (b) the grating is maintained in accordance with the approval,

be taken for the purposes of section 14 of that Act, as substituted by paragraph 13 of Schedule 15 to this Act, to be a screen which complies with the requirements of subsection (2)(a) or (3)(a) of that section, according to the location of the grating, and with the requirements of subsections (4) to (6) of that section.

(7) Any notice given, or objection made, under subsection (2) of section 18 of that Act before the transfer date shall, so far as is required for continuing its effect on and after that date, have effect as a notice given under that subsection as it has effect on and after that date.

(8) In this paragraph—

    "approval" includes a provisional approval;

    "grating" means a device in respect of which there is in force, immediately before the substitution date, an approval given for the purposes of the definition of "grating" in section 41(1) of the Salmon and Freshwater Fisheries Act 1975 as it had effect before that date;

    "the substitution date" means the date on which paragraph 13 of Schedule 15 to this Act comes into force;

    "the transfer date" means the date which, by virtue of section 56(1) of this Act, is the transfer date for the purposes of Part I of this Act as it applies in relation to the Agency.

The Local Government Finance Act 1988

15.—(1) Without prejudice to the generality of subsection (4) of section 64 of this Act, where an order has been made under section 63 of this Act by virtue of section 64(1) of this Act designating a date in relation to a Welsh National Park planning board, the body corporate constituted as that board may at any time before the designated date issue a levy by virtue of section 71 of this Act for a year at or before the beginning of which that body becomes the National Park authority for the National Park in question by virtue of section 64 of this Act as if it were the National Park authority for that National Park, notwithstanding that it has not in fact become a National Park authority at the date when it issues the levy.

(2) Without prejudice to the generality of section 74 of the Local Government Finance Act 1988, where—

    (a) an order is made under section 63 of this Act by virtue of section 64(1) of this Act designating a date in relation to a Welsh National Park planning board; and

    (b) the designated date is a date falling after the beginning, but before the end, of a year in respect of which, at the time the order is made, that board has not issued any levy under that section 74,

that board may nonetheless issue such a levy in respect of that year as if the body corporate constituted as that board was not in fact going to become the National Park authority for the National Park in question by virtue of that order before the end of that year.

(3) Sub-paragraph (5) below applies in a case where a levy is issued in respect of any year by a Welsh National Park planning board under section 74 of the Local Government Finance Act 1988 and—

    (a) that levy is issued by that board at a time when no order has been made under section 63 of this Act by virtue of section 64(1) of this Act designating a date in relation to that board; and

    (b) after the levy is issued, but no later than the end of the year in respect of which it is issued, such an order is so made designating in relation to that board a date falling not later than the end of that year.

(4) Sub-paragraph (5) below also applies in a case where a levy is issued in respect of any year by a Welsh National Park planning board under section 74 of the Local Government Finance Act 1988 and—

    (a) that levy is issued by that board at a time after an order has been made under section 63 of this Act by virtue of section 64(1) of this Act designating a date in relation to that board; and

    (b) the designated date is a date falling after the beginning, but before the end, of that year.

(5) In a case where this sub-paragraph applies, the levy in question or any levy substituted for that levy—

(a) shall have effect or, as the case may be, continue to have effect; and

(b) in particular, but without prejudice to the generality of paragraph (a) above, shall be paid or, as the case may be, continue to be paid,

as if the body corporate constituted as that board was not to, or had not, so become the National Park authority for the National Park in question (but was to continue, or had continued, to be the National Park planning board for that Park for the whole of that year).

(6) Where a body corporate constituted as a Welsh National Park planning board has or is to become the National Park authority for the National Park in question by virtue of an order made under section 63 of this Act by virtue of section 64(1) of this Act, nothing in this paragraph authorises that body corporate to issue for any year both a levy under section 74 of the Local Government Finance Act 1988 and a levy by virtue of section 71 of this Act.

(7) In this paragraph—

"the designated date" has the same meaning as in section 64 of this Act;

"National Park planning board" has the meaning given by section 64(9) of this Act;

"Welsh National Park planning board" means a National Park planning board for the area of a National Park in Wales;

"year" means a period of 12 months beginning with 1st April;

and any reference to the issue of a levy under section 74 of the Local Government Finance Act 1988 by a Welsh National Park planning board is a reference to the issue of a levy under that section by such a board by virtue of subsection (7) of that section.

The Environmental Protection Act 1990

16.—(1) Subject to sub-paragraph (2) below, if, at the transfer date, the content of the strategy required by section 44A of the Environmental Protection Act 1990 has not been finally determined, any plan or modification under section 50 of that Act, in its application to England and Wales, whose content has been finally determined before that date shall continue in force until the contents of the strategy are finally determined, notwithstanding the repeal by this Act of that section.

(2) If the strategy required by section 44A of that Act consists, or is to consist, of more than one statement, sub-paragraph (1) above shall apply as if—

(a) references to the strategy were references to any such statement; and

(b) references to a plan or modification under section 50 of that Act were references to such plans or modifications as relate to the area covered, or to be covered, by that statement.

17. If, at the transfer date, the content of the strategy required by section 44B of that Act has not been finally determined, any plan or modification under section 50 of that Act, in its application to Scotland, whose content has been finally determined before that date shall continue in force until the contents of the strategy are finally determined, notwithstanding the repeal by this Act of that section.

18.—(1) This paragraph applies to—

(a) any resolution of a waste regulation authority under section 54 of that Act (special provision for land occupied by disposal authorities in Scotland);

(b) any resolution of a waste disposal authority having effect by virtue of subsection (16) of that section as if it were a resolution of a waste regulation authority under that section,

which is in force on the transfer date.

(2) A resolution to which this paragraph applies shall continue in force—

(a) where no application is made under section 36(1) of that Act for a waste management licence in respect of the site or mobile plant covered by the resolution, until the end of the period of 6 months commencing with the transfer date;

(b) where an application as mentioned in sub-paragraph (a) above is made, until—

(i) the application is withdrawn;

(ii) the application is rejected and no appeal against the rejection is timeously lodged under section 43 of that Act;

(iii) any appeal against a rejection of the application is withdrawn or rejected; or

(iv) the application is granted.

(3) In relation to a resolution continued in force by sub-paragraph (2) above, the said section 54 shall have effect subject to the amendments set out in the following provisions of this paragraph.

(4) In subsection (2), for paragraph (b) there shall be substituted—

"(b) specified in a resolution passed by a waste regulation authority, or by a waste disposal authority under Part I of the Control of Pollution Act 1974, before the transfer date within the meaning of section 56(1) of the Environment Act 1995".

(5) In subsection (3) for paragraph (b) there shall be substituted—

"(b) by another person, that it is on land which is the subject of a resolution, that it is with the consent of the waste disposal authority and that any conditions to which such consent is subject are within the terms of the resolution."

(6) Subsections (4) to (7) shall cease to have effect.

(7) For subsections (8) and (9) there shall be substituted—

"(8) Subject to subsection (9) below, a resolution continued in force by paragraph 18 of Schedule 23 to the Environment Act 1995 may be varied or rescinded by SEPA by a resolution passed by it.

(9) Before passing a resolution under subsection (8) above varying a resolution, SEPA shall—

(a) prepare a statement of the variation which it proposes to make;

(b) refer that statement to the Health and Safety Executive and to the waste disposal authority in whose area the site is situated or, as the case may be, which is operating the plant; and

(c) consider any representations about the variation which the Health and Safety Executive or the waste disposal authority makes to it during the allowed period.

(9A) The period allowed to the Health and Safety Executive and the waste disposal authority for the making of representations under subsection (9)(c) above is the period of 28 days beginning with that on which the statement is received by that body, or such longer period as SEPA and that body agree in writing.

(9B) SEPA may—

(a) postpone the reference under subsection (9)(b) above so far as it considers that by reason of an emergency it is appropriate to do so;

(b) disregard the Health and Safety Executive in relation to a resolution which in SEPA's opinion will not affect the Health and Safety Executive."

(8) In subsection (10)—

(a) for the words "the authority which passed the resolution" and "the waste regulation authority" there shall be substituted the words "SEPA";

(b) the words "the waste disposal authority to discontinue the activities and of" shall cease to have effect.

(9) Subsections (11) to (15) shall cease to have effect.

The Water Industry Act 1991

19.—(1) Where, before the coming into force of the repeal by this Act of section 151 of the Water Industry Act 1991 (financial contributions to rural services), the Secretary of State has received an application from a relevant undertaker for a contribution under that section, he may, notwithstanding the coming into force of that repeal—

(a) give any such undertaking for any contribution sought by that application as he could have given under that section prior to the coming into force of that repeal;

(b) make any payments provided for in an undertaking given by virtue of this sub-paragraph.

(2) Notwithstanding the coming into force of the repeal by this Act of that section—

(a) the Secretary of State may make any payments provided for in an undertaking given by him under that section prior to the coming into force of that repeal;

(b) subsection (4) of that section (withholding and reduction of contributions) shall—

(i) continue to have effect in relation to contributions which the Secretary of State, before that repeal of that section, gave an undertaking under that section to make; and

(ii) have effect in relation to contributions which the Secretary of State has, by virtue of sub-paragraph (1) above, undertaken to make.

The Water Resources Act 1991

20. Notwithstanding any provision restricting the power of the Agency to grant a licence under Chapter II of Part II of the Water Resources Act 1991 (abstracting or impounding of water), or the power of the Secretary of State to direct the Agency to grant such a licence, the Agency may grant, and the Secretary of State may direct it to grant, such licences as are necessary to ensure that water may continue to be abstracted or impounded by or on behalf of the Crown in the manner in which, and to the extent to which,—

(a) it may be so abstracted or impounded immediately before the coming into force of sub-paragraph (4) of paragraph 2 of Schedule 21 to this Act in relation to that Chapter, or

(b) it has been so abstracted or impounded at any time in the period of five years immediately preceding the coming into force of that sub-paragraph in relation to that Chapter.

21.—(1) This paragraph applies to any consent—

(a) which was given under paragraph 2 of Schedule 10 to the Water Resources Act 1991 (discharge consents), as in force before the transfer date; and

(b) which is in force immediately before that date.

(2) On and after the transfer date, a consent to which this paragraph applies—

(a) shall, for so long as it would have continued in force apart from this Act, have effect as a consent given under paragraph 3 of Schedule 10 to that Act, as substituted by this Act, subject to the same conditions as were attached to the consent immediately before the transfer date; and

(b) shall—

(i) during the period of six months beginning with the transfer date, not be limited to discharges by any particular person but extend to discharges made by any person; and

(ii) after that period, extend, but be limited, to discharges made by any person who before the end of that period gives notice to the Agency that he proposes to rely on the consent after that period.

PART II

TRANSITORY PROVISIONS IN RESPECT OF FLOOD DEFENCE

Disqualification for membership of regional flood defence committee

22. Where a person is disqualified for membership of a regional flood defence committee by virtue of having been adjudged bankrupt before the coming into force of the Insolvency Act 1986, the rules applicable apart from the repeals made by the Consequential Provisions Act or this Act, rather than paragraph 3(2) of Schedule 5 to this Act, shall apply for determining when that disqualification shall cease.

Savings in relation to local flood defence schemes

23.—(1) In any case where—

(a) immediately before the coming into force of section 17 of this Act, any scheme or committee continues, by virtue of paragraph 14 of Schedule 2 to the Consequential Provisions Act, to be treated as a local flood defence scheme or a local flood defence committee, or

(b) immediately before the coming into force of section 18 of this Act, any person continues, by virtue of that paragraph, to hold office,

the scheme or committee shall continue to be so treated or, as the case may be, the person shall continue so to hold office, notwithstanding the provisions of section 18 of, or Schedule 5 to this Act or the repeal of any enactment by this Act.

(2) Where a person is disqualified for membership of a local flood defence committee by virtue of having been adjudged bankrupt before the coming into force of the Insolvency Act 1986, the rules applicable apart from the repeals made by the Consequential Provisions Act or this Act, rather than paragraph 3(2) of Schedule 5 to this Act, shall apply for determining when that disqualification shall cease.

Interpretation

24. In this Part of this Schedule, "the Consequential Provisions Act" means the Water Consolidation (Consequential Provisions) Act 1991.

SCHEDULE 24

REPEALS AND REVOCATIONS

Reference	Short title	Extent of repeal revocation
60 & 61 Vict. c.38.	The Public Health (Scotland) Act 1897.	Sections 16 to 26. Sections 36 and 37.
6 Edw. 7. c.14.	The Alkali, &c, Works Regulation Act 1906.	In section 9, the proviso to subsection (5). Section 25. In section 27(1), the definitions of the expressions "chief inspector" and "inspector". In section 28(b), the words "other than offences under subsection four of section twelve of this Act"; in sub-paragraph (ii), the words from "without the consent" to "direct, nor"; and sub-paragraph (iii).
12, 13 & 14 Geo. 6. c.97.	The National Parks and Access to the Countryside Act 1949.	In section 6(6), the words from "or a local planning authority" to "part of a National Park". Section 11. In section 11A(6)(b), the words "district council". Section 12(2). In section 13(1), the words "and within the area of the authority". In section 111A(3)(b), the words "for the purposes of section 64, 65 and 77".
14 & 15 Geo. 6. c.66.	The Rivers (Prevention of Pollution) (Scotland) Act 1951.	Part II. Section 17. In section 18, in subsection (1), the words "of their area", "in their area" (where first occurring) and "in their area or any part thereof"; and in subsection (3), the words "in their area" and the words from "whose" to "authority" where next occurring; In section 19, in subsection (1), the words "in the area of the authority", subsections (2) to (2B) and, in subsection (4), the words from "any", where first occurring, to "and", where last occurring. In section 35, the definitions of "river purification authority", "river purification board" and "river purification board area".
2 & 3 Eliz. 2. c.70.	The Mines and Quarries Act 1954.	Section 151(5).
8 & 9 Eliz. 2. c.62.	The Caravan Sites and Control of Development Act 1960.	In section 24(8), the words from "and a joint planning board" to "such a National Park".

Reference	Short title	Extent of repeal revocation
1965 c.13.	The Rivers (Prevention of Pollution) (Scotland) Act 1975.	Section 10(6)(a).
1965 c.57.	The Nuclear Installations Act 1965.	In section 3(3)(b), the words "the National Rivers Authority,".
1967 c.13.	The Parliamentary Commissioner Act 1967.	In Schedule 2, the entry relating to the National Rivers Authority and the note 9 inserted by paragraph 11 of Schedule 1 to the Water Act 1989.
1967 c.22.	The Agriculture Act 1967.	In section 50(3), paragraph (e) and the words from "and "National Parks planning authority" means" onwards.
1968 c.41.	The Countryside Act 1968.	In section 6(2), paragraph (c) and the word "or" immediately preceding it. Section 13(11). Section 40. In section 42(1), the words "whether or not within the area of the local planning authority". In section 47A— (a) in subsection (2), the word "18"; and (b) subsection (4).
1968 c.47.	The Sewerage (Scotland) Act 1968.	In section 38(3), the words "river purification authorities". Section 49. In section 59(1), the definition of "river purification authority".
1968 c.59.	The Hovercraft Act 1968.	In section 1(1)(g), the words "Part III of the Control of Pollution Act 1974 or".
1970 c.40.	The Agriculture Act 1970.	In section 92(1), the words "for their area" and "both within (and in the case of a river purification board) outwith, that area". Section 92(2)(c).
1972 c.52.	The Town and Country Planning (Scotland) Act 1972.	Section 251A.
1972 c.70.	The Local Government Act 1972.	Section 101(9)(h). In section 140A(2), in the definition of "local authority", the words "or reconstituted in pursuance of Schedule 17 to this Act". In section 184— (a) in subsection (2), the words "and Schedule 17 to this Act"; (b) in subsection (4), the words "subject to Schedule 17 of this Act"; and

Reference	Short title	Extent of repeal revocation
		(c) subsection (6). In section 223(2), the words "and the National Rivers Authority". In Schedule 16, paragraph 55(2). Part I of Schedule 17.
1972 c.v.	The Clyde River Purification Act 1972.	The whole Act.
1973 c.65.	The Local Government (Scotland) Act 1973.	Sections 135 and 135A. Section 200. In Schedule 16, paragraphs 1 to 5 and 7 to 10. In Schedule 27, in Part II, paragraphs 30 to 32, 37 and 38.
1974 c.7.	The Local Government Act 1974.	Section 7.
1974 c.37.	The Health and Safety at Work etc. Act 1974.	In section 28, in subsection (3)(c)(ii), so far as extending to England and Wales, the words "of the National Rivers Authority or" and the word "Authority" (where next occurring), subsection (3)(c)(iii) and, in subsection (5)(b), so far as extending to England and Wales, the words "the National Rivers Authority".
1974 c.40.	The Control of Pollution Act 1974.	In section 5, in subsection (4), the words following paragraph (b), and subsection (5). In section 7, in subsections (1) and (4), the words "issued by a disposal authority" and, in subsection (2), the words "or, in relation to Scotland, subsection (5)". In section 9(4), the words "issued by the authority". In section 11, subsection (1) to (11). In section 30(1), the words from "and for the purposes" to the end. In section 30A(2)(a), the words "in the area of that authority". In section 30C, in subsection (1), the words "within the area of that authority"; and in each of subsections (4) and (6), the words "in the area of a river purification authority". In section 31, subsections (1) to (3), in subsection (6), the words "in its area" and subsections (7), and (10). Section 31D. Section 32.

Reference	Short title	Extent of repeal revocation
		In section 33(1), the words "in the area of the authority".
		In section 34(3), the words "in its area".
		Section 40(4).
		In section 41(1), in paragraph (c), the words "(except section 40(4))" and paragraphs (d)(ii) and (e).
		In section 46(1), the words "in its area" where they first occur and "in its area or elsewhere".
		In section 47, in subsection (1), the words "in its area" and in subsection (2), the words "in the authority's area".
		In section 48(1), the words "in its area".
		In section 50, the words "in its area".
		Sections 53, 54, 55 and 56(4).
		In section 57, paragraph (a).
		Section 58.
		Section 58A.
		Section 58B.
		Section 59.
		Section 59A.
		In sections 61(9) and 65(8) the words "section 59 of this Act (in relation to Scotland) or" and the words "(in relation to England and Wales)".
		In section 69, in subsection (1), paragraph (a) and, in paragraph (c) the words "section 59(2) or", and in subsection (3) the words "section 59(6) or" and paragraph (i).
		In section 73, in subsection (1), the definition of "equipment" in the definition of "person responsible" paragraphs (b) and (c), and the definition of "road noise", and in subsection (3) the words from "; but a requirement" to the end of the subsection.
		In section 74, the words "Subject to sections 58A(8) and 59A(9) of this Act".
		In section 87(3), the words from the beginning to "offence; and" and the words "in its application to Scotland".
		Section 91(5)(a).
		In section 96(3), the words from "but as if" to the end.
		In section 104(1), the word "59".
		Section 106(2).

Reference	Short title	Extent of repeal revocation
		In Schedule 2, paragraphs 1 to 3. In Schedule 3, paragraphs 12 and 13.
S.I. 1974/2170.	The Clean Air Enactments (Repeals and Modifications) Regulations 1974.	In Schedule 2, paragraph 1.
1975 c.24.	The House of Commons Disqualification Act 1975.	In Schedule 1, in Part II, the entry relating to the National Rivers Authority.
1975 c.25.	The Northern Ireland Assembly Disqualification Act 1975.	In Schedule 1, in Part II, the entry relating to the National Rivers Authority.
1975 c.30.	The Local Government (Scotland) Act 1975.	In section 16, the words "and river purification boards". Section 23(1)(e). In Schedule 3, in paragraph 28(1), the words "or a river purification board".
1975 c.51.	The Salmon and Freshwater Fisheries Act 1975.	In section 5(2), the words following paragraph (b). In section 10, in subsections (1) and (2), the words "with the written consent of the Minister" in each place where they ocur. In section 15, in subsections (1) and (3), the words "with the written consent of the Minister" in each place where they occur. In section 30, the paragraph defining "fish farm". In section 41(1), the definition of "grating".
1975 c.70.	The Welsh Development Agency Act 1975.	In section 16(9), in the definition of "local authority", paragraph (b) and the word "or" immediately preceding it.
1976 c.74.	The Race Relations Act 1976.	In section 19A(2)(a), the words "a special planning board or a National Park Committee".
1980 c.45.	The Water (Scotland) Act 1980.	In section 33(3)(a), sub-paragraph (ii) and the preceding "and". In section 109(1), the definitions of "river purification authority" and "river purification board". In Schedule 1, in paragraph 11(ii) the words "and any river purification authority".
1980 c.65.	The Local Government Planning and Land Act 1980.	In section 52(1), paragraph (b) and the word "and" immediately preceding it. In section 103(2)(c), the word "and" immediately preceding sub-paragraph (ii).

Reference	Short title	Extent of repeal revocation
		In Schedule 2, paragraph 9(2) and (3).
1980 c.66.	The Highways Act 1980.	In section 25(2)(a) the words from "or a joint planning board" to "National Park". In section 27(6), the words from "or any such joint planning board" onwards. In section 29, the words "and joint planning boards". In section 72(2), the words "or joint planning board". Section 118(7).
1981 c.67.	The Acquisition of Land Act 1981.	In section 17, in subsection (3), the words "the Peak Park Joint or Lake District Special Planning Board" and, in subsection (4), in the definition of "a Welsh planning board", paragraph (b) and the word "or" immediately preceding it. In paragraph 4 of Schedule 3, in sub-paragraph (3), the words "the Peak Park Joint or Lake District Special Planning Board" and, in sub-paragraph (4), in the definition of "a Welsh planning board", paragraph (b) and the word "or" immediately preceding it.
1981 c.69.	The Wildlife and Countryside Act 1981.	Section 39(5)(a). In section 44, subsection (1) and in subsection (1A), the words from the beginning to "but". Section 46. In section 52(2), paragraph (a) and, in paragraph (b), the words "in any other provision". Section 72(10).
1982 c.30.	The Local Government (Miscellaneous Provisions) Act 1982.	In section 33(9), in paragraph (a), the words from "or reconstituted" to "1972" and, in paragraph (b), the words "or reconstituted". In section 41(13), in paragraph (b) of the definition of "local authority" the words from "or reconstituted" to "1972". In section 45(2)(b), the words from "or reconstituted" to "1972".
1982 c.42.	The Derelict Land Act 1982.	In section 1(11), in the definition of "local authority", paragraph (b) and the word "or" immediately preceding it.

Reference	Short title	Extent of repeal revocation
1982 c.48.	The Criminal Justice Act 1982.	In Schedule 15, paragraphs 6 and 7.
1983 c.35.	The Litter Act 1983.	In section 4(1)— (a) paragraph (b) and the word "and" immediately preceding it; and (b) the words "the National Park Committee (if any)" in each place where they occur. In section 6(8), the words "or a Park board". In section 10, paragraph (h) of the definition of "litter authority" and the definitions of "National Park Committee" and "Park board".
1984 c.54.	The Roads (Scotland) Act 1984.	In Schedule 9, paragraph 17(3).
1985 c.51.	The Local Government Act 1985.)	In Schedule 3— (a) paragraph 4; (b) in paragraph 5, sub-paragraphs (2) to (8); (c) paragraph 6; and (d) in paragraph 7, sub-paragraph (3) and in sub-paragraph (4), the words "42" and "44".
1985 c.68.	The Housing Act 1985.	In section 573, in subsection (1), the entries relating to the Peak Park Joint Planning Board and the Lake District Special Planning Board and, in subsection (1A), paragraph (b) and the word "or" immediately preceding it.
S.I. 197/180.	The Control of Industrial Air Pollution (Transfer of Powers of Enforcement) Regulations 1987.	Regulations 2 and 4.
1988 c.4.	The Norfolk and Suffolk Broads Act 1988.	In Schedule 6, paragraphs 2 and 13.
1988 c.9.	The Local Government Act 1988.	In Schedule 2, the entries relating to the Lake District Special Planning Board, the Peak Park Joint Planning Board and a special planning board constituted under paragraph 3A of Schedule 17 to the Local Government Act 1972.
1988 c.41.	The Local Government Finance Act 1988.	In section 74(7), paragraph (b) and the word "and" immediately preceding it.
1989 c.14.	The Control of Pollution (Amendment) Act 1989.	Section 2(3)(e). Section 7(2) and (8). Section 11(3).
1989 c.15.	The Water Act 1989.	In Schedule 1, paragraphs 1, 12 and 13.

Reference	Short title	Extent of repeal revocation
		In Schedule 17, paragraphs 3(2) and (3), 5(2), 7(9)(d) and 9(1). In Schedule 25, paragraphs 43(1) and paragraph 48(3) and (4).
1989 c.29.	The Electricity Act 1989.	In Schedule 8, paragraph 2(6) (a)(i).
1989 c.42.	The Local Government and Housing Act 1989.	Section 5(4)(c). Section 13(4)(d). In section 21(1), paragraph (m) and the word "and" immediately preceding it. Section 39(1)(h). Section 67(3)(o). Section 152(2)(k). In Schedule 1, in paragraph 2(1)(b), the word "(m)" and paragraph 2(1)(f).
1990 c.8.	The Town and Country Planning Act 1990.	In section 1, in subsection (5)— (a) in paragraph (a), the words from "and Part I" to "National Parks)"; and (b) in paragraph (c), the words "section 4 and"; and, in subsection (6), the words "section 4(3) and". In section 2(7), the words from "and Part I" to "National Parks)". Section 4. In section 4A(1), the words "instead of section 4(1) to (4)". Section 105. In section 244(1), the words from "or a board" to "1972". In Schedule 1— (a) in paragraph 4(2), the words "or county planning authority" and the words "or, as the case may be, which is"; (b) in paragraph 6, the words from "(including" to "National Park"; (c) in paragraph 13(1), paragraph (d) and the word "or" immediately preceding it; (d) in paragraph 19, sub-paragraph (2); and (e) in paragraph 20(4), paragraph (a) and, in paragraph (b), the word "other".
1990 c.9.	The Planning (Listed Buildings and Conservation Areas) Act 1990.	In section 66(3), the words from "and a board" onwards. In Schedule 4— (a) in paragraph 2, the word "4";

Reference	Short title	Extent of repeal revocation
		(b) in paragraph 3, the words "or county planning authority" and the words "or, as the case may be, which is"; and
		(c) in paragraph 4(1), the words "4(3) and (4)".
1990 c.10.	The Planning (Hazardous Substances) Act 1990.	In section 3— (a) in subsection (1), paragraph (a) and the words after paragraph (c); (b) subsection (2); and (c) in subsections (3) to (5A), the words "or (2)", wherever occurring.
1990 c.11.	The Planning (Consequential Provisions) Act 1990.	In Schedule 2— (a) paragraph 20; (b) paragraph 28(6); and (c) in paragraph 45, sub-paragraph (2) and in sub-paragraph (7), the words "118(7)".
1990 c.43.	The Environmental Protection Act 1990.	In section 4, in subsection (8), the words "or, as the case may be, in the Edinburgh Gazette", in each place where they occur, and, in subsection (11), the words "and Wales" in paragraph (b) and paragraph (c) and the word "and" immediately preceding it. Section 5. In section 7(9), the words from "and, in relation to Scotland," to the end. In section 8, subsection (4) and, in subsection (7) the words from "together with" onwards and subsection (9). Sections 16 to 18. Section 20(3) and (9). In section 23, in subsection (1), paragraphs (d) to (f) and (k), and subsections (4) and (5). In section 28, in subsection (1), the words from "but" onwards and subsections (3) and (4). In section 30, in subsection (4), the words "or regulation authorities" and the words from "establishing authorities" onwards and subsections (6) to (8).

Reference	Short title	Extent of repeal revocation
		Section 31.
		In section 33(1), the words "and, in relation to Scotland, section 54 below,".
		In section 36, subsections (5) and (6), in subsection (11), in the definition of "National Park authority", the words "subject to subsection (12) below" and subsection (12).
		In section 37(5), the words "(5), (6)," and "(8)".
		In section 39, in subsection (7), the words following paragraph (b), subsection (8), in subsection (12), in the definition of "National Park authority", the words "subject to subsection (13) below", and subsection (13).
		Section 41.
		In section 42, subsection (2) and, in subsection (7), the words from "and the power" onwards.
		Section 43(2)(a) and (b).
		Section 50.
		Section 54.
		Section 61.
		In section 64, subsection (1)(l) and, in subsection (4), the words "which is not a waste regulation authority".
		Sections 67 to 70.
		In section 71, subsection (1) and, in subsection (3), paragraph (b) and the word "or" immediately preceding it.
		Section 72.
		Section 75(3).
		In the heading immediately preceding section 79, the words ": England and Wales".
		In section 79, in subsection (7), in the definition of "local authority", the word "and" following paragraph (b).
		Section 83.
		In section 88, in subsection (9), paragraphs (c) and (d), and, in subsection (10), in the definition of "authorised officer", the words from "or in the case" to "on behalf of" and the definitions of "National Park Committee" and "Park board".
		In section 141, in subsection (5)(a), sub-paragraph (ii) and the word "and" immediately preceding it.

Reference	Short title	Extent of repeal revocation
		Section 143. In Schedule 2, in paragraph 17(2), the words "a waste regulation authority or". In Schedule 8— (a) paragraph 1(13); (b) paragraph 3; and (c) in paragraph 4, the words from the beginning to "in Wales)" and". In Schedule 15, paragraphs 5(4) and 16 and, in paragraph 31, in sub-paragraph (2), the word "(6)," where secondly occurring, the word "(2)", where thirdly occurring, and sub-paragraphs (4)(c) and (5)(c).
1991 c.28.	The Natural Heritage (Scotland) Act 1991.	In section 15(3) the words "and a river purification authority of whom such a requirement is made shall make such an application". In Schedule 2, paragraph 10(3). In Schedule 5, in paragraph 2 the words "in their area and". In Schedule 6, paragraph 1(5). In Schedule 8, in sub-paragraph (3) of paragraph 1, in the second column of the Table, in the fourth entry, the words ", river purification authority". In Schedule 10, paragraphs 1, 6, 7(2) and 9(3)(b) and (6).
1991 c.34.	The Planning and Compensation Act 1991.	In Schedule 4, paragraph 39.
1991 c.56.	The Water Industry Act 1991.	In section 4(6), the definition of "National Park authority" and the word "and" immediately preceding it. Section 132(7). Section 151. Section 171(4) and (5). In section 206(2), the words "196 or". In section 219(1), the definition of "the NRA".
1991 c.57.	The Water Resources Act 1991.	Sections 1 to 14. Sections 16 to 19. In section 34, the word "planning", wherever it occurs, and subsection (5). In section 45,— (a) in subsection (2), the word "planning", wherever it occurs; and (b) in subsection (3), the words "and (5)".

Reference	Short title	Extent of repeal revocation
		Section 58. Section 68. Section 69(5). In section 91, in subsection (1), the word "or" immediately preceding paragraph (f). Section 105(1). In section 113(1), in the definition of "drainage", the word "and" immediately preceding paragraph (c). Section 114. Section 117. Section 121 to 124. Section 126(6). Section 129(4). Sections 131 and 132. Section 144. Section 146. Sections 150 to 153. Section 187. In section 190(1), paragraph (d), paragraph (f) and the word "and" immediately preceding it. Section 196. Section 202(5). Section 206(2). Section 209(1), (2) and (4). Sections 213 to 215. Section 218. In section 219, in subsection (2), the words "Subject to subsection (3) below," and subsection (3). In section 221(1), the definitions of "the Authority" and "constituent council". Schedule 1. Schedules 3 and 4.
1991 c.59.	The Land Drainage Act 1991.	In section 61C(5), the definition of "National Park authority" and the word "and" immediately preceding it. In section 72(1), the definition of "the NRA".
1991 c.60.	The Water Consolidation (Consequential Provisions) Act 1991.	In Schedule 1, paragraphs 17, 18(a), 25, 27(2) and 56(3) and (4).
1992 c.14.	The Local Government Finance Act 1992.	Section 35(5)(a) and (b). In Schedule 13, paragraph 95.
1993 c.11.	The Clean Air Act 1993.	Section 3(2)(b) and the word "or" which immediately precedes it. Section 17. Section 42(5). Section 51(1)(b) and the word "or" which immediately precedes it. In Schedule 3, paragraph 4(b).

Reference	Short title	Extent of repeal revocation
1993 c.12.	The Radioactive Substances Act 1993.	Section 4. Section 5. In section 16, in subsection (2), the words "Subject to subsection (3)," subsection (3) and, in subsection (10), the words from "or, as" to "appropriate Minister". Section 17(4). In section 18, in subsection (1), the words "(or, in a case" to "or that Minister)" and "or the appropriate Minister, as the case may be," and, in subsection (2)(b), the words from "(or, where" to "that Minister)". Section 20(3). In section 21, subsection (3) and, in subsection (4), the words from "or, where" to "that Minister". In section 22, subsection (5), in subsection (6), the words from "or, where" to "that Minister" and in subsection (7), the words from "or, where" to "that Minister". In section 25, in subsection (2), the words from "or, in a case" to "Food," and "or their". In section 26, subsection (3)(a) and, in subsection (4), the words "England, Wales or". Section 28. Section 31. Section 35. In section 39, in subsection (2), the words from "or, as" to "and the chief inspector,". Section 42(5). Section 43. In section 47, in subsection (1), in the definition of "the appropriate Minister", paragraphs (a) and (b), in the definition of "the chief inspector", paragraphs (a) and (b), in the definition of "prescribed", the words from "or, in relation to fees" onwards and in the definition of "relevant water body", in paragraph (a), the words "the National Rivers Authority" and, in paragraph (b), the words "a river purification authority within the meaning of the Rivers (Prevention of Pollution) (Scotland) Act 1951".

Reference	Short title	Extent of repeal revocation
		In section 48, in the Table, the entry relating to the chief inspector. Schedule 2. In Schedule 3, in Part II, in paragraph 11 the words "16, 17".
1993 c.25.	The Local Government (Overseas Assistance) Act 193.	Section 1(10)(g).
1993 c.40.	The Noise and Statutory Nuisance Act 1993.	Section 6. Section 13(2). Schedule 1.
1994 c.19.	The Local Government (Wales) Act 1994.	Section 19(2) and (3). Section 59(15). In Schedule 5, in Part III, paragraph 10. In Schedule 6, paragraphs 3 to 12, 18, 23, 24(1), 28 and 29. In Schedule 9, paragraph 17(4) and (12). In Schedule 11, paragraph 3(1) and (2). In Schedule 15, paragraph 64(b). In Schedule 16, paragraph 65(5) and (9). In Schedule 17, paragraph 13.
1994 c.39.	The Local Government etc. (Scotland) Act 1994.	Section 37. Section 54(5). In section 165(6), the words "a river purification board". In Schedule 13, paragraphs 38(2) to (7), 85(3)(a) and (b)(i) and (4), 92(34) and (35), 93(2), 95(2), (4), (8) and (9), and 119(54)(a)(ii) and (h)(iii) and, in paragraph 167, sub-paragraph (2), in sub-paragraph (3) the words "(1) (g),", and sub-paragraphs (4), (5), (7) and (9).
1995 c.25.	The Environment Act 1995.	In section 8, in the definition of "National Park authority" in subsection (5), the words "subject to subsection (6) below" and subsection (6). In Schedule 10, paragraph 22(1) and (7) and, in paragraph 34(1), so much of paragraph (b) as precedes the word "and". In Schedule 11, in paragraph 1, in the definition of "National Park authority" in sub-paragraph (3), the words "subject to sub-paragraph (4) below" and sub-paragraph (4). In Schedule 22, paragraphs 19 to 27, 46(11)(a), 182 and 231.

APPENDIX 1

ENVIRONMENTAL PROTECTION (PRESCRIBED PROCESSES AND SUBSTANCES) REGULATIONS 1991

(S.I. 1991 No. 472)

In force from:

April 1, 1991 (England and Wales) and April 1, 1992 (Scotland)

Enabling power:

Environmental Protection Act 1990, s.2.

Background:

Part I of the Environmental Protection Act 1990 provided for integrated pollution control (IPC) as well as for the control of air pollution by local authorities (LAAPC). Section 2 provides that the Secretary of State may, by regulations, prescribe processes and substances for control. Prescribed processes may not be carried on or prescribed substances released into any environmental medium without prior authorisation after a date which the Secretary of State may prescribe.

These Regulations:
  (a) prescribe processes and substances for control; and
  (b) designate the prescribed process either for central control or for local control. By virtue of ss.2 and 21 of the Environment Act 1995, and consequential amendment to s.1 of the 1990 Act, the Environment Agency is the enforcing authority for processes prescribed for central control in England and Wales, whilst local authorities remain the enforcing authority for processes prescribed for local control. In Scotland, the Scottish Environment Protection Agency is the enforcing authority for all prescribed processes, whether designated for central or local control. (For this reason, "LAAPC" no longer accurately describes the air pollution control regime throughout Great Britain, and therefore this commentary adopts the term "local air pollution control" (LAPC).)

Schedule 1 contains the descriptions of processes prescribed for control and Scheds. 4–6 prescribe the substances. Rules for interpreting Sched. 1 are to be found in Sched. 2. Processes have come under control on a rolling timetable, and Sched. 3 prescribes the date from which authorisation is required for the carrying on of the prescribed processes or the release of the prescribed substances. The last such date for existing processes fell on January 31, 1996.

Statutory reference:

Environmental Protection Act 1990, s.2.

Amendments:

These Regulations have been amended on several occasions. Where changes result in processes moving between IPC and LAPC, or into control for the first time, then transitional provision is made. In some cases such transitional provision does not operate by amendment to these Regulations—in such cases the relevant parts of the amending Regulations are reproduced here immediately after these Regulations.

1991–92 Amendments:

S.I. 1991 No. 836 amended Sched. 3. S.I. 1992 No. 614 amended reg. 4, Scheds. 1 and 2. S.I. 1993 No. 2405 amended Sched. 1 Part A of Section 2.2. Part A of section 4.5, Schedule 2 Parts 2 to 3B; and Schedule 3. S.I. 1993 No. 1749 amended section 6.9 of Schedule 1 and Schedule 3.

Further minor amendments which are essentially clarificatory in nature have been made by the Environmental Protection (Prescribed Processes and Substances) (Amendment) Regulations 1992 (S.I. 1992 No. 614). However, S.I. 1992 No. 614 introduced one substantive amendment; Sched. 1, para. 6 deleted the previous requirement that combustion processes were controlled only where gases were emitted through a common stack, where the emissions arose from two or more boilers or furnaces. See also the Notes below on Sched. 3, Pts. I and II.

1993–94 Amendments:

The 1991 Regulations have been further amended by S.I. 1993 Nos. 1749 and 2405, and by S.I. 1994 No. 1271 and S.I. 1994 No. 1329 (these amendments came into force on two dates, 1st June 1994 and 1st December 1994).

Amendments made by S.I. 1994 No. 1271 which came into force on June 1, 1994 were amendments to paragraphs 2B and 2C of Schedule 2, and the following parts of Schedule 1: Part B of s.1.3, Part B of ss.2.1, 2.2 and 3.4, s.5.1, Part B of ss.6.5 and 6.7, s.6.6, Part B of s.6.8, s.6.9. All the remaining amendments came into force on the 1st December 1994. The transitionals in Schedule 6 were added by S.I. 1994 No. 1329. In addition, Schedule 6 to S.I. 1994 No. 1271 (as subsequently amended by S.I. 1994 No. 1329) contains transitional provisions which do not operate by way of amendment of the 1991 Regulations and must thus be read alongside it. This Schedule is reproduced here, immediately after the 1991 Regulations.

1995 Amendments:

Subject to transitional arrangements in their Sched. 2 (which is printed in this Appendix following the text of the 1991 Regulations), the Environmental Protection (Prescribed Processes and Substances) (Amendment) Regulations 1995 (S.I. 1995 No. 3247) made yet further amendments to the S.I. 1991 No. 472 with effect from January 8, 1996. These amendments moved a number of processes from IPC to LAPC or vice versa and brought certain processes within the scope of Pt. I of the 1990 Act (either IPC or LAPC) for the first time.

Since for the purposes of the application of the transitional provisions it is essential to appreciate which changes were made by the 1995 Regulations, they are printed in the text of the 1991 Regulations within double brackets, thus: [[   ]]. The 1995 Regulations amended the following Sections in Sched. 1, as well as amending Scheds. 2 and 5: sections 1.1, 1.3, 2.2, 4.1, 4.2, 4.5, 4.7, 4.8, 6.1, 6.5 and 6.9.

Note to Sched. 3, Pt. I:

The Environmental Protection (Prescribed Processes and Substances) (Amendment) Regulations 1992 (S.I. 1992 No. 614) amended the Prescribed Processes and Substances Regulations 1991 (S.I. 1991 No. 472) by, among other amendments, those to Sched. 1, s.1.3 (dealing with combustion processes). These amendments brought under control certain existing processes which the previous definition left out of control. The newly affected processes were accordingly required to submit an application for authorisation by July 1, 1992, over a year later than similar processes which were brought under control by the 1991 Regulations. S.I. 1992 No. 614, Sched. 2 therefore amends Pt. I of Sched. 3 to the 1991 Regulations to ensure that the newly affected processes can continue to be carried on if an application for authorisation is made before July 1, 1992. In relation to the newly affected processes therefore, paras. (2)–(7) of this Part (S.I. 1991 No. 472, Sched. 3, Pt. I) must be read as amended by S.I. 1992 No. 614, Sched. 2 as follows:

1. Part I of Schedule 3 to the 1991 Regulations shall apply to a process which by virtue of these Regulations becomes a process to which paragraph (a) of Part A of Section 1.3 of Schedule 1 to the 1991 Regulations applies as if—
   (a) in paragraph 2, for "1st April 1991" there were substituted "1st April 1992";
   (b) in paragraph 3(1)(ii), for the words from "the day after" to the end of the sub-paragraph there were substituted "1st July 1992";
   (c) in paragraph 3(2), for "1st April 1991" there were substituted "1st April 1992";
   (d) paragraph 4 were omitted;
   (e) in paragraph 5, for the words "within the appropriate period specified in paragraph 4" there were substituted "by not later than 30th June 1992";
   (f) in paragraph 6, for "1st April 1991" there were substituted "1st April 1992"; and
   (g) in paragraph 7, for the words from "1st April 1990" to "of that process" there were substituted "1st April 1991 and 30th June 1992".

Note to Sched. 3, Pt. II:

The Environmental Protection (Prescribed Processes and Substances) (Amendment) Regulations 1992 (S.I. 1992 No. 614) amended the Prescribed Processes and Substances Regulations 1991 (S.I. 1991 No. 472) by, among other amendments, those relating to Sched. 1, s.1.3, Pt. B (dealing with combustion processes), Sched. 1, s.2.2 (dealing with non-ferrous metals) and Sched. 1, s.51 (dealing with incineration). These amendments brought under control certain existing processes which the previous definition left out of control. The newly affected processes were accordingly required to submit an application for authorisation by July 1, 1992, over a year later than similar processes which were brought under control by the 1991 Regulations. S.I. 1992 No. 614, Sched. 2 therefore amends Pt. II of Sched. 3 to the 1991 Regulations to ensure that the newly affected processes can continue to be carried on if an application for an authorisation is made before July 1, 1992. In relation to the newly affected processes therefore, paras. (10)–(14) of this Part (S.I. 1992 No. 472, Sched. 3, Pt. II) must be read as amended by S.I. 1992 No. 614, Sched. 2, as follows:

2. Part II of Schedule 3 to the 1991 Regulations shall apply to a process which by virtue of these Regulations becomes a process to which Part B of Section 1.3, 2.2 or 5.1 of Schedule 1 to the 1991 Regulations applies as if—

(a) in paragraph 10, for the words from "the date specified" to the end of the paragraph there were substituted "1st April 1992";

(b) in paragraph 11(1)(ii), for the words from "the day after" to the end of the sub-paragraph there were substituted "1st July 1992";

(c) in paragraph 11(2), for the words from "in the period" to "(when changed)" there were substituted "on or after 1st April 1992 and before 1st July 1992";

(d) paragraph 12 were omitted;

(e) in paragraph 14(i), for the words from "the earlier date" to "falls" there were substituted "1st April 1992"; and

(f) in paragraph 14(ii), for "that earlier date" there were substituted "1st April 1992".

Citation, application and commencement

1.—(1) These Regulations may be cited as the Environmental Protection (Prescribed Processes and Substances) Regulations 1991.

(2) These Regulations shall come into force in England and Wales on 1st April 1991 and in Scotland on 1st April 1992.

Interpretation

2. In these Regulations—

"the Act" means the Environmental Protection Act 1990;

"background concentration" has the meaning given to that term in regulation 4(7);

"Part A process" means a process falling within a description set out in Schedule 1 hereto under the heading "Part A" and "Part B process" means a process falling within a description so set out under the heading "Part B"; and

"particulate matter" means grit, dust or fumes.

Prescribed provisions

3.—(1) Subject to the following provisions of these Regulations, the descriptions of processes set out in Schedule 1 hereto are hereby prescribed pursuant to section 2(1) of the Act as processes for the carrying on of which after the prescribed date an authorisation is required under section 6.

(2) Schedule 2 has effect for the interpretation of Schedule 1.

(3) In paragraph (1), the prescribed date means the appropriate date set out or determined in accordance with Schedule 3.

Exceptions

4.—(1) Subject to paragraph (6), a process shall not be taken to be a Part A process if it has the following characteristics, namely—

(i) that it cannot result in the release into the air of any substance prescribed by regulation 6(1) or there is no likelihood that it will result in the release into the air of any such substance except in a quantity which is so trivial that it is incapable of causing harm or its capacity to cause harm is insignificant; and

[(ii) that it cannot result in the release into water of any substance prescribed by regulation 6(2) except—
  (a) in a concentration which is no greater than the background concentration; or
  (b) in a quantity which does not, in any 12 month period, exceed the background quantity by more than the amount specified in relation to the description of substance in column 2 of Schedule 5; and]
(iii) that it cannot result in the release into land of any substance prescribed by regulation 6(3) or there is no likelihood that it will result in the release into land of any such substance except in a quantity which is so trivial that it is incapable of causing harm or its capacity to cause harm is insignificant.

(2) Subject to paragraph (6), a process shall not be taken to be a Part B process unless it will, or there is a likelihood that it will, result in the release into the air of one or more substances prescribed by regulation 6(1) in a quantity greater than that mentioned in paragraph (1)(i) above.

(3) A process shall not be taken to fall within a description in Schedule 1 if it is carried on in a working museum to demonstrate an industrial process of historic interest or if it is carried on for educational purposes in a school as defined in section 114 of the Education Act 1944 or, in Scotland, section 135(1) of the Education (Scotland) Act 1980.

(4) The running on or within an aircraft, hovercraft, mechanically propelled road vehicle, railway locomotive or ship or other vessel of an engine which propels [or provides electricity for] if it shall not be taken to fall within a description in Schedule 1.

(4A) The running of an engine in order to test it before installation or in the course of its development shall not be taken to fall within a description in Schedule 1.

[(4B) The use of a fume cupboard shall not be taken to fall within a description in Schedule 1 if it is used as a fume cupboard in a laboratory for research or testing, and it is not—
  (a) a fume cupboard which is an industrial and continuous production process enclosure; or
  (b) a fume cupboard in which substances or materials are manufactured.
In this paragraph, "fume cupboard" has the meaning given by the British Standard 'Laboratory fume cupboards' published by the British Standards Institution numbered BS7258: Part 1: 1990.]

(5) A process shall not be taken to fall within a description in Schedule 1 if it is carried on as a domestic activity in connection with a private dwelling.

(5A) [...]

(6) Paragraphs (1) and (2) do not exempt any process described in Schedule 1 from the requirement for authorisation if the process may give rise to an offensive smell noticeable outside the premises where the process is carried on.

[(7) In these Regulations—
"background concentration" means any concentration of the relevant substance which would be present in the release irrespective of any effect the process may have had on the composition of the release and, without prejudice to the generality of the foregoing, includes such concentration of the substance as is referred to in paragraph (8) below; and
"background quantity" means such quantity of the relevant substance as is referred to in paragraph (8) below.]

[(8) The concentration or, as the case may be, quantity mentioned in paragraph (7) above is such concentration or quantity as is present in—

(a) water supplied to the premises where the process is carried on;
(b) water abstracted for use in the process; and
(c) precipitation onto the premises on which the process is carried on.]

Enforcement

5.—(1) The descriptions of processes set out in Schedule 1 under the heading "Part A" are designated pursuant to section 2(4) of the Act for central control.

(2) The description of processes set out in Schedule 1 under the heading "Part B" are so designated for local control.

Prescribed substances: release into the air, water or land

6.—(1) The description of substances set out in Schedule 4 are prescribed pursuant to section 2(5) of the Act as substances the release of which into the air is subject to control under sections 6 and 7 of the Act.

(2) The descriptions of substances set out in [column 1 of] Schedule 5 are so prescribed as substances the release of which into water is subject to control under those sections.

(3) The descriptions of substances set out in Schedule 6 are so prescribed as substances the release of which into land is subject to control under those sections.

Regulation 3(1)   SCHEDULE 1

DESCRIPTIONS OF PROCESSES

CHAPTER 1: FUEL PRODUCTION PROCESSES, COMBUSTION PROCESSES (INCLUDING POWER GENERATION)

Section 1.1 Gasification and associated processes

PART A

[(a) Reforming natural gas.
(aa) Refining natural gas if that process is related to another Part A process or is likely to involve the use in any 12 month period of 1000 tonnes or more of natural gas.]
(b) Odorising natural gas or liquified petroleum gas [if that process is related to another Part A process].
(c) Producing gas from coal, lignite, oil or other carbonaceous material or from mixtures thereof other than from sewage or the biological degradation of waste [unless carried on as part of a process which is a combustion process (whether or not that process falls within Section 1.3 of this Schedule].
(d) Purifying or refining any product of any of the processes described in paragraphs (a), (b) or (c) or converting it into a different product.
In this section, "carbonaceous material" includes such materials as charcoal, coke, peat and rubber.

[PART B

(a) Odorising natural gas or liquified petroleum gas, except where that process is related to a Part A process.
(b) Blending odorant for use with natural gas or liquified petroleum gas.
(c) Any process for refining natural gas not falling within paragraph (aa) of Part A of this Section.]
[[In paragraph (c) of Part B of this Section, "refining natural gas"]] does not include refining mains gas."

Section 1.2 Carbonisation and associated processes

PART A

(a) The pyrolysis, carbonisation, distillation, liquefaction, partial oxidation or other heat treatment of coal [(other than the drying of coal)], lignite, oil, other carbonaceous material (as defined in Section 1.1.) or mixtures thereof otherwise than with a view to gasification or making of charcoal.

(b) The purification or refining of any of the products of a process mentioned in paragraph (a) or its conversion into a different product.

Nothing in paragraph (a) or (b) refers to the use of any substance as a fuel or its incineration as a waste or to any process for the treatment of sewage.

In paragraph (a), the heat treatment of oil does not include heat treatment of waste oil or waste emulsions containing oil in order to recover the oil.

PART B

Nil

Section 1.3 Combustion processes

PART A

[[(a) Burning any fuel in a combustion appliance with a net rated thermal input of 50 megawatts or more;]]

(b) [[...]]

(c) burning any of the following in an appliance with a net rated thermal input of three megawatts or more otherwise than as a process which is related to a Part B process—
  (i) waste oil;
  (ii) recovered oil;
  (iii) any fuel manufactured from, or comprising, any other waste.

[Nothing in this Part of this Section applies to the burning of any fuel in a boiler, furnace or other appliance with a net rated thermal input of less than 3 megawatts.]

[[For the purposes of paragraph (a) above, where—
  (i) two or more boilers or furnaces with an aggregate net rated thermal input of 50 megawatts or more (disregarding any boiler or furnace with a net rated thermal input of less than 3 megawatts); or
  (ii) two or more gas turbines or compression ignition engines with an aggregate net rated thermal input of 50 megawatts or more (disregarding any such turbine or engine with a net rated thermal input of less than 3 megawatts),
are operated by the same person at the same location those boilers or furnaces or, as the case may be, those turbines or engines, shall be treated as a single combustion appliance with a net rated thermal input of 50 megawatts or more.]]

PART B

The following processes unless carried on in relation to [and as part of] any Part A process—
  (a) burning any fuel in a boiler or furnace with a net rated thermal input of not less than 20 megawatts (but less than 50 megawatts);
  (b) burning any fuel in a gas turbine or compression ignition engine with a net rated thermal input of not less than 20 megawatts (but less than 50 megawatts);
  (c) burning as fuel, in an appliance with a net rated thermal input of less than three megawatts, waste oil or recovered oil;
  (d) burning in an appliance with a net rated thermal input of less than three megawatts solid fuel which has been manufactured from waste by a process involving the application of heat;
  (e) burning, in any appliance, fuel manufactured from, or including, waste (other than waste oil or recovered oil or such fuel as is mentioned in paragraph (d)) if the appliance has a net rated thermal input of less than three megawatts but at least 0.4 megawatts or is [used together with (whether or not it is operated simultaneously with)] other appliances which each have a net rated thermal input of less than three megawatts and the aggregate net rated thermal input of all the appliances is at least 0.4 megawatts.

In paragraph (c) of Part A and paragraph (e) of Part B, "fuel" does not include gas produced by biological degradation of waste; and for the purposes of this section—

"net rated thermal input" is the rate at which fuel can be burned at the maximum continuous rating of the appliance multiplied by the net calorific value of the fuel and expressed as megawatts thermal; and

"waste oil" means any mineral based lubricating or industrial oil which has become unfit for the use for which it was intended and, in particular, used combustion engine oil, gearbox oil, mineral lubricating oil, oil for turbines and hydraulic oil; and

"recovered oil" means waste oil which has been processed before being used.

Section 1.4 Petroleum processes

PART A

(a) The loading, unloading or other handling of, the storage of, or the physical, chemical or thermal treatment of—
  (i) crude oil;
  (ii) stabilised crude petroleum;
  (iii) crude shale oil;
  (iv) [if related to another process described in this paragraph, any associated gas or condensate].
  [. . .]
(c) Any process not falling within any other description in this Schedule by which the product of any process described in paragraph (a) above is subject to further refining or conversion or is used (otherwise than as a fuel or solvent) in the manufacture of a chemical.

CHAPTER 2: METAL PRODUCTION AND PROCESSING

Section 2.1 Iron and steel

PART A

(a) Loading, unloading or otherwise handling or storing iron ore except in the course of mining operations.
(b) Loading, unloading or otherwise handling or storing burnt pyrites.
(c) Crushing, grading, grinding, screening, washing or drying iron ore or any mixture of iron ore and other materials.
(d) Blending or mechanically mixing grades of iron ore or iron ore with other materials.
[(e) Pelletising, calcining, roasting or sintering iron ore or any mixture of iron ore and other materials.]
(f) Making, melting or refining iron, steel or any ferrous alloy in any furnace other than a furnace described in Part B in this section.
(g) Any process for the refining or making of iron, steel or any ferrous alloy in which air or oxygen or both are used unless related to a process described in Part B of this section.
(h) The desulphurisation of iron, steel or any ferrous alloy made by a process described in this Part of this section.
(i) Heating iron, steel or any ferrous alloy (whether in a furnace or other appliance) to remove grease, oil or any other non-metallic contaminant (including such operations as the removal by heat of plastic or rubber covering from scrap cable), if related to another process described in this Part of this section.
(j) Any foundry process (including ancillary foundry operations such as the manufacture and recovery of moulds, the reclamation of sand, fettling, grinding and shot-blasting) if related to another process described in this Part of this section.
(k) [. . .]
(l) Handling slag in conjunction with a process described in paragraph (f) or (g).
[(m) Any process for rolling iron, steel or any ferrous alloy carried on in relation to any process described in paragraph (f) or (g), and any process carried on in conjunction with such rolling involving the scarfing or cutting with oxygen of iron, steel or any ferrous alloy.]

Nothing in paragraph (a) or (b) of this Part of this section applies to the handling or storing of other minerals in association with the handling or storing of iron ore or burnt pyrites.

[A process does not fall within paragraph (a), (b), (c) or (d) of this Part of this Section unless—
  (i) it is carried on as part of or is related to a process falling within a paragraph of this Part of this Section other than paragraph (a), (b), (c) or (d); or

(ii) it consists of, forms part of or is related to a process which is likely to involve the unloading in any 12 months period of more than 500,000 tonnes of iron ore or burnt pyrites or, in aggregate, both.]

PART B

(a) Making, melting or refining iron, steel or any ferrous alloy in—
    (i) an electric arc furnace with a designed holding capacity of less than seven tonnes; or
    (ii) a cupola, crucible furnace, reverberatory furnace, rotary furnace, induction furnace or resistance furnace.
[(b) Any process for the refining or making of iron, steel or any ferrous alloy in which air or oxygen or both are used, if related to a process described in this Part of this Section.]
(c) The desulphurisation of iron, steel or any ferrous alloy, if the process does not fall within paragraph (h) of Part A of this section.
(d) Any such process as is described in paragraph (i) of Part A above, if not falling within that paragraph[; but a process does not fall within this paragraph if—
    (i) it is a process for heating iron, steel or any ferrous alloy in one or more furnaces or other appliances the primary combustion chambers of which have in aggregate a net rated thermal input of less than 0.2 megawatts;
    (ii) it does not involve the removal by heat of plastic or rubber covering from scrap cable or of any asbestos contaminant; and
    (iii) it is not related to any other process described in this Part of this Section.]
(e) Any foundry process (including ancillary foundry operations such as the manufacture and recovery of moulds, the reclamation of sand, fettling, grinding and shot-blasting) if related to another process described in this Part of this section.
[(f) Any other process involving the casting of iron, steel or any ferrous alloy from deliveries of 50 tonnes or more at one time of molten metal.]
Any description of a process in this section includes, where the process produces slag, the crushing, screening or grading or other treatment of the slag if that process is related to the process in question.
[In this section "net rated thermal input has the same meaning as in Section 1.3.]
[In this Section and Section 2.2, "ferrous alloy" means an alloy of which iron is the largest constituent, or equal to the largest constituent, by weight, whether or not that alloy also has a non-ferrous metal content greater than any percentage specified in Section 2.2 below, and "non-ferrous metal alloy" shall be construed accordingly.]

Section 2.2 Non-ferrous metals

PART A

(a) The extraction or recovery from any material—
    (i) by chemical means or the use of heat of any non-ferrous metal or alloy of non-ferrous metal or any compound of a non-ferrous metal; or
    (ii) by electrolytic means, of aluminium,
if the process may result in the release into the air of particulate matter or any metal, metalloid or any metal or mettalloid compound or in the release into water of a substance described in Schedule 5 [[and does not fall]] within paragraph (b) of Part B of this section.
In this paragraph 'material' includes ores, scrap and other waste.
(b) The mining of zinc or tin where the process may result in the release into water of cadmium or any compound of cadmium.
(c) The refining of any non-ferrous metal [(other than the electrolytic refining of copper)] or non-ferrous metal alloy except where the process is related to a process falling within a description in paragraphs [[(a), (c) or (d)]] of Part B of this section.
(d) Any process other than a process described in [[paragraph (b), (c) or (d) of Part B]] of this section for making or melting any non-ferrous metal or non-ferrous metal alloy in a furnace, bath or other holding vessel if the furnace, bath or vessel employed has a designed holding capacity of five tonnes or more.
[(e) Any process for producing, melting or recovering by chemical means or by the use of heat lead or any lead alloy, if—

(i) the process may result in the release into the air of particulate matter or smoke which contains lead; and

(ii) in the case of lead alloy, the percentage by weight of lead in the alloy in molten form exceeds 23% if the alloy contains copper and 2% in other cases.]

[(ee) Any process for [. . .] recovering any of the elements listed below if the process may result in the release into the air of particulate matter or smoke which contains any of those elements—

gallium
indium
palladium
tellurium
thallium.]

[(f) Any process for producing, melting or recovering (whether by chemical means or by electrolysis or by the use of heat) cadmium or mercury or any alloy containing more than 0.05 per cent by weight of either of those metals or of both of those metals in aggregate.]

(g) Any manufacturing or repairing process involving the use [manufacture or] of beryllium or selenium or an alloy of one or both of those metals if the process may occasion the release into the air of any substance described in Schedule 4 [; but a process does not fall within this paragraph by reason solely of its involving the melting of an alloy or beryllium if that alloy contains less than 0.1 per cent by weight of beryllium in molten form and the process falls within a description in [[paragraph (a) or (d)]] of Part B of this Section.]

(h) The heating in a furnace or other appliance of any non-ferrous metal or non-ferrous metal alloy for the purpose of removing grease, oil or any other non-metallic contaminant (including such operations as the removal by heat of plastic or rubber covering from scrap cable), if related to another process described in this Part of this Section.

(i) Any foundry process (including ancillary foundry operations such as the manufacture and recovery of moulds, the reclamation of sand, fettling, grinding and shot-blasting) if related to another process described in this Part of this section.

(j) [. . .]

(k) Pelletising, calcining, roasting or sintering any non-ferrous metal ore or any mixture of such ore and other materials.]

PART B

(a) The making or melting of any non-ferrous metal or non-ferrous metal alloy [other than tin or any alloy which in molten form, contains 50% or more by weight of tin] in any furnace, bath or other holding vessel with a designed holding capacity of less than five tonnes (together with any incidental refining).

[[(b) The separation of copper, aluminium, magnesium or zinc from mixed scrap by differential melting.]]

[(bb) The fusion of calcined bauxite for the production of artificial corundum.]

(c) Melting zinc or a zinc alloy in conjunction with a galvanising process.

[[(d) Melting zinc, aluminium or magnesium or an alloy of one or more of these metals in conjunction with a die-casting process.]]

(e) Any such process as is described in paragraph (h) of Part A above, if not related to another process described in that Part [; but a process does not fall within this paragraph if—

(i) it involves the use of one or more furnaces or other appliances the primary combustion chambers of which have in aggregate a net rated thermal input of less than 0.2 megawatts; and

(ii) it does not involve the removal by heat of plastic or rubber covering from scrap cable or of any asbestos contaminant.]

(f) Any foundry process (including ancillary foundry operations such as the manufacture and recovery of moulds, the reclamation of sand, fettling, grinding and shot-blasting) if related to another process described in this Part of this section.

[[. . .]]

The process described in [[paragraphs (a), (c), and (d)]] above include any related process for the refining of any non-ferrous metal or non-ferrous metal alloy.]

[In this section "net rated thermal input" has the same meaning as Section 1.3.]

[Nothing in this Section shall be taken to prescribe the processes of hand soldering or flow soldering.]

Section 2.3 Smelting processes

PART A

[...]

PART B

[...]

CHAPTER 3: MINERAL INDUSTRIES

Section 3.1 Cement and lime manufacture and associated processes

PART A

(a) Making cement clinker.
(b) Grinding cement clinker.
(c) Any of the following processes, where the process is related to a process described in paragraphs (a) or (b), namely, blending cement; putting cement into silos for bulk storage; removing cement from silos in which it has been stored in bulk; and any process involving the use of cement in bulk, including the bagging of cement and cement mixtures, the batching of ready-mixed concrete and the manufacture of concrete blocks and other cement products.
(d) The heating of calcium carbonate or calcium magnesium carbonate for the purpose of making lime where the process is likely to involve the heating in any 12 month period of 5,000 tonnes or more of either substance or, in aggregate, or both.
(e) The slaking of lime for the purpose of making calcium hydroxide or calcium magnesium hydroxide where the process is related to a process described in paragraph (d) above.

PART B

(a) Any of the following processes, if not related to a process falling within a description in Part A of this Section—
    (i) storing, loading or unloading cement or cement clinker in bulk prior to further transportation in bulk;
    (ii) blending cement in bulk or using cement in bulk other than at a construction site, including the bagging of cement and cement mixtures, the batching of ready-mixed concrete and the manufacture of concrete blocks and other cement products.
(b) The slaking of lime for the purpose of making calcium hydroxide or calcium magnesium hydroxide unless related to [and carried on as part of] a process falling within another description in this Schedule.
[(c) The heating of calcium carbonate or calcium magnesium carbonate for the purpose of making lime where the process is not likely to involve the heating in any 12 month period of 5,000 tonnes or more of either substance or, in aggregate, of both.]

Section 3.2 Processes involving asbestos

PART A

(a) Producing raw asbestos by extraction from the ore except where the process is directly associated with the mining of the ore.
(b) The manufacture and, where related to the manufacture, the industrial finishing of the following products where the use of asbestos is involved—
    asbestos cement
    asbestos cement products
    asbestos fillers
    asbestos filters

asbestos floor coverings
asbestos friction products
asbestos insulating board
asbestos jointing, packaging and reinforcement material
asbestos packing
asbestos paper or card
asbestos textiles.
(c) The stripping of asbestos railway vehicles except—
    (i) in the course of the repair or maintenance of the vehicle;
    (ii) in the course of recovery operations following an accident; or
    (iii) where the asbestos is permanently bonded in [cement or in any other material (including plastic, rubber or a resin)].
(d) The destruction by burning of a railway vehicle if asbestos has been incorporated in, or sprayed on to, its structure.

PART B

The industrial finishing of any product mentioned in paragraph (b) of Part A of this section if the process does not fall within that paragraph.
In this section, "asbestos" means any of the following fibrous silicates—
actinolite, amosite, anthophyllite, chrysotile, crocidolite and tremolite.

Section 3.3 Other mineral fibres

PART A

Manufacturing—
    (i) glass fibre;
    (ii) any fibre from any mineral other than asbestos.

PART B

Nil

Section 3.4 Other mineral processes

PART A

Nil

PART B

(a) The crushing, grinding or other size reduction [other than the cutting of stone] or the grading, screening or heating of any designated mineral or mineral product except where—
    (i) the process falls within a description in another section of this Schedule;
    (ii) the process is related to [or carried on as part of] another process falling within such a description; or
    (iii) the operation of the process is unlikely to result in the release into the air of particulate matter.
(b) Any of the following processes unless carried on at an exempt location or as part of a process falling within another description in this Schedule—
    (i) crushing, grinding or otherwise breaking up coal or coke or any other coal product;
    (ii) screening, grading or mixing coal, or coke or any other coal product;
    (iii) loading or unloading [petroleum coke] coal, coke or any other coal product except unloading on retail sale.
(c) The crushing, grinding or other size reduction, with machinery designed for that purpose, of bricks, tiles or concrete.
(d) Screening the product of any such process as is described in paragraph (c).
(e) Coating roadstone with tar or bitumen.
[(f) Loading, unloading, or storing pulverised fuel ash in bulk prior to further transportation in bulk, unless carried on as part of or in relation to a process falling within another description in this Schedule.]

797

In this section—
    "coal" includes lignite;
    "designated mineral or mineral product" means—
        (i) clay, sand and any other naturally occurring mineral other than coal or lignite;
        (ii) metallurgical slag;
        (iii) boiler or furnace ash produced from the burning of coal, coke or any other coal product;
        (iv) gypsum which is a by-product of any process; and
    "exempt location" means—
        [(i) any premises used for the sale of petroleum coke, coal, coke, or any coal product where the throughput of such substances at those premises in any 12 month period is in aggregate likely to be less than 10,000 tonnes; or
        (ii) any premises to which petroleum coke, coal, coke, or any coal product is supplied only for use there;]
    ["retail sale" means sale to the final consumer.]
Nothing in this section applies to any process carried on underground.

Section 3.5 Glass manufacture and production

PART A

The manufacture of glass frit or enamel frit and its use in any process where that process is related to its manufacture [and the aggregate quantity of such substances manufactured in any 12 month period is likely to be 100 tonnes or more].

PART B

    (a) The manufacture of glass at any location where the person concerned has the capacity to make 5,000 tonnes or more of glass in any 12 month period, and any process involving the use of glass which is carried on at any such location in conjunction with its manufacture.
    (b) The manufacture of glass where the use of lead or any lead compound is involved.
    (c) The making of any glass product where lead or any lead compound has been used in the manufacture of the glass except—
        (i) the making of products from lead glass blanks;
        (ii) the melting, or mixing with another substance, of glass manufactured elsewhere to produce articles such as ornaments or road paint;
    (d) Polishing or etching glass or glass products in the course of any manufacturing process if—
        (i) hydrofluoric acid is used; or
        (ii) hydrogen fluoride may be released into the air.
    [(e) The manufacture of glass frit or enamel frit and its use in any process where that process is related to its manufacture if not falling within Part A of this Section.]

Section 3.6 Ceramic production

PART A

    (a) Firing heavy clay goods or refractory [material] in a kiln where a reducing atmosphere is used for a purpose other than coloration.

PART B

    (a) Firing heavy clay goods or refractory [material (other than heavy clay goods)] in a kiln where the process does not fall within a description in Part A of this section.
    [(b) Vapour glazing earthenware or clay with salts.]
  In this section, "clay" includes a blend of clay with ash, sand or other materials [; "refractory material" means material (such as fireclay, silica, magnesite, chrome-magnesite, sillimanite, sintered alumina, beryllia and boron nitride) which is able to withstand high temperatures and to function as a furnace lining or in other similar high temperature applications.]

(See paragraph 4 of Schedule 2 as to cases where processes described in this chapter of the Schedule fall within two or more descriptions.)
[Except where paragraph 2 or 8 of Schedule 2 applies, nothing in this chapter of this Schedule applies to the operation of waste treatment plant.]

Section 4.1 Petrochemical processes

PART A

(a) Any process for the manufacture of [unsaturated hydrocarbons].
(b) Any process for the manufacture of any chemical which involves the use of a product of a process described in paragraph (a).
(c) Any process for the manufacture of any chemical which involves the use of a product of a process described in paragraph (b) otherwise than as a fuel or solvent.
[[(d) Any process for the polymerisation or co-polymerisation of any unsaturated hydrocarbons (other than the polymerisation or co-polymerisation of a pre-formulated resin or pre-formulated gel coat which contains any unsaturated hydrocarbons, or which contains any product of a process mentioned in paragraph (b) or (c) of Part A of this Section) which is likely to involve, in any 12 month period, the polymerisation or co-polymerisation of 50 tonnes or more of unsaturated hydrocarbons or of any such products or, in aggregate, of any combination of those materials and products.]]
[[(e) Any process, if related to and carried on as part of a process falling within another paragraph of this Part of this Section, for the polymerisation or co-polymerisation of any pre-formulated resin or pre-formulated gel coat which contains any unsaturated hydrocarbons, or which contains any product of a process mentioned in paragraph (b) or (c) of Part A of this Section, which is likely to involve, in any 12 month period, the polymerisation or co-polymerisation of 100 tonnes or more of unsaturated hydrocarbons or of any such products or, in aggregate, of any combination of those materials and products.]]

[[PART B

Any process, unless related to and carried on as part of a process falling within Part A of this Section, for the polymerisation or co-polymerisation of any pre-formulated resin or pre-formulated gel coat which contains any unsaturated hydrocarbons, or which contains any product or a process mentioned in paragraph (b) or (c) of Part A of this Section, which is likely to involve, in any 12 month period, the polymerisation or co-polymerisation of 100 tonnes or more of unsaturated hydrocarbons or of any such products or, in aggregate, of any combination of those materials and products.]]
[[In this Section and in Section 4.2, "pre-formulated resin and pre-formulated gel coat" means any resin or gel coat which has been formulated before being introduced into the polymerisation or co-polymerisation process (whether or not the resin or gel coat contain a colour pigment, activator or catalyst).]]

Section 4.2 The manufacture and use of organic chemicals

PART A

Any of the following processes unless falling within a description set out in Section 6.8—
[(a) the manufacture of styrene or vinyl chloride;
[[(aa) the polymerisation or co-polymerisation of styrene or vinyl chloride (other than the polymerisation or co-polymerisation of a pre-formulated resin or pre-formulated gel coat which contains any styrene) where the process is likely to involve, in any 12 month period, the polymerisation or co-polymerisation of 50 tonnes or more of either of those materials or, in aggregate, of both;]]
[[(ab) any process, if related to and carried on as part of a process falling within another paragraph of this Part of this Section, for the polymerisation or co-polymerisation of any pre-formulated resin or pre-formulated gel coat which contains any styrene, which is likely to involve, in any 12 month period, the polymerisation or co-polymerisation of 100 tonnes or more of styrene;]]

(b) any process of manufacture involving the use of vinyl chloride;
(c) the manufacture of acetylene, any aldehyde, amine, isocyanate, nitrile, [any carboxylic acid or any anhydride of carboxylic acid], any organic sulphur compound or any phenol, if the process may result in the release of any of those substances into the air;
[(d) any process for the manufacture of a chemical involving the use of any substance mentioned in paragraph (c) if the process may result in the release of any such substance into the air;]
(e) the manufacture or recovery of carbon disulphide;
(f) any manufacturing process which may result in the release of carbon disulphide into the air;
[(g) the manufacture or recovery of any pyridine, or of any substituted pyridines;]
(h) the manufacture of any organo-metallic compound;
(i) the manufacture, purification or recovery of any [designated] acrylate;
(j) any process for the manufacture of a chemical [which is likely to involve the use in any 12 month period of 1 tonne or more of any designated acrylate or, in aggregate, of more than one such designated acrylate].

[In this Part of this Section, "designated acrylate" means any of the following, namely, acrylic acid, substituted acrylic acids, the esters of acrylic acid and the esters of substituted acrylic acids.]

[[PART B

Any process, unless related to and carried on as part of a process falling within Part A of this Section, for the polymerisation or co-polymerisation of any pre-formulated resin or pre-formulated gel coat which contains any styrene, which is likely to involve, in any 12 month period, the polymerisation or co-polymerisation of 100 tonnes or more of styrene.]]

Section 4.3 Acid processes

PART A

(a) Any process for the manufacture, recovery, concentration or distillation of sulphuric acid or oleum.
(b) Any process for the manufacture of any oxide of sulphur but excluding any combustion or incineration process other than the burning of sulphur.
(c) Any process for the manufacture of a chemical which uses, or may result in the release into the air of, any oxide of sulphur but excluding any combustion or incineration process other than the burning of sulphur [and ...]
(d) Any process for the manufacture or recovery of nitric acid.
(e) Any process for the manufacture of any acid-forming oxide of nitrogen.
(f) Any other process (except the combustion or incineration of carbonaceous material as defined in section 1.1 of this Schedule) [which is not described in Part B of this Section, does not fall within a description in Section 2.1 or 2.2 of this Schedule and is not treated as so falling by virtue of the rules in Schedule 2, and] which is likely to result in the release into the air of any acid-forming oxide of nitrogen.
(g) Any process for the manufacture [or purification] of phosphoric acid.

[PART B

Any process for the surface treatment of metal which is likely to result in the release into the air of any acid-forming oxide of nitrogen and which does not fall within a description in Section 2.1 or 2.2 of this Schedule and is not treated as so falling by virtue of the rules in Schedule 2.]

Section 4.4 Processes involving halogens

PART A

The following processes if not falling within a description in any other section of this Schedule—
(a) any process for the manufacture of fluorine, chlorine, bromine or iodine or of any compound comprising only—

  (i) two or more of those halogens; or
  (ii) any one or more of those halogens and oxygen;
(b) any process of manufacture which involves the use of, or which is likely to result in the release into the air or into water of, any of those four halogens or any of the compounds mentioned in paragraph (a) other than the use of any of them as a pesticide (as defined in Schedule 6) in water;
(c) any process for the manufacture of hydrogen fluoride, hydrogen chloride, hydrogen bromide or hydrogen iodide or any of their acids;
(d) any process for the manufacture of chemicals which may result in the release into the air of any of the four compounds mentioned in paragraph (c);
(e) any process of manufacture (other than the manufacture of chemicals) involving the use of any of the four compounds mentioned in paragraph (c) [or any of their acids] which may result in the release of any of those compounds into the air, other than the coating, plating or [surface treatment] of metal [; and "manufacture of chemical fertilisers" shall be taken to include any process for blending chemical fertilisers which is related to a process for their manufacture.]

PART B

Nil

Section 4.5 Inorganic chemical processes

PART A

(a) The manufacture of hydrogen cyanide or hydrogen sulphide other than in the course of fumigation.
(b) Any manufacturing process involving the use of hydrogen cyanide or hydrogen sulphide.
(c) Any process for the manufacture of a chemical which may result in the release into the air of hydrogen cyanide or hydrogen sulphide.
(d) The production of any compound containing any of [the following]—
  antimony
  arsenic
  beryllium
  gallium
  indium
  lead
  palladium
  platinum
  selenium
  tellurium
  thallium,
where the process may result in the release into the air of any of those elements or compounds or the release into water of any substance described in Schedule 5 [[in a quantity which, in any 12 month period, exceeds the background quantity by more than the amount specified in relation to the description of substance in column 2 of that Schedule]].
(e) The recovery of any [. . .] compound referred to in paragraph (d) where the process may result in any such release as is mentioned in that paragraph.
(f) The use in any process of manufacture, other than the application of a glaze or vitreous enamel, of any element or compound referred to in paragraph (d) where the process may result in such a release as is mentioned in that paragraph.
(g) [The production or recovery of any compound of cadmium or mercury.]
(h) Any process of manufacture which involves the use of cadmium or mercury or of any compound of either of those elements or which may result in the release into the air of either of those elements or any of their compounds.
(i) The production of any compound of—
  chromium
  [. . .]
  manganese
  nickel
  zinc.
(j) The manufacture of any metal carbonyl.

801

  (k) Any process for the manufacture of [a chemical involving the use of a metal carbonyl].
  (l) The manufacture or recovery of ammonia.
 (m) Any process for the manufacture of a chemical which involves the use of ammonia or may result in the release of ammonia into the air other than a process in which ammonia is used only as a refrigerant.
  (n) The production of phosphorus or of any oxide, hydride or halide of phosphorus.
  (o) Any process for the manufacture of a chemical which involves the use of phosphorus or any oxide, hydride or halide of phosphorus or which may result in the release into the air of phosphorus or of any such oxide, hydride or halide.
  (p) The extraction of any magnesium compound from sea water.

PART B

Nil

Section 4.6 Chemical Fertiliser Production

PART A

  (a) The manufacture of chemical fertilisers.
  (b) The conversion of chemical fertilisers into granules.
In this section, "chemical fertilisers" means any inorganic chemical to be applied to the soil to promote plant growth; and "inorganic chemical" includes urea.

PART B

Nil

Section 4.7 Pesticide production

PART A

[The manufacture or the formulation of a medicinal product if the process may result in the release into water of any substance described in Schedule 5 [[in a quantity which, in any 12 month period, exceeds the background quantity by more than the amount specified in relation to the description of substance in column 2 of that Schedule]].]

PART B

Nil

In this section "pesticide" has the same meaning as in Schedule 6.

Section 4.8 Pharmaceutical production

PART A

[The manufacture or the formulation of chemical pesticides if the process may result in the release into water of any substance described in Schedule 5 [[in a quantity which, in any 12 month period, exceeds the background quantity by more than the amount specified in relation to the description of substance in column 2 of that Schedule]].]

PART B

Nil

In this Section, "medicinal product" means any substance or article (not being an instrument,

802

apparatus or appliance) manufactured for use in one of the ways specified in section 130(1) of the Medicines Act 1968.

Section 4.9 The storage of chemicals in bulk

PART A

[Nil]

PART B

The storage in a tank or tanks, other than as part of a Part A process, and other than in a tank for the time being forming part of a powered vehicle, of any of the substances listed below except where the total capacity of the tanks installed at the location in question in which the relevant substance may be stored is less than the figure specified below in relation to that substance;

any one or more designated acrylates	20 tonnes
acrylonitrile	20 tonnes
anhydrous ammonia	100 tonnes
anhydrous hydrogen fluoride	1 tonne
toluene di-isocyanate	20 tonnes
vinyl chloride monomer	20 tonnes
ethylene	8,000 tonnes

In this Section, "designated acrylate" has the same meaning as in Part A of Section 4.2.]

CHAPTER 5: WASTE DISPOSAL AND RECYCLING

Section 5.1 Incineration

PART A

(a) The destruction by burning in an incinerator of any waste chemicals or waste plastic arising from the manufacture of a chemical or the manufacture of a plastic.
(b) The destruction by burning in an incinerator, other than incidentally in the course of burning other waste, of any waste chemicals being, or comprising in elemental or compound form, any of the following—
　　bromine
　　cadmium
　　chlorine
　　fluorine
　　iodine
　　lead
　　mercury
　　nitrogen
　　phosphorus
　　sulphur
　　zinc.
(c) The destruction by burning of any other waste, including animal remains, otherwise than by a process related to [and carried on as part of] a Part B process, on premises where there is plant designed to incinerate such waste at a rate of one tonne or more per hour.
(d) The cleaning for reuse of metal containers used for the transport or storage of a chemical by burning out their residual content.

PART B

(a) The destruction by burning in an incinerator other than an exempt incinerator of any waste, including animal remains, except where related to a Part A process.
(b) The cremation of human remains.

In this section—

"exempt incinerator" means any incinerator on premises where there is plant designed to incinerate waste, including animal remains, at a rate of not more than 50 kgs per hour, not being an incinerator employed to incinerate clinical waste, sewage sludge, sewage screenings or municipal waste (as defined in Article 1 of EC Directive 89/369/EEC; and for the purposes of this section, the weight of waste shall be determined by reference to its weight as fed into the incinerator;

"waste" means solid or liquid wastes or gaseous wastes (other than gas produced by biological degradation of waste; and

"[clinical waste" means waste (other than waste consisting wholly of animal remains) which falls within sub-paragraph (a) or (b) of the definition of such waste in paragraph (2) of regulation 1 of the Controlled Waste Regulations 1992(b) (or would fall within one of those sub-paragraphs but for paragraph (4) of that regulation).]

Section 5.2 Recovery processes

PART A

[(a) The recovery by distillation of any oil or organic solvent.
 (b) The cleaning or regeneration of carbon, charcoal or ion exchange resins by removing matter which is, or includes, any substance described in Schedule 4, 5 or 6.
Nothing in this Part of this Section applies to—
 (i) the distillation of oil for the production or cleaning of vacuum pump oil; or
 (ii) a process which is ancillary and related to another process which involves the production or use of the substance which is recovered, cleaned or regenerated.]

PART B

Nil

Section 5.3 The production of fuel from waste

PART A

Making solid fuel from waste by any process involving the use of heat other than making charcoal.

PART B

Nil

CHAPTER 6: OTHER INDUSTRIES

Section 6.1 Paper and pulp manufacturing processes

PART A

(a) The making of paper pulp by a chemical method if the person concerned has the capacity at the location in question to produce more than 25,000 tonnes of paper pulp in any 12 month period.
(b) Any process [associated with] making paper pulp or paper (including processes connected with the recycling of paper such as de-inking) if the process may result in the release into water of any substance described in Schedule 5 [[in a quantity which, in any 12 month period, exceeds the background quantity by more than the amount specified in relation to the description of substance in column 2 of that Schedule]].

In this paragraph, "paper pulp" includes pulp made from wood, grass, straw and similar materials and references to the making of paper are to the making of any product using paper pulp.

PART B

Nil

Section 6.2. Di-isocyanate processes

PART A

(a) Any process for the manufacture of any di-isocyanate or a partly polymerised di-isocyanate.
(b) Any manufacturing process involving the use of toluene di-isocyanate or partly polymerised toluene di-isocyanate if—
    (i) 1 tonne or more of toluene di-isocyanate monomer is likely to be used in any 12 month period; and
    (ii) the process may result in a release into the air which contains toluene di-isocyanate.]
(c) [...]
[(d) The flame bonding of polyurethane foams or polyurethane elastomers, and the hot wire cutting of such substances where such cutting is related to any other Part A process.]

PART B

[(a) Any process not falling within any other description in this Schedule where the carrying on of the process by the person concerned at the location in question is likely to involve the use in any 12 months period of 5 tonnes or more of any di-isocynate or of any partly polymerised di-isocyanate or, in aggregate, of both.
(b) Any process not falling within any other description in this Schedule involving the use of toluene di-isocyanate or partly polymerised di-isocyanate if—
    (i) less than 1 tonne of toluene di-isocyanate monomer is likely to be used in any 12 month period; and
    (ii) the process may result in a release into the air which contains toluene di-isocyanate.
(c) The hot wire cutting of polyurethane foams or polyurethane elastomers, except where this process is related to any other Part A process.]

Section 6.3 Tar and bitumen processes

PART A

Any process not falling within any other description in this Schedule involving—
    (a) the distillation of tar or bitumen in connection with any process of manufacture; or
    (b) the heating of tar or bitumen for the manufacture of electrodes or carbon-based refractory materials,
where the carrying on of the process by the person concerned at the location in question is likely to involve the use in any 12 month period of 5 tonnes or more of tar or bitumen or, in aggregate, of both.

PART B

Any process not falling within Part A of this Section or within any other description in this Schedule involving—
    (a) the heating, but not the distillation, of tar or bitumen in connection with any process of manufacture; or
    (b) (unless the process is related to and carried on as part of a process falling within Part A of Section 1.4 of this Schedule) the oxidation of bitumen by blowing air through it.
where the carrying on of the process by the person concerned at the location in question is likely

to involve the use in any 12 month period of 5 tonnes or more of tar or of bitumen or, in aggregate, of both.

In this Section the expressions "tar" and "bitumen" include pitch.

Section 6.4 Processes involving uranium

PART A

[. . .]

PART B

[. . .]

Section 6.5 Coating Processes and Printing

PART A

(a) The application or removal of a coating material containing one or more tributyltin compounds of triphenyltin compounds, if carried out at a shipyard or boatyard where vessels of a length of 25 metres or more can be built or maintained or repaired.

(b) The treatment of textiles if the process may result in the release into water of any substance described in Schedule 5 [[in a quantity which, in any 12 month period, exceeds the background quantity by more than the amount specified in relation to the description of substance in column 2 of that Schedule]].

(c) [. . .]

PART B

[(a) Any process (other than for the repainting or respraying of or of parts of aircraft or road or railway vehicles) for the application to a substrate of, or the drying or curing after such application of, printing ink or paint or any other coating material as, or in the course of, a manufacturing process where—

   (i) the process may result in the release into the air of particulate matter or of any volatile organic compound; and

   (ii) the carrying on of the process by the person concerned at the location in question is likely to involve the use in any 12 month period of—

      (aa) 20 tonnes or more applied in solid form of any printing ink, paint or other coating material; or

      (bb) 20 tonnes or more of any metal coatings which are sprayed on in molten form; or

      (cc) 25 tonnes or more of organic solvents in respect of any cold set web offset printing process or any sheet fed offset litho printing process or, in respect of any other process, 5 tonnes or more of organic solvents.

(b) Any process for the repainting or respraying of or of parts of road vehicles if the process may result in the release into the air of particulate matter or of any volatile organic compound and the carrying on of the process by the person concerned at the location in question is likely to involve the use of 1 tonne or more of organic solvents in any 12 month period.

(c) Any process for the repainting or respraying of or of parts of aircraft or railway vehicles if the process may result in the release into the air of particulate matter or of any volatile organic compound and the carrying on of the process by the person concerned at the location in question is likely to involve the use in any 12 month period of—

   (i) 20 tonnes or more applied in solid form of any paint or other coating material; or

   (ii) 20 tonnes or more of any metal coatings which are sprayed on in molten form; or

   (iii) 5 tonnes or more of organic solvents.]

[In this Section—

   "aircraft" includes gliders and missiles;

   "coating material" means paint, printing ink, varnish, lacquer, dye, any metal oxide

coating, any adhesive coating, any elastomer coating, any metal or plastic coating and any other coating material.
the amount of organic solvents used in a process shall be calculated as—
  (a) the total input of organic solvents into the process, including both solvents contained in coating materials and solvents used for cleaning or other purposes; less
  (b) any organic solvents that are removed from the process for re-use or for recovery for re-use.]

Section 6.6 The manufacture of dyestuffs, printing ink and coating materials

PART A

[Any process for the manufacture of dyestuffs if the process involves the use of hexachlorobenzene.]

PART B

Any process [...]
  (a) for the manufacture or formulation of printing ink or any other coating material containing, or involving the use of, an organic solvent, where the carrying on of the process by the person concerned at the location in question is likely to involve the use of 100 tonnes or more of organic solvents in any 12 month period;
  (b) for the manufacture of any powder for use as a coating [material] where there is the capacity to produce 200 tonnes or more of such powder in any 12 month period.
In this section, "coating material" has the same meaning as in Section 6.5, and the amount of organic solvents used in a process shall be calculated as—
  (a) the total input of organic solvents into the process, including both solvents contained in coating materials and solvents used for cleaning or other purposes; less
  (b) any organic solvents (not contained in coating materials) that are removed from the process for re-use or for recovery for re-use.]

Section 6.7 Timber processes

PART A

  (a) The curing or chemical treatment as part of a manufacturing process of timber or of products wholly or mainly made of wood if any substance described in Schedule 5 is used.
  (b) [...]

PART B

The manufacture of products wholly or mainly of wood at any works if the process involves the sawing, drilling, sanding, shaping, turning, planing, curing or chemical treatment of wood ("relevant processes") and the throughput of the works in any [12 month period is likely to exceed—
  (i) 10,000 cubic metres, in the case of works at which wood is sawed but at which wood is not subjected to any other relevant processes or is subjected only to relevant processes which are exempt processes; or
  (ii) 1,000 cubic metres in any other case.]
For the purposes of this paragraph—
  [relevant processes other than sawing are "exempt processes" where, if no sawing were carried on at the works, the activities carried on there would be treated as not falling within this Part of this Section by virtue of regulation 4(2);]
  "throughput" shall be calculated by reference to the amount of wood which is subjected to any of the relevant processes but where, at the same works, wood is subject to two or more relevant processes no account shall be taken of the second or any subsequent process;
  "wood" includes any product consisting wholly or mainly of wood; and
  "works" includes a sawmill or any other premises on which relevant processes are carried out on wood.

Section 6.8 Processes involving rubber

PART A

Nil

PART B

(a) The mixing, milling or blending of—
    (i) natural rubber; or
    (ii) synthetic [organic] elastomers,
    if carbon black is used.
(b) Any process which converts the product of a process falling within paragraph (a) into a finished product if related to a process falling within that paragraph.

Section 6.9 The treatment and processing of animal or vegetable matter

PART A

Any of the following processes, unless falling within a description in another section of the Schedule or an exempt process, namely, the processing in any way whatsoever, storing or drying by the application of heat of any dead animal (or part thereof) or any vegetable matter [[if the process may result in the release into water of any substance described in Schedule 5 in a quantity which, in any 12 month period, exceeds the background quantity by more than the amount specified in relation to the description of substance in column 2 of that Schedule]]: but excluding any process for the treatment of effluent so as to permit its discharge into controlled waters or into a sewer unless the treatment process involves the drying of any material with a view to its use as an animal feedstuff.

PART B

(a) Any process mentioned in Part A, of this section unless an exempt process—
    [(i) where the process has the characteristics described in regulation 4(1)(ii) above;] but
    (ii) may release into the air a substance described in Schedule 4 or any offensive smell noticeable outside the premises on which the process is carried on.
(b) Breeding maggots in any case where five kg or more of animal or of vegetable matter or, in aggregate, of both are introduced into the process in any week.
In this Section—
"animal" includes a bird or a fish; and
"exempt process" means—
    (i) any process carried on on a farm or agricultural holding other than the manufacture of goods for sale;
    (ii) the manufacture or preparation of food or drink for human consumption but excluding—
(a) the extraction, distillation or purification of animal or vegetable oil or fat otherwise than as a process incidental to the cooking of food for human consumption;
(b) any process involving the use of green offal or the boiling of blood except the cooking of food (other than tripe) for human consumption;
(c) the cooking of tripe for human consumption elsewhere than on premises on which it is to be consumed;
    [(iii) the fleshing, cleaning and drying of pelts of fur-bearing mammals;
    (iv) any process carried on in connection with the operation of a knacker's yard, as defined in article 3(1) of the Animal By-Products Order 1992;
    (v) any process for the manufacture of soap not falling within a description in Part A of Section 4.2 of this Schedule;
    (vi) the storage of vegetable matter otherwise than as part of any prescribed process;
    (vii) the cleaning of shellfish shells;
    (viii) the manufacture of starch;
    (ix) the processing of animal or vegetable matter at premises for feeding a recognised pack of hounds registered under article 10 of the Animal By-Products Order 1992;

808

  (x) the salting of hides or skins, unless related to any other prescribed process;
  (xi) any process for composting animal or vegetable matter or a combination of both, except where that process is carried on for the purposes of cultivating mushrooms;
  (xii) any process for cleaning, and any related process for drying or dressing, seeds, bulbs, corms or tubers;
  (xiii) the drying of grain or pulses;
  (xiv) any process for the production of cotton yarn from raw cotton or for the conversion of cotton yarn into cloth;] and]
"green offal" means the stomach and intestines of any animal, other than poultry or fish, and their contents.
["food" includes drink, articles and substances of no nutritional value which are used for human consumption, and articles and substances used as ingredients in the preparation of food;]

Regulation 3(2)   SCHEDULE 2

RULES FOR THE INTERPRETATION OF SCHEDULE 1

1. These rules apply for the interpretation of Schedule 1 subject to any specific provision to the contrary in that Schedule.

2.—(1) Any description of a process includes any other process carried on at the same location by the same person as part of that process; but this rule does not apply in relation to any two or more processes described in different Sections of Schedule 1 which, accordingly, require distinct authorisation.

(2) For the purposes of this paragraph, two or more processes which are described in Part A of different Sections of Chapter 4 of Schedule 1 shall be treated as if they were described in the same Section.

2A. Notwithstanding the rule set out in paragraph 2, where a combustion process described in Part A of Section 1.3 of Schedule 1 is operated, or where one or more boilers, furnaces or other combustion appliances which are operated as part of a process so described are operated, as an inherent part of and primarily for the purpose of a process described in Part A of Section 1.1, Part A of Section 1.4, [[Part A of Section 2.1,]] [Part A of Section 6.3] or Part A of any Section of Chapter 4 of that Schedule ("the other process"), that combustion process or, as the case may be, the operation of those boilers, furnaces or appliances shall be treated as part of the other process and not as, or as part of, a separate combustion process.

[2B. Notwithstanding the rule set out in paragraph 2, where a process of reforming natural gas described in paragraph (a) of Part A of Section 1.1 of Schedule 1 is carried on as an inherent part of and primarily for the purpose of producing a feedstock for a process described in Part A of any Section of Chapter 4 of that Schedule ("the other process"), that reforming process shall be treated as part of the other process and not as a separate process.

2C. Notwithstanding the rule set out in paragraph 2, where the same person carries on at the same location two or more Part B processes described in the provisions of Schedule 1 mentioned in any one of the following sub-paragraphs, those processes shall be treated as requiring authorisation as a single process falling within Part B of the Section first mentioned in the relevant sub-paragraph—
  (a) Section 2.1 and Section 2.2;
  (b) Section 3.1 and Section 3.4;
  (c) Section 3.6 and Section 3.4;
  (d) Section 6.5 and Section 6.6;
  (e) Section 6.7 and paragraph (e) of Part B of Section 1.3 insofar as it relates to any process for the burning of waste wood.]

3. Where a person carries on a process which includes two or more processes described in the same Section of Schedule 1 those processes shall be treated as requiring authorisation as a single process; and if the processes involved are described in both Part A and Part B of the same Section, they shall all be regarded as part of a Part A process and so subject to central control.

3A. Where a person carries on a process which includes two or more processes described in Part A of different Sections of Chapter 4 of Schedule 1, those processes shall be treated as a single process falling within a description determined in accordance with the rule set out in paragraph 4.

3B.—(1) Where paragraph 3A does not apply, but—
  (a) two or more processes falling within descriptions in Part A of any Sections of Chapter 4 of Schedule 1 are carried on at the same location by the same person; and

(b) the carrying on of both or all of those processes at that location by that person is not likely to produce more than 250 tonnes of relevant products in any 12 month period, those processes shall be treated as a single process falling within the description in whichever relevant Section is first mentioned in the sequence set out in paragraph 4.

(2) In sub-paragraph (1), "relevant products" means any products of the processes in question, other than—

(a) solid, liquid or gaseous waste;

(b) by-products, if the total value of all such by-products is insignificant in comparison to the total value of the output of the processes; or

(c) any substance or material retained in or added to the final product formulation, not as an active ingredient, but as a diluent, stabiliser or preservative or for a similar purpose.

4. Where a process falls within two or more descriptions in Schedule 1, that process shall be regarded as falling only within that description which fits it most aptly: but where two or more descriptions are equally apt and a process falls within descriptions in different sections of Chapter 4, it shall be taken to fall within the description in whichever relevant section is first mentioned in the sequence, 4.5; 4.2; 4.1; 4.4; 4.3; 4.6; 4.7; 4.8; 4.9.

5. Notwithstanding the rules set out in paragraphs 2 and 3—

(a) the processes described in Part B of section 1.3 do not include the incidental storage, handling or shredding of tyres which are to be burned;

(b) the process described in paragraph (b) of Part B of section 2.2 does not include the incidental storage or handling of scrap which is to be heated other than its loading into a furnace;

(c) the process described in paragraph (a) in Part B of section 5.1 does not involve the incidental storage or handling of wastes and residues other than animal remains intended for burning in an incinerator used wholly or mainly for the incineration of such remains or residues from the burning of such remains in such an incinerator;

(d) the process described in Part B of section 6.5 does not include the cleaning of used storage drums prior to painting and their incidental handling in connection with such cleaning.

[(e) any description of a Part B process includes any related process which would fall within paragraph (c) of Part A of Section 1.3 if it were not so related.]

[[6. The following activities, that is to say—

(a) the unloading, screening, grading, mixing or otherwise handling of petroleum, coke, coal, lignite, coke or any other coal product;

(b) the unloading of iron ore or burnt pyrites,

for use in a prescribed process by a person other than the person carrying on the process at the place where the process is carried on shall be treated as part of that process.]]

7.—(1) Where by reason of the use at different times of different fuels or different materials or the disposal at different times of different wastes, processes of different descriptions are carried out with the same plant or machinery and those processes include one or more Part A processes and one or more other processes, the other processes shall be regarded as within the descriptions of the Part A processes.

(2) Where by reason of such use or disposal as is mentioned in paragraph (1), processes of different descriptions are carried out with the same plant or machinery and those processes include one or more Part B processes and one or more other processes (but no Part A processes), all those processes shall be regarded as within the descriptions of the Part B processes.

[(3) Where by reason of such use or disposal as is mentioned in sub-paragraph (1), processes of different descriptions are carried out with the same plant and machinery and those processes include Part B processes falling within different Sections of Schedule 1 (but no Part A processes), those processes shall, notwithstanding the rule set out in paragraph 2, be treated as a single Part B process falling within the description in whichever of those Sections first appears in that Schedule.]

(7A) The reference to "any other process" in paragraph 2 and the references to "other processes" in paragraph 7 do not include references to a process (other than one described in Schedule 1) of loading or unloading any ship or other vessel.

[8. Where in the course of, or as a process ancillary to, any prescribed process the person carrying on that process uses, treats or disposes of waste at the same location (whether as fuel or otherwise), the use, treatment or disposal of that waste shall, notwithstanding the rule set out in paragraph 2, be regarded as falling within the description of that process, whether the waste was produced by the person carrying on the process or acquired by him for such use, treatment or disposal.]

9. References in Schedule 1 and this Schedule to related processes are references to separate processes carried on by the same person at the same location.

10. [. . .]

11. References to a process involving the release of a substance falling within a description in Schedule 4 or 5 hereto do not affect the application of paragraphs (1) and (2) of regulation 4.

Regulation 3(1) and (3)   SCHEDULE 3

DATE FROM WHICH AUTHORISATION IS REQUIRED UNDER SECTION 6 OF THE ACT

PART I

Note—Paragraphs 2–7 of this Part should be read subject to the Note to this Part contained in the Introduction to this Appendix.

1. This Part of this Schedule applies in the case of a Part A process carried on in England or Wales.

2. The prescribed date in the case of a Part A process is, except in the case of an existing process, 1st April 1991.

3.—(1) In the case of an existing process, the prescribed date is—

    (i) in a case falling within paragraph (2), the date at which the change mentioned in that paragraph is made unless later than the date applicable in accordance with sub-paragraph (ii);

    (ii) where sub-paragraph (i) does not apply and subject to paragraph 5, the day after that on which the period for applying for authorisation in accordance with the Table in paragraph 4 expires.

(2) A case falls within this paragraph if the person carrying on the process makes a substantial change in the process on or after 1st April 1991 and that change—

    (i) has not occasioned construction work which is in progress on that date; or

    (ii) is not the subject of a contract for construction work entered into before that date.

4. Application for authorisation to carry on an existing process shall be made in the relevant period specified in the following Table—

TABLE

Any process falling within a description set out in—	Application to be made	
	Not earlier than	*Not later than*
Paragraph (a) of Section 1.3	1st April 1991	30th April 1991
Any other paragraph of Chapter 1	1st April 1992	30th June 1992
Section 2.1 or 2.3	1st January 1995	31st March 1995
Section 2.2	1st May 1995	31st July 1995
Chapter 3	1st December 1992	28th February 1993
Section 4.1, 4.2, 4.7 or 4.8	1st May 1993	31st October 1993
[Section 4.3, 4.4 of paragraph (a) of Section 4.6]	1st November 1993	31st January 1994
[Section 4.5, paragraph (b) of Section 4.6, or Section 4.9]	1st May 1994	31st July 1994
Chapter 5	1st August 1992	31st October 1992
Chapter 6	1st November 1995	31st January 1996

5. Where paragraph 3(1)(ii) would otherwise apply and application is duly made in accordance with section 6 of the Act within the appropriate period specified in paragraph 4 for authorisation to carry on a process, the prescribed date as respects the carrying on by the applicant (or other person in his place) of the process to which the application relates is the determination date for that process.

6. Subject to paragraph 7 below, references in this Part to an existing process are to a process—
   (i) which was being carried on at some time in the 12 months immediately preceding 1st April 1991; or
   (ii) which is to be carried on at a works, plant or factory or by means of mobile plant which was under construction or in course of manufacture or in the course of commission at that date, or the construction or supply of which was the subject of a contract entered into before that date.

7. A process shall cease to be an existing process for the purposes of this Part if at any time between 1st April 1990 and the last day by which an application is otherwise required to be made for authorisation for the carrying on of that process, the process ceases to be carried on and is not carried on again at the same location (or with the same mobile plant) within the following 12 months.

8. In this Part and subsequent provisions of the Schedule—
"the determination date" for a prescribed process is—
   (a) in the case of a process for which an authorisation is granted, the date on which the enforcing authority grants it, whether in pursuance of the application or, on an appeal, of a direction to grant it;
   (b) in the case of a process for which an authorisation is refused, the date of the refusal or, on an appeal, of the affirmation of the refusal;
"substantial change" has the same meaning as in section 10 of the Act.

PART II

Note—Paragraphs 10–14 of this Part should be read subject to the Note to this Part contained in the Introduction to this Appendix.

9. This Part of this Schedule applies in the case of a Part B process carried on in England or Wales.

10. The prescribed date in the case of a Part B process is, except in the case of an existing process, the date specified in paragraph 12 below as the date from which application may be made for authorisation to carry on an existing process of the same description.

11.—(1) In the case of an existing process, the prescribed date is, subject to paragraph 13,—
   (i) in a case falling within paragraph (2), the date at which the change mentioned in that paragraph is made;
   (ii) where sub-paragraph (i) does not apply, the day after that on which the period for applying for authorisation in accordance with the Table in paragraph 12 expires.

(2) A case falls within this paragraph if the person carrying on the process makes a substantial change in the process in the period specified in paragraph 12 in relation to the description of processes which comprise that process (when changed) and that change—
   (i) has not occasioned construction work which is in progress at the beginning of that period; or
   (ii) is not the subject of a contract for construction work entered into before the beginning of that period.

12. Application for authorisation for an existing process shall be made in the relevant period determined in accordance with the following Table—

TABLE

Any process falling within a description set out in—	Application to be made	
	Not earlier than	*Not later than*
Paragraph (a), (b), (c) or (e) of Section 1.3, Section 3.5, 3.6, 5.1 or 6.7 or paragraph (b) of Section 6.9	1st April 1991	30th September 1991
Section 2.1, 2.2, 3.1, 3.2 or 3.4	1st October 1991	31st March 1992
Paragraph (d) of Section 1.3, Section 6.2, 6.5, 6.6 or 6.8 or paragraph (a) of Section 6.9	1st April 1992	30th September 1992

13. Where application is duly made in accordance with section 6 of the Act for authorisation for the carrying on of an existing Part B process, the prescribed date as respects the carrying on by the applicant (or another person in his place) of the process to which the application relates is the determination date for that process.

14. References in this Part to an existing process are to a process—
    (i) which was being carried on at some time in the 12 months immediately preceding the earlier date mentioned in paragraph 12 in relation to the description of processes within which the process falls; or
    (ii) which is to be carried on at a works, plant or factory or by means of mobile plant which was under construction or in course of manufacture or in the course of commission at that earlier date, or the construction or supply of which was the subject of a contract entered into before that date.

PART III

15. This Part of this Schedule applies in the case of a Part A process carried on in Scotland.

16. The prescribed date in the case of a Part A process is, except in the case of an existing process, 1st April 1992.

17.—(1) In the case of an existing process, the prescribed date is—
    (i) in a case falling within paragraph (2), the date at which the change mentioned in that paragraph is made unless later than the date applicable in accordance with sub-paragraph (ii);
    (ii) where sub-paragraph (i) does not apply and subject to paragraph 19, the day after that on which the period for applying for authorisation in accordance with the Table in paragraph 18 expires.

(2) A case falls within this paragraph if the person carrying on the process makes a substantial change in the process on or after 1st April 1992 and that change—
    (i) has not occasioned construction work which is in progress on that date; or
    (ii) is not the subject of a contract for construction work entered into before that date.

18. Application for authorisation to carry on an existing process shall be made in the relevant period specified in the following Table—

TABLE

Any process falling within a description set out in—	Application to be made	
	Not earlier than	Not later than
Chapter 1	1st April 1992	30th June 1992
Section 2.1 or 2.3	1st January 1995	31st March 1995
Section 2.2	1st May 1995	31st July 1995
Chapter 3	1st December 1992	28th February 1993
Section 4.1, 4.2, 4.7 or 4.8	1st May 1993	31st October 1993
[Section 4.3, 4.4 or paragraph (a) of Section 4.6]	1st November 1993	31st January 1994
[Section 4.5, paragraph (b) of Section 4.6 or Section 4.9]	1st May 1994	31st July 1994
Chapter 5	1st August 1992	31st October 1992
Chapter 6	1st November 1995	31st January 1996

19. Where paragraph 17(1)(ii) would otherwise apply and application is duly made in accordance with Section 6 of the Act within the period specified in paragraph 18 for authorisation to carry on a process, the prescribed date as respects the carrying on by the applicant (or another person in his place) of the process to which the application relates is the determination date for that process.

20. Subject to paragraph 21 below, references in this Part to an existing process are to a process—
    (i) which was being carried on at some time in the 12 months immediately preceding 1st April 1992; or

(ii) which is to be carried on at a works, plant or factory or by means of mobile plant which was under construction or in course of manufacture or in the course of commission at that date, or, where construction or manufacture had not been begun before that date, the construction or supply of which was the subject of a contract entered into before that date.

21. A process shall cease to be an existing process for the purposes of this Part if at any time between 1st April 1992 and the last date by which an application is otherwise required to be made for authorisation for the carrying on of that process, the process ceases to be carried on and is not carried on again at the same location (or with the same mobile plant) within the following 12 months.

PART IV

22. This Part of this Schedule applies in the case of a Part B process carried on in Scotland.

23. The prescribed date in the case of a Part B process is, except in the case of an existing process, the date specified in paragraph 25 below as the date from which application may be made for authorisation to carry on an existing process of the same description.

24.—(1) In the case of an existing process the prescribed date is, subject to paragraph 26,—
   (i) in a case falling within paragraph (2), the date at which the change mentioned in that paragraph is made;
   (ii) where sub-paragraph (i) does not apply, the day after that on which the period for applying for authorisation in accordance with the Table in paragraph 25 expires.

(2) A case falls within this paragraph if the person carrying on the process makes a substantial change in the process in the period specified in paragraph 25 in relation to the description of processes which comprise that process (when changed) and that change—
   (i) has not occasioned construction work which is in progress at the beginning of that period; or
   (ii) is not the subject of a contract for construction work entered into before the beginning of that period.

25. Application for authorisation for an existing process shall be made in the relevant period specified in the following Table—

TABLE

Any process falling within a description set out in—	Application to be made	
	Not earlier than	*Not later than*
Paragraph (a), (b), (d) or (e) of Section 1.3, Section 3.2, 3.5, 3.6, 5.1 or 6.7 or paragraph (b) of Section 6.9	1st April 1992	31st July 1992
Paragraph (c) of Section 1.3	1st April 1992	30th September 1992
Section 2.1, 2.2, 3.1 or 3.4	1st August 1992	30th November 1992
Section 6.2, 6.5, 6.6 or 6.8 or paragraph (a) of Section 6.9	1st December 1992	31st March 1993

26. Where application is duly made in accordance with section 6 of the Act for authorisation for the carrying on of an existing Part B process, the prescribed date as respects the carrying on by the applicant (or another person in his place) of the process to which the application relates is the determination date for that process.

27. References in this Part to an existing process are to a process—
   (i) which was being carried on at some time in the 12 months immediately preceding the earlier date mentioned in paragraph 25 in relation to the description of processes within which the process falls; or
   (ii) which is to be carried on at a works, plant or factory or by means of mobile plant which was under construction or in course of manufacture or in the course of commission at that earlier date, or the construction or supply of which was the subject of a contract entered into before that date.

Regulation 6(1)   SCHEDULE 4

RELEASE INTO THE AIR: PRESCRIBED SUBSTANCES

Oxides of sulphur and other sulphur compounds
Oxides of nitrogen and other nitrogen compounds
Oxides of carbon
Organic compounds and partial oxidation products
Metals, metalloids and their compounds
Asbestos (suspended particulate matter and fibres), glass fibres and mineral fibres
Halogens and their compounds
Phosphorus and its compounds
Particulate matter.

Regulations 4(1) and 6(2)   SCHEDULE 5

RELEASE INTO WATER: PRESCRIBED SUBSTANCES

(1) Substance	(2) Amount in excess of background quantity released in any 12 month period (Grammes)
Mercury and its compounds	200 (expressed as metal)
Cadmium and its compounds	1000 (expressed as metal)
All isomers of hexachlorocyclohexane	20
All isomers of DDT	5
Pentachlorophenol and its compounds	350 [[(expressed as PCP)]]
Hexachlorobenzene	5
Hexachlorobutadiene	20
Aldrin	2
Dieldrin	2
Endrin	1
Polychlorinated Biphenyls	1
Dichlorvos	0.2
1,2-Dichloroethane	2000
All isomers of trichlorobenzene	75
Atrazine	350*
Simazine	350*
Tributyltin compounds	4 [[(expressed as TBT)]
Triphenyltin compounds	4 [[(expressed as TPT)]]
Trifluralin	20
Fenitrothion	2
Azinphos-methyl	2
Malathion	2
Endosulfan	0.5

* Where both Atrazine and Simazine are released, the figure in aggregate is 350 grammes.]

Regulation 6(3)   SCHEDULE 6

RELEASE INTO LAND: PRESCRIBED SUBSTANCES

Organic solvents
Azides
Halogens and their covalent compounds
Metal carbonyls
Organo-metallic compounds
Oxidising agents
Polychlorinated dibenzofuran and any congener thereof
Polychlorinated dibenzo-p-dioxin and any congener thereof
Polyhalogenated biphenyls, terphenyls and naphthalenes
Phosphorus
Pesticides, that is to say, any chemical substance or preparation prepared or used for destroying

any pest, including those used for protecting plants or wood or other plant products from harmful organisms; regulating the growth of plants; giving protection against harmful creatures; rendering such creatures harmless; controlling organisms with harmful or unwanted effects on water systems, buildings or other structures, or on manufactured products; or protecting animals against ectoparasites.

Alkali metals and their oxides and alkaline earth metals and their oxides.

SCHEDULE 6 to S.I. 1994 No. 1271 (as substituted by S.I. 1994 No. 1329)

TRANSITIONALS

Interpretation

1. In this Schedule—

"the central enforcing authority" means the [Environment Agency] or, in the case of a process carried on in Scotland, [SEPA].

"existing process" means a process—

(a) which was being carried on at some time in the 12 months immediately preceding 1st December 1994; or

(b) which is to be carried on at a works, plant or factory or by means of mobile plant which was under construction or in the course of manufacture or in the course of commission at that date, or the construction or supply of which was the subject of a contract entered into before that date;

"the determination date" for a prescribed process means—

(a) in the case of a process for which an authorisation is granted by the enforcing authority, whether in pursuance of the application or of a direction under section 6(5) of or paragraph 3(5) of Schedule 1 to the Act, the date on which the authorisation is granted;

(b) in the case of a process for which an authorisation is refused by the enforcing authority in pursuance of a direction under section 6(5) of or paragraph 3(5) of Schedule 1 to the Act, the date on which the authorisation is refused;

(c) in the case of a process for which an authorisation is refused by the enforcing authority other than as described in (b) above—

(i) if the applicant appeals against the refusal and the enforcing authority is directed to grant an authorisation, the date on which the authorisation is granted in pursuance of the direction;

(ii) if the applicant appeals against the refusal and the refusal is affirmed, the date of the affirmation of the refusal;

(iii) if no appeal is made against the refusal, the date immediately following the last day, determined in accordance with regulation 10(1) of the Environmental Protection (Applications, Appeals and Registers) Regulations 1991 (S.I. 1991/507), on which notice of appeal might have been given;

"Part A process" and "Part B process" have the same meaning as in the principal Regulations (S.I. 1991/472; *see* regulation 2 for the definition of these terms).

Processes which cease to be prescribed processes

2.—(1) This paragraph applies to a prescribed process—

(a) which, by virtue of regulation 4 above, will cease to be a prescribed process on 1st December 1994; and

(b) in respect of which no authorisation under section 6 of the Act is in force on 1st June 1994.

(2) Regulation 3(3) of the principal Regulations (the prescribed date) shall not apply to a prescribed process to which this paragraph applies.

(3) For the purposes of regulation 3(1) of the principal Regulations, the prescribed date in the case of a prescribed process to which this paragraph applies shall be 30th November 1994.

Processes which become Part A prescribed processes

3.—(1) Where, by virtue of regulation 4 above, an existing process which is not a prescribed process before 1st December 1994 becomes a Part A process on that date, then, with effect from that date—

(a) regulation 3(3) of the principal Regulations (the prescribed date) shall not apply in respect of that process;

  (b) for the purposes of regulation 3(1) of the principal Regulations, the prescribed date in respect of that process shall, subject to paragraph 8 below, be whichever is the latest of the following—
    (i) 30th November 1994; or
    (ii) where application is duly made to the central enforcing authority in accordance with section 6 of the Act before 1st November 1994 for authorisation to carry on the process, the determination date for that process; or
    (iii) the date which would be determined in accordance with Schedule 3 to the principal Regulations (Schedule 3 to the principal Regulations was amended by S.I. 1991/836, S.I. 1993/1749, S.I. 1993/2405) if that Schedule applied with the modifications set out in sub-paragraph (2) below.

  (2) The modifications of Schedule 3 to the principal Regulations referred to in sub-paragraph (1) above are—
    (a) in paragraph 2, for "1st April 1991" substitute "30th November 1994";
    (b) in paragraphs 3(2) and 6, for "1st April 1991" substitute "1st December 1994";
    (c) in paragraph 7, for "1st April 1990" substitute "1st December 1993";
    (d) in paragraph 16, for "1st April 1992" substitute "30th November 1994";
    (e) in paragraphs 17(2) and 20, for "1st April 1992" substitute "1st December 1994";
    (f) in paragraph 21, for "1st April 1992" substitute "1st December 1993".

Processes which transfer from Part B to Part A

  4. Where, by virtue of regulation 4 above, an existing Part B process becomes a Part A process on 1st December 1994, then, with effect from that date—
    (a) regulation 3(3) of the principal Regulations (the prescribed date) shall not apply in respect of that process;
    (b) for the purposes of regulation 3(1) of the principal Regulations, the prescribed date in respect of that process shall, subject to paragraph 8 below, be whichever is the later of the following—
    (i) 31st December 1994; or
    (ii) where application is duly made to the central enforcing authority in accordance with section 6 of the Act before 1st January 1995 for authorisation to carry on the process, the determination date for that process.

Processes which become Part B prescribed processes

  5. Where, by virtue of regulation 4 above, an existing process which is not a prescribed process before 1st December 1994 becomes a Part B process on that date, then, with effect from that date—
    (a) regulation 3(3) of the principal Regulations (the prescribed date) shall not apply in respect of that process;
    (b) for the purposes of regulation 3(1) of the principal Regulations, the prescribed date in respect of that process shall, subject to paragraph 8 below, be whichever is the later of the following—
    (i) 31st May 1995; or
    (ii) where application is duly made to the local enforcing authority in accordance with section 6 of the Act before 1st June 1995 for authorisation to carry on the process, the determination date for that process.

Processes which transfer from Part A to Part B

  6. Where, by virtue of regulation 4 above, an existing Part A process becomes a Part B process on 1st December 1994 and, immediately before that date, that Part A is one for the carrying on of which an application for an authorisation under section 6 of the Act is not yet required to be made, then, with effect from that date—
    (a) regulation 3(3) of the principal Regulations (the prescribed date) shall not apply in respect of that process;
    (b) for the purposes of regulation 3(1) of the principal Regulations, the prescribed date in respect of that process shall, subject to paragraph 8 below, be whichever is the later of the following—
    (i) 31st May 1995; or
    (ii) where application is duly made to the local enforcing authority in accordance with section 6 of the Act before 1st June 1995 for authorisation to carry on the process, the determination date for that process.

7.—(1) Where, by virtue of regulation 4 above, an existing Part A process becomes a Part B process on 1st December 1994 but paragraph 6 above does not apply, then, with effect from that date—

    (a) regulation 3(3) of the principal Regulations (the prescribed date) shall not apply in respect of that process;

    (b) for the purposes of regulation 3(1) of the principal Regulations, the prescribed date in respect of that process shall, subject to paragraph 8 below, be whichever is the later of the following—

        (i) 31st December 1994; or

        (ii) where application is duly made to the local enforcing authority in accordance with section 6 of the Act before 1st January 1995 for authorisation to carry on the process, the determination date for that process.

(2) The requirements of paragraphs 1(2) and 2 of Schedule 1 to the Act (advertisement and consultation) shall not apply in relation to an application made as described in sub-paragraph (1)(b)(ii) above if, in respect of the process to which that application relates—

    (a) an authorisation under section 6 of the Act granted by the central enforcing authority is in force on 30th November 1994; or

    (b) an application for an authorisation under section 6 of the Act has been made to the central enforcing authority and the requirements of those paragraphs have been fulfilled in relation to that application after 31st May 1993.

Substantial changes

8.—(1) This paragraph applies where the person carrying on an existing process described in any of paragraphs 3 to 7 above makes a substantial change in the process on or after 1st December 1994 and that change—

    (i) has not occasioned construction work which is in progress on that date; and

    (ii) is not the subject of a contract for construction work entered into before that date.

(2) Where this paragraph applies, the prescribed date in respect of that process shall be the date at which the change mentioned in sub-paragraph (1) above is made unless later than the date applicable in accordance with paragraphs 3 to 7 above.

(3) In this paragraph "substantial change" has the same meaning as in section 10 of the Act.]

SCHEDULE 2 to S.I. 1995 No. 3247

TRANSITIONALS

Interpretation*

1. In this Schedule—

"the central enforcing authority" means the [Environment Agency] or, in the case of a process carried on in Scotland, [SEPA];

"existing process" means a process—

    (a) which was being carried on at some time in the 12 months immediately preceding 8th January 1996; or

    (b) which is to be carried on at a works, plant or factory or by means of mobile plant which was under construction or in the course of manufacture of in the course of commission at that date, or the construction or supply of which was the subject of a contract entered into before that date;

"the determination date" for a prescribed process means—

    (a) in the case of a process for which an authorisation is granted by the enforcing authority, whether in pursuance of the application or of a direction under section 6(5) of or paragraph 3(5) of Schedule 1 to the Act, the date on which the authorisation is granted;

    (b) in the case of a process for which an authorisation is refused by the enforcing authority in pursuance of a direction under section 6(5) of or paragraph 3(5) of Schedule 1 to the Act, the date on which the authorisation is refused;

    (c) in the case of a process for which an authorisation is refused by the enforcing authority other than as described in (b) above—

        (i) if the applicant appeals against the refusal and the enforcing authority is directed to grant an authorisation, the date on which the authorisation is granted in pursuance of the direction;

---

* *Editor's Note*—References to "the principal Regulations" are references to S.I. 1991 No. 472 as amended.

    (ii) if the applicant appeals against the refusal and the refusal is affirmed, the date of the affirmation of the refusal;

    (iii) if no appeal is made against the refusal, the date immediately following the last day, determined in accordance with regulation 10(1) of the Environmental Protection (Applications, Appeals and Registers) Regulations 1991, on which notice of appeal might have been given;

"Part A process" and "Part B process" have the same meaning as in the principal Regulations.

Processes, other than existing processes, which become Part A or Part B prescribed processes

2. Regulations 3(3) of the principal Regulations (the prescribed date) shall not apply in respect of a process which is not an existing process and which falls within a description of process which, by virtue of regulations 2 above—

    (a) becomes a prescribed process on 8th January 1996 but immediately before that date was not a prescribed process;

    (b) becomes a Part A process on 8th January 1996 but immediately before that date was a Part B process; or

    (c) becomes a Part B process on 8th January 1996 but immediately before that date was a Part A process,

and for the purposes of regulation 3(1) of the principal Regulations the prescribed date in respect of any such process shall be 7th January 1996.

Existing processes which become Part A prescribed processes

3.—(1) Where, by virtue of regulation 2 above, an existing process which immediately before 8th January 1996 is not a prescribed process or is a Part B process becomes a Part A process on that date, then, with effect from that date—

    (a) regulation 3(3) of the principal Regulations (the prescribed date) shall not apply in respect of that process;

    (b) for the purposes of regulation 3(1) of the principal Regulations, the prescribed date in respect of that process shall, subject to paragraph 5 below, be whichever is the later of the following—

      (i) 7th May 1996; or

      (ii) where application is duly made to the central enforcing authority in accordance with section 6 of the Act before 8th May 1996 for authorisation to carry on the process, the determination date for that process.

Existing processes which become Part B prescribed processes

4.—(1) Where, by virtue of regulation 2 above, an existing process which immediately before 8th January 1996 is not a prescribed process or is a Part A process becomes a Part B process on that date, then, with effect from that date—

    (a) regulation 3(3) of the principal Regulations (the prescribed date) shall not apply in respect of that process;

    (b) for the purposes of regulation 3(1) of the principal Regulations, the prescribed date in respect of that process shall, subject to paragraph 5 below, be whichever is the later of the following—

      (i) 7th January 1997; or

      (ii) where application is duly made to the local enforcing authority in accordance with section 6 of the Act after 7th January 1996 and before 8th January 1997 for authorisation to carry on the process, the determination date for that process.

(2) The requirements of paragraphs 1(2) and 2 of Schedule 1 to the Act (advertisement and consultation) shall not apply in relation to an application made as described in sub-paragraph (1)(b)(ii) above if, in respect of the process to which that application relates—

    (a) an authorisation under section 6 of the Act granted by the central enforcing authority is in force on 7th January 1996; or

    (b) an application for an authorisation under section 6 of the Act has been made to the central enforcing authority and the requirements of those paragraphs have been fulfilled in relation to that application after 8th July 1994.

Substantial changes

5.—(1) This paragraph applies where the person carrying on an existing process described in paragraph 3 or 4 above makes a substantial change in the process on or after 8th January 1996 and that change—

(i) has not occasioned construction work which is in progress on that date; and

(ii) is not the subject of a contract for construction work entered into before that date.

(2) Where this paragraph applies, the prescribed date in respect of that process shall be the date at which the change mentioned in sub-paragraph (1) above is made unless later than the date applicable in accordance with paragraphs 3 and 4 above.

(3) In this paragraph "substantial change" has the same meaning as in section 10 of the Act.

APPENDIX 2

ENVIRONMENTAL PROTECTION (APPLICATIONS, APPEALS AND REGISTERS) REGULATIONS 1991

(S.I. 1991 No. 507)

In force from:

April 1, 1991 (England and Wales) and April 1, 1992 (Scotland)

Enabling power:

Environmental Protection Act 1990, ss.10(8), 11(1), (3)–(7), 15(10), 10(1)–(3), (10) and 22(6) and Sched. 1, paras. 1–3, 6 and 7.

Background:

Part I of the Environmental Protection Act 1990 makes provision for Integrated Pollution Control as well as the system of local air pollution control. Section 6 provides that no person shall carry on a prescribed process after the date prescribed or determined for that description of process unless he has applied for and been granted authorisation by the enforcing authority.

These Regulations set out the procedures to be followed and the information to be submitted on an application for authorisation, as well as on an application for a variation of conditions of an authorisation. The regulations provide exemptions from the requirements for reasons of national security and commercial confidentiality. The regulations also set out the procedures and time limits for appeals to the Secretary of State. Finally they prescribe the matters to be included in registers of public information which the enforcing authorities are required to maintain.

Statutory reference:

Environmental Protection Act 1990, ss.6, 15, 20 and 22.

Amendments:

S.I. 1991 No. 836 amended regs. 3 and 5.

S.I. 1994 No. 1271 added reg. 4(1)(i) (now revoked).

The amendments shown in square brackets are those effected by S.I. 1996 No. 667. This amended regs. 2, 3, 4, 5, 11 and 13, substituted regs. 15, 16 and 17, and inserted reg. 15A, all with effect from April 1, 1996 and subject to transitional provisions noted here as footnotes to regs. 4, 5 and 11. To rectify an omission in S.I. 1996 No. 667, S.I. 1996 No. 979 inserted para. (ca) into the substituted reg. 15 with effect from April 24, 1996.

Citation, commencement and interpretation

1.—(1) These Regulations may be cited as the Environmental Protection (Applications, Appeals and Registers) Regulations 1991 and shall come into force in England and Wales on April 1, 1991 and in Scotland on April 1, 1992.

(2) In these Regulations, "the 1990 Act" means the Environmental Protection Act 1990.

Applications for an authorisation

2.—(1) An application to an enforcing authority for an authorisation under section 6 of the 1990 Act shall be in writing and, subject to paragraphs (2) and (3) below, shall contain the following information—

(a) the name of the applicant, his telephone number and address and, if different, any address to which correspondence relating to the application should be sent and, if the applicant is a body corporate, the address of its registered or principal office [and, if that body corporate is a subsidiary of a holding company (within the meaning of section 736 of the Companies Act 1985), the name of the ultimate holding company and the address of its registered or principal office];

(b) in a case where the prescribed process will not be carried on by means of mobile plant—
  (i) the name of any local authority in whose area the prescribed process will be carried on;
  (ii) the address of the premises where the prescribed process will be carried on;
  (iii) a map or plan showing the location of those premises; and
  (iv) if only part of those premises will be used for carrying on the process, a plan or other means of identifying that part;

(c) in a case where the prescribed process will be carried on by means of mobile plant—
  (i) the name of the local authority in whose area the applicant has his principal place of business; and
  (ii) the address of that place of business;

(d) a description of the prescribed process;

(e) a list of prescribed substances (and any other substances which might cause harm if released into any environmental medium) which will be used in connection with, or which will result from, the carrying on of that process;

(f) a description of the techniques to be used for preventing the release into any environmental medium of such substances, for reducing the release of such substances to a minimum and for rendering harmless any such substances which are released;

(g) details of any proposed release of such substances into any environmental medium and an assessment of the environmental consequences;

(h) proposals for monitoring any release of such substances, the environmental consequences of any such release and the use of any techniques described in accordance with sub-paragraph (f) above;

(i) the matters on which the applicant relies to establish that the objectives mentioned in section 7(2) of the 1990 Act (including the objective referred to in section 7(7)) will be achieved and that he will be able to comply with the general condition implied by section 7(4);

(j) any additional information which he wishes the enforcing authority to take into account in considering his application.

(2) Paragraph (1) above shall apply in relation to an application to a local enforcing authority for an authorisation in respect of a prescribed process designated for local control (other than that mentioned in paragraph (3) below) as if the words in brackets in sub-paragraph (i) were omitted and references to the release of substances into any environmental medium were references to the release of substances into the air.

(3) Paragraph (1) above shall apply in relation to an application to a local enforcing authority for an authorisation to carry on any prescribed process involving only the burning of waste oil in an appliance with a net rated thermal input of less than 0·4 megawatts as if the following sub-paragraphs were substituted for sub-paragraphs (d) to (i)—

"(d) the name and number of the appliance (if any) and the name of its manufacturer;

(e) the net rated thermal input of the appliance and whether or not it is constructed or adapted so as to comply with the specification for fixed, flued fan-assisted heaters in Part 2 of the specification for oil-burning air heaters published by the British Standards Institution and numbered BS 4256 1972;

(f) details of the type of fuel to be used and its source;

(g) details of the height and location of any chimney through which waste gases produced by the appliance would be carried away;

(h) details of the efflux velocity of the waste gases leaving such a chimney produced by the appliance in normal operation;

(i) details of the location of the fuel storage tanks of the appliance;".

(4) In this regulation—

"net rated thermal input" is the rate at which fuel can be burned at the maximum continuous rating of the appliance multiplied by the net calorific value of the fuel and expressed as megawatts thermal;

"waste oil" means any mineral based lubricating or industrial oil which—

(a) has become unfit for the use for which it was intended and, in particular, used combustion engine oil, gearbox oil, mineral lubricating oil, oil for turbines and hydraulic oil; and

(b) is generated only as a result of activities carried out by the applicant on the premises where the process is to be carried on.

Variation of conditions of an authorisation

3.—(1) Any notice given to an enforcing authority under section 11(1)(a) of the 1990 Act of a proposed relevant change in a prescribed process shall be in writing.

(2) An application to an enforcing authority under any provision of section 11 of the 1990 Act for the variation of the conditions of an authorisation shall be in writing.

(3) A person making—

(a) a request to an enforcing authority under section 11(1)(b) of the 1990 Act for a determination of the matters mentioned in section 11(2); or

(b) an application to such an authority under any provision of section 11 for the variation of the conditions of an authorisation,

shall furnish the authority with his name, address and telephone number and shall also furnish the authority—

(i) in a case where the prescribed process will not be carried on by means of mobile plant, with the address of the premises where the prescribed process will be carried on;

(ii) in a case where the process will be carried on by means of mobile plant, with the address of his principal place of business;

(iii) in all cases, with a statement of any changes as respects any information supplied under regulation 2(1)(a) to (c) above.

[(iv) in a case where the holder of the authorisation is a body corporate which is a subsidiary of a holding company (within the meaning of section 736 of the Companies Act 1985) and the information has not already been supplied under regulation 2(1)(a) above, with the name of the ultimate holding company and the address of its registered or principal office.]

(4) Subject to paragraph (5) below, a person making—

(a) a request to an enforcing authority under section 11(1)(b) of the 1990 Act for a determination of the matters mentioned in section 11(2); or

(b) an application to such an authority under section 11(5) for the variation of the conditions of an authorisation.

shall also furnish the authority with—

(i) a description of any proposed change in the manner in which the prescribed process will be carried on;

    (ii) a statement of any changes as respects the matters dealt with in regulation 2(1)(e) to (i) above which would result if any proposed change in the manner of carrying on the prescribed process were made;

    (iii) any additional information which he wishes the authority to take into account in considering his application; and

    (iv) in the case of an application under section 11(5) of the 1990 Act, an indication of the variations which he wishes the authority to make.

(5) Paragraph (4) above shall apply in relation to a process mentioned in regulation 2(3) above as if sub-paragraph (ii) were omitted.

(6) A person making an application to an enforcing authority under section 11(3)(b) or (4)(b) of the 1990 Act ... for the variation of the conditions of an authorisation shall also furnish the authority with—

    (a) an indication of the variations which he wishes the authority to make;

    (b) a statement of any changes in any information supplied to the authority under paragraph (3) above; and

    (c) any additional information which he wishes the authority to take into account in considering his application.

(7) A person making an application to an enforcing authority for the variation of the conditions of an authorisation under section 11(6) of the 1990 Act shall also furnish the authority with—

    (a) an indication of the variations which he wishes the authority to make; and

    (b) any additional information which he wishes the authority to take into account in considering his application.

Consultation*

4.—(1) Subject to regulations 6 and 7(2) below, the persons to be consulted under paragraph 2, 6 or 7 of Schedule 1 to the 1990 Act are—

    (a) the Health and Safety Executive, in all cases [except, in the case of a prescribed process designated for local control, where the enforcing authority has, within the period specified in paragraph (2) below, notified the Health and Safety Executive that the application has been made or, as the case may be, that notification has been given pursuant to section 10(5) of the 1990 Act];

    (b) the Minister of Agriculture, Fisheries and Food, in the case of all prescribed processes designated for central control which will be carried on in England;

    (c) the Secretary of State for Wales, in the case of all prescribed processes designated for central control which will be carried on in Wales;

    (d) the Secretary of State for Scotland, in the case of all prescribed processes designated for central control which will be carried on in Scotland;

    [...]

    (f) the sewerage undertaker or, in relation to Scotland, the [sewerage authority], in the case of all prescribed processes designated for central control which may involve the release of any substance into a sewer vested in the undertaker or [the authority];

    (g) the Nature Conservancy Council for England, [Scottish Natural Heritage] or the Countryside Council for Wales—

        (i) in the case of all prescribed processes designated for central control which may involve a release of any substance;

---

* Reg. 4. Where the relevant day referred to in sub-para. (a), (b) or, as the case may be, (c) of reg. 4(2) falls before April 1, 1996, the amendments with which reg. 4 is printed here do not apply (S.I. 1996 No. 667, reg. 3(2)).

(ii) in the case of all prescribed processes designated for local control which may involve a release of any substance into the air,

which may affect a site of special scientific interest within [the body's] area;

(h) the harbour authority, in the case of all prescribed processes designated for central control which may involve a release of any substance into a harbour managed by the harbour authority.

[...]

[(j) the local authority in whose area the process will be carried on, in the case of all prescribed processes (other than those which will be carried on by means of mobile plant) designated for central control, or in respect of which a direction under section 4(4) of the 1990 Act is in force, which will be carried on in England and Wales;

(k) the local authority in whose area the process will be carried on, in the case of all prescribed processes (other than those which will be carried on by means of mobile plant) which will be carried on in Scotland;

(l) the local fisheries committee, in the case of all prescribed processes designated for central control which may involve a release of any substance directly into relevant territorial waters or coastal waters within the sea fisheries district of that committee.]

(2) Subject to regulation 7(5)(a) below, the period for notification under paragraphs 2(1), 6(2) or 7(2) of Schedule 1 to the 1990 Act shall be the period of 14 days beginning with—

(a) in the case of a notification under paragraph 2(1), the day on which the enforcing authority receives the application for an authorisation;

(b) in the case of a notification under paragraph 6(2), the day on which the authority notifies the holder of an authorisation in accordance with section 10(5) of that Act; and

(c) in the case of a notification under paragraph 7(2), the day on which the authority receives the application for a variation of an authorisation.

(3) In paragraph (1)(h) above and regulation 7(3)(c) below, "harbour authority" has the same meaning as in section 57(1) of the Harbours Act 1964.

[(4) In paragraph (1)(f) above "sewerage authority" shall be construed in accordance with section 62 of the Local Government etc. (Scotland) Act 1994.

(5) In paragraph (1)(j) above "local authority" means—

(a) in England—

(i) the council of a county, so far as it is the council of an area for which there are no district councils;

(ii) a district council;

(iii) the council of a London borough;

(iv) the Council of the Isles of Scilly;

(v) the Common Council of the City of London and, as respects the Temples, the Sub-Treasurer of the Inner Temple and the Under-Treasurer of the Middle Temple respectively;

(b) in Wales, the council of a county or county borough.

(6) In paragraph (1)(k) above "local authority" means a council for an area constituted under section 2 of the Local Government etc. (Scotland) Act 1994.

(7) In paragraph (1)(l) above "relevant territorial waters" and "coastal waters" have the same meaning as in Part III of the Water Resources Act 1991].

Advertisements*

5.—(1) Subject to paragraph (4) and regulation 6 below, an advertisement—
  (a) by an applicant under paragraph 1(2) of Schedule 1 to the 1990 Act; or
  (b) by the holder of an authorisation under paragraphs 6(2) or 7(2) of that Schedule,
shall be published in one or more newspapers circulating in the locality in which the prescribed process will be carried on [and also, in the case of a prescribed process designated for central control—
  (i) if the process will be carried on in England and Wales otherwise than by means of mobile plant, or will be carried on by means of mobile plant by a person whose principal place of business in Great Britain is in England and Wales, in the London Gazette;
  (ii) if the process will be carried on in Scotland otherwise than by means of mobile plant, or will be carried on by means of mobile plant by a person whose principal place of business in Great Britain is in Scotland, in the Edinburgh Gazette.].
  (2) Subject to regulation 7(5)(b) below, any such advertisement as is mentioned in paragraph (1) above shall be published within a period of 28 days beginning 14 days after—
  (a) in the case of an advertisement under paragraph 1(2) of Schedule 1 to the 1990 Act, the day on which the application for an authorisation is made;
  (b) in the case of an advertisement under paragraph 6(2) of that Schedule, the day on which the holder of the authorisation is notified in accordance with section 10(5) of that Act;
  (c) in the case of an advertisement under paragraph 7(2) of that Schedule, the day on which the application for a variation is made.
  (3) Subject to regulation 7(4) below, any such advertisement as is mentioned in paragraph (1) above shall—
  (a) state the name of the applicant or, as the case may be, of the holder of the authorisation;
  (b) [except in the case of a prescribed process which will be carried on by means of mobile plant] give the address of the premises on which the prescribed process will be carried on;
  (c) describe briefly the prescribed process;
  (d) state where any register which contains particulars of the application or of the action to be taken may be inspected and that it may be inspected free of charge; and
  (e) explain that any person may make representations in writing to the enforcing authority within the period of 28 days beginning with the date of the advertisement and give the authority's address.
  [(f) explain that any such representations made by any person will be entered in a public register unless that person requests in writing that they should not be so placed, and that where such a request is made there will be included in the register a statement indicating only that representations have been made which have been the subject of such a request.]
  (4) [The requirement in paragraph (1) of this regulation to publish an advertisement in one or more newspapers circulating in the locality in which the prescribed process will be carried on does not apply] in relation to any prescribed process which will be carried on by means of mobile plant.

---

* Reg. 5. Where the relevant day referred to in sub-para. (a), (b) or, as the case may be, (c) of reg. 5(2) falls before April 1, 1996, the amendments with which reg. 5 is here printed do not apply (S.I. 1996 No. 667, reg. 4(2)).

Exemption for waste oil burners

6.—(1) The requirements of paragraphs 1(2), 2, 6 or 7 of Schedule 1 to the 1990 Act shall not apply in relation to any process involving only the burning of waste oil in an appliance with a net rated thermal input of less than 0·4 megawatts.

(2) In this regulation—

"net rated thermal input" has the same meaning as in regulation 2(4) above; and

"waste oil" means any mineral based lubricating or industrial oil which has become unfit for the use for which it was intended and, in particular, used combustion engine oil, gearbox oil, mineral lubricating oil, oil for turbines and hydraulic oil.

National security and confidential information

7.—(1) This regulation applies where in relation to an application or an authorisation—

    (a) a direction given by the Secretary of State under section 21(2) of the 1990 Act applies;

    (b) notice is given to the Secretary of State under section 21(4) of that Act;

    (c) an application is made to an enforcing authority under section 22(2) of that Act; or

    (d) an objection is made to such an authority under section 22(4) of that Act.

(2) Subject to paragraph (3) below, the requirements of paragraphs 2(1), 6(2) or 7(2) of Schedule 1 to the 1990 Act shall not apply in so far as they would require a person mentioned in regulation 4(1)(f), (g), or (h) above to be consulted on information which is not to be included in the register by virtue of sections 21 or 22 of that Act.

(3) Information which is not to be included in the register by virtue of section 22 of the 1990 Act shall not be excluded by paragraph (2) above if—

    (a) in the case of any person mentioned in regulation 4(1)(f) above, it is information about the release of any substance into a sewer vested in that person;

    (b) in the case of any person mentioned in regulation 4(1)(g) above, it is information about the release of any substance—

        (i) designated for central control;

        (ii) designated for local control which may involve a release of any substance into the air,

    which may affect a site of special scientific interest in that person's area; or

    (c) in the case of any person mentioned in regulation 4(1)(h) above, it is information about the release of any substance into a harbour managed by a harbour authority.

(4) The requirements of paragraphs 1(2), 6(2) or 7(2) of Schedule 1 to the 1990 Act shall not apply in so far as they would require the advertisement of information mentioned in regulation 5(3) above which is not to be included in the register by virtue of sections 21 or 22 of that Act.

(5) Where a matter falls to be determined under sections 21 or 22 of the 1990 Act—

    (a) the period for notification under paragraphs 2(1), 6(2) or 7(2) of Schedule 1 to that Act shall be the period of 14 days beginning 14 days after the day on which the matters to be determined under section 21 or 22 of that Act are finally disposed of;

    (b) the period within which an advertisement is to be published in the manner specified in regulation 5(1) above shall be the period of 28 days beginning 14 days after the day on which the matters to be determined under sections 21 or 22 of the 1990 Act are finally disposed of.

(6) For the purposes of paragraph (5) above, the matters to be determined under section 21 or 22 of the 1990 Act are finally disposed of—
- (a) on the date on which the Secretary of State determines under section 21 of that Act whether or not information is to be included in the register;
- (b) on the date on which the enforcing authority is treated under section 22(3) of that Act as having made a determination;
- (c) in a case where the enforcing authority determines under section 22(2) or (4) of that Act that the information in question is commercially confidential, on the date of the authority's determination;
- (d) in a case where the enforcing authority determines under section 22(2) or (4) of that Act that the information in question is not commercially confidential, on the date on which the period for bringing an appeal expires without an appeal being brought or, if such an appeal is brought within that period, on the date of the Secretary of State's final determination of the appeal or, as the case may be, the date on which the appellant withdraws his appeal.

Transmitted applications

8. Where an application for an authorisation is transmitted under paragraph 3(1) of Schedule 1 to the 1990 Act to the Secretary of State for determination, a request by the applicant or the enforcing authority concerned that the Secretary of State exercise one of the powers under paragraph 3(3) of that Schedule shall be made to him in writing within the period of 21 days beginning with the day on which the applicant is informed that the application is being transmitted to the Secretary of State.

Notice of appeal

9.—(1) A person who wishes to appeal to the Secretary of State under sections 15 or 22(5) of the 1990 Act shall give to the Secretary of State written notice of the appeal together with the documents specified in paragraph (2) below and shall at the same time send to the enforcing authority a copy of that notice together with the documents specified in paragraph (2)(a) and (f) below.

(2) The documents mentioned in paragraph (1) above are—
- (a) a statement of the grounds of appeal;
- (b) a copy of any relevant application;
- (c) a copy of any relevant authorisation;
- (d) a copy of any relevant correspondence between the appellant and the enforcing authority;
- (e) a copy of any decision or notice which is the subject-matter of the appeal;
- (f) a statement indicating whether the appellant wishes the appeal to be in the form of a hearing or to be disposed of on the basis of written representations.

(3) If the appellant wishes to withdraw an appeal he shall do so by notifying the Secretary of State in writing and shall send a copy of that notification to the enforcing authority.

Time limit for bringing appeal

10.—(1) Subject to paragraph (2) below, notice of appeal in accordance with regulation 9(1) above is to be given—

(a) in the case of an appeal by a person who has been refused the grant of an authorisation under section 6 of the 1990 Act, before the expiry of the period of six months beginning with—
  (i) the date of the decision which is the subject-matter of the appeal; or
  (ii) in the case of an appeal against a deemed refusal of an application for an authorisation, the date on which the application is deemed under the provisions of paragraph 5(2) of Schedule 1 to the 1990 Act to have been refused;

(b) in the case of an appeal by a person who is aggrieved by the conditions attached to his authorisation or who has been refused a variation of an authorisation on an application under section 11 of the 1990 Act, before the expiry of the period of six months beginning with the date of the decision which is the subject-matter of the appeal;

(c) in the case of an appeal in respect of a decision of an enforcing authority to revoke an authorisation, before the date on which the revocation of the authorisation takes effect;

(d) in the case of an appeal by a person on whom a variation notice, an enforcement notice or a prohibition notice is served, before the expiry of the period of two months beginning with the date of the notice which is the subject-matter of the appeal;

(e) in the case of an appeal in respect of a decision of an enforcing authority that information is not commercially confidential, before the expiry of the period of 21 days beginning with the date of the notice of determination.

(2) The Secretary of State may in a particular case allow notice of appeal to be given after the expiry of the periods mentioned in paragraphs (1)(a), (b) or (d) above.

Action upon receipt of notice of appeal*

11.—(1) Subject to paragraph (4) below, the enforcing authority shall, within 14 days of receipt of the copy of the notice of appeal in accordance with regulation 9(1) above—

(a) in the case of an appeal by a person in respect of a decision of an enforcing authority to revoke an authorisation or on whom a variation notice, an enforcement notice or a prohibition notice is served, give written notice of it to any person who appears to the enforcing authority likely to have a particular interest in the subject-matter of the appeal; and

(b) in any other case given written notice of it—
  (i) to any person who made representations to the authority with respect to the grant or variation of the authorisation; and
  (ii) to any person who was required to be consulted on the application under paragraphs [2 or 7] of Schedule 1 to the 1990 Act pursuant to regulation 4(1) above.

(2) A notice under paragraph (1) above shall—
(a) state than an appeal has been lodged;
(b) give the name of the appellant and—
  (i) where the prescribed process will not be carried on by means of mobile plant, the address of the premises where the prescribed process will be carried on;
  (ii) where the prescribed process will be carried on by means of mobile plant, the address of this principal place of business;

---

* Reg. 11. Where the enforcing authority receives the copy of the notice of appeal in accordance with reg. 9(1) before April 1, 1996, the amendments with which reg. 11 is here printed do not apply (S.I. 1996 No. 667, reg. 5(2)).

(c) describe the application or authorisation to which the appeal relates;

[...]

(e) state that representations with respect to the appeal may be made to the Secretary of State in writing by any recipient of the notice within a period of 21 days beginning with the date of the notice [, and that copies of any representations so made will be furnished to the appellant and to the enforcing authority];

[(ea) explain that any such representations made by any person will be entered in a public register unless that person requests in writing that they should not be so placed, and that where such a request is made there will be included in the register a statement indicating only that representations have been made which have been the subject of such a request; and]

(f) state that if a hearing is to be held wholly or partly in public, a person mentioned in paragraph (1)(a) or b(i) above who makes representations with respect to the appeal and any person mentioned in paragraph (1)(b)(ii) above will be notified of the date of the hearing.

(3) The enforcing authority shall, within 14 days of sending a notice under paragraph (1) above, notify the Secretary of State of the persons to whom and the date on which the notice was sent.

[(3A) In the event of an appeal being withdrawn, the enforcing authority shall give written notice of the withdrawal to every person to whom notice was given under paragraph (1) above.]

(4) The preceding provisions of this regulation do not apply in the case of an appeal brought under section 22(5) of the 1990 Act.

Written representations

12.—(1) Where the appellant informs the Secretary of State that he wishes the appeal to be disposed of on the basis of written representations, the enforcing authority shall submit any written representations to the Secretary of State not later than 28 days after receiving a copy of the documents mentioned in regulation 9(2)(a) and (f) above.

(2) The appellant shall make any further representations by way of reply to any representations from the enforcing authority not later than 17 days after the date of submission of those representations by the enforcing authority.

(3) Any representations made by the appellant or the enforcing authority shall be dated and submitted to the Secretary of State on the date they bear.

(4) When the enforcing authority or the appellant submits any representations to the Secretary of State they shall at the same time send a copy of them to the other party.

(5) The Secretary of State shall send to the appellant and the enforcing authority a copy of any representations made to him by the persons mentioned in regulation 11(1) above and shall allow the appellant and the enforcing authority a period of not less than 14 days in which to make representations thereon.

(6) The Secretary of State may in a particular case—
(a) set later time limits than those mentioned in this regulation;
(b) require exchanges of representations between the parties in addition to those mentioned in paragraphs (1) and (2) above.

Hearings

13.—(1) The Secretary of State shall give the appellant and the enforcing authority at least 28 days written notice (or such shorter period of notice as they may agree) of the date, time and place fixed for the holding of any hearing in respect of an appeal under section 15 or 22(5) of the 1990 Act.

(2) Subject to paragraphs (4) and (5) below, in the case of a hearing which is to be held wholly or partly in public, the Secretary of State shall, at least 21 days before the date fixed for the holding of the hearing, publish a copy of the notice mentioned in paragraph (1) above—

    (a) in a case where the prescribed process will not be carried on by means of mobile plant, in a newspaper circulating in the locality in which the prescribed process which is the subject of the appeal will be carried on; and

    (b) in a case where the appeal is in respect of a decision of an enforcement authority to revoke an authorisation or against a variation notice, an enforcement notice or a prohibition notice in respect of a prescribed process carried on by means of mobile plant, in a newspaper circulating in the locality in which the prescribed process was carried on at the time when the notice of revocation, variation notice, enforcement notice or prohibition notice was served,

and shall serve a copy of the notice mentioned in paragraph (1) above on every person mentioned in regulation 11(1)(a) and (b)(i) above who has made representations in writing to the Secretary of State and on any person who was required under regulation 11(1)(b)(ii) above to be notified of the appeal.

(3) The Secretary of State may vary the date fixed for the holding of any hearing and paragraphs (1) and (2) above shall apply to the variation of a date as they applied to the date originally fixed.

(4) The Secretary of State may also vary the time or place for the holding of a hearing but shall give such notice of any such variation as appears to him to be reasonable.

(5) Paragraph (2) above shall not apply in the case of a hearing in respect of an appeal brought under section 22(5) of the 1990 Act.

(6) The persons entitled to be heard at a hearing are—

    (a) the appellant;

    (b) the enforcing authority; and

    (c) any person required under regulation 11(1)(b)(ii) above to be notified of the appeal.

(7) Nothing in paragraph (6) above shall prevent the person appointed to conduct the hearing of the appeal from permitting any other persons to be heard at the hearing and such permission shall not be unreasonably withheld.

(8) After the conclusion of a hearing, the person appointed to conduct the hearing shall [unless he has been appointed under section 114(1)(a) of the Environment Act 1995 to determine the appeal,] make a report in writing to the Secretary of State which shall include his conclusions and his recommendations or his reasons for not making any recommendations.

Notification of determination

14.—(1) The Secretary of State shall notify the appellant in writing of his determination of the appeal and shall provide him with a copy of any report mentioned in regulation 13(8) above.

(2) The Secretary of State shall at the same time send—

    (a) a copy of the documents mentioned in paragraph (1) above to the enforcing authority and to any persons required under regulation 11(1)(b)(ii) above to be notified of the appeal; and

    (b) a copy of his determination of the appeal to a person mentioned in regulation 11(1)(a) and (b)(i) above who made representations to the Secretary of State and, if a hearing was held, to any other person who made representations in relation to the appeal at the hearing.

Registers

[**15.** Subject to sections 21 and 22 of the 1990 Act, a register maintained by an enforcing authority under section 20 of that Act shall be maintained in accordance with regulation 15A below and shall contain—

(a) all particulars of any application for an authorisation, or for a variation of the conditions of an authorisation, made to the authority;

(b) all particulars of any advertisement published pursuant to regulation 5 above;

(c) all particulars of any notice to the applicant by the authority under paragraph 1(3) of Schedule 1 to that Act and of any information furnished in response to such a notice;

[(ca) all particulars of any representations made by any person required to be consulted under paragraph 2, 6 or 7 of Schedule 1 to the 1990 Act pursuant to regulation 4(1) above;]

(d) all particulars of any representations made by any person in response to an advertisement published pursuant to regulation 5 above which contains the explanation required by paragraph (3)(f) of that regulation, or a notice given pursuant to regulation 11(1) above which contains the explanation required by paragraph (2)(ea) of that regulation, other than representations which the person who made them requested should not be placed in the register;

(e) in a case where any such representations are omitted from the register at the request of the person who made them, a statement by the authority that such representations have been made which have been the subject of such a request (but such statement shall not identify the person who made the representations in question);

(f) all particulars of any authorisation granted by the authority;

(g) all particulars of any written notice of the transfer of an authorisation given to the authority pursuant to section 9(2) of that Act;

(h) all particulars of any notification given to the holder of an authorisation by the authority under section 10(5) of that Act;

(i) all particulars of any revocation of an authorisation effected by the authority;

(j) all particulars of any variation notice, enforcement notice or prohibition notice issued by the authority;

(k) all particulars of any notice issued by the authority withdrawing an enforcement notice or a prohibition notice;

(l) all particulars of any notice of appeal under section 15 of that Act against a decision by the authority, the documents relating to the appeal mentioned in regulation 9(2)(a), (d) and (e) above, any written notification of the Secretary of State's determination of such an appeal and any report accompanying any such written notification;

(m) details of any conviction of any person for any offence under section 23(1) of that Act which relates to the carrying on of a prescribed process under an authorisation granted by the authority, or without such an authorisation in circumstances where one is required by section 6(1) of the 1990 Act, including the name of the offender, the date of conviction, the penalty imposed and the name of the Court;

(n) all particulars of any monitoring information relating to the carrying on of a prescribed process under an authorisation granted by the authority obtained by the authority as a result of its own monitoring or furnished to the authority in writing by virtue of a condition of the authorisation or section 19(2) of that Act;

(o) in a case where any such monitoring information is omitted from the register by virtue of section 22 of that Act, a statement by the authority, based on the monitoring information from time to time obtained by or furnished to them, indicating whether or not there has been compliance with any relevant condition of the authorisation;

(p) all particulars of any other information furnished to the authority on or after 1st April 1996 in compliance with a condition of the authorisation, a variation notice, enforcement notice or prohibition notice, or section 19(2) of that Act;

(q) all particulars of any report published by an enforcing authority relating to an assessment of the environmental consequences of the carrying on of a prescribed process in the locality of premises where the prescribed process is carried on under an authorisation granted by the authority; and

(r) all particulars of any direction (other than a direction under section 21(2) of that Act) given to the authority by the Secretary of State under any provision of Part I of that Act.

15A.—(1) Where an advertisement is required to be published in accordance with regulation 5 above—

(a) in the case of an advertisement under paragraph 1(2) or 7(2) of Schedule 1 to the 1990 Act, the particulars referred to in paragraph (a) of regulation 15 above shall be entered in the register not later than 14 days after the receipt by the enforcing authority of the application to which the advertisement relates;

(b) in the case of an advertisement under paragraph 6(2) of that Schedule, the particulars referred to in paragraph (h) of regulation 15 above shall be entered in the register not later than 14 days after the giving of the notification under section 10(5) of the 1990 Act.

(2) Where an application for an authorisation is withdrawn by the applicant at any time before it is determined, all particulars relating to that application which are already in the register shall be removed from that register not less than two months and not more than three months after the date of withdrawal of the application, and no further particulars relating to that application shall be entered in the register.

(3) Where, by virtue of any regulations made under section 2(1) of the 1990 Act a description of process ceases to be a prescribed process, all particulars relating to processes of that description shall be removed from the register not less than two months and not more than three months after the date on which that description of process ceases to be prescribed.]

[**16.** A register maintained by a local enforcing authority in England and Wales which is not a port health authority shall (in addition to the particulars required by regulation 15 above) contain all particulars of such information contained in any register maintained by the Environment Agency as relates to the carrying on in the area of the local enforcing authority of prescribed processes in relation to which that Agency has functions under Part I of the 1990 Act.]

17. Nothing in regulation 15 or 16 above shall require an enforcing authority to keep in a register maintained by them—

(a) monitoring information relating to a particular process four years after that information was entered in the register; or

(b) information relating to a particular process which has been superseded by later information relating to that process four years after that later information was entered in the register,

but nothing in this regulation shall apply to any aggregated monitoring data relating to overall emissions of any substance or class of substances from prescribed processes generally or from any class of prescribed process.]

APPENDIX 3

A: THE WASTE MANAGEMENT LICENSING REGULATIONS 1994

(S.I. 1994 No. 1056)

In force from:

May 1, 1994

Enabling power:

Section 2(2) of the European Communities Act 1972, sections 30(4) and 104(1) of the Control of Pollution Act 1974, sections 1(3)(a), 2, 8(2) and 9(1) of the Control of Pollution (Amendment) Act 1989, sections 29(10), 33(3), 35(6), 36(1), 39(3), 40(3), 43(8), 45(3), 50(3), 54(14), 64(1), (4) and (8), 74(6), 75(8) and 156 of the Environmental Protection Act 1990.

Background:

Part II of the Environmental Protection Act 1990 ("the 1990 Act") introduced a new waste management licensing system to replace the waste disposal licensing system which operated under Part I of the Control of Pollution Act 1974. The new system expanded the nature of activities requiring a licence to include keeping, treating, depositing and disposing of waste.

1994 Regulations set out the requirements to be met to obtain a waste management licence relating, among others, to relevant offences, technical competence and financial provision. They also grant exemptions for certain activities from the waste management licensing requirements and make provision for the registration of those exempted from the licensing requirement.

The 1994 Regulations also implement in Britain the amendments to the Waste Framework Directive (75/442/EEC) which were introduced by Directive 91/156/EEC). The U.K. definition of controlled waste is modified by reference to the term "Directive waste" to reflect E.C. requirements (subsequent amendments by the Environment Act 1995 of s.75 of the 1990 Act in relation to the definition of waste should be noted in this regard). Finally, the Regulations implement the requirements of the Groundwater Directive (80/68/EEC).

A number of amendments of the 1994 Regulations were introduced by S.I. 1995 No. 288. Chief among these were the replacement of a transitional exemption from waste management licensing for activities involving scrap metal or waste motor vehicles, by a permanent but more limited and conditional exemption for certain such activities.

Subsequent amendments were introduced by S.I. 1995 No. 1950 in order to extend a transitional exemption from waste management licensing and technical competence requirements for certain waste treatment operations. This move was triggered by concerns that on-site trade effluent treatment plants which might merit a permanent exemption might otherwise require a waste management licensing, and the framing of such a permanent exemption or exemptions is understood to be under consideration.

S.I. 1996 No. 634 further extended this transitional exemption to September 30, 1996. It also amended and, in freestanding provisions which are reproduced at the end of this Appendix, modified the provisions in relation to the technical competence of site managers for the purposes of s.74(3)(b) of the Environmental Protection Act 1990. These amendments and modifications took effect on April 1, 1996.

DoE Circular 11/94 (WO 26/94, SOED 10/94), gives guidance on the Regulations and DoE Circular 6/95 gives guidance on the amendments introduced by S.I. 1995 No. 288.

Statutory references:

Section 35 of the Environmental Protection Act 1990.

Amendments:

S.I. 1995 No. 288 (the Waste Management Licensing (Amendment etc.) Regulations 1995) inserted regs. 1(7), 17(1A), 18(1A), (1B), (4A) and (4B), paras. 40(1A), 41(1A), 44 and 45 of Schedule 3, and para. 14(3) of Part I of Schedule 4. It also amended regs. 16(1)(a), 17(2), 18(1), (4) and (6) and paras. 5(1), 42(1)(a) and 43(2) of Schedule 3, substituted reg. 12 and revoked para. 1(6) of Part I of Schedule 5. Without amending the 1994 Regulations, it also (in reg. 4) includes further transitional provisions in addition to those set out in reg. 5 of the 1994 Regulations. Since S.I. 1995 No. 288 is not reproduced in its own right, its reg. 4 is therefore reproduced here immediately after the 1994 Regulations and reg. 5 of the 1994 Regulations should be read in conjunction with it. (S.I. 1995 No. 288 also amends the Controlled Waste Regulations 1992.)

S.I. 1995 No. 1950 (the Waste Management Licensing (Amendment No. 2) Regulations 1995) amended para. 43(2) of Sched. 2 of the 1994 Regulations and S.I. 1995 No. 288, reg. 4.

S.I. 1996 No. 593 (the Environment Act 1995 (Consequential Amendments) Regulations 1996) amended reg. 8, reg. 10, reg. 18(8), Sched. 4, Pt. I (paras. 1, 3(1), 12(9) and 13) and Sched. 5, Pt. I.

S.I. 1996 No. 634 (the Waste Management Regulations 1996) amended reg. 4, paras. (1) and (3), reg. 5, paras. (1) and (2), and inserted reg. 5, paras. (4) to (7); amended reg. 12(1), reg. 18(4A)(d) and Sched. 3, paras. 43(2) and 45(3)(d). Reg. 5 was amended only as it applies to England and Wales: both versions are reproduced here for the reader's convenience.

Citation, commencement, interpretation and extent

1.—(1) These Regulations may be cited as the Waste Management Licensing Regulations 1994 and, except for regulations 4 and 5, shall come into force on 1st May 1994.

(2) Regulations 4 and 5 shall come into force on 10th August 1994.

(3) In these Regulations, unless the context otherwise requires—

"the 1990 Act" means the Environmental Protection Act 1990;

"the 1991 Regulations" means the Environmental Protection (Prescribed Processes and Substances) Regulations 1991;

"construction work" includes the repair, alteration or improvement of existing works;

"the Directive" means Council Directive 75/442/EEC on waste as amended by Council Directives 91/156/EEC and 91/692/EEC;

"Directive waste" means any substance or object in the categories set out in Part II of Schedule 4 which the producer or the person in possession of it discards or intends or is required to discard but with the exception of anything excluded from the scope of the Directive by Article 2 of the Directive, "discard" has the same meaning as in the Directive, and "producer" means anyone whose activities produce Directive waste or who carries out preprocessing, mixing or other operations resulting in a change in its nature or composition;

"disposal" means any of the operations listed in Part III of Schedule 4, and any reference to waste being disposed of is a reference to its being submitted to any of those operations;

"disposal licence" and "disposal authority" have the meaning given by sections 3(1) and 30(2) to (2D) respectively of the Control of Pollution Act 1974;

"enforcing authority" and "local enforcing authority" have the meaning given by section 1(7) and (8) of the 1990 Act;

"exempt activity" means any of the activities set out in Schedule 3;

"inland waters"—

    (a) in England and Wales, has the meaning given by section 221(1) of the Water Resources Act 1991;

    (b) in Scotland, has the meaning given by section 30A of the Control of Pollution Act 1974 except that it includes any loch or pond whether or not it discharges into a river or watercourse;

"operational land" has the meaning given by sections 263 and 264 of the Town and Country Planning Act 1990 or, in Scotland, sections 211 and 212 of the Town and Country Planning (Scotland) Act 1972;

"recovery" means any of the operations listed in Part IV of Schedule 4, and any reference to waste being recovered is a reference to its being submitted to any of those operations;

"scrap metal" has the meaning given by section 9(2) of the Scrap Metal Dealers Act 1964;

"special waste" has the meaning given by regulation 2 of the Control of Pollution (Special Waste) Regulations 1980;

"waste" means Directive waste;

"waste management licence" has the meaning given by section 35(1) of the 1990 Act, and "site licence" has the meaning given by section 35(12) of the 1990 Act;

"waste oil" means any mineral-based lubricating or industrial oil which has become unfit for the use for which it was originally intended and, in particular, used combustion engine oil, gearbox oil, mineral lubricating oil, oil for turbines and hydraulic oil;

"waste regulation authority", "waste disposal authority" and "waste collection authority" have the meaning given by section 30 of the 1990 Act; and

"work" includes preparatory work.

(4) Any reference in these Regulations to carrying on business as a scrap metal dealer has the meaning given by section 9(1) of the Scrap Metal Dealers Act 1964, and any reference, in relation to Scotland, to carrying on business as a metal dealer has the meaning given by section 37(2) of the Civic Government (Scotland) Act 1982.

(5) Regulations 13, 14 and 15, and Schedule 4, shall apply in relation to land in the area of a waste disposal authority in Scotland which is occupied by the authority as if—

(a) references to a waste management licence were references to a resolution under section 54 of the 1990 Act;

(b) references to an application being made for a waste management licence were references to consideration being given to passing such a resolution;

(c) references to granting or issuing a waste management licence were references to passing, and references to rejecting an application were references to not passing, such a resolution;

(d) references to the terms or conditions of a waste management licence were references to the terms or conditions specified in such a resolution; and

(e) references to varying or revoking a waste management licence under section 37 or 38 of the 1990 Act were references to varying or rescinding such a resolution under section 54(8) of that Act.

(6) These Regulations do not extend to Northern Ireland.

[(7) The provisions of section 160 of the 1990 Act shall apply to—

(a) the service or giving of any notice required or authorised by these Regulations to be served on or given to a person; or

(b) the sending or giving of any document required or authorised by these Regulations to be sent or given to a person,

as if the service or giving of any such notice or, as the case may be, the sending or giving of any such document, was required or authorised by or under that Act.]

Application for a waste management licence or for the surrender or transfer of a waste management licence

2.—(1) An application for a waste management licence shall be made in writing.

(2) An application for the surrender of a site licence shall be made in writing and shall, subject to paragraphs (3) and (4) below, include the information and be accompanied by the evidence prescribed by Schedule 1.

(3) Nothing in paragraph (2) above shall require the information

prescribed by paragraphs 3 to 6 of Schedule 1 to be provided to the waste regulation authority if the information has previously been provided by the applicant to the authority or a predecessor of the authority in connection with a waste management licence, or a disposal licence under section 5 of the Control of Pollution Act 1974, in respect of the site in question or any part of it.

(4) In so far as the information prescribed by paragraphs 4, 5(a) and 6(a) of Schedule 1 relates to activities carried on, or works carried out, at the site at a time prior to the applicant's first involvement with the site, paragraph (2) above only requires that information to be included in the application so far as it is known to either the applicant or, where the applicant is a partnership or body corporate, to any of the partners or, as the case may be, to any director, manager, secretary or other similar officer of the body corporate.

(5) An application for the transfer of a waste management licence shall be made in writing and shall include the information prescribed by Schedule 2.

Relevant offences

3. An offence is relevant for the purposes of section 74(3)(a) of the 1990 Act if it is an offence under any of the following enactments—

    (a) section 22 of the Public Health (Scotland) Act 1897;
    (b) section 95(1) of the Public Health Act 1936;
    (c) section 3, 5(6), 16(4), 18(2), 31(1), 32(1), 34(5), 78, 92(6) or 93(3) of the Control of Pollution Act 1974;
    (d) section 2 of the Refuse Disposal (Amenity) Act 1978;
    (e) the Control of Pollution (Special Waste) Regulations 1980;
    (f) section 9(1) of the Food and Environment Protection Act 1985;
    (g) the Transfrontier Shipment of Hazardous Waste Regulations 1988;
    (h) the Merchant Shipping (Prevention of Pollution by Garbage) Regulations 1988;
    (i) section 1, 5, 6(9) or 7(3) of the Control of Pollution (Amendment) Act 1989;
    (j) section 107, 118(4) or 175(1) of the Water Act 1989;
    (k) section 23(1), 33, 34(6), 44, 47(6), 57(5), 59(5), 63(2), 69(9), 70(4), 71(3) or 80(4) of the 1990 Act;
    (l) section 85, 202 or 206 of the Water Resources Act 1991;
    (m) section 33 of the Clean Air Act 1993.

Technical competence

4.—(1) Subject to paragraph (2) and regulation 5 below, a person is technically competent for the purposes of section 74(3)(b) of the 1990 Act in relation to a facility of a type listed in Table 1 below if, and only if, he is the holder of one of the certificates awarded by the Waste Management Industry Training and Advisory Board specified in that Table as being a relevant certificate of technical competence for that type of facility.

Table 1

Type of facility	Relevant certificate of technical competence
A landfill site which receives special waste.	Managing landfill operations: special waste (level 4).
A landfill site which receives biodegradable waste or which for some other reason requires substantial engineering works to protect the environment but which in either case does not receive any special waste.	1. Managing landfill operations: biodegradable waste (level 4); or

Type of facility	Relevant certificate of technical competence
	2. Managing landfill operations: special waste (level 4).
Any other type of landfill site with a total capacity exceeding 50,000 cubic metres.	1. Landfill operations: inert waste (level 3); or 2. Managing landfill operations: biodegradable waste (level 4); or 3. Managing landfill operations: special waste (level 4).
A site on which waste is burned in an incinerator designed to incinerate waste at a rate of more than 50 kilograms per hour but less than 1 tonne per hour.	Managing incinerator operations: special waste (level 4).
A waste treatment plant where [biodegradable, clinical or special waste is subjected to a chemical or physical process].	Managing treatment operations: special waste (level 4).
A waste treatment plant where waste [other than biodegradable, clinical or special waste is subjected to a chemical or physical process].	1. Treatment operations: inert waste (level 3); or 2. Managing treatment operations: special waste (level 4).
A transfer station where— (a) biodegradable, clinical or special waste is dealt with; and (b) the total quantity of waste at the station at any time exceeds 5 cubic metres.	Managing transfer operations: special waste (level 4).
A transfer station where— (a) no biodegradable, clinical or special waste is dealt with; and (b) the total quantity of waste at the station at any time exceeds 50 cubic metres.	1. Transfer operations: inert waste (level 3); or 2. Managing transfer operations: special waste (level 4).
A civic amenity site.	Civic amenity site operations (level 3).

(2) Paragraph (1) above does not apply in relation to a facility which is used exclusively for the purposes of—
  (a) carrying on business as a scrap metal dealer or, in Scotland, as a metal dealer; or
  (b) dismantling motor vehicles.
(3) In this regulation—
  "civic amenity site" means a place provided under section 1 of the Refuse Disposal (Amenity) Act 1978 or by virtue of section 51(1)(b) of the 1990 Act;

"clinical waste" has the meaning given by regulation 1(2) of the Controlled Waste Regulations 1992; and

["landfill site" does not include a site used only for the burial of dead domestic pets;]

"transfer station" means a facility where waste is unloaded in order to permit its preparation for further transport for treatment, keeping or disposal elsewhere.

Technical competence—transitional provisions*

5 (*England and Wales*).—(1) [Subject to paragraph (4),] where before 10th August 1994 a person has applied to the Waste Management Industry Training and Advisory Board for a certificate of technical competence and at any time in the 12 months ending on that date he acted as the manager of a facility of a type listed in Table 1 above for which the certificate is a relevant certificate, then, until 10th August 1999, regulation 4 shall not apply to him in relation to either—

(a) any facility of that type; or

(b) a facility of any other type if—

(i) the certificate is a relevant certificate for that other type of facility; and

(ii) the entry for that other type of facility appears, in Table 1 above, after the entry in that Table for the type of facility in respect of which he acted as the manager,

and he shall be treated as technically competent for the purposes of section 74(3)(b) of the 1990 Act in relation to any such facility.

(2) [Subject to paragraph (4),] where a person is 55 or over on 10th August 1994 and in the 10 years ending on that date he has had at least 5 years experience as the manager of a facility of a type listed in Table 1 above, then, until 10th August 2004, regulation 4 shall not apply to him in relation to either—

(a) any facility of that type; or

(b) a facility of any other type if each certificate which is a relevant certificate for the type of facility in relation to which he has had such experience as manager is also a relevant certificate for that other type of facility,

and he shall be treated as technically competent for the purposes of section 74(3)(b) of the 1990 Act in relation to any such facility.

(3) A person shall be treated as the manager of a facility for the purposes of paragraph (1) or (2) above if at the relevant time he was the manager of activities which were carried on at that facility and which were authorised by a disposal licence under section 5 of the Control of Pollution Act 1974, a resolution under section 11 of that Act or under section 54 of the 1990 Act, or a waste management licence.

[(4) Subject to paragraphs (6) and (7), in their application in relation to a person mentioned in paragraph (5), paragraphs (1) and (2) shall apply as if the following dates were substituted for the dates in those paragraphs which are specified—

(a) in paragraph (1)

(i) for "10th August 1994", "1st October 1996";

(ii) for "10th August 1999", "1st October 2001"; and

(b) in paragraph (2),

(i) for "10th August 1994", "1st October 1996";

(ii) for "10th August 2004", "1st October 2006".

(5) The person mentioned in paragraph (4) is the manager of a facility at

---

* Reg. 5 is here printed first as it applies to England and Wales following amendment by S.I. 1996 No. 634, and then as it applies unamended to Scotland.

which activities were authorised by a resolution under section 11 of the Control of Pollution Act 1974.

(6) Paragraph (4) does not apply to a person who is to be treated as technically competent by virtue of other provisions than those in that paragraph.

(7) Paragraph (4) does not apply in Scotland.]

Notice of appeal

6.—(1) A person who wishes to appeal to the Secretary of State under section 43 or 66(5) of the 1990 Act (appeals to the Secretary of State from decisions with respect to waste management licences or from determinations that information is not commercially confidential) shall do so by notice in writing.

(2) The notice shall be accompanied by—
  (a) a statement of the grounds of appeal;
  (b) where the appeal relates to an application for a waste management licence or for the modification, surrender or transfer of a waste management licence, a copy of the appellant's application and any supporting documents;
  (c) where the appeal relates to a determination under section 66(2) or (4) of the 1990 Act that information is not commercially confidential, the information in question;
  (d) where the appeal relates to an existing waste management licence (including a waste management licence which has been suspended or revoked), a copy of that waste management licence;
  (e) a copy of any correspondence relevant to the appeal;
  (f) a copy of any other document relevant to the appeal including, in particular, any relevant consent, determination, notice, planning permission, established use certificate or certificate of lawful use or development; and
  (g) a statement indicating whether the appellant wishes the appeal to be in the form of a hearing or to be determined on the basis of written representations.

(3) The appellant shall serve a copy of his notice of appeal on the waste regulation authority together with copies of the documents mentioned in paragraph (2) above.

(4) If the appellant wishes to withdraw an appeal, he shall do so by notifying the Secretary of State in writing and shall send a copy of that notification to the waste regulation authority.

Time limit for making an appeal

7.—(1) Subject to paragraph (2) below, notice of appeal shall be given—
  (a) in the case of an appeal under section 43 of the 1990 Act, before the expiry of the period of 6 months beginning with—
    (i) the date of the decision which is the subject of the appeal; or
    (ii) the date on which the waste regulation authority is deemed by section 36(9), 37(6), 39(10) or 40(6) of the 1990 Act to have rejected the application;
  (b) in the case of an appeal under section 66(5) of the 1990 Act, before the expiry of the period of 21 days beginning with the date on which the determination which is the subject of the appeal is notified to the person concerned.

(2) The Secretary of State may in relation to an appeal under section 43 of the 1990 Act at any time allow notice of appeal to be given after the expiry of the period mentioned in paragraph (1)(a) above.

Reports of hearings

8. The person hearing an appeal under section 43(2)(c) of the 1990 Act shall, unless he has been appointed to determine the appeal under [section 114(1)(a) of the Environment Act 1995], make a written report to the Secretary of State which shall include his conclusions and recommendations or his reasons for not making any recommendations.

Notification of determination

9.—(1) The Secretary of State or other person determining an appeal shall notify the appellant in writing of his decision and of his reasons.

(2) If the Secretary of State determines an appeal after a hearing under section 43(2)(c) of the 1990 Act, he shall provide the appellant with a copy of any report made to him under regulation 8.

(3) The Secretary of State or other person determining an appeal shall, at the same time as notifying the appellant of his decision, send the waste regulation authority a copy of any document sent to the appellant under this regulation.

Particulars to be entered in public registers

10.—(1) Subject to sections 65 and 66 of the 1990 Act and regulation 11, a register maintained by a waste regulation authority under section 64(1) of the 1990 Act shall contain full particulars of—

  (a) current or recently current waste management licences ("licences") granted by the authority and any associated working plans;
  (b) current or recently current applications to the authority for licences, or for the transfer or modification of licences, including details of—
    (i) documents submitted by applicants containing supporting information;
    (ii) written representations considered by the authority under section 36(4)(b), (6)(b) or (7)(b) or 37(5) of the 1990 Act;
    (iii) decisions of the Secretary of State under section 36(5), or, in Scotland, section 36(6), of the 1990 Act;
    (iv) notices by the authority rejecting applications;
    (v) emergencies resulting in the postponement of references under section 37(5)(a) of the 1990 Act;
  (c) notices issued by the authority under section 37 of the 1990 Act effecting the modification of licences;
  (d) notices issued by the authority under section 38 of the 1990 Act effecting the revocation or suspension of licences or imposing requirements on the holders of licences;
  (e) notices of appeal under section 43 of the 1990 Act relating to decisions of the authority and other documents relating to such appeals served on or sent to the authority under regulation 6(3) or (4) or 9(3);
  (f) convictions of holders of licences granted by the authority for any offence under Part II of the 1990 Act (whether or not in relation to a licence) including the name of the offender, the date of conviction, the penalty imposed and the name of the Court;
  (g) reports produced by the authority in discharge of any functions under section 42 of the 1990 Act, including details of—
    (i) any correspondence with the National Rivers Authority or river purification authority as a result of section 42(2) of the 1990 Act;
    (ii) remedial or preventive action taken by the authority under section 42(3) of the 1990 Act;

(iii) notices issued by the authority under section 42(5) of the 1990 Act;
(h) any monitoring information relating to the carrying on of any activity under a licence granted by the authority which was obtained by the authority as a result of its own monitoring or was furnished to the authority in writing by virtue of any condition of the licence or section 71(2) of the 1990 Act;
(i) directions given by the Secretary of State to the authority under section 35(7), 37(3), 38(7), 42(8), 50(9), 54(11) or (15), 58 or 66(7) of the 1990 Act;
(j) any summary prepared by the authority of the amount of special waste produced or disposed of in their area;
(k) registers and records provided to the authority under regulation 13(5) or 14(1) of the Control of Pollution (Special Waste) Regulations 1980;
(l) applications to the authority under section 39 of the 1990 Act for the surrender of licences, including details of—
  (i) documents submitted by applicants containing supporting information and evidence;
  (ii) information and evidence obtained under section 39(4) of the 1990 Act;
  (iii) written representations considered by the authority under section 39(7)(b) or (8)(b) of the 1990 Act;
  (iv) decisions by the Secretary of State under section 39(7) or (8) of the 1990 Act; and
  (v) notices of determination and certificates of completion issued under section 39(9) of the 1990 Act;
(m) written reports under section 70(3) of the 1990 Act by inspectors appointed by the authority [or written reports under section 109(2) of the Environment Act 1995 by persons authorised by the authority under section 108(1) or (2) of that Act where the articles or substances seized and rendered harmless are waste];
(n) in Scotland, resolutions made by the authority under section 54 of the 1990 Act, including details of—
  (i) proposals made in relation to land in the area of the authority by a waste disposal authority under section 54(4) of the 1990 Act;
  (ii) statements made and written representations considered by the authority under section 54(4) of the 1990 Act;
  (iii) requests made to, and disagreements with, the authority which are referred to the Secretary of State under section 54(7) of the 1990 Act and his decisions on such references;
  (iv) emergencies resulting in the postponement of references under section 54(4) of the 1990 Act.
(2) The register shall also contain the following—
(a) where an inspector appointed by the authority exercises any power under section 69(3) of the 1990 Act, a record showing when the power was exercised and indicating what information was obtained, and what action was taken, on that occasion;
[(aa) where a person authorised by the authority exercises any power under section 108(4) of the Environment Act 1995 in connection with the authority's functions under Part II of the Environmental Protection Act 1990, a record showing when the power was exercised and indicating what information was obtained, and what action was taken, on that occasion;]
(b) where any information is excluded from the register by virtue of section 66 of the 1990 Act and the information shows whether or not there is compliance with any condition of a waste management

licence, a statement based on that information indicating whether or not there is compliance with that condition.

(3) A register maintained under section 64(4) of the 1990 Act by a waste collection authority in England [or Wales] shall contain full particulars of the following information contained in any register maintained under section 64(1) of the 1990 Act, to the extent that it relates to the treatment, keeping or disposal of controlled waste in the area of the authority—

(a) current or recently current waste management licences;
(b) notices issued under section 37 of the 1990 Act effecting the modification of waste management licences;
(c) notices issued under section 38 of the 1990 Act effecting the revocation or suspension of waste management licences;
(d) certificates of completion issued under section 39(9) of the 1990 Act.

(4) For the purposes of this regulation, waste management licences are "recently" current for the period of twelve months after they cease to be in force, and applications for waste management licences, or for the transfer or modification of such licences, are "recently" current if they relate to a waste management licence which is current or recently current or, in the case of an application which is rejected, for the period of twelve months beginning with the date on which the waste regulation authority gives notice of rejection or, as the case may be, on which the application is deemed by section 36(9), 37(6) or 40(6) of the 1990 Act to have been rejected.

Information to be excluded or removed from a register

11.—(1) Nothing in regulation 10(1)(g) or (m) or (2) shall require a register maintained by a waste regulation authority under section 64(1) of the 1990 Act to contain information relating to, or to anything which is the subject-matter of, any criminal proceedings (including prospective proceedings) at any time before those proceedings are finally disposed of.

(2) Nothing in regulation 10 shall require a register maintained by a waste regulation authority or waste collection authority under section 64 of the 1990 Act to contain—

(a) any such monitoring information as is mentioned in regulation 10(1)(h) after 4 years have elapsed from that information being entered in the register; or
(b) any information which has been superseded by later information after 4 years have elapsed from that later information being entered in the register.

Mobile plant

[**12.**—(1) Plant of the following descriptions, if it is designed to move or be moved by any means from place to place with a view to being used at each such place or, if not so designed, is readily capable of so moving or being so moved, but no other plant, shall be treated as being mobile plant for the purposes of Part II of the 1990 Act—

(a) an incinerator which is an exempt incinerator for the purposes of Section 5.1 of Schedule 1 to the 1991 Regulations;
(b) plant for—
    (i) the recovery, by filtration or heat treatment, of waste oil from electrical equipment, or
    (ii) the destruction by dechlorination of waste polychlorinated biphenyls or terphenyls (PCBs or PCTs);
(c) plant for the vitrification of waste;
(d) plant for the treatment by microwave of clinical waste.
[(e) plant for the treatment of waste soil.]

(2) For the purposes of paragraph (1)(d) above, "clinical waste" has the

meaning given by regulation 1(2) of the Controlled Waste Regulations 1992.]

Health at work

13. No conditions shall be imposed in any waste management licence for the purpose only of securing the health of persons at work (within the meaning of Part I of the Health and Safety at Work etc. Act 1974).

Waste oils

14.—(1) Where a waste management licence or disposal licence authorises the regeneration of waste oil, it shall include conditions which ensure that base oils derived from regeneration do not constitute a toxic and dangerous waste and do not contain PCBs or PCTs at all or do not contain them in concentrations beyond a specified maximum limit which in no case is to exceed 50 parts per million.

(2) Where a waste management licence or disposal licence authorises the keeping of waste oil, it shall include conditions which ensure that it is not mixed with toxic and dangerous waste or PCBs or PCTs.

(3) In this regulation—

"PCBs or PCTs" means polychlorinated biphenyls, polychlorinated terphenyls and mixtures containing one or both of such substances; and

"toxic and dangerous waste" has the meaning given by Article 1(b) of Council Directive 78/319/EEC.

Groundwater

15.—(1) Where a waste regulation authority proposes to issue a waste management licence authorising—

(a) any disposal or tipping for the purpose of disposal of a substance in list I which might lead to an indirect discharge into groundwater of such a substance;

(b) any disposal or tipping for the purpose of disposal of a substance in list II which might lead to an indirect discharge into groundwater of such a substance;

(c) a direct discharge into groundwater of a substance in list I; or

(d) a direct discharge into groundwater of a substance in list II,

the authority shall ensure that the proposed activities are subjected to prior investigation.

(2) The prior investigation referred to in paragraph (1) above shall include examination of the hydrogeological conditions of the area concerned, the possible purifying powers of the soil and sub-soil and the risk of pollution and alteration of the groundwater from the discharge and shall establish whether the discharge of substances into groundwater is a satisfactory solution from the point of view of the environment.

(3) A waste management licence shall not be issued in any case within paragraph (1) above until the waste regulation authority has checked that the groundwater, and in particular its quality, will undergo the requisite surveillance.

(4) In a case within paragraph (1)(a) or (c) above—

(a) where the waste regulation authority is satisfied, in the light of the investigation, that the groundwater which may be affected by a direct or indirect discharge of a substance on list I is permanently unsuitable for other uses, especially domestic and agricultural, the waste management licence may only be issued if the authority is also satisfied that—

(i) the presence of that substance once discharged into ground-water will not impede exploitation of ground resources; and

(ii) all technical precautions will be taken to ensure that no substance in list I can reach other aquatic systems or harm other ecosystems; and

(b) where the waste regulation authority is not satisfied, in the light of the investigation, that the groundwater which may be affected by such a discharge is permanently unsuitable for other uses, especially domestic and agricultural, a waste management licence may only be issued if it is made subject to such conditions as the authority, in the light of the investigations, is satisfied will ensure the observance of all technical precautions necessary to prevent any discharges into groundwater of substances in list I.

(5) In a case within paragraph (1)(b) or (d) above, if a waste management licence is issued, it shall be issued subject to such conditions as the waste regulation authority, in the light of the investigation, is satisfied will ensure the observance of all technical precautions for preventing groundwater pollution by substances in list II.

(6) Where a waste management licence is granted in any case within paragraph (1)(a) or (b) above, the licence shall be granted on such terms and subject to such conditions as specify—

(a) the place where any disposal or tipping which might lead to a discharge into groundwater of any substances in list I or II is to be done;

(b) the methods of disposal or tipping which may be used;

(c) the essential precautions which must be taken, paying particular attention to the nature and concentration of the substances present in the matter to be disposed of or tipped, the characteristics of the receiving environment and the proximity of the water catchment areas, in particular those for drinking, thermal and mineral water;

(d) the maximum quantity permissible, during one or more specified periods of time, of matter containing substances in list I or II and, where possible, of those substances themselves, to be disposed of or tipped and the appropriate requirements as to the concentration of those substances;

(e) the technical precautions required by paragraph (4)(b) or (5) above;

(f) if necessary, the measures for monitoring the groundwater, and in particular its quality.

(7) Where a waste management licence is granted in any case within paragraph (1)(c) or (d) above, the licence shall be granted on such terms and subject to such conditions as specify—

(a) the place where any substances in list I or II are to be discharged into groundwater;

(b) the method of discharge which may be used;

(c) the essential precautions which must be taken, paying particular attention to the nature and concentration of the substances present in the effluents, the characteristics of the receiving environment and the proximity of the water catchment areas, in particular those for drinking, thermal and mineral water;

(d) the maximum quantity of a substance in list I or II permissible in an effluent during one or more specified periods of time and the appropriate requirements as to the concentration of those substances;

(e) the arrangements enabling effluents discharged into groundwater to be monitored;

(f) if necessary, the measures for monitoring the groundwater, and in particular its quality.

(8) Any authorisation granted by a waste management licence for an activity within paragraph (1) above shall be granted for a limited period only.

(9) Any authorisation granted by a waste management licence for an activity within paragraph (1) above shall be reviewed at least every four years.

(10) Waste regulation authorities shall review all waste management licences current on 1st May 1994 which authorise any activity within paragraph (1) above and shall, so far as may be necessary to give effect to Council Directive 80/68/EEC, exercise their powers under sections 37 and 38 of the 1990 Act (variation and revocation etc. of waste management licences) in relation to any such authorisation.

(11) The foregoing provisions of this regulation apply, with any necessary modifications, to the granting or review by disposal authorities of disposal licences under Part I of the Control of Pollution Act 1974 as they apply to the granting or review by waste regulation authorities of waste management licences.

(12) Expressions used both in this regulation and in Council Directive 80/68/EEC have for the purposes of this regulation the same meaning as in that Directive.

Exclusion of activities under other control regimes from waste management licensing

16.—(1) Subject to paragraph (2) below, section 33(1)(a), (b) and (c) of the 1990 Act shall not apply in relation to the carrying on of any of the following activities—

  (a) the [deposit in or on land,] recovery or disposal of waste under an authorisation granted under Part I of the 1990 Act where the activity is or forms part of a process designated for central control under section 2(4) of the 1990 Act;

  (b) the disposal of waste under an authorisation granted under Part I of the 1990 Act where the activity is or forms part of a process within paragraph (a) of Part B of Section 5.1 (incineration) of Schedule 1 to the 1991 Regulations in so far as the activity results in releases of substances into the air;

  (c) the disposal of liquid waste under a consent under Chapter II of Part III of the Water Resources Act 1991 or under Part II of the Control of Pollution Act 1974; and

  (d) the recovery or disposal of waste where the activity is or forms part of an operation which is for the time being either—

   (i) the subject of a licence under Part II of the Food and Environment Protection Act 1985; or

   (ii) carried on in circumstances where such a licence would be required but for an order under section 7 of that Act.

(2) Paragraph (1)(a) and (b) above does not apply in so far as the activity involves the final disposal of waste by deposit in or on land.

Exemptions from waste management licensing

17.—(1) Subject to the following provisions of this regulation and to any conditions or limitations in Schedule 3, section 33(1)(a) and (b) of the 1990 Act shall not apply in relation to the carrying on of any exempt activity set out in that Schedule.

[(1A) Paragraph (1) above does not apply to the carrying on of an exempt activity falling within paragraph 45(1), (2) or (5) of Schedule 3 where the carrying on of that activity is authorised by a waste management licence granted upon an application made after March 31, 1995 under section 36 of the 1990 Act.]

(2) In the case of an exempt activity set out in paragraph 4, 7, 9, 11, 13, 14, 15, 17, 18, 19, 25, 37, [40, 41 or 45] of Schedule 3, paragraph (1) above only applies if—
  (a) the exempt activity is carried on by or with the consent of the occupier of the land where the activity is carried on; or
  (b) the person carrying on the exempt activity is otherwise entitled to do so on that land.

(3) Unless otherwise indicated in Schedule 3, paragraph (1) above does not apply to the carrying on of an exempt activity in so far as it involves special waste.

(4) Paragraph (1) above only applies in relation to an exempt activity involving the disposal or recovery of waste by an establishment or undertaking if the type and quantity of waste submitted to the activity, and the method of disposal or recovery, are consistent with the need to attain the objectives mentioned in paragraph 4(1)(a) of Part I of Schedule 4.

(5) For the purposes of Schedule 3, a container, lagoon or place is secure in relation to waste kept in it if all reasonable precautions are taken to ensure that the waste cannot escape from it and members of the public are unable to gain access to the waste, and any reference to secure storage means storage in a secure container, lagoon or place.

Registration in connection with exempt activities

18.—(1) Subject to [paragraphs (1A), (1B) and (7)] below, it shall be an offence for an establishment or undertaking to carry on, after December 31, 1994, an exempt activity involving the recovery or disposal of waste without being registered with the appropriate registration authority.

[(1A) In the case of an exempt activity falling within paragraph 45(1) or (2) of Schedule 3, paragraph (1) above shall have effect as if "30th September 1995" were substituted for "31st December 1994".

(1B) Paragraph (1) above shall not apply in the case of an exempt activity to which a resolution under section 54 of the 1990 Act relates and which is carried on in accordance with the conditions, specified in the resolution, which relate to it.]

(2) It shall be the duty of each appropriate registration authority to establish and maintain a register for the purposes of paragraph (1) above of establishments and undertakings carrying on exempt activities involving the recovery or disposal of waste in respect of which it is the appropriate registration authority.

(3) Subject to paragraph (4) below, the register shall contain the following particulars in relation to each such establishment or undertaking—
  (a) the name and address of the establishment or undertaking;
  (b) the activity which constitutes the exempt activity; and
  (c) the place where the activity is carried on.

(4) [Subject to paragraphs (4A) and (4B) below, the] appropriate registration authority shall enter the relevant particulars in the register in relation to an establishment or undertaking if it receives notice of them in writing or otherwise becomes aware of those particulars.

[(4A) Paragraph (4) above shall not apply in the case of an exempt activity falling within paragraph 45(1) or (2) of Schedule 3 and, in such a case, the appropriate registration authority shall enter the relevant particulars in the register in relation to an establishment or undertaking only if—
  (a) it receives notice of them in writing;
  (b) that notice is provided to it by that establishment or undertaking;
  (c) that notice is accompanied by a plan of each place at which any such exempt activity is carried on showing—

(i) the boundaries of that place;
(ii) the locations within that place at which the exempt activity is to be carried on;
(iii) the location and specifications of any such impermeable pavements, drainage systems or hardstandings as are mentioned in paragraph 45(1)(c) or (2)(f) or (g) of Schedule 3; and
(iv) the location of any such secure containers as are mentioned in paragraph 45(2)(e) of Schedule 3;

and

(d) that notice is also accompanied by payment of a fee of [£400] in respect of each place where any such exempt activity is carried on.

(4B) Where any fee payable under paragraph 45(3)(d) of Schedule 3 is not received by the appropriate registration authority within two months of the due date for its payment as ascertained in accordance with paragraph 45(4) of Schedule 3—

(a) in a case where the establishment or undertaking is registered for exempt activities falling within paragraph 45(1) or (2) in respect of only one place, or where it is so registered in respect of more than one place and the fee in respect of each such place is then unpaid, the registration of the establishment or undertaking shall be cancelled and the authority shall remove from its register the relevant entry in respect of the establishment or undertaking;

(b) in any other case, the registration of the establishment or undertaking in respect of those activities shall be cancelled insofar as it relates to any place in respect of which the fee is then unpaid and the authority shall amend the relevant entry in its register accordingly,

and where the authority removes or amends an entry from or in its register by virtue of this paragraph it shall notify the establishment or undertaking in writing of the removal or amendment.]

(5) For the purposes of paragraph (4) above, the appropriate registration authority shall be taken to be aware of the relevant particulars in relation to an exempt activity mentioned in paragraph (10)(a), (b) or (c) below.

(6) A person guilty of an offence under paragraph (1) above shall be liable on summary conviction to a fine [not exceeding—

(a) in the case of an exempt activity falling within paragraph 45(1) or (2) of Schedule 3, level 2 on the standard scale; and

(b) in any other case, £10]

(7) The preceding provisions of this regulation shall not apply in the case of an exempt activity to which paragraph 7(3)(c) of Schedule 3 applies, but the appropriate registration authority shall enter in its register the particulars furnished to it pursuant to that provision.

(8) Each appropriate registration authority shall secure that any register maintained by it under this regulation is open to inspection by members of the public free of charge at all reasonable hours and shall afford to members of the public reasonable facilities for obtaining, on payment of reasonable charges, copies of entries in the register.

(9) Registers under this regulation may be kept in any form.

(10) For the purposes of this regulation, the appropriate registration authority is—

(a) in the case of an exempt activity falling within—
(i) paragraph 1, 2, 3 or 24 of Schedule 3; or
(ii) paragraph 4 of Schedule 3 if it involves the coating or spraying of metal containers as or as part of a process within Part B of Section 6.5 (coating processes and printing) of Schedule 1 to the 1991 Regulations and the process is for the time being the subject of an authorisation granted under Part I of the 1990 Act, or if it involves storage related to that process; or

    (iii) paragraph 12 of Schedule 3 if it involves the composting of biodegradable waste as or as part of a process within paragraph (a) of Part B of Section 6.9 (treatment or processing of animal or vegetable matter) of Schedule 1 to the 1991 Regulations, the compost is to be used for the purpose of cultivating mushrooms and the process is for the time being the subject of an authorisation granted under Part I of the 1990 Act, or if it involves storage related to that process,

the local enforcing authority responsible for granting the authorisation under Part I of the 1990 Act for the prescribed process involving the exempt activity, or to which the exempt activity relates;

  (b) in a case falling within paragraph 16 of Schedule 3, the issuing authority responsible for granting the licence under article 7 or 8 of the Diseases of Animals (Waste Food) Order 1973 under which the exempt activity is carried on;

  (c) in a case falling within paragraph 23 of Schedule 3—

    (i) where the exempt activity is carried on by virtue of a licence under article 5(2)(c) or 6(2)(d), or an approval under article 8, of the Animal By-Products Order 1992, the Minister;

    (ii) where the exempt activity is carried on by virtue of a registration under article 9 or 10 of that Order, the appropriate Minister;

    (iii) where the exempt activity is carried on at a knacker's yard in respect of which the occupier holds a licence under section 1 of the Slaughterhouses Act 1974 authorising the use of that yard as a knacker's yard or, in Scotland, in respect of which a licence has been granted under section 6 of the Slaughter of Animals (Scotland) Act 1980, the local authority;

and in this sub-paragraph "the Minister" and "the appropriate Minister" have the meaning given by section 86(1) of the Animal Health Act 1981, and "knacker's yard" and "local authority" have the meaning given by section 34 of the Slaughterhouses Act 1974 or, in Scotland, have the meaning given by section 22 of the Slaughter of Animals (Scotland) Act 1980;

  (d) in any other case, the waste regulation authority for the area in which the exempt activity is carried on.

Waste Framework Directive

   19. Schedule 4 (which implements certain provisions of Council Directive 75/442/EEC on waste) shall have effect.

Registration of brokers

   20.—(1) Subject to paragraphs (2) to (4) below, it shall be an offence for an establishment or undertaking after 31st December 1994 to arrange (as dealer or broker) for the disposal or recovery of controlled waste on behalf of another person unless it is a registered broker of controlled waste.

   (2) Paragraph (1) above shall not apply in relation to an arrangement under which an establishment or undertaking will itself carry out the disposal or recovery of the waste and either—

  (a) it is authorised to carry out the disposal or recovery of the waste by a waste management licence, an authorisation under Part I of the 1990 Act, a consent under Chapter II of Part III of the Water Resources Act 1991 or under Part II of the Control of Pollution Act 1974 or a licence under Part II of the Food and Environment Protection Act 1985; or

(b) the recovery of the waste is covered by an exemption conferred by—
   (i) regulation 17(1) of, and Schedule 3 to, these Regulations; or
   (ii) article 3 of the Deposits in the Sea (Exemptions) Order 1985.

(3) Paragraph (1) above shall not apply in relation to an arrangement for the disposal or recovery of controlled waste made by a person who is registered as a carrier of controlled waste, or who is registered for the purposes of paragraph 12(1) of Part I of Schedule 4, if as part of the arrangement he transports the waste to or from any place in Great Britain.

(4) Paragraph (1) above shall not apply to an establishment or undertaking which—
   (a) is a charity;
   (b) is a voluntary organisation within the meaning of section 48(ii) of the Local Government Act 1985 or section 83(2D) of the Local Government (Scotland) Act 1973;
   (c) is an authority which is a waste collection authority, waste disposal authority or waste regulation authority; or
   (d) applies before 1st January 1995 in accordance with Schedule 5 for registration as a broker of controlled waste but only whilst its application is pending (and paragraph 1(4) and (5) of Part I of Schedule 5 shall apply for the purpose of determining whether an application is pending).

(5) A person guilty of an offence under this section shall be liable on summary conviction to a fine not exceeding level 5 on the standard scale.

(6) Section 157 of the 1990 Act shall apply in relation to an offence under this section as it applies in relation to an offence under that Act.

(7) Schedule 5 (which makes provision for the registration of brokers of controlled waste) shall have effect.

(8) Sections 68(3) to (5), 69 and 71(2) and (3) of the 1990 Act (power to appoint inspectors, powers of entry and power to obtain information) shall have effect as if the provisions of this regulation and Schedule 5 were provisions of Part II of that Act.

Amendment of the Deposits in the Sea (Exemptions) Order 1985

21.—(1) The Deposits in the Sea (Exemptions) Order 1985 shall be amended as follows.

(2) In article 3, before "A licence is not needed", there shall be inserted "Subject to article 4,".

(3) After article 3, there shall be added the following articles—

"Provisions relating to exemptions involving waste

4.—(1) Article 3 only applies to an establishment or undertaking in relation to an operation specified in the Schedule to this Order involving the recovery or disposal of waste if—
   (a) it is carrying out—
      (i) its own waste disposal at the place of production; or
      (ii) waste recovery; and
   (b) the type and quantity of waste involved, and the method of disposal or recovery, are consistent with the need to attain the objective of ensuring that waste is recovered or disposed of without endangering human health and without using processes or methods which could harm the environment and in particular without—
      (i) risk to water, air, soil, plants or animals; or
      (ii) causing nuisance through noise or odours; or
      (iii) adversely affecting the countryside or places or special interest.

(2) In this article and in article 5 below, "disposal", "recovery" and "waste" have the meaning given by regulation 1(3) of the Waste Management Licensing Regulations 1994.

Registration of establishments and undertakings carrying on exempt operations

5.—(1) It shall be an offence for an establishment or undertaking to carry on, after 31st December 1994, an exempt activity without being registered with the licensing authority.

(2) It shall be the duty of each licensing authority to establish and maintain a register for the purposes of paragraph (1) above of establishments and undertakings carrying on exempt activities in the area for which it is the licensing authority.

(3) The register shall contain the following particulars in relation to each such establishment or undertaking—

(a) the name and address of the establishment or undertaking;

(b) the activity which constitutes the exempt activity; and

(c) the place where the activity is carried on.

(4) The licensing authority shall enter those particulars in the register in relation to an establishment or undertaking if it receives notice of them in writing or otherwise becomes aware of those particulars.

(5) A person guilty of an offence under paragraph (1) above shall be liable on summary conviction to a fine not exceeding level 2 on the standard scale.

(6) Each licensing authority shall secure that any register maintained by the authority under this article is available, at all reasonable times, for inspection by the public free of charge and shall afford to members of the public facilities for obtaining copies of entries, on payment of reasonable charges.

(7) Registers under this article may be kept in any form.

(8) In this article, "exempt activity" means any operation specified in the Schedule to this Order involving the disposal or recovery of waste to which article 3 applies.".

Amendment of the Collection and Disposal of Waste Regulations 1988

22.—(1) The Collection and Disposal of Waste Regulations 1988 shall be amended as follows.

(2) At the beginning of regulation 3, there shall be inserted "Subject to regulations 4 and 7A,".

(3) At the beginning of each of regulations 6 and 7, there shall be inserted "Subject to regulation 7A,".

(4) After regulation 7, the following shall be inserted—

"Waste not to be treated as household, industrial or commercial waste

7A.—(1) For the purposes of all the provisions of Part I of the Act, waste which is not Directive waste shall not be treated as household waste, industrial waste or commercial waste.

(2) In this regulation, 'Directive waste' has the meaning given by regulation 1(3) of the Waste Management Licensing Regulations 1994.".

Amendment of the Controlled Waste (Registration of Carriers and Seizure of Vehicles) Regulations 1991

23.—(1) The Controlled Waste (Registration of Carriers and Seizure of Vehicles) Regulations 1991 shall be amended as follows.

(2) For regulation 2(1)(c) there shall be substituted—

"(c) any wholly owned subsidiary of the British Railways Board which has applied in accordance with these Regulations for registration as a carrier of controlled waste but only—
  (i) if it is registered under paragraph 12 of Schedule 4 to the Waste Management Licensing Regulations 1994; and
  (ii) whilst its application is pending;".
(3) At the end of regulation 2(1), there shall be added—
"(i) a person who—
  (i) is the holder of a knacker's yard licence or a licence under article 5(2)(c) or 6(2)(d) of the Animal By-Products Order 1992; or
  (ii) has obtained an approval under article 8 of that Order; or
  (iii) is registered under article 9 or 10 of that Order,
  in relation to the transport of animal by-products in accordance with Schedule 2 to that Order in connection with the activity to which the licence, approval or registration relates."
(4) In regulation 2(2), the following definitions shall be inserted at the appropriate places—
" "animal by-products" has the same meaning as in article 3(1) of the Animal By-Products Order 1992;"
" "knacker's yard licence"—
  (a) in relation to England and Wales, has the same meaning as in section 34 of the Slaughterhouses Act 1974;
  (b) in relation to Scotland, means a licence under section 6 of the Slaughter of Animals (Scotland) Act 1980;"
" "registered broker of controlled waste" has the same meaning as in regulation 20 of, and Schedule 5 to, the Waste Management Licensing Regulations 1994;"
" "wholly owned subsidiary" has the same meaning as in section 736 of the Companies Act 1985.".
(5) At the beginning of regulation 4(9), there shall be inserted "Subject to paragraph 3(11)(a) and (b) of Schedule 5 to the Waste Management Licensing Regulations 1994,".
(6) After regulation 4(9)(b), there shall be inserted—
"(c) in the case of an application by a registered broker of controlled waste for registration as a carrier of controlled waste, £25,".

Amendment of the Controlled Waste Regulations 1992

24.—(1) The Controlled Waste Regulations 1992 shall be amended as follows.
(2) In regulation 1(2)—
  (a) after the definition of "construction", there shall be inserted the following—
  " "Directive waste" has the meaning given by regulation 1(3) of the Waste Management Licensing Regulations 1994;";
  (b) in the definition of "part residential subjects", for "section 26(1) of the Abolition of Domestic Rates etc. (Scotland) Act 1987" there shall be substituted "section 99(1) of the Local Government Finance Act 1992".
(3) In regulation 2(1), for "Subject to paragraph (2)," there shall be substituted "Subject to paragraph (2) and regulations 3 and 7A,".
(4) In regulation 5(1), for "regulation 7" there shall be substituted "regulations 7 and 7A".
(5) In regulation 5(2)(b), for "regulation 7(1)(c)" there shall be substituted "regulation 7(1)(a) or (c)".

(6) In regulation 6, for "regulation 7" there shall be substituted "regulations 7 and 7A".

(7) At the end of regulation 7, there shall be added—

"(3) Animal by-products which are collected and transported in accordance with Schedule 2 to the Animal By-Products Order 1992 shall not be treated as industrial waste or commercial waste for the purposes of section 34 (duty of care etc. as respects waste).

(4) In this regulation, "animal by-products" has the same meaning as in article 3(1) of the Animal By-Products Order 1992."

(8) After regulation 7, the following shall be inserted—

"Waste not to be treated as household, industrial or commercial waste

7A. For the purposes of Part II of the Act, waste which is not Directive waste shall not be treated as household waste, industrial waste or commercial waste.".

(9) In paragraphs 8(b) and 11(a) of Schedule 3 and paragraph 9 of Schedule 4, in each place after "section 22(3) of the Control of Pollution Act 1974" there shall be inserted "or section 25(2) of the Local Government and Planning (Scotland) Act 1982".

Regulation 2(2), (3) and (4)   SCHEDULE 1

INFORMATION AND EVIDENCE REQUIRED IN RELATION TO AN APPLICATION FOR THE SURRENDER OF A SITE LICENCE

1. The full name, address and daytime telephone, fax and telex number (if any) of the holder of the site licence and, where the holder employs an agent in relation to the application, of that agent.

2. The number (if any) of the site licence, and the address or a description of the location of the site.

3. A map or plan—
    (a) showing the location of the site;
    (b) indicating whereabouts on the site the different activities mentioned in paragraph 4 were carried on; and
    (c) indicating relevant National Grid references.

4. A description of the different activities involving the treatment, keeping or disposal of controlled waste which were carried on at the site (whether or not in pursuance of the licence), an indication of when those activities were carried on and an estimate of the total quantities of the different types of waste which were dealt with at the site.

5. Where the site is a landfill or lagoon—
    (a) particulars of all significant engineering works carried out for the purpose of preventing or minimising pollution of the environment or harm to human health as a result of activities carried on at the site, including—
        (i) an indication of when those works were carried out and a copy of all relevant plans or specifications; and
        (ii) details of works of restoration carried out after completion of operations at the site;
    (b) geological, hydrological and hydrogeological information relating to the site and its surrounds, including information about the flows of groundwater;
    (c) monitoring data on the quality of surface water or groundwater which could be affected by the site and on the production of any landfill gas or leachate at the site and information about the physical stability of the site; and
    (d) where special waste has been deposited at the site, a copy of the records and plans relating to the deposits kept under regulation 14 of the Control of Pollution (Special Waste) Regulations 1980;

and any estimate under paragraph 4 of the total quantities of the different types of waste dealt with at the site shall, in particular, differentiate between biodegradable waste, non-biodegradable waste and special waste.

6. Where the site is not a landfill or lagoon—

    (a) details of the contaminants likely to be present at the site having regard to—
        (i) the different activities involving the treatment, keeping or disposal of controlled waste carried on at the site (whether or not in pursuance of the licence); and
        (ii) the nature of the different types of waste dealt with at the site; and
    (b) a report which—
        (i) records the results of the analysis of samples taken in such numbers, and at such locations at the site, that they provide a reliable indication of the locations where contaminants are likely to be present in high concentrations; and
        (ii) shows how many (and from where) samples were taken.

7. Any other information which the applicant wishes the waste regulation authority to take into account.

Regulation 2(5)   SCHEDULE 2

INFORMATION REQUIRED IN RELATION TO AN APPLICATION FOR THE TRANSFER OF A WASTE MANAGEMENT LICENCE

1. The full name, address and daytime telephone, fax and telex number (if any) of the holder of the waste management licence and, where the application is made by an agent of the holder, of the agent.

2. The number (if any) of the waste management licence and, except in the case of mobile plant, the address or a description of the location of the licensed premises.

3. In the case of mobile plant, sufficient information to identify the plant.

4. Where the proposed transferee is an individual, his full name, date of birth, address and daytime telephone, fax and telex number (if any).

5. Where the proposed transferee is a registered company or other body corporate—
    (a) its name and, in the case of a registered company, its registered number;
    (b) the address, telephone, fax and telex number (if any) of its registered or principal office;
    (c) the full name, position, address and date of birth of each director, manager, secretary or other similar officer of the proposed transferee.

6. Where the proposed transferee is a partnership—
    (a) the name of the partnership;
    (b) its address, telephone, fax and telex number (if any);
    (c) the full name, address and date of birth of each partner.

7. If the proposed transferee has a business name different from any name of the transferee mentioned above, the transferee's business name.

8. Where the proposed transferee has appointed an agent to deal with the transfer, the agent's full name, address and daytime telephone, fax and telex number (if any).

9. Details of any conviction of the proposed transferee or of another relevant person for any offence which is relevant for the purposes of section 74(3)(a) of the 1990 Act, including the date of conviction, the penalty imposed and the name of the Court.

10. The full name of the person who is to manage the activities which are authorised by the waste management licence and information to establish that he is technically competent for the purposes of section 74(3)(b) of the 1990 Act, including—
    (a) details of any relevant certificate of technical competence (within the meaning of regulation 4) he holds; or
    (b) in a case where the transferee relies on regulation 5(1) or (2), sufficient information to establish that that provision applies.

11. Details of the financial provision which the proposed transferee has made or proposes to make to discharge the obligations arising from the waste management licence.

12. Any other information which the applicant wishes the waste regulation authority to take into account.

Regulations 1(3) and 17   SCHEDULE 3

ACTIVITIES EXEMPT FROM WASTE MANAGEMENT LICENSING

1.—(1) The use, under an authorisation granted under Part I of the 1990 Act, of waste glass as part of a process within Part B of Section 3.5 (glass manufacture and production) of Schedule 1 to the 1991 Regulations if the total quantity of waste glass so used in that process does not exceed 600,000 tonnes in any period of twelve months.

(2) The storage, at the place where the process is carried on, of any such waste which is intended to be so used.

2.—(1) The operation, under an authorisation granted under Part I of the 1990 Act, of a scrap metal furnace with a designed holding capacity of less than 25 tonnes to the extent that it is or forms part of a process within paragraph (a), (b) or (d) or Part B of Section 2.1 (iron and steel), or paragraph (a), (b) or (e) of Part B of Section 2.2 (non-ferrous metals), of Schedule 1 to the 1991 Regulations.

(2) The loading or unloading of such a furnace in connection with its operation in a manner covered by the exemption conferred by sub-paragraph (1) above.

(3) The storage, at the place where such a furnace is located (but not in cases where that place is used for carrying on business as a scrap metal dealer or, in Scotland, as a metal dealer), of scrap metal intended to be submitted to an operation covered by the exemption conferred by sub-paragraph (1) above.

3. The carrying on of any of the following operations—

   (a) burning as a fuel, under an authorisation granted under Part I of the 1990 Act, of—
      (i) straw, poultry litter or wood;
      (ii) waste oil; or
      (iii) solid fuel which has been manufactured from waste by a process involving the application of heat,
     to the extent that it is or forms part of a process within Part B of any Section of Schedule 1 to the 1991 Regulations;

   (b) the secure storage on any premises of any wastes mentioned in sub-paragraph (a) above, other than waste oil, which are intended to be burned as mentioned in that sub-paragraph, and the feeding of such wastes into an appliance in which they are to be so burned;

   (c) the secure storage of waste oil at the place where it is produced for a period not exceeding twelve months if the waste oil is intended to be submitted to an operation covered by the exemption conferred by sub-paragraph (a) above;

   (d) burning as a fuel, under an authorisation granted under Part I of the 1990 Act, of tyres to the extent that it is or forms part of a process within Part B of Section 1.3 of Schedule 1 to the 1991 Regulations, and the shredding and feeding of tyres into an appliance in which they are to be so burned;

   (e) the storage in a secure place on any premises of tyres where—
      (i) the tyres are intended to be submitted to an operation covered by the exemption conferred by sub-paragraph (d) above;
      (ii) the tyres are stored separately;
      (iii) none of the tyres is stored on the premises for longer than twelve months; and
      (iv) the number of the tyres stored on the premises at any one time does not exceed 1,000.

4.—(1) The cleaning, washing, spraying or coating of waste consisting of packaging or containers so that it or they can be reused if the total quantity of such waste so dealt with at any place does not exceed 1,000 tonnes in any period of seven days.

(2) The storage of waste in connection with the carrying on of any activities described in sub-paragraph (1) above if that storage is at the place where the activity is carried on unless—

   (a) the total quantity of such waste stored at that place exceeds 1,000 tonnes; or
   (b) more than 1 tonne of metal containers used for the transport or storage of any chemical are dealt with in any period of seven days.

5.—(1) Burning waste as a fuel in an appliance if the appliance has a net rated thermal input of less than 0.4 megawatts or, where the appliance is used together with [(whether or not it is operated simultaneously with)] other appliances, the aggregate net rated thermal input of all the appliances is less than 0.4 megawatts.

(2) The secure storage of waste intended to be submitted to such burning.

(3) In this paragraph, "net rated thermal input" means the rate at which fuel can be burned at the maximum continuous rating of the appliance multiplied by the net calorific value of the fuel and expressed as megawatts thermal.

6.—(1) Burning waste oil as a fuel in an engine of an aircraft, hovercraft, mechanically propelled vehicle, railway locomotive, ship or other vessel if the total amount burned of such waste does not exceed 2,500 litres an hour in any one engine.

(2) The storage, in a secure container, of waste oil intended to be so burned.

7.—(1) The spreading of any of the wastes listed in Table 2 on land which is used for agriculture.

(2) The spreading of any of the wastes listed in Part I of Table 2 on—

(a) operational land of a railway, light railway, internal drainage board or the National Rivers Authority; or

(b) land which is a forest, woodland, park, garden, verge, landscaped area, sports ground, recreation ground, churchyard or cemetery.

Table 2

PART I

Waste soil or compost.
Waste wood, bark or other plant matter.

PART II

Waste food, drink or materials used in or resulting from the preparation of food or drink.
Blood and gut contents from abattoirs.
Waste lime.
Lime sludge from cement manufacture or gas processing.
Waste gypsum.
Paper waste sludge, waste paper and de-inked paper pulp.
Dredgings from any inland waters.
Textile waste.
Septic tank sludge.
Sludge from biological treatment plants.
Waste hair and effluent treatment sludge from a tannery.

(3) Sub-paragraphs (1) and (2) above only apply if—

(a) no more than 250 tonnes or, in the case of dredgings from inland waters, 5,000 tonnes of waste per hectare are spread on the land in any period of twelve months;

(b) the activity in question results in benefit to agriculture or ecological improvement; and

(c) where the waste is to be spread by an establishment or undertaking on land used for agriculture, it furnishes to the waste regulation authority in whose area the spreading is to take place the particulars listed in sub-paragraph (4) below—

    (i) in a case where there is to be a single spreading, in advance of carrying out the spreading; or

    (ii) in a case where there is to be regular or frequent spreading of waste of a similar composition, every six months or, where the waste to be spread is of a description different from that last notified, in advance of carrying out the spreading.

(4) The particulars referred to in sub-paragraph (3)(c) above are—

(a) the establishment or undertaking's name and address, and telephone or fax number (if any);

(b) a description of the waste, including the process from which it arises;

(c) where the waste is being or will be stored pending spreading;

(d) an estimate of the quantity of the waste or, in such a case as is mentioned in sub-paragraph (3)(c)(ii) above, an estimate of the total quantity of waste to be spread during the next six months; and

(e) the location, and intended date or, in such a case as is mentioned in sub-paragraph (3)(c)(ii) above, the frequency, of the spreading of the waste.

(5) Subject to sub-paragraph (6) below, the storage, at the place where it is to be spread, of any waste (other than septic tank sludge) intended to be spread in reliance upon the exemption conferred by sub-paragraph (1) or (2) above.

(6) Sub-paragraph (5) above does not apply to the storage of waste in liquid form unless it is stored in a secure container or lagoon and no more than 500 tonnes is stored in any one container or lagoon.

(7) The storage, in a secure container or lagoon (or, in the case of dewatered sludge, in a secure place), of septic tank sludge intended to be spread in reliance upon the exemption conferred by sub-paragraph (1) above.

(8) In this paragraph and paragraph 8, "agriculture" has the same meaning as in the Agriculture Act 1947 or, in Scotland, the Agriculture (Scotland) Act 1948.

(9) In this paragraph and paragraph 30, "internal drainage board" has the meaning given by section 1(1) of the Land Drainage Act 1991 and, for the purposes of the definition of operational land, an internal drainage board shall be deemed to be a statutory undertaker.

(10) In this paragraph and paragraphs 8 and 10, "septic tank sludge" has the meaning given by regulation 2(1) of the Sludge (Use in Agriculture) Regulations 1989.

8.—(1) The storage, in a secure container or lagoon (or, in the case of dewatered sludge, in a secure place) on land used for agriculture, of sludge which is to be used in accordance with the 1989 Regulations.

(2) The spreading of sludge on land which is not agricultural land within the meaning of the 1989 Regulations if—

(a) it results in ecological improvement; and

(b) it does not cause the concentration in the soil of any of the elements listed in column 1 of the soil table set out in Schedule 2 to the 1989 Regulations to exceed the limit specified in column 2 of the table.

(3) The storage, in a secure container or lagoon (or, in the case of dewatered sludge, in a secure place), of sludge intended to be spread in reliance upon the exemption conferred by sub-paragraph (2) above.

(4) In this paragraph, "the 1989 Regulations" means the Sludge (Use in Agriculture) Regulations 1989 and "used", in relation to sludge, has the meaning given by regulation 2(1) of the 1989 Regulations.

(5) In this paragraph, and in paragraphs 9 and 10, "sludge" has the meaning given by regulation 2(1) of the 1989 Regulations.

9.—(1) Subject to sub-paragraph (3) below, the spreading of waste consisting of soil, rock, ash or sludge, or of waste from dredging any inland waters or arising from construction or demolition work, on any land in connection with the reclamation or improvement of that land if—

(a) by reason of industrial or other development the land is incapable of beneficial use without treatment;

(b) the spreading is carried out in accordance with a planning permission for the reclamation or improvement of the land and results in benefit to agriculture or ecological improvement; and

(c) no more than 20,000 cubic metres per hectare of such waste is spread on the land.

(2) The storage, at the place where it is to be spread, of any such waste which is intended to be spread in reliance upon the exemption conferred by sub-paragraph (1) above.

(3) Sub-paragraph (1) above does not apply to the disposal of waste at a site designed or adapted for the final disposal of waste by landfill.

10.—(1) Any recovery operation carried on within the curtilage of a sewage treatment works in relation to sludge or septic tank sludge brought from another sewage treatment works if the total quantity of such waste brought to the works in any period of twelve months does not exceed 10,000 cubic metres.

(2) The treatment within the curtilage of a water treatment works of waste arising at the works from water treatment if the total quantity of such waste which is treated at the works in any period of twelve months does not exceed 10,000 cubic metres.

(3) The storage of waste intended to be submitted to the activities mentioned in sub-paragraph (1) or (2) above if that storage is at the place where those activities are to be carried on.

11. Carrying on at any place, in respect of a kind of waste listed in Table 3, any of the activities specified in that Table in relation to that kind of waste where—

(a) the activity is carried on with a view to the recovery or reuse of the waste (whether or not by the person carrying on the activity listed in that Table); and

(b) the total quantity of any particular kind of waste dealt with at that place does not in any period of seven days exceed the limit specified in relation to that kind of waste in that Table.

Table 3

Kind of waste	Activities	Limit (tonnes per week)
Waste paper or cardboard	Baling, sorting or shredding	3,000
Waste textiles	Baling, sorting or shredding	100
Waste plastic	Baling, sorting, shredding, densifying or washing	100
Waste glass	Sorting, crushing or washing	1,000

Kind of waste	Activities	Limit (tonnes per week)
Waste steel cans, aluminium cans or aluminium foil	Sorting, crushing, pulverising, shredding, compacting or baling	100
Waste food or drink cartons	Sorting, crushing, pulverising, shredding, compacting or baling	100

12.—(1) Composting biodegradable waste at the place where the waste is produced or where the compost is to be used, or at any other place occupied by the person producing the waste or using the compost, if the total quantity of waste being composted at that place at any time does not exceed—

(a) in the case of waste composted or to be composted for the purposes of cultivating mushrooms, 10,000 cubic metres; and

(b) in any other case, 1,000 cubic metres.

(2) The storage of biodegradable waste which is to be composted if that storage is at the place where the waste is produced or is to be composted.

(3) In this paragraph, "composting" includes any other biological transformation process that results in materials which may be spread on land for the benefit of agriculture or ecological improvement.

13.—(1) The manufacture from—

(a) waste which arises from demolition or construction work or tunnelling or other excavations; or

(b) waste which consists of ash, slag, clinker, rock, wood, bark, paper, straw or gypsum, of timber products, straw board, plasterboard, bricks, blocks, roadstone or aggregate.

(2) The manufacture of soil or soil substitutes from any of the wastes listed in sub-paragraph (1) above if—

(a) the manufacture is carried out at the place where either the waste is produced or the manufactured product is to be applied to land; and

(b) the total amount manufactured at that place on any day does not exceed 500 tonnes.

(3) The treatment of waste soil or rock which, when treated, is to be spread on land under paragraph 7 or 9, if—

(a) it is carried out at the place where the waste is produced or the treated product is to be spread; and

(b) the total amount treated at that place in any day does not exceed 100 tonnes.

(4) The storage of waste which is to be submitted to any of the activities mentioned in sub-paragraphs (1) to (3) above if—

(a) the waste is stored at the place where the activity is to be carried on; and

(b) the total quantity of waste stored at that place does not exceed—

(i) in the case of the manufacture of roadstone from road planings, 50,000 tonnes; and

(ii) in any other case, 20,000 tonnes.

14.—(1) The manufacture of finished goods from any of the following kinds of waste, namely waste metal, plastic, glass, ceramics, rubber, textiles, wood, paper or cardboard.

(2) The storage of any such waste intended to be used in reliance upon the exemption conferred by sub-paragraph (1) above if—

(a) the waste is stored at the place of manufacture; and

(b) the total amount of any particular kind of waste stored at that place at any time does not exceed 15,000 tonnes.

15.—(1) The beneficial use of waste if—

(a) it is put to that use without further treatment; and

(b) that use of the waste does not involve its disposal.

(2) The storage of waste intended to be used in reliance upon the exemption conferred by sub-paragraph (1) above insofar as that storage does not amount to disposal of the waste.

(3) This paragraph does not apply to the use or storage of waste if that activity is covered by an exemption conferred by paragraph 7, 8, 9, 19 or 25, or would be so covered but for any condition or limitation to which that exemption is subject by virtue of any provision contained in the paragraph by which that exemption is conferred.

16. The carrying on, in accordance with the conditions and requirements of a licence granted

under article 7 or 8 of the Diseases of Animals (Waste Food) Order 1973, of any activity authorised by the licence.

17.—(1) The storage in a secure place on any premises of waste of a kind described in Table 4 below if—

    (a) the total quantity of that kind of waste stored on those premises at any time does not exceed the quantity specified in that Table;

    (b) the waste is to be reufsed, or used for the purposes of—

        (i) an activity described in paragraph 11; or

        (ii) any other recovery operation;

    (c) each kind of waste listed in the Table stored on the premises is kept separately; and

    (d) no waste is stored on the premises for longer than twelve months.

Table 4

Kind of waste	Maximum total quantity
Waste paper or cardboard	15,000 tonnes
Waste textiles	1,000 tonnes
Waste plastics	500 tonnes
Waste glass	5,000 tonnes
Waste steel cans, aluminium cans or aluminium foil	500 tonnes
Waste food or drink cartons	500 tonnes
Waste articles which are to be used for construction work which are capable of being so used in their existing state	100 tonnes
Solvents (including solvents which are special waste)	5 cubic metres
Refrigerants and halons (including refrigerants and halons which are special waste)	18 tonnes
Tyres	1,000 tyres

(2) In this paragraph, "refrigerants" means dichlorodifluoromethane, chlorotri-fluoromethane, dichlorotetrafluoroethane, chloropentafluoroethane, bromotrifluoro-methane, chlorodifluoromethane, chlorotetrafluoroethane, trifluoromethane, difluoromethane, pentafluoroethane, tetrafluoroethane, chlorodifluoroethane, difluoroethane, trichlorofluoro-methane, trichlorotrifluoroethane, dichlorotrifluoroethane, dichlorofluoroethane and mixtures containing any of those substances.

18.—(1) The storage on any premises in a secure container or containers of waste of a kind described in sub-paragraph (2) below if—

    (a) the storage capacity of the container or containers does not exceed 400 cubic metres in total;

    (b) in the case of waste oil, the storage capacity of any container or containers used for its storage does not exceed 3 cubic metres in total, and provision is made to prevent oil escaping into the ground or a drain;

    (c) there are no more than 20 containers on those premises;

    (d) the waste will be reused, or used for the purposes of—

        (i) any activity described in paragraph 11 carried on at those premises; or

        (ii) any other recovery activity;

    (e) each kind of waste described in sub-paragraph (2) below stored on the premises is kept separately;

    (f) no waste is stored on the premises for longer than twelve months; and

    (g) the person storing the waste is the owner of the container or has the consent of the owner.

(2) Sub-paragraph (1) above applies to the following kinds of waste—

    (a) any waste described in paragraph 17 other than waste solvents, refrigerants or halons;

    (b) waste oil.

19.—(1) The storage on a site of waste which arises from demolition or construction work or tunnelling or other excavations or which consists of ash, slag, clinker, rock, wood or gypsum, if—

    (a) the waste in question is suitable for use for the purposes of relevant work which will be carried on at the site; and

    (b) in the case of waste which is not produced on the site, it is not stored there for longer than three months before relevant work starts.

(2) The use of waste of a kind mentioned in sub-paragraph (1) above for the purposes of relevant work if the waste is suitable for use for those purposes.

(3) The storage on a site of waste consisting of road planings which are to be used for the purposes of relevant work carried on elsewhere if—

(a) no more than 50,000 tonnes of such waste are stored at the site; and

(b) the waste is stored there for no longer than 3 months.

(4) In this paragraph, "relevant work" means construction work, including the deposit of waste on land in connection with—

(a) the provision of recreational facilities on that land; or

(b) the construction, maintenance or improvement of a building, highway, railway, airport, dock or other transport facility on that land,

but not including either any deposit of waste in any other circumstances or any work involving land reclamation.

20.—(1) Laundering or otherwise cleaning waste textiles with a view to their recovery or reuse.

(2) The storage of waste textiles at the place where they are to be so laundered or cleaned.

21.—(1) Chipping, shredding, cutting or pulverising waste plant matter (including wood or bark), or sorting and baling sawdust or wood shavings, on any premises if—

(a) those activities are carried on for the purposes of recovery or reuse; and

(b) no more than 1,000 tonnes of such waste are dealt with on those premises in any period of seven days.

(2) The storage of waste in connection with any activity mentioned in sub-paragraph (1) above at the premises where it is carried on if the total amount of waste stored at those premises does not at any time exceed 1,000 tonnes.

22.—(1) The recovery, at any premises, of silver from waste produced in connection with printing or photographic processing if no more than 50,000 litres of such waste are dealt with on those premises in any day.

(2) The storage, at those premises, of waste which is to be submitted to such a recovery operation as is mentioned in sub-paragraph (1) above.

23.—(1) The keeping or treatment of animal by-products in accordance with the Animal By-Products Order 1992.

(2) In this paragraph, "animal by-products" has the same meaning as in article 3(1) of the Animal By-Products Order 1992.

24.—(1) Crushing, grinding or other size reduction of waste bricks, tiles or concrete, under an authorisation granted under Part I of the 1990 Act, to the extent that it is or forms part of a process within paragraph (c) of Part B of Section 3.4 (other mineral processes) of Schedule 1 to the 1991 Regulations.

(2) Where any such crushing, grinding or other size reduction is carried on otherwise than at the place where the waste is produced, the exemption conferred by sub-paragraph (1) above only applies if those activities are carried on with a view to recovery or reuse of the waste.

(3) The storage, at the place where the process is carried on, of any such waste which is intended to be so crushed, ground or otherwise reduced in size, if the total quantity of such waste so stored at that place at any one time does not exceed 20,000 tonnes.

25.—(1) Subject to sub-paragraphs (2) to (4) below, the deposit of waste arising from dredging inland waters, or from clearing plant matter from inland waters, if either—

(a) the waste is deposited along the bank or towpath of the waters where the dredging or clearing takes place; or

(b) the waste is deposited along the bank or towpath of any inland waters so as to result in benefit to agriculture or ecological improvement.

(2) The total amount of waste deposited along the bank or towpath under sub-paragraph (1) above on any day must not exceed 50 tonnes for each metre of the bank or towpath along which it is deposited.

(3) Sub-paragraph (1) above does not apply to waste deposited in a container or lagoon.

(4) Sub-paragraph (1)(a) above only applies to an establishment or undertaking where the waste deposited is the establishment or undertaking's own waste.

(5) The treatment by screening or dewatering of such waste as is mentioned in sub-paragraph (1) above—

(a) on the bank or towpath of the waters where either the dredging or clearing takes place or the waste is to be deposited, prior to its being deposited in reliance upon the exemption conferred by the foregoing provisions of this paragraph;

(b) on the bank or towpath of the waters when the dredging or clearing takes place, or at a place where the waste is to be spread, prior to its being spread in reliance upon the exemption conferred by paragraph 7(1) or (2); or

(c) in the case of waste from dredging, on the bank or towpath of the waters where the dredging takes place, or at a place where the waste is to be spread, prior to its being spread in reliance upon the exemption conferred by paragraph 9(1).

26.—(1) The recovery or disposal of waste, at the place where it is produced, as an integral part of the process that produces it.

(2) The storage, at the place where it is produced, of waste which is intended to be so recovered or disposed of.

(3) Sub-paragraph (1) above does not apply to the final disposal of waste by deposit in or on land.

27.—(1) Baling, compacting, crushing, shredding or pulverising waste at the place where it is produced.

(2) The storage, at the place where it is produced, of waste which is to be submitted to any of those operations.

28. The storage of returned goods that are waste, for a period not exceeding one month, by their manufacturer, distributor or retailer, where either—
   (a) they are intended for reuse or submission to a recovery operation; or
   (b) they are being stored, at the place where the intention to discard them was formed, pending their disposal.

29.—(1) The disposal of waste at the place where it is produced, by the person producing it, by burning it in an incinerator which is an exempt incinerator for the purposes of Section 5.1 (incineration) of Schedule 1 to the 1991 Regulations.

(2) The secure storage at that place of any such waste intended to be submitted to such burning.

30.—(1) Subject to sub-paragraph (2) below, burning waste on land in the open if—
   (a) the waste consists of wood, bark or other plant matter;
   (b) it is produced on land which is operational land of a railway, light railway, tramway, internal drainage board or the National Rivers Authority, or which is a forest, woodland, park, garden, verge, landscaped area, sports ground, recreation ground, churchyard or cemetery, or it is produced on other land as a result of demolition work;
   (c) it is burned on the land where it is produced; and
   (d) the total quantity burned in any period of 24 hours does not exceed 10 tonnes,

(2) Sub-paragraph (1) above only applies to the burning of waste by an establishment or undertaking where the waste burned is the establishment or undertaking's own waste.

(3) The storage pending its burning, on the land where it is to be burned, of waste which is to be burned in reliance upon the exemption conferred by sub-paragraph (1) above.

31. The discharge of waste onto the track of a railway from a sanitary convenience or sink forming part of a vehicle used for the carriage of passengers on the railway if the discharge in question does not exceed 25 litres.

32. The burial on premises of waste arising from the use on those premises of a sanitary convenience which is equipped with a removable receptacle if the total amount buried in any period of twelve months does not exceed 5 cubic metres.

33.—(1) The keeping or deposit of waste consisting of excavated materials arising from peatworking at the place where that activity takes place.

(2) Sub-paragraph (1) above only applies to the keeping or deposit of waste by an establishment or undertaking where the waste kept or deposited is the establishment or undertaking's own waste.

34.—(1) The keeping or deposit on land at the place where it is produced of spent ballast if the land is operational land of a railway, light railway or tramway and the total amount kept or deposited at that place does not exceed 10 tonnes for each metre of track from which the ballast derives.

(2) Sub-paragraph (1) above only applies to the keeping or deposit of waste by an establishment or undertaking where the waste kept or deposited is the establishment or undertaking's own waste.

35.—(1) The deposit of waste consisting of excavated material from a borehole or other excavation made for the purpose of mineral exploration if—
   (a) it is deposited in or on land at the place where it is excavated; and
   (b) the total quantity of waste so deposited over any period of 24 months does not exceed 45,000 cubic metres per hectare.

(2) Sub-paragraph (1) above only applies if—
   (a) the drilling of the borehole or the making of any other excavation is development for which planning permission is granted by article 3 of, and Class A or B of Part 22 of Schedule 2 to, the Town and Country Planning General Development Order 1988 or,

in Scotland, which is permitted by Class 53, 54 or 61 of Schedule 1 to the Town and Country Planning (General Permitted Development) (Scotland) Order 1992; and

(b) the conditions subject to which the development is permitted are observed.

(3) Expressions used in this paragraph which are also used in the Town and Country Planning General Development Order 1988 or, in Scotland, the Town and Country Planning (General Permitted Development) (Scotland) Order 1992, shall have the same meaning as in the relevant Order.

36.—(1) The temporary storage of waste consisting of garbage, including any such waste which is special waste, at reception facilities provided within a harbour area in accordance with the Merchant Shipping (Reception Facilities for Garbage) Regulations 1988, where such storage is incidental to the collection or transport of the waste and so long as—

(a) the amount of garbage so stored within a harbour area at any time does not exceed 20 cubic metres for each ship from which garbage has been landed; and

(b) no garbage is so stored for more than seven days.

(2) The temporary storage of waste consisting of tank washings, including any such waste which is special waste, at reception facilities provided within a harbour area in accordance with the Prevention of Pollution (Reception Facilities) Order 1984, where such storage is incidental to the collection or transport of the waste and so long as—

(a) the amount of tank washings consisting of dirty ballast so stored within a harbour area at any time does not exceed 30% of the total deadweight of the ships from which such washings have been landed;

(b) the amount of tank washings consisting of waste mixtures containing oil so stored within a harbour area at any time does not exceed 1% of the total deadweight of the ships from which such washings have been landed.

(3) In this paragraph—

"garbage" has the same meaning as in the Merchant Shipping (Reception Facilities for Garbage) Regulations 1988;

"harbour area" has the same meaning as in the Dangerous Substances in Harbour Areas Regulations 1987;

"ship" means a vessel of any type whatsoever operating in the marine environment including submersible craft, floating craft and any structure which is a fixed or floating platform; and

"tank washings" means waste residues from the tanks (other than the fuel tanks) or holds of a ship or waste arising from the cleaning of such tanks or holds.

37.—(1) Subject to sub-paragraph (2) below, the burial of a dead domestic pet in the garden of a domestic property where the pet lived.

(2) This paragraph does not apply if—

(a) the dead domestic pet may prove hazardous to anyone who may come into contact with it; or

(b) the burial is carried out by an establishment or undertaking and the pet did not die at the property.

38. The deposit or storage of samples of waste, including samples of waste which is special waste, which are being or are to be subjected to testing and analysis, at any place where they are being or are to be tested or analysed, if the samples are taken—

(a) in the exercise of any power under the Radioactive Substances Act 1933, the Sewerage (Scotland) Act 1968, the Control of Pollution Act 1974, the 1990 Act, the Water Industry Act 1991 or the Water Resources Act 1991;

(b) by or on behalf of the holder of a waste management licence in pursuance of the conditions of that licence;

(c) by or on behalf of a person carrying on in relation to the waste an activity described in this Schedule or in regulation 16(1);

(d) by or on behalf of the owner or occupier of the land from which the samples are taken;

(e) by or on behalf of any person to whom section 34 of the 1990 Act applies in connection with his duties under that section; or

(f) for the purposes of research.

39.—(1) The secure storage at a pharmacy, pending their disposal there or elsewhere, of waste medicines (including those which are special waste) which have been returned to the pharmacy from households by individuals if—

(a) the total quantity of such returned waste medicines at the pharmacy does not exceed 5 cubic metres at any time; and

(b) any waste medicine so returned to the pharmacy is not stored there for longer than six months.

(2) The storage at the premises of a medical, nursing or veterinary practice of waste (including special waste) produced in carrying on that practice if—

(a) the total quantity of that waste at the premises does not at any time exceed 5 cubic metres; and

(b) no such waste is stored at those premises for longer than three months.

40.—(1) The storage of non-liquid waste at any place other than the premises where it is produced if—

(a) it is stored in a secure container or containers, does not at any time exceed 50 cubic metres in total and is not kept for a period longer than 3 months;

(b) the person storing the waste is the owner of the container or has the consent of the owner;

(c) the place where it is stored is not a site designed or adapted for the reception of waste with a view to its being disposed of or recovered elsewhere; and

(d) such storage is incidental to the collection or transport of the waste.

(1A) Sub-paragraph (1) above does not apply to the storage of waste at a place designed or adapted for the recovery of scrap metal or the dismantling of waste motor vehicles.

(2) The temporary storage of scrap rails on operational land of a railway, light railway or tramway if the total quantity of that waste in any one place does not at any time exceed 10 tonnes and the storage is incidental to the collection or transport of the scrap rails.

41.—(1) The temporary storage of waste, pending its collection, on the site where it is produced.

(1A) Sub-paragraph (1) above does not apply to the storage of waste at a place designed or adapted for the recovery of scrap metal or the dismantling of waste motor vehicles.

(2) Sub-paragraph (1) above shall apply to special waste if—

(a) it is stored on the site for no more than twelve months;

(b) in the case of liquid waste, it is stored in a secure container and the total volume of that waste does not at any time exceed 23,000 litres; and

(c) in any other case, either—

(i) it is stored in a secure container and the total volume of that waste does not at any time exceed 80 cubic metres; or

(ii) it is stored in a secure place and the total volume of that waste does not at any time exceed 50 cubic metres.

42.—(1) The treatment, keeping or disposal by any person at any premises of waste (including special waste) consisting of scrap metal or waste motor vehicles which are to be dismantled if—

(a) he was carrying on the activity in question at those premises before [April 1, 1995]; and

(b) he has applied, before that date, for a disposal licence under Part I of the Control of Pollution Act 1974 authorising that activity and that application is pending on that date.

(2) The exemption conferred by sub-paragraph (1) above, in relation to the carrying on of an activity at any premises, shall cease to have effect in relation to the carrying on of that activity at those premises on the date on which the licence applied for is granted or, if the application is (or is deemed to be) rejected, on the date on which—

(a) the period for appealing expires without an appeal being made; or

(b) any appeal is withdrawn or finally determined.

43.—(1) The treatment, keeping or disposal by any person at any premises of waste (including special waste) if—

(a) he was carrying on the activity in question at those premises before 1st May 1994; and

(b) before that date no disposal licence was required under Part I of the Control of Pollution Act 1974 for that activity.

(2) Subject to sub-paragraph (3) below, the exemption conferred by sub-paragraph (1) above, in relation to an activity carried on by a person at any premises, [shall—

(a) after [30th September 1996], in the case of an activity falling within paragraph 8 or 9 of Part III of Schedule 4;

(b) after 31st July 1995, in any other case,

cease to have effect] in relation to the carrying on of that activity at those premises unless on or before that date he applies for a waste management licence in relation to the activity in question.

(3) Where a person makes such an application as is mentioned in sub-paragraph (2) above, the exemption conferred by sub-paragraph (1) above shall continue to have effect in relation to the activity in question until the date on which the licence applied for is granted or, if the application is (or is deemed to be) rejected, until the date on which—

(a) the period for appealing expires without an appeal being made; or

(b) any appeal is withdrawn or finally determined.

44.—(1) Heating iron, steel or any ferrous-alloy, non-ferrous metal or non-ferrous metal alloy, in one or more furnaces or other appliances the primary combustion chambers of which have in aggregate a net rated thermal input of less than 0.2 megawatts, for the purpose of removing grease, oil or any other non-metallic contaminant.

(2) Sub-paragraph (1) does not apply to the removal by heat of plastic or rubber covering from scrap cable or of any asbestos contaminant.

(3) In the case of a process involving the heating of iron, steel or any ferrous-alloy, sub-paragraph (1) does not apply if that process is related to a process described in any of paragraphs (a) to (h), or (j) to (m), of Part A or paragraphs (a) to (c), or (e) or (f), of Part B of Section 2.1 of Schedule 1 to the 1991 Regulations.

(4) In the case of a process involving the heating of any non-ferrous metal or non-ferrous metal alloy, sub-paragraph (1) does not apply if that process is related to a process described in any of paragraphs (a) to (g), or (i) to (k), of Part A of Section 2.2 of Schedule 1 to the 1991 Regulations.

(5) The secure storage of waste intended to be submitted to heating to which sub-paragraph (1) applies if the waste or, as the case may be, any container in which the waste is stored, is stored on an impermeable pavement which is provided with a sealed drainage system.

(6) In this paragraph, "net rated thermal input" means the rate at which fuel can be burned at the maximum continuous rating of the appliance multiplied by the net calorific value of the fuel and expressed as megawatts thermal.

(7) In this paragraph, "ferrous alloy" means an alloy of which iron is the largest constituent, or equal to the largest constituent, by weight, whether or not that alloy also has a non-ferrous metal content greater than any percentage specified in Section 2.2 of Schedule 1 to the 1991 Regulations, and "non-ferrous metal alloy" shall be construed accordingly.

45.—(1) Subject to sub-paragraph (3) below, the carrying on, at any secure place designed or adapted for the recovery of scrap metal or the dismantling of waste motor vehicles, in respect of a kind of waste described in Table 4A, of any of the activities specified in that Table in relation to that kind of waste if—

    (a) the total quantity of any particular kind of waste so dealt with at that place does not in any period of seven days exceed the limit specified in relation to that kind of waste in that Table;

    (b) the activity is carried on with a view to the recovery of the waste (whether or not by the person carrying on the activity listed in that Table);

    (c) every part of that place upon which the activity is carried out is surfaced with an impermeable pavement provided with a sealed drainage system; and

    (d) the plant or equipment used in carrying on the activity is maintained in reasonable working order.

Table 4A

Kind of Waste	Activities	Seven day limit
Ferrous metals or ferrous alloys in metallic non-dispersible form (but not turnings, shavings or chippings of those metals or alloys)	Sorting; grading; baling; shearing by manual feed; compacting; crushing; cutting by hand-held equipment	8,000 tonnes
The following non-ferrous metals, namely copper, aluminium, nickel, lead, tin, tungsten, cobalt, molybdenum, vanadium, chromium, titanium, zirconium, manganese or zinc, or non-ferrous alloys, in metallic non-dispersible form, of any of those metals (but not turnings, shavings or chippings of those metals or alloys)	Sorting; grading; baling; shearing by manual feed; compacting; crushing; cutting by hand-held equipment	400 tonnes
Turnings, shavings or chippings of any of the metals or alloys listed in either of the above categories	Sorting; grading; baling; shearing by manual feed; compacting; crushing; cutting by hand-held equipment	300 tonnes
Motor vehicles (including any substance which is special waste and which forms part of, or is contained in, a vehicle and was necessary for the normal operation of the vehicle)	Dismantling, rebuilding, restoring or reconditioning, but, in relation to lead acid batteries, only their removal from motor vehicles	40 vehicles

Kind of Waste	Activities	Seven day limit
Lead acid motor vehicle batteries (including those whose contents are special waste), whether or not forming part of, or contained in, a motor vehicle	Sorting (including removal from motor vehicles)	20 tonnes

(2) Subject to sub-paragraph (3) below, the storage, at any secure place designed or adapted for the recovery of scrap metal or the dismantling of waste motor vehicles, of waste of a kind listed in Table 4B if—

(a) the waste is to be submitted to any of the activities specified in Table 4A in relation to that kind of waste, or to a recycling or reclamation operation authorised by a waste management licence or an authorisation under Part I of the 1990 Act;

(b) the total quantity of waste of that kind stored at that place does not exceed the maximum total quantity specified in Table 4B in relation to that kind of waste;

(c) no waste is stored at that place for a period exceeding 12 months;

(d) each kind of waste is either stored separately or is kept in separate containers, but in a case where a consignment consisting of more than one kind of waste is delivered to that place it may be stored unseparated at that place pending sorting for a period not exceeding 2 months;

(e) in the case of waste which is liquid or consists of motor vehicle batteries, it is stored in a secure container;

(f) in the case of waste motor vehicles from which all fluids have been drained, they are, unless stored on a hardstanding, stored on an impermeable pavement;

(g) subject to paragraph (f) above, the waste or, as the case may be, any container in which it is stored, is stored on an impermeable pavement which is provided with a sealed drainage system; and

(h) the height of any pile or stack of waste does not exceed 5 metres.

Table 4B

Kind of waste	Maximum total quantity
Ferrous metals or ferrous alloys in metallic non-dispersible form (but not turnings, shavings or chippings of those metals or alloys)	50,000 tonnes
The following non-ferrous metals, namely copper, aluminium, nickel, lead, tin, tungsten, cobalt, molybdenum, vanadium, chromium, titanium, zirconium, manganese or zinc, or non-ferrous alloys, in metallic non-dispersible form, of any of those metals (but not turnings, shavings or chippings of those metals or alloys)	1,500 tonnes
Turnings, shavings or chippings of any of the metals or alloys listed in either of the above categories	1,000 tonnes
Motor vehicles (including any substance which is special waste and which forms part of, or is contained in, a vehicle and was necessary for the normal operation of the vehicle):	
— where any such vehicle is stored on a hardstanding which is not an impermeable pavement;	100 vehicles
— where all such vehicles are stored on an impermeable pavement:	1,000 vehicles
Lead acid motor vehicle batteries (including those whose contents are special waste) whether or not forming part of, or contained in, a motor vehicle	40 tonnes

(3) Sub-paragraph (1) or (2) above only applies to the carrying on of an activity at a place if—

(a) the person responsible for the management of that place
    (i) has established administrative arrangements to ensure that—
        (A) waste accepted at that place is of a kind listed in Table 4A or, as the case may be, Table 4B; and
        (B) no waste is accepted at that place in such a quantity as would cause there to be a breach of any of the terms and conditions of the exemption;
        and
    (ii) carries out a monthly audit to confirm compliance with the terms and conditions of the exemption;
(b) the records required by paragraph 14 of Part I of Schedule 4 are kept in such a form as to show, for each month, the total quantity of each kind of waste recovered during that month at that place, and details of the total quantity of each kind of waste recovered at that place during the preceding 12 months are sent annually to the appropriate registration authority with the annual fee referred to in paragraph (d) below;
(c) an up to date plan of that place containing the details referred to in regulation 18(4A)(c)(i) to (iv) is sent annually to the appropriate registration authority with the annual fee referred to in paragraph (d) below; and
(d) a fee of [£150] is paid annually in respect of that place to the appropriate registration authority by the due date which shall be ascertained in accordance with sub-paragraph (4) below.

(4) For the purposes of ascertaining the due date in any year for payment of the fee referred in sub-paragraph (3)(d) above in respect of any place—
(a) the appropriate registration authority shall serve notice in accordance with the following provisions of this sub-paragraph on the establishment or undertaking from which notice has been received by the authority under regulation 18(4A) in respect of that place;
(b) a notice required by paragraph (a) above shall be served not later than one month before the anniversary of the date when the notice, plan and fee referred to in regulation 18(4A) were received by the authority in respect of that place and shall specify
    (i) the amount of the payment due,
    (ii) the method of payment,
    (iii) the date of such anniversary,
    (iv) that payment is due on that date or, if later, upon the day falling one month after the date of the notice, and
    (v) the effect of payment not being made by the date on which it is due,
and the due date for payment of the annual fee for that year by that establishment or undertaking in respect of that place shall be the date specified for payment in the notice.

(5) The temporary storage of waste (in this sub-paragraph referred to as "the non-scrap waste"), pending its collection, at a secure place designed or adapted for the recovery of scrap metal or the dismantling of waste motor vehicles if—
(a) the non-scrap waste is not of a kind described in Table 4B;
(b) the non-scrap waste was delivered to that place as part of a consignment of waste of which—
    (i) at least 70 per cent by weight was waste consisting of waste motor vehicles; or
    (ii) at least 95 per cent by weight was waste of any kind described in Table 4B other than waste motor vehicles,
    and is capable of being separated from that waste by sorting or hand dismantling;
(c) the non-scrap waste is stored at that place for no more than 3 months;
(d) in a case where the non-scrap waste is liquid, it is stored in a secure container; and
(e) the non-scrap waste or, as the case may be, the container in which the non-scrap waste is stored, is stored on an impermeable pavement which is provided with a sealed drainage system.

(6) In Table 4A, "shearing" means the cold cutting of metal by purpose-made shears.

(7) For the purposes of this paragraph and paragraph 44 above, "sealed drainage system", in relation to an impermeable pavement, means a drainage system with impermeable components which does not leak and which will ensure that—
(a) no liquid will run off the pavement otherwise than via the system; and
(b) except where they may be lawfully discharged, all liquids entering the system are collected in a sealed sump.]

Regulations 1(3) and 19   SCHEDULE 4

WASTE FRAMEWORK DIRECTIVE ETC.

PART I

GENERAL

Interpretation of Schedule 4
1. In this Schedule, unless the context otherwise requires—
   "competent authority" has the meaning given by paragraph 3;
   "development", "development plan", "government department" and "planning permission" have the same meaning as in the Town and Country Planning Act 1990 or, in Scotland, as in the Town and Country Planning (Scotland) Act 1972;
   "licensing authority" and "the Ministers" have the meaning given by section 24(1) of the Food and Environment Protection Act 1985;
   "local planning authority" and "the planning Acts" have the same meaning as in the Town and Country Planning Act 1990;
   "permit" means a waste management licence, a disposal licence, an authorisation under Part I of the 1990 Act, a resolution under section 54 of the 1990 Act, a licence under Part II of the Food and Environment Protection Act 1985 or a consent under Chapter II of Part III of the Water Resources Act 1991 or under Part II of the Control of Pollution Act 1974 (and, in relation to a permit, "grant" includes give, issue or pass, "modify" includes vary, and cognate expressions shall be construed accordingly);
   "plan-making provisions" means paragraph 5 below, section 50 of the 1990 Act and Part II of the Town and Country Planning Act 1990 or, in Scotland, Part II of the Town and Country Planning (Scotland) Act 1972 [and section 44A of the Environmental Protection Act 1990 or, in Scotland, section 44B of that Act];
   "planning authority" means the local planning authority, the person appointed under paragraph 1 of Schedule 6 to the Town and Country Planning Act 1990 or, as the case may be, the government department responsible for discharging a function under the planning Acts or, in Scotland, the planning authority (as defined in section 172 of the Local Government (Scotland) Act 1973), the person appointed under paragraph 1 of Schedule 7 to the Town and Country Planning (Scotland) Act 1972, or, as the case may be, the government department responsible for discharging a function under the Town and Country Planning (Scotland) Act 1972, and the Secretary of State shall be treated as a planning authority in respect of his functions under the planning Acts or, in Scotland, the Town and Country Planning (Scotland) Act 1972;
   "pollution control authority" means any competent authority other than a planning authority;
   "river purification authority" has the meaning given by section 17 of the Rivers (Prevention of Pollution) (Scotland) Act 1951;*
   "specified action" means any of the following—
   (a) determining—
       (i) an application for planning permission; or
       (ii) an appeal made under section 78 of the Town and Country Planning Act 1990 or, in Scotland, under section 33 of the Town and Country Planning (Scotland) Act 1972, in respect of such an application;
   (b) deciding whether to take any action under section 141(2) or (3) or 177(1)(a) or (b) of the Town and Country Planning Act 1990, or under section 196(5) of that Act as originally enacted, or under section 35(5) of the Planning (Listed Buildings and Conservation Areas) Act 1990 or, in Scotland, under section 85(5)(a), (b) or (c), 91(3) (as enacted prior to its repeal) or 172(2) or (3) of, or paragraph 2(6) of Schedule 17 to, the Town and Country Planning (Scotland) Act 1972;
   (c) deciding whether to direct under section 90(1), (2) or (2A) of the Town and Country Planning Act 1990 or, in Scotland, section 37(1) of the Town and Country Planning (Scotland) Act 1972 or paragraph 7(1) of Schedule 8 to the Electricity Act 1989, that planning permission shall be deemed to be granted;
   (d) deciding whether—

---

* Although the editor is not aware of any formal substitution of reference to SEPA for this reference, section 17 of the 1951 Act was repealed by the Environment Act 1995, Sch. 24, on April 1, 1996 and by s.21 of the 1995 Act, SEPA has exercised the functions of river purification authorities since that date.

(i) in making or confirming a discontinuance order, to include in the order any grant of planning permission; or

(ii) to confirm (with or without modifications) a discontinuance order insofar as it grants planning permission,

and, for the purposes of this sub-paragraph, "discontinuance order" means an order under section 102 of the Town and Country Planning Act 1990 (including an order made under that section by virtue of section 104 of that Act), or under paragraph 1 of Schedule 9 to that Act (including an order made under that paragraph by virtue of paragraph 11 of that Schedule), or, in Scotland, an order under section 49 of the Town and Country Planning (Scotland) Act 1972 (including an order made under that section by virtue of section 260 of that Act);

(e) discharging functions under Part II of the Town and Country Planning Act 1990 or, in Scotland, Part II of the Town and Country Planning (Scotland) Act 1972.

Duties of competent authorities

2.—(1) Subject to the following provisions of this paragraph, the competent authorities shall discharge their specified functions, insofar as they relate to the recovery or disposal of waste, with the relevant objectives.

(2) Nothing in sub-paragraph (1) above requires a planning authority to deal with any matter which the relevant pollution control authority has power to deal with.

(3) In a case where the recovery or disposal of waste is or forms part of a prescribed process designated for local control under Part I of the 1990 Act, and either requires a waste management licence or is covered by an exemption conferred by regulation 17(1) of, and Schedule 3 to, these Regulations, nothing in sub-paragraph (1) above shall require a competent authority to discharge its functions under—

(a) Part I of the 1990 Act in order to control pollution of the environment due to the release of substances into any environmental medium other than the air; or

(b) Part II of the 1990 Act in order to control pollution of the environment due to the release of substances into the air resulting from the carrying on of the prescribed process.

(4) In sub-paragraph (3) above, "prescribed process", "designated for local control", "pollution of the environment due to the release of substances into the air" and "pollution of the environment due to the release of substances into any environmental medium other than the air" have the meaning which they have in Part I of the 1990 Act.

Meaning of "competent authority" etc.

3.—(1) For the purposes of this Schedule, "competent authority" means any of the persons or bodies listed in column (1) of Table 5 below and, subject to sub-paragraph (2) below, in relation to a competent authority "specified function" means any function of that authority listed in column (2) of that Table opposite the entry for that authority.

Table 5

Competent authorities (1)	Specified functions (2)
Any planning authority.	The taking of any specified action.
A waste regulation authority, the Secretary of State or a person appointed under [section 114(1)(a) of the Environment Act 1995].	Their respective functions under Part II of the 1990 Act in relation to waste management licences, including preparing plans or modifications of them under section 50 of the 1990 Act [and preparing the strategy, or any modification of it, under section 44A or 44B of that Act].
A disposal authority or the Secretary of State.	Their respective functions under Part I of the Control of Pollution Act 1974 in relation to disposal licences and resolutions under section 11 of that Act.
A licensing authority or the Ministers.	Their respective functions under Part II of the Food and Environment Protection Act 1985, or under paragraph 5 below.

Competent authorities (1)	Specified functions (2)
An enforcing authority, the Secretary of State or a person appointed under [section 114(1) (a) of the Environment Act 1995].	Their respective functions under Part I of the 1990 Act in relation to prescribed processes except when— (a) the process is designated for local control; and (b) it is an exempt activity carried out subject to the conditions and limitations specified in Schedule 3.
The [Environment Agency] or the Secretary of State.	Their respective functions in relation to the giving of consents under Chapter II of Part III of the Water Resources Act 1991 (offences in relation to pollution of water resources) for any discharge of waste in liquid form other than waste waters.
In Scotland, a river purification authority* or the Secretary of State.	Their respective functions in relation to the giving of consents under Part II of the Control of Pollution Act 1974 (pollution of water) for any discharge of waste in liquid form other than waste waters.

(2) In Table 5 above, references to functions do not include functions of making, revoking, amending, revising or re-enacting orders, regulations or schemes where those functions are required to be discharged by statutory instrument.

Relevant objectives

4.—(1) For the purposes of this Schedule, the following objectives are relevant objectives in relation to the disposal or recovery of waste—

(a) ensuring that waste is recovered or disposed of without endangering human health and without using processes or methods which could harm the environment and in particular without—
   (i) risk to water, air, soil, plants or animals; or
   (ii) causing nuisance through noise or odours; or
   (iii) adversely affecting the countryside or places of special interest;
(b) implementing, so far as material, any plan made under the plan-making provisions.

(2) The following additional objectives are relevant objectives in relation to the disposal of waste—

(a) establishing an integrated and adequate network of waste disposal installations, taking account of the best available technology not involving excessive costs; and
(b) ensuring that the network referred to at paragraph (a) above enables—
   (i) the European Community as a whole to become self-sufficient in waste disposal, and the Member States individually to move towards that aim, taking into account geographical circumstances or the need for specialized installations for certain types of waste; and
   (ii) waste to be disposed of in one of the nearest appropriate installations, by means of the most appropriate methods and technologies in order to ensure a high level of protection for the environment and public health.

(3) The following further objectives are relevant objectives in relation to functions under the plan-making provisions—

(a) encouraging the prevention or reduction of waste production and its harmfulness, in particular by—
   (i) the development of clean technologies more sparing in their use of natural resources;
   (ii) the technical development and marketing of products designed so as to make no contribution or to make the smallest possible contribution, by the nature of their manufacture, use or final disposal, to increasing the amount or harmfulness of waste and pollution hazards; and

---

* See note to the definition of "river purification authority" in para. 1 of this Schedule.

(iii) the development of appropriate techniques for the final disposal of dangerous substances contained in waste destined for recovery; and

(b) encouraging—
(i) the recovery of waste by means of recyclying, reuse or reclamation or any other process with a view to extracting secondary raw materials; and
(ii) the use of waste as a source of energy.

Preparation of offshore waste management plan

5.—(1) Subject to sub-paragraph (2) below, it shall be the duty of a licensing authority to prepare a statement ("the plan") containing the authority's policies in relation to the recovery or disposal of waste for attaining the relevant objectives in those parts of United Kingdom waters and United Kingdom controlled waters for which the authority is the licensing authority.

(2) Two or more licensing authorities may join together to prepare a single statement covering the several parts of United Kingdom waters and United Kingdom controlled waters for which they are the licensing authorities.

(3) The plan shall relate in particular to—
(a) the type, quantity and origin of waste to be recovered or disposed of;
(b) general technical requirements;
(c) any special arrangements for particular wastes; and
(d) suitable disposal sites or installations.

(4) The licensing authority shall make copies of the plan available to the public on payment of reasonable charges.

(5) In this paragraph, "United Kingdom waters" and "United Kingdom controlled waters" have the meaning given by section 24(1) of the Food and Environment Protection Act 1985.

Matters to be covered by permits

6. When a pollution control authority grants or modifies a permit, and the activities authorised by the permit include the disposal of waste, the pollution control authority shall ensure that the permit covers—
(a) the types and quantities of waste,
(b) the technical requirements,
(c) the security precautions to be taken,
(d) the disposal site, and
(e) the treatment method.

Modifications of provisions relating to development plans

7.—(1) Subject to sub-paragraph (2) below, sections 12(3A), 31(3) and 36(3) of the Town and Country Planning Act 1990 or, in Scotland, sections 5(3)(a) and 9(3)(a) of the Town and Country Planning (Scotland) Act 1972, shall have effect as if the policies referred to in those sections also included policies in respect of suitable waste disposal sites or installations.

(2) In the case of the policies referred to in section 36(3) of the Town and Country Planning Act 1990, sub-paragraph (1) above shall have effect subject to the provisions of section 36(5) of that Act.

(3) Section 38(1) of the Town and Country Planning Act 1990 shall have effect as if the definition of waste policies included detailed policies in respect of suitable disposal sites or installations for the carrying on of such development as is referred to in that definition.

Modifications of Part I of the Environmental Protection Act 1990

8.—(1) Subject to section 28(1) of the 1990 Act, Part I of the 1990 Act shall have effect in relation to prescribed processes involving the disposal or recovery of waste with such modifications as are needed to allow an enforcing authority to exercise its functions under that Part for the purpose of achieving the relevant objectives.

(2) Nothing in sub-paragraph (1) above requires an enforcing authority granting an authorisation in relation to such a process to take account of the relevant objectives insofar as they relate to the prevention of detriment to the amenities of the locality in which the process is (or is to be) carried on if planning permission, resulting from the taking of a specified action by a planning authority arter 30th April 1994, is or, before the process is carried on, will be in force.

Modifications of Part II of the Environmental Protection Act 1990

9.—(1) Part II of the 1990 Act shall have effect subject to the following modifications.

(2) Any reference to waste shall include a reference to Directive waste.

(3) In sections 33(1)(a) and (5), 54(1)(a), (2), (3) and (4)(d) and 69(2), any reference to the deposit of waste in or on land shall include a reference to any operation listed in Part III or IV of this Schedule involving such a deposit.

(4) In sections 33(1)(b), 54(1)(b), (2), (3) and (4)(d) and 69(2), any reference to the treatment or disposal, or to the treatment, keeping or disposal, of controlled waste shall be taken to be a reference to submitting controlled waste to any of the operations listed in Part III or IV of this Schedule other than an operation mentioned in sub-paragraph (3) above.

(5) In sections 33(1)(c) and 35, any reference to the treatment or disposal, or to the treatment, keeping or disposal, of controlled waste shall include a reference to submitting controlled waste to any of the operations listed in Part III or Part IV of this Schedule.

(6) Section 33(2) shall not apply to the treatment, keeping or disposal of household waste by an establishment or undertaking.

(7) In section 36(3), the reference to planning permission shall be taken to be a reference to planning permission resulting from the taking of a specified action by a planning authority after 30th April 1994.

(8) In section 50(3), any reference to the disposal of waste shall include a reference to the recovery of waste.

Modifications of Part I of the Control of Pollution Act 1974

10.—(1) Part I of the Control of Pollution Act 1974 shall have effect, in a case where the planning permission referred to in section 5(3) of that Act does not result from the taking of a specified action by a planning authority after 30th April 1994, as if the duty imposed upon the disposal authority by that subsection was a duty not to reject the application unless the authority is satisfied that its rejection is necessary for the purpose of preventing—
 (a) pollution of the environment;
 (b) danger to public health; or
 (c) serious detriment to the amenities of the locality.

(2) In sub-paragraph (1) above, "pollution of the environment" has the same meaning as in Part II of the 1990 Act.

(3) Part I of the Control of Pollution Act 1974 shall have effect as if any reference in that Part to waste included a reference to Directive waste.

References to "waste" in Planning and Water legislation

11. In the Town and Country Planning Act 1990, the Town and Country Planning (Scotland) Act 1972, Part II of the Control of Pollution Act 1974 and Chapter II of Part III of the Water Resources Act 1991, any reference to "waste" shall include a reference to Directive waste.

Registration by professional collectors and transporters of waste, and by dealers and brokers

12.—(1) Subject to sub-paragraph (3) below, if shall be an offence for an establishment or undertaking falling within sub-paragraph (a), (c), (f) or (g) of regulation 2(1) of the Controlled Waste (Registration of Carriers and Seizure of Vehicles) Regulations 1991 after 31st December 1994 to collect or transport waste on a professional basis unless it is registered in accordance with the provisions of this paragraph.

(2) Subject to sub-paragraph (3) below, it shall be an offence for an establishment or undertaking falling within sub-paragraph (a), (b) or (c) of regulation 20(4) after 31st December 1994 to arrange for the recovery or disposal of waste on behalf of another person unless it is registered in accordance with the provisions of this paragraph.

(3) Sub-paragraphs (1) and (2) above do not apply in cases where the establishment or undertaking is carrying on the activities therein mentioned pursuant to, and in accordance with the terms and conditions of, a permit.

(4) An establishment or undertaking shall register with the waste regulation authority in whose area its principal place of business in Great Britain is located or, where it has no place of business in Great Britain, with any waste regulation authority.

(5) Each waste regulation authority shall establish and maintain a register of establishments and undertakings registering with it under the provisions of this paragraph.

(6) The register shall contain the following particulars in relation to each such establishment or undertaking—
 (a) the name of the establishment or undertaking;
 (b) the address of its principal place of business; and
 (c) the address of any place at or from which it carries on its business.

(7) The waste regulation authority shall enter the relevant particulars in the register in relation to an establishment or undertaking if it receives notice of them in writing or otherwise becomes aware of those particulars.

(8) A person guilty of an offence under sub-paragraph (1) or (2) above shall be liable on summary conviction to a fine not exceeding level 2 on the standard scale.

(9) Each waste regulation authority shall secure that any register maintained by it under this paragraph is open to inspection by members of the public free of charge at all reasonable hours

and shall afford to members of the public reasonable facilities for obtaining, on payment of reasonable charges, copies of entries in the register.

(10) Registers under this paragraph may be kept in any form.

(11) In this paragraph, "registered carrier" and "controlled waste" have the same meaning as they have in the Control of Pollution (Amendment) Act 1989, "registered broker" has the same meaning as in regulation 20 and Schedule 5, and "collect" and "transport" have the same meaning as they have in Article 12 of the Directive.

Duty to carry out appropriate periodic inspections

13.—(1) [Subject to sub-paragraphs (3) to (5) below, any] establishment or undertaking which carries out the recovery or disposal of controlled waste, or which collects or transports controlled waste on a professional basis, or which arranges for the recovery or disposal of controlled waste on behalf of others (dealers or brokers), shall be subject to appropriate periodic inspections by the competent authorities.

(2) [Section] 71(2) and (3) of the 1990 Act (power to obtain information) shall have effect as if the provisions of this paragraph were provisions of Part II of that Act and as if, in those sections, references to a waste regulation authority were references to a competent authority.

[(2A) Section 108 of the Environment Act 1995 (powers of entry) shall apply as if the competent authority was an enforcing authority and its functions under this paragraph were pollution control functions.]

(3) Subject to sub-paragraph (4) below, in a case where an establishment or undertaking is carrying on an exempt activity in reliance upon an exemption conferred by regulation 17(1) of, and paragraph 45(1) or (2) of Schedule 3 to, these Regulations, a competent authority which is a waste regulation authority shall discharge its duty under sub-paragraph (1) in respect of any place where such an activity is so carried on by—

    (a) carrying out an initial inspection of that place within two months of having received in respect of that place the notice, plan and fee referred to in regulation 18(4A); and

    (b) thereafter carrying out periodic inspections of that place at intervals not exceeding 12 months.

(4) Where the notice, plan and fee referred to in paragraph (a) of sub-paragraph (3) above are received by the authority before October 1, 1995, that paragraph shall have effect as if for the reference to carrying out an initial inspection within two months of the receipt of such notice, plan and fee there were substituted a reference to carrying out such an inspection within nine months of their receipt.

(5) In the case of any such place as is mentioned in sub-paragraph (3) above, but without prejudice to any duties of waste regulation authorities imposed otherwise than by this paragraph, sub-paragraph (1) above does not require (but does permit) a competent authority which is a waste regulation authority to carry out the periodic inspections referred to in sub-paragraph (3)(b) above at intervals of less than 10 months.]

Record keeping

14.—(1) Subject to [paragraph 45(3)(b) of Schedule 3 and] sub-paragraph (2) below, an establishment or undertaking which carries out the disposal or recovery of controlled waste shall—

    (a) keep a record of the quantity, nature, origin and, where relevant, the destination, frequency of collection, mode of transport and treatment method of any waste which is disposed of or recovered; and

    (b) make that information available, on request, to the competent authorities.

(2) [Subject to sub-paragraph (3) below,] sub-paragraph (1) above does not apply where the disposal or recovery of the waste is covered by an exemption conferred by—

    (a) regulation 17(1) of, and Schedule 3 to, these Regulations; or

    (b) Article 3 of the Deposits in the Sea (Exemptions) Order 1985.

[(3) Sub-paragraph (1) above does apply to an activity subject to an exemption conferred by regulation 17(1) of, and paragraph 45(1) or (2) of Schedule 3 to, these Regulations.]

PART II

SUBSTANCES OR OBJECTS WHICH ARE WASTE WHEN DISCARDED ETC.

1. Production or consumption residues not otherwise specified in this Part of this Schedule (Q1).
2. Off-specification products (Q2).
3. Products whose date for appropriate use has expired (Q3).

4. Materials spilled, lost or having undergone other mishap, including any materials, equipment, etc., contaminated as a result of the mishap (Q4).
5. Materials contaminated or soiled as a result of planned actions (e.g. residues from cleaning operations, packing materials, containers, etc.) (Q5).
6. Unusable parts (e.g. reject batteries, exhausted catalysts, etc.) (Q6).
7. Substances which no longer perform satisfactorily (e.g. contaminated acids, contaminated solvents, exhausted tempering salts, etc.) (Q7).
8. Residues of industrial processes (e.g. slags, still bottoms, etc.) (Q8).
9. Residues from pollution abatement processes (e.g. scrubber sludges, baghouse dusts, spent filters, etc.) (Q9).
10. Machining or finishing residues (e.g. lathe turnings, mill scales, etc.) (Q10).
11. Residues from raw materials extraction and processing (e.g. mining residues, oil field slops, etc.) (Q11).
12. Adulterated materials (e.g. oils contaminated with PCBs, etc.) (Q12).
13. Any materials, substances or products whose use has been banned by law (Q13).
14. Products for which the holder has no further use (e.g. agricultural, household, office, commercial and shop discards, etc.) (Q14).
15. Contaminated materials, substances or products resulting from remedial action with respect to land (Q15).
16. Any materials, substances or products which are not contained in the above categories (Q16).

(Note:— the reference in brackets at the end of each paragraph of this Part of this Schedule is the number of the corresponding paragraph in Annex I to the Directive.)

PART III

WASTE DISPOSAL OPERATIONS

1. Tipping of waste above or underground (e.g. landfill, etc.) (D1).
2. Land treatment of waste (e.g. biodegradation of liquid or sludge discards in soils, etc.) (D2).
3. Deep injection of waste (e.g. injection of pumpable discards into wells, salt domes or naturally occurring repositories, etc.) (D3).
4. Surface impoundment of waste (e.g. placement of liquid or sludge discards into pits, ponds or lagoons, etc.) (D4).
5. Specially engineered landfill of waste (e.g. placement of waste into lined discrete cells which are capped and isolated from one another and the environment, etc.) (D5).
6. Release of solid waste into a water body except seas or oceans (D6).
7. Release of waste into seas or oceans including seabed insertion (D7).
8. Biological treatment of waste not listed elsewhere in this Part of this Schedule which results in final compounds or mixtures which are disposed of by means of any of the operations listed in this Part of this Schedule (D8).
9. Physico-chemical treatment of waste not listed elsewhere in this Part of this Schedule which results in final compounds or mixtures which are disposed of by means of any of the operations listed in this Part of this Schedule (e.g. evaporation, drying, calcination, etc.) (D9).
10. Incineration of waste on land (D10).
11. Incineration of waste at sea (D11).
12. Permanent storage of waste (e.g. emplacement of containers in a mine, etc.) (D12).
13. Blending or mixture of waste prior to the waste being submitted to any of the operations listed in this Part of this Schedule (D13).
14. Repackaging of waste prior to the waste being submitted to any of the operations listed in this Part of this Schedule (D14).
15. Storage of waste pending any of the operations listed in this Part of this Schedule, but excluding temporary storage, pending collection, on the site where the waste is produced (D15).

(Note:— the reference in brackets at the end of each paragraph of this Part of this Schedule is the number of the corresponding paragraph in Annex IIA to the Directive.)

PART IV

WASTE RECOVERY OPERATIONS

1. Reclamation or regeneration of solvents (R1).
2. Recycling or reclamation of organic substances which are not used as solvents (R2).

3. Recycling or reclamation of metals and metal compounds (R3).
4. Recycling or reclamation of other inorganic materials (R4).
5. Regeneration of acids or bases (R5).
6. Recovery of components used for pollution abatement (R6).
7. Recovery of components from catalysts (R7).
8. Re-refining, or other reuses, of oil which is waste (R8).
9. Use of waste principally as a fuel or for other means of generating energy (R9).
10. Spreading of waste on land resulting in benefit to agriculture or ecological improvement, including composting and other biological transformation processes, except in the case of waste excluded under Article 2(1)(b)(iii) of the Directive (R10).
11. Use of wastes obtained from any of the operations listed in paragraphs 1 to 10 of this Part of this Schedule (R11).
12. Exchange of wastes for submission to any of the operations listed in paragraphs 1 to 11 of this Part of this Schedule (R12).
13. Storage of waste consisting of materials intended for submission to any operation listed in this Part of this Schedule, but excluding temporary storage, pending collection, on the site where it is produced (R13).

(Note:— the reference in brackets at the end of each paragraph of this Part of this Schedule is the number of the corresponding paragraph in Annex IIB to the Directive.)

Regulation 20(7)   SCHEDULE 5

REGISTRATION OF BROKERS OF CONTROLLED WASTE

PART I

GENERAL

Interpretation
1.—(1) In this Schedule—
"the Carriers Regulations" means the Controlled Waste (Registration of Carriers and Seizure of Vehicles) Regulations 1991;
"date of expiry", in relation to a broker's registration, in a case to which sub-paragraph (2) or (3) of paragraph 7 applies, has the meaning given by that sub-paragraph, and in any other case means the date on which the period of three years mentioned in paragraph 7(1) expires;
"notice" means notice in writing;
"relevant offence" means an offence under any of the enactments listed in regulation 3; and
"relevant period" means two months or, except in the case of an application for the renewal of his registration by a person who is already registered, such longer period as may be agreed between the applicant and the waste regulation authority.

(2) In determining for the purposes of paragraph 3(13) or 5(1) whether it is desirable for any individual to be or to continue to be authorised to arrange (as dealer or broker) for the disposal or recovery of controlled waste on behalf of other persons, a waste regulation authority shall have regard, in a case in which a person other than the individual has been convicted of a relevant offence, to whether that individual has been a party to the carrying on of a business in a manner involving the commission of relevant offences.

(3) In relation to the applicant for registration or registered broker, another relevant person shall be treated for the purposes of paragraph 3(13) or 5(1) as having been convicted of a relevant offence if—
(a) any person has been convicted of a relevant offence committed by him in the course of his employment by the applicant or registered broker or in the course of the carrying on of any business by a partnership one of the members of which was the applicant or registered broker;
(b) a body corporate has been convicted of a relevant offence committed at a time when the applicant or registered broker was a director, manager, secretary or other similar officer of that body corporate; or
(c) where the applicant or registered broker is a body corporate, a person who is a director, manager, secretary or other similar officer of that body corporate—
(i) has been convicted of a relevant offence; or
(ii) was a director, manager, secretary or other similar officer of another body corporate at a time when a relevant offence for which that other body corporate has been convicted was committed.

(4) For the purposes of this Schedule, an application for registration or for the renewal of a registration as a broker of controlled waste shall be treated as pending—

(a) whilst it is being considered by the waste regulation authority; or

(b) if it has been refused or the relevant period from the making of the application has expired without the applicant having been registered, whilst either—

(i) the period for appealing in relation to that application has not expired; or

(ii) the application is the subject of an appeal which has not been disposed of.

(5) For the purposes of this Schedule, an appeal is disposed of when any of the following occurs—

(a) the appeal is withdrawn;

(b) the appellant is notified by the Secretary of State or the waste regulation authority in question that his appeal has been dismissed; or

(c) the waste regulation authority complies with any direction of the Secretary of State to renew the appellant's registration or to cancel the revocation.

(6) […]

Registers

2.—(1) It shall be the duty of each waste regulation authority to establish and maintain a register of brokers of controlled waste and—

(a) to secure that the register is open for inspection by members of the public free of charge at all reasonable hours; and

(b) to afford to members of the public reasonable facilities for obtaining copies of entries in the register on payment of reasonable charges.

(2) A register under this paragraph may be kept in any form.

Applications for registration

3.—(1) An application for registration or for the renewal of a registration as a broker of controlled waste shall be made to the waste regulation authority for the area in which the applicant has or proposes to have his principal place of business in Great Britain; but if the applicant does not have or propose to have a place of business in Great Britain, the applicant may apply to any waste regulation authority.

(2) Subject to sub-paragraphs (3) to (5) below, a person shall not make an application for registration or for the renewal of a registration whilst—

(a) a previous application of his is pending; or

(b) he is registered.

(3) Sub-paragraph (2) above shall not prevent a person from applying for the renewal of a registration where his application is made within the period of six months mentioned in paragraph 7(5).

(4) An application for registration or for the renewal of a registration in respect of a business which is or is to be carried on by a partnership shall be made by all of the partners or prospective partners.

(5) A prospective partner in a business carried on by a partnership whose members are already registered may make an application for registration as a partner in that business to the waste regulation authority with whom the business is registered.

(6) An application for registration shall be made on a form corresponding to the form of Part II of this Schedule, or on a form substantially to the like effect, and shall contain the information required by that form.

(7) An application for the renewal of registration shall be made on a form corresponding to the form in Part III of this Schedule, or on a form substantially to the like effect, and shall contain the information required by that form.

(8) Where an applicant wishes to apply to be registered both as a carrier and as a broker of controlled waste, he may, instead of making the application on the forms provided for by regulation 4(6) of the Carriers Regulations and sub-paragraph (6) above, make a combined application on a form containing the information required by those forms.

(9) Where an applicant wishes to apply both for the renewal of his registration as a carrier of controlled waste and for the renewal of his registration as a broker of controlled waste, he may, instead of making an application on the forms provided for by regulation 4(7) of the Carriers Regulations and sub-paragraph (7) above, make a combined application on a form containing the information required by those forms.

(10) A waste regulation authority shall provide a copy of the appropriate application form free of charge to any person requesting one.

(11) A waste regulation authority shall charge an applicant in respect of its consideration of his application—

    (a) subject to paragraph (c) below, in the case of either an application for registration as a broker of controlled waste or a combined application for registration as both a carrier and broker of controlled waste, £95;

    (b) in the case of either an application for the renewal of a registration as a broker of controlled waste or a combined application for renewal of registration both as a carrier and as a broker of controlled waste, £65;

    (c) in the case of an application by a registered carrier of controlled waste for registration as a broker of controlled waste, £25,

and the applicant shall pay the charge when he makes his application.

(12) A waste regulation authority shall, on receipt of an application for registration or for the renewal of a registration, ensure that the register contains a copy of the application.

(13) A waste regulation authority may refuse an application for registration or for the renewal of a registration if, and only if—

    (a) there has, in relation to that application, been a contravention of any of the requirements of the preceding provisions of this paragraph; or

    (b) the applicant or another relevant person has been convicted of a relevant offence and, in the opinion of the authority, it is undesirable for the applicant to be authorised to arrange (as dealer or broker) for the disposal or recovery of controlled waste on behalf of other persons.

(14) Where a waste regulation authority decides to refuse an application for registration or for the renewal of a registration, the authority shall give notice to the applicant informing him that his application is refused and of the reasons for its decision.

(15) If an appeal is made under and in accordance with paragraph 6, the waste regulation authority shall, as soon as reasonably practicable, make appropriate entries in its register indicating when the appeal was made and the result of the appeal.

(16) If no such appeal is made, the waste regulation authority shall as soon as reasonably practicable, make an appropriate entry in its register indicating that the application has not been accepted and that no appeal has been made.

(17) A waste regulation authorty may remove from its register—

    (a) a copy of an application included under sub-paragraph (12) above; or

    (b) an entry made under sub-paragraph (15) or (16) above,

at any time more than six years after the application in question was made.

Registration as a broker and amendment of entries

4.—(1) On accepting a person's application for registration or on being directed under paragraph 6(9) to register a person following an appeal in respect of such an application, the waste regulation authority shall make an entry in its register—

    (a) showing that person as a registered broker of controlled waste and allocating him a registered number (which may include any letter);

    (b) specifying the date on which the registration takes effect and its date of expiry;

    (c) stating any business name of his and the address of his principal place of business (together with any telephone, telex or fax number of his) and, in the case of an individual, his date of birth;

    (d) in the case of a body corporate, listing the names of each director, manager, secretary or other similar officer of that body and their respective dates of birth;

    (e) in the case of a company registered under the Companies Acts, specifying its registered number and, in the case of a company incorporated outside Great Britain, the country in which it was incorporated;

    (f) in a case where the person who is registered or another relevant person has been convicted of a relevant offence, giving the person's name, details of the offence, the date of conviction, the penalty imposed, the name of the Court and, in the case of an individual, his date of birth; and

    (g) in a case where the person who is registered or any company in the same group of companies as that person is the holder of a waste management licence, stating the name of the holder of the licence and the name of the authority which granted it.

(2) In the case of a business which is, or is to be, carried on by a partnership, all the partners shall be registered under one entry and only one registration number shall be allocated to the partnership.

(3) On making an entry in its register under sub-paragraph (1) above the waste regulation authority shall provide the registered person or partnership free of charge with a copy of the entry in the register.

(4) On accepting a person's application for the renewal of a registration or on being directed under paragraph 6(9) to register a person following an appeal in respect of such an application, the waste regulation authority shall amend the relevant entry in the register—

    (a) to show the date on which the renewal takes effect and the revised date of expiry of the registration;

    (b) to record any other change disclosed as a result of the application; and

    (c) to note in the register the date on which the amendments are made.

(5) The waste regulation authority shall at the same time as amending the register under sub-paragraph (4) above provide the registered person or partnership free of charge with a copy of the amended entry in the register.

(6) A person who is registered shall notify the waste regulation authority which maintains the relevant register of any change of circumstances affecting information in the register relating to him.

(7) On—

    (a) being notified of any change of circumstances in accordance with sub-paragraph (6) above;

    (b) accepting a prospective partner's application for registration in relation to a business carried on by a partnership whose members are already registered; or

    (c) being directed under paragraph 6(9) to register a prospective partner,

the waste regulation authority shall—

    (i) amend the relevant entry to reflect the change of circumstances or the registration of the prospective partner;

    (ii) note in the register the date on which the amendment is made;

    (iii) provide the registered person or partnership free of charge with a copy of the amended entry in the register.

(8) In this regulation—

    "Companies Acts" has the meaning given by section 744 of the Companies Act 1985;

    "business name" means a name under which a person carries on business and by virtue of which the Business Names Act 1985 applies; and

    "group" has the meaning given by section 53(1) of the Companies Act 1989.

Revocation of registration

5.—(1) A waste regulation authority may revoke a person's registration as a broker of controlled waste if, and only if—

    (a) that person or another relevant person has been convicted of a relevant offence; and

    (b) in the opinion of the authority, it is undesirable for the registered broker to continue to be authorised to arrange (as dealer or broker) for the disposal or recovery of controlled waste on behalf of other persons.

(2) Where a waste regulation authority decides to revoke a person's registration as a broker of controlled waste, it shall give notice to the broker informing him of the revocation and the reasons for its decision.

Appeals

6.—(1) Where a person has applied to a waste regulation authority to be registered as a broker of controlled waste in accordance with paragraph 3, he may appeal to the Secretary of State if—

    (a) his application is refused; or

    (b) the relevant period from the making of the application has expired without his having been registered.

(2) A person whose registration as a broker of controlled waste has been revoked may appeal against the revocation to the Secretary of State.

(3) Notice of an appeal to the Secretary of State under sub-paragraph (1) or (2) above shall be given by the appellant to the Secretary of State.

(4) The notice of appeal shall be accompanied by the following—

    (a) a statement of the grounds of appeal;

    (b) in the case of an appeal under sub-paragraph (1) above, a copy of the relevant application;

    (c) in the case of an appeal under sub-paragraph (2) above, a copy of the appellant's entry in the register;

    (d) a copy of any relevant correspondence between the appellant and the waste regulation authority;

    (e) a copy of any notice given to the appellant under paragraph 3(14) or 5(2);

    (f) a statement indicating whether the appellant wishes the appeal to be in the form of a hearing or to be determined on the basis of written representations.

(5) The appellant shall at the same time as giving notice of appeal to the Secretary of State serve on the waste regulation authority a copy of the notice and a copy of the documents referred to in sub-paragraph (4)(a) and (f) above.

(6) Notice of appeal is to be given before the expiry of the period of 28 days beginning with—

(a) in the case of an appeal under sub-paragraph (1)(a) above, the date on which the appellant is given notice by the waste regulation authority that his application has been refused;

(b) in the case of an appeal under sub-paragraph (1)(b) above, the date on which the relevant period from the making of the application expired without the appellant having been registered; or

(c) in the case of an appeal under sub-paragraph (2) above, the date on which the appellant is given notice by the waste regulation authority that his registration as a broker of controlled waste has been revoked,

or before such later date as the Secretary of State may at any time allow.

(7) If either party to an appeal requests a hearing or the Secretary of State so decides, the appeal shall be or continue in the form of a hearing before a person appointed for the purpose by the Secretary of State.

(8) The person holding such a hearing shall after its conclusion make a written report to the Secretary of State which shall include his conclusions and recommendations or his reasons for not making any recommendations.

(9) On an appeal under this paragraph the Secretary of State may, as he thinks fit, either dismiss the appeal or give the waste regulation authority in question a direction to register the appellant or, as the case may be, to cancel the revocation.

(10) The Secretary of State shall—

(a) notify the appellant in writing of his determination of the appeal and of his reasons for it and, if a hearing is held, shall also provide him with a copy of the report of the person who cnducted the hearing; and

(b) at the same time send a copy of those documents to the waste regulation authority.

(11) Where on an appeal made by virtue of sub-paragraph (1)(b) above the Secretary of State dismisses an appeal, he shall direct the waste regulation authority in question not to register the appellant.

(12) It shall be the duty of a waste regulation authority to comply with any direction under this paragraph.

[(13) This paragraph is subject to 114 of the Environment Act 1995 (delegation or reference of appeals).]

Duration of registration

7.—(1) Subject to the following provisions of this paragraph, a person's registration as a broker of controlled waste shall cease to have effect on the expiry of the period of three years beginning with the date of the registration or, if it has been renewed, beginning with the date on which it was renewed or, as the case may be, last renewed.

(2) Where a registered carrier of controlled waste is registered as a broker of controlled waste otherwise than by way of renewal of an existing registration as a broker, and his registration as a carrier will expire within three years of the date of his registration as a broker, if at the time of making his application for registration as a broker he so requests, his registration as a broker shall expire on the same date as his registration as a carrier.

(3) Where a registered broker of controlled waste is registered as a carrier of controlled waste otherwise than by way of renewal of an existing registration as a carrier, and his registration as a broker will expire within three years of the date of his registration as a carrier, if on the next application for renewal of his registration as a broker which he makes after having been registered as a carrier he so requests, his renewed registration as a broker shall expire on the same date as his registration as a carrier.

(4) Registration as a registered broker shall cease to have effect if the registered broker gives notice requiring the removal of his name from the register.

(5) The waste regulation authority shall, no later than six months before the date of expiry of a broker's registration, serve on a registered broker—

(a) a notice informing him of the date of expiry and of the effect of sub-paragraph (6) below; and

(b) an application form for the renewal of his registration and a copy of his current entry in the register.

(6) Where an application for the renewal of a registration is made within the last six months prior to its date of expiry, the registration shall, notwithstanding the passing of the expiry date, continue in force—

(a) until the application is withdrawn or accepted; or

(b) if the waste regulation authority refused the application or the relevant period from the making of the application has expired without the applicant having been registered, until—

    (i) the expiry of the period for appealing; or

    (ii) where the applicant indicates within that period that he does not intend to make or continue with an appeal, the date on which such an indication is given.

(7) Where a waste regulation authority revokes a broker's registration, the registration shall, notwithstanding the revocation, continue in force until—

(a) the expiry of the period for appealing against the revocation; or

(b) where that person indicates within that period that he does not intend to make or continue with an appeal, the date on which such an indication is given.

(8) Where an appeal is made under and in accordance with the provisions of paragraph 6—

(a) by a person whose appeal is in respect of such an application for the renewal of his registration as was made, in accordance with paragraph 3, at a time when he was already registered; or

(b) by a person whose registration has been revoked,

that registration shall continue in force after its date of expiry or, as the case may be, notwithstanding the revocation, until the appeal is disposed of.

(9) A registration in respect of a business which is carried on by a partnership shall cease to have effect if any of the partners ceases to be registered or if any person who is not registered becomes a partner.

(10) The duration of a registration in respect of a business which is carried on by a partnership shall not be affected if a person ceases to be a partner or if a prospective partner is registered under paragraph 4(7) in relation to the partnership.

(11) Where a waste regulation authority accepts an application for the renewal of a broker's registration before the expiry date, the renewal shall for the purposes of this Schedule take effect from the expiry date.

Cessation of registration

8. Where by virtue of paragraph 6(11) or 7 a registration ceases to have effect, the waste regulation authority—

(a) shall record this fact in the appropriate entry in its register and the date on which it occurred;

(b) may remove the appropriate entry from its register at any time more than six years after the registration ceases to have effect.

PART II

FORM OF APPLICATION FOR REGISTRATION AS A BROKER OF CONTROLLED WASTE

Please read the guidance notes before completing this form

1. Full name of applicant (*note 1*)
Former name (if applicable)
Date of birth (if applicable)

2. Name under which applicant carries on business if (different from 1)

3. Address for correspondence   Post Code

4. Address of principal place of business (if different from 3)   Post Code

5. Telephone/Telex/Fax number   Tel   Telex   Fax

6. If applicant has previously been a registered broker give:
(a) registration number or numbers
(b) name of waste regulation authority or authorities

7. If applicant is a company registered under the Companies Act, give:

(a) company's registered number

(b) address of registered office

Post Code

(c) in the case of a company incorporated outside Great Britain, the country in which it was incorporated

8. If applicant is a registered company or other body corporate, for each director, manager, secretary or other similar officer, give:

Full name	Position held	Address	Date of birth

9. If applicant is a prospective partner in a business carried on by a partnership whose members are already registered brokers, give:

(a) full name of partnership

(b) registration number of partnership

10. Has the applicant or another relevant person (*note 2*) been convicted of any offence listed in regulation 3 of the Waste Management Licensing Regulations 1994 (*notes 3 and 4*)?

Yes ☐ No ☐

If **Yes,** give full details of each offence—

Full name of person convicted	Position held	Name of court	Date of conviction	Offence and penalty imposed

If details of any conviction have been given, use the following space to provide the waste regulation authority with any additional information which you wish the authority to take into account in determining whether or not it is undesirable for the applicant to be authorised to arrange (as dealer or broker) for the disposal or recovery of controlled waste on behalf of other persons—

11. If the applicant is already a registered carrier of controlled waste, does he want his registration as a broker to expire on the same date as that on which his registration as a carrier expires (instead of lasting for 3 years)?

Yes ☐ No ☐

12. Is the applicant or another company in the same group (within the meaning of section 53(1) of the Companies Act 1989) the holder of a waste management licence?

Yes ☐ No ☐

If **Yes,** give details of licence:

Full name of holder of licence	Date of birth (if applicable)	Date of issue of licence	Name of authority which issued the licence

Declaration

I declare that I have personally checked the information given in this application form and that it is true to the best of my knowledge, information and belief. I understand that registration may be refused if false or incomplete information is given and that untrue statements may result in prosecution and could lead to revocation of registration.

Signature: Date:
Position held:

Have you enclosed the fee of £95 (or where you are already a registered carrier of controlled waste, £25)? (*note 5*)   Yes ☐

GUIDANCE NOTES

1. In the case of a partnership or proposed partnership, each partner must apply for registration and his details must be included in this application form.

2. Details of an offence listed in regulation 3 of the Waste Management Licensing Regulations 1994 must be given if the applicant was convicted of the offence or if the person convicted of the offence ("the relevant person")—

    (a) committed it in the course of his employment by the applicant;
    (b) committed it in the course of the carrying on of any business by a partnership one of the members of which was the applicant;
    (c) was a body corporate and at the time when the offence was committed the applicant was a director, manager, secretary or other similar officer of that body;
    (d) was a director, manager, secretary or other similar officer of the applicant (where the applicant is a body corporate);
    (e) was a body corporate and at the time when the offence was committed a director, manager, secretary or other similar officer of the applicant held such an office in the body corporate which committed the offence.

3. The offences listed in regulation 3 of the Waste Management Licensing Regulations 1994 are offences under any of the following provisions—

    section 22 of the Public Health (Scotland) Act 1897;
    section 95(1) of the Public Health Act 1936;
    section 3, 5(6), 16(4), 18(2), 31(1), 32(1), 34(5), 78, 92(6) or 93(3) of the Control of Pollution Act 1974;
    section 2 of the Refuse Disposal (Amenity) Act 1978;
    the Control of Pollution (Special Waste) Regulations 1980;
    section 9(1) of the Food and Environment Protection Act 1985;
    the Transfrontier Shipment of Hazardous Waste Regulations 1988;
    the Merchant Shipping (Prevention of Pollution by Garbage) Regulations 1988;
    section 1, 5, 6(9) or 7(3) of the Control of Pollution (Amendment) Act 1989;
    section 107, 118(4) or 175(1) of the Water Act 1989;
    section 23(1), 33, 34(6), 44, 47(6), 57(5), 59(5), 63(2), 69(9) 70(4), 71(3) or 80(4) of the Environmental Protection Act 1990;
    section 85, 202 or 206 of the Water Resources Act 1991;
    section 33 of the Clean Air Act 1993.

4. Details of a conviction need not be given where under the terms of the Rehabilitation of Offenders Act 1974 the conviction is spent.

5. The fee of £95 (or, if you are already a registered carrier of controlled waste, £25) must be sent with the application. The regulation authority may refuse the application if the fee is not enclosed.

PART III

FORM OF APPLICATION FOR RENEWAL OF REGISTRATION AS A BROKER OF CONTROLLED WASTE

Please read the guidance notes before completing this form

1. Full name of applicant (*note 1*)
   Former name (if applicable)
   Date of birth (if applicable)

2. Address for correspondence   Post Code

3. Telephone/Telex/Fax number   Tel   Telex   Fax

4. Registration number as broker

5. Has the applicant or another relevant person (*note 2*) been convicted of any offence listed in regulation 3 of the Waste Management Licensing Regulations 1994 (*notes 3 and 4*)?
Yes ☐   No ☐
If **Yes,** give full details of each offence—

Full name of person convicted	Position held	Name of court	Date of conviction	Offence and penalty imposed

If details of any conviction have been given, use the following space to provide the waste regulation authority with any additional information which you wish the authority to take into account in determining whether or not it is undesirable for the applicant to be authorised to arrange (as dealer or broker) for the disposal or recovery of controlled waste on behalf of others—

6. Give details of any changes in any other information in the applicant's existing entry in the register (*note 5*)—

7. If the applicant has been registered as a carrier of controlled waste since the commencement of his current registration as a broker, does he want his renewed registration as a broker to expire when his registration as a carrier expires (instead of it lasting for 3 years)?
Yes ☐   No ☐

Declaration

I declare that I have personally checked the information given in this application form and that it is true to the best of my knowledge, information and belief. I understand that registration may be refused if false or incomplete information is given and that untrue statements may result in prosecution and could lead to revocation of registration.

Signature: Date:
Position held:

Have you enclosed the fee of £65 (*note 6*)   Yes ☐

GUIDANCE NOTES

1. In the case of a partnership, each partner must apply for registration and his details must be included in this application form.

2. Details of an offence listed in regulation 3 of the Waste Management Licensing Regulations 1994 must be given if the applicant was convicted of the offence or if the person convicted of the offence ("the relevant person")—

(a) committed it in the course of his employment by the applicant;

(b) committed it in the course of the carrying on of any business by a partnership one of the members of which was the applicant;

(c) was a body corporate and at the time when the offence was committed the applicant was a director, manager, secretary or other similar officer of that body;

(d) was a director, manager, secretary or other similar officer of the applicant (where the applicant is a body corporate);

(e) was a body corporate and at the time when the offence was committed a director, manager, secretary or other similar officer of the applicant held such an office in the body corporate which committed the offence.

3. The offences listed in regulation 3 of the Waste Management Licensing Regulations 1994 are offences under any of the following provisions—

section 22 of the Public Health (Scotland) Act 1897;

section 95(1) of the Public Health Act 1936;

section 3, 5(6), 16(4), 18(2), 31(1), 32(1), 34(5), 78, 92(6) or 93(3) of the Control of Pollution Act 1974;

section 2 of the Refuse Disposal (Amenity) Act 1978;

the Control of Pollution (Special Waste) Regulations 1980;

section 9(1) of the Food and Environment Protection Act 1985;

the Transfrontier Shipment of Hazardous Waste Regulations 1988;

the Merchant Shipping (Prevention of Pollution by Garbage) Regulations 1988;

section 1, 5, 6(9) or 7(3) of the Control of Pollution (Amendment) Act 1989;

section 107, 118(4) or 175(1) of the Water Act 1989;

section 23(1), 33, 34(6), 44, 47(6), 57(5), 59(5), 63(2), 69(9), 70(4), 71(3) or 80(4) of the Environmental Protection Act 1990;

section 85, 202 or 206 of the Water Resources Act 1991;

section 33 of the Clean Air Act 1993.

4. Details of a conviction need not be given where under the terms of the Rehabilitation of Offenders Act 1974 the conviction is spent.

5. Check the information in the copy of the current entry in the register sent with the regulation authority's reminder that registration needs to be renewed or, if no such copy has been received, ask the authority for one.

6. The fee of £65 must be sent with the application. The regulation authority may refuse the application if the fee is not enclosed.

B: WASTE MANAGEMENT LICENSING (AMENDMENT ETC.) REGULATIONS 1995

(S.I. 1995 No. 288)

In force from:

April 1, 1995

Enabling power:

European Communities Act 1972, s.2(2) and the Environment Protection Act 1990, ss.29(10), 33(3), 74(6) and 75(8).

Amendment:

Paragraph 5 of regulation 4 was added by S.I. 1995 No. 1950 and amended by S.I. 1996 No. 634.

Background:

With the exception of regulation 4, which is freestanding and is therefore printed below, these Regulations serve to amend the Waste Management Licensing Regulations 1994 (S.I. 1994 No. 1056) and the Controlled Waste Regulations 1992 (S.I. 1992 No. 588).

Regulation 4 of S.I. 1994 No. 1056 makes provision in respect of technical competence for the purposes of the "fit and proper person" test for waste management licence applicants. Those provisions are subject to transitional exemptions in certain cases, and reg. 4 of these Regulations provides further such transitional exemptions. References to "the Principal Regulations" are to S.I. 1994 No. 1056. Reg. 4(5) was inserted by S.I. 1995 No. 1950 to reflect the extension, for certain activities, of the transitional exemption in para. 43 of Sched. 3 to the 1994 Regulations (see the headnote at the start of this Appendix), and was therefore re-amended by S.I. 1996 No. 634 when that exemption was further extended.

Technical competence—transitional provisions

4.–(1) Where before 10th July 1995 a person has applied to the Waste Management Industry Training and Advisory Board for a certificate of technical competence and at any time in the 23 months ending on that date he acted as the manager of a facility of a type listed in Table 1 in the Principal Regulations for which the certificate is a relevant certificate, then, until 10th August 1999, regulation 4 of the Principal Regulations shall not apply to him in relation to either—

(a) any facility of that type; or

(b) a facility of any other type if—

(i) the certificate is a relevant certificate for that other type of facility; and

(ii) the entry for that other type of facility appears, in Table 1 in the Principal Regulations, after the entry in that Table for the type of facility in respect of which he acted as the manager,

and he shall be treated as technically competent for the purposes of section 74(3)(b) of the 1990 Act in relation to any such facility.

(2) A person shall be treated as the manager of a facility for the purposes of paragraph (1) above if at the relevant time he was the manager of activities which were carried on at that facility and either—

(a) those activities involved the recovery or disposal of waste as or as part of a process designated for central control under section 2(4) of the 1990 Act and were authorised by an authorisation granted under Part I of that Act; or

(b) those activities involved the disposal of waste as or as part of a process designated for local control under section 2(4) of the 1990 Act and falling within paragraph (a) of Part B of Section 5.1 (incineration) of Schedule 1 to the 1991 Regulations and were authorised by an authorisation granted under Part I of that Act.

(3) Where at any time in the 15 months ending on 31st July 1995 a person has acted as the manager of a facility the operation of which at that time was not in breach of section 33(1)(a) or (b) of the 1990 Act solely by virtue of the exemption provided by regulation 17 of, and paragraph 43 of Schedule 3 to, the Principal Regulations, then, until the date specified in paragraph (4) below, regulation 4 of the Principal Regulations shall not apply to him in relation to that facility and he shall be treated as technically competent for the purposes of section 74(3)(b) of the 1990 Act in relation to that facility.

(4) The date referred to in paragraph (3) above as being specified in this paragraph is 31st July 1995 except in the following cases—

   (a) where the facility is of a type listed in Table 1 in the Principal Regulations, and the person has applied on or before 31st July 1995 to the Waste Management Industry Training and Advisory Board for a certificate of technical competence which is a relevant certificate, then the specified date is 10th August 1999;

   (b) where the facility is not of a type listed in Table 1 in the Principal Regulations, and an application is made on or before 31st July 1995 for a waste management licence which, if granted, would authorise the operation of the facility, then the specified date is the day after the day upon which the licence is granted or, if the application is (or is deemed to be) rejected, the day after—

        (i) the day on which the period for appealing expires without any appeal having been made; or

        (ii) the day on which any appeal is withdrawn or finally determined.

[(5) In their application in relation to the manager of a facility at which activities falling within paragraph 8 or 9 of Part III of Schedule 4 to the Principal Regulations are carried on, paragraphs (3) and (4) above shall have effect as if—

   (a) in paragraph (3), for the words "the 15 months ending on 31st July 1995" there were substituted the words ["the 29 months ending on 30th September 1996";]

   (b) in paragraph (4), for the words "31st July 1995" in each place where they occur there were substituted the words ["30th September 1996"].

C: WASTE MANAGEMENT REGULATIONS 1996

(S.I. 1996 No. 634)

In force from:

April 1, 1996 (in so far as included here).

Enabling power:

European Communities Act 1972, s.2(2); Environmental Protection Act 1990, ss.29(10), 33(3), 52(8) and 74(6).

Background:

These regulations make various amendments to the Waste Management Licensing Regulations 1994, the Waste Management Licensing (Amendment etc.) Regulations 1995 and the Environmental Protection (Waste Recycling Payments) Regulations 1992. Regulations 4 and 5, which are printed here, make freestanding provision in relation to the technical competence of site managers for the purposes of s.74(3)(b) of the Environmental Protection Act 1990. Regulation 4 relaxes the technical competence requirements for sites other than landfill sites, and reg. 5 modifies the nature of certain existing transitional provisions in relation to waste treatment, extending the benefit of the exemption in certain cases to include the treatment of special waste.

Pre-qualification technical competence

4.—(1) Where:
   (a) a person has applied to the Waste Management Industry Training and Advisory Board for a certificate of technical competence in relation to one of the types of facility mentioned in paragraph (2);
   (b) an application has been made for a waste management licence to authorise activities whose management is intended to be in that person's hands;
   (c) the activities mentioned in sub-paragraph (b) are to be carried on at a facility of the same type as that in relation to which the application mentioned in sub-paragraph (a) was made; and
   (d) the relevant Agency as defined in paragraph (3) is satisfied that, but for regulation 4 of the Waste Management Licensing Regulations 1994, he would be a technically competent person*;
then, in relation to the facility in respect of which the application mentioned in sub-paragraph (b) was made and until the expiry of two years from the grant of a licence pursuant to that application, regulation 4 of those Regulations shall not apply to that person and he shall be treated as technically competent for the purposes of section 74(3)(b) of the Environmental Protection Act 1990.
   (2) The types of facility mentioned in paragraph (1)(a) are all those listed in Table 1 of regulation 4(1) of the Waste Management Licensing Regulations 1994 other than any type of landfill site.
   (3) The relevant Agency mentioned in paragraph (1)(d) is:
   (a) in relation to England and Wales, the Environment Agency established by section 1 of the Environment Act 1995; and
   (b) in relation to Scotland, the Scottish Environment Protection Agency established by section 20 of that Act.

---

* Section 74(5) Environmental Protection Act 1990 provides that it shall be the duty of the Agencies to have regard to any guidance issued to them by the Secretary of State with respect to the discharge of their functions of making determinations to which section 74 applies.

Transitional provision for certificates of technical competence:

Waste treatment plants

5.—(1) Paragraph (2) of this regulation applies to a person who has made an application to the Waste Management Industry Training and Advisory Board for a "Treatment operations: inert waste (level 3)" certificate of technical competence before 10th August 1994, in a case where that application has not been determined.

(2) Unless he notifies the Board in writing that he does not wish this regulation to apply to him, the person mentioned in paragraph (1) shall be treated for the purposes of regulation 5 of the Waste Management Licensing Regulations 1994 as if the certificate for which he applied was a "Managing treatment operations: special waste (level 4)" certificate of technical competence.

(3) Paragraph (4) of this regulation applies to a person who has made an application to the Waste Management Industry Training and Advisory Board for a "Treatment operations: inert waste (level 3)" certificate of technical competence before 1st April 1996, in a case where that application has not been determined.

(4) Unless he notifies the Board in writing that he does not wish this regulation to apply to him, the person mentioned in paragraph (3) shall be treated for the purposes of regulation 4 of the Waste Management Licensing (Amendment etc.) Regulations 1995 as if the certificate for which he applied was a "Managing treatment operations: special waste (level 4)" certificate of technical competence.

APPENDIX 4

Principal Water Pollution Legislation: Scotland

CONTROL OF POLLUTION ACT 1974 (c. 40)

[PARTS IA AND II

GENERAL NOTE

The principal legislation governing water pollution controls in Scotland, which is contained in Part II of the Control of Pollution Act 1974, has been much amended over the years, for example, by Sched. 23 to the Water Act 1989 and, most recently, by Scheds. 16 and 22 to the Environment Act 1995. The 1995 Act also inserts a new Part IA in respect of abandoned mines into the 1974 Act.

In view of these sweeping amendments, the editor considered that it would be appropriate to provide a consolidated version of Parts IA and II of the 1974 Act for readers north of the border.

It should be noted that as at April 1, 1996, Part IA had only been brought into force in so far as ss.30Y and 30Z conferred power on the Secretary of State to make regulations (S.I. 1995 No. 2649).

In relation to Part II, as at April 1, 1996, all except the following provisions had been brought into force:

     s.46(1A) and (1B); (3A) and (3B) (see footnotes 41 and 48 on p. 915)
     ss.46A-D (see footnote 49 on p. 915)
     ss.49A-B (see footnote 68 on p. 920)

together with the minor amendments to

     s.46(1) made by the 1995 Act, Sched. 22, para. 29(21)(a)(i) (see footnote 34 on p. 914);
     s.46(2) made by the 1995 Act, Sched. 22, para. 29(21)(c) (see footnote 43 on p. 915); and
     s.46(3)(b) made by the 1995 Act, Sched. 22, para. 29(21)(d)(i) and (ii) (see footnotes 46 and 47 on p. 915).

[¹PART IA

Abandoned mines

Introductory

     30Y.—(1) For the purposes of this Part, "abandonment", in relation to a mine,—

     (a) subject to paragraph (b) below, includes—
         (i) the discontinuance of any or all of the operations for the removal of water from the mine;
         (ii) the cessation of working of any relevant seam, vein or vein-system;
         (iii) the cessation of use of any shaft or outlet of the mine;
         (iv) in the case of a mine in which activities other than mining activities are carried on (whether or not mining activities are also carried on in the mine)—
             (A) the discontinuance of some or all of those other activities in the mine; and

---

¹ Sections 30Y–Z inserted by the 1995 Act, s.59. It appears that these sections have been inserted into COPA out of sequence. They should follow s.30J but in fact they are inserted before s.30A by s.59 of the 1995 Act.

889

       (B)   any substantial change in the operations for the removal of water from the mine; but

 (b) does not include—

    (i) the abandonment of any rights, interests or liabilities by the Accountant in Bankruptcy acting as permanent or interim trustee in a sequestration (within the meaning of the Bankruptcy (Scotland) Act 1985); or

    (ii) any disclaimer under section 178 or 315 of the Insolvency Act 1986 (power of liquidator, or trustee of bankrupt's estate, to disclaim onerous property) by the official receiver acting in a compulsory capacity;

and cognate expressions shall be construed accordingly.

(2) In this Part, except where the context otherwise requires—

"acting in a compulsory capacity", in case of the official receiver, means acting as—

  (a) liquidator of a company;

  (b) receiver or manager of a bankrupt's estate, pursuant to section 287 of the Insolvency Act 1986;

  (c) trustee of a bankrupt's estate;

  (d) liquidator of an insolvent partnership;

  (e) trustee of an insolvent partnership;

  (f) trustee, or receiver or manager, of the insolvent estate of a deceased person;

"the official receiver" has the same meaning as it has in the Insolvency Act 1986 by virtue of section 399(1) of that Act;

"relevant seam, vein or vein-system", in the case of any mine, means any seam, vein or vein-system for the purpose of, or in connection with, whose working any excavation constituting or comprised in the mine was made.

(3) This Part extends only to Scotland.

Mine operators to give SEPA six months' notice of any proposed abandonment

30Z.—(1) If, in the case of any mine, there is to be an abandonment at any time after the expiration of the initial period, it shall be the duty of the operator of the mine to give notice of the proposed abandonment to SEPA at least six months before the abandonment takes effect.

(2) A notice under subsection (1) above shall contain such information (if any) as is prescribed for the purpose, which may include information about the operator's opinion as to any consequences of the abandonment.

(3) A person who fails to give notice required by subsection (1) above shall be guilty of an offence and liable—

  (a) on summary conviction, to a fine not exceeding the statutory maximum;

  (b) on conviction on indictment, to a fine.

(4) A person shall not be guilty of an offence under subsection (3) above if—

  (a) the abandonment happens in an emergency in order to avoid danger to life or health; and

  (b) notice of the abandonment, containing such information as may be prescribed, is given as soon as reasonably practicable after the abandonment has happened.

(5) Where the operator of a mine is—

  (a) the Accountant in Bankruptcy acting as permanent or interim trustee in a sequestration (within the meaning of the Bankruptcy (Scotland) Act 1985); or

  (b) the official receiver acting in a compulsory capacity,

he shall not be guilty of an offence under subsection (3) above by reason of any failure to give the notice required by subsection (1) above if, as soon as is reasonably practicable (whether before or after the abandonment), he gives to SEPA notice of the abandonment or proposed abandonment, containing such information as may be prescribed.

(6) Where a person gives notice under subsection (1), (4)(b) or (5) above, he shall publish prescribed particulars of, or relating to, the notice in one or more local newspapers circulating in the locality where the mine is situated.

(7) Where SEPA—
(a) receives notice under this section or otherwise learns of an abandonment or proposed abandonment in the case of any mine, and
(b) considers that, in consequence of the abandonment or proposed abandonment taking effect, any land has or is likely to become contaminated land, within the meaning of Part IIA of the Environmental Protection Act 1990,

it shall be the duty of SEPA to inform the local authority in whose area that land is situated of the abandonment or proposed abandonment.

(8) In this section—
"the initial period" means the period of six months beginning with the day on which subsection (1) above comes into force;
"local authority" means a council constituted under section 2 of the Local Government etc. (Scotland) Act 1994.]

PART II

²**Waters to which Part II applies**

30A.—(1) This part applies to any waters (in this Part referred to as "controlled waters") of any of the following classes—
(a) relevant territorial waters, that is to say, subject to subsection (5) below, the waters which extend seaward for three miles from the baselines from which the breadth of the territorial sea adjacent to Scotland is measured;
(b) coastal waters, that is to say, any waters which are within the area which extends landward from those baselines as far as the limit of the highest tide or, in the case of the waters of any relevant river or watercourse, as far as the fresh-water limit of the river or watercourse, together with the waters of any enclosed dock which adjoins waters within that area;
(c) inland waters, that is to say, the waters of any relevant loch or pond or of so much of any relevant river or watercourse as is above the fresh-water limit;
(d) ground waters, that is to say, any waters contained in underground strata, or in—
(i) a well, borehole or similar work sunk into underground strata, including any adit or passage constructed in connection with the well, borehole or work for facilitating the collection of water in the well, borehole or work; or
(ii) any excavation into underground strata where the level of water in the excavation depends wholly or mainly on water entering it from the strata.

(2) The Secretary of State—
(a) shall deposit maps with [³SEPA] showing what appear to him to be the fresh-water limits of every relevant river or watercourse [⁴...]; and

---

² Sections 30A–42, substituted for ss.31–42 by the Water Act 1989, s.168, Sched. 23, para. 4.
³ Substituted for the words "each river purification authority" by the 1995 Act, s.120 and Sched. 22, para. 29(2).
⁴ The words "in the area of that authority" are repealed by the 1995 Act, s.120; Sched. 22, para. 29(3) and Sched. 24.

(b) may from time to time, if he considers it appropriate to do so by reason of any change of what appears to him to be the fresh-water limit of any river or watercourse, deposit a map showing a revised limit for that river or watercourse;

and in subsection (1) above "fresh-water limit", in relation to any river or watercourse, means the place for the time being shown as the fresh-water limit of that river or watercourse in the latest map deposited for that river or watercourse under this subsection.

(3) It shall be the duty of [⁵SEPA] to keep any maps deposited with it under subsection (2) above available, at all reasonable times, for inspection by the public free of charge.

(4) In this section—

"miles" means international nautical miles of 1,852 metres;

"loch or pond" includes a reservoir of any description;

"relevant loch or pond" means (subject to subsection (5) below) any loch or pond which (whether it is natural or artificial or above or below ground) discharges into a relevant river or watercourse or into another loch or pond which is itself a relevant loch or pond;

"relevant river or watercourse" means any river or watercourse (including an underground river or watercourse and an artificial river or watercourse) which is neither a public sewer nor a sewer or drain which drains into a public sewer;

(5) The Secretary of State may by order provide—

(a) that any area of the territorial sea adjacent to Scotland is to be treated as if it were an area of relevant territorial waters for the purposes of this Part;

(b) that any loch or pond which does not discharge into a relevant river or watercourse or into a relevant loch or pond is to be treated for those purposes as a relevant loch or pond.

(6) The power of the Secretary of State to make an order under subsection (5) above shall be exercisable by statutory instrument subject to annulment in pursuance of a resolution of either House of Parliament; and such an order may—

(a) contain such supplemental, consequential and transitional provision as the Secretary of State considers appropriate; and

(b) make different provision for different cases, including different provision in relation to different persons, circumstances or localities.

Classification of quality waters

30B.—(1) The Secretary of State may, in relation to any description of controlled waters (being a description applying to some or all of the waters of a particular class or of two or more different classes), by regulations prescribe a system of classifying the quality of those waters according to criteria specified in the regulations.

(2) The criteria specified in regulations under this section in relation to any classification shall consist of one or more of the following, that is to say—

(a) general requirements as to the purposes for which the waters to which the classification is applied are to be suitable;

(b) specific requirements as to the substances that are to be present in or absent from the water and as to the concentrations of substances which are or are required to be present in the water;

(c) specific requirements as to other characteristics of those waters;

---

⁵ Substituted for the words "each river purification authority" by the 1995 Act, s.120, Sched. 22, para. 29(2).

and, for the purposes of any such classification, regulations under this section may provide that the question whether prescribed requirements are satisfied may be determined by reference to such samples as may be prescribed.

Water quality objectives

30C.—(1) For the purpose of maintaining and improving the quality of controlled waters the Secretary of State may, by serving a notice on [⁶SEPA] specifying—
(a) one or more of the classifications for the time being prescribed under section 30B above; and
(b) in relation to each specified classification, a date,
establish the water quality objectives for any waters [⁷...] which are, or are included in, waters of a description prescribed for the purposes of that section.
(2) The water quality objectives for any waters to which a notice under this section relates shall be the satisfaction by those waters, on and at all times after each date specified in the notice, of the requirements which at the time of the notice were the requirements for the classification in relation to which that date is so specified.
(3) Where the Secretary of State has established water quality objectives under this section for any waters he may review objectives for those waters if—
(a) five years or more have elapsed since the service of the last notice under subsection (1) or (6) of this section to be served in respect of those waters; or
(b) [⁸SEPA], after consultation with such persons as it considers appropriate, requests a review;
and the Secretary of State shall not exercise his power to establish objectives for any waters by varying the existing objectives for those waters except in consequence of such a review.
(4) Where the Secretary of State proposes to exercise his power under this section to establish or vary the objectives for any waters [⁹...] he shall—
(a) give notice to [¹⁰SEPA] setting out his proposal and specifying the period (not being less than three months from the date of publication of the notice) within which representations with respect to the proposal may be made; and
(b) consider any representations which are duly made;
and if he decides, after considering any such representations, to exercise his power to establish or vary those objectives, he may do so either in accordance with the proposal contained in the notice or in accordance with that proposal as modified in such a manner as he considers appropriate.
(5) A notice under subsection (4) above shall be given—
(a) by publishing the notice in such manner as the Secretary of State considers appropriate for bringing it to the attention of persons likely to be affected by it; and
(b) by serving a copy of the notice on [¹¹SEPA].
(6) If, on a review under this section or in consequence of any representations made following such a review for the purposes of subsection (4) above, the Secretary of State decides that the water quality objectives for

---

⁶ Substituted for the words "a river purification authority" by the 1995 Act, s.120 and Sched. 22, para. 29(2).
⁷ The words "within the area of the authority" are repealed by the 1995 Act, s.120; Sched. 22, para. 29(4)(a) and Sched. 24.
⁸ Substituted for the words "The river purification authority on which that notice has been served" by the 1995 Act, s.120 and Sched. 22, para. 29(4)(b).
⁹ The words "in the area of the river purification authority" are repealed by the 1995 Act, s.120; Sched. 22, para. 29(4)(c)(i); and Sched. 24.
¹⁰ Substituted for the words "that authority" by the 1995 Act, s.120 and Sched. 22, para. 29(4)(c)(ii),
¹¹ Substituted for the words "the authority" by the 1995 Act, s.120 and Sched. 22, para. 29(4)(d).

any waters [12...] should remain unchanged, he shall serve notice of that decision on [13SEPA].

General duties to achieve and maintain objectives etc.

30D.—(1) It shall be the duty of the Secretary of State and of [14SEPA] to exercise the powers conferred on him or it by or under the following provisions of this Part or the provisions of the Rivers (Prevention of Pollution)(Scotland) Acts 1951 and 1965 [15and of the Environmental Protection Act 1990] in such manner as ensures, so far as it is practicable by the exercise of those powers to do so, that the water quality objectives specified for any waters in a notice under section 30C above, or in a notice under [15Asection 83 of the Water Resources Act 1991], are achieved at all times.

(2) It shall be the duty of [16SEPA], for the purposes of the carrying out of its functions under the following provisions of this Part or the provisions of the Rivers (Prevention of Pollution)(Scotland) Acts 1951 and 1965, to monitor the extent of pollution in controlled waters.

Consultation and collaboration

30E. In the performance of [17its] functions in relation to waters partly in Scotland and partly in England [18SEPA] shall, in matters of common interest, consult and collaborate with the [19Environment Agency].

[20Pollution Offences

30F.—(1) A person contravenes this section if he causes or knowingly permits any poisonous, noxious or polluting matter or any solid waste matter to enter any controlled waters.

(2) A person contravenes this section if he causes or knowingly permits any matter, other than trade effluent or sewage effluent, to enter controlled waters by being discharged from a sewer or from a drain in contravention of a prohibition imposed under section 30G below.

(3) A person contravenes this section if he causes or knowingly permits any trade effluent or sewage effluent to be discharged—

    (a) into any controlled waters; or

---

12 The words "in the area of a river purification authority" are repealed by the 1995 Act, s.120; Sched. 22, para. 29(4)(e)(i); and Sched. 24.

13 Substituted for the words "that authority" by the 1995 Act, s.120 and Sched. 22, para. 29(4)(e)(ii).

14 Substituted for the words "each river purification authority" by the 1995 Act, s.120 and Sched. 22, para. 29(2).

15 Words inserted by the Environmental Protection Act 1990, ss.161(1), 164(3), and Sched. 15, para. 15(2).

15A Substituted by the Water Consolidation (Consequential Provisions) Act 1991, s.2 and Sched. 1, para. 27(1).

16 Substituted for the words "each river purification authority" by the 1995 Act, s.120 and Sched. 22, para. 29(2).

17 Substituted for the word "their" by the 1995 Act, s.120 and Sched. 22, para. 29(5)(a).

18 Substituted for the words "river purification authorities" by the 1995 Act, s.120 and Sched. 22, para. 29(5)(b).

19 Substituted for the words "National Rivers Authority" by the 1995 Act, s.120 and Sched. 22, para. 29(5)(c).

20 Sections 30F–J inserted by the 1995 Act, s.106 and Sched. 16, para. 2.

(b) from land in Scotland, through a pipe, into the sea outside the seaward limits of controlled waters.

(4) A person contravenes this section if he causes or knowingly permits any trade effluent or sewage effluent to be discharged, in contravention of any prohibition imposed under section 30G below, from a building or from any plant—

(a) on to or into any land; or

(b) into any waters of a loch or pond which are not inland waters.

(5) A person contravenes this section if he causes or knowingly permits any matter whatever to enter any inland waters so as to tend (either directly or in combination with other matter which he or another person causes or permits to enter those waters) to impede the proper flow of the waters in a manner leading, or likely to lead, to a substantial aggravation of—

(a) pollution due to other causes; or

(b) the consequences of such pollution.

(6) Subject to the following provisions of this Part, a person who contravenes this section shall be guilty of an offence and liable—

(a) on summary conviction, to imprisonment for a term not exceeding three months or to a fine not exceeding £20,000 or to both;

(b) on conviction on indictment, to imprisonment for a term not exceeding two years or to a fine or to both.

Prohibition of certain discharges by notice or regulations

30G.—(1) For the purposes of section 30F above a discharge of any effluent or other matter is, in relation to any person, in contravention of a prohibition imposed under this section if, subject to the following provisions of this section—

(a) SEPA has given that person notice prohibiting him from making or, as the case may be, continuing the discharge; or

(b) SEPA has given that person notice prohibiting him from making or, as the case may be, continuing the discharge unless specified conditions are observed, and those conditions are not observed.

(2) For the purposes of section 30F above a discharge of any effluent or other matter is also in contravention of a prohibition imposed under this section if the effluent or matter discharged—

(a) contains a prescribed substance or a prescribed concentration of such a substance; or

(b) derives from a prescribed process or from a process involving the use of prescribed substances or the use of such substances in quantities which exceed the prescribed amounts.

(3) Nothing in subsection (1) above shall authorise the giving of notice for the purposes of that subsection in respect of discharges from a vessel; and nothing in any regulations made by virtue of subsection (2) above shall require any discharge from a vessel to be treated as a discharge in contravention of a prohibition imposed under this section.

(4) A notice given for the purposes of subsection (1) above shall expire at such time as may be specified in the notice.

(5) The time specified for the purposes of subsection (4) above shall not be before the end of the period of three months beginning with the day on which the notice is given, except in a case where SEPA is satisfied that there is an emergency which requires the prohibition in question to come into force at such time before the end of that period as may be so specified.

(6) Where, in the case of such a notice for the purposes of subsection (1) above as (but for this subsection) would expire at a time at or after the end of the said period of three months, an application is made before that time for a consent in pursuance of section 34 of this Act in respect of the discharge to which the notice relates, that notice shall be deemed not to expire until the result of the application becomes final—

(a) on the grant or withdrawal of the application;
(b) on the expiration, without the bringing of an appeal with respect to the decision on the application, of any period prescribed by virtue of section 39(2) below as the period within which any such appeal must be brought; or
(c) on the withdrawal or determination of any such appeal.

Discharges into and from sewers etc.

30H.—(1) For the purposes of section 30F above where—
(a) any sewage effluent is discharged as mentioned in subsection (3) or (4) of that section from any sewer or works—
    (i) vested in a sewerage authority; or
    (ii) vested in a person other than a sewerage authority and forming (or forming part of) a system provided by him such as is mentioned in section 98(1)(b) of the Local Government etc. (Scotland) Act 1994; and
(b) the authority or, as the case may be, the person did not cause or knowingly permit the discharge but was bound (either unconditionally or subject to conditions which were observed) to receive into the sewer or works matter included in the discharge,
the authority or person shall be deemed to have caused the discharge.

(2) A sewerage authority shall not be guilty of an offence under section 30F of this Act by reason only of the fact that a discharge from a sewer or works vested in the authority contravenes conditions of a consent relating to the discharge if—
(a) the contravention is attributable to a discharge which another person caused or permitted to be made into the sewer or works; and
(b) the authority either was not bound to receive the discharge into the sewer or works or was bound to receive it there subject to conditions but the conditions were not observed; and
(c) the authority could not reasonably have been expected to prevent the discharge into the sewer or works;
and a person shall not be guilty of such an offence in consequence of a discharge which he caused or permitted to be made into a sewer or works vested in a sewerage authority if the authority was bound to receive the discharge there either unconditionally or subject to conditions which were observed.

(3) A person in whom any such sewer or works as is described in subsection (1)(a)(ii) above is vested (such person being in this subsection referred to as a "relevant person") shall not be guilty of an offence under section 30F of this Act by reason only of the fact that a discharge from the sewer or works contravenes conditions of a consent relating to the discharge if—
(a) the contravention is attributable to a discharge which another person caused or permitted to be made into the sewer or works; and
(b) the relevant person either was not bound to receive the discharge into the sewer or works or was bound to receive it there subject to conditions but the conditions were not observed; and
(c) the relevant person could not reasonably have been expected to prevent the discharge into the sewer or works;
and another person shall not be guilty of such an offence in consequence of a discharge which he caused or permitted to be made into a sewer or works vested in a relevant person if the relevant person was bound to receive the discharge there either unconditionally or subject to conditions which were observed.

Defence to principal offences in respect of authorised discharges

30I.—(1) Subject to the following provisions of this section, a person shall not be guilty of an offence under section 30F above in respect of the entry of any matter into any waters or any discharge if the entry occurs or the discharge is made under and in accordance with, or as a result of, any act or omission under and in accordance with—

(a) a consent in pursuance of section 34 of this Act or under Chapter II of Part III of the Water Resources Act 1991 (which makes corresponding provision for England and Wales);

(b) an authorisation for a prescribed process designated for central control granted under Part I of the Environmental Protection Act 1990;

(c) a waste management or disposal licence;

(d) a licence granted under Part II of the Food and Environment Protection Act 1985;

(e) section 33 of the Water (Scotland) Act 1980 (temporary discharge by authorities in connection with the construction of works);

(f) any provision of a local Act or statutory order which expressly confers power to discharge effluent into water; or

(g) any prescribed enactment.

(2) Nothing in any disposal licence shall be treated for the purposes of subsection (1) above as authorising—

(a) any such entry or discharge as is mentioned in subsections (2) to (4) of section 30F above; or

(b) any act or omission so far as it results in any such entry or discharge.

(3) In this section—

"disposal licence" means a licence issued in pursuance of section 5 of this Act;

"local Act" includes enactments in a public general Act which amend a local Act;

"statutory order" means an order, byelaw, scheme or award made under an Act of Parliament, including an order or scheme confirmed by Parliament or brought into operation in accordance with special parliamentary procedure; and

"waste management licence" means such a licence granted under Part II of the Environmental Protection Act 1990.

Other defences to principal offences

30J.—(1) A person shall not be guilty of an offence under section 30F above in respect of the entry of any matter into any waters or any discharge if—

(a) the entry is caused or permitted, or the discharge is made, in an emergency in order to avoid danger to life or health;

(b) that person takes all such steps as are reasonably practicable in the circumstances for minimising the extent of the entry or discharge and of its polluting effects; and

(c) particulars of the entry or discharge are furnished to SEPA as soon as reasonably practicable after the entry occurs.

(2) A person shall not be guilty of an offence under section 30F above by reason of his causing or permitting any discharge of trade or sewage effluent from a vessel.

(3) A person shall not be guilty of an offence under section 30F above by reason only of his permitting water from an abandoned mine or an abandoned part of a mine to enter controlled waters.

(4) Subsection (3) above shall not apply to the owner or former operator of any mine or part of a mine if the mine or part in question became abandoned after 31st December 1999.

(5) In determining for the purposes of subsection (4) above whether a mine or part of a mine became abandoned before, on or after 31st December 1999 in a case where the mine or part has become abandoned on two or more occasions, of which—
(a) at least one falls on or before that date, and
(b) at least one falls after that date,
the mine or part shall be regarded as becoming abandoned after that date (but without prejudice to the operation of subsection (3) above in relation to that mine or part at, or in relation to, any time before the first of those occasions which falls after that date).

(6) Where, immediately before a part of a mine becomes abandoned, that part is the only part of the mine not falling to be regarded as abandoned for the time being, the abandonment of that part shall not be regarded for the purposes of subsection (4) or (5) above as constituting the abandonment of the mine, but only of that part of it.

(7) A person shall not, otherwise than in respect of the entry of any poisonous, noxious or polluting matter into any controlled waters, be guilty of an offence under section 30F above by reason of his depositing the solid refuse of a mine or quarry on any land so that it falls or is carried into inland waters if—
(a) he deposits the refuse on the land with the consent of SEPA;
(b) no other site for the deposit is reasonably practicable; and
(c) he takes all reasonably practicable steps to prevent the refuse from entering those inland waters.

(8) A roads authority obliged or entitled to keep open a drain by virtue of section 31 of the Roads (Scotland) Act 1984 shall not be guilty of an offence under section 30F above by reason of its causing or permitting any discharge to be made from a drain kept open by virtue of that section unless the discharge is made in contravention of a prohibition imposed under section 30G above.]

Control of pollution of rivers and coastal waters etc.

31. [²¹(1)–(3) ...]
(4) Where it appears to the Secretary of State that, with a view to preventing poisonous, noxious or polluting matter from entering any controlled waters, it is appropriate to prohibit or restrict the carrying on in a particular area of activities which he considers are likely to result in pollution of the waters, then, subject to subsection (5) below, he may by regulations—
(a) designate that area; and
(b) provide that prescribed activities shall not be carried on at any place within the area except with the consent (which shall not be unreasonably withheld) of [²²SEPA] and in accordance with any reasonable conditions to which the consent is subject;
(c) provide that a contravention of the regulations shall be an offence and prescribe the maximum penalty for the offence; and
(d) make provision for the imposition by [²³SEPA] of charges in respect of the consent mentioned in paragraph (b) above.

(5) It shall be the duty of the Secretary of State, before he makes any regulations under subsection (4) above—
(a) to publish in the *Edinburgh Gazette* and in at least one newspaper circulating in the area in question a copy of the proposed regulations and a notice specifying—

---

²¹ Repealed by the 1995 Act, s.106, Sched. 16, para. 3 and Sched. 24.
²² Substituted for the words "the river purification authority in whose area the place is situated" by the 1995 Act, s.120 and Sched. 22, para. 29(6)(a).
²³ Substituted for the words "river purification authorities" by the 1995 Act, s.120 and Sched. 22, para. 29(2).

(i) a period of not less than twenty-eight days, beginning with the date on which the notice is first published, within which objections to the proposed regulations may be made, and

(ii) the person to whom such objections may be made; and

(b) to consider any objections to the proposed regulations which are made within that period and, if such an objection is so made by a prescribed person and is not withdrawn, to cause a local inquiry to be held in pursuance of section 96 of this Act with respect to the proposed regulations;

and the Secretary of State may, after considering any such objections as are mentioned in paragraph (b) of this subsection and the report of any person appointed to hold a local inquiry with respect to the proposed regulations, make the regulations either in the form in which a copy of them was published in pursuance of this subsection or in that form with such modifications as he considers appropriate.

(6) [²⁴SEPA] may by byelaws make such provisions as [²⁵it] considers appropriate for prohibiting or regulating the washing or cleaning, in any controlled waters [²⁶...], of things of a kind specified in the byelaws; and a person who contravenes any byelaws made by virtue of this subsection shall be guilty of an offence and liable on summary conviction to a fine not exceeding level 4 on the standard scale or such smaller sum as is specified in the byelaws.

[²⁷(7) ...]

(8) The maximum penalty prescribed in pursuance of subsection (4) of this section shall not exceed the penalties specified in [²⁸section 30F(6) above].

(9) In subsection (4) of this section, the reference to the entry of poisonous, noxious or polluting matter into controlled waters shall not include a reference to the entry of nitrate into controlled waters as a result of, or of anything done in connection with, the use of any land for agricultural purposes.

[²⁸ᴬ(10) ...]

Requirements to take precautions against pollution

31A.—(1) The Secretary of State may by regulations make provision—

(a) for prohibiting a person from having custody or control of any poisonous, noxious or polluting matter unless prescribed works and prescribed precautions and other steps have been carried out or taken for the purpose of preventing the matter from entering controlled waters;

(b) for requiring a person who already has custody or control of, or makes use of, any such matter to carry out such works for that purpose and to take such precautions and other steps for that purpose as may be prescribed.

(2) Without prejudice to the generality of the power conferred by subsection (1) above, regulations under that subsection may—

(a) confer power on [²⁹SEPA]—

(i) to determine for the purposes of the regulations the circumstances in which a person is required to carry out works or take precautions or other steps; and

---

²⁴ Substituted for the words "A river purification authority" by the 1995 Act, s.120 and Sched. 22, para. 29(2).

²⁵ Substituted for the words "the authority" by the 1995 Act, s.120 and Sched. 22, para. 29(6)(b)(i).

²⁶ The words "in its area" are repealed by the 1995 Act, s.120 and Sched. 22, para. 29(6)(b)(ii) and Sched. 24.

²⁷ Repealed by the 1995 Act, s.106, Sched. 16, para. 3 and Sched. 24.

²⁸ Substituted for the words "paragraphs (a) and (b) of the preceding subsection" by the 1995 Act, s.106 and Sched. 16, para. 4.

²⁸ᴬ Repealed by the 1995 Act, s.106, Sched. 16, para. 3 and Sched. 24.

²⁹ Substituted for the words "the river purification authority" by 1995 Act, s.120 and Sched. 22, para. 29(2).

    (ii) by notice to that person, to impose the requirement and to specify or describe the works, precautions or other steps which that person is required to carry out or take;

   (b) provide for appeals to the Secretary of State against notices served by [³⁰SEPA] in pursuance of provisions made by virtue of paragraph (a) above; and

   (c) provide that a contravention of the regulations shall be an offence the penalty for which shall be—

    (i) on summary conviction, imprisonment for a term not exceeding three months or to a fine not exceeding [³⁰ᴬ£20,000] or to both;

    (ii) on conviction on indictment, to imprisonment for a term not exceeding two years or to a fine or both.

Nitrate sensitive areas

31B.—(1) Where the Secretary of State considers that it is appropriate to do so with a view to achieving the following purpose, that is to say, preventing or controlling the entry of nitrate into controlled waters as a result of, or of anything done in connection with, the use of any land for agricultural purposes, he may by order designate that land, together with any other land to which he considers it appropriate to apply the designation, as a nitrate sensitive area.

(2) Where any area has been designated as a nitrate sensitive area by an order under this section and the Secretary of State considers that it is appropriate to do so with a view to achieving the purpose mentioned in subsection (1) above, he may, subject to such restrictions (if any) as may be set out in the order, enter into an agreement under which, in consideration of payments to be made by him—

   (a) [³⁰ᴮthe owner of the dominium utile] of any agricultural land in that area; or

   (b) where any such owner has given his written consent to the agreement being entered into by any person having another interest in that land, that other person,

accepts such obligations with respect to the management of that land or otherwise as may be imposed by the agreement.

(3) Where it appears to the Secretary of State in relation to any area which is, or is to be, designated by an order under this section as a nitrate sensitive area that it is appropriate for provision for the imposition of requirements, prohibitions or restrictions to be contained in an order under this section (as well as for him to be able to enter into such agreements as are mentioned in subsection (2) above), he may, by a subsequent order under this section or, as the case may be, by the order designating that area—

   (a) with a view to achieving the purpose mentioned in subsection (1) above, require, prohibit or restrict the carrying on on or in relation to any agricultural land in that area of such activities as may be specified or described in the order; and

   (b) provide for such amounts (if any) as may be specified in or determined under the order to be paid by the Secretary of State, to such persons as may be so specified or determined, in respect of the obligations imposed in relation to that area on those persons by virtue of paragraph (a) above.

(4) Without prejudice to the generality of subsection (3) above, provision contained in an order under this section by virtue of that subsection may—

   (a) confer power upon the Secretary of State to determine for the purposes of the order the circumstances in which the carrying on of

---

³⁰ Substituted for the words "a river purification authority" by the 1995 Act, s.120 and Sched. 22, para. 29(2).

³⁰ᴬ Substituted by the Environmental Protection Act 1990, s.145(2).

³⁰ᴮ Substituted by the Agricultural Holdings (Scotland) Act 1991, s.88 and Sched. 11, para. 39.

any activities is required, prohibited or restricted and to determine the activities to which any such requirement, prohibition or restriction applies;

(b) provide for any requirement to carry on any activity not to apply in cases where the Secretary of State has consented to a failure to carry on that activity and any conditions on which the consent has been given are complied with;

(c) apply a prohibition or restriction in respect of any activities to cases where the activities are carried on without the consent of the Secretary of State or in contravention of any conditions subject to which any such consent is given;

(d) provide that a contravention of a requirement, prohibition or restriction contained in the order or in a condition of a consent given in relation to or for the purposes of any such requirement, prohibition or restriction shall be an offence the maximum penalties for which shall not exceed the maximum penalties specified in [[31]subsection (6) of section 30F above].

(e) provide for amounts paid in pursuance of any provision contained in the order to be repaid at such times and in such circumstances and with such interest as may be specified in or determined under the order;

(f) provide (subject to any regulations under subsection (6) below) for anything falling to be determined under the order by any person to be determined in accordance with such procedure and by reference to such matters and to the opinion of such persons as may be specified in the order.

(5) The Secretary of State shall not make an order under this section except in accordance with any applicable provisions of Schedule 1A to this Act.

(6) The Secretary of State may, for the purposes of any orders under this section which require his consent to the carrying on of any activities or to any failure to carry on any activity, by regulations make provision with respect to—

(a) applications for any such consent;

(b) the conditions of any such consent;

(c) the revocation or variation of any such consent;

(d) the reference to arbitration of disputes about determinations on any such application;

(e) the imposition of charges where such an application has been made, such a consent has been given or there has been any act or omission in pursuance of any such consent; and

(f) the registration of any such application or consent.

Registering of agreement

31C.—(1) An agreement under subsection (2) of section 31B above may—

(a) where the land is registered in the Land Register of Scotland, be registered in that register;

(b) in any other case, be recorded in the appropriate Division of the General Register of Sasines.

(2) An agreement registered or recorded under subsection (1) above shall be enforceable at the instance of the Secretary of State against persons deriving title to the land (including any person acquiring right to a tenancy by assignation or succession) from the person who entered into the agreement; provided that such an agreement shall not be enforceable

---

[31] Substituted for the words "subsection (7) of section 31 above" by the 1995 Act, s.106 and Sched. 16, para. 5.

against a third party who shall have in good faith and for value acquired right (whether completed by infeftment or not) to the land prior to the agreement being registered or recorded as aforesaid, or against any person deriving title from such third party.

(3) Notwithstanding the terms of any agreement registered or recorded under subsection (1) above, the parties to the agreement or any persons deriving title from them may at any time agree to terminate it; and such an agreement to terminate it shall be registered or recorded in the same manner as was the original agreement.

Powers of entry in relation to agreements under section 31B

31D. [³²...]

Consent of discharges of trade and sewage effluent etc. into rivers and coastal waters etc.

32. [³³...]

Control of sanitary appliances on vessels

33.—(1) [³⁴SEPA] may by byelaws make such provision as [³⁵it] considers appropriate for prohibiting or regulating the keeping or use, on any controlled waters [³⁶...], of vessels of a kind specified in the byelaws which are provided with sanitary appliances; and a person who contravenes any byelaw made by virtue of this section shall be guilty of an offence.

(2) The Secretary of State may by order provide that any byelaws specified in the order which were made by virtue of section 25(1)(c) of the Rivers (Prevention of Pollution) (Scotland) Act 1951 (byelaws) shall have effect, with such modifications (if any) as are so specified, as if made by virtue of the preceding subsection.

(3) In this section "sanitary appliance" means a water closet or other prescribed appliance (except a sink, bath and a shower-bath) which is designed to permit polluting matter to pass into the water on which the vessel in question is for the time being situated.

(4) A person guilty of an offence by virtue of any of the preceding provisions of this section shall be liable on summary conviction to a fine of an amount not exceeding level 4 on the standard scale or such smaller sum as may be specified in the byelaws.

Consents for discharges of trade and sewage effluent etc.

34.—(1) An application to [³⁷SEPA] for consent in pursuance of this section for discharges of any effluent or other matter shall be accompanied or supplemented by all such information as [³⁸SEPA] may reasonably require; and [³⁹SEPA] may if it thinks fit treat an application for consent for discharges at two or more places as separate applications for consent for discharges at each of those places.

(2) Subject to the following section, it shall be the duty of [⁴⁰SEPA, in relation to an application for consent] made in pursuance of this section—

---

³² Repealed by the 1995 Act, s.120, Sched. 22 para. 29(7); and Sched. 24.
³³ Repealed by the 1995 Act, s.106, Sched. 16, para. 3; s.120 and Sched. 24.
³⁴ Substituted for the words "A river purification authority" by the 1995 Act, s.120 and Sched. 22, para. 29(2).
³⁵ Substituted for the words "the authority" by the 1995 Act, s.120 and Sched. 22, para. 29(8)(a).
³⁶ The words "in the area of the authority" are repealed by the 1995 Act, s.120, Sched. 22, para. 29(8)(b) and Sched. 24.
³⁷ Substituted for the words "a river purification authority" by the 1995 Act, s.120 and Sched. 22, para. 29(2).
³⁸ Substituted for the words "the authority" by the 1995 Act, s.120 and Sched. 22, para. 29(9)(a).
³⁹ *ibid.*
⁴⁰ Substituted for the words "a river purification authority to which an application for consent is" by the 1995 Act, s.120 and Sched. 22, para. 29(9)(b)(i).

(a) to give the consent either unconditionally or subject to conditions or to refuse it; and

(b) not to withhold the consent unreasonably;

and if within the period of [⁴¹four] months beginning with the date when an application for consent is received by [⁴²SEPA], or within such longer period as may at any time be agreed upon in writing between [⁴³SEPA] and the applicant, [⁴⁴SEPA] has neither given nor refused the consent nor informed the applicant that the application has been transmitted to the Secretary of State in pursuance of the following section, [⁴⁵the applicant may treat the consent applied for as having been refused].

(3) If it appears to [⁴⁶SEPA] that a person has, without [⁴⁷SEPA's] consent, caused or permitted matter to be discharged [⁴⁸...] in contravention of [⁴⁹section 30F(2) to (4)] of this Act and that a similar contravention by that person is likely, [⁵⁰SEPA] may if it thinks fit serve on him an instrument in writing giving its consent, subject to conditions specified in the instrument, for discharges of a kind so specified; but consent given in pursuance of this subsection shall not relate to any discharge which occurred before the instrument giving the consent was served on the recipient of the instrument.

(4) The conditions subject to which [⁵¹SEPA] may give its consent in pursuance of this section shall be such reasonable conditions as [⁵²SEPA] thinks fit; and without prejudice to the generality of the preceding provisions of this subsection those conditions may include reasonable conditions—

(a) as to the places at which the discharges to which the consent relates may be made and as to the design and construction of any outlets for the discharges;

(b) as to the nature, origin, composition, temperature, volume and rate of the discharges and as to the period during which the discharges may be made;

(c) as to the provision of facilities for taking samples of the matter discharged and in particular as to the provision, maintenance and use of manholes, inspection chambers, observation wells and boreholes in connection with the discharges;

(d) as to the provision, maintenance and testing of meters for measuring the volume and rate of the discharges and apparatus for determining the nature, composition and temperature of the discharges;

(e) as to the keeping of records of the nature, origin, composition, temperature, volume and rate of the discharges and in particular of records of readings of meters and other recording apparatus provided in accordance with any other condition attached to the consent;

(f) as to the making of returns and the giving of other information to [⁵³SEPA] about the nature, origin, composition, temperature, volume and rate of the discharges; and

(g) as to the steps to be taken, in relation to the discharges or by way of subjecting any substance likely to affect the description of matter

---

⁴¹ Substituted for the word "three" by the 1995 Act, s.120 and Sched. 22, para. 29(9)(b)(ii).
⁴² Substituted for the words "the authority" by 1995 Act, s.120 and Sched. 22, para. 29(9)(a).
⁴³ *ibid.*
⁴⁴ *ibid.*
⁴⁵ Substituted for the words "the authority shall be deemed to have refused the consent" by the 1995 Act, s.120 and Sched. 22, para. 29(9)(b)(iii).
⁴⁶ Substituted for the words "the authority" by the 1995 Act, s.120 and Sched. 22, para. 29(9)(a).
⁴⁷ *ibid.*
⁴⁸ The words "in its area" are repealed by the 1995 Act, s.120, Sched. 22, para. 29(9)(c) and Sched. 24.
⁴⁹ Substituted for the words "section 32(1)" by the 1995 Act, s.106 and Sched. 16, para. 6.
⁵⁰ Substituted for the words "the authority" by the 1995 Act, s.120 and Sched. 22, para. 29(9)(a).
⁵¹ *ibid.*
⁵² *ibid.*
⁵³ *ibid.*

discharged to treatment or any other process, for minimising the
polluting effects of the discharges on any controlled waters;
and it is hereby declared that consent may be given in pursuance of this
section subject to different conditions in respect of different periods.

(5) A person who, in an application for consent in pursuance of this
section, makes any statement which he knows to be false in a material
particular or recklessly makes any statement which is false in a material
particular shall be guilty of an offence and liable on summary conviction to a
fine not exceeding the statutory maximum or on conviction on indictment to
a fine.

Reference to Secretary of State of certain applications for consent

35.—(1) The Secretary of State may, either in consequence of representations made to him or otherwise, direct [⁵⁴SEPA] to transmit to him for
determination applications for consent in pursuance of the preceding section
which are specified in the direction or are of a kind so specified, and it shall
be the duty of [⁵⁵SEPA] to comply with the direction and to inform each
relevant applicant that his application has been transmitted to the Secretary
of State.

(2) Before determining an application transmitted to him by [⁵⁶SEPA] in
pursuance of this section the Secretary of State may if he thinks fit, and shall
if a request to be heard with respect to the application is made to him in
accordance with regulations by the applicant or [⁵⁷SEPA], cause a local
inquiry to be held in pursuance of section 96 of this Act into the application
or afford to the applicant and [⁵⁸SEPA] an opportunity of appearing before
and being heard by a person appointed by the Secretary of State for the
purpose.

(3) Where in pursuance of the preceding subsection the Secretary of State
affords to an applicant and [⁵⁹SEPA] an opportunity of appearing before
and being heard by a person with respect to the application in question, it
shall be the duty of the Secretary of State to afford an opportunity of
appearing before and being heard by that person to any person who, in
pursuance of subsection (1)(c) or (5) of the following section, has made
representations relating to the application.

(4) It shall be the duty of the Secretary of State to determine an
application transmitted to him by [⁶⁰SEPA] in pursuance of this section by
directing [⁶¹SEPA] to refuse its consent in pursuance of the preceding
section in consequence of the application or to give the consent either
unconditionally or subject to such conditions as are specified in the direction,
and it shall be the duty of [⁶²SEPA] to comply with the direction.

Provisions supplementary to ss.34 and 35

36.—(1) Where [⁶³SEPA] receives an application for consent in pursuance of section 34 of this Act or serves an instrument in pursuance of
subsection (3) of that section, it shall [⁶⁴subject to subsections (2A) and (2B)

---

⁵⁴ Substituted for the words "a river purification authority" by the 1995 Act, s.120 and Sched. 22, para. 29(2).
⁵⁵ Substituted for the words "the authority" by the 1995 Act, s.120 and Sched. 22, para. 29(10).
⁵⁶ Substituted for the words a river purification authority" by the 1995 Act, s.120 and Sched. 22, para. 29(2).
⁵⁷ Substituted for the words "the authority" by the 1995 Act, s.120 and Sched. 22, para. 29(10).
⁵⁸ *ibid.*
⁵⁹ Substituted for the words "a river purification authority" by the 1995 Act, s.120 and Sched. 22, para. 29(2).
⁶⁰ *ibid.*
⁶¹ Substituted for the words "the authority" by the 1995, s.120 and Sched. 22, para. 29(10).
⁶² *ibid.*
⁶³ Substituted for the words "a river purification authority" by the 1995 Act, s.120 and Sched. 22, para. 29(2).
⁶⁴ Inserted by the 1995 Act, s.120 and Sched. 22, para. 29(11)(a).

below] be the duty of [⁶⁵SEPA], before deciding whether to give or refuse consent in pursuance of the application or, as the case may be, after serving the instrument—

(a) to publish in the prescribed form notice of the application or instrument in two successive weeks in a newspaper or newspapers circulating in—

    (i) the area or areas in which the places are situated at which it is proposed in the application that the discharges should be made or, as the case may be, at which discharges are the subject of consent given by the instrument, and

    (ii) the area or areas appearing to [⁶⁶SEPA] to be in the vicinity of any controlled waters which [⁶⁷SEPA] considers likely to be affected by the discharges,

and, not earlier than the day following that on which the first publication of the notice is completed in all relevant areas in pursuance of the preceding provisions of this paragraph, to publish such a notice in the *Edinburgh Gazette*;

(b) to send copies of the application or instrument to each local authority in whose area [⁶⁸, and to each water authority within whose limits of supply,] it is proposed in the application that a discharge should be made or in whose area [⁶⁹, or within whose limits of supply,] a discharge is the subject of consent given by the instrument and, in the case of an application or instrument relating to coastal waters, relevant territorial waters or an application relating to waters outside the seaward limits of relevant territorial waters, to the Secretary of State; and

(c) to consider any written representations relating to the application or instrument which are made to [⁷⁰SEPA] by any person within the period of six weeks beginning with the date on which the notice of the application or instrument is published in the *Edinburgh Gazette*.

(2) For the purposes of subsection (1) above, "local authority" means [⁷¹council constituted under section 2 of the Local Government etc. (Scotland) Act 1994], and any place at sea at which it is proposed in an application that a discharge should be made shall be treated as situated at the point on land nearest to that place.

[⁷²(2A) A person who proposes to make, or has made, an application to SEPA for consent in pursuance of section 34 of this Act may apply to the Secretary of State within a prescribed period for a certificate providing that subsection (1) above shall not apply to that application.

(2B) If the Secretary of State is satisfied that—

    (i) it would be contrary to the interests of national security; or

    (ii) it would prejudice to an unreasonable degree the commercial interests of any person,

not to issue a certificate applied for under subsection (2A) above, he may issue the certificate and, if he does so, subsection (1) above shall not apply to the application specified in the certificate.]

(3) Where notice of an application is published by [⁷³SEPA] in pursuance

---

⁶⁵ Substituted for the words "the authority" by the 1995 Act, s.120 and Sched. 22, para. 29(10).

⁶⁶ *ibid.*

⁶⁷ *ibid.*

⁶⁸ Inserted by the Local Government etc. (Scotland) Act, Sched. 13, para. 95(3)(a)(i).

⁶⁹ Inserted by the Local Government etc. (Scotland) Act 1994, Sched. 13, para. 95(3)(a)(ii).

⁷⁰ Substituted for the words "the authority" by the 1995 Act, s.120 and Sched. 22, para. 29(10).

⁷¹ Inserted by the Local Government etc. (Scotland) Act 1994, Sched. 13, para. 95(3)(b).

⁷² Inserted by the 1995 Act, s.120 and Sched. 22, para. 29(11)(b).

⁷³ Substituted for the words "a river purification authority" by the 1995 Act, s.120 and Sched. 22, para. 29(2).

of subsection (1)(a) of this section, [⁷⁴SEPA] shall be entitled to recover the costs of publication from the applicant.

(4) [⁷⁵SEPA] shall be entitled to disregard the provisions of subsection (1) of this section in relation to an application (except so much of paragraph (b) of that subsection as requires copies of the application to be sent to the Secretary of State) if [⁷⁶SEPA] proposes to give consent in pursuance of the application and considers that the discharges in question will have no appreciable effect on the water into which they are proposed to be made.

(5) The preceding provisions of this section shall have effect with prescribed modifications in relation to an application which is the subject of a direction in pursuance of subsection (1) of the preceding section.

(6) Where [⁷⁷SEPA] proposes to give consent in pursuance of section 34 of this Act in consequence of an application in respect of which representations have been made in pursuance of subsection (1)(c) of this section then—

(a) it shall be the duty of [⁷⁸SEPA] to serve notice of the proposal on the person who made the representations and to include in the notice a statement of the effect of the following paragraph; and

(b) that person may, within the period of twenty-one days beginning with the day on which the notice of the proposal is served on him, request the Secretary of State in accordance with regulations to give a direction in pursuance of subsection (1) of the preceding section in respect of the application; and

(c) it shall be the duty of [⁷⁹SEPA] not to give consent in consequence of the application before the expiration of that period and, if within that period the said person makes a request in pursuance of the preceding paragraph and serves notice of the request on [⁸⁰SEPA], not to give consent in pursuance of the application unless the Secretary of State has given notice to [⁸¹SEPA] that he declines to comply with the request;

and in calculating in the case of any application period of [⁸²four] months mentioned in section 34(2) of this Act or a longer period there mentioned there shall be disregarded any period during which [⁸³SEPA] [⁸³ᴬto which the application was made] is prohibited by virtue of paragraph (c) of this subsection from giving consent in consequence of the application.

(7) A consent for any discharges which is given in pursuance of section 34 of this Act is not limited to discharges by a particular person and accordingly extends to the discharges in question which are made by any person.

Revocation of consents and alteration and imposition of conditions

37.—(1) [⁸⁴SEPA may from time to time review any consent given in pursuance of section 34 of this Act] and the conditions, if any, to which the consent is subject; and subject to the following section [⁸⁵SEPA] may, by a

---

⁷⁴ Substituted for the words "the authority" by the 1995 Act, s.120 and Sched. 22, para. 29(10).
⁷⁵ Substituted for the words "A river purification authority" by the 1995 Act, s.120 and Sched. 22, para. 29(2).
⁷⁶ Substituted for the words "the authority" by the 1995 Act, s.120 and Sched. 22, para. 29(10).
⁷⁷ Substituted for the words "a river purification authority" by the 1995 Act, s.120 and Sched. 22, para. 29(2).
⁷⁸ Substituted for the words "the authority" by the 1995 Act, s.120 and Sched. 22, para. 29(10).
⁷⁹ *ibid.*
⁸⁰ *ibid.*
⁸¹ *ibid.*
⁸² Substituted for the word "three" by the 1995 Act, s.120 and Sched. 22, para. 29(11)(c).
⁸³ Substituted for the words "the authority" by the 1995 Act, s.120 and Sched. 22, para. 29(10).
⁸³ᴬ These words should have been revoked in the light of the substitution of "SEPA" for the immediately preceding words, "the authority". However, the 1995 Act leaves these redundant words intact.
⁸⁴ Substituted for the words "It shall be the duty of a river purification authority by which a consent is given in pursuance of section 34 of this Act to review from time to time the consent" by the 1995 Act, s.120 and Sched. 22, para. 29(12).
⁸⁵ Substituted for the words "the authority" by the 1995 Act, s.120 and Sched. 22, para. 29(10).

notice served on the person making a discharge in pursuance of the consent, revoke the consent if it is reasonable to do so or make reasonable modifications of the said conditions, or, in the case of an unconditional consent, provide that it shall be subject to reasonable conditions specified in the notice.

(2) Subject to the following section, the Secretary of State may—

(a) for the purpose of enabling Her Majesty's Government in the United Kingdom to give effect to any Community obligation or to any international agreement to which the United Kingdom is for the time being a party;

(b) for the protection of public health or of flora and fauna dependent on an aquatic environment; or

(c) in consequence of any representations made to him or otherwise,

direct [⁸⁶SEPA] to serve a notice in pursuance of the preceding subsection containing such provisions as are specified in the direction and it shall be the duty of [⁸⁷SEPA] to comply with the direction; and if [⁸⁸SEPA] fails to serve the notice within such period as the Secretary of State may allow he may serve the notice on behalf of [⁸⁹SEPA], and it is hereby declared that for the purposes of this Part of the Act a notice served on behalf of [⁹⁰SEPA] by virtue of this subsection is served by [⁹¹SEPA].

Restriction on variation and revocation of consent and of previous variation

38.—(1) Each instrument signifying the consent of [⁹²SEPA] in pursuance of section 34 of this Act shall specify a period during which no notice in pursuance of subsection (1) or (2)(c) of the preceding section is to be served in respect of the consent without the written agreement of a person making a discharge in pursuance of the consent; and the said period shall be a reasonable period of not less than [⁹³four] years beginning with the day on which the consent takes effect.

(2) Each notice served by [⁹⁴SEPA] in pursuance of subsection (1) or (2)(c) of the preceding section (except a notice which only revokes a consent or conditions) shall specify a period during which a subsequent notice in pursuance of that subsection which alters the effect of the first-mentioned notice is not to be served without the written agreement of a person making a discharge in pursuance of the consent to which the first-mentioned notice relates; and the said period shall be a reasonable period of not less than [⁹⁵four] years beginning with the day on which the first-mentioned notice is served.

(3) [⁹⁶SEPA] shall be liable to pay compensation to any person in respect of any loss or damage sustained by that person as a result of [⁹⁷SEPA's] compliance with a direction given in relation to any consent by virtue of section 37(2)(b) of this Act if—

---

⁸⁶ Substituted for the words "a river purification authority" by the 1995 Act, s.120 and Sched. 22, para. 29(2).

⁸⁷ Substituted for the words "the authority" by the 1995 Act, s.120 and Sched. 22, para. 29(10).

⁸⁸ *ibid.*

⁸⁹ *ibid.*

⁹⁰ *ibid.*

⁹¹ *ibid.*

⁹² Substituted for the words "a river purification authority" by the 1995 Act, s.120 and Sched. 22, para. 29(2).

⁹³ Substituted for the word "two" by the 1995 Act, s.120 and Sched. 22, para. 29(13).

⁹⁴ Substituted for the words "a river purification authority" by the 1995 Act, s.120 and Sched. 22, para. 29(2).

⁹⁵ Substituted for the word "two" by the 1995 Act, s.120 and Sched. 22, para. 29(13).

⁹⁶ Substituted for the words "The authority" by the 1995 Act, s.120 and Sched. 22, para. 29(10).

⁹⁷ Substituted for the words "the authority's" by the 1995 Act, s.120 and Sched. 22, para. 29(10).

(a) in complying with that direction [⁹⁸SEPA] does anything which, apart from that direction, it would be precluded from doing by a restriction imposed under subsection (1) or (2) above; and

(b) the direction is not shown to have been in consequence of—

    (i) a change of circumstances which could not reasonably have been foreseen at the beginning of the period to which the restriction relates; or

    (ii) consideration by the Secretary of State of material information which was not reasonably available to [⁹⁹SEPA] at the beginning of that period;

and in this paragraph information is material, in relation to a consent, if it relates to any discharge made or to be made by virtue of the consent, to the interaction of any such discharge with any other discharge or to the combined effect of the matter discharged and any other matter.

(4) A restriction imposed under subsection (1) or (2) of this section shall not prevent the service by [¹SEPA] of a notice by virtue of section 37(1) or (2)(c) of this Act in respect of a consent given under section 34(3) of this Act if—

(a) the notice is served not more than three months after the beginning of the period specified in section 36(1)(c) of this Act for the making of representations with respect to the consent; and

(b) [²SEPA] or, as the case may be, the Secretary of State considers, in consequence of any representations received by it or him within that period, that it is appropriate for the notice to be served.

[³General review of consents

38A.—(1) If it appears appropriate to the Secretary of State to do so he may at any time direct SEPA to review—

(a) the consents given under section 34 of this Act; or

(b) any description of such consents,

and the conditions (if any) to which those consents are subject.

(2) A direction given by virtue of subsection (1) above—

(a) shall specify the purpose for which; and

(b) may specify the manner in which,

the review is to be conducted.

(3) After carrying out the review, SEPA shall submit to the Secretary of State its proposals (if any) for—

(a) the modification of the conditions of any consent reviewed pursuant to the direction; or

(b) in the case of any such consent which is unconditional, subjecting the consent to conditions.

(4) Where the Secretary of State has received any proposals under subsection (3) above in relation to any consent he may, if it appears appropriate to him to do so, direct SEPA, in relation to that consent—

(a) to make modifications of the conditions of the consent; or

(b) in the case of an unconditional consent, to subject the consent to conditions.

(5) A direction given by virtue of subsection (4) above may direct SEPA to do, in relation to any such consent, only—

(a) any such thing as SEPA has proposed should be done in relation to that consent; or

---

⁹⁸ Substituted for the words "the authority" by the 1995 Act, s.120 and Sched. 22, para. 29(10).
⁹⁹ *ibid.*
¹ *ibid.*
² *ibid.*
³ Inserted by the 1995 Act, s.120 and Sched. 22, para. 29(14).

(b) any such thing with such modifications as appear to the Secretary of State to be appropriate.]

Appeals to the Secretary of State

39.—(1) Any question as to whether—
(a) [⁴SEPA] has unreasonably withheld its consent in pursuance of [⁵section 30J(4)] or 34 of this Act or regulations made by virtue of section 31(4) of this Act or has given its consent in pursuance of the said section 34 or such regulations subject to conditions which are unreasonable; or
(b) a notice served in pursuance of section 37(1) of this Act contains terms (other than a term required by subsection (2) of [⁶section 38 of this Act]) which are unreasonable; or
(c) the period specified in any instrument or notice in pursuance of subsection (1) or (2) of [⁷section 38 of this Act] is unreasonable,
shall be determined for the purposes of this Part of this Act by the Secretary of State; but no question relating to a determination of the Secretary of State in pursuance of section 35(4) of this Act shall be referred to him in pursuance of this subsection and any such determination shall be final.

(2) Provision may be made by regulations as to the manner in which and the time within which a question may be referred or a request may be made in pursuance of the preceding provisions of this section and as to the procedure for dealing with such a reference or request.

(3) In any case where—
(a) a question as to whether [⁸SEPA] has unreasonably withheld its consent in pursuance of section 34 of this Act, or has given its consent in pursuance of that section subject to conditions which are unreasonable, is referred to the Secretary of State in pursuance of this section; and
(b) representations relating to the application for the consent in question were made to [⁹SEPA] in pursuance of section 36(1)(c) of this Act, it shall be the duty of the Secretary of State, before he determines the question, to secure that [¹⁰SEPA] has served notice of the reference on the persons who made the representations and to take account of any further written representations relating to the application which are received by him from those persons within a prescribed period.

(4) Where a question is referred to the Secretary of State in pursuance of subsection (1) of this section and he determines that the consent in question was unreasonably withheld or that the conditions or terms or periods in question are or is unreasonable, he shall give to [¹¹SEPA] such a direction as he thinks fit with regard to the consent, conditions, terms or period and it shall be the duty of [¹²SEPA] to comply with the direction.

(5) The withholding by [¹³SEPA] of such a consent as is mentioned in subsection (1) of this section, the conditions subject to which such a consent is given and such [¹⁴period as is] so mentioned shall be treated as reasonable for the purposes of this Part of this Act until the contrary is determined in pursuance of subsection (1) of this section except where a question as to the

---

⁴ Substituted for the words "a river purification authority" by the 1995 Act, s.120 and Sched. 22, para. 29(2).
⁵ Substituted for the words "section 31(3)" by the 1995 Act, s.106 and Sched. 16, para. 7.
⁶ Substituted for the words "the preceding section" by the 1995 Act, s.120 and Sched. 22, para. 29(15)(a).
⁷ *ibid.*
⁸ Substituted for the words "a river purification authority" by the 1995 Act, s.120 and Sched. 22, para. 29(2).
⁹ Substituted for the words "the authority" by the 1995 Act, s.120 and Sched. 22, para. 29(10).
¹⁰ *ibid.*
¹¹ Substituted for the words "the relevant river purification authority" by the 1995 Act, s.120 and Sched. 22, para. 29(10).
¹² Substituted for the words "the authority" by the 1995 Act, s.120 and Sched. 22, para. 29(10).
¹³ Substituted for the words "a river purification authority" by the 1995 Act, s.120, Sched. 22, para. 29(2).
¹⁴ Substituted for the words "terms and period as are" by the 1995 Act, s.120 and Sched. 22, para. 29(15)(b).

reasonableness of the conditions of a consent given in pursuance of regulations made by virtue of section 31(4) of this Act is referred to the Secretary of State in pursuance of this section the consent shall be treated for those purposes as unconditional while the reference is pending.

[¹⁵(5A) Subject to subsection (5B) below, where a question is referred to the Secretary of State in pursuance of subsection (1)(b) above, the revocation of the consent or, as the case may be, the modification of the conditions of the consent or the provision that the consent (having been unconditional) shall be subject to conditions, shall not take effect while the reference is pending.

(5B) Subsection (5A) above shall not apply to a reference where the notice effecting the revocation, modification or provision in question includes a statement that in the opinion of SEPA it is necessary for the purpose of preventing or, where that is not practicable, minimising—

(a) the entry into controlled waters of any poisonous, noxious or polluting matter or any solid waste matter, or

(b) harm to human health,

that that subsection should not apply.

(5C) Where the reference falls within subsection (5B) above, if, on the application of the holder or former holder of the consent, the Secretary of State (or other person determining the question referred) determines that SEPA acted unreasonably in excluding the application of subsection (5A) above, then

(a) if the reference is still pending at the end of the day on which that determination is made, subsection (5A) above shall apply to the reference from the end of that day; and

(b) the holder or former holder of the consent shall be entitled to recover compensation from SEPA in respect of any loss suffered by him in consequence of the exclusion of the application of that subsection;

and any dispute as to a person's entitlement to such compensation or as to the amount of it shall be determined by a single arbiter appointed, in default of agreement between the parties concerned, by the Secretary of State on the application of any of the parties.]

(6) At any stage of the proceedings on a reference to the Secretary of State in pursuance of this section he may, and shall if so directed by the Court of Session, state in the form of a special case for the decision of the court any question of law arising in those proceedings.

[¹⁶(7) This section is subject to section 114 of the Environment Act 1995 (delegation or reference of appeals).

(8) In this section "the holder", in relation to a consent, is the person who has the consent.]

Transitional provisions relating to consents

40.—(1) Regulations may provide—

(a) for any consent for discharges which was given in pursuance of the Rivers (Prevention of Pollution) (Scotland) Acts 1951 and 1965 to have effect for any of the purposes of this Part of this Act as if given in pursuance of prescribed provisions of section 34 of this Act; and

(b) for any conditions to which such a consent was subject in pursuance of any of those enactments to have effect for any of those purposes as if attached to the consent in pursuance of prescribed provisions of this Part of this Act.

(2) Regulations may provide for the terms of a consent for an outlet which was given in pursuance of the Rivers (Prevention of Pollution) (Scotland) Act 1951 and for conditions to which such a consent was subject in pursuance

---

¹⁵ Subsections (5A)–(5C) inserted by the 1995 Act, s.120 and Sched. 22, para. 29(15)(c).
¹⁶ Subsections (7) and (8) inserted by the 1995 Act, s.120 and Sched. 22, para. 29(15)(d).

of that Act or which were imposed with respect to the outlet in pursuance of section 28(4) of that Act—

(a) to have effect, with or without modifications, for any of the purposes of this Part of this Act as if the terms or conditions were conditions attached to a consent given in pursuance of section 34 of this Act for discharges from the outlet; or

(b) to be treated, with or without modifications, for any of those purposes in such other manner as may be prescribed.

(3) An application for such a consent as is mentioned in subsection (1) of this section which is pending immediately before the relevant day shall be treated on and after that day as an application for consent in pursuance of section 34 of this Act which was made on the day on which it was actually made.

[^{17}(4) ...]

(5) Regulations may provide for any appeal which immediately before the relevant day is pending in pursuance of the Rivers (Prevention of Pollution) (Scotland) Acts 1951 and 1965 to be treated on and after that day as an appeal in pursuance of prescribed provisions of this Part of this Act.

(6) In this section "the relevant day" means 31st January 1985.

Registers

41.—(1) It shall be the duty of [^{18}SEPA] to maintain in accordance with regulations, registers containing prescribed particulars of [^{19}or relating to]—

(a) any notices of water quality objectives or other notices served under section 30C above;

(b) application for consents—
  (i) made to [^{20}SEPA] in pursuance of this Part of this Act;
  (ii) sent to the Secretary of State in pursuance of section 34 of this Act (as modified by regulations made under section 55 of this Act);

(c) consents given in pursuance of any provision of this Part of this Act [^{21}...] and the conditions to which the consents are subject;

(d) samples—
  (i) of effluent taken by [^{22}SEPA] in pursuance of section 19 of the Rivers (Prevention of Pollution) (Scotland) Act 1951;
  [^{23}(ii) ...]; and
  (iii) of water taken by [^{24}SEPA];
  and information produced by analyses of the samples and the steps taken in consequence of the information;

[^{25}(e) ...].

[^{26}(f) enforcement notices served under section 49A of this Act;

(g) directions given by the Secretary of State in relation to SEPA's functions under this Part of this Act;

---

^{17} Repealed by the Environment Act 1995, s.120, Sched. 22, para. 29(16) and Sched. 24.
^{18} Substituted for the words "river purification authorities" by the 1995 Act, s.120, Sched. 22, para. 29(2).
^{19} Inserted by the 1995 Act, s.120 and Sched. 22, para. 29(17)(a).
^{20} Substituted for the words "the authorities" by the 1995 Act, s.120 and Sched. 22, para. 29(10).
^{21} The words "(except in section 40(4)" are repealed by the 1995 Act, s.120, Sched. 22, para. 29(17)(b)(i) and Sched. 24.
^{22} Substituted for the words "the authorities" by the 1995 Act, s.120 and Sched. 22, para. 29(10).
^{23} Repealed by the 1995 Act, s.120, Sched. 22, para. 29(17)(b)(ii) and Sched. 24.
^{24} Substituted for the words "the authorities" by the 1995 Act, s.120 and Sched. 22, para. 29(10).
^{25} Paragraph (e) "certificates issued in pursuance of the following section" is repealed by the 1995 Act, s.120, Sched. 22, para. 29(17)(b)(iii) and Sched. 24.
^{26} Paragraphs (f)–(n) are added by the 1995 Act, s.120 and Sched. 22, para. 29(17)(c).

(h) convictions, for offences under this Part of this Act, of persons who have the benefit of consents under section 34 of this Act;

(j) information obtained or furnished in pursuance of conditions of such consents;

(k) works notices under section 46A of this Act;

(l) appeals under section 46C of this Act;

(m) convictions for offences under section 46D of this Act; and

(n) such other matters relating to the quality of water as may be prescribed.]

(2) It shall be the duty of [27SEPA]—

(a) to secure that registers maintained by [28SEPA] in pursuance of the preceding subsection are, after such date as is prescribed with respect to the registers, open to inspection by the public free of charge at all reasonable hours; and

(b) to afford members of the public reasonable facilities for obtaining from [29SEPA], on payment of reasonable charges, copies of entries in the register [30and, for the purposes of this subsection, places may be prescribed at which any such registers or facilities as are mentioned in paragraph (a) or (b) above are to be available or afforded to the public in pursuance of the paragraph in question].

[31(3) The Secretary of State may give SEPA directions requiring the removal from any register maintained by it under this section of any specified information which is not prescribed for inclusion under subsection (1) of this section or which, by virtue of section 42A or 42B of this Act, ought to have been excluded from the registers.]

[32Exclusion from registers of information affecting national security

42A.—(1) No information shall be included in a register kept or maintained by SEPA under section 41 of this Act if and so long as, in the opinion of the Secretary of State, the inclusion in such a register of that information, or information of that description, would be contrary to the interests of national security.

(2) The Secretary of State may, for the purposes of securing the exclusion from registers of information to which subsection (1) of this section applies, give SEPA directions—

(a) specifying information, or descriptions of information, to be excluded from their registers; or

(b) specifying descriptions of information to be referred to the Secretary of State for his determination;

and no information to be referred to the Secretary of State in pursuance of paragraph (b) of this subsection shall be included in any such register until the Secretary of State determines that it should be so included.

(3) SEPA shall notify the Secretary of State of any information it excludes from a register in pursuance of directions under subsection (2) of this section.

(4) A person may, as respects any information which appears to him to be information to which subsection (1) of this section may apply, give a notice to the Secretary of State specifying the information and indicating its apparent nature; and, if he does so—

(a) he shall notify SEPA that he has done so; and

---

27 Substituted for the words "a river purification authority" by the 1995 Act, s.120 and Sched. 22, para. 29(2).

28 Substituted for the words "the authority" by the 1995 Act, s.120 and Sched. 22, para. 29(10).

29 *ibid.*

30 Inserted by the 1995 Act, s.120 and Sched. 22, para. 29(18).

31 Inserted by the 1995 Act, s.120 and Sched. 22, para. 29(19).

32 Sections 42A and B substituted for s.42 (power of Secretary of State to exempt applications, consents and conditions etc. from publicity) by the 1995 Act, s.120 and Sched. 22, para. 29(20).

(b) no information so notified to the Secretary of State shall be included in any such register until the Secretary of State has determined that it should be so included.

Exclusion from registers of certain confidential information

42B.—(1) No information relating to the affairs of any individual or business shall, without the consent of that individual or the person for the time being carrying on that business, be included in a register kept or maintained by SEPA under section 41 of this Act, if and so long as the information—

(a) is, in relation to him, commercially confidential; and

(b) is not required to be included in the register in pursuance of directions under subsection (7) of this section;

but information is not commercially confidential for the purposes of this section unless it is determined under this section to be so by SEPA, or, on appeal, by the Secretary of State.

(2) Where information is furnished to SEPA for the purpose of—

(a) an application for a consent under section 34 of this Act;

(b) complying with any condition of such a consent; or

(c) complying with a notice under section 93 of this Act,

then, if the person furnishing it applies to SEPA to have the information excluded from any register kept or maintained by SEPA under section 41 of this Act, on the ground that it is commercially confidential (as regards himself or another person), SEPA shall determine whether the information is or is not commercially confidential.

(3) A determination under subsection (2) of this section must be made within the period of fourteen days beginning with the date of the application and if SEPA fails to make a determination within that period it shall be treated as having determined that the information is commercially confidential.

(4) Where it appears to SEPA that any information (other than information furnished in circumstances within subsection (2) of this section) which has been obtained by SEPA under or by virtue of any provision of any enactment might be commercially confidential, SEPA shall—

(a) give to the person to whom or whose business it relates notice that that information is required to be included in a register kept or maintained by SEPA under section 41 of this Act, unless excluded under this section; and

(b) give him a reasonable opportunity—

(i) of objecting to the inclusion of the information on the ground that it is commercially confidential; and

(ii) of making representations to SEPA for the purpose of justifying any such objection;

and, if any representations are made, SEPA shall, having taken the representations into account, determine whether the information is or is not commercially confidential.

(5) Where, under subsection (2) or (4) of this section, SEPA determines that information is not commercially confidential—

(a) the information shall not be entered on the register until the end of the period of twenty-one days beginning with the date on which the determination is notified to the person concerned; and

(b) that person may appeal to the Secretary of State against the decision;

and, where an appeal is brought in respect of any information, the information shall not be entered on the register pending the final determination or withdrawal of the appeal.

(6) Subsections (2), (4) and (7) of section 49B of this Act shall apply in relation to appeals under subsection (5) of this section; but

(a) subsection (4) of that section shall have effect for the purposes of this subsection with the substitution for the words from ("which may" onwards of the words "(which must be held in private)"; and

(b) subsection (5) of this section is subject to section 114 of the Environment Act 1995 (delegation or reference of appeals etc.).

(7) The Secretary of State may give SEPA directions as to specified information, or descriptions of information, which the public interest requires to be included in registers kept or maintained by SEPA under section 41 of this Act notwithstanding that the information may be commercially confidential.

(8) Information excluded from a register shall be treated as ceasing to be commercially confidential for the purposes of this section at the expiry of the period of four years beginning with the date of the determination by virtue of which it was excluded; but the person who furnished it may apply to SEPA for the information to remain excluded from the register on the ground that it is still commercially confidential and SEPA shall determine whether or not that is the case.

(9) Subsections (5) and (6) of this section shall apply in relation to a determination under subsection (8) of this section as they apply in relation to a determination under subsection (2) or (4) of this section.

(10) The Secretary of State may prescribe the substitution (whether in all cases or in such classes or descriptions of case as may be prescribed) for the period for the time being specified in subsection (3) above of such other period as he considers appropriate.

(11) Information is, for the purposes of any determination under this section, commercially confidential, in relation to any individual or person, if its being contained in [[32A]...] register would prejudice to an unreasonable degree the commercial interests of that individual or person.]

43. [Repealed by the Water Consolidation (Consequential Provisions) Act 1991, s.3 and Sched. 3.]

44. [Amended by the Water Act 1989, Sched. 8; repealed in part by the Water Act 1989, Sched. 27 and by the Water Consolidation (Consequential Provisions) Act 1991, s.3 and Sched. 3. Does not apply to Scotland].

45. [Repealed by the Water Consolidation (Consequential Provisions) Act 1991, s.3 and Sched. 3].

[33]Operations by SEPA to remedy or forestall pollution of water

46.—(1) [[34]Subject to subsection (1B) below] where it appears to [[35]SEPA] that any poisonous, noxious or polluting matter or any solid waste matter is likely to enter, or is or was present in, any controlled waters [[36]...], [[37]SEPA] may carry out [[38]...] such operations as it considers appropriate—

(a) in a case where the matter appears likely to enter such waters, for the purpose of preventing it from doing so; and

(b) in a case where the matter appears to be or to have been present in such waters, for the purpose of removing or disposing of the matter or of remedying or mitigating any pollution caused by its presence in the waters or of restoring the waters (including the fauna and flora dependent on the aquatic environment of the waters), so far as it is

---

[32A] It would appear that the word "a" should have been inserted here by the 1995 Act.

[33] Sections 46 to 51 substituted by the Water Act 1989, s.168 and Sched. 23, para. 5.

[34] Inserted by the 1995 Act, s.120 and Sched. 22, para. 29(21)(a)(i).

[35] Substituted for the words "a river purification authority" by the 1995 Act, s.120 and Sched. 22, para. 29(2).

[36] The words "in its area" are repealed by the 1995 Act, s.120, Sched. 22, para. 29(21)(a)(ii) and Sched. 24.

[37] Substituted for the words "the authority" by the 1995 Act, s.120 and Sched. 22, para. 29(10).

[38] The words "in its area or elsewhere" are repealed by the 1995 Act, s.120, Sched. 22, para. 29(21)(a)(ii) and Sched. 24.

reasonably practicable to do so, to the state in which they were immediately before the matter became present in the waters; but nothing in this subsection empowers [³⁹SEPA] to impede or prevent the making of any discharge in pursuance of a consent given by [⁴⁰SEPA] by virtue of section 34 of this Act.

[⁴¹(1A) In either case mentioned in subsection (1) of this section, SEPA shall be entitled to carry out investigations for the purpose of establishing the source of the matter and the identity of the person who has caused or knowingly permitted it to be present in controlled waters or at a place from which it was likely, in the opinion of SEPA, to enter controlled waters.

(1B) Without prejudice to the power of SEPA to carry out investigations under subsection (1A) above, the power conferred by subsection (1) above to carry out operations shall be exercisable only in a case where—

(a) SEPA considers it necessary to carry out forthwith any operations falling within paragraph (a) or (b) of subsection (1) above; or

(b) it appears to SEPA, after reasonable inquiry, that no person can be found on whom to serve a works notice under section 46A of this Act.]

(2) Where [⁴²SEPA] carries out any operations [⁴³or investigations] in pursuance of this section [⁴⁴SEPA] shall, subject to the following subsection, be entitled to recover the costs of doing so from any persons who caused or knowingly permitted the matter in question to be present at the place from which it was likely in the opinion of [⁴⁵SEPA] to enter the controlled waters or, as the case may be, to be present in the controlled waters.

(3) No such costs shall be payable by a person—

(a) in so far as he satisfies the court in which it is sought to recover the costs that the costs were incurred unnecessarily; or

(b) for any operations [⁴⁶or investigations] in respect of water from an abandoned mine [⁴⁷or an abandoned part of a mine] which that person permitted to reach such a place as is mentioned in the preceding subsection or to enter the controlled waters.

[⁴⁸(3A) Subsection (3)(b) of this section shall not apply to the owner or former operator of any mine or part of a mine if the mine or part in question became abandoned after 31st December 1999.

(3B) Subsections (5) and (6) of section 30J above shall apply in relation to subsections (3) and (3A) above as they apply in relation to subsections (3) and (4) of that section.]

(4) In determining the damage which a person has suffered in consequence of pollution in respect of which operations have been or may be carried out in pursuance of this section, account shall be taken of the extent to which it is shown that the damage has been reduced by operations in pursuance of this section and of the extent to which it is shown that the damage is likely to be so reduced.

[⁴⁹Notices requiring persons to carry out anti-pollution operations

46A.—(1) Subject to the following provisions of this section where it appears to SEPA that any poisonous, noxious or polluting matter or any

---

³⁹ Substituted for the words "a river purification authority" by the 1995 Act, s.120 and Sched. 22, para. 29(2).

⁴⁰ Substituted for the words "any authority" by the 1995 Act, s.120 and Sched. 22, para. 29(10).

⁴¹ Subsections (1A) and (1B) inserted by the 1995 Act, s.120 and Sched. 22, para. 29(21)(b).

⁴² Substituted for the words "a river purification authority" by the 1995 Act, s.120 and Sched. 22, para. 29(2).

⁴³ Inserted by the 1995 Act, s.120 and Sched. 22, para. 29(21)(c).

⁴⁴ Substituted for the words "the authority" by the 1995 Act, s.120, Sched. 22, para. 29(10).

⁴⁵ *ibid.*

⁴⁶ Inserted by the 1995 Act, s.120 and Sched. 22, para. 29(21)(d)(i).

⁴⁷ Inserted by the 1995 Act, s.120 and Sched. 22, para. 29(21)(d)(ii).

⁴⁸ Subsections (3A) and (3B) inserted by the 1995 Act, s.120 and Sched. 22, para. 29(21)(e).

⁴⁹ Sections 46A, 46B, 46C and 46D inserted by the 1995 Act, s.120 and Sched. 22, para. 29(22).

solid waste matter is likely to enter, or to be or to have been present in, any controlled waters, SEPA shall be entitled to serve a works notice on any person who, as the case may be,—

(a) caused or knowingly permitted the matter in question to be present at the place from which it is likely, the opinion of SEPA, to enter any controlled waters; or

(b) caused or knowingly permitted the matter in question to be present in any controlled waters.

(2) For the purposes of this section, a "works notice" is a notice requiring the person on whom it is served to carry out such of the following operations as may be specified in the notice, that is to say—

(a) in a case where the matter in question appears likely to enter any controlled waters, operations for the purpose of preventing it from doing so; or

(b) in a case where the matter appears to be or to have been present in any controlled waters, operations for the purpose—

(i) of removing or disposing of the matter;

(ii) of remedying or mitigating any pollution caused by its presence in the waters; or

(iii) so far as it is reasonably practicable to do so, of restoring the waters, including any flora and fauna dependent on the aquatic environment of the waters, to their state immediately before the matter became present in the waters.

(3) A works notice—

(a) must specify the periods within which the person on whom it is served is required to do each of the things specified in the notice; and

(b) is without prejudice to the powers of SEPA by virtue of section 46(1B)(a) of this Act.

(4) Before serving a works notice on any person, SEPA shall reasonably endeavour to consult that person concerning the operations which are to be specified in the notice.

(5) The Secretary of State may by regulations make provision for or in connection with—

(a) the form or content of works notices;

(b) requirements for consultation, before the service of a works notice, with persons other than the person on whom that notice is to be served;

(c) steps to be taken for the purposes of any consultation required under subsection (4) above or regulations made by virtue of paragraph (b) above; and

(d) any other steps of a procedural nature which are to be taken in connection with, or in consequence of, the service of a works notice.

(6) A works notice shall not be regarded as invalid, or as invalidly served, by reason only of any failure to comply with the requirements of subsection (4) above or of regulations made by virtue of paragraph (b) of subsection (5) above.

(7) Nothing in subsection (1) above shall entitle SEPA to require the carrying out of any operations which would impede or prevent the making of any discharge in pursuance of a consent given by SEPA by virtue of section 34 of this Act.

(8) No works notice shall be served on any person requiring him to carry out any operations in respect of water from an abandoned mine or an abandoned part of a mine which that person permitted to reach such a place as is mentioned in subsection (1)(a) above or to enter any controlled waters.

(9) Subsection (8) above shall not apply to the owner or former operator of any mine or part of a mine if the mine or part in question became abandoned after 31st December 1999.

(10) Subsections (5) and (6) of section 30J of this Act shall apply in

relation to subsections (8) and (9) above as they apply in relation to subsections (3) and (4) of that section.

(11) Where SEPA—

(a) carries out any such investigations as are mentioned in section 46(1A) of this Act, and

(b) serves a works notice on a person in connection with the matter to which the investigations relate,

it shall (unless the notice is quashed or withdrawn) be entitled to recover the costs or expenses reasonably incurred in carrying out those investigations from that person.

(12) The Secretary of State may, if he thinks fit in relation to any person, give directions to SEPA as to whether or how it should exercise its powers under this section.

Grant of, and compensation for, rights of entry etc.

46B.—(1) A works notice may require a person to carry out operations in relation to any land or waters notwithstanding that he is not entitled to carry out those operations.

(2) Any person whose consent is required before any operations required by a works notice may be carried out shall grant, or join in granting, such rights in relation to any land or waters as will enable the person on whom the works notice is served to comply with any requirements imposed by the works notice.

(3) Before serving a works notice, SEPA shall reasonably endeavour to consult every person who appears to it—

(a) to be the owner or occupier of any relevant land, and

(b) to be a person who might be required by subsection (2) above to grant, or join in granting, any rights,

concerning the rights which that person may be so required to grant.

(4) A works notice shall not be regarded as invalid, or as invalidly served, by reason only of any failure to comply with the requirements of subsection (3) above.

(5) A person who grants, or joins in granting, any rights pursuant to subsection (2) above shall be entitled, on making an application within such period as may be prescribed and in such manner as may be prescribed to such person as may be prescribed, to be paid by the person on whom the works notice in question is served compensation of such amount as may be determined in such manner as may be prescribed.

(6) Without prejudice to the generality of the regulations that may be made by virtue of subsection (5) above, regulations by virtue of that subsection may make such provision in relation to compensation under this section as may be made by regulations by virtue of subsection (4) of section 35A of the Environmental Protection Act 1990 in relation to compensation under that section.

(7) In this section—

"relevant land" means—

(a) any land or waters in relation to which the works notice in question requires, or may require, operations to be carried out; or

(b) any land adjoining or adjacent to that land or those waters;

"works notice" means a works notice under section 46A of this Act.

Appeals against works notices

46C.—(1) A person on whom a works notice is served may, within the period of twenty-one days beginning with the day on which the notice is served, appeal against the notice to the Secretary of State.

(2) On any appeal under this section the Secretary of State—

(a) shall quash the notice, if he is satisfied that there is a material defect in the notice; but

(b) subject to that, may confirm the notice, with or without modification, or quash it.

(3) The Secretary of State may by regulations make provision with respect to—

(a) the grounds on which appeals under this section may be made; or

(b) the procedure on any such appeal.

(4) Regulations under subsection (3) above may (among other things)—

(a) include provisions comparable to those in section 290 of the Public Health Act 1936 (appeals against notices requiring execution of works);

(b) prescribe the cases in which a works notice is, or is not, to be suspended until the appeal is decided, or until some other stage in the proceedings;

(c) prescribe the cases in which the decision on an appeal may in some respects be less favourable to the appellant than the works notice against which he is appealing;

(d) prescribe the cases in which the appellant may claim that a works notice should have been served on some other person and prescribe the procedure to be followed in those cases;

(e) make provision as respects—

(i) the particulars to be included in the notice of appeal;

(ii) the persons on whom notice of appeal is to be served and the particulars, if any, which are to accompany the notice; or

(iii) the abandonment of an appeal.

(5) In this section "works notice" means a works notice under section 46A of this Act.

(6) This section is subject to section 114 of the Environment Act 1995 (delegation or reference of appeals).

Consequences of not complying with a works notice

46D.—(1) If a person on whom SEPA serves a works notice fails to comply with any of the requirements of the notice, he shall be guilty of an offence.

(2) A person who commits an offence under subsection (1) above shall be liable—

(a) on summary conviction, to imprisonment for a term not exceeding three months or to a fine not exceeding £20,000 or to both;

(b) on conviction on indictment, to imprisonment for a term not exceeding two years or to a fine or to both.

(3) If a person on whom a works notice has been served fails to comply with any of the requirements of the notice, SEPA may do what that person was required to do and may recover from him any costs or expenses reasonably incurred by SEPA in doing it.

(4) If SEPA is of the opinion that proceedings for an offence under subsection (1) above would afford an ineffectual remedy against a person who has failed to comply with the requirements of a works notice, SEPA may take proceedings in any court of competent jurisdiction for the purpose of securing compliance with the notice.

(5) In this section "works notice" means a works notice under section 46A of this Act.]

Duty of SEPA to deal with waste from vessels etc.

47.—(1) It shall be the duty of [⁵⁰SEPA]—

(a) to arrange for the collection and disposal of waste from vessels [⁵¹...] which appears to [⁵²SEPA] to need collection in consequence of the provisions of section 33 of this Act; and

(b) to arrange for the provision of facilities for the washing out of prescribed appliances from vessels [⁵³...].

(2) [⁵⁴SEPA] may arrange for the provision of facilities by way of water closets, urinals and wash basins for the use of persons from vessels [⁵⁵...].

(3) A port local authority constituted under Part X of the Public Health (Scotland) Act 1897 shall have power to make arrangements with [⁵⁶SEPA] for the purposes of any of the preceding provisions of this section.

Power of SEPA to exclude unregistered vessels from rivers etc.

48.—(1) Where it appears to [⁵⁷SEPA] to be appropriate to do so for the purpose of preventing the pollution of inland waters [⁵⁸...], [⁵⁹SEPA] may make byelaws providing that vessels shall not be on any such waters which are specified in the byelaws unless the vessels are registered by [⁶⁰SEPA] in accordance with the byelaws or are exempted by the byelaws from registration; and a person who causes or knowingly permits a vessel to be on inland waters in contravention of byelaws made by virtue of this subsection shall be guilty of an offence and liable on summary conviction to a fine not exceeding level 5 on the standard scale or such smaller sum as may be specified in the byelaws.

(2) Byelaws made by [⁶¹SEPA] in pursuance of the preceding subsection may authorise [⁶²SEPA] to make reasonable charges in respect of the registration of vessels in pursuance of the byelaws; and no charges shall be payable, by persons in or from vessels registered by [⁶³SEPA] in pursuance of the byelaws, in respect of the use by those persons of facilities provided in pursuance of the preceding section by or by arrangement with [⁶⁴SEPA].

Deposits and vegetation in rivers etc.

49.—(1) If without the consent of [⁶⁵SEPA], which shall not be unreasonably withheld,—

(a) a person removes from any part of the bottom, channel or bed of any inland waters a deposit accumulated by reason of any dam, weir or sluice holding back the waters and does so by causing the deposit to be carried away in suspension in the waters; or

(b) any substantial amount of vegetation cut or uprooted in any inland waters, or so near to any such waters that it falls into it, is allowed to remain in the waters by the wilful default of any person,

---

⁵⁰ Substituted for the words "each river purification authority" by the 1995 Act, s.120, Sched. 22, para. 29(2).

⁵¹ The words "in its area" are repealed by the 1995 Act, s.120, Sched. 22, para. 29(23)(a) and Sched. 24.

⁵² Substituted for the words "the authority" by the 1995 Act, s.120, Sched. 22, para. 29(10).

⁵³ The words "in its area" are repealed by the 1995 Act, s.120, Sched. 22, para. 29(23)(a) and Sched. 24.

⁵⁴ Substituted for the words "a river purification authority" by the 1995 Act, s.120, Sched. 22, para. 29(2).

⁵⁵ The words "in the authority's area" are repealed by the 1995 Act, s.120, Sched. 22, para. 29(23)(b).

⁵⁶ Substituted for the words "a river purification authority" by the 1995 Act, s.120, Sched. 22, para. 29(2).

⁵⁷ *ibid.*

⁵⁸ The words "in its area" are repealed by the 1995 Act, s.120, Sched. 22, para. 29(24) and Sched. 24.

⁵⁹ Substituted for the words "the authority" by the 1995 Act, s.120, Sched. 22, para. 29(10).

⁶⁰ *ibid.*

⁶¹ Substituted for the words "a river purification authority" by the 1995 Act, s.120, Sched. 22, para. 29(2).

⁶² Substituted for the words "the authority" by the 1995 Act, s.120, Sched. 22, para. 29(10).

⁶³ *ibid.*

⁶⁴ *ibid.*

⁶⁵ Substituted for the words "the relevant river purification authority" by the 1995 Act, s.120, Sched. 22, para. 29(10).

then, subject to the following subsection, that person shall be guilty of an offence and liable on summary conviction to a fine not exceeding level 4 on the standard scale.

(2) Nothing in paragraph (a) of the preceding subsection applies to anything done in the exercise of statutory powers conferred by or under any enactment relating to land drainage, flood prevention or navigation.

(3) Regulations may provide that any reference to inland waters in subsection (1) of this section shall be construed as including a reference to such coastal waters as are prescribed for the purposes of that subsection.

(4) Any question as to whether the consent of [⁶⁶SEPA] in pursuance of subsection (1) of this section is unreasonably withheld shall be determined by the Secretary of State; and any consent given in pursuance of section 24 of the Rivers (Prevention of Pollution) (Scotland) Act 1951 (which is superseded by this section) shall be treated for the purposes of this section as given in pursuance of this section.

[⁶⁷(5) This section is subject to section 114 of the Environment Act 1995 (delegation or reference of appeals).]

[⁶⁸Enforcement notices as respects discharge consents

49A.—(1) If SEPA is of the opinion that the holder of a relevant consent is contravening any condition of the consent, or is likely to contravene any such condition, it may serve on him a notice (an "enforcement notice").

(2) An enforcement notice shall—

(a) state that SEPA is of the said opinion;

(b) specify the matters constituting the contravention or the matters making it likely that the contravention will arise;

(c) specify the steps that must be taken to remedy the contravention or, as the case may be, to remedy the matters making it likely that the contravention will arise; and

(d) specify the period within which those steps must be taken.

(3) Any person who fails to comply with any requirement imposed by an enforcement notice shall be guilty of an offence and liable—

(a) on summary conviction, to imprisonment for a term not exceeding three months or to a fine not exceeding £20,000 or to both;

(b) on conviction on indictment, to imprisonment for a term not exceeding two years or to a fine or to both.

(4) If SEPA is of the opinion that proceedings for an offence under subsection (3) above would afford an ineffectual remedy against a person who has failed to comply with the requirements of an enforcement notice, SEPA may take proceedings in any court of competent jurisdiction for the purpose of securing compliance with the notice.

(5) The Secretary of State may, if he thinks fit in relation to any person, give to SEPA directions as to whether it should exercise its powers under this section and as to the steps which must be taken.

(6) In this section—

(a) "relevant consent" means a consent for the purposes of section 30J(7)(a), 34 or 49(1) of this Act; and

(b) "the holder", in relation to a relevant consent, is the person who has the consent in question.

Appeals against enforcement notices

49B.—(1) A person upon whom an enforcement notice has been served under section 49A of this Act may appeal to the Secretary of State.

(2) This section is subject to section 114 of the Environment Act 1995 (delegation or reference of appeals etc.).

---

⁶⁶ Substituted for the words "a river purification authority" by the 1995 Act, s.120, Sched. 22, para. 29(2).
⁶⁷ Inserted by the 1995 Act, s.120, Sched. 22, para. 29(25).
⁶⁸ Sections 49A–B inserted by the 1995 Act, s.120, Sched. 22, para. 29(26).

(3) An appeal under this section shall, if and to the extent a requirement to do so is prescribed, be advertised in the manner prescribed.

(4) If either party to the appeal so requests or the Secretary of State so decides, an appeal shall be or continue in the form of a hearing (which may, if the person hearing the appeal so decides, be held, or held to any extent, in private).

(5) On the determination of an appeal under this section, the Secretary of State may either quash or affirm the enforcement notice and, if he affirms it, may do so either in its original form or with such modifications as he may in the circumstances think fit.

(6) The bringing of an appeal under this section shall not have the effect of suspending the operation of the notice appealed against.

(7) The period within which and the manner in which appeals under this section are to be brought and the manner in which they are to be considered shall be as prescribed.]

Investigation of water pollution problems arising from closure of mines

50.—(1) [⁶⁹SEPA] shall have the power to carry out studies for the purpose of ascertaining—
 (a) what problems relating to the pollution of controlled waters may arise or have arisen in consequence of the abandonment of any mine [⁷⁰...] or might arise if any such mine were abandoned; and
 (b) what steps are likely to be appropriate for the purpose of dealing with the problems and what the cost of taking those steps would be.

Codes of good agricultural practice

51.—(1) The Secretary of State may by order made by statutory instrument approve any code of practice issued (whether by him or by another person) for the purpose of—
 (a) giving practical guidance to persons engaged in agriculture with respect to activities that may affect controlled waters; and
 (b) promoting what appear to him to be desirable practices by such persons for avoiding or minimising the pollution of any such waters, and may at any time by such an order approve a modification of such a code or withdraw his approval of such a code or modification.

(2) A contravention of a code of practice as for the time being approved under this section shall not of itself give rise to any criminal or civil liability, but [⁷¹SEPA] shall take into account whether there has been or is likely to be any such contravention in determining when and how it should exercise any powers conferred on it by regulations under section 31A of this Act.

(3) The Secretary of State shall not make an order under this section unless he has first consulted [⁷²SEPA].
 [⁷²ᴬ**52.**— ...]
⁷³[⁷⁴**53.**— ....]
 [⁷⁵**54.**— ...]
 [⁷⁶**55.**— ...]

---

⁶⁹ Substituted for the words "Each river purification authority" by the 1995 Act, s.120, Sched. 22, para. 29(2).
⁷⁰ The words "in its area" are repealed by the 1995 Act, s.120, Sched. 22, para. 29(27) and Sched. 24
⁷¹ Substituted for the words "a river purification authority" by the 1995 Act, s.120, Sched. 22, para. 29(2).
⁷² Substituted for the words "the river purification authorities" by the 1995 Act, s.120, Sched. 22, para. 29(2).
⁷²ᴬ Repealed by the Water Act 1989, s.190 and Sched. 27.
⁷³ Sections 53 to 56 substituted by the Water Act 1989, s.168 and Sched. 23, para. 6
⁷⁴ Repealed by the 1995 Act, s.120, Sched. 22, para. 29(28) and Sched. 24.
⁷⁵ *ibid.*
⁷⁶ *ibid.*

Interpretation etc. of Part II

56.—(1) Except where the context otherwise requires, in this Part of this Act—

"agriculture" and "agricultural" have the same meanings as in the Agriculture (Scotland) Act 1948;

"coastal waters", "controlled waters", "ground waters", "inland waters" and "relevant territorial waters" have the meanings given by section 30A(1) above;

[[77]"drain" has the same meaning as in the Sewerage (Scotland) Act 1968;]

"effluent" means any liquid, including particles of matter and other substances in suspension in the liquid;

"micro-organism" includes any microscopic biological entity which is capable of replication;

[[78]"operations" includes works];

[[79]"sewage effluent" includes any effluent from sewage disposal, or sewerage works vested in a sewerage authority];

[[80]"sewer" has the same meaning as in the Sewerage (Scotland) Act 1968];

[[81]"sewerage authority" shall be construed in accordance with section 62 of the Local Government etc. (Scotland) Act 1994];

"substance" includes micro-organisms and any natural or artificial substance or other matter, whether it is in solid or liquid form or in the form of a gas or vapour;

"trade effluent" includes any effluent which is discharged from premises used for carrying on any trade or industry, other than surface water and domestic sewage;

"underground strata" means strata subjacent to the surface of any land;

[[82]"water authority" shall be construed in accordance with section 62 of the Local Government etc. (Scotland) Act 1994];

"watercourse" includes all rivers, streams, ditches, drains, cuts, culverts, dykes, sluices, sewers and passages through which water flows except mains and other pipes which belong to the water authority or are used by a water authority or any other person for the purposes only of providing a supply of water to any premises.

(2) In this Part of this Act—

(a) any reference to the waters of a loch or pond or of any river or watercourse includes a reference to the bottom, channel or bed of any loch, pond, river or, as the case may be, watercourse which is for the time being dry; and

(b) any reference to water contained in underground strata is a reference to water so contained otherwise than in a sewer, pipe, reservoir, tank or other underground works constructed in any such strata.

(3) For the purposes of the definition of "trade effluent" in subsection (1) above any premises (whether on land or not) wholly or mainly used (whether for profit or not) for agricultural purposes or for the purposes of fish farming or for scientific research or experiment shall be deemed to be (and in the case of fish farms, always to have been) premises used for carrying on a trade.

[[83](4) ...]

(5) For the purposes of this Part of this Act a notice imposing conditions

---

[77] Inserted by the 1995 Act, s.106, Sched. 16, para. 8.
[78] Inserted by the 1995 Act, s.120, Sched. 22, para. 29(29).
[79] Substituted by the Local Government etc. (Scotland) Act 1994, Sched. 13, para. 95(5)(a).
[80] Inserted by the 1995 Act, s.106, Sched. 16, para. 8.
[81] Substituted by the Local Government etc. (Scotland) Act 1994, Sched. 13, para. 95(5)(a).
[82] Substituted by the Local Government etc. (Scotland) Act, Sched. 13, para. 95(5)(b).
[83] Subsection (4) is repealed by the 1995 Act, s.120, Sched. 22, para. 29(28).

with respect to discharges which was given by a river purification authority in pursuance of—
 (a) section 28(4) of the Rivers (Prevention of Pollution) (Scotland) Act 1951; or
 (b) section 1(5) of the Rivers (Prevention of Pollution) (Scotland) Act 1965,
shall be treated as having given the authority's consent in pursuance of the Act in question for those discharges subject to those conditions.

[[84](6) Except as provided by regulations made under this subsection, nothing in this Part of this Act applies to radioactive waste within the meaning of the [[85]Radioactive Substances Act 1993]; but regulations may—
 (a) provide for prescribed provisions of this Part of this Act to have effect with such modifications as the Secretary of State considers appropriate for the purposes of dealing with such radioactive waste;
 (b) make such modifications of the [[86]Radioactive Substances Act 1993] and any other Act as the Secretary of State considers appropriate in connection with regulations made under paragraph (a) above.]

[87]SCHEDULE 1A

ORDERS DESIGNATING NITRATE SENSITIVE AREAS: SCOTLAND

PART I

APPLICATIONS BY SEPA FOR DESIGNATION ORDERS

Orders made only on application

1.—(1) Subject to sub-paragraph (2) below, the Secretary of State shall not make an order under section 31B of this Act by virtue of which any land is designated as a nitrate sensitive area, except with the consent of the Treasury and on an application which—
 (a) has been made by [[88]SEPA] in accordance with paragraph 2 below; and
 (b) by virtue of sub-paragraph (2)(a) of that paragraph identifies the controlled waters with respect to which that land is so comprised by the order.
 (2) This paragraph shall not apply to an order which reproduces or amends an existing order without adding any land appearing to the Secretary of State to constitute a significant area to the land already comprised in the areas for the time being designated as nitrate sensitive areas.

Procedure for applications

2.—(1) [[89]SEPA] shall not, for the purposes of paragraph 1 above, apply for the making of any order under section 31B of this Act, by which any land would be comprised in the areas for the time being designated as nitrate sensitive areas unless it appears to [[90]SEPA]—
 (a) that pollution is or is likely to be caused by the entry of nitrate into controlled waters as a result of, or of anything done in connection with, the use of particular land for agricultural purposes; and
 (b) that the provisions for the time being in force in relation to those waters and that land are not sufficient, in the opinion of [[91]SEPA], for preventing or controlling such an entry of nitrate into those waters.
 (2) An application under this paragraph shall identify—
 (a) the controlled waters appearing to [[92]SEPA] to be the waters which the nitrate is entering or is likely to enter; and

---

[84] Substituted by the Environmental Protection Act 1990, ss.162(1), 164(3) and Sched. 15, para. 17.
[85] Substituted for the words "Radioactive Substances Act 1960" by the Radioactive Substances Act 1993, s.49(1), Sched. 4, para. 3.
[86] *ibid.*
[87] Inserted by the Water Act 1989, s.168 and Sched. 23, para. 8.
[88] Substituted for the words "a river purification authority" by the 1995 Act, s.120 and Sched. 22, para. 29(2).
[89] *ibid.*
[90] Substituted for the words "the authority" by the 1995 Act, s.120 and Sched. 22, para. 29(10).
[91] *ibid.*
[92] *ibid.*

923

(b) the land appearing to [93SEPA] to be the land the use of which for agricultural purposes, or the doing of anything in connection with whose use for agricultural purposes, is resulting or is likely to result in the entry of nitrate into those waters.

(3) An application under this paragraph shall be made by serving a notice containing the application on the Secretary of State.

PART II

ORDERS CONTAINING MANDATORY PROVISIONS ETC.

Publication of proposal for order containing mandatory provisions

3.—(1) This paragraph applies where the Secretary of State proposes to make an order under section 31B of this Act which—

(a) makes or modifies any such provision as is authorised by sub-section (3)(a) of that section; and

(b) in doing so, contains provision which is not of one of the following descriptions, that is to say—

    (i) provision reproducing existing provisions without modification and in relation to substantially the same area; and

    (ii) provision modifying any existing provisions so as to make them less onerous.

(2) The Secretary of State shall, before making any such order as is mentioned in sub-paragraph (1) above—

(a) publish a notice with respect to the proposed order at least once in each of two successive weeks, in one or more newspapers circulating in the locality in relation to which the proposed order will have effect;

(b) not later than the date on which that notice is first published, serve a copy of the notice on—

    (i) [94SEPA];

    (ii) every local authority whose area includes the whole or any part of that locality; and

    (iii) in the case of an order containing any such provision as is authorised by section 31B(3)(b) of this Act, such owners and occupiers of agricultural land in that locality as appear to the Secretary of State to be likely to be affected by the obligations in respect of which payments are to be made under that provision; and

(c) publish a notice in the *Edinburgh Gazette* which—

    (i) names every local authority on whom a notice is required to be served under this paragraph;

    (ii) specifies a place where a copy of the proposed order and of any relevant map or plan may be inspected; and

    (iii) gives the name of every newspaper in which the notice required by virtue of paragraph (a) above was published and the date of an issue containing the notice.

(3) The notice required by virtue of sub-paragraph (2)(a) above to be published with respect to any proposed order shall—

(a) state the general effect of the proposed order;

(b) specify a place where a copy of the proposed order and of any relevant map or plan may be inspected by any person free of charge at all reasonable times during the period of forty-two days beginning with the date of the first publication of the notice; and

(c) state that any person may, within that period, by notice to the Secretary of State object to the making of the order.

Supply of copies of proposed orders

4. The Secretary of State shall, at the request of any person and on payment by that person of such charge (if any) as the Secretary of State may reasonably require, furnish that person with a copy of any proposed order of which notice has been published under paragraph 3 above.

Modifications of proposals

5.—(1) Where notices with respect to any proposed order have been published and served in accordance with paragraph 3 above and the period of forty-two days mentioned in sub-paragraph (3)(b) of that paragraph has expired, the Secretary of State may make the order

---

93 *ibid.*

94 Substituted for the words "the river purification authority" by the 1995 Act, s.120 and Sched. 22, para. 29(2).

either in the proposed terms or, subject to sub-paragraph (2) below (but without any further compliance with paragraph 3 above), in those terms as modified in such manner as he thinks fit, or may decide not to make any order.

(2) The Secretary of State shall not make such a modification of a proposed order of which notice has been so published and served as he considers is likely adversely to affect any persons unless he has given such notices as he considers appropriate for enabling those persons to object to the modification.

(3) Subject to sub-paragraph (2) above and to the service of notices of the proposed modification on such local authorities as appear to him to be likely to be interested in it, the modifications that may be made by the Secretary of State include any modification of the area designated by the proposed order as a nitrate sensitive area.

Consideration of objections etc.

6. Without prejudice to section 96 of this Act, where notices with respect to any proposed order have been published and served in accordance with paragraph 3 above, the Secretary of State may, if he considers it appropriate to do so, hold a local inquiry before deciding whether or not to make the proposed order or to make it with modifications.

Consent of Treasury for payment provisions

7. The consent of the Treasury shall be required for the making of any order under section 31B of this Act the making of which does not require the consent of the Treasury by virtue of paragraph 1 above but which contains any such provision as is authorised by subsection (3)(b) of that section.

8. In this Part, "local authority" means [[95]council constituted under section 2 of the Local Government etc. (Scotland) Act 1994].

---

[95] Substituted for the words "regional, islands or district council" by the Local Government etc. (Scotland) Act 1994, Sched. 13, para. 95(10).

INDEX

Generally, references are to the relevant section or Schedule number of either the 1990 or the 1995 Act. References to the commentary to the section or Schedule are denoted by the letter 'N'. Thus the reference 95/1N is to the commentary to section 1 of the 1995 Act, and 95/Sch. 2, para. 2 is to paragraph 2 of Schedule 2 to the 1995 Act.
The Control of Pollution Act 1974 and Statutory Instruments comprise the Appendices to this book and references to them are to the Appendix followed by the relevant section or regulation number. Thus reference App. 4/30Y is to section 30Y of the Act to be found in Appendix 4 of this book.

[1]

Index